Clinical Assessment of Child and Adolescent Intelligence

Clinical Assessment of Child and Adolescent Intelligence

 Springer

To Norma, Ashley, and Natalie—
Thanks for making life meaningful.
And to all of my former assessment students—
Thanks for teaching me how to teach.

Randy W. Kamphaus
Professor of Educational Psychology
University of Georgia
Dept. of Educational Psychology
329 Aderhold Hall
Athens, GA 30602
USA
E-mail: rkamp@arches.uga.edu

Library of Congress Control Number: 2005927416

This book was previously published under the title *Clinical Assessment of Children's Intelligence*.

ISBN-10: 0-387-26299-7   Printed on acid-free paper.

© 2005 Springer Science+Business Media, Inc.

Printed in the United States of America.   (SBA)

10 9 8 7 6 5 4 3 2 1

springeronline.com

CONTENTS

PREFACE

A TEACHING TEXT

This book is born of necessity—my own necessity for a textbook to use for training psychology graduate students in the elementary principles of assessment and diagnostic practice with children and adolescents. I have struggled for years to teach the first graduate course in assessment at two universities. There are many good texts but none that suited my purposes specifically. Some assessment textbooks focus on only one measure. I needed a text that applied the same interpretive system across tests. Other texts and handbooks served my students well as a resource, but they did not provide them with an accessible guide to interpretation. I wrote this text in the hope that it would aid in the assessment training process. I think of this as a *teaching text*, not a resource or reference text.

GOALS

I had the following goals in mind when preparing this book.

1. *Emphasize interpretation.* Intelligence test manuals continue to improve. Newer manuals are not only specific about administration and scoring procedures, but they also include generous interpretive information on every topic from significant profile fluctuations to ability/achievement discrepancy tables. The Binet-4 alone has three manuals and the WISC-III manual also meets high standards. Given the high quality of new manuals, it is no longer necessary to emphasize administration and scoring procedures in a textbook such as this one. Consequently, this book emphasizes the proper interpretation of intelligence tests in the context of a youngster's life circumstances. Interpretation is the crux of the assessment endeavor that is not addressed adequately in many test manuals.

2. *Apply simple step-by-step interpretive methods.* New students of assessment need structure in their early attempts at test interpretation. My book provides a simple method of interpretation that can be applied to *all* measures of intelligence. Several devices are included to enhance the logical processes of assessment, beginning with test selection and concluding with the reporting of results.

3. *Maintain an emphasis on interpretive process over specific tests.* Related to the previous point is the goal to emphasize clear interpretative thinking rather than the use of a particular test. A truly suspect test can be useful in the hands of a gifted clinician. In addition, new tests are being produced at such a rapid rate that it is more important that clinicians have the interpretive skills necessary to adopt a new test and use it properly.

4. *Foster a deeper understanding of the intelligence construct.* Chapters 2 and 3 are devoted to

theory and research findings separately in order to foster a deeper understanding of the nature of the construct that these tests purport to measure. Clinicians receive tough questions from parents and teachers about intelligence tests, and they must be able to respond in an enlightened fashion. Chapter 6 includes an expanded section on test bias to allow clinicians to speak to this topic with authority. If students simply study tests, they may think that Wechsler was famous among intelligence theorists. Not to take anything away from Wechsler, but he was a gifted clinician who made practical contributions to the field. The sophisticated clinician should be able to cite numerous individuals who have made less visible but nonetheless important theoretical contributions that may lead to tests of the future and valid inferences in the present.

5. *Enhance readability.* My text is written to communicate with *beginning* graduate students, not advanced students who have completed previous assessment coursework. I have attempted to write the copy in a conversational style and limit "psychobabble" when possible. Drafts of the text were used in numerous assessment classes prior to publication in order to ensure readability.

6. *Maintain the interest of students.* Several measures were taken to improve student interest and comprehension. Case studies, anecdotes, research reports, and chapter questions are interspersed throughout the text to give students a respite from some of the difficult copy while simultaneously being instructive.

7. *Strive to communicate the state of the art.* While it is impossible to include every test and every new test as it is published, it is desirable to include newer techniques that apply to the interpretation of all tests including intelligence tests. Consequently, this edition is far different from the first.

8. *Emphasize learning by example.* I have found it difficult to teach students about assessment without examples. My students have always forced me to "concretize" the process for them. They crave opportunities to see tests administered and review sample reports. Hence, this text includes case after sample case. These cases provide students with numerous concrete models to emulate.

Uses of the Book

This book was written with several potential uses in mind. While its central purpose is to serve the instructor in a first graduate course in intellectual assessment, it will also be useful as a "refresher" for the clinician who was trained some time ago and seeks some updating. This book may also serve as a companion text in an assessment course. While the book is a teaching text, there is also a need for resource texts, so that the professor can emphasize specific tests or assessment procedures. This book may also be used with Dr. Alan Kaufman's (1990) book, *Assessing Adolescent and Adult Intelligence*, for a course that covers both child and adult intellectual assessment.

Intended Audience

Psychologists have traditionally been charged with the assessment of children's intelligence. This book was intended to communicate to psychologists in training and assumes a certain amount of psychological background. This text may also be used with other trainees, such as educational diagnosticians, who have a similar educational background but are simply not called psychologists. This text may be useful to some educational policy makers and others who are charged with developing assessment or diagnostic guidelines for children and adolescents.

ACKNOWLEDGMENTS

First, I wish to applaud and express my thanks to Cheryl Hendry, Mary Kral, and Ellen Rowe. Their work makes me proud to have them as colleagues. I also wish to express my deep gratitude to the legions of individuals who assisted with either the first or second editions including Dr. Kathy Smith, Dr. Marion Huettner, Dr. Carol Schmitt, Karen Pleiss, Dr. Lori Unruh, Kimberley Wells-Hatton, Dr. Alison Lorys, Dr. Pat Goodyear, Dr. Jose Gonzalez, Dr. Janna Dresden, Dr. Jerry Slotkin, Connie Silberman, Dr. Brian Nicoll, A. Shayne Abelkop, Dr. Leslie Platt, Wanda Sanders, Michael Perla, Carolyn Brennan, and Dr. Nancy Lett.

Many colleagues provided assistance at various stages. Some contributed ideas for psychological reports, and others provided encouragement, feedback and advice on various aspects of the book. I especially appreciate the contributions of Dr. George Hynd, Dr. Paul Frick, Dr. Marion Ego, Dr. Gail Matazow, Dr. Jack Naglieri, Dr. Michael Shapiro, Dr. Janet Martin, Dr. Mary Shapiro, Dr. Roy Martin, Dr. Mark Daniel, and Dr. Ben Lahey.

Invaluable critical feedback came from numerous colleagues, who provided anonymous but skilled reviews. The insights and suggestions of same substantially improved this edition.

Most importantly, this book would not have been possible without the intellectual leadership of colleagues and mentors. In this regard I owe a great debt to Dr. Alan S. Kaufman, Dr. Cecil R. Reynolds, Dr. Ronald Havens, Mr. Pete Prunkl, Dr. Carl Huberty, Mr. Dennis Campbell, Dr. Paul Caillier, and Dr. John Nolan.

Finally, the contributions of Mylan Jaixen, Sue Hutchinson, and Rebecca Pascal of Allyn and Bacon are gratefully acknowledged. Their editorial experience coupled with their considerable expertise served to encourage high-quality work at every step of the writing process.

CHAPTER 1

History

. . . [C]onfusion can arise if one focuses more of the actual tasks assembled in a test than on the underlying ability. This is an issue that bears on matters of test use in predicting educational or occupational success. . . . Perhaps this point can be clarified and reinforced by noting that nobody would challenge the use of opticians' Snellen charts in appraising visual acuity, even though performance in reading such letter charts is unlikely to be directly involved in occupations in which high visual acuity is required. (Carroll, 1993, p. 24)

CHAPTER QUESTIONS

Why were intelligence tests invented?

What are some of the more significant intelligence tests, from a historical perspective?

Who are the creators of modern intelligence tests?

How was the IQ score invented?

The Ubiquitous Nature of Testing

Consider, for example, the typical user of this book. The reader was likely "tested" on a 10-point rating scale of general health status at birth, namely, the Apgar test. Other "tests" soon followed such as measures of height, weight, and, perhaps, physician or other observations of temperament. Medical-related testing then gave way to educational testing in the preschool years. Children are then typically "screened" for kindergarten readiness using scales that assess language development, behavior problems, basic concept knowledge, and other constructs. The educational testing process gathers momentum in elementary school when a child is subjected to teacher-made tests, performance assessments, group-administered, survey-level achievement batteries (often administered in the Spring of alternate academic years), creativity evaluations for gifted program entry, and teacher ratings of classroom behavior among many other evaluations.

Of course, secondary school and university testing is no small matter. The Scholastic Achievement Tests (SAT), American College Testing Program (ACT), high school competency exams, class tests, driving tests, Graduate Record Examination (GRE) and teacher/professor ratings of musical and other talents are significant testing enterprises. Finally, the reader is likely embarking on a professional development track that will result in lifelong testing, including degree-qualifying exams, licensure exams, board specialty examinations, oral ethics examinations, and other "tests." And now, as if this is not enough testing, intelligence and other functions can be "tested" on the World Wide Web at sites such as

Emotional intelligence	www.utne.com/cgl-bin/eq
New age IQ test	www.salemctr.com/iqtest.html
Mensa	www.canada.mensa.org/mensa/workout.html
An easy IQ Test	www.iqtest.com

Intelligence tests are but one component of the substantial testing to which many individuals are exposed over the course of their development. Part of the blame rests with the early intelligence testers who demonstrated that it was possible to systematically assess a variety of human traits. The achievement testing movement, in particular, can easily be identified as having roots in the early intelligence testing movement (French & Hale, 1990). Moreover, intelligence testing, for the most part, predates modern methods of personality assessment. In fact, some personality test items, such as thematic storytelling methods, can be traced directly to research and development in intelligence testing (Kamphaus & Frick, 1996).

Further evidence of the influence of intelligence testing on U.S. culture can be found by perusing the popular media. The term *IQ* enjoys frequent usage in American society in particular. The interested reader can investigate this phe-nomenon by simply recording the number of occasions that the term *IQ* is heard or seen in any given week. One is likely to hear references to basketball IQ, social IQ, exercise IQ, or tax IQ. This chapter summarizes some of the historical events and trends that brings intelligence testing practice to the present day, where in numerous cultures, intelligence testing and its terminology is as prevalent as ever. The reader is cautioned, however, that there are other important milestones that will not be discussed because of space considerations. Other historical events of interest can be found in sources such as Jenkins and Paterson (1961), DuBois (1970), and Thorndike and Lohman (1990).

Historical Knowledge

New intelligence tests and revisions of older tests continue to be released at a steady rate. Some of these tests may purport to assess new abilities, whereas others may claim to be culture fair due to their use of nonverbal test stimuli. Such tests can be evaluated for use according to their research foundation, theory, cost, practicality, and a variety of other considerations, including historical precedent. There are, as the reader will soon know, numerous previous efforts to develop so-called "culture fair" tests and measures of attentional abilities, most of which have not met user expectations for validity evidence. A user with this knowledge of history will be a better and appropriately skeptical consumer of new "innovations" in intelligence testing technology. The history of research and development in intelligence testing is fraught with repeated missteps and failures; with the several attempts to "raise" intelligence being among them (Spitz, 1986a). Every new offering of tests and theories that promises "breakthroughs" challenges the psychologist to be well versed in history. Consequently, this volume begins with an overview of pertinent historical milestones in an attempt to make the reader a better consumer and, of greater importance, a sophisticated test user who aspires to the highest standards of psychological assessment practice.

Knowledge of intelligence testing history also has the potential to enhance psychological assessment practice by improving the ability of the psychologist to answer queries from clients and the public, such as parents and teachers. These consumers of psychological test data can bring historical issues to the meeting with the psychologist who is charged with explaining intelligence test results and other findings. Parents may ask questions about tests that they took as children, and teachers may wish to know the differences between a new test and the method formerly used by the school district.

A perhaps more important advantage of historical knowledge is that it allows the psychologist to develop a depth of understanding of intelligence testing issues that is difficult to attain otherwise. The historically conversant intelligence test user knows how the IQ metric came about and has a better understanding of its limitations. Other equally important perspectives that are developed through such study include an appreciation of the often tenuous relationship of intelligence testing to theory, and a thorough understanding of the initial rationale for intelligence test and item development. Knowledge of these and other historical perspectives allows the test user to interpret modern tests with additional skill.

Knowledge of historical developments is equally important for evaluating changes in the intelligence testing field. E. G. Boring (1929) eloquently described the importance of historical knowledge for evaluating scientific progress in his textbook:

The experimental psychologist, so it has always seemed to me, needs historical sophistication within his own sphere of expertness. Without such knowledge he sees the present in distorted perspective, he mistakes old facts and old views for new, and he remains unable to evaluate the significance of new movements and new methods. In this manner I can hardly state my case too strongly. A psychological sophistication that contains no component of historical orientation seems to me to be no sophistication at all. (p. vii)

EARLY HISTORY

While the roots of psychological testing cannot be traced to a particular culture, individual, or event (Anastasi, 1988), there is considerable agreement that the practice of assessing individual skills and abilities using formal "tests" is an ancient one. The Chinese, for example, were reportedly using civil service examinations as long as 3,000 years ago (DuBois, 1970). The idea of individual differences in human performance was mentioned by great thinkers as diverse as Socrates, Plato, Mohammedan rulers, and Charles Darwin (French & Hale, 1990).

An early intelligence test, described by Sir Anthony Fitzherbert, was published in 1534. This test was intended to differentiate between the "idiot" and the "lunatic." He described his crude measure of intelligence as follows (as cited by Pintner, 1923):

And he who shall be said to be a sot and idiot from his birth, is such a person who cannot account or number 20 pence, nor can tell who was his father or mother, nor how old he is, etc., so as it may appear that he hath no understanding of reason what shall be for his profit, nor what for his loss. But if hath such understanding, that he know and understand his letters, and do read by teaching or information of another man, then it seemeth that he is not a sot nor a natural idiot. (p. 6)

While numerous authors and theoreticians throughout history have mentioned individual differences, it has been only during the last 100 years that formal procedures for the measurement of human abilities have been in widespread use. The relative recency of the development of measures of intelligence may at least partially explain the considerable excitement and satisfaction on the part of early developers of psychometric measures. Emblematic of the excitement of the early test developers is the comment by Goddard (1912) describing the 1905 Binet-Simon scale, when he stated that "the scale would one day take a place in history of science beside Darwin's theory of evolution and Mendel's laws of heredity" (p. 326). The scientific merit of the work of the early test developers has and will continue to be debated. These individuals may be viewed as either true pioneers who changed dramatically the way people think about individual differences, or as scientists who strayed far from the path to scientific truth. It can be said with greater certainty, however, that the introduction of practical intelligence tests spurred the development of a great variety of measures of human abilities and skills, including academic achievement measures and employee selection tests in the 1920s.

Developments in Experimental Psychology

Wundt's Laboratory

The pioneering efforts of early intelligence test researchers were made possible in part by developments in experimental psychology (Anastasi, 1988). It is a well-known fact to students of psychology that intelligence testing is about 100 years old. Not so coincidentally, experimental psychology also traces its roots to the opening of Wilhelm Wundt's lab in Leipzig, Germany, in 1879. Many early efforts at measuring intelligence used tests that were developed in early experimental psychology laboratories. For example, Wundt and his first assistant, the American James McKeen Cattell, found numerous individual differences on measures of sensory abilities and reaction time. These types of measures were later incorporated into intelligence tests developed by Cattell and Sir Francis Galton. Cattell made numerous contributions to the development of the testing movement in the United States, not the least of which was coining the term *mental test*.

It also became clear in early laboratory experiments that experimental conditions had to be carefully controlled in order to achieve reliable findings (Anastasi, 1988). The notion of "control" refers to the need to eliminate the effects of

unwanted variables in the experiment. If one is interested in assessing individual differences in intelligence, then it would be wise to control for unwanted factors such as fatigue by ensuring that the examinee is well rested. Similarly, in Wundt's lab it was discovered that tests of physical skill, such as reaction time, had to be administered under consistent conditions in order to serve as reliable and valid measures of individual differences. The association of experimental control and mental measurement, thus, was established early on. To this day, standardized (carefully controlled) procedures are a hallmark of individual intelligence testing.

Sir Francis Galton

Clearly, numerous early theorists and researchers were convinced that intelligence was an inherited trait. They considered the inheritance of intelligence to be so substantial that intelligence could be measured and studied in much the same way as other inherited characteristics such as height. The Englishman Sir Francis Galton was a contemporary of Cattell's who was keenly interested in the inheritance of mental abilities. Galton (1869/1978) strongly believed that intelligence was inherited and that it could be objectively measured, as is evident from the following quote:

> *I acknowledge freely the great power of education and social influences in developing the active powers of the mind, just as I acknowledge the effect of use in developing the muscles of the blacksmith's arm, and no further. Let the blacksmith labor as he will, he will find that there are certain feats beyond his power that are well within the strength of a man of herculean make, even although the latter may have led a sedentary life. (Jenkins & Paterson, 1961, p. 1)*

Galton developed a battery of tests that he thought would allow him to study the inheritance of intelligence. His tests were similar in content to the tests of sensory and physical skill used by experimental psychologists such as Cattell. Galton viewed the use of these psychophysical measures as sensible because, he reasoned, if all information is obtained through the senses, then intelligent individuals must have very capable sensory abilities (Galton, 1883). Galton's tests were introduced to the public at the 1884 International Exhibition in London, where an individual could get his or her intelligence tested for three pence (Anastasi, 1988).

Galton made many other contributions to the study of individual differences, including laying the groundwork for the understanding of the normal curve. In 1869 he concluded, "Hence we arrive at the undeniable . . . that eminently gifted men are raised as much above mediocrity as idiots are depressed below it . . ." (Jenkins & Paterson, 1961, p. 16). This was an important insight into the nature of individual differences, as it operationalized what many people knew intuitively: There are many more people in the middle of the intelligence distribution than there are at either high or low levels of intelligence. The properties of the normal curve are the foundation of what has been called "classical test theory." The normal curve is also the foundation for much of the interpretive work in intelligence assessment.

Early American Work

Shortly after Galton's original work on intelligence appeared, similar efforts were carried out in the United States. Cattell carried on the tradition of the measurement of sensory and physical characteristics for the purposes of intellectual assessment when he returned to the United States, where he eventually joined the faculty of Columbia College (now Columbia University). The central problem with the use of psychophysical measures of intelligence, their *lack of correlation with school achievement*, became clear in the work at Columbia.

Prior to this time, however, there was not a consensus regarding validity standards (von Mayrhauser, 1992). The concept of criterion-related validity did not gain widespread acceptance until the 1920s. Thus, Wissler's work may

have not been considered conclusive for deciding the utility of Cattell's instruments.

Wissler (1901) reported that every student at Columbia College was required to take an annual psychological examination that was designed by Cattell and his colleagues. This annual psychological exam included the following tests, some of which are direct descendants of measures developed in Wundt's lab:

Perception of Size	Size of Head
Strength of Hand	Fatigue
Eyesight	Color Vision
Hearing	Perception of Pitch
Sensation Areas	Sensitiveness to Pain
Color Preference	Reaction Time
Rate of Perception	Naming Colors
Rate of Movement	Accuracy of Movement
Association	Imagery
Rhythm and Perception of Time	
Perception of Weight or Force of Movement	
Memory (Auditory, Visual, Logical, Retrospective)	

Some interesting results from Wissler's research that highlight the problem of the lack of correlation of early mental tests with academic achievement are given in Table 1.1.

Inspection of Wissler's data in Table 1.1 leads inevitably to the conclusion that the best mental test correlates of achievement are achievement-like measures. Tests of physical attributes are clearly inferior correlates. Specifically, measures of sensory abilities (e.g., reaction time) and physical attributes have very weak correlations with achievement. On the other hand, proficiency in school subjects such as Latin had a considerably more positive relationship with other areas of achievement such as mathematics. The Columbia College study revealed that the challenge remained in 1901 to develop a practical measure of intelligence that would correlate satisfactorily with important criterion variables

TABLE 1.1   Correlations of psychology clinic measures with measures of academic achievement from Wissler's (1901) research

Strength of hand and class standing	−.08
Fatigue and class standing	+.23
Reaction time and class standing	−.02
Association time and class standing	+.08
Naming the colors and class standing	+.02
Logical memory and class standing	+.19
Auditory memory and class standing	+.16
Logical memory and mathematics	+.11
Logical memory and Latin	+.22
Latin and mathematics	+.58
Latin and rhetoric	+.55
Rhetoric and mathematics	+.51
German and mathematics	+.52

such as academic attainment or occupational success. A breakthrough that solved this problem was already in the making in France.

The Societal Need

Like other scientific breakthroughs, the development of intelligence tests was carried out in response to a societal need. Modern intelligence testing can be traced most directly to the concern and need for the *humane treatment of individuals with mental retardation* that was exemplified by the work of pioneers such as Itard (1896–1962) and Sequin (1866–1907) in France and Wilbur and Howe in the United States. Prior to the work of Itard and Sequin, individuals with mental retardation were generally scorned and subjected to inhumane treatment. This lack of respect for individuals afflicted with mental retardation was evident during the Renaissance, when it was commonly believed that mentally retarded individuals were the children of Satan (Pintner, 1923). Logically it followed that if these individuals were possessed by demons, severe forms of treatment were required to drive the evil from them. Frequently, people with mental retardation or illness were whipped, bound with chains, and placed in dungeons until they changed their ways.

Itard and Sequin worked in the days of considerable optimism when they were primarily interested in developing cures for mental retardation. Common to all of their approaches was an emphasis on motor and sensory training to raise the intellectual levels of these individuals (Spitz, 1986a). It is interesting and perhaps not accidental that the emphasis on sensory ability as central to the treatment of mental retardation coincides with the common practice at the time of assessing sensory skills as measures of intelligence.

Interest in the treatment of mental retardation was also strong in the United States at this time. Two special residential schools for the treatment of mental retardation were established in Massachusetts in the mid-1800s. In 1876 the Association of Medical Officers of American Institutions for Idiots and Feeble Minded Persons, now called the American Association on Mental Retardation, was founded. The early special schools in the United States have been cited as early failures, which resulted in considerable pessimism among early American leaders of the movement (J. F. Gardner, 1993).

Of course, to first identify mentally retarded individuals for treatment, it was necessary to develop appropriate diagnostic criteria and procedures. As a result, the need for intelligence tests to diagnose mental retardation was clear. This need for accurate measures of intelligence, particularly measures of children's intelligence, provided an impetus for research and development in intelligence testing.

THE FIRST BREAKTHROUGH

Given the need expressed by European governments (particularly France) for the accurate diagnosis of children's intelligence and the failed efforts of Cattell and Galton at providing measures that correlated adequately with school achievement, the stage was set for some individual or group of individuals to overcome the predictive validity barrier and meet the societal need. In his 1901 presidential address to the American Psychological Association, Joseph Jastrow was optimistic about the prospects of a breakthrough in intelligence testing. He portrayed the future of intelligence testing as bright in the following passage from his speech:

> *The study of normal efficiency of that composite group of processes which contribute to our common humanity has, I confidently believe, an important and a practical future. Its progress is dependent upon careful analysis, upon systematic investigation, upon the cooperative and the coordinate labors of many, upon interpretive skill and psychological insight. An auspicious start has been made; the day of the production of works and fruit cannot be far off. (Jenkins & Paterson, 1961, p. 31)*

It was only a few years later that the breakthrough Jastrow envisioned occurred. Alfred Binet and Theophilius Simon (1905) produced the first technological breakthrough in intelligence testing by developing the first practical intelligence test battery. (See Research Report 1.1 for a history of Binet's earlier work in hypnosis and other areas.) It was practical in the sense that it assessed "higher"-level cognitive skills and, as a result, produced substantial correlations with measures of school achievement. As Boring (1929) observed, "Binet was seeking to measure the intellectual faculties, the complex mental processes, whereas Galton measured only simple capacities, hoping vainly that they might have some significance for the 'intellect.' Binet was right, Galton was wrong . . ." (p. 546).

The 1905 Scale

The 1905 scale consisted of 29 tests. It is notable that Binet and Simon retained some of the psychophysical measures of the past such as "com-

paring two weights." On the other hand, most of the "new" tests departed from past practice by measuring higher-level reasoning abilities. The inclusion of tests such as "reply to an abstract question" and "defining abstract terms" was intended to measure more complex cognitive activities. Some of the tests on the 1905 scale were as follows:

Following a moving object with one's eyes
Grasping a small object which is seen
Finding and eating a square of chocolate wrapped in paper
Naming objects in pictures
Comparing two weights
Susceptibility to suggestion
Defining common words by function
Repeating a sentence of 15 words
Memory for pictures
Drawing a design from memory
Telling how two common objects are alike
Making rhymes
Using three words in a sentence
Reply to an abstract question
Defining abstract terms

Binet validated his tests by administering them to groups of normal and mentally retarded children and determining the ability of each measure to differentiate these two distinct groups. An interesting fact is that Binet used the commonsense judgment of parents and teachers to form his groups of normal and mentally retarded youngsters (Pintner, 1923). As such, society's informal conceptions of who was or was not intelligent played a central role in the validation of this most important measure.

Content Validity

Binet also recognized that if verbal tests were to be used, they should not be too closely related to school tasks. If his tests were too similar to school

RESEARCH REPORT 1.1

Binet's Biography

In a series of articles published in the early 1960s, Theta Wolf (1961, 1964, 1966) documents some of the less well-known aspects of Binet's career and personal life. Through interviews with Binet's faithful colleague, Simon, and reviews of Binet's papers, she gives some valuable insight into the nature of Binet's persona and the early beginnings of intelligence test development. This series of papers must be read by any student of Binet's work.

Binet was in some ways a late bloomer and merely happened upon the area of intellectual assessment. He published his first paper in 1880 at the age of 23. The first 10 years of his career were tumultuous. He began as an "armchair" psychologist who used techniques such as hypnosis to study hysterics. By 1891 his career had reached a low point as is described aptly by Wolf (1964).

> He had become a man almost bereft of theoretical underpinnings, and, what was worse, even of the "facts" on which he had been so sure he could count, whatever theories might be built out of them. . . . They were years in which his own studies and controversies led him into blind alleys and humiliating defeats. (p. 702)

The birth of Binet's children, Madeleine in 1885 and Alice in 1887, may have helped him sharpen his interests in individual differences. First, he noted continuing temperamental differences between his daughters. He described Madeleine as "silent, cool, concentrated, while Alice was a laugher, gay, thoughtless, giddy, and turbulent" (cited in Wolf, 1966). Binet began experimenting with his daughters, studying changes such as dominance (e.g., handedness) and reaction time. He concluded early on that higher-level cognitive tasks would be necessary to differentiate child and adult intelligence. He demonstrated this using a task where the subject was asked to discriminate lines of different lengths; two lines of differing lengths on five cards (Wolf, 1966). He found that his two daughters could discriminate the lines on all of the cards except the last one, and, when he showed the cards to two adults they had the same success rate as the children. This important experiment, showing a lack of age differentiation for a sensory task, thus led him to depart from his contemporaries who were using psychophysical measures of intelligence.

What was Binet like? Wolf (1966) describes him as shy and somewhat uncomfortable in social situations. Some of his colleagues described him as demanding and difficult to work with. He was also very selective about his colleagues. Simon apparently worked diligently to endear himself to Binet in order to get a chance to work in his laboratory. Simon also hypothesized that Binet would not tolerate teaching well as he would likely have had little patience for students. Simon's perseverance, however, was rewarded with the admiration of his mentor. Binet said of Simon,

> I have had many students and collaborators, but I have never had any as sincere and as loyal as Simon. And another thing, never would he say "yes" to me when he thought "no." (p. 247, cited by Wolf, 1961)

---

tasks, then they could be said to measure academic achievement and not intelligence. Consistent with his idea that his test had to be obviously different from achievement tests, he proposed the following three methods of the study of intelligence and showed how intelligence testing differed from other types of assessment:

1. *The medical method*, which aims to appreciate the anatomical, physiological, and pathological signs of inferior intelligence.

2. *The pedagogical method*, which aims to judge the intelligence according to the sum of acquired knowledge.

3. *The psychological method*, which makes direct observations and measurements of the degree of intelligence.

Binet and Simon (1905) stated further:

> Our purpose is to evaluate a level of intelligence. It is understood that we here separate natural intelligence

and instruction. It is the intelligence alone that we seek to measure, by disregarding, insofar as possible, the degree of instruction the subject possesses. He should, indeed, be considered by the examiner as a complete ignoramus knowing neither how to read nor write. This necessity forces us to forego a great many exercises having verbal, literary or scholastic character. These belong to a pedagogical examination. (p. 93)

Binet and Simon, then, placed considerable emphasis on the establishment of content validity for their scale, an emphasis that has been lacking in many subsequent measures. Many modern tests such as the WISC and the latest edition of the Binet, the Binet 4, include arithmetic and other school-related items, whereas the original Binet scale tried to avoid such items (Kamphaus, 1987).

Binet and Simon proposed the purposes outlined below for their test battery in 1905. These purposes have important implications for the interpretation and use of modern tests of intelligence. This is the case because, in many ways, intelligence testing has not changed a great deal since the time of Binet (Kumphaus, 1998).

Our purpose is to be able to measure the intellectual capacity of a child who is brought to us in order to know whether he is normal or retarded. We should, therefore, study his condition at the time and that only. We have nothing to do either with his history or with his future; consequently we shall neglect his etiology, and we shall make no attempt to distinguish between acquired and congenital idiocy; for a stronger reason we shall set aside all consideration of pathological anatomy which might explain his intellectual deficiency. So much for his past. As to that which concerns his future, we shall exercise the same abstinence; we do not attempt to establish or prepare a prognosis and we leave unanswered the question of whether this retardation is curable, or even improvable. We shall limit ourselves to ascertaining the truth in regard to his present mental state. (Jenkins & Paterson, 1961, p. 90)

Binet and Simon elaborated on their earlier work in a 1908 paper where they proposed that one purpose of their measuring scale of intelligence is to be ". . . useful in formulating a course of instruction really adapted to their aptitudes" (Jenkins & Paterson, p. 103).

THE CONTRIBUTIONS OF TERMAN

Lewis Terman (1916) gave one of the first rationales for the use of intelligence tests. He was evidently very optimistic about the value of intellectual assessment. He proposed the use of intelligence tests for individual child study by saying:

Every child who fails in his school work or is in danger of failing should be given a mental examination. The examination takes less than one hour, and the result will contribute more to a real understanding of the case then anything else that could be done. It is necessary to determine whether a given child is unsuccessful in school because of poor native ability, or because of poor instruction, lack of interest, or some other removable cause. (p. 5)

Evidently Terman believed, as did many of his day, that intelligence tests were the best measures available of "innate intelligence." He also believed that if a trait like intelligence was inherited, then it was not malleable. It is important to be aware of the views of early intelligence researchers—that intelligence tests measured an unmalleable and inherited trait—because those views have shaped the opinions of some scientists and society at large.

Terman (1916) produced the most successful of the English translations of Binet's work. His scale, the Stanford-Binet, met high psychometric standards for the time. He took great pains, for example, to collect a U.S. norming sample. He also introduced the concept of the *intelligence quotient* (IQ), which was originally the invention of a German scientist named William Stern (Boring, 1929). Hence, the IQ score is one of Terman's contributions to intelligence testing and not a contribution of Binet. In fact, Simon stood in opposition to the use of the intelligence quotient (Wolf, 1961). This original IQ was called a Ratio IQ, using the formula IQ = 100 × MA/CA, where MA equals the child's mental age (as typically determined by the number of tests a child passed that were designated for a particular age group of children) and CA equals the child's chronological age in years and months. When this formula was used, a child who passed few of the tests designated for his or her age group would have a lower MA than CA, which would result in an IQ less than 100. Conversely, the child who passed all of the tests designated for his or her age group and perhaps some for an older age group would obtain an IQ higher than 100. Unfortunately, this Ratio IQ metric has some rather severe psychometric limitations (Davis, 1964). It was soon replaced by Wechsler's so-called Deviation IQ (actually a standard score; see Chapter 5).

Terman participated in the development of several subsequent revisions of the Stanford-Binet. The various editions of the Stanford-Binet are listed below:

YEAR	TEST	AUTHORS
1916	Stanford-Binet Intelligence Scale This was the version that popularized the term *IQ*.	L. Terman
1937	Stanford-Binet Intelligence Scale This version of the Binet had two forms (versions) L and M.	L. Terman, M. Merrill
1960	Stanford-Binet Intelligence Scale Form L-M For this scale the two 1937 forms were combined into one again.	L. Terman, M. Merrill
1972	Stanford-Binet Intelligence Scale Form L-M This version was revised under the direction of Robert L. Thorndike.	L. Terman, M. Merrill
1986	Stanford-Binet Intelligence Scale Fourth Edition	R. L. Thorndike, R. Hagen, J. M. Sattler

Early workers in intelligence testing were also keenly aware of the limitations of the popular tests of the day. Terman called for intelligence tests that gave more than just global estimates of ability. He noted the need for tests of specific abilities. Terman (1916) compared the need for more specific tests of ability to medical diagnosis by proposing:

It is necessary to have a definite and accurate diagnosis, one which will differentiate more finely the many degrees and qualities of intelligence. Just as in the case of physical illness, we need to know not merely that the patient is sick, but also why he is sick, what organs are involved, what course the illness will run, what physical work the patient can readily undertake . . . .(p. 23)

Terman stated further that Binet also agreed with this point of view. Terman (1916) believed that "Binet fully appreciated the fact that intelligence is not homogeneous, that it has many aspects, and that no one kind of test will display it adequately" (p. 36). It is interesting that one of the "modern" trends in intelligence theory today is to speak of multiple intelligences (e.g. Sternberg, 1987). Terman argued this same point of the multifaceted nature of intelligence over a half century ago!

Terman also agreed with other intellectual assessment pioneers such as Binet and Simon who emphasized the importance of devising tests that limit the impact of formal schooling on the results. Terman (1916), in describing the development of verbal comprehension items, stated, "In developing tests of this kind we should, of course, have to look out for the influences of formal instruction" (p. 337). This problem of the overlap of the assessment of school achievement and intelligence remains as a nagging interpretive dilemma for users of these tests even today.

WORLD WAR I

Intelligence testing received considerable attention in the United States during World War I. During the war, Robert Yerkes directed an assessment committee of the American Psychological Association that was eventually charged with the screening of about a million and a half potential soldiers (Anastasi, 1988). It was this group of psychologists that developed the first group-administered tests of intelligence.

A Graduate Student's Insight

As it turns out, this group of researchers benefited greatly from the pioneering work of a student of Lewis Terman's by the name of Arthur Otis (Lennon, 1985). Otis began as an engineering student who switched majors to psychology and became intrigued with the work of Terman. While Otis was convinced that Terman was correct in arguing that every schoolchild should receive an individual evaluation in order to understand him/her better, Otis wondered if this was truly practical. He reasoned that if children could be tested in groups that they could, in fact, all receive an evaluation of their intelligence. Otis describes how he became involved in this undertaking in a 1959 television interview with Walter Durost. Otis describes his involvement in a response to a question by Durost as follows (as cited by Lennon, 1985):

Otis: Yes. Well, when World War I began, Major Yerkes, a psychologist at Yale University, conceived the idea that it would be very desirable to test the intelligence of the draftees as soon as they came into the Army so that the superior officers could pick out officer material and could place the men in the various functions of the Army to the best advantage. So he invited some other psychologists, Drs. Whipple, Terman, and Haggerty, to form with him a committee to consider the possibility of doing this testing. It was Major Yerkes' idea at the time that they would have to train a lot of psychologists to give the Binet. He didn't know anything about any group tests. . . . So, fortunately perhaps, Dr. Terman presumably had a copy of my test in his pocket with him at the time. You see this incident occurred, this incident of World War I—just at the time that I was finishing my doctor's degree, and I had this manuscript of the test and it was pretty well standardized. Dr. Terman had been convinced that it was fairly sound and workable, and so he probably told him that they needn't bother with giving the Binet to everybody because there's a young fellow out at the University in my class who has made up a group test. He presumably convinced them that they should send for me and make up some group tests which, of course, was done. They enlisted the help of perhaps 100 or so psychologists from all over the country and we got together and made up as many items as we could. They just followed my group test. They said, "Wess, he made up opposites, we'll do that, and he made up analogies, we'll do that," and they made up groups of tests just of personnel of the Army. Very much to the surprise of everyone, including our psychologists, we found that the privates did the most poorly, and the corporals did better, and the sergeants did better, and the second lieutenants did better, and the first lieutenants did better, and the captains did better, and the majors did better, and the lieutenant colonels did better, and the colonels did better, and the majors, and the generals did the best of all. Well, that sold intelligence testing to the Army completely, of course. . .

Some insight into the inner workings of the eminent psychologists involved in the World War I testing effort is provided by von Mayrhauser (1992), a historian. Procedures that we consider settled by consensus today, such as basic issues regarding the demonstration of reliability, had to be worked out to the satisfaction of committee members and the military. The following quote by von Mayrhauser (1992) sheds some light on the early development and reliability and validity evidence that fostered acceptance of the committee's efforts.

> *During the summer of 1917, after Yerkes and Terman could not agree on whether to use the Stanford-Binet or the Yerkes point scale to demonstrate the reliability of alpha, Yerkes asked [E. L.] Thorndike and a statistical unit to settle the issue. Thorndike delivered two reports on August 15, which set the precedent for separating experimental reliability from a method of legitimation that required a criterion extrinsic to test construction. For his colleagues he demonstrated the consistency between alpha's component tests and previous test results. For the military, he correlated alpha's components with the officer ratings of "intelligence" that Scott had collected with his "Rating Scale for Selecting Captains." That scale sold the military on approving a Committee on Classification of Personnel in the Army. . . . Although the check against concurrent judgments did not impress Yerkes and Terman, it salvaged development of the instrument that would become the professions' most influential contribution to American Society. (p. 252)*

The Army Alpha (See Box 1.1) was used to screen most recruits, while the Army Beta, a non-verbal test, was used with nonreaders and those who did not speak English. Among other things, these tests highlighted the practical and cost-efficient nature of multiple-choice item types. As a result, these first group intelligence tests spawned the creation of similar tests for a variety of age groups and populations. Group intelligence testing soon became standard fare in American classrooms. The army recruit screening effort was seen as being so successful that the invention of these tests was cited as one of many factors that contributed to the winning of the war (French & Hale, 1990).

Controversy has surrounded intelligence testing since its inception. The use of tests to screen recruits led to some of the first controversial stances taken based on intelligence test results. It was found, for example, after the test results from the recruits were analyzed, that there were distinct group differences. After the war, it was reported that the recruits with the highest scores

were from England, Scotland, Canada, and Scandinavia, and those with the lowest scores were from Russia, Italy, and Poland (Eysenck & Kamin, 1981). Consequently, it was concluded that "Nordics" were genetically superior to their counterparts from "Alpine" and "Mediterranean" races (Eysenck & Kamin, 1981). In these early years it was a commonly held belief that intelligence tests measured genetic potential—a position not held by all psychologists of the day, including Binet (Eysenck & Kamin, 1981). Evidently, the stage was set early on for the nature/nurture debate regarding the determination of intelligence.

THE SECOND 50 YEARS

The 1920s

One of the most influential early theories of intelligence was popularized by Spearman (1927). In his frequently cited 1927 text, *The Abilities of Man*, Spearman defined his hierarchical model of intelligence. This model emanates largely from Spearman's pioneering work in factor analysis. At the top of Spearman's hierarchy is the *general factor* (general intelligence or "g"), the factor that explains most of the variance in the factor analytic solutions conducted by Spearman. While "g" is frequently the most important determinant of an individual's performance on a particular test, every test also required a *specific factor* ("s") or mental ability for the particular test. In Spearman's (1927) own words, the concepts of "g" and "s" are explained in the following manner:

> *The one part has been called the "general factor" and denoted by the letter g; it is so named because, although varying freely from individual to individual, it remains the same for any one individual in respect of all the correlated abilities. The second factor has been called the "specific factor" and denoted by the letter s. It not only varies from individual to individual, but even for any*

Box 1.1 A POST WORLD WAR I VERSION OF THE ARMY ALPHA

Prepared by
ELSIE O. BREGMAN, PH.D.

Copyright 1925
THE PSYCHOLOGICAL CORPORATION
522 FIFTH AVENUE
NEW YORK, N. Y.

REVISION OF ARMY ALPHA EXAMINATION
FORM A

Name _____ Date _____
Address _____ City _____ State _____ Age _____ Sex _____
In what country or state born? _____ Years in U. S. _____ Race _____
Draw a circle around the highest grade of school reached.
  Grades 1, 2, 3, 4, 5, 6, 7, 8; High or Prep School, Year 1, 2, 3, 4; College, Year 1, 2, 3, 4.

Occupation: From   To   Weekly Salary
  Present _____ Month _____ Year _____   Month _____ Year _____ $ _____
  Preceding _____ Month _____ Year _____   Month _____ Year _____ $ _____
  Preceding _____ Month _____ Year _____   Month _____ Year _____ $ _____
Remarks _____

Printed in U.S.A.   46-116T

Test 2

Get the answers to these examples as quickly as you can.
Place the answer to each example in the parentheses after the example.
Use the side of this page to figure on if you need to.

SAMPLES
{
1   How many are 5 men and 10 men? ....Answer (15   )
2   If you walk 4 miles an hour for 3 hours, how far do
    you walk? ....Answer (12   )

1   How many are 60 hats and 5 hats? .... (   )
2   If you save $9 a month for 3 months, how much will you save? .... (   )
3   If 48 men are divided into groups of 8, how many groups will there be? .... (   )
4   Mike had 11 cigars. He bought 2 more and then smoked 7. How many cigars did he have
    left? .... (   )
5   A man walked 8 miles and then walked back 2 miles. How far was he then from where he
    started? .... (   )
6   How many hours will it take a truck to go 42 miles at the rate of 3 miles an hour? .... (   )
7   How many pencils can you buy for 60 cents at the rate of 2 for 5 cents? .... (   )
8   A company of Boy Scouts marched 40 miles in five days. The first day they marched 9
    miles, the second day 6 miles, the third 10 miles, the fourth 6 miles. How many miles did
    they march the last day? .... (   )
9   If you buy 2 packages of tobacco at 8 cents each and a pipe for 65 cents, how much change
    should you get from a two-dollar bill? .... (   )
10 If it takes 4 men 3 days to dig a 120-foot drain, how many men are needed to dig it in half
    a day? .... (   )
11 A dealer bought some mules for $2,000. He sold them for $2,400, making $50 on each
    mule. How many mules were there? .... (   )
12 A rectangular bin holds 200 cubic feet of lime. If the bin is 10 feet long and 5 feet wide,
    how deep is it? .... (   )
13 A recruit spent one-eighth of his spare change for post cards and twice as much for a box
    of letter paper, and then had $1.00 left. How much money did he have at first? .... (   )
14 If 3½ tons of clover cost $14, what will 6½ tons cost? .... (   )
15 A ship has provisions to last her crew of 700 men 2 months. How long would it last 400
    men? .... (   )
16 If an aeroplane goes 250 yards in 10 seconds, how many feet does it go in a fifth of a sec-
    ond? .... (   )
17 A submarine makes 8 miles an hour under water and 20 miles on the surface. How long
    will it take to cross a 100-mile channel, if it has to go two-fifths of the way under water? (   )
18 If 134 men are to dig 3,618 yards of ditch, how many yards must be dug by each man?.... (   )
19 A certain division of the army contains 5,000 artillery, 15,000 infantry, and 1,000 cavalry.
    If each branch is expanded proportionately until there are in all 23,100 men, how many
    will be added to the artillery? .... (   )
20 A commission house which had already supplied 1,897 barrels of apples to a wholesaler
    delivered the remainder of its stock to 37 retailers. Of this remainder each retailer received
    54 barrels. What was the total number of barrels supplied? .... (   )

Score ....

Test 3

This is a test of common sense. Below are sixteen questions. Three answers are given to each question. You are to look at the answers carefully; then make a cross in the square before the best answer to each question, as in the sample:

Why do we use stoves? Because

SAMPLES $\left\{\begin{array}{l}\square \text{ they look well} \\ \boxtimes \text{ they keep us warm} \\ \square \text{ they are black}\end{array}\right.$

Here the second answer is the best one and is marked with a cross. Begin with No. 1 and keep on until time is called.

1   Cats are useful animals, because
   ☐ they catch mice
   ☐ they are gentle
   ☐ they are afraid of dogs

2   Shoes are made of leather, because
   ☐ it is tanned
   ☐ it is tough, pliable and warm
   ☐ it can be blackened

3   If it rains when you are starting to go for the doctor, what should you do?
   ☐ stay at home
   ☐ take an umbrella
   ☐ wait until it stops raining

4   The main reason why stone is used for building purposes is because
   ☐ it makes a good appearance
   ☐ it is strong and lasting
   ☐ it is heavy

5   Why is beef better food than cabbage? Because
   ☐ it tastes better
   ☐ it is more nourishing
   ☐ it is harder to obtain

6   If someone does you a favor, what should you do?
   ☐ try to forget it
   ☐ steal for him if he asks you to
   ☐ return the favor

7   Why is wheat better for food than corn? Because
   ☐ it is more nutritious
   ☐ it is more expensive
   ☐ it can be ground finer

8   The main thing the farmers do is to
   ☐ supply luxuries
   ☐ make work for the unemployed
   ☐ feed the nation

9   If a man who can't swim should fall into a river, he should
   ☐ yell for help and try to scramble out
   ☐ dive to the bottom and crawl out
   ☐ lie on his back and float

10   The feathers on a bird's wing help him to fly because they
   ☐ make a wide, light surface
   ☐ keep the air off his body
   ☐ keep the wings from cooling off too fast

11   All traffic going one way keeps to the same side of the street because
   ☐ most people are right handed
   ☐ the traffic policeman insists on it
   ☐ it avoids confusion and collisions

12   Why are criminals locked up?
   ☐ to protect society
   ☐ to get even with them
   ☐ to make them work

13   Why should a married man have his life insured? Because
   ☐ death may come at any time
   ☐ insurance companies are usually honest
   ☐ his family will not then suffer if he dies

14   In Leap Year February has 29 days because
   ☐ February is a short month
   ☐ some people are born on February 29th
   ☐ otherwise the calendar would not come out right

15   If you are held up and robbed in a strange city, you should
   ☐ apply to the police for help
   ☐ ask the first man you meet for money to get home
   ☐ borrow some money at a bank

16   Why do some men who could afford to own a house live in a rented one? Because
   ☐ they don't have to pay taxes
   ☐ they don't have to buy a rented one
   ☐ they can make more money by investing the money the house would cost

Score _____

Test 4

If the two words of a pair mean the same or nearly the same, draw a line under **same**. If they mean the opposite, or nearly the opposite, draw a line under **opposite**. If you cannot be sure, guess. The two samples are already marked as they should be.

SAMPLES $\Big\{$ good—bad ....same—<u>opposite</u>
little—small ....<u>same</u>—opposite

1	no—yes	same—opposite
2	day—night	same—opposite
3	go—leave	same—opposite
4	begin—commence	same—opposite
5	bitter—sweet	same—opposite
6	assume—suppose	same—opposite
7	command—obey	same—opposite
8	tease—plague	same—opposite
9	diligent—industrious	same—opposite
10	corrupt—honest	same—opposite
11	toward—from	same—opposite
12	masculine—feminine	same—opposite
13	complex—simple	same—opposite
14	sacred—hallowed	same—opposite
15	often—seldom	same—opposite
16	ancient—modern	same—opposite
17	enormous—gigantic	same—opposite
18	confer—grant	same—opposite
19	acquire—lose	same—opposite
20	compute—calculate	same—opposite
21	defile—purify	same—opposite
22	apprehensive—fearful	same—opposite
23	sterile—fertile	same—opposite
24	chasm—abyss	same—opposite
25	somber—gloomy	same—opposite
26	vestige—trace	same—opposite
27	vilify—praise	same—opposite
28	finite—limited	same—opposite
29	contradict—corroborate	same—opposite
30	immune—susceptible	same—opposite
31	credit—debit	same—opposite
32	assiduous—diligent	same—opposite
33	transient—permanent	same—opposite
34	palliate—mitigate	same—opposite
35	execrate—revile	same—opposite
36	extinct—extant	same—opposite
37	pertinent—relevant	same—opposite
38	synchronous—simultaneous	same—opposite
39	supercilious—disdainful	same—opposite
40	abstruse—recondite	same—opposite

Score (R-W) _____

Test 5

The words 'A EATS COW GRASS' in that order are mixed up and don't make a sentence; but they would make a sentence if put in the right order: 'A COW EATS GRASS,' and this statement is true.

Again, the words 'WHEELS SQUARE ARE ALL' would make a sentence if put in the order 'ALL WHEELS ARE SQUARE,' but this statement is false.

Below are twenty-four mixed-up sentences. Some of them are true and some are false. When I say 'begin,' take these sentences one at a time. Think what each **would** say if the words were straightened out, but don't write them yourself. Then, if what it **would** say is true, draw a line under the word 'true'; if what it **would** say is false, draw a line under the word 'false.' If you cannot be sure, guess. The two samples are already marked as they should be. Begin with No. 1 and work right down the page until time is called.

SAMPLES { a eats cow grass .... <u>true</u>—false
{ wheels square are all.. true—<u>false</u>

1 lemons yellow are..true—false

2 hear are with to ears..true—false

3 harness paper of made is..true—false

4 trees in nests build birds ....true—false

5 oil water not and will mix ....true—false

6 and cows from honey come bread...true—false

7 fuel wood are coal and for used ....true—false

8 moon earth the only from feet twenty the is.............................true—false

9 to life water is necessary ....true—false

10 are clothes all made cotton of...true—false

11 horses automobile an are than slower ....true—false

12 tropics is in the produced rubber ....true—false

13 leaves the trees in lose their fall...true—false

14 place pole is north comfortable a the ....true—false

15 sand of made bread powder and is..true—false

16 sails is steamboat usually by propelled a...................................true—false

17 is the salty in water all lakes..true—false

18 usually judge can we actions man his by a.................................true—false

19 men misfortune have good never ....true—false

20 tools valuable is for sharp making steel....................................true—false

21 due sometimes calamities are accident to..................................true—false

22 forget trifling friends grievances never ....true—false

23 feeling is of painful exaltation the...true—false

24 begin a and apple acorn ant words with the..............................true—false

Score (R−W) _____

Test 6

Look at each row of numbers below, and on the two dotted lines write the two numbers that should come next as in the samples.

2	4	6	8	10	12	14	16
9	8	7	6	5	4	3	2
2	2	3	3	4	4	5	5
1	7	2	7	3	7	4	7

SAMPLES {

3	4	5	6	7	8	____	____
8	7	6	5	4	3	____	____
10	15	20	25	30	35	____	____
9	9	7	7	5	5	____	____
3	6	9	12	15	18	____	____
8	1	6	1	4	1	____	____
5	9	13	17	21	25	____	____
8	9	12	13	16	17	____	____
27	27	23	23	19	19	____	____
1	2	4	8	16	32	____	____
19	16	14	11	9	6	____	____
11	13	12	14	13	15	____	____
2	3	5	8	12	17	____	____
18	14	17	13	16	12	____	____
29	28	26	23	19	14	____	____
20	17	15	14	11	9	____	____
81	27	9	3	1	$\frac{1}{3}$	____	____
1	4	9	16	25	36	____	____
16	17	15	18	14	19	____	____
3	6	8	16	18	36	____	____

Score _____

Test 7

In each of the lines below, the first two words are related to each other in some way. What you are to do in each line is to see what the relation is between the first two words, and underline the word in heavy type that is related in the same way to the third word. Begin with No. 1 and mark as many sets as you can before time is called. The samples are already marked as they should be.

SAMPLES
{
sky—blue :: **grass—table <u>green</u> warm big**
fish—swims :: **man—paper time <u>walks</u> girl**
day—night :: **white—red <u>black</u> clear pure**
}

1 shoe—foot :: **hat—kitten head knife penny**
2 pup—dog :: **lamb—red door sheep book**
3 spring—summer :: **autumn—winter warm harvest rise**
4 devil—angel :: **bad—mean disobedient defamed good**
5 finger—hand :: **toe—body foot skin nail**

6 legs—frog :: **wings—eat swim bird nest**
7 chew—teeth :: **smell—sweet stink odor nose**
8 lion—roar :: **dog—drive pony bark harness**
9 cat—tiger :: **dog—wolf bark bite snap**
10 good—bad :: **long—tall big snake short**

11 giant—large :: **dwarf—jungle small beard ugly**
12 winter—season :: **January—February day month Christmas**
13 skating—winter :: **swimming—diving floating hole summer**
14 blonde—light :: **brunette—dark hair brilliant blonde**
15 love—friend :: **hate—malice saint enemy dislike**

16 egg—bird :: **seed—grow plant crack germinate**
17 dig—trench :: **build—run house spade bullet**
18 agree—quarrell :: **friend—comrade need mother enemy**
19 palace—king :: **hut—peasant cottage farm city**
20 cloud-burst—shower :: **cyclone—bath breeze destroy West**

21 success—joy :: **failure—sadness success fail work**
22 parents—command :: **children—men shall women obey**
23 diamond—rare :: **iron—common silver ore steel**
24 yes—affirmative :: **no—think knowledge yes negative**
25 hour—day :: **day—night week hour noon**

26 eye—head :: **window—key floor room door**
27 clothes—man :: **hair—horse comb beard hat**
28 draw—picture :: **make—destroy table break hard**
29 automobile—wagon :: **motorcycle—ride speed bicycle car**
30 granary—wheat :: **library—read books paper chairs**

31 quarrel—enemy :: **agree—friend disagree agreeable foe**
32 razor—sharp :: **hoe—bury dull cuts tree**
33 esteem—despise :: **Friends—Quakers enemies lovers men**
34 abide—stay :: **depart—come hence leave late**
35 abundant—scarce :: **cheap—buy costly bargain nasty**

36 whale—large :: **thunder—loud rain lightning kill**
37 reward—hero :: **punish—God everlasting pain traitor**
38 music—soothing :: **noise—hear distracting sound report**
39 book—writer :: **statue—sculptor liberty picture state**
40 wound—pain :: **health—sickness disease exhilaration doctor**

Score _____

Test 8

Notice the sample sentence:

People hear with the   eyes   <u>ears</u>   nose   mouth

The correct word is **ears,** because it makes the truest sentence.

In each of the sentences below you have four choices for the last word. Only one of them is correct. In each sentence draw a line under the one of these four words which makes the truest sentence. If you cannot be sure, guess. The two samples are already marked as they should be.

SAMPLES { People hear with the   eyes   <u>ears</u>   nose   mouth
France is in   <u>Europe</u>   Asia   Africa   Australia

1   The **apple** grows on a   shrub   vine   bush   tree
2   **Five hundred** is played with   rackets   pins   cards   dice
3   The **Percheron** is a kind of   goat   horse   cow   sheep
4   The most prominent industry of **Gloucester** is   fishing   packing   brewing   automobiles
5   **Sapphires** are usually   blue   red   green   yellow
6   **Salsify** is a kind of   snake   fish   lizard   vegetable
7   **Timothy** is a kind of   corn   rye   wheat   hay
8   **Coral** is obtained from   mines   elephants   oysters   reefs
9   The **tuna** is a kind of   fish   bird   reptile   insect
10   The **rutabaga** is a   lizard   vegetable   fish   snake
11   **Artichoke** is a kind of   hay   corn   vegetable   fodder
12   **Chard** is a   fish   lizard   vegetable   snake
13   The **penguin** is a   bird   fish   reptile   insect
14   **Buenos Aires** is a city of   Spain   Brazil   Portugal   Argentina
15   **Ivory** is obtained from   elephants   mines   oysters   reefs
16   **Maise** is a kind of   corn   hay   oats   rice
17   The **armadillo** is a kind of   ornamental shrub   animal   musical instrument   dagger
18   The **tendon of Achilles** is in the   heel   head   shoulder   abdomen
19   **Cypress** is a kind of   machine   food   tree   fabric
20   An **aspen** is a   machine   fabric   tree   drink
21   The **sabre** is a kind of   musket   sword   cannon   pistol
22   The **mimeograph** is a kind of   typewriter   copying machine   phonograph   pencil
23   **Maroon** is a   food   fabric   drink   color
24   The **clarinet** is used in   music   stenography   book-binding   lithography
25   **Denim** is a   dance   food   fabric   drink
26   The author of **"Huckleberry Finn"** is   Pie   Mark Twain   Stevenson   Hawthorne
27   **Faraday** was most famous in   literature   war   religion   science
28   **Cerise** is a   color   drink   fabric   food
29   **Rubber** is obtained from   ore   petroleum   trees   hides
30   **Pasteur** is most famous in   politics   literature   war   science
31   **Arson** is a term used in   medicine   law   theology   pedagogy
32   **Turpentine** comes from   petroleum   ore   hides   trees
33   **Habeas corpus** is a term used in   medicine   law   theology   pedagogy
34   **Ensilage** is a term used in   fishing   athletics   farming   hunting
35   **Bile** is made in the   spleen   kidneys   stomach   liver
36   **General Lee** surrendered at Appomattox in   1812   1865   1886   1832
37   **Mauve** is the name of a   color   drink   fabric   food
38   **Mica** is a   vegetable   mineral   gas   liquid
39   **Napoleon** defeated the Austrians at   Friedland   Wagram   Waterloo   Leipzig
40   **Darwin** is most famous in   literature   science   war   politics

Score _____

one individual from each ability to another.... Although, however, both of these factors occur in every ability, they need not be equally influential in all.... At one extreme lay the talents for classics, where the ratio of the influence of "g" to "s" was rated to be as high as 15 to 1. At the other extreme was the talent for music, where the ratio was only 1 to 4 (p. 75)

The notion of intellectual abilities being hierarchically organized is an alluring one that has been embraced by a number of influential intelligence theorists. Spearman's influence can also be found in the everyday practice of assessing intelligence, where psychologists may be observed discussing the "g"-loading of a particular subtest from an intelligence test battery. In addition, Spearman's introduction of factor analytic methods into intelligence research has resulted in a continuing emphasis on factor analytic procedures for, among other things, establishing the validity of intelligence measures. A final example of the enduring influence of Spearman's theorizing is the continuing research into the nature of "g" (Jensen, 1986).

It was also at about this time that scientists were expressing a great deal of doubt about the practice of intelligence testing. Respected scientists such as E. L. Thorndike (1927) questioned whether anyone knew what intelligence tests measured. Furthermore, writers such as Pintner (1923) were wholly dissatisfied with vague concepts of general intelligence. In fact, Pintner (1923) argued the following:

We may say rather that the psychologist borrowed from everyday life a vague term implying all-round ability and knowledge, and in the process of trying to measure this trait, he has been and still is attempting to define it more sharply and endow it with a stricter scientific connotation. (p. 53)

Wechsler's Tests

David Wechsler was a clinical psychologist at Bellevue Psychiatric Hospital in New York. He was to adult intelligence testing what Binet was to children's intelligence testing (see Research Report 1.1). He used some of the same tests as Binet, and he introduced and adapted other tasks for the purpose of assessing adult intelligence.

Most importantly, Wechsler was the beneficiary of the World War I testing experience. In many ways his tests mimic the methods used in the war effort. One of the contributions of his scale was the inclusion of separate verbal and performance scales akin to the Army Alpha/Beta measures that he used in the war. Wechsler popularized other innovations in individual intelligence testing, including the use of the Deviation IQ (standard score) in lieu of the old Ratio IQ and the provision of subtest scores in addition to composite scores. His children's test batteries differed substantially from Binet's test. Wechsler did not order his subtests sequentially by developmental age as Binet did. Instead, Wechsler created subtests that possessed enough range of item difficulty to span the entire age range of the scale. Hence, there was much less switching from one subtest to another when administering the Wechsler scales, making them easier for examiners to master. The Wechsler-Bellevue I, an adult intelligence test published in 1939, was Wechsler's first test. The chronology of Wechsler's prolific test development career is given below.

Year	Test
1939	Wechsler-Bellevue I
1946	Wechsler-Bellevue II
1949	Wechsler Intelligence Scale for Children (WISC)
1955	Wechsler Adult Intelligence Scale (WAIS)
1967	Wechsler Preschool and Primary Scale of Intelligence (WPPSI)
1974	Wechsler Intelligence Scale for Children-Revised (WISC-R)
1981	Wechsler Adult Intelligence Scale-Revised (WAIS-R)

YEAR	TEST
1989*	Wechsler Preschool and Primary Scale of Intelligence-Revised (WPPSI-R)
1991*	Wechsler Intelligence Scale for Children-III (WISC-III)
1997*	Wechsler Adult Intelligence Scale-III (WAIS-III)

One aspect of the Wechsler tradition that has resulted in considerable misunderstanding is the offering of the Verbal and Performance scales. Wechsler (1974) ascribed to a notion of general intelligence. He states that, "Intelligence is the overall capacity of the individual to understand and cope with the world around him" (p. 5). What is often misunderstood is that the Verbal and Performance scales were constructed not to represent distinct abilities but as "two languages" through which the underlying general intelligence may express itself. Stated in Wechsler's own words, "This dichotomy is primarily a way of identifying two principle modes by which human abilities express themselves" (p. 9).

The Age of Theory

In the 1950s many psychologists turned to the development of theories that explained the concept of intelligence. Up until this time intelligence testing was more empirical than theoretical in nature. Binet and Simon recognized the independence of theory and practice by stating their view on the nature of the intelligence testing controversy in this excerpt from a 1908 paper.

> Some psychologists affirm that intelligence can be measured; others declare that it is impossible to measure intelligence. But there are still others, better informed, who ignore these theoretical discussions and apply themselves to the actual solving of the problem. (p. 96)

*The latter three scales were published without the benefit of Wechsler's involvement in the project.

Similarly, in his APA presidential address of 1946, Henry Garrett made the following statement showing his recognition of the separation of intelligence testing and theory:

> . . . it may be well to recall that the measurement of intelligent behavior began as a practical enterprise and that theory has in general followed rather than preceded application. Perhaps, had theory come first, we might have been saved much argument and many intelligence tests. (1946/1961, p. 573)

This lack of theory has led to the common criticism of intelligence being defined as "what the test measures." This criticism is very understandable when one reads the manuals of older tests and finds no explicit theory behind the selection of items or subtests. The gap between theory and intelligence testing began to close in the 1950s, when many theories were offered to explain intelligence. Some of the most influential theories of the day included Cattell's (1971) theory of Fluid and Crystallized intelligence, Guilford's (1967) Structure of Intellect Model, and Vernon's (1950) Hierarchical Model of Intelligence. Unfortunately, while these numerous theories spawned a great deal of research, they have not yet produced popular intelligence tests that could compete with the Binet and Wechsler scales. These theories have been used primarily to interpret tests such as the Wechsler scales (Kaufman, 1979a) that were based on practical and clinical rather than theoretical concerns. The true merger of intelligence testing and theory does not occur until the 1980s (see Chapter 2).

Intelligent Testing

The 1960s were another era of concern about intelligence tests. There were questions about test bias and test misuse. In 1968, an article by Alexander Wesman, "Intelligent Testing," appeared in *American Psychologist*. Among other things, Wesman pointed out the need for psychologists to be very clear about the nature of intelligence tests and what they measure. Wesman stated unequivocally that intelligence tests measured "previous learnings," not ability to learn. He offered the following conclusions regarding intelligence that he described as "obvious":

1. Intelligence is an attribute, not an entity.
2. Intelligence is the summation of the learning experiences of the individual.

Given these conclusions, he then argued that the separation of intelligence, ability, and achievement measures was more artificial than real. This is a dramatic departure from the early part of the century when many psychologists were convinced that some sort of innate intellectual ability could be measured.

Wesman's article has also proven to be so influential because of the adoption of many of Wesman's tenets by Alan Kaufman (1979b) in his book *Intelligent Testing with the WISC-R*. In this very popular text, Kaufman emphasized flexibility in WISC-R interpretation. His updated volume for the WISC-III (Kaufman, 1994) provides a logical and systematic approach to test interpretation and many alternative theories to the Wechsler Verbal/Performance model for WISC-III interpretation. In this way interpretation is fit to the child rather than the child being forced to fit the theoretical model of a particular test. Anastasi (1988) lauded Kaufman's approach to WISC interpretation by saying:

> The basic approach described by Kaufman undoubtedly represents a major contribution to the clinical use of intelligence tests. Nevertheless, it should be recognized that its implementation requires a sophisticated clinician who is well informed in several fields of psychology. (p. 484)

Kaufman's approach to interpretation has proven popular, as aspects of it have been incorporated into modern tests such as the Vineland Adaptive Behavior Scales (Sparrow, Balla, & Cicchetti, 1984), and the Kaufman Assessment Battery for Children (Kaufman & Kaufman, 1983a & b).

The Contributions of Dorothea McCarthy

The McCarthy Scales of Children's Abilities was published in 1972. The McCarthy scale was a welcome change in the assessment of young children. First and foremost, the scale was more sensitive to the needs of young children than tests such as the WPPSI. It included full color artwork and tasks such as a bean bag toss that were inherently appealing to young children. The examiner directions for the McCarthy scale were also hailed as an improvement because their simple wording did not require preschoolers to understand basic concepts that were beyond their comprehension (Kaufman & Kaufman, 1977).

McCarthy also took a very bold move with her scale by eschewing the term *IQ*. It was the first popular test not to call the overall composite score an IQ. Instead, it used the term *General Cognitive Index (GCI)*. This was a risk in that it made some potential users question whether the McCarthy was an intelligence test. It appears now that McCarthy was ushering in a new era, as many popular tests of today do not use the term *IQ*.

A CENTURY OF CONTROVERSY

American and other societies are of two minds regarding intelligence testing. Even critics of intelligence testing cite their development as the signature contribution of psychology to American society. Von Mayrhauser (1992) concluded that intelligence testing is ". . . the profession's most influential contribution to American Society" (p. 252). Although sales figures are not readily available, there is substantial evidence that these tests enjoy widespread use. The release of many new tests, which will be discussed in subsequent chapters, indicates that the desire for new and better tests is ever present. At the same time, tests of this nature have always served as a lightning rod for criticism from both within and outside of psychology. All indications are that this love–hate relationship with such tests will continue. Witness some of the more strident protests of the 1960s.

The sidewalk in front of the headquarters of the American Psychological Association served as the platform for about a dozen protesters. Their placards read:

"Help stop grants from your tax money given to the American Psychological Association"

"Support Congressional investigations of Psychological sex tests in Government
Private Employment
School"

"Where did the millions come from to build this APA building?"

"Don't be brainwashed by some Ph.D. See your clergyman or doctor."

"These tests are supported by the American Psychological Association. They admit they 'do not know what a psychologist is.' Do they know what a test is?"

This protest took place in 1965, but the concerns about testing have been expressed throughout the century-old history of intelligence testing (American Psychological Association [APA], 1965). Although intelligence tests have been linked with controversy almost from their beginning, American society has decided to continue using them in spite of their inadequacies (Neisser, 1979). During the protests of the 1960s, Amrine (1965) reached a conclusion that rings true today.

Tests and testers are thus attacked by the right and the left, from outside psychology and inside. Meanwhile, the sale and use of tests increases steadily because to thousands of users of psychological tests even as presently designed appear to be better than the alternative of no tests. (p. 859)

The first century of intelligence testing continues to be both celebrated and derided, dichotomous views that remain in sharp contrast. The controversial book by Hernstein and Mur-

ray (1994) and the virulent reactions to it are further testimony to a continuing legacy of contentious debate.

RECENT HISTORY

The Demise of the IQ

The term *intelligence quotient* has been outdated for some time. Once the use of standard scores became widespread, the IQ was no longer descriptive; the score from an intelligence test was not a "quotient" but rather a standard score. Yet the IQ was retained on popular tests such as the Wechsler scales. Several writers have also proposed that the IQ fostered misunderstanding and misuse of intelligence tests. Plotkin (1974), for example, observed that, "In a sense there is a certain personal worth interpretation that is put on the results of an IQ test," and furthermore, "the IQ, however, has much more of a final, unquestioned, and innate sort of sound to it. . . ." The IQ score has even been found to have a substantial impact on family relationships (Dirks, Bushkuhl, & Marzano, 1983). Dirks et al. (1983) found that parents who were told that their child had an average IQ were less accurate in their memory of the test results and reported few positive consequences from the testing. The parents of above-average children, on the other hand, reported that they experienced considerable pride and self-confidence as a result of finding out about their child's high IQ.

Today, most modern intelligence tests no longer use the term *IQ* to describe an overall intelligence test score. The Wechsler Scales still do. The Stanford-Binet Fourth Edition, which was a substantial revision of previous editions, now calls the overall score a Composite Standard Score. The Kaufman Assessment Battery for Children (K-ABC) calls its overall score a Mental Processing Composite (MPC). This is also the case for group-administered tests where only a few retain names such as "intelligence" or "mental ability" (Lennon, 1985). The days of the use of the term *IQ* appear numbered. While renaming the composite scores of intelligence tests is not revolutionary, it is symptomatic of the changing intellectual assessment scene.

It is also conceivable that the term *intelligence test* may fall into disuse. Long ago, group-administered tests of intelligence dropped the term *intelligence* from their titles, using other terms such as *cognitive skills* or *scholastic ability* instead. It would not be surprising to see tests of the future opting for alternate terms to intelligence.

Individuals with Disabilities Education Act (IDEA)

In 1974 the Education for all Handicapped Children Act (PL 94-142) was passed by Congress. This federal law mandated that school districts provide a "free and appropriate" public education for all handicapped children living in their jurisdiction. Now referred to as IDEA, Public Law 94-142 mandated the identification of all children eligible for special education services. This "child find" effort created a great need for examiners of children and enhanced the demand for intelligence testing of children.

This law also carried with it some very explicit guidelines for the use of tests, including intelligence tests, in the diagnostic process. The important aspect of these regulations for intelligence testing was that, in many ways, this was the first time that federal standards for the use of intelligence tests in the schools were instituted.

The IDEA standards, for example, make it clear that intelligence test results should not outweigh other test results in making diagnostic decisions. They should be viewed as but one piece of evidence to be considered when making diagnoses. This is an important point to remember when interpreting intelligence tests to parents and others who may focus almost exclusively on intelligence test data in order to gauge their child's needs. The IDEA emphasizes the point that other tests may be equally or more impor-

tant in making decisions and that they should not be undervalued because of the presence of intelligence test scores. Furthermore, the IDEA also created a need for translations and modifications of popular intelligence tests. This occurred because of the standard indicating that a test should be administered in the child's native language or "other means" should be used to assess intelligence without undue influence from linguistic difference.

Larry P. v. Riles

The case of *Larry P. v. Riles* is of significance in the annals of intellectual assessment. As a result of the testimony at this trial, intelligence tests were found to be biased against African American children, and the San Francisco public schools were enjoined from using intelligence tests when evaluating African American children (Elliot, 1987). In 1986, the *Larry P.* decision was reiterated and clarified (Landers, 1986). Judge Peckham, who presided over the original *Larry P.* trial, made his decision quite clear in this most recent statement. He said, "School districts are not to use intelligence tests in the assessment of Black pupils who have been referred for special education services."

This trial and the associated testimony brought into clear focus all of the data, and the lack of data, on issues of test bias. As a result, this case provided the impetus for considerable research and discussion of issues of test bias that may not have taken place otherwise. This case is a landmark because it is also the only case where intelligence tests were found to be invalid for use with a particular cultural group. More on this issue will be presented in later chapters.

Mergers of Theory and Intelligence Testing

The marriage between intelligence testing and psychological theory has always been a tenuous one. In fact, intelligence testing began primarily as an empirical effort relatively uninfluenced by theory. The separation of test development and theory was recognized by many psychologists and is reflected in the following quote by Henry Garrett (1946/1961) in his presidential address to the American Psychological Association in 1946:

> The trial and error period in mental measurement is, I believe, drawing to a close. Much progress has been made over the war years in the construction and use of mental tests. I think that we can anticipate a bright future for psychometrics, and by no means the smallest achievement will be an increase in the number of valid tests capable of measuring precisely defined aptitudes and traits. (p. 581)

It appears that Garrett's prediction was accurate but its fulfillment belated. Up to this point it has been difficult to argue that intelligence tests are measures of precisely defined traits. The traits being measured by the Wechsler scales and older editions of the Binet scales have not been clearly delineated in the test's manuals. The Kaufman Assessment Battery for Children (K-ABC) ushered in a new era with its publication in 1983 by devoting a great deal of space in its manual to discussing the theory underlying the test development process and interpretation of results. More recently, the Stanford-Binet Fourth Edition, Differential Ability Scales (DAS), and Cognitive Assessment System (CAS) devote considerable attention in their various manuals to discussing the theory underlying their scales. The pendulum, however, should not be allowed to tilt too far toward theory without scientific support. Cronbach (1986) wisely cautions against this outcome by concluding,

> we don't have much theory, and I don't favor using the word loosely for almost any abstraction of point of view. . . . I would reserve the word theory for substantial, articulated, somewhat validated constructions. Rather than an emperor with no clothes, we have theory being used as an imperial cloak that has no emperor inside. (p. 23, cited in Messick, 1992)

New measures of intelligence will need to take further strides in this regard in order to gain acceptance among users. These new tests are likely to use methods described as rational-theoretical approaches to test development where theoretical and empirical methods, mutatis mutandis, produce tests that benefit from the use of both methods.

The pace of change, however, is frustratingly slow (Sternberg & Kaufman, 1996). The history of innovation in intelligence testing is marked by minor, seemingly glacial, changes in the technology. Such incremental change is likely to continue, and change will not be welcomed unless the new test is proven to have some enhanced value over its competitors (Daniel, 1997). Intelligence tests and intelligence testing has faced many challenges and, yet, it remains a widely practiced enterprise. Many "innovations" have been offered over the course of the first 100 years and most have been discarded in favor of the standard bearers. Considerable time, money, and energy will be needed to make the next bonafide breakthrough.

Intelligence Tests of the Future

The major breakthroughs of the near future are likely to be an increase in the number of available tests and a further rapprochement between theory and intelligence testing. New tests are likely to expand on the precedents of the 1980s and 1990s set by the Kaufman Assessment Battery for Children (K-ABC), and Woodcock-Johnson (WJ-R), which have clear-cut theoretical foundations. There are likely to be a variety of tests available because of the increasing diversity of theories of intelligence. Some of this diversity is reflected in Table 1.2, where a sampling of definitions of intelligence is given.

It is also important to consider that it may not be necessary, or even desirable, to achieve unanimity on the definition of intelligence. Jensen (1987) likened the term *intelligence* to other

TABLE 1.2   Definitions of intelligence from the distant past to the present

Alfred Binet and Theophilius Simon (1905). "It seems to us that in intelligence there is a fundamental faculty, the alteration or the lack of which, is of the utmost importance for practical life. This faculty is judgment, otherwise called good sense, practical sense, initiative, the faculty of adapting one's self to circumstances. To judge well, to comprehend well, to reason well, these are the essential activities of intelligence" (Jenkins & Paterson, 1961, p. 93).

Rudolf Pintner (1923). "It includes the capacity for getting along well in all sorts of situations. This implies ease and rapidity in making adjustments and, hence, ease in breaking old habits and in forming new ones. . . . The intelligent person has a multiplicity of responses; the unintelligent few. The intelligent organism responds to a great number of situations; the unintelligent few. Intelligent behavior leads one from one thing to another in ever-widening circles; unintelligent behavior is narrow and restricted, and leads to repetition or cessation."

C. Spearman (1927). "This is to regard 'g' as measuring something analogous to an 'energy'; that is to say, it is some force capable of being transformed from one mental operation to another different one. Even on the physiological side, there are some grounds for hoping that some such energy will sooner or later be discovered in the nervous system, especially the cerebral cortex."

Henry E. Garrett (1946/1961). ". . . intelligence as I shall use the term in this paper includes at least the abilities demanded in the solution of problems which require the comprehension and use of symbols. By symbols I mean words, numbers, diagrams, equations, formulas, which represent ideas and relationships ranging from the fairly simple to the very complex. For simplicity we may call the ability to deal with such stimuli *symbol or abstract intelligence.*"

Frederick B. Davis (1964). "From time immemorial, men have observed that their fellows differ greatly in the ease and accuracy with which they perceive facts and ideas, remember them, draw logical conclusions and inferences from them, and benefit or learn from experiences."

Alexander G. Wesman (1968). "Intelligence as here defined is a summation of learning experiences. The instances in which intelligent behavior is observed may be classified in various ways that appear to be logical or homogeneous, but they are individual instances all the same. Each instance represents a response the organism has learned; each learned response in turn predisposes the organism for learning additional responses which permit the organism to display new acts of intelligent behavior."

J. P. Guilford (1979). ". . . Intelligence is defined as a systematic collection of abilities or functions for processing different kinds of information in various ways. Intelligence is thus concerned both with kinds of information and kinds of operations performed with information. Regarding the brain as 'that computer between our ears' is a useful conception, at least by analogy. Like computers, brains also possess information in storage and programs for dealing with that information."

Jaan Valsiner (1984). ". . . We can operationalize it in terms of the process structure—the dynamic organization of the actor's goal-directed actions in the particular (possibly dynamic) ecological niche."

Phillip A. Vernon (1985). ". . . individual differences in mental ability can be thought of as being a function of what appears to be a rather general factor of neural efficiency. At one level, neural efficiency allows information to be processed quickly, preventing an overload of the limited capacity of working memory. At another level, the factor is expressed as neural adaptability, again relating to an efficient use of limited neural resources. At still a third level, neural efficiency will at some time undoubtedly be identified with some sort of neuronal biochemical processes. . . ."

Robert J. Sternberg (1997): "Intelligence comprises the mental abilities necessary for adaptation to, and shaping and selection of, any environmental context."

broadly defined scientific terms. He concluded, "Scientists don't actually try to define 'nature' or to construct 'theories of nature.' 'Intelligence' ought to be regarded like 'nature' in this respect" (p. 196). This school of thought suggests that intelligence be viewed as a field of study with many potentially appropriate lines of inquiry.

It is unlikely, and probably undesirable, that one definition of intelligence will be found. It is probable, however, that new intelligence tests, based on a variety of theoretical approaches, will measure more precisely defined intellectual skills, abilities, traits, styles, or behaviors. Intelligence and cognition researchers are frequently calling for future tests to assess very precisely defined cognitive activities (Pellegrino, 1986; Richardson & Bynner, 1984). Richardson and Bynner (1984), for example, suggest that intelligence researchers ". . . follow in the footsteps of more rigorous sciences by seeking precise definitions of the different elements of cognitive functions and processes . . ." (p. 521). We will wait with eager anticipation to see the new tests offered and their associated theories. It appears that, regardless of the theories that will be favored, the criticism that intelligence is "what the test measures" will no longer apply as we move from the empirical to the theoretical age of intellectual assessment.

CONCLUSIONS

The development of intelligence tests remains a major technological advance in psychological assessment. These measures have been cited as breakthroughs because they provided a means for assessing a particularly intriguing construct (Davis, 1964). While there may be natural curiosity about measuring levels of intelligence, there is also great societal concern about the use of these measures for diagnostic or placement decisions. Because intelligence tests have been used to make potentially life-changing decisions

about individual's lives, such as the diagnoses and services they receive, and the educational opportunities they are afforded, these tests are likely to continue to be controversial. Hence, any discussion of the history of intelligence testing must consider not only the scientific aspects of these measures, but the sociopolitical aspects as well (Elliot, 1987).

The last century of intelligence assessment has been marked by changes in the tests themselves, including their theoretical foundations, and guidelines for test use. In addition, significant scientific progress has been made in understanding the nature of intelligence (Hunt, 1999). There is no indication from history that this pace of change in this vibrant field of inquiry and practice is slowing. On the contrary, the pool of available measures and theories continues to expand rapidly. The next century of intelligence assessment should continue to differentiate itself from the first 100 years. The pace of change is likely to be consistent but not convulsive. Some strive for an upheaval of the status quo. Such upheaval may not occur in the nature of intelligence tests themselves but rather in their normal usage. Current psychological research gives clear evidence that current tests should be used in different ways than is often the case. These alterations in test usage are the practicing clinician's best hope of avoiding some of the mishaps of the past, usages that have been characterized by making inferences that are not consistent with the current state of psychological knowledge.

CHAPTER SUMMARY

- The first intelligence testers were parents, preschoolers, employers, teachers, spouses, grandparents, and philosophers, among others.
- There is considerable agreement that the practice of assessing individual skills and abilities is an ancient one.

- Many early efforts at measuring intelligence used tests that were developed in early experimental psychology laboratories.

- Galton viewed the use of psychophysical measures to assess intelligence as sensible because, he reasoned, ·if all information is obtained through the senses, then intelligent individuals must have very capable sensory abilities.

- The central problem with the use of psychophysical measures of intelligence was their *lack of correlation with school achievement.*

- The development of intelligence tests was carried out in response to a societal need. Modern intelligence testing can be traced to the concern for the *humane treatment of mentally retarded individuals* that was exemplified by the work of pioneers such as Itard and Sequin during the 19th century.

- Alfred Binet and Theophilius Simon (1905) produced the first technological breakthrough in intelligence testing by developing the first practical intelligence test battery.

- The Binet-Simon scale assessed higher-level cognitive skills and, as a result, produced substantial correlations with measures of school achievement.

- Binet and Simon placed considerable emphasis on the establishment of content validity for their scale, an emphasis that has been lacking in many subsequent measures.

- Terman (1916) produced the most successful of the English translations of Binet's work. His scale, the Stanford-Binet, met high psychometric standards for the time.

- Terman also introduced the concept of the intelligence quotient (IQ), which was originally the invention of a German scientist named William Stern.

- There were four editions of the Stanford-Binet. The 1972 version was simply a renorming.

- During the war, Robert Yerkes directed an assessment committee of the American Psychological Association that was eventually charged with the screening of about a million and a half potential soldiers (Anastasi, 1988). It was this group of psychologists that developed the first group-administered tests of intelligence. The Army Alpha was used to screen most recruits, while the Army Beta, a nonverbal test, was used with nonreaders and those who did not speak English.

- In 1927 Spearman introduced an influential hierarchical theory of intelligence. At the top of Spearman's hierarchy is the "general factor" (general intelligence or "g"), the factor that explains most of the variance in the factor analytic solutions conducted by Spearman.

- David Wechsler was a clinical psychologist at Bellevue Psychiatric Hospital in New York who developed adult and children's intelligence tests. He used some of the same tests as Binet, and he introduced and adapted other tasks for the purpose of assessing adult intelligence.

- In the 1950s, many psychologists turned to the development of theories that explained the concept of intelligence. Some of the most influential theories of the day included Cattell's (1971) theory of Fluid and Crystallized intelligence, Guilford's (1967) Structure of Intellect Model, and Vernon's (1950) Hierarchical Model of Intelligence.

- Wesman (1968) stated unequivocally that intelligence tests measured "previous learnings," not ability to learn. He offered the following conclusions regarding intelligence that he described as "obvious": (1) Intelligence is an attribute, not an entity. (2) Intelligence is the summation of the learning experiences of the individual.

- The McCarthy Scales of Children's Abilities is a preschool intelligence test that was published in 1972.

- The term *intelligence quotient* is outdated. Once the use of standard scores became widespread, the IQ was no longer descriptive; the score from an intelligence test was not a "quotient" but rather a standard score.

- In 1975 the Education for all Handicapped Children Act (PL 94-142) was passed by Congress. This law also carried with it some very explicit guidelines for the use of tests, including intelligence tests, in the diagnostic process.

- The case of *Larry P. v. Riles* is of significance in the annals of intellectual assessment. As a result of the testimony at this trial, intelligence tests were found to be biased against African American children, and the San Francisco public schools were enjoined from using intelligence tests when evaluating African American children.

- New measures of intelligence are promising to continue the trend of measuring intelligence from a stronger theoretical basis.

CHAPTER 2

Theory

The problem of definition is an embarrassment to all of science. Edgar Doll (1953, p. 60)

CHAPTER QUESTIONS

What is a latent trait?

How has favor analysis contributed to intelligence theory?

What is the relationship between specific and general intellectual abilities?

Which theories are used widely for intelligence test development?

Why Theory?

Theoretical knowledge is important because it can affect behavior—in this case the interpretive behavior of the clinician using an intelligence test. Our interpretations of test results, either in writing or presented orally in a parent conference or other venue, are expressions of our theoretical knowledge or biases. Similarly, a person's reaction to being called into the boss's office is influenced by theory depending on whether one thinks that the boss is calling the meeting to offer congratulations or a reprimand. So too, in intellectual assessment, a psychologist may offer either a dismal prognosis for or a favorable one depending on the examiner's theories of intelligence. This is one crucial reason psychologists should have a clear understanding of intelligence theory.

Another reason for theoretical knowledge is to allow implementation of the "intelligent testing" approach to interpretation (Kaufman, 1990, 1994). This interpretive method is highly sophisticated and individualized, requiring substantial theoretical knowledge on the part of examiners. Take, for example, the case of a child who is referred for an evaluation subsequent to receiving a head injury in a car wreck. If this child's intelligence test score is considerably lower than premorbid estimates (estimates of the child's intelligence before the injury), a psychologist would be hard pressed to argue that the child's scores are now lower due to changes in reinforcement contingencies (behavioral theory).

More than likely a neuropsychological model of intelligence would best explain the score decrement in this case. The variety of problems and circumstances presented by children call for a clinician who is well versed in a variety of disciplines and possesses knowledge of several theories if interpretation is going to be truly "intelligent." A psychologist who does not individualize interpretation is easily "found out" by referral sources. If all children are found to have brain damage, or task-intrinsic motivation deficits, or long-term memory problems, the consumers of reports such as teachers, psychiatrists, and parents will soon realize the limited knowledge of the psychologist and stop referring cases or only refer those that fit the psychologist's theoretical leanings. Perhaps the worst eventuality that can befall a psychologist bereft of theory is to simply report scores without any interpretation. This practice will not satisfy parents and others, and it poses peril to the well-being of children and adults. The mere "tester" of children offers no advice for helping a child and perhaps produces scores that can be misunderstood by others since they are not connected to useful interpretation.

The remainder of this chapter is designed to help foster the theoretical sophistication necessary to be a capable interpreter of scores by focusing primarily on factor analytic theory. It has been said that trait theory associated with intelligence and personality measurement, which has as its foundation factor analytic findings, is one of the most significant "fruits" of the psychological science of individual differences (Harkness & Lilienfeld, 1997). To that end, this chapter is devoted to providing an overview of the substantial fruits of the labors of the legions of individual-difference researchers of the past 100 years.

COLLOQUIAL THEORY

The original "testers" were parents, preschoolers, employers, teachers, spouses, grandparents, and philosophers. They were people like you and me who for whatever reason labeled an individual as intelligent or less than intelligent. The lexicon of intelligence and its assessment has been commonly used for centuries, long before the availability of intelligence tests. Individuals have always categorized others as "bright," "dull," "gifted," and the like. In fact, humans have a natural tendency to categorize (Kamphaus, Reynolds, & Imperato-McCammon, 1998). Even preschoolers "assess" their own intelligence and that of their peers. Parents of young children know that children make their own diagnoses of intelligence in the early school grades by saying such things as, "Lanier is smart, she's in the cardinal's reading group." Teachers also know that the names they use to deemphasize differences in instructional groups are usually decoded by children within minutes of their application. Children in early grades know full well that if all the good readers are in one group that this is the "advanced group." Actually, intelligence tests simply formalize a common practice used by humans to identify individual differences between people—they assess intelligence. Hopefully, the science of intelligence research has allowed for the development of intelligence tests that are more objective than intuitive classification practices.

We all have our own implicit theories of what constitutes intelligent individuals and intelligent behavior (Weinberg, 1989). When commuters waiting for a train, shoppers in a supermarket, and university students were asked, "What is intelligence?," there were three general areas of agreement: (1) practical problem-solving ability, (2) verbal ability, and (3) social intelligence (Weinberg, 1989). It has also been found that adults consider problem solving and reasoning to become increasingly important markers of intelligence with increasing developmental age. In addition, perceptual and motor abilities are seen as measures of intelligence for infants and younger children, whereas verbal ability is perceived as important from age 2 through adulthood (Weinberg, 1989). Weinberg (1989) also makes the point that these public conceptions of the nature of intelligence are quite similar to the conceptualizations commonly held by professionals such as psychologists.

The idea that something such as "intelligence" exists also appears to be universal. Neisser (1979) made the following observations about African conceptions of intelligence and their similarity to Western definitions.

> The notion that some people are intelligent (or clever, or cunning, or bright, or smart, or wise, or insightful, or brilliant, or intellectual, or . . .) is widespread indeed. I suspect that every language must have some such galaxy of cognitive terms. It is at least certain that the existence of intelligence-related words does not depend on technology or education, or testing. E. F. Dube (1977) recently conducted an inquiry into the meaning of such concepts among non-literate traditional villagers in Botswana. He used 13 Setswana words which had been suggested by translators as possible equivalents of "intelligent" and other related words in English. The elders of the villages were easily able to "define" these terms, by giving examples of the behaviors and characteristics that justify using a given word. Moreover, their attributions were genuinely predictive of behavior. At Dube's request, the elders pointed out which of the children were definitely "botlhale" (the Setswana word closest to "intelligent") and which ones were not. These attributions were powerful predictors of the children's subsequent performance in an experiment on memory for stories. (p. 222)

The universality of the concept of intelligence, not just intelligence testing, perhaps explains why the tests are viewed with such reverence by some and disdain by others. The idea that the construct of intelligence can be measured is intriguing to many. The search for a definitive theory of intelligence is equally alluring.

Binet's Rationale

Though Binet's efforts aimed at developing the first intelligence test were mostly practical and empirical, he did theorize about the nature of intelligence. His theoretical stance, however, seems to vary from citation to citation (Thorndike & Lohman, 1990). By most accounts he did seem to ascribe to the notion of intelligence as a single entity. One of his most recognized statements on his views of the nature of intelligence is given in this excerpt:

> It seems to us that in intelligence there is a fundamental faculty, the alteration or lack of which, is of the utmost importance for practical life. This faculty is judgement, otherwise called good sense, practical sense, initiative, the faculty of adapting one's self to circumstances. To judge well, to comprehend well, to reason well, these are the essential activities of intelligence. A person may be a moron or an imbecile if he is lacking in judgment; but with good judgement he can never be either. Indeed the rest of the intellectual faculties seem of little importance in comparison with judgement. (Binet & Simon, 1905, pp. 42–43)

Even in this statement Binet seems to waiver. While emphasizing the preeminence of judgment he then begins to retreat and mention that this is but one of many faculties. This retreat suggests that he considers other abilities or skills as aspects of intelligence. This lack of precise definition, however, is not only a characteristic of Binet's work but also Wechsler's (1958) and other definitions of intelligence. Binet's emphasis on a single global entity is consistent with the *zeitgeist* of the times in that numerous workers emphasized an "intelligence" as opposed to distinct intelligences, abilities, or faculties. Additional theories that emphasized a global ability are exemplified by the work of the British.

Measurement Assumptions

This chapter focuses primarily on factor analytic theory for several reasons. Factor analysis, at its essence a correlational method, has proven to be the dominant research methodology for intelligence theory development for decades. In addition, many modern intelligence tests are based on factor analytically derived theories and/or they made extensive use of factor analysis during various phases of test construction. Consequently, factor analytic theories are likely to be applicable to the intelligence test interpretation process. The forthcoming discussion of factor analytic theories will serve as the backbone for an interpretive system to be offered in later chapters. Still other theories will be introduced in this and other chapters as deemed relevant. Knowledge of theories, other than those developed via factor analysis, is not to be viewed as irrelevant. On the contrary, new and alternate theories provide the fertile ground on which new approaches can be germinated.

Latent Traits

There are many well-known psychological traits including anxiety, extroversion, distractibility, and yes, intelligence. The theories presented in this chapter explicate the latter construct. Some terminology must be introduced, however, to further clarify the intelligence trait(s). A *trait* may be defined as, "*A characteristic feature of mind or character; a distinguishing quality, especially of a person, culture, or social group*" (Brown, 1997). Consistent with this definition, a psychological trait has several key characteristics.

First, a psychological trait is a construct, not a palpable entity. In other words, traits of the nature that will be discussed in this volume cannot be directly perceived through the senses. Traits are merely inferred based on test scores, observations, and other referents. In classical test theory traits are inferred in a three-step process beginning with the observed score (i.e., the intelligence test scores). These scores, however, are known to possess some degree of imperfection (error). Theoretically, an estimated true score can be calculated based on the observed score. The third step involved in measuring a trait is to make an inference based on the true score; that is to say, a person is identified as having a particular level of the unobservable trait (Suen, 1990). Since it cannot be observed, a psychological trait

can be referred to as "*latent.*" In addition, since psychological tests are not direct measures of intelligence, they are sometimes referred to as "*indicators*" of the trait. To reiterate, when we say that an individual has high or low or average intelligence, we are making an inference based on observed scores or estimated true scores, which are indirect measures of the trait.

Second, traits are often thought of as residing within the individual. People are said to possess average intelligence, introversion, sociability, and the like. As a result much of the psychological testing enterprise is aimed at measuring the person, as opposed to the person's environment. This statement does not imply that measurement of environments is unimportant, rather that the measurement of environments rests on theories other than trait theory.

Third, traits are presumed to be relatively stable; otherwise they cannot be measured with accuracy. Certainly, the amount of trait that a person possesses can change due to a variety of circumstances, but a trait possesses adequate stability so as to be measurable.

Finally, traits typically take a monotonic (nearly linear form) in that performance on a test usually indicates a level of the latent trait (Thorndike, 1982). Items are typically, as is the case for intelligence tests, ordered by item difficulty. Therefore, mastery of item content on an intelligence test is associated with increasingly high levels of a trait.

Since latent traits of the intelligence nature are inferred and not measured directly, their existence cannot be proven or disproved definitively. The existence of traits can only be confirmed via the accumulation of substantial evidence and through "logical deductions and mathematical proofs" (p. 8, Suen, 1990). The process of accumulating such evidence will be elaborated in later chapters. The premise introduced at this point is that the practical utility of all measures of latent traits is a function of the variety of evidence currently available—the scientific ebb and flow of supportive, clarifying, and disconfirming evidence. Just as is the case in physical science where theories of temperature, evolution, and other constructs are the subjects of vigorous debate so too is intelligence testing, perhaps even more so given the association of this trait with controversy.

Moreover, various types of validity evidence are required to support test interpretations. While factor analysis is a popular statistical technique for evaluating the validity of a test, it is by no means the only or best method for all circumstances. At the risk of being repetitive, it is important to punctuate the notion that validity emanates from the accumulation of a variety of types of evidence (Messick, 1989).

Abilities

Some psychological traits are identified as *abilities* because individuals differ in terms of the amount of the latent trait that they possess. In other words, an ability can be defined as "*suitable or sufficient power; capacity*" (Brown, 1997). The term *ability* does not presume a particular explanation for its development. Likewise, precursors of any given ability may be either innate or experiential, or a dynamic combination thereof. Lastly, ability tests may measure a variety of dimensions and appear on intelligence, achievement, temperament, or other test batteries. Cognitive abilities may serve as but one set of abilities of interest to psychologists and others.

Cognitive abilities are those that require the "*processing of mental information*" (p. 10, Carroll, 1993). This mental processing is requisite to successful performance on the cognitive ability test. According to this definition, a test of verbal reasoning ability would presumably qualify as a cognitive measure. Scales of behavioral impulsivity or introversion by contrast would likely not fall into the category of "cognitive" but, in contrast, would lay in the realm of emotion, temperament, or similar area of study. The cognitive versus noncognitive distinction, however, does depend on consensus at some point since a large array of abilities may require some type of mental processing. The correlational relationships among test scores have proven helpful for defining the universe of cognitive abilities. Traditionally, tests that have not been found to correlate to some extent with widely recognized intelligence tests have difficulty being accepted as measures of cognitive abilities.

Skills

Skills may also be defined as the capacity to do something, and the term can apply to ability to "*reason as a mental faculty*" (Brown, 1997). The term, however, has a slightly different connotation in that it refers to an ability that is "*acquired through practice or learning.*" This meaning of the term *skill* is especially appropriate with reference to intelligence testing in the sense that these tests share so many similarities with achievement measures of a great variety. The term *cognitive skills* may be most appropriate for use in describing the results of intelligence tests. This point will be buttressed further as intelligence testing research is covered in more detail in the next and later chapters.

The assumptions of traits and abilities are central to the work of Charles Spearman, who studied the correlations among cognitive tests as a means of developing an influential theory of intelligence.

GENERAL INTELLIGENCE THEORY

Spearman's theory exemplifies an approach to conceptualizing intelligence that has sometimes been called the "British approach" (Minton & Schneider, 1980). This approach is exemplified by the work of Spearman (1927), Burt (1950), and Vernon (1950), among others. Weinberg (1988) describes these theorists as "lumpers" or those who tend to focus on a single general intelligence as the major concept. Spearman is usually credited as the first to offer a hierarchical theory of intelligence.

It could be said that the invention of the correlation coefficient by Charles Spearman set the stage for the development of the construct of *general intelligence* ("g"). Spearman made the insightful observation that cognitive tests tended to positively correlate with one another (Carroll, 1993). This "positive manifold," as it is sometimes called, suggested to Spearman that performance on cognitive tests was in large part determined by a common latent trait that is causing all of the cognitive tests to correlate. He identified this central trait as "g" and theorized that the observed positive manifold supports the idea that this is the most important intellectual trait. Consequently, he placed "g" at the top of a hierarchical model of intelligence. He also hypothesized that "g" represents an underlying "mental energy" that is central to all intelligent problem solving and called for further research to better identify the biological roots of this "energy." Spearman recognized that performance on a cognitive task also requires a *specific factor* or "s"; it is, however, the general ability that is clearly viewed as most important for producing intelligence test performance.

The relative influence of both "g" and "s" can be crudely demonstrated by reviewing a set of correlations such as those in the matrix shown in Table 2.1. These data show that the three tests can be ordered according to their "g" saturation

TABLE 2.1 Hypothetical intercorrelation matrix for a set of three cognitive tests

	Vocabulary	Memory	Spatial
Vocabulary		.50	.60
Memory	.50		.40
Spatial	.60	.40	

Average Correlation of Vocabulary with Two Other Tests = .55 [(.50 + .60)/2]

Average Correlation of Memory with Two Other Tests = .45 [(.50 + .40)/2]

Average Correlation of Spatial with Two Other Measures = .50 [(.60 + .40)/2]

(i.e., average correlation with other cognitive tests). In this example, Vocabulary has the most saturation and Memory the least. It may be said then that performance on the Vocabulary test is determined to a greater extent by "g" than in the case for Memory. In addition, all three of the tests are positively correlated to a significant degree indicating that "g" is an important influence on performance on a variety of cognitive tasks.

In Support of "g"

A well-known proponent of the British approach to the study of intelligence is the American researcher Arthur Jensen. Jensen (1969) proposed a theory of intelligence that hypothesized the existence of two mental processes. Level I processing (associative ability) typically does not require manipulation or transformation of the stimulus input prior to producing a response. Level I ability is tapped by rote learning tasks such as digit recall and paired associate learning. Level II processing (conceptual ability), on the other hand, requires considerable manipulation and elaboration of the stimulus input in order to produce a response. Level II processing is tapped by tests such as concept learning and spatial problem solving. Level II processing is clearly the higher level of processing in Jensen's hierarchy of intelligence, whereas Level I processing does not require very complex problem solving. While only hypothesizing two mental processes, Jensen's earlier theorizing clearly resembles a hierarchical approach where reasoning is considered to be an indicator of better intelligence than measures of rote recall.

Jensen (1982) has since turned his attention to "g" and its definition. He has also responded to the criticism that psychometric "g," the positive correlation among mental tests, is a statistical artifact. After a careful review of research studies, he concluded:

Evidence is summarized showing that g is correlated more highly than any other factor with a number of phenomena that are wholly independent of both psychomet-

rics and factor analysis. Relationships have been found between g and the heritability of test scores, the effects of inbreeding depression on test scores, reaction times to elementary cognitive tasks which have virtually no intellectual content, evoked electrical potentials of the cerebral cortex, and other physical correlates. This evidence of biological correlates of g supports the view that g is not a biological artifact but is a fact of nature. However, the causal nature of g itself is not yet scientifically understood. That goal awaits further advances in neuroscience. (p. 157)

Additionally, Jensen (1982) has declared a revival for theories of reaction time (RT) as measures of general intelligence. Previously, reaction time and simple psychophysical measures were found to not correlate highly with criterion measures, especially academic achievement. Jensen, however, has concluded that Galton was in fact correct, but that he lacked the technology necessary to assess reaction time adequately. He also argued that much of the RT research suffered from other experimental design problems, such as not using enough trials so as to obtain reliable estimates of reaction time. Jensen (1982) cited numerous studies and research paradigms as indicative of renewed interest in RT as a measure of general intelligence. Jensen (1987) himself has shown correlations as high as .98 between dual RT measures and the "g" (general intelligence) factor of an aptitude battery.

There are also studies that have not found high correlations between RT measures and intelligence tests. Ruchala, Schalt, and Bogel (1985) found only a complex RT task to correlate somewhat with a German test of intelligence, the "Intelligenz-Strukturtest." However, even the correlation of the complex RT task with the intelligence test was significant, but unimpressive. The highest correlation found was only .16.

One should not presume, based on the foregoing discussion, that RT research and its variants are no longer of interest. Inspection time, a significant variant from the RT measure, continues to be studied with vigor (Deary, 1999). The inspection time paradigm differs from the RT methodology in numerous ways. The stimulus is

visual (such as an incomplete drawing that has vertical lines of differing length on both the right and left sides); it is exposed for 10 milliseconds or less but, in contrast to RT tasks, the correctness of the individual's judgment of the line length (Which one is longer, the right or the left?) is taken as the item response (Deary & Stough, 1996). The examinee can take as much time as possible to offer a response since speed of response is irrelevant.

Deary and Stough (1996) contend that meta-analyses of correlations of inspection time measures with intelligence tests such as the Wechsler series have consistently found coefficients to be in the range of .40 to .50. However, these coefficients are higher for the Wechsler Performance scale than for the Verbal scale, and the correlations may be better for elderly populations of those with cognitive impairments. The interested reader is referred to Deary and Stough (1996) for an overview of inspection time research.

The overall intelligence index, the practical expression of the measurement of "g," has also been shown to be stable over the course of development (Moffit, Caspi, Harkness, & Silva, 1993). In fact, Moffit et al. (1993) demonstrated that the popular alternative to the composite score, the profile of scores represented by a variety of intelligence test subtests, is unstable when analyzing data from a large longitudinal study of change. Such findings further buttress the conception of "g" based on its practical interpretive value.

Recent work has pointed to two mechanisms that may serve as the essence of psychometric "g"—reasoning ability and working memory (Gustafsson, 1999). Reasoning ability, as alluded to earlier, is best represented by measures of "fluid" ability (to be discussed later). Working memory capacity (also discussed later) has also been cited as a central mechanism of "g" (Kyllonen, 1996). These intriguing possibilities bring us closer to an understanding of "g" than has been possible in the first century of intelligence testing. We are presuming, however, that there is general agreement that the concept of "g" exists. Some prominent researchers and theoreticians think that not only is "g" an epiphenomenon but much time has been wasted in pursuit of a better understanding of this unimportant concept. A sampling of these views are aired next.

Counter Arguments to "g"

Detterman (1987) has taken issue with the concept of "g" using the modern large university as an analogy. He proposed that intelligence tests currently in use are made up of complex tasks that when summed or averaged produce an estimate of overall system (intellectual) functioning. This estimate is similar to the size of a university's endowment or library holdings in that it is a gross estimate of the quality of a university (Detterman, 1987). This information is helpful to the high school senior who intends to select among various colleges so long as the student is interested in the overall quality of the institution. But a prospective student may be interested in a specific program at the university, say the Journalism school. It is conceivable that the university is excellent overall but the Journalism school for some reason is in turmoil. In this case the overall university rating or "g" is of no value. So too is the case with intelligence testing where a child may receive a particularly high or low composite score. A child may have a rather unique skill or weakness that is masked because the focus is on the composite score. Taking this argument one step further, a case could be made that both Galton and Binet were incorrect. Galton had a good idea to measure discrete basic cognitive skills, but he erred by not demonstrating how combining these skills can be used to solve certain problems. Binet too may have erred by using only complex tasks, making it difficult to determine how cognitive skills may interact to solve problems.

Vandenberg and Vogler (1985) question the concept of "g" from a different vantage point by concluding:

Against the argument that all ability tests correlate positively and therefore measure the same ability, one can point out that height and weight also correlate, and rather substantially, yet we consider them to be separate characteristics. (p. 6)

Detterman's ideas are provocative in that they are one way of reconciling the differences between Weinberg's "lumpers" and "splitters." He suggested that both points have something to contribute to our understanding of intelligence that may be greater than either theory individually.

More condemning criticisms of the concept of "g" are made by Horn (1988), Stankov (1999), and others. One of the most problematic pieces of evidence that detracts from the validity of "g" is that many different combinations of tests yield the same "g" factor. For example, a reasonable estimate of general intelligence can be obtained from the many short-term memory (labeled *sequential processing* by the test authors) and spatial ability (labeled *simultaneous processing*) subtests of the K-ABC. On the other hand, the verbal, spatial, and sequential and quantitative reasoning scales of the DAS, when combined, also produce a good estimate of general intelligence. Such findings do indeed make "g" look like a statistical artifact of cognitive testing. Based on data such as these, the criticisms of "g" can be stinging. Stankov (1999) stated the spirit of most of these criticisms by saying:

First, there has been an unjustified tendency to overemphasize the role of the general factor at the expense of broad (e.g., Gf [fluid intelligence], Gc [crystallized intelligence], and so forth) and primary factors (Jensen, 1997). A logical conclusion on the part of the decision makers is that research into the usefulness of a variety of tasks is unnecessary—virtually any cognitive task that has satisfactory psychometric properties will do. This is not only an impoverished view of human cognition but is also scientifically dubious because it ignores a large body of contrary evidence. (p. 316)

Stankov (1999) is not only arguing that the study of "g" is of little value, but also theorizing that such research could lead those who fund cognitive science research to falsely believe that further scientific work is unnecessary. Basically, an emphasis on "g" may give the false impression that much of human intelligence and cognition is understood. This latter outcome would truly be disastrous as there is clear evidence that other factors of intelligence are highly related to a variety of life outcomes. First, however, it is important to understand the factor analytic tradition that has produced much of the knowledge base regarding intelligence and its measurement.

FACTOR ANALYTIC THEORIES

Factor Analysis

At its simplest level, factor analysis is an analytical technique that reduces a given set of variables (or tests) to a smaller number in order to simplify the interpretation of data. As Spearman observed, the subtests included in a larger battery of intelligence tests correlate with one another; a phenomenon that he referred to as the "positive manifold." As such, it is theorized that this correlation between subtests is the result of one or more common factors. The purpose of factor analysis is to reduce the correlations between all subtests in an intelligence test to a smaller set of common factors. This smaller set of factors will presumably be more interpretable than considering all of the subtests in an intelligence test battery as measures of unrelated individual traits.

The output from a factor analysis is a factor matrix showing the factor loading of each subtest on each factor. A *factor loading* is in many cases the correlation between a subtest and a factor.[1] Factor loadings range from −1 to +1 just as do correlation coefficients, and they can be squared to compute the amount of shared variance be-

TABLE 2.2 Hypothetical factor loadings for four cognitive tests

Test	Factor 1	Factor 2
Vocabulary	.71	−.22
Definitions	.60	−.11
Copying Designs	.10	.59
Visual Closure	.18	.66

tween a subtest and a factor. In this way one can determine the extent to which a subtest is an indicator of, or measures, the latent trait represented by the factor. The factor loadings for a hypothetical data set are shown in Table 2.2. The four subtests and their respective loadings can be plotted as shown in Figure 2.1, and the relative amount of specific variance, that which cannot be presumed to be influenced by "g," is given for two tests in Figure 2.2.

Note that there are two axes, marked by heavy lines, depicted in Figure 2.1 to represent the two

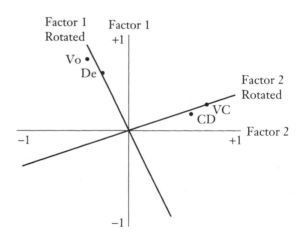

Vo = Vocabulary, De = Definitions, CD = Copy Designs, and VC = Visual Closure

FIGURE 2.1

Depiction of hypothetical factor loadings for four subtests

[1]When orthogonal (independent or uncorrelated) rotation techniques are used (and these techniques are very frequently used in test validation research), the factor loading represents the correlation between the subtest and a factor. This is not the case when oblique or correlated methods of factor analysis are used (Anatasi, 1988).

Vocabulary (excellent measure of "g" with little "subtest specificity," i.e., "s")

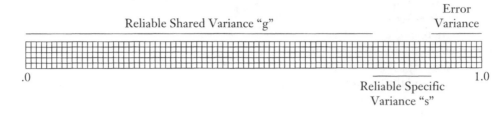

Copying Designs (relatively poor measure of "g" with more "subtest specificity," i.e., "s")

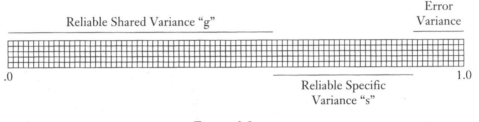

FIGURE 2.2

Relative influence of "g" and "s" on two cognitive tests

factors (i.e., latent traits) that underlie the correlations among these four tests. The factor loadings for each test on each factor are shown in the preceding table (the loading for the factor of which it is a member is given first for each test). Also observe that the higher factor loadings approach a value of 1.0 while lower loadings nearer to the juncture of the factor vectors are 0. While the initial factor loadings place the four tests near the vectors representing their factors, the solution can be improved by "rotating" the axes, a procedure designed to maximize the loadings of tests on factors. The rotation procedure provides a better fit of the tests to the factors, thus making the factor a better estimate of the underlying latent trait. Now the difficult part involves identifying the latent trait and defining it in a manner that fosters usage of the factor as a derived score.

Once the factor matrix, as is shown in Table 2.2, is obtained, the reseacher must provide an interpretation and label for the obtained factors. This labeling is done not based on statistical procedures but based on theoretical considerations on the part of the individual researcher (Anastasi, 1988). In the case of the WISC there is a long tradition associated with the names of the first two factors. The first factor is typically referred to as Verbal Comprehension, and the second as Perceptual Organization. The labels for these factors have, however, been debated and the naming of the third factor has been particularly controversial (Lowman, Kamphaus, & Schwanz, 1996). For many tests such as the K-ABC and Binet 4, there is considerable disagreement as to the traits being measured by the obtained factors (Kamphaus, 1990; Thorndike, 1990).

The logical procedures for identifying the trait associated with a factor are not consistently elucidated or utilized. A trait may be identified based on the content of the items themselves (e.g., verbal versus nonverbal) or the nature of the stimulus input or output (e.g., expressive versus receptive). Traits may also be hypothesized using the theory of information processing underlying the test as was the case for the K-ABC, where the two major factors were labeled simultaneous and sequential processing (Kaufman & Kaufman, 1983b). Research from areas such as cognitive psychology and neuropsychology may also be used to label a factor. Digit recall tests, for example, have been called memory span or working memory by various researchers. This knowledge may be used by a factor analyst to then label a factor that, among other properties, is characterized by high factor loadings for a digit recall task. Finally, tradition certainly plays a role in this naming process. One of my colleagues once described himself as a "practicing and devout chicken" when referring to his naming of factors for a research study. Perhaps there is some safety in naming factors based on precedents that have been set by famous factor analysts of the past.

Conservatism notwithstanding, the identification of the latent trait underlying performance on a factor is a crucial inferential step in the intelligence testing process. Failure to provide a clear interpretation of a factor has a direct and detrimental impact on the interpretability of the obtained score associated with a factor. This lack of interpretive clarity makes the utility of many intelligence test scores questionable. For example, although most psychologists are familiar with the term *perceptual organization*, a consensual definition of the term eludes the field. More alarmingly, few psychologists can offer an operational definition of this construct, thus reinforcing the perception that intelligence is "what the test measures."

Therefore, it is incumbent on the field to identify consensual definitions of the constructs measured by various intelligence test factors. Debate can continue to rage among researchers but clinicians must have some commonly understandable trait definitions and labels. Consensual definitions have emerged for some psychological traits such as depression. The use of this term connotes some meaning to clients and colleagues alike. In direct contrast, when one speaks of a strength in perceptual organization the meaning is less clear. One standard that clinicians may apply to assess the clarity of their interpretations is the parental standard that has been applied in fields such as journalism—that is, "you say that your mother loves you, now prove it." If test results cannot be explained successfully to your mother or father, who are presumed to not be psychologists, then your identification of the latent trait underlying test performance is of questionable value to other consumers.

Factor Analytic Theories

Vernon (1950) expanded on the hierarchical model proposed by Spearman by offering a more detailed hierarchy of intellectual abilities as is shown in Figure 2.3. At the top of this hierarchy is the major group factor, general intelligence, which is highly consistent with the theorizing of Spearman. Next in the hierarchy are the minor group factors, which are of two varieties: verbal/educational (*v:ed*) and spatial/mechanical (*k:m*) types of intelligence. Within these two group factors then are several specific factors of intelligence.

Vernon (1984) supports the further division of "g" into the verbal/educational and spatial/mechanical dimensions primarily with factor analysis. His studies have shown that when overall "g" is held constant, verbal tests intercorrelate and visual/spatial tests intercorrelate, but the correlation between the two types is usually negative. Vernon, however, finds little evidence to support focusing on particular cognitive styles including the verbal/spatial dichotomy, as most of the variance in intelligence tests is still attributable to the major group factor—"g." Vernon's

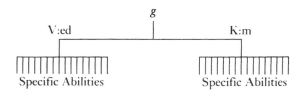

FIGURE 2.3

Vernon's (1950) hierarchical model

theory is of greater interest today than perhaps at any time because his work foreshadowed the refinement of so-called hierarchical theories of intelligence.

Thurstone's Primary Mental Abilities

Thurstone's theory has often been cited as standing in direct opposition to that of Spearman. While Spearman used factor analysis to "prove" the existence of "g," Thurstone used factor analytic techniques to prove the opposite, that intelligence was made up of a rather large number of faculties, the so-called primary mental abilities (PMAs). Performance of an individual on a particular cognitive task was not then a function of "g" and the "s," or specific cognitive ability, required for the task; rather performance was dictated by the primary mental abilities required for successful completion of the cognitive task. As such, Thurstone's theory was not hierarchical in nature as was Spearman's.

The PMAs

Thurstone (1938) first identified nine, then seven (Thurstone & Thurstone, 1941), then six (Thurstone, 1961/1941) primary mental abilities through factor analytic investigations. The seven abilities most frequently attributed to Thurstone include those listed below (Minton & Schneider, 1980).

Space (S)	Facility in spatial or visual imagery.
Perceptual Speed (P)	Quick and accurate noting of visual details.
Number (N)	Speed and accuracy in making arithmetic computations.
Verbal Meaning (V)	Understanding ideas and meanings of words.
Word Fluency (W)	Speed in manipulating single and isolated words.
Memory (M)	Facility in rote memory of words, numbers, letters, and other materials.
Inductive Reasoning (I)	Ability to abstract a rule common to a set of particulars.

Cattell's Fluid and Crystallized Abilities

At about the same time as the development of the first publication of the Wechsler scale, Cattell's factor analytically based intelligence theory was garnering recognition (Cattell, 1940). Cattell, as is seemingly common for intelligence theorists, hypothesized two types of intelligence. Essentially, Cattell found that the ideas of Spearman's "g" and Thurstone's primary mental abilities were not irreconcilable (Cattell, 1979). He proposed reconciling the two approaches by designating two types of "g." The first type is "g_f," or fluid intelligence. This is similar to Spearman's "g" in that it affects all types of problem solving. As Cattell (1979) states, "it flows with unrestricted expression into all fields of relation perception." Fluid intelligence has been found to develop rapidly to about age 15 (regardless of education) and decline thereafter. It is also more related to physiological factors and more highly influenced by genetic factors (Cattell, 1979). Crystallized intelligence, "g_c," by contrast, is related to some particular area of expertise that an individual has specifically learned or experienced (e.g., arithmetic, vocabulary, general information).

Presumably, a culture-free intelligence test could be devised using only "g_f" tests. This has proved difficult in practice, and some expert academicians such as Anastasi (1988) have advised against it, saying it is not possible to separate the two.

Horn (1979), a colleague of Cattell's, has expanded on the "g_f" and "g_c" dimensions by adding second-order factors. He has further identified factors, including "g_v," *visualization*.

Abilities that are part of this factor include visualization, spatial orientation, flexibility of closure, and speed of closure. Another factor, "g_a," *general auditory organization*, includes abilities such as speech perception under distraction/distortion, auditory cognition of relationships, and temporal tracking. The *short-term acquisition and retrieval* (SAR) factor measures the ability of the individual to learn and retain information over the span of a few seconds or minutes. A final factor is labeled *tertiary storage and retrieval* (TSR), and abilities it assesses include associational fluency, ideational fluency, and expressional fluency. This factor assesses the ability to make association with material recalled from the distant past. Horn's (1979) approach to the study of individual differences has received considerable attention since it serves as the basis for the cognitive assessment portion of the Woodcock-Johnson Psychoeducational Test Battery—Revised.

Carroll's Tour de Force

The three-stratum theory of intellectual abilities is based on the already classic 1993 text by John B. Carroll. This text represents one of the most ambitious undertakings in the history of factor analytic research. Carroll (1993) gathered hundreds of sets of correlational data for cognitive tests, both experimental and clinical, and reanalyzed the data using factor analysis. This compilation of factor analytic findings is of such breadth and depth that no distillation of his findings will suffice, including that which follows. The serious student of intellectual assessment is ill-informed if he or she has not read the text in its entirety.

In its simplest form the three-stratum theory derives from data, not the clinical or theoretical musings of Dr. Carroll. The data utilized to generate the theory are the results of numerous hierarchical factor analyses that yielded three "strata" of factors for interpretation. The first "narrow" stratum consists of factors that measure relatively discrete cognitive abilities such as Piagetian reasoning, lexical knowledge, spelling ability, visual memory, spatial scanning, speech sound discrimination, ideational fluency, rate of test taking, and simple reaction time.

The second "broad" stratum in the hierarchy represents measures of traits that are combinations of stratum-one measures. The stratum-two construct of crystallized intelligence, for example, is produced by measuring first-stratum traits such as tests of language development, verbal language comprehension, lexical knowledge, etc. In other words, crystallized intelligence represents a trait that is measured substantially by all of these first-stratum traits. The complete list of second-stratum traits hypothesized by Carroll includes fluid intelligence, crystallized intelligence, general memory and learning, broad visual perception, broad auditory perception, broad retrieval ability, broad cognitive speediness, processing speed (i.e., reaction time decision speed). Each of these factors will be discussed, in turn, as they have numerous implications for the interpretation of intelligence tests.

The ground rules for interpreting Carroll's work in this section are as follows. First, the marker tests for each of the second-order factors are given with special emphasis devoted to those tests that are currently part of commercially available intelligence tests. Whether one considers the current crop of tests to be of sufficient practical value is not a consideration. These tests are likely to continue to be applied for the foreseeable future, making clear interpretation of their results a continuing professional need. Second, Carroll's and related works will be integrated and interpreted in the context of other findings so as to deepen the clinician's knowledge of the major factors of intelligence tests (stratum-two factors). The second-stratum factors will then be linked conceptually to popular tests and definitions offered for each. This joining of these factors to popular tests will serve as an important foundation for an interpretive system that will be offered in a later chapter.

Fluid Intelligence

The tests and first-order factors comprising this ability are previously referred to as measures of reasoning, including tests of general sequential reasoning, induction, syllogisms, series tasks, matrix tasks, analogies tasks, quantitative reasoning tasks, etc. (Carroll, 1993). Sample reasoning test items include

1. Verbal analogy item—Shoe is to foot, as hat is to? *Head*
2. Figural analogy item—Half square is to square as half circle is to? *Circle*

Tasks of this nature have high loadings on the stratum-three general intelligence factor, higher than those of any other second-order factor. Fluid intelligence tasks, however, are not particularly well represented in widely used tests of intelligence such as the WISC-III. If fact, none of the WISC-III subtests can be easily identified as belonging to this group. Some of the matrices tasks on the Binet 4, DAS, W-J, and K-ABC could be considered to be members of this second-order factor. On the other hand, a matrix reasoning task in isolation does not meet the typical standard of having two indicators of a latent trait in order to define a factor. If this standard is applied, the fluid ability second-order factor is lacking a sufficient number of indicators on most intelligence tests.

The fluid ability label may be of questionable value for two reasons: (1) psychologists may not have a general consensual definition of the construct that allows for clear communication among clinicians, and (2) the fluid ability terminology may communicate some superfluous meaning to others. For example, fluid ability theory has been associated with genetic causation, an oversimplification of the nature/nurture debate (see next chapter). For these reasons, I prefer to refer to this second-order factor in a manner consistent with its constituent indicators, that is, reasoning.

A review of marker test items provides one vehicle for communicating the essence of the trait that is assessed by a factor, and an operational definition of the trait enhances communication further. For the purposes of this text, reasoning may be defined as "that follows as a reasonable inference or natural *consequence; deducible or defensible on the grounds of consistency; reasonably believed or done"* (Brown, 1997).

Crystallized Intelligence

First-order factors of crystallized ability typically have one central characteristic; they involve language abilities. The language abilities involved range from vocabulary knowledge to spelling, foreign-language proficiency, and reading comprehension. It is not reasonable, however, to dismiss this ability as a general academic achievement factor. Carroll (1993) identified a separate set of factors of school achievement and knowledge comprised of tests of specific academic subject areas (e.g., English, History), among other tasks. The linguistic influence on these tasks is evident especially in the tasks comprising the first-order language development factor.

The item types included in measures of language development are readily identifiable by psychologists due to their prevalence on popular measures of intelligence such as the Wechsler series. Carroll (1993) cited Wechsler Vocabulary and Similarities subtests as premier measures of language development. Sample items include

1. How are a book and a newspaper alike?
2. What does the word *pusillanimous* mean?

It can be concluded then that the Verbal scales of numerous intelligence tests may have two or more indicators of the language development factor. Consequently, this factor generally may be interpretable for many popular intelligence tests.

Other factors within the crystallized intelligence domain can be differentiated from language development, but with some difficulty (Carroll, 1993), thus supporting the interpretability of the second-order factor. It is important then to turn attention to the labeling of this factor.

The crystallized ability label possesses some of the same problems with clarity as is endemic to the fluid ability factor: (1) psychologists may not have a general consensual definition of the construct that allows for clear communication among clinicians, and (2) the term *crystallized ability* is often accompanied by simplistic interpretations. Specifically, crystallized ability theory has been associated with environmental causation (see next chapter). Therefore, it may be defensible and, in fact, advantageous to the need for effective communication to relabel the second-order factor so as to fully recognize the centrality of language processes represented by all of the first-order factors. With this objective in mind, it is now necessary to identify a language-related label and propose an accompanying operational definition.

In the interpretive scheme introduced later, this secondary factor will adopt the name *verbal* so as to enhance communication between clinicians and consumers. This characterization recognizes the centrality of language and yet the variety of tasks found to measure this latent trait (e.g., word reading and spelling). In addition, the term *verbal* has often been used by the general public when describing types of intelligence, suggesting that this label may be helpful for communicating the results derived from such measures. Finally, for the purposes of this text, the *verbal latent trait* is defined as *oral and written communication skills that follow the system of rules associated with a language*. This definition is intended to apply to various forms of oral and written expression and to both forms of comprehension.

General Memory and Learning

The vast majority of tests of memory included in popular intelligence tests are of the *memory span* variety. The popular digit span, sentence recall, geometric design recall, bead recall, and similar measures loaded consistently on a first-order factor that, in turn, can be subsumed under this sec-

ond-order factor (Carroll, 1993). All of these tasks have the common characteristics of recalling the identity of stimuli and, in most cases, doing so in serial order. Typical item types for such measures include

1. The examiner asks a child to repeat these numbers in sequence, "9-2-6-8."
2. The examiner asks a child to repeat these words in sequence, "It is very cold when the wind blows."
3. After showing a stalk with 6 differing colored beads on it an examiner asks the child to repeat the pattern using a separate stalk and set of beads.

Carroll (1993) observed that all *memory span* subtests require "*attention to temporally ordered stimulus, registration of the stimulus in immediate memory, and output of its repetition*" (p. 259). This quote serves as a good operational definition of the trait assessed by the majority of these tests in current use. Furthermore, Carroll (1993) did not identify any differences in factor loadings that could be attributed to requiring the presentation of digits in reverse sequence (i.e., WISC-III Digits Backward), or differences due to verbal versus visual presentation of the stimuli. These data suggest that the more global term *memory* may be applicable to the naming of this factor and serve to describe the central underlying latent trait.

Some intelligence tests have a limited number of measures of this variety (e.g., WISC-III), whereas others have two or more such measures allowing for the ready identification of a memory span factor (e.g., the Binet 4 has both Bead Memory and Memory for Sentences subtests among others). Given this situation, clinicians are often able to have adequate indicators of the first-stratum memory span factor, which they may use to make an inference about the stratum-two memory trait.

Memory, however, is a complex function that can be subdivided into a lengthy list of component processes or, so we think (see information processing theory described later in this chapter). Carroll's data, on the other hand, indicate that a general memory trait is the primary determinant of performance on the variety of first-order factor marker tasks.

Broad Visual Perception

The major level factor here is referred to as Visualization by Carroll (1993). This factor is of potential importance for the practicing psychologist because it has been identified in numerous factor analytic studies and, as will be shown in later chapters, factor analysis of popular intelligence tests have long produced a similar factor. Tests of this factor may require the ability to accurately perceive and transform stimuli in either two- or three-dimensional space, including items that require

1. building a block tower that matches a model.
2. accurately reproducing Greek letters.
3. folding paper and asking the examiner to select a picture, among a set of options, that best depicts the appearance of the paper (the folds) when unfolded.

This ability was defined in the 1963 ETS Kit of Factor Reference Cognitive Tests as "the ability to manipulate or transform the image of spatial patterns into other visual arrangements" (p. 316, cited in Carroll, 1993). This definition, however, implies that some visual manipulation may be necessary to solve the test item correctly; however, many test items that factor in this domain merely require reproduction of a model design (e.g., the population Block Design task and its variants). In these tasks the ability to "see" the model (or stimulus) accurately is likely a necessary precursor to successful problem solving. Consistent with this observation, the definition of *visualization* could be expanded to include problems where the examinee must first *form a mental image of a visual stimulus and then correctly arrange the response stimuli in space.*

Broad Auditory Perception

The first-order factors and subtests that contribute to their measurement are more likely found on speech tests used by speech pathologists and audiologists than those used by psychologists. Sample test items may include

1. identifying whether two auditorily presented speech sound stimuli (e.g., phonemes) are the same or different.
2. indicating whether tones of various frequencies are heard.
3. identifying speech sounds that are in some way distorted.

This factor will be deemphasized to some extent in this volume for two reasons. First, few intelligence measures (the Woodcock-Johnson Cognitive is a notable exception) include subtests of this nature. Some of these tests also require specialized equipment, which may partially explain their absence on popular tests. Second, many psychologists likely do not possess the competencies necessary to interpret these tests, which require specialized training in the communication sciences and disorders.

Broad Retrieval Ability

The level factor of this second-order factor is given as originality/creativity by Carroll (1993). The word *retrieval* is likely included to describe this dimension due to the requirement that multiple responses be elicited for this task. A test of creativity, such as the Torrance Tests of Creative Thinking, may include items such as

1. using a pencil to make as many designs/solutions as possible within a specified time limit using a simple design, such as a square.
2. creating as many unusual (rare) solutions to a problem as possible within a generous time limit.

This factor is also not emphasized in later chapters since tests of this variety are rarely included in popular test batteries. These tests are more frequently encountered on creativity tests and related measures.

Broad Cognitive Speediness

This factor, on the other hand, is measured by subtests that are common to intelligence tests. Moreover, this ability is characteristically a speed as opposed to level ability due to the supposition that differences between individual performances are typically not due to correct or incorrect responding but, rather, to slow or fast responding. Therefore, tests within this domain customarily involve simple test stimuli that merely need to be replicated at a rapid pace in order to obtain a high score. In addition, little decision making is required in order to complete the individual components of the task. Speed or rate of test taking tasks find their roots in the World War I testing movement in the United States. Item types for rate of test taking measures include

1. copying designs according to a prespecified code. For example, the code may be 1=g, 2=r, 3=y, 4=b, 5=a, etc.
2. indicating whether pairs of stimuli are alike or different. An example may be 1 vs. 5, 4 vs. 3, 9 vs. 9, 10 vs. 12, 2 vs. 2, etc.

This factor is important to distinguish from other intelligence factors because of its relative emphasis on speed. The primacy placed on speed is consistent with the prototypical relatively low "g" loadings of these tasks. Mediocre to poor "g" loadings may in turn indicate that intelligence (broadly defined) is best considered a level variable (Carroll, 1993). The reader will find that several popular tests contain measures of the factor (e.g., WISC-III Coding and Symbol Search subtests). An operational definition of *broad cognitive speediness* is offered as *the speed with which simple stimuli are reproduced by an examinee.*

Processing Speed

The marker tests for the processing speed factor differ from the previous speed factor in several ways. First, these tasks typically involve the measurement of reaction time and, second, they often require decision making. Prototypical tasks include

1. tapping a device in response to the perception of stimulus.
2. making a choice in response to a stimulus as quickly as possible.

While there is a long history of questionable correlations between measures of reaction time and general intelligence, modern reaction time measures, such as the so-called Elementary Cognitive Tasks (ECTs), do correlate moderately with "g."

Stratum Three

The third "general" stratum represents the familiar construct of general intelligence (Carroll, 1993). This highest-order factor is believed, in agreement with Spearman and others, to account for much of the variance in intelligence test performance.

The relationship among the three strata is, however, a complex one (see Figure 2.4). Carroll hypothesizes that the hierarchy is necessary since the differing levels contribute differentially to successful performance on intelligence, achievement, and related measures. Specifically, measures of first-strata traits are "dominated" by second-strata traits which, in turn, are dominated by stratum-three "g." By way of example, much of the variance in vocabulary knowledge (a stratum-one marker task) is accounted for by the other strata. Logically then this theory predicts that scores on a vocabulary test are determined first by general intelligence, second by crystallized ability, and third by specific vocabulary knowledge.

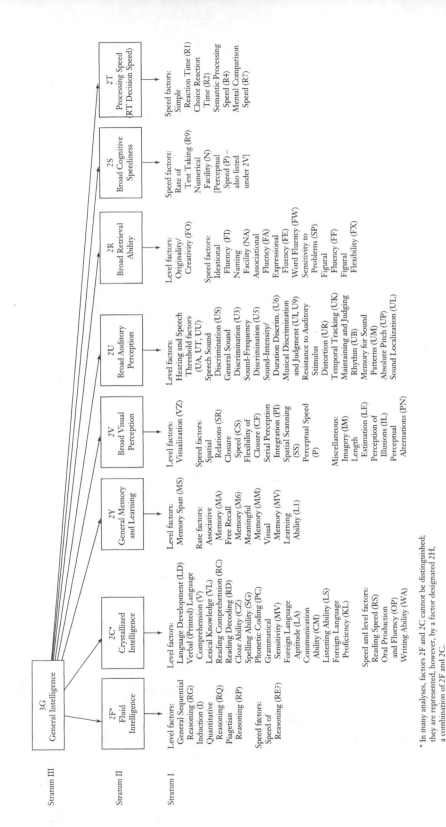

FIGURE 2.4

Hierarchical organization of Carroll's (1993) three-stratum theory (Reprinted with permission)

* In many analyses, factors 2F and 2C cannot be distinguished;
they are represented, however, by a factor designated 2H,
a combination of 2F and 2C.

The essence of "g" can be inferred to some extent based on inspection of Figure 2.4. The second-order factors most related to the first factor are fluid and crystallized ability, while measures of auditory perception, retrieval, rate of test taking, and processing speed are further removed. Such findings suggest that "g" is comprised primarily of tests that are already common on popular measures of intelligence. Further delineation of the "g" construct, however, is difficult to achieve given the varied nature of the second-stratum tasks that contribute to its measurement. In fact, the psychologist is more likely to be able to successfully explain the first- and second-stratum factors since these are less removed from their marker tasks.

Carroll's monumental compilation of data takes further support from related research by other factor analysts. His findings are not surprising to the student of factor analytic theories of intelligence. These results are, in fact, reassuring in that they confirm the earlier findings of factors of fluid and crystallized ability, memory span, and visual perception that are encountered in many popular tests of intelligence to be discussed in this volume.

Stratum One Revisited

The importance of stratum-one factors cannot be overlooked in spite of the premise that it accounts for less variance in score determination. While tests within the crystallized abilities domain, for example, presumably measure the same construct, reading specialists and others are unlikely to adopt the view that reading decoding, reading comprehension, phonemic awareness, and spelling tests measure the same constructs. Simply put there are other types of evidence, in addition to factor analysis, that shed light on the abilities measured by tests. Experimental investigations also demonstrate that stratum-one tests can function quite dissimilarly for select populations of children (Baddeley, 1999). In a series of investigations Baddeley (1999) has shown that a stratum-one test of phonological encoding in

working memory quite adeptly identified children with language impairments. More significantly, this stratum-one task appears to cause problems in language acquisition—the abilities assessed at stratum two by measures of crystallized intelligence.

While it is tempting to reify a particular level (or stratum) of interpretation, "g," stratum two, or narrowly defined stratum-one factors, to do so would likely be simplistic. Individuals may display dysfunction or strength at each level, making interpretation dependent on the clinician's knowledge of relevant research.

Developed Abilities

Factor analytic evidence clearly indicates that intelligence and academic achievement tests often correlate highly, suggesting that the distinction between the two types of tests is based primarily on differences in content, not factor structure or other psychometric evidence. One needs only to witness Carroll's second-stratum crystallized intelligence factor to see this relationship. This factor includes numerous indicators that are shared between intelligence and achievement measures, with spelling and reading comprehension tests as noteworthy examples.

Although these findings are long standing, intelligence test performance is still typically presumed to be predictive of and underlie academic achievement test results. Similarly, intellectual abilities are thought to be the result of a multitude of factors, including genetic predisposition, parental stimulation, schooling, and other influences whereas achievement test results are viewed as resulting from formal school instruction. Depending on the ability being assessed, both of these suppositions may be untenable (Anastasi & Urbina, 1997). Perhaps it is best to consider intelligence test results as developed abilities just as is typically the case for academic achievement tests.

In addition, one can say that intelligence tests currently in vogue are measures of "academic intelligence" or "scholastic aptitude" (p. 296,

Anastasi & Urbina, 1997). They measure a limited range of cognitive abilities that, in some cases, such as quantitative or crystallized abilities, are highly related to academic achievement measures. The distinction between intelligence and achievement tests is a subtle one that requires further clarification throughout this volume. At this point one distinction is clear: Binet as well as his successors have merely attempted to differentiate the item content of intelligence and achievement measures in order to aspire to the "psychological" as opposed to the "pedagogical" method.

A TAXONOMY

Guilford's (1967) book, *The Nature of Human Intelligence*, offered an alternative, comprehensive, and complex theory of intelligence designed to explain the great variety of human cognition. According to Guilford's (1979) "structure of intellect" (SI) model, intelligence is

a systematic collection of abilities or functions for processing different kinds of information in different ways. Intelligence is thus concerned both with kinds of information and kinds of operations performed with information. Regarding the brain as "that computer between our ears" is a useful conception, at least by analogy. Like computers, brains also possess information in storage and programs for dealing with that information. (p. 33)

The three components of the SI model are contents, operations, and products. *Content* refers to a kind of information. The five contents are shown in Table 2.3. *Products* are items of information from the same content category (see Table 2.3). Guilford (1979) proposed that humans are constantly striving to organize related content for more efficient search and processing. As an example, it is much easier to retrieve information about hieroglyphics, a question that has been included on intelligence tests for some time, if one has a category for "languages" that

TABLE 2.3 Categories of the structure of intellect model

Operations	Contents	Products
Cognitive	Visual	Units
Memory	Auditory	Classes
Divergent Production	Symbolic	Relations
Convergent Production	Semantic	Systems
Evaluation	Behavioral	Transformations
		Implications

SOURCE: Adapted from Guilford (1979).

can be systematically searched for the information. *Operations* are rules of logic or mental procedures that act on content to solve problems.

Two of the more well-known operations from Guilford's theory are convergent and divergent production. *Convergent production* is a "focused search for a particular item of information that satisfies well-defined specifications" (Guilford, 1979, p. 35). *Divergent production* differs substantially in that it is "a broad search of the memory store, scanning it for alternative items of information all of which could possibly satisfy the same need" (Guilford, 1979, p. 35). A convergent question might be something like, "Who sells the brand X mousetrap?" versus a more divergent question, "How does one catch mice?" Divergent production has been used as the basis for the assessment of creativity (Torrance, 1965).

It is important to recall, however, that Guilford's theory is not based in factor analysis, although this may appear to be the case. A taxonomy refers to a classification of cognitive abilities based on either theoretical or empirical findings. In the case of the SI model the foundation is largely theoretical, yet the theory has contributed substantially to some aspects of cognitive assessment practice.

New "Factors"

Multiple Intelligences

The explication of H. Gardner's theory of *multiple intelligences* (1993) served to renew interest in the breadth of factors that may be considered to fall within the intelligence domain. Interestingly, Gardner proposes a similar number of intelligences to those that have been offered by Thurstone and others. The similarities of Gardner's intelligences to other multifactor theories are primarily superficial.

Gardner (1993) defined intelligence as "the ability to solve problems, or to create products, that are valued within one or more cultural settings" (p. x). He offers seven different intelligences, including linguistic, logical-mathematical, musical, spatial, bodily-kinesthetic, interpersonal, and intrapersonal. Gardner also attempts to broaden the types of assessment procedures used to measure these various abilities. Multiple intelligence theory proposes that linguistic and logical-mathematical intelligences are assessed to some extent by current test batteries to the exclusion of the other five abilities. Each intellectual ability, however, should be assessed within its context with "authentic" measures. Musical talent, for example, must be assessed "directly" by assessing performances.

Gardner's particular theory differs from numerous other theories discussed thus far in one central way. He offers that the seven intelligences are, for the most part, unrelated in terms of their polygenetic determination and their neurological locus. Additionally, the intelligences are not subserved by central processing abilities such as attention, memory, spatial ability, etc. (Chen & Gardner, 1997). It is this latter proposition that is difficult to support with empirical evidence. One can imagine the difficulties doing so given the tendency of a great many tests to be correlated. At any rate, Gardner remains firm in the conviction that multiple intelligences are in-

dependent functions. He observes that few individuals have equally developed abilities citing cases of idiot savants, focal brain injuries, and other phenomena as examples.

Gardner's theory has served to refocus efforts on entertaining the possibility that a variety of abilities may still be candidates for inclusion in intelligence theory and practice. Empirical support for the theory, in particular, the strict independence of the seven intelligences, is lacking. Messick (1992) states doubts about the theory more forcefully by concluding it ". . . is simply counterfactual" (p. 379).

Practical Intelligence

Practical intelligence derives from Sternberg's "contextual" subtheory (Sternberg, 1997). This type of intelligence is correlated poorly with traditional measures of intelligence, which can be considered an asset by its supporters or a weakness by detractors. Sternberg supports the utility of the practical intelligence construct by producing data showing that it is predictive of some school and employment criterion variables above and beyond the prediction offered by traditional intelligence tests.

This work has already resulted in curricular interventions for children. An educational program designed to teach practical intelligence skills to 9- to 11-year-old children in "reading, writing, homework, and test taking" has already resulted in some supportive outcome data (Sternberg, 1997). Watch for more writings on practical intelligence and its application in the future.

Emotional Intelligence

The 1990s produced another candidate for intelligence tests, namely, *emotional intelligence*. Mayer and Salovey (1993) define the construct as

a type of social intelligence that involves the ability to monitor one's own and others' emotions, to discriminate among them, and to use the information to guide one's thinking and actions. . . . The scope of emotional intelligence includes the verbal and nonverbal appraisal and expression of emotion, the regulation of emotion in the self and others, and the utilization of emotional content in problem solving. (p. 433)

Emotional intelligence has been proposed to be similar to other types of intelligence, such as spatial abilities, in that it is correlated with "g" and yet is distinct. Wechsler's more global conceptualization of intelligence (see Chapter 1) can serve as a broad intelligence umbrella under which the construct of emotional intelligence can easily be accommodated (Salovey & Mayer, 1989–90).

Mayer and Salovey (1995) later proposed that effective individuals display a number of characteristics that allow them to regulate emotions effectively. Clarity relates to the ability of an individual to clearly identify mood. Measures of clarity include items such as "I don't know how I feel." Greater clarity has been found to predict more positive judgments. Another emotional intelligence factor is referred to as attention, which refers to a person's tendency to attend to their moods. Ambivalence is another factor that includes items that assess uncertainty or regret about the expression of anger or other emotions. Further factor analytic studies have identified "meta-regulatory" mechanisms of mood, including mood repair, mood maintenance, and mood dampening. Scores derived from scales of these measures have been related to important health outcomes. Mood repair, for example, has been found to correlate with optimism (Mayer & Salovey, 1995).

The derivation of emotional intelligence theory is still in its early stages although it is yet another variant of older notions of social intelligence. Social intelligence theory have been part of intelligence theory for most of the 20th century (Mayer & Salovey, 1995). Joint factor analyses of the new breed of emotional intelligence measures and traditional cognitive indicators are needed to help articulate the relationship of these newer constructs to the old.

DEVELOPMENTAL PERSPECTIVES

Jean Piaget

Piaget's theory of cognitive development has had a profound influence on the way professionals view the thinking of young children. Most undergraduate students are at least somewhat familiar with his insightful observations of young children's thinking. Perhaps his most famous contribution is his delineation of a series of stages of cognitive development.

Piaget also theorized about the nature of intelligence. He proposed that children progress to successively higher stages of intellectual development through the use of two intellectual functions that promote cognitive growth. One of these processes is called *assimilation*. The process of assimilation is used by a child to incorporate a stimulus into an existing cognitive representation or schema. This is the process whereby a young child may take a piece of candy that she has never seen before and unwrap it and eat it. This child was able to fit the new stimulus, a new type of candy, into an existing schema and eat it, as opposed to fitting the new stimulus to an inappropriate schema, such as ball, and trying to bounce it. So what is a child to do when a new stimulus cannot be incorporated into an existing schema? In this case the child uses the other intellectual process called *accommodation*. Accommodation is said to occur when a child has to create a new schema or significantly alter an existing schema in order to incorporate a new stimulus. Say an infant is given a book for the first time. The infant is likely to try to first use assimilation in order to incorporate the stimulus into an existing schema. The child would put the book in his mouth. Should he be unsuccessful at ingesting the book he will likely form a new schema for "book" through the process of accommodation. It is easy to see how the use of assimilation and accommodation produces cognitive growth in order to allow the child to move through Piaget's cognitive stages.

Piaget's theory has only infrequently been used as a model for the development of intelligence tests. An attempt was made by Uzgiris and Hunt (1989) to develop an intelligence measure based on Piaget's theory of cognitive development. Other attempts to measure intelligence with Piagetian tasks have depended heavily on conservation tasks. This approach resulted in considerable disagreement as to whether Piagetian intelligence differs significantly from so-called psychometric intelligence as measured by the Wechsler or Binet scales (Carroll, Kohlberg, & DeVries, 1984) (see Research Report 2.1). In one large-scale investigation, however, it was

RESEARCH REPORT 2.1

Piagetian Intelligence and Binet's Test

Carroll, Kohlberg, and DeVries (1984) tried to discern the difference, or lack of it, between the intelligence measured by practical tests such as the Binet and Wechsler scales and intelligence as measured by tasks inspired by Piaget's theory and used in his clinical method. Carroll et al. (1984) reanalyzed data from two samples that were administered using the Stanford-Binet form LM and a variety of Piagetian tasks in order to assess the degree of overlap in the measures. The Piagetian tasks included Magic, Class Inclusion, Dream Concepts, L-R Perspectives, Number Conservation, Conservation—Liquid, Conservation—Length, Mass Conservation, Ring Segment, Generic Identity, Sibling Egocentrism, Length Transitivity, Guessing Game, and Object Sorting.

Scores on these various measures were then submitted, along with the Binet, to a series of factor analyses where age was partialled out. The loadings of the measures on a two-factor solution are shown below.

Test	Factor A	Factor B
Stanford-Binet	.78	.01
Magic	.49	.06
Class Inclusion	.58	−.12
Dream Concepts	.44	.20
L-R Perspectives	.51	−.19
Number Conservation	.06	.68
Conservation—Liquid	.04	.69
Conservation—Length	.07	.60
Mass Conservation	−.07	.62
Ring Segment	.37	.41
Generic Identity	.28	.24
Sibling Egocentrism	.15	.14
Length Transitivity	.37	−.09
Guessing Game	.41	.07
Object Sorting	.08	.00

The authors observed that since the conservation tasks have their highest loadings on a separate factor from the Binet that these tests measure something that is not part of traditional test batteries. Carroll et al. (1984) likened this conservation factor to other group factors that have been identified for cognitive tests such as spatial, verbal, or numerical abilities. They also concluded, however, that the majority of the Piagetian tests are like other tasks on intelligence measures in that there is a significant correlation among the measures or "g" factor. Based on these results the authors offered the proposition that Piagetian and traditional "psychometric" intelligences were similar and yet distinct and that current intelligence tests did not assess some of the important milestones of cognitive development such as conservation.

concluded that traditional intelligence tests and tests based on Piagetian tasks measure the same construct (Humphreys & Parsons, 1979).

A recent investigation used Piagetian theory as a basis for an intervention program with children of low socioeconomic status (SES) (Campbell & Ramey, 1990). The Concept Assessment Kit-Conservation (CAK) was used to assess the conservation skills of eighty-six 5-, 6-, and 7-year-olds in a longitudinal investigation. The low SES children did show a favorable response to conservation training. More germane to this discussion, however, were the findings of significant relationships between CAK scores and WISC-R and mathematics achievement scores. CAK scores correlated .49 with the Full Scale and Verbal scores of the WISC-R and .37 with the Performance Scale. Similarly, the CAK scores correlated .46 with a measure of mathematics achievement (Campbell & Ramey, 1990). These results provide empirical support for the continued study of Piaget's theory in order to assess its contribution to intelligence theory and measurement. On a practical level, it appears that despite the profound influence of Piaget's theorizing on education, his views have had relatively little influence on the day-to-day practice of intellectual assessment.

Transactional Theory

Transactional theory as proposed by Haywood and Switzky (1986) presents a theory of intelligence that attempts to explain the nature of the genetic/environmental interaction that produces various levels of performance on intelligence tests. A central premise of this theory, which is the same as other transactional notions of intelligence offered long ago, is that current intelligence tests, such as the Wechsler scales, are confounded measures in that they measure two constructs. One of the constructs measured by the Wechsler scales is intelligence, or native ability, which Haywood and Switzky attribute almost exclusively to genetic factors. The other construct is cognitive functions, or "learned cognitive operations, principles, processes, and strategies,

as well as a host of 'non-intellective' variables such as attitude toward learning, work habits, and motives."

Haywood and Switzky's ideas build on the writings of McCall (1983). One central feature of this theory is the concept of canalization, which McCall (1983) describes as follows:

Canalization postulates a species typical path, called a creod, *along which nearly all members of the species tend to develop. However, a given characteristic follows the creod only so as long as the organism is exposed to species-typical, appropriate environments. In the presence of such environments, development proceeds "normally"; when the environment deviates markedly from the typical, development may stray from the creod. (pp. 113–114)*

Davis (1964) also agrees with the transactional viewpoint. He gives a more practical application of the notion of deviation from a genetically determined path (or creod) in the following quotation.

Of course, the predictive accuracy of an aptitude test is poorest for individuals of high native ability who have had exceptionally barren or stultifying environments and for individuals of low native ability who have had exceptionally rich and stimulating environments. (p. 130)

In a simplified way, transactional theory stipulates that everyone has a creod for intelligence. If, for example, a child's genetic endowment includes a creod for high intelligence, this may or may not be evident in the child's scores. If the child has had a minimally supportive environment (e.g., adequate parental stimulation and schooling), then high intelligence will be expressed on the intelligence test. If, however, the child has been reared in a harsh and unstimulating environment, then the child may get lower scores on the intelligence test. In this latter situation, a child's creod for high intelligence is "masked." Haywood and Switzky (1986) site this idea of the "masking" of intelligence as the reason current intelligence tests are seriously flawed in that in many cases they underestimate the intelligence of children from nonsupportive environments. This idea, however, is not supported by research on test bias.

Some of the basic tenets of the way intelligence is conceptualized by transactional theory are given below.

1. Intelligence is largely transmitted genetically through a polygenetic inheritance system.

2. Certain genetic and environmental characteristics occur fairly consistently together. Thus, children who inherit polygenes for high IQ from their parents are often reared in psychologically stimulating environments, and the reverse is often true of children who inherit polygenes associated with low IQ.

3. Persons differ in the extent to which their intellectual functioning is affected by more-or-less standard environmental variations. Thus, some children gain many IQ points from participation in a preschool education program, while other children in the same classes gain very little.

4. Other biological events such as clinical (and even subclinical) malnutrition and anomalies of the nervous and metabolic systems often produce dramatic effects on intellectual development.

5. These biological events often are correlated with specific environmental circumstances that alter their effects on intellectual development. A child's response to malnutrition and premature birth are dependent on the qualities of the rearing environment.

6. The greatest intellectual deficits can be expected to occur among children who have the combination of poor nutrition, poor biomedical history, and poor environment. (Haywood, 1986, pp. 5–6)

Haywood (1986) hypothesizes further that there are equally important factors that should be considered when evaluating children and their intelligence test scores. The most important of these are environmentally determined cognition

and task-intrinsic motivation. It is these latter two constructs that Haywood has attempted to modify in his experimental preschool programs. Haywood, Tzuriel, and Vaught (1992) explain further:

> . . . *intelligence is largely genetically determined, whereas cognitive processes must be acquired. Intelligence is modestly modifiable, but cognitive processes are highly modifiable (having been acquired through learning in the first place). Components of intelligence include general, group, and specific factors—all related to "pure" ability variables, but components of cognitive processes may include both cognitive "structures" and motivational/attitudinal/affective variables. (p. 47)*

Transactional theory, however, does not yet have an extensive research base. Its major offshoot, dynamic assessment, has spawned both research and disagreement, as is discussed later in the text.

A Cognitive-Developmental Model

An alternative developmental model has been offered by Borkowski (1985), who has elaborated on the work of Campione and Brown (1978), and has drawn heavily from information processing research to propose a theory of intelligence and methods for its assessment. This is a hierarchical model with two levels (Borkowski, 1985).

1. The *architectural system*, which includes capacity for memory span, durability of stimulus traces, and efficiency or speed of encoding-decoding information.

2. The *executive system*, which includes retrieval of knowledge from long-term memory, Piagetian schemes, control processes (e.g., rehearsal strategies), and metacognitive states.

One of the interesting aspects of this theory is its emphasis on the development of these systems and their components over the life span. The developmental trajectories for several components

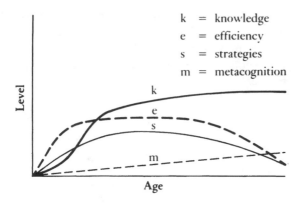

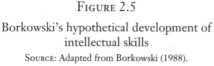

FIGURE 2.5

Borkowski's hypothetical development of
intellectual skills
SOURCE: Adapted from Borkowski (1988).

of the architectural and executive systems are
shown in Figure 2.5. Efficiency, for example,
peaks very early, perhaps by age 5, and declines
in late adulthood. Knowledge, on the other hand,
increases throughout the life span. Interestingly,
these predictions are somewhat consistent with
research on the assent and decline of intelligence
test scores (see next chapter).

INFORMATION PROCESSING
THEORY

Information processing approaches to the study
of human cognition burst onto the scene in the
late 1960s and early 1970s. A central characteristic of information processing theories is the use
of the computer and the way it processes information as a metaphor for human cognition. A
classic information processing model that may be
used for understanding performance on intelligence tests is depicted in Figure 2.6.

A simplified description of how the system
works is as follows. The processing begins in
response to an environmental stimulus, which
could be a test question. The question, asked of

the child by the examiner, must first be correctly
encoded by the sensory register. Note that the
sensory register must be capable of encoding a
variety of types of stimuli. In this case auditory
sensory capabilities are most important. The sensory register holds the stimuli intact, but only for
a short period of time—milliseconds (Bjorklund,
1989). At this point the question is transferred to
the short-term memory store or working memory for further processing. Here there is a limited
capacity, but the stimulus trace is more durable—
lasting for seconds (Bjorklund, 1989). It is in
short-term memory that a great deal of "thinking" is done. Perhaps this is why it is sometimes
called "working memory." It is also in short-term

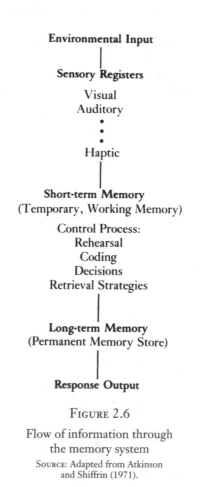

FIGURE 2.6

Flow of information through
the memory system
SOURCE: Adapted from Atkinson
and Shiffrin (1971).

memory where a number of strategies can be used to process information efficiently. In the case of an intelligence test item, it will probably be necessary for retrieval strategies to be generated in order to find the answer to our question. A retrieval cue such as a related concept or mental image may be used to search for information related to the item. In order to carry out this search, one has to go to the last component of the system, long-term memory. It is here where memory traces are placed for extended periods of time—hours, days, or years for that matter. Surely the answer is in there somewhere! Once the answer to the test item is found in long-term memory, it is transferred back to short-term memory and given in a vocal response to the examiner.

Long-Term Memory

The basic information processing model has been expanded by a number of researchers. Kyllonen and Alluisi (1987), for example, divide long-term memory into two components—declarative memory and procedural memory. *Declarative memory* is similar to traditional notions of long-term memory in that it is characterized by long-term storage and slow decay of memory

traces, and it stores acquired facts. *Procedural memory* differs in a number of ways but most importantly in that it stores rules for problem solving or production knowledge. Procedural memory stores knowledge about how to solve problems or apply information (Kyllonen & Alluisi, 1987). These two types of long-term storage then work in concert with working (short-term) memory to solve problems. Currently there are no commercially produced tests of these two types of long-term storage. Much needs to be learned about these and other aspects of memory, including how procedural memory develops (Kyllonen & Alluisi, 1987).

Metacognition

The basic human information processing system has been expanded by others. Flavell and Wellman (1977) subsequently offered the idea of metacognition. As the name implies, metacognition is knowledge about how thinking works. Metacognition may include knowledge about one's own cognitive strengths and weaknesses, about how to keep memory working efficiently, or about how to size up the demands of a cognitive task (Bjorklund, 1989). An important finding for understanding children's intelligence test performance

TABLE 2.4   Characteristics of declarative and working memories

	Declarative	Procedural
PRIMARY FUNCTION	Stores meaning of inputs	Stores how-to knowledge
CAPACITY	Unlimited	Unlimited
CONTENTS	Semantic codes Spatial codes Acoustic codes Motor codes Temporal codes	Semantic codes Spatial codes Acoustic codes Motor codes Temporal codes
INFORMATION UNITS	Concepts Propositions Schemata/frames/scripts	Productions (if-then rules) Specific to general

Adapted from Kyllonen and Alluisi (1987).

is that metacognitive knowledge increases with age.

More recently, the focus of information processing research has begun to shift emphasis from process to knowledge and its organization and use (Curtis & Glaser, 1984). Some researchers have proposed that knowledge may even be prerequisite to the use of some strategies (Bjorklund, 1989). This intermingling of the concepts of knowledge and process to the study of children's intelligence is described in the following excerpt from Curtis and Glaser (1984).

> . . . individual differences in the ability to learn can be attributed to differences in the content and structure of the knowledge base, and to differences in the way that knowledge is accessed, applied, and modified. It must be noted that this view is in sharp contrast to one in which skilled learners are thought to differ from those who are less-skilled simply because of superior mental ability. Instead, cognitive models view intellectual competence as a much more complex function of the knowledge that has been acquired and the processes that act on that knowledge. (p. 481)

This point of view is not an isolated one. Additionally, it may also serve to reiterate the point that it is simplistic to make a strict differentiation between intelligence and achievement testing, at least in the current manner in which these two constructs are assessed. The skilled psychologist can make inferences about the interplay of knowledge and cognitive skills that affect a child's performance on a great variety of cognitive tasks encountered in academic and other settings.

CONTEXTUAL/ECOLOGICAL THEORIES

Triarchic Theory

As proposed by Robert Sternberg, *triarchic theory* is an attempt to produce an integrative theory of intelligence (Sternberg, 1987). Sternberg has thoroughly reviewed the so-called psychometric and other approaches to the study of intelligence in the process of proposing his model. His theory has a distinctly information processing flavor to it, making it resemble various aspects of cognitive theories. Perhaps the greatest contribution of Sternberg is his attempt to "decompose" intellectual performance into the various strategies, procedures, and processes used to solve a problem. In a sense it could be said that his theory allows for a detailed task analysis of problem solving, fostering better understanding of the *reasons* a child may perform well or poorly on a problem.

This theory hypothesizes three types of information processing components that are necessary for competent problem solving. One type of process consists of *metacomponents*. These are executive processes that plan, monitor, and evaluate problem solving. Clearly, there is some relationship here to the cognitive term *metacognition*. Metacomponential processes include the following (Sternberg, 1987).

1. Deciding on the nature of the problem.
2. Selecting a set of lower-order processes to use to solve a problem.
3. Selecting a strategy for combining processes to solve a problem.
4. Selecting a mental representation on which the processes and strategy can act.
5. Allocating mental resources.
6. Monitoring problem solving

Performance components are a second level of cognition that consists of lower-order mental processes that are controlled by metacomponents. Inductive reasoning is one type of performance component. The third part of Sternberg's theory involves knowledge acquisition components that are used to learn the metacomponents and components processes. According to Sternberg, these skills are not well researched at this point, but they are crucial for acquiring important factual information needed for problem solving. Knowledge acquisition components include selective encoding, selective combination, and selective comparison.

Another part of triarchic theory, *experiential subtheory*, has two characteristics. It deals with the effects of experience on the expression of intelligent behavior. As Sternberg (1987) and others have correctly observed, all tasks used to assess intelligence have some level of familiarity to the individual being tested. As such, the ability to deal with novelty becomes a factor in intelligence test performance. Sternberg (1987) proposes that one reason cultural groups may have different mean scores on intelligence tests is due to the cultural group's experiences, or lack of same, with novel stimuli.

The second ability that is central to this experiential subtheory is the ability to automatize information processing. This ability refers to the common finding that problem solving occurs more expeditiously with repeated trials.

The *contextual subtheory* of triarchic theory states that intelligent behavior is directed toward the achievement of three behavioral goals: adaptation to an environment, shaping of an environment, and selection of an environment (Sternberg, 1987). The idea that intelligence has to be understood in relationship to environmental context makes this and other recent theories of intelligence (e.g., Valsiner, 1984) very distant cousins to early intelligence theories in that the vast majority of early intelligence theories emphasize the internal world of the person being tested. An example of how intelligent behavior can be defined differently based on culture or context is provided by Cole, Gay, Glick, and Sharp (1971) as described by Sternberg (1987) in the following quote:

> These investigators asked adult Kpelle tribesmen to sort 20 familiar objects into groups of things that belong together. Their subjects separated the objects into functional groupings (e.g., a knife with an orange), as children in western societies would do. This pattern of sorting surprised investigators, who had expected to see taxonomic groupings (e.g., tools sorted together and food sorted together) of a kind that would be found in the

> sortings of western adults. Had investigators used the sorting task as a measure of intelligence in the traditional way, they might well have labeled the Kpelle tribesmen as intellectually inferior to western adults. However, through persistent exploration of why the Kpelle were sorting in this way, they found that the Kpelle considered functional sorting to be the intelligent form of sorting. When the tribesmen were asked to sort the way a stupid person would do so, they had no trouble sorting taxonomically. In short, they differed on this test not in their intellectual competence vis-à-vis western adults, but in their conception of what was functionally adaptive. Indeed, it takes little thought to see the practicality of sorting functionally: people do, after all, use utensils in conjunction with foods of a given category (e.g., fruits) on a frequent basis. (p. 159)

Sternberg (1997) continues to clarify and expand his theory in numerous ways. He makes a case for the importance of his theory to lifelong learning and success in an article in *American Psychologist*. In this article he differentiates three constructs: "intelligence, intelligent behavior, and tested intelligence" (p. 1031). Tested intelligence is reflected in the set of scores obtained from a formal measure administered by a qualified examiner. Intelligence is conceptualized as the mental processes used by an individual to learn as reflected by the use of metacomponents, for example. Intelligent behavior is something quite different from tested intelligence and intelligence. Intelligent behavior is the behavior exhibited by the individual that is largely determined by environmental context as in the case of the Kpelle cited previously. Thus when psychologists draw inferences regarding a person's intelligence, Sternberg suggests that there may often be conceptual confusion. Tested intelligence may reflect deficient intelligence or intelligent behavior that is simply different from that of the expectation of the examiner due to contextual factors. Most important, Sternberg attempts to "stretch" the factor analytic theories of intelligence (e.g., Carroll) to include constructs such as practical intelligence or intelligence behavior. Other theoreticians and researchers stretch the construct much further, as will be seen.

Sternberg's theoretical work is one of the most recognized of the latter half of the 20th century. Moreover, his work has had an impact on the public due to his prolific writing. On the other hand, triarchic theory needs considerable research to support it—research that is lacking as of the time of this writing. One eminent reviewer of his work cites the clarity of Sternberg's theory as an impediment to its testability. Messick (1992), in a detailed review, found triarchic theory wanting by concluding that

> . . . *several aspects of Sternberg's theory appear to be simply nonfactual, in the sense that the ratio of constructs invoked to constructs measured is very high. . . . Furthermore, the ratio of interconstruct nomological relations entailed in the theory to the number examined empirically appears to be even higher. Hence, relative to the degree of empirical grounding, the triarchic theory is construct dense. (p. 379)*

Nevertheless, Sternberg's theory does bring to mind some potential test interpretations. An example of the application of Sternberg's contextual "subtheory" of intelligent behavior in interpreting the profile of an undergraduate student may be found in Box 2.1. The notion of the contextualist nature of intelligence is receiving increasing attention by recent theorists. In fact, the theorizing of Jaan Valsiner (1984) may place the greatest premium on understanding intelligence in context.

Intelligence Is the Interaction

Valsiner (1984) takes an interesting approach to conceptualizing intelligence by disavowing the vast majority of approaches to understanding intelligence. Valsiner (1984) observes, as did Sternberg, that definitions of intelligence and in-

Box 2.1

Application of Sternberg's Theory to Interpretation of a Young Adult's WAIS Results

The various theories described in this chapter may seem somewhat removed from the realm of everyday intelligence test interpretation. I beg to differ. On the contrary, I find myself labeling children as little Jensen's, Sternberg's, Cattell's, or the like. One of the clearest cases of the application of a theory comes from a coed who volunteered to take the WAIS-R for a student in my graduate assessment course.

The student who tested this young lady brought the results to my class for presentation and discussion. My student's concern about the young lady was obvious shortly after the case was presented. The young lady had achieved a WAIS-R Full Scale of *only* 86. We then launched into a discussion of whether we should tell this person about her "low IQ" despite our policy to the contrary and commitment to confidentiality. I then interrogated my student to produce the following profile of the coed.

She had a B+ college GPA, she was well liked by all, her major was recreation studies, she planned to open a health club after graduation, she was engaged and looking forward to getting married, and she was an elected member of student government. It then struck me that this lady's profile was a perfect example of one of Sternberg's contextual notions of adult intelligence. Namely, intelligent people shape and adapt to their environments by making maximum use of their strengths and deemphasizing their weaknesses.

By traditional measures of intelligence, the WAIS-R, this student had "problems," was "below average—dull" or "at risk" to say the least. However, when broadening the concept of intelligence to include adaptation, this lady was clearly clever, and I thought to myself, she will definitely be physically healthier, if not happier and wealthier than myself! She was clearly behaving quite adaptively as was indicated by her choice of major field of study. She must have some strengths in this area to have a good GPA, and she avoided majors that could have perhaps highlighted whatever cognitive limitations that she may possess. My suggestion to the class was to review Sternberg's ideas, to continue to strive to integrate theory and practice so as to avoid being merely a producer of intelligence test scores, and to *not attempt to seek this young woman out and tell her that she has a low IQ.*

telligent behavior are frequently culture specific (remember the Kpelle). Many Western cultures, for example, refer to intelligence as a stable property of the individual (e.g., "she's intelligent"). According to Valsiner (1984), this traditional approach assumes that intelligence is an internal characteristic of the individual. The traditional view also conceptualized intelligence as static, with a level of intelligence for any one individual that is relatively stable.

Valsiner (1984) argues that in order for an intelligence theory to be relevant to a host of cultures, it must be set in an ecological framework. In other words, intelligence theory must move from being internal/static in nature to being relationship/dynamic. Viewed in this way, intelligence cannot be attributed to the individual *or* the environment, but to the relationship between the two. Valsiner (1984) cites the mother/child relationship as an example. If two mothers are observed trying to calm their crying children and one mother is much more successful more quickly, is she the intelligent one (an internal/static attribution)? As mothers know, however, frequently the key to calming a crying child is determined by cues given by the child that allow the mother to ascertain if the child is tired, is hungry, or has soiled pants. Perhaps the mother who calmed her child first was more successful not because *she* is intelligent, but because her child has very distinct cries that allow her to easily discern the source of the child's discomfort. Valsiner (1984) argues for this latter viewpoint, that it is the ecology of this relationship that needs to be studied if we are going to be able to define intelligence in a cross-culturally meaningful way.

Vygotsky

Valsiner and others (Belmont, 1989) have cited Vygotsky's (1968) theory regarding the zone of proximal development (ZPD) as the theoretical basis for an ecological point of view. Briefly, the ZPD is the difference between how a child may perform on an intelligence test in isolation and how the child would perform given some hints,

clues, and suggestions by the examiner. Some children, then, may have identical IQs but very different ZPDs based on how they benefit from social interaction with a competent adult. Characteristics of the ZPD include the notion that all learning is interpersonal and ecological in nature. A child does not have a ZPD per se, but rather a ZPD exists between the adult and child in an interpersonal interaction (Belmont, 1989). The concept of the ZPD has been used to support the development and use of dynamic assessment models (Belmont, 1989). These models (see Chapter 6) hold out the promise of a strong link between cognitive assessment and intervention planning since "teaching" is an integral part of the assessment process.

Ecological models are also better able to capture the full range of intelligent behavior (Frederiksen, 1986). Group-administered measures of intelligence are most limited in the range of behavior they assess. Three major limitations of these measures include (Frederiksen, 1986):

1. The basic format of intelligence tests is unable to access the full range of real-life behavior, especially when multiple-choice formats are used.

2. A particular problem with intelligence tests is their inability to diagnose the various processes that underlie a person's performance on a test. Individual children may use a host of different strategies for responding to the same stimuli. A child may respond to a puzzle-solving item nonverbally and use spatial skills to solve it, or a child may speak out loud while solving the item and use verbal mediation to assemble the puzzle.

3. There is little variation in the situations in which intelligence test data are collected, thus precluding the possibility of novel responses to problem solving. In a sense, the standardized procedures that enhance reliability may force a limited range of intellectual assessment. In less structured settings a child may respond to a challenge very differently than in an academic-like setting.

In ecological fashion, Frederiksen (1986) has also proposed numerous alternatives to group tests of intelligence that use different formats, including tests of hypothesis testing using real-life types of problems, interviewing to assess intelligence, and "in-basket" tests.

Conclusions

Jensen (1987) and Baltes (1986) proposed that intelligence not be viewed as an elusive construct that requires one definition on which everyone agrees. They offered that intelligence be a more global construct that defines a field of study. Jensen (1987) similarly argued that the term *intelligence* be treated in the same way as the term *nature*, in that it be viewed as a broadly descriptive term of an area of inquiry. Intelligence, like nature, includes a variety of different phenomena to be studied. Baltes (1986) eloquently described this view of intelligence as an area of investigation.

> *First, intelligence should not be used as a "theoretical" construct, but as the label for a field of scholarship. . . . Second, if one is interested in formulating theoretical accounts of facets of the field, then it is necessary to introduce qualifiers to be added to the term* intelligence. *Otherwise, surplus meaning and metatheoretical discord will continue to be paramount. For example, rather than speak of intelligence per se, my preference is to speak of constructs such as innate intellectual capacity* (Anlage), *intellectual reserve capacity, learning capacity, intellectual abilities, intelligent systems, problem-solving ability, and knowledge systems. Each of these compound terms permits the generation of more theoretical specificity and precision. (cited in Detterman & Sternberg, p. 24)*

While a single theory of intelligence will not in the near future (Eysenck, 1988) be deemed the "correct" one, current data suggest problems and promise for some theories. The psychometric theories that have dominated the 20th century continue to do so. Remarkably, they have not only stood the test of time but also gained renewed vigor due in large part to Carroll's herculean effort to map the factor analytic terrain. It also appears that there is no clear successor to this tradition despite proposals for a number of alternatives (Daniel, 1997). It could very well be that further attempts to refine and extend the work of Carroll will be the focus of study for some time to come.

All of this theoretical work must eventually collide with practice, because, whether or not one thinks that intelligence testing practice has preceded adequate science, the application takes place daily on a grand and global scale. This consideration increases the appeal of the body of factor analytic research to serve as an anchor for test interpretation. In fact, new interpretive procedures are being offered based on the recent work of Carroll, Horn, and others. Hence, this text will detail an interpretive procedure in Chapter 17 that attempts to align the popular tests with factor analytic theory while leaving room for the use of other theories. In fact, the potential utility of some of the factor analytic results becomes apparent in the next chapter, which presents and discusses selected empirical findings.

Chapter Summary

- A psychologist's interpretations of test results, either written in a report or orally presented in a parent conference or other venue, are expressions of the psychologist's theoretical knowledge or biases.

- The idea that something such as "intelligence" exists appears to be universal.

- Binet seemed to ascribe to the notion of intelligence as a single entity.

- Spearman hypothesized the existence of "g" or general intelligence, an underlying "mental energy" that is central to all intelligent problem solving. There are also specific or "s" factors that are of lesser importance.

- Vernon (1950) offered a more detailed hierarchy of intellectual abilities where general intelligence is at the top of the hierarchy. Next in the hierarchy are the major group factors, which are of two varieties: verbal/educational (*v:ed*) and spatial/mechanical (*k:m*) types of intelligence.

- Jensen (1969) proposed a theory of intelligence that hypothesized the existence of two mental processes. Level I processing (associative ability) typically does not require manipulation or transformation of the stimulus input prior to producing a response. Level II processing (conceptual ability) requires considerable manipulation and elaboration of the stimulus input in order to produce a response.

- Thurstone (1938) first identified nine, then seven (Thurstone & Thurstone, 1941), then six (Thurstone, 1951) primary mental abilities through factor analytic investigations.

- The complete list of second-stratum traits hypothesized by Carroll include fluid intelligence, crystallized intelligence, general memory and learning, broad visual perception, broad auditory perception, broad retrieval ability, broad cognitive speediness, and processing speed (i.e., reaction time decision speed).

- Weinberg (1989) offered the broad categories of "lumpers" and "splitters," those who propose that intelligence is a general ability and those who prefer to consider it as a set of abilities respectively.

- Piaget's theory has only infrequently been used as a model for the development of intelligence tests (e.g., Uzgiris & Hunt, 1989).

- David Wechsler views intelligence as a complex interaction of abilities that produce intelligent behavior that reflects "g."

- Cattell proposed two types of intelligence: fluid and crystallized. His follower, John Horn, has expanded the model to include other factors such as visualization and short-term memory.

- Transactional theory, as proposed by Haywood and Switzky (1986), presents a theory of intelligence that attempts to explain the nature of the genetic/environment interaction that produces various levels of performance on intelligence tests.

- Transactional theory stipulates that everyone has a creod, a species specific developmental path, for intelligence.

- Jensen (1987) has shown significant correlations between dual reaction time measures and the "g" (general intelligence) factor of an aptitude battery.

- The three components of Guilford's structure of intellect model are contents, operations, and products.

- A central characteristic of information processing theories is the use of the computer, and the way it processes information, as a metaphor for human cognition.

- Declarative memory is similar to traditional notions of long-term memory in that it is characterized by long-term storage and slow decay of memory traces, and it stores acquired facts. Procedural memory stores rules for problem solving or production knowledge.

- Robert Sternberg has proposed his triarchic theory in an attempt to produce an integrative theory of intelligence.

- Valsiner argues that intelligence theory must move from being internal/static in nature to being relationship/dynamic.

- Frederiksen (1986) has proposed numerous alternative methods for assessing intelligence, including tests of hypothesis testing using real-life types of problems, interviewing to assess intelligence, and "in-basket" tests.

- Anastasi and Urbina (1997) view intelligence as a type of developed ability similar to academic achievement.

- Intelligence can be conceptualized as a global construct that defines a field of study.

CHAPTER 3

Research Findings

The concepts of average child and average environment have no utility whatever for the investigation of dynamics. . . . An inference from the average to the particular case is . . . impossible. (Lewin, 1931, p. 95; cited in Richters, 1997)

CHAPTER QUESTIONS

How stable are intelligence test scores?

How potent are environmental effects on intelligence?

Can we "cure" low intelligence?

Intelligence test research serves the practicing psychologist in many ways. Research has shown, for example, that children with intelligence test scores below 55 do not respond as well to psychostimulant therapy (e.g., Ritalin) (Brown, Dreelin, & Dingle, 1997). In addition, while clinical depression does have adverse affects on cognition these effects are not as pervasive or de-

bilitating as is revealed by research indicating that clinical depression does not lower composite intelligence test scores (Grossman, Kaufman, Mednitsky, Scharff, & Dennis, 1994). It is also interesting to note that children with higher intelligence test scores are at less risk for engaging in criminal behavior (Neisser, et al., 1996). These are among many of the compelling findings yielded in the last century of a vigorous research effort, where intelligence tests have served a critical role in advancing knowledge.

In order to fully understand the implications of such research, some definitional issues must first be put to rest. In order to gauge the generalizability of this repository of knowledge, it is important to understand the typical research design utilized. Most of the research studies that have used intelligence tests have been conducted in the United States, utilizing a Wechsler scale, and featuring interpretation of the overall composite score (i.e., measure of "g"). Consequently, this same large body of research can simultaneously be viewed as limited. The defacto definition of intelligence, intelligence test scores, psychometric intelligence, intellectual abilities, and similar terms used by researchers is the Full Scale composite score of a Wechsler scale. Although this point represents an overgeneralization, it does cause the reader of such research to think carefully about the meaning of the results reported. It may be inappropriate to conclude, for example, that "intelligence" is affected or unaffected by some variable under study. It is, therefore, important to consider the scores under study. These may be subtest, composite, stratum II, item, or other scores yielded by a great variety of intelligence tests.

Throughout this chapter, I attempt to refer to *changes in intelligence test scores as opposed to changes in intelligence*. This distinction is important because of the aforementioned scientific debate regarding whether or not current intelligence tests measure "intelligence." Just as the original roentgen ray (X ray) machines may have been difficult to read because of "shadows" and other factors, so too modern intelligence tests may in some cases not measure intelligence well because of technical inadequacies, socioeconomic, motivational, and other individual factors. All of the findings in this chapter refer to results obtained with the current technology, which likely is not the ultimate measures of the intelligence con-

struct. In those cases where the word *intelligence* is used it is only offered as a short form for *intelligence test score*.

Alas, the title of this chapter may constitute a misrepresentation of its contents. No single chapter, book, or subdiscipline in psychology can claim to summarize intelligence research. This field, which also evades easy definition, is simply too substantial to be easily summarized. Hence, this chapter will provide only a glimpse of a few key issues and findings. I aspire, however, to ensure that you, the reader and test user, will be well informed regarding scientific findings that affect your interpretations. In this spirit I recommend some additional readings to you. These readings, which I highly recommend, will cause you to think differently and deeply about the intellectual assessment process. My annotated bibliography is given in Research Report 3.1 accompanying this chapter.

STABILITY

Age and Test Interval

There are three major findings of importance on this topic. First, intelligence test scores are less

---

RESEARCH REPORT 3.1

Additional Scientific Readings

Burchinal, M. R., Campbell, F. A., Bryant, D. M., Wasik, B. H., & Ramey, C. T. (1997). Early intervention and mediating processes in cognitive performance of children of low-income African-American families. *Child Development, 68*, 935–954.

Carroll, J. B. (1997). The three stratum theory of cognitive abilities. In D. P. Flanagan, J. L. Genshaft, & P. L. Harrison (Eds.), *Contemporary intellectual assessment: Theories, tests, and issues* (pp. 122–130). New York: Guilford Publications.

Fergusson, D. M., & Horwood, L. J. (1995). Early disruptive behavior, IQ, and later school achievement and delinquent behavior. *Journal of Abnormal Child Psychology, 23*, 183–199.

Grossman, I., Kaufman, A. S., Mednitsky, S., Scharff, L., & Dennis, B. (1994). Neurocognitive abilities for a clinically depressed sample versus a matched control group of normal individuals. *Psychiatry Research, 51*, 231–244.

Neisser, U., Boodoo, G., Bouchard, T. J., Boykin, A. W., Brody, N., Ceci, S. J., Halpern, D. F., Loehlin, J. C., Perloff, R., Sternberg, R. J., & Urbina, S. (1996). Intelligence: Knowns and Unknowns. *American Psychologist, 51*, 77–101.

Schwean, V. L., Saklofske, D. H., Yackulic, R. A., Quinn, D. (1994). WISC-III performance of ADHD children. *Journal of Psychoeducational Assessment, Monograph*, 56–70.

stable for infants and preschoolers than for older children (Goodman, 1990). Second, the longer the interval between tests the greater the instability (Schuerger & Witt, 1989). Finally, high scores for young children are less stable than low scores (Bauman, 1991).

Infant intellectual assessment is a special problem area. The instability of infant intelligence test scores has led some to question the continued practice of testing young children (Goodman, 1990). The lack of stability for infant intelligence test scores is most apparent for samples of nondisabled children. Some typical results are shown in Table 3.1. These results clearly demonstrate that the stability of the obtained scores increases dramatically as a result of the child being older at the time of initial assessment.

The stability of scores for infants and preschoolers with developmental disabilities, however, is considerably better than for nondelayed children (Goodman, 1990). Whereas the stability coefficients in Table 3.1 were only in the .30 to .50 range at best, coefficients for samples of children with disabilities of this same age range are generally above .50 when retested at 5 to 7 years of age. Some studies have found stability coefficients as high as .80 and .90 (Goodman, 1990).

Given this contrast in findings a single statement cannot be made about the stability of intelligence test scores for infant and preschool children. Therefore, two statements are in order.

1. Intelligence test scores should generally be considered as unstable for nonreferred, otherwise normally developing preschool and, seemingly, precocious children.
2. Intelligence test scores are fairly stable for children with disabilities, particularly infants and preschoolers with mental retardation.

What about the stability of scores for older children? At this age the results are much less interesting. Intelligence test scores seem to stabilize at about age 6. Schuerger and Witt (1989) reviewed 34 studies of test-retest reliability for the WAIS, WAIS-R, WISC, WISC-R, and several editions of the Stanford-Binet, exclusive of the Binet 4. Using multiple regression procedures they found that age and interval between tests were the two variables most predictive of changes in intelligence test scores. Gender was not a significant variable, nor was treatment status (i.e., patient versus nonpatient). These results reinforced the previous findings of studies regarding age, but they also demonstrate a relationship between age and test interval for elementary grade samples and samples of adults.

Schuerger and Witt (1989) found stability coefficients to be high, even for 6-year-olds. The coefficients for 6-year-olds ranged from .85 for a 1-week interval to .67 for a 20-year interval. Stability was still better for 39-year-olds where coefficients ranged from .99 for 1 week to .82 for 20 years. This relationship between age/interval and stability of test scores is depicted graphically in Figures 3.1 and 3.2. Stability is maximized as age increases and interval between test administration decreases.

Wechsler Verbal, Performance, and Full Scale scores have all been found to be very stable for children participating in special education classes (Canivez & Watkins, 1998). Cassidy (1997) com-

TABLE 3.1   Average correlations between infant and later intelligence test scores for nondisabled children

Age in Months at Initial Test	Age in Years at Childhood Test		
	3–4	5–7	8–18
1–6	.21	.09	.06
7–12	**.32**	.20	.25
13–18	**.50**	**.34**	**.32**
19–30	**.59**	**.39**	**.49**

Correlations of .30 and above are in boldface.
SOURCE: Adapted from McCall (1979).

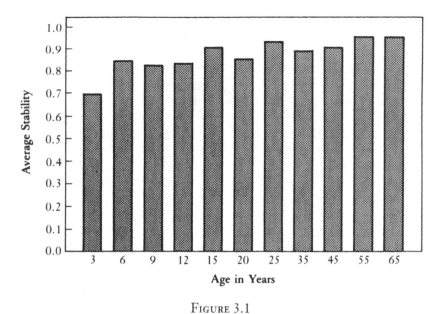

FIGURE 3.1

Graph depicting the relationship between age and stability
SOURCE: Adapted from Schuerger and Witt (1989).

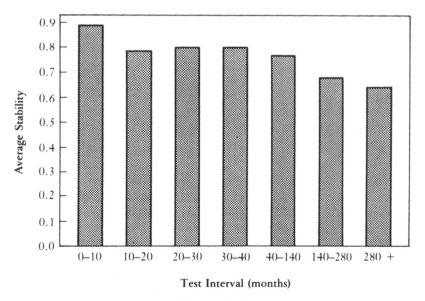

Test Interval (months)

FIGURE 3.2

Graph depicting the relationship between test interval and stability
SOURCE: Adapted from Schuerger and Witt (1989).

pared the Wechsler scores for 592 children who were enrolled in special education classes for a 3-year period. She found that for the group as a whole the scores did not significantly differ over this time period. There was also a tendency for deviant scores to regress toward the mean upon retest. Children with Full Scale scores below 90 score higher upon retest by 1 or 2 points, whereas children with scores above 109 scored lower by 3 to 5 points when retested.

These same Wechsler scores are remarkably consistent in late adulthood. A study of 70-year-olds (mean age = 72) who were administered the WAIS-R one year apart produced a remarkably high test-retest coefficient of .90 (Raguet, Campbell, Berry, Schmitt, & Smith, 1996). Of particular interest is the finding that there was a slight rise in scores from time one to time two of about 3 standard score points for the Full Scale (mean = 111.5 at time one and mean = 114.7 at time two). The authors attributed this mild increase to practice effects, that is, the tendency for scores to improve due simply to familiarity with the item types.

It is important to be mindful of the fact that all of the results cited are based on group, not single-case data (see opening quote for this chapter). Schuerger and Witt (1989) also calculated the percentage of each sample that would show a change in intelligence test score of 15 points or more. They found that for 6-year-olds evaluated 1 year apart fully 13% of the sample changed scores by at least one standard deviation—a big change by any standard! Even 7% of the 30-year-olds changed their scores by more than 15 standard score points. In another study of changes in intelligence test scores from age 6 to 18 years stability coefficients were high, but considerable changes in the *magnitude* of scores were noted (Anastasi, 1988). One study found 59% of the children to change by 15 or more standard score points, 37% by 20 or more points, and 9% by 30 or more points (Honzik, Macfarlane, & Allen, 1948). In another investigation of 170 children with learning disabilities who were tested 3 years apart, the changes were less dramatic than in the studies just cited (Oakman & Wilson, 1988).

However, 4% of the sample experienced changes of at least 15 points on the WISC-R. The practicing psychologist has to identify the "changers" in order to make predictions with precision. It is up to the experience and acumen of the psychologist to identify the children who will change significantly, an unenviable task indeed.

A search for guidance for identifying "changers" has largely been unsuccessful. Moffitt et al. (1993) tested children every 2 years between the ages of 3 and 11 for a longitudinal sample of 794 children who were participants in the Dunedin (New Zealand) Multidisciplinary Health and Development Study. This research group studied the relationship between a variety of contextual and child variables and intelligence test score change. Some of these variables included two-parent families, number of address changes, number of siblings, SES, family relations, maternal health, perinatal problems, impaired vision or audition, and a variety of behavior problems. With regard to contextual variables the authors concluded,

> *Contrary to conventional wisdom about environmental influences on changes in children's test performance, there were no such systematic relations in our data. There was also no evidence of a systematic temporal relation between naturalistic environmental change and IQ change. (p. 489)*

In a smaller scale investigation (N = 169) of "disadvantaged" children, Pianta and Egeland (1994) concluded that the environmental variables of maternal social support, maternal interactions with others, and child internalizing problems (although this latter variable accounted for only 2% of the variance accounted for at age 8) were predictive of intelligence test score change. This study differs from the Moffitt et al. (1993) investigation in numerous ways, including smaller sample size, use of a high-risk sample, and a smaller number of data points (2 as opposed to 4). An attempt to reconcile the differences among these studies may be to conclude that *intelligence test scores change little over the course of development for most individuals. Moreover, when scores change the specific variables implicated may be unpredictable and variable between individuals.*

Perhaps one of the reasons for the lack of change in intelligence test scores is the stability of environmental characteristics. Sameroff, Seifer, Baldwin, and Baldwin (1993) found measured intelligence at 4 years of age to correlate .72 with intelligence at 13 years of age, whereas the correlation between cumulative risk factors across this same period was equally high at .76. Their sample, including many disadvantaged families, was taken from the Rochester Longitudinal Study. The risk factors studied were minority group status, occupation of head of household, maternal education, family size, father absence, stressful life events (e.g., deaths, job losses), parental perspectives on child development, and maternal mental health, among others. Sameroff, Seifer, Baldwin, and Baldwin (1993) concluded that cumulative risk was more predictive of child intelligence than pattern of risk. In other words, *it is far more difficult to implicate a specific risk factor that may be associated with intelligence change than to suggest that a child with many risk factors is at risk for obtaining lower scores and maintaining low scores.* It is possible that the lack of change in scores for most children is due to more than one "fixed" entity (i.e., genetics). Environments may be "fixed" for most children as well (Reiss, et al., 2000).

Growth and Decline

Early research and theory gave a pessimistic view of the trajectory of intellectual development beyond adolescence. Pintner (1923) reviewed the research on the intelligence test scores of World War I recruits in order to determine when intelligence test scores reached an asymptote in adulthood. As far as the maximum level of mental development he concluded that

At present, it is customary to assume the fourteen-year-old level in view of the general results of the mental testing in the army, where it was found that the average

recruit had a mentality about equal to a mental age of 13.8 on the Stanford Revision. (p. 67)

Fortunately, the outlook for adult intelligence has become more optimistic since the early days of testing. The pessimistic views regarding the growth and decline of intelligence were in ascendance in the 1940s and 1950s. At that time a number of research investigations using cross-sectional methods made the claim that intelligence test scores declined, in some cases, dramatically in old age (Dixon, Kramer, & Baltes, 1985). This finding generated a great deal of controversy and resulted in the onset of a number of longitudinal investigations of intellectual growth. These longitudinal investigations did not produce such pessimistic outcomes (Dixon et al., 1985). One study, using a longitudinal research design, found that one of the few reliable decrements before age 60 was in word fluency. On the contrary, there was a reliable increment in verbal meaning to the age of 39 years. Why, then, is there a seeming disagreement between longitudinal and cross-sectional studies? The most likely hypothesis is that differences in educational attainment are a potent factor in cross-sectional investigations. The average level of education for the American population has increased over the generations, resulting in older individuals in a cross-sectional design having lower levels of educational attainment than younger individuals. Of course, the effect of educational attainment can be more easily controlled in a longitudinal investigation.

There are, however, some reliable decrements in intelligence (Schaie & Hertzog, 1983). Schaie and Hertzog (1983) found a reliable decrement in overall intelligence between the ages of 60 and 80 years of about one standard deviation. In addition, when these same individuals were placed in an intervention program, their intelligence test scores gained by about the same amount, one standard deviation. Remarkably, they returned to predecline levels. The decrement in intelligence test scores in late adulthood has been attributed to both biological and social factors. The effects of cardiovascular disease

(Hertzog, Schaie, & Gribbin, 1978) and social deprivation (Gribbin, Schaie, & Parham, 1975) have both been implicated.

Fluid and Crystallized Theory

The application of the fluid/crystallized dichotomy still seems to be useful for conceptualizing the rise and fall of specific cognitive skills. Recent investigations have replicated previous findings regarding the decline of WAIS-R IQs (Kaufman, Reynolds, & McClean, 1989). Wechsler Verbal scores, typically considered to be measures of crystallized ability, tend to show little decline over the course of adulthood, while Performance scores, considered by some to be measures of fluid abilities, decline precipitously (see Figure 3.3). These data do support the relationship between fluid ability and physical well-being. Kaufman (1990) provides a very detailed analysis of this issue and summarizes relevant research on changes in adult intelligence.

A large-scale cross-sectional investigation produced some intriguing clues as to which of Cat-

tell/Horn's abilities remain stable or decrease with age (Kaufman, Kaufman, Chen, & Kaufman, 1996). This investigation of a U.S. nationally representative norming sample of individuals aged 15 to 94 years evaluated the stability of six abilities from Cattell/Horn's work, many of which are analogous to several of Carroll's (1993) Stratum II abilities. The abilities under investigation included "g_c" (crystallized), "g_f" (fluid), "g_q" (quantitative reasoning, which was not found adequate for inclusion in Carroll's Stratum II), "g_v" (visualization or in Carroll's terms broad visual perception), SAR (short-term acquisition and retrieval, which is roughly equivalent to Carroll's general memory and learning Stratum II ability), and TSR (long-term storage and retrieval, which is similar to Carroll's Stratum II broad retrieval ability). Age was controlled in all analyses to account for the fact that older individuals generally have less formal education.

Kaufman et al. (1996) found some predictable results in that crystallized and quantitative abilities showed less deterioration with age. "g_c", for example, produced a mean of 89.1 at ages 15–16,

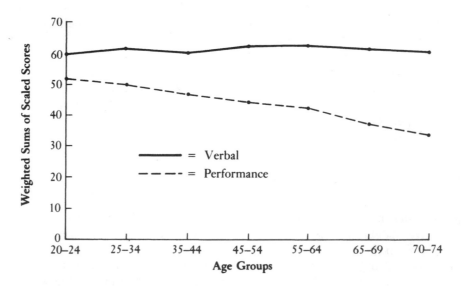

FIGURE 3.3

Data from the Kaufman, Reynolds, and McClean (1989) investigation on changes in intelligence in adulthood reached an asymptote of 105.8 at ages 40–44, and reverted to a mean of 90.0 at ages 70–94. "g_f", on the other hand, showed considerable decrement with a mean of 102.2 at ages 15–16, a high point of 107.4 at 20–24, and a decline to a mean of 82.6 at ages 75–94. These findings are highly consistent with Cattell/Horn theory, which hypothesizes that "g_f" is much more vulnerable to the effects of aging. One interesting finding from the investigation was a suggestion that "g_v" is also quite vulnerable. Using a gestalt closure subtest (an incomplete drawing that must be named by the examinee) Kaufman et al. (1996) found a mean of 104.9 at ages 15–16 and only 82.1 at age group 70–94. This finding does require cross-validation, but it does imply that research on the effects of aging on all Stratum II abilities are in order if we are going to develop a more thorough understanding of the growth and decline of cognitive function.

These findings have resulted in reframing the question, do intelligence test scores decline in late adulthood? There are now a host of questions about which intelligence test scores decline, the causes of the decline, and its permanence. Similarly, why do some scores show great resistance to decline? Some of these findings may have relevance for understanding the declining scores of some children. If, for example, physical well-being is associated with intelligence test scores in adulthood, then this may also be the case for children. (See Chapter 19 for related research on the effects of brain injury on children's intelligence test scores.)

Cumulative Deficits

The cumulative deficit phenomenon is a more distressing type of instability that psychologists have to face all too often. There is a tendency for children from low SES environments to have their intelligence test scores gradually decrease over the course of development in relationship to the normative mean (Anastasi, 1988; Saco-Pollitt, Pollitt, & Greenfield, 1985). Jensen (1974,

1977) has defined cumulative deficits as the tendency for the effects of an unfavorable environment to compound with time. Jensen explains that new learning is dependent on previous learning. When initial learning is inadequate, considerable effort must be expended in order to reverse the inadequate course of cognitive development. This conceptualization is consistent with Piaget's and other developmental theories. A lack of early stimulation may inhibit opportunities for accommodation and inhibit cognitive growth. Haywood (1986) has noted this phenomenon with children with mental retardation and labeled it the MA (mental age) deficit.

Evidence for the existence of the cumulative deficit phenomenon comes from a variety of sources. One of the first studies was conducted with impoverished mountain children in Appalachia (Sherman & Key, 1932). Cumulative deficits in performance have also been identified for low SES children in India (Misra, 1983), low SES African American children (Jensen, 1977), and disadvantaged children from England and Wales (Cox, 1983).

The cumulative deficit is often explained based on environmental variables. It has been documented that low SES children who have not participated in a preschool intervention program are at higher risk for special education placement, and "as a result, their parents, their teachers, and they themselves come to expect less of themselves, and thus the twig is bent" (Bouchard & Segal, 1985, p. 451). This scenario, in turn, creates a spiral of decelerating school performance, resulting in cumulative deficits in test scores.

This type of instability in test scores is of particular importance for psychologists given that in a number of settings the primary type of referral will be high-risk children from impoverished environments. When these children are retested by psychologists, the cumulative deficit phenomenon may be observed. Unfortunately, the cure for this disturbing phenomenon is not yet readily apparent as we do not yet have a clear understanding of the salient environmental effects on intelligence test scores. Although the nature/

nurture debate has been vigorous for decades, relatively little is understood about environmental effects.

NATURE VERSUS NURTURE

Environmental Determinants

Sometimes research merely confirms conventional wisdom. The idea that good care leads to better development of children is intuitive. Proper child care, including being affectionate and meeting the social and physical needs of children, is associated with positive developmental outcomes (Horney, 1939). Research on the relationship between environmental effects and intelligence dates at least as far back as the 1930s, with numerous studies producing evidence of environmental effects.

Skodak and Skeels

A classic study was conducted by Skodak and Skeels (1949). This study suggested that environmental effects might be important by conducting follow-up evaluations of children who were adopted in infancy. In its day it was one of very few studies reporting longitudinal data. This study does have methodological flaws, since it was conducted as a service project as opposed to a research study. Regardless, the data were intriguing then and they are now.

The children who were placed (adopted) were generally from low SES backgrounds, whereas the adoptive parents were "above the average of their communities in economic security and educational and cultural status" (Skodak & Skeels, 1949). The children were tested at five intervals ranging from an average age at the first evaluation of 2 years, 2 months, to an average at the fifth follow-up evaluation of 13 years, 6 months. The major finding of the study was that the average IQ score of this group remained remarkably stable across development from a mean of 117 at the first test to a mean of 117 at the last follow-up. Based on these findings Skodak and Skeels (1949) concluded:

> The intellectual level of the children has remained consistently higher than would have been predicted from the intellectual, educational, or socioeconomic level of the true parents, and is equal to or surpasses the mental level of children in environments similar to those which have been provided by the foster parents. (p. 650)

Other Studies of Environmental Effects

One could easily attack this study on methodological bases. Other recent studies have, however, produced consistent results. A well-known study by Scarr and Weinberg (1976) investigated groups of African American and "interracial" children who were adopted at a young age by upper-middle-class families who were of European descent. These authors found that the adopted children performed well above average in intelligence tests and on school achievement measures, and considerably better than African American and interracial children from similar genetic backgrounds who were not adopted.

Using a different approach, Hanson (1975) found significant correlations between a number of environmental factors and intelligence test scores. Significant variables produced correlations of .26 and higher, and these included freedom to engage in verbal expression, direct teaching of language behavior, parental involvement with the child, emphasis on school achievement, emphasis on performing independently, models of intellectual interests, and models of language development. Nonsignificant variables included emphasis on female sex role development, freedom to explore the environment, and models of task orientation. It is also noteworthy that correlations were higher for girls than for boys in many cases.

Harnqvist (1968) investigated the results of tracking in Swedish schools. He concluded that when variables such as initial estimates of ability were held equal, pupils who chose a more challenging academic track gained as much as two-thirds of a standard deviation more than students who chose a vocationally oriented track. These results suggest that the greater intellectual demands of the college preparatory curriculum promoted intellectual development. These findings may be interpreted as indicating that increased knowledge provides the necessary schemata for optimal cognitive growth and problem solving.

Glaser (1984) advocated for this point of view by first critiquing the educational movement aimed at teaching problems-solving and reasoning skills in a decontextualized manner. He concluded that training cognitive processes such as memory strategies and reasoning heuristics have failed to generalize to nontarget problems thus rendering processing training approaches failures. In studies of novices and experts he found that expert problem solvers did not possess better strategies, rather they possessed more knowledge relevant to the task. In his own words,

> In our studies, high-aptitude individuals appear to be skillful reasoners because of the level of their content knowledge as well as because of their knowledge of the procedural constraints of a particular problem form, such as inductive or analogical reasoning. This suggests that improvement in the skills of learning, such as required on aptitude and intelligence tests, takes place through the exercise of conceptual and procedural knowledge in the context of specific knowledge domains. Learning and reasoning skills develop not as abstract mechanisms of heuristic search and memory processing. Rather, they develop as the content and concepts of a knowledge domain are attained in the learning situations that constrain this knowledge to serve certain purposes and goals. (p. 99)

If, in fact, knowledge continues to be found to be influential in the cognitive development as seems to be the case (Hunt, 1999), then one more brick has been added to the foundation of science revealing that environmental effects are potent. Perhaps more than one brick has been added to this foundation by the work of James Flynn, who has provided compelling evidence for environmental effects.

The Flynn Effect

Flynn (1984) studied changes in intelligence test scores across generations of U.S. citizens and found a 14 standard score point increase (for overall composite score) from 1932 to 1978. This finding has been so influential as to have it described as the "Flynn Effect," which is testimony to its potential importance. Briefly, the Flynn Effect is best summarized in Flynn's (1998) own words.

> Massive IQ gains began in the late 19th century as early as the industrial revolution, and have affected 20 nations, all for whom data exist. Not doubt, different nations have enjoyed different rates of gain, but the best data do not provide an estimate of the differences. Different kinds of IQ tests show different rates of gain: Culture-reduced tests of fluid intelligence show gains of as much as 20 points per generation (30 years); performance tests show 10–20 points; and verbal tests sometimes show 10 points or below. Tests closest to the content of school-taught subjects, such as arithmetic reasoning, general information, and vocabulary, show modest or nil gains. More often than not, gains are similar at all IQ levels. Gains may be age specific, but this has not yet been established and they certainly persist into adulthood. The fact that gains are fully present in young children means that causal factors are present in early childhood but not necessarily that they are more potent in young children than among older children or adults. (p. 61)

He, and many others (e.g., Neisser, 1998), concluded that a change in the gene pool of the American or other populations is not a plausible explanation for these gains. Rather, he asserts that these data support the hypothesis that intelligence test scores are clearly affected by environmental influences by saying, "The period in question shows the radical malleability of IQ during a time of normal environmental change; other times and other trends cannot erase that fact" (Flynn, 1984, p. 48). Several theories regarding causal environmental variables have been offered but there is no commonly accepted explanation. Increased test-wiseness, nutrition, TV time, urbanization, educational opportunities, and SES have all been found wanting for explanatory power (Flynn, 1998). Several additional intriguing possibilities exist for explaining the environmental mechanisms that cause the Flynn Effect including environmental complexity (Schooler, 1998), peer influences (Steinberg, Dornbusch, & Brown, 1992), and early enrichment experiences (Burchinal, Campbell, Bryant, Wasik, & Ramey, 1997). While the exact mechanism(s) is unknown there is, with dissenters duly recognized, a consensus among many investigators that the ultimate cause will be an environmental one (Neisser, 1998).

Some researchers who are interested in environmental effects assert that there is a technological vacuum that is hindering the study of environmental factors on intelligence and other traits (Bloom, 1964; Bouchard & Segal, 1985; Horowitz & O'Brien, 1989). There are no well-developed and normed measures of "environment" that are as respected as those used to measure intelligence. There may be many unexplored aspects of environmental effects that are awaiting the development of interviews, participant observational systems, or tests. Considerable progress continues to be made giving hope that several plausible environmental mechanisms are nearing discovery.

Genetic Effects

The evidence for the heritability of intelligence is equally weighty. Many researchers are willing to attribute at least some of the variance in intelligence test scores to genetic factors (Snyderman & Rothman, 1987). Much of the evidence rests on the evaluation of correlations between biologically related relatives. The first studies to point to the likelihood of a strong genetic effect on intelligence test performance were twin studies.

Bouchard and McGue (1981) reviewed all of the research comparing monozygotic and dizygotic twins. Monozygotic twins are the so-called identical twins that emanate from one fertilized ovum. Dizygotic twins, better known to the public as fraternal twins, are those that are the results of two fertilized ova. In behavior genetics research, it is important to note that correlation coefficients are described in particular ways. The two words that are used to describe correlational relationships are *concordant* and *discordant*. A concordant relationship means that there is a high correlation between relatives, and discordant means that there is a low or perhaps even negative correlation between relatives. Twins tend to be concordant for intelligence with monozygotic twins having higher concordance rates than dizygotic twins. As Bouchard and McGue (1981) reported, the average correlation for monozygotic twins between their intelligence test scores is .86, whereas for dizygotic twins the correlation is only .60. These values show the tendency for intelligence test performance to be related to degree of genetic similarity among individuals.

Another large-scale analysis of twin studies again showed a substantial relationship between genetic similarity and intellectual similarity (Osborne, 1980). Osborne (1980) also separated the twin correlations for various specific types of abilities. Skills with greater heritability included spatial visualization, reasoning, and clerical speed and accuracy. Skills that are least affected by hereditary factors are verbal fluency and divergent thinking. Vandenberg and Vogler (1985) suggest cautious interpretation of these data by noting that if all of the variance was due to genetic factors, the correlation for monozygotic twins would be near 1.0., which is clearly not the case.

Twin studies, however, have frequently been criticized because twins share not only genetics, but frequently they also share environmental influence. This situation is changing, however, as more and more data are becoming available on twins that have been reared apart. These data also show a strong genetic component in the inheritance of intelligence, since the correlations between twins and their adoptive parents tend to be smaller than those between twins and their biological parents with whom they do not share any environmental circumstances. Studies of this nature and their results are shown in Table 3.2. In a study by Bouchard at the University of Min-

TABLE 3.2   Parent–child IQ correlations in four adoption studies

Study		Adoptive		Biological	
		r	**N**	**r**	**N**
Scarr & Weinberg (1976)	Fathers	.27	170	**.39**	142
	Mothers	.23	174	**.34**	141
Scarr & Weinberg (1978)	Fathers	.15	150	**.39**	237
	Mothers	.04	150	**.39**	237
Horn (1979)	Fathers	.17	457	**.42**	162
	Mothers	.19	455	.23	162
Labuda et al. (1986)	Fathers	.16	133	**.46**	133
	Mothers	.16	133	.23	133

Correlations above .30 are in **boldface**.

nesota (as cited by Vandenberg & Vogler, 1985) the correlation between twins reared apart on the Wechsler Adult Intelligence Scale was .66.

As the state of science currently stands, it appears that there is considerable evidence of the heritability of intelligence from a host of different types of investigations. Based on numerous twin studies, Vandenberg and Vogler (1985) estimate that 30% to 40% of the variance in intelligence test scores is due to hereditary factors.

Plomin (1989) notes further that there is not only a strong relationship between genetic inheritance and intelligence, but that this relationship gets stronger with increasing age (see Table 3.3).

In some of his own investigations he has found that the correlation between biological parents and their adopted away infants increases with increasing age of the child (Plomin, 1989). This tendency was demonstrated in a study by LaBuda, DeFries, Plomin, amd Fulker (1986). In this study 133 adopted children were followed and their intelligence test scores correlated with those of their biological and adoptive mothers and fathers (see Table 3.3).

The results of the Labuda et al. (1986) study suggest a strong hereditary component to intelligence. With the exception of year three, the correlations are significantly higher between

TABLE 3.3   Relationship between intelligence test scores of biological and adoptive parents and offspring

AGE IN YEARS	Adoptive MOTHER	Adoptive FATHER	Biological MOTHER	Biological FATHER
1	.11	.10	.18	.48
2	.02	.08	.11	.49
3	.16	.21	.15	.25
4	.16	.16	.23	.46

SOURCE: These correlations are pooled estimates adapted from Labuda et al. (1986).

biological parents and offspring than between adoptive parents and offspring (see Table 3.3).

Another convincing bit of evidence for the genetic point of view is the lack of correlation of intelligence test results and other scores for individuals in the same environment. Plomin (1989) summarizes the research on the correlations between children who are adopted into the same family (shared environment, not shared inheritance).

> *Results are clear in showing little influence of shared environment. For personality, adoptive sibling environments are about .05 on the average. Genetically unrelated individuals adopted together show no-greater-than-chance resemblance for psychopathology. For cognitive abilities, although adoptive siblings are similar in childhood (correlations of .25), by adolescence, their correlations are near zero, suggesting that the long-term impact of shared family environment is slight. (p. 109)*

There is a potential problem with the increased willingness on the part of the scientific community to consider genetic determinants of intellectual abilities (Plomin, 1988; Weinberg, 1988). Some may search for a single gene that mediates the inheritance of intelligence. A single gene is an unlikely explanation. According to at least one well-known researcher in the area of behavior genetics, this is misguided (Plomin, 1989). Plomin (1989) notes, for example, that early reports of a single gene determining spatial ability have turned out to be unfounded. He asserts, furthermore, that researchers have not been able to find a single gene that is associated with susceptibility to disorders such as schizophrenia and depression. Intelligence is a very complex construct, and the search for a single gene that determines intellectual abilities is likely to prove fruitless. As such, intelligence is likely determined polygenetically (by a number of genes) (Plomin, 1989). In addition, genetic effects on intelligence are likely to be probabilistic, as opposed to deterministic (Plomin, 1989). In comparison, diseases such as sickle cell anemia are determined by a single gene and express themselves regardless of environment or genetic

background of the individual. Intelligence is not likely to follow this pattern because of the complexity of intellectual behaviors that are assessed. Environmental factors will still be considered to play an important role in affecting the expression of the genetic potential of the individual. As Plomin (1989) notes:

> *As the pendulum swings from environmentalism, it is important that the pendulum be caught mid swing before its momentum carries it to biological determinism. Behavioral genetic research clearly demonstrates that both nature and nurture are important in development. (p. 110)*

Anastasi (1988) gives additional caveats regarding research on the heritability of intelligence citing specific problems with the use of heritability coefficients. Heritability estimates, the percentage of variance in a trait that is due to genetic factors, are affected by the nature of the sample on which the index was calculated. More important, heritability indices are based on group not individual data, and the psychologist is most concerned with the individual client. One child with mild mental retardation could suffer from Down syndrome, a genetic disorder, whereas another mildly retarded child may have been adversely affected by an extremely stultifying environment. For these two cases the heritability index in the population is irrelevant; of greatest importance to the psychologist seeking to understand these cases is the "heritability index" *for each case*. As is the situation with other aspects of clinical assessment, the group-based research aids primarily in giving a set of probabilities for the case, but the psychologist has to decide if these probabilities apply.

Confusing Malleability and Genetic Determination

The conventional wisdom, and perhaps one of the causes for the polemics associated with intellectual assessment, is that if a trait such as intelligence is at least partly genetically determined then the trait is affected very little by environmental factors. This viewpoint is a fallacy. A number of authors have shown convincingly that the relationship between genetic determination of a characteristic, such as intelligence, to its malleability is a tenuous one (Anastasi, 1988; Angoff, 1988; Plomin, 1989).

Angoff (1988) observes, for example, that even characteristics that are thought to have heritability coefficients near 1.0 can be malleable. He uses height as an example of a trait that is considered by most people to be 100% genetically determined. Yet a number of studies have shown remarkable changes in height due to environmental variation. As an example, some research has shown that American and British adolescents are about 6 inches taller today than their peers of a century ago (Angoff, 1988). Other data are cited showing that Japanese children born in California were taller, heavier, and more long-legged than children born in Japan (Angoff, 1988). It is also important to remember that some of these changes noted in a characteristic over time are masked by correlation coefficients. This is the case because a correlation coefficient between two groups of related individuals, such as twins, indicates only the rank ordering of the individuals on the characteristic being studied. Angoff (1988) observes that "the correlations between heights of fathers and heights of their sons would be unaffected whether the sons were two, three, or five inches taller, or shorter, than their fathers" (p. 714). Hence, since correlation coefficients between biologically related individuals do not assess mean differences, they may mask important changes in a characteristic under study. In other words, correlation coefficients can be high as well and yet mean differences between groups can be large.

Statistical caveats aside, the important notion regarding heritability is that the construct for the most part should be considered separately from the issue of malleability. Neisser (1998) cites Lewinton's (1970) view that genetic cause and environmental malleability may be orthogonal by describing a field of corn.

Imagine that two fields of corn have been planted with the same strain of genetically varied seeds but that only one field is adequately watered and fertilized. The result will be an entirely environmental between-field difference, together with a large and entirely genetic within-field variance. (p. 18)

Neisser (1998) goes on to say,

Whatever the merits of the various explanations, they may all soon be out of date. This is for two reasons. The first reason, of course, is the rise in test scores. As we have seen, the 3-point-per-decade gain documented by Flynn means that the test performance of Black Americans today is roughly equivalent to that of Whites in the 1940s. Even if the mean test scores [between the two groups] are still 15 points apart, it is now clear that a gap of this size can easily result from environmental differences, specifically, from the differences between the general American environment of 1940 and 1990. (p. 18)

CAN WE "CURE" LOW INTELLIGENCE?

The noble goals of Seguin, Itard, and others to cure mental retardation remain largely unfulfilled. This is not to say that immense progress has not been made in the prevention and treatment of the disability. Thanks largely to the use of intelligence tests by researchers, expecting mothers routinely receive counsel to limit alcohol and other substance intake, eliminate smoking, and take other measures to avoiding prenatal destruction of cognitive ability. Laws restricting the use of lead-based paint are another example of the influence of research that has used intelligence tests. It may be a bold statement to make but I think that the invention of the intelligence test provided a readily available and practical measurement technology for gauging the effects of many variables on cognitive development. Therefore, failure to find a cure for low intelligence test scores should be placed in the larger perspective that substantial progress has been made while simultaneously recognizing that much needs to be done. This section is focused exclusively on efforts to train intelligence in order to improve intelligence test scores, which is an exceedingly narrow focus that has produced disappointing results. Nevertheless, this tradition is of historical import because of its failure.

Nineteenth-century pioneers in mental retardation treatment tried a variety of sensory and motor training tasks to improve intelligence. In this century the movement to train intelligence continues in various theoretical guises. The work of Feuerstein, Rand, and Hoffman (1979) on dynamic assessment (see Chapter 6) has garnered a great deal of attention in this regard. Feuerstein's theory of cognitive modifiability assumes that intelligence is a highly malleable trait. He advises that after intellectual assessment pupils receive his instrumental enrichment program to improve their intelligence and, hence, their academic success in school.

Despite these seemingly sensible theories, research does not show that intelligence, as measured by current intelligence tests, is substantively trainable. Glutting and McDermott (1990) elucidated several statistical problems with research on the training of intelligence. For example, some of the positive results shown for the training of intelligence may be explained by regression to the mean. Since the subjects of these investigations tend to be individuals with test scores far below the mean, it may be that gains in performance over time are not the result of a training program such as instrumental enrichment, but rather simply regression to the mean (see Chapter 5 for a discussion of regression effects). Given that intelligence tests are not perfectly reliable measures, the amount of the regression effect can be predicted based on a test's reliability coefficient. Glutting and McDermott (1990) have done just this. They concluded that the vast majority of gains in performance shown in intelligence training studies are within the range of improvement that could be explained by regression effects alone.

One of the most disconcerting aspects of the intelligence training movement is the lack of generalization of improvements in intelligence to improvements in academic performance (Glutting & McDermott, 1990). Perhaps the focus of this type of research is misguided in that it emphasizes intelligence (the predictor variable), when the real question of import is how well the child is doing in school (the criterion variable). A similarly illogical situation would occur when an individual does perfectly well in college when admitted on a probationary basis without admission test scores and later obtains an admission test score that is so low that it resulted in the individual's suspension from school. Logic of this nature has led to the use of the term *overachiever*—a very dubious concept.

This same confounding of predictor and criterion variables may be evident in intelligence training research, suggesting that the focus of research should be on developing new instructional technologies for improving the achievement test scores of individuals with low intelligence test scores rather than on improving intelligence per se. There is also a remarkable lack of data on the Feuerstein methodology. It may be the case that there is simply not yet enough data available on the Feuerstein approach to evaluate its validity (Brody, 1985).

Lidz and Mearig (1989) take issue with criticisms of Feuerstein's so-called dynamic assessment by emphasizing the differing emphasis that this approach embodies. They argue that the virtues of Feuerstein's approach are numerous, including

1. an emphasis on the link between assessment and intervention.

2. a deemphasis on passive placement and prediction.

They cite disillusionment with current approaches by saying, "It is historical fact that many children have been misclassified by static, 'objective,' standardized tests, and on this basis have been assigned to programs with minimal content, low expectations, and restricted (rather than enriched) teaching approaches" (p. 83). This point may be argued, but it is emblematic of the concern over the use of intelligence tests and their association with special education programs of questionable value. While reforms in special education are under way, changes in intellectual assessment should also be sought. Though Feuerstein's Learning Potential Assessment Device (LPAD) method lacks empirical support, a cure for low intelligence should still be pursued earnestly (Spitz, 1986a).

Early Intervention Research

Another important evaluation of the malleability of intelligence test scores concerns the evaluation of Head Start and a variety of other preschool intervention programs designed primarily for impoverished preschool-age children. The federally sponsored Head Start program was initiated in 1965, and it is unusual in that it continues to enjoy bipartisan political support (Ramey, 1999). Head Start programs also distinguish themselves from various state-sponsored preschool programs due to the comprehensive nature of services provided (Ripple, Gilliam, Chanana, & Zigler, 1999). Interventions and services are not limited to the classroom, and parental involvement, for example, is an integral component. After a careful review, Hoskins (1989) drew the following four conclusions regarding research on the effectiveness of Head Start programs at improving intelligence and academic achievement test scores.

1. Both model programs and Head Start produce significant and meaningful gains in intellectual performance and socioemotional development by the end of a year of intervention.

2. For both types of programs, gains on standardized IQ and achievement tests as well as on tests of socioemotional development decline within a few years (or even less in the case of Head Start programs).

3. On categorical variables of school performance, such as special education placement and grade retention, there is very strong evidence of positive effects for the model programs and modest evidence of the effects for Head Start programs.

4. On measures of life-success, such as teen pregnancy, delinquency, welfare participation, and employment, there is modest evidence of positive impacts for model programs but virtually no evidence for Head Start. (p. 278)

There are, however, potential confounds to keep in mind when evaluating this research. Hoskins (1989) has noted that in the comparison between Head Start and control-group children, the Head Start sample seemed to be a more high-risk sample than the control groups. It consisted of children with mothers with fewer years of schooling, homes that were more crowded, larger families, and other characteristics that have been associated with at-risk children.

Head Start has also been thoroughly evaluated in a study conducted by the General Accounting Office (1997). This review again called into question the lasting beneficial effects of Head Start programs. Regardless, the clear evidence of shorter-term effects are frequently cited as important for helping so-called at-risk children achieve readiness for formal schooling. Moreover, school readiness involves much more than cognitive development (Ripple et al., 1999).

> To be ready to learn, children need to be in good physical and mental health, be socially well-adjusted, and possess age-appropriate cognitive competencies. They need to have an idea of how to behave in the classroom by knowing how to follow instructions, to be sensitive to the feelings of others, to communicate their thoughts and feelings, and not to disrupt the classroom. (p. 329)

Thus, while current evidence of effects on intelligence test scores are either short-lived or negligible it is important for the clinician to impart to parents, teachers, and other caregivers of preschool children that intelligence is but one variable that affects preschool readiness. A child with below-average intelligence but who is well liked, hardworking, attentive, physically robust, and has had good cognitive stimulation at home is likely to have differing outcomes in comparison to the child with the same intelligence test scores, ill-temper, hyperactivity, aggression toward peers, juvenile diabetes, and chronic exposure to domestic violence and drug abuse at home.

Other preschool intervention programs shed additional light on the effects of early intervention on intelligence test scores. An early review by Bouchard and Segal (1985) provided the following summary of the effects of preschool intervention as studied by the Consortium for Longitudinal Studies founded in 1975. This group combined data from 11 major preschool projects and reached the following conclusions. Program children scored higher than control children at immediate posttesting (7.42 points), 1 year follow-up (4.32), 2 year follow-up (4.62), and 3 to 4 year follow-up (3.04). By the time the children were followed at 10 to 19 years of age, however, there were no significant differences in WISC scores between control and program children (Bouchard & Segal, 1985). Even at these older ages, however, there were differences in favor of the program children, but they were not IQ variables. Bouchard and Segal (1985) describe these other program outcomes as follows.

> Some superiority in achievement test scores was maintained by program children, especially in mathematics, in grades three through six. Some other benefits were in the areas of achievement orientation, school competence, educational attainment, and career accomplishments. For example, at age 15 years, program participants cited a school-related activity when asked to name something that makes them proud (achievement orientation). Parents of these children voiced high aspirations for these children. Furthermore, only 13% of the program children, compared with 31% of the nonprogram children, were eventually enrolled in special education classes. (p. 451)

Bouchard and Segal (1985) presented considerable data to show that while school accounts for some of the variance in intelligence test scores, the effects of family context are as potent or more potent as suggested earlier. These findings are consistent, then, with the Head Start results showing school effects but primarily during the phases of intensive intervention.

There is, however, some relationship (Bouchard & Segal, 1985) between the amount of schooling and intelligence test scores. Correlations in the .60s and .70s between the intelligence test scores of adult males and number of years of schooling are typical. The effect of education, however, may not be as dramatic as the correlations indicate, since the typical effect of one year of education is to produce one standard score point improvement in general intellectual level (Bouchard & Segal, 1985).

Perhaps the now-dated conclusion drawn by the Coleman report (1966) on the relationship between schooling and outcomes for a child speaks most clearly to this issue. The report concluded:

> Taking all these results together, one implication stands out above all: the schools bring little influence to bear on a child's achievement that is independent of his background and general social context; and that this very lack of an independent effect means that the inequalities imposed on children by their home, neighborhood, and peer environment are carried along to become the inequalities which control life at the end of school. For equality of educational opportunity through the schools to be effective, one must imply a strong effect of schools that is independent of the child's immediate social environment, and that strong independent effect is not present in American schools. (Coleman et al., 1966, p. 325)

In addition to the influence of family factors, and this point is frequently overlooked, it may be that Head Start intervention is too brief, as it is primarily focused on the preschool years. It may be necessary to continue intervention throughout a child's lifetime of schooling in order to produce positive outcomes. This point of view is eloquently stated in the following quotation (Horowitz & O'Brien, 1989):

Development is not a disease to be treated. It is a process that needs constant nurturance. There is no reason to expect that an intensive program of early stimulation is an inoculation against all further developmental problems. No one would predict that a child given an adequate amount of Vitamin C at two years of age will not have Vitamin C deficiency at 10 years of age. Currently, according to the most viable model of development that applies to both at-risk and normal children, developmentally functional stimulation is desirable at every period of development and not only in early years. (p. 444)

Unfortunately, for practicing examiners, the research aimed at identifying environmental factors that affect intelligence is at about the same stage as the search for specific genes that may play a role in intellectual development. Now that it is clearly recognized that genetic and environmental factors are crucially important in affecting intellectual development, the call is out for researchers to determine the exact interplay of these factors (Horowitz & O'Brien, 1989).

OTHER FACTORS AFFECTING INTELLIGENCE

Ethnic Differences and Intelligence

Since the time of Galton there has been theorizing about the differences observed between various racial/ethnic/linguistic groups. For example, the results of the Army Alpha and Beta examinations after World War I were used to construct a hierarchy of various ethnic groups with Scandinavian groups being considered more intellectually competent (see Box 3.1).

In a 1922 study there was great concern about the genetic differences between the various "stocks" found in different areas of the United States (see Box 3.1). In 1923 Pintner noted that there was great concern about the genetic inferiority of farmer's children, African Americans, and American Indians. Cautions about these findings

Box 3.1

The Beginnings of Controversy over Genetic Differences

After World War I, Alexander (1922) published the results of the Army Alpha testing program. This article is an excellent example of the type of article to engender polemics regarding intelligence testing. One can imagine the consternation of politicians over such an article. Alexander drew several controversial conclusions after reviewing the average Alpha scores of the states including the following, "It may be argued that the best blood tends to be attracted to the cities, that good endowment assures success in economic advancement, and that states having the better stocks build the better schools" (p. 183). The rankings of top five and bottom five states are given below.

State	Rank (Highest to Lowest)	State	Rank (Highest to Lowest)
Oregon	1	North Carolina	37
Washington	2	Georgia (my home)	38
California	3	Arkansas	39
Connecticut	4	Kentucky	40
Idaho	5	Mississippi	41

Of course, at this time there were fewer than 50 states.

were also delineated back in these early days, although these were often ignored. One such caution regarding the lower intelligence test scores of rural children was that, "Lincolns come from rural districts, but they never go back" (Pintner, 1923, p. 250). Of course, polemics arise when the difference between various groups is attributed to genetic factors alone. Over the years there have been many hypotheses offered about the genetic inferiority of various racial and ethnic groups. The only change has been the target groups of the hypotheses (see Box 3.1). After World War I, one of the first targets were the Italians. Later in the 1920s there was great concern about the inferiority of rural children (Pintner, 1923). Also in the 1920s there was concern about the genetic inferiority of American Indians (Pintner, 1923), and there has been continuing hypotheses offered about African Americans (Jensen, 1969).

Comparisons between American children as a group, American White children, and various Asian groups have also received considerable attention. This controversy asserted itself in a study by Lynn (1977), who compared the standardization data for older versions of the Wechsler scales that were normed in both the United States and in Japan. The Japanese outperformed the American children consistently, leading the author to conclude that the Japanese were genetically superior in intelligence.

Stevenson, Stigler, Lee, Lucker, Kitamura, and Hsu (1985) tried to eliminate potential methodological problems by developing cognitive and academic tests specifically for cross-cultural study. Their tests were constructed to be as comparable as possible for Taiwanese, Japanese, and American children. In contrast to Lynn (1977), Stevenson et al. (1985) found no significant differences in overall cognitive (intelligence) test scores for the two groups. The most striking difference was the American children's inferiority in mathematics achievement. These findings could be interpreted as ruling out genetic differences in intelligence in favor of other factors that may give some Asian groups an advantage in quantitative skills.

Sue and Okazaki (1990) proposed a theory of relative functionalism to explain Asian and American differences in achievement. They noted the consistent finding that Asian children show higher educational attainment than other American minority groups, and they proposed that this is true because it is more "functional" for Asians. Their theory of relative functionalism has three premises:

1. Every cultural group has a drive for upward mobility that is shaped by environmental factors.

2. When opportunities for a cultural group are limited in most areas but educational attainment, a cultural group will choose educational attainment as a goal.

3. Having other cultural groups adopt Asian educational values will likely be unsuccessful since other cultural groups have outlets for attainment other than education.

Sue and Okazaki (1990) concluded that Asian American children seek educational attainment in part because of premise 2. Unlike other cultural groups that have opportunities in areas such as politics, government, entertainment, sports, and the like, Asian American children do not have such opportunities readily available to them, leaving education and the professions as avenues for realizing their strivings.

Given our current knowledge of research on the nature/nurture question, these hypotheses about racial and ethnic group differences should be clearly identified as such, hypotheses as opposed to conclusions that can be strongly reinforced by research data. The only conclusion that can be drawn is that there are mean differences between various ethnic groups worldwide and in the United States. Even on newer intelligence tests that have virtually eliminated individually biased items mean differences persist. Kaufman and Kaufman (1983b) note that on the WISC-R the commonly found difference between Black and White children was about 15 standard score points. On the K-ABC, the difference was somewhat less, about 7 to 9 standard score points (Kamphaus & Reynolds, 1987). Even though we know that this difference exists, we are still a long way from understanding the phenomenon. The different cultural rates of teratogens, family factors and values, poverty, social status, societal opportunities, and a long list of other factors must be studied in order to understand group differences. Hence, to say that the difference between groups of children (and just defining the group members is not an easy task) is due to genetic or environmental factors is likely a gross oversimplification of the complex factors that may produce an intelligence test score. Furthermore, general conclusions are frequently going to be useless to psychologists who must strive to understand the complex interplay of biological and environmental factors affecting children's cognitive development. What conclusions can be drawn, for example, for the case where a child's mother and father are both products of multiracial backgrounds? The "dual ocular test of race" (i.e., the physical characteristics of the examinee) frequently is not of great help in understanding the individual case.

Zuckerman (1990) challenged much of the work on group differences as being based on flawed research studies. He argued that the difficulties involved in diagnosing race for research purposes are not appreciated by many researchers and not recognized as a confounding variable in many investigations on group differences. In Zuckerman's (1990) words:

Studying distributions of blood types shows that some groups with common blood-type frequencies do not resemble each other in classical racial features, whereas others, like Africans and Oceanic Negroids, who have common features of color and hair form, differ in blood types. Australoid aborigines resemble American Indians far more than they do Africans, Asians, or Europeans in their low frequencies of the type B gene even though they are markedly different in physical type. The modern anthropology of population genetics raises serious questions about the old concepts of race based on phenotypes. (p. 1298)

So how do most researchers assess race for research purposes? They usually make a judgment of the subject's phenotype or they ask the subject to evaluate his or her own phenotype. Zuckerman (1990) also cited data to show that within-group variability is larger than between-group variability for some traits, which further calls into question some findings on racial group differences. There is a continuing need to identify the biological and environmental variables that affect cognitive development so that treatment and preventive measures can be taken. This research agenda is likely a more fruitful endeavor in the long term than studying group differences (Zuckerman, 1990).

Currently much of the focus on racial or ethnic group differences has changed to the evaluation of cultural effects on behavior and/or performance in the assessment session. It has been found, for example, that the ethnicity of the evaluating psychologist and the language used to conduct the evaluation has an impact on the psychologist's rating of presenting symptom severity (Malgady & Costantino, 1998). In their study Malgady and Costantino (1998) evaluated 148 low SES Hispanic patients of primarily Puerto Rican and Dominican Republic origin. These adult patients were eventually diagnosed primarily with schizophrenia, depression, and anxiety disorders according to DSM criteria. All patients included in the research study were evaluated with semistructured interviews by a team of psychiatrists and psychologists, all bilingual, who had to achieve 100% blind agreement on the Axis I Diagnosis. Patients were also reevaluated again after 2 weeks of treatment to ensure accuracy of the initial diagnosis. A new team of 6 psychiatrists and 23 psychologists then evaluated each patient in order to assess their presenting symptomatology. Four groups of patients were formed for diagnostic interview purposes: English only—non-Hispanic Clinician; Spanish only—Hispanic clinician; English only—Hispanic clinician; and Bilingual—Hispanic clinician. All four patient groups were matched on a variety of variables, including gender, diagnosis, and acculturation.

No differences were found in symptom ratings between psychologists and psychiatrists. Among many findings, the authors noted that patients in the Spanish-only and Bilingual interview conditions were rated as having the most symptomatology (Malgady & Costantino, 1998). These results, according to the authors, raise at least two possibilities: (1) interviews conducted in the patient's native language by a Hispanic clinician may result in "overly pathologizing" the patient's condition, or (2) Hispanic clinicians are more sensitive than non-Hispanic clinicians in this circumstance to the presence of symptomatology. While more research is needed to test these hypotheses, studies of this nature show clearly that language and culture can affect the diagnostic process, perhaps in unanticipated ways. Malgady and Costantino also observed that given the failure to recruit large numbers of Hispanics to the field, more training is needed for non-Hispanic psychologists.

Research of this nature has implications for the assessment process and interpretation of results. Intelligence test results per se have been found to measure the same constructs for a variety of cultural groups (test bias will be discussed in a later chapter) (Neisser et al., 1996). It is the interpretation of these results in the context of culture and language that can make intellectual assessment either a stigmatizing or enabling process.

Gender Differences

Boys and girls show consistent differences on children's intelligence measures, and again psychologists disagree over the attribution of these differences to genetic factors. The differences, however, are extremely small in comparison to racial/ethnic group differences. As an example, Kaufman (1979b) found that girls outperform boys by about 1 1/2 scaled score points on the Coding subtest of the WISC-R (this is a half standard deviation difference). On all other WISC-R Performance scale subtests boys scored slightly higher than girls, about a half scale score

point for each subtest (this is only a 1/6 standard deviation difference). As a result, the girls' advantage on the Coding subtest, and the boys' slighter advantage on the other Performance subtests resulted in approximately equal Performance IQs for boys and girls.

Vandenberg and Vogler (1985) have investigated the possibility of genetic differences existing in the performance of females and males on spatial subtests. They agree with the conclusions of Plomin (1989) that the data does not quite give adequate support for a genetic explanation for the relative superiority of boys on spatial tests. Jacklin (1989) offers the point of view that sex differences on various measures of intelligence, especially measures of verbal ability, has shown a closing of the gap between girls and boys over the years. Perhaps another reason why there are only a few sex differences between boys and girls on intelligence measures is that as far back as the 1916 version of the Stanford Binet attempts were made to search out and eliminate items that appeared to be gender biased. The most reasonable conclusion is that a child's gender is not likely to be a worthwhile explanation for a child's profile of scores. The differences between boys and girls on tests such as the WISC-R, while statistically significant (primarily due to large sample sizes), are not clinically significant or meaningful. The gender issue seems to be of more theoretical than immediate practical importance due to the fact that results to date have produced small differences that are inconsistent across a variety of abilities (Neisser et al., 1996).

Socioeconomic Status and Intelligence

During the long history of the development of intelligence tests, there has been a consistent and robust relationship noted between measures of socioeconomic status, such as parental occupation, levels of parental educational attainment, and median family income, and the intelligence test scores. As far back as 1942, McNemar found that the average intelligence test score of 15- to 18-year-old children whose parents were classified as professionals was 116.4, while that of children whose parents were classified as day labor urban and rural workers was 97.6.

Intelligence and SES are so intertwined that they cannot be separated, much like genetic and environmental influences (Brody, 1985). Individuals with higher intelligence test scores obtain more schooling, and educational attainment is the most potent predictor of occupational status (Brody, 1985). This fact suggests that SES can be viewed as a proxy variable for intelligence and vice versa.

Birth Order and Intelligence

Birth order is another variable related to intelligence test scores. Apparently, if one has a choice it is best to be born first. Bouchard & Megue (1981) draws the following conclusions regarding this field of research:

1. IQ declines with increasing family size.

2. Within each family size, IQ declines with increasing birth order.

3. Excluding last-borns, the data assume the form of a quadratic function. This means that, until the last-born child, there is a progressive reduction in IQ decrement, and an eventual upswing for families of eight and nine children.

4. Within each family size, last-borns show a greater decline than do children of any other birth rank.

5. Only children score at about the same level as second-borns in two-child families, or first-borns in four-child families. (p. 478)

The theories as to why this association between birth order and intelligence test scores occurs are numerous and none widely accepted. The Confluence Model of Zajonc and Markus (1975) has been frequently cited as one explanation for the decline in intelligence test scores with increasing family size. Presumably, as family size increases parents have less and less time to devote to each child. Thus, while the first-born child receives a great deal of parental attention and interaction with competent adult models, second-, and later-born children have less access to more competent models and more access to their siblings, who are presumably not maximally intellectually developed. The finding of an eighth or ninth child having a higher intelligence score than some of the earlier children is also explained by this particular model. By this point in time the older children of the family are adults and are able to give more individual attention to the later-born children. Others, most notably Hurnst and Ankst (1983) in a review of the literature, contend that the confluence model does not really explain the observed phenomena. They note that the reason why children born to larger families tend to have lower average intelligence test scores is because larger families are associated with lower levels of socioeconomic status. In this scenario, a first-born child may be more representative of the society at large, whereas a fourth- or fifth-born child is born into a family suffering considerably more financial strain.

Regardless of the theories offered, the pecking order of siblings for intelligence test scores has been a fairly robust finding. Given that it requires a certain intellectual level to be using a graduate-level text, such as this one, it may be interesting to know the number of first-borns that are in the intellectual assessment course using this textbook. If more intellectually capable individuals enroll for graduate coursework, there should be a large number of first-borns in the class using this text.

The effects of birth order, however, typically do not warrant interpretation for intelligence tests. This is a phenomenon similar to gender differences, where the findings are more provocative for theory building than for clinical assessment practice. This is because the changes from child to child in a family are relatively small, only a standard score point or two. The only reason that the phenomenon is worth mentioning is that the finding of small differences between siblings is so consistent across studies.

Teratogens and Trauma

Malnutrition

Malnutrition may be a powerful teratogen affecting development. There are, however, dramatic differences in the way malnutrition affects the development of various organs. Naeye, Diener, Dellinger, and Blancs (1969) compared the organ weights of 445 consecutive stillbirths for poor and "nonpoor" children. They found that all major organs were smaller for the malnourished children. Of those affected the thymus was only 66% of normal size for these offspring and the adrenal gland was 77% of normal. Of particular interest was the finding that the only organ that was expected size was the brain (101% of normal for the poor group and 107% of normal for the nonpoor group). This surprising finding is consistent with research on the intellectual development of malnourished children, suggesting that children seem to be resilient.

An investigation of Korean children who experienced severe malnutrition during their first two or three years of life and were later adopted into relatively prosperous American families before the age of 3 showed a reversal of the effects of malnutrition. They showed dramatic gains in height and weight and in intelligence and achievement test performance (Winick, Meyer, & Harris, 1975). This finding was cross-validated by a study of nutritionally deprived children from Colombian families (McKay, Sinisterra, McKay, Gomez, & Lloreda, 1978). Malnutrition and other potential teratogens may be responsible for the lower-than-average intelligence test scores seen in samples of homeless children (Rafferty & Shinn, 1991).

Low Birth Weight

The relationship between low birth weight and intelligence test scores is also not as permanent and immutable as was initially hypothesized. Bouchard and Segal (1985) conclude, based on an exhaustive review of the research, that the correlation between IQ and birth weight is due to differences between families, such as socioeconomic status, not to birth weight per se. Children from impoverished families who are of low birth weight tend to have lower-than-average intelligence test and other scores. The lower scores, however, are more likely due to the multiple effects of impoverishment rather than the low birth weight or, for that matter, malnutrition, specifically.

Anoxia

Similarly, children suffering anoxia (a significant lack of oxygen) shortly after birth have been hypothesized to have a higher incidence of mental retardation (Gottfried, 1973). However, on further analysis of longitudinal data it was found that while there was an intelligence test score decrement for anoxic children, the decrement had all but disappeared by the age of 7 (Bouchard & Segal, 1985).

Findings regarding the relationship between prenatal and perinatal insults, malnutrition, and intelligence suggest a great deal of resiliency on the part of children. If an insult, such as anoxia, occurs at a fairly young age and is not of a sufficient nature to be particularly life threatening or result in easily documented physical damage, the prognosis for recovery of intelligence test performance in the early elementary grade years is remarkably good. These results should not, however, rule out the possible effects of early trauma on obtained intelligence test scores. When the trauma is fairly substantial or occurs later in life than infancy, there may be a substantial impact on scores.

Fetal Alcohol Exposure

Two recent studies highlight the detrimental effects of maternal alcohol use during pregnancy on cognitive (Coles, Brown, Smith, Platzman, Erickson, & Falek, 1991) outcomes. The Coles et al. (1991) investigation followed three groups of high-risk mothers from an impoverished inner city environment. One group of 21 mothers reported never drinking alcohol during pregnancy. A group of 22 mothers drank during part of the pregnancy but quit after being advised of the risk to the fetus. This group averaged 11½ ounces of alcohol per week up until the time they quit drinking. The third group of 25 mothers continued drinking an average of 12 ounces of alcohol per week in spite of being advised not to. Numerous measures were taken on the offspring.

The results revealed a direct relationship between maternal alcohol use and cognitive function with the never-drank and stopped-drinking groups being similar and the continued-drinking group showing significant cognitive impairment. The composite intelligence test scores (the composite for the K-ABC is called the Mental Processing Composite or MPC) for the K-ABC taken at follow-up for the three groups were significantly different. The mean MPC for the no-drinking and stopped-drinking groups were similar at 92 and 89, whereas the mean MPC for the continued-drinking group was 84. These results show the clear teratogenic effects of alcohol use during pregnancy.

Other traumas and physical problems may adversely affect intelligence test scores. The above research suggests that child clinicians should be alert for any such conditions that may affect current performance. Among other things the child clinician should simply inquire about the current health status of a child during the administration of an intelligence test. In a study of adults, Field, Schaie, and Leino (1988) found a significant relationship between the adult's self-reported health and intelligence test scores.

Cumulative Family Risks

A study by Liaw and Brooks-Gunn (1994) outlined an approach to gauging risk based on the consideration of the accumulative effects of various risks. In an investigation of 704 children, who were followed from birth to 3 years, they found that individual risk factors were not as helpful for assessing teratogenic effects on intelligence test results as multiple risks.

Specifically, they hypothesized that the number of risk factors may be more important to know than the types. A total of 13 risk factors were collected for two classifications of families—poor and nonpoor. The risk factors studied included birth weight, neonatal health, race/ethnicity, unemployment of head of household, maternal education, maternal verbal ability, maternal mental health, stressful life events, maternal social support, teenage motherhood, father absence, high family density, and parental beliefs such as holding a simplistic and rigid view of child development. Poor families were found to have a greater prevalence of 11 of these 13 risk factors. The risk factors shown to be associated with overall intelligence estimates at age 3 included poverty status (poor versus nonpoor), neonatal health, race/ethnicity, maternal education, maternal verbal ability PPVT-R scores (a measure of hearing vocabulary), and maternal depression. Generally, the children of poor African American and Hispanic American families, and those with depressed mothers, were at greatest risk for low intelligence test scores. Interestingly, an intervention that included home visits, parent group meetings, and full-day attendance at a child development center produced significant gains in intelligence test scores over a 3-year period. The intervention group that benefited most included poor children that had the fewest risk factors. Also noteworthy was the finding that the treatment group of poor children scored higher than those of the no-treatment nonpoor group.

This study produces several implications for further research and practice including:

First, poor families may be more likely to be exposed to multiple risks, which, in turn, have detrimental effects on child and parent well-being, highlight the importance of looking at cumulative risks rather than focusing on single risk factors. Second, the finding that being classified as above the poverty line does not prevent a family from experiencing risk factors—or prevent the adverse effects of risk factors—suggests that income per se should not be taken as the single criterion for negative outcomes or be used as a marker for a range of family conditions. (Liaw & Brooks-Gunn, 1994, p. 369)

Motivation, Temperament, and Intelligence

Research that addresses the relationship between motivational and temperament variables and intelligence test scores is minimal (Brody, 1985). Anastasi (1988) cites some research showing a relationship between personality characteristics and intelligence test performance. She notes that some studies show that when personality test scores are added to intelligence test scores in order to predict a person's subsequent academic achievement, they do add a significant amount of variance to the prediction.

Martin (1988) reports some studies assessing the relationship between his Temperament Assessment Battery for Children (TABC) and cognitive criterion variables such as school grades and achievement tests that are good correlates of intelligence measures. In one sample of 43 first-grade children, some TABC scales were stronger correlates of achievement than others. Emotional intensity was a relatively low correlate of reading grades, whereas adaptability and persistence had strong positive correlations in the .60s and distractibility had a negative correlation of –.63. A similar pattern was found for mathematics grades. These findings were cross-validated in a second study of 104 first-grade children where reading and mathematics achievement test scores and grades were used as criterion variables. These findings suggest that certain temperament variables may be related to intelligence test scores. Adaptability and persistence may by positively related and distractibility may be negatively related. This does appear, however, to be a remarkably understudied topic that requires further research.

Some potential causal links are also beginning to emerge between early behavior problems and later intelligence test results. Fergusson and Horwood (1995), for example, using a large longitudinal sample, found that early disruptive behavior problems such as aggression, hyperactivity, and conduct and oppositional behavior were significantly correlated with later intelligence test scores. They implicate disruptive behavior as one potential cause of score decrements. Additional research of this nature will hopefully reveal the full extent of behavioral "teratogens" that may affect cognitive development.

Intelligence and Academic Achievement

If, as transactional theory dictates, psychologists are trying to measure intelligence as opposed to achievement, then intelligence tests should be substantially different from measures of academic achievement, or as Binet called achievement, "the pedagogical method." Generally, there is a significant overlap in variance between the two types of measures (Anastasi, 1988; Wright, 1987).

This overlap in variance has led Anastasi (1988) and others (Kaufman, 1990) to propose that intelligence and achievement are not unique and, therefore, intelligence tests should be interpreted as specialized types of achievement measures (Anastasi, 1988; Kaufman, 1990). Correlations between the two measures, however, cannot be used as sole evidence that these measures are redundant. In another, but virtually identical context, Vandenburg and Vogler (1985) eschew the substantial correlation argument as evidence against the construct called "g" by pointing out that "Against the argument that all ability tests correlate positively and therefore measure the same ability, one can point out that height and weight also correlate, and rather substantially, yet we consider them to be separate characteristics" (p. 6). Similarly, measures of reading and mathematics achievement also correlate highly, and we do not consider reading and mathematics to be the same construct.

The problem with the relationship between intelligence and scholastic achievement is the "chicken and egg" phenomenon. Since intelligence is called such, people often assume that it is the causative agent for academic achievement. It is equally likely that poor achievement "causes" poor intelligence test scores, since intelligence tests, especially the more verbal ones, have vocabulary, mathematical, and other achievement item types. At high levels of occupational attainment, knowledge becomes very specialized and more important than intelligence test results per se. "Knowledge also counts" according to Hunt (1999) who observed that several studies have shown that people who, in a modern industrial or postindustrial society requiring specialized skills, learn the most become the most successful. Hunt (1999) pointedly describes the importance of knowledge in adulthood in the following quote:

Today there is a great deal of talk about "learning how to learn" but little discussion about precisely how teachers are supposed to teach people to learn. Teachers certainly can teach specific skills, "g_c" in its broadest framework. Students who complete a course in psychological statistics will be able to solve problems that baffled Gauss or Pascal. Does this mean that today's students are more intelligent than Blaise Pascal? In a sense, no, but who cares? They are better statisticians. (p. 24)

Thus, the conceptual separation of the notions of intellectual ability and achievement can be said to be unnecessary for some referral questions. In the case of competent performance, be it job- or school-related, the question of ability is mute. Assessment of the predictor variable, intelligence, is unneeded since performance on the criterion variable, achievement, is already known. Similarly, as will be discussed in detail in later sections on test interpretation, even when assessment of intelligence is warranted, the focus of intervention needs to be directed at achievement.

Intelligence and Adaptive Behavior

There are numerous similarities in definitions of adaptive behavior. Edgar Doll, an illustrious psychologist at the Vineland State Training School in New Jersey, introduced the construct in the

1930s as central to the process of assessing mental retardation. He believed that social maturity (an older term for adaptive behavior) was as important in the assessment of mentally retarded individuals as was intelligence. He published the first edition of what is now called the Vineland Adaptive Behavior Scales (Sparrow, Balla, & Cicchetti, 1984). His definition of adaptive behavior is similar to modern ones. He states:

Social competence is the functional ability of the human organism for exercising personal independence and social responsibility. (Doll, 1953, p. 10)

Doll's test and subsequent scales measure a host of skills needed for personal independence. The Vineland, for example, includes scales that assess Communication, Daily Living Skills, Socialization, and Motor Skills.

The relationship between intelligence and adaptive behavior measures is well researched, although there is considerable variability among studies (Destefano & Thompson, 1990). Overall though, the evidence reveals modest relationships (correlations in the .30 to .60 range) with adaptive behavior scales (Kamphaus, 1987; Keith, Fehrmann, Harrison, & Pottebaum, 1987).

Keith et. al. (1987) conducted an exhaustive study of the relationship between the Vineland and the K-ABC involving 556 children in grades 1 through 8 from a variety of locations around the United States. Three confirmatory factor models were fit to the data. Model 1 was constrained so that the relationship was assumed to be low (r = .39). Model 2 assumed no correlation between intelligence and adaptive behavior. This model assumes that the two constructs are completely independent. Model 3 hypothesized a perfect relationship between the two constructs, which assumes that both constructs are subserved by the same general ability. The various fit statistics for the models are given in Table 3.4. The fit statistics show Model 1 to be the best fit to the data. This model had the smallest Chi-square, the largest fit index, and the smallest root mean square residual, all indications of better fit to the

TABLE 3.4   Fit statistics for the three factor models compared in the Keith et al. (1987) study

	Model 1	Model 2	Model 3
Chi-Square	83.01	134.36	379.91
Adjusted Fit Index	.876	.843	.521
Root Mean Square Residual	.072	.160	.153

model. This study exemplifies a more sophisticated approach than comparing simple zero order correlations between the two variables, but the results are the same—intelligence tests are separate but related constructs (Keith et al., 1987).

This relationship is notable in that it differs significantly from the relationship between intelligence and academic achievement in which correlations tend to range from .55 to .90, depending on the study and achievement domain (e.g., reading, writing). This modest relationship does leave considerable room for variability between intelligence and adaptive behavior scores for a particular child, making interpretation a challenge.

One of the reasons for variability among studies is the nature of the adaptive behavior scale being used. Some scales use teachers as informants, and these produce larger correlations between intelligence and adaptive behavior (Kamphaus, 1987). Also, scales that assess academic types of adaptive behavior tend to produce more overlap between intelligence and achievement measures (Destefano & Thompson, 1990). Hence, the agreement between intelligence and adaptive behavior scales, or lack thereof, depends on the nature of the adaptive behavior test's item content as well as the informant. Psychologists are likely to find adaptive behavior to differ from intelligence test scores when the items pertain to nonschool behavior and parents serve as the informant. Even though the correlations of intelligence with adaptive behavior are lower than for achievement, they will often be statistically significant and moderate in magnitude. This fact begs psychologists not to consider these measures as independent and calls for interpretation of intelligence test scores and adaptive behavior scores in combination. Psychologists should, for example, look for an integration of results between verbal intelligence test scores and communication domains of adaptive behavior. Use of these multiple measures are most likely to produce the greatest insight into the child's referral problems.

CONCLUSIONS

The cause(s) of intelligence of various kinds must be delineated in order for intelligence assessment to be deemed desirable by society (Hunt, 1999). Jencks (1992) observed that *the nonscientific public dislikes the argument that genes cause intelligence because the mechanism for doing so has not been delineated by research*. It is only in the last decade, as the fields of behavior genetics and neuropsychology have grown in sophistication and application, that we have begun to develop an understanding of the biological causes, moderators, and mediators of intelligent performances (Reiss, Neiderhiser, Hetherington, & Plomin, 2000). Analogously, Hunt (1999) rings a hopeful note, based on recent research progress, that explanations will be found. He offered the analogy that Columbus did not bring any gold back to Spain but his successors, the conquistadors, were entirely successful at doing so. Referring to the known fact that intellectual variation exists in humans, Hunt (1999) highlights the importance of future research by observing:

> We need to know the biological mechanisms by which this is achieved. This is partly because we want to understand the gene-performance relationships. In part, and equally important, it is because we want to understand what other physical factors can affect mental competence and how we can avoid or ameliorate them. The persistence of recreational drugs, including alcohol, stands high on the list of danger factors to be investigated, but they are by no means alone. We need a better understanding of nutritional effects and deterioration of intellectual competence associated with aging and disease. We do not need to know the value of the heritability coefficient to the third decimal place, or even the second. (p. 24)

Much progress has been made along these lines and preventive measures (e.g., admonishments against alcohol consumption during pregnancy) have been implemented to societal benefit. Perhaps more important, personality, motivational (see Research Report 3.2), and ecological factors that affect intelligence have yet to be substantially defined (Ackerman, 1999). And, as aptly pointed out by Hunt (1999), this progress will not be made by "gazing" at correlation coefficients or factor analytic solutions. Other research paradigms (e.g., experimental cognitive) and disciplines (e.g., anthropology) will be needed to make substantive research progress. Fortunately, for the next generation, such realizations are now commonplace in the psychological science community, making the potential for progress better than at any time before.

RESEARCH REPORT 3.2

Praise Effort, Not Intelligence

Sara Solovitch

(*San Jose Mercury News*, May 18, 1999, Reprinted with permission)

Your 3-year-old daughter fits the last piece into a 20-piece puzzle, and what do you tell her? That she's the smartest little girl in the world, of course.

It's the most natural thing in the world to tell your child how smart she is. All parents do it. (And some insufferable ones tell everybody who comes into sight.)

But as it turns out, this kind of praise may not be the most constructive you can give your child. It may even undermine her motivation to work hard and meet new challenges.

It is far better to praise for hard work. That is the conclusion of new research looking at children's motivation, and many psychologists believe it may help explain why some intelligent kids never meet their potential.

Carol Dweck, a psychology professor at Columbia University, studied fifth-graders and kindergartners from diverse economic and social backgrounds from Indiana to New York. She gave them an easy pattern-recognition test, praising one group for its innate intelligence and another group for its good effort. The schoolchildren praised for intelligence "got these little proud smiles, but that was their high point," said Dweck. After failing a more difficult test, they tended to give up, lose pleasure in their work and show a general loss in confidence. Their intelligence was viewed as a fixed trait; once lost, they didn't know how to get it back.

The process of learning

By comparison, the students who were praised for their hard efforts tended to focus on the process of learning. In the face of criticism, they adopted new strategies and consistently refused to take their failures personally.

"Children who are vulnerable are very focused on their intelligence," concluded Dweck. "Am I smart? Am I not smart? Is this test going to make me look smart?" They are enmeshed in it. Whereas, the kids who are really hardy don't think of it that much. They see it as a set of skills that can be developed, but they don't worry how it looks at any given moment."

(Continued)

RESEARCH REPORT 3.2 (CONTINUED)

Cross-cultural studies reveal huge differences in the motivational factors that govern U.S. and Japanese students. Hazel Marcus, a psychologist at Stanford, has found that when U.S. students are told that they've performed well in a test, they are motivated to work harder. When they learn they've done poorly, they lose interest. Japanese students, on the other hand, respond in the opposite way. Those who are told they've done poorly work hard to improve themselves.

Mark Lepper, another Stanford psychologist, has spent 20 years studying motivation in children. He has looked at both intrinsic and extrinsic learning and concluded that a student's motivation makes all the difference. An intrinsically motivated student who pursues an activity for its own sake ultimately works harder and reaches for higher challenges. The extrinsically motivated student who works for stickers, happy smiles or the ultimate reward —money—often puts forth the minimal amount of effort necessary to get the maximal reward.

'Inherently rewarding'

"With young children it's just so obvious that the process of learning is inherently rewarding," says Lepper. "No one has ever seen a 3-year-old with a motivational deficit. Parents are more likely to complain of their child being overly curious, always asking 'why,' exploring here and there. Yet, four or five years later, a substantial number of children are diagnosed as having 'motivational problems.'

"When we get into school, because of the constraints of wanting to educate everybody we now have to teach everybody the same thing at the same time, and we have to do it on a schedule. That means that you're not learning right at the point when you're most excited, but because it's the middle of March, you're in second grade, and that's when we study subtraction with borrowing."

All too often, it is second grade when children get their first real taste of failure. Streamlined into reading groups with fuzzy-sounding names of birds and animals, the kids quickly figure out the score — who among them are good readers and who aren't.

"Giving up is a long process," says Lepper. "A lot of it depends on the child's theory of success and failure. Do you believe it's because you're dumb and you'll never be able to change? Or do you believe it's because you didn't work hard enough or have the right strategy?"

There's a lesson in all this for parents and teachers, which is to teach children to focus on the process and to delight in challenges, what William Butler Yeats, the great Irish poet, called "the fascination of what's difficult." And, of course, children need praise.

"But it needs to be sincere, not condescending," says Karen Friedland-Brown, director of parent education at the Children's Health Council in Palo Alto. "Let's say they're trying to make their bed. Say, 'I like your effort.' Not 'You did a beautiful job.' Use as few words as possible; us parents tend to over-talk."

CHAPTER SUMMARY

- Intelligence test scores are more stable for handicapped than nonhandicapped preschoolers.

- Intelligence test scores are less stable for preschoolers than for school-aged children and adults.

- Intelligence test scores are fairly stable for adults yielding coefficients in the .60s over a 20-year time span.

- In some cases, intelligence test scores can change by a standard deviation or more, even in adulthood.

- Early researchers believed that intelligence test scores peaked in adolescence and declined together. Recent research suggests that intelligence test scores peak in adulthood, and some scores do not show substantial decline in the late adult years.

- The term *cumulative deficit* refers to the theory that the ill effects of an impoverished early environment accumulate over the course of development to reveal decreasing intelligence test scores with increasing age. There is some research to support the phenomenon.

- Early adoption studies suggested that environmental factors played a very important role in intellectual development. Recent studies have shown that genetic endowment is a more important determinant of intelligence test scores.

- Intelligence is likely determined polygenetically, as opposed to being linked to a single gene.

- The issues of the genetic causation and malleability are often confused. It is often assumed that if intelligence is genetically determined it is not malleable.

- Research to date shows that intelligence test scores are not highly malleable, at least with short-term intervention. There is not yet a "cure" for low intelligence although there may be some day.

- Race/cultural group differences in intelligence test scores persist. Traditionally, these differences have been attributed to genetic differences and this has caused great controversy.

Today, it is recognized that these differences are so intertwined with SES, values, family constellation, and other factors that it is difficult to determine the extent of the differences due to genetic factors.

- Gender differences in intelligence test scores are small and not clinically meaningful.

- SES differences in intelligence test scores are large and clinically significant.

- The effects of birth order on intelligence test scores are consistent but small. Oldest children tend to have slightly higher scores.

- Prenatal and postnatal teratogens adversely affect intelligence test scores. There is evidence of resiliency whereby the effects of teratogens such as low birth weight can be overcome by the time a child reaches elementary school.

- The relationship of personality to intelligence test scores is not yet well understood.

- Intelligence and academic achievement tests show substantial intercorrelations. These measures covary a great deal in clinical assessment practice.

- Intelligence and adaptive behavior scales correlate moderately at best.

CHAPTER 4

The Assessment Process

In these terms a test presumably is like an x-ray: regardless of the conditions external to the patient (the immediate environment) the 'thing' being studied (e.g., a bone, intelligence, fantasy) can be observed in splendid isolation—a statement which is true neither for a test nor for an x-ray" (Sarason, 1954, p.59).

CHAPTER QUESTIONS

How do examiners test infants and young children?

What is "standardized procedure"?

The clinical skill required to properly administer an intelligence test cannot be overemphasized. Clinical skill is especially needed when assessing children, since they are highly influenced by adult behavior. The psychologist who acquires the necessary knowledge to use intelligence tests but not the requisite clinical skill is ill prepared.

This individual will find intelligence testing to be arduous, unrewarding, and perhaps punishing. The clinician who is skilled in interacting with children will be capable of making the often stilted test directions used by some intelligence tests seem like ordinary conversation to a child. She will make the intellectual evaluation a pleasant experience for the child rather than an onerous one.

It is also not possible to acquire clinical skill by reading a book chapter. Clinical skill may be a personality related factor leading to the old question, are clinicians born or are they trained? While this debate is far from settled, there are steps that trainees can take to enhance their clinical skill in addition to reading chapters. Useful activities for acquiring clinical skill include the following:

1. Observe a variety of children in a variety of settings. Trainees in intellectual assessment should be keenly aware of the developmental characteristics of children. Such awareness can

be gained by observing children in preschool and other school settings, on playgrounds, and in other public settings such as shopping centers. Trainees should also notice how children interact with parents and other adults in these settings.

2. Observe master teachers interacting with children. This will allow the trainee to acquire a host of skills for interacting effectively with children and adolescents. Experienced teachers can model a number of important skills for establishing and maintaining rapport with children.

3. Observe experienced psychologists administering tests to normal and disabled children when possible. Clinicians may also see the differences, and lack of them, between normal and disabled children and adolescents.

4. Observe a special education teacher administering tests to children. Special education teachers have to work with children intensively for long time periods and develop an exhaustive repertoire of skills for dealing effectively with them.

5. Practice administering intelligence tests to cooperative individuals before giving a test for clinical or course grading purposes. This practice will allow the new examiner to work out minor problems in a nonthreatening atmosphere prior to testing a "real" case.

6. If videotape equipment is available, it can serve as an important self-evaluation tool. If such equipment is not available, audiotapes of several testing sessions can also be helpful. Using these methods, examiners frequently find that they are using repetitive wording, or they can discover why a session was so difficult when the reasons were not apparent at the time.

These exercises and others will go a long way toward supplementing this text in order to develop necessary clinical assessment skills. One key to acquiring good assessment skills, which has little to do with the personal qualities of the examiner, is to know the test well before testing.

Collecting Background Information

There are a number of psychological, social, and medical factors that are either related to or have an effect on intelligence test scores. These variables include SES, ethnicity, dominant language, low birth weight, head trauma, and others. As a result, examiners must collect information regarding these variables when gathering background information. A lack of such background information puts the evaluator at a disadvantage when it is time to interpret the obtained scores. Hence, it is important to conduct a thorough interview of a child's or adolescent's parents or caregivers in order to understand the meaning of her scores.

An example of the importance of even minimal background information for interpreting a child's scores is evident in the following case. I once had a case where there seemed to be little resemblance between parent and child. The parents brought their 10-year-old daughter to be evaluated for academic problems. The parents were high-achieving individuals, both holding Ph.D. degrees. The daughter obtained an average score on the K-ABC and had little interest in academic endeavors. In addition, the daughter did not look like her parents. She had red hair and fair skin in contrast to her parents, who had brown hair and darker complexion. The differences in intellectual level and physical appearance between parents and child did not seem readily understandable given the background information obtained using a standard form, until I asked if they had adopted their daughter. They indicated that they had adopted her a couple of years prior to the evaluation. This case was very puzzling until I had complete background information. Prior to uncovering the child's complete history, I questioned the validity of my obtained scores because they seemed at odds with the scores one would expect given parental characteristics.

Now the question is which pieces of background information are important to obtain? The clinician should collect information on all of the relevant variables that are known to affect intelligence test scores. In addition to these variables, however, it is also important to collect information on variables that may be specific to the clientele that the clinician usually assesses. For example, if a clinician works in a rehabilitation facility for brain-injured children, it will be vitally important for him to gather detailed information on the nature of the trauma that caused the injury, including such things as the time of the insult and the medical interventions carried out to treat the condition. Oftentimes, examiners will use a two-stage process for obtaining background information; the first stage involving collecting general information about the child's background and the second stage involving collecting very detailed information about a specific episode or condition that may be especially germane to the testing. The latter type of information usually centers around the referring problem.

There are numerous forms and interview formats for use with children and their families for obtaining background information. Some topics that are often part of questionnaire/interview schedules are shown in Figure 4.1. It is probably wise for the new examiner to use standard forms or outlines for collecting information to ensure that important aspects of behavior are not missed. This information will prove crucial in the final stages of test interpretation.

Demographic Information
Name, birthdate, address, parents' names, educational attainment, and occupation, etc.

Referral Information
Source and nature of referral

Family Structure and History
Siblings, parenting style, history of medical/psychiatric illnesses, dwelling, family activities, etc.

Pre- and Perinatal History
Conception, maternal care or problems, type of delivery, complications, etc.

Child's Medical History
Respiratory, gastrointestinal, neuropsychiatric, vision, hearing, etc.

Developmental History
Motor and language milestones, toilet training, sleep habits, etc.

Social History
Hobbies, friends, behavior, etc.

School History
Preschool, elementary, high school, retentions, special education, etc.

FIGURE 4.1

Topics/content that are typically part of background information questionnaires

THE TESTING ENVIRONMENT

Test Setting

Environmental variables are as important to the intelligence testing process as they are for some medical procedures. Consequently, physicians and psychologists alike try to control for the effects of extraneous factors.

To provide an optimal testing environment:

1. The testing room should
   - be free from interruptions.
   - be pleasantly, but minimally, decorated so as not to distract the child.
   - be well lit, without being too bright and with no glare.
   - have adequate ventilation.
   - be quiet with no noise from adjoining rooms.
   - be a few degrees cooler than a room meant for adults, as children have higher body temperatures than adults.

- be sparsely furnished to minimize possible distractions.

2. The furniture should
   - be comfortable.
   - be child sized—a table 36″ long and 20–24″ wide and adjustable in height is best. The child's elbows should rest on the table and his feet on the floor—if his feet do not touch the floor, put a box under the feet to avoid a restless feeling.

3. The materials should
   - be child sized (i.e., large crayons).
   - be well-organized and accessible to the examiner.
   - be set up so that the child can only reach the materials needed for the current task. These materials should be directly in front of the child.
   - be set up so that the examiner can effectively use the manual without it becoming a barrier between the child and the examiner.
   - be set up so that the examiner can efficiently use the scoring sheet, but so the child cannot see it.

Timing

Another important environmental variable is the timing of the assessment. Young children may still take naps and show fatigue quickly in an assessment situation. For most purposes it is best to test children and adolescents when they are best able to give their optimal performance. In most instances this is going to be in the morning, the same time when the most demanding work is offered in schools. If a young child does need to take a break because of fatigue or for toileting needs, *it is important to break in between tests or subtests in order to not spoil a test.* One common pitfall that I have seen a number of trainees encounter is not recognizing when a young child needs a break. Usually my students will ask a child about halfway through the testing session if

they need a break, and many children who are very compliant will deny the offer. The examiner then pays a price for the child's compliance by having to help the child clean his soiled pants.

In order to avoid this embarrassment it is important for examiners to develop the skills to "read" a child's behavior. One way of doing this is to observe the child's behavior closely and take a break if the child's behavior changes from being calm to fidgety, or from being alert to yawning. It is also helpful for the examiner to monitor her own behavior. If the examiner feels that the room is getting stuffy or finds herself yawning, the child may also be experiencing these problems, and a break will be in order. In other words, examiners should not always make the decision to take a break in the testing based on the verbal report of the child.

In addition to considering sleeping and eating routines, examiners need to consider the possible impact of activities that precede the assessment (Anastasi, 1988). Children are likely to behave differently in an assessment situation if the preceding activity has been a boisterous outdoor time or a quiet story time (Kamphaus, Dresden, & Kaufman, 1993).

Other Participants

A final environmental variable involves the presence of other people, particularly parents, in the testing room. Psychologists generally agree that having parents present is not advisable for children, especially those over the age of 3. There is some suggestion, however, that for very young children parental presence may, in fact, be beneficial (Sattler, 1988). With young children an examiner must weigh the potential distraction caused by an additional person in the testing room against the problems caused by separation anxiety. More valid assessments of young children may be obtained when a parent is with the child in the testing room but is sitting quietly out of the child's line of vision (Kamphaus, Dresden, & Kaufman, 1993). Most importantly, when addressing the issue of parental presence, examiners must treat parents with respect, not as unwanted intruders. If a parent wants to observe the testing session, an examiner must take the time necessary to fully explain the pros and cons of observing. It may be helpful, for example, to explain how difficult it is for parents to observe their child being tested. Parents who are allowed to observe may find the experience very stress provoking. Parents want their child to do well, and when they do not, it can be extremely punishing to a parent, especially when they know that their child is taking an intelligence test. To some parents it is helpful to simply be aware that such stress is universal.

Physical Arrangements

Examiners are typically well advised to keep test materials out of sight from the child so as to avoid distracting the child from the task at hand and to keep the young or obstreperous child from destroying the organization of the materials. Examiners also should have all of the materials arranged prior to the child's entering the testing room. This preparation will allow the examiner to focus on his interaction with the child when he enters the testing room as opposed to arranging materials.

For some examiners the choice of seating arrangements is influenced by their personal preference. Some examiners, for example, prefer to sit across the table from the child. This allows the examiner to easily keep the materials and the record form out of the child's view. For many examiners who work with children, it is either necessary and/or preferable to sit next to the child. For young children this allows the examiner to more closely monitor the child during testing (in other words, this allows the examiner to grab the child if he starts to run) and direct his attention as necessary.

One advantage of sitting across the table from the child is that it makes it more likely that the examiner will orient materials correctly for the child's viewing or manipulation. I have seen many anxious novices who are so concerned about reading instructions correctly that they pay little attention to the child. Therefore, they sometimes do not place materials in the correct orientation, which is usually in a parallel fashion to the child. Note, also, that an examiner can also produce a psychological barrier between herself and the child by placing a test manual between her and the child. In such a circumstance, the test manual appears to be protecting the examiner from intrusion by the child. This situation should be avoided as it hinders working comfortably with the child and perhaps also hinders rapport.

Finally, and perhaps most importantly, it is important for the child to be seated comfortably regardless of the examiner's physical stature. Young children should be seated in chairs and at tables that are appropriate to their size. This arrangement is necessary to ensure that the child can easily see and manipulate the test materials.

ESTABLISHING RAPPORT

Rapport is the process of establishing a comfortable working relationship with a child (Anastasi, 1988). More than anything else, the practical advice given earlier in this chapter on familiarizing oneself with the developmental characteristics of children will be most helpful to the new examiner in learning how to establish rapport. In addition this section will provide some sage wisdom on the topic. Binet and Simon (1905) give recommendations on the establishment of rapport. As the inventors of modern intelligence testing, their words are worthy of our attention.

> *The examination should take place in a quiet room, quite isolated, and the child should be called in alone without other children. It is important that when a child sees the experimenter for the first time, he should be reassured by the presence of someone he knows, a relative, an attendant, or a school superintendent. The witness should be instructed to remain passive and mute, and not to intervene in the examination by either word or gesture. The experimenter should receive each child with a friendly familiarity to dispel the timidity of early years.*

Greet him the moment he enters, shake hands with him and seat him comfortably. If he is intelligent enough to understand certain words, awaken his curiosity, his pride. If he refuses to reply to a test, pass to the next one, or perhaps offer him a piece of candy; if his silence continues, send him away until another time. These are little incidents that frequently occur in an examination of the mental state, because in its last analysis, an examination of this kind is based upon the good will of the subject. (Jenkins & Paterson, 1961, p. 94)

Binet and Simon (1908) give additional recommendations on the conduct of an intellectual assessment.

The subject to be examined should be kindly received; if he seems timid he should be reassured at once, not only by a kind tone but also by giving him first the tests which seem most like play, for example—giving change for 20 sou., constantly encourage him during the tests in a gentle voice; one should show satisfaction with his answers whatever they may be. One should never criticize nor lose time by attempting to teach him the test; there is a time for everything. The child is here that his mental capacity may be judged, not that he may be instructed. Never help him by supplementary explanation which may suggest the answer. Often one is tempted to do so, but it is wrong. (Jenkins & Paterson, 1961, p. 97)

It has also been argued that the intelligence test itself (Glasser & Zimmerman, 1967) is often effective at building rapport for the school-age child. This comment highlights a major difference between establishing rapport and establishing a therapeutic relationship. Some students confuse the two. Perhaps because of their therapeutic training and good intentions, they try to develop something more akin to a therapeutic relationship in lieu of a working relationship. For the purposes of assessing a child's intelligence, a therapeutic relationship is not necessary unless the testing session is a prelude to or occurs in the context of psychotherapy. Many of my students have found that trying too hard to establish a relationship has proved counterproductive. They have found that after spending a half hour trying to develop a relationship that the child may then be too weary to take the test.

Young Children

Kamphaus, Dresden, and Kaufman (1993) delineate several characteristics of young children that make them more of a challenge in the assessment setting. These include the following characteristics.

1. Young children view the world differently from adults and older children and so have a different view of the assessment process (Goldman, Stein, & Querry, 1983). More specifically, children under the age of 5 or 6 tend to be egocentric and are unable to take the perspective of another person. Because young children are only able to understand their own feelings and needs, they are less likely to be motivated by extrinsic rewards and are often less compliant than older children (Goldman et al., 1983; Lidz, 1983).

2. The physical development of young children requires a high level of activity, and they may have trouble sitting still for long periods of time (Lidz, 1983). Dealing with this straightforward problem may require considerable ingenuity on the part of the examiner.

3. Many children of this age require naps and/or frequent snacks, so testing sessions must be scheduled to accommodate these needs.

4. One of the major developmental tasks of the preschool years is the ability to separate successfully from significant adults. As many children continue to struggle with this issue, the assessment process will be complicated by the difficulties involved in being away from a parent or trusted teacher (Lidz, 1983).

5. The cognitive capabilities of young children also differ from those of older children and create challenges for the examiner. Preschool-aged children are beset with several cognitive limitations: (a) they are only able to perceive or focus on one dimension of an object at a time (e.g., height *or* width); (b) they are only able to remember a few pieces of information at a time (and don't know how to use mnemonic strategies to increase their memory capacity);

(c) they do not understand the principle of transitivity (knowing that A > B, and B > C does not, to them, imply that A > C); (d) they may not understand concepts of time, or even such relational terms as alike or different; and (e) they often do not have well-developed verbal expressive skills (Goldman et al., 1983; Lidz, 1983).

6. The behavior of young children is simply more variable than that of older children (Lidz, 1983) and, in addition, young children are much more susceptible to the influence of extraneous variables. The characteristics of the examiner and of the environment exert more control over the performance of children, especially young children, than they do on the performance of adults (Anastasi, 1988, p. 38).

In addition to child characteristics, it is also important to consider the effects of examiner characteristics on children's behavior, especially the more variable behavior of young children. Unfortunately, while opinions abound on the potential effects of examiner characteristics on a child's intelligence test performance (Anastasi, 1988; Barber, 1973; Epps, 1974; Sarason, 1954), the research literature provides very little guidance on the impact of examiner variables. Concern has been voiced on the effects of a mismatch between examiner and child on characteristics such as race (Epps, 1974) and linguistic background (Figueroa, 1990). There appears to be a consensus, even without research data, that it is desirable for examiner and child to share as many background characteristics as possible in order to establish rapport.

Several suggestions have been offered for developing a personality style that is optimal for the development of rapport, especially with young children. Kamphaus et al. (1993) have gleaned the following suggestions from the literature on this topic.

1. Examiners should be friendly, cheerful, relaxed, warm, and natural (Anastasi, 1988).

2. Examiners should be reassuring and encouraging (Anastasi, 1988; Epps, 1974).

3. Examiners should be patient with the child's efforts.

In addition to the style used by the examiner to interact with the child, the appearance of the examiner may even come into play. Exceedingly elaborate clothing or jewelry may receive more interest from the child than the test materials. All of this information is not intended to make the new trainee obsess unduly about her personality style or appearance prior to her first testing session. Examiners will find that most children and adolescents will respond to any adult who is sincerely interested in their well-being.

Some specific suggestions for examiner behaviors that may be helpful for establishing rapport with particularly young children include the following (Kamphaus et al., 1993).

1. Place yourself at the child's eye level before you begin talking to them (Sattler, 1988); squatting is preferable to bending over because you are then truly at their level.

2. Introduce yourself to the child, avoiding use of the title "Dr.," and ask what you should call him or her (Kaufman & Kaufman, 1983a).

3. Do not be overly demonstrative or intrusive; allow the child to make the first move (Anastasi, 1988).

4. Be honest and direct, explain to the child exactly what will happen during the session.

5. Speak clearly—avoid both a "cutesy," high-pitched approach and an overly technical, adult style of conversation (Paget, 1983).

The astute examiner will notice that there are basically two methods for establishing rapport, talking and doing. For many school-age children and adolescents talking will suffice. The examiner may be able to quite satisfactorily develop rapport by asking her about her family, hobbies, toys, friends, and school. For the younger child, on the other hand, doing may be more important than talking. Many preschool and early elementary grade children may present themselves as mutes when initially greeted by the examiner. It is often difficult to counteract their reticence by asking them questions. I have a "magic wand" once given to me by a colleague. I have found that many young children readily overcome their reticence when they are given the wand and its uses are explained to them. The point being made here is that the examiner should have at her disposal objects such as toys, puppets, or even pencil and paper that may be used to draw out the reticent child.

Conducting an Assessment

The process of conducting an assessment is complex, requiring all of the clinical and interpersonal skill an examiner can muster. Several practical aspects of the skills required and process of conducting an effective intellectual assessment will be discussed in this section.

If the examiner must go to the child's classroom or day care room to get her, he or she should not ask the child to leave in the middle of an activity or at the beginning of a preferred activity (Kamphaus et al., 1993). To the extent possible, the examiner should spend some time in the classroom just watching the child. This observation time will facilitate the familiarization process *and* will likely add a great deal to the examiner's understanding of the assessment results. When it is time to begin the session, the child should not be asked if he or she is ready to go—this violates the old adage of never giving a child a choice unless they do, in fact, have a choice. Instead, the examiner should approach the child with positive, confident anticipation and simply state that now it is time to go (Paget, 1983). The examiner may wish to tell the child that she will be playing some games and that her help is needed to gather some information. Specific words are not particularly important; it is the way you approach the child that will make a difference (see Research Report 4.1).

If the child is brought to the examiner, it is helpful to begin the conversation with a neutral or "easy" topic such as the weather. Especially useful for starting conversations in these situations are concrete objects like fish tanks or appealing toys.

Creating Interest and Motivation

Motivating the child requires the examiner to understand how the child perceives the assessment and how the child feels about being assessed. This knowledge will enable the examiner to present the various tasks in a manner that is both interesting and nonthreatening.

In addition, the attitude of the examiner toward the assessment process will have an impact on the child's level of interest and motivation. An examiner with a cheerful and friendly attitude will convey to the child the message that the assessment process will be enjoyable for both of them (Kaufman & Kaufman, 1983a).

The plan for the entire session and the requirements of each task as it is presented should be thoroughly explained to the child. Testing should begin as soon as the child seems ready, in order to maximize the time before the child gets tired (Kaufman & Kaufman, 1983). Tasks should be presented as shared activities, and it is generally useful to begin with subtests that are appealing and relatively easy (Anastasi, 1988).

How to Start

One of the most frequent questions of new examiners is how to start. Glasser and Zimmerman (1967) provide an introduction to the WISC that may be used to introduce any test of intelligence. They advise beginning the session by saying the following:

> *I will be giving you this test which, as you see, is divided into eleven parts (here demonstrate this by showing the selections on the blank). Each part starts out with easy questions which then get harder as we go along. This is because the test is made up to test children from the first grade on, up through high school. Don't worry if you*

RESEARCH REPORT 4.1

Reinforcement and Testing

A 1988 article by Joseph M. Fish reviewed the issue of reinforcement in testing. The review assessed the research findings regarding the assumption "that a subject's performance [on an intelligence test] can be changed by enhancing motivation." Clinicians generally assume that a child is giving maximum effort when taking an intelligence test. If substantial reinforcement effects could be shown, then clinicians would have to question the accuracy of their obtained scores more frequently and evaluate examiner, rapport, and other environmental effects on intelligence test scores more carefully.

This review of the literature included a total of 35 studies. Studies were included only for nonhandicapped samples, and data on children with intelligence test scores below a standard score of 70 were omitted. The studies included an ample representation of boys, girls, ethnic groups, and SES levels. All studies used control groups, and children were randomly assigned to experimental groups. Some studies used reinforcers, including verbal praise with words such as "good," "you're smart," and "excellent" and tangible rewards included candy and toys. All rewards were given in response to correct responses on various editions of the Binet and Wechsler scales.

Of the 35 studies 18 showed some effect for reinforcement and 17 did not. Two of these 18 studies showed effects for only one experimental group. The effect sizes for the 18 supportive studies were relatively small. A chi square of .47 for the overall effects was not significant. Fish (1988) concluded that

> *Considering the number of studies conducted to date, tests administered, and subject variables, the findings are not substantial. The literature does not lend itself to an adequate determination of whether rewards influence performance, under what conditions, and for whom. (p. 214)*

Fish (1988) does recognize that individual children may not be putting forth maximum effort and proposes the use of reinforcement as a procedure for "testing the limits." An examiner could retest a child on portions or all of an intelligence test if the child's motivation on the first test is suspect. If scores obtained under reinforcement conditions are significantly higher (higher than one would expect by chance) than previous scores, the examiner will be able to more confidently interpret a child's profile and how it may be affected by motivational factors.

---

can't get all the questions right—I don't expect you to. But I do want you to do the best you can. (p.11)

I use a similar statement to introduce intelligence tests. My little speech is as follows:

I will be administering you this test to determine how you think and solve problems. Your job in taking this test is to try as hard as you can. You will probably find some of the items easy and others to be hard. This is to be expected since this test has items for both very young and older children. The important thing is that you just give your best effort. Let me know if you get tired or for whatever reason you need to take a break.

I do recommend that the examiner be flexible in the wording she uses to introduce the test. Some children will require considerable assurance while others do not. As children differ so should the introduction.

Using Praise

In attempting to encourage children, examiners should praise effort instead of correctness. The new trainee should know that this advice is awkward to follow. I have found that new students have an extremely difficult time avoiding the use of phrases such as "that's right" or "you got it." This temptation to praise correctness is particularly difficult after a child has worked very hard on a very demanding item. This situation may tempt the examiner to stand up and cheer, let alone praise correctness. Of course, the reason why it is desirable for the examiner not to praise correctness is because the child may then become demoralized when his behavior is not praised.

There are some steps that the new examiner can take to avoid the temptation to praise correctness. These include the following.

1. Make a point to praise effort on items that the child *did not get correct* as well as on items that the child did get correct.

2. Use phrases such as the following to praise effort.

   "You are working very hard."

   "Keep up the good effort."

   "I really appreciate the hard work you are doing on this."

   "Thanks for your hard work."

   "You are really concentrating well."

   "That was a tricky one, thanks for sticking with it."

3. Avoid praising effort by using the following phrases.

   "You got it right."

   "Good answer."

   "Right."

   "That's correct."

It is also important to not give "faint praise" (undeserved praise). Even the youngest examinees can detect false praise, and the examiner risks the possibility of rewarding uncooperative behavior. I was recently reminded again of the savvy of young children when my 5-year-old brought home her first report card from school. She pointed to the "excellent" that she received in reading and said, "That's an A."

The new examiner can gauge his skill at praising effort in lieu of correctness by observing the reactions of young elementary-grade children to the testing session. If the trainee used praise appropriately, most young children will speak positively or at least not negatively of the testing session. If many children are demoralized and apparently upset at the end of a testing session, then the examiner is likely doing something wrong that may have something to do with the appropriate use of praise.

Keeping the Child on Task

The primary tool for keeping children on task is simply the reinforcement of on-task behavior. Social approval or praise may be used liberally, but again, praise should be directed at process, *not* the product (Anastasi, 1988; Sattler, 1988). Such comments as "I see you're really thinking hard," or "I can tell you're really trying," can be valuable reinforcers. Praise of this type, however, should be spontaneous and genuine, not redundant or perfunctory. Physical contact, used appropriately, can also be reinforcing and motivating to a child. A pat on the arm, or even a hug, can show children that you like them and want them to try to do their best.

Keeping children on task will be easier if the testing sessions are brief (Anastasi, 1988) and if the examiner makes allowances for different needs wherever possible. Some subtests can be done on the floor or in a different part of the room, and the order of the tasks can be varied to suit the individual needs of the child. For example, shy or anxious children are likely to perform best when the initial tasks are unstructured, play-type procedures that do not have obvious right and wrong answers, while highly active children benefit from beginning with structured activities that help them to focus their attention. For most children, however, alternating tasks demanding close attention with those that are more play-like and/or emphasize motor skills makes good sense.

Another area where testing sessions can be modified to suit the needs of individual children is in the area of the pacing or tempo of the assessment (Sattler, 1988). Some children do best with a slow and relaxed pace, while other children need to move very swiftly from one subtest to the next in order to keep their attention on the tasks. Examiners should be attentive to signs of boredom, fatigue, or overstimulation and should adjust the tempo or length of the testing session accordingly.

Children should also be allowed to respond in their own way and at their own pace. It takes a great deal of sensitivity to know how to handle children who are very slow to respond or who frequently say that they don't know the answer. On the one hand, children should not be urged to respond before they are ready, but on the other hand children who respond that they don't know should generally be encouraged to try again (Sattler, 1988). It is sometimes difficult to know what to do, but when children hesitate or say, "I don't know," it is usually a good idea to make sure that they have understood the directions and then to encourage them to try again.

A final technique for keeping children on task is the judicious use of breaks. Some children will be refreshed by a chance to get up and stretch for a moment, others will lose their concentration and have difficulty getting back to work. It is the examiner's job to use breaks in such a way that they maximize the child's ability to perform well on the tests. Although it is advisable to let children work steadily if they seem to be doing fine, it is the examiner's responsibility to watch for any signs of discomfort and to offer the shy child an opportunity to use the bathroom or get a drink of water. Active or restless children will frequently request breaks or the opportunity to play again with some favorite materials. These requests can be granted upon completion of other tests thus serving as rewards for appropriate behavior. For example, "You may have another drink of water as soon as we finish this game." In this way the examiner maintains control while being responsive to the needs of the child (see Research Report 4.2).

Cuing Responses

Examiners are not permitted to query responses in such a way as to give hints as to the correct response. As with the use of praise, examiners are again asked to respond to children in the assessment setting in an unusual and awkward manner. Examiners have to elicit more information regarding a child's response by asking the child for elaboration without giving hints as to the correct response.

The need for cuing responses usually comes into play in the following circumstances.

1. When a child responds to an item very quickly by saying, "I don't know."
2. When a child refuses to respond to an item and communicates this nonverbally (by perhaps shaking his head no), or by saying something like, "That's too hard for me" or "I can't do it."
3. When the child asks for help with the problem.
4. When the child responds in a matter that is not clearly correct or incorrect, but is ambiguous.

In the first two situations when a child does not seem to be giving her best effort or even some effort the child may be masking her own intelligence by not responding at a level that she may be capable of. This behavior does not allow the examiner to view the child's maximum performance and may result in scores that are invalid in the sense that they do not reflect the child's ability. Hence, the examiner should help the child give his or her best effort by cuing responses. Examiners should use neutral phrases such as the following that do not give hints as to the correct response.

Suggested cues include:

1. "Tell me more about it."
2. "Explain what you mean."
3. "Explain more fully."
4. "Tell me more."

None of these statements are given in the form of a question so as not to allow the child to respond to a query by saying "no" (Wechsler, 1974). Questions such as "Can you tell me more about it" are thus discouraged.

The queries suggested above are also to be used to elicit more complete explanations of verbal responses. This situation is particularly germane

---

RESEARCH REPORT 4.2

Validity of Test Session Behavior

A study by Glutting, Oakland, and McDermott (1989) studied the validity of clinicians' observations and ratings of children's behavior during a test session. The purposes of the study were given in the following manner.

> *Empirical inquiry is needed concerning both the intra- and exosession validity of observations, where* intrasession validity *refers to the degree of concurrence between conclusions derived from observations and from the formal tests they accompany and* exosession validity *represents the degree of generality of test observations to conditions outside the test situation. (p. 156)*

Subjects for the study were 311 children ranging in age from 7 years 6 months to 14 years 4 months with a mean of 10.5 years. Each child was administered the WISC-R, the Adaptive Behavior Inventory for Children (ABIC) (administered to parents), and the California Achievement Test (CAT). The Test Behavior Observation Guide (TBOG) was used as the measure of test session behavior. The items of interest from the TBOG included performance rate, orientation to examination, initial adjustment, interest, cooperation, expressive ability, attention, self-confidence, motivation, effort, persistence, ability to shift, reaction to praise and encouragement, reaction to failure, and self-criticism. Each item was rated by examiners on a 5-point scale where 1 represents optimal behavior.

The TBOG was submitted to an exploratory factor analysis procedure, and three factors were identified as the most parsimonious explanation of the item set. The first factor was labeled *Task Attentiveness*, the second *Task Confidence*, and the third as *Cooperative Disposition*. These three factors of the TBOG were used in all subsequent analyses.

The correlations between the TBOG and the WISC-R were moderate (.40 to .50 range). The TBOG correlations with the ABIC and CAT were generally smaller. The correlations of the TBOG with the ABIC ranged from .08 to .29, and with the CAT .04 to .36. Cannonical correlation analyses were then used to study the overlap in variance between these variables further.

The higher correlations of the TBOG with the WISC-R were interpreted as supportive of the intrasession validity of observations during testing. The lower correlations of the TBOG with the ABIC in particular were taken as evidence of a lack of exosession validity of test session observations. The authors caution that these findings suggest that test session behaviors may not generalize to other settings thus limiting the ability of the clinician to confidently draw hypotheses about exosession behavior. These results also argue for the importance of taking samples of behavior from multiple environments as standard operating procedure for child examiners.

---

to the Wechsler scales, which use a multipoint scoring system for many verbal subtests. Examples of responses to items that would require cuing include the following.

Item: Tooth

Unclear Response: Mouth

Item: Who was the first United States president?

Incomplete Response: He was a Virginian.

In these situations, the examiner would use one of the cues given above to get the child to elaborate on his response. As Wechsler (1974) recognized, cuing responses requires considerable skill since it is important that the cuing be nonthreatening and nonevaluative. If a number of children tested by a new examiner do not respond favorably to cuing, then the examiner should reevaluate her efforts. In addition, she should evaluate her nonverbal behavior when cuing responses, which to some children may be punitive.

Following Standardized Procedures

Perhaps one of the most difficult and awkward set of skills that new examiners must acquire is that of adhering to standardized procedures. The importance of adhering to standardized procedures cannot be overemphasized, however, since it is one of the hallmarks of intelligence testing. Why are standardized procedures important? They are crucial because they ensure that the testing was conducted under similar circumstances for both the child currently being tested and the children tested in order to develop the norm tables. The examiner can then feel confident that comparing the child's scores to the norm for his age is justified. So *if an examiner does not use standardized procedures, then he or she should not use the norm tables.* A recent study highlights the importance of using standardized procedures. Hutchens and Thomas (1990) administered the same digit span test to 82 undergraduate students under two conditions. In the first condition the examiner administered the stimuli monotonically without dropping his voice at the end of the stimulus string. In the second condition the same examiner (actually test administration was done by audiotape for better control) administered the items while dropping his voice after the last stimulus digit was given. The scores on the digit span test differed significantly across conditions with the monotonic administration being significantly more difficult. This finding shows how even seemingly minor changes in administration procedure affect test results (Hutchens & Thomas, 1990).

One of the best ways for new examiners to understand the importance of standardized procedures is to think of their own experience taking tests. Most examiners recall taking a college and/or graduate school entrance exam. They also recall that there was a great deal of time at the beginning of the test session that was devoted to explaining the "rules" to be followed in taking the test. Examiners probably also remember that the proctor read instructions word for word from an instruction sheet and that they may have sounded stilted and uninteresting. These instructions that were read verbatim were an important part of the standardized method for the test in addition to other procedures such as time limits, the number of proctors, and the seating arrangements of examinees.

This same level of rigid adherence to standardized procedures has to be followed by a user of intelligence tests. The critical difference for intelligence test users is that they have to achieve the difficult balance of rigid adherence to procedure, and yet not sound stilted or rigid. This is a difficult task indeed! One suggestion I give my students is to try and smile as they read instructions. I hope that this will force them to think about having to portray a warm and friendly attitude when administering a test. I think, however, that the ability to be rigid and yet warm develops only after considerable practice. New examiners should practice as if they were actors preparing for a performance.

GENERAL ADMINISTRATION PROCEDURES

There are also some administration procedures that apply to most tests. One of the common prohibitions is to not allow memory items to be repeated. Whether it be digit, sentence, or object recall, if the goal is to assess memory, it is not sensible to repeat the stimuli for the child.

A frequent situation encountered by examiners is the child who asks, "Did I get it right?" The examiner is not allowed to answer this question, as it effectively gives away too much information about the test's content, an act prohibited by the Ethical Principles of Psychologists (American Psychological Association, 1992). Releasing test content is prohibited by principle 2, which states: ". . . Psychologists make reasonable effort to maintain the integrity and security of tests and other assessment techniques consistent with law . . ." (standard 2.10).

Another nuance of test administration that can be problematic for trainees is the use of a stopwatch. New examiners are advised to handle the stopwatch as they do a wristwatch, as if it is a very normal tool to use. Unfortunately, I have seen many new examiners attempt to hide the stopwatch. This makes use of the watch seem nefarious.

Testing the Limits

Now I would like to contradict everything that I just said in the previous section, or a least it will seem that way to the reader, because this section deals with using nonstandardized procedures to assess intelligence. In common usage this procedure is called testing the limits. More than anything else, testing the limits allows the professional examiner to test hypotheses. An example would be a fire alarm interrupting the testing session at the end of a subtest where a child had missed several items in a row and was near to meeting the discontinue criterion. The null hypothesis that the examiner may want to test here is that the interruption caused by the fire alarm did not adversely affect the child's performance and cause her to discontinue prematurely thus inappropriately lowering her score on the subtest.

In this case the examiner would go back and readminister these items in order to test her hypothesis. This will allow the sophisticated examiner to qualify her test results appropriately in her written and verbal reports. If the child were to get several of the previously missed items correct during limit testing, then the null hypothesis would be disproved. If this occurred the examiner would have to carefully describe the potential detrimental impact of the interruption on the child's performance. If the impact were such that the child's intelligence were severely underestimated by the test, then limit testing may provide enough evidence to discard the entire test. In this situation the examiner would likely administer a new intelligence test to the child.

The examiner who readministers items for the purposes of testing limits should, however, follow these guidelines.

1. Items should be readministered *only after the entire intelligence test has been administered.*

2. Items that are readministered using nonstandardized procedures or for the purposes of limit testing *should not be counted in any way in the scoring of the test.*

One important point that a new examiner should take from this discussion is that testing the limits is a very powerful procedure in the hands of an experienced and sophisticated examiner. Limit testing is not likely to be as valuable a method for the new examiner.

General Scoring Principles

There are a few principles of item scoring that apply to virtually all major intelligence tests. One of these is the importance of adherence to time limits. Generally speaking, a correct response given after the time limit allowed for the item has expired is scored as a failure. Examiners may not reason that the response was given "close enough" to the time limit and give credit as this would likely be a violation of standardized scoring procedures.

A more difficult scoring dilemma occurs when a child gives multiple verbal responses to an item. The question in the examiner's mind then is which item to score, and what to do if a child gives an incorrect and a correct response. It is generally agreed that in the case of multiple verbal responses to an item that the examiner should score the response that the child clearly indicates is her final response. Consider the following example.

Vocabulary Item: Bird

Response: "A small animal with fur; no it has feathers and can fly."

In this case the child clearly intended his last response to replace the first. This situation, however, is relatively clear cut. In some cases it is not clear at all if a child intends a later response to replace an earlier one. If a child gives a laundry list of responses with no clear indication of which one he prefers, then the examiner may have to ask something like *"Which one is it?"* (Wechsler, 1974; Kaufman & Kaufman, 1983a)

It is also possible for a child to spoil a response by replacing a correct response with an incorrect response. This event may occur on both verbal and nonverbal items. An examiner can get very frustrated watching a child construct something like a Wechsler Block Design item correctly and then dismantle it. If the child indicates that her incorrect Block Design construction is intended to replace the previous correct construction, then it is the incorrect one that is scored. Similarly, if a child responds correctly to a verbal item but replaces her response with an incorrect one, she does not receive credit. The following example illustrates this point.

Vocabulary Item: Roach

Response: "An insect; no, a style of clothing.

Examiners often have difficulty reading a child's intentions. They can develop a better sense for this with training and experience. A more frequently encountered scoring problem is the case where a child gets an item correct but does so after the time limit for the item has expired. This situation occurs on subtests such as Block Design of the Wechsler Scales, Triangles of the K-ABC, and Pattern Analysis of the Stanford-Binet Fourth Edition. In most cases, where a child solves an item correctly after the time limit is expired, a child does not receive credit.

Recording Responses

To the extent that it is practical, a detailed written record of the child's responses to the individual items needs to be kept. This record is important for a number of reasons. A written record is invaluable for use by the examiner in interpretation and report writing. Moreover, the written record will provide valuable details to enhance the examiner's memory of the child's performance for the purposes of report writing.

Unfortunately, there is frequently a time delay between testing a child and writing a report. This delay of hours, days, or even weeks can cause the memory of a child's performance to fade.

A written record of responses is also important when an examiner needs to report on the child's performance at some time in the future. For example, an examiner may be asked to give considerable detail about a child's performance at a court proceeding that is called years after the child was originally tested. A written record also serves as proof that services were in fact delivered, should this ever be questioned.

The examiner needs to take the process of recording responses seriously. While this endeavor may seem an arduous one for the trainee, it is in the long-term interest of the child and the examiner to do so. Fortunately, some time can be saved by using a "shorthand" system for recording the child's responses. A sample system is shown below.

1. All of the child's verbal responses to items should be recorded verbatim.

2. If a response is unclear or incomplete and is cued by the examiner, he or she should enter a *"Q" (Query)* and record the child's response to the cue.

3. Many tests require an examiner to model correct responses especially on easy items. If, for example, a child responds to the question, "Who discovered the north pole" incorrectly, the examiner may be instructed to give the child a correct response to this question before proceeding to the next question. When an examiner models a response per standardized procedure, an *"M" (model)* should be entered by the item on the record form.

4. If a child exceeds the time limit allowed for an item, the examiner should enter a *"T" (time)* on the record form.

5. If the examiner repeats an item at the child's request (note that this is not allowed on a number of subtests, especially memory tests—this is typically allowed on arithmetic and vocabulary

tests), then an *"R" (repeat)* should be entered on the record form.

6. If a child points to indicate a correct response in lieu of a verbal response (this is allowed on the Picture Completion subtest of the WISC-III and the Expressive Vocabulary subtest of the K-ABC), the examiner should enter *"pts" (points)* on the record form.

7. A *"Ro" (rotation)* is noted when a child constructs a design correctly but rotates it significantly (about 30 to 40 degrees or more). This notation is used on tests such as WISC-III Block Design and Stanford-Binet Fourth Edition Pattern Analysis.

8. The notation *"OT" (over time)* is used to signify when a child solved an item correctly but did so after the time limit for the item had expired.

9. The letters *"DK" (don't know)* are written to signify when a child said something like "I don't know" in response to an item.

Making and Recording Observations

The child's behavior during testing is frequently a crucial variable for testing hypotheses that may explain a child's performance. Hence, making relatively detailed behavioral observations eases somewhat the interpretive work of the examiner by providing a considerable amount of data against which to test hypotheses. The richness of interpretive information yielded by detailed observations is shown in the psychological report excerpts given in Figures 4.2 and 4.3. Note that like a good novel the detailed description of the child yields a vivid portrayal in the reader's mind. The lucidness of the portrayal assists the reader in understanding the child's results more fully.

Several informal procedures for recording behavioral observations have been offered (e.g., Aylward & MacGruder, 1986). Guides such as the *Test Behavior Checklist* are particularly helpful to the new examiner because they provide

her with a framework for observing behavior during the session. Among other possibilities, some of the typical aspects of child test-taking behavior that are observed by examiners include the following.

- A description of the examinee, which may include aspects such as appearance, physical limitations, and posture.

- Speech, including quality of the individual's voice, amount and quality of verbalization, and a general impression of the ability of the child to express himself verbally.

- Vision and hearing, including any signs of deficiencies in these areas such as squinting or asking that questions be repeated frequently.

- Attitude toward the testing, including observations of a lack of cooperation.

- Gross and fine motor skills, including the individual's gait, the presence or absence of motor ticks.

- Activity level, ranging from high activity levels to very low levels of energy or activity.

- Self-confidence, including any self-deprecating statements made by the child.

- Attention, concentration, achievement motivation, and effort.

- Persistence, tenacity, and the child's reaction to praise or encouragement.

These are just a few of the variables that examiners typically note about the child's behavior during testing. More structured behavioral observation systems are also available, such as the *Test Behavior Checklist* (Aylward & MacGruder, 1986).

Whether the examiner chooses to use one of the systems mentioned or not, the new examiner should use some sort of system for recording observations during testing. This forces the new examiner to think more critically about a variety of aspects of child behavior that may affect children's obtained scores.

Brad was eager to be tested. He met the examiner at the door of the clinic room and enthusiastically escorted her into the room. He was ready immediately to begin testing.

It was apparent early on that Brad is a highly verbal child. He chattered incessantly before, during, and after testing, and he particularly enjoyed the tests that required verbal responses. He occasionally bragged about how much he knew, and commented on how easy some of the questions were. However, his thoughts often became tangential and he had to be directed back onto task frequently. For example, when asked to answer questions that required comprehension of certain concepts, he would answer the question and then start telling a story either about the question, or about something that had nothing to do with the question at all. He was particularly excited over the stopwatch, and many of his stories revolved around how fast he could run, how fast he could ride his bike, and how fast the race cars would be going at the Talladega 500.

Brad's behavior was marked by drastic changes from one subtest to the other; a change that was usually brought about by moving from a Verbal subtest to a Performance test. On the Verbal items, he appeared comfortable and at ease, and when confronted with an item he did not know, he simply said he forgot or he had not done that in school yet. When presented with Performance tasks, he became irritated and frustrated. On an item on which he was asked to assemble pieces of a puzzle together, he accused the examiner of not giving him all of the pieces. He continually insisted that he could not do what was being asked, and that the tasks were not fair. However, he eventually did complete the puzzles, only giving up completely when the task clearly was too difficult for him. He grew frustrated at another subtest that required him to assemble blocks to match a picture, and at one point he stood up and pushed the pieces across the table. This mood did not seem to spill over onto the immediately succeeding test, however, as Brad became calm again with the introduction of a more verbally oriented task.

One final note—Brad went on four self-imposed breaks. The examiner felt these were necessary in order to get optimal performance for the remaining test items. It was clear that he could not stick to the testing for prolonged periods of time, as during testing he occasionally got out of his chair and began walking around. His conversation became most tangential at these times, and it was relatively easy for the examiner to predict when his next break would be.

FIGURE 4.2

Behavioral observation—WISC-III

PROBLEMS IN THE ASSESSMENT PROCESS

Most problems in the assessment process can be avoided by following the guidelines outlined thus far, by providing clear limits, and by redirecting any inappropriate behavior. When a child is uncooperative and is clearly not doing his or her best, the examiner should confront the child directly, but not angrily, and verbally acknowledge the situation. The examiner should attempt to discuss the situation with the child but should not try to change the child's behavior through negative comments or comparisons with other children (Sattler, 1988).

If an assessment is proving totally unproductive, the examiner may want to terminate the session before the child is completely miserable or before the examiner has lost control. However, the examiner's offer to terminate a session and reschedule may have a variety of results. The offer to end the current session and reschedule may cause the child to begin to cooperate more fully; the child may accept the offer and a subsequent session may prove more productive;

Sharon is an attractive and friendly 9-year-old female, who was tested in her home. Throughout the assessment session, Sharon was cooperative and helpful. For example, she offered the examiner a soft drink several times during the assessment session. In addition, she offered to help transport testing material from the examiner's car into Sharon's home. Sharon maintained excellent eye contact during the course of the assessment and excellent rapport was established.

Prior to testing, Sharon appeared concerned that she would not do well on the test. She asked the examiner several questions such as, "What grade do most kids get on the test?" and "If I don't do very good, can I take it again?" Consequently, Sharon appeared to work hard on each test item. Before answering a question, she often spent several seconds thinking intently. While contemplating an answer, Sharon would wrinkle her forehead and repeat the question to herself before answering. On several items, she asked the examiner to repeat the question. During the Number Recall subtest, a test that requires the examinee to repeat a string of numbers back in a certain sequence, and the Word Order subtest, a test that requires the examinee to identify a series of pictures from memory, Sharon demonstrated rehearsal strategies. She repeated items softly to herself several times before answering. At one point during the Word Order subtest, Sharon stated, "I'm trying to figure out the best way to remember these." Sharon appeared to work especially hard during the Triangle subtest, in which the examinee uses triangles to reproduce abstract designs. On most of the items, Sharon would not give up until she was able to reproduce the appropriate design. For example, after working for several minutes on a particular design, the examiner suggested that Sharon try another pattern. Sharon would not agree to move on to the next item until she was told that she would be allowed to come back to the item on which she was working. After the Triangle subtest was completed, Sharon stated that she had enjoyed the subtest. She said, "It's kind of fun doing this to see how well you can match the picture (copy the abstract design with the blocks)."

FIGURE 4.3

Behavioral observation—K-ABC

or the termination may simply reinforce the child's uncooperative behavior and cause future testing sessions to be even more difficult (Goldman et al., 1983). Thus the examiner must evaluate the situation very carefully before offering to terminate a session (see Research Reports 4.3 and 4.4 and Box 4.1).

Debriefing

At the close of the assessment, the examiner should discuss the testing session with the child and elicit his or her feelings about it (Goldman et al., 1983). The examiner might ask how the child felt about participating in the assessment, whether the child enjoyed it, which parts the child liked best, and so forth. The examiner should also honestly acknowledge the way the

RESEARCH REPORT 4.3

Additional Scientific Readings

Grossman, I., Kaufman, A. S., Mednitsky, S., Scharff, L., & Dennis, B. (1994). Neurocognitive abilities for a clinically depressed sample versus a matched control group of normal individuals. *Psychiatry Research, 51,* 231–244.

Schwean, V. L., Saklofske, D. H., Yackulic, R. A., & Quinn, D. (1994). WISC-III performance of ADHD children. *Journal of Psychoeducational Assessment, Monograph,* 56–70.

child behaved during the session by saying something like, "I realize that you were a little unhappy about being here today, but you tried hard to do what I asked and I really appreciate that." Such a discussion will provide a sense of closure for what has probably been an intense, if not difficult,

RESEARCH REPORT 4.4

The *Non*effects of Methylphenidate and Clinical Depression on Intelligence Test Scores

It is intuitive that frankly symptomatic behavior in a test session should significantly affect intelligence test results. It is equally logical that the well-known effects of psychostimulant medication on behavior would also translate into significant effects on intelligence test results. These hypotheses, however, have been shown to be equally incorrect.

A clever study by Schwean, Saklofske, Yackulic, and Quinn (1994) compared the WISC-III performance of 45 ADHD children both on and off medication. They found no effect for medication status on subtest, Index, or Full Scale intelligence test scores. In fact, the means were strikingly similar between conditions. The Full Scale, for example, was 98.21 when on medication and 97.67 when not taking methylphenidate. The corresponding val.:es for the Verbal IQ were 96.17 and 94.76, respectively. The Performance IQ was virtually identical at 101 for the two conditions. As one can imagine with composite scores this close the subtest and Index scores were strikingly similar. These data are, of course, based on groups so it is possible that an individual child or adult will show clinically meaningful differences under various medication conditions. These data do suggest, however, that such medication effects would constitute an exception to the rule.

In another well-controlled study Grossman, Kaufman, Mednitsky, Scharff, and Dennis (1994) tested a well-matched group of 44 adults hospitalized for clinical depression with controls selected from a large national norming study of the Kaufman Adolescent and Adult Intelligence Test (KAIT; Kaufman & Kaufman, 1996). This study, like earlier ones with the WAIS-R, showed no effects for depression. The Composite score was 103 for both groups and the fluid and crystallized scores for the two groups were also identical at 102 (when rounded to whole numbers). In addition, the authors found no significant differences between groups on five memory tests administered as part of the KAIT battery. They concluded, "The most important finding in this study was that the depressed patients displayed no significant neurocognitive deficits, relative to a carefully selected control group, on a well-normed test battery with excellent psychometric properties" (p. 238).

These studies, combined with others, demonstrate a consistent pattern of findings indicating that the expression of clinical symptomatology, perhaps even during a test session as is often the case with children with ADHD, does not affect the results of standardized intelligence tests for most examinees. Hence, our null hypothesis in such situations should likely be that there is no effect of symptomatology on intelligence test scores. We will then have to mount considerable evidence to reject the null in individual cases. The next chapter provides a potential explanation of this lack of impact of symptomatology—the use of standardized procedure, long a hallmark of experimental psychology.

---

experience for the child. It also may help the child gain a better understanding of the experience and place it in some kind of context.

Assessing Infants

The assessment of children under 24 months of age typically involves different psychometric instruments (as is discussed in Chapter 12) and some further modifications in the standard assessment procedure. The most notable difference in the assessment of infants is that their mothers are typically present during the testing session and are an integral part of the process. Parents are crucial in the assessment of infants because of

their ability to translate the "baby talk" of their children. Thus, infant assessment requires that the examiner develop a good rapport with the mother as well as with the baby. In fact, rapport with the mother is probably more important. Rapport with the mother will be facilitated by making eye contact, smiling, and approaching her in a direct and friendly manner. The reason for the assessment and/or more neutral topics such as the weather and parking difficulties may provide good material for an opening conversation. It is also important to explain the testing procedures thoroughly to the mother and to continue to explain what you are doing as you go along.

The examiner should be aware of the context surrounding the individual testing session. This is particularly important when testing infants because the examiner has the opportunity to provide the parent with some information about her child. For example, the examiner may use the session to model appropriate interaction with an infant for a parent whose parenting skills need strengthening, or may highlight the child's capabilities in order to reassure an overly anxious parent.

Scheduling, though an important consideration with preschoolers, is crucial with infants. Young infants may have only an hour or two of alert time each day, and it is imperative that examiners attempt to schedule testing for this time. Unfortunately, predicting these alert times is often very difficult, making the testing of infants very tricky indeed. In any case, a testing session should not be scheduled during a regular nap or feeding time.

Recommendations regarding the environment are essentially the same for infants as for preschoolers, with the addition of several suggestions. The floor should be carpeted, and there should be comfortable places for the young infant—a quilt on the floor and an infant seat, for example. If infant seats are not available, the mother can be asked to bring the infant to the testing session in his or her car seat and the car seat can be used instead.

Because infants generally have such brief periods when they are happy and alert, the examiner must pace the session carefully and be extremely flexible. The pace of the session must be very

Box 4.1 Testing Children or Friends

Remember the old saying, "No good deed goes unpunished"? I remember it all too well. The year was 1975 and I was taking my first graduate-level course in intellectual assessment. I learned the meaning of this old saying on two occasions that summer.

The first mistake I made was to volunteer to take a 5-year-old to the university for testing in order to meet course requirements. The child's mother was perfectly willing to bring the young boy into the university, but I was sure that I could handle it. I was wrong. I did not have children of my own at the time and knew precious little about the little creatures. I picked up the boy at home. He was well scrubbed and polite. I drove him to the university amid sweltering summer heat. Since "parking on campus" is a true oxymoron, we had to walk several blocks in the heat to reach the building. Immediately upon entering the building, I offered the lad a soft drink (a Coke), and those who know young children can imagine what happened next. He quaffed the Coke and proceeded to have an emesis (i.e., "vomit"). Of course, I panicked and took him home immediately.

There was, however, an important lesson to be learned from this. Clinicians who test children have to have more than academic knowledge of their intended victims. They have to also have practical experience with children. I recommend to my students without extensive child-rearing experience that they spend a few hours a week volunteering in schools, preschools, and churches in order to acquire more experience with children. I had to learn the hard way so that my students will not.

The second lesson that I learned in this first course was to never test a friend, spouse, relative of any sort, or other significant other who wants to know his or her "IQ." I had a friend (a fellow psychology student) who wanted to know his IQ. Despite my professor's admonitions regarding this issue I decided to test him with the 1955 WAIS. Well, I knew that I was in trouble before we even finished the Information (the first) subtest. His response to, "What is the Vatican," was, "I think it's a big bird isn't it"? Well, needless to say his scores were not as high as he had hoped, and I had to break the news.

I also admonish my students not to test significant others because of their own preconceptions of the IQ score, but they often do it anyway. If I didn't know better, I would say that some students in my classes have been testing potential suitors for their fitness!

rapid in order to catch as much optimal behavior as possible, *and* very calm and gentle in order not to overstimulate the baby. Too many repetitions of an item or too many items in too little time can cause the baby to be overwhelmed and fall apart. Flexibility is also necessary—the examiner may have to follow a toddler around the room administering whatever item seems most likely to attract the child's attention. The key to flexible, swift, yet relaxed administration of a test is a very thorough knowledge of the test and total familiarity with the materials. This preparedness enables the examiner to move rapidly from one item to another while focusing on the child and maximizing the likelihood that the child will perform up to the level of his or her true capability.

Conclusions

Acquiring clinical assessment skills can be a daunting task, especially for the new clinician who has little experience with children. A lack of experience with children, however, is easily remedied through experimental means. It behooves the new examiner to seek out these experiences in order to ease the process of testing.

Strong clinical interaction skills are also important to parents who are seeking evaluations for their children. A clinician without strong interpersonal skills has the same difficulties as a physician without "bedside manner." Parents are especially sensitive to how a child responds to a professional, and they may become dissatisfied if a clinician cannot develop a good working relationship with their child.

Chapter Summary

- Substantial clinical skill is required to properly administer an intelligence test.

- Observing other child professionals can be a useful activity for acquiring clinical skills for assessing young children.

- It is important to conduct a thorough interview of a child's or adolescent's parents or caregivers in order to collect relevant background information.

- It is helpful for the new examiner to use a standard form for collecting background information in order to ensure that no important aspects of behavior are missed.

- Environmental variables can be crucial for determining the success or failure of an intelligence testing session.

- If a parent wants to observe the testing session, an examiner must take the time necessary to fully explain the pros and cons of observing.

- Rapport refers to the process of establishing a comfortable working relationship with a child.

- Examiners should have at their disposal objects such as toys, puppets, or even pencil and paper that may be used to draw out the reticent child.

- If the child is brought to the examiner, it is helpful to begin the conversation with a neutral or "easy" topic such as the weather. Especially useful for starting conversations in these situations are concrete objects like fish tanks or appealing toys.

- Motivating the child requires the examiner to understand how the child perceives the assessment and how the child feels about being assessed.

- Examiners should praise the child's effort instead of the correctness of the child's response.

- The primary tool for keeping children on task is simply the reinforcement of on-task behavior.

- It is not permissible for examiners to query responses in such a way as to give hints as to the correct response.

- Examiners must adhere to standardized procedures.

- Testing the limits allows the professional examiner to test hypotheses.

- A correct response given after the time limit allowed for the item has expired is scored as a failure.

- A detailed written record of the child's responses to the individual items should be kept.

- Detailed behavioral observations ease somewhat the interpretive work of the examiner by providing a considerable amount of data against which to test hypotheses.

- At the close of the assessment the examiner should discuss the testing session with the child and elicit his or her feelings about it.

- Mothers, fathers, and other caretakers are crucial in the assessment of infants because of their ability to translate the "baby talk" of their children.

CHAPTER 5

Psychometric Principles and Issues

The task for research in individual differences in cognitive abilities is one of mapping a large territory. Some 350 years after the New World was opened up by Columbus, the British Admiralty, with the voyage of the Beagle, was still engaged in making more adequate maps to sail ships around its waters; the task of mapping the terrain of the New World is still going on—using cameras in satellites, space shuttles, and other modern gadgetry. The task we have of mapping the terrain and the waters of cognitive individual differences is even more immense. If it is ever completed—even to a reasonable approximation—we will find that we have completed a large part of the task of psychological science itself. (Carroll, 1983, pp. 29–30)

CHAPTER QUESTIONS

How do scientists assess the reliability of intelligence tests?

How are intelligence tests validated?

Users of intelligence tests should have a thorough understanding of statistics, scaling, and measurement principles. The discussion to follow, however, would hardly qualify as "thorough." This chapter is merely a reminder of what students have already covered in previous coursework that is central to the use of intelligence tests. It is assumed that the user of this text has had, at a minimum, undergraduate courses in statistics and tests and measurement. If a user of this text is not acquainted with some of the principles discussed here, then a statistics and/or measurement textbook should be consulted. There are a number of excellent measurement textbooks available including Anastasi and Urbina (1997).

This chapter begins with a review of basic principles of statistics and measurement including topics ranging from measures of central tendency to factor analysis. The last portion of the chapter introduces measurement issues that are more specific to the use and interpretation of intelligence tests.

MEASURES OF CENTRAL TENDENCY

Mode

Measures of central tendency are useful for describing the performance of a group of individuals. Everyone is interested in the "average" obtained for a particular group of individuals. Examples are the average SAT score for a particular high school or the typical size of the modern family unit. One such measure of central tendency is the *mode* (Mo), the most frequently occurring score in a distribution of scores. This most frequently occurring score is, however, not what most consumers of test data want in terms of the "average." As a result, the mode is not a frequently used test statistic in psychological measurement.

Median

An alternative measure of central tendency is the *median* (Md), the midpoint of a distribution of scores. The Md is the point in a distribution that divides it into equal halves, with 50% of the cases falling below the Md and 50% of the cases above the Md.

Mean

The Md, however, is also not the statistic that most consumers have in mind when inquiring about average test scores. Most people want to know the arithmetic average of the distribution of scores, the *mean* (M). Most people frequently compute means as part of their everyday work. Professors frequently compute mean test scores for students in their classes. Students in these same classes compute their mean test score in order to decide whether or not they want to drop the professor's class. Meteorologists may compute mean temperatures. Doctors compute the mean number of patients they see in a week.

Farmers compute the mean amount of feed consumed by their livestock. The mean, then, is the most widely used measure of central tendency, as will be the case in this textbook.

MEASURES OF VARIABILITY

Range

While the public is interested in the average test score, they are also sometimes interested in more specific information. Similarly, parents may inquire about how their child compares to the average for an age group, but, most importantly, they want to know *how far below or above average* their child performed. This latter question has to do with the variability of a distribution of scores. A rather crude measure of variability is the *range*, the difference between the highest and lowest scores in a distribution. The range is an imprecise measure of variability in that it rarely pinpoints exactly where a child's score lies (unless a child's score is extremely high or low).

Standard Deviation

The preferred statistic for measuring variability is the *standard deviation* (SD), the square root of the average squared deviation from the mean in a group of scores (Nitko, 1983). The SD is large when there is much variability (a large range) of scores, and small when there is little variability.

If, for example, a researcher collects a sample of all children living in Alaska, the intelligence test scores are likely to be very heterogeneous, or highly variable. If, however, an intelligence test researcher collects test scores for a sample of 30 gifted children from the same classroom, then the standard deviation is likely to become more homogeneous, less variable, smaller. The SD is useful for intelligence test interpretation since it pinpoints more exactly how far a child's score falls from the center of a distribution. The SD is also important because it helps in understanding the normal curve.

The Normal Curve

The normal curve refers to the graphic depiction of distributions of test scores that is symmetrical (normal), resembling a bell (hence, the term *bell-shaped*). Sometimes researchers do not obtain normal distributions of scores in their samples, but when large samples of intelligence test performance are collected, and there is little sampling error, the distributions approximate normality very closely (see Figure 5.1). In a normal distribution there are a few people with very low scores (these people are represented by the tail of the curve on the left), a few with very high

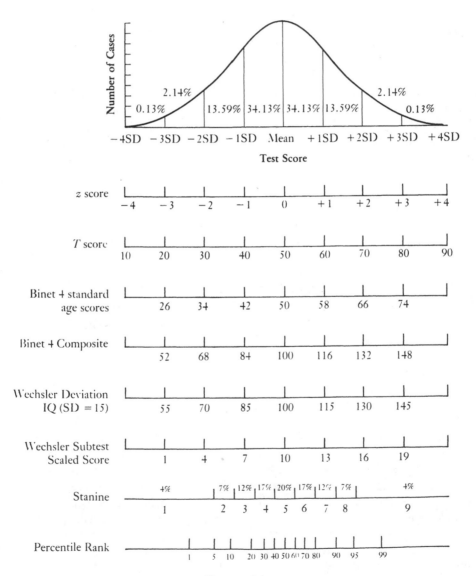

Figure 5.1

scores (the tail on the right), and many individuals with scores about the average (the highest point in the curve).

When a distribution is normal or bell-shaped, as is the case in Figure 5.1, the SD always divides up the same proportion of a normal distribution. More specifically, ±1 SD always includes approximately 68% of the cases in a normal distribution, and ±2 SD always includes approximately 95% of the cases, as is shown in Figure 5.1. The normal curve is also sometimes referred to as the *normal probability* or *Gaussian curve*.

NORM-REFERENCED SCORES

Intelligence test interpretation focuses on *norm-referenced interpretation*, the comparison of children's scores to some standard or norm. For the purposes of intelligence test interpretation, scores are usually compared to those of children the same age. Achievement tests may compare children's scores to those of others in the same grade. College admission counselors may compare an incoming student's GPA to that of freshmen who entered the year before. Just as people frequently compute means, they also engage in norm-referenced interpretation. Students may compare their performance to others in the same class or compare their professors to others they have had in the past.

TYPES OF SCORES

There are a great variety of scores, most of which are norm-referenced, that are yielded by intelligence tests.

Raw Scores

The first score that the clinician encounters after summing item scores is usually called a *raw score*.

Raw scores on most tests of intelligence are simply comprised of the number of items correct, or they are a summation of the number of points earned on individual items. The term *raw* is probably apropos for these scores in that they give little information about the child's performance as compared to his/her peers. As such, raw scores are not helpful for norm-referenced interpretation.

Standard Scores

The most popular type of score for intelligence tests is the *standard score*. Standard scores convert raw scores to a distribution with a set mean and standard deviation, with equal units along the scale. The typical standard score scale used for intelligence tests is what Wechsler termed the *Deviation IQ*, where the mean is set at 100 and the standard deviation is set at 15. By having equal units along the scale, standard scores are very powerful for statistical analyses and useful for making comparisons across tests. The equal units (or intervals) that are characteristic of standard scores are shown in Figure 5.1 for the various Deviation IQ scores, where the distance between 55 and 70 is the same as that between 70 and 85, which is the same as between 85 and 100, and so on.

Standard scores are also particularly useful for intelligence test interpretation because they allow comparisons among various subtests or composites yielded by the same intelligence test. In other words, they facilitate interpretation of a child's profile of scores. Most modern intelligence tests use standard scores for their composites that have a mean of 100 and a standard deviation of 15. This metric is used for popular tests such as the WISC-III, K-ABC, and WAIS-III. The notable exception to this standard score scale is the Binet 4, which yields a standard score scale with a mean of 100 and standard deviation of 16 for its composite scores (see Figure 5.1). Fortunately, a number of tables (see Table 5.1) are available for equating one scale to another.

TABLE 5.1   Standard score and percentile rank conversion table

Standard Score M = 100 SD = 15	Standard Score M = 100 SD = 16	T-score M = 50 SD = 10	Binet Subtest Score M = 50 SD = 8	Subtest "Sealed Score" M = 10 SD = 3	Percentile Ranks
160	164	90	82		99.99
159	163	89			99.99
158	162	89	81		99.99
157	161	88			99.99
156	160	87	80		99.99
155	159	87			99.99
154	158	86	79		99.99
153	157	85			99.98
153	156	85	78		99.98
152	155	85			99.97
151	154	84	77		99.96
150	153	83			99.95
149	152	83	76		99.94
148	151	82			99.93
147	150	81	75		99.91
146	149	81			99.89
145	148	80	74	19	99.87
144	147	79			99.84
143	146	79	73		99.80
142	145	78			99.75
141	144	77	72		99.70
140	143	77		18	99.64
139	142	76	71		99.57
138	141	75			99
138	140	75	70		99
137	139	75			99
136	138	74	69		99
135	137	73		17	99
134	136	73	68		99
133	135	72			99
132	134	71	67		98
131	133	71			98
130	132	70	66	16	98
129	131	69			97
128	130	69	65		97
127	129	68			97
126	128	67	64		96
125	127	67		15	95
124	126	66	63		95
123	125	65			94
123	124	65	62		93
122	123	65			92
121	122	64	61		92

TABLE 5.1   Standard score and percentile rank conversion table (Continued)

Standard Score M = 100 SD = 15	Standard Score M = 100 SD = 16	T-score M = 50 SD = 10	Binet Subtest Score M = 50 SD = 8	Subtest "Sealed Score" M = 10 SD = 3	Percentile Ranks
120	121	63		14	91
119	120	63	60		89
118	119	62			88
117	118	61	59		87
116	117	61			86
115	116	60	58	13	84
114	115	59			83
113	114	59	57		81
112	113	58			79
111	112	57	56		77
110	111	57		12	75
109	110	56	55		73
108	109	55			71
108	108	55	54		69
107	107	55			67
106	106	54	53		65
105	105	53		11	65
104	104	53	52		62
103	103	52			57
102	102	51	51		55
101	101	51			52
100	100	50	50	10	50
99	99	49			48
98	98	49	49		45
97	97	48			43
96	96	47	48		40
95	95	47		9	38
94	94	46	47		35
93	93	45			33
93	92	45	46		31
92	91	45			29
91	90	44	45		27
90	89	43		8	25
89	88	43	44		23
88	87	42			21
87	86	41	43		19
86	85	41			17
85	84	40	42	7	16
84	83	39			14
83	82	39	41		13
82	81	38			12
81	80	37	40		11
80	79	37		6	9

(Continues)

TABLE 5.1   Standard score and percentile rank conversion table (Continued)

Standard Score M = 100 SD = 15	Standard Score M = 100 SD = 16	T-score M = 50 SD = 10	Binet Subtest Score M = 50 SD = 8	Subtest "Sealed Score" M = 10 SD = 3	Percentile Ranks
79	78	36	39		8
78	77	35			8
78	76	35	38		7
77	75	35			6
76	74	34	37		5
75	73	33		5	5
74	72	33	36		4
73	71	32			3
72	70	31	35		3
71	69	31			3
70	68	30	34	4	2
69	67	29			2
68	66	29	33		2
67	65	28			1
66	64	27	32		1
65	63	27		3	1
64	62	26	31		1
63	61	25			1
63	60	25	30		1
62	59	25			1
61	58	24	29		.49
60	57	23		2	.36
59	56	23	28		.30
58	55	22			.25
57	54	21	27		.20
56	53	21			.16
55	52	20	26	1	.13
54	51	19			.11
53	50	19	25		.09
52	49	18			.07
51	48	17	24		.06
50	47	17			.05
49	46	16	23		.04
48	45	15			.03
48	44	15	22		.02
47	43	15			.02
46	42	14	21		.01
45	41	13			.01
44	40	13	20		.01
43	39	12			.01
42	38	11	19		.01
41	37	11			.01
40	36	10	18		.01

NOTE: I appreciate the assistance of Dr. Gary Robertson with obtaining some of the raw data for this table.

There are other popular standard score scales. Wechsler also popularized the *scaled score* metric for intelligence test subtest scores. Scaled scores have a mean of 10 and a standard deviation of 3 (see Figure 5.1). A standard score scale that is commonly used in personality assessment is the *T-score* scale (see Figure 5.1). The *T*-score scale has a mean of 50 and standard deviation of 10. The Binet 4 Standard Age Scores are a variant of the *T*-score scale having the same mean of 50, but a standard deviation of only 8 (Thorndike, Hagen, & Sattler, 1986; see Figure 5.1).

A more unusual type of standard score scale is the *normal curve equivalent*, better known as the NCE. The NCE was developed to produce a standard score that ranges from 1 to 99. In order to achieve this end, the NCE scale has a mean of 50 and a rather unusual standard deviation of 21.06 (Nitko, 1983)!

A less popular type of standard score is referred to as *stanines*, which stands for "standard nines." This scale was used heavily by the armed forces and was rather convenient because it is the lone standard score scale that uses only one digit and ranges from a low of 1 to a high of 9. The stanine scale is also shown in Figure 5.1. Stanines are rarely used in modern intelligence test interpretation.

The important thing to remember about this great variety of standard scores is that they are simply different ways of doing the same thing, expressing children's scores in terms of their distance from the mean or average. All standard scores that reflect a normal distribution divide up the same proportions of the normal curve. As can be seen in Figure 5.1, a Deviation IQ of 85, a *T* score of 40, a Scaled Score of 7, and a Standard Age Score of 42 all represent the same level of performance! These scores are also all at the 16th percentile rank (see Figure 5.1).

Percentile Ranks

A score that is particularly useful for intelligence test interpretation is the percentile rank. A percentile rank gives an individual's relative position within the norm group (Lyman, 1965). Percentile ranks are very useful for communicating with parents, administrators, educators, and others who do not have an extensive background in scaling methods (Lyman, 1963). It is very easy for parents to understand that if their child received a percentile rank of 50 he or she scored better than approximately 50% of the norm group and worse than approximately 50% of the norm group. This type of interpretation works well so long as the parent understands the difference between percentile rank and percent of items passed.

As can be seen from inspection of Figure 5.1, percentile ranks have one major disadvantage in comparison to standard scores: percentile ranks have unequal units along their scale. Note in Figure 5.1 that the difference between the first and fifth percentile rank is *larger* than the difference between the 40th and 50th percentile ranks. In other words, percentile ranks in the middle of the distribution tend to *overemphasize* differences between standard scores, whereas percentile ranks at the tails of the distribution tend to *underemphasize* differences in performance.

Here is an example of how confusing this property of having unequal units can be. Every time I teach my intellectual assessment course, I ask my students the following question: "How would you describe a child who obtained a percentile rank of 25 on an intelligence test: well above average, above average, average, below average, or well below average?" Most often the majority of the class responds with "*below average*." Then I ask, "How would you rate the intelligence of a child with a standard score of 90 using the same classification system?" In this latter case most students describe the child as being "*average*" or "*below average*." Usually, however, one or two students are not fooled, and they correctly point out that a *percentile rank of 25 equals a standard score of 90* (see Figure 5.1). This is one graphic method of portraying one of the interpretive problems with percentile ranks, their unequal scale units. An average standard score, for example, can be made to sound much worse when converted to a percentile rank. As a result, when percentile ranks may be misleading when used to describe a child's performance, they should not be used, despite some of their obvious advantages.

Age Equivalents

Individual intelligence tests have a long history of the use of *age equivalents (AE), developmental ages,* or *mental ages (MA).* These terms all refer to the same type of score. Age equivalents are computed based on the performance of every age group used in the norming of the test. For example, if the average raw score for 7-year-olds on an intelligence test is 24, then 24 becomes the raw score that yields an age equivalent of 7 years. If the average raw score on the same intelligence test for 10-year-olds is 32, then 32 becomes the raw score corresponding to an age equivalent of 10 years. If a 7-year-old obtains a raw score on an intelligence test of 32, the child's age equivalent on this intelligence test is 10 years, and he or she is considered above average for his age group. The 10-year-old who obtains a raw score of 24 is assigned an age equivalent of 7 years and is deemed as being below average in comparison to other 10-year-olds. The important thing to remember about the derivation of age equivalents is that they describe nothing more than the number of raw score points obtained by a particular age group.

Since age equivalents merely reflect whether or not a child obtained a high or low raw score, they are typically prone to overinterpretation (Lyman, 1963). A frequent scenario would be for the 7-year-old who obtained an age equivalent of 10 years to be considered to have the "mind of a 10-year-old." This, in fact, may or may not be the case. What is true is that the 7-year-old has certainly obtained *more items correct* than the average 7-year-old. Whether or not he or she has the "mind" of a 10-year-old is open to debate and is not measured directly by the mental age score.

Perhaps a more extreme case would better illustrate this point. Say an 18-year-old moderately mentally retarded individual is working in a sheltered workshop setting and living in a group home for retarded individuals. This person is responsible for some of his own cooking and all of his housekeeping duties. He maintains his own room and laundry, and he is responsible for taking public transportation to and from the sheltered workshop every day. He is currently dating another resident of the group home and plans to get married. This individual is tested with an intelligence test and obtains an age equivalent of 7-4 (7 years-4 months). This score indicates that he obtained a relatively low score on the intelligence test in comparison to other 18-year-olds. This score does not, however, mean that this 18-year-old has the "mind" of a 7-year-old. He is involved in a host of activities that may or may not even occur to a 7-year-old child. This tendency to ascribe superfluous psychological meaning to age equivalents is a major reason for their deemphasis in test interpretation.

On a technical level, age equivalents are also problematic since they have different standard deviations at each age level, with a trend for larger standard deviations with increasing age (Anastasi, 1988). As such, age equivalents have unequal units along their scale and, just as is the case with percentile ranks, powerful statistical methods cannot be used with them.

Grade Equivalents

Grade equivalents (GE) are another type of developmental norm. These were derived specifically for plotting growth through the academic curriculum. Unfortunately, grade equivalents may not be the best score for this purpose as they share all of the interpretive and technical weaknesses of age equivalents. Grade equivalents are computed in identical fashion to age equivalents and have the same central interpretive problem in that they do not indicate a particular level of curricular knowledge. They simply indicate whether or not a child obtained a higher or lower raw score than her particular grade-reference group. The following example illustrates the problem with grade equivalents.

Suzie is a student in the first grade who is very intelligent. She obtained a grade equivalent of 3-4 (third grade-fourth month) on the mathematics portion of an academic achievement test. Her performance on every item is shown below.

Item	Score
1	1
2	1
3	1
4	1
5	1
6	0
7	0
8	0

Raw Score = 5

Amy is a student in the third grade who is of about average intelligence, and she also obtained a grade equivalent of 3-4 (third grade-fourth month) on the same mathematics test. Her performance is shown below.

Item	Score
1	1
2	0
3	0
4	1
5	0
6	1
7	1
8	1

Raw Score = 5

Note that Suzie and Amy obtained the same raw scores on the achievement test and, consequently, the same grade equivalents. Suzie's parents, however, may easily misinterpret her grade equivalent by thinking that, if she has a third-grade equivalent, then perhaps she should be advanced to that grade level in mathematics. This course of action, however, does not appear to be warranted because although the two children received the same raw score and grade equivalents, they achieved them in very different ways, with Amy showing considerably more mathematical knowledge (albeit with a tendency to make some "silly" errors) than Suzie. Suzie has also clearly not mastered the higher-level skills. Grade equivalents thus do not necessarily indicate the level of curricular knowledge or expertise that an individual child possesses. They simply indicate a level of performance. In addition, as was the case with age equivalents, grade equivalents do not have equal units along their scale.

Latent Trait Scores

A proposed solution to the problems of age equivalents and grade equivalents is *latent trait methodology*, also referred to as *item response theory* (Anastasi, 1988). The terms most frequently used to describe these scores are *scaled scores, latent trait scores, Rasch scaling techniques, one-, two-,* or *three-parameter scaling techniques,* or *item response theory scaling methods*. Latent trait scores are developmental norms like GEs and AEs with one exception: these scores have equal units along their scale. These scores, frequently referred to as "scaled scores" on academic achievement tests, are designed for the same purposes as GEs, tracking growth through the curriculum. At this point in their development, they do not solve the interpretive problems of grade equivalents or age equivalents as far as providing an estimate of curricular knowledge goes. They do, however, solve one interpretive problem in that obtaining the same difference between scaled scores from year to year indicates a similar level of growth. Again, an example is in order here. Say that Jimmy obtained the grade equivalents and scaled scores shown below:

	First Grade	Second Grade	Third Grade	Fourth Grade
Grade Equivalent	1-7	2-7	3-7	4-7
Scaled Score	240	260	280	300

One can say, based on scaled score information, that Jimmy does seem to be progressing at about the same rate from year to year. This statement can be made since scaled scores have equal units along the scale. A teacher, however, cannot say that Jimmy is making the same gains every year based on GEs because GEs have unequal units along their scale.

Another notable characteristic of scaled scores is that they are not useful for making comparisons across subtests or composites. If a child, for example, obtains a scaled score of 392 in mathematics and 377 in reading, it does not necessarily follow that he or she is better in mathematics than in reading.

Latent trait derived scores are creeping onto the clinical assessment scene. The DAS (Elliott, 1991) is one example. Users of individually administered intelligence tests and other clinical measures will soon have to become more familiar with their properties.

CORRELATION

Correlation Coefficients

A *correlation coefficient* ($r_{x.y}$) expresses the degree to which two variables, in this case test scores, covary or go together. The range of values for expressing this covariance is from –1 to +1. The value –1 is a perfect negative correlation in that as one test score increases the other decreases, and +1 is a perfect positive correlation in that as one variable increases so does the other. In addition to being expressed numerically, the correlation between two variables can also be expressed graphically with a scatterplot. A *scatterplot* is a graph of a group of children's scores in which each child's scores on the two variables being correlated are plotted as shown in Figures 5.2, 5.3, and 5.4.

An example of a negative correlation between two tests is shown in Figure 5.2, in which the relationship between psychoticism and intelligence is depicted in a scatterplot. In this case higher levels of intelligence are associated with lower levels of psychoticism and vice versa. (The correlation coefficient will approximate 1.0.)

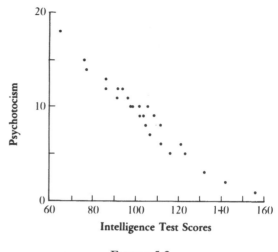

FIGURE 5.2

In the second example, shown in Figure 5.3, the opposite situation is displayed—a strong positive correlation between intelligence and mathematics achievement. Here the correlation coefficient will approximate +1.0. The third example, shown in Figure 5.4, is of a poor correlation between hair length and intelligence, where the resulting coefficient will be near 0.

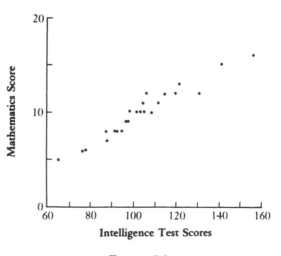

FIGURE 5.3

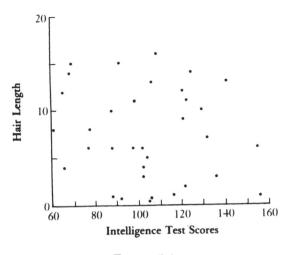

FIGURE 5.4

Correlations between two variables occur because two variables share some common variance. Correlations can be squared to calculate the exact amount of variance shared by the two tests or variables being correlated. If, for example, tests A and B correlate .70 with each other, the amount of shared variance equals 49% ($.70^2$).

In this book, as in most others, the plus sign (+) is assumed for correlation coefficients when it is not present. An important understanding is that correlation coefficients assess rank ordering, not agreement (Lyman, 1963). For example, the correlation between two sets of scores may be high, and yet the means of the two sets of scores can be very different. The comparison of the concepts of correlation and agreement can be better appreciated by computing an example. If a correlation was computed between the numbers 2, 4, 6, 8, 10 and the squares of these numbers, the resulting correlation is .95, and yet the means are 6 and 44, respectively. Since correlations do not necessarily reflect agreement, a high correlation between two scores does not suggest that a child will obtain highly similar scores on the two measures.

Multiple Correlation

A *multiple correlation* ($R_{x.yz...}$) is the correlation between one variable and two or more other vari-

ables (Nitko, 1983). In contrast to the correlation just described (in which scores were obtained for only two variables), a multiple correlation can only be computed when scores on three or more scales are available on the same sample of children. An example is the correlation of SAT score (variable 1) *and* high school GPA (variable 2) with college GPA (variable 3). This multiple correlation serves as the basis for formulas using SAT scores and high school GPA to predict college GPA. Multiple correlations are otherwise similar to other correlations in that they range from –1 to +1, and the amount of variance shared between one variable and two or more others is computed by squaring the coefficient (R^2). Using the example above, R^2, indicates the amount of variance shared by the predictors (SAT and high school GPA) and the criterion (college GPA).

RELIABILITY

When attempting to quantify a sample of behavior, *reliability* refers to the consistency of such measurements when the testing procedure is repeated on a population of individuals or groups (AERA, 1999, p. 25). The type of reliability that is of particular interest to intelligence test users is stability, or the degree to which a child's intelligence test scores are likely to be similar from one measurement to the next. The various theories of intelligence all suggest that it is a fairly stable trait over the course of development. If an individual has an extremely high level of intelligence, it is likely to remain this way barring any unusual circumstances.

The Reliability Coefficient

The reliability of an intelligence test is expressed by the computation of a reliability coefficient, which is a special type of correlation coefficient (Anastasi, 1988). One essential difference between a reliability coefficient and a correlation coefficient is that reliability coefficients are typically not negative, while negative correlation coefficients are eminently possible. Reliability coefficients range, then, from 0 to +1. Reliability coefficients represent the amount of reliable variance associated with a test. In other words, a reliability coefficient is not squared, as is the case with correlation coefficients, to calculate the amount of reliable variance (Anastasi, 1988). For example, the reliable variance of a test with a reliability coefficient of .90 is 90%, an unusually easy computation (Anastasi, 1988)!

The error variance associated with a test is also easy to calculate. It is done by subtracting the reliability coefficient from 1 (perfect reliability). Taking the previous example, the error variance for a test with a reliability coefficient of .90 is 10% (1–.90).

Test-Retest Method

The most popular method for computing the stability of intelligence test scores is the *test-retest method*. In this method the same test, for example the WISC, is administered to the same group of individuals under the same or similar conditions over a brief period of time (typically 2 to 4 weeks). The correlation between the first and second administrations of the test is then computed, yielding a test-retest reliability coefficient that is typically very close to 1.0, usually somewhere between .90 and .98.

Internal Consistency Coefficients

Another type of reliability coefficient that is typically reported in intelligence test manuals is an internal consistency coefficient. This is very different from test-retest or stability coefficients in that it does not assess directly the stability of the measure of intelligence over time. Internal consistency coefficients assess what the name implies—the average correlation among the items in an intelligence test, or in other words, the homogeneity of the test item pool. Internal consistency coefficients are primarily valuable because they are inexpensively produced, since they only require one administration of the test, and serve as *good estimates* of test-retest or stability coefficients. Typical formulae used for the computation of internal consistency coefficients include split-half coefficients, Kuder Richardson 20, and Coefficient Alpha (Anastasi, 1988).

On occasion there are differences between internal consistency and test-retest coefficients that can affect intelligence test interpretation. A test may, for example, have a relatively poor internal consistency coefficient, and yet have a strong test-retest coefficient. An example is the Gestalt Closure subtest of the K-ABC, which has a very heterogeneous item pool. Its internal consistency coefficients are in the .60 to .70 range, but its test-retest coefficient is in the .80 range. Because internal consistency coefficients are imperfect estimates of stability coefficients, both types of coefficients should be recorded in the manual for an intelligence test (see also AERA, 1999).

Variables That Affect Reliability

Clinicians who use intelligence tests should be especially cognizant of factors that can affect reliability. Foremost among these is test length (Nitko, 1983). The longer the test, the more likely the clinician is to obtain an accurate assessment of a child's intelligence. For this reason, short forms of intelligence tests are generally frowned upon. Other factors that the clinician should keep in mind when estimating the reliability of a test for a particular child include the following:

1. Reliability is affected by homogeneous ability levels. Differentiating among the very gifted or severely impaired may be difficult since these individuals represent a very small range of scores (Nitko, 1983).

2. Reliability can change for different ability levels. A test that is very reliable for gifted students is not necessarily as reliable for mentally retarded students without research evidence to support its use (Nitko, 1983).

3. Reliability can suffer when there is a long interval between assessments (Nitko, 1983).

4. Characteristics of the child can affect reliability including age, fatigue, and other factors. Reliability of intelligence measurement drops precipitously at preschool-age levels.

Reliable Specific Variance

Another reliability coefficient that has become more popular in recent years is the estimate of reliable specific variance more commonly referred to as subtest specificity (Kaufman, 1979b). *Subtest specificity* is the amount of reliable specific variance that can be attributed to a single subtest. Kaufman (1979b) popularized the use of subtest specificity in clinical assessment as a way of gauging the amount of confidence a clinician should have in conclusions that are based on a single subtest. In effect, knowledge of subtest specificity makes clinicians more cautious about drawing conclusions based on single subtest scores.

A reliability coefficient represents the amount of reliable variance associated with a test. An example would be a quantitative reasoning test taken from a larger battery of 13 tests, all of which are part of a major intelligence test battery. The quantitative reasoning test has a test-retest reliability coefficient of .82. On the surface this test looks reliable. If this test produces the child's lowest score, the examiner may wish to say that the child has a problem with quantitative reasoning. The examiner can then make this statement with confidence because the test is relatively reliable, right? Not necessarily. As Kaufman (1979b) points out, the conclusion being drawn by the clinician is about some skill or ability (in this case quantitative reasoning) that is specific or *measured only by this one subtest*. The reliability coefficient, on the other hand, reflects not just reliable specific variance but also reliable shared variance. As such, Kaufman (1979b) presents revised reliability estimates for the WISC-R that reflect only subtest specificity. He computes and evaluates subtest specificity in the following way:

1. Compute the multiple correlation (R) between the test in question and all other tests in the battery and square it (R^2). This computation yields the amount of reliable shared variance between the test in question, in this case quantitative reasoning, and the other tests in the battery.

2. Subtract the squared multiple correlation coefficient from the reliability coefficient or r_{tt}. If $R^2 = .30$, $.82 - .30 = .52$. This formula yields the reliable specific variance.

3. Compare the amount of reliable specific variance (.52) to the amount of error variance ($1 - .82 = .18$). If the reliable specific variance exceeds the error variance by .20 or more, then the test is considered to have adequate specificity for interpretive purposes. If the reliable specific variance exceeds the error variance by .19 or less, then the test lacks specificity, and it should be cautiously interpreted. If the reliable specific variance does not exceed the error variance, then very cautious interpretation of the subtest is advised.

Fortunately, subtest specificity values are already computed for most tests, and summary tables are provided. New clinicians should remember that the observed reliability coefficients for a subtest are not adequate for gauging the reliable specific variance of a subtest.

Standard Error of Measurement

The *standard error of measurement* (SEM) gives an indication of the amount of error associated with test scores. In more technical terms, the SEM is the standard deviation of the error distribution of scores. The reliability coefficient of an intelligence test is one manner of expressing the amount of error associated with an intelligence test score in order to allow the user to gauge the level of confidence that she should place in the obtained scores. An examiner may report an intelligence test score for a child as being 113 with a test reliability coefficient of .95.

This practice, however, is unorthodox and clumsy. The typical practice is to report an intelligence test score along with the test's standard error of measurement. This procedure is frequently done for opinion polls that are conducted by the popular media. In a poll, a national sample may be surveyed to determine what percentage of the population eats rutabagas on a daily basis. A news reporter may report the results of the poll by saying, "Rutabagas are a less than popular vegetable in that only 5% of the respondents to our poll indicate that they eat rutabagas at any time. The error rate of this poll is 3%." The *error rate reported by newscasters is typically the standard error of measurement* for the poll that was taken. The standard error of measurement simply is another way of reflecting the amount of error associated with a test score.

In theory, if a child were administered an intelligence test 100 times under identical conditions, he or she would not get the same composite score on all 100 administrations. The child would not obtain the same composite score because the reliability of an intelligence test is imperfect. Rather, the child would obtain a distribution of scores that approximates a normal curve. Hence, in theory, *error is also normally distributed.* This error distribution would have a mean. The mean of this theoretical distribution of scores is the child's "true score." *A true score is a theoretical construct that can only be estimated.* This error distribution, like other normal distributions, not only has a mean, but also can be divided into standard deviations. In an error distribution, however, instead of being called a standard deviation it is called the SEM. As one would predict then, in this error distribution of scores ±1 SEM divides up the same portion of the normal curve (68%) as does a standard deviation and ±2 SEMs divides up the same proportion of the error distribution (95%) as ±2 standard deviations does for a normal distribution of obtained scores.

Confidence Bands

A *confidence band* is a probability statement about the likelihood that a particular range of scores includes a child's true score. Just as is done with the televised opinion polls, clinicians use the SEM to show the amount of error, or unreliability, associated with obtained scores on intelligence tests. Obtained scores are banded with error. Banding is accomplished by subtracting 1 SEM from and adding 1 SEM to the obtained score. If, for example, the child obtained a standard score of 103 on the WISC, one could apply the theory of standard error of measurement to band this score with error. With most age groups the standard error of measurement for the WISC rounds to about three standard score points (Wechsler, 1991). Given that ±1 SEM includes approximately 68% of the error distribution of scores, the clinician could then say that there is a 68% likelihood that the child's true score lies somewhere in the range of 100 to 106. Or, if an examiner wanted to use a more conservative ±2 SEMs, he could say that there is a 95% probability that the child's true score lies somewhere between 97 and 109. Confidence bands may be obtained for a variety of levels. Most manuals include confidence bands for the 68%, 85%, 90%, 95%, and 99% levels of confidence.

Regression Effects

Regression effects refer to the well-known phenomenon of discrepant scores tending to regress toward the mean upon retesting. Using the obtained score to make a probability statement about the child's true score is probably a very reasonable practice for scores in the middle of the distribution—that is, for those children with scores near the average. However, at the tails of the distribution for the developmentally delayed or the exceedingly precocious, use of the obtained score with its associated confidence band is more questionable because of regression effects. In theory and in everyday practice, scores at the tails of the distribution are less reliable and, as such, they are more likely to regress (move) toward the mean upon retesting.

If, for example, a child has an obtained score of 103 on a test with a reliability coefficient of

.95, there is little regression to the mean when a theoretical true score is computed. The resulting true score is 102.85 which rounds to 103. On the other hand, for a child who has a standard score of 65, when the true score is computed there is considerable regression toward the mean.

Most test manuals ignore this fact of regression and simply use what are called *symmetrical confidence bands*, where the *obtained score* is assigned a confidence band. This practice has become customary for at least two reasons. First, many clinicians are accustomed to using symmetrical bands and have not been introduced to the computation of true scores and their underlying theory. Secondly, some children upon retesting violate what would be predicted based upon test theory and obtain scores that are even further from the mean! This result has been the frequently noted case with data associated with the cumulative deficit hypothesis where children's scores upon retesting actually move *further* from the mean (see Chapter 3).

A few tests such as the Wechsler Intelligence Scale for Children—Third Edition (WISC-III) use *asymmetrical confidence bands*. When true score confidence bands are used, the obtained score is not banded with error; rather, the child's estimated true score is banded with error. This procedure takes into account regression effects, which results in confidence bands about the obtained score that are *asymmetrical*, especially at the tails of the distribution. Clinicians should understand the difference between symmetrical and asymmetrical confidence bands, because some tests do prefer the latter, most notably the PPVT-III and WISC-III. In addition, many more computer programs offer true scores and/or asymmetrical confidence bands as output.

VALIDITY

Validity is the foundation upon which the use of modern tests of intelligence is based. *Validity* is defined as *the degree to which a test measures the construct that it purports to measure*. There are a number of different ways of evaluating the validity of a test. A variety of the more common types of validity evidence will be discussed in this section. Validity is the most important psychometric characteristic that an intelligence test must possess. A test can be extremely well normed and extremely reliable, and yet have no validity for the assessment of intelligence. One could, for example, develop a very good test of algebra knowledge, but if one were to try to call this a test of general intelligence, there would likely be a number of opponents to this point of view.

Recently, uniform theories of construct validity have held sway over partitioning approaches (Suen, 1990). Traditionally, distinctions have been made between various types of validity evidence. Some types of validity—for example, construct validity—have been distinguished from factor analysis, which has been considered to be a test of construct validity per se. Messick's (1989) influential work has resulted in a blurring of distinctions between types of validity evidence and resists reifying one type of validity evidence in favor of others. At the time of this writing many types of validity evidence are deemed necessary to support score interpretation.

Benson (1998) has described modern approaches to construct validation in an article that defines a "strong program of construct validation." This approach to construct validation, a program for combining various forms of validity evidence, will be described in detail after several types of validation procedures are described.

Content Validity

One of the reasons that many people would disagree with using a test of algebra knowledge as a measure of intelligence is that it does not appear to possess valid content. *Content validity* refers to the appropriate sampling of a particular content domain (Anastasi, 1988). Content validity has been most closely associated with the development of tests of academic achievement for use in school settings (Anastasi, 1988). Typically,

procedures for the establishment of content validity are judgmental in nature (Petersen, Kolen,
& Hoover, 1989). In the process of developing
an academic achievement test, a test publisher
will hire a number of consulting editors to define
the appropriate content for reading, mathematics, spelling, and other areas included in the battery. This board of editors will define the content
and in addition to that, determine the agreement
between the content used in the test and the cur-
ricula typically used in the schools.

Unfortunately, intelligence test developers,
until recently, have paid little or no attention to
the establishment of content validity (Kamphaus,
1998). This oversight is perhaps why the construct of intelligence has been criticized as being
"what the test measures." Intelligence tests were
first developed for empirical purposes. More recently, attention has been given to the content
validity issue.

The K-ABC, for example, took a very strong
theoretical stand in the test's manuals and then
selected the content for individual subtests based
upon this theoretical model. As such, the authors
attempted to define content domains and select
subtests and items to assess the domains. Older
tests, however, included very little information
regarding the theory behind the test in the test
manuals. Consequently, the purposes behind the
selection of items and subtests were never clearly
explained. It is hoped that new tests and revisions
of older tests will now pay more attention to the
establishment of content validity.

Criterion-Related Validity

Criterion-related validity assesses the degree to
which intelligence tests relate to other tests in a
theoretically appropriate manner. Some of the
types of criterion-related validity studies are described next.

Concurrent Validity

This type of validity stipulates that an intelligence
test should show substantial correlations with
other measures to which they are theoretically

related. One of the important criteria for the evaluation of intelligence measures since their inception was that they show a substantial correlation
with measures of academic achievement. The
typical concurrent validity investigation involves
administering a new intelligence test and an academic achievement test to a group of students. If
a correlation of .20 was obtained, then the concurrent validity of the intelligence test would be
in question. A .75 correlation, on the other hand,
would be supportive of the validity of the intelligence test. Other possible criterion measures that
may be used in concurrent validity studies include
measures of psychomotor skills, speech/language
tests, and tests of information processing.

Composite scores for more narrowly defined
abilities can also be assessed to determine whether
or not they correlate with criteria in predictable
ways. The third factor of the WISC-III, which
produces a *freedom from distractibility* (FFD) index
score, has been predicted to relate to criterion
measures of inattention. Cohen, Becker, and
Campbell (1990) conducted such a study in which
they correlated FFD scores with the Revised Behavior Problem Checklist (RBPC), Conners
Teacher Rating Scale, and Conners Parent Rating
Scale for 135 consecutive referrals to a pediatric
neuropsychology clinic. They found that, contrary
to prediction, the FFD factor did not correlate
significantly with any behavioral measure of inat-
tention/distractibility. The highest correlation
noted was a −.31 between the FFD score and
teacher-rated anxiety. The FFD scale never correlated significantly with parent or teacher ratings of attention problems as rated by parents or
teachers with the Conners. The result of this
type of investigation is straightforward to interpret in that it clearly demonstrates a lack of concurrent validity for the FFD scale in relationship
to a criterion construct that it has been hypothesized to assess.

Correlations with Similar Tests

One can use correlations with other tests in order
to evaluate the validity of an intelligence test. In a

sense this method is a special type of concurrent validity study. The difference here is that the correlation is not between an intelligence measure and some criterion variable, such as academic achievement, but between an intelligence test and a measure of the same construct, another intelligence measure. If a new intelligence test comes onto the scene, it should show a substantial relationship with previous measures, but not an extremely high relationship (Anastasi, 1988). If a new intelligence test correlates .99 with a previous intelligence test, then it is not needed as it is simply another form of an existing test and does not contribute to increasing our understanding of what is, at times, the seemingly nebulous construct of intelligence (Anastasi, 1988). If a new intelligence test correlates only .15 with existing intelligence tests, it is likely also to not be a good measure of intelligence. New intelligence tests should show a moderate to strong relationship with existing tests of intelligence, yet contribute something new to our understanding of the intelligence construct.

Predictive Validity

The other important type of criterion-related validity is *predictive validity*—the ability of an intelligence test to predict (as shown by its correlation) some later criterion of success. This type of research investigation is conducted in a very similar manner to a concurrent validity study with one important exception. The important difference is that in a predictive validity study the intelligence test is first administered to a group of children, and then sometime in the future, perhaps 2 months, 3 months, or even 2 years, a criterion measure is administered to the same group of children. Usually some measure of academic achievement is administered as the criterion measure since this is the criterion variable that is frequently of interest. With regard to measures of academic achievement, correlations have typically been found to be in the .50 to .75 range (Anastasi, 1988). Of course, correlations tend to be higher the closer the interval between the administration of the intelligence and achievement measures.

Age Differentiation Validity

One aspect of the construct validity of an intelligence test is the degree to which raw scores show theoretically lawful increases or decreases with age, or age differentiation validity. Intelligence test raw scores tend to increase with age, especially in childhood and adolescence. One aspect of the validity of an intelligence test would be for it to show increases in mean raw scores for the age groups for which the test is designed. In the example shown in Figure 5.5, Test A shows good evidence of age differentiation validity, whereas Test B does not.

Convergent/Discriminant Validity

Convergent validity is established when an intelligence test construct correlates with constructs with which it is hypothesized to have a strong relationship. Discriminant validity is supported when an intelligence measure has a poor correlation with a construct with which it is hypothesized to be unrelated. This type of assessment of validity is shown clearly in Table 5.2, taken from an investigation from the K-ABC *Interpretive Manual* (Kaufman & Kaufman, 1983b).

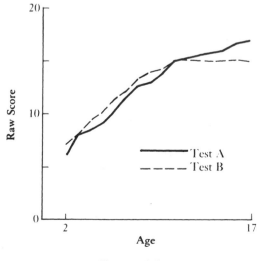

FIGURE 5.5

TABLE 5.2　Correlations between K-ABC scores and factor scores on the Das-Kirby-Jarman Successive-Simultaneous Battery

Correlations with Das-Kirby-Jarman Factors Learning Disabilities Referrals (N = 53)	Successive	Simultaneous
Global Scales		
Sequential Processing	**.50**	.32
Simultaneous Processing	.12	**.54**
Sequential Processing Subtests		
3. Hand Movements	**.30**	.31
5. Number Recall	**.46**	.27
7. Word Order	**.48**	.33
Simultaneous Processing Subtests		
1. Magic Window		
2. Face Recognition		
4. Gestalt Closure	−.10	**.43**
6. Triangles	.27	**.51**
8. Matrix Analogies	.03	**.52**
9. Spatial Memory	.37	**.47**
10. Photo Series	.23	**.42**

Correlations of .30 and above are in **boldface**.
SOURCE: Adapted from Kaufman & Kaufman (1983b).

It is evident from this table that the Simultaneous and Sequential scales of the K-ABC show evidence of convergent and discriminant validity. To show evidence of convergent/discriminant validity the following pattern of correlations should hold:

1. The K-ABC Simultaneous scale should correlate highly with the Das Simultaneous scale and poorly with the K-ABC Sequential and Das Successive scales.

2. The K-ABC Sequential scale should correlate highly with the Das Successive scale and poorly with the Simultaneous scales of both tests.

The results are generally consistent with these predictions. The Simultaneous scale of the K-ABC correlates with a measure of the same construct on the other test battery substantially, which is indicative of evidence of convergent validity. Yet, the Simultaneous scale of the K-ABC did not correlate as highly with measures of dissimilar constructs, including the Sequential scale of the K-ABC and the successive scale of the other test battery. The predicted pattern also emerged for the K-ABC Sequential scale. This table shows an excellent example of the establishment of convergent and discriminant validation, a type of validity evidence that is all too frequently missing from test manuals.

Factor Analysis

Factor analysis is a popular technique used in the process of validating modern tests of intelligence that traces its roots to the work of the eminent statistician Karl Pearson (1901). Factor analysis has become increasingly popular as a technique for test validation because of the onset of high-speed computers that greatly facilitate what was formerly a very laborious statistical procedure. Hence, there are a wealth of factor analytic studies beginning with the widespread availability of computer systems in the 1960s.

Factor analysis is a very difficult topic to broach in only a few paragraphs although an attempt was made in Chapter 2. Those readers who are interested in learning factor analysis require a separate course on this particular technique and a great deal of independent reading and experience. A very thorough discussion of factor analytic techniques can be found in Gorsuch (1988). An introductory-level discussion may be found in Anastasi and Urbina (1997).

Confirmatory Factor Analysis

The procedures discussed in Chapter 2 are generally referred to as *exploratory factor analytic procedures*. A newer factor analytic technique, utilizing structural equation modeling, is referred to as *confirmatory factor analysis*. These two factor analytic procedures differ in some very important ways. In exploratory factor analysis, the number of factors to be yielded is typically dictated by the characteristics of the intercorrelation matrix. That is, the number of factors selected is based upon the amount of variance that each factor explains in the correlation matrix. If a factor, for example, explains 70% of the variance in the correlation matrix, then it is typically included as a viable factor in further aspects of the factor analysis. If, on the other hand, the factor only accounts for 2% of the variance in a factor matrix, then it may not be included as a viable factor.

In direct contrast, in confirmatory factor analysis the number of factors is not dictated by data, but rather by the theory underlying the test under investigation. In confirmatory factor analysis the number of factors is selected a priori, and the factor loadings of each subtest on the a priori designated number of factors is then analyzed.

In addition, the general fit between the factor structure dictated a priori and the obtained data are assessed. If there is a great deal of correspondence between the hypothesized structure and the obtained factor structure, then the validity of the intelligence test is supported (hence the term *confirmatory*), and the theory is confirmed. If, for example, a researcher hypothesized the existence of four factors in a particular intelligence test, the confirmatory factor analysis will, in fact, yield four factors. Statistics assessing the fit of these four factors to the data may, however, indicate a lack of congruence (correlation) between the hypothesized four factors and the obtained four factors.

More thorough confirmatory factor analytic studies use a variety of statistics to assess the fit of the hypothesized factor structure to the data. These statistics may include a Chi-square statistic, goodness-of-fit index (GFI), adjusted goodness-of-fit index (AGFI), and root mean square residual (RMR) among others. Several statistics are desirable for checking the fit of a confirmatory factor analysis because all of these statistics have strengths and weaknesses. The Chi-square statistic, for example, is highly influenced by sample size (Glutting & Kaplan, 1990). Some general guidelines for assessing the fit of a confirmatory factor analysis may include the following (Kline, 1989):

1. Nonsignificant Chi-square statistic
2. Goodness-of-fit index > .90
3. Adjusted goodness-of-fit Index > .80
4. Root Mean square residual < .10

Consequently, confirmatory factor analytic procedures may yield the number of factors hypothesized by the test developer, which, in exploratory factor analysis, would lend support to the theory and structure of the test. In confirmatory factor analysis, however, consumers of the research have to evaluate the statistics that assess the fit between the hypothesized and the obtained factor structure. These statistics will indicate whether or not the evidence is strong or weak for the validity of the scores yielded by the test under study.

Another issue in confirmatory factor analysis is that many researchers use it in an exploratory factor analytic manner (Thorndike, 1990). Some authors specify a model a priori and then modify that model numerous times until adequate fit statistics are obtained. Thorndike (1990) contends that this is a misuse of the methodology that dilutes the theoretical importance of the obtained results. Ideally, researchers should conduct studies comparing competing theoretical models (see Kline, 1989, for such an example) in order to evaluate the theoretical structure of a test (Thorndike, 1990).

The Validation Process

It is always inappropriate to refer to tests as being either valid or invalid, although this is often the case in conversation among individual test users and, in fact, references of this nature are difficult to avoid. Validation is not a condition but, rather, it is a process (Benson, 1998) whereby evidence is continually collected to support or refute particular test uses. Benson (1998) describes her interpretation of the validation process as follows:

> *The belief in a strong program of validation also was reflected in the early writing of Loevinger (1957) and later by Nunnally (1978) who described the process of construct validation as consisting of three aspects: a substantive component, a structural component, and an external component. The substantive component is where the theoretical domain of the construct is specified and then operationally defined in terms of the observed variables (e.g., the behaviors that reflect the construct). The structural component involves relating the items to the structure of the construct by determining to what extent the observed variables relate to one another and the construct. It is the external component that begins to give meaning to test scores by determining whether or not the measures of a given construct relate in expected ways with measures of other constructs. (p. 11)*

The conclusion that theory development has commonly lagged in intelligence test development is irrefutable (Kaufman & Sternberg, 1997). It logically follows then that studies of structural and external validation will be hindered by a lack of clarity. It is impossible, for example, to definitively prove the existence of "g" or challenge the theory when the construct is vaguely defined as a first principle component or first factor yielded by exploratory factor analysis. Supporters of "g" can claim validity for the construct given the certainty that factor analysis will produce a first factor that accounts for more variance than other factors and detractors can justifiably claim that the finding is an artifact of the statistical methodology. This type of study, based on inadequate theory and irrefutable hypotheses, only contributes to a continuous loop of fruitless discussion and debate.

An example of a more scientifically valuable approach to test validation is provided in a study of "g" theory by Jensen (1983), who reviewed the K-ABC shortly after its release. He offered a refutable hypothesis, based on theory, that the K-ABC would not measure "g" as well as some competitors. His theory-based hypothesis was incorrect.

The related problems of construct irrelevance and construct underrepresentation (Messick, 1989) can plague definitions of intelligence constructs. Construct irrelevance may become problematic if an intelligence construct is defined too broadly. For example, many non-psychologists are surprised to discover that several intelligence tests include measures of basic arithmetic skills. In a sense, the public is concluding that mathematics skills are irrelevant to the intelligence construct. Factor analysis or structural equation modeling (of which confirmatory factor analysis is subset) may be used to determine if mathematics subtests are good measures of intelligence. Some studies have found "g" loadings for such measures to be adequate (Kaufman & McLean, 1987), and a relatively new test, the Differential Ability Scales, has included some mathematics items along with figural matrices items to measure "nonverbal reasoning." These findings reveal that some items that may first appear inappropriate for intelligence measures are not construct irrelevant in that they measure at least the "g" and reasoning constructs. Some mathematics items, however, may not function as well, such as knowledge of geometry, which loads on an achievement factor (Carroll, 1993). Geometry items may represent construct irrelevancy.

Construct underrepresentation may pose equally serious problems for the definitional stage of the validation process (Benson, 1998). A spelling measure, for example, may be inadequate to measure the verbal ability represented by Carroll's (1993) crystallized factor. Construct underrepresentation may still be obtained if a second indicator of spelling ability is added. Two spelling measures would lead to adequate assessment of the first-order spelling factor, but they may not adequately represent the second-order verbal skills construct, which includes language development, reading, and other first-order factors. Construct underrepresentation would be particularly likely if two spelling measures were utilized to measure the verbal skills of preschoolers.

Most of the popular procedures for test validation are utilized during the structural stage, where the relationships among test variables are compared to the theoretical organization of the constructs (Benson, 1998). Factor analysis, generalizability theory, item response theory, item-test intercorrelations, multitrait-multimethod matrix procedures, and confirmatory factor analysis are commonly used for such purposes.

STANDARDIZATION SAMPLING

Intelligence test scores are rather meaningless without the use of norm groups. Generally speaking, individuals are to be compared to norm groups of their peers. Intelligence test developers thus strive to collect norm samples that are reflective of a child's peers.

The ideal for developing intelligence test norms for an American test would be to test all children in the United States in order to compare individual children with the national norm. This procedure would be used for any country that would be using a particular intelligence test, thus allowing a child to be compared to a common norm regardless of the municipality in which she resides in a country. Unfortunately, this process is not possible, so test developers collect samples of children that are representative of the national population, much in the same way that pollsters collect samples of the population in order to gauge the political will of voters prior to an election.

In order to select a representative sample of the national population for any country, test developers typically use what are called *stratification variables*. These stratification variables are assumed to have important effects upon intelligence test scores, which necessitates their inclusion as sample selection variables. Two of the most important stratification variables in the United States are some indication of socioeconomic status and ethnic/racial identification. Differences in SES and ethnicity produce significant differences in intelligence test scores (Vanderploeg, Schinka, Baum, Tremont, & Mittenberg, 1998). Some stratification variables such as gender and geographic region are included based more upon tradition, since they do not produce substantial differences in intelligence test scores.

In the United States, the stratification variables are based upon U.S. Census Bureau statistics. If the census, for example, says that 75% of the United States population is made up of white children, then test developers will typically try to include 75% white children in the norming sample. Some typical stratification variables are age, gender, parental socioeconomic status (tests have traditionally used either parental educational attainment or occupation), race or ethnic group, community size, and geographic region.

In many cases a psychologist will wish to compare intellgence test results with other measures such as adaptive behavior or academic achievement. A comparison of intelligence to adaptive behavior may be important for making the mental retardation diagnosis and a comparison to achievement may be utilized to make a learning disability diagnosis. In these cases, error is introduced into the comparison process if the two tests utilized are normed on different samples of children taken at different points in time (Cicchetti, 1994). Some tests are normed together (e.g., K-ABC and Vineland Adaptive Behavior Scales—Survey Form) but others are not. Examiners must then be aware of the possibility of noncomparable norms when making cross-construct comparisons (Cicchetti, 1994).

Local Norms

Occasionally, a clinician may want to have local norms available (Kamphaus & Lozano, 1981). Local norms are those based on some subset of the national population. Say, for example, a child was transferring from an impoverished area of a city to a school system in a high-SES area. The child from the impoverished environment may have obtained an intelligence test composite score of 100. This child, however, may be at considerable risk for school problems if she is moved to a highly competitive school system where the average intelligence test composite score is 117. In this case, the national norms are of some benefit in that they indicate that the child has average intelligence, but local norms based on a sample from a high-SES school district may be even more enlightening and might assist with planning the transition of this child from one school system to another. Local norms, however, are rarely available for clinical tests because they are time consuming and somewhat expensive to develop.

WHY TEST SCORES DIFFER

A frequently perplexing problem for clinicians is having to explain why two or more sets of intelligence test scores for the same child differ, sometimes substantially. There are a number of psychometric reasons for changes in scores, including the age of the norms, floor and ceiling effects, selection bias/regression effects, age at which the child was first tested, item content differences, and reliability of gain/difference scores.

Age of Norms

One of the most important characteristics of norm tables is the necessity that they be recent. A comprehensive analysis of changes in Stanford-Binet and Wechsler norms from the years 1932 to 1978, by James Flynn (1984), highlights the problem of using antiquated norms. Flynn's conclusion, as noted in Chapter 3, was that the American population became about one standard deviation (15 standard score points) "smarter" over an approximately 50-year period. In other words, the norm tables became "tougher" with each succeeding decade in the sense that a child had to obtain a higher raw score every time a test was renormed to obtain the same standard score that he had obtained previously. If a child, for example, took the WISC (normed in the 1940s) in 1956 and correctly answered 13 Vocabulary items, she may obtain a scaled score of 10. If a child took the Vocabulary test on the WISC-R (normed in the early 1970s) and answered 13 items correctly, her scaled score may be only 8 or 9. One of the most interesting aspects of the Flynn investigation is that he provides a rule of thumb for this change in the difficulty of American intelligence test norms. He concludes that intelligence test norms for the United States increase in difficulty by about three standard score points every decade. A test, for example, that was normed in 1980, would have "softer" or easier norms. This test would yield standard scores that, on the average, are about three standard score points (based on a mean of 100 and a standard deviation of 15) higher than for a comparable or the same test with norms collected in 1990. This statement assumes, of course, that the norm samples for both tests are representative of the national population.

Based on data other than Flynn's, it is striking how aptly this rule of thumb of a change of three standard score points applies. A perusal of the WISC-R manual shows that it produced scores about 2 points lower than the 1967 WPPSI. Similarly, the 1981 edition of the WAIS-R produces standard scores about 6 points lower than the 1955 WAIS. Finally, the Binet-4, and K-ABC, both normed in the 1980s, produced standard scores anywhere from about 2 to 4 points lower than the WISC-R, which was normed in the 1970s (Kamphaus & Reynolds, 1987).

Though this rule of thumb may not be in effect forever, at this time when a clinician selects an intelligence test for use, one of the first things to look for is the date of the data collection for the sample. *If the standardization sample is 10 years old or more, then the clinician has to become wary of the accuracy of the norms for current use.*

This psychometric hypothesis is one of the first to entertain when a difference is observed between intelligence test scores gathered on separate occasions. Clinicians, for example, can expect to see WISC-III scores that are 2 to 4 standard score points lower than K-ABC and Binet 4 scores for the same child.

Floor and Ceiling Effects

Floor effects occur when the test being administered to a child lacks enough easy items to allow the child to obtain a raw score (i.e., the child gets all of the items wrong). Conversely, *ceiling effects* occur when a test lacks difficult items, resulting in the child obtaining a perfect score. These problems of a lack of an adequate range of difficulty are frequently encountered in clinical assessment. Floor and ceiling effects are problematic in that if a child obtains either a perfect score or a zero raw score, his intelligence has not been measured adequately. The examiner then does not know how far his ability lies below the lowest item or how far he is above the last item.

Clinicians are most likely to encounter problems with insufficient floor and ceiling near the extremes of a test's age range. The WISC-III age range, for example, is 6 to 16 years. The WISC-III is likely to exhibit ceiling effects for 15-year-olds of average to above-average ability and floor effects for 6- and 7-year-olds who are developmentally delayed. Some tests, however, may be more prone to floor effects than others. The clinician can identify these problems through experience with a particular test. Another way to identify the presence of floor and ceiling effects, however, is to inspect P-values for a particular test. A *P-value* is the percentage of children passing an item (e.g., 45% of 2-year-olds passed the first item on a test). Unfortunately, publishers usually do not include P-values in their test manuals (P-values for the K-ABC are available in Kamphaus & Reynolds, 1987). Publishers are, however, likely to publish raw score descriptive statistics by age group, including means and standard deviations. Floor effects can be gauged by reviewing the relationships of the mean to the standard deviation for the younger age ranges of a test. If the standard deviation exceeds the mean at an age group, this suggests that the test is too difficult (Kamphaus & Reynolds, 1987).

Similarly, the age differentiation validity of a test can indicate whether or not ceiling effects are present. If the mean raw score for the oldest age group is similar to or less than the preceding age group, the test has poor age differentiation validity and an associated ceiling effect. Ceiling effects are a problem for all tests at their extreme age ranges. The best way to avoid ceiling effects if little is known about the nature of the referral is to not use a test with an age range that will increase the likelihood of a lack of item difficulty. For example, for a 14-year-old use a test with an upper age limit of 18, instead of using a test that has an upper age limit of only 16.

Correlations Between Tests

Certainly one of the most straightforward reasons for test score differences is the possibility that the two tests are not highly correlated. Intelligence test composite scores typically have reliability coefficients in the .90 range. As a result, when a child is tested with the same test twice his scores are likely to be similar. If, on the other hand, a child is administered two different intelligence tests, his scores are likely to differ simply because an intelligence test typically correlates more with itself than it does with other intelligence tests.

Selection Bias

The regression effect for extreme scores is frequently compounded by selection bias, which is also a plausible explanation for score differences. *Selection bias*, as coined by Richard Woodcock (1984), occurs when the regression effect is compounded for the second test administered to a child who is at the extremes of the normal distribution. Say, for example, that children are selected for mental retardation classes using the WISC-III and these children are reevaluated with the Differential Ability Scales (DAS). Selection bias predicts that the mean score for the DAS will be higher (closer to the mean) than for the WISC-III since the WISC-III was used as the selection test.

The selection bias phenomenon for this scenario is shown graphically in Figure 5.6. This figure is a scatterplot, divided into four quadrants

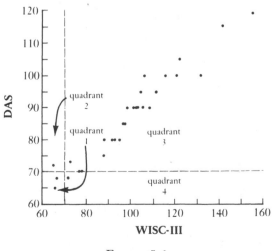

FIGURE 5.6

representing the relationship between the WISC-III and DAS. If the sample of mentally retarded children is selected based on having WISC-III scores less than 70 (these are the children whose scores are represented in quadrants 1 and 2), then some children with DAS composite scores of less than 70 (and WISC-III scores greater than 70) were not diagnosed as mentally retarded and not included in the sample (these cases are in quadrant 4). The use of the WISC-III as selection test therefore lowers the mean of the WISC-III for the sample and raises the mean of the DAS since the children's scores in quadrant 4 with DAS composites below 70 and WISC-III scores above 70 were excluded from the sample. The phenomenon of selection bias suggests that the scores of children who are diagnosed because of being at the tails of the normal distribution can be quite discrepant on two tests of intelligence.

Reliability and Age

Generally, intelligence tests are less reliable for preschool-aged children (Anastasi, 1988). This unreliability is a plausible hypothesis for differences between intelligence test scores for a preschool child and for differences between scores when a child is tested in the preschool years and again at a later date.

Test length can also be a plausible hypothesis for differences between intelligence tests. The K-ABC, for example, is shorter than either the WISC-III or Binet 4 by about two subtests. Similarly, short forms of intelligence tests can produce differences between tests.

Content Differences

Intelligence tests can be based on a variety of theories that dictate item and subtest selection. Some tests may place a premium on verbal skills, others on motor skills. The child with cerebral palsy, for example, may perform very differently on two intelligence measures depending on the content of the items—verbal versus nonverbal.

Reliability of Gain/Difference Scores

Gain scores are computed by subtracting a child's first score on an intelligence test from her second score. They are commonly referred to as gain scores because scores tend to be slightly higher on the second testing (a gain) in test-retest reliability studies. Difference scores subsume gain scores. The term *difference score*, however, is usually used in conjunction with comparing composite scores within a test or across tests. An example of a difference score would be the difference between Verbal and Performance scores on the WISC. It is important when interpreting score differences to keep in mind that difference scores and gain scores are inherently less reliable than composite or subtest scores (Anastasi, 1985). Specifically, a gain or loss from one test administration to another is a difference score. *Difference scores possess the error variance of both tests used* in producing the difference. If, for example, each test has a reliability coefficient of .90, then the error variance associated with the difference score is .20 (.10 + .10). Being aware of the increased error associated with difference scores, clinicians frequently attribute small differences between composite scores to chance variation.

Practice Effects

Practice effects may explain small differences in scores between intelligence tests. *Practice effects* are observed when scores improve (a gain score) due to familiarity with the test items. The size of practice effects is usually less than 10 standard score points (2/3 SD).

Interpreting Score Differences

Based on the previous discussion, the following list of psychometric hypotheses should be considered when differences between intelligence tests occur.

1. Age of norms
2. Floor and ceiling effects
3. Correlations between tests
4. Selection bias
5. Reliability and age
6. Content differences
7. Reliability of difference (gain) scores
8. Practice effects

These hypotheses are primarily psychometric. Scores may differ due to other factors. Say, for example, a child is tested on two occasions, once when she is taking medication and once when she is not. This situation could have a dramatic impact on the two test scores that is independent of psychometric reasons.

CONCLUSIONS

Knowledge of psychometric principles is becoming an increasingly important issue since this type of coursework has been deemphasized in many psychology programs leading to a "crisis in measurement literacy" (Lambert, 1991). Yet psychologists have a continuing reputation for assessment expertise that is well known to the public and other professions. A strong background in psychometrics is a necessary prerequisite for the assessment process, as are knowledge of specific tests and clinical skill. Fortunately, psychometric information is now readily available in numerous formats including the internet (see Box 5.1).

CHAPTER SUMMARY

- The mode (Mo) is the most frequently occurring score in a distribution of scores.
- The median (Md) is the midpoint of a distribution of scores.

Box 5.1   World Wide Web Sites

Assessment and Testing Web Sites

American Psychological Association	http://www.apa.org/science/test.html
The National Council on Measurement in Education	http://www.iupui.edu/NCME/
The ERIC Clearinghouse on Assessment and Evaluation	http://ericae.net/scripts/cat/catdemo.htm
Educational Testing Services (ETS)	http://www.ets.org/cbt/index.html
MESA Psychometric Laboratory, University of Chicago	http://mesa.spc.uchicago.edu/
The Buros Institute of Mental Measurements	http://www.UNL.edu:80/buros/
Center for Research on Evaluation, Standards and Student Testing (CRESST)	http://www.cse.ucla.edu
Educational Testing Service	http://ets.org/
Rasch Measurement	http://rasch.org/
National Association of Test Directors Home Page	http://www.natd.org/

Psychological and Educational Test Publishers

AGS (American Guidance Service)	http://www.agsnet.com/
California Test Bureau	http://www.cpp-db.com/
Educational and Industrial Testing Service	http://www.edits.net/
Institute for Personality and Ability Testing	http://www.ipat.com/
Pro-ed	http://proedinc.com/
Riverside Publishing	http://www.riverpub.com/
The Psychological Corporation	http://www.hbtpc.com/
PAR (Psychological Assessment Resources	http://www.parinc.com/
Western Psychological Services	http://www.wpspublish.com/

- The mean (M) is the arithmetic average of the distribution of scores.

- The range is the difference between the highest and lowest scores in a distribution.

- The standard deviation (SD) is the square root of the average squared deviation in a group of scores. The SD is large when there is a great deal of variability (a large range) of scores, and it is very small when there is little variability.

- Raw scores on most tests of intelligence are simply comprised of the number of items correct, or they are a summation of the number of points earned on individual items.

- The most popular type of score for intelligence tests is the standard score. Standard scores convert raw scores to a distribution with a set mean and standard deviation, with equal units along the scale.

- Scaled scores are standard scores that have a mean of 10 and a standard deviation of 3.

- A *T* score is a standard score that has a mean of 50 and standard deviation of 10.

- A normal curve equivalent (NCE) is a standard score that has a mean of 50 and a rather unusual standard deviation of 21.06.

- Stanines, which stands for "standard nines," were used heavily by the armed forces and were rather convenient because they represent the lone standard score scale that uses only one digit and ranges from a low of 1 to a high of 9.

- A percentile rank gives an individual's relative position within the norm group.

- Age and grade equivalents are computed based upon the performance of every age/grade group used in the norming of the test.

- Latent trait scores are developmental norms like GEs and AEs with one exception: these scores have equal units along their scale.

- A correlation coefficient ($r_{x.y}$) expresses the degree to which two variables (test scores) covary.

- A multiple correlation ($R_{x.yz...}$) is the correlation between one variable and two or more other variables.

- The reliability of a test refers to the degree to which its scores are free from errors of measurement.

- Subtest specificity is the amount of reliable specific variance that can be attributed to a single subtest.

- The standard error of measurement (SEM) is the standard deviation of the error distribution of scores.

- A confidence band is a probability statement about the likelihood that a particular range of scores includes a child's true score.

- Regression effects refer to the well-known phenomenon of discrepant scores tending to regress toward the mean upon retesting.

- Validity is defined as the degree to which tests measure what they purport to measure.

- Content validity refers to the appropriate sampling of a particular content domain.

- Concurrent validity stipulates that an intelligence test should show substantial correlations with other measures that should theoretically correlate with intelligence tests.

- Predictive validity refers to the ability of an intelligence test to predict (as shown by its correlation) some criterion of success.

- The age differentiation validity of an intelligence test is the degree to which raw scores show theoretically lawful increases or decreases with age.

- Convergent validity is established when an intelligence test construct correlates with constructs with which it is hypothesized to have a strong relationship. Discriminant validity is supported when an intelligence measure has a poor correlation with a construct with which it is supposed to have a poor correlation.

- Factor analysis is a data reduction technique that attempts to explain the variance in an intelligence test in a parsimonious fashion.

- A factor loading is in most cases the correlation between a subtest and a factor.[1]

- In confirmatory factor analysis, consumers of the research have to evaluate the statistics that assess the fit between the hypothesized and the obtained factor structure.

- In order to select a representative sample of the national population for any country, test developers typically use what are called stratification variables.

- Local norms are those based on some subset of the national population.

- One of the most important characteristics of norm tables is the necessity that they be based on recent data.

- Floor effects occur when the test being administered to a child lacks enough easy items to allow the child to obtain a raw score (i.e., the child gets all of the items wrong).

---

[1] When orthogonal (independent or uncorrelated) rotation techniques are used (and these techniques are very frequently used in test validation research), the factor loading represents the correlation between the subtest and a factor. This is not the case when oblique or correlated methods of factor analysis are used (Anastasi, 1988).

- Conversely, ceiling effects occur when a test lacks difficult items, resulting in the child obtaining a perfect score.
- A P-value is the percentage of children passing an item (e.g., 45% of 2-year-olds passed the first item on a test).
- Selection bias occurs when the regression effect is compounded for the second test administered to a child who is at the extremes of the normal distribution.
- Gain scores are computed by subtracting a child's first score on an intelligence test from her second score.
- Practice effects are observed when scores improve (a gain score) due to familiarity with the test items.

Chapter 6

Culture and Bias

The social problem of alienation between technical psychology and the mainstream of cultural understanding cannot be resolved by merely selling the ideas of science to the general public. Because intelligence is itself a culturally constructed aspect of the human mind, scientific theories of intelligence need to incorporate the common-sense intuitions of the society at large. Professional psychologists need to adapt their definitions, their assessment methods, and their interventions in the light of open and constructive discourse with other participants of the culture. (Serpell, 1994, p. 163)

CHAPTER QUESTIONS

What were the outcomes of litigation related to intelligence tests and special education?

How would one assess the intelligence of a non-English-speaking child when only English-language tests are available?

Several issues have led to concern about the use of intelligence tests with children from cultures different from that of the test developers. The traditions of Galton, Binet, Wechsler, Cattell, and others underlie all modern tests of intelligence. These tests emanated from French, British, German, North American, and other similarly European cultures. Intelligence testing, however, became unusually popular in the United States, a society that is perhaps unusually multicultural, being characterized by diverse values, languages, and religious beliefs.

The utility of intelligence tests for U.S. children of non-European descent or non-English-speaking background has been questioned since the early days of intelligence testing (French & Hale, 1990). Since intelligence tests have resembled academic achievement tests, their content has always been easily criticized as being culturally specific. The essential question is, can an intelligence test serve the same purpose as measures for the physical sciences?

Intelligence tests have come under great scrutiny because of their *uses*. The seemingly arbitrary and capricious nature of special education diagnosis brought the use of intelligence measures to the attention of the courts in the 1970s.

TEST BIAS AND THE COURTS

History

Psychologists have learned a great deal about intelligence test bias in the decades of the 1970s and 1980s. The premier reason for this greater understanding has been the litigation of the 1970s. Court cases forced organized psychology to study test bias issues with greater urgency. Research in this area was substantial in the late 1970s and early 1980s so that today we know a great deal about the statistical properties of intelligence tests for various cultural groups.

More importantly, the issues regarding intelligence test misuse have been clarified. This clarification has led to numerous publications advising clinicians how to use intelligence, and other, tests appropriately in multicultural settings (Sandoval & Irvin, 1990).

Court Cases

One can imagine how these court cases came about. Put yourself in the shoes of a parent for a moment. Imagine receiving a letter from your child's school saying that your child has been evaluated and you need to come to school for a meeting to decide what to do with your child. You arrive at school and are ushered into a room with a half dozen school personnel, some of whom you may not know, including the principal, your child's teacher, a school psychologist, a social worker, a guidance counselor, and a special education teacher. Is it not clear to you at this point that you are going to hear some very bad news? These people are not gathered here to give you a parenting award. Then they tell you that your 12-year-old son has some school problems, which, by the way, is not news to you. You were already aware that his achievement motivation has become worse from year to year, and you have

tried your best to resolve the problem. Now they tell you that your child was given "some tests" and that these showed that his ability was poor, to the point that he qualified as "mildly mentally handicapped," which you know means that they are calling him "retarded." Note that it is easier for the professionals to emphasize the test's role rather than the role of the professionals. It is easier to say, "The test indicates . . ." than "I think . . .". You may now have several thoughts running through your mind such as, "I know he can do better," "Why didn't they tell me about it in grade school, how can he suddenly be retarded?," "Is it my fault?," and, finally, "What are these intelligence tests, I know that he can figure things out at home if he wants to—he handles his own lawn mowing service?"

The foregoing vignette provides a concrete example of the frustration and tension surrounding special education placement decisions. The consternation of parents and others came to a boiling point in the late 1960s when a number of well-known court cases were filed in order to deal with the very thorny special education placement issue. More specifically, special education aimed at children with mental retardation was the focus of numerous court cases.

The folk definition of intelligence is that it is an innate capacity. Hence, there is an extraordinary stigma associated with low scores on intelligence measures. This stigmatization is even more clearcut and abhorrent to many individuals when the term *mentally retarded* is used. It is the diagnosis of mental retardation and the associated educational placement of children in classes for the mentally retarded that has created a search for an alternative or remedy to what has been viewed by many as a stigmatizing and ineffective enterprise.

Hobson v. Hanson

One of the first cases to question the use of so-called ability tests to make special education decisions for mental retardation placement—the oft-used term is *educable mentally retarded*

(EMR)—was the case of *Hobson v. Hansen* (1967). This decision resulted in the dissolution of a tracking system in the Washington, DC, public schools that depended on the use of group-administered achievement tests. It was determined that as a result of the tracking system, many African American children were placed in the lower tracks in a proportion that exceeded the proportion of African American children in the total school population. Some 90% of the school population was Black, but Black children accounted for approximately 95% of the children in the "mental retardation" track (Elliott, 1987). Judge Wright in this case was concerned that in addition to the use of tests that were not true measures of innate ability, the tracking system resulted in children being placed in tracks that provided a lower-quality educational experience. These tracks also had the potential to be stigmatizing and produce expectations on the part of teachers and students alike for low academic achievement. One of Judge Wright's concerns was that this self-fulfilling prophecy would lead to children staying in this track for the remainder of their school career.

Diana

A second case filed in 1970 in northern California was the case of *Diana v. State Board of Education* (1970). There were nine plaintiffs in this particular case, all of Latino descent. These nine children were placed in an EMR class based upon individually administered intelligence test results. Upon retesting however, eight of the nine children scored outside the EMR range. The case of *Diana* resulted in consent decrees that served to clarify the appropriate and inappropriate uses of intelligence measures and special education assessment procedures in general with children for whom English was not their primary language. Some of the decrees of this case are strikingly similar to the regulations later included in Public Law 94-142 (now known as the Individuals with Disabilities Education Act, IDEA).

Some important practices that were to be implemented as a result of this case included using more than one assessment device to make the diagnosis of mental retardation. Related to this directive was a stipulation that adaptive behavior scores should also be used in the mental retardation diagnostic process. Although it had long been standard practice to diagnose mental retardation on the basis of concurrent deficits in intelligence and adaptive behavior (see Chapter 20), apparently this standard practice was not routine practice for the school system involved in this particular case. Hence, by emphasizing multiple measures and the use of adaptive behavior scales, the consent decree was reiterating long-standing practices of sound psychological assessment and diagnosis. The *Diana* decision also required the periodic reevaluation of the EMR students in order to allow for their passage out of the EMR program should improvements obtain.

Another result of the *Diana* case was to clearly identify the criterion of two standard deviations below the mean as the cutoff for mental retardation special education placement. This decision resulted in a reduction in the total number of EMR enrollment in California schools from a high of 57,148 in 1968–1969 to 38,208 in 1971–1972 after the *Diana* decision (Elliott, 1987). This reduction of EMR enrollment because of the new standard, however, did not solve the continuing problem of overrepresentation of minority, especially African American, children in proportion to the total population. In 1968 and 1969, African Americans constituted 25.5% of the EMR enrollment and in 1971–72, they constituted 26.7% of the EMR enrollment. Even as late as 1976–77 when EMR enrollment was only about 19,000 students, 25% of these students were African American (Elliott, 1987).

After *Hobsen v. Hansen* and the case of *Diana*, section 504 of the Rehabilitation Act of 1973 and PL 94-142, the Education for all Handicapped Children Act of 1975, clarified some of the standards of nondiscriminatory assessment and, more importantly, specified criteria for the selection and use of measures such as intelligence tests.

These regulations essentially borrowed the principles that were discovered as part of litigation over employment testing of a decade earlier. As a consequence of this litigation, the Equal Employment Opportunity Commission (EEOC) developed guidelines and regulations that *a test must be specifically validated for the purpose for which it is being used* (Anastasi, 1988). This is the standard to which intelligence tests would be held in later cases. In the case of employment testing, it was necessary for every employer to show that a particular selection test was appropriate for a specific job classification. For example, an employer could not use an intelligence test to select individuals for secretarial and managerial positions unless the test was specifically validated (through traditional predictive validity types of studies) separately for managerial applicants and for secretarial applicants.

Larry P.

The *Larry P. v. Riles* case began in 1971 when the plaintiffs representing Black children who were overrepresented in classes for the mentally retarded asked for an injunction against the use of intelligence tests in the San Francisco public schools. The injunction was granted by Judge Peckham in June of 1972 (Elliott, 1987). The injunction suggested that before the trial began, there was the presumption that the intelligence tests were culturally biased. The trial did not actually occur until 1977 and 1978. Many well-known psychologists testified at the hearing. Dr. Leon Kamin, the author of the book *The Science and Politics of IQ* (1974), provided some compelling testimony about the history of intelligence testing. He provided quotations from such luminaries as Lewis Terman, Henry Goddard, and Robert Yerkes that revealed clearly racist viewpoints. These viewpoints were so strident that they could not be differentiated from the viewpoints of modern groups such as the Klu Klux Klan (Elliott, 1987). This sort of testimony certainly created concern about the intentions of early intelligence test developers. Additional damaging evidence against the use of the WISC-R was provided by Dr. Jane Mercer of the University of

California at Riverside. She suggested that intelligence tests were unable to predict school grades, especially those of minority children. This belief is reflected in the development of her own SOMPA (as is discussed later in this chapter). She proposed that minority group children should routinely have their scores adjusted in order to preclude placement in classes for the mentally retarded (the adjusted score is called an ELP, estimated learning potential, score). Conceptually, the use of the ELP is similar to a veteran's preference (Elliott, 1987).

Many noted psychologists also provided testimony supporting the use of intelligence tests. Well-known measurement experts such as Dr. Lloyd Humphries, Dr. Robert Thorndike, and Dr. Jerome Doppelt testified in the case. Measurement experts provided considerable evidence that the WISC-R was not biased. Dr. Nadine Lambert of the University of California at Berkeley testified in support of the use of intelligence tests, suggesting that teachers were the most important variable in making placement decisions and that because of the high teacher referral rate of minority group children, there was overrepresentation in classes for the mentally retarded.

Data in support of teacher referral as a biasing factor were collected by Ashurst and Meyers (1973) (as cited in Elliott, 1987). These data from the Riverside, California, school system showed that the population of the school system at the time was 80% White, 8% Black, and 11% Latino. Of the 257 children referred and studied in the investigation, 48% were Anglo, 20% were Black, and 31% were Latino. The percentage of different ethnic groups actually placed in special education classes were 41% White, 20% Black, and 30% Latino. These results supported Lambert's argument that teacher referral is the major arbiter in the special education decision for the mental retardation placement.

PASE

The 1980 *PASE* case came to the opposite conclusion of the *Larry P.* case, although much of the testimony was the same. The acronym PASE stands for Parents in Action on Special Education. Most of the individuals involved in the lawsuit were Latino. The organizer of the case, Dan Merquez, was a student interning in an EMR classroom in a heavily Latino area of the city. He thought that many of the students were inappropriately placed in the class because of linguistic differences (Elliott, 1987). Elliott (1987) provides interesting information on the social milieu of the *PASE* case and its differences from that of the *Larry P.* case. For example, by the time of the filing of the *PASE* case, most of the central office administration of the Chicago Public Schools were minority group members. In addition, the vast proportion of students in the Chicago public schools were minorities.

Judge Grady was very interested in obtaining data on the individual Wechsler items, and his interest was clearly peaked by the controversy over the famous WISC-R "fight" item. This comprehension item asked what a boy or girl should do if a child much smaller than himself or herself should start to pick a fight. This item was identified in the *Larry P.* case as an inappropriate item for a Black child from a ghetto, because these children would customarily get the item wrong because the most adaptive response in their harsh environment would be to fight back. Judge Grady was very impressed by the research on this item. Contrary to the testimony in the *Larry P.* case, the item was found to be easier for African American than for Anglo children (Elliott, 1987). Judge Grady apparently expended considerable time on his own study of Wechsler and Stanford-Binet items and identified some as potentially biased. Regardless, Judge Grady decided in favor of the Chicago Board of Education, indicating that the bias identified in the Wechsler and Binet items was not substantial.

The issue of overrepresentation, which was central to many of these cases, can also be overstated by the use of statistics. For example, while 10% of the population in a particular school system might be minority, it sounds like a gross amount of overrepresentation to have 20% of the children in EMR classes to be minority. However, when one looks at the absolute numbers, this is still a relatively small proportion of African American children. Consider the hypothetical example where 90% of the children are Anglo and 10% are minority, and 100 of the children in the school district were placed in EMR classes in a given year. If minority children were 100% overrepresented, then the make-up of the class of mentally retarded children would be 20% minority children and 80% White children. If there were 10,000 students in the entire school system, of the 1,000 minority children in the school system (10% of the 10,000 children), 20 are in classes for the mentally retarded. The 20 children represent 2% of the entire minority population. When the statistics are presented in this fashion, the rate of special education placement whereby minority children are 100% overrepresented in classes for the mildly retarded does not sound nearly as aberrant. Because of such caveats the statistics offered in these court cases had to be considered very carefully since only a small proportion of the school-age population is identified as having mental retardation.

Marshall v. Georgia (1984)

This case was brought against rural school districts in the state of Georgia by the NAACP. It argued that instructional grouping and placement practices were discriminatory. The *Marshall* case heard considerable testimony by numerous experts in assessing mental retardation and intellectual development. As was the case with Judge Grady, the grouping and placement practices were upheld.

Elliott (1987), in his extensive and thoughtful review of these and other court cases, drew the conclusion that court decisions regarding the use of tests have not substantially helped minority group children nor have they impacted test use. He suggested that what is needed is strong leadership, patience, and the expenditure of large sums of money to help disadvantaged children of all ethnic groups.

Effects of Court Decisions

One of the clearest impacts of these cases has been an increase in research on test bias issues.

Judge Grady's consternation at a lack of item bias data for the WISC-R (Elliott, 1987) was one factor that undoubtedly spawned a number of studies on WISC-R item bias. Now it is ordinary and customary practice for new tests of intelligence to have investigated bias in judgmental and statistical fashion prior to publication. Furthermore, it will be increasingly likely that new tests will assess construct validity bias prior to publication. Some good examples of the consideration of bias in the development of item pools are given in the K-ABC and DAS manuals.

There has for many years been a hesitancy to place minority group children in classes for the mentally retarded. This reluctance had to be reinforced by the attention that intelligence testing received in the courts in the 1970s. This in turn may be one of the factors that has decreased placement rates in classes for the mildly retarded. Potentially another factor is a lack of convincing effectiveness research for special education of the mildly retarded. EMR enrollment in California went from an all-time high of 58,000 children in EMR classrooms for the years 1968–69 to only 12,000 to 13,000 in 1984 (Elliott, 1987). This prevalence rate for EMR children is lower than the rate for moderate mental retardation. Elliott (1987) has argued that many of these children have been picked up for services in the less stigmatizing learning disabilities program or other remedial programs.

These court cases also spawned a search for new assessment approaches. One of the most favored assessment approaches to come from this era was the SOMPA (described in the next section). These trials also increased interest in test-teach-test assessment paradigms. The most popular such paradigm of the 1970s was Feuerstein's Learning Potential Assessment Device (LPAD). The dynamic assessment model of Feuerstein emphasizes the malleability of intelligence. This paradigm emphasizes an initial assessment, then the application of the intervention program, and a subsequent posttesting.

Another popular adaptation of intelligence tests that could potentially be related to the litigation of the 1970s is the increasing availability of nonverbal scales. Nonverbal scales presumably would allow the scores to be less influenced by cultural and linguistic differences. There has been a burst of new entries in the nonverbal intelligence market (see Chapter 16).

THE SOMPA ALTERNATIVE

One proposed solution to the issues posed by the *Larry P.* case was the *System of Multicultural Pluralistic Assessment (SOMPA)* (Mercer, 1979). The SOMPA, created by Dr. Jane Mercer, had several aims for attacking the overrepresentation problem, including (1) adjusting IQ scores based on social and cultural differences in order to prevent overrepresentation, (2) offering a variety of domains of assessment to consider when making special education decisions, and (3) using Spanish-language materials for the assessment of Latino children and their families.

To fulfill these goals the SOMPA had to be comprehensive, including the medical, social, and pluralistic components. These included:

MEDICAL

1. Physical Dexterity Tasks
2. Bender-Gestalt Test
3. Visual Acuity
4. Auditory Acuity
5. Health History Inventory

SOCIAL

1. Adaptive Behavior Inventory for Children (ABIC) (a parent report adaptive behavior scale)
2. Wechsler Intelligence Scale for Children—Revised (WISC-R)

PLURALISTIC

1. *Sociocultural scales.* These assess the degree to which a child's culture differs from the dominant Anglo culture.

2. *Estimated learning potential.* This score is computed based on multiple regression techniques that use the sociocultural scales to "adjust" the child's WISC-R IQs according to his or her own culture (Anglo, Latino, African American). This score is intended to project how a child may perform if all impediments to learning, such as language differences, were removed.

The SOMPA was normed in the early 1970s on a California sample of 2,100 public school children aged 5 to 11 years. There were 700 Latinos, 700 African Americans, and 700 Anglos. Parent interviews were conducted by fluent bilingual examiners, and child testing was completed by qualified examiners.

While the SOMPA originally seemed like a reasonable approach, it has fallen into disuse. Why is this? The predictive validity of the ELP score is the primary culprit. Say, for example, a child obtains a Full Scale IQ score of 78 and an ELP of 94. What does this mean? Many psychologists had trouble grappling with this issue because they knew that the child was referred because of academic problems and that the Full Scale was fairly predictive of school achievement. How could the more optimistic prediction of the ELP be brought about? This question and others did not have clear answers. There are, however, clear answers to the predictive validity question regarding the ELP score.

The most impressive study in this area was conducted by Figueroa and Sassenrath (1989). These researchers were able to find 1,184 of the original SOMPA standardization participants and retest them approximately a decade later in 1981–83. At this point the children were all in high school. This sample does have some problems, however, since it only includes children that were still in school. Certainly this is a skewed sample since the dropout rates, especially for impoverished children, are distressingly high. The original Full Scale and ELP scores were correlated with student's reading and mathematics scores from the Stanford Achievement Test and various GPAs.

The results are generally congruent with clinician's impressions that the ELP score would not show better predictive validity than the regular Wechsler IQs. Predictive validities for the IQs and ELPs were consistently in the .40s and .50s. There were no differences across ethnic group or level of SES with one exception. For the African American children at the lowest level of SES there was some slight superiority for the predictive validity of the ELP. This finding, however, could be explained by sampling error. Since these were impoverished children who did not drop out of school, they may have some special characteristics that allowed them to "beat the odds." Figueroa and Sassenrath (1989) concluded that

> For all three ethnic groups, VIQ correlated slightly but consistently higher with all the achievement measures than did VIQ-ELP.... Consequently, VIQ rather than VIQ-ELP generally appears to be the more sensitive predictor of school achievement. (p. 17)

It is also possible that the ELP is a viable construct but was simply poorly executed (Figueroa & Sassenrath, 1989). It could also be that the value of the ELP does not rest with prediction but with focusing treatment goals. Both the Wechsler Full Scale and ELP long-term predictive validity coefficients found in the Figueroa and Sassenrath (1989) investigation are low to moderate. Although it sounds axiomatic, these results show that there are factors above and beyond the Wechsler scores that are important to consider when gauging a child's needs in order to provide educational/cognitive intervention.

A. R. van den Berg (1986) proposed a score similar to an ELP but offered it for very different uses. He essentially advocated computing a "range of reaction" for each child tested. He first computed an SEDIQ (socioeconomically deprived IQ). This is the norm-referenced score for the low-SES child living in an English-dominant society. It is presumed that this score is depressed in these cases because of the known relationship between environmental factors and intelligence scores. Van den Berg (1986) cited the environmental factors identified by Thorndike and Hagen (1977) as the causative agents for this low score. These factors included

1. a home language other than "standard" English.

2. home values that do not emphasize school learning.

3. home, social, and economic factors that may interfere with development.

4. undereducated parents that cannot function as teachers for their children.

5. a feeling of separation and alienation from the dominant culture.

The next score derived by van de Berg is the PROIQ (projected IQ). This score is like an ELP. It is an SEDIQ (obtained IQ) that is adjusted by a measure of the child's difference from the norm based on the socioeconomic factors identified by Thorndike and Hagen (1977) above. Van den Berg (1986), however, departed from Mercer's notion of the ELP. He stated that

I am not in favour of the notion that the IQ score of a socioeconomically deprived testee should be adjusted routinely in the hope that this will compensate for his handicap. This kind of "compensation" is simply an illusion because it can make no real change in the testee's ability to solve intellectual problems in the scientifically and technologically based culture. (p. 20)

He continued by describing the PROIQ by saying that

The PROIQ index estimates the IQ that could be expected for the deprived pre-adolescent if intensive long-term remedial treatment, which would include improving his environment but exclude direct training in answering IQ tests, were given to him. (p. 21)

If this sounds familiar, it should. Van den Berg is advocating "peeling" the phenotype just as was proposed by Haywood in his transactional theory (see Chapter 2). Van den Berg (1986) also maintains that successful achievement of the

PROIQ is rare in reality because interventions are not strong or lengthy enough. Preschool interventions, for example, often result in the child going home after school to an environment that still has one of the risk factors identified above. Environments work both ways, both to gradually foster or hamper intellectual development (van den Berg, 1986). The range of reaction notion is important for test interpretation. This concept, supported by the nearly equivalent predictive validity of obtained and adjusted IQ scores (Figueroa & Sassenrath, 1989), means that outcomes may differ considerably for individuals with the same scores.

DEFINING THE ISSUES

In addition to suggesting new methodologies for assessing intelligence, court cases have served to define the issues of intelligence test use more clearly. Test bias has always been a difficult issue to discuss because it is so imbedded in other issues. Hence, in order to consider issues of test bias one must first define the issues involved. One source of confusion is the nature/nurture debate. The public, and some professionals, seem to take the news that one cultural group has a higher mean score than another cultural group as evidence of either genetic inferiority or superiority. The conclusion of genetic differences has nothing to do with the issue of whether or not a test is biased (Reynolds & Kaiser, 1990).

Another common source of confusion is the relationship between special education and test bias. If one cultural group scores lower than others, then more members of this group would be diagnosed as mildly retarded—a label considered abhorrent by many parents, including myself. Not only is the label stigmatizing, but as a parent I would be concerned that my child not be "warehoused" and thus not receive a quality instructional program. Here the issue of the effectiveness of special education becomes intertwined with intelligence test bias. This source of confusion highlights the relationship between test bias and differential impact. It is this latter issue that has led to many of the court cases regarding the use of intelligence tests.

Unfortunately, most of the research on intelligence tests does not address directly these "larger" issues. The wealth of data available focuses on the properties of tests per se, rather than on some equally interesting issues such as the reasons for referring more children from one cultural group for a psychological evaluation than others, the effectiveness of special education, stigmatization associated with being diagnosed as mentally retarded, and the relationship between stigmatization and a child's achievement motivation.

The point of this prelude is to emphasize that *there is much more to the test bias issue than the research on bias in intelligence tests*. It is for this reason that the last section of this chapter focuses on test use. There is a specific concern about the overuse of intelligence tests by less qualified individuals who may misuse the results or let tests make the decisions rather than depend on the judgment of a highly trained professional (Kaufman, 1990).

Even a moratorium on the use of intelligence tests would likely not eliminate injustice and poor instruction of children. Unfortunately, such assaults on children predate the invention of intelligence tests. Jensen (1980) explained why the elimination of tests will not solve child problems:

> The answers to questions about test bias surely need not await a scientific consensus on the so-called nature-nurture question. A proper assessment of test bias, on the other hand, is an essential step towards a scientific understanding of the observed differences in all the important educational, occupational, and social correlates of test scores. Test scores themselves are merely correlates, predictors, and indicators, of other socially important variables, which would not be altered in the least if tests did not exist. The problem of individual differences and group differences would not be made to disappear by abolishing tests. One cannot treat a fever by throwing away a thermometer. (p. xi)

SCIENTIFIC STUDIES OF BIAS

Mean Score Differences

One of the conventional pieces of wisdom regarding test bias is that if two cultural groups, linguistic groups, or racial groups obtain mean score differences on a test, then the test is biased against one group or another. It is difficult to determine how this logic became applied to intelligence tests, but this has been this case. This view has served to distort somewhat the issue of intelligence test bias because essentially the issue of mean score differences between cultural groups is irrelevant (Reynolds & Kaiser, 1990; Thorndike, 1971). If intelligence tests did not produce mean score differences between groups such as younger children and older children, they would be worthless. The essence of any type of psychological or physical test is for the measure to be able to discriminate among individuals and groups of individuals. In almost all other types of measures, mean score differences between cultural groups exist. For example, it is well documented that certain groups of children are on average shorter than others. Similarly, men are consistently taller than women as indicated by tests of height. In all these incidences, we do not say that the test is biased because it measures height, medical condition, or whatever. However, when it comes to intelligence and academic achievement testing, the lay public is much more willing to consider mean score differences as evidence of bias in the test.

The Psychometric Approach

In some cases, however, even the mean differences in intelligence are small between groups. Jensen and Whang (1993) found few significant differences in reaction time between Chinese American and Anglo-American children. Psychometric studies of test bias do not consider the issue of mean score differences as a meaningful test of bias. Hence, when people talk of test bias, they may be talking about vastly different issues than lay individuals or others who are unfamiliar with the science of measurement. The psychometrician is assessing the validity of an intelligence test across groups as opposed to evaluating mean score differences. In this approach to bias, there would have to be evidence that the *construct validity* for an intelligence test differs across groups. Numerous studies have addressed these technical issues. For the purpose of this chapter, the definition of test bias offered by Reynolds and Kaiser (1990) is most appropriate.

> *"Test bias" refers in a global sense to* systematic *error in the estimation of some "true" value for a group of individuals. The key word here is "systematic"; all measures contain error, but this error is assumed to be random unless shown to be otherwise. Bias investigation is a statistical inquiry that does not concern itself with culture loading, labeling effects, or test use/test fairness. (p. 624)*

Content Validity Bias

Bias in content validity was one of the first areas of investigation of intelligence test bias. This is highly understandable given that the scoring criteria for many intelligence test items seem arbitrary and were devised primarily by Anglo males and females. WISC-III comprehension items are especially prone to arguments of inappropriate content or bias. Again, a very helpful definition of content validity bias may be taken from Reynolds and Kaiser (1990).

> *An item or subscale of a test is considered to be biased in content when it is demonstrated to be relatively more difficult for members of one group than for members of another in a situation where the general ability level of the groups being compared is held constant and no reasonable theoretical rationale exist to explain group differences on the item (or subscale) in question. (p. 625)*

Numerous procedures have been proposed for assessing bias in individual items, but the logic behind item bias detection techniques is fairly simple. The central aspect of most statistical methods that assess for bias across cultural or gender groups is at the first step in the procedure, which is to match the groups on overall score (ability) level. If one, for example, was looking for gender bias in a pool of intelligence test items, one would first match boys and girls on their overall intelligence test score, be it standard or raw score. So if one wanted to evaluate biased items in the Differential Ability Scales, for example, one would first statistically group the cases with perhaps all of the boys and girls with composite standard scores above 150 as one group, those between 140 and 149 as another group, those between 130 and 139 as another group and so on (it should be understood that this is not the exact procedure used by most item bias techniques but an oversimplification of such procedures). Then some statistical test of significance is applied to see if within these various ability groups there are still significant differences in difficulty for the items for one gender group or another. A similar approach to this was used in the development of the K-ABC. Most of these items were removed from the K-ABC; however, some were retained (Kamphaus & Reynolds, 1987). For example, Item 15 of Gestalt Closure was biased against boys at age 7 only and item 37 of the Arithmetic subtest was biased against girls only at age 11. These items were likely retained because although they were biased, it was only at a particular age group. Item 15 on Gestalt closure is a crown, and item 37 on Arithmetic requires the child to round a four-digit number.

As is obvious from these examples, it is oftentimes difficult to interpret the results of the statistical analysis of item bias on a particular test. Why would the crown item be biased against boys, and only 7-year-old boys, and why is only one Arithmetic rounding item, the second-most difficult on the test, biased only against girls who are age 11? Why not 10-year-old or 12-year-old girls? It appears that it would require a rather rich imagination on the part of the test developer to determine why some of these items are biased against one gender or cultural group.

This discussion relates to another popular item bias technique, that of using judgmental bias reviews. The procedure used by many publishers is to have groups of individuals review the items carefully. This procedure ensures that members of a number of cultural groups review the items to determine not only potential bias but also items that may be insulting or inappropriate for various cultural groups. Many tests in the past such as the K-ABC used Anglo male and female reviewers, African American reviewers, and Latino item reviewers. This procedure resulted in a few items being removed from the K-ABC (Kamphaus & Reynolds, 1987). One of these items so removed was a vacuum cleaner from the Gestalt Closure subtest. One of the Latino reviewers remarked that in the inner-city environment where she worked, many Latino children lived in apartments where brooms were used in lieu of vacuum cleaners. There is, however, a great deal of disagreement between judgmental reviews of items and statistical analyses of bias. It appears that statistical analyses of bias are more reliable (Reynolds & Kaiser, 1990). In another investigation of judgmental bias reviews, Sandoval and Mille (1979) compared the ratings of 45 WISC-R items by 38 African American, 22 Mexican American, and 40 Anglo undergraduate students. Their study found that minority and nonminority judges did not differ in their ability to identify culturally biased items. The conclusions of Sandoval and Mille (1979) were that "(1) judges are not able to detect items which are more difficult for a minority child than for an Anglo child, and (2) the ethnic background of the judges makes no difference in accuracy of item selection for minority children" (p. 6). It should also be noted that in the Sandoval and Mille investigation, the most biased items were used from the WISC-R to try to make it easier for the judges to select biased items.

Now the most important question regarding this line of research is not these technical issues but whether or not very popular tests of intelligence such as the WISC-III are riddled with biased items for cultural groups, gender, geographic region, or whatever. Results suggest that this is not the case. Numerous studies (Jensen,

1976; Mille, 1979; Sandoval, 1979) have found that anywhere from 2% to 5% of the variance in the WISC-R was due to biased items. Also, it is important to note that the biased items in the WISC-R seemed to work in various directions: against boys, in favor of boys, against Anglos, in favor of Anglos, and so on.

Substitute Canadian item content for the WISC Information subtest has been added for Canadian examiners. Yet Beal (1988) found no empirical justification for doing so.

Construct Validity Bias

A workable definition of construct validity bias by Reynolds and Kaiser (1990) suggests that

Bias exists in regard to construct validity when a test is shown to measure different hypothetical traits (psychological constructs) for one group or another, or to measure the same trait but with differing degrees of accuracy. (p. 632)

The most popular method used for the study of construct validity bias is factor analysis. Numerous researchers have used similar procedures. The central characteristic of these procedures is to conduct factor analyses separately for various cultural and gender groups. Since the WISC-R was the target of early court cases in the 1970s, it was the recipient of the largest number of factor analytic investigations. Reschly (1978) compared the factor structure of the WISC-R for groups of Anglo, African American, Mexican American, and Native American children. All of these children were from the southwestern United States. Reschly compared two factor solutions across the various cultural groups and found substantially high correlations among the factor solutions across groups. The most popular procedure used for assessing the agreement between the factor structures across groups is a coefficient of congruence, which is interpreted similarly to a correlation coefficient. Reschly found coefficients of congruence across groups to range from .97 to .99, in other words, near perfect congruence of factors across these four cultural groups for the WISC-R. These findings suggest that in terms of factor structure, the WISC-R was virtually identical across these four groups and no evidence of bias was present. Other studies have come to the identical conclusions of Reschly (Vance & Wallbrown, 1978; Wherry & Wherry, 1969). Oakland and Feigenbaum (1979) factor analyzed the WISC-R separately for samples of nonhandicapped African American, Anglo, and Mexican American children from an urban area in the southwestern United States. Pearson coefficients were used to assess the similarity of factors for each group. The first unrotated "g" factor showed an Anglo/African American correlation of .95 and a Mexican American/Anglo correlation of .97. The lowest correlation among factors to be found in this investigation was still high at .94. The authors concluded that there is no evidence of construct validity bias for the WISC-R in this investigation. Gutkin and Reynolds (1980, 1981) conducted two large-scale investigations of construct validity bias for the WISC-R. The first investigation (1980) involved comparing the factor structure of the WISC-R for samples of referred children including Anglo American and Mexican American children. Coefficients of congruence for this investigation ranged from .91 to .99. Similarly, the second investigation (Gutkin & Reynolds, 1981) of the WISC-R standardization sample comparing African American and Anglo American children produced coefficients of congruence in the 90s. Similar studies of construct validity bias have been conducted for the WISC-III (Roid & Warrall, 1997), the WISC-R and Chinese children (Dai & Lynn, 1994), McCarthy Scales (Kaufman & DiCuio, 1975), the WPPSI (Kaufman & Hollenbeck, 1974), and the K-ABC (Reynolds, Willson, & Chatman, 1985). There is also one factor analytic study of the K-ABC for separate groups of boys and girls (Kamphaus & Kaufman, 1986). All of these investigations have resulted in similar findings—a great deal of similarity of factor structure across ethnic and gender groups. These results then mimic the findings for content validity bias in that evidence of bias is difficult to find and erratic when it does occur. The final type of bias that has received a great deal of attention in the adult personnel selection literature is bias in predictive validity.

Predictive Validity Bias

A working definition of predictive validity bias as adapted from Cleary, Humphreys, Kendrick, and Wesman (1975) by Reynolds and Kaiser (1990) is as follows:

A test is considered biased with respect to predictive validity if the inference drawn from the test score is not made with the smallest feasible random error or if there is constant error in an inference for prediction as a function of membership in a particular group. (p. 638)

The issue regarding predictive or criterion-related validity is that these coefficients should not differ significantly across cultural or gender group. One of the typical procedures in this research literature is to compare the predictive validity coefficients across groups. A study by Glutting (1986) is an excellent example of such an investigation. This investigation studied the predictive validity of the K-ABC for 146 Anglo, African American, and Puerto Rican children from the New York City metropolitan area. In addition, the Puerto Rican sample was subdivided into English-dominant children and into Spanish-dominant children. The predictive validity coefficients found for this investigation were strikingly similar across ethnic and linguistic groups. That is, the magnitudes of the coefficients were very similar. Comparing the magnitude of the coefficients as Glutting did by collecting a sample, administering an intelligence test, and administering a criterion test, such as an achievement test at some subsequent date, is a common procedure. If Glutting would have found, for example, that the predictive validity coefficient for the K-ABC for the Anglo group was .90 and for the other groups was .30, this would be evidence of significant predictive validity bias and that the test is more predictive for the Anglo than for the other groups. This result, however, did not occur in this investigation. If it were to occur, this type of bias (different predictive validity coefficients) would be called *slope bias*. In order to understand the concept of slope bias, it is helpful to recollect how correlation coefficients are learned in introductory statistics courses. Such procedures are typically taught by having the students collect data on two variables and plotting the scores of a group of individuals on these two variables. This plot results in a scatter plot (see Chapter 5). Then students compute a correlation coefficient and draw a line of best fit through the scatter plot. This line of best fit is a visual representation of the slope (see Chapter 5). A correlation coefficient (predictive validity coefficient) of .90 would produce a very different slope than a correlation coefficient of .30. This is why this type of bias in predictive validity is referred to as slope bias. Studies of the WISC-R again have produced little evidence of slope bias.

Reynolds and Hartlage (1979) conducted a study of the predictive validity of the Full Scale standard scores from the WISC-R for African American and Anglo children who were referred for psychological services. In addition, they used the Potthoff (1966) technique to test for identity of the slopes or regression lines for the two groups for predicting reading and mathematics achievement. This study did not yield significant evidence of bias for the two groups. In a series of studies, Reynolds and colleagues (Reynolds & Gutkin, 1980a) conducted a predictive validity study of bias for Anglo and Mexican American children from the southwestern United States and found no evidence of bias. In another study by Reynolds, Gutkin, Dappen, and Wright (1979), no evidence of predictive validity bias was found for groups of boys and girls on the WISC-R. The WISC-III appears to vary little from its predecessors showing no evidence of slope bias for African American and Hispanic children or for gender (Weiss, Prifitera, & Roid, 1992).

There is one study that is something of an outlier as far as predictive validity bias goes, and this is a study by Goldman and Hartig (1976). This study used the 1949 WISC and compared predictive validity coefficients for African American, Mexican American, and Anglo children. It found adequate predictive validity coefficients for the Anglo children, but coefficients were not adequate for African American and Mexican American children. This is the only study to show such substantial evidence of predictive validity or slope bias. But it has been criticized on methodological grounds (Reynolds & Kaiser, 1990). This study is one of a very few to use "academic GPA" or school grades as a criterion measure of academic achievement. There were significant differences in the variances or range of scores between the Anglo children and the two other groups. This fact alone could account for the difference in predictive validity coefficients (see the discussion of restriction of range and how this may deflate correlation coefficients in Chapter 5). In addition, however, Reynolds and Kaiser suggest that the study may also be an outlier because of the use of GPA, a questionable and frequently unreliable measure of performance. They point out that academic GPA in this particular study also included grades in music, health, art, and physical education and that in these particular courses, it looked as if the students received exceedingly high grades producing little variability.

These studies of slope bias are strikingly similar to the studies of content validity and construct validity bias. Evidence of predictive validity bias is infrequent. When it does occur, it is often counterintuitive and inexplicable, as in the case of the Glutting analysis of the K-ABC. Thus the wealth of findings suggest that as far as most major tests of intelligence go, evidence of internal test bias is exceedingly difficult to document. Moreover, studies of personality test bias have produced similar results. A meta-analysis of 25 comparative studies of the MMPI for various ethnic groups over a 31-year period produced no evidence of bias, and highly similar mean scores, for all major U.S. ethnic groups (Hall, Bansal, & Lopez, 1999).

Summary Comments on Bias

The results of bias studies, many of which were conducted from the mid-1970s to the mid-1980s as a consequence of the numerous court cases in the 1970s, have turned up little substantial evidence of bias in modern tests of intelligence. This evidence suggests that intelligence tests are measures very similar to medical tests that have shown significant group differences. Group differences between intelligence test scores are likely real, but what they mean and the implications of the findings remain open to debate.

One view is that these results sound an alarm regarding the cognitive development of children. Just as differences in the prevalence rates of breast cancer, blood pressure, diabetes, and school dropout raise alarms as they afflict cultural groups differentially, so too, intelligence test scores that may differ across cultural groups should be a call to arms for those individuals concerned about the welfare of children. As van den Berg (1986) states aptly:

> *Inappropriate acceptance of the test bias hypothesis could therefore inadvertently maintain the poverty cycle; inadvertently for those who wish to break the cycle but perhaps advertently for those who might wish to maintain it. (p. 16)*

Another point of view is that intelligence testing and schooling is a cultural construction that should be aligned more closely with a culture's view of cognitive and social competency (Serpell, 1994). A study of rural Zambian children revealed that they systemmatically avoided school and labeled themselves unintelligent. They did so because they saw no chance of success in a rigidly hierarchical system with examinations required for promotion from one grade level to the next. They knew that often fewer than 20% of the children would typically be advanced to the next grade level. Yet, these children and families had

shown considerable adaptation to harsh environmental circumstances (Serpell, 1994). In this view intelligence testing, as is the case for schooling, may be viewed as an irrelevant enterprise for large groups of children if it is seen as disconnected from the culture's views. It is perhaps for this reason that the recent theory of multiple intelligences has captured the fancy of the public and some school personnel. Multiple intelligence theory may appeal to the public view that intelligence is a multifaceted construct (Sternberg, Conway, Ketron, & Bernstein, 1981) that includes social and practical intelligences that are not assessed by most tests. Toward this end, psychologists are beginning to strive to develop cultural and linguistic competencies to allow themselves to better understand the application of intelligence testing for diagnosis and treatment planning within various cultural contexts.

MULTICULTURAL EXPERTISE

Cultural plurality has posed a challenge to assessment and diagnostic practice since the early days of the "mental testers." The testing movement was forced early on to change tests and testing practice in the United States because of the tremendous influx of new immigrants. Between 1901 and 1910 over 9 million immigrants entered the United States. This figure represented more immigrants than the combined populations of New York, Maryland, and New Hampshire in 1900 (French & Hale, 1990).

The creation of new tests (e.g., SOMPA and nonverbal measures) has not proved sufficient to meet the assessment and diagnostic needs of a multicultural society because new tests cannot preclude poor interpretation. In many cases clinicians choose the wrong test and make inappropriate interpretations of the data (Shepard, 1989). Interpretations have often been simplistic and culturally bound, showing a lack of appreciation for cultural differences and traditions (see Research Report 6.1).

RESEARCH REPORT 6.1

Different Intelligences for Different Societies

Dasen (1984) proposes that while all cultures have terms roughly similar to the term *intelligence* (see Chapter 2), their emphasis on the component skills or abilities of this construct vary substantially. His expectation regarding the study of the Baoulé, an African culture, was that this illiterate cultural group would have a term corresponding to the Western term *intelligence*, but that its connotations would differ substantially. His study found that the Baoulé do have a comparable term for intelligence that is called *n'glouélê*. Dasen found several aspects of this term that differ from Western notions of intelligence. He found that among the adult Baoulé that were interviewed regarding the use of this term and its meaning the characteristic identified by most of the group members was that an individual with n'glouélê displayed a "readiness to carry out tasks in the service of the family and the community." This emphasis on social aspects of intelligence is characteristic of other research findings regarding African cultures. It is also interesting that the Baoulé refer to n'glouélê primarily in the future tense. He notes that they are reluctant to assess children in the present feeling that this particular characteristic is relatively malleable and may change through a variety of interventions. Similar to Western societies, however, they are willing to use current behavior as something of a predictor of future behavior. The various descriptors of n'glouélê that were given by the adults interviewed include the following:

Serviceableness and responsibility

Politeness, obedience, and respect

To retell a story with precision; verbal memory

To speak in a socially appropriate way

To act like an adult

Reflection, responsibility, and memory

Observation, attention, fast learning, and memory

Literacy, school intelligence

To be lucky, to bring luck

Manual dexterity, writing, and drawing

Dasen notes that there is some distinction in these descriptors of intelligent behavior between the social and the academic. Among this particular culture, the academic is deemed relatively useless unless it is applied to enhance the social well-being of the cultural group. Dasen (1984) thinks that it is this integration of the social and cognitive intelligences that makes this culture's view of intelligent behavior unique from that of Western societies.

The next part of the investigation was to test these adult conceptualizations of child intelligence by determining the extent to which Baoulé children show knowledge of concrete operations. Another interesting observation regarding cultural differences was that Dasen and his colleagues could not praise children as they performed the tasks as is typical of Piaget's clinical method. In this particular culture, praising a child may bring bad luck. After assessing the concrete operation skills of a sample of Baoulé children, the authors then had parents rate the children on the extent to which they possess n'glouélê (intelligence). These ratings were then correlated with performance on the Piaget concrete operation tasks. The correlations between three Piagetian tasks of space, conservation, and elementary logic yielded small and frequently negative correlations with the parents ratings of n'glouélê. School intelligence, for example, correlated –.74 with parent ratings of n'glouélê. The only consistent positive correlation between parent ratings of n'glouélê were with regard to otikpa (serviceableness). These correlations ranged from .03 to .23. The logical conclusion from these results was that parent ratings of n'glouélê value social intelligence to a greater extent, resulting in low and frequently negative correlations between parent ratings and Piagetian cognitive task performance. Further analyses of the data showed that parents were generally not concerned about a child's school marks and that spatial skills were not prized.

(Continues)

RESEARCH REPORT 6.1 (Continued)

Different Intelligences for Different Societies

While the results showed that certain cognitive skills were valued in the culture, they were only valued if they were put into the service of the culture group. Dasen (1984) made the following comments on cultural differences in intelligence based on these results.

> But are these implications valid only for African cultures? Could we, in the overindustrialized west, not learn something from the African definition of intelligence? . . . Our society values mainly intellectual skills, and uses these selfishly, in particular for developing more deadly weapons, over-exploiting non-renewable sources, and increasing its wealth at the expense of the third world. Wouldn't these skills be more useful if they were more integrated with social skills, in the service of the world as a community? (p. 431)

Few technological gains have been made in devising specific tests for specific populations. As Figueroa (1990) observes:

> Currently, bilingual testing is an art form. The tester must infer and estimate the impact of language, culture, and schooling in the English versions of intelligence tests, and then do the same with even more marginal tests in another language. (p. 687)

Inappropriate, ill-informed, or insensitive interpretations also apply to "clinical" data. An examiner may conclude that a 13-year-old girl of Asian heritage is socially introverted, shy, and perhaps in need of assertiveness training because of her behavior during an interview with a male clinician. She may have been demure and made no eye contact. The examiner may draw such a conclusion despite the fact that she appeared friendly and outgoing when she was observed on the school playground and seemed to interact more openly with her family members. This client may not in fact be pathologically shy, rather she may be adhering to a prohibition against making eye contact with a male because of her cultural values, which suggest that this is a highly sexually seductive behavior (or an indication of a lack of respect) that is deemed inappropriate for her (Hasegawa, 1989). In this case the clinician was simply ignoring relevant data, and the clinician's lack of familiarity with the child's culture resulted in an erroneous interpretation.

Malgady and Constantino (1998) found that bilingual Hispanic examiners identified significantly more symptoms in bilingual Hispanic patients than Anglo examiners. One of their conclusions was that Anglo clinicians lacked adequate cultural knowledge, resulting in underdiagnosis.

Another example of the importance of multicultural knowledge may help clarify the need for such knowledge. Perhaps a psychologist is working in a multicultural neighborhood where most of the inhabitants are children of African and Indian/Pakistani decent and Italian American children are in the minority. Yet the Italian immigrant children are making up a large percentage of the referrals for mental health services, much larger than would be expected based on their proportions in the neighborhood. A psychologist who is not schooled in multicultural research may conclude that there is something awry with the Italian American family, physical constitution, or whatever. However, the psychologist who is familiar with multicultural issues may more appropriately conclude that community/preventive interventions may be most appropriate since research shows that *minority status itself is a stressor* for any cultural group. Mintz and Schwartz (1964, cited in Gibbs & Huang, 1989), for example, found that Whites living in Black areas had an incidence of psychosis about 313% higher than Whites who lived in communities where they were the majority.

Within cultural groups, variability can also be substantial (Zuckerman, 1990). It may be assumed by some that Vietnamese and Chinese children have similar values due to earlier Chinese domination and inculcation with Confucian ethic. There have also been other influences on this culture that may affect a child's behavior including European Roman Catholicism brought by the French conquest of 1958, the influence of American culture from the Vietnam War, and Buddhist influences from neighboring Cambodia (Huang, 1990). Classifying children by race, culture, or language background is an appealing approach for researchers and clinicians alike that is fraught with errors primarily due to the tendency to overgeneralize about a particular group of people (Zuckerman, 1990).

Incla'n and Herron (1989) cite the "culture of poverty" as another subculture that may affect a variety of groups. This "culture" is formed by a clash between those who have achieved material wealth and prosperity and those who struggle to achieve economic parity with little hope of doing so. Children reared in a culture of poverty possess characteristics such as an orientation to present time, inability to delay gratification, impulsivity, sense of predetermined fate, resentment of authority, alienation and distrust of others, and lack of emphasis on rigor, discipline, and perseverance (Incla'n & Herron, 1989). Incla'n and Herron (1989) note that some impoverished parents of adolescents may be assessed by a therapist as being too rigid and controlling of their youngsters at a time when parents should be allowing their children more freedom. It is possible, however, that poor parents may be all too familiar with the culture of poverty, and they may be seeking control not for its own sake but rather to ensure that their child or adolescent does not fall prey to the negative consequences of behavior associated with a culture of poverty (Incla'n & Herron, 1989).

More than anything else clinicians have to develop an enlarged knowledge base in order to deal effectively with their referral population. Just as clinicians have to have knowledge of behavioral principles, psychometrics, child development, child psychopathology, and physiological psychology to conduct an evaluation competently, it is increasingly clear that they must know the history, culture, and language of their community extremely well in order to not use assessment procedures inappropriately and make naive interpretations. One source of such knowledge may be university coursework in the history and culture of Appalachia, Puerto Rico, Cuba, Uganda, Korea, Hungary and the like, depending on the nature of the local population being served by the clinician.

Assessing Multilingual Children

One advised alternative for the assessment of children for whom English is not their primary language is to use a translation of a popular intelligence test. This practice, however, is fraught with problems, including the fact that once the test is translated its psychometric properties are unknown (Figueroa, 1989) (see Research Report 6.2). It may be that if the WISC-R were to be used with a Spanish-speaking population, for example, it would have to be created anew. In fact, problems of translation can occur even if minor changes are made in an item. I was reminded of this when I attended a conference in Canada where the metric system is used. There was concern expressed about an Arithmetic item on an intelligence test that involved calculating miles per hour from the miles driven in a specified time period. Would this item remain in the same difficulty order on the test if the metric were changed to kilometers? I don't know, but the item would definitely involve larger numbers. At any rate, if there are difficulties with changes within the English language, one can imagine the potential problems when an entire test is translated.

A second popular assessment choice is to use a nonverbal test with non-English-speaking children. This practice, however, has also been questioned, as it has been argued that these measures are less predictive of future academic achievement (Figueroa, 1990).

A third approach is to take an English test and administer it via a translator. As one can imagine

RESEARCH REPORT 6.2

Problems in Constructing Equivalent Tests

A fascinating and detailed study by Valencia and Rankin (1985) highlights the difficulty involved in creating equivalent instruments in different cultural and linguistic groups. The authors conducted a study of the standard English version of the McCarthy Scales of Children's abilities and a Spanish translation of the McCarthy. The subjects of their study were 304 children with a mean age of 4 1/2 years. All of these were Head Start children or children from public school-sponsored preschool programs. The Hollingshead two-factor index of social position was used to determine socioeconomic status. The majority of the children were from working-class backgrounds, and their socioeconomic status was determined to be very low by the Hollingshead.

The language status of the children was evaluated using teacher judgment, knowledge of parental language, language spoken to the child by the parents, examiner judgment as determined by conversation repertoire established the day before testing, and child preference. For a child to be classified as either English or Spanish speaking, there had to be total agreement for these five sources of information. In addition, the verbal subtest protocols of the McCarthy were evaluated to determine if there were any language switching on individual items. An extremely small number of children were judged to be bilingual based upon this review and were eliminated from the study. The resulting sample included 142 children who were classified as English-language dominant and 162 children who were classified as Spanish dominant.

The English-language children were administered the standard McCarthy scale. The Spanish-language children were administered a translated version of the McCarthy that was developed for research purposes. This Spanish-language McCarthy was developed by researchers with the assistance of bilingual preschool teachers and a Spanish professor. The goal was to develop a Spanish-language version that was as close as possible to the English-language McCarthy. The examiners were bilingual Mexican American women. The motor tasks were not administered to either group.

An item-by-group partial correlation was used to determine item bias. This method basically determines the proportion of variance of any individual item that is due to language differences because total score (ability), age, and gender are partialed out. This method seems to do a good job of controlling for overall ability level.

The results reveal that 6 of the 16 McCarthy subtests showed some evidence of bias. Bias is indicated by a significant partial correlation between language and subtest score. The two drawing tests of the McCarthy showed a mild bias effect in favor of the Spanish-speaking children. Four of the tests showed more substantial and consistent bias in favor of English-speaking children. In particular, the Numerical Memory I test had 16% of its variance attributed to the language the child speaks ($r = .40$). In order to explore the nature of the observed bias in greater detail, the

this introduces further complications into the interpretation of the results. As Figueroa (1989) states:

> When a psychologist uses an interpreter, the child is at risk and the psychologist is at risk. There is no empirically validated model for training or using an interpreter. There is no data indicating the operative conditions necessary to insure that the one-on-one experience of an English-speaking child is comparable to the one-on-one experience of an LEP [limited English proficient] child with her/his psychologist and interpreter. There is no information on which tests to use in this process, though

> some have argued that only with psychometrically valid tests in the child's primary language can an interpreter be used. There is no cross-cultural data on how children from different cultures and languages respond to two unknown adults asking decontextualized questions and presenting progressively more complex problems. Finally, there is no recognition of the legal distinctions that can be raised about which linguistic groups may have to be tested with an interpreter. (p. 19)

So what is a clinician to do? Well, it seems intuitive that a clinician will undoubtedly encounter a situation where cultural/linguistic differences

RESEARCH REPORT 6.2 (Continued)
Problems in Constructing Equivalent Tests

authors investigated item bias on the McCarthy. Of the 157 McCarthy items, they identified 23 that were biased. Of these, 6 were biased against the English-language group and 17 were biased against the Spanish-language group. Notably, the 6 items biased against the English-language group were spread across a variety of subtests suggesting a more random effect. The bias against the Spanish-language children was centralized on 2 measures of Serial Order Short-term Memory: Verbal Memory I and Numerical Memory I.

The authors reviewed research on variables affecting memory performance in order to explain this significant bias. They cite two effects, the Word Length effect and the Acoustic Similarity effect, as explanations for this difference. The Word Length effect states that words with more syllables increase the short-term memory load and thus reduce the number of words that may be recalled. They tested for the presence of this effect by reviewing the number of syllables involved in the English and Spanish words included on these two subtests. They cite the well-known phenomenon that Spanish words typically contain more syllables than their English equivalent. The number of English syllables in Verbal Memory I items was 44 for the English- and 73 for the Spanish-language version. Similarly, on Numerical Memory I, the English version included 28 syllables and the Spanish version, 48 syllables. These results indicate that the word length effect may be a plausible explanation for the poor performance of the Spanish-speaking children on these two subtests.

The Acoustic Similarity effect maintains that when words sound similar, they create confusion on part of the examinee. This lack of distinctiveness between stimuli on a memory task makes the memory task more difficult. The authors note that the Spanish language is less complex, involving only a 5-vowel system. On the other hand, the English language is considerably more complex, including an 11-vowel system. The authors made a count of the number of phonemes on Verbal Memory I and found that 23 Spanish phonemes were represented 160 times on this test whereas the 36 English phonemes were represented only 117 times. Again, there is evidence for the Acoustic Similarity effect in that the Spanish-speaking child heard more phonemes repeated thus decreasing the distinctiveness of the memory items.

The authors conclude by saying that Spanish versions of popular intelligence measures are likely to be developed and used. They also maintain that "It is critical that these tests meet the minimal psychometric properties of reliability and validity and are free of bias" (p. 206). Evidently, considerable care and sophisticated research and development will be necessary to construct equivalent forms of tests that are administered in different languages.

---

will be magnified (see Box 6.1). If possible (unfortunately, it usually is not) it would be best to refer to a psychologist that may share some linguistic similarity with the child. Frequently, linguistic differences are associated with cultural differences and a psychologist may unwittingly behave in a way that is insulting or intimidating to a child. In some cultures, for example, it is viewed as impolite or improper to show your teeth (as in smiling), a very high frequency behavior for those who assess children. López (1999) suggests that carrying out the evaluation in both English and the clients' other language yields more information than using one language alone.

It is also overly simplistic to give guidelines for cultural groups such as Hispanic, African American, Asian, and other cultural groups. These groups are not monoliths. The cultural and linguistic differences among Hispanic children, for example, are numbing. In constructing prediction equations for academic achievement for Asian American children, Sue and Abe (1988) found significant differences among Asian groups, including Chinese, Japanese, Koreans, Filipinos,

Box 6.1   Culturologic Interview

One way of gathering cultural information that may affect test score interpretation is to interview the client and/or a caregiver. Johnson-Powell (1997) provides just such an interview outline. My adaptation of her culturologic interview includes the following components.

Country of origin

Reason for immigration and time of arrival in new country

Number of generations in country

Language proficiency(ies)

Perceptions of social resources and family support

Proximity to members of their own cultural group

Religious beliefs and beliefs about causality of problems

Child-rearing practices of client or child perceptions

Sex roles

Kind of community of current residence (perceived cohesiveness, minority status, crime rate, housing patterns, etc.)

Life space (number of rooms and residents in household, numbers of children and adults)

Reasons for seeking help

Descriptions of help-seeking process/behavior

Socioeconomic (financial) status

Educational attainment

Current and/or former occupation

Experiences with rejection or racism

Degree of acculturation (food, attire, social activities)

Degree of cultural conflicts

---

and East Indians/Pakistanis. A comparable American example would be the various Native American tribes and their languages and cultures. For these reasons psychologists cannot expect to memorize a few simple rules about cultural values. Assessment situations will have to be individualized and perhaps improvised by the savvy clinician.

Here are some suggestions for dealing with linguistic differences in the intellectual assessment process.

1. Collect detailed background information on each case. Clinicians already typically collect various types of developmental, medical, and social history information. Multicultural expertise, however, requires the collection of information that may not be part of traditional history questionnaires. Castaneda (1976) gives an example of additional information that would be desirable for proper interpretation of the assessment data for a Mexican American child. He proposed that the following factors

may affect the acculturation and behavior of Mexican American students.

a. Length of residence in the United States

b. Distance from the Mexican border

c. Degree of urbanization

d. Degree of economic and political strength of Mexican Americans in the community

e. Identity with Mexican and/or Mexican American history

f. Degree of prejudice toward Mexican Americans in the community

Efforts to improve services in multicultural societies include the recruitment of multicultural providers and the use of intercultural teams (Gibbs & Huang, 1989).

2. Attempt to refer the child to a psychologist who speaks the child's native tongue. This examiner could use tests designed specifically for the child's linguistic group (e.g., there could

be some from the child's homeland, although often there will not be any) or administer non-verbal measures.

3. Failing this, the psychologist should consult with a community resource about the child's language and culture before proceeding with the evaluation. There are usually others in the community who speak the same language. Potential resources could include a parent, shopkeeper, office of bilingual education, or minister. One could also contact professional organizations such as the American Psychological Association for advice. These individuals could give advice as to how to interact with the child. They may also be willing to join the test session, much in the same way that parents will sometimes join a session, to help make the child feel more at ease. The examiner could then use a nonverbal measure of intelligence.

In these circumstances, however, the results may still be speculative. Hence, psychologists should make greater use of "therapeutic testing" with children who speak a language other than English. Many of us remember visits to the physician when the doctor told us to take an over-the-counter medication and get bed rest. In most cases we get better soon after. This is one type of therapeutic testing where the physician takes an educated guess that we are suffering from the common cold, prescribes treatment, and tells us to call back if we don't get better. If the therapy works, then the diagnosis must have been correct, hence, the term *therapeutic testing*. If the bilingual child scores extremely well on the intelligence test, we may want to have him or her try some enrichment classes to mitigate against boredom. If the child scores poorly, classes for children in need of remedial work could be advised. Regardless, these should be *tentative, short-term, therapeutic tests* that should be reevaluated consistently by consulting with teachers and parents in an ongoing fashion (probably at least once a week) to make modifications in the "treatment" as necessary. This process will also allow the psychologist to collect more long-term data on the

child and assess the trajectory of his or her cognitive development. In this paradigm the administration and scoring of the intelligence test is the *beginning of the assessment process, not the end result*. Actually, all children could likely benefit from such careful case management, but particularly those children for whom the psychologist feels less certain of the results.

CONCLUSIONS

Much progress has been made in exploring the issue of test bias. Litigation regarding assessment practices, and intelligence testing specifically, has created needed motivation to carefully consider the nature and use of such tests with children from diverse backgrounds. While bias internal to intelligence tests is rare, test overuse, misuse, and differential impact remain relatively commonplace.

Linguistic and cultural issues in the assessment process are the new fruitful areas for research and practice innovation. Clearly, the role of affluence and its impact on schooling and test performance is one of many areas needing study (Campbell, 1996; van deVijver, 1997). In the interim, consensual guidelines such as the *Guidelines for Providers of Psychological Services to Ethnic, Linguistic, and Culturally Diverse Populations* (APA, 1993) are advised.

CHAPTER SUMMARY

- The utility of intelligence tests for children of non-European descent or non-English-speaking background has been questioned since the early days of intelligence testing (French & Hale, 1990).

- Psychologists learned a great deal about intelligence test bias in the decades of the 1970s and 1980s.

- One of the first cases to question the use of so-called ability tests to make special education decisions for mental retardation placement—

the oft-used term is *educable mentally retarded* (EMR)—was the case of *Hobson v. Hansen* (1967).

- One result of the *Diana* case was to clearly identify the criterion of two standard deviations below the mean as the cutoff for mental retardation special education placement.

- The *Larry P. v. Riles* case began in 1971 when the plaintiffs representing Black children who were overrepresented in classes for the mentally retarded asked for an injunction against the use of intelligence tests in the San Francisco public schools.

- The 1980 *PASE* case came to the opposite conclusion of the *Larry P.* case, although much of the testimony was the same.

- The statistics offered in these court cases had to be considered very carefully since only a small proportion of the school-age population is identified as suffering from mental retardation.

- One proposed solution to the issues posed by the *Larry P.* case was the *System of Multicultural Pluralistic Assessment (SOMPA)* (Mercer, 1979).

- The ELP score does not show better predictive validity than the regular Wechsler scores.

- If intelligence tests did not produce mean score differences between groups such as younger children and older children, they would be worthless. Psychometric studies of test bias typically do not consider the issue of mean score differences as a meaningful test of bias.

- The central aspect of most statistical methods that assess for bias across cultural or gender groups is that the first step in the procedure is to match the groups on overall score (ability) level.

- There is a great deal of disagreement between judgmental reviews of items and statistical analyses of bias. It appears that statistical analyses of bias are more reliable (Reynolds & Kaiser, 1990).

- Numerous studies (Jensen, 1976; Mille, 1979; Sandoval, 1979) have found that anywhere from 2% of 5% of the variance in the WISC-R is due to biased items. Biased items in the WISC-R seem to work in various directions: against boys, in favor of boys, against Anglos, in favor of Anglos, and so on.

- The most popular method used for the study of construct validity bias is factor analysis.

- Content validity bias is difficult to find and erratic when it does occur.

- The results of bias studies, many of which were conducted from the mid-1970s to the mid-1980s as a consequence of the numerous court cases in the 1970s, have turned up little substantial evidence of bias in modern tests of intelligence.

- Between 1901 and 1910 over 9 million immigrants entered the United States. This figure represented more immigrants than the combined populations of New York, Maryland, and New Hampshire in 1900 (French & Hale, 1990).

- Mintz and Schwartz (1964, cited in Gibbs & Huang, 1989) found that Whites living in Black areas had an incidence of psychosis about 313% higher than Whites who lived in communities where they were the majority.

- Incla'n and Herron (1989) cite the "culture of poverty" as another subculture that may affect a variety of groups. This "culture" is formed by a clash between those who have achieved material wealth and prosperity and those who struggle to achieve economic parity with little hope of doing so.

- Translation of popular intelligence test such as the WISC for children for whom English is not their primary language is fraught with problems, including the fact that once the test is translated its psychometric properties are unknown (Figueroa, 1989).

CHAPTER 7

Practice Standards and Test Selection

When making inferences about a client's past, present, and future behaviors and other characteristics from test scores, the professional reviews the literature to develop familiarity with supporting evidence. (AERA, APA, NCME, 1999, p. 121)

CHAPTER QUESTIONS

Is it permissible to demonstrate the use of an intelligence test to a group of parents at a PTA meeting by administering a few items from the WISC-III?

How should a psychologist respond to a judicial mandate to release copies of test protocols (i.e., record forms)?

This chapter addresses three important areas of practice: test standards, ethics, and test selection. The first two topics are routinely considered in assessment texts but often not in a separate chapter so as to give them substantial emphasis. The issue of test selection is oft ignored. Intelligence

tests are becoming available in numerous shapes, sizes, and varieties. The last section of this chapter suggests to the clinician a framework for selecting a test in order to maximize the effectiveness of a given evaluation.

STANDARDS

The practicing clinician will be assaulted with new intelligence test offerings that will promise phenomenal results or features (Buros, 1963). Thus clinicians will have to know psychometric principles well in order to judge the quality of new methods. As Buros (1963) laments, clinicians are left to their own devices when judging the qualities of new measures (see Research Report 7.1) as publishers and test authors will sometimes make exaggerated claims that may confuse the uncritical clinician.

In order to make an informed decision about the purchase and use of a particular instrument, a standard is needed. Fortunately, considerable

RESEARCH REPORT 7.1

Buros' Lament

This is a rather unusual research report in that it is not a study per se but a statement by O. K. Buros on the relationship (or lack of it) between psychometric quality and test popularity. The amazing thing about this quote is its timeless nature. The same problems persist today, so test users should consider themselves forewarned.

At present, no matter how poor a test may be, if it is nicely packaged and if it promises to do all sorts of things which no test can do, the test will find many gullible buyers. When we initiated critical test reviewing (1938) we had no idea how difficult it would be to discourage the use of poorly constructed tests of unknown validity. Even the better informed test users who finally become convinced that a widely used test has no validity after all are likely to rush to use a new instrument which promises far more than any good test can possibly deliver. Counselors, personnel directors, psychologists, and school administrators seem to have an unshakable will to believe the exaggerated claims of test authors and publishers. If these users were better informed regarding the merits and limitations of their testing instruments, they would probably be less happy and less successful in their work. The test user who has faith—however unjustified—can speak with confidence in interpreting test results and in making recommendations. The well informed test user cannot do this; he knows that the best of our tests are still highly fallible instruments which are extremely difficult to interpret with assurance in individual cases. Consequently, he must interpret test results cautiously and with so many reservations that others wonder whether he really knows what he is talking about. Children, parents, teachers, and school administrators are likely to have a greater respect and admiration for a school counselor who interprets test results with confidence even though his interpretations have no scientific justification. The same applies to psychologists and personnel directors. Highly trained psychologists appear to be as gullible as the less well trained school counselor. It pays to know only a little about testing; furthermore, it is much more fun for everyone concerned—the examiner, examinee, and the examiner's employer.

It is difficult to allocate the blame for the lack of greater progress. We think, however, that the major blame rests with test users. The better test publishers would like to make more moderate claims for their tests. Unfortunately, test buyers don't want tests which make only moderate claims. Consequently, even the best test publishers find themselves forced by competition to offer test users what they want. Bad usage of tests is probably more common than good usage. Must it always be this way? We are afraid so.

From O. K. Buros. (1961). *Tests in Print: A Comprehensive Bibliography of Tests for Use in Education, Psychology and Industry*. Highland Park, New Jersey: Gryphon Press. Reprinted with permission of the Buros Institute, University of Nebraska, Lincoln, NE.

---

attention has been directed of late to setting standards for intelligence and other measures. The next section highlights the application of some standards to test selection and use.

TEST STANDARDS

The *Standards for Educational and Psychological Testing* (AERA, APA, NCME, 1999, hereafter referred to as the "*Test Standards*"), a much-needed revision of an earlier edition, serves as an invaluable compendium of guidance for test users, producers, consumers, and other stakeholders. These standards are so widely cited that they are likely to influence litigation and legislation related to testing in school, business, and clinical settings, including intelligence testing. Hence, they are mandatory reading for all psychologists

and other professionals who engage in any type of assessment. The new *Test Standards* are divided into three substantive sections: test construction, evaluation, and documentation; fairness in testing; and testing applications. A few of the standards will be highlighted here as they relate specifically to intelligence testing applications.

A central theme of the new *Test Standards* is evidentiary-based interpretation as alluded to in the opening quote of this chapter. Several standards are offered related to the issue of evidence-based interpretations. The second standard for test users (Standard 11.2), for example, states that

When a test is used for a purpose for which little or no documentation is available, the user is responsible for obtaining evidence of the test's validity and reliability for this purpose. (AERA, APA, NCME, 1999, p. 113)

This evidentiary-based interpretation theme has been present in the *Test Standards* and other publications for some time, but its meaning and centrality to the assessment enterprise is highlighted significantly in the revision. It is also noteworthy in Standard 11.2 that users have to take responsibility for their interpretations and validation of same. The major implication of these standards is that modern interpretation of intelligence tests must depend more on sound psychometric evidence than has been the case in the past. A few examples may help clarify the meaning of these standards relating to evidence-based interpretation.

A psychologist, for example, may wish to begin using the Differential Ability Scales (DAS) for the diagnosis of intellectual problems of children who are suspected of having moderate to severe levels of mental retardation. The *Test Standards* suggest that the DAS manual or *Handbook* (Elliott, 1990b), or an independent research study, should provide evidence for the validity of the DAS for making such a diagnosis. The DAS seems well suited to this use, since it has an extended score scale that appears ideal for the diagnosis of such a population. In addition, the DAS *Handbook* includes an impressive array of prepublication research with special populations of children, yet a study with children with moderate to severe mental retardation is lacking. It is therefore conceivable that, if an independent study of the use of the DAS with this population cannot be found, the use of the DAS for making the diagnosis of moderate or severe mental retardation could be construed as inappropriate in the light of the *Test Standards*.

The *Test Standards*, however, do offer a fairly generous definition of evidence. They note that support for an interpretation may come from both empirical and theoretical literatures. They also do not restrict clinicians from offering hypotheses based on observations during test sessions and other data that are indiosyncratic to the case. Clinicians are cautioned to label hypotheses, including those that may be contraindicated by the research literature as "tentative." In addition, "Interested parties should be made aware of the potential limitations of the test scores in such situations" (p. 114).

It is particularly difficult to amass validity evidence for interpretations associated with the diagnosis of low incidence disorders. Turner's syndrome, Asperger's syndrome, Rasmussen's syndrome, and cognitive impairment associated with tuberous sclerosis are only a few of the many syndromes that are typically lacking validity evidence in a test's manual. Children from remote areas (e.g., northern Alaska) and those who speak lesser known languages (e.g., Euskera from the Basque region) are also not likely to have been studied systematically as part of the test validation process either prior to or after publication of the scale. In all of these cases the *Test Standards* suggest that conclusions be offered as tentative hypotheses pending further assessment or follow-up assessment at a later date. This theme of evidence-based interpretation serves as the foundation for the interpretation methodology to be offered in Chapter 17.

Another recurring theme of the revised *Test Standards* is full disclosure. Test user Standard 11.5, for example, states,

> *Those who have a legitimate interest in an assessment should be informed about the purposes of testing, how tests will be administered, the factors considered in scoring examinee responses, how the scores are typically used, how long records will be retained, and to whom and under what conditions the records may be released. (AERA, APA, NCME, 1999, p. 114)*

In the case of child examinees these explanations should likely be given to the child and caregivers at a minimum. This standard, and related ones, require that clinicians themselves enter the clinical assessment process fully informed in order to explain the points above to examinees and others. It may be helpful to prepare a written guide to be handed to parents, children, and other interested parties in the assessment. The act of preparing such a document will help examiners clarify their thinking about these issues.

Some of these issues, such as the release of records, are at least partially governed by state statutes in the United States. Laws regarding privileged communication between client and psychologist, for example, are not uniform across all jurisdictions.

Examiners also must carefully plan an assessment in order to aspire to this standard. The tests and other assessment procedures must be specified in order to provide accurate information regarding test administration, scoring procedures, and the use of scores for diagnostic, treatment planning, classroom consultation, or other purposes.

The *Test Standards* are clear regarding the disclosure of actual test items. Standard 11.7 indicates that the security of test content should be maintained in order to ensure the validity of the test with future examinees. This standard reads

> *Test users have the responsibility to protect the security of tests, to the extent that developers enjoin users to do so.* (AERA, APA, NCME, 1999, p. 115)

The case law in this area is ever changing, making the 1996 *Statement on Disclosure of Test Data* of the APA somewhat dated. Most of the advice offered in this statement is still of value (APA, 1997). When involved in litigation, however, some legal consultation will be necessary to guide the psychologist in this matter. The clear will of the profession, however, is to limit the unnecessary disclosure of test content in order to maintain the long-term usefulness of the measure.

The *Test Standards* also address issues specific to several domains of assessment, including "psychological" assessment with standards regarding introducing biases into test selection, suitability of tests for the characteristics of examinees, the validity of combining tests, practice within the clinician's scope of expertise and training, validity evidence for differential diagnosis between clinical groups, supervision of psychometric assistants, communication with the examinee in her or his native language, confidentiality of results, assessment under less-than-optimal environmental conditions, familiarity with the reliability and validity evidence associated with the tests used, inclusion of qualitative data in interpretation,

appropriate use of computer-generated interpretations, interpretations of relationships among tests in the absence of evidence, necessity of criterion-related validity, use of convergent evidence to make interpretations, inclusion of alternative hypotheses in a report, and the sharing of results with the "test taker."

Some of these standards require psychologists to aspire to a higher standard of practice than has been the case in the past. For example, Standard 12.6 requires that studies of differential diagnosis for a test show that the test can differentiate one condition from others not just from so-called normal groups. For example, a research study showing that children without a diagnosis obtain higher scores than children with a diagnosis of a reading disability would be considered inadequate for making the reading disability diagnosis, unless this same intelligence test shows that children with a reading disability can also be distinguished from children with early infantile autism, mathematics disability, and so on, as well. Consequently, the professional psychologist must now be keenly aware of the quality of validity studies of differential diagnosis available for a particular test.

Standard 12.16 also requires an empirical basis for relating intelligence test results to other "test results, prescribed interventions, and desired outcomes" (p. 134) with the support of "empirical evidence." An often-heard interpretive remark is that this scale or that scale is the "best indicator" of a child's future academic performance. This prognostic statement is sometimes made based on nonverbal measures of intelligence when empirical evidence is clear that nonverbal measures show less predictive validity than verbal measures for a variety of samples and populations (see Chapter 17). The new *Test Standards*, because of standards such as 12.16, will probably be used to question the utility of conclusions that are based on colloquial intuition but are nevertheless contrary to empirical results. In fact, Standard 12.13 suggests that not only is empirical support necessary for interpretations but, in addition, "a logical analysis" of the inferences made should be offered. Moreover, any inferences lacking evidence of validity through prior research should be identified as such.

Psychologists are also now clearly prohibited from selecting tests and interpreting results as a result of bias that is introduced by colleagues, attorneys, other health care professionals or others who may have a vested interest in a particular outcome (Standard 12.2). As the psychological assessment process has become more visible in litigation, school placement, and other circumstances the potential for bias, even unarticulated bias, is large. It is indeed helpful that the *Test Standards* have addressed this sometimes unrecognized source of influence on the testing process.

The aforementioned entries are merely some of the standards that appear to be "raising the standard" of psychological assessment practice, including the use of intelligence tests. The specifics of each are better understood by reading the original source. It may be helpful to the practitioner, however, to have a short-form reminder of the major standards to use as a mental checklist during an evaluation. In this spirit the following self-assessment questions are offered as a guide to encourage compliance with the *Test Standards* specifically related to "psychological assessment."

1. Am I competent by virtue of my "education, supervised training, experience, and appropriate credentialing" (p. 131) to use this test? Exemplar: I have completed a 2-year postdoctoral experience in neuropsychology, which qualifies me to conduct an assessment of memory and learning for this adolescent.

2. Did I select this test primarily because of the influence of others more so than for its appropriateness to the case? Exemplar: I administered the Wechsler scale because this test was requested by the parents.

3. Am I making this interpretation primarily as the result of the influence of others rather than based on the test findings? Exemplar: I made the diagnosis of mental retardation

because this diagnosis would preclude my client from receiving the death penalty.

4. Is this test appropriate for use given the examinee's "culture, language, and/or physical requirements of the tests" (p. 131)? Exemplar: I chose the K-ABC because it has been shown to be less influenced by linguistic factors for Hispanic bilingual children (Kaufman & Kaufman, 1983b).

5. Is there validity evidence to support my combining these scores from two measures to make an interpretation? Exemplar: I cannot make the determination of a learning disability based on a simple discrepancy between my Binet-4 and measures of reading achievement when the achievement scores are in the average or above range (Siegel, 1999; Stanovich, 1999).

6. Does the combination of tests that I have selected have adequate evidence of sensitivity and specificity for detecting the child's problem or problem areas? Exemplar: I cannot make the diagnosis of Asperger's syndrome based solely on the results of this test because no validity evidence exists.

7. Is there adequate validity evidence to show that this test is capable of differentiating the diagnostic group of interest from other diagnostic groups? Exemplar: I cannot use DAS results in isolation to differentiate early infantile autism from mental retardation in this case because no validity evidence exists for doing so.

8. Do I have a defensible operational definition of the diagnostic terms that I am employing to conceptualize and report the diagnostic results? Exemplar: I am using the DSM-IV definition of ADHD to report my diagnostic findings both orally and in writing.

9. When I am supervising a group administration of a test (e.g., a screening measure), have I ensured that the individuals who interpret the scores are properly trained for this purpose? Exemplar: I have taught the

psychology assistant how to properly administer and score the Otis Lennon School Ability Test in a small-group format. I have also supervised her work with 20 cases, and I am confident that she will make appropriate referrals for comprehensive intellectual assessments when necessary.

10. Prior to testing, have I explained the testing procedures to my client using the language that he or she understands best, and have I explained any procedures for obtaining retesting? Exemplar: I have communicated with my client in Spanish because this is his preferred language for everyday use. He is, however, bilingual due to the requirements of his job where he has spoken English exclusively for the past 10 years. I have therefore also explained the testing procedures in English.

11. Do I maintain the confidentiality of test results and materials as dictated by my ethical guidelines? Exemplar: When called by the noncustodial parent of my client, I informed her that I would share information about her daughter after I received written permission from the custodial parent.

12. Before testing did I examine available norms, follow administration instructions (including calibrating any technical equipment and verifying scoring accuracy and replicability), and arrange for an optimal testing setting? Exemplar: I arranged for administration of the WISC-III in an administrative office in the hospital in order to conduct the testing in a less-distracting setting than the patient's room. I followed standardized procedures throughout the administration.

13. If the testing setting was nonoptimal, did I report the reason for using such a setting and did I ". . . conduct the testing under optimal conditions to provide a comparison" (p. 133)? Exemplar: When I administered the DAS to her in the hospital, she was very tearful and uncooperative, and she refused to take one of the subtests resulting in one prorated composite score. The DAS was administered in the hospital in order to rule out suspected mental retardation, a finding that may have significantly impacted discharge plans. I scheduled an appointment with her after discharge to administer the Wechsler Abbreviated Scale of Intelligence (WASI; Wechsler, 1999) which, by the way, produced an overall composite score very similar to that of the DAS that was administered under less-optimal conditions.

14. Am I fully aware of the validity evidence associated with the inferences that I wish to draw from the test, and can I articulate a "logical analysis" that supports the inferences drawn? Exemplar: I have concluded that my client's potential for academic achievement in school is quite good based on the finding that he possesses above-average verbal abilities as assessed by the WISC-III. The Verbal scale of the WISC-III has been shown to be a better predictor of academic achievement than its composite scores (see Chapter 8).

15. Did I incorporate observations, interviews, and historical and qualitative data into my interpretations? Exemplar: Her high scores on the Kaufman Adolescent and Adult Intelligence Test (KAIT; 1993) were matched by her good attention to tasks, persistence in difficult tasks, and expressions of motivation to perform well.

16. When I use computer-based interpretations, have I systematically evaluated the quality of the interpretations and the appropriateness of the norm samples on which the interpretations are based? Exemplar: I do not use this output, which suggests that certain patterns of intelligence test results may be diagnostic of ADHD, because this conclusion is based only on studies differentiating ADHD from "normal" samples. They did not test the ability of the test to differentiate ADHD from learning disability or other similar clinical groups.

17. Did I avoid making inferences regarding the relationships among test results, ". . . prescribed interventions, and desired outcomes" when empirical evidence for same was not available for individuals similar to my client? Exemplar: I cannot confidently predict my client's performance in school based on the results of WASI, because I could not identify predictive validity studies utilizing Navajo samples drawn from Navajo schools such as the one that this child is attending.

18. Did I avoid making actuarial-based interpretations when criterion-related validity was unavailable? Exemplar: I cannot state that your child has a 50% chance of success in his new residential school. Any such conclusion would be merely conjecture since such actuarial data are not available.

19. Did I use multiple sources of convergent evidence to draw inferences about my client? Exemplar: I think that your child requires intensive academic intervention given that her DAS results, school grades, local criterion-referenced test results, and teacher's appraisal of her cognitive abilities are all consistently below average.

20. Do I have ". . . appropriate education, supervised experience, and an appreciation of procedural, theoretical, and empirical limitations of the tests" (p. 134) to draw appropriate inferences? Exemplar: I have not begun using the DAS because I do not have any formal training in its use. I will be attending a workshop next week in order to learn how to administer it properly and become introduced to the theory and psychometric evidence related to the DAS.

21. Am I fully aware of the many factors that may have influenced my client's performance on this test? Exemplar: I noted that she was very irritable and inattentive during administration of the WAIS-III.

22. When appropriate, did I report alternative hypotheses to my inferences that may also explain the results? Exemplar: It could very well be the case that his intelligence is above average, but in this testing circumstance, his symptoms associated with depression may explain his average scores.

23. Did I share the results with my client? Exemplar: I met with Janine and her mother to share the test results.

The new *Test Standards* also address issues of linguistic and cultural diversity and their consideration in the assessment process.

Fairness in Testing

Issues not adequately addressed by the prior *Test Standards* are thoroughly treated in the revision. Some of these issues include guidelines for the encouragement of a fair interaction between psychologist and client, establishment of subgroup validity when necessary, offensiveness of test content and sensitivity to cultural differences, and assessment of multiple domains for individuals suspected of having disabilities.

The goal of the intelligence assessment is to assess the intelligence constructs of interest and, relatedly, avoid the assessment of construct irrelevant variance (i.e., nonintelligence constructs) (Standard 7.2, AERA, APA, NCME, 1999). It is necessary then to be cognizant of the potential influence of other sources of variance on the test scores. One source of construct irrelevant variance is membership in a subgroup that is known to typically solve test items in a manner not anticipated by the test developers. For example, I once worked on a project where a test item used a photograph of the Leaning Tower of Pisa. We noticed that one group of children was giving the response "leaning tower of the YMCA." Upon further investigation, we noted that these children were all from the Evanston, Illinois, test site where a replica of the tower resides near the entrance to the YMCA. The item was discarded since it was not assessing knowledge of world architecture but rather attendance at the local YMCA.

It is for this reason that the previous chapter cited the results of many factor analytic investigations of the Wechsler scales for a variety of different cultural, ethnic, or racial groups. For the most part the Wechsler scales withstood such scrutiny well by yielding the same intelligence factors across groups. If this were not the case, the test should not be used for some subgroups or a new test developed that would not assess construct-irrelevant variance for the subgroup. The *Test Standards* do not specifically require validation evidence for every subgroup recognizing the lack of feasibility of this endeavor. It is, however, important for the test user to routinely consider the possibility of subgroup inappropriateness and act accordingly by exercising "thoughtful professional judgment." By doing so the clinician increases the likelihood that the evaluation will be "fair."

An issue related to subgroup relevance is the need to refrain from unnecessarily insulting a client by using potentially offensive item content (Standard 7.4; AERA, APA, NCME, 1999). Most test developers make a significant effort to eliminate such content, but not all potentially problematic items can be identified. The identification of offensive content can serve as a factor to be considered in test selection. Fortunately, the large array of available tests allows modern examiners to choose tests with item content that is most appropriate for the groups that they serve.

Examiners are also cautioned to attend to the interpersonal issues associated with this very invasive assessment process. They should be cognizant of the effects of their behavior and the examination on the client and ". . . be professional, courteous, caring, and respectful." Clinicians should be aware of the potential for influence due to the power differential in the testing relationship. Moreover, remarks, behaviors, and the conclusions of the examiner have the potential to markedly alter the life circumstances of the client. Examiners should also be aware of any negativity that they hold toward the client. Sufficient negative attitudes by the examiner would warrant referral to someone who is less likely to bias the assessment results and conclusions.

The issue of fairness also looms large for the examination of individuals with disabilities or those who are suspected of disabilities. Clinicians are cautioned to not use a single score, such as a composite from an intelligence test, as the "sole indicator" of an examinee's functioning (Standard 10.12; AERA, APA, NCME, 1999). The multidimensional nature of human functioning must be recognized and considered when making diagnostic or prognostic decisions that may have a profound influence on the life of a person with a disability. In addition, psychologists should realize that a team of multidisciplinary examiners is often needed to fully evaluate the functioning of an individual with a disability.

Another characteristic of an examination that is "fair" is an adequately prepared examinee. Although written consent for child testing is routinely obtained, some children may not have been made aware of the specific day or time of day of the assessment by their parents or the examining psychologist. Unprepared children may be less likely to display their intellectual abilities, particularly in the presence of a stranger in a new environment.

Some young children may require multiple exposures to a psychologist before they become comfortable enough to respond. Psychologists may have to schedule two or more appointments in order to ensure that they are getting the optimal performance of a child on an intelligence test.

Test developers have also become more sensitive to preparing examinees for taking an intelligence test by building sample items into the tests themselves. The Binet-4 and WISC-III, for example, include more sample unscored items than was the case for their earlier editions.

Efforts to prepare examinees need to be made, however, prior to the test session. Parents should be informed in advance of intelligence testing that is being done at school including the exact date of the testing. This knowledge will help the parents prepare the child for the testing by ensuring that the child obtains adequate sleep the evening before the testing and nourishment to encourage stamina during the test session.

ASSESSMENT ETHICS

In addition to the *Test Standards* a variety of professional organizations have developed ethical principles with provisions regarding the use of educational and psychological tests. Many of the users of intelligence tests are members of the American Psychological Association and are, therefore, responsible for following the *Ethical Principles of Psychologists and Code of Conduct* (APA, 1992).

This ethics code overlaps considerably with the *Test Standards* in that it addresses the following issues, most of which are covered in greater detail in the *Test Standards*.

2.01 Evaluation, Diagnosis, and Interventions in Professional Context

2.02 Competence and Appropriate Use of Assessments and Interventions

2.03 Test Construction

2.04 Use of Assessment in General and with Special Populations

2.05 Interpreting Assessment Results

2.06 Unqualified Persons

2.07 Obsolete Tests and Outdated Test Results

2.08 Test Scoring and Interpretation Services

2.09 Explaining Assessment Results

2.10 Maintaining Test Security

Ethical guidelines produced by professional membership organizations do differ in one very important way from the *Test Standards* in that they do possess associated enforcement procedures for members of the association. A member found in violation of the ethical guidelines may be subjected to disciplinary actions including expulsion from the organization. More on the APA standards and their enforcement for members may be found at the association's Web site at www.apa.org.

TEST SELECTION

The premise underlying this chapter is consistent with the premise underlying the *Test Standards*—not all intelligence tests are valid for all children all of the time. This section assumes that intelligence tests have accumulated various types of validity evidence that makes them useful for particular purposes. It is also not likely that a single intelligence test will prove useful for all assessment purposes. This last section builds on the assumption of a lack of universal validity for an intelligence test by giving guidance to test selection. Having considered this issue, the clinician will be able to choose an intelligence test more wisely in the future. There are a number of variables that may influence test selection for an individual case. Among the variables that clinicians should consider are the following (see Box 7.1).

Purpose of the Assessment

Is the purpose screening or diagnosis? A screening measure would require only a few subtests from a major test of intelligence with the focus of the assessment on deriving a global estimate of intellectual functioning. Screeners such as the Kaufman Brief Intelligence Test (K-BIT; Kaufman & Kaufman, 1990) or the Vocabulary and Pattern Analysis subtests of the Binet-4 might suffice.

An assessment that is aimed at diagnostic decision making, by contrast, calls for an in-depth evaluation that measures multiple domains of intelligence. Cognitive domains of interest might include verbal, spatial, or short-term memory skills.

The diagnostic assessment of intelligence also requires a measure of intelligence that is highly reliable and valid. Screening measures are less reliable because of their brief nature. A diagnostic decision should never be based on a measure with low reliability. Diagnostic decision making requires that a measure have reliability estimates in the .90 and above range.

Box 7.1   Questions to Consider When Evaluating a New Intelligence Test

New intelligence assessment measures are constantly being released, and clinicians have to be savvy consumers. Here are some questions that the clinician may ask in order to help make a purchase decision.

1. Is the premise of the test reasonable? Is its theory based on some supportive citations of previous research?
2. Are the test development goals clearly delineated?
3. Are the manuals complete, including topics ranging from theory to interpretation of the results?
4. Are administration and scoring guidelines complete and easy to follow?
5. Are the test materials attractive to children? Are they sturdy and practical?
6. Are all of the items derivatives of those on other tests? Are some of them new?
7. Were the items subjected to judgmental bias reviews so as to not be offensive to test users or takers?
8. Is the test easy to administer so that the examiner can focus on the child's behavior during testing?
9. Is there evidence of content validity? Were cognitive science experts consulted? Does the item content seem consistent with the theory?
10. Were statistical item bias studies undertaken?
11. Was the test norming sample collected recently?
12. Does the norming sample closely match the stratification statistics selected? Was there some measure of SES used for stratification?
13. Are the internal consistency and stability coefficients high—above .90 for the composite?
14. Is there evidence of good factorial, predictive, and concurrent validity?
15. Are several derived scores offered, such as standard scores and percentile ranks, in order to enhance interpretation?
16. Are interpretive tables for determining intraindividual strengths and weaknesses offered?
17. Are the scaling methods (i.e., norm-development procedures) described in detail?
18. Have early reviews been either favorable or optimistic?
19. Is the test appropriate for the population of children that I serve? For example, does it have extended norms for a severely mentally handicapped population?

The screening versus diagnosis test selection decision then requires the clinician to weigh the need for a highly reliable estimate of intelligence that considers multiple intelligence domains versus a global estimate of intelligence with lower reliability. A third possibility is to assess only global capacity with an intelligence measure that has strong reliability estimates. The Binet-4 subtests, for example, are rather long and combining two of them in many cases will result in reliability estimates that approach or exceed .90.

There are several reasons for choosing screeners over a longer examination. One reason is triage.

All children who are evaluated by the psychologist may receive a screener in order to assess the need for administration of a diagnostic measure. One colleague of mine always uses the Draw-a-Person (DAP) as a screener for children referred for school problems. The DAP serves as a screener for spatial/visual-motor skills. While the DAP in particular is a fairly poor correlate of comprehensive measures (see Chapter 14), she has found this set of measures helpful for planning the remainder of the evaluation. This psychologist found screeners to be extremely powerful in one case. In this case she had a boy referred for school problems who drew a sexually explicit DAP. When asked how he had learned to draw like this, he indicated that the girl seated next to him in class had taught him how to do this. Further investigation revealed the girl *seated next to him* was being sexually abused at home. This is an unusually powerful result for a screener. The screener served a triage function in this case by helping decide which child needed the most immediate attention.

Screeners may also be used when abundant information about intelligence is already available for the child. A child may have received the DAS on two separate occasions in the past year and received similar scores both times. If the child were evaluated a third time, a shorter form may be adequate.

Screeners may also be useful when intelligence is not central to the referral problem. If, for example, a child were referred for depression but was obtaining good grades in school, the focus of the evaluation would likely be on the referral problem. A screener for intelligence may be administered just to ensure that no unidentified problems lay in the cognitive realm. If screener results are suspicious, then a more comprehensive measure would be in order.

Age/Score Range

For some assessment purposes an extended score range is necessary. An example would be differentiation among levels of mental retardation—mild, moderate, severe, and profound. Many tests simply do not have the score range necessary for such differential diagnoses. In fact, some intelligence measures do not possess a wide enough range of scores to differentiate mental retardation from below-average intelligence or giftedness from above-average intelligence.

Tests are most likely to pose floor and ceiling problems near the "tails" of their age range. Hence, age is merely a proxy variable for score range. It appears that test developers have become sensitized to the need for extended score ranges,

as some of the newer tests have impressive ranges (e.g., the DAS; see Research Report 7.2).

Practicality

To some this issue seems trite, but this is a central issue with infants and preschoolers, especially those who exhibit behavior problems. Practicality can include several components. One component is interest level to children. Interest level may not only be important for the practicality of administration but also because a high level of interest may enhance validity. Children who are highly motivated will presumably put forth their best effort for the examiner. While interest level is somewhat of an intangible, there is accumulated clinical experience to suggest that some instruments are more childlike and inherently more interesting to young children than others. The McCarthy and K-ABC appear to be more attractive, for example, than the WPPSI-R. Realistically, clinicians will have to decide which tests are more interesting and attractive to their clientele especially in the light of multicultural issues. Although the K-ABC is attractive to many children, some items may be offensive or inappropriate for children from some cultural groups. An attendee at a workshop that I once presented suggested that the "clapping hands" item on the Reading Understanding subtest was inappropriate for some of the Russian immigrant children with whom she was working because they were members of a religious sect that did not allow hand clapping.

Another aspect of practicality is ease of administration. If a child is exhibiting substantial behavior problems, administration of a complex instrument may be difficult. The extensive follow-up questioning required on the Vocabulary, Similarities, and Comprehension subtests of the WISC-III, for example, may be interpreted by some children as an unnecessary inquisition. Some obstreperous children may respond to this administration format by refusing to complete the test. Similarly, a test with complex instructions

RESEARCH REPORT 7.2

Individual Assessment Accuracy

Lawrence Rudner (1983) conducted an interesting simulation study where he compared nine statistics that assess individual assessment accuracy. These statistics are generally unheard of in the realms of clinical assessment practice. This is an oversimplification, but basically these statistics assess the degree to which a child's item responses on a test compare to those of the standardization sample. Essentially, "high ability examinees are expected to get few easy items wrong, low ability examinees are expected to get few difficult items right" (p. 207).

In order to test the accuracy of nine statistical methods, Rudner created two data sets through computer-simulation methods. The first data set was based on 80 verbal items from the Scholastic Aptitude Test (SAT). The second data set consisted of 45 items from a general biology test. Rudner then generated large samples of examinees, over 2,000, for each of these tests. In order to test the comparative accuracy of the nine statistics, however, he created several subsamples of 100 cases each. These various hypothetical subsamples consisted of groups that received inordinately high scores or low scores on the two tests. In this way, the relative accuracy of each of the nine measures to identify spuriously high and low scores could be directly tested.

The nine statistics that were used for assessing individual accuracy included a variety of procedures. Among them were Rasch model approaches, Birnbaum model approaches, correlational approaches, and sequence approaches. The least complicated approaches are the correlational methods. One method utilized a personal point-biserial correlation statistic. This is a correlation between a child's correct and incorrect responses on a set of items and the item difficulty indices (P-values) for the norming population for the same test.

The results of the study showed that all of the nine approaches were able to identify irregular item response sets at a statistically significant level. However, some of the approaches were more suited to the longer SAT examination and some were better suited to the shorter examination. The Rasch model statistic, for example, tended to work better on the shorter test. The various point-biserial correlational methods also seemed to work better on the shorter examination.

Rudner (1983) concluded that while all nine approaches were relatively effective, their accuracy was not startlingly different. These remained a number of spuriously high and low scores that were not detected by these various methods. He concluded that these techniques would not be valid for developing a particularly useful cut score that would be indicative of a flawed response pattern. He stated rather, "Professional judgement must be used in selecting an approach, determining critical values, and in using the statistics" (p. 217).

Many an examiner has scratched his or her head in puzzlement when viewing the subtest performance of a child who gets easy items incorrect and difficult items correct, and vice versa. The techniques described by Rudner allow the clinician to obtain a quantitative index of the irregularity of a specific response pattern. This could be useful for a number of purposes, including determining when a second measure of intelligence should be administered, and whether or not a child from another culture may not be understanding the directions of a test. The statistics, however, are relatively complex and will likely be most useful when intelligence tests of the future become computer based.

---

may not be welcomed by the impatient child with attention difficulties.

There are many aspects of practicality, ranging from the size of the test kit to administration time to cost to ease of scoring. One would not think that ease of scoring could be a factor, but it can be. The W-J Cognitive, for example, is a poor choice for emergency work because it is so complex to score that many people prefer using computer scoring routinely. This makes the W-J less desirable for emergency cases in a hospital or other setting where the psychologist needs to score all tests immediately and does not have access to the software scoring back at the office.

Even administration time may become important in some assessment situations. The WISC-III, for instance, possesses numerous strengths, including a broad sampling of intelligence. The DAS takes a narrower swath, but it provides an estimate of cognitive development in a more time efficient manner when time is at a premium.

Examiners will have to gauge the practicality of individual tests in the light of the clientele they serve. Although frequently neglected these can be crucial issues to the practitioner.

Clinicians, however, have to balance the needs for practicality against the need to enhance the validity of the results. Clinicians could be encouraged by administrators to emphasize issues such as cost and time that may hinder the ability to the clinician to do a thorough job (see Box 7.1).

Revisions versus Old Editions

Often clinicians debate whether or not to switch from an old edition of a test to a revision. Reference to the *Test Standards* would lead the clinician to *always use tests with the strongest validity evidence* for the assessment purpose. If a revision has better evidence of validity, then it should be adopted. This scenario is the most frequent one. In most cases the new edition of a test does possess strengths over the old one.

In some cases, however, the issue of whether or not to use a new edition of a test clouds the essential issue of choosing the best test for the assessment situation. A clinician, for example, may wish that the old Stanford-Binet—Form LM were still available for assessing young children with developmental problems. There may be another option here that is less obvious, and that is the DAS. The DAS has some Binet-LM item types and it has more "floor" than either the Binet-LM or the Binet-4. In other words, in some cases the clinician may feel that the only choice is between a new or old edition when, in fact, an entirely new measure should be considered.

Domains Assessed

Assessment domain is becoming a more crucial variable as new intelligence tests are offered that include an enlarged sampling of children's cognitive performance. The clinician needs to gauge

beforehand which domains of intelligence require assessment and select the test(s) that best assesses these domains. A sample case would be a child who is referred for a short-term memory deficit. In this case the current status of the deficit is important to assess. In this situation the clinician would likely choose to use the Binet-4, DAS, K-ABC, or W-J, all of which possess more short-term memory subtests. If, on the other hand, a child is referred for a possible processing speed problem, then the WISC-III, DAS, or W-J would likely serve this purpose best.

Someone may query, however, what would happen if a clinician assesses weaknesses and this serves to lower the child's composite score and qualify a child for mental retardation placement when this would be inappropriate? *Intelligence test scores should never "qualify" any child for placement. Professional judgment and consultation should be the only vehicles used to decide what services a child may need.* I refer back to my previous example of a physician only being allowed to prescribe a medication for high blood pressure if a person's systolic pressure is beyond a certain level. This latter scenario is an example of uninspired medicine just as the former scenario is a example of poor psychological assessment practice.

Intelligence tests may also be selected so as to assess for the presence of cognitive strengths. If a child were referred for an evaluation for giftedness and is reported to have strong quantitative skills, the Binet-4 may be the test of choice because of its Quantitative Reasoning scale. The clarification of this strength may be helpful for emphasizing its presence so that it could be considered as a strength to be capitalized on in curriculum planning.

Test Strengths and Weaknesses

The strong and weak points of individual tests are crucial elements in the test selection process (see Research Report 7.3). It is for this reason that specific mention of same is made in later chapters.

RESEARCH REPORT 7.3

The Case Against Intelligence Testing

Asa Hilliard, a well-known critic of the use of intelligence tests, particularly in the schools, questions the use of intelligence measures (Hilliard, 1989). Hilliard's critique focuses primarily on the use of such measures for intervention planning in the schools. In commenting on the question of bias Hilliard remarks, "Unfortunately, the bias and fairness debate obscures the more fundamental issue of the pedagogical utility of the IQ test, not just for minority cultural groups, but for everyone" (p. 125). Hilliard's concern about the relevance of IQ testing to designing instructional interventions is expressed clearly in the following quote.

> There is little, if any, evidence that test designers, producers, and administrators are any more pedagogically prepared today. To the extent that professional educators were skilled and insightful, the record does not show that they were a part of the design of diagnostic instruments that were to be used for their benefit. In fact, one clear thing stands out in the abundant effective teacher and effective schools research literature. *In no studies of successful teachers and successful schools is there ever any mention of reliance on IQ measures.* In other words, IQ is irrelevant to successful instruction. (p. 129)

Hilliard's comments are not isolated. Objections to the widespread use of intelligence tests for "placement" purposes in public schools have been expressed since the time of Terman's original work (see Chapter 1). Hilliard's remarks, and those of others, should caution all clinicians to evaluate carefully the situations in which tests are used.

SAMPLE CASES
OF TEST SELECTION

Case 1

Alexandra is a 6-year-old who is referred for attention deficit. She is also suspected to have below-average intelligence.

Test Selection Considerations

Such a referral would require a high-interest test that is not too lengthy. Tests lacking considerable appeal for young children would be ruled out, including the Binet-4, DAS, W-J, and WPPSI-R. Other high-appeal tests available for this age group would include the K-ABC and McCarthy. While the K-ABC is appealing, this is a "crossover" age for the scale in that a number of new tests begin at ages 5 and 6 (e.g., Matrix Analogies, Photo Series, and Reading/Decoding). Where new tests begin for an age group, they may be difficult. Since Alexandra is suspected of below-average intelligence, some of the K-ABC subtests may prove too difficult for her resulting

in too many raw scores of 0. In this case the McCarthy would be a good test to attempt with Alexandra because it should have enough easy items, administration time is reasonable, and the test provides built in "breaks" (i.e., the Motor scale) for children with limited attention spans.

Case 2

Alai is an 11-year-old boy who is referred for reading problems. He has a history of above-average grades in all school subjects except for reading and spelling.

Test Selection Considerations

The K-ABC would be ruled out quickly in this case because of a lack of difficult items for this age group. The WISC-III, Binet-4, DAS, and W-J may all be useful in this case.

Case 3

Janine is a 16-year-old who is seeking assistance in choosing a college. She has always been in gifted classes and she is attending an elite boarding school for high school.

Test Selection Considerations

The WICS-III would be a poor choice here because of a lack of difficulty. The Binet-4 also lacks some difficulty at this age. The DAS, W-J, and WAIS-III may be reasonable options.

Case 4

Pablo is an 8-year-old who is referred for poor academic performance. His performance began to deteriorate about a year ago subsequent to a head injury incurred in an automobile accident. His family speaks Spanish at home. Pablo speaks English most of the time.

Test Selection Considerations

The English-language demands of the WISC-III, Binet-4, DAS, and W-J may be an impediment here. The brief oral instructions of the K-ABC may help ensure that Pablo understands what is expected of him in the test session.

It is important to understand that these test selection examples are based on the examiner's predictions that have emanated from extensive knowledge of numerous test instruments. As a result these predictions will occasionally be flawed. Hopefully, the word "occasionally" is the operative term here. Regardless of the "hit rate," the importance of examiner foresight in test selection cannot be emphasized too much.

CONCLUSIONS

As is eminently clear from reading the *Test Standards*, the modern-day user of intelligence tests has to aspire to an entirely new level of practice in comparison to previous generations of clinicians. Users of modern intelligence tests have to be extremely well informed about the tests they use and about appropriate practices for their use. It is likely that should there be a problem with the use of an individual's intelligence test results, the clinician will be held accountable for compliance to relevant standards and guidelines. Readers of this text would be well advised to discuss the implications of various standards and guidelines in order to ensure that they are using children's intelligence tests appropriately.

CHAPTER SUMMARY

- Clinicians have to know psychometric principles well in order to judge the quality of new methods.

- The *Standards for Educational and Psychological Testing* (AERA, APA, NCME, 1999) discusses numerous types of validity evidence.

- Clinicians should customarily make efforts to explain how test results will be used and how they may be released to others.

- Not all intelligence tests are valid for all children all of the time.

- An assessment that is aimed at diagnostic decision making, as opposed to screening, requires an in-depth evaluation that measures multiple domains of intelligence.

- Screening measures may be preferred for use, including triage, in situations when abundant information about intelligence is already available for the child and when intelligence is not central to the child's referral problem(s).

- The practicality of an intelligence test can include several components such as interest level to children, administration time, and ease of administration and scoring.

- Another factor to consider in test selection is assessment domain, which is becoming a more crucial variable as new intelligence tests are offered that include an enlarged sampling of children's cognitive performance.

CHAPTER 8

The Wechsler Intelligence Scale for Children—Third Edition (WISC-III)

"Dr. Wechsler possessed a rare blend of humility and grandeur." (Kaufman, 1992, p. 4)

CHAPTER QUESTIONS

What features have served to make the Wechsler scales so popular?

What are the strengths and weaknesses of the WISC-III?

WECHSLER'S VIEWS

David Wechsler placed a great deal of emphasis on the assessment of general intelligence even though his original test featured both Verbal and Performance scales. Wechsler viewed intelligence as a complex interaction of abilities that produce intelligent behavior that reflects "g." He explained:

But Vocabulary is a better test of intelligence than a Form Board, primarily because people can express themselves more meaningfully in verbal than in geometric symbols. This, of course, would not hold in the case of deaf-mutes or individuals who are in the habit of thinking spatially, manipulatively or in any other way. Hence, as a general principle, an effective test of intelligence should be made up of tasks calling upon as many "abilities" as possible. This was intuitively perceived by Binet, who was the first to devise an effective test of general intelligence. (p. 16, 1958)

Wechsler (1958) also took a stand on the issue of the localization of intelligence. He said that essentially intelligence will never be localized in a particular area of the brain. Since intelligence, in Wechsler's view, is basically the "perception of relations" among stimuli, then the modality of neural representation of these stimuli is unimportant. The perception of relations then will be independent of the localization of specific stimuli.

Just as it is important to understand the history and original purposes of the Binet scale, it is equally important to understand Wechsler's purposes in order to appropriately use his tests. Binet's test was designed solely for the purpose of diagnosing mental retardation, yet it and other intelligence measures have become centerpieces of neuropsychological and learning disability diagnosis, purposes for which they were not specifically designed. In similar fashion there is a great deal of discussion in the literature about verbal and nonverbal (or performance) intelligence, yet these scales were formed based on practical considerations, not theoretical ones (see Chapter 1). The Verbal and Performance scales of the Wechsler series were similarly not designed to assess laterality of cerebral function. With these points of view in mind it is probably best for modern psychologists to use the Wechsler scales as they were originally intended, as measures of general intelligence designed primarily for use with adolescents and adults.

WISC History

The Wechsler scales enjoy unprecedented popularity and have a rich clinical and research tradition. The publication of the Wechsler-Bellevue in 1939 was a bold stroke on the part of David Wechsler in even attempting to challenge the hallowed Binet scales (Reynolds & Kaufman, 1990). Somewhat surprisingly, from the outset the Wechsler scales were welcomed. The Wechsler/Bellevue offered a number of features that were not available in previous editions of the Binet scales, including separate norms for children and adults; the provision of subtest standard scores, which made the test more amenable to profile interpretation; the inclusion of a separate Performance scale to allow for the assessment of linguistic and cultural minorities; and a Standard Score (Deviation IQ) that solved many of the psychometric problems associated with ratio IQ scales (Zimmerman & Woo-Sam, 1985).

The Wechsler scales also enjoyed immediate credibility because of the reputation of David Wechsler himself. In contrast to Binet, who was known as a researcher, Wechsler was a clinical psychologist who had a wealth of experience in the individual study of psychiatric patients at the Bellevue Psychiatric Hospital (Zimmerman & Woo-Sam, 1985). For many reasons, at the time the Wechsler/Bellevue was published, it was clearly differentiated from the Binet scales and offered a number of advantages that were attractive to practicing psychologists.

This extensive popularity has led to the publication of a variety of scales by Wechsler, including his most famous children's scale, the Wechsler Intelligence Scale for Children–Revised (WISC-R). The original WISC was published in 1949 and its revision, the WISC-R, was published in 1974. The WISC-R also enjoyed a great deal of popularity with researchers. As a result, it is a very well-known test both clinically and empirically, with over 1,100 publications that assess various aspects of its clinical utility and validity (Reynolds & Kaufman, 1990). The Wechsler scales promise to be popular for the foreseeable future, especially with the publication of the WISC-III. Through all of these revisions, the structure of the Wechsler scales has not changed appreciably. The most daring changes in the WISC were made in the WISC-III when a new subtest, Symbol Search, was added.

Detterman (1985) attributes the popularity of the WISC to its ease of administration. This relative ease of administration is fostered by the organization of the tests into subtests that are brief yet long enough to be reliable and have long clinical histories (Detterman, 1985). Detterman's (1985) major complaint about the WISC is that it clings to the tradition of offering "only one interpretable score." He acknowledges the need for an intelligence test that assesses more specific skills so that it will lend itself better to treatment planning.

Opinions about the WISC run the gamut from ebullient praise to condemnation. A review by Witt and Gresham (1985) concluded that the WISC-R was overrated. Specifically, they suggest that the WISC is outdated and that it lacks treatment validity.

The WISC-III, however, remains the most popular and respected test in the world with separate standardization samples for Canada,

Australia, and the United Kingdom and at least 11 translations for major language groups (Prifitera, Weiss, & Saklofske, 1998).

WECHSLER'S VIEW OF INTELLIGENCE

David Wechsler's conceptualization of intelligence is consistent with that of other well-known theorists of his day. He, as well as Spearman, Galton, and others, emphasized the concept of general intelligence. An excerpt from Wechsler's WISC-R manual (1974) best describes his view:

> Intelligence is the overall capacity of an individual to understand and cope with the world around him. Stated in these general terms, this definition may impress the reader perhaps as not too radically different from any other definitions that might be cited. A careful comparison with these, however, would reveal that it differs from most of them in two important respects: (1) it conceives of intelligence as an overall or global entity; that is, a multidetermined and multifaceted entity rather than an independent, uniquely-defined trait. (2) It avoids singling out any ability, however esteemed (e.g., abstract reasoning), as crucial or overwhelmingly important. In particular, it avoids equating general intelligence with intellectual ability. (p. 5)

Wechsler designed his scale with subtests in order to give numerous opportunities for the clinician to assess this global entity. He spoke of these subtests as different "languages" that may be used to assess the expression of intelligence. He also points out that he *did not consider the Verbal and Performance scales to represent separate abilities*, but, rather, he regarded them as two additional "languages" through which the underlying general intelligence may express itself.

STRUCTURE OF THE WISC-III

The primary test development goals for the WISC-III included (a) enhancing, and perhaps clarifying, the WISC factor structure, (b) im-

proving the subtests, (c) minimizing test bias, and (d) developing supplementary materials such as a conormed achievement test (Roid, 1990). It appears that another overriding goal was to keep the basic structure of the WISC intact.

The WISC-III is comprised of 10 mandatory and 3 supplementary subtests, all of which span the age range of 6 through 16 years. The 5 mandatory subtests on the Verbal scale include Information, Similarities, Arithmetic, Vocabulary, and Comprehension. The supplementary subtest on the Verbal scale is Digit Span. Traditionally, Digit Span is administered with the remainder of the Verbal subtests, although it is not included in the computation of the Verbal IQ unless one of the Verbal subtests is spoiled or invalidated, at which point it may be substituted in the computation of the Verbal IQ. Wechsler (1974) points out clearly, however, that the Digit Span score may not be substituted for a Verbal scale subtest simply because a Verbal scale subtest score may be low.

Similarly, the Performance scale of the WISC-III is comprised of 5 subtests, including Picture Completion, Picture Arrangement, Block Design, Object Assembly, and Coding. The two supplementary subtests on the Performance scale are Mazes and Symbol Search, which (as was the case with Digit Span) are not included in the computation of the Performance IQ. The Symbol Search subtest, however, is somewhat unique in that it may only be substituted for the Coding subtest. The Mazes subtest, however, may be substituted for any Performance scale subtest.

The Verbal and Performance IQs are then combined in order to compute the Full Scale IQ. In the computation of the composite scores of the WISC-III, all subtests and composites are weighted equally, reflecting Wechsler's belief that all of the Wechsler subtests and scales have an equal opportunity of uncovering an individual's intelligence. The WISC-III uses standard scores for interpretation. The subtest scaled (standard) scores have a mean of 10 and standard deviation of 3, whereas the IQs have a mean of 100 and standard deviation of 15.

Administration and Scoring Improvements

Enhancements to Subtests

The subtests of the WISC-III were targeted for substantial revision. Efforts were made to modernize artwork, reduce biased or offensive content, ease administration and scoring, and add items so as to allow the tests more range of item difficulty for the assessment of 6 and 16 year olds (Wechsler, 1991).

The great variety of item and administration and scoring changes for the subtests are discussed in detail in the WISC-III manual (Wechsler, 1991). One of the more substantial administration changes is the placement of Picture Completion as the first test. This is a much needed reorganization, particularly for young children, who no longer will be queried in a manner that seems like an onerous inquisition to many children. The Picture Completion is more innocuous and more interesting to youngsters.

Symbol Search

This new subtest was added in an attempt to clarify the controversial WISC-R third factor, often called *freedom from distractibility* (Wechsler, 1991). The WISC-R third factor included the Arithmetic, Digit Span, and Coding subtests (Kaufman, 1979b). The controversy surrounding the labeling of this third factor in a manner that best describes the major abilities assessed by the factor is legendary (this controversy will be discussed in detail in later sections). The rationale for adding the Symbol Search test was that this addition might clarify the nature of the third factor by determining whether or not attention/distractibility, short-term memory, or some other ability is central to successful performance on the third factor subtests (Wechsler, 1991). To some extent the addition of this new test clarifies the third factor; however, it also produced a new fourth factor. The answer to the third factor puzzle is provided later.

Other enhancements to the WISC included modernizing artwork, expanding floor and ceiling (the number of easy and difficult items per subtest), and reordering subtests so that the less threatening Picture Completion subtest is administered first.

PSYCHOMETRIC PROPERTIES OF THE WISC-III

Item and Subtest Development

Item Tryout 1

The WISC-III was first pilot tested with a sample of 119 children. One of the goals of this first data collection effort was to test the value of the Symbol Search subtest as a measure of memory or attention that could clarify the nature of the WISC-III third factor (Wechsler, 1991).

Item Tryout 2

The second field testing of the WISC-III was conducted in 1988 with a sample of 450 children (Wechsler, 1991).

Norming

The WISC-III was normed in early 1989 using a stratified sampling procedure. The stratification variables used included age, sex, race/ethnicity, geographic region, occupation of head of household, and urban-rural residence. The sample included 200 children in each of 11 age groups from 6 through 16 years. This sampling plan produced a total of 2,200 cases in the standardization sample.

The stratification percentages for the WISC-III sample are based upon 1988 United States Census Bureau Data. There is a very close match between the standardization sample and Census Bureau statistics on all of the stratification variables.

Reliability

The internal consistency of the WISC-III is exemplary. The average internal consistency coefficient for the Full Scale IQ is .96; the Verbal IQ, .95; and the Performance IQ, .91. Average subtest coefficients range from .70 for Mazes to .87 for Vocabulary and Block Design. Mazes has particular problems at older age levels where its internal consistency coefficient falls to .61 at age 15 and .67 at age 16. The internal consistency of Index scores is also adequate, varying from .94 for the Verbal Comprehension Index to .85 for Processing Speed.

Test-Retest Reliability

The test-retest studies described in the WISC-III manual produce stability coefficients, very close to the internal consistency coefficients, however, some estimates of reliability drop precipitously. The reliability of the Performance IQ drops to .87 and the Freedom From Distractibility Index drops to .82. Several subtest coefficients drop considerably, including Picture Arrangement to .64, Object Assembly to .66, and Mazes to .57. These subtest stability coefficients are worrisome in that they suggest that many of the subtest scores are likely to be unstable. These findings should make clinicians appropriately cautious in interpreting WISC-III subtest scores.

Gain Scores

An instructive aspect of the research on the test-retest reliability of the WISC-III is the information that it provides on practice effects. The WISC-III manual shows the changes in test scores for individuals who were tested on two different occasions (an average of 23 days apart) with the WISC-III. These data suggest that the Verbal IQ changes relatively little from the first to second administration. For the study for ages 6 to 7 the Verbal IQ changed from 100.8 on the first testing to 102.5 on the second test. The Verbal IQ changes for the 10- to 11-year-olds and 14- to 15-year-olds were 100.3 to 102.2 and 99.4

to 102.7, respectively. A gain of two to three points seems to be the typical practice effect for the Verbal IQ over the short term.

In contrast, having familiarity with Performance scale subtests is advantageous as the gain from first to second testing on the Performance scale is more in the range of 11 to 13 points. The changes in the Performance IQ from first to second testing for the 6–7, 10–11, and 14–15-year-old-age groups was 102.7 to 114.2, 99.0 to 112.0, and 99.6 to 112.1, respectively (see Tables 5.3 through 5.5 in Wechsler, 1991). These data suggest that if a child's scores are higher by only a few points from one administration of the WISC-III to the next, the gain is likely attributable to familiarity with the test materials or *practice effects*. It is also more sensible to attribute small gains in performance to practice effects, since gain scores are like difference scores in one very important respect—they are more unreliable than the composite scores themselves (see Chapter 5).

Coding and Picture Arrangement appear to be "driving" the Performance IQ gain upon retest. These tests gained anywhere from 2/3 to a full standard deviation upon retest. If these scores were expressed in the traditional IQ metric of mean = 100 and SD = 15, the gains could be as much as a change of 100 to 115. This gain is impressive. These results indicate that a child's performance could change substantially upon retest, which can be crucial for some diagnostic decisions. A child with a WISC-III profile where Verbal = 73, Performance = 73, and Full Scale = 71 is very close to the diagnosis of mental retardation. The results of the test-retest studies portend that this child's Performance score upon retest could easily change to 84, which, in turn, could change the Full Scale to 77. This prediction also assumes that the Verbal scale would not change, which is not an accurate assumption. This child's first set of scores are very close to the mental retardation range (usually considered as a Full Scale of about 70 or below) but the second set of scores is clearly outside this range. In fact, the child's second Performance score is only somewhat below average. The Performance scale gain scores suggest that while the first score obtained is reliable the second score may be significantly higher. This is an important distinction to draw because it makes the examiner more cautious when interpreting the Performance score the first time it is administered.

The Performance scale gain scores are only rivaled by the Perceptual Organization and Processing Speed Index scores. These scores produce gains ranging from about 9 to 11 points in the three test-retest studies (see Tables 5.3 through 5.5 in Wechsler, 1991). These scores should also be expected to improve perhaps significantly on a second test.

Standard Error of Measurement

The standard error of measurement (SEM) is simply another way of expressing the amount of error associated with a test score (see Chapter 5). The average standard error of measurement for the Full Scale IQ across all age groups for the WISC-III is 3.20 (Wechsler, 1991). The standard error of measurement is larger for the Performance IQ (4.54) than for the Verbal IQ (3.53). A value of 3 standard score points for the SEM of the Full Scale IQ is a good rule of thumb to keep in mind when reporting scores from the WISC-III.

WISC-III SEMs for the Index scores are somewhat higher (Table 5.2, Wechsler, 1991). The SEM values range from 3.78 for the Verbal Comprehension Index to 5.83 for the Processing Speed Index.

Validity

Bias

The manual reports that efforts were made to eliminate item bias using both statistical and judgmental methods (Wechsler, 1991). Tryout and standardization data were both analyzed to detect items that were exceedingly difficult for one group of children despite controlling for overall ability

level. Analyses were conducted to assess ethnic, gender, and regional bias. This procedure resulted in the elimination and modification of items primarily on the Information, Vocabulary, and Comprehension subtests (Wechsler, 1991). Judgmental bias reviews were also conducted.

The results of predictive validity bias studies indicate that this version differs little from its predecessors in that it produces equivalent predictive validity coefficients for Caucasian American, Hispanic American, and African American groups that were self-identified or identified by adults (Weiss, Prifitera, & Roid, 1995; Weiss, Prifitera, & Roid, 1993). Furthermore, no significant bias in prediction of academic achievement was found between the Canadian, British, and American norming samples (Prifitera et al., 1998).

Age Differentiation

Mean raw scores by age group are not provided in the WISC-III manual. Hence, age differentiation validity has to be inferred from the norm tables. The norm tables do provide a good range of scores for each subtest with the IQ scores producing a range of 40 to 160. The index scores, however, do not produce much differentiation at low and high score levels with scores ranging from 50 to 150.

Concurrent Validity

Correlations between the WISC-III and other intelligence tests are high. Concurrent validity studies reported in the manual show the WISC-III Full Scale to correlate .89 with the WISC-R, .86 with the WAIS-R, .85 with the WPPSI-R, and .92 with the Differential Ability Scales.

While the rank orders of these scores for various tests are likely to be similar, there are consistent mean score differences. In these same studies the Full Scale score of the WISC-III was 5 points lower than for the WISC-R, 4 points lower than WAIS-R, 4 points higher than WPPSI-R, and 2 points higher than the DAS. Weiss (1991) explains that the WISC-III should produce lower scores than the WISC-R because of the out-of-date standardization sample of the latter. Weiss (1991) provides a sample explanation for parents about the changes in norms, which may also be helpful to others trying to conceptualize the issue:

> *Often the pediatrician will tell the parent that their child's height or weight is in a certain percentile for children his/her age. These charts are (or should be) based on a contemporary sample. Using older charts, the same child would have a higher percentile ranking. This is because children are generally taller now than they were 20 years ago, so an average child today will appear tall when compared to average children 20 years ago. The same is true of intelligence. Children are generally smarter now than they were 20 years ago. So, children need to do better than before just to get an average score. (p. 8)*

This point of view is highly consistent with the Flynn effect, showing the generational changes in norms. Moreover, the differences between the two sets of Wechsler scale norms are mostly due to changes in the difficulty of Performance scale items. WISC-III Performance scale scores were found to be about 8 points lower than for WISC-R and Verbal scores were only about 3 points lower than their WISC-R counterpart.

On the other hand, why would the WAIS-R score be so much lower than the WISC-III? And why would the WPPSI-R, published in 1989, score lower than the WISC-III? These differences are likely due to differences in content, ceiling and floor effects, and other factors. Such routine differences between the WISC-III and other test scores should be taken into account when making diagnostic decisions, in addition to considering the SEM of the WISC-III and other measures.

The manual data for exceptional samples are also revealing. The WISC-III produced a Full Scale score approximately 9 points lower than the WISC-R for a sample of 43 children diagnosed with mental retardation. In direct contrast, the WISC-III produced a FSIQ approximately 5 points lower than the WISC-R for a sample of 23 children who were identified as gifted. These results suggest that while on the average WISC-III scores may be 5 points lower

than on the WISC-R the differences may be more substantial for children diagnosed with mental retardation. More detail on these investigations may be found in the WISC-III manual.

Predictive Validity

A central issue in intellectual assessment is the importance of showing that intelligence measurement is highly related to some important criterion, which in most cases is school achievement. The WISC-III follows in the tradition of other intelligence tests by showing substantial correlations between its IQ scores and measures of academic achievement. A number of investigations have shown that the WISC-R is predictive of future school achievement as measured by achievement tests (Kaufman, 1979b; McGrew & Pehl, 1988; Reilly, Drudge, Rosen, Loew, & Fischer, 1985). Typically, predictive validity coefficients are in the range of .50 to .65. While these correlations are not overwhelming, they are significant and stable over a number of investigations (Kaufman, 1979b). More recently, Figueroa and Sassenrath (1989) found the WISC-R Full Scale IQ to have predictive validity coefficients ranging from .49 to .64 when predicting reading and mathematics scores over a *10-year period*.

A study of 358 children cited in the WISC-III manual produced significant correlations with a variety of group-administered achievement tests. Scores from the various tests were combined to achieve the total sample of 358 cases. Correlations of WISC-III scores with total achievement were .74 for the Full Scale and .74 for the Verbal scale. The Performance scale correlation with achievement was considerably lower at .57.

An important finding from concurrent and predictive validity studies is that the Verbal scale of the WISC-R and WISC-III is more highly correlated with school achievement than the Performance scale (Figueroa & Sassenrath, 1989). This relationship is sensible from a number of vantage points, especially considering the content that is included in the Verbal scale subtests. The Arithmetic subtest, for example, includes items that are highly related to school instruction.

Similarly, Information and Vocabulary contain items that are likely influenced by various aspects of school instruction. These findings give further credence to Anastasi's (1988) conceptualization of intelligence tests as measures of developed abilities (see Chapter 2). The Verbal IQ of the WISC-III in particular should be regarded as a specialized type of achievement measure. Kaufman (1994) argues that the Performance IQ should be conceptualized similarly—that is, as a measure of what a child has learned.

Another investigation of several age groups reinforces the view that the Verbal scale is likely to routinely be a better predictor of academic achievement in reading, mathematics, and spelling than the Performance score. In a multi-age-group study of the relationship of the WISC-III with the Kaufman Test of Educational Achievement (K-TEA; Kaufman & Kaufman, 1985b) for four age groups, the Verbal scale correlated more highly with K-TEA achievement scores than the Performance score and often as well as the Full Scale score. Some sample correlations are shown below.

WISC-III Scale	Reading Composite	Mathematics Composite	Spelling
Ages 6–7			
Verbal	.55	.65	.51
Performance	.46	.58	.44
Full Scale	.60	.72	.56
Ages 8–10			
Verbal	.82	.78	.76
Performance	.65	.65	.59
Full Scale	.79	.77	.73
Ages 11–13			
Verbal	.83	.84	.61
Performance	.69	.73	.57
Full Scale	.82	.84	.64
Ages 14–16			
Verbal	.84	.80	.68
Performance	.69	.69	.59
Full Scale	.79	.78	.66

NOTE: These correlations are taken from unpublished Research Report KT-2 that is available from AGS, 4201 Woodland Road, Circle Pines, MN 55014-1796.

These data raise some interesting questions. Specifically, why administer the Performance scale if one is only interested in predicting achievement? And why administer the subtests necessary to compute the Full Scale if one is only interested in prediction of achievement? Answers will be proposed to these questions at later points, particularly in Chapter 17.

These relationships with academic achievement are clarified somewhat by the correlations of the WISC-III Index scores with achievement. In the aforementioned investigation of 358 youngsters the Verbal Comprehension Index (VCI) correlated highest with total achievement at .70. The Freedom from Distractibility Index (FDI) was next at .63. The Perceptual Organization Index (POI) and the Processing Speed Index (PSI) were the poorest correlates with achievement with coefficients of .56 and .50. In another study with the Wide Range Achievement Test—Revised (WRAT-R) the VCI and FDI were again higher correlates with achievement than the POI and PSI. There was an exception to this rule in that the PSI was a high correlate of mathematics scores on the WRAT (.73) (Wechsler, 1991).

Factor Analysis: WISC-R

The factor structure of the WISC-R is important to understand as a backdrop to factor studies of the WISC-III. There are many studies, using many samples, that have evaluated the factor structure of the WISC and WISC-R (Reynolds & Kaufman, 1990).

Like many intelligence tests, the WISC-R produced a large first or general intelligence "g" factor (see Chapter 5). The large WISC-R "g" factor also supported the WISC-R, yielding an overall composite score, or to use WISC-R terminology, the Full Scale IQ (the combination of the Verbal and Performance IQs) (Wallbrown, Blaha, Wallbrown, & Engin, 1975). The results of studies of "g" loadings suggest that tests such as Digit Span, Coding, and Mazes prove to be interpretive challenges, as they may frequently be deviant from the overall trend in a child's scores.

One of the consistent findings in the WISC-R factor analytic literature was the robust nature of its three-factor structure (Reynolds & Kaufman, 1990). Kaufman's (1975a) seminal investigation showed the WISC-R to have a very comparable factor structure to its predecessor, the 1949 WISC (Silverstein, 1982a; Silverstein & Legutki, 1982), including three factors that are easily labeled Verbal Comprehension, Perceptual Organization, and Freedom from Distractibility. The 12 subtests of the WISC-R correspond to the three factors as shown below.

Verbal Comprehension	Perceptual Organization	Freedom from Distractibility
Information	Picture Completion	Arithmetic
Similarities	Picture Arrangement	Digit Span
Vocabulary	Block Design	Coding
Comprehension	Object Assembly	
	Mazes	

The three-factor structure of the WISC-R has been shown to be consistent for a variety of populations. These same three factors have emerged for children with learning disabilities (Naglieri, 1981b), children with learning disability (LD) tested on two occasions 3 years apart (Juliano, Haddad, & Carroll, 1988), and mildly mentally retarded children (Cummins & Das, 1980). Another consistent finding in these investigations is that the Freedom from Distractibility factor is small. It accounts for a small proportion of variance in comparison to the first two factors. As a result, the Verbal and Performance scales of the WISC-R have long been considered to have adequate construct validity as assessed by factor analysis. The third factor, or Freedom from Distractibility factor, was the only blemish on this otherwise favorable picture of validity for the Verbal and Performance scales. The Freedom from Distractibility label comes from the work of Cohen (1959) on the original WISC. The Freedom from Distractibility factor (hereafter referred to as the WISC-R "third factor") has been enigmatic (Kaufman, 1979b), with a number of alternative names for this factor being proposed, including attention/distractibility, anxiety, symbolic ability, sequential processing, and memory (Reynolds & Kaufman, 1990).

Some researchers voiced dissenting opinions on the labels applied to the WISC-R factors. Most notably, Wallbrown et al. (1975) proposed application of Vernon's (1950) hierarchical model (see Chapter 2) of intelligence to the WISC-R. At the top of the hierarchy is "g" or general intelligence. The two lower levels in the hierarchy, the major group factors according to Vernon, are Verbal-Educational-Numerical (V:ed) and Spatial-Practical-Manual-Mechanical (K:m). In the Wallbrown et al. (1975) investigation, the Verbal Conceptualization and Perceptual Organization factors were renamed Verbal-Educational and Spatial-Mechanical, consistent with Vernon's theory. Silverstein (1982a) concluded that there was only a slight advantage for three-versus two-factor WISC-R solutions.

The label of Verbal-Educational for the first WISC-R factor was also supported by an investigation by Kaufman and McClean (1987). These researchers performed a joint factor analysis for 212 children without known disabilities on the WISC-R and the K-ABC. The Verbal subtests of the WISC-R and the Achievement subtests of the K-ABC showed a great deal of congruence; all loaded on the same first factor. The term *educational* from Vernon's theory seems comparable to the term *achievement* from Kaufman's conceptualization for the K-ABC, implying that there is a heavy emphasis on the assessment of academic skills for the Verbal subtests. These findings are also consistent with the aforementioned predictive validity data on the WISC-R, showing that the Verbal scale is considerably more predictive of future school success than the Performance scale.

In summary, there are several important lessons to be learned from the factor analytic research on the WISC-R. The more pertinent of these findings include:

1. There was strong factor analytic support for the Full Scale IQ.
2. There was strong factor analytic support for the Verbal and Performance IQs.
3. There was strong support for the third factor, but little agreement as to what it measured. The third factor was also smaller in comparison to the Verbal and Performance factors.
4. Some subtests such as the Coding, Picture Arrangement, and Digit Span subtests would more frequently emerge as deviant subtests that were difficult to interpret.

Factor Analysis: WISC-III

The factor analysis of the WISC-III reported in the manual produces some interesting findings (Wechsler, 1991) in that there are numerous points of agreement with tradition and yet some disagreement. Findings of agreement will be considered first.

The WISC-III produces two factors that correspond to some extent with the Verbal and Performance scales. The verbal factor has strong average loadings for the Information (.72), Similarities (.72), Vocabulary (.79), and Comprehension (.65) subtests. The Arithmetic subtest also loads on this factor at .41.

The perceptual organization factor remains intact, but it is less well supported, consisting primarily of three subtests. The factor is defined by strong loadings for Picture Completion (.53), Block Design (.70), and Object Assembly (.69). As was the case with the WISC-R, Picture Arrangement has a mediocre loading on this factor (.37), as does Mazes (.36).

Picture Arrangement (PA) not only loads poorly on the perceptual organization factor, but it also does not affiliate itself with any WISC-III factor. Picture Arrangement loaded .33 on the verbal factor, .37 on the performance factor, .08 on the third factor, and .25 on the processing speed factor. These data suggest that PA will continue to be difficult to interpret because of its allegiance to numerous factors and composites.

Digit Span (DS) is similar to PA in that it is not strongly linked with a particular factor. This test loads .26 on verbal, .19 on performance, .34 on the third factor, and .18 on the processing speed factor. These results suggest that Digit Span will also not consistently align itself with a particular composite.

The addition of the Symbol Search subtest did not strengthen the "distractibility" factor as was anticipated. The Symbol Search subtest helped create a new fourth factor (based on an exploratory factor analysis with varimax rotation) labeled processing speed, which is marked by high loadings for Coding (.79) and Symbol Search (.46). No other subtests have substantial loadings on this factor. This finding of a new fourth factor next raises the question of the clarity of the third factor.

The WISC-III third factor differs substantially from that of the WISC-R. This factor is now marked by only two subtests—Arithmetic (.73) and Digit Span (.34). The label now assigned to this factor is "freedom from distractibility." This label is questionable at best given the history of controversy surrounding the identification of the unifying ability underlying it (Kaufman, 1979b). Little (1991) argued for dropping the freedom from distractibility label by commenting, "Would it not therefore make more sense to abandon this terminology now so that individuals would be less likely to make faulty assumptions" (p. 24). The WISC-III third factor seems even more difficult to label because of the pattern of loadings of its two component subtests. The loadings for the Arithmetic subtest are consistently high, ranging from .54 for 8- to 10-year-olds to .85 for ages 14 to 16. The Arithmetic subtest also has consistent secondary loadings on the verbal factor (average = .41). As was previously cited, the Digit Span loadings show no particular allegiance to a factor. While its mean loading on the third factor is .34, its average loading on the verbal factor is .26, which is not a substantial difference. There is no evidence

that the WISC-III third factor is any more interpretable than the third factor for the WISC-R.
Researchers can still argue for previous interpretations, ranging from numerical facility to auditory short-term memory. It is now abundantly
clear, however, that the third factor is a poor
measure of distractibility (Kamphaus, 1998). Riccio, Cohen, Hall, and Ross (1997) studied the
correlation of the third factor with behavioral
measures of inattention and hyperactivity for
controls and children with ADHD subtypes. Correlations of the third factor with the Continuous
Performance Test were nonsignificant. Correlations with the Wisconsin Card Sorting Test (a
measure of executive functioning) were also insignificant for 7 of 8 comparisons. Correlations
were insignificant with the Conners parent and
teacher rating scales for all 8 comparisons and
with the Behavior Assessment System for Children (BASC) parent and teacher ratings for all
26 comparisons; for the Revised Behavior Problem Checklist, the correlations were insignificant
for 6 of 8 comparisons. These results, taken in
the context of other findings (Lowman, Schwanz,
& Kamphaus, 1997), lead clearly to the conclusion that *the WISC-III third factor is one of the
worst measures of distractibility that a psychologist
could utilize.*

Keith and Witta (1997) propose that the third
factor be considered to be a measure of quantitative reasoning. This hypothesis is similar to that
of Carroll's (1993), who proposed that the third
factor measures facility with numbers. Kranzler
(1997) disagrees with these interpretations and
makes a compelling case for labeling the third
factor as working memory. He reviews previous
literature by Baddeley (1996) and others and
notes that there are two aspects of short-term
memory: (1) primary memory, which is a passive
store that simply holds information for the purposes of further processing, and (2) working
memory (WM), where the actual processing of
information occurs. It is WM then that is more
highly correlated with "g" thus explaining why
Arithmetic (a measure of WM capacity that requires active processing of information) correlates

more highly with "g" than Digit Span (passive
storage in primary memory). Thus, Kranzler
(1997) proposes that *working memory efficiency* is
a better label for the latent trait assessed by the
third factor. This point of view is logical and consistent with previous research. The only caveat
remaining to consider is that the third factor was
not explicitly designed to measure WM, suggesting that better measures of the WM construct
may be available. Said another way, it is nevertheless troublesome that Digit Span has a mediocre loading on the third factor in comparison
to Arithmetic. Further studies are needed comparing the third factor to measures of numerical
facility, WM, etc., to assist the clinician in interpretation of this factor. In the interim I think
that *working memory efficiency is the most logically
consistent label for the latent trait assessed by the
third factor.*

Similarly, the labeling of the new fourth factor
as processing speed should be considered as tentative pending the outcome of future studies of
the relationship of this factor to other measures
of processing speed and other cognitive ability
constructs. The relationship of processing speed
to "g" has a long research tradition in individual differences inquiry (Deary, 1999) with one
prominent finding—measures of reaction time
and inspection time correlate significantly and
moderately with measures of "g." In the case of
the fourth factor of the WISC-III, this typical
pattern of results does not occur (Kranzler,
1997). Coding and Symbol Search may be a less
cognitively complex processing task in comparison to the typical processing speed paradigms, thus attenuating their relationship to
"g" (Kranzler, 1997). In fact, Carroll (1993)
noted this distinction in task demands and assigned Coding-like tasks to the stratum II factor
of broad cognitive speediness, which is far removed from better measures of "g" at stratum
II (see Chapter 2). Kranzler (1997) cites the
modest loading of these component subtests as
a rationale for not using the processing speed
label espoused for this factor. In his own words
he observed:

Further research on what this factor measures is obviously needed, but in the meantime other names should be considered, because labeling this factor "Processing Speed" is inconsistent with the results of contemporary theory and research on the cognitive underpinnings of g and may mislead those unfamiliar with the literature. (p. 114)

The implications of these findings for interpretive purposes are myriad. The clinician who understands these findings has a clear sense of how the WISC-III subtests are likely to covary for most children. This allows the clinician to know when test results are likely attributed to normal variation and when they are anomalous and therefore clinically meaningful. At a minimum the WISC-III factor analyses teach us the following lessons about expected variation on the WISC-III.

1. The Verbal and Performance scales lack the internal validity evidence of the new Index scores. Generally speaking, the VOI and POI Index scores are a better choice for routine assessment of verbal and spatial abilities. The PA subtest, however, does not appear to belong on the POI.

2. The third factor should be routinely referred to as *working memory*, which has broad meaning. This label is suggested with two cautions: (1) the third factor has only the minimum of two indicators to measure the WM trait, and (2) only the Arithmetic subtest may involve WM, whereas the Digit Span subtest may measure primary memory (Kranzler, 1997) and working memory (i.e., digits backwards) (Reynolds, 1997). Clinicians will only be able to interpret the factor in light of other data. If, for example, a child with a mathematics disability has a depressed third factor score then numerical facility may be a plausible reason for the low score. This type of case-by-case interpretation is the only reasonable course of action until convincing validation studies are done to elucidate the latent trait underlaying this factor or the factor is reconstructed in a

manner to improve its validity as a measure of WM.

3. The fourth factor possesses evidence of factorial validity but not substantial evidence of criterion-related or predictive validity. Pending such research, this factor should also be considered as supplementary and only interpreted in the context of case data that are compelling.

4. Arithmetic is the marker task for the third factor, yet it has a substantial secondary loading on the verbal comprehension factor. The Arithmetic subtest is only, therefore, slightly more likely to align itself with the third factor than with the Verbal IQ. As such, clinicians evaluating the profile for a particular child should not be surprised to see the Arithmetic subtest align itself with either the Verbal IQ or the third-factor subtests, Digit Span and potentially Coding.

5. Also noteworthy from these factor analytic results is that Digit Span bears little relationship to the Verbal IQ, despite the fact that it is placed on this scale. The Digit Span subtest, therefore, is not a good substitute for other verbal tests that have been spoiled or have somehow been invalidated. Perhaps *prorating*, the process of computing an estimated IQ when one or more subtests are missing for either the Verbal or Performance IQ, is a better option than substituting a Digit Span score (see the WISC-III manual for discussion of prorating procedures).

6. Clearly, Block Design and Object Assembly are the marker Perceptual Organization tasks contributing to the Performance IQ. Picture Arrangement, on the other hand, has a mediocre loading on the Perceptual Organization factor (.37). Picture Arrangement is less likely than other Performance subtests to align itself with the Performance IQ. In addition, the Picture Arrangement subtest has slightly smaller secondary loadings on the fourth factor and on the verbal comprehension factor. Consequently, *the Picture Arrangement subtest score is more likely than most WISC-III subtests*

to be a maverick in the profile for an individual child. This subtest could easily produce a scaled score that is an outlier from the rest of the WISC-III.

7. The Coding subtest, despite its placement as an alternative Performance scale test, is not a strong member of the Performance IQ, similar to the way Digit Span shares little variance with the Verbal IQ, making it a poor substitute if one of the Performance scale subtests is spoiled. Coding, then, may frequently be found to be deviant from the rest of the Performance subtests.

8. The new Symbol Search test actually has a better perceptual organization factor loading (.35 versus .13) than the Coding subtest. This subtest may be a more suitable Performance scale alternate than Coding.

9. Given the preliminary nature of the processing speed factor and the controversial nature of the third factor, these factors are only advised for use by experienced WISC-III examiners, and only by these individuals if future validity studies are supportive of these factors.

ADMINISTRATION

The WISC-III administration procedures are consistent with the history of psychological assessment. For example, while many newer tests such as the K-ABC, Woodcock-Johnson, and Binet-4 use an easel format where the various stimuli and instructions are self-contained, the WISC-III test stimuli and manual are separate from one another. The WISC-III, in contrast to the WISC-R, obviates the need for purchasing a bookstand because of the "crack back" manual that stands on its own. Administration of the WISC-III can be rather awkward for the new examiner, since both the manual and the test stimuli have to be manipulated separately.

The WISC-III also places a premium on the use of a stopwatch. The stopwatch has also been supplanted by newer tests that place more emphasis on power than speed. Since the WISC-III makes heavy use of a stopwatch, it is incumbent on the examiner to develop skill in its use. Examiners should not expect use of the stopwatch to come naturally, as it takes a great deal of practice for most.

Some of the examiner instructions on the WISC-III are wordy. Examiners have to therefore do their best to make the testing seem less contrived in spite of this. Examiners have to do this, however, without shortcutting or modifying the standardized wording. *The standardized wording must be used.*

The new examiner must also study the starting points and discontinue rules for each subtest carefully. On the WISC-III these differ considerably for each subtest. On Information, for example, there are four different starting points depending on a child's age. By contrast, on Comprehension every child begins with Item 1.

SCORING

For the most part the WISC-III is easy and objective to score. The scoring of some subtests can still be tricky for new examiners. While the scoring of Mazes is objective, it does take some time and practice. Similarly, awarding partial credit for the Object Assembly items can be tricky. For partially complete items, the raw score is equal to the "number of correct junctures." New examiners would benefit from practice in giving partial credit for various arrangements of puzzle pieces.

Scoring Verbal Responses

The WISC-R Similarities, Vocabulary, and Comprehension tests were particularly difficult for new examiners to score correctly (Slate & Chick, 1989). It is not clear how much easier the scoring of these verbal tests will be for the WISC-III. These tests are unusual because of their use of a trichotomous scoring system (scores of 2,1,0). Most modern tests eschew such a system and use dichotomous scoring for vocabulary and similar tests. The WISC-III tries to ease scoring of these tests by placing scoring criteria adjacent to the item. The advantage of such a trichotomous system is that it requires more verbal expression on the part of the child, which provides the examiner with rich observations of the child's verbal skills.

In order to use the discontinue rules for each of these tests appropriately, one should commit the scoring criteria for each item to memory. This task, however, is difficult to accomplish. A frequent error made by my students is to score a questionable response from memory when the exact response given by the child is listed verbatim in the scoring criteria accompanying the item. I suggest that for a questionable response, new examiners should *read every response given in the scoring criteria for the item before assigning a score to the response.*

Computing Derived Scores

The Computation of WISC-III raw and derived scores is simple. Clinicians do have to be careful when adding item scores to obtain a raw score. A frequently made mistake is to fail to give a child credit for items not administered *prior* to the starting point for a particular subtest.

Subtest scaled scores (standard scores with a mean of 10 and SD of 3) are easily obtained from Table A.1 of the WISC-III manual. The Wechsler IQ equivalents (standard scores with a mean of 100 and SD of 15) are then computed based on the sums of scaled scores using Tables A.2 through A.4. Index scores are provided in Tables A.5 through A.7. The Index scores are the alternative "IQ equivalents" for the four factor scores. These standard scores also use the mean = 100 and SD = 15 metric.

One oft-made mistake of new examiners is to pick raw scores off the front of the record form when writing a report. New examiners may want to highlight the standard scores to avoid this frequent and embarrassing mistake.

Confidence bands for the WISC-III are included with the composite score norm tables in the manual. Examiners will note that the WISC-

III offers asymmetrical confidence bands (see Chapter 5). For most cases a 90% confidence level is reasonable to use (Kaufman, 1979b).

Age equivalents and prorating tables are also given in the WISC-III manual. The numerous WISC-III interpretive tables will be discussed later in this chapter.

THE WECHSLER SUBTESTS

This section discusses some of the distinctive aspects of each subtest. Most of the WISC-III subtests have a long and rich clinical history. Understanding the origins of the item types and formats of the individual subtests is crucial to an integrative approach to interpretation. The description of each subtest will begin with an overview of the nature of the task, its history, and any distinctive aspects. Any noteworthy characteristics having to do with administration and scoring will then be addressed. Common problems and tips for beginners are also delineated. This section, however, is not a substitute but a supplement to the WISC-III manual.

Next some important psychometric characteristics for each test that have implications for interpretation are listed. The reliability coefficients reported are median internal consistency coefficients from the WISC-III manual (Wechsler, 1991). The factor analytic results are median loadings taken from the factor analysis of the WISC-III standardization sample cited in the manual (Wechsler, 1991). The "g" loadings and reliable specific variance (subtest specificity) estimates were computed based on the intercorrelation matrix of the WISC-III subtests for all ages combined[3] (Wechsler, 1991).

---

[3] The "g" loadings used for this chapter represent the loading for each subtest on the unrotated first principal component. The subtest specificities were computed in the same fashion as Kaufman (1979b). These values were computed by subtracting the squared multiple correlation of each subtest from its average internal consistency coefficient. I am indebted to Dr. Leslie Oliver Platt for her expeditious computation of these values.

A list of noteworthy behaviors for examiners to observe during testing is also provided. These behaviors can be helpful for testing hypotheses about a child's performance. Finally, hypotheses regarding variables that may influence subtest performance are provided. The interpretive process that is used to test these hypotheses will be discussed in detail in the following chapter. These lists are offered in this chapter to help the examiner better understand the range of possible skills and behaviors that influence each WISC-III subtest.

Picture Completion

On Picture Completion the child has to identify the missing part in a picture. This test is also an analog of a similar test from the Army examinations from World War I (Reynolds & Kaufman, 1990). Picture Completion is a nonthreatening introduction to the Performance scale (Zimmerman & Woo-Sam, 1985) and to the WISC-III as a whole. This test has a sample item that allows the child ample opportunity to understand the nature of the test demands. Similarly, for young children beginning with item 1 the examiner may model the correct response for the child who misses either item 1 or 2.

A stopwatch or other timing device is used on the Picture Completion subtest to time the 20-second maximum response time, resulting in associated anxiety by some children and adolescents. Children sometimes approach the task impulsively by giving a response before taking the time to survey the picture. The examiner should note whether or not a child tends to respond verbally or prefers pointing, for which credit is also given.

A child's negativism may also be observed on this scale (Zimmerman & Woo-Sam, 1985). This tendency is reflected for some children with comments such as, "nothing is missing." This comment results in the examiner having to practice the art of encouraging the child to try without giving clues or pushing the child to respond to

the point of frustration. The examiner has to "read" carefully the child's reaction to encouragement and discontinue prodding when it is clear that the child is getting frustrated.

Edelman (1996) harshly criticizes the "Orange" item of this test. He notes:

The worst item on this subtest is the Orange. . . . It has been my experience that more children say that the seeds were missing than the sector line. Apparently, this was a problem during the standardization, because the examiner must ask for another response and allow for an additional 20 seconds when the child says that the seeds are missing. This causes one to wonder whether the item was included because the substitution of a different item would have been too much of a bother. (p. 221)

Administration and Scoring Pointers

1. Practice using a stopwatch for timing short intervals (20 seconds).
2. Practice the verbal cues used to follow up responses.

Psychometric Properties

Average reliability = .77

"g" loading = .60

Loading on verbal comprehension factor = .38

Loading on perceptual organization factor = .53

Loading on third factor = .10

Loading on fourth factor = .08

Subtest specificity = .39 (ample)

Behaviors to Note

1. Squinting or other behavior suggesting difficulty seeing the stimuli
2. Excessive concern and interest in turning the cards
3. Excessive attention to the timing device

COGNITIVE HYPOTHESES TO INVESTIGATE

1. Knowledge base
2. Holistic (simultaneous) processing (Luria, Das)
3. Coping with novelty (Sternberg)
4. Perceptual organization (factor analysis)
5. Spatial ability (Carroll)
6. Part-whole relationships
7. Perceptual speed (Thurstone)
8. Executive system (Borkowski)

BIOGRAPHICAL AND BEHAVIORAL HYPOTHESES TO INVESTIGATE

1. Anxiety related to the timing device
2. Willingness to venture a response or guess when uncertain
3. Attention span/impulsivity
4. Visual acuity and discrimination

Information

Information requires the child to answer factual questions presented by the examiner. This test is an adaptation of tests developed by the Army to screen recruits for World War I (Reynolds & Kaufman, 1990).

The Information subtest gives the examiner a sense of the child's cultural, linguistic, and educational background. A foreign-born child, for example, may be unable to identify Christopher Columbus (Item 13). Similarly, a child whose primary language is Spanish may have difficulty articulating some of the responses such as months and seasons of the year in English. A child who is the product of an impoverished family or a poor educational experience may show substantial gaps in his or her knowledge base.

The Information items for the most part are perceived as being innocuous. Accordingly, a child's indignant response or refusal to complete the task is highly significant (Zimmerman & Woo-Sam, 1985).

Edelman (1996) has much practical administration advice for examiners of low-SES children or children from non-English-speaking cultures who may not clearly understand the question. He suggests the following:

If a child gives the amount of a coin rather than naming it say: "What is a 25-cent coin called?"

If a child says "eggs" in response to the "dozen" item say: "How many eggs make a dozen?"

If a child says there are "eight" hours in a day say: "How many hours are there in a whole day?"

If a child says that the stomach "growls" say: "What is the stomach used for?"

ADMINISTRATION AND SCORING POINTERS

1. Be prepared to give the supplemental queries associated with some items (e.g., 26).

PSYCHOMETRIC PROPERTIES

Average reliability = .84
"g" loading = .78
Loading on verbal comprehension factor = .72
Loading on perceptual organization factor = .29
Loading on third factor = .25
Loading on fourth factor = .09
Subtest specificity = .25 (adequate)

BEHAVIORS TO NOTE

1. Seeming familiarity with the item but struggles to remember the specific response
2. Self-deprecating statements
3. Comments about schooling
4. Comments about the difficulty of the items
5. Long response latency
6. Unwillingness to respond or guess when uncertain
7. Strong desire to know the correct answer
8. Requesting repetitions from examiner

Cognitive Hypotheses to Investigate

1. Knowledge base (acquired knowledge or fund of information)
2. Verbal expressive skill
3. Long-term memory
4. Knowledge acquisition components (Sternberg)
5. Verbal comprehension (factor analysis)
6. General intelligence (factor analysis)
7. Verbal meaning (Thurstone)
8. Crystallized ability (Cattell)
9. Executive system (Borkowski)
10. Social science knowledge

Biographical and Behavioral Hypotheses to Investigate

1. Quality of schooling
2. English-language proficiency
3. Acculturation (familiarity with American culture)
4. Parental cognitive stimulation
5. Achievement motivation
6. Interest in reading

Coding

Coding requires a child to copy letter and number-like symbols according to a specified pattern as quickly as possible. This test measures a great deal of motor skill akin to clerical aptitude tests that have been used in military and employment testing for generations. It requires some visual perception skill to recognize the code, and the ability to remember the code can be quite advantageous to success. Some fine motor skill is also required to complete the items expeditiously. This test has unnecessarily long instructions. Examiners will find it very difficult to read the instructions verbatim when a child obviously understands what to do. The examiner must persevere nonetheless.

Although motivation has been cited as a significant influence on Coding performance, this variable is unlikely to be relevant for older examinees. A well-controlled study by Lindley and Smith (1992) administered a Coding analog under incentive and nonincentive conditions to college students. Two groups were administered an alphanumeric coding task over several trials varying the order of the incentive and nonincentive conditions and instructions to participants to try and improve their performance. A third control group was administered several trials with no incentives. None of the conditions affected the relationship between task performance and an intelligence measure, thus casting into serious doubt the hypothesis that motivation affects performance. Lindley and Smith (1992) concluded, "The relationship between information processing speed and IQ appears to be cognitive and not motivational" (p. 25). Although motivation is offered as a potential explanation for Coding performance in this section, this is done primarily in consideration of the possibility that this variable may be important in some unusual case where test behaviors and background information strongly support such an interpretation. In most cases this hypothesis will be of little value.

Administration and Scoring Pointers

1. Be sure to use a pencil without an eraser.
2. Use only the standardized instructions given.

Psychometric Properties

Average reliability = .79

"g" loading = .41

Loading on verbal comprehension factor = .11

Loading on perceptual organization factor = .13

Loading on third factor = .09

Loading on fourth factor = .79

Subtest specificity = .49 (ample)

Behaviors to Note

1. Rechecking the code, indicating that it is not memorized
2. Squinting or other evidence of difficulty seeing
3. Poor motor control

Cognitive Hypotheses to Investigate

1. Fluid ability (Cattell)
2. Clerical speed and accuracy
3. Sequencing or successive processing (Luria, Das)
4. Coping with novelty (Sternberg)
5. Pencil and paper skill
6. Short-term memory (information processing theory)
7. Following instructions
8. Level I processing (Jensen)
9. Visual-motor coordination

Biographical and Behavioral Hypotheses to Investigate

1. Visual acuity and discrimination
2. Anxiety related to the stopwatch
3. Attention span/impulsivity
4. Achievement motivation
5. Fatigue or boredom

Similarities

On this test the child has to orally identify a unifying attribute for two verbal concepts. Similarities can trace its roots to the work of Binet, who used similar tasks at the turn of the century (Reynolds & Kaufman, 1990). This subtest is a rather unusual test of concept formation in that all of the verbal stimuli used, even on the more difficult items, are familiar to most children. As such, vocabulary knowledge is not as much of a factor on this test as it may first appear. The crucial issue for the child to grasp is the notion of "sameness." Some young children never fully grasp this concept.

Administration and Scoring Pointers

1. Become extremely familiar with the trichotomous scoring system prior to administration.

Psychometric Properties

Average reliability = .81
"g" loading = .77
Loading on verbal comprehension factor = .72
Loading on perceptual organization factor = .29
Loading on third factor = .23
Loading on fourth factor = .09
Subtest specificity = .23 (adequate)

Behaviors to Note

1. Preponderance of 1-point responses indicative of more concrete thinking
2. A tendency to "talk around" the issue

Cognitive Hypotheses to Investigate

1. Verbal expression
2. Categorical thinking
3. Level II processing (Jensen)
4. Knowledge base
5. Verbal comprehension (factor analysis)
6. Inductive reasoning (Thurstone)
7. Verbal meaning (Thurstone)
8. Executive system (Borkowski)

Biographical and Behavioral Hypotheses to Investigate

1. Quality of schooling
2. English-language proficiency

3. Achievement motivation

4. Interest in reading

5. Parental cognitive stimulation

Picture Arrangement

This test requires the child to arrange cards depicting a scene from a story in their correct sequence. Picture Arrangement was also originally developed during the World War I screening effort (Reynolds & Kaufman, 1990). This test assesses whether or not the child can follow a story line given in pictures. This fact is probably one of the reasons why this test has a significant factor loading on the verbal comprehension factor in some investigations. Clearly, children will be helped if they are able to verbally identify the plot (although this is usually done subvocally by children taking the test) and to explain the order of the pictures. Generally, however, this test can be difficult to interpret as it has mediocre loadings on three of the four WISC-III factors (save factor 3). In fact, when five-factor exploratory factor analysis solutions were computed for the WISC-III, the Picture Arrangement subtest occasionally produced its own factor, particularly at younger age groups. This failure to align itself clearly with a factor makes it enigmatic.

Administration and Scoring Pointers

1. Always replace pictures in the box *in layout order* so that they are ready for the next administration.

2. Practice the procedures for modeling and giving second trials.

Psychometric Properties

Average reliability = .76

"g" loading = .53

Loading on verbal comprehension
   factor = .33

Loading on perceptual organization
   factor = .37

Loading on third factor = .08

Loading on fourth factor = .25

Subtest specificity = .48 (ample)

Behaviors to Note

1. Gives several responses in reverse sequence

2. Does not survey the cards before responding

Cognitive Hypotheses to Investigate

1. Social judgment (See Chapter 17)

2. Knowledge base

3. Inferring cause-and-effect relationships

4. Executive system (Borkowski)

5. Fine motor skill

6. Successive processing (Luria, Das)

Biographical and Behavioral Hypotheses to Investigate

1. Anxiety related to the stopwatch

2. Experience with comic strips

3. Experiences with social interaction

4. Attention span/impulsivity

5. Visual acuity and discrimination

Arithmetic

Arithmetic requires the child to answer applied mathematical questions that are, for the most part, presented orally by the examiner. This subtest is probably the most school-like of any subtest on the WISC-III. It is essentially a test comprised of "word problems." Arithmetic, however, does differ from mathematics testing in school in a number of ways. This test has a distinct speed component. Rarely is a child's mathematics problem solving clocked by a stopwatch. For the child who is insecure about his or her mathematics ability, the timing of performance may be especially threatening.

This test is also rather unusual in that the child is not allowed to use aids such as pencil and paper or a calculator. This makes the task unrealistic in comparison to everyday mathematics calculation tests.

Finally, the Arithmetic test is not a comprehensive test of mathematics knowledge, and in some cases it may not even serve well as a screener. This situation is primarily due to the fact that the Arithmetic test lacks evidence of content validity. Evidence has not been presented to support the item selection for Arithmetic or to assess the degree to which the items reflect the content domain of mathematics. This lack of content validity is most clearly seen for adolescents. Adolescents are not asked to use estimation, measurement, graphing, or a host of other skills that they have been taught. Hence, while the Arithmetic test is very school-like, performance depends primarily on whether or not the child has acquired basic skills. It does differ enough from the arithmetic tests that children encounter in school that clinicians should not expect scores from this test to always agree with mathematics scores from the child's school, or even with parent's or teacher's report of a child's mathematics performance in school. Clinicians have often evaluated adolescents who are failing mathematics coursework and yet achieve an average score on the Arithmetic subtest.

The Arithmetic subtest also has a significant and consistent secondary factor loading on the verbal comprehension factor (see below). Hence, although this test marks the third factor it may also be influenced to some extent by verbal skills, perhaps above and beyond mental calculation skills.

ADMINISTRATION AND SCORING POINTERS

1. Be sure to time each item.

PSYCHOMETRIC PROPERTIES

Average reliability = .78
"g" loading = .76

Loading on verbal comprehension
factor = .41

Loading on perceptual organization
factor = .27

Loading on third factor = .73

Loading on fourth factor = .15

Subtest specificity = .30 (adequate)

BEHAVIORS TO NOTE

1. Self-deprecating statements about mathematics skills
2. Comments about schooling
3. "Rushes" to beat the stopwatch

COGNITIVE HYPOTHESES TO INVESTIGATE

1. Mathematics knowledge
2. Number (Thurstone)
3. Crystallized ability (Cattell)
4. Short-term memory (information processing)
5. Long-term memory (information processing)
6. Knowledge acquisition components (Sternberg)
7. Level II processing (Jensen)
8. Architectural system (Borkowski)

BIOGRAPHICAL AND BEHAVIORAL HYPOTHESES TO INVESTIGATE

1. Anxiety related to mathematics or stopwatch
2. Quality of schooling
3. Attention span/impulsivity
4. Achievement motivation
5. Auditory acuity and discrimination
6. Attitude toward mathematics
7. English-language proficiency

Block Design

On this task the child is required to construct designs out of blocks to match a model. Block Design is a variant of a test developed in the early part of last century by Kohs (1923). Block Design has a distinctly spatial component and requires a minimal level of fine motor skill to make the necessary constructions. The spatial aspects of the task are emphasized in the scoring in which rotations of greater than 30 degrees are scored as incorrect. This suggests that rotations are pathological (possibly indicative of something like a brain insult), although there are no data to document this. Again, speed becomes an important factor on this test as additional points are awarded for quick responses. Consequently, it is crucial to use the standardized procedures, as these make it clear that a child should not dawdle. Some very intelligent children may obtain average scores on this test because they were more concerned with accuracy than speed. Two children can obtain average scores on this test in very different ways. A child can achieve a scaled score of 10 by working quickly and getting a few items wrong. A child can also work slowly, get all of the items correct, and still get a 10.

This test has been raised to preeminence somewhat by research on split-brain patients (Springer & Deutsch, 1981) (see Chapter 2). In a number of studies Block Design was used as a marker task of right brain (holistic) processing. Schorr, Bower, and Kiernan (1982) tested two strategies for solving Block Design items: "an analytic strategy in which subjects mentally segment each block in the design to be constructed and a synthetic strategy, which involves wholistic pattern matching" (p. 479). These authors found that the analytic strategy was dominant in a series of four experiments. Schorr et al. (1982) also theorize that it is the inability to employ an analytic strategy that adversely affects the Block Design performance of brain-injured individuals.

ADMINISTRATION AND SCORING POINTERS

1. Practice modeling and administering second trials.
2. Practice scoring rotations.

PSYCHOMETRIC PROPERTIES

Average reliability = .87

"g" loading = .71

Loading on verbal comprehension factor = .29

Loading on perceptual organization factor = .70

Loading on third factor = .24

Loading on fourth factor = .17

Subtest specificity = .34 (ample)

BEHAVIORS TO NOTE

1. Attempts to align the sides of the blocks in addition to the tops
2. Excessive frustration over failures on difficult items

COGNITIVE HYPOTHESES TO INVESTIGATE

1. General intelligence (factor analysis)
2. Spatial ability
3. Holistic (simultaneous) processing (Luria, Das)
4. Coping with novelty (Sternberg)
5. Fine motor coordination
6. Visual-motor coordination
7. Fluid ability (Cattell)
8. Executive system (Borkowski)
9. Perceptual organization (factor analysis)
10. Right hemisphere processing (split-brain research)

BIOGRAPHICAL AND BEHAVIORAL
HYPOTHESES TO INVESTIGATE

1. Attention span/impulsivity
2. Anxiety related to the stopwatch
3. Achievement motivation
4. Visual acuity and discrimination

Vocabulary

This test requires a child to orally define words presented by the examiner. The Vocabulary test follows in the tradition of Binet's emphasis on the assessment of higher-level cognitive skills. This format creates the opportunity for the examiner to assess how eloquently a child expresses his or her thoughts. The open-ended response format of the test also allows the child to express information of great clinical importance (e.g., "a knife is for killing people").

ADMINISTRATION AND SCORING POINTERS

1. Read the scoring guide completely before scoring a questionable response.

PSYCHOMETRIC PROPERTIES

Average reliability = .87

"g" loading = .80

Loading on verbal comprehension
  factor = .79

Loading on perceptual organization
  factor = .22

Loading on third factor = .18

Loading on fourth factor = .16

Subtest specificity = .24 (adequate)

BEHAVIORS TO NOTE

1. Word retrieval (finding) problems
2. Preponderance of 1-point responses
3. Misarticulation

COGNITIVE HYPOTHESES TO INVESTIGATE

1. Knowledge base
2. Verbal expression
3. Long-term memory
   (information processing)
4. Knowledge acquisition components
   (Sternberg)
5. Verbal comprehension (factor analysis)
6. General intelligence (factor analysis)
7. Verbal meaning (Thurstone)
8. Crystallized ability (Cattell)
9. Executive system (Borkowski)
10. Vocabulary knowledge

BIOGRAPHICAL AND BEHAVIORAL HYPOTHESES TO INVESTIGATE

1. Parental cognitive stimulation
2. Quality of schooling
3. Achievement motivation
4. Interest in reading
5. English-language proficiency

Object Assembly

This test is also an analog of a test from the World War I effort (Reynolds & Kaufman, 1990). Object Assembly, like Block Design, has a strong spatial component and a minor fine motor component. The stimuli used are relatively common, so knowledge base is rarely a factor.

Object Assembly is a rather unique test in the annals of intellectual assessment because it has only five items (plus a sample item that is completed by the examiner). Based on the relationship between reliability and test length, one may think that the test is wholly unreliable. The reliability problem, however, has been conquered by awarding partial credit and bonus points for speedy performance for each item. Because of the small number of items it is, nevertheless, important to note how a child obtained his or her raw score. A careless error on one of the items may have a dramatic effect on the overall score. As was the case with Block Design, a child may be punished for having very careful work habits, as speed is integral to obtaining a high score.

ADMINISTRATION AND SCORING POINTERS

1. Practice the rules for assigning partial credit to imperfect responses.

PSYCHOMETRIC PROPERTIES

Average reliability = .69

"g" loading = .61

Loading on verbal comprehension factor = .26

Loading on perceptual organization factor = .69

Loading on third factor = .11

Loading on fourth factor = .14

Subtest specificity = .26 (inadequate)

BEHAVIORS TO NOTE

1. Overconcern with the stopwatch
2. Inability to verbally "label" an item, resulting in a failure

COGNITIVE HYPOTHESES TO INVESTIGATE

1. Perceptual organization (factor analysis)
2. Spatial ability (Carroll)
3. Holistic (simultaneous) processing (Luria, Das)
4. Fine motor coordination
5. Visual-motor coordination
6. Executive system (Borkowski)
7. Puzzle-solving skill

BIOGRAPHICAL AND BEHAVIORAL HYPOTHESES TO INVESTIGATE

1. Visual acuity and discrimination
2. Anxiety related to the stopwatch
3. Achievement motivation
4. Attention span/impulsivity

Comprehension

This test requires the child to respond orally to questions posed by the examiner. This verbal test places a premium on the child's verbal expression skills. Also, Comprehension more than any other WISC-III subtest is known as having the potential to elicit rich clinical cues about a child's personality (Zimmerman & Woo-Sam, 1985). This test is clinically rich in that it assesses not only knowledge but also conformity to societal conventions. Every child begins with Item 1 on this test regardless of age, which creates the opportunity for older children to respond to very easy items. An adolescent with a conduct disorder may respond in a socially deviant manner.

ADMINISTRATION AND SCORING POINTERS

1. Remember to cue items requiring a second response when necessary.
2. Read the scoring guide completely before scoring a questionable response.

PSYCHOMETRIC PROPERTIES

Average reliability = .77

"g" loading = .68

Loading on verbal comprehension factor = .65

Loading on perceptual organization factor = .19

Loading on third factor = .17

Loading on fourth factor = .19

Subtest specificity = .30 (adequate)

BEHAVIORS TO NOTE

1. Word retrieval (finding) problems
2. Responses that are deviant from societal norms

COGNITIVE HYPOTHESES TO INVESTIGATE

1. Knowledge base
2. Verbal expression
3. Long-term memory
4. Verbal comprehension (factor analysis)
5. Knowledge acquisition components (Sternberg)
6. Verbal meaning (Thurstone)
7. Executive system (Borkowski)
8. Crystallized ability (Cattell)

BIOGRAPHICAL AND BEHAVIORAL HYPOTHESES TO INVESTIGATE

1. Quality of schooling
2. English-language proficiency
3. Acculturation
4. Parental cognitive stimulation
5. Achievement motivation
6. Interest in reading
7. Fatigue (the child has taken several tests at this point and Comprehension is among the least interesting)
8. Values and moral development

Symbol Search

This test measures mental processing speed and visual search skills akin to Coding. Symbol Search also has two levels like Coding (under 8, and 8 and over), and its oral instructions are rather lengthy. This test is reminiscent of the speed of processing test of the Differential Ability Scales (see Chapter 13).

The clinical value of this test is not well known nor is its distinctiveness from the Coding subtest. Symbol Search does covary with Coding, yet it has a significant secondary loading on the perceptual organization factor, unlike Coding (see below and section on factor analysis). This finding reveals that the Symbol Search test shares more with the Performance scale than Coding, making it a more suitable substitute for another Performance scale subtest than the Wechsler original—Coding. While such a substitution is warranted by the data, the advice in the manual is contrary, in that Symbol Search is only allowed to be substituted for the Coding test. The logic of the position taken in the manual is, therefore, not clear.

ADMINISTRATION AND SCORING POINTERS

1. Be sure to have two pencils without erasers.
2. Use only the standardized instructions given.

PSYCHOMETRIC PROPERTIES

Average reliability = .76
"g" loading = .56
Loading on verbal comprehension factor = .20
Loading on perceptual organization factor = .35
Loading on third factor = .19
Loading on fourth factor = .56
Subtest specificity = .34 (adequate)

BEHAVIORS TO NOTE

1. Rechecking the target symbols, indicating that they are not memorized
2. Squinting or other evidence of difficulty seeing

COGNITIVE HYPOTHESES TO INVESTIGATE

1. Fluid ability (Cattell)
2. Clerical speed and accuracy

3. Sequencing or successive processing (Luria, Das)

4. Coping with novelty (Sternberg)

5. Pencil and paper skill

6. Short-term memory (information processing theory)

7. Following instructions

8. Level I processing (Jensen)

9. Visual-motor coordination

10. Processing speed

Digit Span

This test requires the child to orally reproduce a string of numbers that are dictated by the examiner. Digit Span has a long history as part of intellectual assessment (Reynolds & Kaufman, 1990). Digit Span requires the child to attend at least briefly, and the child will benefit from rehearsal of the numbers in short-term memory. Some children rehearse more overtly than others—one can hear them or see their lips move. Other children show no evidence of rehearsal. This test also requires adequate auditory perception and discrimination skills.

For the first time the cumulative frequency of raw scores for the Digits Forward and Digits Backward items is included in the manual (Table B.6, Wechsler, 1991). Clinicians have always noted that some children are much more adept at repeating forward digits than at backward digits although no data have been available to allow clinicians to check their informal impressions. The data presented in the manual do suggest that the forward digits are in fact considerably easier than the backward digits. The average longest string of forward digits for the entire sample was 5.81 whereas a mean of only 4.01 was obtained for the backward digits.

The factor loadings for Digit Span lead one to conclude that it is the most unique subtest on the WISC-III in that it loads poorly on all factors and only slightly better on factor three than on factor one. It is almost as if Digit Span is dependent on a rather unique skill (auditory short-term memory) that is simply not measured well by other WISC-III subtests. This lack of covariation with the remainder of the WISC-III will make this test more likely to deviate from other tests as a strength or weakness.

Digit Span interpretation is more difficult due to a lack of complementary measures of memory on the WISC-III. Hence, we have only one indicator of auditory short-term memory, making hypotheses associated with this ability more prone to error. In fact, experienced clinicians have often seen a Digit Span score that was not corroborated by other memory measures. In addition, the Digit Span score is reflective of two memory abilities rather than one (Reynolds, 1997). When factor analyzed with other memory measures, digits forward and backward were found to load on two distinct factors. Reynolds (1997) found digits and letters forward tasks to load on one factor, whereas digits and letters backward tasks load on a second factor. These results convincingly make the point that the Digit Span subtest is a confounded measure of two latent traits, making interpretation uncertain. This finding is yet another reason to assign a rather general *working memory* label to the third factor and exercise some caution when drawing both Digit Span and third-factor hypotheses.

ADMINISTRATION AND SCORING POINTERS

1. Practice the 1-second administration interval between stimuli in order to develop a "rhythm."

2. Do not take pains to make eye contact during administration of the stimuli. One research study has found that routine eye contact significantly *detracted* from performance (Goldfarb, Plante, Brentar, & DiGregorio, 1995).

PSYCHOMETRIC PROPERTIES

Average reliability = .85

"g" loading = .47

Loading on verbal comprehension
   factor = .26

Loading on perceptual organization
  factor = .19

Loading on third factor = .34

Loading on fourth factor = .18

Subtest specificity = .63 (ample)

BEHAVIORS TO NOTE

1. Absence of evidence of rehearsal

2. Comments about their memory skills

3. Responds before examiner gives complete
   stimulus suggesting impulsivity

COGNITIVE HYPOTHESES TO INVESTIGATE

1. Fluid ability (Cattell)

2. Architectural system (Borkowski)

3. Knowledge of numbers

4. Sequencing or successive processing
   (Luria, Das)

5. Short-term memory span
   (information processing theory)

6. Level I processing (Jensen)

BIOGRAPHICAL AND BEHAVIORAL HYPOTHESES TO INVESTIGATE

1. Auditory acuity and discrimination

2. English-language proficiency

3. Attention span/impulsivity

4. Anxiety

5. Fatigue or boredom

Mazes

Mazes, another component of the old Army examinations (Reynolds & Kaufman, 1990), assesses the ability of a child to complete a series of mazes with pencil and paper. This task is not unlike the mazes that many children complete for their own enjoyment. It requires adequate spatial ability and fine motor skill to guide the pencil through each maze.

This test can also be difficult to score, especially if a child changes his or her mind frequently or is sloppy. Mazes also lacks difficulty (ceiling) for older children, resulting in lower reliability coefficients for older age groups. In fact the test-retest coefficients (corrected for variability) for Mazes for the 10–11 and 14–15 age groups were .56 and .57, respectively. These factors have contributed to its lack of popularity with practicing clinicians. This test is rarely used in clinical practice.

ADMINISTRATION AND SCORING POINTERS

1. Practice scoring a variety of responses.

PSYCHOMETRIC PROPERTIES

Average reliability = .70

"g" loading = .30

Loading on verbal comprehension
  factor = .06

Loading on perceptual organization
  factor = .36

Loading on third factor = .11

Loading on fourth factor = .12

Subtest specificity = .57 (ample)

BEHAVIORS TO NOTE

1. Numerous changes of course indicative
   of impulsivity

2. Squinting or other evidence of vision
   problems

COGNITIVE HYPOTHESES TO INVESTIGATE

1. Short-term memory
   (information processing)

2. Spatial ability (Thurstone)

3. Holistic (simultaneous) processing
   (Luria, Das)

4. Fine motor coordination

5. Visual-motor coordination

6. Pencil and paper skill

7. Executive system (Borkowski)

BIOGRAPHICAL AND BEHAVIORAL
HYPOTHESES TO INVESTIGATE

1. Visual acuity and discrimination

2. Anxiety related to the stopwatch

3. Attention span/impulsivity

4. Achievement motivation

5. Fatigue or boredom

6. Experience with mazes

BASIC INTERPRETATION

Hypotheses for V/P Differences

Theories abound regarding the abilities and skills assessed by the Verbal and Performance scales, some of which were discussed earlier in the section on factor analysis. This section explores a variety of explanations for score differences between the scales as a prelude to competent WISC-III interpretation (to be discussed later in this chapter and in Chapter 17).

What are the factors that contribute to V/P discrepancies, and how do these factors affect diagnosis, prognosis, treatment plans, and the like? Kaufman (1979b) suggested several possible hypotheses for interpreting WISC V/P discrepancies. These and some additional hypotheses are discussed next. Along with a discussion of each hypothesis, some "suggestive evidence" will be offered. Such evidence refers to behaviors, background information, other test scores, and information that may be consistent with a child's performance on these scales.

Verbal versus Nonverbal Content (V>P or P>V)

It is quite possible that a child may simply be more adept at responding to verbal stimuli than nonverbal stimuli. This hypothesis should always be considered when entertaining reasons for verbal/performance discrepancies on the WISC-III, because this distinction does enjoy a history of factor analytic support (Kaufman, 1994). Vernon (1984) labels verbal and nonverbal abilities as "major group factors" because they have emerged in countless factor analytic investigations.

The distinction between the ability to apply cognitive operations to verbal as opposed to more nonverbal content is an ideal one for application to the WISC-III. This hypothesis is supported not only by factor analytic findings but by the fact that it was the basis upon which the Wechsler tradition is premised. Wechsler's development of a clinical test of intelligence mirrors the experience of World War I psychologists, who found that many non-English-speaking immigrants to this country obtained inappropriately low scores on the primarily verbal Army Alpha. As a result of this experience, the requirement to access intelligence through the use of nonverbal procedures was adopted by the military through the creation of the Army Beta. Hence, the measurement of intelligence has a long tradition of conceptualization based upon the nature of the content to be processed cognitively.

Even when there is a substantial Verbal/Performance discrepancy, some subtests may still not align themselves with either the Verbal or Performance scales. In fact, this misalignment is probable given that the Arithmetic, Coding, and Digit Span subtests have their primary loadings on the third and fourth factors and Picture Arrangement does not load well on any WISC-III factor. These subtests may frequently not align themselves with the Verbal and Performance scales. The examiner, then, should not expect unanimity of performance within the Verbal and Performance scales given these findings. The clinician will more commonly find a trend for most of the Verbal and Performance subtest scores to fall together. In other words, *the Verbal/Performance distinction may still be the most parsimonious explanation for a child's scores, even when some of the subtests do not support this distinction.*

Ancedotally, I have seen a number of children display a P>V pattern that seemed to center on the child's preference for dealing with nonverbal stimuli. The children who come to mind when thinking of this pattern have been reticent during the testing. They seem to be genuinely enthusiastic about the Performance tests (as indicated by moving closer to the table and working intently) and dread the Verbal scale tests. Less frequently, I have observed children who obtain a V>P pattern who take delight in the Verbal tests and appear confident in their verbal skills. On Performance tests, by contrast, their confidence withers, and they seem unsure as to how to solve the problems. Frequently, these children will express interest in highly Verbal activities, such as reading. Test behavior such as these may be helpful in corroborating verbal or nonverbal content differences.

Suggestive Evidence

1. Poor (or strong) academic achievement record

2. Poor (or good) articulation

3. Delayed (or precocious) language development

4. Interest (or lack of interest) in mechanical skills or hobbies

5. Interest (or lack of interest) in reading

6. Good (or poor) conversational skills

7. Strong (or poor) school achievement

Linguistic Differences (P>V)

Related to the notion of a verbal/nonverbal content distinction is the hypothesis that a V/P discrepancy is the result of linguistic differences (limited English proficiency in most cases). Numerous research studies have noted a P>V profile for groups of children for whom English is not their primary language (Fourqurean, 1987; Gerken, 1978; Shellenberger & Lachterman, 1976). This hypothesis is reasonable for a P>V profile whenever information documenting linguistic differences in home and/or the school setting is available.

A linguistic difference hypothesis should enter clinician's minds when testing any non-English-speaking child, including Spanish-speaking, Asian American, and Native American children. There may also be forms of English that differ somewhat from the terminology used on the WISC-III. I once tested an impoverished black child from rural Appalachia with whom I had considerable difficulty communicating. I remember having difficulty interpreting his responses to Verbal scale items. One response sounded to me like "bo dolla," which turned out to be a dollar bill. The causative factors were unclear, whether it be poverty, Black dialect, or rural location, but his English clearly departed substantially from that required to get a high Verbal score (see Chapter 17). A linguistic difference hypothesis may also be confounded by cultural differences. A child may conceivably be self-conscious about his or her lack of English proficiency and make a limited attempt to use English. An examiner could assess this possibility before the evaluation by observing the child in school or other social setting, or by asking the child's teacher or parent to describe the child's English-language proficiency. Examiners may also assess the impact of English proficiency on the child's test scores by obtaining information from other sources about his or her knowledge and use of English.

Suggestive Evidence

1. Non-English first language

2. Primary language of the home is not English

3. Immigrant from non-English culture

4. Was reared with "nonstandard" form of English (e.g., Cajun)

5. Poor reading skills

Speech or Language Impairment (P>V)

The presence of a speech or language impairment may also depress Verbal scores in relationship to Performance scores. This hypothesis, like the linguistic difference hypothesis, is again typically suggested based upon thorough knowledge of background information regarding the child being assessed. Clearly, a child who has a verbal expression problem will have difficulty on the Verbal scale more than on the Performance scale.

SUGGESTIVE EVIDENCE

1. Delayed language development
2. History of speech/language services
3. Poor reading skills
4. Poor Vocabulary test scores

Hearing Impairment (P>V)

Common sense and research findings support a clear Performance > Verbal profile for children with significant hearing impairments. Sullivan and Burley (1990) state that typical practice involves using the WISC Performance scale only in the assessment of the cognitive skills of hearing-impaired children.

A clinician may also encounter children with mild or undetected hearing loss that produce a P>V pattern. Behaviors that may suggest hearing loss include unclear, loud, or delayed speech; requests to repeat items or instructions; or difficulty understanding instructions. Children who have been prescribed hearing aids should wear them for the evaluation. When a child's speech is not easily interpretable, or the child uses sign language, a specialist should conduct the intellectual evaluation.

SUGGESTIVE EVIDENCE

1. History of hearing impairment
2. Does not hear well during evaluation
3. Wears hearing aids
4. Uses sign language
5. Poor Vocabulary test scores

Novelty (V>P)

Sternberg (1987) contends that some children, especially some minority group children, have trouble coping with novelty. This hypothesis may explain why African American children showed a V>P profile on the WISC-R (Reynolds, 1981a). The Performance scale poses a number of unfamiliar item types to children in contrast to the familiar words used on the Verbal scale. Perhaps children who are not used to having novel stimuli presented to them, as is more likely to be the case for impoverished children or children from cultural groups with a history of a high incidence of poverty, may not possess coping skills for dealing with novelty.

Clinicians can "test the limits" in order to assess the effects of novelty on WISC-III Performance scores. An examiner could ask the child, once testing is completed, if certain items were more familiar to him or her than others.

SUGGESTIVE EVIDENCE

1. Uses unsystematic (trial and error) approach to Performance items
2. Seems uncomfortable in test setting (e.g., reluctant to speak or make eye contact)
3. Low scores on other nonentrenched tests such as Ravens Progressive matrices
4. Adequate to good school achievement

Achievement Motivation (V>P or P>V)

Since the Verbal scale of the WISC-III is more highly correlated with school achievement than the Performance scale, a child may have a V>P profile that is due to a high level of achievement motivation and associated academic achievement. A relatively high Verbal score could not only be the cause of a high level of academic achievement, but also be the product of high levels of academic achievement, especially on tests highly related to in-school achievement, such as Information and Arithmetic.

A child who is the product of a striving family may exhibit this profile. Behaviors that may be exhibited by the child include tenacity, great concern about whether or not he or she gave correct responses, and curiosity about correct responses for items solved incorrectly.

A contrasting lack of achievement motivation could be associated with a P>V profile. While this is theoretically possible, it may be more clinically rare. The unmotivated child or adolescent may also not put forth good effort during administration of the Performance scale, resulting in a lack of bonus points. This scenario could produce an overall underestimate of the child's skills. This hypothesis could be tested by readministering some tests, or a new intelligence test, and giving rewards (e.g., toys, money, praise, etc.) for competent performance (see Chapter 5, Research Report). If a child's scores increase dramatically (beyond what would be expected based on the standard error of estimate for the subtest or composite score) on retesting, then an achievement motivation weakness may be suspected as contributing to low scores or a P>V split.

This hypothesis is more likely to be sensible for older children. It assumes that the child has already had ample opportunity to demonstrate tenacity, hard work, or apathy in school.

Suggestive Evidence

1. Parents (do or do not) emphasize education and achievement

2. Academic achievement scores higher (or lower) than Performance score

3. Good (or poor) effort in school

4. Child expresses like (or dislike) for school

5. Lack (or excess) of behavior problems in school

6. Low (or high) level of aspiration as indicated by career goals

Hemispheric Specialization (V>P or P>V)

Researchers have hypothesized for some time that the Verbal scale of the WISC-III measures primarily left-brain processing, and the Performance scale right-brain processing (Kaufman, 1979b), based upon the groundbreaking research of Sperry, Gazzaniga, and Bogen (1969) (see Chapter 2). The hypothesis that left-hemisphere processing is more related to Verbal scale performance is due to the theorizing that the left brain is specialized for language and the right hemisphere is primarily nonverbal (Gazzaniga, 1975) (see Chapter 19). The right hemisphere has been associated with Performance scale abilities because tests such as Block Design were included by split-brain researchers as exemplary measures of the spatial-holistic processing abilities of the right hemisphere. Unfortunately, while this left hemisphere versus right hemisphere dichotomy seems logical and intuitively appealing, it is apparently not consistently documented in children (Kamphaus & Reynolds, 1987). A number of research investigations have shown no clear-cut relationship between Verbal and Performance IQs and left- and right-hemisphere functioning for children (Kaufman, 1979b; Morris & Bigler, 1985; Shapiro & Dotan, 1985) (see also Chapter 19). Part of the problem is that the attribution of a child's problems to one hemisphere is an oversimplification of a dynamic and complex system. There are cases where this model may be at least partially helpful.

One of the more salient cases in my memory is of a child who displayed a P>V profile shortly after recovering from a drug-induced coma. The child was given the wrong medication by his pharmacy. He lost almost all speech but did recover much of it. Later, he still showed a P>V profile that was statistically significant, although his speech had apparently returned to normal.

Suggestive Evidence

1. History of head trauma

2. History of seizures

3. Delayed early developmental milestones

4. History of medical condition associated with neurological damage (e.g., tuberous sclerosis)

Spatial Ability (P>V or V>P)

Due to the preponderance of visual stimuli on the Performance scale, performance deficits relative to the Verbal scale may be explained by poor spatial problem-solving abilities. Related to this the clinician may, in fact, find evidence of visual problems that could certainly interfere with Performance scale results. Alternately, well-developed spatial skills may explain a P>V profile.

A colleague told me of a child with mild cerebral palsy who had a V>P difference of 50 points! Even on visual perception measures that did not require motor skill he had extreme difficulty. According to physician reports, his eyesight was normal. He just had extraordinary difficulty interpreting most spatial stimuli. As one would expect, his major school problem was in mathematics. Visual acuity could also be the explanation for a V>P profile. Children should always be assessed for vision problems prior to an evaluation. Clinicians should also check to ensure that a child with corrective lenses is wearing them during the evaluation.

SUGGESTIVE EVIDENCE

1. History of vision problems (V>P)
2. Difficulty (or success) in academic areas requiring spatial skills (e.g., geometry, fine motor skills)
3. Congenital or traumatic neurological insult to visual/spatial processing areas of brain (V>P)
4. Poor scores on visual-motor tests such as Bender or Beery

Motor Problem (V>P)

A child with a motor deficit, particularly a fine motor deficit, may have extraordinary difficulty with Performance scale subtests, resulting in a Verbal > Performance profile. I once had a case where I was asked to assess a hydrocephalic child. This child, even at age 12, was still suffering cerebral damage due to marginally controlled hydrocephaly. Occasionally her cerebral shunt would clog, resulting in an exacerbation of her physical condition. Among the sequelae of her hydrocephaly was a significant gross and fine motor coordination problem. This individual showed a very clear pattern of V>P intelligence on the WISC-III. This hypothesis may also apply to other conditions with associated motor problems. These conditions may include cerebral palsy and muscular dystrophy.

SUGGESTIVE EVIDENCE

1. Sloppy construction of Performance items
2. Frustration during construction
3. History of motor disability (cerebral palsy, muscular dystrophy, etc.)
4. Poor scores on visual-motor tests such as Bender or Beery

Deliberate Response Style (V>P)

A child may also obtain a V>P profile because of a very deliberate response style. A child may achieve nearly perfect scores but receive few bonus points on Performance scale subtests. Sometimes, a child may have solved a Block Design item correctly but will then spend considerable time "tidying" up the design. Some children will not leave any blocks out of perfect alignment. These compulsive behaviors can preclude a child from earning bonus points for quick performance.

Kaufman (1979c) demonstrated the clear effects of speed on WISC performance and concludes that speed of response becomes increasingly important for obtaining high Performance scale scores with increasing age. In parallel fashion, a deliberate response style hypothesis should become more viable for older children and adolescents.

SUGGESTIVE EVIDENCE

1. Compulsive neatness when constructing designs
2. Child earns few, if any, bonus points

Time Pressure (V>P)

Since the only timed items are on the Performance scale, a V>P pattern may occur because of an inability to handle the pressure associated with being timed by a stopwatch. Some children become visibly upset, with hands shaking, and face flushed on tests such as Block Design and Object Assembly.

Underlying anxiety may set the stage for responding to time pressures. The following observations taken from a WISC-III evaluation of a 13-year-old exemplify this pattern. "Significant weight loss lately. Many, many self-deprecating statements throughout exam despite continuous successes. Extreme somatic tenseness: cracking vertebrae, clenching jaw, trembling hands, sitting rigidly in his seat, breathing heavily. Careless mistakes on portions of timed tests. Too much pressure for him." This individual obtained a Verbal score of 137 and Performance of 121!

SUGGESTIVE EVIDENCE

1. Signs of anxiety during timed tests (e.g., sweating, increased respiration)
2. Rushes through timed tests

Learning Disability (P>V)

The general trend for children with learning disabilities is to have a P>V profile (Kavale & Forness, 1984). The differences in a number of investigations, however, are small. In the Kavale and Forness (1984) meta-analytic investigation of 94 studies of learning disabled children, the average Verbal standard score was 94 and the Performance standard score average was 98. This difference of a few standard score points, although small, is persistent.

A trend toward a P>V profile for learning disabled children is intuitive since the Verbal scale is more highly correlated with school achievement. Children are referred for learning disability services because they are performing poorly in the classroom (Kaufman, 1979b). More recent investigations have also corroborated the findings of a P>V profile (Fourqurean, 1987; Rethazi & Wilson, 1988). This profile, however, is of virtually *no value in making the diagnosis of a learning disability* since the crux of learning disability diagnosis is the determination of an ability/achievement discrepancy (see Chapters 17 and 20).

SUGGESTIVE EVIDENCE

1. Delayed acquisition of basic academic skills, particularly in reading
2. History of diagnosis of reading disability in immediate family members
3. Teacher and parent suspicions of a learning disability

Long-Term Memory/Word Retrieval (V<P or V>P)

A V/P discrepancy could be highly influenced by long-term memory processes if one subscribes to an information processing perspective (see Chapter 2). The efficiency with which a child solves Verbal scale items is determined to a large extent by his or her ability to store and retrieve information from long-term memory. A child who does not use good strategies to store verbal information or lacks retrieval cues may display a P>V profile. The Performance scale does not require a child to retrieve substantial amounts of information from memory.

Children sometimes struggle through a variety of Verbal tests making comments like, "I know that." One hypothesis that this type of statement suggests is that the child did not do a good job of storing the class material and, therefore, was unable to efficiently retrieve the information (P>V profile). A child may also have word retrieval problems that are due to neuropsychological insults (see Chapter 19).

SUGGESTIVE EVIDENCE

1. Good (or poor) school performance
2. Exhibits obvious memory strategies during the evaluation (V>P) (e.g., repeats numbers on Digit Span)

3. Spontaneously expresses knowledge of memory strategies (V>P) (e.g., "I repeat names to myself so I can remember them better")

4. Good (or poor) performance on delayed recall tests such as those on the Woodcock-Johnson or Differential Ability Scales

Classification of the Full Scale and Other Composites

The classification scheme that I use is as follows (see Chapter 18 for other systems).

1. 130 and above—significantly above average
2. 110–129—above average
3. 90–109—average
4. 71–89—below average
5. 70 and below—significantly below average

I use two classifications to describe a Full Scale or other composite score if the score is borderline—that is, within 3 standard score points (about 1 SEM) of the adjoining category. If, for example, a significantly below-average Full Scale of 69 is obtained, then the score is described as "below to significantly below average." The same two classifications are given for a score of 73.

Compare Composite Scores to Assess Their Meaningfulness

The interpretive value of the Full Scale score may be gauged in two ways. The first procedure is to test the statistical significance (or reliability; Silverstein, 1981) of the difference between Verbal and Performance standard scores. In this way the examiner can determine if the difference between Verbal and Performance scores is likely accurate and not a statistical artifact (i.e., due to chance). The average values across ages are a Verbal/Performance difference of 12 standard score points at the .05 level and 15 points at the .01 level (Wechsler, 1991). In other words, a difference of

12 points between the Verbal and Performance scales is likely a reliable one that is not due to chance factors. Said another way, there is only a 5% probability (.05) that the difference is due to chance and there is a 95% probability that it is an accurate difference.

Because of the difference between statistical significance and clinical significance, Kaufman (1979b) advised that examiners also consider the relative rarity of discrepancy scores in the normal population. Values for determining the proportion of the WISC-III standardization sample that obtained a given discrepancy score or larger are given in the WISC-III manual. As a general guide, I suggest that *a discrepancy of 25 points that occurs in 5% or less of the standardization sample is rare* (see Table B.2, Wechsler, 1991) and renders the overall composite standard score, in this case the Full Scale standard score, as relatively useless as an overall estimate of intelligence. When a difference this unusual, and this large, occurs in an individual's intelligence test performance at the composite score level, the child's intelligence is simply too multifaceted to be summarized with a single number (see section on Illusory V/P differences discussed later for an exception).

Differences between Index scores may also be hypothesized and tested (see Research Report 8.1). Tables B.1 and B.2 of the WISC-III manual (Wechsler, 1991) allow examiners to test for reliable and rare differences between many pairwise comparisons of Index scores. An examiner may hypothesize, for example, that the Processing Speed Index will be lower than the Perceptual Organization Index because a child is said to be extremely slow to complete written work in the classroom. A reading of Table B.1 reveals that a 15-point difference between these two Index scores is reliable (i.e., statistically significant at the .05 level), and Table B.2 shows that a difference between these scores of 31 points or more occurs in less than 5% of the population.

Interpretation of the WISC-III composites is confusing at first blush due to the preponderance of composite scores now available. Clinicians can choose to interpret the traditional VIQ/PIQ and

RESEARCH REPORT 8.1

Characteristic WISC-III Profile Types

Donders (1996) utilized cluster analysis to identify core profile types in the WISC-III standardization sample. By doing so one can determine if a given child's profile of scores is different from one that may be relatively common in the population. If, for example, a child's profile looks unique or interesting, yet it is shared by 20% of the normative sample it is unwise to conclude that the child's profile of scores is in some way deviant.

The cluster analysis conducted by Donders (1996) identified five profile types that seemed to differentiate the members of the normative sample. Of greater interest is the finding that three of these types are differentiated not by shape of their profile of WISC-III Index scores but, rather, by their overall level of performance. In other words, the overall FSIQ would suffice for summarizing these three types.

The mean Index scores for the three "level" types were as shown below.

Type	Verbal Comprehension	Perceptual Organization	Freedom from Distractibility	Processing Speed
2	81	81	84	87
3	117	119	118	118
4	96	95	97	91

The two "shape" types produced the following means.

Type	Verbal Comprehension	Perceptual Organization	Freedom from Distractibility	Processing Speed
1	96	99	99	113
5	112	109	109	100

It is interesting that the two "shape" profiles may also be differentiated by level for the first three Index scores. Only the Processing Speed Index adds "shape" to these profiles. In the absence of this finding the five clusters of children in the sample could be easily classified as ranging from below average to above average.

The relative importance of the Processing Speed finding is also unclear since the clusters have not been validated against external criteria (e.g., child academic performance). The average socioeconomic status of the families of the five types were calculated by Donders as one test of external validation. Consistent with intuitive predictions (and empirical findings cited in Chapter 3) the SES associated with the types were predicted by FSIQ. Type one, for example, would be expected to be of lower SES than type 5, and this finding was obtained. Approximately 10% of the parents of type 1 cases had 16 or more years of education versus 22% of type 5.

This investigation suggests that the Processing Speed Index requires further study. Until results of importance are obtained the level of performance seems to be of greater importance than shape for most members of the standardization sample which is, after all, intended to serve as a microcosm of the U.S. population of children between 6 and 16.

Full Scale or the newer four Index scores and the even newer General Ability Index (GAI) (Prifitera et al., 1998). The new GAI is merely an eight subtest short form Full Scale composite (excluding Arithmetic and Coding) based on the four scores that enter the Verbal Comprehension Index and the four that make up the Perceptual Organization Index. I advise the following simple prioritization rules.

First, *utilize the traditional Full Scale score for most purposes*. The GAI is not particularly short, consisting of eight subtests, so it offers few practical advantages. In addition, the traditional Full Scale will ensure comparability with prior results. I realize, however, that differences between the GAI and Full Scale will likely be small in everyday assessment practice. Therefore, for most purposes, the choice of overall composite score is not of critical importance.

Secondly, *utilize the newer Index scores for most purposes.* Granted, the traditional VIQ and PIQs have a substantial research base. It is also clear, however, that this research base has clearly shown that the WISC, WISC-R, and now WISC-III are better described as assessing more than two latent traits (see Appendix A). Hence, the large number of available studies contradict Wechsler's original conceptualization for children. It should also be recalled that Wechsler did not have modern statistical methods available to thoroughly test the factorial validity of the original scales.

Unfortunately, the nature of the latent traits assessed by the four Index scores is likely to be debated for some years to come. The latent trait assessed by the third factor, for example, is alternatively considered to be a measure of "working memory" (Prifitera et al., 1998) or two traits: "short-term memory" (Digit Span) and "quantitative ability" (Arithmetic) (McGrew & Flanagan, 1998). The VCI and POI indexes will be easier to interpret, regardless of the name utilized, since they have apt descriptions from a variety of theoretical perspectives ranging from the seminal factor studies of Philip E. Vernon (Verbal/Educational versus Spatia/Mechanical) to the comprehensive factor analyses of John B. Carroll (crystallized versus visualization). Working definitions of these traits and the Processing Speed Index may be obtained from Chapter 2.

The clear caveat to the clinician is that some or all of the Index scores can be of little value in a case if the component subtests of the Index score produce highly variable results, otherwise known as "scatter." If, for example, a child obtains third factor Index subtest scores of 14 for Arithmetic and 7 for Coding, then the FFD Index score is of no value for describing a latent trait at Stratum II (Carroll, 1993).

Consider Shared Subtest Hypotheses

Experienced examiners will be able to merely glance at the subtest scores for an individual child and discover significant fluctuations in the profile (see Box 8.1). The new examiner, however, requires specific guidelines for determining when a

---

Box 8.1 WISC-III Basic Interpretation Methods

1. Collect background information
2. Offer Hypotheses
   A. Full Scale (Global) composite
   B. Other composites (e.g., V and P)
   C. Profiles (i.e., 2 or more subtests)
   D. Single subtest
3. Test Hypotheses
   A. Full Scale (Global) composite against descriptive category
   B. Other composites against composite score significant and rare differences
   C. Profiles against subtest strengths and weaknesses
   D. Single subtest against subtest strengths and weaknesses
4. Draw conclusions

---

fluctuation in a child's profile may be of significance. Kaufman (1979b) produced tables for determining the statistical significance of profile fluctuations. This principle is the same as was used in determining significant or reliable differences between Verbal and Performance scores. The difference in this case is determining whether or not there are reliable peaks or valleys, or strengths or weaknesses, in a child's profile of Wechsler subtest scores.

The common procedure for determining significant strengths and weaknesses in Wechsler subtest profiles is to consult Table B.3 of the WISC-III manual (Wechsler, 1991). The WISC-III manual offers a bewildering number of possibilities for determining subtest strengths and weaknesses—eight to be exact, depending on the number of subtests administered and whether or not one uses the mean of all subtests for comparison or the mean of the Verbal and Performance scales separately (the issue of which subtest mean is preferable will be discussed later). The values needed for this section are given on page 264 of the WISC-III manual.

The advised procedure for determining significant fluctuations in a profile is as follows:

1. Compute the mean scaled score of all 12 subtests (or 10 or 13 subtests as appropriate) combined and round this value to the nearest whole number.

2. Compute the difference between each subtest scaled score and the mean scaled score.

3. Compare each difference score to the corresponding subtest difference score value for the .05 level (the second column in the table) presented in Table B.3 (p. 264) of the WISC-III manual. Round the values in Table B.3 to make these comparisons. If a difference between a subtest score and the mean *meets or exceeds the rounded tabled value*, then it is marked as a strength (S). Mark a weakness (W) if the subtest scaled score is lower than the mean but at least as large as the tabled value.

The WISC-III profile for Connie in Figure 8.1 will serve as an example of how subtest strengths and weaknesses are determined. This child obtained a mean scaled score for 12 tests of 11. The subtest scores are compared to the mean, revealing the strengths and weaknesses shown in Figure 8.1.

In order to confirm shared subtest hypotheses in the sample profile *all, or virtually all, of the scores for the subtests that are a part of the hypothesis should be at or below the subtest mean of 11*. In Connie's case such a hypothesis would be supported by the Coding and Symbol Search scores of 4 and 9, respectively.

Shared subtest hypotheses for Wechsler Subtests are given in Table 8.1. This table is given to assist clinicians in the process of generating hypotheses as to why a child's score may be particularly high or low.

Table 8.1 also includes cognitive factors, background variables, test behaviors, and emotional traits and states that may affect performance. This list is also provided for the purpose of generating hypotheses during interpretation.

For a number of reasons these lists should not be treated as a "cookbook." Lists of this nature can be misleading because many of the hypotheses may not possess scientific support. They do help new clinicians think through a profile, yet trainees can easily become too dependent on them. These lists emanate from theory and experience more so than research. They are based primarily on the work of Kaufman (1979b), Zimmerman and Woo-Sam (1985), the larger body of WISC-R literature, and on my own experiences and those of my colleagues and students with the WISC-III. Another important realization is that each item in these lists is relative. For example, quality of schooling probably influences performance on every WISC-III subtest, but it is not listed for all. By inference then these lists are suggestive and certainly not all inclusive.

The significant fluctuations in this profile give some guidelines as to where to search for profiles that may be of importance for understanding a

CONNIE

The basics of interpretation are now demonstrated with a sample case. Connie is a 16-year-old female who was evaluated subsequent to receiving hospital treatment for drug dependency. Her scores and significant profile fluctuations are shown below. Connie's significant profile fluctuations were determined using the aforementioned procedures.

Composite Scores

Full Scale Standard Score	108
Verbal Standard Score	117
Performance Standard Score	96

Subtest Scores

VERBAL SCALE		MEAN	DIFFERENCE	SIGNIFICANCE VALUE (TABLE B.3)	S OR W
Information	13	11	2	3	—
Similarities	13	11	2	4	—
Arithmetic	13	11	2	4	—
Vocabulary	12	11	1	3	—
Comprehension	13	11	2	4	—
Digit Span	13	11	2	4	—

PERFORMANCE SCALE		MEAN	DIFFERENCE	SIGNIFICANCE VALUE (TABLE B.3)	S OR W
Picture Completion	14	11	3	4	—
Picture Arrangement	10	11	−1	4	—
Block Design	10	11	−1	3	—
Object Assembly	10	11	−1	5	—
Coding	4	11	−7	4	W
Symbol Search	9	11	−2	4	
Overall Mean = 11 (11.36)					

Drawing Conclusions

One can easily corroborate the hypothesis of average to above-average intelligence. First, Connie's achievement test scores were average to above average, and secondly, the examiner noted that she was highly motivated to do well on the tests. For example, she frequently asked whether or not she solved items correctly. She also appeared somewhat confident of her skills.

Connie's V>P profile of a relative strength in verbal skills and weakness in nonverbal skills is also easily corroborated. It is noteworthy that her highest score on the Performance scale was on the only subtest on that scale that elicits a verbal response (Picture Completion).

It is also possible to support the hypothesis of a deficit in pencil and paper (writing) skill. According to her teacher she has particular difficulty expressing herself in writing. She also had a difficult time on the spelling test that was administered as part of the test battery. She erased frequently, which resulted in a messy written product. Connie's weakness in written expression was also shown in the following written responses to the sentence completion blank.

"I want to be like myself off of drugs."

FIGURE 8.1
Sample cases

"I hate to hear people say that I ain't tall."

"My greatest fault is to be avoiding."

In summary, in Connie's case there are only two reasonable hypotheses at the composite score level (average to above-average intelligence and verbal >nonverbal content skills) and one at the single subtest level (pencil and paper or writing skill). Hence, the task here is to take the pencil and paper skill hypothesis and try to attribute it to the more reliable and valid relative weakness in nonverbal areas. The goal here is to say that Connie's pencil and paper skill weakness is merely a reflection of her overall relative weakness in nonverbal areas.

In this case such a statement is not logical. While ideally one would like to err in the direction of "higher" levels of interpretation, the evidence for the weakness in pencil and paper skill is compelling. The following evidence supports interpreting the Coding test separately for Connie:

1. Coding is one of only two test on the WISC requiring the child to use a pencil.

2. Coding is not slightly lower than the other tests but considerably lower. The next highest scaled score is 6 points higher. This is more than a standard deviation and a half difference.

3. Writing problems were obvious on other tests administered as part of the evaluation.

4. A written expression weakness is well documented by teacher report.

5. Coding and Symbol Search possess ample subtest specificity.

In the light of the aforementioned considerations, the following *conclusions* will be listed in Connie's report.

1. Connie's measured intelligence is in the average to above-average range.

2. Connie's verbal skills are stronger than her nonverbal skills. Her verbal skills are above average and her nonverbal skills are average.

3. Connie's written expression weakness was also reflected on the WISC-III where she performed most poorly (well below average) on a test requiring her to copy nonsense symbols with a pencil as rapidly as possible. While this conclusion is consistent with a written expression weakness, more testing would be recommended to document a bonafide learning disability.

JERRY

Jerry is a third-grader who was referred by his teacher for academic problems in all areas.

Composite Scores

Full Scale Standard Score	69
Verbal Comprehension Index	68
Performance Perceptual Organization Index	85
FFD Index	64
Processing Speed Index	50

Subtest Scores

VERBAL SCALE		MEAN	DIFFERENCE	SIGNIFICANCE VALUE (TABLE B.3)	S OR W
Information	3	5	–2	3	—
Similarities	5	5	0	4	—

FIGURE 8.1

Sample cases (Continued)

(Continues)

VERBAL SCALE		MEAN	DIFFERENCE	SIGNIFICANCE VALUE (TABLE B.3)	S OR W
Arithmetic	4	5	−1	4	—
Vocabulary	4	5	−1	3	—
Comprehension	4	5	−1	4	—
Digit Span	3	5	−2	4	—

PERFORMANCE SCALE		MEAN	DIFFERENCE	SIGNIFICANCE VALUE (TABLE B.3)	S OR W
Picture Completion	8	5	−3	4	—
Coding	1	5	−4	4	W
Picture Arrangement	7	5	−2	4	—
Block Design	6	5	1	3	—
Object Assembly	8	5	−3	5	—
Symbol Search	1	5	−4	4	W

Overall Mean = 5 (4.5)

Drawing Conclusions

The bulk of evidence suggests that Jerry's intelligence is significantly below average. This consistent evidence makes it reasonable to emphasize the composite score conclusion in a report.

In Jerry's case, however, the WISC-III Index scores give the clearest picture of his intellectual strengths and weaknesses. The Index scores are also strikingly consistent with previous information. Because of the clarity with which the Index scores describe Jerry's cognitive skills, these should be highlighted in written reports along with the Full Scale.

Many implications could be drawn from Jerry's WISC-III results. The relative strength in perceptual organization, for example, may be of benefit on some academic or vocational tasks.

JANINE

Janine is an 8-year-old female who is well liked by everyone. She is described by her parents and teacher as cheerful, cooperative, and hardworking. She is, however, having significant difficulties in school. She was retained in kindergarten due to her lack of academic progress, and she is currently being evaluated by school personnel to determine her eligibility for special education and related services. A prior evaluation did not produce a diagnosable condition.

Janine's intelligence and achievement test results produce a consistent picture of a child with below-average cognitive skill development. These results stand in stark contrast to her interpersonal and adaptive strengths. She occasionally produces test scores in the average range; however, these scores are not as highly related to successful school performance.

Of greater concern is Janine's developing negative attitude toward school, as revealed on the BASC Self-Report of Personality where she reported significant evidence of negative attitude toward school and her teacher. She also reported feelings of inadequacy regarding her school performance.

FIGURE 8.1
Sample cases (Continued)

Janine requires academic instruction that fosters her academic growth and, simultaneously, her academic motivation. Currently, she does not appear to be making adequate progress toward meeting either objective.

Interpretive Notes

The case of Janine points out several interpretive principles. Note that WISC-III Coding emerges as a strength of dubious value. First, this result is not surprising given that Coding, a member of the rate of test-taking factor as alluded to by Carroll (1993), is distant from "g." Consequently, this strength is likely to be of limited value for supporting her academic success.

Note also that most of the visualization factor subtests are below average save one: Visual Closure from the W-J Test of Cognitive Abilities. Other equally strong tests of visualization, such as the WISC-III PIQ and DAS Spatial, are consistently below average. There are then two possible interpretations for the Visual Closure score: (1) it is anomalous, representing a single indicator of a trait when two indicators are needed to adequately assess a trait, or (2) it is an accurate identification of a level I specific factor of cognitive ability. Even if this finding is accepted as a valid indicator, interpretation of this score may not need to be emphasized. In the context of the entire case this finding, like the Coding result, represents overinterpretation that does not contribute substantially to either diagnosis or case planning for Janine. Certainly, academic skill development requires a complex array of cognitive abilities utilized in combination, and a curricular intervention cannot be based on such an isolated skill that is not highly correlated with general academic achievement in the early elementary grades.

Analogously, emphasizing Janine's Coding and/or Visual Closure results would be similar to a neurologist concluding that a pediatric stroke victim who has incurred damage to Broca's area and thus has lost speech has an intact olfactory nerve. The importance of this result pales in comparison to the fact that numerous neurological systems, some of which are highly valued for functioning in society, are substantially impaired and in need of treatment. It is sufficient in Janine's case to merely identify the Visual Closure result as a finding of unknown value at this time, but it is reported for future reference if needed.

WISC-III

Composite Scores

Full Scale Standard Score	69
Verbal Standard Score	66
Performance Standard Score	75

Subtest Scores

VERBAL SCALE

Information	5	Vocabulary	5
Similarities	4	Comprehension	4
Arithmetic	9	Digit Span	8

PERFORMANCE SCALE

Picture Completion	5	Block Design	6
Coding	11	Object Assembly	5
Picture Arrangement	9	Symbol Search	8

FIGURE 8.1
Sample cases (Continued)

(Continues)

DAS

GCA	77	Nonverbal Reasoning	79
Verbal	81	Spatial	81

Verbal

Similarities	24	Word Definitions	39

Spatial

Recall of Designs	34	Pattern Construction	39

Nonverbal Reasoning

Matrices	42	Sequential & Quantitative Reasoning	34

Diagnostic Subtests

Recall of Digits	42	
Speed of Information Processing	42	

W-J TCA

Memory for Sentences	79	Visual Closure	100
Visual Matching	86	Picture Vocabulary	86
Incomplete Words	89	Analysis-Synthesis	72

Wechsler Individual Achievement Tests

Composite Score	81	Mathematics	75
Reading	77	Language	87

Subtests

Basic Reading	83	Numerical Operations	85
Mathematics Reasoning	76	Listening Comprehension	93
Spelling	78	Oral Expression	88
Reading Comprehension	78		

W-J Tests of Achievement

Broad Written Language	55	Skills	75
Broad Mathematics	87	Mathematics Reasoning	89
Broad Knowledge	94	Broad Reading	81

Subtests

Letter-Word Identification	80	Writing Samples	18
Passage Comprehension	85	Science	97
Calculation	92	Social Studies	104
Applied Problems	89	Humanities	83
Dictation	71		

FIGURE 8.1
Sample cases (Continued)

BASC SRP

School Maladjustment	67	Personal Adjustment	41
Clinical Maladjustment	38	Emotional Symptoms Index	46

SCALES

Attitude to School	65	Depression	49
Attitude to Teacher	67	Sense of Inadequacy	60
Atypicality	36	Relations with Parents	42

FIGURE 8.1
Sample cases (Continued)

TABLE 8.1   Shared and single subtest hypotheses for WISC-III strengths and weaknesses

Hypotheses	Inf	Sim	Arith	Voc	Comp	DS	PC	PA	BD	OA	Cod	Maz
Knowledge Base	√	√	√	√	√		√	√		√		
Sequencing			√			√					√	
Short-Term Memory			√			√					√	
Long-Term Memory	√	√	√	√	√		√			√		
Achievement Motivation		√		√								√
Level II Processing		√	√						√			
Verbal Comprehension		√	√		√	√						
Verbal Expression	√	√		√	√							
Knowledge Acquisition Components	√		√	√								
Auditory Acuity and Discrimination			√			√						
Categorical Thinking		√										
Mathematics Knowledge			√									
Social Studies Knowledge	√											
English Vocabulary				√								
Commonsense Reasoning					√							
Short-Term Memory Span						√						
Perceptual Organization								√	√	√		√
Visual Acuity and Discrimination							√	√	√	√	√	√
Holistic Processing							√		√	√		√
Spatial Ability							√		√	√		√
Fine Motor Coordination								√	√	√	√	√
Coping with Novelty		√				√	√		√		√	
Visual-Motor Coordination								√	√	√	√	
Distinguishing Essential from Nonessential Details							√					

(Continues)

Table 8.1   Shared and single subtest hypotheses for WISC-III strengths and weaknesses (Continued)

Hypotheses	Inf	Sim	Arith	Voc	Comp	DS	PC	PA	BD	OA	Cod	Maz
Inferring Cause-and-Effect Relationships								√				
Right-Hemisphere Processing										√		
Clerical Speed and Accuracy											√	
Pencil and Paper Skill										√	√	
Following Instructions										√		
Quality of Schooling	√	√	√	√	√							
English-Language Proficiency	√	√	√	√	√	√						
Acculturation (to American Culture)	√	√	√	√	√							
Parental Cognitive Stimulation		√	√	√	√	√						
Interest in Reading	√	√		√	√							
Anxiety Related to Stopwatch							√	√	√	√	√	√
Willingness to Guess							√					
Attention Span/Impulsivity			√				√	√	√	√	√	√
Experience with Comic Strips							√					
Experience with Social Interaction							√					
Fatigue/Boredom						√	√				√	√
Values and Moral Development							√					
Distractibility							√					
Experience with Mazes												√

child's cognitive skills. The profile in Figure 8.1 has only one significant fluctuation—a weakness for the Coding subtest. The next step is to enter Table 8.1 and *write down all shared subtest hypotheses* for Coding.

For a hypothesis to be listed as potentially viable, it has to include, of course, Coding, and all, or nearly all, of the subtests that are lower than the subtest mean of 11. If one enters Table 8.1 the following hypotheses may be listed as plausible for shared subtest weaknesses that include Coding. The first hypothesis that includes the Coding subtest is sequencing. Looking across the page there are two other subtests that are hypothesized as placing a premium on this skill—Arithmetic and Digit Span. As alluded to earlier, in order to list sequencing as a hypothesis worth investigating further *all, or virtually all, of the scores for the subtests that are a part of this hypothesis should be at or below the subtest mean* of 11. Arithmetic does not lend support because of its score of 13. Digit Span mitigates further against listing this hypothesis because of its score of 13. Given this state of affairs the sequencing hypothesis is discarded as a possible weakness and the search continues.

The next step is to reenter Table 8.1 and check the next hypothesis that includes the Coding subtest—short-term memory. This hypothesis will also not work because it includes the same subtests as the prior hypothesis—Arithmetic and Digit Span. This process continues until all shared subtest hypotheses are exhausted.

One more caution regarding scatter analysis is necessary, whether one is discussing Index score differences, differences between lowest and highest subtest scores, or other indices of deviance. *Most clinicians tend to underestimate the amount of scatter that is normal in the population* (Kaufman, 1990) which, in turn, can result in overdiagnosis of pathology. On the face of it, for example, a subtest score range of 5 to 14 for the 12 subtest administration of the WISC-III is not well within normal limits, but it was obtained by 39% of the norming sample. A range of 5 to 17 may be more unusual but this variability was seen in about 13% of the norming sample cases (Schinka, Vanderploeg, & Curtiss, 1997). The normal base rate of occurrence of scatter must always be considered prior to drawing a conclusion regarding the presence of cognitive pathology.

Consider Single Subtest Hypotheses

These hypotheses are considered if the subtest score upon which the hypothesis is based is determined to be a statistically significant (or nearly significant) strength or weakness. Ideas for these hypotheses are provided with the detailed descriptions of the WISC-III subtests and in Table 8.1.

This level of interpretation was saved for last because it is the most treacherous as it lacks reliability and validity support even more so than the shared subtest level (see Chapter 17). This step involves taking the subtests that emerge as strengths or weaknesses and entering Table 8.1 in order to generate hypotheses for the Coding subtest in isolation. Entering Table 8.1 with Coding in mind the following list of hypotheses can be written: weaknesses in clerical speed and accuracy, following instructions, and fatigue or boredom. A hypothesis not offered in Table 8.1 is dysgraphia (a written expression learning disability that could be secondary to a brain insult). This is but one of many potential hypotheses that is not offered in Table 8.1 because it is low incidence, lacks research support, or is speculative. It is, however, an example of a hypothesis that may be offered based on the examiner's knowledge of the case.

Examiners also need to refer back to information on subtest specificity when offering a single subtest hypothesis. It would be helpful to record the subtest specificity on the sheet used for making case notes and listing hypotheses. The subtest specificity for Digit Span may bolster the clinician's confidence in the hypothesis, and for Object Assembly the clinician may decide a priori to not even entertain single subtest hypotheses.

Draw Conclusions

Now the clinician must determine which hypotheses have the most support by "testing" each hypothesis listed against background information, observations during testing, interview information, school or clinic records, reports of parents and teachers, other test scores, and WISC research findings.

Each hypothesis should be taken in turn and the corroborating or conflicting evidence recorded. *Two pieces of evidence* are generally adequate to corroborate or reject a hypothesis. In some cases one strong piece of evidence may corroborate a hypothesis. If, for example, a child was brought to a clinic setting for a suspected mathematics learning disability, and the Arithmetic subtest of the WISC-III emerged as a lone weakness, then the referral problem (mathematics learning disability) may be a strong piece of evidence that explains the Arithmetic weakness. A more cloudy case would be the situation where Arithmetic is the lone weakness in a profile and there is no evidence of a mathematics problem.

The disconfirming evidence for a hypothesis can also be compelling. Low scores on Object Assembly and Block Design could be used to form a shared subtest hypothesis having to do with part–whole relationships. This is a difficult hypothesis to corroborate as is, but if the child had strengths on Pattern Analysis (a Block Design look-alike on the Stanford-Binet), the Bender (a design drawing task), and no problems with part–whole relationships are noted by parents or teachers, then the disconfirming evidence forces the clinician to attribute the hypothesis to chance variation or some other factor. This hypothesis is then not offered to others as being important.

The final step in the interpretive process is to consider the hypotheses that have been corroborated and determine which ones, if any, should be reported orally or in writing. The important rule at this stage is to *subsume less reliable and valid hypotheses under more reliable and valid ones.* By doing so examiners are erring in the direction of drawing conclusions based on greater evidence of reliability and validity (see Appendix A).

If a child had a lone weakness on the Information test, one may be tempted to interpret this as a single subtest weakness and say something about fund of general information in an oral or written report. This same child, however, could also have a P>V discrepancy. In most cases it will be more sensible to subsume the Information weakness under the Verbal standard score and conclude that the child simply has a relative weakness in verbal skills. This conclusion is more psychometrically robust than the single subtest conclusion (again, see Appendix A).

Similarly, if a child obtains an Information relative strength, this too could be subsumed under high composite scores. If this same child has a high Full Scale score, it would be best to attribute the Information strength to overall strong cognitive skills.

This emphasis on composite scores (whether overall composite or other composites such as Index scores), and shared hypotheses over single test hypotheses, is an interpretive bias that shows respect for psychometric properties. Shared or single subtest hypotheses may still be viable, but they should be corroborated to the point that they are *clearly superior* to composite score hypotheses.

It is also possible to draw conclusions at all levels of interpretation for the same case. A composite score and single subtest conclusion can coexist, as will be seen in some of the sample cases. In fact, in some situations, it will be eminently reasonable to draw conclusions at all three levels of interpretation.

A second overriding rule for drawing conclusions is to favor hypotheses that are based on background information. Most importantly, they are "ecologically" valid in that they are directly related to the referral questions. In addition, these hypotheses can be highly valid because they are frequently based on considerable historical data. If, for example, a child has a history of language delays, is receiving speech/language services, and her teacher observes language weaknesses, then a relative weakness on the Verbal scale is predictable and important to interpret.

OTHER WISC-III INTERPRETIVE ISSUES

Factor Analysis and WISC-III Interpretation Revisited

The case studies presented in Figure 8.1 demonstrate the importance of factor analysis for competent WISC-III interpretation. In many of the cases which are a representative sample of children with a great variety of presenting problems, the factor structure of the WISC-III is supported. For most cases the Verbal and Performance scales are relatively unitary. When they are not, the results mimick more closely the four-factor structure of the WISC-III. Specifically, when subtests deviate from the child's average, they tended to be those that correlated least with the Full Scale score, such as Coding, Symbol Search, and Digit Span. These and other factor analytic findings are probably *the clinician's most potent weapons* for making sense of WISC-III results.

Illusory V/P Differences and Subtest Scatter

One way of evaluating whether or not a Verbal/ Performance discrepancy is illusory is to investigate scatter within the Verbal and Performance scales. The normal range of scaled scores (the difference between the lowest subtest scaled score and the highest scaled score within the Verbal and

Performance Scales) is approximately 6 points for six Verbal tests and six Performance tests (Table B.5, Wechsler, 1991). If the intrascale scatter is somewhat unusual, then it becomes difficult to interpret the Verbal and Performance scales as unitary dimensions. With considerable scatter the Verbal and Performance scales are best considered as assessing a variety of cognitive skills. When within-scale scatter is fairly large, reasonable conclusions may not lie in the Verbal/Performance scales or at the composite score level but at the shared or single subtest levels of interpretation.

Jerry's case (see Figure 8.1) provides a good example of the meaningfulness of intrascale scatter. Jerry's level of scatter within the Verbal and Performance scales is 2 (scaled scores of 3 to 5) and 7 (scaled scores of 1 to 8), respectively. The Verbal scale scatter is not unusual in that a difference of 2 points or larger between the lowest and highest subscale score occurred in 99.5% of the WISC-III norm sample (Table B.5, Wechsler, 1991). A difference of 7 points or more for the Performance scale occurred in 46% of the norming sample (Table B.5, Wechsler, 1991). The 7-point scatter on the Performance scale is not unusual by any standard, but it does hint that there is more diversity of skills on this scale than on the Verbal scale. A difference of 11 points on the Performance scale would indicate significant scatter, as a difference this large or larger occurred in 5% or less of the norming sample (Table B.5, Wechsler, 1991).

Supplementary Procedures for Profile Analysis

Kaufman (1979b) popularized a method of WISC-R hypothesis generation involving determining subtest strengths and weaknesses *separately* for the Verbal and Performance scales. This procedure requires the examiner to compute separate mean scaled scores for the Verbal and Performance scales, then compare each subtest to its respective means. In order to use this procedure the following means must be computed.

1. Compute the mean scaled score of the Verbal scale subtests administered and round it to the nearest whole number.
2. Compute the mean of the Performance scale subtests administered and round it to the nearest whole number.

The examiner then computes significant strengths and weaknesses (Table B.3, Wechsler, 1991) and then uses shared ability tables (see Table 8.1) to develop hypotheses.

The within scale approach may be useful for testing the homogeneity of a child's performance on that scale. *This approach is most likely to be useful when there is a significant V/P discrepancy (a V/P discrepancy of 11 points or more).*

The WISC-III manual does include all of the data necessary to determine strengths and weaknesses separately for the Verbal and Performance scales in Table B.3 (Wechsler, 1991). Examiners may want to initially use both methods for determining strengths and weaknesses particularly if they are using computer scoring, which makes computation easy.

WISC-III Strengths and Weaknesses

Clinicians must be familiar with the strengths and weaknesses of the WISC-III in order to decide when to use it. This premise of test selection assumes that there is no such thing as a perfect intelligence test that should be used with all children under all circumstances. In fact, this point of view is a consistent bias underlying this textbook. Just as there are numerous word processing programs available for writing a textbook such as this one, there are also an increasing number of intelligence tests and procedures, all of which have some virtues and problems. It is hoped that by having a clear understanding of the strengths and weaknesses of each test discussed in this book, examiners can make informed choices that meet their assessment needs and serve their clients best.

Strengths

Glasser and Zimmerman (1967) noted that one advantage of the WISC is the Verbal/Performance division of subtests. This enhances the assessment of children with vision, hearing or orthopedic impairments, children with language-based LD (Stanovich, 1986), and bilingual children. This organization allows the examiner to administer nonpenalizing portions of the WISC to a variety of children.

The WISC-III and its predecessors possess an extraordinary research base that can be used to guide assessment practice (Reynolds & Kaufman, 1990). The collection of well over a thousand research studies in the scholarly literature allows clinicians to predict how children will perform and alerts the examiner to inconsistencies between a child's scores and previous research, thus allowing the examiner to engage in more sophisticated interpretation of scores. Much of this research applies to the WISC-III. The WISC-III also possesses a comprehensive manual that includes considerable evidence of reliability and validity.

The factorial validity of the WISC-III is better than that of the WISC-R. The third and fourth factors are clearcut but small and, consequently, they do not play a large role in interpretation due to limited validity evidence (see Chapter 17).

The WISC-III can effectively diagnose mental retardation and giftedness (Wechsler, 1991). Such findings establish the WISC-III as a competent intelligence test in the tradition of Binet's early work and that of the Army mental testers.

The WISC-III measures verbal expression to a greater extent than several other intelligence tests. The WISC-III allows the examiner the opportunity, in a sense, to hear the child think aloud when trying to verbally reason through a word definition, verbal concept, or practical problem-solving situation. Allowing the child or adolescent greater opportunity to "reveal" himself or herself provides valuable clinical insight into the nature of a child's problems or assets.

The WISC-III possesses many admirable psychometric properties. It is a good measure of "g," has ample concurrent validity, and has excellent reliability estimates for the composite scores. The new norming sample is consistent with current high standards.

Weaknesses

A major weakness of the WISC-III is its lack of theoretical clarity. This limitation is shared by a variety of intelligence tests that were developed prior to the 1980s when (see Chapter 1) no premium was placed on the use of theory in the test development process. Glasser and Zimmerman (1967) eloquently describe this limitation:

> In many ways, the WISC is essentially a revamped Binet, composed of various tasks (most of which are also found on the Binet) which are assumed to be components of intelligence. The WISC is thus based solely on the pragmatic inferences about the nature of intelligence first advanced by Binet. The rationale for interpreting subtest scores remains obscure. (p. 7)

Another weakness of the WISC-III is its low interest level for early elementary grade children. Most of the tasks are merely downward extensions of Wechsler's original adult scale and some of the subtests, such as Comprehension, are still too lengthy.

The verbal instructions given by the WISC-III examiner are still too long, and they require too much verbal comprehension on the part of the child (Kaufman, 1977). This English language comprehension requirement makes the test, including performance tests, more difficult to administer to some children than some other measures.

CONCLUSIONS

The WISC has a long clinical and research history that supports interpretation by clinicians. The WISC-III is yet another milestone in the development of the Wechsler series that promises to receive widespread acceptance. Its longevity is testimony to the accuracy of Wechsler's original ideas about the practical needs of clinicians involved in intellectual assessment. Other assets of the WISC-III are its long clinical and research history. This legacy has led to the development of strong interpretive systems (Kaufman, 1994) that further enhance the utility of the scale. The WISC-III possesses numerous strengths that enhance the Wechsler tradition, including a clarification of the WISC factor structure that promises to enhance interpretation.

The WISC-III's history and lack of change over the generations is also its greatest liability (Sternberg & Kaufman, 1996). Much has been learned about children's cognitive development since the conceptualization of the Wechsler scales, and yet few of these findings have been incorporated into revisions. New tests that capitalize on current research findings will be the greatest challenge to the WISC-III. The popularity of the WISC, however, cannot be overstated.

CHAPTER SUMMARY

- The Wechsler-Bellevue offered a number of features that were not available in previous editions of the Binet scales, including separate norms for children and adults, the provision of subtest standard scores, a separate Performance scale to allow for the assessment of linguistic and cultural minorities, and a Standard Score (Deviation IQ) that solved many of the psychometric problems associated with ratio IQ scales. The Wechsler series of tests are the only widely used measures of intelligence that continue to use the term *IQ*. Most modern tests have dropped the terminology.

- Wechsler did not consider the Verbal and Performance scales to represent separate abilities, but, rather, he considered them as two additional "languages" through which the underlying general intelligence may express itself.

- The WISC-III is comprised of 10 mandatory and 3 supplementary subtests, all of which span the age range of 6½ through 16½ years. The 5 mandatory subtests on the Verbal scale include Information, Similarities, Arithmetic, Vocabulary, and Comprehension. The supplementary subtest on the Verbal scale is Digit Span. Traditionally, Digit Span is administered with the remainder of the Verbal subtests.

- The Performance scale of the WISC-III is comprised of 5 subtests, including Picture Completion, Picture Arrangement, Block Design, Object Assembly, and Coding. The Supplementary subtests on the Performance scale are Mazes and Symbol Search.

- The WISC has been criticized for not being in tune with modern research in cognition and neuropsychology (Witt & Gresham, 1985).

- Wechsler subtest scaled (standard) scores have a mean of 10 and standard deviation of 3, whereas the IQs have a mean of 100 and standard deviation of 15.

- The WISC-III norming sample was stratified so as to match 1990 U.S. Census statistics.

- The reliability of the WISC is exemplary.

- The average standard error of measurement for the Full Scale IQ across all age groups for the WISC-III is 3.19.

- Gain scores for the Verbal scale are small (2–4 points), whereas on the Performance scale the average gain upon short-term retesting is in the 8- to 11-point range.

- WISC-III predictive validity coefficients are in the range of .50 to .60 for most investigations.

- The WISC-III produces a large first or general intelligence "g" factor.

- Kaufman's (1975a) seminal investigation showed the WISC-R to have a very comparable factor structure to its predecessor, the 1949 WISC, including three factors labeled verbal comprehension, perceptual organization, and freedom from distractibility.

- There was considerable controversy over the naming of the WISC-R freedom from distractibility factor. Alternate names that were proposed for this factor included symbolic ability, sequential processing, and short-term memory (Reynolds & Kaufman, 1990).

• WISC-III factor analytic findings are probably *the clinician's most potent weapons* for interpreting WISC-III results.

• Some of the examiner instructions on the WISC-III are wordy and inappropriate for early elementary-grade children.

• The WISC-III Verbal tests of Similarities, Vocabulary, and Comprehension seem to be particularly difficult for new examiners to score correctly.

• The WISC-III also possesses an extraordinary research base that can be used to guide assessment practice.

• The WISC-III possesses many admirable psychometric properties. It is a good measure of "g," has ample predictive validity, and has excellent reliability estimates for the composite scores.

• A major weakness of the WISC-III is its lack of theoretical clarity.

• Hypotheses for V/P differences may include:

Verbal versus Nonverbal Intelligence (V>P or P>V)
Linguistic Differences (P>V)
Speech or Language Impairment (P>V)
Hearing Impairment (P>V)
Novelty (P>V)
Achievement Motivation (P>V)
Hemispheric Specialization (V>P or P>V)
Spatial Ability (P>V or V>P)
Motor Problem (V>P)
Deliberate Response Style (V>P)
Time Pressure (V>P)
Learning Disability (P>V)
Long-Term Memory (V<P or V>P)
Third-Factor Hypotheses

• The typical procedure for determining significant strengths and weaknesses in Wechsler subtest profiles is to consult a table of values for determining the significance of a difference between a subtest score and the child's average subtest score.

• Kaufman (1979b) popularized a method of WISC-R hypothesis generation involving determining strengths and weaknesses *separately* for the Verbal and Performance scales.

CHAPTER 9

Stanford-Binet–Fourth Edition (Binet-4)

This essentially new instrument . . . is not much like the Stanford-Binet of former years. (Cronbach, 1989, p. 773)

CHAPTER QUESTIONS

How does this Binet differ from its predecessors?

How does factor analytic research for the Binet-4 affect interpretation of its composite scores?

The latest (fourth) edition of the Stanford-Binet in some ways follows in the tradition of Alfred Binet's original work and Terman's American revision of his scale (see Chapter 1). Some of the items found on the Binet-4 have long histories and can be traced directly to Binet's original work. On the other hand, this newest version of the Binet departs from its predecessors to such an extent, especially in terms of its structure and theory, that it should be considered a new test, as

opposed to what is typically considered a mere revision of an earlier scale. The Binet-4, however, does remain a significant achievement in intelligence test technology and, as such, it warrants serious consideration by individuals who use these measures.

THEORETICAL BASIS

The Binet-4 differs from its forbearers by proposing a theoretical model that was used to guide test development endeavors, and which is described in detail in the Binet-4 *Technical Manual* (Thorndike, Hagan, & Sattler, 1986). This theoretical model had not been used in any previous editions of the Binet scales. In this hierarchical model, "g," or general intelligence, remains the premier cognitive ability at the top of the hierarchy (Thorndike et al., 1986). The Binet-4 authors observed: "Still, the general ability factor, g, refuses to die. Like a phoenix, it

231

keeps rising from its ashes and will no doubt continue to be an enduring part of our psychometric theory and psychometric practice" (Thorndike et al., 1986, p. 6).

Regarding whether to assess "g" with a single test or a variety of tests, the authors (Thorndike et al., 1986) decided to side with the wisdom of Wechsler, as is shown in the following quotation.

It is our strong belief that the best measure of g—and consequently broad effective prediction—will stem from a diverse set of cognitive tasks that call for relational thinking in a diversity of contexts. We have tried to provide this both in CogAT and in the Fourth Edition of the Stanford-Binet. (p. 6)

The second level of the Binet hierarchy is based on the work of Cattell and his fluid and crystallized dimensions of intelligence (see Chapter 2). The crystallized abilities, those abilities that are most influenced by schooling, familial, and other environmental factors, are measured by subtests from the Verbal Reasoning and Quantitative Reasoning areas. The fluid analytic abilities at the second level of the hierarchy consist of primarily abstract/visual reasoning tasks. The authors of the Binet-4 added a third theoretical construct to this second most important level of interpretation. Short-term memory is a theoretical construct that is more associated with human information processing theories than the theories of Cattell (Glutting & Kaplan, 1990). Nevertheless, it is added to Cattell's work to create a triumvirate, so to speak, at the second level of the Binet-4 theoretical hierarchy. This hierarchical framework of intelligence is highly consistent with the British approach to intelligence.

The third level in the Binet theoretical hierarchy consists of finer discriminations of the fluid and crystallized abilities. The crystallized abilities are subdivided into Verbal Reasoning and Quantitative Reasoning areas. The Abstract/Visual Reasoning area or group of subtests represents the assessment of fluid analytic abilities. This third level of interpretation—Verbal Reasoning,

Quantitative Reasoning, and Abstract/Visual Reasoning—was designed to receive less emphasis in interpretation than the two higher levels (Thorndike et al., 1986). Finally, the Binet-4 consists of 15 subtests, 4 subtests each for Verbal Reasoning, Abstract/Visual Reasoning, and Short-Term Memory, and 3 subtests for Quantitative Reasoning.

Some of the areas assessed by the Binet-4, such as Verbal Reasoning and Abstract/Visual reasoning, are also reminiscent of Vernon's (1950) well-known hierarchical model of intelligence (see Chapter 2 and Glutting & Kaplan, 1990). In many ways, then, the Binet interpretive hierarchy is based upon a confluence of theories from a variety of individuals who wrote extensively on theories of intelligence in this past century. As such, the Binet-4 theory should in no way be considered as new or novel or, for that matter, modern. The emphasis on an overall composite score dates back to Spearman's work in the 1920s; the second level of interpretation based upon the fluid/crystallized dichotomy dates back to the 1940s; and the third level of interpretation, which is reminiscent of Vernon's theory, dates back to the 1940s and 1950s. Hence, the Binet-4 is based on several well-known theoretical traditions.

PSYCHOMETRIC PROPERTIES

Standardization

The Stanford-Binet—Fourth Edition was normed on 5,013 children between the ages of 2 and 23 years. Cases were drawn from 47 states in the United States, including Alaska and Hawaii, so as to be representative of the 1980 U.S. Census. A stratified random sampling procedure was employed, with stratification variables that included geographic region, community size, gender, ethnicity, and socioeconomic status. Parental occupation and education were used as the measures of SES (Thorndike et al., 1986).

One of the early controversies that occurred shortly after the release of the Binet-4 was the apparent mismatch between Census Bureau statistics and the Binet-4 standardization sample. The Binet-4 *Technical Manual* (Thorndike et al., 1986) showed clearly that the sample was biased toward the inclusion of children from higher socioeconomic status families than would be indicated by the appropriate census statistics. This oversampling of high-SES groups and undersampling of low-SES children could have contributed dramatically to the development of norms of inappropriate difficulty level. In order to counteract this sampling problem the authors weighted the norming cases to create a proper SES distribution. In other words, since high-SES children were overrepresented, the scores of children from high-SES families counted as less than one case in the development of norms. On the other hand, the scores of children from low-SES families were counted as greater than one—thus weighting them more heavily in the development of norms for the individual subtests. This weighting procedure, then, served to change the composition of the sample to match very closely 1980 Census figures. Weighting samples this way is not typical of clinical tests of intelligence such as the WISC (Wechsler, 1991) and the K-ABC (Kaufman & Kaufman, 1983b). Consequently, questions arise as to the appropriateness and accuracy of the weighting procedure.

All indications are, however, that the weighting procedure was effective in producing norm-referenced scores that are consistent and predictable in relationship to other tests of intelligence (Glutting & Kaplan, 1990). Several studies of nondisabled children have shown the Binet-4 norm-referenced scores to be slightly lower (2–3 standard score points) than those of older tests normed in previous eras (see Table 9.1; the Binet-4 *Technical Manual*; and Sattler, 1988).

TABLE 9.1   Mean differences between the Binet-4 and other test composites

Authors/Date	Sample	N	Means
Carvajal, Gerber, Hewes, & Weaver (1987)	ND	32	WAIS-R = 103.5 Binet-4 = 100.9
Carvajal & Weyand (1986)	ND	23	WISC-R = 115.0 Binet-4 = 113.3
Hartwig, Sapp, & Clayton (1987)	ND	30	Binet-LM = 113.1 Binet-4 = 114.4
Prewett & Matavich (1994)	ND	73	WISC-III = 74.6 Binet-4 = 82.9
Rothlisberg (1987)	referred	32	WISC-R = 112.3 Binet-4 = 105.5
Thorndike, Hagen, & Sattler (1986)	ND	139	Binet-LM = 108.1 Binet-4 = 105.8
Thorndike, Hagen, & Sattler (1986)	ND	205	WISC-R = 105.2 Binet-4 = 102.4
Thorndike, Hagen, & Sattler (1986)	ND	75	WPPSI = 110.3 Binet-4 = 105.3
Thorndike, Hagen, & Sattler (1986)	ND	47	WAIS-R = 102.2 Binet-4 = 98.7

(Continues)

TABLE 9.1   Mean differences between the Binet-4 and other test composites (Continued)

Authors/Date	Sample	N	Means
Thorndike, Hagen, & Sattler (1986)	ND	175	K-ABC = 107.4 Binet-4 = 112.7
Thorndike, Hagen, & Sattler (1986)	gifted	82	Binet-LM =135.3 Binet-4 = 121.8
Thorndike, Hagen, & Sattler (1986)	gifted	19	WISC-R = 117.7 Binet-4 = 116.3
Thorndike, Hagen, & Sattler (1986)	LD	14	Binet-LM = 76.9 Binet-4 = 79.9
Thorndike, Hagen, & Sattler (1986)	LD	90	WISC-R = 87.8 Binet-4 = 84.8
Thorndike, Hagen, & Sattler (1986)	LD	30	K-ABC = 94.2 Binet-4 = 92.5
Phelps, Bell, & Scott (1988)	LD	35	WISC-R = 95.6 Binet-4 = 92.3
Thorndike, Hagen, & Sattler (1986)	MR	22	Binet-LM = 49.5 Binet-4 = 50.9
Thorndike, Hagen, & Sattler (1986)	MR	61	WISC-R = 67.0 Binet-4 = 66.2
Thorndike, Hagen, & Sattler (1986)	MR	21	WAIS-R = 73.1 Binet-4 = 63.8

ND = no diagnosis

Reliability

Internal Consistency

Reliability, as measured by indices of internal consistency for the Binet-4 composite score, is extraordinarily high over the 2- to 23-year age span of the Binet-4. Internal consistency reliabilities for the composite score range from .95 to .99. The reliabilities for the four area scores of the Binet-4 are also extremely high, ranging from .80 to .97. The reliabilities of the Binet-4 subtests are also strong. These high reliabilities are likely due to their length, resulting in a larger sampie of behavior. Consider, for example, the Pattern Analysis subtest of the Binet-4, which has 41 items in comparison to the similar Block

Design subtest on the Wechsler scales, which contains only 12 items. In virtually all cases, the Binet-4 subtests are considerably longer than subtests typically found on intelligence batteries such as the Wechsler series or the K-ABC.

Test-Retest

Test/retest reliabilities for the Binet-4 are somewhat lower than the internal consistency coefficients. The test-retest reliability of the quantitative subtest is especially noteworthy in that a study of 55 elementary-grade children (Thorndike et al., 1986) yielded a reliability coefficient of only .28. In the same investigation, reliability coefficients for the four area scores ranged from a .51 for the Quantitative Reasoning scale to a

.87 for the Verbal Reasoning scale. The composite score reliability coefficient for this investigation was .90. Since stability coefficients are of practical importance, these test-retest coefficients should be kept clearly in mind. This advice is particularly true for problematic tests such as those on the quantitative scale. Further test-retest studies on the Binet-4 could yield higher test-retest coefficients. Unfortunately, the single study included in the *Technical Manual* (Thorndike et al., 1986) is all that is currently available.

Validity

The Binet-4 has amassed considerable validity evidence to date, particularly evidence of concurrent and factorial validity. Some of the earliest studies of concurrent validity are reported in the *Technical Manual* and Table 9.2. These studies show a strong correlational relationship between the Binet-4 and its predecessors, suggesting that the Binet-4 is very much like other well-respected intelligence measures. Studies reported in the *Technical Manual* (Thorndike et al., 1986) and elsewhere have produced coefficients for non-disabled samples ranging from .72 to .91. The focus of these studies, however, is on the composite score of the Binet-4. The area scores of the test are less well-known entities, particularly the Short-Term Memory and Quantitative scales, since these are not offered on tests such as the WISC-III.

TABLE 9.2 Concurrent validity studies of the Binet-4 composite and other test composites

Authors / Date	Sample	N	r with Binet-4
Carvajal, Gerber, Hewes, & Weaver (1987)	ND	32	WAIS-R = .91
Carvajal & Weyand (1986)	ND	23	WISC-R = .78
Hartwig, Sapp, & Clayton (1987)	ND	30	Binet-LM = .72
Prewett & Matavich (1994)	ND	73	WISC-III = .81
Rothlisberg (1987)	ND	32	WISC-R = .77
Thorndike, Hagen, & Sattler (1986)	ND	139	Binet-LM = .81
Thorndike, Hagen, & Sattler (1986)	ND	205	WISC-R = .83
Thorndike, Hagen, & Sattler (1986)	ND	75	WPPSI = .80
Thorndike, Hagen, & Sattler (1986)	ND	47	WAIS-R = .91
Thorndike, Hagen, & Sattler (1986)	ND	175	K-ABC = .89
Thorndike, Hagen, & Sattler (1986)	gifted	82	Binet-LM = .27
Thorndike, Hagen, & Sattler (1986)	gifted	19	WISC-R = .69
Thorndike, Hagen, & Sattler (1986)	LD	14	Binet-LM = .79
Thorndike, Hagen, & Sattler (1986)	LD	90	WISC-R = .87
Thorndike, Hagen, & Sattler (1986)	LD	30	K-ABC = .74
Bell, Phelps, & Scott (1988)	LD	35	WISC-R = .92
Thorndike, Hagen, & Sattler (1986)	MR	22	Binet-LM = .91
Thorndike, Hagen, & Sattler (1986)	MR	61	WISC-R = .66
Thorndike, Hagen, & Sattler (1986)	MR	21	WAIS-R = .79

ND = no diagnosis

Exceptional Children

The relationship of the Binet-4 to other tests for samples of children with disabilities is less clear, however. The findings of the Thorndike, Hagen, and Sattler (1986) study of gifted children are particularly striking. This study involved 82 children who were administered both the Binet-4 and the Binet-LM. The resulting means differed greatly, with the Binet-4 mean being 13 points lower than the Binet-LM mean. This finding did not occur in the other Thorndike, Hagen, and Sattler (1986) study of gifted children that used the WISC-R. In this study the Binet-4 mean was only 1 point lower than the WISC-R. A first hypothesis to consider for the difference between the two Binet scales is simple regression toward the mean. One may then ask, however, why was no regression apparent in the WISC-R study? It could also be that the old and new Binet measure very different things that belie their high correlation. The item content of the scales are different, with the old Binet being more verbally loaded and the Binet-4 giving more weight to spatial, memory, and quantitative skills in addition to verbal skills. This hypothesis of content differences is supported by some of the concurrent validity studies. In the Thorndike, Hagen, and Sattler (1986) study of 82 gifted children, the correlation between the Binet-4 Verbal Reasoning scale and Binet-LM composite (.40) was higher than that between the two test composites (.27). This result also occurred for the study of 19 children in which the correlation between the Binet-4 and WISC-R verbal scores was .71 and the correlation between the two composites was lower at .62. These results suggest that the older Binet may be more influenced by verbal skills than the new one, and when the two tests differ, the verbal ability of the sample (or child for that matter) may be the culprit.

The Binet-4 produces results very similar to the WISC-R for mentally retarded and learning-disability samples, with the Binet-4 consistently yielding slightly lower scores (see Chapter 20). A reasonable question, however, is why doesn't the Binet-4 exhibit regression effects for mental retardation samples? Regression effects would certainly be expected given the low WISC-R scores for these groups. The studies for mentally retarded children are consistent with those for the WISC-R in a number of respects. As is the case with the WISC-R (Kaufman, 1979b), the mental retardation samples had a relative strength in the Abstract/Visual area (Thorndike et al., 1986). For children with mental retardation, however, the Binet-4 is not simply another form of the WISC-R, given the modest correlations between the two (see the Binet-4 *Technical Manual*). Seeing the range of scores for the samples on both measures would also be more helpful. It could be that because the Binet-4 norms extend to 35, as opposed to the WISC-R's lowest possible score of 45, that the Binet could "allow" more low scores thus mitigating against regression effects. Only one investigation, however (Thorndike et al., 1986), gives evidence of a larger standard deviation on the part of the Binet-4. For the moment the Binet-4 must be assumed to yield similar mean scores to the WISC-R for groups of children with mental retardation regardless of the reason for it.

Prewett and Matavich (1994) showed, however, that at-risk children of low socioeconomic status scored about 8 points lower on the WISC-III than the Binet-4. They suggested that the verbal scales of the respective scales did produce similar measurement.

Factor Analysis

For clinicians one of the most confusing aspects of the Binet-4 is the disagreement over the amount of factor analytic support for the various scales. It is important that composite scores show some evidence of factor analytic support in order to allow psychologists to use them for interpretive purposes. For the Binet-4, most of the subtests ideally would have high loadings on a large first factor (or general intelligence factor). Such a finding would lend support to the use of the test composite for interpretive purposes. Similarly, there are four other featured composites on the

Binet-4: Verbal Reasoning, Abstract/Visual Reasoning, Quantitative Reasoning, and Short-Term Memory. Since these are the four featured area scores, supportive factor analytic studies should show four factors that intuitively correspond to these groupings of subtests.

Factor analytic studies have created some confusion because various researchers, using similar procedures, have produced different conclusions. Keith, Cool, Novak, White, and Pottebaum (1988) used confirmatory factor analytic procedures to conclude that there was general support for the four area scores, while Kline (1989) used these same procedures to conclude that Sattler's (1988) two- and three-factor models were a better fit to the data. Upon closer inspection one can find considerable agreement among these studies. The agreement across studies will be captured next in an effort to develop an interpretive system for the Binet-4.

"g" Loadings

General intelligence ("g") loadings are typically defined as the loading of each test on an unrotated first factor. Analyses of the Binet-4 suggest that tests such as Vocabulary, Quantitative, Number Series, Comprehension, and Matrices are likely to produce scores that are consistent with one another (i.e., they have high "g" loadings) (Reynolds, Kamphaus, & Rosenthal, 1988; Sattler, 1988; Thorndike et al., 1986). On the other hand, Memory for Digits, Memory for Objects, and Copying are likely to produce discrepant scores from the remainder of the test battery (i.e., they have low "g" loadings) (Reynolds et al., 1988; Sattler, 1988; Thorndike et al., 1986).

The Area Score Controversy

While all factor analytic researchers have concluded that the Binet-4 test composite is a good measure of "g" (Glutting & Kaplan, 1990), there is not unanimity on the factorial validity of the four area scores: Verbal Reasoning, Abstract/ Visual Reasoning, Quantitative Reasoning, and Short-Term Memory. Several researchers have used confirmatory factor analytic methods to support the validity of the area scores (Keith et al., 1988; Ownby & Carmin, 1988; Thorndike et al., 1986), and yet, several studies using both comfirmatory and exploratory methods have concluded that some of the four area scores lack factor analytic support (Kline, 1989; Reynolds et al., 1988; Sattler, 1988). These contrasting findings do provide a dilemma for the clinician who needs to know how much faith can be placed in the area scores. Fortunately, despite the obvious differences, consistency can be found across many of these studies when one looks closely at the results of these articles and chapters.

First, there is agreement that the Verbal Reasoning and Abstract/Visual Reasoning areas show strong evidence of factorial support (Keith et al., 1988; Kline, 1989; Ownby & Carmin, 1988; Reynolds et al., 1988; Sattler, 1988; Thorndike et al., 1986). This is hardly surprising given the well-known verbal/nonverbal factors that have been well documented since World War I.

There is also considerable agreement that the Quantitative scale lacks clear evidence of a corresponding factor (Kline, 1989; Reynolds et al., 1988; Sattler, 1988). This observation is true even when one inspects the results of "supportive" studies. The analysis of Thorndike, Hagen, and Sattler (1986) that generally supports the area scores shows some problems with the Quantitative Reasoning scale. In this analysis the Quantitative and Number Series subtests have paltry loadings of .21 and .26, respectively, on the Quantitative factor. The Quantitative Reasoning area score is also suspect because it is most appropriate for older children. The typical procedure used by many clinicians is to only administer one or two subtests from this domain. If a clinician uses the general-purpose six-subtest battery, then only one subtest (Quantitative) from this area is used. Finally, it could be argued that the Quantitative area, although certainly measuring aspects of intelligence, is so similar to mathematics tests that it is difficult to establish its content validity as an intelligence measure (Kaufman & Kaufman, 1983b).

The Short-Term Memory area score is a mixed bag. Some researchers have found support for it (Keith et al., 1988; Ownby & Carmin, 1988; Thorndike et al., 1986), others have not (Reynolds et al., 1988), and some have found support for it at elementary and secondary age groups but not for preschoolers (Kline, 1989; Sattler, 1988). There are two subtests that seem to contribute to the disagreement regarding this area score: Memory for Sentences and Bead Memory.

Memory for Sentences loads as highly, and in some cases higher, on the verbal reasoning factor as on the memory factor. Sattler (1988), for example, found Memory for Sentences to have an average loading of .57 on the memory factor and .58 on the verbal factor. Keith et al. (1988), although generally supportive of the Binet-4 structure, found that in their "relaxed" confirmatory model, Memory for Sentences loaded .43 on the memory factor and .40 on the verbal factor.

The scenario for Bead Memory is strikingly similar. Sattler (1988) found the average loading for this test on the memory factor to be .36, and on the abstract/visual factor its loading was higher at .51. Again, in the Keith et al. (1988) relaxed model, Bead Memory loaded higher on the abstract/visual (.49) than on the memory factor (.27). These results all bring into question the routine interpretation of the Quantitative Reasoning and Short-Term Memory area scores as homogeneous scales. These results do suggest that the Verbal and Abstract/Visual area scores are sound.

Developmental Differences in Factor Structure

Sattler (1988), Kline (1989), Gridley and McIntosh (1991), and Moltese et al. (1992) call attention to possible developmental factors in the interpretation of the Binet-4 by concluding that two factors (Sattler calls them verbal comprehension and nonverbal reasoning/visualization) constitute the most parsimonious solution for children ages 2 through 6, and three factors for ages 8 and above (where a memory scale is added). This structure is also supported by the confirmatory factor structure of Kline (1989). The finding of developmental differences in factor structure is also consistent with the factor analytic findings for the K-ABC (Kaufman & Kaufman, 1983b). These findings also cast further doubt on the robustness of the Quantitative and Short-Term Memory area scores.

Binet-4 and Wechsler Research

Perhaps one way of reconciling this overwhelming amount of data is to compare these findings to those for other tests and three-stratum theory. The literature is replete with the findings of two and three factors for multisubtest intelligence measures. Of course, the Wechsler scales are notable for this finding. The well-known verbal and spatial visualization constructs are again evident.

Certainly the Binet-4 is not a Wechsler clone. It has many new subtests that measure a great variety of skills. It could well be that although the Quantitative score lacks support, it could be extremely useful for identifying the mathematically gifted, or perhaps other uses.

Implications for Interpretation

With these findings in mind, the following applications of the Binet-4 factor analytic results are offered.

1. The Binet-4 test composite can be interpreted in much the same way as other tests that have been shown to be good measures of general intelligence, such as the WISC-III.

2. The Quantitative Area Score has little factor analytic support and would have to be congruent with other data in order to be emphasized in the interpretive process.

3. The Short-Term Memory Area Score may have more validity at ages 7 and above.

4. Tests such as Memory for Digits, Memory for Objects, and Copying have poor "g" loadings. Therefore, they are more likely to deviate from the remainder of the profile.

Administration and Scoring

Administration and scoring of the Binet-4 departs dramatically from the l972 Stanford-Binet Form LM. The 1972 version and all previous editions of the Binet-4 had a number of brief subtests or small clusters of items that were different for every age level. The current edition conforms more closely to modern intelligence tests such as the Wechsler, K-ABC, and Woodcock-Johnson. The Binet-4 consists of 15 subtests, only a portion of which are administered to each age group. This design is laudable in that it shows some developmental sensitivity on the part of the Binet designers.

While Binet-4 subtests and items were devised in accordance with its theoretical model, an attempt was also made to include as many item types as possible from previous editions of the Binet scales (Anastasi, 1988). To some extent, however, this decision has complicated the administration of some of the individual subtests. On some subtests two different item types from earlier versions of the Binet were, in a sense, collapsed in order to form one subtest with different item types used at different age levels. This situation creates problems from an administration standpoint because the examiner may have to become familiar with two distinct sets of procedures for an individual subtest. One example is the Copying subtest, on which items for preschoolers require the examiner to become facile with the administration of items using single-color blocks. The item type then switches at older ages, requiring the child to use pencil and paper skills. Perhaps more important than the issue of adding an additional "wrinkle" to the administration of this particular subtest, this switch in item type makes the interpretation of the scores on the Copying subtest more difficult. Another example of this situation is the Pattern Analysis subtest, on which early items use a three-piece form board. The next set of items requires a child to match a model made of single-color cubes, and more difficult items involve constructing intricate designs. Internal consistency coefficients for the Binet subtests, which are typically very impressive, do not preclude an individual

child responding very differently to different item types. No evidence, such as other measures of internal consistency, is reported to suggest that the different item types used in some Binet-4 subtests measure comparable or the same skills.

The Binet-4 items are more attractive than its predecessors', and the manipulatives and the stimuli involved are more easily stored and used by the examiner than in previous editions. For example, Form LM's version of Bead Memory required the examiner and child to string wooden beads on a shoestring. This apparatus was difficult for young children to handle, and many of them spilled considerable numbers of small beads. The newer version is somewhat more manageable, requiring the child to place beads on a stalk (stick). The stimuli used on the Bead Memory subtest, however, still have been criticized because at least two of the pieces are able to be pushed through a "choke-tube," a device that indicates whether or not an object is small enough to easily be swallowed and induce choking in a young child (Glutting & Kaplan, 1990). Concern has also been expressed that a couple of items on the Binet-4 may not be readily interpreted by children with color blindness. Glutting and Kaplan (1990) identify item 1 of the Vocabulary test, which depicts a red car on a brown background, as potentially extremely difficult for the color-blind child to interpret. Similarly, the form-board items of the early portion of the Pattern Analysis subtest depict red pieces against a green background, making this item difficult to interpret for children with red/green color blindness.

One aspect of Binet-4 administration that is potentially troublesome is the question of which subtests to administer. The Binet-4 differs in that the use of short forms is discussed in its various manuals, including short forms for mental retardation and gifted diagnosis. A six-subtest, general-purpose, abbreviated battery includes Vocabulary, Bead Memory, Quantitative, Memory for Sentences, Pattern Analysis, and Comprehension. The various reliability and validity data reported in the *Technical Manual* (Thorndike et al., 1986), however, are based on research studies in which each child was administered the number of subtests deemed appropriate by his or her scores on the Vocabulary routing test—usually about eight subtests. Binet-4 short forms, and those for other tests, should likely be used as screening or backup procedures as opposed to batteries of first choice for diagnosis (see Chapter 14).

Adaptive Testing

The Binet-4 uses an adaptive testing design. This design was one of the unique features of previous editions of the Binet. Adaptive procedures are included primarily to make testing efficient and brief (Thorndike et al., 1986). The basic procedure is to administer the Vocabulary subtest first to all children. This Vocabulary subtest then serves as a "routing" subtest to appropriate entry points on subsequent subtests that are administered to the child. The Vocabulary test is an excellent candidate for a routing test because traditionally it has been an excellent measure of "g" (Kamphaus & Reynolds, 1987), and on the Binet-4 it is an extremely high correlate of all the other subtests in the battery (Reynolds et al., 1988). If a test is a high correlate of various other tests in the battery, then it will do a good job of routing the examiner to items of appropriate difficulty level on subsequent subtests.

Consistent with theories of adaptive testing, the Vocabulary test serves as an initial estimate of the child's ability. Based upon this initial estimate of ability, the examiner can be routed to the various levels of the Binet (that are signified by letters of the alphabet) that are most likely to be of appropriate difficulty for the child. This procedure should facilitate starting at appropriate points on individual subtests so as to quickly identify basal and ceiling levels in order to reduce testing time. This approach is in contrast to others such as those used on the Wechsler and the K-ABC, on which starting points for children are designated by the child's chronological age. The Binet-4 routing procedure may be a very efficient procedure for a child whose mental age is very different from his or her chronological age.

If a child is precocious, beginning at a point appropriate for his or her chronological age is not a wise use of testing time. The Binet-4 adaptive testing strategy using the Vocabulary subtest is intended to counteract this problem by basing starting points for individual subtests on ability rather than on chronological age.

The efficiency of this adaptive testing strategy, however, is dependent on the correlation of the Vocabulary subtest with the other subtests of the Binet-4. Consequently, the Vocabulary subtest is going to be a better routing test for some tests than for others. It is likely to be an excellent routing test for the Comprehension subtest, with which it shares a high intercorrelation (Thorndike et al., 1986). On the other hand, the Vocabulary subtest is likely to be an inefficient and perhaps inaccurate routing test for a test such as Bead Memory, which has a considerably lower correlation with Vocabulary. This is the reason why, in everyday practice, the wisdom of an adaptive testing strategy is not overwhelmingly evident. The Binet-4 is likely ushering in a new era in children's intellectual assessment where eventually many tests will be administered and scored via computers and routing procedures can then be made more efficient.

Comprehension of Instructions

Glutting and Kaplan (1990) reviewed the comprehension level of Binet-4 directions for preschoolers by evaluating the number of basic concepts that are used by the instructions to children. They used the same procedure as Kaufman (1978), who found that several preschool tests require children to understand basic concepts that may be too difficult for the typical preschooler. Kaufman (1978) found, for example, that the McCarthy Scales of Children's Abilities (McCarthy, 1972) included 7 basic concepts in the instructions. By comparison, the Glutting and Kaplan (1990) analysis of the Binet-4 revealed that 8 basic concepts were included in the instructions for this measure. This review suggests that the comprehension level of Binet-4 instructions is about the same as that of other popular pre-school measures of intelligence.

Differences from WISC-III

Some Binet-4 administration and scoring procedures differ significantly from those of the WISC-III. Dichotomous scoring was used on the Vocabulary subtest of the Binet-4, as opposed to the three-point system used on the Wechsler scales. In fact, all of the Binet-4 subtests use a dichotomous scoring system. Also, the Binet-4 makes extensive use of sample items. This practice creates the opportunity for a child to make mistakes on initial items without having his or her score affected. Similarly, it allows the examiner greater opportunity to explain the nature of the various tasks to the child before continuing with the test.

Derived Scores

One of the complications of the Binet-4 for examiners is the use of a standard score metric that is not comparable with other modern tests of intelligence and, for that matter, with tests of academic achievement. While virtually all the tests discussed in this volume use standard score metrics with a mean of 100 and standard deviation of 15, the Binet-4 defies this trend. The Binet-4, in a sense, goes "back to the future" and resurrects an older metric in which the mean of the standard score distribution is set at 100 and the standard deviation is set at 16. This metric is used for the Binet-4 test composite score and for the four area scores. This scaling procedure can be an annoyance. For example, the standard score to percentile rank conversion table for all tests that use normalized standard scores with the mean of 100 and standard deviation of 15 is universal. One can use the percentile rank tables for the WISC-III, K-ABC, or the Woodcock-Johnson, for example. However, because of the standard deviation of 16, the percentile rank distribution for the Binet-4 is different from that of other

measures. A conversion table is presented in the Binet-4 *Expanded Guide for Scoring and Interpretation* (Delaney & Hopkins, 1987) and the *Technical Manual* (Thorndike et al., 1986).

Perhaps the most confusing of the different metrics used by the Binet-4 is that used for the subtest scores. These are normalized standard scores with a mean of 50 and a standard deviation of 8. This metric seems to be wholly idiosyncratic and is not used by any other popular tests. It is reminiscent of the *T*-score method used heavily in personality assessment, where the mean is 50 and the standard deviation 10. However, this subtest score metric on the Binet-4 differs enough from the *T*-score metric to make for little transfer of training. As a result, examiners have to think very differently when interpreting Binet-4 composite, area, and subtest standard scores since these scores have different percentile rank conversions than those of other popular tests.

A scoring procedure that is unique to the Binet-4 is the use of common area score norm tables regardless of the tests used to assess the child. For example, the manual includes only one norm table for converting the sum of the Short-Term Memory subtest score to an area composite score, and yet, anywhere from one to four of the Short-Term Memory subtests may be used to enter the table and derive a composite. A clinician may use Bead Memory and Memory for Sentences, or Memory for Digits and Memory for Objects to enter the norm table and obtain a composite score. Without separate tables for the specific tests used, one basically assumes that all subtests intercorrelate equally—an untenable assumption.

BINET-4 SUBTESTS

The Binet-4 subtests are described next in the same manner that was used for the WISC-III. The reliabilities, "g" loadings, and specificities are from Thorndike, Hagen, and Sattler (1986), and factor loadings are from Table 19 of Thorndike (1990).

Verbal Reasoning Area

Vocabulary

For the first 15 items in the Vocabulary subtest, the child has to point to a picture named by the examiner. Items 16 through 46 require the child to define words given by the examiner. While the word definition portion of this test appears similar to that of the Wechsler scales, scoring of the individual items has been simplified. Instead of the more complex 2-1-0 scoring system used by the Wechsler scales, only dichotomous scoring is used on this particular subtest (1 or 0), thus simplifying scoring.

Performance on this test may be affected by language stimulation at home, school, and among peers. Scores may also be impacted by linguistic and schooling differences and language-based handicapping conditions such as oral expression learning disabilities. Information about the child's language development and environmental stimulation may be helpful in corroborating hypotheses.

ADMINISTRATION AND SCORING POINTERS

1. Study the scoring criteria carefully in order to be able to query responses appropriately.
2. Be sensitive to cultural/linguistic differences and local dialects.
3. Record actual responses if possible to assist with report writing.
4. Check the pronunciations of unclear words with the child's parent.

PSYCHOMETRIC PROPERTIES

Average reliability = .87

"g" loading = .76

Loading on verbal factor = .86

Loading on memory factor = .06

Loading on quantitative factor = −.00

Loading on abstract/visual factor = .03

Subtest specificity = .25 (adequate)

BEHAVIORS TO NOTE

1. Poor or misarticulation
2. Description of the word or examples of use of the word in lieu of a definition
3. Word retrieval problems (follow up with a word retrieval test if necessary)
4. Reticence to speak, point, or use gestures ("test the limits" by readministering items if the child becomes more expressive on later items than on earlier items)

Comprehension

For the first six items, a child is required to identify body parts on a card with a picture of a child. For items 7 through 42, the child has to respond to Wechsler-like questions about everyday problem situations ranging from survival behavior to civic duties.

Performance on this test may be particularly affected by oral expression skills and language stimulation at school and at home. Acclimation to American culture is also an important determining factor. This test should not be used in situations where cultural factors may be preeminent. Information about the child's language development, environmental stimulation, and culture may be helpful in corroborating hypotheses.

ADMINISTRATION AND SCORING POINTERS

1. Study the scoring criteria carefully in order to be able to query responses and score them appropriately.
2. Be sensitive to cultural/linguistic differences and local dialects.
3. Record actual responses if possible to assist with scoring and report writing.
4. Check the pronunciations of unclear words with the child's parent.

PSYCHOMETRIC PROPERTIES

Average reliability = .89

"g" loading = .71

Loading on verbal factor = .70
Loading on memory factor = .07
Loading on quantitative factor = –.00
Loading on abstract/visual factor = .11
Subtest specificity = .47 (adequate)

BEHAVIORS TO NOTE

1. Poor or misarticulation
2. Use of words or phrases from another language in responses
3. Word retrieval problems (follow up with a word retrieval test if necessary)

Absurdities

The child has to point to inaccurate pictures that show a situation that is contrary to common sense or that is false for items 1 through 4. For items 5 through 32 the child has to describe the absurdity that is depicted.

Absurdities items are especially prone to idiosyncratic or creative interpretations. Performance on this test may be affected by a child's tendency toward conformity or nonconformity to societal expectations. Interpretation of this test can be difficult because of the confounding of visual and verbal skills and its lack of research or substantial clinical history. Reynolds, Kamphaus, and Rosenthal (1988) found this test to load on its own factor, which further suggests that it possesses some unique properties.

ADMINISTRATION AND SCORING POINTERS

1. Study the scoring criteria carefully in order to be able to query responses and score them appropriately.
2. Be sensitive to cultural differences that may influence interpretation of the stimuli.
3. Record actual responses if possible to assist with scoring and report writing.

PSYCHOMETRIC PROPERTIES

Average reliability = .87
"g" loading = .67

Loading on verbal factor = .40
Loading on memory factor = .03
Loading on quantitative factor = -.14
Loading on abstract/visual factor = .45
Subtest specificity = .57 (ample)

BEHAVIORS TO NOTE

1. Reluctance to respond to the stimuli that may be due to an inability to respond when uncertain
2. Creative responses to stimuli that are not included in the scoring criteria and are yet somewhat plausible (such responses may violate the validity of this test for a particular child)

Verbal Relations

Given four words by the examiner, the child has to state how three words out of the four-word set are similar. This test assesses aspects of concept development—specifically, the ability to relate concepts to one another. Certainly a strong fund of verbal information is necessary to solve these items correctly. Subtleties of meaning are central to obtaining correct items, making linguistic and cultural differences a potential confound. Research on concept development may be helpful in interpreting scores on this test (see, for example, Bruner, Olver, & Greenfield, 1966). Information on SES and quality of schooling may be helpful in corroborating hypotheses.

ADMINISTRATION AND SCORING POINTERS

1. Study the scoring criteria carefully in order to be able to query responses appropriately.
2. Be sensitive to cultural/linguistic differences.
3. Record actual responses if possible to assist with report writing.

PSYCHOMETRIC PROPERTIES

Average reliability = .91
"g" loading = .66
Loading on verbal factor = .74

Loading on memory factor = –.07
Loading on quantitative factor = .18
Loading on abstract/visual factor = –.01
Subtest specificity = .54 (ample)

BEHAVIORS TO NOTE

1. Questions about the meanings of words used in the stimuli

Quantitative Reasoning Area

Quantitative

In the Quantitative subtest, children are required to solve applied mathematics problems and show knowledge of mathematics concepts. This test uses visual as well as oral stimuli, making it perhaps more similar to the Arithmetic subtest of the K-ABC than to the Arithmetic test of the WISC-III. In addition, the child is allowed to use scratch paper and pencil on this test.

Quantitative scores are likely affected by the child's mathematics knowledge, which in turn may be determined by interest, quality of schooling, and other factors. Scores on this test can be compared to scores from other mathematics measures to test hypotheses. Scores for young children on this test may be difficult to interpret since a different item type is used for items 1 to 3 and 6 to 8. These early items place a premium on spatial perception and reasoning skills. While the items used in this test assess a variety of mathematics skills, the authors do not suggest that the test is a comprehensive measure of mathematics ability.

ADMINISTRATION AND SCORING POINTERS

1. Be sure to give the child scratch paper beginning with item 19.

PSYCHOMETRIC PROPERTIES

Average reliability = .88
"g" loading = .78

Loading on verbal factor = .25
Loading on memory factor = .20
Loading on quantitative factor = .37
Loading on abstract/visual factor = .21
Subtest specificity = .48 (adequate)

BEHAVIORS TO NOTE

1. Self-deprecating statements about mathematics skills
2. Limited or no use of the scratch paper on difficult items (this may indicate poor achievement motivation or lack of confidence)
3. Impulsive responding
4. Sweating, tearfulness, shaking, or other signs of anxiety
5. Statements suggesting low self-esteem (e.g., "I can't do this, I'm not as smart as my friends")

Number Series

The child has to review a series of four or more numbers presented by the examiner, identify the principle underlying the series of numbers, and then generate the next two numbers in the series consistent with the principle.

This test is also affected by academic achievement in mathematics. Scores on this test may also be affected by related factors such as achievement motivation and academic self-concept. Scores on this test may be compared to scores from other mathematics measures to test hypotheses.

ADMINISTRATION AND SCORING POINTERS

1. Record responses as an aid to understanding the nature of a child's reasoning errors.

PSYCHOMETRIC PROPERTIES

Average reliability = .90
"g" loading = .79
Loading on verbal factor = .05
Loading on memory factor = .26

Loading on quantitative factor = .42

Loading on abstract/visual factor = .33

Subtest specificity = .45 (adequate)

<hr>

BEHAVIORS TO NOTE

<hr>

1. Self-deprecating statements about mathematics skills
2. Indicators of poor achievement motivation or lack of confidence (e.g., an expressed dislike for schoolwork)
3. Impulsive responding

Equation Building

The child has to take numerals and mathematical signs and resequence them in order to produce a correct solution (equation). This test is clearly a measure of advanced mathematics skill. It may be wholly inappropriate as a measure of intelligence for a 12-year-old who has not yet taken related coursework such as algebra. This test may be more useful for assessing the mathematically precocious child who is a candidate for some type of advanced coursework.

<hr>

ADMINISTRATION AND SCORING POINTERS

<hr>

1. Brush up on your algebra! The manual states that not all of the correct solutions may be given.

<hr>

PSYCHOMETRIC PROPERTIES

<hr>

Average reliability = .91

"g" loading = .65

Loading on verbal factor = .13

Loading on memory factor = .11

Loading on quantitative factor = .71

Loading on abstract/visual factor = .01

Subtest specificity = .49 (ample)

<hr>

BEHAVIORS TO NOTE

<hr>

1. Responses to failure
2. Level of interest in the task

Abstract/Visual Reasoning Area

Pattern Analysis

The first six items require the child to place puzzle pieces into a form board. Items 7 through 42 require the child to reproduce patterns with blocks. This test is a clone of Wechsler's Block Design, which was a clone of Kohs's (1923) Block Design from earlier in this century (see Chapter 8). The test, however, can be somewhat confounded for younger children because of the use of the form board. The task effectively changes from puzzle solving to abstract design reproduction.

This test can be dramatically affected by speed of performance. A large number of time failures (three or more items) would call into question the obtained score for this test. This test may also serve as a marker of right-hemisphere skills, as is the case of Block Design.

<hr>

ADMINISTRATION AND SCORING POINTERS

<hr>

1. Practice timing items

<hr>

PSYCHOMETRIC PROPERTIES

<hr>

Average reliability = .92

"g" loading = .67

Loading on verbal factor = .00

Loading on memory factor = .00

Loading on quantitative factor = .08

Loading on abstract/visual factor = .74

Subtest specificity = .22 (adequate)

<hr>

BEHAVIORS TO NOTE

<hr>

1. Attempts to align the sides of the blocks in addition to the tops
2. Frequent time failures
3. Impulsive responses where the child does not survey the stimulus before constructing the design

Copying

For the first 12 items the child is required to produce models with single-color blocks. For items 13 through 28 the child has to use pencil and paper to draw a variety of geometric and similar designs to match a model. This test follows in the tradition of visual-motor skill assessment popularized by Lauretta Bender (1938). These item types (i.e., drawing geometric designs) have, however, been included on previous editions of the Binet. As with all visual-motor tests, the Copying test items are most appropriate for younger children. The skills required for this type of test evidently develop early and peak by about the middle of the elementary school years. Performance on this test can be affected by visual activity, motor problems, or neurodevelopmental problems.

Administration and Scoring Pointers

1. The Copying test has two item types: blocks are used for early items and pencil and the record form for older ages.

2. Scoring of the design items may take some practice.

Psychometric Properties

Average reliability = .87

"g" loading = .60

Loading on verbal factor = .09

Loading on memory factor = .13

Loading on quantitative factor = −.08

Loading on abstract/visual factor = .54

Subtest specificity = .69 (ample)

Behaviors to Note

1. Poor pencil grip

2. Frequent erasures

3. Failure to scan the stimuli adequately before responding (impulsive responding)

Matrices

The child is presented figural matrices in which one portion of the matrix is missing. The child has to identify the missing element from multiple-choice alternatives.

The Matrices test uses a format similar to that used by Ravens Progressive Matrices and the Matrix Analogies of the K-ABC. Tests of this nature are known for strong correlations with composite scores or "g" loadings. This test requires strong spatial skills.

Administration and Scoring Pointers

1. Although this test is difficult for younger children, it may be appropriate for some younger precocious children.

Psychometric Properties

Average reliability = .90

"g" loading = .75

Loading on verbal factor = .12

Loading on memory factor = .16

Loading on quantitative factor = .27

Loading on abstract/visual factor = .39

Subtest specificity = .57 (ample)

Behaviors to Note

1. Good success on early items compared with no success on the later pencil and paper items

Paper Folding and Cutting

The child has to choose the correct picture from a multiple-choice format that shows how a piece of paper might look if it were folded as shown in a drawing. This test has a long history with the Binet and is relatively unique. It assesses spatial skills with little confound from motor skills.

Administration and Scoring Pointers

1. Administration of this test can be inefficient if the examiner has not practiced folding and

cutting the paper. Examiners should practice this if they have not used the test in some time.

Average reliability = .94

"g" loading = .69

Loading on verbal factor = .09

Loading on memory factor = .09

Loading on quantitative factor = .35

Loading on abstract/visual factor = .55

Subtest specificity = .60 (ample)

BEHAVIORS TO NOTE

1. Excessive help (teaching) required in order for the child to grasp the nature of the task

Short-Term Memory Area

Bead Memory

For the first 10 items, the child has to recall which of one or two beads was exposed briefly by an examiner. For items 11 through 42 the child has to place beads on a stick in the same sequence as shown by the examiner in a picture.

Bead Memory can be a challenge to interpret because of its tendency to not correlate with the remainder of the Short-Term Memory area subtests. The substantial loading by Bead Memory on the abstract/visual factor suggests that frequently this test will produce a score more similar to the A/V than the STM subtests. Evidently the spatial aspects of this task loom large as a factor affecting performance.

ADMINISTRATION AND SCORING POINTERS

1. Do not present the box of beads before being ready to begin the test because access to the beads may be difficult for many children to resist.

PSYCHOMETRIC PROPERTIES

Average reliability = .87

"g" loading = .69

Loading on verbal factor = .04

Loading on memory factor = .31

Loading on quantitative factor = .05

Loading on abstract/visual factor = .44

Subtest specificity = .59 (ample)

BEHAVIORS TO NOTE

1. Inability to resist "playing" with the beads
2. Motor coordination problems (e.g., child has difficulty placing beads on the stalk)

Memory for Sentences

The child has to repeat a sentence exactly as it was stated by the examiner. This test seems to possess "ecological" validity in that it assesses an important and practical cognitive skill—the ability of a child to recall a series of words. This is similar to the task of following directions given by teachers or parents. This is a classic example of a fluid ability task that may be adversely affected by medical or neurodevelopmental problems. This test may be a poor test of memory for a child whose first language is not English.

ADMINISTRATION AND SCORING POINTERS

1. Practice may be required in order to read the items at an even rate.

PSYCHOMETRIC PROPERTIES

Average reliability = .89

"g" loading = .67

Loading on verbal factor = .44

Loading on memory factor = .52

Loading on quantitative factor = −.06

Loading on abstract/visual factor = −.07

Subtest specificity = .53 (ample)

1. Heavy use of colloquial language, which results in low scores

Memory for Digits

The child has to repeat digits exactly as they were stated by the examiner and, for some items, in reverse order. This is a clone of Wechsler's Digit Span test, a classic short-term memory test that traces its roots to the earliest days of intellectual assessment.

1. The 1-second presentation rate may require practice in order to administer the items in consistent fashion.

Average reliability = .83

"g" loading = .58

Loading on verbal factor = .01

Loading on memory factor = .70

Loading on quantitative factor = .13

Loading on abstract/visual factor = −.02

Subtest specificity = .49 (adequate)

1. Little evidence of rehearsal
2. Impulsivity, as shown by the child responding before the examiner completes the stimuli

Memory for Objects

The examiner presents a group of objects on a page and the child has to identify the objects in the correct order from a larger array. In some ways this test resembles Spatial Memory of the K-ABC. This test may require adequate verbal skills to encode the stimuli properly.

1. Practice may be required to flip the stimulus pages quickly.

Average reliability = .73

"g" loading = .51

Loading on verbal factor = .00

Loading on memory factor = .50

Loading on quantitative factor = .00

Loading on abstract/visual factor = .18

Subtest specificity = .50 (adequate)

1. Inattention
2. Absence of rehearsal strategies

INTERPRETATION

The Binet-4 is amenable to the same interpretive approach described in Chapter 17; however, because of its relative "youth" it is a less well-known entity. An example of a lack of research is the Absurdities subtest, which, although present on previous editions, is not well researched and is factorially unclear (Sattler, 1988). Considerably more research will help the Binet-4 user discern the meaning of its subtest, area, and composite scores.

The Binet-4 authors are also in general agreement with the interpretive approach of this test (Thorndike et al., 1986). They clearly emphasize the importance of the composite score and relegate the area and subtest scores to a lesser status. Factor analytic findings generally support this approach, with one exception: the equal treatment of the area scores. The Verbal Reasoning and Abstract/Visual area scores are factorially more viable than the Quantitative and Short-Term

Memory scores. Given the lack of validity evidence for these latter two scales, they are more similar to shared hypotheses than composite score hypotheses. The three levels of Binet-4 interpretation may then be conceptualized as follows.

COMPOSITE SCORE HYPOTHESES

Composite
Verbal Reasoning area
Abstract/Visual area

SHARED SUBTEST HYPOTHESES

Combinations of two or more subtests
Short-Term Memory area
Quantitative area

SINGLE SUBTEST HYPOTHESES

Individual subtest scores

An alternative approach to placing two area scores at the composite score level and two area scores at the shared subtest level is to use a factor score interpretation approach. For various reasons (see Chapter 8), the factor score approach is eschewed in this text. The factor score method of interpreting the Binet-4 is particularly unattractive given the availability of numerous factor analytic studies upon which a factor score method could be based.

Composite Score Hypotheses

Tables for determining significant composite score differences and the rarity of differences can be found in Delaney and Hopkins (1987), Spruill (1988), and Rosenthal and Kamphaus (1988). The average differences between the A/V and V/R area scores for the norming sample are shown in Table 9.3.

Hypotheses for the Test Composite, Verbal Reasoning, and Abstract/Visual area scores can be generated based on information in previous

TABLE 9.3 Clinical rarity of differences between abstract/visual and verbal reasoning area scores for two age groups

A/V vs V/R DIFFERENCE	Percentage of Norm Sample Obtaining a Difference This Size or Larger	
	AGES 2–10	AGES 11–23
10 points	48	39
15 points	29	20
20 points	16	8
25 points	8	3
30 points	3	1
35 points	1	1

Table values were computed based on data provided by Rosenthal and Kamphaus (1988).

chapters, particularly the WISC-III chapters. By now scores of this variety are familiar, as are the factors that may influence them. Various composite score hypotheses will be offered and interpreted in the case studies to follow.

Shared Subtest Hypotheses

Table 9.4 offers a number of shared subtest hypotheses for Binet-4 subtests that are adapted from Delaney and Hopkins (1987) and from factor analytic results. As always, these hypotheses should be considered cautiously because of their lack of validity evidence. Additionally, something unique to the Binet-4 is the listing of the Quantitative and Short-Term Memory area scores as shared, *not* composite, score hypotheses.

Subtest strengths and weaknesses may be determined using the rule of thumb offered by Delaney and Hopkins (1987). They suggest using +/–7 points as indicative of a significant subtest deviation from the overall subtest mean.

The Binet-4 subtests are relatively lengthy. This subtest length—and its associated reliability—is

TABLE 9.4   Shared subtest hypotheses for the Stanford-Binet—Fourth Edition

	Verbal Reasoning Area				Abstract/Visual Reasoning Area				Quantitative Reasoning Area				Short-Term Memory Area			
	Voc	Com	Abs	VR	PA	Cpy	Mat	PF&C	Qun	NS	Eq	Bld	BM	MfS	MfD	MfO
Vocabulary knowledge	√	√		√										√		
Verbal expression	√	√	√	√										√		
Verbal concept formation	√			√												
Verbal comprehension		√												√		
Part-to-whole synthesis					√	√										
Visual analysis					√	√	√	√					√			√
Mathematics knowledge									√	√		√				
Fluid ability					√		√	√					√	√	√	√
Crystallized ability	√	√	√	√					√							
Memory strategies													√	√	√	√
Short-term auditory memory														√	√	
Short-term visual memory													√			√
Visual-motor coordination					√	√										
Knowledge of social conventions		√	√													
Attention													√	√	√	√
Response to novelty							√	√								
Manual dexterity					√	√							√			
Time pressure					√											

unusual. It also may produce some quite high ratios of subtest specificity to error variance for several subtests (e.g., .59 for Bead Memory), suggesting that some of the Binet-4 subtests are amenable to interpretation as assessing some relatively unique cognitive skill or set of skills. The validity of such interpretations, however, is still dependent on the clinician's judgment rather than an available body of validity research. Single subtest hypotheses are also given in Table 9.4.

Report Writing

The Binet-4 poses several interesting challenges for report writing. It is one of the few tests where the subtests administered to a child should be clearly listed. Since the array of subtests that may be administered is large, the reader of a Binet report will likely question which "version" of the Binet was used. I recommend that each report *list the Binet-4 subtests administered* and any that were spoiled or eliminated for whatever reason. Report writers should explain why subtests were eliminated in order to ensure that subtests were not eliminated capriciously.

The Binet report also needs an introductory paragraph. Here is one example of such an introduction.

The Stanford-Binet Intelligence Scale—Fourth Edition (Binet-4) is a major test of intelligence that yields a composite that is comparable to the overall score of other major intelligence tests and similar to the traditional IQ score. The Binet-4 subtests are divided into four subscales—Verbal Reasoning, Abstract/Visual Reasoning, Quantitative Reasoning, and Short-Term Memory. Typically a minimum of two subtests from each area are administered, although the specific subtest used and scores interpreted may vary depending on the case.

For the Binet-4 it may also be necessary to describe the nature of a particular subtest when writing about it. Some of the Binet items, such as those on the Number Series test, are infrequently used and/or new to this edition of the Binet. This situation creates the possibility that even other psychologists may be unfamiliar with the task.

Case Study

The Binet-4 case study of Jerri (see Box 9.1) differs from those of earlier chapters. This case is presented as a final report with a priori hypotheses offered. This format assumes that the new clinician has progressed to the point that he or she can apply an integrative approach to a larger set of data that includes information in addition to intelligence test data.

Jerri is referred for school difficulties. There is concern about her poor academic performance. She is currently being served in a special education program on a resource basis with an emphasis on basic academic skill development. She was retained once for academic failure and she has received after-school tutoring. She also has a history of head injury and questionable prenatal care or environment. All of these factors are associated with lower-than-average intelligence test scores. A reasonable a priori hypothesis is that her Binet scores will be below average. Jerri also estimated her intelligence to be below average, as was indicated by her numerous self-deprecating statements during testing.

Box 9.1   Psychological Evaluation

Name: Jerri
Grade: Fifth
Sex: Female
Age: 12 years, 3 months
School: East End Middle School

Assessment Procedures

Parent, teacher, and child interviews
Parent rating scales
  Parenting Stress Index (PSI)
  Parent Achenbach Child Behavior Checklist (Parent Achenbach)
Teacher rating scale
  Teacher Achenbach Child Behavior Checklist (Teacher Achenbach)
Child rating scales
  Piers-Harris Children's Self-Concept Scale (Piers-Harris)
  Revised Children's Manifest Anxiety Scale (RCMAS)
  Reynolds Adolescent Depression Scale (RADS)
Stanford-Binet Intelligence Scale—Fourth Edition (Binet-4)
Bender Gestalt
Kaufman Test of Educational Achievement/Comprehensive Form (K-TEA)
Draw-a-Person (DAP)
Thematic Apperception Test (TAT)

Reason for Referral

Jerri was referred for evaluation by her mother and teachers for poor performance in many academic areas.

(Continues)

Box 9.1   **Psychological Evaluation** (Continued)

Background Information

Background information was provided by Jerri's mother. Her mother reports that throughout her pregnancy she smoked cigarettes and experienced significant depression and crying spells. Jerri's birth was uneventful except for the use of forceps during the delivery. Developmental milestones were reported as achieved within normal limits.

Significant head injuries occurred on two occasions. At age 20 months, Jerri fell from her bed, resulting in a concussion. While at her preschool at age 2, she again experienced a head injury, but her mother was not aware of specific details of the accident. Jerri was toilet trained at 24 months, yet she continued to wet the bed periodically until age 7. Her mother attributes this problem to frequent kidney infections.

Jerri currently lives with her mother, stepfather, and two brothers, one 14 years of age and one 5 years of age. Her mother and biological father have been divorced for several years. Jerri's mother says that Jerri is emotionally close to her stepfather. She also gets along well with her brothers.

Jerri's mother reports a number of emotional problems in the past. In the first grade Jerri was sexually fondled by an adult male.

Jerri attends regular classes for a portion of the school day with the remainder of the day spent in a resource classroom for behavior-disordered children. In the resource room she is receiving remedial instruction in reading and math. She also receives some voluntary after-school tutoring. She was retained in the third grade.

Test Observations

Jeri was extremely cooperative during testing. She was compliant and attentive. She did, however, display a poor academic self-concept. She called herself "stupid" and "dumb" on numerous occasions.

Assessment Results

The Binet-4 intelligence scale comprises 15 subtests, of which usually 6 to 9 are administered to a given child or young adult. These tests are divided into four areas, including Verbal Reasoning, Abstract/Visual Reasoning, Quantitative Reasoning, and Short-Term Memory. The Verbal Reasoning area contains tests such as defining words and answering commonsense questions. Abstract/Visual Reasoning tests include items such as constructing puzzles, assembling abstract designs with blocks, and drawing figures. The Quantitative Reasoning area includes test items that assess applied mathematical problem solving and advanced mathematical skills such as algebra. Finally, Short-Term Memory items require children to recall digits, sentences, and arrangements of multicolored and multishaped beads. The subtests in each area are combined to produce an area score (e.g., Abstract/Visual). These area scores in turn are combined to derive a Test Composite Score. Jerri obtained a Test Composite in the well-below-average range. Her Test Composite score corresponds to a percentile rank of 7, indicating that she performed better than approximately 7% of other 12-year-olds taking the test and worse than approximately 93%. Jerri's performance on this measure is highly consistent with her mother's report of Jerri being "low" in all skill areas.

These results are also highly consistent with those from the K-TEA. Individual academic area and composite standard scores for Jerri ranged from 70 to 85, which corresponds to percentile ranks ranging from 2 to 16 (see psychometric summary). No significant pattern of strengths and/or weaknesses were evident between subtest areas; rather, all skill areas assessed were below average. Again, this result is supported by maternal reports and school records of Jerri's past and present academic achievement.

Social/Emotional Area

According to results of the Parenting Stress Index, areas of stress revealed between Jerri and her mother appear to be related to her mother's frustration with what she perceives as her daughter's excessive activity level and lack of fulfillment of her mother's expectations for her. On the Achenbach Child Behavior Checklist (CBCL), the only clinically significant area was attention problems. Interview information obtained from Jerri's mother confirms these findings, with her reporting that she sees Jerri as extremely distractable and overactive.

Box 9.1 Psychological Evaluation (Continued)

Jerri's teacher ratings revealed no significant scale elevations. Her teacher says that Jerri cannot concentrate long enough to complete her schoolwork and that she is constantly asking for assistance for even the simplest assignments. Socially, she reports that Jerri has few friends.

Rating scales and an interview were used to determine Jerri's personal perception of her social and emotional functioning. Jerri's Piers-Harris scores in all areas assessed were extremely low, with the exception of the area of Happiness and Satisfaction. This profile tends to be associated with an adolescent who feels incompetent but denies it when directly questioned about it. A significant amount of inconsistency in Jerri's responses was noted on the RCMAS, which is usually associated with an adolescent having a distorted or inaccurate view of themselves and their current level of emotional stability. Finally, RADS results indicate that she does not see herself as depressed at this time.

On the DAP and TAT, Jerri tended to give responses that were considered developmentally immature. Interview information from Jerri supports these findings. She relates that she is anxious and that she gets upset easily "like her mother." She is concerned about not having any close friends, and she feels that the other children in school "talk about her behind her back." Surprisingly, she reports that she is generally a happy person. Regarding her poor performance in school subjects, she says that she is "real slow" and that it takes her a long time to learn things. She, like her mother and teacher, feels that she has a very hard time concentrating and that it is easy for her to be distracted.

Conclusions and Recommendations

Jerri is a 12-year-old female who was referred for evaluation for determination of significant factors related to her academic problems. Intellectual and achievement testing indicate that she functions as a "slow learner" with below-average skills evident in all achievement areas assessed. Evaluation of social-emotional areas indicates that Jerri is an extremely distractable child. She has a poor self-image and may be experiencing significant feelings of anxiety and apprehension at this time. Recommendations based on assessment results include:

1. Jerri's behavior meets the diagnostic criteria for attention deficit disorder, as specified by the Diagnostic and Statistical Manual of Mental Disorders (4th ed., hyperactivity—primary inattentive type). This diagnostic category seems appropriate for Jerri because of her high level of inattention and distractibility without hyperactivity. This diagnosis suggests that Jerri will need some type of intervention to control her distractibility at school.

2. A number of risk factors appear to be present in areas related to Jerri's emotional functioning. It is recommended that individual counseling and group counseling be sought to lessen the risk of Jerri's development of future emotional problems.

3. Jerri has been identified as a slow learner in academic areas. A formal tutorial program is recommended to enhance her development of academic skills. In conjunction with tutoring, curriculum-based assessment is advised to help pinpoint specific areas of academic weakness.

Psychometric Summary
Stanford-Binet Intelligence Scale—Fourth Edition

AREA/SUBTEST	STANDARD AGE SCORE
Verbal Reasoning	73
Vocabulary	36
Comprehension	39
Abstract/Visual Reasoning	86
Pattern Analysis	43
Copying	43

(Continues)

Box 9.1   Psychological Evaluation (Continued)

AREA/SUBTEST	STANDARD AGE SCORE
Quantitative	84
Quantitative	42
Short-Term Memory	74
Bead Memory	36
Memory for Sentences	42
Composite	76, 7th percentile

Kaufman Test of Educational Achievement

SUBTESTS	STANDARD SCORE	PERCENTILE RANK	GRADE EQUIVALENT
Mathematics Applications	80	9	3.9
Reading Decoding	79	8	3.6
Spelling	70	2	2.6
Reading Comprehension	85	16	4.5
Mathematics Computation	77	6	4.1
Composites			
Reading	81	10	4.0
Mathematics	78	7	4.0

Bender Gestalt Test

Errors = 5

Age Equivalent = 7-6 –7-11

Percentile = less than 5th

Achenbach Child Behavior Checklist (CBCL)

	MOTHER		TEACHER
Internalizing Scale	57	Internalizing Scale	61
Anxious/Depressed	57	Anxious/Depressed	59
Somatic Complaints	67	Social Problems	63
Social Problems	67	Thought Problems	64
Thought Problems	55	Somatic Complaints	62
Attention Problems	74*	Attention Problems	68
Externalizing Scale	59	Externalizing Scale	69
Delinquent Behavior	66	Delinquent Behavior	63
Aggressive Behavior	55	Aggressive Behavior	69

Box 9.1   Psychological Evaluation (Continued)

Piers-Harris Children's Self-Concept Scale

Clusters	Raw Scores	Percentile	Stanine	T-score
Behavior	10	25	4	43
Intellectual & School Status	5	6	2	34
Physical Appearance & Attributes	4	11	2	37
Anxiety	8	37	4	47
Popularity	3	5	2	34
Happiness & Satisfaction	9	72	6	56
Total Score	18	1	1	27

Child Subscale Scores		Parent Subscale Scores	
Adaptability	26	Dependent	21
Acceptability	19	Attentive	14
Demonstrative	21	Restraint	16
Mother	12	Competent	30
Distractibility	32	Isolation	13
Reinforcement	10	Health	10

Sum of Child Domain Score = 120
Sum of Parent Domain Score = 121
Total Stress Index = 241

Revised Children's Manifest Anxiety Scale (RCMAS)

Clusters	Percentile	T-score or Scaled Score
Total Anxiety	38	47
Lie	90	13

Reynolds Adolescent Depression Scale

Raw Score = 53
Total Percentile = 28
Only one critical item noted (# 30)

RESEARCH REPORT 9.1

The Binet Factor Structure Arbitrated

Robert M. Thorndike (the son of the late Robert L. Thorndike) has attempted to tie together all of the factor analytic research on the Binet—Fourth Edition. This is a monumental task given the considerable disagreement in the research literature. Thorndike (1990) begins by making critical comments about existing factor analytic studies of the Binet-4. He cites problems with the exploratory analyses of Thorndike, Hagen, and Sattler (1986); Reynolds, Kamphaus, and Rosenthal (1988); and Sattler (1988). He then proposes an exploratory factor analytic procedure as the "right" answer.

He used a principal axis factor analytic method where squared multiple correlations were used in the diagonal of the correlation matrix as initial communality estimates. His first analysis was conducted on 17 correlation matrices corresponding to the age groups of the Binet-4. Two- and three-factor solutions were rotated using the Oblimin (Oblique, see Chapter 5) rotation procedure. For ages 2–6, the first factor yielded relatively large eigenvalues, ranging from a low of 3.46 for age 2 to a high of 4.72 for age 5. Similarly, the eigenvalues for the second factor were substantial at most ages, ranging from .80 at age 5 to 1.18 at age 2. By comparison, however, the eigenvalues for the third factor were considerably lower, ranging from .55 at age 3 to .81 at age 2. Thorndike (1990) concluded that a three-factor solution was the best fit for the 2-year-olds but a two-factor solution representing primarily verbal and nonverbal subtests was the most sensible for ages 3 through 6. Hence, he concluded that at ages 2 through 6, a two-factor solution representing primarily verbal and nonverbal skills was most supportable for the Binet-4. Subtests with high loadings on the verbal factor included Vocabulary (loadings from .83 to .89), Comprehension (loadings from .62 to .98), Absurdities (loadings from .34 to .75), and Memory for Sentences (loadings from .56 to .71). The subtests that marked the nonverbal factor included Pattern Analysis (loadings of .63 to .82), Copying (loadings of .61 to .76), Quantitative (loadings from .39 to .73), and Bead Memory (loadings of .59 to .78). These results gained some additional support because they are consistent with the analysis favored by Sattler (1988).

Thorndike used the same procedures to evaluate the factor structure for the middle age group, ages 7 through 11 years. In this age group, the first factor produced eigenvalues ranging from 4.97 for 7-year-olds to 6.62 for 11-year-olds. The second factor yielded eigenvalues ranging from .83 for 11-year-olds to 1.24 for 7-year-olds. The third factor produced eigenvalues ranging from .71 for 11-year-olds to 1.02 for 9-year-olds. The fourth factor was considerably and inconsistently smaller, with eigenvalues ranging from .66 for 8-year-olds to .78 for 7-year-olds. Thorndike interpreted these results as supporting a three-factor solution. This solution was also supported by evaluation of Scree plot results.

Thorndike identified the first factor as verbal ability because it included strong loadings for subtests such as Vocabulary (loadings of .43 to .94), Comprehension (loadings of .41 to .87), and Memory for Sentences (loadings of .45 to .73). The Absurdities subtest takes a minor role in the verbal factor at this age, producing loadings ranging from .14 to .45. The second factor is interpreted as a nonverbal factor that is marked by subtests, including Pattern Analysis (loadings of .58 to .88), Copying (loadings of .52 to .59), Matrices (loadings of .15 to .75), Bead Memory (loadings of .36 to .63), and Absurdities (loadings of .43 to .88). At this age range, the Absurdities subtest switches factors from its place on the verbal factor at the preschool ages. Thorndike attributes this switch to the use of visual stimuli on this primarily verbal subtest. It is also noteworthy, however, that as was the case with the analyses of younger children, there is a melding of quantitative and short-term memory tests (Bead Memory) with the abstract/visual factor.

The new factor to emerge at this age is labeled as "Memory" by Thorndike. This factor is marked primarily by Memory for Digits, with loadings ranging from .52 to .83. Memory for Objects contributes somewhat to this factor, with loadings ranging from .15 to .58. Similarly, Memory for Sentences contributes some variance to this factor, with loadings ranging from .21 to .58. Memory for Sentences, however, continues to have considerably higher loadings at this age range on the verbal factor.

RESEARCH REPORT 9.1 (Continued)

The final age range to be investigated was ages 12 through 23 years (the last age group is 18–23). Again, three factors were obtained using the Kaiser criterion and Scree plots. Eigenvalues for the first factor ranged from 6.79 for 15-year-olds to 7.91 for ages 18 to 23. Eigenvalues for the second factor ranged from .92 for 14-year-olds to 1.36 for 12-year-olds. Eigenvalues for the third factor ranged from .83 for 16-year-olds to 1.15 for 12-year-olds. All of the eigenvalues for the fourth factor were below 1, with a range of .63 for 17-year-olds to .86 for 12-year-olds.

The first factor was marked by loadings for verbal subtests and was identified as a verbal factor. It had uniformly high loadings by Vocabulary (loadings of .61 to .88), Comprehension (loadings of .34 to .78), and Memory for Sentences (loadings of .32 to .94) subtests. Again, the loadings for the Absurdities subtest were equivocal, ranging from .30 to .71 for ages 12 through 14 years. The abstract/visual factor for ages 12–23 was marked by high loadings on the part of Pattern Analysis (loadings of .25 to .89), Matrices (loadings of .25 to .68), Paper Folding and Cutting (loadings of .68 to .82), Number Series (loadings of .31 to .84), Equation Building (loadings of .07 to .85), and to a lesser extent, Bead Memory (loadings of .06 to .48). The memory factor again was marked by the Memory for Digits subtest with factor loadings ranging from .17 to .78. This factor was supported to a lesser extent by Memory for Sentences with loadings of .14 to .69 and Memory for Objects with loadings of .12 to .68. The Bead Memory subtest contributed very little to the memory factor, with a median factor loading of .28.

Most apparent from these factor analytic results is that they agree with those of researchers such as Sattler (1988) and Reynolds, Kamphaus, and Rosenthal (1988) in that a quantitative factor could not be identified. As Thorndike (1990) states, "Attempts to clarify this situation by finding a factor common to the three quantitative tests were not successful" (p. 427).

Thorndike concludes that these factors are also identified by Sattler (1988). He also notes, however, that the strong correlation of about .40 to .70 between the factors suggests a strong "g" component. A dissertation study by Wilson (1995) also notes the strong "g" component. He also concluded that the Binet-4 is best used as a test of general ability for children with LD.

Thorndike then turns his attention to reviews of the confirmatory factor analyses. He concludes that "Although the evidence from these confirmatory analyses may be gratifying to those who have an interest in four factors, the support is rather weak" (p. 433). He also criticizes the method used by some confirmatory factor analytic researchers who are using these models in an "exploratory" fashion.

Other studies have shown that a two-factor verbal/nonverbal model is best for preschoolers and young children (Gridley & McIntosh, 1991; Molfese, Yaple, Helwig, Harris, & Connell, 1992). Both studies called into question the validity of the memory factor for young children.

There are numerous practical implications of these research findings. One can follow the road taken by Sattler (1988) and reinvent the Binet-4 by using factor scores for interpretive purposes. Another approach is to use the existing Binet-4 with the lessons from these factor analytic findings clearly in mind. These lessons suggest that a Verbal Reasoning area score is most homogeneous and distinct from other area scores when it is made up of the Vocabulary and Comprehension subtests. Similarly, the Short-Term Memory area score is most robust when it includes Memory for Digits. The Abstract/Visual area score is most sound when using Pattern Analysis, Copying, Paper Folding and Cutting, and Matrices. The Abstract/Visual score comes closest to the original conceptualization of the Binet developers. The Quantitative area score of the Binet-4 is a wash. These results are all too familiar. The Binet-4 area scores resemble the Verbal and Performance standard scores from the WISC when supplemented by a Digit Span subtest to assess short-term memory.

Binet-4 Strengths and Weaknesses

Strengths

1. The age and standard score ranges of the Binet-4 are strengths that make it useful in a wide variety of applications. The large age range allows for some continuity of assessment to track development. The larger-than-usual standard score range makes the test more useful for children at the tails of the normal distribution (i.e., children with mental retardation and giftedness).

2. The flexibility of administration is helpful for devising a test that is customized for use with a client.

3. Some Binet-4 subtests, such as Number Series, are unprecedented in individual intellectual assessment. Novel tests such as this one create the opportunity for specialized clinical and research uses.

4. The Binet-4 concurrent validity and reliability research is solid and impressive.

5. The dichotomous scoring system of the Binet-4 facilitates the scoring of verbal response item types.

6. Factor analytic support for the Test Composite and Verbal Reasoning and Abstract/Visual area scores is good.

Weaknesses

1. Factor analytic support for the Short-Term Memory and Quantitative area scores is unusually poor.

2. The current Binet does not have as much ceiling and floor as its predecessor. It is not unusual for adolescents to obtain perfect scores on tests such as Pattern Analysis. Nor is it unusual for a 2-year-old to obtain raw scores of zero on one or more tests.

3. The Copying test drawing items are relatively difficult to score in comparison to other visual-motor tests.

Conclusions

The Binet-4 represents a significant step forward in the development of Binet's original technology. The new scale is so comprehensive and different from its predecessors that it cannot draw upon its earlier research base; hence, it may take several years of research to understand the nature of its contributions and limitations. Unfortunately, this research base is developing slowly due to the relative unpopularity of the Binet-4. The Binet-4 is due for revision which could significantly alter the scale yet again.

Chapter Summary

- The Binet-4 departs from its predecessors to such an extent, especially in terms of its structure and theory, that it should be considered a new test, as opposed to what is typically considered a mere revision of an earlier scale.

- In the Binet-4 hierarchical model, "g," or general intelligence, is the premier cognitive ability at the top of the hierarchy.

- The second level of the Binet hierarchy is based on the work of Cattell and his fluid and crystallized dimensions of intelligence.

- The third level in the Binet theoretical hierarchy consists of finer discriminations of the fluid and crystallized abilities. This level includes the area scores and subtests.

- The weighting procedure used to correct for norming sampling problems was effective in producing norm-referenced scores that are consistent and predictable in relationship to other tests of intelligence.

- Internal consistency reliability for the Binet-4 Composite score is extraordinarily high over the 2- to 23-year age span of the test.

- Concurrent validity studies show a strong correlational relationship between the Binet-4 and its predecessors, suggesting that the Binet-4 is very much like other well-respected intelligence measures.

- Factor analytic studies of the Binet-4 have created some confusion because various researchers, using similar procedures, have produced different conclusions.

- Vocabulary, Quantitative, Number Series, Comprehension, and Matrices have high "g" loadings. Memory for Digits, Memory for Objects, and Copying have poor "g" loadings.

- The Verbal Reasoning and Abstract/Visual Reasoning area scores show strong evidence of factorial support.

- The Quantitative area score lacks clear evidence of a corresponding factor.

- The Short-Term Memory area score receives support in some factor analytic studies yet not in others.

- The Binet-4 consists of 15 subtests, only a portion of which are administered to each age group.

- Until more research support exists for the Binet-4 short forms, they should likely be used as secondary or backup procedures as opposed to batteries of first choice.

- The Binet-4 uses an adaptive testing design. The Vocabulary subtest then serves as a "routing" subtest to appropriate entry points on subsequent subtests that are administered to the child.

- The comprehension level of Binet-4 instructions is about the same as that of other popular preschool measures of intelligence.

- The Binet-4 uses a standard score metric that is not comparable with other modern tests of intelligence and, for that matter, with tests of academic achievement.

- In a report, clinicians should list the Binet-4 subtests administered and any that were spoiled or eliminated for whatever reason.

Kaufman Assessment Battery for Children (K-ABC)

CHAPTER QUESTIONS

Who created the K-ABC and how is it different from other popular tests?

With what groups of children is the K-ABC likely to be most useful?

The Kaufman Assessment Battery for Children (K-ABC) (Kaufman & Kaufman, 1983a) has been the subject of scores of research investigations (at least several hundred). A book published in 1987 by Kamphaus and Reynolds containing a rich collection of research indicates that the pace of K-ABC research shows no sign of slowing.

The K-ABC is also becoming a frequently used test in everyday assessment practice. In a nationwide survey of school psychologists conducted in 1987 by Obringer (1988), respondents were asked to rank the following instruments in order of their usage: Wechsler's scales, the K-ABC, and both the old and new Stanford-Binets. The Wechsler scales earned a mean rank of 2.69, followed closely by the K-ABC with a mean of 2.55; then came the old Binet (1.98) and the Stanford-Binet—Fourth Edition (1.26). This survey revealed that 41% of the practitioners used the McCarthy Scales of Children's Abilities with preschoolers (see Chapter 15), 28% used the Binet-4, and 25% used the K-ABC. For ages 5 to 11 years the WISC-R was endorsed by 82%, the K-ABC by 57%, and the Binet-4 by 39% of the practitioners. Flanagan (1995) identified the K-ABC as the test of choice for young children who are bilingual English speakers. These results argue that child clinicians should have at least some familiarity with the K-ABC. Whether its relative popularity stems from the novelty of the instrument (it differs from other scales in theory, organization of subtests, and other ways), its ease of use, or other factors is not clear. It does, however, appear to be around for the long haul.

From the outset the K-ABC has been the subject of great controversy, as attested to by the strongly pro and con articles written for a special issue of the *Journal of Special Education* devoted to

RESEARCH REPORT 10.1

Use of the K-ABC with children diagnosed with attention-deficit hyperactivity disorder

A study by Carter and colleagues (1990) used 38 consecutive clinic referrals. Girls were, however, subsequently eliminated from the sample because there were a disproportionate number of females in the clinic control sample and the girls tended to be younger than the boys. Consequently, two male-only groups were formed. One group was composed of 23 children who were diagnosed as attention deficit hyperactivity disorder (ADHD) and who had a mean age of 9.1 years. The other group consisted of 15 clinic control subjects with a mean age of 9 years. The average grade level for the ADHD group was 3.70 and for the clinic control group was 3.33. Children were eliminated from either group if they had any evidence of neurological impairment or seizures, chronic mental illness, major psychiatric disorder, significantly subnormal intelligence, or other evidence of developmental disabilities.

Children were diagnosed as ADHD based upon a variety of criteria. One of the criteria included a score of 15 or more on the Parent 10-item Conners Abbreviated Symptom Questionnaire. The same criteria were used for the Teacher's Conners. Additional criteria included a T-score above 60 on the hyperactivity scale of the Personality Inventory for Children and a score in the "significant" range or higher on the attention scale of the Burke's Behavioral Rating Scale that was completed by the children's fathers. When there was more than one rater on a particular measure, the ratings were averaged. All of the subjects were dependents of military personnel who were seen at an outpatient pediatric clinic of an Air Force Medical Center. The two groups did not differ significantly on socioeconomic status or ethnicity. The vast majority of the children in the sample were of Anglo-culture origin. The scores on the various ratings scales for the ADHD group and the clinic control group differed substantially. For example, the mean Parent Conner's rating for the ADHD group was 19.26, versus 11.87 for the control group. On the PIC Hyperactivity Scale, the mean for the ADHD group was 72.13, versus 52.40 for the clinic controls. Fifteen of the 23 ADHD children were subsequently prescribed stimulant medication. In order to control for the possible confounding effects of medication on K-ABC and WISC-R performance, a 48-hour abstinence period from medication was required prior to the cognitive testing. The children were tested by a psychometrist or clinical psychologist and examiners were blind to group membership for the study.

The K-ABC composite scores and the WISC-R composite scores were used for all analyses. In addition, a WISC-R freedom from distractibility factor score was computed for the purposes of analysis. A multivariate analysis of variance was used to determine whether the two groups differed on various composite scores of the WISC-R and the K-ABC. There were statistically significant differences between the ADHD and clinical groups on only two composite scores—the sequential scale of the K-ABC and the freedom from distractibility factor of the WISC-R. The Sequential standard scores for the ADHD group produced a mean of 91.44; the mean for the clinic control group was 100.87. Similarly, the mean freedom from distractibility score for the ADHD group was 87.65, versus 100.00 for the clinic control group. Although not statistically significant, the groups did differ in overall intelligence score. The mean MPC for the control group was 104.87, versus 105.33 for the WISC-R. In contrast, the mean MPC for the ADHD group was 99.83, versus 107.44 for the WISC-R. The correlation between the MPC and Full Scale score was also very high at .77. In order to more clearly determine the contribution of the individual subtests to the group differences, subtest group comparisons for the K-ABC Sequential scale were conducted. All of the Sequential scale subtests were lower for the ADHD than for the control group, but only the Word Order test was statistically significant, with a mean of 8.39 versus a mean of 10.53 for this same subtest for the control group.

The authors interpret these findings as suggesting that the Sequential scale of the K-ABC is adversely affected by attentional problems. This, in turn, results in a correspondingly lower MPC than Full Scale score. While the freedom from distractibility subtests of Arithmetic, Coding, and Digit Span were also adversely affected, their effect on total score is diluted by the fact that only two of these subtests influence the Full Scale score. It is also interesting that the MPC and the subtest scores on the Sequential scale subtests are still within the average range for this particular sample.

A major interpretive problem for these results is produced by the low correlation of .38 between the Sequential scale of the K-ABC and the freedom from distractibility factor of the WISC-R for the sample of ADHD children.

(Continues)

RESEARCH REPORT 10.1 (Continued)

Use of the K-ABC with children diagnosed with attention-deficit hyperactivity disorder

This suggests that these scales are depressed for different reasons. It could be that the distractibility factor of the WISC-R is assessing something different for the ADHD sample from the Sequential scale of the K-ABC. Is one scale adversely affected by distractibility and the other by sequential processing problems? The answer is currently unknown, and examiners will have to interpret results for individual children based upon their clinical acumen. Given the small sample size and some of the controversy regarding the appropriate methods for diagnosing ADHD, these results require replication.

the K-ABC (Miller & Reynolds, 1984) (see Box 10.1). Many of the controversies, especially those regarding the validity of the K-ABC theory, will likely endure unresolved for some time. In the meantime, however, a wealth of research can lead clinicians in interpreting the K-ABC because so much is known about how it correlates with other measures.

Despite its apparent nuances, the K-ABC should be viewed as a logical outgrowth of the history of intelligence testing. The K-ABC authors have extensive experience with other measures, notably the WISC-R. Alan Kaufman had a major impact on the assessment of children's intelligence in his role as a researcher at The Psychological Corporation. Kaufman was project director for development of the WISC-R and the McCarthy scales, tasks to which he was well suited because of his studies at Columbia under the tutelage of the famed psychometrician Robert L. Thorndike.

The Kaufmans' first book, *Clinical Evaluation of Young Children with the McCarthy Scales* (1977), provided a training ground for their work on the K-ABC by immersing them in the work of Dorothea McCarthy, a well-respected child clinician. Alan Kaufman is probably best known for his text *Intelligent Testing with the WISC-R* (1979b). This text laid the groundwork for modern intelligence test interpretation, much of which is incorporated into early chapters of this book. As Anastasi (1988) observes: "The basic approach described by Kaufman undoubtedly represents a major contribution to the clinical use of intelligence tests. Nevertheless, it should be recognized

that its implementation requires a sophisticated clinician who is well informed in several fields of psychology" (p. 484).

One can readily see that the Kaufmans entered the arena of intelligence test development with well-deserved laurels. This fact may explain in part why the K-ABC has enjoyed some acceptance.

THEORETICAL FRAMEWORK

The K-ABC intelligence scales are based on a theoretical framework that differs greatly from the approach of Wechsler, who emphasized the assessment of "g" (see Chapter 2). The Kaufmans put much more emphasis on their subscales, Sequential and Simultaneous information processing, which are roughly equivalent to the Verbal and Performance scales. Wechsler used the Verbal and Performance scales as means to an end, that end being the assessment of general intelligence. The Kaufmans, however, elevate the Sequential and Simultaneous scales so that they rather than the overall score—the Mental Processing Composite (MPC)—are the focus of interpretation.

The theoretical underpinnings of the Sequential and Simultaneous scales are really an updated version of a variety of theories (Kamphaus, 1990). They were gleaned from a convergence of research and theory in diverse areas including clinical and experimental neuropsychology and

Box 10.1

Now I'm really confused

Reviews of tests by experts are important sources of information when making intelligence test purchase and use decisions. The clinician should, however, read more than one review as experts often disagree, as shown in the examples below that were taken from a 1984 special issue of the *Journal of Special Education* devoted entirely to reviews of the K-ABC. Often intelligence test users will have to read several reviews and even try out a new test before deciding on its utility. While at first these reviews of the K-ABC appear confusing, they are enlightening in at least several respects. They highlight the controversial nature of the K-ABC when it was first published and they show that the K-ABC appeared at the time to be different from its predecessors.

Dean (1984)

The K-ABC represents a theoretically consistent battery of tests that offers insights into children's cognitive processing beyond presently available measures of intelligence.

Sternberg (1984)

The creators of the Kaufman Assessment Battery for Children have attempted to put together a unique, innovative test that will solve the problems created by existing tests. Unfortunately, the test generates more problems than it solves. It is based upon an inadequate conception of intelligence, and as a result, it is not a good measure of intelligence. The data of others cited to support the conception do not in fact support it, and the data collected specifically to evaluate the K-ABC also do not support it. The external validations, if anything, contraindicate the validity of the theory, and the internal validations are inadequate. I cannot think of any circumstance under which I would advocate use of this test over its major competitors, such as the WISC-R or the Stanford-Binet. I am sorry to have to conclude with such a negative evaluation, because ideally, innovation should be rewarded. In the present case, the innovation did not succeed, and the value of the test appears to be a media phenomenon rather than a new measure of intelligence.

Majovsky (1984)

The K-ABC appears to have adequate construct validity as supported by its theoretical basis from the research of cognitive psychology, clinical neuropsychology, cerebral lateralization studies, and other psychological supporting evidence. Secondly, the K-ABC can be most useful in research studies on normal neuropsychological development in young children, as well as impaired brain-behavior functions in diverse childhood populations. Thirdly, the K-ABC is seen to be useful in neuropsychological investigations offering the experienced clinician to see how the information processing style of a child is utilized and on what kinds of tasks. The K-ABC can give a wider degree of information that is not readily obtained by other intelligence measures or test batteries. Fourthly, the K-ABC can be used to supplement a child's clinical neuropsychological evaluation of the level at which the child is processing specific kinds of information, what cognitive strategies are employed, and the efficiencies of the child's information processing styles. The K-ABC in the hands of an experienced clinician offers qualitative observation plus well-standardized and well-defined reliability and validity for making generalizations when and where appropriate.

Salvia and Hritko (1984)

We take the position that there should be empirical validation before ability training is introduced in the schools. In the absence of such empirical validation, the educational uses that the Kaufmans advocate for the K-ABC are currently unacceptable. Ysseldyke and Salvia (1974) argued that implementation of unvalidated educational programs on the basis of theoretical derivation, speculation, and good intentions (rather than data) constituted experimentation. Experimentation should be governed by the procedures for research with human subjects, including obtaining informed consent and systematically collecting data. Those requirements seem appropriately employed with the K-ABC.

Anastasi (1984)

The use of multiple scores and profile analysis are a commendable feature of the K-ABC, a feature that enhances the diagnostic value of the battery and facilitates the planning of individualized educational programs. But such multiple assessments can be implemented without introducing a distinction that encourages misuse. In the hands of a highly qualified professional, the K-ABC is a promising instrument for dealing with important practical testing needs. It should be presented to the testing community with adequate safeguards against popular misinterpretation.

Box 10.1 (Continued)

Jensen (1984)

The diminished black-white difference on the K-ABC seems to be largely the result of psychometric and statistical artifacts: lower g loadings of the mental processing scales and greater heterogeneity of the standardization sample, which causes mean group differences to be smaller when they are expressed in standard score units. The general factor measured by the K-ABC is essentially the same g as that of the Stanford-Binet and Wechsler scales. But the K-ABC yields a more diluted and less valid measure of g than do the other tests. The K-ABC factors of successive and simultaneous mental processing, independent of the g factor, constituted only a small fraction of the total variance in K-ABC scores, and the predictive validity of these small factors per se is probably nil.

Kaufman (1984)

If the widespread use of the K-ABC shows that the WISC-R/Binet monopoly can be challenged, and if that realization spurs the development of numerous new well-normed and well-conceived intelligence tests from a plethora of practical, clinical, and theoretical perspectives, then I will be the first to applaud. That, to me, would be the K-ABC's finest legacy.

cognitive psychology. The Sequential and Simultaneous theory was distilled primarily from two lines: the information processing approach of Luria (e.g., Luria, 1966a) and the cerebral specialization work done by Sperry (1968, 1974), Bogen (1969), Kinsbourne (1975), and Wada, Clarke, and Hamm (1975).

Simultaneous Processing

Simultaneous processing refers to the mental ability of the child to integrate input all at once to solve a problem correctly. Simultaneous processing frequently involves spatial, analogic, or organizational abilities (Kaufman & Kaufman 1983b; Kamphaus & Reynolds, 1987). Often there is a visual aspect to the problem and visual imagery may be involved in solving it. The Triangles subtest on the K-ABC (an analogue of Wechsler's Block Design task) is a prototypical measure of simultaneous processing. To solve these items correctly one must mentally integrate the components of the design to "see" the whole. Such a task seems to match up nicely with Luria's qualifying statement of synthesis of separate elements (each triangle) into spatial schemes (the larger pattern of triangles, which may form squares, rectangles, or larger triangles). Whether the tasks are spatial or analogic in nature, the unifying

characteristic of simultaneous processing is the mental synthesis of the stimuli to solve the problem, independent of the sensory modality of the input or the output. Simultaneous processing is also required on the Photo Series subtest of the K-ABC. This finding is sometimes a surprise to the new user because of the similarities between this test and Wechsler's Picture Arrangement. The Photo Series test, however, is a marker task of the Simultaneous scale, as it is tied with Triangles for having the best factor loading on the simultaneous factor (Kaufman & Kamphaus, 1984). Hence, even though the Photo Series subtest appears to have a sequential component (and the Kaufmans theorized that it was a sequential task but were surprised themselves [Kamphaus & Reynolds, 1987]), the process that most children elect to use places it on the Simultaneous scale. Evidently the more crucial aspect of solving Photo Series items correctly involves developing a sense of the whole series of pictures and how they connect to one another.

Sequential Processing

Sequential processing, on the other hand, emphasizes the arrangement of stimuli in sequential or serial order for successful problem solving. In every instance each stimulus is linearly or temporally related to the previous one (Kaufman & Kaufman, 1983b), creating a form of serial interdependence within the stimulus. The K-ABC includes sequential processing subtests that tap a variety of modalities. The Hand Movements subtest involves visual input and a motor response; the Number Recall subtest involves auditory input with an auditory response. Word Order involves auditory input and a visual response. Therefore, the mode of presentation or mode of response is not what determines the scale placement of a task, but rather the *mental processing demands* are important (Kaufman & Kaufman, 1983b).

Process versus Content

Unfortunately, this distinction between type of mental process as opposed to type of content or stimulus makes the K-ABC theory more difficult to grasp than the verbal/nonverbal content distinction of the WISC. The logic of the Wechsler scales as to why subtests belong on either the Verbal or Performance scale is easy to understand. In the case of the Wechsler scales, if it "looks like a duck, and walks like a duck, it is probably a duck." Alternatively, the K-ABC subtests were placed on the Sequential and Simultaneous scales empirically regardless of the authors' intuitions or hopes. Consequently, the K-ABC intelligence scales require a higher level of inference than the Wechsler scales, making them more difficult for the student to understand. In the case of the K-ABC theory, if it "looks like a duck, and walks like a duck, it may in fact be a groundhog!"

Achievement versus Intelligence

While the empirical nature of the intelligence scales of the K-ABC may be novel, an equally controversial move was to take the equivalent of the WISC-III Verbal scale and say that these types of tests are no longer intelligence tests—they are now achievement tests (Kamphaus & Reynolds, 1987), which is what the Kaufmans did by taking analogues of Wechsler tests such as Information

(Faces and Places), Vocabulary (Riddles and Expressive Vocabulary), and Arithmetic (Arithmetic) and putting them on their own scale as achievement tests. The K-ABC authors (Kaufman & Kaufman, 1983b) give the following rationale for this move.

> *Unlike the theoretically based mental processing scales, the K-ABC Achievement Scale was derived from only rational and logical considerations. . . . We see these diverse tasks as united by the demands they place on children to extract and assimilate information from their cultural and school environment. Regardless of more traditional approaches to the definition and measurement of intelligence, the K-ABC is predicated on the distinction between problem solving and knowledge of facts. The former set of skills is interpreted as intelligence; the latter is defined as achievement. This definition presents a break from other intelligence tests, where a person's acquired factual information and applied skills frequently influence greatly the obtained IQ. (p. 2)*

The label "achievement" may, however, not be the best for this scale (Kamphaus & Reynolds, 1987) because of its similarity to the WISC-III Verbal scale. In some cases this scale may function as two—verbal intelligence and reading (Kamphaus & Reynolds, 1987). This division of the Achievement scale is especially appealing in the light of the factor analytic data on the K-ABC, which suggests that the K-ABC possesses three factors that are very similar to those of the WISC-III.

ORGANIZATION OF THE K-ABC

The intelligence scales of the K-ABC consist of subtests that are combined to form scales of Sequential Processing, Simultaneous Processing, and the Mental Processing Composite, a summary score reflective of the Sequential and Simultaneous scales. On the separate Achievement scale, subtests are combined to form a global Achievement score.

The K-ABC differs greatly from the WISC-III in its developmental focus. Instead of giving all subtests to all children, the K-ABC has subtests that are designed only for specific age groups. As a result, children at different ages not only are administered different subtests but also different numbers of subtests, with young children receiving far fewer subtests than older children.

The K-ABC also includes a special short form of the Mental Processing Composite, known as the Nonverbal scale (composed of tasks that can be administered in pantomime and that are responded to motorically) to assess the intelligence of children with speech or language handicaps, of hearing-impaired children, and of those who do not speak English. It is particularly useful as part of the assessment of children suspected of aphasias or other expressive or receptive language disorders. However, the Nonverbal scale is useful as an estimate of general intellectual level only and cannot be subdivided into Sequential or Simultaneous Processing scales.

Supplementary Scales

Kamphaus and Reynolds (1987) proposed new supplementary scales for Verbal Intelligence, Reading Composite, and a Global Intelligence Composite. These supplementary scales are intended for specialized uses (see Table 10.1).

TABLE 10.1   Kamphaus and Reynolds supplementary scales

	Verbal	Reading
Expressive Vocabulary	x	
Faces & Places	x	
Arithmetic	x	
Riddles	x	
Reading/Decoding		x
Reading/Understanding		x
Global Intelligence = Seq + Sim + Verbal		

Norms for these scales can be found in Kamphaus and Reynolds (1987).

All of the K-ABC global scales (Sequential Processing, Simultaneous Processing, Mental Processing Composite, Achievement, and Nonverbal) yield standard scores, with a mean of 100 and standard deviation of 15, to provide a commonly understood metric and to permit comparisons of mental processing with achievement for children suspected of learning disabilities. Furthermore, use of this metric allows for easy comparison of the K-ABC global scales to other major tests of intelligence and to popular individually administered tests of academic achievement. The Mental Processing subtests yield standard scores with a mean of 10 and standard deviation of 3, modeled after the familiar Wechsler scaled score. Achievement subtests, on the other hand, yield standard scores with a mean of 100 and a standard deviation of 15, which permits direct comparisons of the Mental Processing global scales with individual achievement areas. The K-ABC achievement tests are also longer than similar tests on the WISC-III, which allows them to support a more familiar metric.

PSYCHOMETRIC PROPERTIES OF THE K-ABC

Standardization

The K-ABC was standardized on a sample of 2,000 children, using primarily 1980 U.S. Census figures. The sample was stratified by age, gender, geographic region, race/ethnic group, parental educational attainment (used as a measure of SES), community size, and educational placement (regular class placement versus placement in a variety of programs for exceptional children). In the past, exceptional children have been excluded from the standardization samples for individually administered tests (Kaufman & Kaufman, 1983b). The K-ABC authors attempted to include representative proportions of learning-disabled, mentally retarded, gifted and talented, and other special populations in the standardization sample according to data provided by the National Center for Education Statistics and the U.S. Office of Civil Rights. Overall, the match of the sample to Census statistics is quite good, although high-SES minorities (specifically African Americans and Hispanics) were statistically significantly oversampled (Bracken, 1985). The effect of this sampling, however, was probably rather small (Kamphaus & Reynolds, 1987).

Reliability

Split-half reliability coefficients for the K-ABC global scales range from 0.86 to 0.93 (mean = 0.90) for preschool children and from 0.89 to 0.97 (mean = 0.93) for children age 5 to 12½. All of the K-ABC subtests show internal consistencies that are comparable to those of other measures except one—Gestalt Closure. This test had mean internal consistency coefficients of .72 for preschoolers and .71 for school-age children. These results suggest that this test has a relatively heterogeneous item pool.

I have seen this heterogeneity reflected in my own clinical assessment practice, where I will frequently see children perform inconsistently on this test. A child may solve easy items incorrectly and later, more difficult, items correctly. The Gestalt Closure subtest is also a good example of the difference between internal consistency coefficients and test-retest coefficients. The stability or test-retest coefficients are considerably higher for this test (.74 for preschoolers, .84 for early elementary grades, and .86 for later elementary grades) than the internal consistency estimates. These data suggest that although this test has a heterogeneous item pool, the overall scores obtained by a child are relatively stable over time.

A test-retest reliability study was conducted with 246 children retested after a 2- to 4-week interval (mean interval = 17 days). The results of this study showed good estimates of stability that improved with increasing age. For the Mental Processing Composite, coefficients of .83, .88, and .93 were obtained for each age group (for preschoolers, for early elementary grades, and for later elementary grades). Achievement scale composite reliabilities for these same age ranges were .95, .95, and .97, respectively. (Further details of the test-retest study can be found on pp. 81–84 of the *Interpretive Manual* for the K-ABC [Kaufman & Kaufman, 1983b]).

The test-retest reliability coefficients for the global scales—and to a lesser extent the internal consistency (split-half) coefficients—show a clear developmental trend, with coefficients for the preschool ages being smaller than those for the school-age range. This trend is consistent with the known variability over time that characterizes preschool children's standardized test performance in general (Kamphaus & Reynolds, 1987).

Validity

The eagerness to conduct research on the K-ABC may have been spurred by the Kaufmans themselves. The *Interpretive Manual* for the K-ABC (Kaufman & Kaufman, 1983b) includes the results of 43 validity studies, an impressive amount of prepublication research that at the time was all too uncommon in test manuals. Studies were conducted on aspects of construct, concurrent, and predictive validity. In addition, several of the studies were conducted with samples of exceptional children, including samples classified as hearing impaired, physically impaired, gifted, mentally retarded, and learning disabled.

Developmental Changes

The K-ABC yields satisfactory growth curves for most age groups (Kamphaus & Reynolds, 1987). It has, however, some problems with a lack of easy items for preschoolers (inadequate floor) and difficult items for older children (inadequate ceiling) (Kamphaus & Reynolds, 1987). At the preschool level the K-ABC generally lacks difficulty for 2½- and 3-year-olds with below-average intelligence. Since children are usually referred at this age for developmental problems, a child will likely obtain at least one raw score of zero. A child who obtains more than one raw score of 0 has not been measured because the examiner does not know how far below 0 this child's skill or ability lies. When this situation occurs, it makes interpretation of the child's scores difficult and results in the examiner having to engage in a high level of inference. The examiner would do better to avoid such problems by choosing a test with more floor. The problem with this age group is that there are not many alternatives to the K-ABC with evidence of adequate floor (see Chapter 15).

The parallel problem is the lack of ceiling for older age groups, which occurs for children beginning at about 10 years of age. The major problem here is on the Simultaneous scale, on which a child may obtain a perfect score on tests such as Photo Series and Matrix Analogies. If this eventuality occurs, then, again, the child has not been measured. The K-ABC is perhaps not the test of choice for gifted children 10 years old or older.

In summary, age differentiation validity is an issue of greater relevance to the K-ABC than to the WISC-III. The K-ABC introduces new tests at a variety of ages and spans the preschool and school-age ranges, and both of these factors make the scale more prone to zero and perfect raw scores than the WISC-III. Clinicians have to keep knowledge about age differentiation validity clearly in mind in order to use this test effectively.

Item Bias/Content Validity

The K-ABC has an extremely well-scrutinized set of items. Many items were removed at various stages of the test development process due to concern over gender, regional, or racial/ethnic group bias. A more thorough discussion of this issue and examples of biased items can be found in Kamphaus and Reynolds (1987).

Correlations with Other Tests

Despite the fact that the K-ABC differs in numerous ways from tests such as the WISC, overwhelming evidence shows that these measures correlate very highly (Kamphaus & Reynolds, 1987). In a study of 182 children enrolled in regular classrooms, the Mental Processing Composite (MPC) correlated 0.70 with WISC-R Full Scale IQ (FSIQ) (Kaufman & Kaufman, 1983b). Hence, the K-ABC Mental Processing scales and the WISC-R share a 49% overlap in variance. They correlate similarly to the relationship between older versions of the Wechsler and Binet scales. The correlations between the K-ABC and WISC-R for numerous nonhandicapped and exceptional populations shown in the *Interpretive Manual* range from .57 to .74. The K-ABC overlaps with the WISC-R a good deal, and yet it also shows some independence. Also of interest in the sample of 182 children is the standard score difference between the MPC and FSIQ. The K-ABC, based on 1980 U.S. Census data, was shown to be about 3 points "tougher" (mean MPC = 113.6) than the WISC-R (mean FSIQ = 116.7) based on this sample of children from regular classes (Kaufman & Kaufman, 1983b). These findings suggest that *just because the K-ABC and WISC-R correlate relatively highly with one another does not mean that they will yield the same score.*

Predictive Validity

Predictive validity evidence for the K-ABC is generally comparable to that of the WISC-III (Kaufman & Kaufman, 1983b). Murray and Bracken (1984), for example, evaluated the predictive validity of the K-ABC over an 11-month interval for a group of 29 children. They found the MPC to predict Peabody Individual Achievement Test (PIAT) Total Test scores at a .79 level over this time period. The Achievement scale composite from the K-ABC was an even better predictor, with a validity coefficient of .88. In a 6-month predictive validity study by Childers and colleagues (1985) the MPC was found to correlate .65 with the Total score on the California Achievement Test (CAT). The relationship of the K-ABC Achievement scale to the CAT was .77. These studies, along with those in the *Interpretive Manual* for the K-ABC (Kaufman & Kaufman, 1983b), suggest good predictive validity evidence for the MPC and exemplary predictive validity evidence for the K-ABC Achievement scale.

Factor Analysis

The K-ABC initially sparked a flurry of factor analytic investigations. These studies are helpful for understanding the K-ABC better, and because of similar results, they have the potential to enhance interpretation of the WISC-III and Binet-4. The factor structures of these three measures are looking more similar with each new factor analytic investigation.

A first point to consider is the "g," or unrotated first factor, loadings of the K-ABC in comparison to the WISC-R. Initially researchers thought that the K-ABC, particularly the Sequential scale, was a more diluted measure of "g"—that the Mental Processing subtests measured more simple memory and spatial skills than high-level intellectual abilities (Jensen, 1984; Sternberg, 1984). Subsequently these researchers have been proven wrong, as the similarity between the "g" factors of the K-ABC and the WISC-R have proved strikingly similar (Kamphaus & Reynolds, 1987). Also of interest is the finding that the Sequential and Simultaneous scales measure "g" to the same extent (Kamphaus & Reynolds, 1987). This is a somewhat surprising finding given that for most children the Simultaneous scale has two more tests than the Sequential scale and is slightly more reliable. A study by Kline, Guilmette, Snyder, and Castellanos (1992) concluded that the K-ABC assessed less cognitive complexity than the WISC-R.

The first well-known factor analytic evidence offered in support of the Sequential and Simultaneous scales was by Kaufman and Kamphaus (1984). These authors identified three factors for the K-ABC and labeled them as sequential, simultaneous, and achievement.

Some problems with the sequential/simultaneous model, however, were apparent even in this early investigation. Hand Movements had a split loading, particularly at the school-age level. Even though Hand Movements was consistently the third-best measure of the sequential factor, it had a consistent and significant secondary loading on the simultaneous factor. In addition, Photo Series, long thought to be a sequential task, loaded consistently higher on the simultaneous factor. As a result, after norming, this test was switched from the Sequential to the Simultaneous scale (Kaufman & Kaufman, 1983b). There was, however, some support for the K-ABC theoretical model that emerged from the "nonloadings" in this investigation for Hand Movements and Spatial Memory. The Hand Movements subtest had an insignificant loading on the simultaneous factor for preschoolers. Similarly, Spatial Memory never had an important loading on the sequential factor. These two sets of loadings support the processing (versus content) distinction of the Kaufmans. Hand Movements has an obvious visual component, and yet it never loads higher on the more visual simultaneous factor than it does on the sequential factor. Spatial Memory, with its obvious short-term memory component (it has a 5-second exposure of the stimuli before their placement must be recalled), never joins the sequential factor. These two findings suggest that there may be problems applying hierarchical (memory versus reasoning) and content (verbal versus nonverbal) models to the K-ABC.

Kamphaus and Kaufman (1986) conducted an exploratory factor analysis for boys and girls. This investigation yielded similar results to the Kaufman and Kamphaus (1984) study, finding virtually no differences in factor structure attributable to gender. There was a tendency for Hand Movements to have a higher simultaneous loading for girls at the school-age level than for boys. Again, however, Hand Movements and Spatial Memory remained aligned with their respective scales, providing some support for the Kaufmans' processing distinction.

In a series of studies, Keith and his colleagues (Keith, 1985; Keith & Dunbar, 1984; Keith, Hood, Eberhart, & Pottebaum, 1985) have called the K-ABC processing model into question by applying Wechsler-like content labels to the K-ABC scales. Keith (1985) has used labels such as "non-verbal/reasoning" (Simultaneous), "achievement/verbal reasoning" (Achievement), and "verbal memory" (Sequential) for the K-ABC, factors, making the scales similar to the tradition of psychological assessment. In a study of a sample of 585 referred children (Keith et al., 1985) three factors emerged in an exploratory factor analysis. Virtually all of the factor analyses were similar to those found in previous studies, but their interpretation differed greatly. Hand Movements, for example, loaded highest on the verbal memory factor, and Faces & Places, Riddles, and Arithmetic had substantial secondary loadings on the nonverbal/reasoning factor. The issue of what to call the K-ABC factors remains debated but unresolved (see, for example, Kamphaus, 1990).

Kaufman and McLean (1987) conducted a factor analytic investigation for a sample of learning-disabled children and obtained a factor structure that was similar to the model proposed by Keith. Findings of this nature suggest that the interpretive model applied to the K-ABC may depend on sample (child) characteristics. In this way, K-ABC interpretation is entirely consistent with Kaufman's (1979b) intelligent testing model.

One confirmatory factor analytic investigation has provided strong support for the two-factor sequential and simultaneous processing model (Wilson, Reynolds, Chatman, & Kaufman, 1985) but less enthusiastic support of a distinct Achievement scale. The subtests of the Achievement scale do show their largest loadings on a separate factor, as Kaufman and Kaufman (1983b) proposed, yet each shows large secondary loadings on the two mental processing factors.

ADMINISTRATION AND SCORING

Administration and scoring procedures for the K-ABC are available in the *Administration and Scoring Manual* for the K-ABC (Kaufman & Kaufman, 1983a). One important aspect of K-ABC administration that deserves special mention, however, is the notion of *teaching items*. The first three items of each Mental Processing subtest (the sample and the first two items appropriate for a child's age group) are designated as teaching items. On these items the examiner is required to teach the task if the child fails on the first attempt at solving the item. The phrase "teaching the task" means that the examiner is allowed the flexibility to use alternate wording, gestures, physical guidance, or even a language other than English to communicate the task demands to the child. The examiner is not allowed to teach the child a specific strategy for solving the problem, however. This built-in flexibility was designed to be particularly helpful to preschoolers, minority-group children, and exceptional children, who sometimes perform poorly on a task from a traditional IQ test not because of a lack of ability but because of an inability to understand the instructions given. Kaufman and Kaufman (1983b) discuss the concept of teaching items in greater detail and note that this built-in flexibility has not adversely affected the reliability of the K-ABC. Sample items are now common fare, as they were subsequently embraced by both the Binet-4 and WISC-III.

The K-ABC basal and ceiling rules, referred to as *starting and stopping points* in the *Administration and Scoring Manual* for the K-ABC (Kaufman & Kaufman, 1983a), also differ from those of many existing intelligence tests. The first rule for administering the K-ABC subtests is straightforward: Examiners are instructed to start and stop testing at the items designated as starting and stopping points for the child's age group. The set of items between the starting and stopping points are, therefore, designed based on standardization data to represent a full range of difficulty for the child's age group. This first basal and ceiling rule is very straightforward, but it is also rigid. Hence, several supplemental rules are given to allow examiners to find items of appropriate difficulty for children at the ends of the distribution of ability (Kaufman & Kaufman, 1983a). The K-ABC also incorporates a very simple discontinue rule (discontinue testing after

1 unit of incorrect items) that is the same for all K-ABC subtests.

The K-ABC Subtests

In contrast to the WISC-III, the K-ABC subtests are a rather unique collection. The WISC-III subtests, for example, were taken primarily from the early Army group tests. The K-ABC subtests are taken from a wider range of sources including the WISC-III (Number Recall and Triangles), experimental cognitive science (Face Recognition), neuropsychology (Hand Movements), and early psychometricians such as Raven (Matrix Analogies), among other sources. In addition, some of the K-ABC subtests are novel, such as Magic Window and Faces & Places.

The K-ABC subtests, however, do have a common lineage in the K-ABC theoretical model, the division of the Sequential, Simultaneous, and Achievement scales. The K-ABC subtests had to show a great deal of consistency with the test's theoretical model in order to be retained. This philosophy is illustrated by the large number of tests that were discarded in the developmental process (Kaufman & Kaufman, 1983b). This section is organized in the same manner as for the WISC-III; a test overview, administration and scoring pointers, noteworthy observations, and psychometric properties.

Psychometric properties are taken from the *Interpretive Manual* for the K-ABC (Kaufman & Kaufman, 1983b). Some factor analytic results are from Jensen (1984).

Magic Window (Ages 2½– 4)

Magic Window requires the child to identify a picture that the examiner exposes by moving it past a narrow slit or "window" (making the picture only partially visible at any one point in time). This subtest appears to be one of the few subtests that can justifiably be described as novel, as it has no clear counterpart in the history of intellectual assessment. This test is designed as the first measure of simultaneous processing and

the first test to be administered to preschoolers. It appears to be appropriately placed as the first subtest for preschoolers, as viewing through the window to try to discover the object behind it is a genuinely intriguing task for young children.

It is also an interesting task from the standpoint that while the stimulus is visual, the response is clearly verbal, demonstrating again the relative independence of test content from the mental process used to solve the item. This task was found to be one of the best measures of simultaneous processing for preschoolers (Kaufman & Kaufman, 1983b).

ADMINISTRATION AND SCORING POINTERS

1. Practice the 5-second exposure interval used on this subtest. While the marks on the back of the window are a helpful guide, it does take some experience to get used to this exposure interval.

PSYCHOMETRIC PROPERTIES

Average reliability = .72

"g" loading = N/A

Loading on sequential factor = .24

Loading on simultaneous factor = .53

Loading on achievement factor = .23

Subtest specificity = .40 (ample)

BEHAVIORS TO NOTE

1. Squinting or other indication that the child is having extraordinary difficulty seeing the items
2. A lack of curiosity about the task
3. Poor articulation
4. Curiosity as to the correct answer
5. An ability to describe the correct answer yet not name it accurately (for example, it has tires and doors)

Face Recognition (ages 2½–4)

This test requires a child to select from a group photograph the one or two facts that were shown briefly in a preceding photograph. This task is also a good early task on the K-ABC, as children seem to have a natural curiosity about photographs. This test has its roots in neuropsychological assessment, in which it has been used for the diagnosis of cerebral dominance (Benton, 1980). The Kaufmans (Kaufman & Kaufman, 1983b) chose this task not only because it was a good measure of simultaneous information processing but also because it was a measure that produced few group differences for children from disparate cultures (Kagan & Klein, 1973).

The Face Recognition subtest was excluded from the school-age level of the K-ABC because it switched factor loadings for older children. For older children it became more of a measure of sequential processing, suggesting a developmental change in the way that children process these types of photographs. Perhaps young children process faces more as a whole and older children try to break them down into component parts and describe them verbally.

ADMINISTRATION AND SCORING POINTERS

1. Practice the 5-second exposure to develop a rhythm.

PSYCHOMETRIC PROPERTIES

Average reliability = .77
"g" loading = N/A
Loading on sequential factor = .24
Loading on simultaneous factor = .44
Loading on achievement factor = .33
Subtest specificity = .48 (ample)

BEHAVIORS TO NOTE

1. Squinting or some indication that the child is having difficulty seeing the photographs

Hand Movements (2½–12½ years)

For this test the child has to imitate a series of hand movements in the same sequence as the examiner performed them. This test is taken directly from the work of Luria (1966a), who used a similar test to assess motor function as part of his neuropsychological evaluation. This test also gives the examiner a clinical sense of the child's fine motor skill (Kaufman & Kaufman, 1983b) and eye-hand coordination.

ADMINISTRATION AND SCORING POINTERS

1. This test unfortunately requires fine motor skill also on the part of the examiner. Be sure to practice using your right hand to administer the items.

2. Be especially vigilant during the most difficult items, as they may become rather difficult to score.

PSYCHOMETRIC PROPERTIES

Average reliability—preschool = .78
Average reliability—school age = .76
"g" loading = .54
Loading on sequential factor = .46
Loading on simultaneous factor = .31
Loading on achievement factor = .18
Subtest specificity—preschool = .49 (ample)
Subtest specificity—school age = .41 (ample)

BEHAVIORS TO NOTE

1. Inability of the child to form the three different hand movements adequately

2. Demonstrating all of the correct movements but failing the items primarily because of difficulty in sequencing

3. Vocalization or subvocalization being used as a strategy to solve the items correctly

Gestalt Closure (2½–12½)

The child is required to name an object or scene pictured in a partially completed "inkblot" drawing. Not unlike some Rorschach items, this test requires a child to visually "complete" drawings. On the face of it, this test is another classic measure of simultaneous/holistic right-brain types of processing. This is borne out by factor analytic findings (Kaufman & Kaufman, 1983b; Kaufman & Kamphaus, 1984).

This test has a long history, dating back to the early 1930s (Street, 1931), and yet the Kaufmans were the first to include it in a major test of intelligence.

ADMINISTRATION AND SCORING POINTERS

1. Study the scoring criteria for each item carefully before administering the test.
2. It is important to remember that a nonverbal response can be considered correct (in lieu of a verbal response) on this subtest.

PSYCHOMETRIC PROPERTIES

Average reliability—preschool = .72
Average reliability—school age = .71
"g" loading = .47
Loading on sequential factor = .10
Loading on simultaneous factor = .49
Loading on achievement factor = .28
Subtest specificity—preschool = .39 (ample)
Subtest specificity—school age = .38 (ample)

BEHAVIORS TO NOTE

1. Squinting or other indications that the child is having difficulty seeing the items
2. Seeming realization of the identity of the item but having difficulty naming it
3. Describing parts of the item but inability to label the whole
4. An unwillingness to guess
5. Bizarre responses (e.g., "A frog with blood on it")

Number Recall (2½–12½)

This task is a familiar adaptation of Digits Forward from the WISC-III. Of course, this type of task has been part of intelligence testing since the days of Binet (see Chapter 1). This test is, however, different from Wechsler's in at least a few respects. Most importantly, it includes only Digits Forward.

ADMINISTRATION AND SCORING POINTERS

1. Remember that the examiner's voice may not be dropped at the end of each item.

PSYCHOMETRIC PROPERTIES

Average reliability—preschool = .88
Average reliability—school age .81
"g" loading = .55
Loading on sequential factor = .66
Loading on simultaneous factor = .16
Loading on achievement factor = .24
Subtest specificity—preschool = .51 (ample)
Subtest specificity—school age = .34 (ample)

BEHAVIORS TO NOTE

1. Recalls all of the digits correctly but errs because of an incorrect sequence
2. Unwillingness to respond or guess when uncertain
3. Self-deprecating statements about memory ability

Triangles (4–12½)

The Triangles subtest is also an adaptation of Wechsler's Block Design task—which is an adaptation of Kohs's (1927) Block Design test. Like Gestalt Closure, this test, too, seems to be a clear measure of simultaneous processing. This supposition is also borne out by factor analytical results (Kaufman & Kaufman, 1983b; Kaufman & Kamphaus, 1984; Kamphaus & Reynolds, 1987).

Wechsler's Block Design task has also been used in split-brain research investigations as a marker task of right-brain processing (see Chapter 19) (see Chapter 2).

Although the Triangles test is obviously related to Wechsler's Block Design test, the absolute correlations between these two tests is not all that high, generally in the .50s (Kaufman & McLean, 1987). It appears that these two tests, while tending to correlate with one another, should not be viewed by clinicians as interchangeable.

ADMINISTRATION AND SCORING POINTERS

1. Remember that there are no time bonus points for these items.

2. Remember that the child is not allowed to stand the triangles on end.

3. Remember that there is no penalty for rotations.

PSYCHOMETRIC PROPERTIES

Average reliability—preschool = .89

Average reliability—school age = .84

"g" loading = .65

Loading on sequential factor = .21

Loading on simultaneous factor = .63

Loading on achievement factor = .27

Subtest specificity—preschool = .51 (ample)

Subtest specificity—school age = .37 (ample)

BEHAVIORS TO NOTE

1. Squinting or other indications that the child is having difficulty seeing the stimulus pictures

2. Dependence on one hand or difficulty using hands to construct the designs

3. Numerous 90° rotations

Word Order (4–12½)

Word Order is the third and last Sequential Processing subtest on the K-ABC. It ranks behind Number Recall as the premier measure of sequential processing. This task requires a child to touch a series of pictures in the same sequence as they were named by the examiner. On more difficult items a color interference task is used. The Kaufmans (Kaufman & Kaufman, 1983b) see this task as an auditory-vocal test of the McCarthy (1972) Verbal Memory ilk. This task is also similar to tests such as Memory for Sentences on the Stanford Binet-4. The Kaufmans borrowed some aspects of this test, including the interference task component, from a clinical neuropsychological test used by Luria (1966a).

The color interference task of Word Order may also provide some valuable clinical information. Denckla (1979) observed that disabled readers perform more poorly than capable readers on rapid naming tests that include the naming of colors, letters, and objects.

ADMINISTRATION AND SCORING POINTERS

1. Remember that examiners are not allowed to drop their voice at the end of each sequence.

2. The color interference task can be especially awkward, and the examiner requires some practice in order to administer it properly.

PSYCHOMETRIC PROPERTIES

Average reliability—preschool = .84

Average reliability—school age = .82

"g" loading = .64

Loading on sequential factor = .68

Loading on simultaneous factor = .22

Loading on achievement factor = .29

Subtest specificity—preschool = .33 (ample)

Subtest specificity—school age .28 (ample)

BEHAVIORS TO NOTE

1. Recalls the stimuli correctly but misses items because of recalling them in incorrect sequence

2. Self-deprecating statements about memory ability

3. Considerable anxiety at the introduction of the color interference task and failing of all items thereafter

Matrix Analogies (5–12½)

The Matrix Analogies test requires the child to select a picture or abstract design that completes a visual analogy. In many ways the Matrix Analogies test resembles Raven's Progressive Matrices (1956, 1960). As such, Matrix Analogies is one of the better measures of simultaneous processing skills. In fact, Raven's Progressive Matrices was used by Das, Kirby, and Jarman (1979) as part of their simultaneous/successive test battery.

One of the interesting aspects of this task is that it may also have a sequential component at older age groups. A separate factor analysis conducted for boys and girls in the K-BC standardization sample found that when the sample was divided by gender, Matrix Analogies began to take on more substantial loadings on the Sequential Scale for 11- and 12-year-olds, especially for girls. This result suggests that children may apply different, perhaps more sequential/analytic, skills to solving the matrices at older ages. This occurrence may be inferred through observation of the child during testing.

ADMINISTRATION AND SCORING POINTERS

1. Be sure to lay out the "chips" in the same sequence as shown on the easel.

PSYCHOMETRIC PROPERTIES

Average reliability = .85
"g" loading = .62
Loading on sequential factor = .30
Loading on simultaneous factor = .50
Loading on achievement factor = .26
Subtest specificity = .44 (ample)

BEHAVIORS TO NOTE

1. Use of verbal strategies to solve the items

Spatial Memory (5–12½)

Saptial Memory requires the child to recall the placement of pictures on a page that was exposed for a 5-second interval. Although memory tasks such as this one have not previously appeared on popular tests of intelligence, they have suddenly appeared on the K-ABC and on the Stanford Binet-4. This test serves to round out memory assessment on the K-ABC in that it provides for a nonverbal stimulus and response, like Hand Movements. This subtest, however, is somewhat unique from the other K-ABC memory tasks in that it shows a substantial loading on the simultaneous processing factor. This test, along with Face Recognition at the preschool level, makes it difficult to apply a memory versus reasoning dichotomy to the Sequential/Simultaneous Processing scales. This relatively large number of memory tests, however, provides the basis for a strong measure of children's memory.

ADMINISTRATION AND SCORING POINTERS

1. Like Hand Movements, this task can become extremely difficult to score at more advanced difficulty levels.

PSYCHOMETRIC PROPERTIES

Average reliability = .80
"g" loading = .56
Loading on sequential factor = .26
Loading on simultaneous factor = .58
Loading on achievement factor = .15
Subtest specificity = .39 (ample)

BEHAVIORS TO NOTE

1. Strategies such as a child configuring his or her fingers while watching the stimulus page

and then applying this configuration on the response page

2. Focusing more attention on the content of the stimuli (e.g., naming the stimuli or asking questions about them) than on the location of the stimuli on the page per se

3. Difficulty in rapid naming of the colors

Photo Series (6–12½)

Photo Series requires the child to place photographs of an event in chronological order. This test, on the face of it, looks similar to Wechsler's Picture Arrangement subtest. However, several investigations of these two batteries show modest to poor intercorrelations between these two subtests (Kaufman & Kaufman, 1983b; Kaufman & McLean, 1987). The Photo Series test also appears to have a distinctly sequential component. However, factor analyses of the K-ABC have shown that this subtest, along with Triangles, is a marker task of simultaneous processing ability (Kamphaus & Reynolds, 1987). One hypothesis is that in the case of Photo Series the sequential response is anticlimactic to the holistic processing of the stimuli that is required prior to producing a response. In other words, a child has to first visually interpret and verbally label the series (e.g., as a car backing up) before he or she can put the pieces in their correct sequence in the examiner's hand.

ADMINISTRATION AND SCORING POINTERS

1. Examiners must hold the cards in their hands so that they are visible to the child at all times.

2. This test has a number of administration and scoring procedures that share nothing in common with Wechsler's Picture Arrangement task.

PSYCHOMETRIC PROPERTIES

Average reliability = .82
"g" loading = .67
Loading on sequential factor = .25

Loading on simultaneous factor = .64
Loading on achievement factor = .26
Subtest specificity = .33 (ample)

BEHAVIORS TO NOTE

1. Impulsive responding, where the child does not survey the stimulus cards adequately prior to producing a response

2. Trial-and-error responding, where the child obviously does not have a Gestalt for how the picture should be placed together and tries to compare each card to every other card.

Expressive Vocabulary (2½–4)

Expressive Vocabulary requires the child to name objects that are pictured in photographs. This test is the first one encountered by preschoolers on the Achievement scale. The Expressive Vocabulary test is intended to follow in the tradition of Wechsler and Binet Vocabulary tests (Kaufman & Kaufman, 1983b). The Kaufmans propose that the assessment of verbal intelligence is essential as part of an intellectual evaluation, but they prefer that the "verbal intelligence" subtests on the K-ABC be included on the Achievement scale and not labeled intelligence as such (Kaufman & Kaufman, 1983b; Kamphaus & Reynolds, 1987).

ADMINISTRATION AND SCORING POINTERS

1. Poorly articulated responses that are otherwise correct can be accepted as correct responses.

PSYCHOMETRIC PROPERTIES

Average reliability = .85
"g" loading = N/A
Loading on sequential factor = .25
Loading on simultaneous factor = .61
Loading on achievement factor = .77
Subtest specificity = .27 (ample)

1. Poor articulation
2. Responses in languages other than English
3. Word retrieval problems

Faces & Places (2½–12½)

Faces & Places involves having a child name a well-known person, fictional character, or place pictured in a photograph or illustration. This test is designed as an analogue of Wechsler's Information subtest. It is sensitive, just as is the Information subtest, to factors such as linguistic and cultural background. This test is also sensitive to academic stimulation in school.

This test, however, presents general information items in a novel format. This format has led to considerable criticism of some of the items, the main complaint being that some of them are out of date (most notably Mohammed Ali) (Kamphaus & Reynolds, 1987). Although the content of the individual items is controversial, the test still correlates rather highly with Wechsler's Information subtest (Kamphaus & Reynolds, 1987).

ADMINISTRATION AND SCORING POINTERS

1. Correct last names can be accepted as correct responses even if the first name is not given.

PSYCHOMETRIC PROPERTIES

Average reliability—preschool = .77
Average reliability—school age = .84
"g" loading = .69
Loading on sequential factor = .21
Loading on simultaneous factor = .39
Loading on achievement factor = .67
Subtest specificity—2.5–4 = .27 (ample)
Subtest specificity—school age = .24 (ample)

BEHAVIORS TO NOTE

1. Responses given in languages other than English

2. A pattern of correct responses for the preschool cartoonlike items and incorrect responses for school-age items that assess more academic/school-related knowledge

Arithmetic (3–12½)

The Arithmetic subtest of the K-ABC requires a child to answer questions that assess knowledge of math concepts or the manipulation of numbers. This Arithmetic subtest resembles more the Arithmetic subtest of Wechsler's genre as opposed to pencil and paper subtests found on clinical measures of mathematics achievement. As such, this test should be considered as a measure of verbal intelligence or a screening measure of mathematics as opposed to a mathematics subtest per se (Kamphaus & Reynolds, 1987). While designed as an analogue of Wechsler's Arithmetic test, this test is somewhat unique because it is considerably longer and assesses a wider range of mathematics skills and content than Wechsler's. This test does show substantial correlations with more traditional mathematics achievement tests (Kamphaus & Reynolds, 1987).

ADMINISTRATION AND SCORING POINTERS

1. Remember that the child is not allowed to use pencil and paper for this subtest.

PSYCHOMETRIC PROPERTIES

Average reliability—preschool = .87
Average reliability—school age = .87
"g" loading = .82
Loading on sequential factor = .46
Loading on simultaneous factor = .48
Loading on achievement factor = .49
Subtest specificity—preschool = .28 (ample)
Subtest specificity—school age = .20 (adequate)

Behaviors to Note

1. Failures on items that are part of a particular content domain (e.g., all subtraction items or multiplication or division items are failed)
2. Self-deprecating statements regarding academic or mathematics achievement

Riddles (3–12½)

Riddles requires a child to name an object or concept that is described by a list of three of its characteristics. From a psychometric standpoint it appears to be a close analogue of vocabulary tests that have always been a part of intelligence tests (Kamphaus & Reynolds, 1987). While this subtest does not require the eloquent multiword expression of the Vocabulary test of the WISC-III, it does seem to require a high level of vocabulary knowledge. This test mimics vocabulary tests from other batteries in other ways, including the fact that it is one of the premier measures of general intelligence ("g") on the K-ABC.

Administration and Scoring Pointers

1. This test uses only a 1-0 scoring system with no bonus points.

Psychometric Properties

Average reliability—preschool = .83
Average reliability—school age = .86
"g" loading = .78
Loading on sequential factor = .34
Loading on simultaneous factor = .42
Loading on achievement factor = .62
Subtest specificity—3–8 = .23 (adequate)
Subtest specificity—9–12½ = .19 (inadequate)

Behaviors to Note

1. Word retrieval problems
2. Self-deprecating statements regarding academic achievement

Reading/Decoding (5–12½)

This test requires a child to read words out of context. This is a simple word recognition task similar to those found on screening measures of academic achievement such as the Wide Range Achievement Test—Revised. This test is intended as a measure of basic reading skill.

This test may not serve as a substitute for other clinical tests of reading achievement, in spite of its high correlations with these measures. This prohibition is primarily because of questionable content validity. There are, for example, a number of items with silent consonants. These items may lack "social validity" or utility since they may not be frequently used by children or appear regularly in their reading materials.

Administration and Scoring Pointers

1. Pronunciation is crucial, and the child's response cannot be scored as correct unless pronounced correctly.

Psychometric Properties

Average reliability = .92
"g" loading = .79
Loading on sequential factor = .39
Loading on simultaneous factor = .26
Loading on achievement factor = .68
Subtest specificity = .21 (adequate)

Behaviors to Note

1. Frustration on the part of the child with his/her reading ability
2. Self-deprecating statements regarding reading ability
3. Reversals
4. Problems with particular item types (e.g., silent consonants)

Reading/Understanding (7–12½)

This task requires a child to act out commands that are given in words or sentences. While intended as a measure of reading comprehension, it is an extraordinarily novel way of assessing reading comprehension. In contrast to many academic achievement measures, this task requires a child to follow commands. While this approach makes the task somewhat controversial, it correlates in the expected fashion with other measures of basic reading skills and reading comprehension (Kamphaus & Reynolds, 1987).

This test also has the potential to yield some insights into the child's personality. A child's refusal to do the task or demonstration of no reluctance whatsoever may be used to corroborate findings from personality measures.

This test should be interpreted cautiously if a child seems reticent, and perhaps more so at the older ages (10 and above) since the reliability tends to dip somewhat.

ADMINISTRATION AND SCORING POINTERS

1. Older children may require considerable encouragement to act out commands.

PSYCHOMETRIC PROPERTIES

Average reliability = .91

"g" loading = .71

Loading on sequential factor = .37

Loading on simultaneous factor = .28

Loading on achievement factor = .76

Subtest specificity = .11 (adequate)

BEHAVIORS TO NOTE

1. Refusal to act out commands
2. Self-deprecating statements regarding reading skills

INTERPRETATION

The K-ABC is amenable to the same interpretive framework that was espoused for the WISC-III.

The following steps should be taken to begin the K-ABC interpretive process.

1. Offer a priori hypotheses.
2. Assign a verbal classification to the MPC (e.g., average).
3. Band the MPC with error (the 90% level of confidence is recommended)
4. Assign verbal classifications to the Sequential and Simultaneous scales.
5. Band the Sequential and Simultaneous scales with error.
6. Test the difference between the Sequential and Simultaneous scales for statistical significance (a reliable difference at the .05 level) using Table 10 of the *Administration and Scoring Manual* for the K-ABC (Kaufman & Kaufman, 1983a).
7. Test the difference between the Sequential and Simultaneous scales for clinical rarity (where a difference that occurred in 5% of the population or less is considered rare) using Table 5.12 (p. 193) of the *Interpretive Manual* for the K-ABC (Kaufman & Kaufman, 1983b).
8. Test a priori hypotheses.
9. Develop a posteriori hypotheses at the composite, shared subtest, and single subtest level.
10. Test a posteriori hypotheses.
11. Draw conclusions.

Interpretation

In order to offer a priori hypotheses, one must know the cognitive and behavioral factors that affect K-ABC composite and subtest scores. The characteristics of subtests have already been discussed. Now the Sequential and Simultaneous scales will be considered.

Hypotheses for Sequential/Simultaneous (Seq/Sim) Differences

While the K-ABC is built around a fairly explicit theoretical stance, Kaufman's own intelligent testing philosophy (Kamphaus & Reynolds, 1987) would encourage examiners to entertain other possible reasons for Seq/Sim differences. Various explanations for such differences are offered next.

SEQUENTIAL VERSUS SIMULTANEOUS PROCESSING (SEQ > SIM OR SIM > SEQ) The relatively clear factor structure of the K-ABC Mental Processing scales makes a difference in Sequential and Simultaneous Processing a necessity to investigate (Kaufman & Kamphaus, 1984). The major question regarding the K-ABC is in regard to the range of application of the Seq/Sim model. Just how many and what types of children have Seq/Sim discrepancies? The answer to the latter question is only recently becoming apparent. Learning-disabled or mentally retarded children do not show clear patterns (Kamphaus & Reynolds, 1987). Hence, the meaning of a Seq/Sim discrepancy is going to be difficult to establish in many cases, thereby testing the clinical acumen of the examiner to the same extent as V/P differences did.

LINGUISTIC DIFFERENCES (SIM > SEQ) Two of the three Sequential scale subtests have English-language content (Number Recall, Word Order). In contrast, the one test with obvious English-language content on the Simultaneous scale (Gestalt Closure) makes up only one-fifth of that composite (versus two-thirds for the Sequential scale) for school-age children. Consequently, where English-language proficiency is in question a Sim > Seq pattern is likely. A Navajo sample cited in the *Interpretive Manual* demonstrated this problem (Kaufman & Kaufman, 1983b). The sample spoke the Navajo language both at home and at school. They obtained a mean Sequential score of 88 and a mean Simultaneous score of 100. This pattern of Sim > Seq for a linguistically different group was also found by Valencia (1985) in an investigation of 42 Mexican American preschoolers. Here the mean Sequential score of 100 was again lower than the Simultaneous score of 106.5. Another interesting finding from this investigation was the WISC-R Verbal score of only 96 compared to a Performance score of 109, suggesting that the WISC-III Verbal scale is even more sensitive to linguistic difference than the Sequential scale of the K-ABC.

Whether or not a Sim > Seq pattern can be attributed to a linguistic difference can be checked by the Achievement scale. For that same Navajo group the K-ABC analogue of Wechsler's Vocabulary, Riddles, was the group's lowest Achievement score, with a score of 75 (where mean = 100 and SD = 15).

These findings regarding linguistic differences on the K-ABC are also enlightening from a test design standpoint. The Kaufmans clearly wanted to limit the influence of cultural and linguistic factors on the K-ABC intelligence (Mental Processing) scales. As is clear from these data, the effects of language may be deemphasized on the K-ABC Mental Processing scales, but its influence may still be powerful, especially on the Sequential scale.

MOTOR PROBLEM (SIM < SEQ) Motor problems may adversely affect a child's performance on the Simultaneous scale of the K-ABC. While the K-ABC Simultaneous scale requires only minimal fine motor skill, it does require enough dexterity that children with substantial motor involvement may produce lower scores on this scale due to a motor problem as opposed to a simultaneous processing weakness.

A potentially difficult aspect of evaluating the potential effects of a motor deficit is teasing out the effects of visual problems or simultaneous processing problems. This "unmasking" or clarification process can be aided by administering additional tests. One case I observed involved a child with cerebral palsy who obtained a whopping 55 standard score point discrepancy in favor of sequential processing. In order to determine if the simultaneous weakness was only the result of motor problems, the clinicians involved administered the Motor Free Visual Perception Test (MVPT) to assess visual perception skills relatively independently of motor skill. The MVPT score was very similar to the Simultaneous score, suggesting that the child's visual perception problems were more important than the motor problem in determining the low Simultaneous score. This finding was also sensible in the light of the K-ABC profile, which showed that even tests such as Gestalt Closure, which has a visual perceptual component but no motor involvement, were also depressed.

For some children with motor problems *both* the Simultaneous and Sequential scales may be well below the mean of 100. This possibility is exemplified by a study of hemiplegic children (Lewandowski & DiRienzo, 1985). In this study a group of children with cerebral palsy (and documented congenital neurodevelopmental delays localized primarily to one of the cerebral hemispheres) were compared to a group of control children without neurodevelopmental problems. These children with obvious hemiplegia on one side achieved mean K-ABC Sequential and Simultaneous scores that were significantly below that of the control group, which achieved means near 100. The mean Sequential scores of the two brain-injured groups with associated motor problems were 95 and 95, whereas their Simultaneous scores were 84 and 95. These data hint that the Simultaneous sale may be more sensitive to motor problems, but they also suggest that the Sequential scale, with tests such as Hand Movements, may show some depression due to severe motor problems.

AUDITORY SHORT-TERM MEMORY PROBLEM (SIM > SEQ) This profile seems to be all too frequent and tests the interpretive savvy of clinicians (Kamphaus & Reynolds, 1987). It occurs relatively frequently because it is consistent with the factor structure of the K-ABC. The Hand Movements test "switches allegiance" because of its equivocal factor loadings for school-age children

(Kamphaus & Reynolds, 1987). This test's loading on the Sequential factor is consistently *but not considerably* higher than its loading on the Simultaneous factor.

The often observed consequence of this factor structure is that the Number Recall and Word Order tests will yield similar scores that are both discrepant from the rest of the profile. The difficult call in this instance is to determine if these two tests are reflecting sequential processing or auditory short-term memory. Several suggestions for testing these hypotheses are:

1. If a child's responses on these two tests indicate good recall but poor sequencing, then a sequencing hypothesis is supported. For example, a child who responds to the stimulus "8-2-5-1" with "2-5-1-8" may have greater problems with sequencing in recall than memory span per se.

2. If Spatial Memory and Hand Movements scores are more in line (not necessarily strong or weak to the same degree) with Number Recall and Word Order than with the Simultaneous scale subtests, then hypotheses related to a memory problem are more plausible.

3. Teacher reports can also help test an auditory short-term memory versus sequencing hypothesis. A child's teacher may produce evidence of sequencing problems from worksheets or other student products. The child's teacher should also be asked whether or not examples of significant memory failure can be cited.

VERBAL VERSUS NONVERBAL INTELLIGENCE (ACH > SEQ > SIM) Factor analyses of all K-ABC subtests have consistently produced three factors similar to the Sequential, Simultaneous, and Achievement scales. Factor labels, however, are dictated to a large extent by the theoretical orientation of the test author or researcher conducting the investigation (Kamphaus, 1990). Kamphaus and Reynolds (1987) have taken this work one step further by developing new scores for the K-ABC that facilitate the application of a verbal/nonverbal intelligence dichotomy. Use of the Wechsler model, however, is not only a change in labels but a change from a process to a content distinction.

Kamphaus and Reynolds (1987) divide the Achievement scale into two components: verbal intelligence, which includes all of the Achievement scale subtests exclusive of the two reading tests, and a reading composite, which consists of the two reading subtests. Even without the use of these supplementary procedures (see Kamphaus & Reynolds, 1987) the verbal/nonverbal distinction may be of some value.

Two of the Sequential tests (Number Recall and Word Order) use verbal stimuli, and so do the Achievement scale subtests. A child with an oral expression deficit, speech problem, language processing problem, or similar difficulty that may adversely impact performance on Verbal subtests may produce a profile of Ach < Seq < Sim. Similarly, a child with strong verbal skills may produce the reverse.

Examples

Examples of hypotheses for the K-ABC are given next. The reader will note that many of these overlap with WISC-III hypotheses because the K-ABC possesses a similar research base.

Background Information	Hypothesis
Jesse is a first-grader who is referred for a suspected reading disability. His teacher reports that he is slow to acquire phonics skills and has difficulty sequencing.	Sim > Seq
Jack is referred for language delays by his social worker. His native language is Navajo, although he speaks primarily English at school. His mother is concerned because he spoke much later than her other children and his Navajo and English articulation are poor.	MPC > Ach
Peter was diagnosed with fetal alcohol syndrome shortly after birth. His mother used alcohol daily during pregnancy and she smoked one to two packs of cigarettes per day. His developmental milestones were delayed and he was retained in kindergarten for next year. His family is poor. His mother and father cannot read.	below avg Seq, Sim, MPC, and Achievement scores
Monja is in the gifted class at her school. She was referred by her teacher for behavior problems in class and inattention.	Ach > Sim > Seq
Cheng was born with cerebral palsy.	Ach & Seq > Sim
Gina has missed 60 days of school this past year due to frequent relocations of her family.	MPC > Ach. Arithmetic may be particularly low

Shared Subtest Hypotheses

The *Interpretive Manual* for the K-ABC (Kaufman & Kaufman, 1983b) uses the same procedure for determining strengths and weaknesses as was outlined previously for the WISC-III in Chapter 8. Rounded values for determining subtest strengths and weaknesses are again advised.

This interpretive step is analogous to the WISC-III. Numerous possible hypotheses are given on pages 197–201 of the *Interpretive Manual* for the K-ABC (Kaufman & Kaufman, 1983b).

Single Subtest Hypotheses

The K-ABC Mental Processing subtests are rather brief, like those of the WISC-III, and produce similar reliabilities. This fact suggests that a similar amount of caution be used when interpreting K-ABC subtests. The same process for generating single subtest hypotheses should also be used.

When recording single subtest hypotheses from the *Interpretive Manual for the K-ABC* (Kaufman & Kaufman, 1983b), the amount of subtest specificity associated with the test should also be noted. Specificity values and ratings were given earlier in this chapter, and more information can be found in Tables 5.9, 5.10, and 5.11 of the *Interpretive Manual for the K-ABC* (Kaufman & Kaufman, 1983b).

SAMPLE CASE—WALTER

Referral Information

Walter is a 3-year-old male who was referred for hyperactivity and attention problems. His pediatrician wanted to know if he suffered from attention deficit hyperactivity disorder.

Behavioral Observations

Walter was brought to the clinic by his birth father. It was clear in the waiting room that his father had trouble controlling him. Walter immediately opened the candy jar on the receptionist's desk upon entering the waiting area. He unwrapped and ate a piece of candy despite his father's protests. He talked almost constantly to whomever would listen. He tried to strike up a conversation with every adult in the waiting room. He removed most of the toys from the toy box, and he refused to replace any of them.

After entering the testing room, Walter grabbed several games and a whistle from a shelf. He asked to play with these rather than "your games." He protested taking the test at least once during every subtest. At the end of Number Recall, for example, he said, "I told you I don't want to do this anymore." During Gestalt Closure he feigned illness by slouching in his chair and complaining of a stomach ache. After the examiner asked him about his not feeling well, he perked up and said, "Gotcha! You thought I was sick, didn't you." After Gestalt Closure, Walter ran from the room, saying that he had to use the restroom. He played with water in the restroom for several minutes before agreeing to come out.

Walter required continuous monitoring and reminders to stay in his seat and pay attention. He missed some Number Recall items because the examiner could not maintain his attention. On some Gestalt Closure items he gave the impression that he preferred to not put forth an effort. When Walter was asked where his mother was, he responded. "Doin' drugs."

Background Information

Walter's maternal grandmother currently has custody of him. Custody was removed from his birth mother because of numerous accusations of child abuse and neglect. His mother has a long-standing history of chemical dependency.

Walter's grandmother's account of his early development was sketchy. She was able, however, to provide vivid descriptions of his current behavior problems. She reports that Walter is highly active, strong-willed, manipulative, disobedient, accident-prone, and disorganized. He has had conduct problems, including setting another child's hair ablaze.

Drawing Conclusions

With a child is this age one has few pieces of data to use for corroboration. In such a case even the conclusions of above-average intelligence and achievement should be presented cautiously and additional testing recommended. These scores could be a fairly drastic underestimate of Walter's cognitive development given his misbehavior during testing. In this case the scores serve an important function as baselines for further evaluations.

The Number Recall test could be interpreted as a unique strength, but such an interpretation would be highly speculative for the following

K-ABC Scores

	Standard Score	Mean	Diff.	Diff.	Significant S or W
Sequential Scale					
Hand Movements	10	11	−1	3	
Number Recall	14	11	3	3	S
Simultaneous Scale					
Magic Window	11	11	0	4	
Face Recognition	10	11	−1	3	
Gestalt Closure	10	11	−1	4	
Achievement Scale					
Expressive Vocabulary	128	117	11	13	
Faces & Places	130	117	13	15	
Arithmetic	90	117	−27	12	W
Riddles	122	117	5	13	

Global Scales	Standard Scores
Sequential Processing	112
Simultaneous Processing	104
Mental Processing Composite	109
Achievement	121

reasons: (1) there is no corroborating evidence for this strength; (2) more cautious interpretation of Walter's profile is advised because of his age and the potential confounding of his behavior problems; and (3) the Number Recall strength is consistent with his overall above-average performance, making it easy to subsume this under the global scale hypothesis.

Any interpretation of the Arithmetic weakness would be similarly highly speculative. This weakness, however, is more plausible because it flies in the face of the above-average trend in the profile. The child's history of neglect provides some corroborating evidence for this hypothesis. On the other hand, why did the neglect not affect his other measures of knowledge acquisition? This hypothesis also requires further corroboration.

The main conclusions are above-average intelligence and academic achievement. A hypothesis of an Arithmetic weakness could either not be offered or offered as a hypothesis that requires further evaluation. Walter's volatile living situation and behavior beg for ongoing monitoring of treatment and periodic reevaluation of numerous domains including intelligence. In Walter's case, intelligence and achievement may be bright spots. In this situation the psychologist will likely focus attention on other domains and let intelligence fade into the background for the time being.

Assessing Exceptional Children with the K-ABC

Given that for most children the K-ABC correlates substantially with the WISC-R, it is likely that the K-ABC and WISC-III will covary to a great extent when used for evaluating exceptional children. Some groups of children, however, show substantial differences. For these groups the selection of one test over another can be crucial in the diagnostic process. Moreover, the clinician has to be especially alert when dealing with individual cases where research does not apply or is lacking. This section summarizes research on the utility of the K-ABC for assessing exceptional children, with special emphasis on its assets and liabilities as identified by Kamphaus and Reynolds (1987).

Mental Retardation

There is a tendency for children with mental retardation to have higher K-ABC than WISC-R scores (Naglieri, 1985a). K-ABC data for samples of previously identified (usually with the WISC-R) children with mental retardation (Kamphaus & Reynolds, 1987) (see Chapter 20) show mean Mental Processing Composite scores ranging from the mid-60s to about 70. Naglieri (1985a) administered the K-ABC to 37 children who were diagnosed previously as mildly mentally retarded. When these children were reevaluated, the K-ABC and WISC-R were administered in counterbalanced fashion. The resulting WISC-R Full Scale mean was 58 and the K-ABC mean was 65. The correlation of the K-ABC and WISC-R for this sample was very high (.83), suggesting that the rank order of the children on these two tests was highly similar, but the K-ABC distribution of scores was tilted more toward the normative mean of 100.

The K-ABC has some practical limitations that examiners must consider in using the test to diagnose mental retardation. First is the issue of subtest floor. Kamphaus and Reynolds (1987) observed that the K-ABC lacks easy items for some developmentally delayed children. In other words, a 5-year-old mentally retarded child may obtain too many raw scores of zero. This risk of a lack of floor, however, is less likely to occur for an 8-, 9-, or 10-year-old mildly retarded child. For moderately to severely mentally retarded

children, however, there is a substantial risk of a lack of floor for most ages, as the K-ABC has new subtests introduced at virtually every age group from 2½ through 7. Second, the K-ABC composite score norms usually do not extend below a standard score of 55, which makes the K-ABC less useful for the diagnosis of moderate or severe levels of mental retardation. Tests such as the Stanford-Binet Fourth Edition and the DAS may be better suited for the purpose since their composite score norms often extend down below 55 (see Chapter 13).

The availability of sample and teaching items and the intuitive nature of the K-ABC task demands are advantages for the assessment of delayed children. A potential benefit of the use of teaching items is that they allow the examiner to see how a child responds to instruction. This opportunity can be a primitive assessment of a child's zone of proximal development (ZPD) (Vygotsky, 1962; see Kamphaus & Reynolds, 1987), where the ZPD is the difference in performance on a task with and without instruction.

Learning Disabilities

Mean K-ABC global scale and subtest scores for a number of samples of learning-disabled children suggest that children with learning problems tend to score in the below-average to average ranges, exhibit a "mild" Simultaneous greater than Sequential profile (6 to 8 standard score points), and have their lowest scores on the Achievement and Sequential scales (Kamphaus & Reynolds, 1987). There is also a consistent trend for the average MPC to be greater than the average Achievement scale score. This is consistent with the operational definition of learning disabilities, where a discrepancy between "ability" and achievement must be identified.

Fourquean (1987) identified a substantial pattern of underachievement for a sample of limited English proficient Latino learning-disabled children. These results support the hypothesis that the K-ABC Achievement scale is adversely affected not only by learning problems but also by cultural and/or linguistic differences. In addition, the MPC in this study appeared to be less influenced or confounded by linguistic or cultural differences. This study highlights the theoretical differences between the K-ABC and the WISC-R. The mean WISC-R Verbal IQ of 68.1 for these children, for example, was almost identical to their mean Achievement scale score on the K-ABC of 67.7. As a result, the MPC for this sample was considerably higher (82.9) than the Full Scale IQ (76.7). The K-ABC may prove valuable in cases where a clinician is trying to differentiate among intellectual, cultural, and linguistic influences on learning.

Intellectually Gifted Children

No typical global scale profile emerges for samples of gifted children (Kamphaus & Reynolds, 1987). Gestalt Closure is one of the worst subtests for gifted children. Relative strengths on Triangles and Matrix Analogies may suggest that the higher the "g" loading of the subtest, the more likely the gifted samples will score higher (Kamphaus & Reynolds, 1987). The K-ABC MPC is consistently lower than Stanford-Binet and Wechsler scores for these children. Naglieri and Anderson (1985), for example, obtained a K-ABC means of 126.3 and WISC-R mean of 134.3. McCallum, Karnes, and Edwards (1984) obtained a mean Stanford-Binet LM IQ (1972 edition) that was about 16.19 points higher than the mean K-ABC MPC. One explanation for the difference between the 1972 Stanford-Binet and the K-ABC for gifted children is that the 1972 Stanford-Binet may give higher bound estimates of intelligence for academically capable children. This is suggested by a study by Zins and Barnett (1984) that showed an extremely high correlation (.86) between the 1972 Stanford-Binet and the K-ABC Achievement scale. In addition, a study in the Stanford-Binet—Fourth Edition *Technical Manual* (1986) indicates that the 1972 Stanford-Binet produces much higher scores (mean IQ = 135.3) than the 1986 Fourth Edition (mean IQ = 121.8). It may be that the 1972 Stanford-

Binet shared extensive overlap with measures of academic achievement.

EDUCATIONAL REMEDIATION RESEARCH

The K-ABC is unique in that one of the test development goals was to produce a test that is helpful in the educational remediation process (Kaufman & Kaufman, 1983b). This is an ambitious goal that is similar to saying that a cure exists for low intelligence (i.e., mental retardation). Hence, the mere statement of intent to be useful for educational remediation was controversial and led to immediate attack (Salvia & Hritcko, 1984).

The Kaufmans went much further than their predecessors by including an entire chapter on educational translation of K-ABC scores in the *Technical Manual* (Kaufman & Kaufman, 1983b). They reviewed some models of special education intervention, identified problems, and proposed solutions. They offered a "strength" model of remediation (Reynolds, 1981a) that borrows heavily from neuropsychological models of remediation. The Kaufmans' model proposed that one should not try to remediate weaknesses (e.g., prescribe exercises that would improve a child's simultaneous weakness), but rather a child's cognitive strengths should be utilized to improve academic skills. This model is a familiar one in medical rehabilitation. A stroke victim, for example, may never regain the strength of his dominant hand that he used to dress himself. In cases such as this an occupational therapist will teach the patient dressing skills that capitalize on the patient's strengths. The therapist may show the patient clever ways to fasten fasteners partially before the garment is worn. Similarly, the Kaufmans propose that a child with reading problems and a sequential deficit not be taught sequencing skills (this would be nonsensical since sequencing is the predictor variable not the criterion variable), but rather be taught how to use simultaneous skills to compensate for sequential weaknesses in the reading process.

Recently the whole idea of using intelligence tests with the goal of a *direct* link to intervention has been questioned (Kamphaus, 1990). As Kamphaus (1990) observed: "I think that intelligence tests will never have *direct*, and I emphasize the word *direct*, effects on treatment planning. . . . Take, for example, measures of height, such as feet and inches. Do these measures have 'treatment validity' for measuring height?" (p. 366).

Kamphaus (1990) proposes that intelligence tests will be more likely to have *indirect* effects on treatment. Medical tests such as the MRI scan do not possess strong evidence of treatment validity, but they do allow for more sophisticated research on a disorder that may indirectly lead to treatment. This discussion calls into question the inclusion of a "remediation" chapter in the K-ABC manual.

Some pilot data presented in the *Interpretive Manual* for the K-ABC (Kaufman & Kaufman, 1983b) suggested that the K-ABC may be useful for designing educational interventions. In direct contrast, a study by Ayres, Cooley, and Severson (1988) suggested that the K-ABC will not be useful for treatment planning. Both of these pieces of research have methodological weaknesses. The Kaufman and Kaufman (1983b) studies were based on small samples and they were not well controlled. The Ayres, Cooley, and Severson (1988) investigation used criterion measures of sequential and simultaneous processing that had no strong evidence of validity. The question of whether or not the K-ABC remedial model is effective is still not answered. There are simply no large-scale, well-controlled studies available on this topic.

K-ABC Short Forms

Kaufman and Applegate (1988) developed short forms of the K-ABC that may be useful when only general estimates of mental processing and achievement that can be administered in relatively brief amounts of time are needed. Examples of uses of short forms include preschool screening for identification of at-risk or potentially gifted children, research, and certain clinical or educational circumstances. Although the administration of a short form can never replace the multiple scores and clinical evaluations obtained from administration of a complete battery, short forms of the K-ABC demonstrate excellent psychometric properties and offer useful estimates of functioning.

Extensive analysis of the reliability and validity of various combinations of subtests led to the selection of the following short forms for age 4 through 12½ years. (Short forms were not developed for younger children because the K-ABC is already relatively brief for those ages.)

Mental Processing Dyad: Triangles, Word Order

Mental Processing Triad: Triangles, Word Order, Matrix Analogies

Mental Processing Tetrad: Hand Movements, Triangles, Word Order, Matrix Analogies

Mean reliability coefficients for the short forms are excellent and range from .88 to .93. Although the corrected validity coefficient between the Mental Processing dyad and the complete K-ABC is a marginal .80, the remaining short forms demonstrate excellent validity, with corrected coefficients of .86 for the Mental Processing triad, .88 for the Mental Processing tetrad, and .93 for an Achievement dyad. Applegate and Kaufman (1988) recommended using either the Mental Processing triad or tetrad along with an Achievement dyad whenever a short form of the K-ABC, is needed. Tables for computing *Estimated* Mental Processing Composites and Achievement standard scores (X = 100, SD = 15) based on the sum of subtest scaled or standard scores are provided in Kaufman and Applegate (1988). The word *estimated* should be used whenever scores from short forms are reported.

NONVERBAL SCALE

The Nonverbal scale is intended for use with children for whom administration of the regular K-ABC (and virtually all other well-normed, standardized measures of intelligence) would be inappropriate: those who are hearing impaired, have speech or language disorders or other communication handicaps, or have limited English proficiency. The Nonverbal scale yields a global estimate of intelligence.

K-ABC STRENGTHS AND WEAKNESSES

Strengths

1. The theory underlying the K-ABC is explicit, making it easier to understand why the test is organized as it is. The theory also yields a predictable factor structure that is the beneficiary of some research support.

2. The K-ABC is lawfully related to other intelligence measures. It does differ from other measures when language is an important variable for a child.

3. The K-ABC is relatively fun and easy to administer and score. The newer and more portable and lighter version is also a boon to the mobile clinician.

4. The psychometric properties of the K-ABC, including norming, reliability, and validity, are strong.

5. The K-ABC assesses more memory functions than the WISC-III.

Weaknesses

1. While the MPC may be easily interpreted, the meaning of the Sequential and Simultaneous scores is not as clear, making the test more of an interpretive challenge for clinicians.

2. The K-ABC suffers from floor and ceiling effects at a number of ages. This problem is compounded by changing subtests at various ages.

3. The K-ABC Achievement scale is enigmatic. It is a Wechsler-like verbal intelligence scale in some regards, but it also resembles clinical measures of achievement that are used for diagnosing learning disabilities. The Achievement scale, then, seems to require some experience if one is to interpret it properly.

4. The Kaufmans' remedial model should be used cautiously until some research is available to support it.

5. The K-ABC item content and norming need revision.

CONCLUSIONS

The K-ABC is a unique contribution to the intellectual assessment scene that has resulted in polarized viewpoints on the instrument—either you like it or you do not. The K-ABC has made some important contributions to children's intellectual assessment. The most important one is that it has served as a catalyst for research on children's intellectual assessment. The K-ABC has also been adopted by clinicians, suggesting that it has proven clinical value for some children in some settings. This is a well-known test because of all of its related research, which will likely foster its use for the foreseeable future (see Appendix A).

CHAPTER SUMMARY

- Surveys have found that the K-ABC is still heavily used by practitioners.

- The K-ABC has been the subject of great controversy, as attested to by the strongly pro and con articles written for a special issue of the *Journal of Special Education* devoted to the K-ABC.

- Simultaneous processing is the mental ability of the child to integrate input all at once to solve a problem correctly.

- Sequential processing, on the other hand, emphasizes the arrangement of stimuli in sequential or serial order for successful problem solving. In every instance, each stimulus is linearly or temporarily related to the previous one.

- A controversial move was to take the equivalent of the WISC-III Verbal scale and say that these types of tests are no longer intelligence tests—they are now achievement tests.

- Kamphaus and Reynolds (1987) proposed new supplementary scales for verbal intelligence, reading composite, and a global intelligence composite.

- The K-ABC global scales (Sequential Processing, Simultaneous Processing, Mental Processing Composite, Achievement, and Nonverbal) yield standard scores, with a mean of 100 and standard deviation of 15.

- The K-ABC was standardized on a sample of 2,000 children, using primarily 1980 U.S. Census figures.

- Split-half reliability coefficients for the K-ABC global scale range from 0.86 to 0.93 (mean = 0.90) for preschool children, and from 0.89 to 0.97 (mean = 0.93) for children age 5 to 12½.

- The K-ABC yields satisfactory growth curves (age differentiation validity) for most age groups.

- The K-ABC has an extremely well-scrutinized set of items, which benefited from item bias studies.

- In a study of 182 children enrolled in regular classrooms, the Mental Processing Composite (MPC) correlated 0.70 with WISC-R Full Scale IQ (FSIQ).

- Predictive validity evidence for the K-ABC is comparable to that of the WISC-III.

- The first well-known factor analytic evidence offered in support of the Sequential and Simultaneous scales was by Kaufman and Kamphaus (1984). These authors identified three factors for the K-ABC and labeled them as sequential, simultaneous, and achievement.

- In a series of studies, Keith and his colleagues have called the K-ABC processing model into question by applying Wechsler-like content labels to the K-ABC scales.

- The following steps are advised to begin the K-ABC interpretive process.

  1. Assign a verbal classification to the MPC (e.g., average).

  2. Band the MPC with error (the 90% level of confidence is recommended).

  3. Assign verbal classifications to the Sequential and Simultaneous scales.

  4. Band the Sequential and Simultaneous scales with error.

  5. Test the difference between the Sequential and Simultaneous scales for statistical significance (a reliable difference at the .05 level) using Table 10 of the *Administration and Scoring Manual* for the K-ABC (Kaufman & Kaufman, 1983b).

  6. Test the difference between the Sequential and Simultaneous scales for clinical rarity (where a difference that occurred in 5% of the population or less is considered rare) using Table 5.12 (p. 193) of the *Interpretive Manual* for the K-ABC (Kaufman & Kaufman, 1983b).

  7. Develop hypotheses for reliable (not necessarily rare) differences between Sequential and Simultaneous scores.

- Hypotheses for Sequential/Simultaneous (Seq/ Sim) differences include:

  Sequential versus Simultaneous Processing (Seq > Sim or Sim > Seq)

Linguistic differences (Sim > Seq)

Motor problem (Sim < Seq)

Auditory short-term memory problem
(Sim > Seq)

Verbal versus nonverbal intelligence
(Ach > Seq > Sim)

- The question of whether or not the K-ABC remedial model is effective is still not answered.
- Kaufman and Applegate (1988) developed short forms of the K-ABC.

CHAPTER 11

Assessment of Adolescent and Adult Intelligence

Ellen W. Rowe

The University of Georgia

CHAPTER QUESTIONS

In what ways is the WAIS-III similar to previous Wechsler adult intelligence scales and to the WISC-III?

What do these similarities mean in terms of generalizing previous research findings to the WAIS-III and for interpretation?

What are the theoretical underpinnings of the Kaufman Adolescent and Adult Intelligence Test?

In general adult and adolescent intelligence is assessed for reasons similar to those for children. In a survey of American Psychological Association (APA) members, Harrison, Kaufman, Hickman, and Kaufman (1988) found that the main reason for the use of intelligence tests

with adults was to measure an individual's cognitive potential or capacity. This is usually the overarching reason that children are assessed. The second reason cited by respondents in the Harrison et al. study was to gather clinically useful information. Respondents also listed assessment of the functional integrity of the brain as important. In this survey, respondents indicated that they assess a rather normal distribution of adults across all IQ levels, except for a relative bulge in the category listed as below 70. Fewer than half of the APA respondents used intelligence tests for the purpose of either educational or vocational placement or intervention. As most school-age children and adolescents are tested for the purpose of educational placement and intervention, this last finding clearly highlights a difference between the assessment of children or adolescents and adults.

RECENT DEVELOPMENTS IN ADOLESCENT AND ADULT INTELLECTUAL ASSESSMENT

As noted in the chapter on theory, the past few decades have witnessed a resurgence of interest and development in the area of intelligence theory (e.g., Carroll, 1993; Das, Naglieri, & Kirby, 1994; Gardner, 1993; Horn, 1994; Sternberg, 1985b). Parallel to these theoretical advances are a growing number of options for the assessment of children's intelligence. In fact, Esters, Ittenbach, and Han (1997) noted that important and useful theories of intelligence now often give rise to new instruments. The Kaufman Assessment Battery for Children (K-ABC; Kaufman & Kaufman, 1983a) and the Woodcock-Johnson Tests of Cognitive Ability—Revised (WJ-R COG; Woodcock & Johnson, 1989b) were among the first in this direction, and the Differential Abilities Scale (DAS; Elliott, 1990c), and the Cognitive Assessment System (CAS; Das & Naglieri, 1997) have continued the trend (Esters et al., 1997; Harrison, Flanagan, & Genshaft, 1997). These recent developments in children's intellectual assessment offer clinicians an array of practical and theoretical options.

The area of instrument development for adolescent and adult intellectual assessment has not experienced the same degree of growth. However, this situation may be changing. In 1993 Alan and Nadeen Kaufman published the Kaufman Adolescent & Adult Intelligence Test (KAIT), which is based on a theoretical framework of "g_f"–"g_c." The WJ-R, Tests of Cognitive Ability, also based on the "g_f"–"g_c" theory, was developed and normed for use up to the age of 90 (Woodcock & Johnson, 1989b). In addition, the most recent revision of the Wechsler Adult Intelligence Scale (WAIS; Wechsler, 1955), the Wechsler Adult Intelligence Scale—Third Edition (WAIS-III; Wechsler, 1997a) was completed as well. Recently, then, clinicians have begun to see more options for the assessment of adolescents and adults, and perhaps the next

decade will bring further developments. This chapter presents two currently available tests for use solely with adolescents and adults: the WAIS-III and the KAIT.

THE WECHSLER ADULT INTELLIGENCE SCALES: HISTORY

Like the WISC-III for children, the Wechsler scales for the assessment of adult and adolescent intelligence are, and have been for the past several decades, the most commonly used instruments in the assessment of adults and adolescents. As Kaufman (1990) pointed out in the introduction to his book, *Assessing Adolescent and Adult Intelligence*, the main question faced by most examiners was not if one should use the Wechsler Adult Intelligence Scale—Revised (WAIS-R; Wechsler, 1981), but what tests and means of assessment should be used to supplement the WAIS-R. As one might expect, these scales also have generated an enormous amount of research.

Several surveys of test use in the past decade have confirmed the popularity of the Wechsler scales in adult and adolescent assessment. In the Harrison et al. (1988) survey of psychologists, 93% of respondents indicated they commonly used either the WAIS or its revision, the WAIS-R (Harrison et al., 1988). In addition, 92% of respondents reported that these instruments provided information of great importance. The authors of this study concluded that the WAIS-R (or WAIS) totally dominated the intelligence category of assessment and that the WAIS-R was clearly the instrument of choice for the assessment of adult intelligence. A 1990 survey (Archer, Maruish, Imhof, & Piotrowski, 1991) that focused on the assessment of adolescents found results similar to those of the Harrison et al. survey. The survey of adolescent assessors revealed that 88% of respondents used the Wechsler scales, and these scales were the most

Box 11.1   Testing in China

Interestingly, the response patterns in the Ryan et al. (1994) survey in China were very different from those of the Harrison et al. (1988) study conducted in the United States. To begin, the response rate in the China survey was over twice that of the response rate in the U.S. survey. The response rate in the Ryan et al. study was 59% without a follow-up mailing, while that of the Harrison et al. study was 22.4%. Also of interest is the fact that in the Ryan et al. study physicians completed 70% of the questionnaires, and only 18.5% were returned by psychologists. Ryan and his colleagues observed that while the practice of psychological testing is active in the People's Republic of China, it is the province of medical doctors, not academic or applied psychologists. The authors noted that this may have come about, at least in part, because psychology as a scientific and professional discipline was virtually eliminated on mainland China during the political upheaval of the 1960s and 1970s. Now that a number of Chinese universities and medical schools have reinstated graduate training programs in psychology, Ryan et al. predicted that psychologists will assume principal responsibility for the development and use of psychological tests. Future surveys of psychological testing in mainland China will determine the accuracy of this prophecy.

---

frequently cited measure (91%) in clinicians' batteries. Even in other cultures, the Wechsler scales are often the instruments of choice for assessment of adults. Ryan, Dai, and Zheng (1994) found that the Chinese version of the WAIS was the most popular and frequently used test, regardless of assessment domain, in their survey of medical, psychiatric, and educational facilities in the People's Republic of China (see Box 11.1).

From the W-B I to the WAIS and the WAIS-R: Similarities and Differences

Knowledge of the many revisions and extensions of the Wechsler scales is important not only from a historical perspective, but as Kaufman (1990) observed, also for interpretive purposes. Researchers have designed and carried out thousands of studies on the WAIS-R and its predecessors, but the ability to generalize these findings from one revision to another depends on the degree of change from revision to revision. Because the most recent revision, the WAIS-III,

has been published recently, this issue is particularly germane at this time. Therefore, this section begins with an introduction of the WAIS-III predecessors.

As discussed elsewhere in this text, Wechsler's first test was the Wechsler-Bellevue Intelligence Scale Form I (W-B I) published in 1939 (Wechsler, 1939). The WAIS was published in 1955 (Wechsler, 1955) as a revision to the W-B I. The WAIS-R appeared in 1981 (Wechsler, 1981), and the most recent revision, the WAIS-III (Wechsler, 1997a) became available in 1997. When learning the Wechsler intelligence tests, it is helpful to keep in mind that all are based, in some form, on the Wechsler-Bellevue or one of the revisions. Hence there is a great deal of similarity and continuity across ages and revisions of the Wechsler intelligence tests (Thorndike, 1997).

Similarities in Format and Content for the W-B I, the WAIS, and the WAIS-R

Through the first two revisions, the Wechsler intelligence scales for adults retained a format was relatively like that of Wechsler's original scale. The W-B I, the WAIS, and the WAIS-R all provide an IQ score as well as Verbal and Performance scales. Furthermore, all three contain the same 11 subtests. In addition, all of these subtests or an analogous one also appear on the WISC-III and the WAIS-III. As discussed in the chapter on the WISC-III, Wechsler did not actually develop his subtests, but selected various tasks from the tests available in the 1930s, such as the Army Alpha and Army Beta (Kaufman, 1990; Thorndike, 1997). Wechsler's theoretical orientation and reasons for selecting each subtest are discussed earlier in this text. While Wechsler's theoretical orientation is important, one should keep in mind that his approach was primarily a practical one. He chose a set of tasks that were suitable across a broad span of ages, were easy to administer and score, and had documented ability to discriminate at both the item and subtest level (Zachary, 1990). The fact that these same 11 subtests still appear on the most widely used intelligence tests to date is a testament to Wechsler's acumen and insight.

About two-thirds of the items on the W-B I appeared on the WAIS and almost three-fifths remained on the WAIS-R (Wechsler, 1955, 1981). At the same time, a number of new items, 42.8%, appeared on the WAIS that had not appeared on the W-B I. From the WAIS to the WAIS-R, however, the changes were minor. Only 13.2% of WAIS-R items were totally new. Changes in content from the WAIS to the WAIS-R were made primarily to delete or modify dated or ambiguous items, to add more items relevant to women and minorities, and to remove very easy items (Wechsler, 1981). Interestingly, in the revision of the WAIS-R to the WAIS-III, the developers added a number of easier items across several subtests (this issue is discussed further in a following section).

Reliabilities and Normative Samples for the W-B I, the WAIS, and the WAIS-R

One of Wechsler's main goals in revising the W-B I was to achieve better score distributions and greater reliability (Kaufman, 1990; Matarazzo,

1972). The increase in reliability from the W-B I to the WAIS and the continued high reliability for the WAIS-R (.97 for Full Scale IQ) are evidence of his success. Another goal in Wechsler's revisions was to improve the quality of the standardization samples. The original W-B I sample consisted mainly of white, urban New Yorkers, age 17–70 years (Wechsler, 1939). This sample was roughly stratified on education, but not on gender, race, or occupation. Although these norms seem extremely limited by today's standards, Wechsler did not have financial backing, so a nationwide norming was virtually impossible. Wechsler, however, did recognize the importance of stratification on education (Wechsler, 1939). Furthermore, Wechsler, an innovator in many areas, was among the first to stratify by age for adults. Previously, adults over the age of 16 had often been considered a single age group. Years later, Kaufman (1994) speculated on what Dr. Wechsler would have thought about the revised WISC-III. These comments are probably applicable to revisions of Wechsler's adult scales also. According to Kaufman (1994), "he'd be impressed by the immaculate standardization and supersophisticated psychometric treatment of the data, but he wouldn't admit it to anyone. Instead he'd argue that his all–Coney Island standardization of the original Wechsler-Bellevue was pretty darn good" (pp. xiii–xiv).

Both the WAIS (ages 16–64) and the WAIS-R (16–74) were normed on a sample stratified for age, gender, race, geographic region, urban versus rural households, education, and occupation (Wechsler, 1955, 1981). The norms for the WAIS-R represented an extension of those for the WAIS by providing stratified norms up to age 74.

Correlations: The W-B I with the WAIS; the WAIS and the WAIS-R

Matarazzo (1972) reviewed the results of five studies that compared IQ scores from the W-B I or the W-B II and the WAIS in samples of Air

Force flyers, college students, brain-injured patients, and high school students. Although several statistically significant differences existed, the differences were often not clinically significant. In most cases, the WAIS scores were slightly lower. Given the findings of Flynn (1984), however, one would expect lower mean scores on a restandardization of a test.

In the *WAIS-R Manual*, Wechsler (1981) reported correlations between the WAIS and the WAIS-R of .91 for the Verbal scale, .79 for the Performance scale, and .88 for the Full Scale. These results were not substantially lower than those for the WAIS-R IQs in a test-retest format. The high correlations among the WAIS and WAIS-R IQs are not surprising, however, given the degree of similarity between items on the two tests. Later investigations explored the relationship between the WAIS and the WAIS-R IQs with such various populations as college students, intellectually disabled individuals, psychiatric patients, neurological patients, and Mensa Society members (Edwards & Klein, 1984; Lewis & Johnson, 1985; Simon & Clopton, 1984; Zarantonello, 1988). In 1987, Ryan, Nowak, and Geisser reviewed a large number of studies comparing the WAIS and the WAIS-R. In general, IQs were lower on the WAIS-R than on the WAIS. The mean differences across the studies in the Ryan et al. (1987) paper were 6.6 for the Verbal scale, 6.4 on the Performance scale, and 6.8 on the Full Scale. Again, one would expect lower scores with a revised test and updated norms. These differences, then, may be viewed as highlighting the importance of updating the normative samples for tests and of using the most recent versions of tests, but not as an indication of lack of consistency between the WAIS and the WAIS-R IQ scores (Kaufman, 1990).

Factor Analytic Studies of the Wechsler Adult Scales

Following Cohen's (1952, 1957) seminal factor analytic studies of the W-B I and the WAIS, the question of how many constructs underlie the Wechsler adult batteries generated an enormous amount of interest and attention from psychometric researchers (Kaufman, 1990). Much of this interest was undoubtedly due to the fact that a definitive solution to the question was not reached. In fact, different factor analytic studies produced differing results, and the number and structure of constructs to interpret was debated from the W-B to the WAIS-R. Various researchers and writers argued for the interpretation of one-factor (O'Grady, 1983), two-factor (Silverstein, 1982c), and three-factor (Geary & Whitworth, 1988; Kaufman, 1990; Leckliter, Matarazzo, & Silverstein, 1986; Waller & Waldman, 1990) solutions. The one-factor solution represented the hypothesis that the Wechsler adult scales were primarily a measure of "g." The two-factor solutions usually corresponded to Wechsler's Verbal and Performance scales. In a three-factor solution, a third factor of just a few subtests (usually Digit Span, Arithmetic, and Digit Symbol) emerged in addition to Verbal and Perceptual factors. In spite of the disagreement over an optimal factor solution and structure, Kaufman (1990) concluded that strong similarities were present in the factor structures of the W-B I, the WAIS, and the WAIS-R. As a result, factor analytic studies with the W-B I and the WAIS could be generalized to the WAIS-R. In other words, the constructs that underlie the three tests, appeared to be the same.

Developmental Trends

An additional means of supporting the construct validity of a test is with theoretically expected or anticipated developmental trends (Kaufman, 1990). For example, intelligence test raw scores (not age-corrected scores) should increase with age during childhood and adolescence due to factors such as increases in levels of education. For the WAIS-R 16 to 20 age group, the normative sample failed to show the anticipated developmental trend, while the WAIS 16 to 20 sample did evidence an expected developmental trend (Kaufman, 1990). In Table 7 of the *WAIS-R*

Manual, Wechsler (1981) presents the sum of scaled scores (not age corrected on the WAIS-R) for the nine age groups. As Kaufman pointed out, the 18- to 19-year-olds showed little increase in scores above the 16 to 17 age group although they had more education. Furthermore, the average scaled scores for the Performance, Verbal, and Full scales in the WAIS-R sample were much lower for ages 16 to 19 than those for the WAIS (Kaufman, 1990). This difference was particularly striking for the 18- to 19-year-olds. For all ages 20 or above, the scores between the WAIS and WAIS-R were comparable. Kaufman reasons that some type of error in the WAIS-R standardization sample procedure for ages 16 to 19 resulted in these problems. According to Kaufman, because of this issue, the construct validity of the WAIS-R for ages 16 to 19 was not supported, and one could not generalize findings from the W-B I or the WAIS to the WAIS-R for samples of adolescents. Kaufman warned that interpretation of WAIS-R scores for 16- to 19-year-olds should be done with caution.

Conclusions: W-B I to WAIS-R

Overall, however, the findings imply that a great degree of continuity existed from the W-B I to the WAIS-R (Kaufman, 1990). As a result, research findings based on earlier instruments could be applied to the WAIS-R. The one exception to this continuity was the 16 to 19 age group for the WAIS-R. Having established the continuity and reviewed the similarities of these first three Wechsler adult tests, the focus of the chapter now turns to the latest version, the WAIS-III.

WAIS-III

The WAIS-III consists of 14 subtests for the assessment of individuals age 16 to 89. In Wechsler fashion, the 14 subtests are grouped into Verbal and Performance sections (Wechsler, 1997c). The six standard verbal subtests are Vocabulary, Similarities, Arithmetic, Digit Span, Information, and Comprehension. Letter-Number Sequencing is a supplementary subtest for the Verbal or Full Scale IQs that can replace a spoiled Digit Span subtest. The standard five Performance subtests are Picture Completion, Digit Symbol-Coding, Block Design, Matrix Reasoning, and Picture Arrangement. Symbol Search is a supplementary subtest that can substitute only for a spoiled Digit Symbol-Coding in calculating Performance or Full Scale IQs. Object Assembly is an optional subtest that can take the place of any spoiled Performance subtest for individuals between 16 and 74. The *WAIS-III Administration and Scoring Manual* (Wechsler, 1997c) indicates that analyses of the standardization data suggest that Performance IQs in which Object Assembly was used as a replacement for each of the other Performance subtest scores were roughly equivalent to Performance scores without using Object Assembly.

Verbal and Performance IQs are added to compute a Full Scale IQ. All of the IQ and Index scores have a mean of 100 and a standard deviation of 15. The subtests have a mean scaled score of 10 and a standard deviation of 3.

In a presentation at the 1996 American Psychological Association annual conference a year before the WAIS-III was released, the WAIS-III project directors stressed that the WAIS-III would resemble its predecessors (Tulsky, Zhu, & Prifitera, 1996). The WAIS-III does resemble the previous Wechsler adult intelligence scales. The WAIS-III, like its predecessors, provides clinicians with Verbal, Performance, and Full Scale IQ scores, and all 11 of the traditional subtests are present. Of the actual items, more than 68% of the WAIS-R items appear in their original or a slightly modified form on the WAIS-III (Wechsler, 1997c).

At the same time, there are clear differences between the WAIS-R and the WAIS-III. One of the most obvious changes is the addition of three new subtests, Matrix Reasoning, Symbol Search, and Letter-Number Sequencing. Approximately 57% of the items on the WAIS-III are new (this does not include new Digit Symbol items) (Wechsler, 1997c). Of the 159 new items on the WAIS-III, 93 are on the three new subtests. The WAIS-III includes 31 reversal items, scattered across selected subtests that are administered only if an individual does not get the first two core items correct. The familiar Object Assembly, though present, is optional. In addition to the IQ scores, clinicians also have the option of calculating and interpreting four Index scores from the test protocol. As with the WISC-III, the four Index scores represent factors identified in factor analytic studies. The four Index scores are Verbal Comprehension Index (VCI), Perceptual Organization Index (POI), Working Memory Index (WMI), and Processing Speed Index (PSI). With this format, clinicians can interpret IQ scores, Index scores, or both.

A further difference between the WAIS-R and the WAIS-III is that all examinees were administered the same battery of 11 subtests on the WAIS-R. The 11 subtests were used to compute the IQ scores. On the WAIS-III examinees are not necessarily administered every subtest. The set of subtests administered depends on the scores an examiner wishes to interpret. Only 11 of the 14 WAIS-III subtests are used to determine IQ scores (Wechsler, 1997c). In this way the WAIS-III is similar to the WISC-III. On the WAIS-III, however, a different set of 11 subtests are used for the Index scores (see Table 11.1). When a clinician wants to interpret both IQ and Index scores for an individual, 13 subtests are administered. A final change is that the WAIS-III and the Wechsler Memory Scale—Third Edition (WMS-III; Wechsler, 1997b) were normed together and share the same technical manual (The Psychological Corporation, 1997).

TABLE 11.1   Composition of WAIS-III IQ and Index Scores

Subtest	IQ and Index Scores						
	Verbal IQ	Performance IQ	Full Scale IQ	Verbal Comprehension	Perceptual Organization	Working Memory	Processing Speed
Picture Completion		X	X		X		
Vocabulary	X		X	X			
Digit Symbol		X	X				X
Similarities	X		X	X			
Block Design		X	X		X		
Arithmetic	X		X			X	
Matrix Reasoning	X	X			X		
Digit Span	X		X			X	
Information	X		X	X			
Picture Arrangement		X	X				
Comprehension	X		X				
Symbol Search							X
Letter-Number Sequencing						X	
Object Assembly							

Reasons for Revision and Enhancements

The *WAIS-III—WMS-III Technical Manual* (The Psychological Corporation, 1997) lists numerous reasons for revision of the WAIS-R, and these reasons provide logical explanations for the obvious and not so obvious changes evident in the WAIS-III. The first reason cited is the need for updated normative data. The WAIS-R was normed in 1980, and a restandardization of the norms was needed. In addition to updating the normative data, test items themselves need to be updated. The *WAIS-III—WMS-III Technical Manual* (The Psychological Corporation, 1997) indicates that significant steps, based on methodologies such as item response theory, were taken to select items for the WAIS-III in order to limit the amount of bias in the test.

Furthermore, the artwork and stimuli were updated and enlarged, and steps were taken to make them more attractive (The Psychological Corporation, 1997). In this way the WAIS-III resembles the WISC-III more than it does the WAIS-R. For example, the Picture Arrangement cards have been redrawn, and the items from dated comic strips were removed. Occasionally, an older individual who took the WAIS-R would chuckle and note that some of the Picture Arrangement items look like a cartoon figure, the Little King, which was popular when they were younger. However, most individuals do not recognize these figures, and these dated cartoon figures do not appear on the WAIS-III. In addition, Picture Completion items are larger and in color. According to the manual, colored pictures were thought to be more relevant and closer to real-life items (The Psychological Corporation, 1997). The WAIS-III Digit Symbol test also has more space between the key and the items. This is a welcome change for left-handed examinees who were often covering the WAIS-R key with their arm as they worked.

The WAIS-III developers also cited a need to extend the age range of the norms and make the test more accommodating for an older population

as reasons for the revision (The Psychological Corporation, 1997). The WAIS-R had normative information for individuals up to 74 years of age. However, the life expectancy of those living in the United States is increasing, and currently 6% of the U.S. population is over the age of 75 (The Psychological Corporation, 1997). Furthermore, policy makers, researchers, and clinicians have recognized the need for and importance of evaluation and research with older populations. In recognition of these trends, the WAIS-III norms extend to age 89. Adaptations like larger pictures and stimuli have made the test more conducive to use with an older population or individuals with visual problems.

Another change that will make the test more appropriate for older adults is a decreased reliance on timed performance (The Psychological Corporation, 1997). Six of the WAIS-R subtests had time limits and three subtests award extra points for quick, correct solutions. The new Matrix Reasoning subtest is without a time limit or bonus points for fast solutions. Matrix Reasoning was added to the Performance scale and now replaces Object Assembly in the calculation of WAIS-III IQ and Index scores.

In addition to reducing the emphasis on timed performance, the Matrix subtest was added to strengthen the measurement of fluid or abstract reasoning. Matrix reasoning types of tasks are usually considered a measure of fluid ability (Carroll, 1993; McGrew, 1997). As discussed in the chapter on theory, several current theories of intelligence, such as Cattell and Horn's model or Carroll's, stress the role of fluid reasoning in human intelligence. The WAIS-R was criticized for not providing adequate measures of fluid reasoning (McGrew, Flanagan, Keith, & Vanderwood, 1997; The Psychological Corporation, 1997).

As indicated earlier in this chapter, disagreement exists concerning the number of WAIS-R factors to interpret. The *WAIS-III—WMS-III Technical Manual* (The Psychological Corporation, 1997) states that attempts were made from the beginning to incorporate new subtests that would strengthen hypothesized third (Working

Memory) and fourth factors (Processing Speed). Hypotheses of these four factors emerged from the data supporting a four-factor model of the WISC-III. The new Letter-Number Sequencing subtest was designed as a measure of working memory, and Symbol Search was added as a measure of processing speed.

One criticism often leveled against the WAIS-R was the lack of an adequate floor (The Psychological Corporation, 1997). In other words, the IQ scores do not extend low enough. Because of this, clinicians could not use the WAIS-R to discriminate adequately among individuals with various levels of mental retardation. Moreover, many of the subtests did not have enough easy items to permit accurate scaling at lower levels. To correct these problems, easier, "reversal" items were added to several WAIS-III subtests. As a result of these additions, the WAIS-III IQ scores have been extended downward to 45 for the Full Scale IQ, 48 for the Verbal IQ, and 47 for the Performance IQ. This will allow clinicians to distinguish between mild and moderate levels of mental retardation when intelligence test scores are included as criteria.

Today, the developmental phase of most new tests or major revisions of existing tests includes reassessment of reliability and validity. The WAIS-III is certainly no exception, and the results of these studies are presented in the technical manual (The Psychological Corporation, 1997). In addition, WAIS-III means are reported for samples of individuals with schizophrenia, neurological disorders (including Alzheimer's disease and traumatic brain injury), and alcohol-related disorders. Finally, the conorming of the WAIS-III and the WMS-III allows clinicians to compare an individual's performance on the two measures directly.

Psychometric Properties of the WAIS-III

Norming

The norming data for the WAIS-III was collected beginning in the summer of 1995 from a representative, national sample stratified on the variables of age, race/ethnicity, gender, education level, and geographic region (Tulsky et al., 1996). The standardization sample closely matches the 1995 U.S. Census Bureau statistics on all the stratification variables. The total sample consists of 2,450 individuals in 13 age bands (16–17, 18–19, 20–24, 25–29, 30–34, 35–44, 45–54, 55–64, 65–69, 70–74, 75–79, 80–84, 85–89) (The Psychological Corporation, 1997). Each age group except the two oldest included 200 participants. The 80 to 84 age group had 150 adults, and the 85 to 89 group had 100. Thus, the WAIS-III follows in the tradition of the WAIS and the WAIS-R with a large, representative normative sample.

Reliability

As with the WAIS-R and the WISC-III, the internal consistency of the WAIS-III is superb. The average internal consistency for the Full Scale is .98, the Verbal is .97, and the Performance is .94 (The Psychological Corporation, 1997). The Index scores also have good internal consistency with averages of .96 for Verbal Comprehension, .93 for Perceptual Organization, .94 for Working Memory, and .88 for Processing Speed. The average reliabilities for individual subtests range from .93 for Vocabulary to .70 for Object Assembly. Matrix Reasoning (average reliability of .90) replaces Block Design (average reliability of .86) as the most reliable subtest on the Performance scale.

In the test-retest reliability studies presented in the technical manual, participants in four age groups (16–29, 30–54, 55–74, and 75–89) were tested twice after an average interval of 34.6 days (The Psychological Corporation, 1997). The average stability coefficients across ages for the three IQs were high: .96 for Full Scale IQ, .96 for Verbal IQ, and .91 for Performance IQ. Index score test-retest reliabilities were also high: .95 for Verbal Comprehension, .88 for Perceptual Organization, and .89 for both Working Memory and Processing Speed. Of the subtests,

Picture Arrangement had the lowest average stability coefficient at .69 and Information had the highest at .94. Across all age groups the mean changes upon retest were about 2.5–3.2 points for the Verbal IQ, 2.5–8.3 for the Performance IQ, and 2.0–3.2 points for the Full Scale IQ. These differences probably reflect practice effects, and it is not surprising that the difference is greater for the Performance scale. Overall, then, clinicians can be assured that the WAIS-III provides extremely reliable IQ scores.

Standard Error of Measurement

The average SEM for all 13 age groups is 2.30 for the Full Scale IQ, 2.55 for the Verbal IQ, and 3.67 for the Performance IQ (The Psychological Corporation, 1997). From this information it is clear that one can have more confidence in the Full Scale IQ than in either the Verbal or Performance IQs. The average SEMs for the Index scores are 3.01 for Verbal Comprehension, 3.95 for Perceptual Organization, 3.84 for Working Memory, and 5.13 for Processing Speed.

Comparisons between the SEM of subtests and IQ or Index scores should not be made due to the difference in standard deviation units. On average, Verbal scale subtests tend to have lower standard errors of measurement than do Performance scale subtests. On the Verbal scale, Vocabulary has the lowest average SEM (.79), while Matrix Reasoning has the lowest (.97) on the Performance scale.

Validity

Because the WAIS-III was released so recently, no independent studies of WAIS-III validity are yet available. However, the *WAIS-III—WMS-III Technical Manual* (The Psychological Corporation, 1997) presents the results of several concurrent validity studies. Evidence of construct validity is available from the factor analyses and the intercorrelations among subtests and scales presented in the *Technical Manual*.

CONCURRENT VALIDITY, WAIS-R AND WAIS-III. To assess the relationship between the WAIS-R

and the WAIS-III, 192 individuals between the ages of 16 and 74 were administered the two tests in counterbalanced order (The Psychological Corporation, 1997). The correlation coefficients for the three IQs are .94 for Verbal, .86 for Performance, and .93 for Full Scale. These coefficients are even higher than those between the WAIS and WAIS-R. As was the case with the WAIS-R and WAIS correlations, the coefficients for the WAIS-R and the WAIS-III are not much lower than those from the WAIS-III test-retest reliability data. In general, Verbal scale subtests tended to have higher correlations than did Performance subtests. The range for Verbal subtests was .76 to .90, while the range for Performance was .50 to .77. Because Index scores do not appear in a standard format on the WAIS-R, correlations for these scores are unavailable.

The IQ scores on the WAIS-III were predictably lower than those of the WAIS-R. The difference was greatest for the Performance IQs (4.8 points), and least for the Verbal IQs (1.2 points). The difference on Full Scale IQs was 2.9 points. These differences are within an anticipated range, given Flynn's (1984) findings. Future studies will undoubtedly examine the relationship between the WAIS-R and the WAIS-III in a variety of populations, but these initial findings appear to support the similarity between the WAIS-III and the WAIS-R.

CONCURRENT VALIDITY, WAIS-III AND WISC-III. The WISC-III and the WAIS-III overlap for the 16-year-old age group, and either test may be used with this age group. The relationship between the two tests was examined by administering the tests in counterbalanced order to 184 16-year-olds (The Psychological Corporation, 1997). The correlations between IQ scores on the two tests were high. The coefficient for Verbal IQ was .88, for Performance .78, and for Full Scale .88. The correlations of Index scores are also available since both tests produce four Index scores. These values are .87, .74, .80, and .79 for Verbal Comprehension, Perceptual Organization, Working Memory, and Processing Speed, respectively.

It is clear that the two tests produce similar IQ scores as well as Index scores. These findings are not surprising, however, due to the degree of similarities between the two tests. As discussed earlier, both tests are derivatives of the early Wechsler-Bellevue Scales. In fact, of the 14 subtests available to WAIS-III users, 12 appear in an analogous format on the WISC-III. Furthermore, the factor structure of the two instruments is comparable. The factor structure of the WAIS-III will be discussed below.

CONCURRENT VALIDITY, WAIS-III AND STANFORD-BINET—FOURTH EDITION. Both the Stanford-Binet—Fourth Edition (Binet-4) and the WAIS-III were administered to a sample of 26 adults from age 16 to 45 (The Psychological Corporation, 1997). The mean Full Scale IQ on the WAIS-III was 113.3, while that on the Binet-4 was 114.8. The correlations between Full Scale IQs on the two tests was .88. This correlation is comparable to that found between the WAIS-R and the Binet-4 (.91).

CRITERION VALIDITY, WAIS-III AND WIAT. The WAIS-III and the Wechsler Individual Achievement Test (WIAT; The Psychological Corporation, 1992) were administered to 142 individuals from age 16 to 19 (The Psychological Corporation, 1997). Generally, the correlations between the WAIS-III IQ scores and the WIAT composite scores are moderate to high, with a range from .53 to .81. The correlations between WAIS-III Index scores and WIAT composite scores also range from moderate to high (.42 to .77). Altogether, most of the correlations between composite scores are in the .60s or .70s. These findings are consistent with the correlations found between the WIAT and the WAIS-R and between most intelligence and achievement tests.

FACTOR ANALYTIC RESULTS. To date the only factor analytic studies on the WAIS-III are those discussed and presented in the *WAIS-III—WMS-III Technical Manual* (The Psychological Corporation, 1997). The factor analytic studies in the manual include both exploratory and confirmatory factor analyses. In the first stage, the test developers conducted exploratory factor analyses of the overall sample to decide if a factorial pattern similar to that of the WISC-III could be replicated in the WAIS-III. The WISC-III pattern replicated, and further analyses supported the inclusion of Letter-Number Sequencing to strengthen the third factor, labeled Working Memory. The four subtests that loaded most highly on the first factor, Verbal Comprehension, were Vocabulary (loading .89), Information (.82), Comprehension (.79), and Similarities (.76). The second factor, Perceptual Organization, also had four subtests with relatively high loadings. These were Block Design (.71), Matrix Reasoning (.61), Picture Completion (.56), and Picture Arrangement (.47). The Working Memory factor consisted of three subtests: Digit Span (.71), Letter-Number Sequencing (.62), and Arithmetic (.51). Processing Speed had two subtests: Digit Symbol (.68) and Symbol Search (.63). Object Assembly was excluded from this analysis.

Following the analysis of the overall sample, the standardization sample was split into five age groups (16–19, 20–34, 35–54, 55–74, and 75–89) in order to test the factor structure across age groups (The Psychological Corporation, 1997). In the four youngest age bands, the factor structure was generally supported. In the 75–89 age group, however, the results were not consistent with those of the overall sample or the four younger age groups. In this older age group, the first (Verbal Comprehension) and third factors (Working Memory) did appear similar to those in the overall sample and the other age groups. However, the Perceptual Organization and Processing Speed factors were not replicated in a similar form. Only one subtest, Matrix Reasoning, had a loading on Perceptual Organization above .40. At the same time, five subtests Picture Completion, Block Design, Picture Arrangement, Digit Symbol, and Symbol Search had loadings above .40 on the Processing Speed factor. Given these findings, the factor structure of the WAIS-III at this age group remains in question. Future studies undoubtedly will examine the stability of this four-factor solution across various populations.

At the next step, five different models were compared and evaluated in confirmatory factor analyses to consider which model best fit the data (The Psychological Corporation, 1997). These analyses were run for an overall sample and at five age bands. The first model examined was one general factor with all 13 subtests (again, Object Assembly was excluded from the analyses). The second model was that of two factors: seven Verbal subtests and six Performance subtests. The third model contained three factors consisting of five Verbal Comprehension subtests, four Perceptual Organization subtests, and four Attentional subtests. The fourth model was the four-factor model discussed in the paragraph above. The fifth model included the four factors, Verbal Comprehension, Perceptual Organization, Memory, and Processing Speed, with an added fifth factor, Quantitative Ability/Numerical Ability. In the fifth model, the arithmetic subtest no longer contributed to the third factor (Working Memory) but was the only subtest on a Quantitative Ability factor. The goodness-of-fit indices suggest that the fourth and fifth models best fit the data. For the most part, the improvement of the fifth model over the fourth was slight to not at all. The case was made that the four-factor solution was more parsimonious than the five-factor solution, and therefore, the four-factor solution was determined to be the optimal solution (The Psychological Corporation, 1997).

In the last step of the factor analyses, the final composition of the factors was considered. Analyses were conducted to decide if all 13 subtests were needed in the factor structure (The Psychological Corporation, 1997). The results of a hierarchical regression analysis revealed that three subtests were sufficient to assess the abilities measured by the Verbal Comprehension and Perceptual Organization indices. Therefore, Comprehension, which takes longer to administer than Vocabulary, Information, or Similarities, was not included on the Verbal Comprehension index. Also, Picture Arrangement, which tends to have a high loading on Verbal Comprehension as well as Perceptual Organization, was dropped from the Perceptual Organization index. Working Memory and Processing Speed, which have three and two subtests respectively, retained the same structure.

Overall, these analyses provide support for the interpretation of the four factors up to the age of 75. Missing from these analyses, however, is a presentation of the two-factor solution along Verbal and Performance domains from an exploratory factor analysis and the loadings of each subtest on the Verbal and Performance factors. Although numerous studies have examined the Verbal and Performance factors in previous Wechsler adult intelligence tests, the composition of the Performance IQ is slightly different on the WAIS-III. It would be helpful to know if, or how, this change affects the two-factor solution. Future studies with the WAIS-III will likely address these questions.

INTERCORRELATIONS AMONG SUBTESTS AND SCALES
The pattern of intercorrelations among the WAIS-III subtests, IQ, and Index scores is similar to that of the WAIS-R. Overall, most of the subtests correlate at least moderately with one another. The *WAIS-III—WMS-III Technical Manual* (The Psychological Corporation, 1997) asserts that this supports the idea of a "g" factor underlying the WAIS-III. The correlations between subtests range from a low of .26 between Object Assembly and Digit Span to a high of .77 between Vocabulary and Information. Verbal subtests tend to have stronger correlations with other Verbal subtests than with Performance subtests. Performance subtests show the same tendency but not to the degree of the Verbal subtests. According to the *WAIS-III—WMS-III Technical Manual* (The Psychological Corporation, 1997), Performance subtests with high "g" loadings tend to have moderate correlations with Verbal subtests as well as Performance subtests. Generally, Verbal subtests tend to have higher correlations with the Full Scale IQ. The exceptions

Box 11.2   WAIS and Education

The validity of an intelligence measure can also be considered by examining its relationship to measures such as levels of education, grade point averages, and placement tests. Although no information is available concerning the relationship between the WAIS-III and level of educational attainment, this information is available for the WAIS-R. Two separate studies found significant differences between the mean Full Scale IQs among various levels of educational achievement (Matarazzo & Herman, 1984; Reynolds, Chastain, Kaufman, & McLean, 1987). In the Reynolds et al. study, the mean Full Scale IQ for college graduates was 115, the mean Full Scale IQ for high school graduates was 100, and the mean for those with an elementary school education was 91. The overall correlation between education level and the WAIS-R Verbal Scale IQ was .60, for the Performance scale .44, and .57 for the Full Scale (Reynolds et al., 1987). Although a strong relationship exists between education and IQ, one should keep in mind that this does not imply causality, and the nature of this relationship is unclear (Kaufman, 1990; Matarazzo & Herman, 1984).

Another study with a sample of master's level graduate students explored the relationship among WAIS-R IQ scores, undergraduate grade point averages (UGPA) from the last 60 hours, and Graduate Record Examination (GRE) scores (Carvajal & Pauls, 1995). In this study, Verbal IQ correlated highly with Verbal GRE (.73), Quantitative GRE (.71), Analytical GRE (.57), and UGPA (.53). Full Scale IQ also had strong correlations with examination scores and UGPA. The correlations were .63 between Full Scale IQ and Verbal GRE, .71 with Quantitative GRE, and .52 with Analytical GRE. Interestingly, the lowest correlation for Full Scale IQ was with UGPA (.42). The correlations with Performance IQ were generally lower than those for Verbal IQ or Full Scale. Performance IQ correlated most strongly with Quantitative GRE (.58). The lowest, and only nonsignificant correlation among these measures and IQ scores, was between UGPA and Performance IQ (.22). In spite of the possible interest of this study for graduate students, one should keep in mind that the sample was small and from one regional, midwestern university and therefore, not necessarily representative of graduate students in general.

---

are Digit Span (r = .52 with Full Scale IQ) and Letter-Number Sequencing (r = .64). The range for correlations between Performance subtests and Full Scale IQ is .59 for Object Assembly to .69 for Matrix Reasoning.

ADMINISTRATION AND SCORING

The administration procedures for the WAIS-III are similar to those of the WAIS-R and the WISC-III. Like the WISC-III and the WAIS-R, the WAIS-III administration manual is separate from the testing stimuli. Also like the WISC-III, the WAIS-III manual is designed to stand on its own. The WAIS-III requires the use of a stopwatch for most Performance subtests, and as with all Wechsler intelligence tests, examiners should adhere to standardized wording. Instructions for

the WAIS-III are printed in blue in the *WAIS-III Administration and Scoring Manual* (Wechsler, 1997c). Guidelines for teaching tasks, repeating items, probing responses, and queries are similar to those on the WISC-III.

Subtest Sequence

The recommended order for administration of the WAIS-III subtests is different from that of the WAIS-R. On the WAIS-III, the first subtest to be administered is Picture Completion. Following Picture Completion, the subtests generally alternate between the Verbal and Performance scales. Because Object Assembly is an optional subtest and is not used to calculate IQ or Index scores, it is administered last. The *WAIS-III Administration and Scoring Manual* (Wechsler, 1997c) advises examiners to administer all of the remaining 13 subtests whenever possible. If a clinician is interested in only IQ or Index scores but not both, he or she should follow the order on the Record Form and skip subtests that are not necessary for the relevant composite scores. If breaks are needed, they should take place between subtests.

Administration Time

Administration time of the WAIS-III depends on the subtests administered and, as always, the experience level of the examiner. The *WAIS-III Administration and Scoring Manual* (Wechsler, 1997c) states that the subtests required for the three IQ scores take about 80 minutes to administer, while the subtests for the Index scores require about 60 minutes. Administration of the 13 subtests for both IQ and Index scores requires about 85 minutes. Clinicians who wish to administer Object Assembly should allocate an additional 10 to 15 minutes. Examiners with less testing experience or less familiarity with the WAIS-III may want to allocate up to 2 hours.

Starting and Discontinue Rules

Six of the WAIS-III subtests begin with the first item. Easier, reversal items are included in the other eight subtests. Those subtests with reversal items are Picture Completion, Vocabulary, Similarities, Block Design, Arithmetic, Matrix Reasoning, Information, and Comprehension. On these eight subtests if an examinee does not obtain a perfect score (full credit, excluding bonus points) on the first two items designated by the starting point, previous items are administered in reverse order. Unlike Block Design and Picture Arrangement on the WISC-III, items before a starting point on the WAIS-III are administered in reverse (not normal sequence) order for every subtest. On subtests with reversal items, full credit is awarded for all previous items not administered once the criterion of two correct is met.

Eleven subtests have discontinue rules based on the criteria of consecutive failures. The specific

number required for each subtest are given on the Record Form. The discontinue rules were determined by empirical data from the standardization sample. Of the remaining three subtests, Digit Symbol and Symbol Search are discontinued after 120 seconds. All Object Assembly items are administered.

Scoring Responses

The scoring guidelines for the WAIS-III resemble those of the WISC-III. Scoring for most subtests is relatively objective. However, scoring of Similarities, Vocabulary, and Comprehension is on a 3-point scale (0, 1, 2) which makes scoring more challenging. As advised for the WISC-III, read all responses given in the manual before determining a score.

Computing Derived Scores

The process for converting raw scores to scaled scores and composite scores for the WAIS-III is like that for the WISC-III. This process represents a change from the WAIS-R, where scaled scores for all ages were based on those of the reference group, ages 20–34. To obtain raw subtest scores, simply sum the points awarded and remember to include credit for reverse items not administered. Raw scores are converted to scaled scores, based on the examinee's age, by using Table A.1 in the *WAIS-III Administration and Scoring Manual* (Wechsler, 1997c). Each page of Table A.1 gives the scaled scores for one of the 13 age groups. Once the sum of scaled scores are calculated, the IQ and Index score equivalents are found in Tables A.3 to A.9.

Other Options on Record Form

The WAIS-III Record Form also gives examiners the options of calculating subtest strengths and weaknesses on the Score Conversion Page. Subtest scaled scores may be compared to the overall mean scaled score, a Verbal mean, or Performance mean. The differences required for statistical significance at the .05 and the .15 are available in Table B.3 of the *WAIS-III Administration and Scoring Manual* (Wechsler, 1997c). Frequencies for differences obtained by the standardization sample are also given in Table B.3 at levels of 1%, 2%, 5%, 10%, and 25%. Clinicians should find these frequency tables helpful in determining the degree to which significant differences should be interpreted.

The Discrepancy Analysis Page provides examiners with space on the Record Form to compare differences between Verbal and Performance IQs, among Index scores, and the longest correct Digit Span Forward and Backward. The required differences for statistical significance at the .05 and .15 between IQ and among Index scores are listed in Table B.1 by age group. The frequencies of these differences in the standardization sample are found in Table B.2. Again, these frequency tables provide important information for interpretive purposes. Tables B.6 and B.7 provide information on percentages correct and difference percentages on for Digits Forward and Digits Backward.

WAIS-III Subtests

Twelve of the 13 WISC-III subtests appear in an analogous form on the WAIS-III. Mazes is the only WISC-IIII subtest that does not have a parallel on the WAIS-III. The descriptions, administrative and scoring pointers, behaviors to note, and hypotheses to investigate for the 12 subtests are similar to those for the WISC-III. All of the psychometric information except "g" loadings and subtest specificities is from the *WAIS-III and WMS-III Technical Manual* (The Psychological Corporation 1997). The "g" loadings and subtest specificities are from Sattler and Ryan (1999).

Picture Completion

This subtest is similar to Picture Completion on the WISC-III. On the WAIS-III Picture Completion consists of 25 items, 5 of which are reverse

items. All examinees start with item 6 and the discontinue rule is 5 consecutive failures. Teaching, in the form of providing the correct response, is allowed on items 6 and 7 only. The examinee must respond to each item within 20 seconds. Three caution statements are allowed, once each. These statements are included on the Record Form as well as in the Administration Manual. Each item is scored 0 or 1. This subtest is used in the calculation of both IQ and Index scores.

Psychometric Properties

Mean split-half reliability = .83

Average test-restest reliability = .79

Correlation with Performance Scale = .60

Correlation with Full Scale IQ = .60

Correlation with Verbal Scale = .53

Correlation with Perceptual Organization Index = .55

Factor loading on Perceptual Organization = .56

"g" loading = .64

Mean subtest specificity is ample

Vocabulary

Vocabulary on the WAIS-III is comparable to the Vocabulary subtest on the WISC-III. The WAIS-III Vocabulary subtest contains 33 words that the examiner reads and presents concurrently in printed format. Examiners should be aware that presentation on the WAIS-III is different than on the WISC-III where words are read, but not presented written. The subtest begins on item 4, and the discontinue rule is 6 consecutive scores of 0. Items 1 through 3 are reverse items. All responses are scored 0, 1, or 2. This subtest is used in the calculation of both IQ and Index scores.

Psychometric Properties

Mean split-half reliability = .93

Average test-retest reliability = .91

Correlation with Verbal Scale = .83

Correlation with Full Scale IQ = .80

Correlation with Performance Scale = .65

Factor loading on Verbal Comprehension
= .89

"g" loading = .83

Mean subtest specificity is adequate

Digit Symbol-Coding

Digit Symbol-Coding is analogous to Coding on the WISC-III. There are 133 items with a time limit of 120 seconds. Unlike the WISC-III, the WAIS-III Digit Symbol sheet is not removed from the record form. Examiners simply hand the booklet to the examinee for this subtest. Credit is awarded for any items the examinee spontaneously corrects but not items completed out of order. This subtest is used in the calculation of both IQ and Index scores.

An incidental learning trial that includes Pairing and Free Recall trials is optional after the standard administration. The form for these trials is found at the back of the Symbol Search booklet. On the Pairing trial, the examinee is asked to fill in the appropriate symbol for numbered boxes without the key available. For the Free Recall trial, the examinee is asked to recall as many symbols as he or she can spontaneously without the numbers. These tasks allow the examiner to assess the examinee's ability to remember symbols and pair them with the correct numbers.

PSYCHOMETRIC PROPERTIES[4]

Average test-retest reliability = .86

Correlation with Performance Scale = .50

Correlation with Full Scale IQ = .53

Correlation with Verbal Scale = .49

Factor loading on Processing Speed = .68

"g" loading = .59

Mean subtest specificity is ample

[4]*The WAIS-III—WMS-III Technical Manual* (The Psychological Corporation, 1997) notes that because Digit Symbol-Coding is a speeded subtest, the split-half coefficient is not an appropriate estimate of reliability.

Similarities

This subtest is much like Similarities on the WISC-III. The subtest begins with item 6, and items 1–5 are reverse items. There are 19 pairs of words, and the discontinue rule is 4 consecutive scores of 0. Examiners should note that reverse items (1–5) are scored on a scale of 0 or 1, while items 6–19 are scored 0, 1, 2. This can lead to incorrect tabulation of a Similarities raw score if one is not careful when adding credit for reversal items not administered. This subtest is used in the calculation of both IQ and Index scores.

PSYCHOMETRIC PROPERTIES

Mean split-half reliability = .86

Average test-retest reliability = .83

Correlation with Verbal Scale = .77

Correlation with Full Scale IQ = .76

Correlation with Performance Scale = .65

Factor loading on Verbal Comprehension = .76

"g" loading = .79

Mean subtest specificity is adequate

Block Design

A comparable Block Design subtest is present on the WISC-III. Administration starts with item 5 on the WAIS-III. The discontinue rule is 3 consecutive scores of 0. There are 14 designs, but designs 1–4 are reverse items. On designs 1–5, the examinee copies the examiner's model, and no picture is presented. On item 6, a picture of the design is presented, and the examiner demonstrates with the examinee's blocks. After item 6, the examiner presents only the picture. Demonstrations are not allowed following item 6. This subtest is required and is used in the calculation of both IQ and Index scores.

PSYCHOMETRIC PROPERTIES

Mean split-half reliability = .86

Average test-retest reliability = .82

Correlation with Performance Scale = .66

Correlation with Full Scale IQ = .66

Correlation with Verbal Scale = .59

Factor loading on Perceptual Organization = .71

"g" loading = . 72

Mean subtest specificity is ample

Arithmetic

The WAIS-III Arithmetic format is similar to that of the WISC-III. Examiners administer item 5 first, and there are 20 items total (items 1–4 are reverse items). Only items 19 and 20 offer an extra point for quick performance. The discontinue rule is 4 failures. This subtest is used in the calculation of both IQ and Index scores.

PSYCHOMETRIC PROPERTIES

Mean split-half reliability = .88

Average test-retest reliability = .86

Correlation with Verbal Scale = .70

Correlation with Full Scale IQ = .72

Correlation with Performance Scale = .63

Factor loading on Working Memory = .51

"g" loading = .75

Mean subtest specificity is ample

Matrix Reasoning

A matrix-type subtest has not traditionally been part of the Wechsler intelligence tests. As discussed previously, this subtest was added to provide a measure of Fluid Reasoning and to decrease the importance of time on the Performance scale. The examiner presents a series of incomplete patterns from the stimulus booklet. The examinee responds by giving the number for or pointing to the correct response. There are five possible choices for each item. This subtest is similar to Matrix Analogies on the K-ABC (Kaufman & Kaufman, 1983a) or Matrices on the DAS (Elliott, 1990c).

The examiner administers the three sample items in order of A, B, C and then proceeds to item 4. Items 1–3 are reverse items. This subtest consists of 26 items, and all are scored 0 or 1.

The discontinue rule is slightly different in that there are two possible discontinue conditions: after 4 consecutive failures or 4 failures out of 5 consecutive items. This subtest is used in the calculation of both IQ and Index scores.

PSYCHOMETRIC PROPERTIES

Mean split-half reliability = .90

Average test-retest reliability = .77

Correlation with Performance Scale = .65

Correlation with Full Scale IQ = .69

Correlation with Verbal Scale = .64

Factor loading on Perceptual Organization = .61

"g" loading = .72

Mean subtest specificity is ample

Digit Span (Digits Forward and Digits Backward)

This subtest is much like the one on the WISC-III. The subtest has two sections, Digits Forward and Digits Backward. All examinees begin with item 1 on Digits Forward. There are 8 items in Digits Forward and 7 in Digits Backward for a total of 15 items. Each item has two trials. To discontinue either section, an examinee must have a score of 0 on both trials of any item. As on the WISC-III, the examiner drops his or her pitch at the end of an item, and numbers are administered at the rate of one per second. This subtest is used in the calculation of both IQ and Index scores.

PSYCHOMETRIC PROPERTIES

Mean split-half reliability = .90

Average test-retest reliability = .83

Correlation with Verbal Scale = .51

Correlation with Full Scale IQ = .52

Correlation with Performance Scale = .47

Factor loading on Working Memory = .71

"g" loading = .57

Mean subtest specificity is ample

Information

There are 28 Information questions, similar in form to those on the WISC-III. Item 5 is the starting point, with items 1–4 as reverse items. The subtest is discontinued after 6 consecutive failed items. This subtest is required and is used in the calculation of both IQ and Index scores.

Psychometric Properties

Mean split-half reliability = .91
Average test-retest reliability = .94
Correlation with Verbal Scale = .79
Correlation with Full Scale IQ = .76
Correlation with Performance Scale = .63
Factor loading on Verbal Comprehension = .81
"g" loading = .79
Mean subtest specificity is adequate

Picture Arrangement

This subtest is like Picture Arrangement on the WISC-III. There are 11 sets of pictures to arrange. The starting point is item 1, and the discontinue rule is 4 consecutive scores of 0 starting with item 2. As with WISC-III, the cards are arranged in numerical order starting on examiner's left. The time limits range from 30 to 120 seconds. Six items are scored on a 0, 1, or 2 point scale, and 5 items are scored 0 or 1. Picture Arrangement is used to calculate IQ scores but not Index scores.

Psychometric Properties

Mean split-half reliability = .74
Average test-retest reliability = .69
Correlation with Performance Scale = .60
Correlation with Full Scale IQ = .63
Correlation with Verbal Scale = .59
"g" loading = .66
Mean subtest specificity is inadequate

Comprehension

The questions and scoring of the Comprehension subtest are similar to those on the WISC-III. The test begins with item 4, so items 1–3 are reverse items. Items 5, 6, 7, 10, and 13 require an answer that reflects more than one general concept. Note that these items are marked by an asterisk to the right of the identifying word on the record form. As on the WISC-III, if the examinee's spontaneous response reflects only one general concept, the examiner is to query for a second response. The discontinue rule is 4 consecutive scores of 0. Comprehension scores are used to calculate IQ but not Index scores.

Psychometric Properties

Mean split-half reliability = .84
Average test-retest reliability = .81
Correlation with Verbal Scale = .76
Correlation with Full Scale IQ = .75
Correlation with Performance Scale = .62
"g" loading = .77
Mean subtest specificity is adequate

Symbol Search

The WAIS-R did not have a Symbol Search task, but this subtest is parallel to the one on the WISC-III. On the WAIS-III, there is only one form for all ages. The Symbol Search response booklet is separate from the record form. As on the WISC-III, the raw score is the number of correct minus the number of incorrect. There are 60 items and the time limit is 120 seconds. Symbol Search scores are typically used to calculate Index but not IQ scores. However, Symbol Search can substitute for a spoiled Digit Symbol-Coding in calculating IQ scores.

Psychometric Properties[5]

Average test-retest reliability = .79
Correlation with Performance Scale = .69
Correlation with Full Scale IQ = .66
Correlation with Verbal Scale = .57
Factor loading on Processing Speed = .63
"g" loading = .70
Mean subtest specificity is adequate

[5]*The WAIS-III—WMS-III Technical Manual* (The Psychological Corporation, 1997) notes that because Symbol Search is a speeded subtest, the split-half coefficient is not an appropriate estimate of reliability.

Letter-Number Sequencing

A letter-number sequencing task did not appear on the WAIS-R nor is there a similar subtest on the WISC-III. For this task, the examiner reads a combination of letters and numbers, and the examinee is asked to recall the numbers first in ascending order, and then the letters in alphabetical order. There are seven sets of letters and numbers in increasing length, and each set consists of three trials. The subtest begins with item 1. Five practice items appear in the *WAIS-III Administration and Scoring Manual* (Wechsler, 1997c) but are not on the record form. The scoring is 0 or 1 per trial. If an examinee responds with letters first, then numbers but all of them in correct sequence, credit is awarded. Discontinue after all three trials of an item are scored 0. Usually Letter-Number Sequencing scores are used to calculate Index but not IQ scores. However, Letter-Number Sequencing can take the place of a spoiled Digit Span in calculating IQ scores.

PSYCHOMETRIC PROPERTIES

Mean split-half reliability = .82

Average test-retest reliability = .75

Correlation with Verbal Scale = .62

Correlation with Full Scale IQ = .64

Correlation with Performance Scale = .57

Factor loading on Working Memory =.62

"g" loading = .65

Mean subtest specificity is ample

Object Assembly

This subtest is similar to Object Assembly on the WISC-III. There is no sample item on the WAIS-III, but if an examinee does not arrange item 1 correctly, the examiner demonstrates the correct solution. There are 5 items, and all items are administered. The last two designs are new ones. This subtest is now optional and is not used in the calculation of IQ or Index scores. Object Assembly can take the place of any spoiled Performance subtest for ages 16–74.

PSYCHOMETRIC PROPERTIES

Mean split-half reliability = .70

Average test-retest reliability = .76

Correlation with Performance Scale = .64

Correlation with Full Scale IQ = .59

Correlation with Verbal Scale = .50

"g" loading = .62

Mean subtest specificity is inadequate

INTERPRETATION OF THE WAIS-III

A sample testing case utilizing the WAIS-III is presented in Box 11.3. Generally, interpretation of the WAIS-III follows the same guidelines as those for the WISC-III (see Chapters 8 and 17). The WAIS-III now shares a factor structure and composition like that of the WISC-III, and 12 of the 14 subtests are the same. Also, the similarities between the WAIS-III and the WAIS-R are substantial. As a result, much of the extensive research literature on previous Wechsler adult intelligence tests can be applied to the WAIS-III. One criticism of the WAIS-R made by Kaufman (1990) was the lack of an expected developmental trend for the normative sample at ages 16 to 19. In his recent book on the WAIS-III, however, Kaufman (1999) reports that he examined the WAIS-III standardization data. He concludes that the norms for ages 16 to 17 are definitely valid, and those for ages 18 to 19 are probably valid. Thus, it appears that for these ages, clinicians can interpret WAIS-III results with greater assurance than they could WAIS-R results.

In spite of the similarities, the WAIS-III has features not shared with the WISC-III or the WAIS-R that influence interpretation. The new Matrix Reasoning subtest is unique to the WAIS-III. The addition of this subtest provides clinicians with a measure of fluid reasoning, "g_f." Previously, it was thought that Performance IQ was a measure of "g_f" (Daniel, 1997; Kaufman, 1990), but recent data analyses have not supported

Box 11.3   Psychological Evaluation Using the WAIS-III

Name: Dan

Age: 46 years

Gender: male

Referral Question

Dan contacted the clinic to inquire about testing for attention deficit hyperactivity disorder (ADHD). He wanted to know more about ADHD and whether his behavior was characteristic of others who have this disorder. Also, he questioned his academic fitness for graduate studies due to the fact that he has had long-standing difficulties with academic achievement.

Assessment Instruments

  Wechsler Adult Intelligence Scale—Third Edition (WAIS-III)

  Woodcock-Johnson Cognitive Ability—Revised (WJ-R Cog.)

  Woodcock-Johnson Achievement Test—Revised (WJ-R Ach.)

  Wide Range Achievement Test—Third Edition (WRAT-III)

  Revised NEO Personality Inventory (NEO-PI-R)

  Symptom Checklist-90-R (SCL-90-R)

  Millon Clinical Multiaxial Inventory-II

  Beck Depression Inventory-II (BDI-II)

  Brown ADD Scales

  Self-Report ADHD Checklist

  Clinical Interview

  Clinical Observation

Background

Social History

Dan is a 46-year-old male, who lives alone. At this time, he is self-employed as a communications consultant. He has been married once, to a teacher for three years. This relationship ended in a divorce 10 years ago. Dan has no children.

  Dan is the only child of an affluent family. His mother is a lawyer specializing in estate planning. She was the primary caregiver for Dan. His father is a physicist who traveled frequently during the time Dan lived at home. Dan described his parents as pillars of the community and extremely gifted intellectually. He commented that he feels substantial pressure from his parents to become financially successful and to pursue advanced degrees. At times he believes these expectations are unrealistic. Although Dan had many same-age friends growing up, he remembered constantly being around his parents' friends and other adults. Presently, he has few friends his age. He commented that people are "attracted to me." His friends are usually younger or older than he.

Developmental and Educational History

Dan reported that his birth and developmental history was unremarkable. He was a full-term baby weighing 9 lbs. and 9 ounces at birth. His development was typical of other children. He noted that he has never been hospitalized for any illness or accident and has never taken any long-term medication. Dan's present health is excellent. He refrains from drug and alcohol use. It should be noted that he drinks about 4 cups of coffee a day, usually in the morning.

  Dan attended public school in New York. He commented that he always got the message that he was not as smart as his peers. On specific occasions, he can remember teachers telling him that he was not smart and should not have such high aspirations for himself. He described himself as the "class clown" who had a "problem with petty

Box 11.3   Psychological Evaluation Using the WAIS-III (Continued)

authority." He remembered being in the lowest academic level of classes. He received mostly Cs and graduated with a C average. He stated that his academic strength was science because the subject was "authentic and real, uncomplicated by man." He had more difficulty with math. He was tutored in math throughout his schooling. He said that he spent a lot of time daydreaming during school; for example, he would be singing a song in his head. His elementary school teachers often reported that he did not seem to pay attention in class.

Because Dan's high school grades were not adequate to attend a university, he enrolled in a small two-year college and then transferred to a private college. He completed a masters degree in theater from Eastern University. Then he worked for a number of years as a theater manager in New York. He started his own theater company and served as artistic director for 9 years before returning to graduate school to obtain a masters in fine arts. Dan would like to return to school for a doctoral degree in adult education. He is currently applying for programs in this area of study but has been unsuccessful due to his GRE scores. Dan reported that he made a 250 in Math, 475 in Verbal, and 400 in Analytic Reasoning on the GRE.

Behavioral Observations

For the purposes of this evaluation, Dan spent 11 hours completing rating scales and the assessment battery. Upon arrival at the clinic, Dan appeared extremely tense and anxious. Most notably, he avoided making eye contact with the graduate clinician. During the interview, Dan revealed that he felt some nervousness and hesitation about coming to the clinic, but he would go through with the testing because he had already made the appointment. After approximately 1 hour, Dan seemed more acclimated to the environment. Throughout the interview and testing sessions, Dan was extremely honest and forthcoming with details and examples of his difficulties. He presented as insightful and introspective about his growth and current functioning. He listed his strengths as bright, articulate, compassionate, generous, accessible, dependable, sensitive, and hardworking.

An additional observer during the testing process commented that Dan was very animated. He constantly used his hands and became increasingly restless as the testing progressed. However, he was cooperative and put forth good effort throughout the process. Despite some inattention and/or tiredness, this evaluation appears a valid assessment of Dan's performance.

Test Interpretation

Intelligence
Cognitive functioning is estimated to be in the average to high average range. His WAIS-III Full Scale score places him in the average range. Dan's cognitive skills are typical for someone his age. During the testing sessions, it was obvious to the examiner that Dan enjoyed verbal tasks, such as defining words and discussing how two words were similar. Dan's performance on the WAIS-III evidenced a relative strength on the Verbal Comprehension Index, suggesting that his verbal conceptual skills are well developed.

He appeared more tense during tasks when he had to hold and transform information in his head. As an illustration, when solving word problems in his head, Dan needed items to be repeated so that he could remember the numbers with which he had to work. He began apologizing and making self-deprecating statements such as, "I'm spacing out on these, and this is so embarrassing because these problems are so elementary." However, Dan's performance for subtests that tap working memory suggested that he has typical skills in that area. He was able to recall digits in forward and backward order correctly and transform a series of numbers and letters in correct order. Dan lost points during the testing for failing to complete items within the time limit. In most of the instances, he correctly solved the problem soon after the time limit.

To further examine Dan's cognitive strengths and weaknesses, he was administered the Woodcock-Johnson Tests of Cognitive Ability—Revised. Overall, his performance was typical of others his age. His reasoning skills on this test are consistent with average to above-average cognitive ability. Specifically, Dan's processing speed was somewhat slower when he had an array of complex figures to scan. For example, in one subtest he had to mark all the like symbols in a row of many different symbols. His relatively poorer performance may be the result of age-related decrements in his vision. Dan had to hold some of the picture arrangement cards up close to his face to note

(Continues)

Box 11.3   Psychological Evaluation Using the WAIS-III (Continued)

the detail in the cards. In addition, his auditory acuity was not precise. As he repeated a tape-recorded list of words, he made substitutions for words with like sounding words, suggesting that he had misheard the word. However, Dan did not have any other indication in his communication with the examiner that he was not able to hear clearly.

Achievement

Dan's academic achievement, as measured by the Woodcock-Johnson Tests of Achievement and the Wide Range Achievement Test, is within the average to above-average range. His strengths were in reading comprehension. Dan's arithmetic skills appear typical of others his age. Despite his apparent anxiety in math performance, his math reasoning is within the average range. He was able to add, subtract, multiply, and divide equations with ease. It became more difficult for him when mixed numbers, fractions, and percentages were introduced. Dan's performance revealed some faulty understanding of mathematical operations. For example, he was unsure where to put the decimal when multiplying numbers. He did not attempt any of the algebraic equations, explaining that he had never done that kind of problem before. As stated previously, Dan became frustrated with his math performance when the questions were presented orally without paper and pen. He commented that he was not able to hold the information in his head. He was slightly more confident when he had paper and pencil to work out the problems.

Social-Emotional

Dan completed a number of self-report rating scales that assessed social-emotional functioning and provided a description of his personality. These measures included the Brown ADD scales, the Revised NEO-Personality Inventory, the Symptom Checklist-90-Revised, Millon Clinical Multiaxial Inventory-II, and the Beck Depression Inventory-II. Dan endorsed a number of statements that suggest he has difficulty with attention, hyperactivity, and impulsivity, including frequently shifting from one task to another, avoiding tasks that require mental effort, talking too much, not listening to others, blurting out answers, and difficulty organizing tasks and activities. Almost daily Dan reported that he gets lost in daydreaming or is preoccupied with his own thoughts almost daily. Dan stated that he loses interest in projects quickly, which is also substantiated by his work history. He commented that the "dreary routine is awful for me." He described himself as a butterfly, who is easily sidetracked. Being alone for Dan is especially difficult. He frequently is distracted when by himself. In the company of other people, however, Dan reports being able to concentrate and focus when provided with the expectations of others that he should be attending to them. Interestingly, Dan discussed his ability to solve problems in multiple ways as a creative strength; however, at times this creative ability could also be described as distractibility. In addition, he procrastinates excessively. For example, when his parents requested that he purchase a book, he put this off for months until his parents eventually sent him a copy. During the testing session, Dan asked for breaks every 2 hours. He purchased a cup of coffee during the lunchtime break. He stated that he usually does not drink in the afternoon but that he felt like he needed it.

Dan is not concerned with his level of energy or his memory. Although he has difficulty sleeping throughout the night, Dan said that he is ready to go in the morning. He stated that he has a photographic memory.

Dan reported fluctuating moods. He described feeling lonely, blue, and worrying too much about things. He can't get any pleasure from the things he used to enjoy. At times he feels like a failure or that he is the "end of a defective line." He has had thoughts of committing suicide but said he would never do it. Dan stated that both his parents have struggled with depression in their lives. The lowest point for him was his divorce 10 years ago. Although Dan indicated a depressive tendency, he did not report any functional impairment or major depressive episodes. His high rating of positive emotions is contraindicated for depression. In addition, there is some indication that Dan has a tendency to cycle from depressive moods to elevated moods. After further exploration of these themes, Dan did evidence some expansive thoughts, but he denied behaviors that are characteristic of individuals with bipolar disorder.

Dan reported that he feels different from everybody else, like he is an observer in the world. He described himself as an "alien." His behavioral ratings suggest that his personality dimensions include some histrionic and narcissistic tendencies. That is, Dan strives to give the impression to others that he is clever and artful but beneath this exterior he is constantly searching for acceptance and assurance. Dan is extremely perceptive of his own feelings and

Box 11.3   Psychological Evaluation Using the WAIS-III (Continued)

emotions. In this way, his energies are focused on his view of the world. He believes others are stuck in mediocrity; however, he wishes he could just be a plumber and be happy. He commented that he does not have friends his own age because they all want to engage in base activities like drinking. His ratings suggested that he is extremely open to new experiences and appreciates aesthetic pursuits like art and theatre. Furthermore, he enjoys outside activities such as hiking, baseball, and backpacking.

Summary and Conclusions

Dan is a 46-year-old man who presents with academic self-doubts, significant attention problems, and some concerns about mood states. The cognitive and academic testing performed revealed that Dan's skills are typical of others his age. He is functioning in the average to above-average range in cognitive and academic ability. His math skills are somewhat weaker than his verbal reasoning skills, but they are still within the average range for someone his age. Dan reports significant difficulty with attention, distractibility, and impulsivity. There is enough evidence based on history, self-ratings, observer ratings, and clinical impairment based on DSM-IV criteria to diagnose Dan with attention deficit hyperactivity disorder—predominately inattentive type. Dan's ratings of personality indicate that he is generally a sociable person who has a tendency to have depressive feelings. It is not clear the degree to which Dan's mood states affect his functioning. At this time, he does not show any clinical impairment.

   Diagnosis: 314.00 attention deficit hyperactivity disorder—predominately inattentive type

Recommendations

1. As a result of Dan's average performance on tests of cognitive ability, it is apparent that his difficulty with attention and hyperactivity are interfering with his performance on the Graduate Record Exam. In addition, Dan's distractibility makes it hard for him to complete items within the required time limit. Thus, it is recommended that the Educational Testing Service allow Dan some accommodations that will provide him the opportunity to perform to the best of his ability. Specifically, he would benefit from an extended time limit that would allow him to gather his thoughts and to reason through items. Also, he may need time for multiple breaks to allow him to regain an appropriate level of attention.

2. Dan may benefit from consultation with a physician about the pharmacological treatment of ADHD. A variety of medications have been useful for others diagnosed with this disorder. A blind placebo trial of medication will help Dan know if the treatment is effective for him.

3. Dan may enjoy reading a book about adults with ADHD, *You Mean I'm Not Crazy, Lazy. or Stupid?* by Kate Kelly and Peggy Ramundo, published by Fireside in 1993.

4. Dan should contact a counselor or psychologist to begin a therapeutic relationship in order to discuss some of his concerns about self-worth, personal relationships, career-related issues, and family-of-origin issues.

5. As soon as Dan arrives at his new university, he should make contact with the office of disability services. The professionals will be able to provide academic and emotional support for him as he completes doctoral work. The following modifications are recommended if available: extended time on exams, permission to tape class, notetakers, and the use of a calculator for math assignments and tests.

Psychometric Summary

WECHSLER ADULT INTELLIGENCE SCALE—THIRD EDITION (WAIS-III)
The WAIS-III is an individually administered clinical instrument for assessing the intellectual ability of adults over the age of 16. The adult's performance on the 13 subtests are summarized in three composite scores: the Verbal, the Performance, and the Full Scale Standard Scores.

   The following composite scores have a mean score of 100 with a standard deviation of 15. Scores between 90 and 109 are considered average.

(Continues)

Box 11.3   **Psychological Evaluation Using the WAIS-III** (Continued)

	Standard Score	90% Confidence Interval
Full Scale Score	110	106–113
Verbal IQ	113	108–117
Performance IQ	105	99–110

	Standard Score	90% Confidence Interval
Verbal/Comprehension Index	122	116–126
Perceptual/Organizational Index	103	97–109
Working Memory Index	99	93–105
Processing Speed Index	99	92–107

The following subtest scores have a mean of 10 with a standard deviation of 3. Scores between 7 and 13 are considered average.

Information	12	Picture Completion	14
Digit Span	11	Matrix Reasoning	10
Vocabulary	13	Block Design	8
Arithmetic	9	Picture Arrangement	12
Comprehension	11	Digit Symbol	10
Similarities	17	Symbol Search	10
Letter-Number Sequencing	10		

WOODCOCK-JOHNSON TESTS OF COGNITIVE ABILITIES

The Woodcock-Johnson Tests of Cognitive Abilities is an individually administered standardized test used to measure cognitive processes. The scores are reported in standard score form with a mean of 100 and a standard deviation of 15. Standard scores between 90 and 110 are considered average.

	Standard Score	90% Interval
Visual Auditory Learning	96	92–100
Short-Term Memory	103	98–108
Memory for Sentences	107	111–121
Memory for Words	96	90–102
Processing Speed	90	85–95
Visual Matching	86	80–92
Cross Out	97	90–104
Sound Blending	93	88–98
Visual Closure	103	96–110
Fluid Reasoning	103	100–106
Analysis-Synthesis	97	93–101
Concept Formation	110	106–114
Verbal Analogies	115	111–119

WOODCOCK-JOHNSON TESTS OF ACHIEVEMENT (WJTA-R)

The WJTA-R is an individually administered achievement test containing various subtests. The subtest scores are combined into composite scores: Broad Reading, Basic Reading Skills, Broad Mathematics, Broad Written Language,

Box 11.3 **Psychological Evaluation Using the WAIS-III** (Continued)

and Broad Knowledge. The Woodcock-Johnson yields standard scores with a mean of 100 and a standard deviation of 15. Standard scores between 90 and 110 are considered average.

	Standard Score	90% Interval
Letter-Word Identification	103	100–106
Passage Comprehension	118	114–122
BROAD READING	**110**	**107–113**
Calculation	97	94–100
Applied Problems	98	94–102
Quantitative Concepts	91	86–96
BASIC MATH SKILLS	**93**	**90–96**
BROAD MATHEMATICS	**98**	**95–101**

WIDE RANGE ACHIEVEMENT TEST REVISION 3 (WRAT 3)
The WRAT-3 is a general screener for academic achievement. The test consists of three subtests: reading, spelling, and arithmetic. The WRAT-3 yields standard scores with a mean of 100 and a standard deviation of 15. Standard scores between 85 and 115 are considered average.

	Standard Score	Percentile
Reading	111	77
Spelling	100	50
Arithmetic	89	23

REVISED NEO PERSONALITY INVENTORY (NEO-PI-R)
The NEO-PI-R is a rating scale designed to measure dimensions of personality. This instrument yields T-scores with a mean of 50 and a standard deviation of 10. Scores between 45 and 55 are average. Scores between 55 and 65 are high. Scores above 65 are considered very high.

	T-score	Description
Neuroticism	64	High
Extraversion	59	High
Openness to Experience	75	Very High
Agreeableness	46	Average
Conscientiousness	52	Average

BROWN ADD SCALES
The Brown ADD scales are a diagnostic system for the identification of adolescents and adults with attention deficit hyperactivity disorder. Clients are interviewed about symptomatology that is consistent with ADHD. The ADD Scales yield T-scores with a mean of 50 and a standard deviation of 10. Scores above 70 may suggest some clinical impairment.

	T-score
Activation	75
Attention	68
Effort	58
Affect	83
Memory	58
Total Score	72

that hypothesis (Carroll, 1993; Daniel, 1997; McGrew, 1997). Instead, Performance IQ tests appear to measure visual ability or "g_v" (Carroll, 1993; McGrew, 1997). If Matrix Reasoning does prove to be a measure of "g_f," then its addition affords a broader measure of the "$g_f–g_c$" abilities. Another unique characteristic of the WAIS-III is the extension of normative data up to the age of 89. As stated earlier, the four-factor structure for the 75–89 age group does not appear consistent with that for other age groups or the sample as a whole. Therefore, interpretation of the four factors for ages 75 to 89 should be made with caution.

WAIS-III STRENGTHS AND WEAKNESSES

The WAIS-III is a sound instrument that shares many of the strengths and weaknesses of the other Wechsler intelligence tests. To begin, the WAIS-III rests on an extensive body of research dating from the original W-B I. This base of research has contributed greatly to the fields of school psychology, clinical psychology, and special education (Harrison et al., 1997). The WAIS-III is similar to its predecessors so that much of this knowledge can be applied. This similarity also allowed the legions of clinicians who had used or were familiar with the WAIS-R to adapt easily to the newest battery. Most clinicians probably view the changes in artwork, spacing, and addition of color as improvements. Moreover, the calculation of IQs from scaled scores based on age instead of the reference group is more intuitive.

The psychometric properties of the WAIS-III are very strong. The normative sample is consistent with the high standards David Wechsler hoped to achieve when he revised his original W-B I. These standards of a representative, national sample are now customary for broadly marketed intelligence tests. Like the WAIS-R before it, the WAIS-III Full Scale IQ is extremely reli-

able, with an average reliability of .98 (The Psychological Corporation, 1997). Also, the concurrent validity studies of the WAIS-III with various other measures support the criterion-related validity of the WAIS-III. Based on the factor analytic studies in the manual, it appears that one can interpret a four-factor structure with confidence for all but the oldest age group.

Furthermore, the relationship between the WAIS-III and other measures or constructs has been more firmly established. Due to conorming with the WMS-III, differences in memory and cognitive abilities can be stated with greater confidence. The similarity in structure between the WISC-III and the WAIS-III enhances the continuity between these two measures. One can use a Wechsler cognitive measure at almost any age. Finally, the linking between the WAIS-III and the WIAT results in technically valid aptitude-achievement discrepancy norms (Harrison et al., 1997).

As is the case with the other Wechsler tests (Carroll, 1993; Harrison et al., 1997; McGrew et al., 1997), one of the main weaknesses of the WAIS-III is its lack of a clear theoretical framework. Attempts to fit the WAIS-III into current accepted theories of intelligence are often awkward and inelegant. Although the data do support a four-factor solution, neither this nor the two-factor, Verbal/Performance structure, fit well with currently accepted models of intelligence. If one ascribes to the psychometric Carroll/Horn-Cattell model, for example, the WAIS-III appears to have no subtests that measure Auditory processing ("g_a") or Long-Term Retrieval ("g_{lr}").

One criticism from several practitioners is the length and time for administration. Since most practitioners are interested in gaining as much information as possible, administration of 13 subtests seems to be the standard. This can often take up to an hour and a half. Another criticism is the continued emphasis on speed in many of the subtests. Although Matrix Reasoning is not a timed task, the other four Performance subtests, as well as Arithmetic, are.

In summary, one can say the WAIS-III is a battery that provides clinicians with a reliable measure of "g." The four Index scores, though new to the WAIS-III, seem valid in the light of the factor analyses presented in the *Technical Manual* (The Psychological Corporation, 1997). At the same time, the WAIS-III does not fit well into the psychometrically based theoretical frameworks like those of Carroll or Horn-Cattell. Clinicians operating from this perspective may decide not to rely solely on the WAIS-III for the intellectual assessment of adolescents and adults.

KAUFMAN ADOLESCENT AND ADULT INTELLIGENCE TEST

KAIT Theoretical Foundations

As noted in the previous section of this chapter, the WAIS-III and the WISC-III share a similar format and factor structure. In fact, the WAIS-III is essentially an extension of the WISC-III. Because of this, learning to administer the WAIS-III is relatively easy if one has been trained to administer the WISC-III. However, the Kaufmans' intelligence test for adults, the Kaufman Adolescent and Adult Intelligence Test (KAIT; Kaufman & Kaufman, 1993a) is a very different test from the Kaufman's intelligence test for children, the K-ABC (Kaufman & Kaufman, 1983a). Early in the *KAIT Manual*, Kaufman and Kaufman (1993b) stress that the KAIT was not designed as an upward extension of the K-ABC. The Kaufmans contend that adolescent and adult intelligence is based on constructs different from those of children. Hence, the KAIT has a different set of theoretical foundations (Brown, 1994; Kaufman & Kaufman, 1993b). Many of the differences between the KAIT and the K-ABC are a result of these different theoretical underpinnings. It should be noted that the KAIT is also very different from the Wechsler tests.

The KAIT is based on a synthesis of three developmental models of intelligence (Kaufman & Kaufman, 1993b). In discussing factors that guided the design of tasks appropriate for adolescents and adults, Kaufman and Kaufman (1993b) refer to two theories that address developmental and neurological changes posited to begin in early adolescence. Kaufman and Kaufman (1993b) cite the work of Golden and Luria in describing neurological developments in the prefrontal cortex occurring around age 12. According to Golden (as cited in Kaufman & Kaufman, 1993b), neurological developments at this age in the tertiary areas of the frontal lobes correspond to the development of functions such as decision making, hypothesis testing, and emotional control so critical to Luria's notion of planning ability. In addition, Kaufman and Kaufman consider aspects of Piaget's theory in which the abstract skills of formal operations begin at 11 or 12. Together these theories served as the initial impetus for the development of new tasks requiring abstract thinking and decision-making skills appropriate for adolescents and adults (Kaufman & Kaufman, 1993b, 1997c). As Brown (1994) points out, many of the KAIT subtests are designed to measure deductive rather than inductive reasoning. Finally, these theories provide the rationale for the lower bound age limit of 11 on the KAIT.

The main theoretical underpinnings of the KAIT, however, are found in the Cattell-Horn "g_f-g_c" model of intelligence (Kaufman & Kaufman, 1993b). Although the WJ-R COG is also based on "g_f-g_c" theory (Woodcock & Mather, 1989), Kaufman and Kaufman point out that the KAIT differs from the WJ-R COG in substantive ways. A main distinction between the WJ-R Cog and the KAIT is that the KAIT is tied to the fluid–crystallized dichotomy. The WJ-R COG, on the other hand, was designed to assess the eight abilities included in Horn's (1994) expanded theory (Woodcock & Mather, 1989). Because of its basis in the fluid–crystallized dichotomy, the KAIT consists of a Crystallized scale and a Fluid scale (Kaufman & Kaufman, 1993b). The tasks on the Crystallized scale are in line with Horn's current writings on crystallized intelligence (see Chapter 2 on theory). The Fluid scale, however, reflects abilities closer to Cattell and Horn's earlier conceptualization of fluid intelligence rather than the newer definitions found in Horn's (Horn, 1994; Horn & Noll, 1997) more recent work (Kaufman & Kaufman, 1993b). In their earlier writings, Horn and Cattell included the influence of short-term acquisition and retrieval, response speed, and long-term storage and retrieval in their conceptualization of fluid intelligence (Flanagan, Alfonso, & Flanagan, 1994; Kaufman & Kaufman, 1993b). Consistent with this broader definition, the KAIT Fluid scale includes tasks that incorporate memory and speed components.

Structure of the KAIT

The KAIT Core Battery consists of six subtests, three for the Crystallized scale and three for the Fluid scale. The three subtests comprising the Crystallized scale are Definitions, Auditory Comprehension, and Double Meanings. Those for the Fluid scale are Rebus Learning, Logical steps, and Mystery Codes. The Crystallized and Fluid scales yield Crystallized and Fluid IQ scores and combine to produce the Composite Intelligence scale, a measure of overall intellectual functioning. The KAIT also contains four additional subtests that, together with the Core Battery, make up the Extended Battery. The four additional subtests are Memory for Block Designs, Famous Faces, Rebus Delayed Recall, and Auditory Delayed Recall. Memory for Block Designs can be substituted for one of the three subtests on the Fluid scale, while Famous Faces is an alternative subtest on the Crystallized scale. Memory for Block Designs and Famous Faces are used in the calculation of IQ scores only when another subtest from the Core Battery is not used. The Rebus Delayed Recall and the Auditory Delayed Recall are not used in the calculation of IQs but can be used to make comparisons between immediate and delayed memory (Flanagan et al., 1994; Kaufman & Kaufman, 1993b). These two delayed memory tasks also provide a measure of Horn's Long-Term Storage and Retrieval ability (Kaufman &Kaufman, 1997c). The final component of

the KAIT battery is a short Mental Status subtest, which consists of 10 items.

The KAIT has been normed for use with adolescents and adults from age 11 to 85 or older. Each of the three intelligence scales (Crystallized, Fluid, and Composite) has a mean of 100 and a standard deviation of 15. The mean for each subtest is 10, and the standard deviation is 3.

KAIT Subtests

As alluded to previously, few of the KAIT subtests are found in an analogous format on the K-ABC. In fact, the KAIT subtests seem new and interesting, even though many are adaptations from other sources. The psychometric information listed below for each subtest is taken directly from the *KAIT Manual* (Kaufman & Kaufman, 1993b).

Definitions

On this subtest, the examinee figures out a word based on a clue about the word's meaning and a presentation of the word with some letters missing. An example of a clue is, "It's awfully old." The examiner points to the line "_ N T _ Q _ _" and asks, "what word goes here?" The answer, of course, is "ANTIQUE." Examinees have 30 seconds to respond to each item. Like other tests of vocabulary, Definitions was developed to assess verbal concept formation and word knowledge (Kaufman & Kaufman, 1993b). In addition to Samples A and B, items 1 and 2 can serve as teaching items. Examiners discontinue this subtest after five consecutive scores of 0. Of course, this subtest cannot be administered to examinees who cannot read or spell. Definitions is on the Crystallized scale and is one of the six core subtests. Kaufman and Kaufman (1993b) point out that as with other tests of vocabulary, Definitions is an excellent measure of "g."

PSYCHOMETRIC PROPERTIES

Mean split-half reliability = .90
Average test-retest reliability = .95.

Correlation with Crystallized Scale = .76

Correlation with Composite Intelligence Scale = .75

Correlation with Fluid Scale = .64.

Factor loading on Crystallized Scale = .80

"g" loading = .82 (highest in the battery)

Mean subtest specificity is ample

Rebus Learning

On Rebus Learning, the examinee learns the word or concept associated with a rebus drawing and then attempts to read sentences or phrases made from the drawings. Rebus Learning is similar in format to Visual-Auditory Learning on the WJ-R. However, unlike Visual-Auditory Learning, the examiner does not correct each error on Rebus Leaning. Instead, all symbols but the last few are presented twice, once initially and again to review with the next new set of symbols. The discontinue rules for Rebus Learning are based on the number correct per block of items and are provided on the easel pages and on the test record. Rebus Learning is a Fluid subtest and is one of the six core subtests.

PSYCHOMETRIC PROPERTIES

Mean split-half reliability = .93

Average test-retest reliability = .81

Correlation with Fluid Scale = .61

Correlation with Composite Intelligence Scale = .68

Correlation with Crystallized Scale = .63

Factor loading on Fluid Factor = .55

"g" loading = .72.

Mean subtest specificity is ample

Logical Steps

For Logical Steps, the examiner gives the examinee a set of logical facts both visually and in spoken format. The examinee then answers a question based on the information presented.

For example, the examinee might be told that a staircase has seven steps. On the staircase Bob is always one step above Ann, and Bob is on step 6. What step is Ann on? Paper and pencil are allowed to help work problems, but the subtest has a 30-second time limit for each item. This subtest does not have a parallel on other tests of intelligence. In fact, this subtest was inspired by a section of the *Law School Admissions Test* (LSAT). Kaufman and Kaufman (1993b) state that Logical Steps was designed to measure deductive reasoning and syllogistic thinking, both of which are associated with formal operations and planning ability. The discontinue rule for this subtest is based on the number correct per block of items. The corresponding easel pages and the test record have reminders about when to discontinue. Logical Steps is a core subtest and is on the Fluid scale.

PSYCHOMETRIC PROPERTIES

Mean split-half reliability = .90

Average test-retest reliability = .76

Correlation with Fluid Scale = .64

Correlation with Composite Intelligence Scale = .67

Correlation with Crystallized Scale = .61

Factor loading on Fluid Scale = .66

"g" loading = .72

Mean subtest specificity is ample overall but merely adequate at ages 70–85+

Auditory Comprehension

On Auditory Comprehension, the examinee listens to a tape of fictitious news stories and responds to both literal and inferential questions about the stories. Unlike similar tasks involving memory for stories on tests like the WMS-III and the WJ-R, the examinee is not asked to repeat the entire story, only respond to questions. The discontinue rule for Auditory Comprehension is based on the subtotal of correct responses per set of items. These rules are listed on the record form and on the easel pages. Auditory Comprehension is a Crystallized subtest and is one of the six core subtests.

PSYCHOMETRIC PROPERTIES

Mean split-half reliability = .89

Average test-retest reliability = .77

Correlation with Crystallized Scale = .70

Correlation with Composite Intelligence Scale = .72

Correlation with Fluid Scale = .63

Factor loading on Crystallized Scale = .69

"g" loading = .79

Mean subtest specificity is ample

Mystery Codes

On this subtest the examinee studies a set of codes associated with pictorial stimuli. The examinee is then asked to figure out the code for a new stimulus based on the information provided. Items 1–6 and a–e are found in the easel, but items 7–18 are in a separate Mystery Codes Item Booklet. Examiners should note that some of the items on Mystery Codes are scored 2, 1, or 0. If the examinee gets fewer than 3 points on the first 6 items, items a–e are administered and then the subtest is discontinued. Otherwise, items 7–18 are administered in the Mystery Codes Item Booklet. If items 7–18 are started, all those items should be administered, and the subtest is discontinued following item 18. Items 1–6 have a 1-minute time limit; items a–e do not have a time limit. An examinee is allowed a 3-minute interval to work items 7–12 and another 3-minute interval for items 13–18. Brown (1994) notes that this subtest can require an extensive amount of teaching in order for the examinee to understand the task. Mystery Codes is the fifth core subtest and is on the Fluid scale.

PSYCHOMETRIC PROPERTIES

Mean split-half reliability = .87

Average test-retest reliability = .72

Correlation with Fluid Scale = .63

Correlation with Composite Intelligence Scale = .64

Correlation with Crystallized Scale = .56

Factor loading on the Fluid Scale = .71

"g" loading = .69

Mean subtest specificity is ample

Double Meanings

On the Double Meanings subtest, the examinee considers two sets of word clues and then is asked to generate a word with two meanings that relates to both sets of presented clues. For example, the two sets of words displayed might be "Animal/Vampire" and "Baseball/Stick," with the correct response being "bat." The time limit for each item is 30 seconds. Examiners discontinue testing after four consecutive scores of 0. Double Meanings is the sixth and final core subtest. It is on the Crystallized scale.

PSYCHOMETRIC PROPERTIES

Mean split-half reliability = .89

Average test-retest reliability = .79

Correlation with Crystallized Scale = .74

Correlation with Composite Intelligence Scale = .74

Correlation with Fluid Scale = .64

Factor loading on Crystallized Scale = .69

"g" loading = .80

Mean subtest specificity is ample

Rebus Delayed Recall

On the delayed task, the examinee reads a new set of phrases and sentences made from the rebus drawings presented earlier in the battery in subtest 2. Examiners give no prior warning that a delayed subtest will occur. This subtest is administered about 45 minutes after subtest 2, following the intervening subtests. In the manual, Kaufman and Kaufman (1993b) stress that the two measures of delayed recall, Rebus Delayed Recall and Auditory Delayed Recall (see below), are not to be considered true KAIT subtests. These two measures were developed and included in the battery only to allow comparisons between a Rebus Learning score and a Rebus Delayed Recall score and between Auditory Comprehension and Auditory Delayed Recall. Chapter 5 of the manual provides tables and rules for making comparisons and for interpreting these comparisons. Neither of the delayed tasked is intended to measure fluid or crystallized intelligence or a specific ability. As a result, the delayed tasks were not included in the KAIT factor analyses and the only psychometric information available is reliability.

RELIABILITY INFORMATION

Mean internal consistency = .91

Auditory Delayed Recall

For this delayed recall subtest, the examinee answers further questions about the fictitious news stories introduced in subtest 4, Auditory Comprehension. This task is also administered without warning, following a 25-minute delay in which the intervening subtests are administered.

RELIABILITY INFORMATION

Mean internal consistency = .71

Memory for Block Designs

Memory for Block Designs is similar in format to the block design subtests found on other tests of intelligence. On the KAIT block design task, however, the examinee is allowed to examine the pictorial design only 5 seconds before it is removed. At that point, the examinee is asked to make the design from memory. The examinee is allowed 45 seconds to complete the design, and no bonus points are awarded for quick responses. In fact, if the examinee is working toward a correct solution (four blocks placed correctly with no incorrectly placed blocks), he or she may continue another 45 seconds. If the examinee produces the design correctly in the additional time, he or she is still given credit for a correct response. Items 1 and 2 are worth 2 points. The remaining items are scored 0 or 1. Memory for Block Designs is a supplemental Fluid subtest and is not normally used to compute the Fluid IQ or the Composite Intelligence scale. This subtest can be used as a substitute for other Fluid subtests.

PSYCHOMETRIC PROPERTIES

Mean internal consistency = .79

Average test-retest reliability = .73

Correlation with Fluid Scale = .61

Correlation with Composite Intelligence Scale = .58

Correlation with the Crystallized Scale = .47

Factor loading on Fluid Scale = .76

"g" loading = .61 (lowest among the subtests and possibly a reason for its status as a supplemental subtest)

Mean subtest specificity is ample

Famous Faces

Famous Faces is similar to the Faces & Places subtest on the K-ABC. On Famous Faces, the examinee is asked to name famous people based on their picture and a short verbal clue about them. Unlike Faces & Places where the child is shown one picture per item, on Famous Faces the examinee is to respond to one out of two or two out of three famous faces per item. This is the only KAIT subtest besides the two delayed recall subtests without teaching items. The discontinue rule for Famous Faces is four consecutive scores of 0. Famous Faces is a supplemental subtest on the Crystallized scale. Because it is supplemental, this subtest is not routinely used to calculate the Crystallized or Composite IQs.

PSYCHOMETRIC PROPERTIES

Mean split-half reliability = .92

Average test-retest reliability = .84

Correlation with Crystallized Scale = .69

Correlation with Composite Intelligence Scale = .64

Correlation with Fluid Scale = .49

Factor loading on Crystallized Scale = .84

"g" loading = .69 (this is the lowest of a Crystallized subtest on the first factor and is probably among the reasons Famous Faces is a supplemental test)

Mean subtest specificity is ample

Mental Status

The Mental Status subtest consists of 10 simple questions that are similar in format to questions found on many mental status examinations. Example questions are, "Right now, who is the president of the United States?" and "What city are we in right now?" Kaufman and Kaufman (1997c) point out that most adolescents and adults will answer at least 9 of the items correctly. Normative information for Mental Status raw scores is found in Table D.5 of the *KAIT Manual* (Kaufman & Kaufman, 1993b). This subtest can be helpful with individuals who have neurological impairment. The subtest can also be used as a screener to help determine if the KAIT can be administered validly.

CORRELATIONAL INFORMATION Mental Status correlates .31 with Crystallized IQ and .25 with Fluid IQ. The correlation between Mental Status and the Composite scale is .30.

McGrew and Flanagan (1996) have also conducted a set of independent analyses looking at the factor loadings of KAIT subtests on the first unrotated factor, "g," as well as the subtest specificity of each subtest. In general, the findings of McGrew and Flanagan were similar to those in the *KAIT Manual* (Kaufman & Kaufman, 1993b). The few overall differences of consequence related to subtest specificity. In their analyses, McGrew and Flanagan found that both Auditory Comprehension and Rebus Learning had adequate specificity as opposed to Kaufman and Kaufman's (1993b) findings of ample specificity for these two subtests. The only subtest with less than adequate subtest specificity from the McGrew and Flanagan work was Auditory Delayed Recall. However, Kaufman and Kaufman (1993b) stress that this subtest should be interpreted only in relation to the second subtest, Auditory Recall.

Psychometric Properties of the KAIT

Standardization

The national standardization data for the KAIT were collected from April 1988 to October 1991 (Kaufman & Kaufman, 1993b). A representative sample of 2,000 individuals between the ages of 11 and 85+ years was obtained from the four major regions of the United States. The sample was stratified on gender, geographic region, socioeconomic status, and race or ethnic group according to 1988 U.S. Census data projections. There was a slight overrepresentation of individuals from the West and underrepresentation from the Northeast. The sample was organized into 13 age bands (11, 12, 13–14, 15–16, 17–19, 20–24, 25–34, 35–44, 45–54, 55–64, 65–69, 70–74, 75–85+) with 100 to 250 subjects at each level. The three oldest groups had 100 subjects each, while the two groups between ages 25 and 44 were the largest with 250 per group. Each of the four youngest groups consisted of 125 individuals, the two groups between 17 and 24 both had 150, and the two groups from 45 to 64 had 250 subjects. In their review of the KAIT, Flanagan et al. (1994) concluded that the normative sample is large and matches the U.S. Census Bureau predictions of the U.S. population on the stratification variables. At the same time, Brown (1994) suggested that the sample size for ages 11 to 24, while adequate, could be larger, given the variability in developmental rates at these ages.

Reliability

INTERNAL CONSISTENCY. The split-half reliability coefficients for the three KAIT IQ scores are high: .95 for Crystallized IQ; .95 for Fluid IQ; and .97 for Composite IQ (Kaufman & Kaufman, 1993b). Typically, scores above .90 are considered good. For the six core subtests, reliability coefficients range from .87 for Mystery Codes to a .93 on Rebus Learning. The two auxiliary tests, Famous Faces and Memory for Block Designs, have reliability coefficients of .92 and .79, respectively. The reliability coefficients for the two delayed recall tests are .91 for Rebus Delayed recall and .71 for Auditory Delayed Recall.

TEST-RETEST STABILITY. One hundred and fifty-three adolescents and adults in three age groups (11–19, 20–54, and 55–85+) were administered the KAIT twice over an interval of 6 to 99 days. The mean interval was 31 days. The mean test-retest coefficients were high for the Crystallized (.94) and the Composite (.94) IQs. Although the .87 for Fluid IQ is lower, it is still adequate. Average coefficients for the core subtests ranged from .72 for Mystery Codes to .95 for Definitions. In this sample, five of the core subtests and one subtest from the extended battery had test-retest coefficients below .80. These subtests were Auditory Comprehension, Double Meanings, Logical Steps, Mystery Codes, Memory for Block Designs, and Auditory Delayed Recall. As a result of the relatively low stability coefficients for these subtests, Kaufman and Kaufman (1993b) recommend that clinicians attempt interpretation of the KAIT by focusing on subtest groupings and not on individual subtests (Dumont & Hagberg, 1994).

In the *KAIT Manual*, Kaufman and Kaufman (1993b) also present the results of an independent test-retest study by Pinion with an interval of about one year (as cited in Kaufman & Kaufman, 1993b). In this study, the test-retest coefficient for Composite IQ was .92, for Crystallized .85, and for Fluid .79. The practice effects were naturally lower over this extended period with an average gain of 2.7 on the Composite IQ, and

2.4 on both the Crystallized and Fluid IQs. Flanagan et al. (1994) observe that these one-year stability coefficients are excellent.

Standard Error of Measurement

The mean SEM across the 13 age groups is 2.5 for the Composite Intelligence score. For both the Fluid and Crystallized IQs the average SEM is 3.2. The mean SEMs for subtests on the Crystallized scale are similar to the subtests on the Fluid scale. In the core battery the SEMs range from .8 on Rebus Learning to 1.1 on Mystery Codes. Rebus Delayed Recall and Auditory Delayed Recall have average SEMs of .9 and 1.6 respectively.

Validity

The *KAIT Manual* (Kaufman & Kaufman, 1993b) provides several types of evidence that support the validity of the KAIT, the Fluid and Crystallized scales, and the placement of each subtest in its respective scale. The first evidence is correlations of the KAIT and other tests of intelligence. The *KAIT Manual* also includes results from both exploratory and confirmatory factor analyses. Finally, the manual contains information about age changes in the raw scores of subtests and IQ scales.

CONCURRENT VALIDITY, KAIT AND WECHSLER SCALES. Unfortunately, correlational studies of the KAIT with the WISC-III or the WAIS-III could not be located. However, the *KAIT Manual* presents the results of correlations of the KAIT with the WISC-R and the WAIS-R. A sample of 461 individuals in five age groups (11–16, 16–19, 20–34, 35–49, and 50–83) were administered the KAIT and either the WISC-R or the WAIS-R. Correlations between the KAIT Composite IQ and the WISC-R or WAIS-R Full Scale are high and ranged from .82 to .88. The mean correlation across age groups was .84. The Crystallized IQs correlated more highly with WISC-R/WAIS-R Verbal IQ (range .78–.85) than with Performance IQs (range .57–.74). As

Box 11.4   **Comparison of WAIS-R and KAIT Scores on a Sample of College Students**

A study conducted at the University of Georgia Learning Disabilities Center (Morgan, Sullivan, Darden, & Gregg, 1997) compared WAIS-R and KAIT scores for a sample of college students that included 30 students with learning disabilities (LD) and 30 students without learning disabilities. On the composite scores, the researchers found no interaction between group and test and no significant differences between tests or groups. Likewise, a comparison of the WAIS-R Verbal scale and the KAIT Crystallized scale yielded no significant findings. In other words, in this sample the WAIS-R Full Scale and the KAIT Composite IQs produced essentially equivalent results. The same was true for the WAIS-R Verbal and the KAIT Crystallized. However, a comparison of the WAIS-R Performance scale and the KAIT Fluid scale revealed significant differences between the tests. In both the LD and non-LD groups, the average KAIT Fluid score was significantly below the WAIS-R Performance score. The difference in the LD group was 3.17 points and the difference in the non-LD group was 5.23 points.

The authors discuss several possible explanations for their findings. One explanation is the age difference of the norms. The WAIS-R norms are 10 years older than the KAIT norms. This is certainly a reasonable hypothesis, yet it is surprising that the effect appeared only in the Performance versus Fluid scale comparison. Though not discussed by the authors, an alternative explanation might be differences in the abilities measured by each scale. The KAIT Fluid scale is reported to be a measure of fluid intelligence. The exact ability measured by the WAIS-R Performance subtests remains an issue of debate (Kaufman & Kaufman, 1997c). Carroll (1993) states that the WAIS-R Performance scales "can be taken as an approximate measure of Factor Gv, or somewhat less validly, of factor Gf" (p.702). Whatever abilities the WAIS-R Performance scale measures, Kaufman and Kaufman (1997c) conclude that the two scales measure different abilities. This difference in abilities measured may account for the findings of differences in scores on the Performance and Fluid scales for both LD and non-LD college students.

Kaufman and Kaufman (1993b) observe, this is expected given the idea that the Wechsler Verbal scale is considered to be a good measure of crystallized ability. The KAIT Fluid IQs correlated about equally with Verbal and Performance IQs. Kaufman and Kaufman propose three possible explanations for this finding: (1) the Wechsler Performance subtests may not be measuring fluid ability; (2) two of the KAIT fluid subtests have strong verbal requirements (Logical Steps and Rebus Learning); (3) some of the Wechsler Verbal subtests may demand fluid ability. The mean differences between IQ scores on the KAIT and the Wechsler tests were within the range that would be predicted based on the Flynn (1987) effect.

CONCURRENT VALIDITY, KAIT AND K-ABC. Correlations among the scales of the KAIT and the K-ABC were obtained with a sample of 124 adolescents aged 11 and 12. The correlation for the KAIT Composite Intelligence and

the K-ABC Mental Processing Composite is moderate, .66. Interestingly, the correlation between the KAIT Composite IQ and the K-ABC Achievement score is higher, .82. The KAIT Crystallized scale had its highest correlations with the K-ABC Achievement scale. Because the Achievement scale is the only scale on K-ABC with tests of crystallized ability, this finding would be predicted. Based on these same hypotheses, one would expect the KAIT Fluid scale to correlate more highly with the K-ABC Mental Processing Composite (MPC) than the Achievement scale. This was not the case. The KAIT Fluid scale correlated about equally with the MPC and Achievement scales. As with the Wechsler Performance scale, it may be that the MPC is not a measure of fluid ability (Kaufman & Kaufman, 1993b). Overall, KAIT IQs are about 4 points lower than the K-ABC scores. This difference is slightly more than one would expect with a restandardized test (Kaufman & Kaufman, 1993b).

CONCURRENT VALIDITY, KAIT AND STANFORD-BINET—FOURTH EDITION. The KAIT Composite IQ correlated highly with the Binet-4 Test Composite (.87). The Crystallized IQ had higher correlations with the Binet-4 Verbal Reasoning (.78) and Quantitative Reasoning (.77) than with Abstract/Visual Reasoning (.66). This is consistent with expectations due to the fact that Verbal and Quantitative Reasoning were developed as measures of crystallized ability and Abstract/Visual Reasoning as a measure of fluid ability. Again, the Fluid scale did not conform to predictions. The KAIT Fluid scale had a slightly higher correlation with the Binet-4 Verbal and Quantitative Reasoning than with the Abstract/Visual Reasoning scale. This pattern of correlations with the Binet-4 may be related to the findings suggesting that the Abstract/Visual Reasoning scale lacks construct validity (Kaufman & Kaufman, 1993b).

FACTOR ANALYTIC RESULTS. The results of both exploratory and confirmatory factor analyses are presented in the *KAIT Manual* (Kaufman & Kaufman, 1993b). The first set of factor loadings from an exploratory analysis are the loadings of each subtest on the first, unrotated factor "g" when two factors (Fluid and Crystallized) were extracted. Across all age groups, the factor loadings for the subtests on the "g" factor ranged from a low of .61 for Memory For Block Designs to a high of .82 for Definitions. The three core subtests of the Crystallized scale had loadings of about .80 and the three core Fluid subtests had loadings around .70. One can conclude, therefore, that the six core subtests are good measures of general intelligence, "g."

Exploratory analyses were also used to consider two-, three-, and four-factor solutions across age groups. The two-factor solution emerged as the most meaningful. In the total sample, Crystallized subtests had loadings on the Crystallized scale from .69 for Auditory Comprehension and Double Meanings to .84 for Famous Faces. The loadings of these subtests on the Fluid scale ranged from .07 to .16. Overall, the Fluid subtests had loadings on the Fluid scale from .55 for Rebus Learning to .76 for Memory for Block Designs and loadings on the Crystallized scale below .23. In particular age groups, several of the subtests had moderate secondary loadings on the alternative factor. For example, in the 15 to 19 age group Double Meanings had a loading of .44 on the Crystallized factor and .41 on the Fluid factor. Usually, secondary loadings should not exceed .30, and clinicians may want to use caution in interpreting an individual's profile at those age levels (Flanagan et al., 1994). Generally, though, the results of these exploratory factor analyses support the validity of the battery.

Confirmatory factor analyses provided further evidence for the validity of the two-factor model (Kaufman & Kaufman, 1993b). In analyses that compared one-factor "g," two-factor (crystallized and fluid), and three-factor (crystallized, fluid, and memory) models, the goodness-of-fit indices suggested that the two-factor model provided an acceptable fit for the data. This was true for all ages except the 70 to 85 age group. For this group, none of the models fit the data particularly well. It is interesting to note that the three-factor solution in all age groups except the eldest also yielded goodness-of-fit indices indicative of an acceptable model fit. In this model, the Crystallized factor remained the same as in the two-factor model, but the Fluid factor was divided into two factors. The first of these factors was a "pure" fluid factor more in line with Horn's (1994) more recent writings that consisted of Logical Steps and Mystery Codes. The next factor was a memory factor consisting of Rebus Learning and Memory for Block Designs. However, this three-factor model did not improve the fit significantly and was therefore rejected in favor of the more parsimonious two-factor model. In summary, then, the exploratory and confirmatory factor analyses supported the construct validity of the Crystallized and Fluid scales, up to the age of 70, as well as for the placement of subtests on one scale or another.

The finding of a two-factor solution was replicated in a later study in separate samples of Caucasian, African American, and Hispanic adolescents and adults using exploratory factor analysis (Kaufman, Kaufman, & McLean, 1995). It would be interesting to see a similar across-groups study using confirmatory factor analysis, so that factor structure could be constrained across groups.

AGE CHANGES AND DEVELOPMENTAL TRENDS ON SUBTESTS AND IQ SCALES. Most of the data on age changes for the KAIT were as one would predict. Mean raw scores on all subtests increased relatively steadily from age 11 to the 20- to 24-year-old age group. Given the general advances in education across these ages, one would expect increases in raw scores. Raw scores on the Crystallized subtest were at their highest in the 20–24 age group and remained stable until about 50–54. After age 54, average scores on the Crystallized subtests dropped slowly but steadily. For the Fluid subtests, mean raw scores reached a peak at ages 20–24. Fluid raw scores dropped slightly at 25 to 29 and then remain stable until age 54. After 54, these raw scores decline steeply. As Kaufman and Kaufman (1993b) note, these Fluid and Crystallized changes are in line with predictions from the Horn-Cattell theory.

INTERCORRELATIONS AMONG SUBTESTS AND SCALES. The correlation between the Fluid and Crystallized scales is .72. As Kaufman and Kaufman (1993b) point out, this denotes an overlap in variance of about 52%. The correlation for these two scales is similar to that of the Verbal and Performance scales of the WAIS-III (r = .75). For the total KAIT standardization sample, the intercorrelation among the four Crystallized subtests was about .64 and about .53 for the Fluid subtests.

Administration and Scoring

Administration

Administration time for the six subtests of the KAIT core battery is approximately an hour.

Inclusion of the two supplemental tests and two recall tests increases the administration time to about an hour and a half. The KAIT is organized in an easel format. Easel 1 consists of the six core subtests, and Easel 2 contains the additional four subtests from the expanded battery as well as the Mental Status questions. Directions for the subtests are included on the easel pages, so no additional manuals are needed during administration. However, a stopwatch is necessary. None of the items on the KAIT have bonus points for quick responses, but five of the subtests require a response within a time limit.

Both easels have tabbed starting pages for each subtest, but subtests are presented in the order recommended for administration. The recommended order is particularly important if the delayed memory subtests are to be administered. All subtests except the delayed recall tasks and Famous Faces include teaching items. On these items, the examiner is allowed to explain or teach an approach if the examinee does not respond correctly. Items that are considered teaching items are so designated on the easel page for that item. All examinees begin with sample items and start testing with item one. In other words, there are no age-specific starting points on the KAIT. Discontinue rules vary from subtest to subtest and are marked on the record form.

Scoring

Scoring on the KAIT is relatively straightforward, and most items are scored either 0 or 1. The exceptions to the 0/1 scoring are on Rebus Learning, Rebus Recall, and Mystery Codes, where points may be earned for partially correct responses. In addition, items 1–3 on Double Meanings are scored 2, 1, or 0. Scoring on Auditory Comprehension can be slightly tricky, as some subjectivity is required. The manual provides sample responses, but as is always the case, examinees sometimes give responses that are not in the manual.

The protocol permits the examiner to obtain raw score summations easily for each subtest.

When computing a raw score for Mystery Codes, though, examiners need to remember to award credit for items a–e, which are not administered but are given credit with a correct response on items 1 through 6. If all items are administered on the two delayed subtests, raw scores are obtained by simply summing item scores. If, however, an examinee is not given all of the delay items, the examiner uses a chart found in the test record to convert an observed raw score to a total raw score.

Once the subtest raw scores are obtained, the examiner has the option of using the norms tables in the manual and the profile page on back of the protocol to calculate scores by hand or of using the computerized scoring. If scoring by hand, the procedure is similar to that for other standardized intelligence tests. The examiner transfers raw scores to the front page of the test record and obtains subtest scaled scores. After the examiner calculates sums of subtest scaled scores, he or she can use Tables D.2, D.3, and D.4 in Appendix D of the manual to get IQ scores for each scale. Confidence intervals, percentile ranks, mean scaled scores, and descriptive categories for IQ scores are also found in the same tables. At this point, the examiner can compare Crystallized versus Fluid IQs, and if desired, a pattern of subtest strengths and weaknesses.

The Profile Analysis page on the back of the test record has all the necessary information to determine significant subtest strengths and weaknesses. In determining subtest strengths and weaknesses, Kaufman and Kaufman (1993b) recommend comparing subtest scaled scores with the mean from the six core subtests. If, however, a significant difference between Crystallized and Fluid IQs is found, Kaufman and Kaufman (1993b) advise clinicians to compare Crystallized subtest scores with the mean scaled score on the Crystallized scale. This Crystallized mean is derived from only the three core Crystallized subtests, even if all four were administered. Likewise, with a significant Crystallized/Fluid difference, clinicians are advised to compare Fluid subtests with the mean of the three core Fluid subtests.

Interpretation of the KAIT

The *KAIT Manual* (Kaufman & Kaufman, 1993b) provides a substantial amount of information to assist clinicians in their interpretation of the KAIT. After completing the front of the test record, Kaufman and Kaufman recommend beginning by examining the difference between the Crystallized and Fluid IQs. If the difference is not significant, then interpretation of the Composite Intelligence Scale is appropriate. Kaufman and Kaufman write that the Composite IQ is intended as a unitary measure to show the overall intellectual functioning of an individual who evidences no significant difference between the Crystallized and Fluid scales. With no significant difference, one may conclude that an individual's cognitive abilities, as measured by the KAIT, are relatively equal. On the other hand, if a significant difference does exist between the Crystallized and Fluid scales, the Kaufmans strongly admonish clinicians not to interpret the Composite IQ. They reason that individuals who demonstrate meaningful differences on their Crystallized and Fluid IQs should be described by two separate IQs.

Because the empirical evidence does support the validity of the Fluid and Crystallized scales on the KAIT, interpretation of these two scales appears warranted. According to Kaufman and Kaufman (1993b), the Fluid scale measures an individual's intelligence when faced with novel problems, and the Crystallized scale measures ability when faced with academic and experience-related problems. Clearly, a significantly higher score on one scale or the other indicates a significantly stronger ability in that area. When significantly different, clinicians can further describe the discrepancy between the Fluid and Crystallized IQs in terms of the unusualness of that difference in a normal population of individuals using Table 5.3 of the manual. Once the clinician has examined possible differences between the Crystallized and Fluid IQs, Kaufman and Kaufman advise clinicians to identify subtest strengths and weaknesses.

Box 11.5   KAIT Subtests According to Current Horn-Cattell Theory

As has been emphasized, one of the main theoretical underpinnings of the KAIT is fluid and crystallized intelligence. However, Horn and Cattell (Horn, 1994; Horn & Cattell, 1966) have expanded their theory beyond the original dichotomy. One might naturally wonder how the KAIT subtests fit with the more expanded theory that posits 8 to 10 broad abilities. To explore this question, McGrew (1997) presents the results of an unpublished manuscript (Flanagan and McGrew, as cited in McGrew, 1997) involving a factor analysis of the KAIT with the WJ-R. These researchers used the WJ-R because it was designed in accordance with the expanded Horn-Cattell theory. All of the subtests on the Crystallized scale appeared to be measures of crystallized intelligence "g_c." At the same time, all but one of the Crystallized subtests turned out to be mixed measures of more than one factor. Of the four Crystallized subtests, only Famous Faces was a pure measure of "g_c." Both Definitions and Double Meanings appear to measure Reading/Writing "g_{rw}" ability as well as "g_c." Interestingly, in Carroll's (1993) theory reading and writing abilities are subsumed under crystallized intelligence. Auditory Comprehension seems to measure Short-Term Memory "g_{sm}" in addition to "g_c."

On the KAIT Fluid scale, all of the subtests were strong or pure measures of their respective factors. Two subtests seemed to be pure measures of fluid intelligence "g_f," while the other two appeared to be measures of memory. Logical Steps and Mystery Codes were the two subtests that loaded clearly on a "g_f" factor. Rebus Leaning appeared to be a measure of Long-Term Memory "g_{lr}," and Memory for Block Designs loaded on the "g_{sm}" factor. Overall, these findings not only help place the KAIT in relation to current theory, but they can also aid clinicians in the process of interpretation.

The Profile Analysis page on the back of the test record allows clinicians to determine significant subtest strengths and weaknesses at the .05 level. However, Flanagan and her colleagues (1994) encourage examiners to use the tables in Appendix B of the manual for this purpose, because the tables provide more complete information. Once significant strengths and weaknesses have been identified, Kaufman and Kaufman (1993b) recommend that clinicians generate hypotheses about an examinee's intellectual abilities based on groupings of subtests. The use of subtest groupings seems particularly important, as five of the KAIT subtests have test-retest reliabilities under .80. Chapter 6 of the manual presents several tables of abilities believed to be shared by two or more subtests. Furthermore, the tables list the test-retest reliabilities of the subtest groupings. For example, Logical Steps and Mystery Codes are listed in Table 6.2 as sharing the ability of "Hypothetico-deductive reasoning (planning) with novel stimuli." Separately, these two subtests have test-retest reliabilities below .80. Together, though, their test-retest reliability is an adequate .83.

If hypotheses of abilities based on subtest groupings cannot be found, Kaufman and Kaufman (1993b) suggest that clinicians consider interpreting individual subtest strengths and weaknesses. In fact, the subtests generally demonstrate ample subtest specificity for this purpose. However, Kaufman and Kaufman do urge caution in the practice of interpreting unique abilities measured by a single subtest. Moreover, some researchers argue against the interpretation of single subtest strengths or weaknesses (McDermott, Fantuzzo, Glutting, Watkins, & Baggaley, 1992). Given the test-retest reliabilities under .80 for five subtests, the use of caution does seem appropriate when interpreting an individual subtest (Flanagan et al., 1994; Kaufman & Kaufman, 1993b). As always, additional information should be considered when evaluating hypotheses of an individual's cognitive strengths or weaknesses (see Chapter 17).

Neither of the delayed recall tasks (Rebus Delayed Recall and Auditory Delayed Recall) was included in the factor analyses of the KAIT. Kaufman and Kaufman (1993b) state that these two tasks were not developed as measures of Fluid or Crystallized abilities, nor are they meant to be measures of specific mental abilities. The sole purpose of these tasks is for comparison with either Rebus Leaning or Auditory Comprehension. No other interpretation of the delayed recall scores is recommended. In fact, Kaufman and Kaufman (1993b) did not combine these two delayed recall tasks into a delayed memory scale because the factor analytic results did not support the validity of such a scale. It seems that retention of rebus symbols over time is not related to the retention of information from stories. Therefore, interpretation of immediate versus delay should be done separately for the two sets of subtests. The authors go on to say that the assessment of memory on the KAIT is intended merely as a screening device. Possible problems with memory as indicated on the KAIT by poor performance on the memory subtests or significant differences between immediate and delayed recall subtests should be investigated further with a thorough assessment of memory.

Strengths and Weaknesses of the KAIT

As is the case with the WAIS-III, the KAIT is a sound instrument that offers users both advantages and disadvantages. Probably the most obvious advantage to clinicians, particularly for examiners or examinees who are thoroughly familiar with the Wechsler Scales, is that the KAIT subtests are innovative and new. Examiners find the KAIT to be relatively easy to administer, and examinees find it interesting (or at least different). Another advantage of the KAIT is that it can usually be administered in an hour. In these days of managed care, the administration time for any test is often an issue for consideration.

The psychometric properties of the KAIT are excellent. The standardization sample is of the caliber one would expect for a measure of intelligence intended for national or international use. The internal reliabilities for the three IQ scales are at .95 or above (Kaufman & Kaufman, 1993b). Furthermore the test-retest reliabilities for the

three scales are very good. The subtests also have good internal reliabilities, and the subtest test-retest reliabilities are in line with those from other batteries. Also, information in the manual does support the validity of the KAIT, the Crystallized and Fluid scales, as well as the placement of the subtests on their respective scales.

The fact that the Crystallized and Fluid scales are based on the early Horn-Cattell theory is a major advantage. This foundation provides clinicians with a theoretical framework from which to interpret and understand results. Moreover, as Flanagan et al. (1994) point out, this is one of the few measures of intelligence, besides the WJ-R COG, that combines theories of cognitive, psychometric, and neurological development. The tables of shared abilities in the manual are a further advantage for interpretive purposes.

At the same time, findings like those of Carroll (1993) provide support for a more expanded theory of intelligence that is in line with the more recent writings of Horn and his colleagues (Horn, 1994; Horn & Noll, 1997). With an appreciation for a broader set of eight or more abilities, the fluid–crystallized dichotomy seems almost truncated. In addition, the information presented in a recent chapter by McGrew (1997) raises the question of the abilities actually measured by some of the subtests on the Fluid scale. Clearly, more research is needed.

This last sentence raises a final limitation of the KAIT. More research is needed. Although the *KAIT Manual* (Kaufman & Kaufman, 1993b) provides ample evidence to support the KAIT, continuing research is also important. This research should include information on the abilities measured, as well as on the diagnostic validity. The manual provides some evidence of diagnostic validity but additional research is needed.

To date, one can conclude that the KAIT is a viable, innovative option for the assessment of adolescent and adult intelligence. The test provides reliable measures of intelligence, with a theoretical base, in a reasonable amount of time. As Brown (1994) notes, however, the KAIT may suffer from a lack of use due to the profession's seeming blindness to all but the Wechsler scales, particularly in the assessment of adolescents and adults.

CHAPTER SUMMARY

- Like the WISC-III for children, the Wechsler scales for the assessment of adult and adolescent intelligence are, and have been for the past several decades, the most popular and commonly used instruments in adult assessment.

- The WAIS-III consists of 14 subtests for the assessment of individuals age 16 to 89. In Wechsler fashion, the 14 subtests are grouped into Verbal and Performance sections.

- The six standard Verbal subtests are Vocabulary, Similarities, Arithmetic, Digit Span, Information, and Comprehension. Letter-Number Sequencing is a supplementary subtest for the Verbal or Full Scale IQs that can replace a spoiled Digit Span subtest.

- The standard five Performance subtests are Picture Completion, Digit Symbol-Coding, Block Design, Matrix Reasoning, and Picture Arrangement. Symbol Search is a supplementary subtest that can substitute only for a spoiled Digit Symbol-Coding in calculating Performance or Full Scale IQs. Object Assembly is an optional subtest that can take the place of any spoiled Performance subtest for individuals between 16 and 74.

- Like the WISC-III, the WAIS-III yields four index scores. These are the Verbal Comprehension Index (VC), the Perceptual Organization Index (PO), the Working Memory Index (WM), and the Processing Speed Index (PS).

- Clinicians should allow 80 minutes to administer the subtests required for the three IQ scores. The subtests for the Index scores take about 60 minutes to administer. Administration of the 13 subtests for both IQ and Index scores requires about 85 minutes. Clinicians

who wish to also administer Object Assembly should allocate an additional 10 to 15 minutes.

- Interpretation of the WAIS-III is now similar to that for the WISC-III. The WAIS-III shares a factor structure and composition like that of the WISC-III, and twelve of the fourteen subtests are the same.

- The similarities between the WAIS-III and the WAIS-R are also substantial. As a result, much of the extensive research literature on previous Wechsler adult intelligence tests can be applied to the WAIS-III.

- The psychometric properties of the WAIS-III are excellent. For example, the WAIS-III Full Scale IQ is extremely reliable. Furthermore, the relationship between the WAIS-III and other measures or constructs has been firmly established. Based on the factor analytic studies in the manual, it appears that one can interpret a four-factor structure with confidence for all but the oldest age group.

- As is the case with other Wechsler tests, one of the main weaknesses of the WAIS-III is its lack of a clear theoretical foundation.

- The KAIT was not designed as an upward extension of the K-ABC, and the KAIT is a very different test from the Kaufman's intelligence test for children, the K-ABC.

- The main theoretical underpinnings of the KAIT are found in the Cattell-Horn Gf-Gc model of intelligence, and the KAIT is tied to the fluid-crystallized dichotomy.

- As a result of its theoretical framework, the KAIT consists of a Crystallized Scale and a Fluid Scale. The KAIT also yields a measure of overall intellectual functioning, the Composite Intelligence scale.

- The KAIT has been normed for use with adolescents and adults from age 11 to 85 or older.

- The KAIT Core Battery consists of six subtests. The three subtests comprising the Crystallized scale are Definitions, Auditory Comprehension, and Double Meanings. Those for the Fluid scale are Rebus Learning, Logical steps, and Mystery Codes.

- The KAIT also contains four additional subtests that, together with the Core Battery, make up the Extended Battery. The four additional subtests are Memory for Block Designs, Famous Faces, Rebus Delayed Recall, and Auditory Delayed Recall.

- Administration time for the six subtests of the KAIT core battery is approximately an hour. Inclusion of the two supplemental tests and two recall tests increases the administration time to about an hour and a half.

- The tasks on the Crystallized scale are in line with Horn's current writings on crystallized intelligence. The Fluid scale, however, reflects abilities closer to Cattell and Horn's earlier conceptualization of fluid intelligence, and the Fluid scale includes tasks that incorporate memory and speed items.

- The psychometric properties of the KAIT are excellent. The standardization sample is of the caliber one would expect, and the internal reliabilities for the three IQ scales are at .95 or above. The information in the manual does support the validity of the KAIT, the Crystallized and Fluid scales, as well as the placement of the subtests on their respective scales.

- Continuing research on the KAIT is needed.

CHAPTER 12

Woodcock-Johnson Tests of Cognitive Ability (W-J)

Tradition and veneration are not hallmarks of technological advancement; rather, progress evolves from the search to replace old ways with new ones. The technology of intelligence assessment should be no exception. (Woodcock,1997, p. 230)

CHAPTER QUESTION

What theory drove development of the Woodcock-Johnson?

OVERVIEW

The WJ-R Cog was published in 1989 as a revision to the 1977 edition. While this chapter focuses on the cognitive battery, the W-J actually represents one of the most comprehensive test batteries available for the clinical assessment of children and adolescents. The W-J Tests of Achievement have enjoyed considerable popularity since their original release, probably more so than the cognitive battery. The system also includes the W-J Scales of Independent Behavior (SIB), an adaptive behavior scale, among other components.

The current WJ-R Cog, however, differs significantly from its predecessor in many ways. Most obvious is its closer tie to John Horn's work with Cattell's fluid/crystallized model of intelligence (see Chapter 2). Woodcock aligns the subtests of the W-J with seven of the cognitive abilities isolated by Horn as shown in Table 12. 1 although additional abilities continue to be isolated and scores offered (e.g., quantitative).

The WJ-R Cog is extensive as is revealed by the breadth of its theoretical model. The scale also includes two sets of subtests: standard and supplemental. Each of the seven featured cognitive abilities have two subtests (or indicators) which constitute the minimum necessary to measure a latent trait.

Some of the WJ-R Cog abilities are already familiar to readers because they have been used

TABLE 12.1   Cognitive factors and subtests of the Woodcock-Johnson

Cognitive Factor		Subtests
Long-Term Retrieval	Stand. Supp.	1. Memory for Names 8. Visual-Auditory Learning 15. Delayed Recall—Memory for Names 16. Delayed Recall—Visual Auditory Learning
Short-Term Memory	Stand. Supp.	2. Memory for Sentences 9. Memory for Words 17. Numbers Reversed
Processing Speed	Stand. Supp.	3. Visual Matching 10. Cross Out
Auditory Processing	Stand. Supp.	4. Incomplete Words 11. Sound Blending 18. Sound Patterns
Visual Processing	Stand. Supp.	5. Visual Closure 12. Picture Recognition 19. Spatial Relations
Comprehension Knowledge	Stand. Supp.	6. Picture Vocabulary 13. Oral Vocabulary 20. Listening Comprehension 21. Verbal Analogies
Fluid Reasoning	Stand Supp.	7. Analysis-Synthesis 14. Concept Formation 19. Spatial Relations 21. Verbal Analogies

Stand. = Standard Battery
Supp. = Supplemental

in other tests and/or they are described in earlier chapters. The greater dependency of the WJ-R Cog revision on an explicitly stated theoretical orientation is a major improvement over the original W-J and many other measures for that matter. The closer tie between the WJ-R Cog subtests and theory enhance the ability of the new WJ-R Cog user to learn to interpret the test. In addition, the theoretical orientation should allow the user to interpret the scales with greater confidence and accuracy. Some data are presented in the manual to support the theoretical organization of the subtests, and independent factor analytic and other investigations have generally been supportive (Bickley, Keith, & Wolfe, 1995).

Standardization

The WJ-R Cog was normed on 6,359 cases using a stratified sampling procedure to match U.S. Census Bureau statistics. The sample for ages 2 to 5 consisted of 705 cases, while the sample for grades Kindergarten through 12th grade included 3,245 cases. Stratification variables included gender, geographic region, community size, and race (White, Black, Native American, Asian Pacific, Other and Hispanic origin). The WJ-R Cog used a different approach from the other tests discussed thus far to control for family SES. Communities were selected for the standardization program based on SES. Community SES was gauged by adult educational attainment, type of occupation, occupational status, and household income. Educational attainment and occupation were used as direct measures of SES for the adult norming sample. Overall, there is a relatively close match between Census statistics and the characteristics of the norming sample.

The WJ-R Cog was normed concurrently with the WJ-R Tests of Achievement. Because of the conorming of the WJ-R Tests of Cognitive Ability and Achievement, the WJ-R Cog fosters ability/achievement comparisons. Ability/achievement discrepancies, which may be particularly useful for learning disability diagnosis, may be computed based on the frequency of occurrence of these discrepancies in the standardization sample. The manual and software program provide for the systematic evaluation of such discrepancies (see Chapter 20 for a discussion of the issue of ability/achievement discrepancies and learning disability diagnosis). This conorming is particularly necessary in the case of the WJ-R Cog since the Quantitative cluster is comprised of two subtests from the WJ-R Tests of Achievement.

Reliability

Internal consistency estimates for the standard battery subtests are quite high. The median coefficients are above .80 for five of the seven subtests. It is noteworthy that the Visual Closure subtest yields coefficients in the .60s for ages 6 through 39. This test is similar to the Gestalt Closure subtest of the K-ABC, which has some of the lowest internal consistency coefficients for that battery. At other ages the Visual Closure subtest has some coefficients in the .80s, but the most use of the test will occur in the age range with the worst coefficients. The Visual Closure subtest may produce some difficult scores to interpret as is the case with the K-ABC. The

other test with lower coefficients is Visual Matching. Reliability estimates in the .70s for this test, however, are comparable to those for the WISC-III Coding subtest. (These coefficients are test-retest coefficients since internal consistency coefficients are inappropriate for timed tests.)

The Broad Cognitive Ability (BCA) composite score for the seven standard battery subtests yields a median internal consistency coefficient of .94. The Broad Cognitive Ability Early Development scale is also highly reliable for preschoolers with a coefficient of .96 at ages 2 and 4. Internal consistency reliabilities for the clusters (composites) that are derived when supplemental scales are used are also high. They range from a median coefficient of .80 for Fluid Reasoning to .96 for Short-Term Memory. While composites on the WISC-III and other tests produce consistent reliability estimates in the .90s, some of the WJ-R Cog Cluster scores do not produce estimates this high. The Auditory Processing, Visual Processing, Comprehension-Knowledge, and Fluid Reasoning clusters all have coefficients that average in the .80s. With this finding in mind, these clusters may represent something of an intermediate score that is more reliable that the typical intelligence test subtest and yet somewhat less reliable than the typical intelligence test composite score. Depending on the nature of validity evidence, these scores should be interpreted in like fashion—that is, receive more emphasis than a subtest score but less emphasis than a composite score.

Validity

Some attention was paid to the establishment of content validity for the WJ-R Cog, but no evidence is presented. According to the *Examiner's Manual* (Woodcock & Mather, 1989a), "Items included in the various tests were selected using item validity studies as well as expert opinion" (p. 7). Some results of the expert's judgments or description of the methods and results of the studies would have been desirable.

Several prepublication concurrent validity studies were also completed. The concurrent validity coefficients show some overlap with existing measures, but the magnitude of the correlations is somewhat less than one would expect for a multisubtest measure of intelligence. For a study of 64 3-year-olds the WJ-R Cog BCA Early Development score correlated .69 with the K-ABC MPC, .62 with the McCarthy GCI, and .69 with the Binet-4 Composite. For a sample of 9-year-olds the BCA Standard Battery composite correlated .57 with K-ABC MPC, .68 with Binet-4 Composite, and .68 with the WISC-R Full Scale. These relationships are lower and less impressive than some would have hoped. Correlations with the WAIS-R also stayed below .70 in a study involving 51 17-year-olds. The WJ-R Cog BCA Standard Battery correlated .65 with the Binet-4 and .64 with the WAIS-R Full Scale. All of these coefficients are slightly lower than one would expect based on correlations among previously published measures where coefficients have often been above .70. This typical finding still shows substantial overlap with the existing general intelligence assessment technology.

The factor analytic validity of the WJ-R Cog has been evaluated by Woodcock (1990), Reschly (1990), and Ysseldyke (1990). Woodcock (1990) presented the results of several factor analytic studies. He found support for eight factors underlying the WJ-R Cog, which corresponded closely to Horn-Cattell theory. He also argued that other tests are underfactored and made the point that many tests do not possess enough breadth and depth of measurement of intelligence (Woodcock, 1990).

The tendency to emphasize breadth in the intellectual assessment process is emphasized in the following remarks from Woodcock (1990). He proposed that

Horn (1988) conceptualizes intellectual functioning as a "Milky Way" of human abilities. Just as we do not know how many stars make up the Milky Way, we also do not know precisely how many unique intellectual abilities

exist. In the Milky Way, we infer constellations. In the "Milky Way of intellectual abilities," we infer common-factor concepts of constellations that help us describe and understand human intellectual functioning. (p. 233)

Woodcock (1990) first presented a confirmatory factor analysis of 16 subtests with eight factors identified. The fit indices were all strong (above .95) and the root mean square residual was only .02. Details regarding the specifications of the model (e.g., whether some or all tests were allowed to have coloadings although some were apparently allowed to coload) were not given. The factor loadings themselves are also supportive of the WJ-R Cog model, although there are some hints of problems. Picture Recognition does not appear to be a marker of the Visual Processing cluster as its loading was .38 on this scale and .24 on the Long-Term Retrieval cluster. This finding is also consistent with the lower reliability coefficients for this cluster.

An exploratory factor analysis using oblique rotation replicated these findings in that there was considerable resemblance to the WJ-R Cog model, but there were also some inconsistencies (Woodcock, 1990). Picture Recognition again was a poor measure of the Visual Processing cluster with a small loading (less than .20 although the actual coefficient is not given) on this cluster and a loading of .25 on the Long-Term Retrieval cluster. In effect, the Visual Processing cluster looks like a one-subtest cluster where Visual Closure devours the lion's share of the variance. Some questions are also raised by this analysis for the Quantitative Ability cluster, as the Applied Problems test had loadings of .44 on Quantitative, .20 on Fluid Reasoning, and .27 on Comprehension-Knowledge. Remember the Binet-4? The WJ-R Cog may be having similar problems identifying a homogeneous quantitative scale. It is also noteworthy that Carroll's (1993) landmark work could not find ample evidence for a Stratum II Quantitative Reasoning ability.

Reschly (1990) and Ysseldyke (1990) lauded the WJ-R Cog factor analytic data. Reschly (1990) observed, "The psychometrically sound, relatively clean measures of the eight factors are a major accomplishment" (p. 265). Ysseldyke (1990) similarly pointed out that, "it appears that the WJ-R adequately represents many of the major components of human ability as suggested by the extant factor analytic research in intelligence" (p. 274). Independent factor analyses of the WJ-R Cog are difficult to come by. The Bickley et al. (1995) study is an exception but the purpose of this study was to assess aspects of Carroll's (1993) theory, not the validity of the WJ-R Cog per se.

Administration

The WJ-R Cog is designed for ages 2 to 90+ and is administered in an easel format. The cognitive battery consists of 21 subtests, only 7 of which are considered as part of the standard battery (see Table 12.1). Many of the WJ-R Cog subtests are familiar ones. Visual Matching, for example, is highly similar to the Coding subtest of the WISC-R. On the other hand, Memory for Names uses a novel and clever format (i.e., teaching the child the names of space creatures) that is interesting, time efficient, and clinically rich in that it allows the examiner to actually observe the child "learning." The administration of several tests is also aided by the use of an audiotape for administration. For the Incomplete Words test the word fragments are presented by a female voice on the tape. This procedure not only fosters the use of uniform administration procedures, but it also hastens the pace of administration.

The following comment may seem peculiar. The easel format of the WJ-R Cog makes it so easy to administer that it does not resemble other tests of intelligence. It resembles academic achievement measures to a greater degree. For example, manipulatives (or toy-like materials) are not available for the assessment of preschoolers. Similarly, while most intelligence tests have a visual-motor measure (e.g., Block Design,

Triangles, or Pattern Analysis), the WJ-R Cog does not. While the WJ-R Cog is extremely easy to administer, its lack of similarity to other well-known tests may deter transfer of training from other measures. On a practical level, the test may also not be as inviting as others (e.g., McCarthy) for preschoolers who require manipulatives to maintain their attention. The WJ-R Cog does have an Early Development scale for preschoolers consisting of the Memory for Names, Incomplete Words, Visual Closure, and Picture Vocabulary subtests.

Scoring

The scoring options for the WJ-R Cog are limitless, so much so that they may be bewildering, especially to clinicians who primarily use standard scores for interpretation. The composite or IQ-like score is called Broad Cognitive Ability, thus avoiding the inappropriate connotations of the IQ score. The overall composite for preschoolers is called Early Development. Latent trait scores ("W" scores) are offered as intermediate scores for later score calculations. The composites and individual subtest scores have a mean of 100 and standard deviation of 15, and percentile ranks are offered. Cluster scores are available for the seven cognitive factors shown in Table 12.1. Other scores offered include T-scores, normal curve equivalents (NCEs), and stanines. Grade-based scores where grade is used as the norm or reference group are offered in addition to the traditional age-based scores.

One of the novel scores offered by the WJ-R Cog, which has previously been used more in achievement testing, is the Relative Mastery Index (RMI). The RMI is similar to a ratio with the second part of the ratio set at a value of 90. Sample RMIs look like the following: 40/90, 55/90, 95/90. The 90 is based on the performance of the norm sample (either age or grade reference groups). The denominator means that children in the norm sample can perform the intellectual task with 90% accuracy. The first number of the ratio represents the child's performance in relationship to the 90% level of accuracy (mastery). If a child obtained an RMI of 45/90, it would mean that the child's proficiency on the subtest is at a 45% level, whereas the typical child of his or her age (or grade) mastered the material at a 90% level. The RMI is similar to the rationale behind the Snellen Chart used for visual screening. Some of us have vision of 20/20, some 20/60, and so on. In the case of the Snellen Chart, however, the first number is fixed and the second one varies. The rarity of the use of the RMI score in intellectual assessment makes it difficult to gauge its value in everyday cognitive assessment practice. No other major test of intelligence offers such a score. As noted earlier the notion of "mastery" is more common for achievement testing.

The WJ-R Cog also offers extended age and grade equivalent scales that may facilitate the evaluation of children at the tails of the normal distribution. Instead of having a lowest possible age equivalent of 2-0 (2 years, 0 months), the WJ-R Cog offers an age equivalent of $2\text{-}0^1$, where the superscript one represents the first percentile rank. An age equivalent of $2\text{-}0^{48}$ means that the child obtained a score at the 48th percentile rank for 2-year-olds.

The easel format of administration and scoring is assisted by a user-friendly and fast software program. The foregoing paragraphs make handscoring of the WJ-R Cog sound formidable and, in fact, it is. This fact undoubtably makes the software of the WJ-R Cog very popular.

Interpretation

Descriptive terms for levels of WJ-R Cog performance are modern in that they describe levels of performance as opposed to offering a diagnosis. The WJ-R Cog descriptive labels corresponding to standard scores are given in the next column.

Standard score	Label
131 and above	Very Superior
121–130	Superior
111–120	High Average
90–110	Average
80–89	Low Average
70–79	Low
69 and below	Very Low

One caveat to consider when interpreting WJ-R Cog scores is the relatively small number of items per subtest. The WJ-R Cog covers an extraordinarily large age range with a small number of items. If a child is not attending on a few of the items of a subtest, the derived scores could change rather dramatically. On Memory for Sentences, for example, a raw score of 49 corresponds to an age equivalent of 16.3, but a raw score of 50 corresponds to an AE of 20. Incomplete Words is another brief subtest. For this test a raw score of 24 corresponds to an AE of 7-0 and a raw score of 26 corresponds to an AE of 8-5. These conversions hint that some of the WJ-R Cog subtests may have too few items to assess such a large age range. This situation results in some unexpected relationships between raw scores and derived scores where small increases in raw scores may produce larger-than-expected differences in derived scores, thus creating more opportunity for test behavior, such as inattention, to influence scores.

In lieu of providing extensive tables of difference score values for profile interpretation, the WJ-R Cog advises using confidence bands to compare cluster and subtest scores. The rules for comparing scores via this method are given on page 82 of the *Examiner's Manual* (Woodcock & Mather, 1989a).

Woodcock (1997) continues to refine the WJ-R Cog theoretical model in order to enhance interpretation. He has collapsed nine Stratum II-like abilities to produce four intermediate categories of abilities referred to as a Cognitive Performance

Model (CPM)—namely, Short-Term Memory, Acquired Knowledge, Thinking Abilities, and Facilitator-Inhibitors. Operational definitions of these four categories, their graphically depicted relationship, and definitions of the subtests that enter into each are presented in Figure 12.1 and Table 12.2. This model is, not surprisingly, unique in comparison to its competitors. Woodcock (1997) clearly emphasizes the assessment of multiple abilities in the interpretation process. For him, ". . . the primary purpose of testing should be to find out more about the problem—not to determine an IQ" (p. 235).

Sample Case

This case demonstrates the use of the WJ-R Cog in a test battery for an adolescent who is being evaluated upon admission to an inpatient treatment unit of a general hospital. The report is written in a style that may be more appropriate for hospital practice where a brief stay is

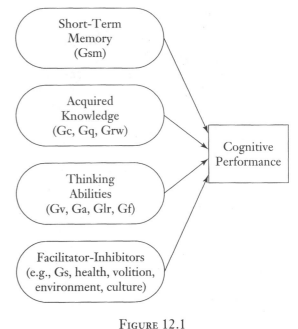

FIGURE 12.1

WJ-R Cog Cognitive Processing Model (Woodcock, 1997 with permission)

TABLE 12.2   WJ-R Cog Cognitive Processing Model: Categories, subtests, and definitions (Woodcock, 1997 with permission)

Functional category of the CPM	
TEST NAME	DEFINITION
Short-Term Memory	
Test 2: Memory for Sentences	Measures the ability to remember and repeat simple words, phrases, and sentences presented auditorily by a tape player; test is a measure of Short-Term Memory (Gsm)
Test 9: Memory for Words	Measures the ability to repeat lists of unrelated words in the correct sequence; words are presented by audiotape; test is a measure of Short-Term Memory (Gsm)
Test 17: Numbers Reversed	Measures the ability to repeat a series of random numbers backward; number sequences are presented by audiotape; test is a mixed measure of Short-Term Memory and Fluid Reasoning (Gsm and Gf)
Stores of Acquired Knowledge	
Test 6: Picture Vocabulary	Measures the ability to name familiar and unfamiliar pictured objects; a measure of Comprehension-Knowledge (Gc)

TABLE 12.2 WJ-R Cog Cognitive Processing Model: Categories, subtests, and definitions (Woodcock, 1997) (Continued)

	Functional category of the CPM
TEST NAME	DEFINITION
Test 13: Oral Vocabulary	Measures knowledge of word meanings in Part A: Synonyms, the subject must say a word similar in meaning to the word presented; in Part B: Antonyms, the subject must say a word that is opposite in meaning to the word presented; test is a measure of Comprehension-Knowledge (Gc)
Test 20: Listening Comprehension	Measures the ability to listen to a short tape-recorded passage and to verbally supply the single word missing at the end of the passage; test is a measure of Comprehension-Knowledge (Gc)
Test 24: Calculation	[WJ-R ACH] measures the subject's skill in performing mathematical calculations ranging from simple addition to calculus; subject is not required to make any decisions about what operations to use or what data to include; test is a measure of Quantitative Ability (Gq)
Test 25: Applied Problems	[WJ-R ACH] measures the subject's skill in analyzing and solving practical problems in mathematics; subject must decide not only the appropriate mathematical operations to use but also which of the data to include in the calculation; test is a measure of Quantitative Ability (Gq)

Thinking Abilities

Test 5: Visual Closure	Measures the ability to name a drawing or picture of a simple object that is altered or obscured in one of several ways; test is a measure of Visual Processing (Gv)
Test 12: Picture Recognition	Measures the ability to recognize a subset of previously presented pictures within a larger set of pictures; test is a measure of Visual Processing (Gv)
Test 19: Spatial Relations	Measures the ability to visually match and combine shapes; subject must select from a series of shapes, the component parts composing a given whole shape; test is a mixed measure of Visual Processing and Fluid Reasoning (Gv and Gf)
Test 4: Incomplete Words	An audiotape subtest that measures auditory closure: after hearing a recorded word with one or more phonemes missing, subject names the complete word; test is a measure of Auditory Processing (Ga)
Test 11: Sound Blending	Measures the ability to integrate and then say whole words after hearing parts (syllables and/or phonemes) of the word; audiotape presents word parts in their proper order for each item; test is a measure of Auditory Processing (Ga)
Test 18: Sound Patterns	Measures the ability to indicate whether parts of complex sound patterns are the same or different: patterns may differ in pitch, rhythm, or sound content; sound patterns are presented by an audiotape; test is a mixed measure of Auditory Processing and Fluid Reasoning (Ga and Gf)
Test 1: Memory for Names	Measures the ability to learn associations between unfamiliar auditory and visual stimuli (an auditory-visual association task): task requires learning the names of a series of space creatures; test is a measure of Long-Term Retrieval (Glr)

(Continues)

TABLE 12.2   WJ-R Cog Cognitive Processing Model: Categories, subtests, and definitions (Woodcock, 1997) (Continued)

Functional category of the CPM	
TEST NAME	DEFINITION
Test 8: Vocal-Auditory Learning	Measures the ability to associate new visual symbols (rebuses) with familiar words in oral language and to translate a series of symbols presented as a reading passage (a visual–auditory association task); test is a measure of Long-Term Retrieval (Gir)
Test 15: Delayed Recall—Memory for Names	Measures the ability to recall (after 1 to 8 days) the space creatures presented in Memory for Names; test is a measure of Long-Term Retrieval (Glr)
Test 16: Delayed Recall—Visual-Auditory Learning Retrieval	Measures the ability to recall (after 1 to 8 days) the symbols (rebuses) presented in Visual-Auditory Learning; test is a measure of Long-Term (Glr)
Test 7: Analysis-Synthesis	Measures the ability to analyze the components of an incomplete logic puzzle and to determine and name the missing components; test is a measure of Fluid Reasoning (Gf)
Test 14: Concept Formation	Measures the ability to identify and state the rule for a concept about a set of colored geometric figures when shown instances and noninstances of the concept; test is a measure of Fluid Reasoning (Gf)
Test 21: Verbal Analogies	Measures the ability to complete phrases with words that indicate appropriate analogies; although the vocabulary remains relatively simple, the relationships among the words become increasingly complex; test is a mixed measure of Fluid Reasoning and Comprehension-Knowledge (Gf and Gc)
Facilitator—Inhibitors	
Test 3: Visual Matching	Measures the ability to quickly locate and circle the two identical numbers in a row of six numbers: task proceeds in difficulty from single-digit numbers to triple-digit numbers and has a 3-minute time limit; test is a measure of Processing Speed (Gs)
Test 10: Cross Out	Measures the ability to quickly scan and compare visual information: subject must mark the 5 drawings in a row of 20 drawings that are identical to the first drawing in the row; subject is given a 3-minute time limit to complete as many rows of items as possible; test is a measure of Processing Speed (Gs)

anticipated. Intelligence is not the major referral question and therefore is not highlighted in the report.

Kathy demonstrates few risk factors for low intelligence test scores. Her development and medical histories are unremarkable. She has not been in special education nor has she been retained. On the other hand, there are not suggestions of high intelligence test scores either. She has not been identified as precocious, and she is not in the college preparatory curriculum at her school. Kathy's test behavior suggested at least average intelligence test scores. Her effort in the test session was good despite her depression. All of these factors argue for a prediction that she will possess general intelligence.

In addition, Kathy worked extremely hard on the Visual Matching test. This test is a Wechsler

Box 12.1   Psychological Evaluation/Consultation

Name: Kathy
Age: 16 years, 8 months
Grade: 11
School: Comprehensive High School
Class: Regular
Occupation: Part-time employment at a fast-food restaurant approximately 25 hours per week

Assessment Procedures

Diagnostic Interview

K-TEA Comprehensive Form

Achenbach Youth Self-Report

Woodcock-Johnson Tests of Cognitive Ability

Sentence Completion Test

Rorschach

Thematic Apperception Test

Referral Information

Kathy was referred by her attending physician for a psychological evaluation subsequent to admission to the hospital. Her admitting diagnosis was major depression, single episode, moderate. The referral question was whether or not psychological evaluation would confirm this diagnosis.

Background Information

Kathy has been experiencing symptoms of depression for the past 6 months. These symptoms have included withdrawal, feelings of hopelessness, depressed affect, crying spells, periodic suicidal ideation (without a specific plan), difficulty falling asleep, and declining school grades. Kathy sought help from her high school English teacher and was subsequently referred to the hospital.

Kathy lives with her birth father, mother, and three younger siblings. Her father works as a custodian and her mother as a seamstress. She has never been retained nor has she received special education. She enjoys math and art class. Kathy works 25–30 hours a week and seems to enjoy this activity. She reports that she has many friends. She says that she is experiencing difficulty in her relationship with her mother. She feels that her mother is not giving her appropriate attention or care. As an example, she cited that occasionally she has come home after drinking some alcohol with friends and that although there was a notable change in her behavior, she received no comment from her mother.

Observations During Testing

Kathy displayed depressed mood throughout the test session. She was, however, compliant and exceedingly polite. Her effort during the testing sessions was commendable and suggestive of good achievement motivation. She exhibited some confidence in her mathematics and spelling skills. She showed good concentration and attention.

Test Results and Conclusions

All of Kathy's cognitive test scores were within the average range. Her percentile ranks on the Woodcock-Johnson Cognitive ranged from a low of 30 to a high of 86 with no significant strengths or weaknesses being evident. She obtained her highest percentile rank of 86 on the Visual Matching subtest. She worked extremely hard on this test showing good manual speed, dexterity, and motivation to comply with the demand for speed. On the K-TEA her percentile ranks were also average, ranging from a low of 47 to a high of 66.

(Continues)

Box 12.1　Psychological Evaluation/Consultation　(Continued)

Kathy gave numerous indications of dysthymic tendencies in her personality test results. She seems plagued by anxiety, low self-concept, emotional dependency, ruminations, and perhaps compulsive tendencies. She, for example, admitted to some excessive hand-washing and concern with cleanliness. There is also some indication that she is willing to suppress her own feelings and desires in favor of those of others. She may also engage in passive-aggressive behaviors in order to meet her emotional needs. There are also indications in the personality test results that she may be a "well-compensated" depressive. In other words, she may have been hiding feelings of depression considerably longer than the past 4–6 months.

Recommendations

The current findings suggest that Kathy may require long-term (more than a few weeks) psychotherapeutic intervention and that she may be passively resistant to it. She may require fairly aggressive approaches to psychotherapy. There are also suggestions of family difficulties, indicating a need for family assessment with the potential requirement for family therapy. Regardless of therapeutic modality, there are suggestions that while Kathy may appear to be rather forthcoming, it may not be easy for her to change her behavior patterns.

Diagnosis

Major depression, single episode, moderate.

Coding subtest analogue where a premium is placed on speed of performance. Kathy responded well to the demands of the task and seemed to push herself hard to respond. This test also seemed to elicit Kathy's tendency to be extremely compliant and to try to meet the demands of others. Her behavior on this test leads one to predict that this would be one of her higher subtest scores. We will see.

CONCLUSIONS

The WJ-R Cog is clearly the product of a thorough test development process. The result is a test with substantial psychometric support. This edition of the WJ-R Cog deserves serious research attention and a clinical trial by psychologists. In a thorough review Cummings (1995) concluded:

> . . . the WJ-R merits the attention of all engaged in norm-referenced psychoeducational assessment. (p. 1116)

Ever the innovator, Woodcock has created one of the first full Spanish versions of a U.S.-developed cognitive test, the *Bateria Woodcock-Munoz-Revisada* (Woodcock & Munoz-Sandoval, 1996). Reviews of this innovation, however, have not been so positive. Lintel (1998), in fact, says that the instrument should not be used, and she gives numerous suggestions for creating a Spanish edition for use in the United States.

The forthcoming revision of the W-J Cog, which is near release at the time of this writing, has a substantial foundation on which to build. Therefore, many of us eagerly await further refinements and improvements.

CHAPTER SUMMARY

- The WJ-R Cog is designed for ages 2 to 90+ and is administered in an easel format. The test battery consists of 21 subtests, only 7 of which are considered as part of the standard battery.

- The WJ-R Cog was normed on 6,359 cases using a stratified sampling procedure to match U.S. Census Bureau statistics.

- The WJ-R Cog concurrent validity coefficients show some overlap with existing measures but the magnitude of the correlations is somewhat less than one would expect for a multisubtest measure of intelligence.

- Reschly (1990) and Ysseldyke (1990) lauded the WJ-R Cog factor analytic data.

- One caveat to consider when interpreting WJ-R Cog scores is the relatively small number of items per subtest, which may compromise the reliability and validity of scores for an inattentive child.

Differential Ability Scales (DAS)

"*Although there is so much that is new in the DAS, paradoxically it recaptures the child-centered approach and appeal of the old Stanford-Binet L-M (Terman & Merrill, 1960)*" *(Elliott, 1997, p. 204)*

CHAPTER QUESTION

How does the DAS use item sets to reduce child frustration?

The Differential Ability Scales (DAS; Elliott, 1990c) is a comprehensive battery of cognitive and achievement tests that are designed for children and adolescents between the ages of 2½ and 17 years. The DAS is a revision and U.S. adaptation of the British Ability Scales (BAS; Elliott, Murray, & Pearson, 1979). There were, however, several changes made in the DAS from its progenitor. In addition to the collection of the U.S. normative sample, several new subtests were developed and a standard "core" battery

was created. The DAS Cognitive Battery has both a preschool level (see Chapter 15) and a school-age level. For school-aged children, there are also reading, mathematics, and spelling achievement tests that are described primarily as "screeners." All of these measures were normed on the same sample to make the comparison of cognitive and achievement domains more appropriate (see Chapter 14).

Theory and Features

The DAS is built on a number of test development goals, theoretical traditions, and assumptions about cognition. Elliott (1990b) describes his approach to the development of the DAS as "eclectic," having borrowed from the work of Cattell, Horn, Das, Jensen, Thurstone, Vernon, and Spearman. Elliott (1990b) appeals to Thurstone's notion of primary mental abilities. He agrees with Thurstone's ideas that the emphasis in intellectual assessment should be on the assessment and interpretation of distinct abilities as opposed to the assessment process focusing exclusively on an overall composite score. For this reason the DAS subtests were constructed in order to enhance their subtest specificity which, in turn, should make the subtests more interpretable as measures of unique abilities. Elliott (1997) presents evidence of higher subtest specificities by about a third, than for the WISC-III, K-ABC, and W-JR Cog. Presumably, higher specificities would lead to clearer profiles (Elliott, 1990b).

Empirical evidence of meaningful DAS profiles for types or subtypes of clinical populations, however, is just emerging and, only for samples of children with LD. McIntosh and Gridley (1993) found that the addition of DAS Diagnostic (i.e., optional) subtests and achievement subtests was necessary to better differentiate subtypes.

Elliott (1990b) also appeals to the theoretical stance of Spearman and others of the British school (see Chapter 2). He suggests that:

1. *All ability measures are intercorrelated and, thus, are likely to yield a general factor, "g."*

2. *Ability measures, if developed to be homogeneous, are likely to form subgroupings at a lower level of generality than "g," as well as showing a proportion of reliable specific variance. The structure of abilities is, therefore, likely to be hierarchical, with "g" at the apex, followed by group factors and subtests at the lowest level.*

3. *The hierarchical structure will differentiate and develop with age. (p. 378)*

Elliott (1990a) defines the "g" measured by the DAS in the following manner:

Psychometric "g" is the general ability of an individual to perform mental processing that involves conceptualization and the transformation of information. (p. 380)

This definition is strikingly similar to Jensen's definition of Level II processing (reasoning ability; see Chapter 2), especially the emphasis on the transformation of information. Such a definition

also clearly makes Elliott's work consistent with that of Spearman, Vernon, Jensen, and others (see Chapter 2).

It appears that Elliott reaches far and wide adopting theoretical notions from hierarchical models and those espousing the value of assessing specific abilities with greater emphasis on the latter (see Chapter 2). This eclecticism reveals Elliott's (1990b) grasp of the issues and provides support for the inclusion of the General Conceptual Ability (GCA), Cluster, and Diagnostic subtest scores. Elliott's approach is also consistent with the three-stratum theory of Carroll (1993).

Although the theoretical structure of the DAS presages the publication of three-stratum theory, the scale provides a thorough assessment of general intelligence at Stratum III. At Stratum II the DAS provides an assessment of Nonverbal Reasoning (fluid ability) (Elliott, 1997), Verbal (crystallized ability), and Spatial (visualization) abilities (see Table 13.1). The diagnostic subtests offered provide at least some indicators of Stratum II memory and processing speed abilities. In fact, the DAS allows for a more thorough sampling of Stratum II abilities than the majority of available tests save the WJ-R Cog. Finally, Elliott's (1990b) attempt to enhance subtest specific is potentially advantageous for the assessment of some Stratum I abilities.

Above all, Elliott (1997) desired to create a test that would meet the needs of the practitioner. In his own words he addressed this central goal as follows:

Two principles—self-evident truths to many practitioners—drove the development of the DAS. The first is that professionals assessing children with learning and developmental disabilities need information at a finer level of detail than an IQ score. IQ tests in the past have had a primary, disproportionate focus on global composite scores. The second principle is that psychometric assessment has much to offer the practitioner: Psychometric tests of cognitive abilities not only have well-established qualities of reliability, validity, time efficiency, objectivity, and lack of bias, but often give us information critical to our understanding of a child's learning styles and characteristics. (p.183)

TABLE 13.1   Differential Ability Scale subtests and three Stratum Theory Abilities measured (Elliott, 1997)

Ages	Cluster Subtests	Diagnostic Subtests
2–6 to 3–5	Block Building (gv) Picture Similarities (gf) Naming Vocabulary (gc) Verbal Comprehension (gc)	Recall of Digits (gsm) Recognition of Pictures (gsm, gv)
3–6 to 5–11	*Nonverbal*: Copying (gv) Pattern Construction (gv) Picture Similarities (gf) *Verbal*: Naming Vocabulary (gc) Verbal Comprehension (gc) Early Number Concepts (gq)	Block Building (gv) Matching Letter-like Forms (gv) Recall of Digits (gsm) Recall of Objects (glr) Recognition of Pictures (gsm, gv)
6 to 17	*Nonverbal Reasoning*: Matrices (gf) Sequential and Quantitative Reasoning (gf) *Spatial*: Pattern Construction (gv) Recall of Designs (gv, gsm) *Verbal*: Similarities (gc) Word Definitions (gc)	Recall of Digits (gsm) Recall of Objects (glr) Speed of Information Processing (gs)

Administration and Scoring

The DAS manual is exceedingly well written and helpful. The DAS norm tables, however, use a small typeface and are "busy." The small font is a particular problem for the achievement tests, where it seems that this typeface could lead to the incorrect calculation of scores.

There are two sets of subtests on the cognitive scales of the DAS. One set is a group of "core" subtests that are used to derive the GCA composite score and cluster scores. In addition to these there are a number of "diagnostic" subtests that are intended to measure relatively independent abilities. The "core" battery is made up of four to six subtests, depending on the child's age. These subtests were selected because they were "the best measure of reasoning and conceptual

abilities" that were available in the test battery. They include a balance of verbal and nonverbal content and are administered in a prescribed sequence. The General Conceptual Ability (GCA) score is a summary score for the cognitive domains that is similar to what is typically called a Full Scale IQ or overall cognitive score for other intelligence tests.

Subtest norms employ a nonstandard metric in intellectual assessment using *T*-scores with a mean of 50 and a standard deviation of 10. This metric is commonly used in personality assessment but may provide a challenge for the intelligence examiner who is used to a metric with a mean of 100 and a standard deviation of 15 or subtest scores with a mean of 10 and standard deviation of 3. The GCA score uses the more familiar metric of mean of 100 and standard deviation of 15. The various diagnostic and "core" subtests for the DAS are shown in Table 13.1.

Like the Stanford-Binet, the administration of the DAS is somewhat flexible allowing for out-of-level testing and selection of diagnostic subtests. This practice of using diagnostic subtests is especially appealing since administration of the core subtests is relatively brief, anywhere from 25 to 65 minutes in comparison to the typical one hour or greater administration of a test such as the WISC-III. This flexibility allows the examiner the opportunity to supplement the core DAS with additional diagnostic subtests.

The DAS is designed to ensure that each child is administered a set of items that is most appropriate for his or her ability level. This task can be difficult to carry out with the DAS as it is with other tests (e.g., Binet-4) that use forms of adaptive testing. The DAS tries to mimic adaptive testing practices by having varied starting points for age groups and using "decision points." Children begin at a point that is designated for their age group, and they respond to items until a decision point is reached. At this decision point the examiner uses the child's performance as a basis for deciding to stop testing, administer more difficult items, or return to easier items. In addition to designated stopping points, there are also "alternative" stopping points that should be used when a child is failing numerous items in succession. Some DAS subtests do not use these procedures but revert to using the traditional basal and ceiling approach. This variety of procedures is unusually burdensome to the new user but, once mastered, users will find the DAS item sets preferable to the use of the typical basal and ceiling rules. The use of item sets for administration, however, makes it less likely that a child will experience significant failure prior to reaching a discontinue point. Unlike other tests, a child may miss only a few items or even discontinue after passing an item, thus not interfering with achievement motivation.

The implementation of these various approaches to item administration also requires a record form that is very "busy" by comparison to

tests such as the WISC-III. A raw score to ability score conversion for the subtests contributes further to the complexity of the record form. Once the DAS has been mastered, however, the wealth of information offered on the record form will likely be valued. It is also unusual to have separate record forms for the preschool and school-age ranges. Examiners must, therefore, keep track of supplies of two record forms as opposed to one for tests such as the Binet-4. The DAS also uses many manipulatives that may require some practice to handle in a facile manner.

The three achievement tests on the DAS include arithmetic computation, spelling, and word recognition (decoding). These subtests use the convenient standard score metric where mean = 100 and SD = 15. Grade-based percentile ranks, NCEs, and grade equivalents are available in addition to the usual age-based scores. The estimated administration time for these subtests is anywhere from 15 to 25 minutes. Like the K-ABC, the DAS makes provisions for out-of-level testing. This option is especially helpful for preschoolers of either very high or very low ability levels and for low-scoring children age 6 and older. Examiners may select particular subsets of items in order to get the best match between the items and the child's ability level. In addition, examiners may select a set of subtests normally given at younger or older ages.

The DAS also includes a nonverbal scale to allow for even greater flexibility in the assessment of children with limited verbal abilities, linguistic differences, hearing impairments, or for whatever other reason the examiner feels that administration of a verbal test may be confounded by language-related factors. The nonverbal scale, however, is relatively brief, producing a slightly lower reliability coefficient than when using the core subtests (see Chapter 16).

Standardization

The DAS was normed on a representative national sample of 3,475 children tested between 1987 and 1989. The normative sample included

200 cases per 1-year age group between the ages of 5 and 17 years. At the younger age groups the sample includes 350 cases between 2½ and 4–11 per year. Exceptional children were also included in this standardization to make it as representative as possible of the population of U.S. children. Socioeconomic status was gauged using the average educational level of the parent or parents living with the child. Sex, race/ethnicity, geographic region, community size, and enrollment (for ages 2–5 through 5–11) in an educational program were also controlled.

One of the difficulties in the assessment of individuals with mental retardation is the problem of differentiating levels of cognitive dysfunction. The DAS attempts to address this dilemma by developing extended GCA norms. The extended GCA norms, which extend to a standard score of 25, are obtained by scoring each subtest on norms for a younger age, and then converting the sum of subtest scores to an appropriate standard score for the child's chronological age.

Out-of-level norms are also provided to allow the examiner to use subtests that are designed for a particular age group at a lower level in order to provide the child with an easier set of items. These out-of-level norms can be interpreted in the same way as other norms because they were based on the complete standardization sample.

Reliability

Composite score reliabilities for the GCA are generally quite good ranging from .89 to .95 depending on the age range studied. Internal consistency reliability estimates for the cluster scores (a second tier of composites similar to Binet-4 area scores) range from .83 for Nonverbal Reasoning at age 5 to .94 for Spatial at several ages (although Elliott cautions that the values for Spatial Ability are slightly inflated). The mean internal consistency estimates for the clusters at the school-age level are .88 for Verbal Ability, .90 for Nonverbal Reasoning Ability, and .92 for Spatial Ability. These coefficients are high for composites that each comprise only two subtests.

Internal consistency reliabilities of the subtests are also relatively strong with a few exceptions. The mean reliability coefficient for Recall of Objects, for example, is only .71 and for Recognition of Pictures only .73.

Test-retest coefficients for the composite scores are slightly lower primarily at the preschool ages. At the preschool level the test-retest reliability of the overall GCA is still a respectable .90. However, the reliability of the Verbal and Nonverbal Reasoning composites are .84 and .79, respectively. Some of the individual subtest reliabilities are also low at these young ages. For example, Picture Similarities obtained a test-retest coefficient at the preschool level of only .56, and Recognition of Pictures obtained a reliability coefficient of only .58. The average test-retest coefficient for the subtests is .78. The trade-off of lower reliabilities at the preschool ages may well be worth the reduction in testing time.

Subtest specificities for the school-age level of the DAS are given in the *Handbook* (Elliott, 1990b). Recall of Digits and Speed of Information Processing have particularly favorable ratios of subtest specificity to error variance. Speed of Information Processing, for example, has a mean specificity of .82 and error variance of only .09.

Item bias was systematically assessed during the test development process as is now the case for most tests. There is no detailed information provided, however, only a few items were eliminated (Elliott, 1997).

Validity

Several correlational studies show good evidence of concurrent validity for the DAS. Studies with school-age children have yielded strong GCA correlations with the WISC-R Full Scale (.84 for 8- to 10-year-olds and .91 for 14- and 15-year-olds), Binet-4 Composite (.88 for 9- and 10-year-olds and .85 for a sample of gifted children), and K-ABC MPC (.75) for 5- to 7-year-olds. The DAS did produce lower mean scores than the criterion test in each of these investigations.

The GCA was 6 points lower than the WISC-R Full Scale score in one study and 8 points lower in another. The DAS was only 3 points lower than the Binet-4 composite in one study but 6 points lower in the study for gifted children. The GCA was 9 points lower than the K-ABC MPC. It is difficult to explain these differences based on the norming samples since some of these measures have older norms and some do not. Score differences of about 5 points with the WISC-R and about 2 points with the K-ABC would be expected because of the time intervals between norming, but the actual differences exceed these expectations. A study by Dumont, Cruse, Price, and Whelley (1996) demonstrated strikingly similar mean scores for WISC-III VIQ and DAS Verbal, and WISC-III PIQ and DAS Spatial. The Nonverbal Reasoning score was lower than the WISC-III and DAS composites for this LD sample. We have seen the same trend clinically in that Nonverbal Reasoning tends to differ more than other DAS composites from the WISC-III. This observation is well explained by factor analytic results to be discussed later.

The correlations of the DAS ability measures and achievement tests with academic achievement tests mimic closely those results found for the K-ABC. Namely, the achievement tests are consistently more highly correlated with other achievement measures than are the ability measures. A correlational study of the DAS with the BASIS (Basic Achievement Skills Individual Screener) clearly demonstrated this finding (Elliott, 1990b). Correlations of the GCA with the three achievement subtests of the BASIS ranged from .46 (Spelling for 11-year-olds) to .66 (Reading for 7-year-olds). In direct contrast, the DAS achievement test correlations ranged from .64 (DAS Word Reading and BASIS Reading) to .88 (DAS Spelling and BASIS Spelling). The .64 coefficient was the only one in the .60s; all others were .75 and above. This trend was repeated in a study of the DAS and K-TEA (Kaufman Test of Educational Achievement) with 7- to 11-year-old gifted education referrals. In this study the GCA correlated .56 with the K-TEA composite and the DAS Basic Number Skills, Spelling, and Word Reading skills correlated .71, .78, and .81, respectively, with the K-TEA composite. The DAS Achievement scale advantage was even obtained when school grades were used as the criterion of achievement. In a study of approximately 626 cases (some of the Ns for individual comparisons were smaller) the correlation between Mathematics grades and GCA was .40, and between Mathematics grades and Basic Number Skills .43. The pattern was more striking for Spelling and Word Reading, where the correlations with their grades in these areas and GCA were .25 and .38, and grades with the achievement tests were .60 and .48, respectively. These results suggest that when one is only interested in the passive prediction of school achievement, the DAS achievement test scores are superior.

Factor analyses of the DAS were conducted using confirmatory and exploratory factor analytic techniques. At the school-age level the first factor (a confirmatory factor that could also be interpreted as a "g" factor) was marked by core subtests including Word Definitions, Similarities, Matrices, Sequential and Quantitative Reasoning, and Pattern Construction. At ages 2½ to 3½ the Verbal Comprehension and Naming Vocabulary subtests are the premier measures of "g." At ages 4 and 5 Verbal Comprehension and Early Number Concepts are premier measures (Elliott, 1990b). These results hint that there may be a developmental component to "g" since there is a tendency for the "g" factor to be marked by verbal tests at younger ages and spatial/nonverbal reasoning tests at older ages. This developmental trend may require the clinician to ascribe different interpretations to the GCA depending on the child's age. Subtests with low "g" loadings included Speed of Information Processing, Recognition of Pictures, Recall of Digits, and Recall of Objects. These results corroborate the subtest specificity and intercorrelation findings for Recall of Digits and Speed of Information Processing, showing that these subtests measure discrete skills that overlap little with other tests in the battery.

Elliott (1990b) interpreted these results as supporting the idea that "g" is a "mental complexity factor." The paltry "g" loadings for the Speed of Information Processing test attest to its specificity. Hence, this test may be an interesting supplemental clinical or research tool.

Elliott (1990b) incorporated findings regarding general intelligence factor loadings into the computation of the GCA score which provides a parsimonious measure of "g." At ages 2½ through 3½ the GCA only includes four subtests, and at ages 3½ and above six subtests are included. In contrast to the WISC-III, for example, where subtests with small first factor loadings such as Coding were included in the computation of the Full Scale, the DAS only includes tests in the computation of the GCA if they have substantial first factor loadings. The day-to-day advantage of this approach is that it reduces testing time and calculations when one is solely interested in testing for "g." It is also a theoretically defensible practice that is loyal to the factor analytic data.

The factor analytic study of the DAS included in the *Handbook* (Elliott, 1990b) is as thorough as in any intelligence test manual. At ages 2½ through 3½ Elliott (1990b) concluded that a single general factor was the most appropriate explanation for the intercorrelation matrix. Elliott (1990b) and colleagues tried to fit two- and three-factor models to the data with less success. The DAS scores remain loyal to these data by offering only the GCA at these ages, without lower-level "cluster" scores.

At ages 3–6 through 5–11 a two-factor model was proposed as the best fit to the data. These two factors were labeled as verbal and nonverbal. Confirmatory factor analyses that included the memory subtests in a third factor did not produce an increase in fit. It was concluded that not only were the memory subtests relatively independent of the verbal and nonverbal factors, but, in addition, they were relatively independent of one another. Elliott (1990b) cited some information processing research to support his view that a conceptualization of memory as a unitary dimension is not defensible at this age. This finding of

a lack of a clear memory factor is also consistent with the research for the Binet-4 where the memory factor has been disputed for younger children (see Chapter 9), and for the K-ABC where Spatial Memory never joins the other short-term memory subtests (see Chapter 10). So far, the DAS factors resemble closely those of other tests, which should enhance transfer of training and competent interpretation.

At the school-age level of the DAS, three factors were deemed most appropriate (Elliott, 1990b). These factors were identified as representing verbal, nonverbal reasoning, and spatial abilities. The verbal factor seems intuitive and familiar in that it is marked by loadings for the Word Definitions and Similarities subtests. The nonverbal reasoning and spatial factors were also consistent with the existence of separate Stratum II abilities.

Finally, for clinical assessment purposes, it is important to keep in mind that some subtests are complex. Pattern Construction, for example, could align itself with either the Spatial or Nonverbal Reasoning Cluster depending on the extent to which a child's performance is subserved by either spatial or fluid reasoning abilities.

Interpretation

The DAS manual provides interpretive information and a framework for interpretation for the composite scores and subtests. The DAS offers yet another classification system for intelligence test scores. This system is similar to newer systems in that it offers categories that are more descriptive than diagnostic. The classification system is as follows.

GCA AND CLUSTER SCORES	CATEGORY
130 and above	Very High
120–129	High
110–119	Above Average
90–109	Average
80–89	Below Average
70–79	Low
69 and below	Very Low

The DAS manual then proposes an interpretive system including appropriate tables of statistical values. For example, values are given on the record form for determining the statistical significance of a difference between cluster scores. The values given in conjunction with the cluster scores indicate that a 9-point difference is required to have a statistically significant difference between any of the three cluster scores and the GCA. Similarly, a 16-point difference is required for a statistically significant difference between two cluster scores. The DAS difference values are adjusted for multiple comparisons.

Values for determining significant strengths and weaknesses within a cluster are also given on the DAS record form. A difference of 12 points or more between the two verbal tests is statistically significant. Finally, values are given for comparing a child's subtest score to the mean of all core subtest scores in order to determine significant strengths and weaknesses. Although there is potential for confusion by including all of these interpretive values on the record form, some would likely argue that for the frequent DAS user the advantages of speed and convenience far outweigh any disadvantages.

Supplementary interpretive methods and associated values are offered for evaluating the child's diagnostic subtest performance. Tables of shared subtest hypotheses are also offered, as shown on pages 101 and 102 of the *Handbook* (Elliott, 1990b). These tables allow the examiner to apply numerous theories to the interpretation of the DAS. For example, Elliott (1990b) shows how the K-ABC simultaneous/sequential distinction may be applied to the DAS.

The DAS also offers tables and procedures for interpreting ability/achievement discrepancies for the purposes of learning disability diagnosis. The *DAS Manual* and *Handbook* offer values for determining the statistical significance and frequency of a difference between the DAS ability and achievement tests. Similarly, the *Manual* and *Handbook* provide tables of the frequency and significance of differences in the population between a child's *expected* achievement level and his or her actual achievement. This *regression* approach is not offered by all tests but is of potential value as it is a popular method for the determination of ability/achievement discrepancies (see Chapter 20).

The DAS manual also includes some validity study research for samples of exceptional children. The mean scores for a sample of gifted children were rather low (Mean GCA = 118.1). This finding, however, may be due to selection bias since all of the children were previously identified with other tests based on high intelligence test scores (see Chapter 5). The mean GCA was 59.4 for a sample of 25 students who were previously identified as mildly retarded. A sample of 110 children who were identified by their school as learning disabled obtained a mean GCA of 89.6 with a consistent composite score pattern. There was, however, a discrepancy in that DAS Achievement test scores were consistently lower than the ability scores especially in Spelling (mean = 78.2) and Word Reading (mean = 76.5). This finding suggests that the GCA/Achievement test discrepancy may be consistent with much of current practice in the assessment of learning problems.

Testimony to the thoroughness of the DAS manual is the fact that a cluster analytic study was included. The researchers selected 136 children from the DAS standardization sample who had GCA scores >85, Word Reading scores <85, and Word Reading scores at least 15 points below the score predicted by their GCA. These children were considered reading disabled, and their scores submitted to a cluster analysis. The cluster analysis produced four clusters. Three of the clusters were marked by a relative strength in spatial ability and one by a relative strength in verbal ability. All mean GCAs were in the middle to high 90s. Although the sample was selected on the basis of reading scores, spelling scores were also low. Spelling scores for the four clusters ranged from 77.1 to 82.1. Basic Numbers Skills scores were not as depressed, but they were consistently lower than the GCAs with means in the high 80s to low 90s. The ranks of the achievement tests in this study are the same as those for the school-selected sample cited previously.

The ability/achievement discrepancy profile is striking in this study, and the cluster scores are consistent with one another.

Interpretive notes to keep in mind for the DAS might include the following:

1. Be aware of the slightly lower reliabilities of clusters and composites at the preschool level.

2. When WISC-III and DAS overall composite scores differ, it may be due to two factors: (a) more of the FSIQ (1/2) is comprised of verbal content compared to 1/3 for the DAS, and (b) the DAS Nonverbal Reasoning score may be deviant since reasoning (i.e., fluid) abilities are not well assessed by the WISC-III.

3. The Speed of Information Processing test may be difficult to support with other test results because many tests do not include similar measures. This test may relate to scores on other tests such as the WISC-III because of its enhanced speed of processing component.

4. The Pattern Construction subtest may be a good analogue of Wechsler's Block Design since two studies produced correlations of .80 and .86 between these two measures (Elliott, 1990b).

DAS SAMPLE CASE

The following is a report of a psychological evaluation in which the DAS was used as part of a comprehensive test battery. This case is interesting in that the DAS and WISC-III scores do not correspond closely with one another.

Dahlia's background and test behavior may be described as erratic. She has not failed a grade, been retained, or placed in special education, and yet her academic performance has been inconsistent. Her test behavior was similarly inconsistent suggesting that she may achieve high

Box 13.1   Psychological report

Name: Dahlia
Age: 12 years, 10 months
Gender: Female

School: County Middle
Grade: 7

Assessment Procedures

Differential Ability Scale (DAS)
Wechsler Intelligence Scale for Children—Third Edition (WISC-III)
Woodcock-Johnson Tests of Achievement-Revised (WJ-R)
Kaufman Test of Educational Achievement—Comprehensive Form (K-TEA)
Bender-Gestalt Test of Visual-Motor Development (Bender)
Achenbach Youth Self-Report (YSR)
Social Skills Rating System—Student Form (SSRS)
Sentence Completion Survey
Reynolds Adolescent Depression Scale (RADS)
Kinetic Family Drawing (KFD)
Achenbach Child Behavior Checklist (CBCL)
Social Skills Rating System—Parent Form (SSRS)
Parenting Stress Index (PSI)
Behavior Assessment System for Children-Structured Developmental History (BASCSDH)
Achenbach Child Behavior Checklist—Teacher Report Form (TRF)

Box 13.1 Psychological report (Continued)

Reason for Referral

Dahlia was evaluated at her parent's request because of concerns about her achievement motivation, failure to complete assignments, poor organizational skills, inattention, and deterioration in grades. Parents and teachers alike feel that Dahlia is an underachiever. Her parents in particular want to rule out the presence of a learning disability.

Background Information

Dahlia lives with her birth mother and father. Both her mother and father are faculty members at a local junior college. The parents could not describe any particular strife at home with the exception of some arguments over homework.

Dahlia's mother reports a normal pregnancy and delivery. At age 3, Dahlia contracted chicken pox, which is the only childhood illness that was reported.

According to her mother, Dahlia's developmental milestones were delayed. However, once she acquired these skills, she did not differ noticeably from her peers. Her mother also reported that she was given a readiness test before entering kindergarten, on which she did very poorly. The school decided to admit Dahlia, contingent upon her performance.

Dahlia's academic performance has been inconsistent, which has been of considerable concern to her parents. They stated that after approximately 3 weeks of this school year, her attitude seemed to change for the worse and she seemed "stressed." Of all her academic subjects, Dahlia's mother is most concerned with mathematics. After an initial parent–teacher conference at the beginning of the school year, Dahlia's teachers decided to help her work on her organizational skills and completion of assignments. They have incorporated a plan of initialing her assignment list to verify that Dahlia had copied her assignments.

Dahlia's most recent vision and hearing exams were given in the fall of this year. The results were negative.

Behavioral Observations

Dahlia was pleasant and well mannered during the testing session. She was reticent at first, but rapport was quickly established. A notable observation was her attempt to control her inattention and impulsivity. On one test she said aloud "think," which seemed to be aimed at ensuring a nonimpulsive response. On some tests she seemed disinterested (e.g., she sat far away from the test table), and on some she responded impulsively by not surveying problems before responding.

Assessment Results

Cognitive

Dahlia's performance on the intelligence measures was variable, making it difficult to summarize her performance with a single score. Her WISC-III revealed a Verbal greater than Performance profile with a difference of 19 points. Her Verbal score was a relative strength with a score in the above-average range with her Performance score in the average range.

The Differential Abilities Scales (DAS) includes subtests that assess Verbal, Nonverbal Reasoning, and Spatial skills. Dahlia's summary score on this measure, the General Conceptual Ability score (GCA), was also less relevant (as were WISC composites) because of variability in her subtest scores. Her WISC-III and DAS scores taken together suggest that Dahlia has problems with subtests that require sustained effort and concentration. These tests happen to be on nonverbal reasoning scales of the DAS and WISC-III. These tests usually involve manual activities and good spatial skills in which the child has to copy a pattern or solve figural analogies. Her performance is somewhat better, by contrast, when she solves verbal items. These items involve tasks such as defining words or giving oral descriptions of how to solve practical problems.

Academic Achievement

Dahlia's academic achievement was evaluated with the WJ-R and the K-TEA. Both of these measures contain subtests similar to school-related tasks, such as reading comprehension, mathematics calculation, and spelling.

(Continues)

Box 13.1   **Psychological report** (Continued)

Dahlia's scores on both achievement measures are commensurate with her intellectual skills in that all of her scores hover in the average to above-average ranges. There was also no suggestive evidence of a specific learning disability or a particular academic weakness.

Visual-Motor Skills

Dahlia's visual-motor skills were evaluated by using the Bender and the Recall of Designs subtest of the DAS. These tests are similar and consist of copying several designs that are presented to the examinee.

Dahlia's performance was below average on the Bender. This low score may be due to the fact that she drew each design quickly without referring back to the stimulus. Her performance on the Recall of Designs subtest of the DAS meets or exceeds 82% of the children her age. Again, she was quick to reproduce these designs, which is consistent with previous observations of impulsive tendencies. Dahlia's scores on the Recall of Designs test may be higher because there is also a memory component for this test. Impulsive tendencies may have worked to her benefit somewhat as she responded quickly, which may have allowed her adequate access to the memory traces.

Social-Emotional Status

Self-Report Information

Dahlia completed the Reynolds Adolescent Depression Scale (RADS), Social Skills Rating System (SSRS), Achenbach Youth Self-Report (YSR), Kinetic Family Drawing (KFD), and the Sentence Completion Survey. There were no apparent problems indicated on these measures.

According to the SSRS, Dahlia views herself as cooperative, assertive, empathic, and as having self-control. Dahlia's responses on the YSR also support these views of herself; however, these self-reports are in direct contrast to the way her parents view her behavior. The KFD, RADS, and the Sentence Completion Survey did not indicate that there are any emotional or family problems of significance.

Parent Information

Dahlia's mother completed the Parenting Stress Index (PSI), Social Skills Rating System (SSRS), and the Achenbach Child Behavior Checklist (CBCL). The scores obtained on the CBCL indicated that she views Dahlia's behavior as being in the normal range. She did, however, endorse items such as inattention and disorganization as were noted in the original referral.

Teacher Information

All of Dahlia's teachers completed the Achenbach Child Behavior Checklist—Teacher's Report Form. There were no problems indicated in the areas of adaptive functioning or classroom behavior.

Summary and Conclusions

Dahlia is a 12-year-old female who was evaluated at her parent's request to determine if she has a learning or motivational problem that may explain a perceived problem with academic underachievement. Dahlia is functioning in the average to above-average ranges of intelligence, with a relative weakness in attention that becomes apparent on tests that require concentrated and sustained effort and planful problem solving. This estimate is commensurate with her estimates of achievement. There is no evidence currently of a specific learning disability. Although Dahlia views herself as socially and emotionally well-adjusted, her parents are concerned about her tendencies to appear stressed and make self-deprecating statements.

All assessment results indicate that Dahlia seems unable, rather than unwilling, to perform up to her ability in school. This tendency was most apparent on tasks requiring sustained attention. She has difficulty attending and poor organizational skills that she is aware of and tries to control occasionally through self-talk. No evidence of motor hyperactivity is present.

Diagnosis

Dahlia's long-standing symptoms of inattention and impulsivity without motor hyperactivity are consistent with the diagnosis of attention deficit hyperactivity disorder primary inattentive type.

Box 13.1   Psychological report (Continued)

Recommendations

1. Consultation should be sought by her district's school psychologist and student support team in order to develop further instructional interventions.

2. Dahlia's parents should receive some professional consultation in order to help them manage Dahlia's homework assignments.

3. Dahlia should be reevaluated a few months after the initiation of school-based treatment to assess her progress, confirm the diagnosis, and initiate other treatments as indicated.

Psychometric Summary

Wechsler Intelligence Scale for Children—Revised (WISC-III)

Composite scores	Standard scores	PR
Full Scale	111	77
Verbal Scale	119	90
Performance Scale	100	50

Subtests	Scaled scores
Verbal	
Information	14
Similarities	11
Arithmetic	14
Vocabulary	9
Comprehension	18
Digit Span	6
Performance	
Picture Completion	11
Picture Arrangement	15
Block Design	8
Object Assembly	6
Coding	10
Mazes	13

Differential Ability Scales (DAS)

Subtests	T-score	PR
Recall of Designs	59	82
Word Definitions	50	50
Pattern Construction	50	69
Matrices	37	10
Similarities	56	73
Sequential & Quantitative Reasoning	51	54

(Continues)

Box 13.1   **Psychological report** (Continued)

COMPOSITE SCORES	STANDARD SCORES	PR
Verbal	104	61
Nonverbal Reasoning	89	23
Spatial	111	77
General Conceptual Ability	102	55

Kaufman Test of Educational Achievement (K-TEA)

COMPOSITE SCORES	STANDARD SCORE	PR
Reading	105	63
Mathematics	120	91
Battery	112	79
Subtests		
Mathematics Applications	130	98
Reading Decoding	110	75
Spelling	102	55
Reading Comprehension	100	50
Mathematics Computation	107	68

Woodcock-Johnson Psychoeducational Battery (WJ-R)

COMPOSITE SCORES	STANDARD SCORES	PR
Broad Reading	111	77
Broad Math	111	77
Broad Written Language	100	50
Skills	108	70
Subtests		
Letter-Word Identification	118	88
Passage Comprehension	100	50
Calculation	103	59
Applied Problems	115	84
Dictation	90	25
Writing Samples	125	95

Bender-Gestalt Test of Visual-Motor Development (Bender)
Score = 2   Age equivalent 9:0 to 9:11

Reynolds Adolescent Depression Scale (RADS)

SCALE	RAW SCORE	PR
Depression	36	4

Social Skills Rating System—Student Form

SCALE	STANDARD SCORE	PR
Social Skills	108	70

Box 13.1 Psychological report (Continued)

Achenbach Youth Self-Report (YSR)

	T-SCORE
Depressed	55
Unpopular	55
Somatic Complaints	55
Self-Destructive	55
Thought Disturbances	55
Delinquent	55
Aggressive	55
Sum	33
Activities	**48**
Social	55
Total Competence	52

Parenting Stress Index (PSI)

	PR
Child Domain Score	**78**
Adaptability	17
Acceptability	12
Demandingness	19
Mood	3
Distractibility/Hyperactivity	20
Reinforces Parent	7
Parent Domain Score	**90**
Depression	12
Attachment	11
Restriction of Roles	5
Sense of Competence	25
Social Isolation	10
Relation with Spouse	10
Parent Health	10
Total Stress Score	5

Social Skills Rating System—Parent Form

	STANDARD SCORES	PR
Social Skills	120	91
Problem Behaviors	92	30

CASE NOTES Dahlia's WISC-III shows a relative verbal strength and the DAS does not. The WISC-III and DAS scores were also somewhat erratic. On the DAS, for example, there is a relative Nonverbal Reasoning weakness, but it occurs as a result of one test (Matrices) and the other nonverbal test, Sequential and Quantitative Reasoning, is average. Hence, several of Dahlia's composite scores are comprised of heterogeneous subtest performances. Even scores that typically correlate highly, namely Block Design and Pattern Construction, are inconsistent. What's wrong here? I suspect that the answer lies in Dahlia's behavior. She is inattentive, disorganized, and her motivation wavers. The report does not make a great deal of her intelligence test profile because it seems secondary to social/emotional/behavioral issues *and* tainted by them.

scores on some tests and low scores on others. Given her lack of "risk" factors, an a priori hypothesis of average intelligence test scores seems warranted.

CONCLUSIONS

The DAS is yet another promising intelligence test instrument. There is every indication that the developers of the DAS erred in the direction of quality at every turn. The manual is extraordinarily thorough, the psychometric properties are strong, and the test materials are of high quality. This test deserves more research attention than it has received and a clinical trial by all who assess children. The extended range of scores to a standard score of 25 make this an especially appealing test to those who are trying to differentiate among levels of mental retardation. Other unique features include the Nonverbal scale and provisions for out-of-level testing. The learning curve for administration and scoring seems steep, but for some if not many clinicians the effort may be well worth it. In fact, the DAS is favored by our students as it provides a very time efficient assessment of "g" and of several important Stratum II abilities. Moreover, our examinees experience less frustration and failure due to the use of item sets.

Aylward (1992) identified numerous features of the DAS by concluding:

The DAS contains many subtle "perks" such as performance analysis in Word Reading, the Informal Behavior Scale, and scoring templates for drawing tests. Comparison can be made between Cluster scores, the GCA, subtest scores, and achievement, thereby allowing for more precision in the identification of strengths and weaknesses. (p. 282)

CHAPTER SUMMARY

- The DAS is a comprehensive battery of cognitive and achievement tests that are designed for children and adolescents between the ages of 2½ and 17 years.
- The DAS borrows from numerous theorists and research findings.
- There are two sets of subtests on the cognitive scales of the DAS. One set is a group of "core" subtests that are used to derive the GCA composite score. In addition to these there are a number of "diagnostic" subtests that are intended to measure relatively independent abilities.
- There are three achievement tests on the DAS. These include arithmetic computation, spelling, and word recognition (decoding).
- The DAS also includes a nonverbal scale to allow for even greater flexibility in the assessment of children.
- The DAS was normed on a representative national sample of 3,475 children tested between 1987 and 1989.
- Several correlational studies show good evidence of concurrent validity for the DAS.
- The DAS GCA should not be used for predicting school achievement if the DAS achievement test scores are available.
- The learning curve for DAS administration and scoring may be steep.

CHAPTER 14

Intelligence and Achievement Screeners

Cheryl Nemeth Hendry
The University of Georgia

CHAPTER QUESTIONS

What are some purposes of intelligence and achievement screening?

What is the difference between broadband and diagnostic achievement testing?

This chapter focuses primarily on relatively brief, individually administered, norm-referenced measures or "screeners" of intelligence and academic achievement. Screeners are useful for a myriad of purposes when the administration of more comprehensive instruments is impractical. Some such circumstances include:

- *Reevaluation*: Individuals who have previously been administered a comprehensive psychoeducational battery for the purpose of determining eligibility for special education or other services may not require a detailed reassessment to determine whether or not services should be continued. Screeners can often provide quick, reliable indicators of current functioning.

- *Differing referral questions*: In cases of some evaluations, comprehensive measures of intelligence and achievement are not necessary, as these areas may not be central to the referral question at hand. For example, a child who is referred to a psychologist for treatment of anxiety may not benefit from a comprehensive evaluation of intelligence and achievement. However, the psychologist may desire some general information pertaining to the child's performance in these areas prior to treatment.

- *Large-scale screenings*: Screeners of intelligence and achievement can be used to identify individuals in a variety of settings (e.g., educational, vocational, and clinical) who may be in need of a comprehensive psychoeducational evaluation.

- *Supporting evidence*: Screeners may also be used for the purpose of confirming other assessment results.

Caveat: It is emphasized that screening measures alone are not sufficient to form definitive diagnoses, but that they are considered to be useful preliminary and/or ancillary measures in the assessment process. This chapter consists of two primary sections: intelligence screeners and academic achievement screeners in which specific instruments and their purposes are described. Not all tests of this nature are covered in this text, and exclusion of a test is not a comment on its quality. Instruments were selected for discussion primarily according to both their frequency of use and technical adequacy.

INTELLIGENCE SCREENERS

Peabody Picture Vocabulary Test—Third Edition (PPVT-III)

The PPVT-III (Dunn & Dunn, 1997a, 1997b) is the successor to the PPVT-R (Dunn & Dunn, 1981) and the original PPVT (Dunn, 1959). The PPVT-III is perhaps one of the shortest screening measures of intelligence ever developed. It is an unusual test in that it has an identity problem of sorts. In its first edition, the test was offered to clinicians as a quick screening measure of general intellectual ability. This claim, however, was attacked by a number of reviewers because of the brevity of the measure as well as the limited skills it assessed. Therefore, this assertion of being a screening measure of general intelligence was withdrawn with the publication of the PPVT-R in 1981. Most recently, the authors of the PPVT-III purport that the instrument is an achievement measure of receptive language or "hearing vocabulary" acquisition for standard English and a screening measure of verbal ability for those individuals who speak English as a first language across home, school, and community

settings. One may conjecture, however, that some clinicians continue to use the PPVT-III as a brief screening measure of overall intellectual ability or cognitive development. The authors of the PPVT-III also mention that it is considered to be a good rapport-building instrument for assessment in that it requires little or no oral response. It can also be used with success for some individuals with autism, cerebral palsy, and reticent behavior for this same reason. The PPVT-III also has specialized uses in the area of speech and language assessment. For example, nonreaders and children who may have normal hearing but impaired oral communication skills could be assessed with the PPVT-III since the items require only a pointing response. The PPVT-III can serve as a screening device for verbal ability in preschool-age children, a measure of English-language proficiency in those who use English as a second language, giftedness, mental retardation, and language disorders. However, the authors caution against overgeneralizing the results of PPVT-III administrations, stressing that the specific skill measured is hearing or receptive vocabulary. The PPVT-III contains some new features that improve upon previous editions, including extended age-based norms (ranges from 2 years, 6 months through 90+ years), updated item content with refined ethnic and gender balance, numerous new stimulus words, arrangement of items into sets grouped by difficulty, and improved packaging. This instrument is also available in Spanish, TVIP: Test de Vocabulario en Imágenes Peabody (Dunn, Lugo, Padilla, & Dunn, 1986), and measures the receptive vocabulary of Spanish-speaking children ages 2 years, 6 months to 18 years.

Administration and Scoring

The construction of the PPVT-III is relatively simple in that it is an untimed, individually administered test having an easel format. It consists of two equivalent forms, IIIA and IIIB, with 204 items per form, and items are grouped by difficulty level into 17 sets of 12 items each. Each item consists of a "PicturePlate" or page having four black-and-white illustrations and a stimulus word to be read by the examiner. The examiner dictates a stimulus word, and the examinee is required to point to one of the four pictures that best describes the meaning of the word dictated. The examiner then uses basal and ceiling rules to determine, based upon the individual's performance, the appropriate sets of the 204 items to be administered. Training or teaching items are also included. Alternatively, the PPVT-III manual also includes useful guidelines for adapting administration for those with severe motor and/or speech impairment. In such a case, the examiner may point to each of the four pictures and have the examinee use a head shake, other signal, or communication board to indicate a yes/no response. Total standard test administration time is generally 11 to 12 minutes. Scoring procedures are relatively quick and simple and do not require extensive psychometric training and/or experience. Responses to each item are scored as pass or fail, and the total raw score is converted to a single age-based standard score with a mean of 100 and standard deviation of 15. A normal-curve graphic display of score classification schemes is provided on the PPVT-III protocol. Scores are classified in a symmetrical fashion: Extremely High Score (130 and above), Moderately High Score (115–129), High Average Score (100–114), Low Average Score (85 to 99), Moderately Low Score (70–84), and Extremely Low Score (69 and below). The combination of quick, simple administration and scoring and a broad age range serve to make the PPVT-III an attractive screening measure.

Standardization

The PPVT-III norming sample consisted of 2,725 individuals between the ages of 2 years, 6 months through 90+ years, with 2,000 children and adolescents and 725 individuals over the age of 19. Due to the rapidity of language development in young children, 6-month intervals were used for children between the ages of 2 years, 6 months and 6 years.

Whole-year intervals were used for children between the ages of 7 and 16 years, as language development occurs at a steadier rate. Accordingly, multiyear intervals were used for individuals over age 16, as language acquisition at this time is relatively stable. Standardization was conducted during 1995 and 1996, and the sample was selected to correspond proportionately to the U. S. Census data as presented in the March 1994 *Current Population Survey*. The sample was stratified according to variables of age, gender, race/ethnicity, socioeconomic status (as defined by education level of self or parent), geographic region, and special education category. Overall, the standardization sample of the PPVT-III appears to be closely representative of the U.S. population.

Reliability

Internal consistency estimates for the PPVT-III are stronger than those found for the PPVT-R overall. Split-half reliability coefficients for Form IIIA ranged from .89 to .97 with a median of .94 and ranged from .86 to .96 with a median of .94 for Form IIIB across the standardization sample. Alpha coefficients are also reported, ranging from .93 to .98 with a median of .95 for Form IIIA and .92 to .98 with a median of .95 for Form IIIB. Test-retest reliability coefficients were computed for a sample of 226 individuals ages 2 years, 6 months to 57 years, 11 months, ranging from .91 to .93 for Form IIIA and from .91 to .94 for Form IIIB with an approximate 1-month administration interval. In addition, alternate-forms reliability coefficients for the standard scores of the standardization sample are presented, ranging from .88 to .96 with a median of .94. These figures suggest a high degree of item uniformity within each form and throughout the test overall, as well as stability of scores.

Validity

The PPVT-III manual presents a variety of types of validity, including content, construct, internal, and concurrent or criterion-related validity. In terms of content validity, the PPVT-III appears to measure what it claims to measure (i.e., hearing or receptive vocabulary for standard English). Examination of the test items in addition to the methodology used to select these items as described in the manual provides evidence for content validity. Construct validity is used to support the claim that the PPVT-III is a screening measure of verbal ability. References to studies indicating that Vocabulary subtests of intelligence instruments such as the WISC-III correlate most highly with composite intelligence scores are used to demonstrate evidence of construct validity. However, as the PPVT-III only measures one mode of vocabulary knowledge (i.e., receptive only versus receptive and expressive), this defense is not infallible. Documentation of internal validity is presented in terms of age differentiation, item growth curves, Rasch models, and item homogeneity. However, the bulk of evidence concerning the validity of the PPVT-III relies on concurrent or criterion-related validity, at least in terms of its ability to serve as a screening measure of verbal intelligence. Correlations between standard scores on both forms of the PPVT-III and the WISC-III were calculated for a sample of 41 children between the ages of 7 years, 11 months and 14 years, 4 months. These figures ranged from .82 to .84 for Performance IQ, .91 to .92 for Verbal IQ, and .90 for Full Scale IQ. As expected, PPVT-III scores were found to correlate higher with the WISC-III Verbal IQ. Scores on the PPVT-III and the KAIT for a sample of 28 adolescents between the ages 13 years and 17 years, 8 months were correlated. The correlations ranged from .87 to .91 for Crystallized IQ, .76 to .85 for Fluid IQ, and .85 to .91 for Composite IQ. As anticipated, it was found that PPVT-III scores were more highly correlated with Crystallized IQ scores on the KAIT. Further, for a sample of 80 adults between the ages of 18 years and 71 years, 1 month, scores on the PPVT-III and the Kaufman Brief Intelligence Test (K-BIT) were correlated. Specifically, these figures ranged from .80 to .82 for Vocabulary, .62 to .65 for Matrices,

and .76 to .78 for the K-BIT IQ Composite. As can be seen, PPVT-III scores correlated higher with the Vocabulary scores on the K-BIT. Overall, these figures appear to be adequate, as most intelligence tests seem to correlate with each other in the .70s and sometimes in the .80s.

In addition, two studies were conducted for the purpose of correlating the PPVT-III with the Oral and Written Language Scales (OWLS). For a sample of 41 children ranging in age from 3 years to 5 years, 8 months, correlations were .63 to .66 for Listening Comprehension, .77 to .83 for Oral Expression, and .77 to .82 for Oral Composite. For a sample of 43 children ages 8 years, 1 month to 12 years, 10 months, correlations were .70 to .77 for Listening Comprehension, .67 to .68 for Oral Expression, and .75 to .77 for Oral Composite. On the surface, it appears that the correlations between the PPVT-III and the OWLS are less robust than they should be; however, the OWLS measures several skills associated with oral language, whereas the PPVT-III measures only receptive vocabulary. Lastly, a summary of validity studies conducted with the PPVT-III's predecessors, the PPVT and PPVT-R, is presented, as these studies are more plentiful than what is yet available on the PPVT-III. A summary of selected studies correlating scores on the PPVT-R and scores on intelligence tests is presented, including the Columbia Mental Maturity Scale (N=44, r=.23); the DAS Verbal Ability Cluster (N=103, r=.70); the K-ABC Mental Processing Composite (N=2,790, r=.58) and Achievement Composite (N=2,822, r=.75); the KAIT Composite IQ (N=192, r=.76), Crystallized IQ (N=192, r=.78), and Fluid IQ (N=192, r=.67); the McCarthy Scales of Children's Abilities General Cognitive Index (N=155, r=.69), Verbal (N=155, r=.65), Perceptual (N=155, r=.58), Quantitative (N=155, r=.56), and Memory (N=155, r=.43); the Raven's Coloured Progressive Matrices (N=60, r=.56); the SB-IV Test Composite (N=424, r=.58), Verbal (N=329, r=.69), Abstract/Visual (N=329, r=.43), Quantitative (N=208, r=.29), and Short-Term Memory (N=329, r=.44); the WAIS-R Full Scale IQ

(N=314, r=.73), Verbal IQ (N=283, r=.74), and Performance IQ (N=262, r=.64); the WISC-R Full Scale IQ (N=1,099, r=.70), Verbal IQ (N=1,345, r=.69), and Performance IQ (N=1,034, r=.51); the WPPSI-R Full Scale IQ (N=154, r=.68), Verbal IQ (N=154, r=.68), and Performance IQ (N=154, r=.50). Additionally, a comprehensive review by Bracken, Prasse, and McCallum (1984) indicates that the PPVT-R yields correlation coefficients with popular intelligence tests in the general range of the .70s, although in some individual studies, the correlations have been poor. A summary of studies correlating the PPVT-R with a variety of Vocabulary tests and subtests is provided in the manual, including the WISC-R Vocabulary subtest (N=640, r=.70), the Beery Picture Vocabulary Test (N=146, r=.65), the Boehm Test of Basic Concepts (N=99, r=.64), the Boston Naming Test (N=305, r=.59), the Bracken Basic Concepts Scale (N=247, r=.76), the DAS Naming Vocabulary subtest (N=79, r=.73), the Expressive One-Word Picture Vocabulary Test (N=1,283, r=.62), the SB-IV Vocabulary subtest (N=207, r=.66), the Test of Language Development Picture Vocabulary subtest (N=201, r=.63), and the WPPSI-R Vocabulary subtest (N=154, r=.40). Validity evidence presented for the PPVT-III appears to be adequate, although more information would be useful. It should be noted that since the PPVT-III represents a significant revision of the PPVT-R, the numerous validity studies from the PPVT-R may not necessarily hold true for the PPVT-III. Certainly, there is a need for more studies of concurrent or criterion-related validity to be conducted with the PPVT-III.

Summary

The PPVT-III has a long tradition as a screening measure of intelligence. Its simple format, administration, and scoring have proved enticing to psychologists and others who have used the test as a screening measure. Some psychologists, for example, may use the PPVT-III as an initial screener for children, and then use this information to select a comprehensive test battery for use in the complete evaluation. This practice seems acceptable in that the PPVT-III in this case is being used truly as a screener. One must keep in mind, however, that the PPVT-III measures only one facet of intelligence: crystallized or verbal ability from Carroll's (1993) theory. Consequently, the PPVT-III may not be useful for screening for reasoning, visualization, or other problems. One of the pitfalls of the PPVT-III and its forerunners is that its brevity has made it apt for misuse and overuse by clinicians. Occasionally, the PPVT-III has been used as a substitute for a more comprehensive measure of intelligence, a practice that is not suggested by its authors. Overall, the PPVT-III appears to be well normed and technically adequate, even though more criterion-related validity studies and independent studies would be beneficial. As with any test, however, clinicians should take care to use this test for the purposes for which it was intended, a measure of hearing vocabulary or, a screening measure of crystallized ability.

Slosson Intelligence Test— Revised (SIT-R)

The SIT-R (Slosson, 1991a, 1991b) is the latest revision of its predecessor, the SIT (Slosson, 1963). As a screening instrument, the SIT-R was designed to provide a quick estimate of verbal, crystallized intelligence for individuals between the ages of 4 and 18+ years. The author cautions the test-user against interpreting the SIT-R as anything but a screener, suggesting that follow-up assessment is necessary to confirm results. Suggested uses of the SIT-R include large-scale screening, tentative diagnosis, and corroboration of other assessment results. More specifically, the SIT-R was "designed to be an individual test for use in screening or estimating the cognitive ability of an individual, public school student, college student, mental patient, or mentally handicapped person" (Sloson, 1991a, p. 1). Lastly, although during the trial and standardization phase, the SIT-R was administered to "blind, learning disabled, cerebral palsy, orthopedically handicapped, emotionally disturbed, mentally handicapped, and behavior disordered subjects" (Slosson, 1991a, p. 9), the author strongly cautions against interpretation of scores obtained for persons with disabilities. These two statements, therefore, appear to be conflicting and could be potentially confusing for the examiner. Further, it is stated that as the SIT-R was only administered to individuals fluent in English, it should not be used for those lacking proficiency with the English language. The SIT-R reflects the following improvements upon previous editions: More even distribution of item types, updated language, updated and expanded standardization sample, more extensive reliability and validity studies, scoring guidelines allowing for English or metric responses, and changing the term *Intelligence Quotient (IQ)* to *Total Standard Score (TSS)*. Further, in this revision, Slosson departed from his prior use of the Stanford-Binet as a model for developing the SIT-R. The development of the instrument was not guided by any one test, but by a theoretical rationale of the construct of intelligence as described by experts in the field such as Thurstone, Guilford, Wechsler, Thorndike, and Cattell. The SIT-R model consists of global ability "g" at the top of the hierarchy, with crystallized intelligence and memory at the second level of the hierarchy. Crystallized intelligence is further subdivided into verbal and quantitative components. Per this model, several types of items from six domains are found on the SIT-R. Crystallized intelligence, verbal includes Vocabulary (VO), General Information (GI), Similarities and Differences (SD), and Comprehension (CO); crystallized intelligence, quantitative includes Quantitative (QN); memory includes Auditory Memory (AM). The SIT-R is designed such that at least one item from each of these domains is present within every group of ten items with the exception of two groups of ten items.

Administration and Scoring

Overall, the SIT-R is easy to administer and to score and requires minimal competency in psychometrics to interpret. The SIT-R is an untimed, individually administered test that consists of one form containing 187 items. Within the test, six domains, or types of items are included: Vocabulary (VO)—33 items, General Information (GI)—29 items, Similarities and Differences (SD)—30 items, Comprehension (CO)—33 items, Quantitative (QN)—34 items, and Auditory Memory (AM)—28 items. Items are arranged by level of difficulty, and unlike more extensive intelligence tests such as the WISC-III, item types are dispersed throughout the test rather than separated into subtests. Items are administered in a straightforward question-and-answer format. Training or teaching items are not included. The SIT-R manual offers some suggestions for testing persons with disabilities, such as excluding items requiring visual ability for those with visual impairment. However, it should be noted that no norms including testing modifications are included for the SIT-R, thus weakening the interpretation of such scores. Total standard test administration time ranges from 10 to 30 minutes. Responses to items are scored as pass or fail, and basal and ceiling rules are used to determine the appropriate number of items to be administered. Computerized scoring is available. The total raw score on the SIT-R is converted to a single Total Standard Score (TSS) with a mean of 100 and a standard deviation of 16. These scores may also be converted to standard scores having a mean of 100 and a standard deviation of 15. The SIT-R also provides a "Slosson Classification Chart," which presents a "classification" of ability levels as well as a description of "school accomplishment and placement." For example, any individual with a TSS of 148 and above is classified as "very superior" and school accomplishment and placement is described as "gifted programs, college, and graduate work." At the other extreme, any individual with a TSS of 35 and below is classified as "severe/profound M/H" and school accomplishment and placement is described as "classes for severe/profound" (Slosson, 1991a, p. 41). This classification chart is evaluative in nature and may likely encourage the overinterpretation of scores, a practice that the author cautions the test consumer against in other sections of the manual. Further, Kamphaus (1995) indicates that this chart may suggest that the TSS can be used to diagnose persons with syndromes such as mental retardation or giftedness. However, to rely wholly on intelligence scores for any type of diagnosis is an unsound practice. The inclusion of this classification chart conflicts with the delineated purposes of the SIT-R and may confound appropriate test use. Nevertheless, the fact that the SIT-R is quick and easy to administer and score makes it an inviting choice for practitioners.

Standardization

The SIT-R norming sample consisted of 1,854 subjects between the ages of 4 years and 18+ years. Interestingly, the SIT-R was administered to a total pool of more than 2,400 persons, and the final subjects to be included in the sample were subsequently chosen according to demographic characteristics. Attempts were made to approximate the sample to the U. S. population as described in the 1990 World Almanac as opposed to U. S. Census data. The sample was stratified according to gender, geographic region, occupational category, education level, size of population center, and race. However, the standardization sample underrepresents minorities for the total sample as well as individuals living in areas with populations below 5,000 and above 500,000. Further, the norms do not present the number of individuals per stratification variable by age group. Such information should have been presented, as the Total Standard Scores were delineated by age group in the normative tables. In this same vein, it is unclear why separate age group norms are not presented for those 18 years of age and over, as 517 cases ranging in age from 18 years to 64 years, 9 months are depicted in the reliability section of the SIT-R. Recently, calibrated

norms were published for the SIT-R to correct this problem. The normative information is the same, except that the norms tables are divided into 3-month intervals up to age 64 years, 9 months as opposed to 18+ as presented in the first edition of the norms tables. Additionally, individuals with disabilities were either not included in the sample or omitted in the presentation of the normative information. The omission of individuals with disabilities is inconsistent with the aforementioned purposes and uses of the SIT-R. Overall, although improved from the previous edition, the norming sample of the SIT-R is not adequately representative of the U. S. population in all areas described. Further, the SIT-R does not offer sufficient information pertaining to age without the newly calibrated norms.

Reliability

Internal consistency estimates for the SIT-R were computed by age levels (4 years to 64 years, 9 months) for 1,793 subjects from the norming sample using the Kuder-Richardson Formula 20 (KR-20), an estimate of coefficient alpha (i.e., the mean of all possible split-half reliability coefficients). These figures ranged from .88 to .97, indicating a high degree of item consistency. Further, KR-20 was computed for the entire standardization sample, yielding a coefficient of .96. Split-half reliability was also calculated for the entire sample, yielding a coefficient of .97 using both the Spearman-Brown correction and the Rulon procedure. Test-retest reliability was estimated to be .96. However, this coefficient was computed using a 1-week administration interval for a small (N=41) sample having an unspecified age range. The reported reliabilities for the SIT-R appear to be adequate; however, more extensive studies of test-retest reliability using longer test administration intervals would be more informative.

Validity

Information on construct, content, and criterion-related or concurrent validity is presented for the SIT-R. In terms of construct validity, the authors pulled from a number of theories of intelligence to develop a theoretical model for the SIT-R. The model consists of global ability "g" at the top of the hierarchy, and crystallized intelligence and memory at the second level of the hierarchy. Crystallized intelligence is further subdivided into verbal and quantitative. Content validity is described, as well, and primarily described in terms of similarities between SIT-R items and items on other well-known tests of intelligence such as the WISC-R and the SB-IV. As mentioned previously, the SIT-R includes items in the following domains: General Information (GI), Vocabulary (VO), Similarities and Differences (SD), Comprehension (CO), Quantitative (QN), and Auditory Memory (AM), with approximately 30 items per domain. Incidentally, over half of the items on the SIT-R were also included in the original SIT. These two types of validity could profit from more explanation. Limited documentation of concurrent criterion-related validity is provided. For example, it was found that the SIT-R correlated .82, .88, and .73 with the WAIS-R Full Scale IQ, Verbal IQ, and Performance IQ, respectively, in a sample of 10 subjects of unspecified age. Further, scores on the SIT-R and the WISC-R were correlated for a sample of 234 children ranging in age from 6 to 16 years. The overall average correlations for this group were .84 with the WISC-R Full Scale IQ, .89 with the Verbal IQ, and .63 with the Performance IQ. This sample was further broken down by age. For a sample of 53 children ages 6 to 8, correlations were .92, .91, and .84 with the WISC-R Full Scale IQ, Verbal IQ, and Performance IQ, respectively. Correlations were .61, .89, and .61 with the WISC-R Full Scale IQ, Verbal IQ, and Performance IQ scores for a sample of 74 children ages 9 to 11 years. In a sample of 78 children ages 12 to 14 years, correlations with the WISC-R Full Scale IQ, Verbal IQ, and Performance IQ were .74, .83, and .43, respectively. Lastly, for a sample of 29 children ages 15 to 16 years of age, correlations with the WISC-R Full Scale IQ, Verbal IQ, and Performance IQ were .85, .83, and .38, respectively. Another study was conducted

for the purpose of comparing scores on the SIT with scores on the SIT-R for a sample of 32 individuals of unspecified age. As a result, the correlation between the two tests was .87.

In an independent study, Smith, Klass, and Stovall (1992) found that the SIT-R Total Standard Score (TSS) and the K-BIT IQ Composite correlated at .61 for a sample of 32 gifted students. Further, a correlation of .62 was found between K-BIT Vocabulary and the TSS, and a correlation of .40 was found between K-BIT Matrices and the TSS. Kunen, Overstreet, and Salles (1996) conducted a study for the purpose of providing concurrent validity data on the SIT-R in relation to an abbreviated form of the SB-IV for a sample of 191 persons ranging in age from 5 to 69 years, including 61 individuals with mental retardation. For the total sample, the correlation between these two measures was .92, and for the sample of persons with mental retardation, the correlation was .63. The study also included a comparison of IQ classification according to the SIT-R and the abbreviated form of the SB-IV. Of those previously diagnosed with moderate mental retardation (n=23), 95.6% were classified as such using both the SIT-R and the SB-IV. In contrast, only 23.7% of those with a prior diagnosis of mild mental retardation were classified as such with the SIT-R and the SB-IV. In general, it was found that the SIT-R did not adequately match IQ classification as assigned by the SB-IV. Thus, although the SIT-R correlated highly with this form of the SB-IV overall, the authors caution against the use of the SIT-R for assigning persons to IQ categories. Thus, the use of the "Slosson Classification Chart" may be inappropriate. Although the given validity results are for the most part adequate, additional studies of concurrent validity with a wider variety of tests and age groups would be useful.

Summary

The SIT-R is considered to be a fairly popular screener of intelligence. However, it does suffer from some significant weaknesses. According to a review by Kamphaus (1995), these include "limited evidence of concurrent validity, lack of evidence of a match of the norming to U. S. Census statistics, dependence on a classification system for total scores that may encourage misuse, and excessive dependence on English-language fluency" (p. 956). Watson (1995) moreover cites a lack of adequate reliability data and the omission of data pertaining to individuals with disabilities in the norming sample as being problematic. Thus, Kamphaus (1995) suggests that although the SIT-R is not entirely without merit as an intelligence screener, there are alternatives with better psychometric properties, such as the Kaufman Brief Intelligence Test (K-BIT).

Kaufman Brief Intelligence Test (K-BIT)

The K-BIT (Kaufman & Kaufman, 1990) is a relatively new instrument designed to provide a brief measure of verbal (crystallized) and nonverbal (fluid) intelligence for individuals from 4 to 90 years of age. The fact that the K-BIT measures both verbal and nonverbal abilities differentiates it from the PPVT-III and the SIT-R. However, the authors emphasize that this instrument is not to be considered a substitute for a more comprehensive measure of intelligence. The authors indicate that among other purposes, the K-BIT is a useful instrument for reevaluating the intellectual status of individuals who have previously received comprehensive evaluations, large-scale screenings for at-risk children or children who may be gifted, obtaining estimates of intelligence for persons referred for psychiatric assessments, and assessing persons in need of vocational evaluation.

Administration and Scoring

The K-BIT is an individually administered test having an easel format that consists of two subtests, Vocabulary and Matrices. The Vocabulary subtest is designed to measure verbal or crystallized ability through assessing knowledge of words

and their definitions, as well as general information. It consists of two parts: Part A, Expressive Vocabulary, which has 45 items, and Part B, Definitions, which has 37 items, and both types of items are grouped by difficulty. The Expressive Vocabulary portion requires the individual to name a pictured object presented by the examiner. Responses to these items may be made in English, sign language, or other languages, such as Spanish. The Definitions portion requires the individual to supply a word that best suits two clues (a short description of the word as well as a partial spelling of the word). Responses to these items are permitted in English only, and a maximum of 30 seconds is allowed to answer. Whereas Expressive Vocabulary is administered to all individuals, Definitions is administered to those aged 8 years and above only. The second subtest, Matrices, is designed to measure nonverbal or fluid ability through assessing the ability to solve novel problems that involve understanding relationships and completing analogies. This subtest consists of 48 items having a multiple-choice format that are grouped by difficulty level. The items utilize pictures and abstract designs as to limit the need for language skills. For example, Matrices items include having the individual choose which one of five pictures goes with the stimulus picture presented by the examiner and choosing which one of a number of alternatives best completes a visual analogy or matrix. Teaching items are included for both subtests. The items are scored as correct or incorrect, and the clinician uses set basal and ceiling rules to determine the appropriate number of items to be administered. Total test administration time takes 15 to 30 minutes, and it is relatively easy to administer and score. Raw scores for each subtest are converted to standard scores with a mean of 100 and a standard deviation of 15. A K-BIT IQ composite that combines the subtest scores may also be computed. A normal-curve graphic display of descriptive categories is provided in the manual. Scores are classified in a symmetrical, nonevaluative fashion: Upper Extreme (130 and above), Well Above Average (120–129), Above

Average (110–119), Average (90–109), Below Average (80–89), Well Below Average (70–79), and Lower Extreme (69 and below). Significant differences between Vocabulary and Matrices standard scores may also be calculated. However, it is recommended that these discrepancies be interpreted with caution as the K-BIT only consists of two subtests (Cohen & Spenciner, 1998). In addition, a three-page report template is provided in the manual as a guide for examiners.

Standardization

The K-BIT was standardized on 2,022 individuals between the ages of 4 and 90 years. This instrument was both codeveloped and conormed along with the Kaufman Adolescent and Adult Intelligence Test (KAIT) for those ages 11 to 90 years, allowing for direct comparisons between the measures. Also, construction of items on the K-BIT for young children ages 2 to 6 years was done in conjunction with the development of AGS Early Screening Profiles. The norming process took place during 1988 and 1989, and the sample was selected to correspond with the most current U. S. Census data (1985 estimates or 1990 projections). The sample was stratified according to gender, geographic region, socioeconomic status (as defined by education level of self or parent), and race/ethnicity. The bulk of the sample was within the age range of 7 to 19 years, and the sample sizes decreased significantly with age. On most stratification variables, the K-BIT standardization sample appears to be an adequately close match with U. S. population statistics. However, the Northeast region was slightly underrepresented, and those with 1 to 3 years of college or technical school education were slightly overrepresented. There was no mention of accounting for individuals with disabilities, and samples sizes for adults were somewhat small in comparison with younger age groups.

Reliability

Split-half reliability coefficients were computed for both subtests as well as the K-BIT IQ Composite as estimates of internal consistency across the standardization sample. On the Vocabulary subtest, split-half reliability coefficients ranged from .89 to .98 with a mean of .92. Coefficients for the Matrices subtest ranged from .74 to .95 with a mean of .87. The K-BIT IQ Composite split-half reliability coefficients ranged from .88 to .98 with a mean of .93. Test-retest reliability coefficients were also computed for a sample of 232 individuals ages 5 to 89 years, with the interval between testing being 21 days on average. Across this sample, the mean test-retest coefficients for Vocabulary, Matrices, and the K-BIT IQ Composite were .94, .85, and .94, respectively. This sample was also subdivided into four groups. For a subsample of 53 children ages 5 to 12, the test-retest coefficients were .86, .83, and .92 for Vocabulary, Matrices, and the K-BIT IQ Composite, respectively. Test-retest coefficients for a subsample of adolescents ages 13 to 19 (N=60) were .96, .80, and .93 for Vocabulary, Matrices, and the K-BIT IQ Composite, respectively. For a subsample of 69 adults ages 20 to 54, the coefficients were .97, .86, and .95 for Vocabulary, Matrices, and the K-BIT IQ Composite. Lastly, for a subsample of 50 adults ages 55 to 89, the test-retest reliability values were .95 for Vocabulary, .92 for Matrices, and .95 for the K-BIT IQ Composite. These estimates of reliability indicate a high degree of item consistency and stability between test administrations.

Validity

The K-BIT manual presents a variety of information pertaining to validity. To establish test validity, the test developers used a process that provided for the careful selection of the subtests, item analysis, and internal and external test analysis. The construct validity of the K-BIT was described in terms of its relationship to comprehensive intelligence tests such as the Wechsler scales, the K-ABC, and the SB-IV. The Vocabulary and Matrices subtests were chosen to reflect the Verbal/Performance split in the WISC-R, the Achievement/Mental Processing structure of the K-ABC, and the crystallized/fluid differentiation in the SB-IV. Further, vocabulary and matrices tasks have been found to be good measures of "g." Construct validity was also examined in terms of correlating the K-BIT with the K-ABC, the WISC-R, and the WAIS-R. Scores on the K-BIT were correlated with K-ABC scores for three samples of children, including children aged 4 to 6 years (N=41), 7 to 9 years (N=70), and 10 years to 12 years, 6 months (N=39). Correlations with the K-BIT Vocabulary subtest across these samples of children were .29 to .56 with Sequential Processing, .34 to .55 with Simultaneous Processing, .47 to .63 with the Mental Processing Composite, .66 to .87 with Achievement, and .41 to .50 with Nonverbal. Correlations with the K-BIT Matrices subtest across these samples of children were .37 to .57 with Sequential Processing, .38 to .54 with Simultaneous Processing, .44 to .62 with the Mental Processing Composite, .44 to .63 with Achievement, and .34 to .61 with Nonverbal. Finally, correlations with the K-BIT IQ Composite across these samples of children were .41 to .65 with Sequential Processing, .50 to .61 with Simultaneous Processing, .58 to .69 with the Mental Processing Composite, .74 to .76 with Achievement, and .48 to .58 with Nonverbal. Correlations for a sample of 35 children ranging in age from 6 to 15 years were calculated using the WISC-R and the K-BIT. Correlations between the K-BIT Vocabulary subtest and the Verbal IQ, Performance IQ, and Full Scale IQ were .78, .54, and .75, respectively. Correlations between the K-BIT Matrices subtest and the Verbal IQ, Performance IQ, and Full Scale IQ were .48, .50, and .56, respectively. Lastly, correlations between the K-BIT IQ Composite and the Verbal IQ, Performance IQ, and Full Scale IQ were .77, .63, and .80, accordingly. In addition, correlations for a sample of 64 adults aged 16 to 47 years were calculated using the WAIS-R and the K-BIT. Correlations between the K-BIT Vocabulary subtest and the Verbal IQ, Performance IQ, and Full Scale IQ were .60, .45, and .61, respectively. Correlations between the K-BIT Matrices subtest and the Verbal IQ, Performance

IQ, and Full Scale IQ were .58, .52, and .61, respectively. Lastly, correlations between the K-BIT IQ Composite and the Verbal IQ, Performance IQ, and Full Scale IQ were .73, .60, and .75, accordingly. These correlations provide moderate support for the construct validity of the K-BIT, but additional studies would be useful in confirming these preliminary findings.

Concurrent validity was examined in relation to other brief tests of intelligence as well as achievement tests. For a sample of 54 children ages 7 to 11, correlations between the Test of Nonverbal Intelligence (TONI) Quotient and the K-BIT Vocabulary, Matrices, and IQ Composite scores were –.04, .36, and .23, respectively. Scores on the K-BIT were correlated with Slosson Intelligence Test (SIT) scores for four samples of individuals, including children aged 4 to 5 years (N=62), 6 to 11 years (N=70), 12 to 17 years (N=42), and 18 to 47 years (N=53). Across these samples, correlations between the Slosson IQ and the K-BIT Vocabulary subtest ranged from .46 to .73, for the Matrices subtest they ranged from .37 to .61, and for the K-BIT IQ Composite they ranged from .50 to .76. Correlations between the SIT and the K-BIT were also computed for a sample of 55 gifted children ages 8 to 13. Correlations between the Slosson IQ and the scores on the K-BIT Vocabulary subtest, Matrices subtest, and IQ Composite were .50, .25, and .44, accordingly. These figures indicate moderate support for concurrent validity. Further, the Kaufman Test of Educational Achievement (K-TEA), Comprehensive and Brief Forms and the Wide Range Achievement Test—Revised (WRAT-R) were correlated with the K-BIT to illustrate concurrent validity with achievement tests. Scores on the K-BIT and the K-TEA Brief Form were correlated for two samples of children, including children 6 to 9 years of age (N=50) and 12 to 17 years of age (N=38). Correlations between the K-BIT Vocabulary subtest and the K-TEA Brief Form across these samples were as follows: Math (r=.40 to .72), Reading (r=.47 to .80), Spelling (r=.36 to .69), and Battery Composite (r=.47 to .86). Correlations between the K-BIT Matrices subtest and the K-TEA Brief Form for these samples were as follows: Math (r=.29 to .73), Reading (r=.31 to .63), Spelling (r=.31 to .43), and Battery Composite (r=.31 to .70). Correlations between the K-BIT IQ Composite and the K-TEA Brief Form for these samples were as follows: Math (r=.46 to .80), Reading (r=.53 to .78), Spelling (r=.44 to .60), and Battery Composite (r=.53 to .86). Next, correlations between the K-BIT and the K-TEA Comprehensive Form are presented for a sample of 49 children ages 6 to 12 years and a sample of 39 adolescents ages 12 to 17 years. Here, representative correlations between the K-BIT Vocabulary subtest and the K-TEA Comprehensive Form were as follows: Reading Composite (r=.57 to .78), Math Composite (r=.57 to .69), and Battery Composite (r=.61 to .82). For the K-BIT Matrices subtest, representative correlations were Reading Composite (r=.43 to .50), Math Composite (r=.62 to .67), and Battery Composite (r=.52 to .58). Correlations between the K-BIT IQ Composite and the K-TEA Comprehensive Form included Reading Composite (r=.53 to .71), Math Composite (r=.66 to .77), and Battery Composite (r=.61 to .78). In addition, correlations for two samples of children with learning disabilities, one consisting of 49 children ages 6 to 14 years and the other consisting of 48 children ages 11 to 17 years, were calculated using the K-TEA Comprehensive Form and the K-BIT. Correlations between the K-BIT Vocabulary subtest included Reading Composite (r=.69 to .70), Math Composite (r=.56 to .74), and Battery Composite (r=.72 to .74). Correlations between the K-BIT Matrices subtest included Reading Composite (r=.33 to .77), Math Composite (r=.61 to .78), and Battery Composite (r=.45 to .80). Lastly, correlations between the K-BIT IQ Composite included Reading Composite (r=.53 to .80), Math Composite (r=.65 to .83), and Battery Composite (r=.62 to .84). Correlations were also calculated using the K-BIT and the Wide Range Achievement Test—Revised (WRAT-R) for a sample of 49 children with learning disabilities ages 12 to 19 years, 41 normal adults ages 19 to 24 years, and 34 school dropouts ages 18 to 49 years. Across these samples, the K-BIT Vocabulary subtest correlated with the WRAT-R Reading (r=.32 to .82), Spelling (r=.42 to .74), and Arithmetic (.28 to .60). The K-BIT Matrices subtest correlated with the WRAT-R Reading (r=.18 to .42), Spelling (r=.19 to .46), and Arithmetic (r=.31 to .63). The K-BIT IQ Composite correlated with the WRAT-R Reading (r=.34 to .65), Spelling (r=.35 to .64), and Arithmetic (r=.35 to .69). Further, intercorrelations between the Matrices and Vocabulary subtests across the standardization sample are also presented as measures of convergent validity. These values ranged from .38 to .75 with a mean of .59. These coefficients show that each subtest makes a unique contribution to the K-BIT as a whole.

Other validity studies on the K-BIT have been published. Prewett (1995) examined the concurrent validity of the K-BIT with the WISC-III for a sample of 50 students ages 6 years, 1 month to 14 years, 2 months, all of whom were referred for psychoeducational evaluation. Per the results, the K-BIT IQ Composite correlated .78 with the WISC-III Full Scale IQ. Prewett (1992a) also found that the K-BIT IQ Composite correlated .69, .36, and .64 with the WISC-R Verbal, Performance, and Full Scale IQ, respectively, in a sample of 40 incarcerated adolescent males. Further, K-BIT Vocabulary correlated .70, .27, and .60 with the WISC-R Verbal, Performance, and Full Scale IQ, respectively. Finally, K-BIT Matrices correlated .46, .29, and .45 with the WISC-R Verbal, Performance, and Full Scale IQ, accordingly. In a sample of 35 referred students ranging in ages from 7 years to 16 years, 4 months, the K-BIT IQ Composite correlated .79, .69, and .81 with the WISC-R Verbal, Performance, and Full Scale IQ scores, accordingly. K-BIT Vocabulary correlated .83, .58, and .77 with the WISC-R Verbal, Performance, and Full Scale IQ, respectively. K-BIT Matrices correlated .62, .70, and .72 with the WISC-R Verbal, Performance, and Full Scale IQ, respectively (Prewett, 1992b). Naugle, Chelune, and Tucker (1993) investigated the concurrent validity of the

K-BIT with the WAIS-R for a sample of 200 clinical patients ranging in age from 16 to 74 years. The WAIS-R Verbal IQ and the K-BIT Vocabulary subtest correlated .83, the Performance IQ and the Matrices subtest correlated .77, and the Full Scale IQ and the K-BIT IQ Composite correlated .88. Canivez (1995) investigated the concurrent validity of the K-BIT with the WISC-III for a sample of 137 children ages 6 to 15 who were referred for psychoeducational evaluation. K-BIT Vocabulary correlated .80, .62, and .76 with the WISC-III Verbal, Performance, and Full Scale IQ. Further, K-BIT Vocabulary correlated .79, .62, .65, and .36 with the Verbal Comprehension, Perceptual Organization, Freedom From Distractibility, and Processing Speed Indices on the WISC-III, respectively. K-BIT Matrices correlated .67, .74, and .75 with the WISC-III Verbal, Performance, and Full Scale IQ, respectively. Further, K-BIT Matrices correlated .66, .70, .60, and .47 with the Verbal Comprehension, Perceptual Organization, Freedom from Distractibility, and Processing Speed Indices on the WISC-III, respectively. Lastly, the K-BIT IQ Composite correlated with the WISC-III Verbal, Performance, and Full Scale IQ .84, .79, and .87, respectively. Further, the K-BIT IQ Composite correlated .83, .76, .71, and .48 with the Verbal Comprehension, Perceptual Organization, Freedom from Distractibility, and Processing Speed Indices on the WISC-III, respectively. Canivez (1996) also investigated the concurrent validity of the K-BIT with the WISC-III and the Woodcock Johnson Psycho-Educational Battery-Revised, Tests of Achievement (WJ-R ACH) for a sample of 75 students with learning disabilities, ages 6 to 15 years. Here, correlations for K-BIT Vocabulary were .72 with Verbal IQ, .51 with Performance IQ, .67 with Full Scale IQ, .73 with Verbal Comprehension, .55 with Perceptual Organization, .48 with Freedom from Distractibility, and .18 with Processing Speed. Correlations for K-BIT Matrices were .60 with Verbal IQ, .64 with Performance IQ, .67 with Full Scale IQ, .56 with Verbal Comprehension, .62 with Perceptual Or-

ganization, .56 with Freedom from Distractibility, and .26 with Processing Speed. Lastly, the K-BIT IQ Composite correlated .81 with Verbal IQ, .71 with Performance IQ, .82 with Full Scale IQ, .78 with Verbal Comprehension, .72 with Perceptual Organization, .64 with Freedom from Distractibility, and .27 with Processing Speed. Scores on the K-BIT correlated with selected tests and composites of the WJ-R ACH in the .50s. Further, a high rate of agreement was found between the K-BIT and the WISC-III in determining achievement–ability discrepancies for learning disability criteria with scores on the WJ-R ACH. These initial findings pertaining to validity appear promising. However, additional studies of this nature are warranted.

Summary

The K-BIT is a comparatively new screening measure of intelligence. Other measures such as the PPVT-III and the SIT-R have undergone revisions and considerable more research that have served to improve these instruments. However, the K-BIT seems to hold promise as a strong competitor. In a review of this test, Miller (1995) notes that the K-BIT appears to be a sound instrument overall, but that it would benefit from additional subjects in the older age ranges of the standardization sample and further validation studies.

Wechsler Abbreviated Scale of Intelligence (WASI)

As a new addition to the market, the WASI (The Psychological Corporation, 1999) is the first commercially published screening measure of intelligence to emerge from the Wechsler series. This instrument is designed to provide a quick, reliable measure of intelligence for individuals 6 to 89 years of age. In the Wechsler tradition, the WASI yields information pertaining to both verbal and performance abilities. The test creators specifically indicate that the WASI is not a substitute for more comprehensive measures of intelligence and that comprehensive tests should be used for making diagnostic decisions. Instead, the WASI is purported to be useful in screening for mental retardation and giftedness, reassessment of persons having received a comprehensive evaluation previously, obtaining estimates of current cognitive functioning for psychiatric, vocational, or rehabilitation purposes, and for estimating intellectual ability for large samples of individuals. However, the WASI is linked to the Wechsler Intelligence Scale for Children, Third Edition (WISC-III) and the Wechsler Adult Intelligence Scale, Third Edition (WAIS-III), and tables are included in the WASI manual that allow the examiner to estimate IQ score ranges or "prediction intervals" on the WISC-III and the WAIS-III.

Administration and Scoring

The WASI is an individually administered instrument that consists of a total of four subtests. Importantly, the WASI was developed as an independent scale. All items are new, albeit parallel to their full WISC-III and WAIS-III counterparts. Vocabulary and Similarities subtests comprise the Verbal scale, and Block Design and Matrix Reasoning comprise the Performance scale. These Wechsler subtests were chosen for inclusion on the WASI as they have the highest "g" loadings and also "tap various facets of intelligence, such as verbal knowledge, visual information processing, spatial and nonverbal reasoning, and crystallized and fluid intelligence" (The Psychological Corporation, 1999, p. 3). Unlike the WISC-III and WAIS-III version of the Vocabulary subtest, the WASI Vocabulary subtest, consisting of 42 items, involves both the oral and visual presentation of words. Further, picture items were added to extend the floor of the subtest. Items 1–4 require the examinee to name individually presented pictures, while items 5–42 require the examinee to orally define both orally and visually presented words. The Vocabulary subtest is considered to be a good measure of crystallized as well as general intelligence, as it assesses

one's expressive vocabulary, fund of information, and verbal knowledge. The Similarities subtest of the WASI, which comprises 26 items, is parallel to the counterpart WISC-III and WAIS-III versions, but also includes picture items to enhance the floor of the subtest. The first four items require the individual to identify the one of four picture choices that best goes with a given set of similar pictures, while for the remaining 22 verbal items, the examinee is required to explain the similarity between two orally presented words. The Similarities subtest is considered to be a measure of abstract verbal reasoning, general intelligence, and verbal concept formation. Block Design, which has 13 items, is similar to the WISC-III and WAIS-III version and is included as a measure of visual-motor coordination skills, spatial visualization, perceptual organization, and general intelligence. Each item is either a modeled or pictorially presented geometric design that the examinee is required to replicate using cubes within a specified time limit. The Matrix Reasoning subtest, consisting of 35 items, is similar to that of the WAIS-III and is intended to assess nonverbal fluid abilities as well as general intelligence. The items of this subtest consist of incomplete patterns for which the examinee is to complete the pattern by choosing from one of five possible choices. Teaching items are provided for the WASI and starting and stopping points are determined by examinee age. Reversal rules are also provided. Scoring guidelines are clear, as are the test instructions, making the WASI fairly simple to administer and score. Guidelines for testing examinees with physical or language challenges are also included in the manual. The WASI may be given in a four-subtest or two-subtest format. The four-subtest format takes approximately 30 minutes to administer. Here, Vocabulary and Similarities comprise the Verbal scale that yields a Verbal IQ (VIQ), representing a measure of crystallized abilities. Block Design and Matrix Reasoning form the Performance scale that yields a Performance IQ (PIQ) score. Altogether, the four-subtest format yields a Full Scale IQ (FSIQ-4), as well. The two-subtest version is composed of Vocabulary and Matrix Reasoning. This format takes 15 to 20 minutes for administration. The FSIQ score (FSIQ-2) is provided for this abbreviated format. Each subtest is scored in terms of T scores having a mean of 50 and a standard deviation of 10. FSIQ, VIQ, and PIQ scores are presented as standard scores having a mean of 100 and a standard deviation of 15. Qualitative descriptions for WASI IQ scores are provided in the manual: Very Superior (130 and above), Superior (120–129), High Average (110–119), Average (90–109), Low Average (80– 89), Borderline (70–79), and Extremely Low (69 and below). Significant differences between VIQ and PIQ scores may also be computed for the four-subtest format.

Standardization

The WASI was standardized on a sample of 2,245 individuals between the ages of 6 and 89 years. The national standardization sample was stratified on variables of sex, race/ethnicity, geographic region, and socioeconomic status (as defined by education level of self or parent) according to the 1997 U. S. Census data. The bulk of the sample was comprised of children within the age range of 6 to 16 years, with 100 participants of each year of age (N=1,100). For adults, 75 to 100 participants were included for each specified age group (N=1,145). The manual included exclusionary criteria for the standardization process. For example, persons with insufficient English-language proficiency, persons requiring treatment for alcohol and/or drug dependence, persons with uncorrected hearing and/or vision loss, and persons with any medical or psychiatric condition that could potentially affect cognitive functioning (e.g., Alzheimer's dementia) were not included in the standardization sample. On most stratification variables, the WASI standardization sample appears to be an adequately close match with U. S. population statistics. However, children in the West region were slightly underrepresented. Correlational research data link the WASI with the WISC-III, WAIS-III, and the Wechsler Individual Achieve-

ment Test (WIAT). This serves to increase the clinical utility of the WASI, allowing the evaluator to estimate FSIQs on the corresponding comprehensive batteries and to calculate ability/achievement discrepancies. Further, the clinical utility of the WASI was assessed using data from various clinical samples (e.g., mental retardation, learning disabilities, Attention-Deficit/Hyperactivity Disorder), and results are presented in the manual.

Reliability

A variety of information pertaining to reliability is available for the WASI. Split-half reliability coefficients were calculated for all four subtests, as well as VIQ, PIQ, and FSIQ-4 for the four-subtest version and FSIQ-2 for the two-subtest version for each age group from the standardization sample. First, reliability coefficients are presented for the children's sample (ages 6–16, N=1,100). For the Vocabulary subtest, the coefficients ranged from .86 to .93 with a mean of .89. For Similarities, coefficients ranged from .81 to .91 with a mean of .87. Reliability coefficients for the Block Design subtest ranged from .84 to .93 with a mean of .90. For Matrix Reasoning, the reliability coefficients ranged from .86 to .96 with a mean of .92. The IQ split-half reliability coefficients for the children's sample are higher, as would be expected. For VIQ, the coefficients ranged from .92 to .95 with a mean of .93. Coefficients ranged from .92 to .95 for PIQ, yielding a mean of .94. For FSIQ-2, the coefficients ranged from .92 to .95 with a mean of .93. Finally, for FSIQ-4, the coefficients ranged from .95 to .97 with a mean of .96. Next, split-half reliability coefficients are presented for the adult sample (ages 17–89, N=1,145). Overall, these figures are slightly higher than those computed for the children's sample. For the Vocabulary subtest, the coefficients ranged from .90 to .98 with a mean of .94. For Similarities, coefficients ranged from .84 to .96 with a mean of .92. Reliability coefficients for the Block Design subtest ranged from .90 to .94 with a mean of .92. For

Matrix Reasoning, the reliability coefficients ranged from .88 to .96 with a mean of .94. The IQ split-half reliability coefficients for the adult sample are also higher, as would be expected. For VIQ, the coefficients ranged from .92 to .98 with a mean of .96. Coefficients ranged from .94 to .97 for PIQ, yielding a mean of .96. For FSIQ-2, the coefficients ranged from .93 to .98 with a mean of .96. Finally, for FSIQ-4, the coefficients ranged from .96 to .98 with a mean of .98. Further, the WASI manual also presents standard errors of measurement by subtests and IQ composites by age group. Test-retest reliability coefficients were also computed for a sample of 222 participants representing each of the age groups. The interval between testing sessions was 31 days on average. The test-retest stability coefficients were calculated for four separate age ranges: 6–11, 12–16, 17–54, and 55–89. Results are also presented in terms of an overall children's sample (ages 6–16, N=116) and adult sample (ages 17–89, N=106). Subtest stability coefficients per the children's sample were .85, .86, .81, and .77 for Vocabulary, Similarities, Block Design, and Matrices, respectively. Stability coefficients are higher for the IQ composite scores: VIQ (.92), PIQ (.88), FSIQ-2 (.85), FSIQ-4 (.93). Subtest stability coefficients per the adult sample were .90, .88, .86, and .79 for Vocabulary, Similarities, Block Design, and Matrices, respectively. Stability coefficients are higher in general for the IQ composite scores: VIQ (.92), PIQ (.87), FSIQ-2 (.88), FSIQ-4 (.92). A study of interscorer agreement was also conducted to assess scoring of the Vocabulary and Similarities subtest, as these two subtests require more judgment in the scoring process. For this study, 60 cases (30 children and 30 adult cases) were randomly selected from the standardization sample. A total of four raters, two with extensive experience and two with limited experience, scored each of the 60 protocols independently. The resulting interrater reliability coefficients across the raters were .98 for Vocabulary and .99 for Similarities. Overall, the presented estimates of reliability for the WASI indicate a strong degree of item consistency and stability between test administrations.

Validity

Numerous types of evidence concerning validity are depicted in the WASI manual. In terms of content validity, the WASI subtests were chosen on the basis of both their high "g" loadings and the cognitive functions assessed by each, as the WASI's purpose is to be a screening measure of intelligence. Parallel items were designed for the WASI based on content analyses of the counterpart WISC-III and WAIS-III subtests. In addition, expert reviewers were utilized to ensure that the WASI items were indeed parallel to their counterpart comprehensive batteries and that item content was similar. Information pertaining to convergent and discriminant validity is also presented. To determine the degree of these types of validity, correlational studies were conducted comparing the WASI to the WISC-III, WAIS-III, and the Wechsler Individual Achievement Test (WIAT). First, the WASI and the WISC-III were given in counterbalanced order to a nonclinical sample of children 6 to 16 years of age (N=176), with approximately 14 to 18 participants representing each of the age groups. On average, the time between testing sessions was 23 days. Correlations between the WASI and WISC-III Vocabulary, Similarities, and Block Design subtests were .72, .69, and .74, respectively. Correlations could not be computed for the Matrix Reasoning subtest, as there is no counterpart on the WISC-III. For the IQ composites, correlations for VIQ, PIQ, FSIQ-2, and FSIQ-4 were .82, .76, .81, and .87, respectively. These results suggest that the subtests and IQ composites of the WASI measure constructs similar to those assessed by the WISC-III. Because of this, the obtained data from this study were used to develop prediction intervals for the WISC-III FSIQ based on WASI FSIQ-4 scores. Next, the WASI and the WAIS-III were given in counterbalanced order to a sample of adults 16 to 89 years of age (N=248), with approximately

17 to 21 participants representing each of the age groups. On average, the time between testing sessions was 28 days. Correlations between the WASI and WAIS-III Vocabulary, Similarities, Block Design, and Matrix Reasoning subtests were .88, .76, .83, and .66, respectively. For the IQ composites, correlations for VIQ, PIQ, FSIQ-2, and FSIQ-4 were .88, .84, .87, and .92, respectively. As with the WISC-III study, these results suggest that the subtests and IQ composites of the WASI measure constructs similar to those assessed by the WAIS-III. Likewise, because of this, the obtained data from this study were used to develop prediction intervals for the WAIS-III FSIQ based on WASI FSIQ-4 scores. Finally, the WASI and the WIAT were administered to a sample of 210 nonclinical participants 6 to 19 years of age. For this study, counterbalancing was unnecessary, and the WIAT was administered following the WASI on the same day. Overall, moderate correlations were found between the WASI and WIAT. For VIQ, correlations were as follows with WIAT subtests and composites: Basic Reading (.60), Mathematics Reasoning (.58), Spelling (.57), Reading Comprehension (.66), Numerical Operations (.48), Listening Comprehension (.58), Oral Expression (.42), Written Expression (.57), Reading Composite (.69), Mathematics Composite (.58), Language Composite (.60), and Writing Composite (.70). For PIQ, correlations were as follows with WIAT subtests and composites: Basic Reading (.50), Mathematics Reasoning (.54), Spelling (.46), Reading Comprehension (.60), Numerical Operations (.53), Listening Comprehension (.41), Oral Expression (.41), Written Expression (.55), Reading Composite (.59), Mathematics Composite (.56), Language Composite (.53), and Writing Composite (.57). For FSIQ-2, correlations were as follows with WIAT subtests and composites: Basic Reading (.61), Mathematics Reasoning (.64), Spelling (.57), Reading Comprehension (.67), Numerical Operations (.60), Listening Comprehension (.52), Oral Expression (.47), Written Expression (.64), Reading Composite (.69), Mathematics Composite (.66), Language

Composite (.63), and Writing Composite (.72). For FSIQ-4, correlations were as follows with WIAT subtests and composites: Basic Reading (.63), Mathematics Reasoning (.64), Spelling (.59), Reading Comprehension (.71), Numerical Operations (.56), Listening Comprehension (.57), Oral Expression (.47), Written Expression (.64), Reading Composite (.72), Mathematics Composite (.64), Language Composite (.64), and Writing Composite (.72).

Construct validity of the WASI was examined in terms of intercorrelations of the WASI subtests and IQ composites as well as by factor analyses. Predictions were made that each of the WASI subtests would have moderate to high correlations with each other and that Verbal subtests would have higher correlations with each other than with the Performance subtests. The intercorrelation study was conducted using the entire standardization sample. Figures are presented according to each age group, in addition to the averages for the children's sample, the adult sample, and the total sample. For the children's sample (N=1,100), the Vocabulary subtest correlations with Similarities, Block Design, and Matrix Reasoning were .71, .46, and .50, respectively. The correlations of Vocabulary with VIQ, PIQ, FSIQ-2, and FSIQ-4 were .71, .54, .50, and .68, respectively. The Similarities subtest correlations with Vocabulary, Block Design, and Matrix Reasoning were .71, .47, and .48, respectively. The correlations of Similarities with VIQ, PIQ, FSIQ-2, and FSIQ-4 were .71, .54, .69, and .68, respectively. The Block Design subtest correlations with Vocabulary, Similarities, and Matrix Reasoning were .46, .47, and .54, respectively. The correlations of Block Design with VIQ, PIQ, FSIQ-2, and FSIQ-4 were .50, .54, .57, and .58, respectively. The correlations of Matrix Reasoning with Vocabulary, Similarities, and Block Design were .50, .48, and .54, respectively. The Matrix Reasoning subtest correlations with VIQ, PIQ, FSIQ-2, and FSIQ-4 were .53, .54, .50, and .60, respectively. In terms of composite scores for the children's sample, the intercorrelation for VIQ and PIQ was .59. VIQ correlated .85 and .90 with FSIQ-2 and FSIQ-4, respectively. PIQ correlated .81 and .89 with FSIQ-2 and FSIQ-4, respectively. The intercorrelation for FSIQ-2 and FSIQ-4 was .93. For the adult sample (N=1,145), the Vocabulary subtest correlations with Similarities, Block Design, and Matrix Reasoning were .79, .54, and .61, respectively. The correlations of Vocabulary with VIQ, PIQ, FSIQ-2, and FSIQ-4 were .79, .64, .61, and .76, respectively. The Similarities subtest correlations with Vocabulary, Block Design, and Matrix Reasoning were .79, .55, and .59, respectively. The correlations of Similarities with VIQ, PIQ, FSIQ-2, and FSIQ-4 were .79, .63, .77, and .75, respectively. The Block Design subtest correlations with Vocabulary, Similarities, and Matrix Reasoning were .54, .55, and .63, respectively. The correlations of Block Design with VIQ, PIQ, FSIQ-2, and FSIQ-4 were .58, .63, .65, and .65, respectively. The correlations of Matrix Reasoning with Vocabulary, Similarities, and Block Design were .61, .59, and .63, respectively. The Matrix Reasoning subtest correlations with VIQ, PIQ, FSIQ-2, and FSIQ-4 were .64, .63, .61, and .71, respectively. In terms of composite scores for the adult sample, the intercorrelation for VIQ and PIQ was .67. VIQ correlated .88 and .92 with FSIQ-2 and FSIQ-4, respectively. PIQ correlated .86 and .91 with FSIQ-2 and FSIQ-4, respectively. The intercorrelation for FSIQ-2 and FSIQ-4 was .95. For the total sample (N=2,245), the Vocabulary subtest correlations with Similarities, Block Design, and Matrix Reasoning were .75, .50, and .56, respectively. The correlations of Vocabulary with VIQ, PIQ, FSIQ-2, and FSIQ-4 were .75, .60, .56, and .72, respectively. The Similarities subtest correlations with Vocabulary, Block Design, and Matrix Reasoning were .75, .51, and .54, respectively. The correlations of Similarities with VIQ, PIQ, FSIQ-2, and FSIQ-4 were .75, .59, .73, and .72, respectively. The Block Design subtest correlations with Vocabulary, Similarities, and Matrix Reasoning were .50, .51, and .59, respectively. The correlations of Block Design with VIQ, PIQ, FSIQ-2, and FSIQ-4 were .54, .59,

.62, and .62, respectively. The correlations of Matrix Reasoning with Vocabulary, Similarities, and Block Design were .56, .54, and .59, respectively. The Matrix Reasoning subtest correlations with VIQ, PIQ, FSIQ-2, and FSIQ-4 were .59, .59, .56, and .66, respectively. In terms of composite scores for the total sample, the intercorrelation for VIQ and PIQ was .63. VIQ correlated .87 and .91 with FSIQ-2 and FSIQ-4, respectively. PIQ correlated .84 and .90 with FSIQ-2 and FSIQ-4, respectively. The intercorrelation for FSIQ-2 and FSIQ-4 was .94. Overall, these results support the "g" factor, and evidence of convergent and discriminant validity amongst the subtests and composites of the WASI is confirmed.

Both confirmatory and exploratory factor analyses were performed to assess the degree to which the WASI measures the constructs of verbal and performance (nonverbal) cognitive abilities. Exploratory joint factor analyses were conducted using the data from the WASI/WISC-III (N=176) and the WASI/WAIS-III (N=248) correlational studies. As expected, the results supported a factor pattern that separated verbal from nonverbal subtests. For the WASI/WISC-III joint factor pattern, the WASI Vocabulary and Similarities subtests loaded on the Verbal Comprehension factor of the WISC-III .87 and .66, respectively. The WASI Block Design and Matrix Reasoning subtests loaded on the Perceptual Organization factor of the WISC-III .60 and .54, respectively. Similarly, for the WASI/WAIS-III joint factor pattern, the WASI Vocabulary and Similarities subtests loaded on the Verbal Comprehension factor of the WAIS-III .90 and .75, respectively. The WASI Block Design and Matrix Reasoning subtests loaded on the Perceptual Organization factor of the WAIS-III .73 and .68, respectively. However, it is noted in the manual that although the four-subtest version of the WASI is the better screening tool as opposed to the two-subtest format, the WASI lacks useful information that can be derived from the third and fourth factors of the WISC-III/WAIS-III (Working Memory and Processing

Speed). The WASI standardization data were used for the confirmatory factor analyses. These analyses were conducted using the total sample, all adults, all children, and six more specified age groupings. Here, a one-factor model (all four subtests on a general factor) and a two-factor model (two Verbal subtests and two Performance subtests) were compared. Results indicated that the two-factor model provided the best fit for all groups, including the total standardization sample.

Additionally, evidence of clinical validity is presented for the WASI. At the outset, it is mentioned that the clinical samples are indeed convenience samples that are not intended to be absolute representations of these groups. The WASI was administered to a group of 119 persons diagnosed with mental retardation. More specifically, the sample included 57 individuals with mild mental retardation, 30 individuals with moderate mental retardation, and 32 persons with Down syndrome. Results supported the diagnoses, with the mean FSIQ-4 WASI scores being 63, 55, and 56 for the samples of persons with mild mental retardation, moderate mental retardation, and Down syndrome, respectively. Interestingly, all groups performed best on the Block Design subtest. However, further analysis of the data revealed that 61% of the individuals with mild mental retardation obtained WASI FSIQ-4 scores of 56 to 70, 67% of those with moderate mental retardation obtained scores of 55 or below, and 97% of those with Down syndrome scored in the range of 52 to 69. These results suggest that although the WASI may be useful as a screening instrument for mental retardation, the WASI is not able to adequately assess the degree of mental retardation. As such, a comprehensive intelligence test as well as a measure of adaptive behavior should be used for purposes of determining a diagnosis of mental retardation. The WASI was also administered to a sample of 33 children and adolescents classified as being gifted. The mean WASI FSIQ-4 performance for this group was 129, and 67% of the sample obtained a FSIQ-4 of 125 or above.

These results indicate that the WASI may be a useful tool for screening children who may be intellectually gifted. Moreover, the WASI was administered to 46 children diagnosed with Attention-Deficit/Hyperactivity Disorder (ADHD) and a matched control group. Results showed that the group with ADHD scored only slightly lower (FSIQ-4 = 101) than the control group (FSIQ-4 = 103). This was expected as the WASI is considered to be a measure of "g" that does not include subtests associated with the third and fourth factors (Working Memory and Processing Speed). The WASI was also given to 89 children and adolescents with learning disabilities. Of this sample, 23 individuals were diagnosed with a mathematics disability, 47 were diagnosed with a reading disability, and 19 were diagnosed as having both a mathematics and a reading disability. A matched control group was selected from the WASI standardization sample for each of these groups. The average FSIQ-4 score for the individuals with mathematics disabilities was 90. No significant performance differences were noted amongst subtests or score composites. The matched control group achieved a mean FSIQ-4 score of 97, yet the difference between this group and the group with mathematics disabilities was not considered significant. The average FSIQ-4 score for those with reading disabilities was 94. Although the mean VIQ score was slightly lower than the mean PIQ score, this difference was not significant. However, the group performed significantly more poorly on Vocabulary than on Block Design. The matched control group scored significantly higher (103) than the group with reading disabilities. The average FSIQ-4 score for individuals with reading and mathematics disabilities was 88. Here, the mean VIQ score was significantly lower than the mean PIQ score, and the mean Vocabulary score was significantly lower than the average Block Design and Matrix Reasoning scores. The control group scored substantially higher (98) than the group with reading and mathematics disabilities. Further, WISC-III IQ scores were calculated for 35 of the individuals with learning disabilities. The differences between the WISC-III IQ and WASI FSIQ-4 scores were marginal, ranging from 0.2 to 1.1 points. Therefore, the WASI can yield a comparatively accurate estimate of WISC-III IQ scores for those with learning disabilities. Nevertheless, it is suggested that comprehensive instruments be used for diagnostic purposes. Finally, the WASI was administered to a sample of 14 adolescents and adults who had incurred a moderate to severe traumatic brain injury (TBI). A matched control group was also evaluated. As anticipated, the group with TBI scored significantly lower (81) than the matched control group (97) on the WASI FSIQ-4. However, it is again noted that useful information may be lost using the WASI with persons with TBI as tasks representing the Working Memory and Processing Speed factors are not included. Overall, "the studies involving special groups show that although the WASI can provide reliable and relatively accurate estimates of general intellectual functioning for some clinical groups, it cannot provide some important clinical information due to its lack of measures related to the third and fourth factors . . . for the purpose of diagnosis and placement, clinicians should use comprehensive measures, such as the WISC-III and WAIS-III" (The Psychological Corporation, 1999, p. 153). Generally speaking, the findings related to validity seem encouraging. However, additional studies of this type are warranted.

Summary

The WASI is one of the latest additions to the field of intelligence screening. In accordance, few psychologists have had the opportunity to review or research this instrument. Nevertheless, from this review, the WASI appears to be sound as a screening measure of intelligence. Further, as the Wechsler testing tradition maintains its popularity, the WASI will likely be a contender in the testing market, and researchers will no doubt conduct numerous studies using this instrument.

ACADEMIC ACHIEVEMENT SCREENERS

Achievement Screeners versus Diagnostic Tests

It is sometimes difficult to classify the many academic achievement testing selections that are available. Generally speaking, there are two classes of achievement tests that exist along a continuum from screeners or broadband measures of achievement to diagnostic tests. Screeners survey a broad range of content areas such as mathematics, reading, and writing at a wide range of skill levels. Ordinarily, no one content area is probed in-depth. However, achievement screeners can be useful in identifying general weak areas for individuals. Once a weak area is identified, skilled psychologists will follow-up with diagnostic testing that addresses that weak area. For example, if a child scores poorly on the Reading Recognition subtest of the Peabody Individual Achievement Tests—Revised (PIAT-R), a diagnostic achievement test such as the Woodcock Reading Mastery Test—Revised (WRMT-R) would be administered for the purpose of identifying more specifically which discrete skill(s) is (are) deficient. The following sections will cover achievement tests that are considered to be screeners or broadband measures.

Wide Range Achievement Test—3 (WRAT-3)

The WRAT-3 (Wilkinson, 1993) is the latest revision of the original WRAT, which was published in 1936 as an adjunct to the Wechsler-Bellevue Scales. The WRAT-3 was developed to assess the "codes which are needed to learn the basic skills of reading, spelling, and arithmetic" (p. 10). According to Cohen and Spenciner (1998), the precise definition of the word "codes" is unclear, although it is generally assumed that it refers to basic academic skills that are essential in reading, spelling, and arithmetic. This basic tenet of the WRAT-3 has not been changed since its original publication over 60 years ago. Also, many of the items found on the WRAT-3 were first constructed for previous editions of the test. For these reasons, this test has been criticized as being outdated. There is also substantial confusion regarding the name of the test and the skills that it purports to measure. At first glance, a test consumer may assume that the name "Wide Range" implies that a wide range of skills is assessed. However, the name refers to the fact that a wide range of ages is covered (5 years to 74 years, 11 months). Further, the names of the subtests, Reading, Spelling, and Arithmetic, may imply that a broad range of skills is assessed within each of these areas. Upon closer examination of the rationale and descriptions in the test manual, it is found that this is not the case.

Administration and Scoring

The WRAT-3 is an individually administered test of academic skills. It consists of two forms, Blue and Tan, with the same number of items for each subtest per form. Additionally, both Blue and Tan forms can be administered (i.e., Combined form). The test consists of three subtests:

1. Reading. This subtest is essentially a test of word recognition alone, as opposed to a test that measures more than one reading skill. Here, the individual is required to recognize and name 15 letters and 42 words as presented on a card. Ten seconds are allowed for the individual to respond to each item.
2. Spelling. This subtest is a test of written encoding that requires an individual to write his/her name and to write letters (15 items) and words (40 items) from dictation. 15 seconds are allowed per item.
3. Arithmetic. The Arithmetic subtest is basically a test of computation. The subtest consists of an untimed Oral Arithmetic section in which the examinee is required to read numbers and

solve problems that are dictated (15 items), and a timed Written Arithmetic section in which the examinee is required to perform arithmetic computations (40 items) within a 15-minute time limit.

Items are scored as correct or incorrect, and set basal and ceiling rules are used to determine the appropriate number of items to administer. Computerized scoring is available. The total test administration time takes from 15 to 30 minutes, and the test is relatively quick and simple to score. Raw scores can be converted to standard scores having a mean of 100 and a standard deviation of 15. Scores for each subtest can be computed for the Blue, Tan, and Combined forms. Profile/Analysis forms may be used to graphically display scores. In addition, a score classification scheme is presented in the manual: Very Superior (130 and up), Superior (120 to 129), High Average (110 to 119), Average (90 to 109), Low Average (80 to 89), Borderline (70 to 79), and Deficient (69 and below).

Standardization

The standardization sample of the WRAT-3 consisted of 4,433 individuals between the ages of 5 years and 74 years, 11 months. The norming process took place during 1992 and 1993, and the sample was selected to approximate 1990 U. S. Census data. The sample was stratified according to variables of age, gender, geographic region, ethnicity, and socioeconomic level (as defined by occupational category). It is unclear how many individuals with disabilities, if any, were included in the sample. Overall, it appears that the obtained normative sample resembles that of the U. S. population.

Reliability

Internal consistency estimates for the WRAT-3 were determined using coefficient alpha for each test across the standardization sample and for each form (Blue, Tan, and Combined). For the Combined form of the Reading subtest, coefficients ranged from .91 to .97 with a median of .95. On the Blue form, the values ranged from .88 to .95 with a median of .91. On the Tan form, the coefficients ranged from .88 to .94 with a median of .90. For the Combined form of the Spelling subtest, the coefficients ranged from .89 to .97 with a median of .95. On the Blue form, the values ranged from .83 to .95 with a median of .91. On the Tan form, the coefficients ranged from .83 to .94 with a median of .89. On the Combined form of the Arithmetic subtest, the coefficients ranged from .72 to .96 with a median of .92. On the Blue form, the values ranged from .69 to .82 with a median of .86. On the Tan form, the coefficients ranged from .70 to .92 with a median of .85. Alternate form correlations were also computed to compare the Blue and Tan forms of the WRAT-3. On Reading, correlations ranged from .87 to .99 with a median of .92. Spelling correlations ranged from .86 to .99 with a median of .93, and Arithmetic correlations ranged from .82 to .99 with a median of .89. Further, the stability of the WRAT-3 was assessed using test-retest reliability, with an average of 37.4 days in between test administrations, for a sample of 142 individuals between the ages of 6 and 16 years for each form. These coefficients ranged from .91 to .98 overall, with a range of .96 to .98 for Reading, .93 to .96 for Spelling, and .91 to .94 for Arithmetic. Altogether, the presented reliability estimates for the WRAT-3 appear to be adequate.

Validity

Content and construct validity are addressed in the WRAT-3 manual. In terms of content validity, it is reemphasized that the test intends to measure basic academic skills, specifically, word recognition, spelling from dictation, and arithmetic computation. However, evidence of adequate content validity is not well delineated. The author (Wilkinson, 1993) claims that the subtests of the WRAT-3 measure the domains of "all the words in the English language for reading and spelling and the arithmetic computation problems

taught in grades Kindergarten through high school for arithmetic" (p. 176). The Rasch statistic of item separation was used to indicate whether or not adequate numbers of items at varying levels of difficulty were chosen for the test. However, item separation does not directly measure the content validity of a domain. Therefore, it appears that more evidence of content validity is in order. Construct validity is presented in terms of developmental skills, intercorrelations of the WRAT-3 tests, and relationships with measures of intelligence and achievement. Intercorrelations suggest that the subtests of the WRAT-3 are moderately to highly related to one another. Median intercorrelations were .87, .66, and .70, respectively for Reading and Spelling, Reading and Arithmetic, and Spelling and Arithmetic. WRAT-3 Combined form scores were correlated with results on the WISC-III for a sample of 100 children ages 6 to 16 years. The WISC-III Verbal IQ scores correlated .70, .69, and .71, respectively, with the WRAT-3 Combined scores on Reading, Spelling, and Arithmetic. WISC-III Performance IQ scores correlated .52, .53, and .67, respectively, with the WRAT-3 Combined scores on Reading, Spelling, and Arithmetic. The Full Scale IQ scores correlated .66, .66, and .73, respectively, with the WRAT-3 Combined scores on Reading, Spelling, and Arithmetic. Correlations for the WRAT-3 Combined scores and WISC-III subtests are also presented: Picture Completion (Reading r=.47, Spelling r=.46, Arithmetic r=.49), Information (Reading r=.71, Spelling r=.63, Arithmetic r=.66), Coding (Reading r=.44, Spelling r=.55, Arithmetic r=.54), Similarities (Reading r=.68, Spelling r=.60, Arithmetic r=.66), Picture Arrangement (Reading r=.33, Spelling r=.31, Arithmetic r=.48), Arithmetic (Reading r=.54, Spelling r=.59, Arithmetic r=.66), Block Design (Reading r=.41, Spelling r=.42, Arithmetic r=.64), Vocabulary (Reading r=.64, Spelling r=.64, Arithmetic r=.58), Object Assembly (Reading r=.37, Spelling r=.30, Arithmetic r=.45), Comprehension (Reading r=.53, Spelling r=.60, Arithmetic r=.59), and Digit Span (Reading r=.58, Spelling r=.64,

Arithmetic r=.52). In a separate study, WRAT-3 scores were correlated with WAIS-R scores for a sample of 40 adolescents and adults 16 to 63 years of age. The WAIS-R Verbal IQ scores correlated .63, .59, and .53 with the WRAT-3 Combined scores on Reading, Spelling, and Arithmetic. WAIS-R Performance IQ scores correlated .31, .28, and .54 with the WRAT-3 Combined scores on Reading, Spelling, and Arithmetic. WAIS-R Full Scale IQ scores correlated .53, .49, and .60, respectively, with the WRAT-3 Combined scores on Reading, Spelling, and Arithmetic. Correlations for the WRAT-3 Combined scores and WAIS-R subtests are also presented: Picture Completion (Reading r=.35, Spelling r=.19, Arithmetic r=.26), Information (Reading r=.52, Spelling r=.44, Arithmetic r=.34), Similarities (Reading r=.47, Spelling r=.52, Arithmetic r=.46), Picture Arrangement (Reading r=.39, Spelling r=.42, Arithmetic r=.43), Arithmetic (Reading r=.36, Spelling r=.36, Arithmetic r=.46), Block Design (Reading r=.32, Spelling r=.32, Arithmetic r=.49), Vocabulary (Reading r=.62, Spelling r=.58, Arithmetic r=.46), Object Assembly (Reading r=.05, Spelling r=.05, Arithmetic r=.25), Comprehension (Reading r=.48, Spelling r=.43, Arithmetic r=.46), Digit Symbol (Reading r=.09, Spelling, r=.24, Arithmetic r=.48), and Digit Span (Reading r=.45, Spelling r=.41, Arithmetic r=.35).

Relationships between the WRAT-3 and the WRAT-R are also presented for a sample of 77 children. Here, each form of the WRAT-3 was administered on average 82 days after the WRAT-R was given. As a result, correlations between Reading on the WRAT-3 and the WRAT–R ranged from .90 to .95, correlations between Spelling on the WRAT-3 and the WRAT–R ranged from .96 to .99, and correlations between Arithmetic on the WRAT-3 and the WRAT-R ranged from .79 to .85. Correlations of the WRAT-3 Combined form with standardized group achievement tests, e.g., the California Test of Basic Skills—4th edition (CTBS-4), California Achievement Test Form E (CAT), and the Stanford Achievement Test (SAT)

are also presented. First, WRAT-3 and CTBS-4 scores were correlated for a sample of 46 children ages 8 to 16 years. Here, the WRAT-3 Reading subtest correlated .69 with Total Reading on the CTBS-4, WRAT-3 Spelling correlated .84 with CTBS-4 Spelling, and WRAT-3 Arithmetic correlated .79 with Total Math on the CTBS-4. Next, scores on the WRAT-3 and the CAT were correlated for a sample of 49 children ages 8 to 16 years. Results yielded correlations of .72 between WRAT-3 Reading and CAT Total Reading, .77 between WRAT-3 Spelling and CAT Total Spelling, and .41 between WRAT-3 Arithmetic and CAT Total Math. Finally, scores on the WRAT-3 and the SAT were correlated for a sample of 31 children ranging in age from 9 to 15 years. WRAT-3 Reading correlated .87 with SAT Total Reading, WRAT-3 Spelling correlated .76 with SAT Spelling, and WRAT-3 Arithmetic correlated .81 with SAT Total Math. Discriminant analysis was used to determine the utility of the WRAT-3 in special education placement. Of a sample of 222 persons, the WRAT-3 grouped gifted children at 85% accuracy, children with learning disabilities at 72% accuracy, children with mental handicaps (mildly mentally retarded) at 83% accuracy, and "normal" at 56% accuracy. As a result, the test developer purports that the WRAT-3 can be a useful tool in making special education placement decisions, although it should not be the only criteria utilized.

Independent validity investigations have been done with the WRAT-3. Vance and Fuller (1995) examined the validity of the WRAT-3 in relationship to the WISC-III for a sample of 60 children ages 6 years to 15 years, 8 months who were referred for special education. WRAT-3 Reading correlated with the WISC-III Verbal IQ, Performance IQ, and Full Scale IQ .71, .62, and .72, respectively. WRAT-3 Spelling correlated with the WISC-III Verbal, Performance, and Full Scale IQ .66, .59, and .68, respectively. Finally, WRAT-3 Arithmetic correlated with the Verbal, Performance, and Full Scale IQ .79, .73, and .82, respectively. Smith, Smith, and Smithson

(1995) examined the relationship between the WRAT-3 and the WISC-III for a sample of 37 rural children ages 6 to 16 years whom were referred for psychoeducational evaluation. Combined Reading scores on the WRAT-3 correlated with the WISC-III Verbal, Performance, and Full Scale IQ .59, .45, and .59, respectively. Combined Spelling scores on the WRAT-3 correlated with the WISC-III Verbal, Performance, and Full Scale IQ .51, .51, and .58, accordingly. Combined Arithmetic scores on the WRAT-3 correlated with the WISC-III Verbal, Performance, and Full Scale IQ .66, .48, and .66, respectively. Although most of the figures pertaining to construct validity of the WRAT-3 appear adequate, there are problems pertaining to the definition of the constructs themselves and with the limited variety of instruments and the limited sample sizes upon which the validity evidence is based.

Summary

The WRAT-3 has a long history, as well as an ample number of users. Its brevity and ease of use make it popular instrument. However, it does appear to be riddled with numerous problems. First, the terminology used throughout the test (i.e., Reading, Spelling, Arithmetic, and Wide Range) can be problematic. Such terms may imply to some test consumers that the WRAT–3 covers a wide array of skills, which it clearly does not. Instead, it assesses three discrete skills: word recognition, spelling from dictation, and arithmetic computation. Although these skills are outlined in the manual, the test would benefit from revised terminology that better reflects the test content. Also, it should be noted that the WRAT-3 differs from many other screeners of academic achievement in that it assesses considerably fewer skills. In a sense, the WRAT-3 could be considered a "screener of a screener." Clinicians should take care to see that the WRAT-3 is used for screening purposes only. Mabry (1995) criticizes the WRAT-3 for its obsolescence, test content, lack of underlying rationale and philosophy, and insufficient evidence

of validity, among other concerns. Cohen and Spenciner (1998) suggest that although the WRAT-3 possesses adequate norms and reliability, that this test should be used solely as a "screening instrument, if at all" (p. 148).

Woodcock-McGrew-Werder Mini-Battery of Achievement (MBA)

The MBA (Woodcock, McGrew, & Werder, 1994) is a relatively new brief academic achievement screening measure that may be used with children and adults from 4 to 95 years of age. This test is designed to expand upon content that is generally found in brief achievement screening measures such as the WRAT-3. Specifically, the MBA contains tests of reading, mathematics, writing, and general knowledge. These tests are highly similar in format and content of the WJ-R ACH, which is discussed later in this chapter. In fact, WJ-R ACH counterparts for the MBA are presented in the manual, and MBA items were drawn from WJ-R ACH item banks. Each of the MBA tests covers more than one skill, thus providing "more extensive coverage of basic and applied skills than any other brief achievement battery" (Woodcock, MacGrew, & Werder, 1994, p. 219). The authors of the MBA suggest several applications of this instrument: Screening for special education referrals; intake screenings in pediatric, geriatric, psychological, medical, and other clinical settings; hiring and job placement decisions; initial screenings of new students in educational settings; and research uses. However, the authors of this instrument also point out that the MBA should be not used without corroborating information to make placement or treatment decisions. Instead, it is recommended that MBA results be utilized to identify potential need for more in-depth evaluations using instruments such as the Woodcock-Johnson Psycho-Educational Battery—Revised (Woodcock & Johnson, 1989a).

Administration and Scoring

The MBA is an individually administered test of basic academic skills and knowledge designed for use with children and adults ages 4 through 95 years. It consists of a single form and four tests that can be given separately or in any combination. The MBA consists of four tests presented in an easel format:

1. Reading. This test contains three parts. Part A: Identification, has 28 items that assess reading recognition skills. Here, the individual is required to recognize and name letters and words as presented by the examiner. Part B: Vocabulary, has 22 items that assess skills in reading words and supplying correct meanings. The individual is required to read a stimulus word and supply a word that is opposite in meaning. Part C: Comprehension, consists of 23 items. Here, an individual is required to point to a picture that describes a written phrase and/or read passages and identify a missing word. All items on the Reading test are presented in order of difficulty and are not timed. The counterpart for the MBA Reading test is the Broad Reading Cluster of the WJ-R ACH.

2. Writing. This test consists of two parts. Part A: Dictation, measures skills in writing responses to questions that involve knowledge of letters, spelling, capitalization, punctuation, and usage. This part contains 32 items and is administered in a traditional spelling test format using the provided MBA Worksheet. Part B: Proofreading, contains 26 items. This task is designed to assess skills in identifying errors in writing, requiring the individual to both identify and specify how errors should be corrected in printed passages as presented by the examiner. Items on the Writing test are organized according to level of difficulty and are not timed. The counterpart for the MBA Writing test is the Basic Writing Skills Cluster on the WJ-R ACH.

3. Mathematics. The Mathematics test consists of two sections. Part A: Calculation, has 29 items intended to measure basic mathematical computations such as addition, subtraction, multiplication, and division. Geometry, trigonometry, and calculus problems are also included. The items are completed on the MBA Worksheet. Part B: Reasoning & Concepts, has 50 items that measure skills in analyzing and solving problems, as well as knowledge of mathematical concepts and terminology. Unlike Calculation, this section requires that the individual decide which mathematical operations to use and which information to include in solving the problems. Examinees may use scratch paper if needed. Items on the Mathematics test are arranged in the order of difficulty and are not timed. The counterpart of the MBA Mathematics test is the WJ-R ACH Broad Mathematics Cluster.

4. Factual Knowledge. This test assesses knowledge of social studies, science, and the humanities (literature, music, and art). Factual Knowledge contains 59 items that are arranged according to difficulty level and is not timed. The counterpart of the MBA Factual Knowledge test is the WJ-R ACH Broad Knowledge Cluster.

The four MBA subtests can be given separately or in any combination thereof. The scores from the Reading, Writing, and Mathematics subtests are combined into a Basic Skills Cluster score as an indicator of general overall achievement. The counterpart of the MBA Basic Skills Cluster is the Skills Cluster on the WJ-R ACH. Items are scored as correct or incorrect. Set basal and ceiling rules are used to determine the appropriate number of items to administer. The total test administration time takes approximately 30 minutes. The MBA includes a computerized program that calculates and reports standard scores having a mean of 100 and a standard deviation of 15, as well as other scores based on entered raw scores. This program also generates a brief narrative report. Hand scoring of the MBA is not an option for anything other than raw scores.

Standardization

The standardization sample of the MBA consisted of 6,026 individuals between the ages of 4 and 95 years. The norming data were collected from 1986 to 1988 and are based on data from a common norming sample with the WJ-R. The sample was stratified according to variables of age, gender, geographic region, race, community size, origin (Hispanic, non-Hispanic), funding of college/university (public, private), type of college/university (university and 4-year college, 2-year college), distribution of adult occupation in the community, distribution of adult occupational status in the community (e.g., employed or unemployed), and distribution of adult education in the community. It is unclear whether or not individuals with disabilities were included in the sample. The norming sample was selected to approximate 1980 U.S. Census data. Descriptive standardization data is adequately presented in the MBA manual, and the authors refer the test consumer to the normative information presented in the WJ-R. A more detailed description of norms is provided in the WJ-R ACH section of this chapter. Overall, it appears that the obtained normative sample for the MBA closely resembles that of the U. S. population of 1980. However, these norms are relatively old, especially for a test published in 1994. Kamphaus (1993) suggests a rule of thumb that if the standardization sample is 10 or more years old, that the examiner should be cautious of the accuracy of the norms for current use.

Reliability

Internal consistency reliability coefficients for the MBA were calculated for the four tests as well as the Basic Skills Cluster for individuals ages 5 through 79 years using the split-half method. It is unclear as to why data is presented only for individuals in this age range from the standardization sample. Across a sample of 2,675 individuals ages 5 to 79, reliability coefficients for the Reading test ranged from .88 to .98 with a median of .94. For a sample of 2,666 individuals ages 5 to 79, the Writing test reliability coefficients ranged from .79 to .97 with a median of .92. For a sample of 2,673 individuals ages 5 to 79, the Mathematics test reliability coefficients ranged from .70 to .98 with a median of .93. Reliability coefficients for the Factual Knowledge test ranged from .80 to .96 with a median of .87 for a sample of 2,854 individuals ages 5 to 79. Lastly, the Basic Skills Cluster had reliability coefficients ranging from .90 to .98 with a median of .93 for a sample of 2,838 individuals ages 5 to 79. Further, the stability of the MBA was assessed using test-retest reliability, with an interval of one week separating the two administrations for three samples. For a sample of 52 sixth-grade students, test-retest reliability coefficients were .89 for Reading, .85 for Writing, .86 for Mathematics, .88 for Factual Knowledge, and .96 for the Basic Skills Cluster. In a sample of 53 college students, test-retest reliability coefficients were .86 for Reading, .93 for Writing, .90 for Mathematics, .88 for Factual Knowledge, and .94 for the Basic Skills Cluster. In a sample of 56 adults, test-retest reliability coefficients were .90 for Reading, .94 for Writing, .89 for Mathematics, .89 for Factual Knowledge, and .97 for the Basic Skills Cluster. Overall, the presented reliability estimates for the MBA appear to be adequate. However, internal consistency estimates would have been more informative if the entire standardization sample had been used, and additional studies of stability with larger samples and longer administration intervals would be useful.

Validity

Content, concurrent, and construct validity are addressed in the MBA manual. In terms of content validity, it is emphasized that the items included in the MBA were chosen for the purpose of offering a brief, but extensive sampling of knowledge and basic academic skills. Items were also selected to cover a wide range of ability levels. Though this explanation makes sense, more information pertaining to content validity would be beneficial. Concurrent validity studies were conducted with other popular tests of achievement using three different samples. Selected correlations are presented here. For a sample of 55 sixth-grade students, MBA Reading test scores correlated .79 with WJ-R ACH Broad Reading, .75 with K-TEA Brief Form Reading, .82 with PIAT-R Total Reading, and .64 with WRAT-R Reading. MBA Writing test scores correlated .53 with WJ-R ACH Broad Written Language, .62 with K-TEA Brief Form Spelling, .64 with PIAT-R Written Language Composite, and .57 with WRAT-R Spelling. MBA Mathematics test scores correlated .72 with WJ-R ACH Broad Mathematics, .67 with K-TEA Brief Form Mathematics, .62 with PIAT-R Mathematics, and .66 with WRAT-R Arithmetic. MBA Factual Knowledge test scores correlated .74 with WJ-R ACH Broad Knowledge and .64 with PIAT-R General Information. The MBA Basic Skills Cluster correlated .82 with the WJ-R ACH Skills Cluster. For a sample of 58 college students, MBA Reading test scores correlated .70 with WJ-R ACH Broad Reading, .60 with K-TEA Brief Form Reading, .68 with PIAT-R Total Reading, and .66 with WRAT-R Reading. MBA Writing test scores correlated .74 with WJ-R ACH Broad Written Language, .80 with K-TEA Brief Form Spelling, .70 with PIAT-R Written Language Composite, and .67 with WRAT-R Spelling. MBA Mathematics test scores correlated .84 with WJ-R ACH Broad Mathematics, .75 with K-TEA Brief Form Mathematics, .82 with PIAT-R Mathematics, and .72 with WRAT-R Arithmetic. MBA Factual Knowledge test scores correlated .77 with WJ-R ACH Broad Knowledge and .53 with PIAT-R General Information. The MBA Basic Skills Cluster correlated .85 with the WJ-R ACH Skills Cluster. In a sample of 59 adults, MBA Reading test scores correlated .75 with WJ-R ACH Broad Reading, .70 with K-TEA Brief Form Reading, .73 with PIAT-R Total Reading, and .70 with WRAT-R Reading. MBA Writing test scores correlated .78 with WJ-R ACH Broad Written Language, .76 with K-TEA Brief Form Spelling, .59 with

PIAT-R Written Language Composite, and .78 with WRAT-R Spelling. MBA Mathematics test scores correlated .88 with WJ-R ACH Broad Mathematics, .76 with K-TEA Brief Form Mathematics, .83 with PIAT-R Mathematics, and .75 with WRAT-R Arithmetic. MBA Factual Knowledge test scores correlated .77 with WJ-R ACH Broad Knowledge and .69 with PIAT-R General Information. The MBA Basic Skills Cluster correlated .88 with the WJ-R ACH Skills Cluster.

Further, MBA subtest and Basic Skills Cluster intercorrelation patterns for those individuals between the ages of 5 and 79 are reported for the purpose of contributing evidence for construct validity. The median correlations were Reading with Writing (r=.80), Reading with Mathematics (r=.66), Reading with Factual Knowledge (r=.74), Writing with Mathematics (r=.65), Mathematics with Factual Knowledge (r=.68), Writing with Factual Knowledge (r=.68), Basic Skills Cluster with Reading (r=.90), Basic Skills Cluster with Writing (r=.93), Basic Skills Cluster with Mathematics (r=.82), and Basic Skills Cluster with Factual Knowledge (r=.76). The figures show that the four MBA subtests measure different but related academic skills. No studies relating the MBA to measures of intelligence are presented. Altogether, there needs to be more clarification pertaining to content and construct validity. Further, despite the fact that the figures pertaining to concurrent validity appear adequate, studies having a wider variety of instruments and increased sample sizes would enhance claims of validation.

Summary

The MBA is a new brief screening measure of academic achievement. It appears to be technically adequate in some respects. However, more recent norms and enhanced reliability and validity studies would certainly be beneficial. Unfortunately, little independent research has been conducted using the MBA. The content of the MBA covers a broader range of skills than do other brief screeners of achievement such as the

WRAT-3, but it still might be considered a "screener of a screener" as there are yet more comprehensive screening measures of academic achievement. The instrument appears to be quick and easy to use, has close ties with the WJ-R, and comes with a computerized scoring program. Michael (1998) concluded in a review of the MBA that "this reviewer would consider the MBA to be a practical measure requiring a relatively short time (about 30 minutes) to administer and in light of the supporting reliability and validity data would recommend its use" (p. 1142). As always, clinicians should take care to use the MBA for the purposes for which it was intended.

Differential Ability Scales School Achievement Tests (DAS ACH)

The DAS ACH (Elliott, 1990a, 1990b) is a portion of the Differential Ability Scales, a comprehensive instrument designed to assess cognitive ability and achievement. Although the DAS covers an age range of 2 years, 6 months to 17 years, 11 months overall, the DAS ACH tests are designed to cover an age range of 6 years to 17 years, 11 months. The DAS ACH consists of three school achievement tests that measure the basic skills of word reading, spelling, and arithmetic, similar to the WRAT-3. An advantage of the DAS School Achievement Test component is that it shares a common normative sample with the DAS Cognitive Battery, thus enhancing ability-achievement comparisons. The test author cautions against misuse of the DAS ACH, stating that these tests should not be considered as measures of general achievement in their respective areas.

Administration and Scoring

The DAS ACH is an untimed, individually administered test of basic academic skills. It consists of three school achievement tests:

1. Basic Number Skills. This test consists of a total of 48 items and is generally administered to children ages 6 years to 17 years, 11 months. Skills assessed include the recognition and naming of numbers, as well as computation using the four basic arithmetic operations with whole numbers, fractions, decimals, and percentages. Items are presented on the Basic Number Skills worksheet. Low scores on this test may indicate that a child has poor understandings of mathematical operations, numeration, and/or poor attention or motivation.

2. Spelling. Like Basic Number Skills, Spelling is administered to children ages 6 years to 17 years, 11 months. This 70-item test assesses knowledge and recall of spellings by requiring the child to write words that are dictated to him or her onto the Spelling worksheet. Low scores on the Spelling test may indicate poor knowledge of phonological skills, poor auditory and/or visual memory, or poor auditory discrimination.

3. Word Reading. The usual age range for administering Word Reading is 6 years to 17 years, 11 months, but on occasion, this test is administered to children as young as 5 years old. On this 90-item test, word recognition is assessed by having the individual read aloud printed words as presented on the Word Reading card. Low scores on this test may reflect similar difficulties as those described for Spelling.

The DAS ACH tests may be given separately, or in any combination desired. Items on each of these tests are scored as correct or incorrect, and set basal and ceiling rules are used to determine the appropriate number of items to administer. The total test administration time takes about 15–25 minutes, and the test is relatively simple to score. Raw scores for each test are first converted to "Ability Scores," and these can be further converted to standard scores having a mean of 100 and a standard deviation of 15. Computerized scoring is also available. Further, each of these tests can be subjected to a performance analysis. Performance analysis calls for the clinician to examine the child's responses for the purpose of identifying strengths and weaknesses in terms of more discrete skills. For example, discrete academic skills presented in the Basic Number Skills subtest include multiplying simple fractions and naming a two-digit number. Performance analysis guidelines are presented on the test record forms as well as in the manual. The DAS ACH includes guidelines for testing children with disabilities and children who are not proficient in English. Instructions and suggestions for computing ability-achievement discrepancies are presented, as well.

Standardization

The standardization sample of the DAS, hence the DAS ACH, consisted of 3,475 children, including 175 children for each 6-month interval for ages 2 years, 6 months to 4 years, 11 months, and 200 children for each 1-year interval for ages 5 years to 17 years, 11 months. The standardization process took place from 1987 to 1989, and the sample was selected to approximate U. S. Census data as presented in the March 1988 *Current Population Survey*. The sample was stratified according to variables of age, gender, geographic region, race/ethnicity, and socioeconomic status (as defined by education level of parent(s) or guardian(s)), and preschool enrollment. Students enrolled in special education classes, with the exclusion of children with severe disabilities, were also included in the normative sample. Overall, it appears that the obtained normative sample for the DAS is representative of the U. S. population.

Reliability

Internal consistency reliabilities based on item-response theory were computed for the DAS ACH using individuals ages 6 years to 17 years, 11 months from the standardization sample. Two hundred cases at each 1-year age level were used in the calculations (N=2,400). These coefficients ranged from .82 to .90 with a mean of .87 for Basic Number Skills, .91 to .94 with a mean of .92 for Spelling, and .88 to .95 with a mean of

.92 for Word Reading. In addition, the coefficient was computed as .68 for the 5 year to 5 year, 11 months age group (N=200) for Word Reading. Indicators of test-retest reliability were also computed. The interval separating the test administrations spanned 2 to 6 weeks. For children ages 5 years, 9 months to 6 years, 11 months (N=67), test-retest reliability was .79 for Basic Number Skills. On this same test, the reliability was .85 for children ages 12 years to 13 years, 11 months (N=121). Test-retest reliability for Spelling was .89 for children ages 5 years, 9 months to 6 years, 11 months (N=62), and for children ages 12 years to 13 years, 11 months (N=118), it was .94. For children ages 5 years, 9 months to 6 years, 11 months (N=79) test-retest reliability was .97 for Word Reading. On this same test, the reliability was .94 for children ages 12 years to 13 years, 11 months (N=121). These figures suggest a high degree of item consistency and score stability.

Validity

Internal validity of the DAS as a whole is described in terms of intercorrelations of tests and composites. Correlations between the DAS School Achievement Tests and the Cognitive Battery General Conceptual Ability (GCA) composite are moderate. Intercorrelations are reported for 2,400 individuals ages 6 years to 17 years, 11 months with 200 cases per 1-year age level. Basic Number Skills, Spelling, and Word Reading correlated with the GCA .60, .52, and .60, respectively. For Verbal Ability on the DAS, correlations were .48, .49, and .59 for Basic Number Skills, Spelling, and Word Reading. For Nonverbal Reasoning Ability, correlations were .59, .49, and .52 for Basic Number Skills, Spelling, and Word Reading. For Spatial Ability, correlations were .45, .34, and .40 for Basic Number Skills, Spelling, and Word Reading. Further, the correlation for Basic Number Skills with Spelling was .56, for Basic Number Skills with Word Reading was .53, and Word Reading with Spelling was .81. Several concurrent validity studies are also reported. Correlations of the DAS ACH and the WISC-R were calculated for a sample of 66 children 8 to 10 years of age. Basic Number Skills was found to correlate with the WISC-R Verbal IQ, Performance IQ, Full Scale IQ, and Freedom from Distractibility .62, .53, .68, and .69, respectively. Spelling correlated with the Verbal IQ, Performance IQ, Full Scale IQ, and Freedom from Distractibility .57, .34, .50, and .47, respectively. Word Reading correlated with the Verbal IQ, Performance IQ, Full Scale IQ, and Freedom from Distractibility .68, .50, .66, and .50, respectively. Further, Basic Number Skills correlated .66 with Arithmetic on the WISC-R. For a sample of 60 children 14 to 15 years of age, Basic Number Skills correlated with the WISC-R Verbal IQ, Performance IQ, Full Scale IQ, and Freedom from Distractibility .66, .40, .68, and .63, respectively. Spelling correlated with the Verbal IQ, Performance IQ, Full Scale IQ, and Freedom from Distractibility .57, .34, .55, and .47, respectively. Word Reading correlated with the Verbal IQ, Performance IQ, Full Scale IQ, and Freedom from Distractibility .74, .38, .72, and .63 respectively. In addition, it was found that Basic Number Skills correlated .67 with Arithmetic on the WISC-R. Correlations of the DAS ACH and the SB-IV were calculated for a sample of 55 children 9 to 10 years of age. Basic Number Skills correlated .55 with Verbal Reasoning, .56 with Abstract/Visual Reasoning, .69 with Quantitative Reasoning, .28 with Short-Term Memory, and .66 with the Test Composite. Spelling correlated .34 with Verbal Reasoning, .44 with Abstract/Visual Reasoning, .50 with Quantitative Reasoning, .39 with Short-Term Memory, and .49 with the Test Composite. Word Reading correlated .58 with Verbal Reasoning, .48 with Abstract/Visual Reasoning, .63 with Quantitative Reasoning, .45 with Short-Term Memory, and .66 with the Test Composite. For a sample of 29 children having gifted referrals 7 to 11 years of age, Basic Number Skills correlated .28 with Verbal Reasoning, .52 with Abstract/Visual Reasoning, .64 with Quantitative Reasoning, .37 with Short-Term Memory, and .57 with the Test Composite. Spelling corre-

lated .24 with Verbal Reasoning, .36 with Abstract/Visual Reasoning, .43 with Quantitative Reasoning, .35 with Short-Term Memory, and .46 with the Test Composite. Word Reading correlated .50 with Verbal Reasoning, .51 with Abstract/Visual Reasoning, .52 with Quantitative Reasoning, .43 with Short-Term Memory, and .61 with the Test Composite. Correlations of the DAS ACH and the K-ABC were calculated for a sample of 18 to 27 children ages 5 to 7. Correlations of K-ABC Sequential Processing and the DAS ACH yielded values of .58, .49, and .34 for Basic Number Skills, Spelling, and Word Reading, respectively. Accordingly, correlations were computed with K-ABC Simultaneous Processing, yielding values of .38, .38, and .38 for Basic Number Skills, Spelling, and Word Reading, respectively. Correlations with K-ABC Mental Processing Composite were .66, .51, and .38 for Basic Number Skills, Spelling, and Word Reading, accordingly. For K-ABC Achievement, correlations were .64, .60, and .83 for Basic Number Skills, Spelling, and Word Reading, respectively. Correlations between scores on the DAS ACH and the PPVT-R were also reported for a sample of 64 children ages 6 years to 10 years, 9 months. The PPVT-R and Basic Numbers Skills correlated .31, Spelling and the PPVT-R correlated .42, and Word Reading and the PPVT-R correlated .48.

In addition, correlations are reported using both individually administered and group administered achievement tests. Correlations were calculated for a sample of 198 children of age 7 years and 157 children of age 11 years using the Basic Achievement Skills Individual Screener (BASIS). Basic Number Skills correlated .75 to .79 with the BASIS Mathematics subtest, Spelling correlated .87 to .88 with the BASIS Spelling subtest, and Word Reading correlated .64 to .79 with the BASIS Reading subtest. In a sample of 100 children ages 8 to 11 years, a correlation of .83 was found between Word Reading and the Total Reading score on the Woodcock Reading Mastery Tests—Revised (WRMT-R). Correlations for a sample of 29 children ages 7 to 11 years having gifted referrals were calculated with the K-TEA. Basic Number Skills correlated .84

with the K-TEA Mathematics Composite, Spelling correlated .85 with the K-TEA Spelling, and Word Reading correlated .85 with the K-TEA Reading Composite. Correlations were also calculated to compare the scores on the DAS ACH with group achievement test results collected from the standardization sample. The group tests included measures such as the California Achievement Test, the California Test of Basic Skills, the Stanford Achievement Test, and the Iowa Test of Basic Skills. Basic Number Skills correlated at .62 with total mathematics scores on the group tests, Word Reading correlated at .67 with total reading scores, and Spelling correlated with spelling scores at .77. Further, DAS ACH scores and school grades were correlated for the standardization sample. Basic Number Skills and mathematics grades correlated at .43, Spelling and spelling grades correlated at .60, and Word Reading and reading grades correlated at .48. Overall, these figures lend adequate support for the validity of the DAS ACH. However, additional studies with larger sample sizes would be more informative.

Summary

The DAS ACH appears to be a useful tool for measuring basic academic achievement skills. Because the DAS ACH examines a limited range of skills, not unlike the WRAT-3, it may be best considered a "screener of a screener." However, the DAS ACH possesses several characteristics that make it worthy of use, including an adequate standardization sample and the ability to make direct comparisons with the DAS Cognitive Battery, adequate reliability and validity data, and the availability of performance analysis procedures. Aylward (1992) indicates that DAS as a whole is a psychometrically sound, well-constructed test.

Peabody Individual Achievement Test—Revised (PIAT-R)

The PIAT-R (Markwardt, 1989) is the revision of the original PIAT (Dunn & Markwardt, 1970). Recently, a normative update was released for the PIAT-R (Markwardt, 1997). The only difference

between the 1989 and 1997 versions of the PIAT-R is that the 1997 update contains a more current standardization sample. The PIAT-R includes a greater number of items and more contemporary items than its predecessor, and a new subtest, Written Expression, was also added. The PIAT-R is an individually administered achievement test designed to provide a wide range of assessment in six content areas: General Information, Reading Recognition, Reading Comprehension, Mathematics, Spelling, and Written Expression. According to the test author, the PIAT-R is useful in providing a survey of an individual's academic achievement. As such, results of the PIAT-R may be used to determine the need for diagnostic testing. Other purposes include individual evaluation, program planning, school admissions and placement, ability grouping, guidance and counseling, personnel selection, and follow-up evaluation, as well as research uses. Several caveats are presented in the manual, cautioning the test consumer against the limitations of the PIAT-R—for example, that the PIAT-R is not designed to be a diagnostic test of achievement or to provide highly precise measurements of achievement, that it is not based on any one curriculum used in schools, and that the qualifications of the test consumer may influence the interpretation of the test.

Administration and Scoring

The PIAT-R is an individually administered test of academic achievement constructed for use with individuals ages 5 years to 18 years, 11 months. The PIAT-R consists of one form having six subtests presented in an easel format:

1. General Information. This subtest contains 100 items. The examinee answers open-ended questions as read aloud by the examiner. Items cover general encyclopedic knowledge in the areas of science, social studies, the humanities, and recreation.

2. Reading Recognition. This subtest contains 100 items comprising two distinct types. Items 1–16 are multiple choice in format (4 alternatives per item) and assess readiness skills. Here,

the student is to choose the correct word or picture to demonstrate knowledge of phonics skills. Items 17–100 require the examinee to read aloud words as presented by the examiner.

3. Reading Comprehension. The Reading Comprehension subtest contains 82 items designed to measure the individual's understanding of what is read. Each item covers two pages in the Book of Plates. On the first page, the examinee reads a sentence silently, and on the second page, chooses one of four pictures that best illustrates the sentence.

4. Mathematics. This subtest consists of 100 items in which the examiner reads aloud each item while displaying the four choices to the subject. The content of this test focuses on application of mathematical concepts rather than computation, and the level of difficulty ranges from recognizing numbers to solving trigonometry problems.

5. Spelling. Unlike other tests of this nature, the Spelling subtest of the PIAT-R is presented in a multiple-choice format. This subtest consists of 100 items requiring the examinee to accurately recognize letters and correct spellings of words from four given choices.

6. Written Expression. This subtest consists of two levels. Level I (19 items) is designed for use with kindergarten and first-grade students and measures readiness skills, including writing one's name, copying letters and words, and writing letters, words, or sentences as dictated by the examiner. Level II is designed for use with students in grades 2 to 12. Here, the student is asked to write a story in response to one of two picture prompts (A or B) with a time limit of 20 minutes. Stories are scored on 24 criteria relating to content, organization, and mechanics.

Items on the first five subtests are scored as correct or incorrect, and set basal and ceiling rules are used to determine the appropriate number of items to administer. Training exercises or teaching items are provided. The Written Expression subtest is scored differently, and the manual presents a detailed scoring guide for examiner use. A computerized scoring program is also available. The total test administration time takes about 60 minutes. Raw scores can be converted to standard scores having a mean of 100 and a standard deviation of 15 among other scores. These scores can be calculated for each subtest. Written Expression is an exception to this, and yields a "developmental scaled score," which ranges from 1 to 15, as well as grade-based stanines. In addition, a Total Test Composite score comprising General Information, Reading Recognition, Reading Comprehension, Mathematics, and Spelling, a Total Reading Composite comprising Reading Recognition and Reading Comprehension, and an optional Written Language Composite comprising Spelling and Written Expression can also be computed. Instructions for determining significant differences between scores are given in the manual. Guidelines for testing individuals with disabilities are also provided for reference. Further, a Report to Parents form is included in the manual and can be used as an aide in communicating scores.

Standardization

The PIAT-R was renormed between October 1995 and November 1996 to match U. S. Census data as depicted in the March 1994 *Current Population Survey*. These updated norms were published in 1997. The standardization sample is linked to those of the Kaufman Test of Educational Achievement, the Woodcock Reading Mastery Tests—Revised, and the KeyMath—Revised. The sample consisted of 3,429 individuals, including 3,184 students in kindergarten through grade 12 and 245 young adults ages 18 to 22 years. The sample was stratified according to variables of age, gender, socioeconomic status (i.e., parent education level), race/ethnicity, and geographic region. Gifted and special education status was also considered when constructing the sample. Overall, the sample appears to adequately match census statistics. However,

Caucasians are slightly overrepresented, as are individuals from the Southern and North Central regions of the country.

Reliability

In looking at reliability, it should be noted that the original PIAT-R norms from 1989 were used, not those from 1997. Split-half reliability coefficients were calculated for a sample of 1,563 students ages 5 to 18 years from the original PIAT-R normative sample. Reliability information is also presented according to grade level in the manual, but is not presented here. For the General Information subtest, split-half coefficients ranged from .92 to .96 with a median of .94. Coefficients for Reading Recognition ranged from .94 to .98 with a median of .97. For Reading Comprehension, coefficients ranged from .90 to .96 with a median of .93. The Total Reading Composite coefficients ranged from .95 to .98 with a median of .97. The Mathematics subtest coefficients ranged from .83 to .98 with a median of .94. Coefficients for Spelling ranged from .91 to .97 with a median of .95. Coefficients for the Total Test Composite ranged from .98 to .99 with a median of .99. Kuder-Richardson reliability coefficients were also calculated for that same sample. For the General Information subtest, coefficients ranged from .93 to .97 with a median of .96. Coefficients for Reading Recognition ranged from .93 to .97 with a median of .96. For Reading Comprehension, coefficients ranged from .92 to .98 with a median of .95. The Total Reading Composite coefficients ranged from .96 to .99 with a median of .97. The Mathematics subtest coefficients ranged from .87 to .98 with a median of .95. Coefficients for Spelling ranged from .90 to .97 with a median of .95. Coefficients for the Total Test Composite ranged from .98 to .99 with a median of .99. Test-retest reliability was calculated for a sample of 225 individuals ages 6 to 16 years, with the testing interval being 2 to 4 weeks long. For the General Information subtest, coefficients ranged from .83 to .97 with a median of .90. Coefficients for

Reading Recognition ranged from .94 to .98 with a median of .96. For Reading Comprehension, coefficients ranged from .65 to .97 with a median of .90. The Total Reading Composite coefficients ranged from .87 to .98 with a median of .96. The Mathematics subtest coefficients ranged from .67 to .94 with a median of .90. Coefficients for Spelling ranged from .78 to .97 with a median of .90. Coefficients for the Total Test Composite ranged from .88 to .99 with a median of .96. Item response theory reliability coefficients are presented for a sample of 1,560 children ages 5 to 18 years, as well. For the General Information subtest, coefficients ranged from .95 to .98 with a median of .97. Coefficients for Reading Recognition ranged from .96 to .99 with a median of .98. For Reading Comprehension, coefficients ranged from .94 to .98 with a median of .96. The Total Reading Composite coefficients ranged from .97 to .99 with a median of .98. The Mathematics subtest coefficients ranged from .91 to .99 with a median of .96. Coefficients for Spelling ranged from .93 to .98 with a median of .97. Coefficients for the Total Test Composite were all .99. Reliability information pertaining to Written Expression is also presented. Coefficient alpha reliabilities for Level I of Written Expression were calculated for a sample of 437 children in kindergarten and first grade. These values ranged from .60 to .69. For a sample of 45 first-graders, test-retest reliability coefficients were calculated for Level I Written Expression with a testing interval of 2 to 4 weeks. The overall coefficient was .56. Further, interrater reliability was calculated. For a sample of 299 kindergarten children, the interrater reliability was .90, and for a sample of 138 first graders, the interrater reliability was .95. Coefficient alpha reliabilities were also calculated for Level II of Written Expression for samples of children in grades 2 to 12. For Prompt A (N=530), these values ranged from .69 to .89 with a median of .86, and for Prompt B (N=541) these values ranged from .76 to .91 with a median of .88. Interrater reliability for Prompt A (N=537) ranged from .30 to .81 with a median of .58, and for Prompt B (N=550) ranged from

.53 to .77 with a median of .67. Alternate-forms reliability coefficients were also presented for a sample of 168 children in grades 3, 5, 7, 9, and 11. The coefficients ranged from .44 to .61 for these grades, and for the total sample, was .63. Overall, the reliability estimates for the PIAT-R are adequate, but this information would be improved if it had been based on the more recent standardization sample. As expected, coefficients are not as impressive for Written Expression as this subtest requires more subjective scoring.

Validity

As with the reliability information, validity information for the PIAT-R is based on the 1989 norms. Content validity of the PIAT-R is addressed in terms of the development process for each subtest. Also, the test author asserts that the internal consistency coefficients indicate that each subtest measures a clear content domain. Further, intercorrelation data support the content validity of each subtest. For a total sample of 715 children ages 5, 7, 9, 11, 13, 15, and 17 years, intercorrelations between subtests and composites with the Total Test Composite are presented: General Information (r=.78 to .86), Reading Recognition (r=.78 to .95), Reading Comprehension (r=.85 to .93), Total Reading Composite (r=.90 to .96), Mathematics (r=.66 to .87), and Spelling (r=.66 to .92). Construct validity is evidenced through age differentiation of scores, correlations with other tests, and factor analysis. Correlations between scores on the original PIAT and the PIAT-R were calculated for a sample of 273 children ages 6 to 17. Correlations for Mathematics ranged from .54 to .93 with a median of .78, correlations for Reading Recognition ranged from .68 to .95 with a median of .88, correlations for Reading Comprehension ranged from .63 to .90 with a median of .79, correlations for Spelling ranged from .59 to .92 with a median of .76, correlations for General Information ranged from .46 to .86 with a median of .78, and correlations for the Total Test Composite ranged from .82 to .97 with a median of .91. As further evidence of construct validity, scores on the PIAT-R were correlated with PPVT-R scores for a sample of 1,522 children ages 5 to 18. For General Information, correlations ranged from .61 to .81 with a median of .72. For Reading Recognition, correlations ranged from .51 to .70 with a median of .62. Correlation coefficients ranged from .54 to .75 with a median of .66 for Reading Comprehension. For the Total Reading Composite, correlations ranged from .52 to .78 with a median of .69. For Mathematics, correlations ranged from .50 to .69 with a median of .56. Correlation coefficients ranged from .28 to .58 with a median of .50 for Spelling. For the Total Test Composite, correlations ranged from .62 to .81 with a median of .72.

Further, the underlying constructs of the PIAT-R were examined via a factor analysis of subtest intercorrelations for those in grades 2 through 12 in the standardization sample. Six factors were identified, but three of these factors were found to account for 64.3% of the total variance. Factor I had high loadings for General Information (.71), Reading Comprehension (.52), and Mathematics (.70), appearing to represent a general verbal-educational ability factor. Factor II was characterized by high loadings for Reading Recognition (.73) and Spelling (.75), appearing to represent a more specific verbal factor involving knowledge of letters and phonics. Factor III was marked by modest loadings for Reading Comprehension (.39) and Written Expression, Level II (.39). This factor appears to represent a more complex verbal factor involving knowledge of grammar and syntax. Although the inclusion of factor analyses lends unique evidence of construct validity for the PIAT-R, other forms of validity are certainly missing. For example, no correlations with other measures of achievement or intelligence are provided in the manual. Instead, numerous validity studies on the original PIAT are provided. The utility of this information is questionable as only about 35% of the items on the PIAT-R are found on the PIAT.

In an independent investigation, Prewett and Giannuli (1991) investigated the relationships among the reading subtests of the PIAT-R, WJ-R ACH, K-TEA, and the WRAT-R for a sample of 118 students referred for psychoeducational evaluation ages 6 years, 5 months to 11 years, 11 months. The correlations amongst these subtests ranged from .78 to .98. Specifically, the Total Reading Composite of the PIAT-R correlated .88 with Broad Reading on the WJ-R ACH, .93 with the Reading Composite of the K-TEA Comprehensive Form, and .92 with Reading on the WRAT-R. Daub and Colarusso (1996) examined the validity of the reading subtests of the PIAT-R, WJ-R ACH, and the Diagnostic Achievement Battery-2 (DAB-2) for a sample of 35 children ages 9 years, 3 months to 10 years, 11 months identified as having reading disabilities. The Total Reading Composite of the PIAT-R correlated .82 with Broad Reading on the WJ-R ACH and .88 with the Reading Composite on the DAB-2. Although the evidence presented in the PIAT-R manual for validity is supportive, more studies using a wider variety of tests and populations would be worthwhile.

Summary

The PIAT-R is a widely used test of academic achievement. Some clinicians find that the multiple-choice formats of many of the subtests are relatively nonthreatening for special populations of students. Others may criticize this type of response format in that students are often asked to supply or produce their own answers for most tasks encountered in school. Costenbader and Adams (1991) indicate that more extensive research with the PIAT-R needs to be conducted with other major instruments. Likewise, Rogers (1992) suggests that although more evidence to support concurrent validity is needed, that "the PIAT-R appears to be a useful instrument both to practitioners in the schools and to researchers" (p. 654).

Kaufman Test of Educational Achievement (K-TEA)

The K-TEA (Kaufman & Kaufman, 1985a, 1985b) is an individually administered test of academic achievement that consists of two forms: Brief and Comprehensive. Recently, a normative update was released for the K-TEA (Kaufman & Kaufman, 1997a, 1997b). The sole difference between the 1989 and 1997 versions of the K-TEA is that the 1997 update contains a more current standardization sample. The Brief Form consists of three subtests: Mathematics, Reading, and Spelling. The Comprehensive Form consists of five subtests: Mathematics Applications, Reading Decoding, Spelling, Reading Comprehension, and Mathematics Computation. Some items have been taken from or are highly similar to ones on the K-ABC. The authors propose several uses appropriate for both forms of the K-TEA, including a contribution to a psychoeducational battery, program planning, research, pretesting and posttesting, placement decisions, student self-appraisal, use by government agencies such as social services, personnel selection, and as a measure of adaptive functioning. In addition, the Comprehensive Form is useful in analyzing strengths and weaknesses and for error analysis. Generally, it is recommended that the Brief Form be used for screening and prereferral and that the Comprehensive Form be used when more detailed information is warranted.

Administration and Scoring

The K-TEA Brief Form is an individually administered test of academic achievement that is designed for use with children ages 6 years to 18 years, 11 months. This test consists of a single form and easel format and contains items that are completely different than the ones on the K-TEA Comprehensive Form. The K-TEA Brief Form consists of the following subtests:

1. Mathematics. This subtest contains 52 items that assess basic arithmetic concepts, applications, numerical reasoning, and computational skills. Items 1–25 are comprised of computational problems that are completed on the Mathematics Worksheet. Items 26–52 consist of concepts and applications problems in which each problem is presented orally along with an accompanying picture. The examinee

may use paper and pencil to complete necessary calculations, but must respond orally.

2. Reading. This subtest also consists of 52 items that assess reading decoding and comprehension. Items 1–23 assess decoding skills, requiring the examinee to identify printed letters and words as presented. Items 24–52 assess comprehension and require the examinee to respond orally or in gestures to printed instructions as presented by the examiner.

3. Spelling. The Spelling subtest consists of 40 items. Here, the examiner reads aloud a word both in isolation and as used in a sentence, and the examinee writes each word on the Spelling Sheet. Alternatively, the examinee may spell the word aloud.

The K-TEA Brief Form generally takes 30 minutes to administer. Items are grouped into units and are scored as correct or incorrect. Verbal responses may be made in languages other than English provided that the correctness of such responses is easily determined. Set basal and ceiling rules are used to determine the appropriate number of items to administer. Extensive psychometric training is not a prerequisite for administering and scoring the K-TEA Brief Form, although practice is recommended. Separate subtest scores as well as a Battery Composite may be calculated. Among other scores, the K-TEA Brief Form yields standard scores having a mean of 100 and a standard deviation of 15. Computerized scoring is available. The K-TEA Brief Form also allows for subtest comparisons for the purpose of identifying general strengths and weaknesses. A graphic display of descriptive categories is presented in the manual for the purpose of interpreting standard scores: Upper Extreme (130 and above), Well Above Average (120–129), Above Average (110–119), Average (90–109), Below Average (80–89), Well Below Average (70–79), and Lower Extreme (69 and below). A K-TEA Brief Form Report to Parents is also available for use to report test results.

The K-TEA Comprehensive Form is an individually administered test of academic achievement that is designed for use with children ages 6 years to 18 years, 11 months. This test consists of a single form and contains items that are completely different than the ones on the K-TEA Brief Form. The K-TEA Comprehensive Form consists of the following subtests presented in an easel format:

1. Mathematics Applications. This subtest contains 60 items that assess arithmetic concepts and problem-solving applications. Each problem is presented orally along with an accompanying picture, graph, etc. The examinee may use paper and pencil to complete necessary calculations, but must respond orally.

2. Reading Decoding. This subtest also consists of 60 items that assess decoding skills, requiring the examinee to identify and read aloud printed letters and words as presented to them.

3. Spelling. The Spelling subtest consists of 50 items. Here, the examiner reads aloud a word both in isolation and as used in a sentence, and the examinee writes each word on the Spelling Sheet. Alternatively, the examinee may spell the word aloud.

4. Reading Comprehension. This subtest consists of 50 items. Here, for some items, the student is to read passages and answer questions about them. Other items require the student to read printed instructions and to respond orally or in gestures, accordingly.

5. Mathematics Computation. This subtest consists of 60 items that measure computational skills involving the four basic arithmetic operations to more complex (e.g., algebraic) operations. The examinee completes the problems on the Mathematics Computation Worksheet.

The K-TEA Comprehensive Form generally takes 60 to 75 minutes to administer. Items are grouped into units and are scored as correct or incorrect. Verbal responses may be made in languages other than English provided that the correctness of such responses is easily determined. Set basal and ceiling rules are used to determine the appropriate number of items to administer. Extensive psychometric training is not a prerequisite for administering and scoring the K-TEA Comprehensive Form, although practice is recommended. Separate subtest scores as well as a Reading Composite, Mathematics Composite, and Battery Composite may be calculated. Among other scores, the K-TEA Comprehensive Form yields standard scores having a mean of 100 and a standard deviation of 15. Computerized scoring is available. The K-TEA Comprehensive Form also allows for subtest comparisons for the purpose of identifying general strengths and weaknesses. Further, detailed error analysis procedures are available to provide more refined information pertaining to specific skills. Further, the same graphic display of descriptive categories is presented in the K-TEA Comprehensive Form manual for the purpose of interpreting standard scores, and a K-TEA Comprehensive Form Report to Parents is also available for use to report test results.

Standardization

The K-TEA was renormed between October 1995 and November 1996 to match U. S. Census data as depicted in the March 1994 *Current Population Survey*. These updated norms were published in 1997. The standardization sample is the same for the K-TEA Brief Form and Comprehensive Form and is linked to those of the Peabody Individual Achievement Test—Revised, the Woodcock Reading Mastery Tests—Revised, and the KeyMath—Revised. The sample consisted of 3,429 individuals, including 3,184 students in kindergarten through grade 12 and 245 young adults ages 18 to 22 years. The sample was stratified according to variables of age, gender, socioeconomic status (i.e., parent education level), race/ethnicity, and geographic region. Gifted and special education status was also considered in constructing the sample.

Overall, the sample appears to adequately match census statistics. However, Caucasians are slightly overrepresented, as are individuals from the Southern and North Central regions of the country.

Reliability

Reliability data are based on the original K-TEA norms from 1985. Internal consistency reliability coefficients for the K-TEA Brief Form were calculated for each subtest as well as the Battery Composite across 589 individuals ages 6 to 18 years from the standardization sample. Coefficients were also presented in the manual according to grade level, but are not presented here. Reliability coefficients for the Mathematics subtest ranged from .81 to .92 with a mean of .87. For the Reading subtest, the coefficients ranged from .83 to .97 with a mean of .91. For the Spelling subtest, reliability coefficients ranged from .79 to .96 with a mean of .89. Reliability coefficients for the Battery Composite ranged from .91 to .98 with a mean of .95. Test-retest reliability was also assessed for a sample of 153 students in grades 1 to 12, with an average testing interval of 1 week. In a sample of 79 first through sixth grade students, test-retest coefficients were .88 for Mathematics, .84 for Reading, .90 for Spelling, and .94 for the Battery Composite. In a sample of 74 students in grades 7 to 12, test-retest coefficients were .85 for Mathematics, .85 for Reading, .84 for Spelling, and .92 for the Battery Composite. A sort of "alternate forms" reliability is also presented using the Brief Form (Mathematics, Reading, Spelling, and Battery Composite) and the Comprehensive Form (Mathematics Composite, Reading Composite, Spelling, and Battery Composite) for a sample of 576 children ages 6 to 18 years. For Mathematics, correlations ranged from .79 to .90 with a mean of .85. For Reading, correlations ranged from .68 to .95 with a mean of .83. Correlations on Spelling ranged from .86 to .94 with a mean of .90. Finally, correlations for the Battery Composite ranged from .90 to .97 with a mean of .93.

As with the K-TEA Brief Form, reliability data pertaining to the K-TEA Comprehensive form are based on the 1985 norms. Internal consistency reliability coefficients for the K-TEA Comprehensive Form were calculated for each subtest and composite for 2,476 individuals ages 6 to 18 years from the normative sample. Coefficients were also presented in the manual according to grade level, but are not presented here. Reliability coefficients for the Mathematics Applications subtest ranged from .86 to .94 with a mean of .92. For the Mathematics Computation subtest, the coefficients ranged from .83 to .97 with a mean of .92. These two tests combine to form the Mathematics Composite, for which reliability coefficients ranged from .93 to .98 with a mean of .95. For the Reading Decoding subtest, the coefficients ranged from .91 to .97 with a mean of .95. Coefficients for the Reading Comprehension subtest ranged from .89 to .96 with a mean of .93. These two subtests combine to form the Reading Composite, for which reliability coefficients ranged from .94 to .98 with a mean of .97. For the Spelling subtest, reliability coefficients ranged from .88 to .96 with a mean of .94. Finally, reliability coefficients for the Battery Composite ranged from .97 to .99 with a mean of .98. As a measure of stability, test-retest coefficients are presented for a sample of 172 individuals in grades 1 to 12 with an average testing interval of about 1 week. In a sample of 85 first-through sixth-grade students, test-retest coefficients were .90 for Mathematics Applications, .83 for Mathematics Computation, .93 for the Mathematics Composite, .95 for Reading Decoding, .92 for Reading Comprehension, .96 for the Reading Composite, .95 for Spelling, and .97 for the Battery Composite. In a sample of 87 students in grades 7 to 12, test-retest coefficients were .94 for Mathematics Applications, .92 for Mathematics Computation, .96 for the Mathematics Composite, .91 for Reading Decoding, .90 for Reading Comprehension, .94 for the Reading Composite, .96 for Spelling, and .97 for the Battery Composite. The information pertaining to a variety of "alternate forms" reliability is the same as that presented for the Brief Form (see above). Altogether, the estimates of reliability for the K-TEA appear to be strong. However, such information needs to be calculated with the normative update to make it more current.

Validity

Content validity for the K-TEA Brief Form was described in terms of the item selection process. The test authors indicated that content validity was in part established through consultation with curriculum experts in each subject area. In addition, item analysis procedures such as the Rasch-Wright and Angoff methods were utilized. Mean intercorrelations are presented for the K-TEA Brief Form for a sample of 589 individuals ages 6 to 18 years from the normative data. Mathematics correlated with Reading and Spelling .63 and .55, respectively, and Spelling correlated .65 with Reading. Evidence of construct validity is presented in terms of age differentiation in the K-TEA Brief Form. Also, correlations were computed between the subtests and the Battery Composite for a sample of 589 children ages 6 to 18 years. Correlation coefficients for Reading and the Battery Composite ranged from .62 to .86 with a mean of .79. Correlations for Mathematics ranged from .75 to .93 with a mean of .84. For Spelling, correlations ranged from .68 to .90 with a mean of .81. Evidence of concurrent validity is also presented. For a sample of 198 students in grades 1 to 12, correlations between Reading on the K-TEA Brief Form and Reading on the WRAT ranged from .61 to .74. For Mathematics on the K-TEA Brief Form and Arithmetic on the WRAT, correlations ranged from .42 to .84 in a sample of 200 students in grades 1 to 12. For K-TEA Brief Form Spelling and WRAT Spelling, correlations ranged from .43 to .87 in a sample of 200 students in grades 1 to 12. For a sample of 52 students in grades 1 to 12, correlations were calculated between the K-TEA Brief Form and the PIAT. The correlation between the K-TEA Brief Form Mathematics subtest and Mathematics on the PIAT was .59. Reading on the K-TEA

Brief Form correlated .78 with Reading Recognition and .80 with Reading Comprehension on the PIAT. Spelling on the K-TEA Brief Form correlated .68 with Spelling on the PIAT. Finally, the K-TEA Brief Form Battery Composite correlated .84 with the Total Test score on the PIAT.

Correlations between the K-TEA Brief Form and the K-ABC are also presented for a sample of 105 children ages 6 to 12 years. For this total sample, Mathematics on the K-TEA Brief Form correlated .39 to .45 with Sequential Processing, .36 to .58 with Simultaneous Processing, .52 to .60 with the Mental Processing Composite, .19 to .66 with Nonverbal, .60 to .71 with Achievement, .26 to .37 with Faces & Places, .71 to .78 with Arithmetic, .32 to .42 with Riddles, .26 to .55 with Reading/Decoding, and .57 to .66 with Reading/Understanding. Reading on the K-TEA Brief Form correlated .27 to .38 with Sequential Processing, .36 to .46 with Simultaneous Processing, .46 to .48 with the Mental Processing Composite, .22 to .59 with Nonverbal, .73 to .82 with Achievement, .28 to .43 with Faces & Places, .55 to .63 with Arithmetic, .30 to .54 with Riddles, .45 to .90 with Reading/Decoding, and .78 to .95 with Reading/Understanding. Spelling on the K-TEA Brief Form correlated .37 to .41 with Sequential Processing, .11 to .21 with Simultaneous Processing, .23 to .39 with the Mental Processing Composite, .21 to .23 with Nonverbal, .52 to .75 with Achievement, .32 to .33 with Faces & Places, .42 to .50 with Arithmetic, .18 with Riddles, .63 to .86 with Reading/Decoding, and .46 to .79 with Reading/Understanding. The Battery Composite on the K-TEA Brief Form correlated .44 to .48 with Sequential Processing, .33 to .47 with Simultaneous Processing, .51 to .54 with the Mental Processing Composite, .22 to .60 with Nonverbal, .77 to .84 with Achievement, .34 to .39 with Faces & Places, .63 to .76 with Arithmetic, .26 to .45 with Riddles, .58 to .90 with Reading/Decoding, and .78 to .92 with Reading/Understanding. Lastly, for a total sample of 580 children in grades 1 to 12, scores on the K-TEA Brief Form and the PPVT-R were correlated. For Mathematics, correlations with

PPVT-R scores ranged from .25 to .46. For Reading, correlations with PPVT-R scores ranged from .42 to .66. For Spelling, correlations with PPVT-R scores ranged from .25 to .42. Correlations between the Battery Composite and PPVT-R scores ranged from .35 to .59.

Content validity for the K-TEA Comprehensive Form was also described in terms of the item selection process. The test authors indicated that content validity was in part established through consultation with curriculum experts in each subject area. In addition, item analysis procedures such as the Rasch-Wright and Angoff methods were utilized. Mean intercorrelations are presented for the K-TEA Comprehensive Form for 2,476 individuals ages 6 to 18 years from the standardization sample. The Mathematics Composite correlated with the Reading Composite and Spelling .74 and .64, respectively. Spelling correlated .81 with the Reading Composite. Evidence of construct validity is presented in terms of age differentiation in the K-TEA Comprehensive Form. Also, correlations were computed between the subtests and the Battery Composite for a sample of 2,476 children ages 6 to 18 years. Correlation coefficients for Reading Decoding and the Battery Composite ranged from .83 to .93 with a mean of .87. For Reading Comprehension, correlations ranged from .84 to .92 with a mean of .88. Correlations for Mathematics Applications ranged from .72 to .91 with a mean of .84. Correlations for Mathematics Computation ranged from .73 to .90 with a mean of .82. For Spelling, correlations ranged from .76 to .91 with a mean of .85.

Evidence of concurrent validity is also presented for the K-TEA Comprehensive Form. For a sample of 199 students in grades 1 to 12, correlations were computed between Reading on the WRAT and reading scores on the K-TEA Comprehensive Form. For Reading Decoding, correlations ranged from .67 to .90, Reading Comprehension from .51 to .78, and the Reading Composite .65 to .89. For a sample of 201 students in grades 1 to 12, correlations between Arithmetic on the WRAT and Mathematics

Applications, Mathematics Computation, and the Mathematics Composite were .35 to .66, .34 to .52, and .37 to .66, respectively. For a sample of 201 students in grades 1 to 12, correlations ranged from .43 to .84 for the K-TEA Comprehensive Form Spelling and WRAT Spelling. For a sample of 52 students in grades 1 to 12, correlations were calculated between the K-TEA Comprehensive Form and the PIAT. The correlation between Mathematics on the PIAT and Mathematics Applications, Mathematics Computation, and the Mathematics Composite were .72, .63, and .75, respectively. Correlations between Reading Recognition on the PIAT and Reading Decoding, Reading Comprehension, and the Reading Composite were .84, .73, and .82, respectively. For Reading Comprehension on the PIAT, correlations were .81, .74, and .82 with Reading Decoding, Reading Comprehension, and the Reading Composite, respectively. Spelling on the PIAT correlated .78 with Spelling on the K-TEA Comprehensive Form. Finally, the K-TEA Comprehensive Form Battery Composite correlated .86 with the Total Test score on the PIAT.

Correlations between the K-TEA Comprehensive Form and the K-ABC are also presented for a sample of 106 children ages 6 to 12 years, 6 months. For this total sample, the Mathematics Composite on the K-TEA Comprehensive Form correlated .39 to .55 with Sequential Processing, .43 to .66 with Simultaneous Processing, .63 to .67 with the Mental Processing Composite, .29 to .68 with Nonverbal, .69 to .76 with Achievement, .25 to .32 with Faces & Places, .79 to .85 with Arithmetic, .38 to .54 with Riddles, .34 to .59 with Reading/Decoding, and .63 to .66 with Reading/Understanding. The Reading Composite on the K-TEA Comprehensive Form correlated .45 to .54 with Sequential Processing, .34 to .54 with Simultaneous Processing, .50 to .64 with the Mental Processing Composite, .19 to .56 with Nonverbal, .80 to .84 with Achievement, .27 to .48 with Faces & Places, .59 to .69 with Arithmetic, .24 to .61 with Riddles, .75 to .89 with Reading/Decoding, and .74 to .92 with Reading/Understanding. Spelling on the K-TEA Comprehensive Form correlated .45 with Sequential Processing, .14 to .30 with Simultaneous Processing, .30 to .47 with the Mental Processing Composite, .19 to .23 with Nonverbal, .51 to .77 with Achievement, .28 to .30 with Faces & Places, .45 to .56 with Arithmetic, .17 to .19 with Riddles, .60 to .88 with Reading/Decoding, and .43 to .83 with Reading/Understanding. The Battery Composite on the K-TEA Comprehensive Form correlated .51 to .55 with Sequential Processing, .38 to .58 with Simultaneous Processing, .56 to .67 with the Mental Processing Composite, .25 to .61 with Nonverbal, .83 to .84 with Achievement, .27 to .43 with Faces & Places, .73 to .80 with Arithmetic, .28 to .55 with Riddles, .65 to .85 with Reading/Decoding, and .76 to .86 with Reading/Understanding. Next, for a total sample of 1,054 children in grades 1 to 12, scores on the K-TEA Comprehensive Form and the PPVT-R were correlated. For the Reading Composite, correlations with PPVT-R scores ranged from .45 to .67. For the Mathematics Composite, correlations ranged from .41 to .54. For Spelling, correlations with PPVT-R scores ranged from .29 to .46. Correlations between the Battery Composite and PPVT-R scores ranged from .47 to .63. For a second sample of 1,402 children in grades 1 to 12, scores on the K-TEA Comprehensive Form and the PPVT-R were correlated. For the Reading Composite, correlations with PPVT-R scores ranged from .57 to .68. For the Mathematics Composite, correlations ranged from .49 to .64. For Spelling, correlations with PPVT-R scores ranged from .40 to .51. Correlations between the Battery Composite and PPVT-R scores ranged from .57 to .70.

Lastly, concurrent validity studies involving group achievement tests are presented. The correlations between Reading on the Stanford Achievement Test (N=53), Metropolitan Achievement Test (N=41), and the Comprehensive Test of Basic Skills (N=43) and the K-TEA Comprehensive Form Reading Composite were

.79, .75, and .73, respectively. The correlations between Mathematics on the Stanford Achievement Test (N=54), Metropolitan Achievement Test (N=41), and the Comprehensive Test of Basic Skills (N=43) and the K-TEA Comprehensive Form Mathematics Composite were .78, .74, and .87, respectively. The correlations between Composite scores on the Stanford Achievement Test (N=42), Metropolitan Achievement Test (N=30), and the Comprehensive Test of Basic Skills (N=35) and the K-TEA Comprehensive Form Battery Composite were .85, .80, and .90, respectively. Lavin (1996b) examined the relationship between the WISC-III and the K-TEA Comprehensive Form for a sample of 72 children ages 7 to 16 years with emotional handicaps. WISC-III Full Scale IQ correlated .66 with Mathematics Applications, .54 with Mathematics Computation, .38 with Spelling, .51 with Reading Decoding, .53 with Reading Comprehension, .53 with the Reading Composite, and .65 with the Mathematics Composite. WISC-III Verbal IQ correlated .64 with Mathematics Applications, .52 with Mathematics Computation, .55 with Spelling, .63 with Reading Decoding, .67 with Reading Comprehension, .60 with the Reading Composite, and .57 with the Mathematics Composite. WISC-III Performance IQ correlated .37 with Mathematics Applications, .27 with Mathematics Computation, .05 with Spelling, .13 with Reading Decoding, .10 with Reading Comprehension, .19 with the Reading Composite, and .42 with the Mathematics Composite. Overall, the presented indices of validity appear to be adequate, although more studies using a wider variety of tests and including the updated norms would be desirable. Specifically, some studies should be conducted using special populations, as these are included in the normative sample.

Summary

The K-TEA is a relatively new measure of academic achievement in that it is still in its first edition. Worthington (1987) describes the K-TEA as a technically strong instrument with more than adequate reliability and validity. As such, the K-TEA holds promise as a prominent competitor in the field of achievement assessment.

Woodcock-Johnson Psycho-Educational Battery—Revised, Tests of Achievement (WJ-R ACH)

The WJ-R ACH (Woodcock & Johnson, 1989a; Woodcock & Mather, 1989) is one of two components of the Woodcock-Johnson Psycho-Educational Battery—Revised (WJ-R; Woodcock & Johnson, 1989a). The original Woodcock-Johnson Psycho-Educational Battery was published in 1977 (WJ; Woodcock & Johnson, 1977). The other component of the battery is the Woodcock-Johnson Psycho-Educational Battery-Revised Tests of Cognitive Ability (WJ-R COG). The WJ-R COG was developed according to the Horn-Cattell "g_f"–"g_c" (fluid and crystallized abilities) theory as noted elsewhere. Certain portions of the WJ-R ACH are also supportive of this framework. The WJ-R COG and WJ-R ACH were conormed, allowing the examiner to make meaningful ability-achievement comparisons. In comparison to the original WJ ACH, the WJ-R ACH has been improved in a number of ways and includes two parallel achievement batteries, as well as four new subtests. The WJ-R ACH is an individually administered test of achievement designed to provide a complete assessment of reading, mathematics, written language, and general knowledge. Specific tests may be selected to suit a variety of testing purposes. The test authors purport several uses of the WJ-R ACH in the manual, including diagnosis, determination of psychoeducational discrepancies, individual program planning, program placement, guidance, assessment of growth, program evaluation, and research. A Spanish-language version of the entire battery is also available: Batería Woodcock-Muñoz-Revisada (Woodcock & Muñoz-Sandoval, 1996).

Administration and Scoring

The WJ-R ACH is an individually administered test of academic achievement that was designed for use with individuals ages 2 to 95 years of age. The WJ-R ACH consists of two parallel forms, A and B in an easel format. Each form, in turn, consists of a Standard Battery and a Supplemental Battery. Clinicians may select a variety of combinations of tests to administer for any given situation, and a Selective Testing Table is provided in the manual for reference. The Standard Battery contains nine tests as follows:

1. Letter-Word Identification (Test 22). This test consists of 57 items. The first five items require the individual to match a rebus with an actual picture of an object. The remaining items require the individual to orally identify letters and words presented in isolation.

2. Passage Comprehension (Test 23). This test consists of 43 items. The first four items require the individual to point to a picture represented by a phrase. The remaining items require the individual to read a short passage and identify a missing word.

3. Calculation (Test 24). The Calculation test consists of 58 items. Here, the individual solves problems in a paper-and-pencil format as presented in the Subject Response Booklet. Problems involve basic arithmetic operations up to trigonometric and calculus operations.

4. Applied Problems (Test 25). This test consists of 60 items requiring the individual to solve practical mathematical problems. If needed, the examinee may make calculations on the provided Applied Problems Worksheet portion of the Subject Response Booklet, but the response must be given orally.

5. Dictation (Test 26). The Dictation test consists of 56 items, and responses are written in the designated portion of the Subject Response Booklet. Items 1–6 assess prewriting skills such as drawing and copying. The remaining items assess the subject's skill in providing written responses to questions pertaining to knowledge of letters, spelling, punctuation, capitalization, and word usage.

6. Writing Samples (Test 27). This test consists of 30 items that require the individual to write responses to a variety of instructions. Responses are recorded in the designated section of the Subject Response Booklet.

7. Science (Test 28). The Science test consists of 49 items covering content in the biological and physical sciences. The first eight items require pointing responses from the examinee, whereas for the remainder of the items, the examinee must respond orally to questions posed by the examiner.

8. Social Studies (Test 29). Like the Science test, Social Studies consists of 49 items. The items cover content from history, government, geography, economics, and the like. The first six items require pointing responses, whereas the remainder of the items require oral responses to questions read aloud by the examiner.

9. Humanities (Test 30). The Humanities test consists of 45 items that assess an individual's knowledge in art, music, and literature. The first five items require pointing responses, whereas the remainder of the items require oral responses to questions read aloud by the examiner.

The Supplemental Battery contains the following five tests:

1. Word Attack (Test 31). This test consists of 30 items that assess the individual's ability to apply rules of phonics and structural analysis in reading aloud unfamiliar or nonsense words.

2. Reading Vocabulary (Test 32). Part A, Synonyms, consists of 34 items in which the examinee must state a word similar in meaning to the one presented. Part B, Antonyms, consists of 35 items in which the examinee must state a word opposite in meaning to the one presented.

3. Quantitative Concepts (Test 33). This test consists of 48 items that require the examinee to respond to questions involving mathematical concepts and terminology.

4. Proofing (Test 34). Proofing consists of 36 items in which the examinee must identify and explain how to correct a mistake (e.g., punctuation, spelling, etc.) in a printed passage.

5. Writing Fluency (Test 35). This test consists of 40 items in which the examinee must write a sentence that relates to a given stimulus picture and includes three given words. Answers are recorded in the designated portion of the Subject Response Booklet, and there is a 7-minute time limit.

Additional test scores may be obtained for Punctuation & Capitalization (P), Spelling (S), and Usage (U). Responses from the Dictation and Proofing tests are used to obtain these scores. Further, a Handwriting (H) test score may be obtained from the Writing Samples test.

Various combinations of tests from the WJ-R ACH Standard Battery yield five cluster scores: Broad Reading (Letter-Word Identification and Passage Comprehension), Broad Mathematics (Calculation and Applied Problems), Broad Written Language (Dictation and Writing Samples), Broad Knowledge (Science, Social Studies, and Humanities), and Skills (Letter-Word Identification, Applied Problems, and Dictation). Supplemental Battery cluster scores may also be computed: Basic Reading Skills (Letter-Word Identification and Word Attack), Reading Comprehension (Passage Comprehension and Reading Vocabulary), Basic Mathematics Skills (Calculation and Quantitative Concepts), Mathematics Reasoning (Applied Problems), Basic Writing Skills (Dictation and Proofing), and Written Expression (Writing Samples and Writing Fluency). Of further note, the following tests and clusters can be used as a measure of quantitative ability "g_q" when analyzing cognitive factors of the WJ-R COG: Calculation, Applied Problems, Quantitative Concepts, and Broad Mathematics. Writing Fluency may be used as a measure of processing speed "g_s," and Word Attack may be used as a measure of auditory processing "g_a." Science, Social Studies, and Humanities may be used as measures of comprehension-knowledge "g_c." Further, Letter-Word Identification, Applied Problems, Dictation, Science, Social Studies, Humanities, the Broad Knowledge, and Skills cluster scores may be used as Early Development (EDev) measures.

Items on most of the tests are scored as correct or incorrect, with the exception of Writing Samples, which is scored 2, 1, or 0. Writing Fluency, Punctuation & Capitalization, Spelling, Usage, and Handwriting also have differing scoring criteria. Set basal and ceiling rules are used to determine the appropriate number of items to administer. Teaching items are provided. The total test administration time varies according to how many tests are administered, but generally ranges from 20 minutes to over an hour. As the WJ-R ACH is lengthier and somewhat more complex than other measures of achievement, the authors recommend that the training steps outlined in the manual be followed before attempts are made to administer the test. Raw scores can be converted to standard scores having a mean of 100 and a standard deviation of 15, among other scores. These scores can be calculated for each individual test and for each cluster, provided that the appropriate tests are given. Further, instructions for determining significant intra-achievement and ability-achievement discrepancies are outlined in the manual. A standard score and percentile rank classification guide is provided in the manual: Very Superior (131 and above), Superior (121–130), High Average (111–120), Average (90–110), Low Average (80–89), Low (70–79), and Very Low (69 and below). Alternate descriptive labels are also provided, for example, Mentally Deficient (69 and below), but these are excessively evaluative in nature. Guidelines for testing preschoolers, individuals with disabilities, and those with language differences are also provided for reference.

However, it should be noted that if English is not the primary language of the examinee, attempts to translate the WJ-R ACH should not be made. As mentioned previously, a Spanish-language version has been published for use with persons having Spanish as their primary language. Many clinicians find the WJ-R ACH somewhat cumbersome to score. However, computerized scoring and reporting are available to ease the scoring process.

Standardization

The WJ-R ACH was conormed with the WJ-R COG. As mentioned previously in this chapter, the normative sample for the MBA was also derived from this sample. The WJ-R ACH was normed between September 1986 and August 1988. The standardization sample was selected to match 1980 U. S. Census statistics. The sample consisted of 6,359 individuals in over 100 communities of the U. S. The preschool sample consisted of 705 subjects ages 2 to 5, the school-age sample consisted of 3,245 individuals in kindergarten through 12th grade, the college/university sample was composed of 916 subjects, and the nonschool adult sample consisted of 1,493 subjects ages 14 to 95 years. The sample was stratified according to variables of age, gender, geographic region, race, community size, origin (Hispanic, non-Hispanic), funding of college/university (public, private), type of college/university (university and 4-year college, 2-year college), distribution of adult occupation in the community, distribution of adult occupational status in the community (e.g., employed or unemployed), and distribution of adult education in the community. It is unclear if individuals with disabilities were accounted for in the sample. Overall, it appears that the obtained normative sample for the WJ-R ACH closely resembles that of the U. S. population of 1980. However, these norms are relatively old. As with the MBA, Kamphaus (1993) suggests a rule of thumb that if the standardization sample is 10 or more years old, that the examiner be cautious of the accuracy of the norms for current use.

Reliability

The split-half method corrected by the Spearman-Brown formula was used to estimate internal consistency for the WJ-R ACH. Figures are presented for each age level based on the data for all subjects at that level in the norming sample who took each test. Average reliabilities for Form A and Form B are presented. It should be noted that although the norming sample is based on persons ages 2 to 95 years, reliability information is presented only for those ages 2 to 79 years of age. First, reliabilities are presented for the Standard Battery. For Letter-Word Identification, reliability coefficients ranged from .88 to .98 with a median of .92. For Passage Comprehension, the coefficients ranged from .78 to .96 with a median of .90. Coefficients for Calculation ranged from .89 to .98 with a median of .93. For Applied Problems, the coefficients ranged from .84 to .97 with a median of .91. For Dictation, the values ranged from .83 to .96 with a median of .92. Coefficients for Writing Samples ranged from .85 to .98 with a median of .93. For Science, values ranged from .79 to .94 with a median of .87. For Social Studies, the coefficients ranged from .75 to .96 with a median of .87. Coefficients for Humanities ranged from .83 to .95 with a median of .87. Next, reliability information is presented for the Supplemental Battery. For Word Attack, the split-half reliability coefficients ranged from .87 to .95 with a median of .91. Reading Vocabulary coefficients ranged from .88 to .97 with a median of .93. For Quantitative Concepts, the values ranged from .76 to .91 with a median of .86. For Proofing, the coefficients ranged from .85 to .96 with a median of .91. The coefficients for Writing Fluency ranged from .59 to .87 with a median of .76. For Punctuation & Capitalization, the values ranged from .78 to .95 with a median of .86. For Spelling, the coefficients ranged from .85 to .96 with a median of .89. The coefficients for Usage ranged from .81 to .94 with a mean of .84. Further, reliability coefficients are presented for cluster scores. For Broad Reading, the coefficients ranged from .90

to .98 with a median of .95. The coefficients for Broad Mathematics ranged from .93 to .99 with a median of .95. The coefficients for Broad Written Language ranged from .85 to .98 with a median of .94. For Broad Knowledge, the values ranged from .91 to .98 with a median of .94. For Skills, the coefficients ranged from .94 to .99 with a median of .96. For Basic Reading Skills, the values ranged from .93 to .98 with a median of .96. Coefficients for Reading Comprehension ranged from .90 to .97 with a median of .95. For Basic Mathematics Skills, the values ranged from .89 to .97 with a median of .94. For Mathematics Reasoning, the coefficients ranged from .84 to .97 with a median of .91. Coefficients for Basic Writing Skills ranged from .91 to .98 with a median of .94. Lastly, coefficients for Written Expression ranged from .87 to .97 with a median of .93. These indices of internal consistency are quite adequate. Test-retest reliability information is not presented in the manual; however, more detailed information pertaining to reliability can be found in the WJ-R Technical Manual (McGrew, Werder, & Woodcock, 1991).

Validity

Content, concurrent, and construct validity are addressed for the WJ-R ACH. Content validity is described in terms of the item selection process. The authors indicated that expert opinion was used in developing the test content and that the tests were designed to provide a sampling of skills in a number of areas. This area of validity could profit from more explanation. Concurrent validity investigations are presented in the test manual. For a sample of 62 children ages 2 years, 6 months to 3 years, 7 months, correlations with the Boehm Test of Basic Concepts—Preschool Version of .61 and .53 were found for the WJ-R ACH Broad Knowledge Cluster and Skills Cluster, respectively. For this same sample, the Broad Knowledge Cluster and Skills Cluster correlated .61 and .49 with the Bracken Basic Concepts Scale, respectively. Also for this same sample, the Broad Knowledge and Skills Cluster correlated

.63 and .52 with the PPVT-R, respectively. Broad Knowledge and Skills correlated .32 and .29, respectively, with Expressive Vocabulary on the K-ABC for this same sample. Broad Knowledge and Skills correlated .29 and .10 accordingly with Faces & Places on the K-ABC. For a sample of 30 children ages 2 years, 6 months to 3 years, 7 months, correlations were .72 and .63 with Broad Knowledge and Skills for Arithmetic on the K-ABC. For this same sample, correlations of .47 and .24 were found with Broad Knowledge and Skills for Riddles on the K-ABC. Lastly, for the sample of 62 children of this same age group, Broad Knowledge and Skills correlated .61 and .52, respectively, with the Total Achievement score on the K-ABC. Next, concurrent validity studies are presented for a sample of 70 nine-year-old children. Selected correlations are presented here. Broad Reading correlated as follows with the following measures: BASIS Reading (r=.63), K-ABC Reading Composite (r=.80), K-TEA Reading Composite (r=.85), PIAT Reading Composite (r=.86), and WRAT-R Reading (r=.83). Broad Mathematics correlated as follows with the following measures: BASIS Math (r=.71), K-ABC Arithmetic (r=.71), K-TEA Mathematics Composite (r=.83), PIAT Mathematics (r=.41), and WRAT-R Mathematics (r=.63). Broad Written Language correlated as follows with the following measures: BASIS Spelling (r=.63), K-TEA Spelling (r=.68), PIAT Spelling (r=.53), and WRAT-R Spelling (r=.69). Further, Broad Knowledge correlated .64 with General Information on the PIAT. Concurrent validity studies are also presented for a sample of 51 17-year-olds. Broad Reading correlated as follows with these measures: BASIS Reading (r=.36), K-TEA Reading Composite (r=.49), PIAT Reading Composite (r=.68), and WRAT-R Reading (r=.57). Broad Mathematics correlated as follows with these measures: BASIS Mathematics (r=.65), K-TEA Mathematics Composite (r=.73), PIAT Mathematics (r=.74), and WRAT-R Mathematics (r=.72). Broad Written Language correlated as follows: BASIS Spelling (r=.48), K-TEA Spelling (r=.53), PIAT Spelling (r=.62), and WRAT-R Spelling (r=.69). Further, Broad Knowledge correlated .66 with General Information on the PIAT.

Construct validity is presented in terms of intercorrelation patterns. Although other indices of construct validity would be useful, these intercorrelations are supportive of the domains represented on the WJ-R ACH. Intercorrelations are presented for the individual tests and the cluster scores. Selected figures are presented here. For children of age 6 in the standardization sample, Broad Reading correlated .94 and .96 with Basic Reading Skills and Reading Comprehension, respectively. At this same age, Broad Mathematics correlated .93 and .82 with Basic Mathematics Skills and Mathematics Reasoning, respectively. Further, Broad Written Language correlated .87 and .96 with Basic Writing Skills and Written Expression, respectively. Further evidence of construct validity would be desirable with other measures using a variety of populations. In an independent study, Lavin (1996a) examined the relationship between the WJ-R ACH and the WISC-III for a sample of 85 children ages 6 to 16 years with emotional handicaps. WISC-III Full Scale IQ scores correlated as follows: Letter-Word Identification (r=.34), Passage Comprehension (r=.39), Calculation (r=.46), Applied Problems (r=.58), Broad Reading (r=.36), and Broad Mathematics (r=.52). WISC-III Verbal IQ scores correlated as follows: Letter-Word Identification (r=.41), Passage Comprehension (r=.51), Calculation (r=.47), Applied Problems (r=.60), Broad Reading (r=.47), and Broad Mathematics (r=.54). WISC-III Performance IQ scores correlated as follows: Letter-Word Identification (r=.16), Passage Comprehension (r=.14), Calculation (r=.32), Applied Problems (r=.38), Broad Reading (r=.13), and Broad Mathematics (r=.36). As expected, higher correlations were found with Verbal IQ. Although more information pertaining to validity is presented in the WJ-R technical manual (McGrew et al., 1991), additional studies of concurrent validity and construct validity would be informative.

Summary

The WJ-R ACH is a popular broadband achievement test. It is a flexible instrument in that the clinician may choose a variety of combinations of tests to administer for varying purposes. Although much of the reliability and validity information presented for the WJ-R ACH is strong, additional information would be beneficial for the test consumer. It also appears that the WJ-R ACH could benefit from a normative update since current norms are based on a decade-old sampling using 1980 U. S. Census data. In fairness, however, the third edition of the Woodcock-Johnson Psycho-Educational Battery is in the final stages of completion as of press time. Publication is anticipated in the fall of 2000. Until then, despite these problems, Lee (1995) suggests that the WJ-R "represents a significant advancement in the field of cognitive and achievement testing" (p. 1117).

Wechsler Individual Achievement Test (WIAT)

The WIAT (The Psychological Corporation, 1992) is a comparatively new, individually administered test of academic achievement, in that it is in its first edition. The WIAT was designed to cover all of the achievement areas of learning disability as defined in the Individuals with Disabilities Education Act: Oral expression, listening comprehension, written expression, basic reading skills, reading comprehension, mathematics calculation, and mathematics reasoning. The WIAT Comprehensive Battery contains eight subtests overall, and a WIAT Screener consisting of three of the eight subtests is also published. It is stated in the manual that the WIAT is to be considered as a single piece in the assessment context, and that the clinician should take care to gather client information from multiple sources. In this context, the WIAT can be used to assist in diagnosis, placement, program planning, and intervention. Of further note, the WIAT is the only achievement test that is directly linked to the WISC-III, WPPSI-R, and WAIS-R. This advantage allows for more precise ability-achievement comparisons.

Administration and Scoring

The WIAT is an individually administered test having an easel format that is designed for use with children and adolescents ages 5 years to 19 years, 11 months. This test consists of a single form with the following subtests:

1. Basic Reading. This subtest contains 55 items that assess decoding and word reading ability. The first seven items contain picture cues and require pointing responses only. Items 8–55 require the examinee to read aloud printed words as presented by the examiner. Items are scored as correct or incorrect.

2. Mathematics Reasoning. This subtest contains 50 items that assess one's ability to reason mathematically. Here, the examinee is to respond orally, point, or write answers to questions posed by the examiner. For some problems, visual stimuli are provided. If needed, the examinee may use pencil and paper. Items are scored as correct or incorrect.

3. Spelling. This subtest consists of 50 items. Items 1–6 require the examinee to write single letters, and items 7–50 require the examinee to write words as dictated by the examiner. Responses are written in the designated section of the Response Booklet. Items are scored as correct or incorrect.

4. Reading Comprehension. The items on this 38-item subtest are designed to measure an individual's ability to comprehend printed passages. Items 1–8 contain a one-sentence passage accompanied by a picture. The remaining items contain longer passages without picture cues. For all items, the examinee is to read the passage and respond orally to a question asked by the examiner. Items are scored as correct or incorrect.

5. Numerical Operations. This subtest contains 40 problems that the examinee is to answer in the provided Response Booklet. The first four items require the examinee to write numerals dictated by the examiner. The remaining items require the examinee to solve problems covering basic arithmetic operations to algebraic equations. Items are scored as correct or incorrect.

6. Listening Comprehension. This subtest consists of 36 items that assess one's ability to comprehend orally presented information. Items 1–9 require the individual to point to one of four pictures correctly describing a word spoken by the examiner. The remaining items require the examinee to listen to a passage read aloud by the examiner and to answer one or more questions about it. A corresponding stimulus picture is presented for each of these items. Items are scored as correct or incorrect.

7. Oral Expression. This subtest contains 16 items intended to assess one's ability to express words, give directions, and describe scenes. For items 1–10, the examiner presents a picture depicting a word and defines the word. In turn, the examinee is to orally respond to these clues with the correct word. Items 11–12 require the individual to orally describe a scene depicted in a stimulus picture, items 13–14 require the individual to look at a map and describe how to get to one location from another, and items 15–16 require the examinee to describe the steps needed in order to complete an action. Items are scored according to sets of criteria for a total possible raw score of 40 points.

8. Written Expression. This subtest is administered only to students in grades 3 to 12. Here, the examinee is given 15 minutes to write in response to one of two prompts. Responses are written in the designated section of the Response Booklet. The Written Expression subtest is scored analytically and holistically according to a given set of criteria for a total possible raw score of 24 points.

The WIAT Comprehensive Battery takes 30 to 60 minutes to administer in general, depending on the age of the individual. Written Expression is the only timed subtest, although suggested time limits are given for the other subtests. Items on Basic Reading, Mathematics Reasoning, Spelling, Numerical Operations, Reading Comprehension, and Listening Comprehension are scored as correct or incorrect. However, Reading Comprehension and Listening Comprehension, as well as Oral Expression and Written Expression, are scored somewhat subjectively in nature. Scoring guidelines and examples are provided in the manual. Teaching is allowed for certain items. Set basal and ceiling rules are used to determine the appropriate number of items to administer. Guidelines for testing special populations are provided. Extensive psychometric training is not a prerequisite for administering and scoring the WIAT, although practice is recommended. The WIAT also includes Skills Analysis procedures allowing for more in-depth examination of the individual's performance. Further, detailed procedures for determining ability-achievement discrepancies are provided. Among other types of scores, the WIAT yields standard scores having a mean of 100 and a standard deviation of 15. These scores can be calculated for each of the eight subtests, in addition to a Reading Composite, Mathematics Composite, Language Composite, Writing Composite, and Total Composite for the Comprehensive Battery. The WIAT Screener consists of the identical Basic Reading, Mathematics Reasoning, and Spelling subtests as found on the WIAT Comprehensive Battery. The Screener takes about 10 to 15 minutes to administer. Although not really necessary, separate WIAT Screener test protocols are marketed. Computerized scoring and reporting programs are available.

Standardization

The standardization sample of the WIAT was selected to match March 1988 U. S. Census data. The sample was composed of 4,252 individuals ages 5 years to 19 years, 11 months, in grades kindergarten through 12. The sample was stratified according to variables of age, grade, sex, race/ethnicity, geographic region, and parent education. In addition, it is noted that 6% of the normative sample consisted of children classified as learning disabled, speech/language impaired, emotionally disturbed, or physically impaired. Children served in gifted programs comprised 4.3% of the sample, and those classified as borderline or mildly mentally retarded comprised 1.4% of the sample. Separate norms are not presented for these groups. Further, the linking sample is described. This sample consisted of 1,284 children who were administered the WPPSI-R, the WISC-III, or the WAIS-R. The sample slightly overrepresents those with parents having higher education levels and those living in the southern region of the United States. Weighting procedures were used to adjust race/ethnicity proportions to U. S. Census data. Overall, the WIAT standardization sample closely matches the U. S. population as described in the 1988 Census.

Reliability

Split-half reliability coefficients were used to estimate internal consistency across the standardization sample for the WIAT. These are presented according to both age and grade. Age-based coefficients are presented here. For Basic Reading, reliability coefficients ranged from .87 to .95 with a mean of .92. Coefficients for Mathematics Reasoning ranged from .74 to .92 with a mean of .89. Spelling coefficients ranged from .80 to .93 with a mean of .90. Reading Comprehension coefficients ranged from .81 to .93 with a mean of .88. Numerical Operations had coefficients ranging from .69 to .91 with a mean of .85. For Listening Comprehension, values ranged from .80 to .88 with a mean of .83. Oral Expression coefficients ranged from .88 to .92 with a mean of .91. Written Expression coefficients ranged from .76 to .84 with a mean of .81. Coefficients for the Reading Composite ranged from .90 to .97 with a mean of .95. For the Mathematics Composite, coefficients ranged from .83 to .95 with a mean of .92. Coefficients for the Language Composite ranged from .88 to .93 with a mean of .90. For the Writing Composite, the values ranged from .89 to .92 with a mean of .90. The Total Composite coefficients ranged from .94 to .98 with a mean of .97. For the Screener, coefficients ranged from .91 to .97 with a mean of .96.

In addition, test-retest reliability was assessed for a sample of 367 children in grades 1, 3, 5, 8, and 10. The median interval between testing was 17 days, ranging from 12 to 52 days. The average test-retest reliability coefficients across this sample were as follows: Basic Reading (r=.94), Mathematics Reasoning (r=.89), Spelling (r=.94), Reading Comprehension (r=.85), Numerical Operations (r=.86), Listening Comprehension (r=.76), Oral Expression (r=.68), Written Expression (r=.77), Reading Composite (r=.93), Mathematics Composite (r=.91), Language Composite (r=.78), Writing Composite (r=.94), Total Composite (r=.96), and Screener (r=.95). As the Reading Comprehension, Listening Comprehension, Oral Expression, and Written Expression subtests require more judgment in scoring, studies of interscorer agreement were conducted. Fifty protocols were randomly selected from the standardization sample, including protocols from each grade level. Four raters independently scored responses on all 50 protocols for these four subtests. For Reading Comprehension and Listening Comprehension, the mean interscorer agreement was .98. The mean for Oral Expression was .93. Average correlations for Written Expression were .89 for Prompt 1 and .79 for Prompt 2. Overall, indices for reliability on the WIAT appear quite adequate.

Validity

Information pertaining to content, construct, and criterion-related validity is presented in the WIAT manual. Several goals guided the development of the WIAT. One of the aims was to develop an achievement test that reflected current curricular trends. Second, a goal was to link the WIAT to the Wechsler scales to promote meaningful ability-achievement comparisons. Third, the WIAT was designed to reflect the seven areas of achievement specified in the Individuals with Disabilities Education Act that may be used to identify children with learning disabilities. Subtest and item specifications, field testing, and item analysis procedures are described at length in the manual, and a clear scope and sequence chart of curricular objectives addressed is included. Overall, the information pertaining to content validity appears to be adequate. Construct validity is evidenced by intercorrelations amongst the subtests, correlations with the Wechsler scales, and in studies of group differences. As a whole, the intercorrelation patterns confirm expected relationships amongst the subtests and composites. For example, at age 7 years, the Reading Composite correlated .98 with Basic Reading and .95 with Reading Comprehension. At this same age, the Mathematics Composite correlated .96 with Mathematics Reasoning and .91 with Numerical Operations. The Language Composite correlated .82 with Listening Comprehension and .90 with Written Expression. As an additional measure of construct validity, correlations with the Wechsler scales are presented. For children in the linked sample at age 5 years to 5 years, 11 months, scores on the WPPSI-R and the WIAT were correlated. Verbal IQ correlated as follows: Mathematics Composite (r=.65), Language Composite (r=.65), Screener (r=.62), and Total Composite (r=.70). Performance IQ correlated as follows: Mathematics Composite (r=.61), Language Composite (r=.54), Screener (r=.53), and Total Composite (r=.59). Full Scale IQ correlated as follows: Mathematics Composite (r=.70), Language Composite (r=.67), Screener (r=.63), and Total Composite (r=.71). For children ages 6 to 16 years, scores on the WIAT were correlated with scores on the WISC-III. Verbal IQ correlated as follows: Reading Composite (r=.50–.81), Mathematics Composite (r=.62–.78), Language Composite (r=.40–.71), Writing Composite (r=.49–.67), Screener (r=.59–.84), and Total Composite (r=.69–.84).

Performance IQ correlated as follows: Reading Composite (r=.31–.55), Mathematics Composite (r=.44–.63), Language Composite (r=.30–.55), Writing Composite (r=.32–.45), Screener (r=.41–.61), and Total Composite (r=.46–.61). Full Scale IQ correlated as follows: Reading Composite (r=.48–.75), Mathematics Composite (r=.65–.79), Language Composite (r=.49–.68), Writing Composite (r=.51–.60), Screener (r=.55–.81), and Total Composite (r=.53–.80). Lastly, correlations were calculated between the WIAT and WAIS-R for the sample of adolescents ages 17 years to 19 years, 11 months. Verbal IQ correlated as follows: Reading Composite (r=.77), Mathematics Composite (r=.73), Language Composite (r=.57), Writing Composite (r=.63), Screener (r=.76), and Total Composite (r=.83). Performance IQ correlated as follows: Reading Composite (r=.54), Mathematics Composite (r=.66), Language Composite (r=.27), Writing Composite (r=.52), Screener (r=.64), and Total Composite (r=.62). Full Scale IQ correlated as follows: Reading Composite (r=.74), Mathematics Composite (r=.77), Language Composite (r=.49), Writing Composite (r=.64), Screener (r=.78), and Total Composite (r=.81). Further, several studies were conducted with various clinical groups (e.g., mental retardation). Scores for such groups were compared with those of the standardization sample. Expected differences were found, verifying the construct validity of WIAT interpretations. Overall, these indices of construct validity appear adequate. Studies using other major measures of intelligence would also be of interest, however.

Criterion-related validity evidence is demonstrated through comparisons with other achievement tests, grades, and special education classification. The BASIS was administered to a sample of 80 children in grades 3 and 8. Across this group, correlations between BASIS Reading were .80 with Basic Reading and .81 with Reading Comprehension. Correlations with BASIS Mathematics were .82 with Mathematics Reasoning and .79 with Numerical Operations. BASIS Spelling correlated .88 with Spelling on the WIAT. Scores on the WIAT and the K-TEA were correlated for a sample of 28 children ages 6 to 16 years. K-TEA Reading Decoding and Basic Reading correlated .86, K-TEA Reading Comprehension and Reading Comprehension on the WIAT correlated .78, K-TEA Mathematics Applications and Mathematics Reasoning correlated .87, K-TEA Mathematics Computation and Numerical Operations correlated .81, and K-TEA Spelling and WIAT Spelling correlated .73. Scores on the WRAT-R and the WIAT were correlated for a sample of 251 children ages 7 to 19 years of age. WRAT-R Reading correlated .84 with Basic Reading, WRAT-R Arithmetic correlated .77 with Numerical Operations, and WRAT-R Spelling correlated .84 with WIAT Spelling. Further, scores on the WJ-R ACH and the WIAT were correlated for a sample of 43 children ages 7 to 14 years. Here, WJ-R ACH Letter-Word Identification correlated .79 with Basic Reading, WJ-R ACH Passage Comprehension correlated .74 with Reading Comprehension, WJ-R ACH Calculation correlated .68 with Numerical Operations, WJ-R ACH Applied Problems correlated .67 with Mathematics Reasoning, and WJ-R ACH Dictation correlated .72 with Written Expression and .88 with Spelling. Scores on the DAS ACH and the WIAT were correlated for a sample of 29 children ages 8 to 13. DAS ACH Word Reading correlated .82 with Basic Reading and .42 with Reading Comprehension, DAS ACH Basic Number Skills correlated .75 with Mathematics Reasoning and .70 with Numerical Operations, and DAS ACH Spelling correlated .86 with WIAT Spelling. For a sample of 51 children ages 6 to 16 years, scores on the WIAT and the PPVT-R were correlated, as well. Basic Reading, Reading Comprehension, and Listening Comprehension correlated .68, .68, and .75 with the total score on the PPVT-R, respectively. Correlations between the composite scores of the WIAT and composite scores of group-administered achievement are also presented. Nine hundred forty-four children ages 6 to 19 years were administered the Stanford Achievement Test, the Iowa Tests of Basic Skills, or the California Achievement Test in addition to the WIAT. Average correlations between the WIAT Reading Composite and the Total Reading scores on these group measures ranged from .72 to .78, average correlations between the WIAT Mathematics Composite and the Total Mathematics scores on the group measures ranged from .64 to .77, and WIAT Spelling and the Spelling scores on the group measures correlated from .70 to .77. In addition, teacher-assigned grades were obtained for a sample of 897 children 6 to 19 years of age. Here, reading grades correlated .42 with scores on the WIAT Reading Composite and mathematics grades correlated .43 with scores on the WIAT Mathematics Composite.

Independent validity studies of the WIAT have also been conducted. Gentry, Sapp, and Daw (1995) compared scores on the WIAT and the K-TEA Comprehensive Form for a sample of 27 emotionally disturbed children ages 12 years, 9 months to 18 years, 1 month. As a result, K-TEA Reading Decoding correlated .88 with Basic Reading, K-TEA Reading Comprehension correlated .79 with Reading Comprehension on the WIAT, K-TEA Mathematics Applications correlated .89 with Mathematics Reasoning, K-TEA Mathematics Computation correlated .91 with Numerical Operations, and K-TEA Spelling correlated .85 with WIAT Spelling. Slate (1994) compared WISC-III and WIAT scores for a sample of 202 students with specific learning disabilities (mean age 11 years, 4 months), 115 students with mental retardation (mean age 11 years, 5 months), and 159 students who did not qualify for special education (mean age 9 years, 8 months). The following correlations were found across these groups (N=476) for the WIAT and the WISC-III Full Scale IQ: Basic Reading (r=.52), Reading Comprehension (r=.71), Mathematics Reasoning (r=.81), Numerical Operations (r=.70), Spelling (r=.57), Listening Comprehension (r=.70), Oral Expression (r=.45), and Written Expression (r=.36). For the WISC-III Verbal IQ, the correlations were Basic Reading (r=.62), Reading Comprehension (r=.73), Mathematics Reasoning (r=.81), Numerical Operations (r=.66),

Spelling (r=.63), Listening Comprehension (r=.69), Oral Expression (r=.52), and Written Expression (r=.42). For the WISC-III Performance IQ, the correlations were Basic Reading (r=.30), Reading Comprehension (r=.49), Mathematics Reasoning (r=.65), Numerical Operations (r=.59), Spelling (r=.38), Listening Comprehension (r=.55), Oral Expression (r=.28), and Written Expression (r=.20). For the WISC-III Verbal Comprehension Index, correlations were Basic Reading (r=.62), Reading Comprehension (r=.72), Mathematics Reasoning (r=.73), Numerical Operations (r=.61), Spelling (r=.59), Listening Comprehension (r=.66), Oral Expression (r=.47), and Written Expression (r=.39). For the WISC-III Perceptual Organization Index, correlations were: Basic Reading (r=.25), Reading Comprehension (r=.46), Mathematics Reasoning (r=.53), Numerical Operations (r=.39), Spelling (r=.25), Listening Comprehension (r=.44), Oral Expression (r=.14), and Written Expression (r=.08). For the WISC-III Freedom from Distractibility Index, correlations were: Basic Reading (r=.64), Reading Comprehension (r=.73), Mathematics Reasoning (r=.75), Numerical Operations (r=.50), Spelling (r=.66), Listening Comprehension (r=.43), Oral Expression (r=.51), and Written Expression (r=.43). Although the WIAT manual includes numerous informative validity studies, additional investigations using a wider variety of populations and instruments would be of use.

Summary

The WIAT is a comparatively new screener or broadband measure of academic achievement. The WIAT appears to have a representative standardization sample, adequate to strong psychometric characteristics, as well as a sensible rationale. Further, its connection to the Wechsler intelligence scales makes the WIAT an appealing choice for use with learning problems referrals. In a review of this test, Ackerman (1998) indicates that the WIAT seems to be an instrument worthy of use, but that additional "empirical evidence supporting its effectiveness needs to be gathered" (p. 1128). It is highly likely that the WIAT will become a mainstay in the arena of academic achievement. The second edition of the WIAT is due to arrive on the test market in the spring of 2001.

SAMPLE CASE

The report in Box 14.1 is the report of a psycho-educational evaluation in which screening measures of intelligence and achievement were used as components of a comprehensive battery.

CONCLUSIONS

This chapter has taken the reader on a tour of numerous screening measures of intelligence and academic achievement. Again, even more testing options than the ones presented here are available. Screening instruments, when used appropriately, can be useful assessment tools for a variety of purposes. Time constraints imposed by school systems and managed healthcare have certainly contributed to the increasing popularity and use of screening instruments. It is highly likely that screening measures will continue to improve and that new ones will be developed and researched.

Box 14.1   Psychoeducational report using screening measures of intelligence and achievement

Name:	Ben	**Birthdate:**	4/20/82
Gender:	Male	**Age:**	15 years, 7 months
School:	Suburban High	**Grade:**	10

Assessment Procedures

Differential Ability Scales (DAS)

Slosson Intelligence Test-Revised (SIT-R)

Beery-Buktenica Developmental Test of Visual-Motor Integration (VMI)

Wechsler Individual Achievement Test (WIAT)

Test of Written Language—Third Edition (TOWL-3)

Woodcock Reading Mastery Tests—Revised (WRMT-R)

Behavior Assessment System for Children—Parent, Teacher, and Self-Report (BASC)

Behavior Assessment System for Children—Structured Developmental History (BASC-SDH)

Parent Interview

Adolescent Clinical Interview

Review of Records

Referral and Background Information

Ben, a 15-year, 7-month-old tenth-grader, was referred by his parents for psychoeducational evaluation. The purpose of the evaluation was to explore parental concerns about his learning progress and to ascertain his current intellectual functioning. Specifically, Ben's parents expressed concern regarding Ben's spelling, grammatical, and copying errors, as well as his composition skills. Concerns were also expressed regarding his reading fluency and articulation, and his lack of interest in reading and writing.

Ben resides in Atlanta, Georgia, with his birth mother and father as well as a sister, age 12. Ben's mother is a homemaker, and his father is a physician. They indicated a family history of cancer, high blood pressure, and diabetes. Ben's younger sister has been diagnosed with Attention-Deficit/Hyperactivity Disorder, Combined Type. With this exception, no other learning or attentional problems in the family were reported.

Box 14.1 Psychoeducational report using screening measures of intelligence and achievement (Continued)

Ben's mother reported that his prenatal development was fairly unremarkable. Ben met developmental milestones such as crawling, walking, and talking within normal limits. She noted that Ben has suffered from allergies since an early age and that he experiences frequent sinus infections as a result of this. Ben also had several ear infections as a child and contracted chicken pox at age 6. Ben's mother indicated that he seemed to be ambidextrous at a young age, but that teachers over the years had instructed him to write with his right hand. Further, Ben exhibited normal hearing and vision during a recent screening.

Ben was evaluated for the gifted education program while in first grade. Results from this evaluation indicated that Ben's intellectual functioning was in the very superior range, and he qualified for the gifted program. When he was in sixth grade, his mother had him evaluated by a psychologist in private practice to address concerns that she had with his reading and writing abilities, although Ben was ranked high in his class. This report indicated that Ben's intelligence level was in the superior to very superior range and that he had learning disabilities in the areas of attention and reading decoding. Ben's parents also sought assistance for him through his school under Section 504 of the Rehabilitation Act based on the information found by his previous evaluations. As a result, Ben is provided with the following modifications as needed: Extra time to complete reading and writing assignments and the use of a spell checker on his work. Ben is currently enrolled in 10th grade, and takes Pre-calculus, history, biology, English, French, and electives, including band. He has a 3.5 cumulative grade point average. His parents indicated that he at times has a short temper, particularly when asked about grades. Ben's parents acknowledge his scholastic achievements, but feel that due to learning disabilities that he is not living up to his full academic potential.

General Observations and Impressions

Ben was seen for one day, including 3 hours before lunch and 3 hours after lunch. He was neat in appearance, polite, and cooperative throughout the session. He seemed healthy and demonstrated no hearing or vision difficulties. He did show some fatigue toward the end of the day. Overall, Ben was pleasant to work with, and the results of this evaluation should be considered valid.

Assessment Results and Interpretations

Intelligence

Ben's cognitive functioning, as measured by the Differential Ability Scales (DAS), an individually administered comprehensive intelligence test, was in the very high or significantly above-average range. Specifically, Ben obtained a General Conceptual Ability (GCA) score of 134. There is a 90% chance that the range from 128 to 139 includes Ben's true GCA, and his performance was equal to or exceeded that of about 99% of individuals in his age range in the general population. The GCA consists of three different scores: Verbal, Nonverbal Reasoning, and Spatial. Verbal and nonverbal ability involve complex processing and inductive reasoning, whereas spatial ability measures a student's skills in perceiving, remembering, and replicating visual-spatial relationships and shapes. Ben's Verbal, Nonverbal Reasoning, and Spatial scores were 133, 131, and 120, respectively. The differences between these scores are not significant in nature. There was some slight variability in the individual subtest scores. In particular, a relative psychological processing weakness was noted on the Pattern Construction subtest, a task involving the reconstruction of designs with blocks, which assesses one's ability to replicate visual-spatial designs.

A second, brief, intelligence measure, the Slosson Intelligence Test—Revised (SIT-R), was administered to confirm or deny Ben's score on the DAS. His total standard score on the SIT-R was 141, which is also in the superior or significantly above average range. On this measure, there is a 95% chance that the range from 134 to 148 contains Ben's true score. Furthermore, Ben's performance was equal to or exceeded that of 99% of individuals in his age range in the general population.

Visual-Motor

In order to assess visual perceptual ability, Ben was administered the Beery-Buktenica Developmental Test of Visual-Motor Integration (VMI). On this test, a student is to reproduce geometric figures. His performance on this

(Continues)

Box 14.1   Psychoeducational report using screening measures of intelligence and achievement (Continued)

task falls in the average range, with a score of 107. His performance was equal to or exceeded that of 68% of individuals in his age range in the general population. However, it should be noted that Ben got 26 of the 27 items correct. With older children, this test demonstrates a ceiling effect. Ceiling effect means that there are not enough difficult items on the test to adequately measure the skill, thus causing the score to appear lower than it actually should be.

Achievement

In order to assess achievement capabilities, Ben was administered the Wechsler Individual Achievement Test (WIAT), the Test of Written Language—Third Edition (TOWL-3), and the Woodcock Reading Mastery Tests—Revised (WRMT-R).

Ben's scores on the mathematics portion of the WIAT were all in the superior range. Specifically, his Mathematics Composite score was 125. As such, Ben's achievement in mathematics is consistent with his intelligence and school performance.

Ben's scores on the language portion of the WIAT were all in the above average to superior range. Specifically, his score on the Language Composite, which measures listening comprehension and oral expression, was 133. His achievement in language skills is therefore consistent with his intelligence and academic accomplishments.

Ben's scores on the writing portion of the WIAT were all in the above average to superior range. Specifically, his Writing Composite score was 123. As writing was an area of concern, the TOWL-3, a diagnostic instrument for written language, was administered as a second measure. His Spontaneous Writing Quotient on the TOWL-3 was also 123. These two scores are also essentially consistent with Ben's intelligence and school performance.

Finally, Ben was administered the reading portion of the WIAT and selected subtests of the WRMT-R. All of his reading scores were in the average to above average range. His overall Reading Composite score on the WIAT was 108, being lower than what would be expected compared with his intelligence and school performance. Ben's WIAT Reading Comprehension subtest score was 121, more commensurate with his intelligence and school performance. Ben's WIAT Basic Reading subtest score of 93 was below what would be expected considering his intelligence and academic accomplishments. The Basic Skills Cluster of the WRMT-R, a diagnostic reading test, was administered to further assess Ben's reading skills. His Basic Skills Cluster score was 95, with his performance on this measure equal to or above that of 38% of individuals in his age range in the general population. This score is also lower than what would be expected when compared to Ben's intelligence and school performance.

Social-Emotional

To gather information regarding Ben's social-emotional status, the examiner conducted an adolescent interview. Here, Ben indicated that he is satisfied with his school performance and his social life. He admitted to sometimes getting angry with his parents over curfew and doing chores. He likes his friends and enjoys participating on the tennis team and band. Ben wishes to participate in the state tennis tournament and then attend college and graduate school. He aspires to be a lawyer or an accountant. Ben reported that he has to work more diligently in English and that he sometimes gets "stressed out" about grades.

Ben also completed the Behavior Assessment System for Children Self-Report of Personality (BASC-SRP) form to assess his own perceptions of himself. He rated himself as essentially "problem-free." However, he had an elevated score on the Lie Index, indicating that he may have marked items to make himself look good. Thus, these scores should be interpreted with caution.

Behavioral

Parent. Behavioral ratings were obtained from Ben's parents using the Behavior Assessment System for Children Parent Rating Scales (BASC-PRS). Both parents rated Ben as average overall, indicating no significant problems in any areas such as depression, conduct problems, attention, and so on. Further, his adaptive skills such as leadership were rated as being average to above average.

Teacher. A teacher interview was conducted by telephone with Ben's English teacher, Ms. Costanza. She indicated that he is a solid student academically, has no significant behavior problems, and is popular with others.

Box 14.1   Psychoeducational report using screening measures of intelligence and achievement (Continued)

She expressed concern that Ben seems to feel pressured to do his best in school. She indicated that he is eligible to receive modifications under Section 504, and that he requests these as often as he needs. Ms. Costanza also completed the BASC Teacher Rating Scales (BASC-TRS). Her ratings of his behavior were all in the average range, with the exception of slightly elevated scores relating to anxiety and depression.

Summary

Ben is a 15-year, 7-month-old male who was referred for an evaluation of his learning capabilities. He currently lives with both of his parents. He has undergone evaluations in the past, which have yielded some evidence of a possible learning disability. However, with modifications, Ben demonstrates a solid performance in school, maintaining a 3.5 grade point average.

Intellectual testing indicates that Ben's cognitive functioning is in the significantly above average range as compared to his peers. However, he did demonstrate a relative weakness in visual-spatial processing. His academic achievement test scores overall are commensurate with his intelligence. However, lower scores on reading subtests indicate relative weaknesses in this area. Scores in the area of basic reading skills were low enough to indicate the presence of a reading disability. In spite of this, Ben's high intelligence as well as his usage of classroom modifications enable him to compensate for this weakness. Further, no remarkable emotional or behavioral problems were noted.

Diagnosis

Reading Disorder (DSM-IV Code 315.00)

Recommendations

This report should be shared with the school to assess eligibility for special education services and modifications. Additional information may need to be gathered.

Ben should be allowed extra time to complete reading and writing assignments when needed.

Ben should receive extra time on both informal and standardized tests as needed.

Ben should receive extra assistance in learning to identify mistakes in his writing and should be provided with extra practice in essay writing.

High-interest reading material should be provided to Ben to promote better appreciation of reading.

Ben should be allowed to consult aides such as a dictionary, thesaurus, or spell checker as needed to complete assignments.

Psychometric Summary

Differential Ability Scales (DAS)

COMPOSITE SCORES	STANDARD SCORES	90% CONFIDENCE BANDS	PERCENTILES
GCA	**134**	**128–139**	**99**
Verbal	133	122–140	99
Nonverbal	131	122–137	98
Spatial	120	112–126	91

(Continues)

Box 14.1   Psychoeducational report using screening measures of intelligence and achievement (Continued)

Subtest scores	T-scores
Verbal	
Word Definitions	74
Similarities	64
Nonverbal Reasoning	
Matrices	66
Sequential & Quantitative Reasoning	70
Spatial	
Recall of Designs	70
Pattern Construction	53

Slosson Intelligence Test—Revised (SIT-R)

	Standard scores	95% Confidence Bands	Percentiles
Total Standard Score	141	134–148	99

Beery-Buktenica Developmental Test of Visual-Motor Integration (VMI)

Standard score	Percentile
107	68

Wechsler Individual Achievement Test (WIAT)

	Standard scores	95% Confidence Bands	Percentiles
Basic Reading	93	83–103	31
Reading Comprehension	121	109–133	92
Reading Composite	**108**	**99–117**	**69**
Mathematics Reasoning	125	115–135	94
Numerical Operations	121	109–133	92
Mathematics Composite	**125**	**116–134**	**95**
Listening Comprehension	139	126–152	99
Oral Expression	119	110–128	89
Language Composite	**133**	**123–143**	**99**
Spelling	123	112–134	93
Written Expression	120	108–132	91
Writing Composite	**123**	**112–134**	**94**
Total Composite	**128**	**122–134**	**97**

Box 14.1   Psychoeducational report using screening measures of intelligence and achievement (Continued)

Test of Written Language—Third Edition (TOWL-3)

	STANDARD SCORE	PERCENTILE
Spontaneous Writing Quotient	**123**	**94**
	SCALED SCORES	PERCENTILES
Contextual Conventions	13	84
Contextual Language	16	98
Story Construction	15	95

Woodcock Reading Mastery Tests—Revised (WRMT-R)

	STANDARD SCORES	PERCENTILES
Word Identification	96	40
Word Attack	92	29
Basic Skills Cluster	**95**	**38**

Behavior Assessment System for Children—Parent Rating Scales (BASC-PRS)

	T-SCORES	
CLINICAL SCALES	MOTHER	FATHER
Hyperactivity	51	54
Aggression	49	53
Conduct Problems	47	51
Externalizing Problems Composite	48	53
Anxiety	36	38
Depression	38	54
Somatization	36	36
Internalizing Problems Composite	34	41
Atypicality	39	39
Withdrawal	39	40
Attention Problems	41	50
Behavioral Symptoms Index	40	47
ADAPTIVE SCALES		
Social Skills	53	50
Leadership	58	61
Adaptive Skills Composite	55	53

Behavior Assessment System for Children—Teacher Rating Scales (BASC-TRS)

CLINICAL SCALES	T-SCORES
Hyperactivity	47
Aggression	54
Conduct Problems	44

(Continues)

Box 14.1   Psychoeducational report using screening measures of intelligence and achievement (Continued)

Externalizing Problems Composite	48
Anxiety	57
Depression	58
Somatization	44
Internalizing Problems Composite	54
Attention Problems	40
Learning Problems	48
School Problems Composite	44
Atypicality	45
Withdrawal	40
Behavioral Symptoms Index	45

ADAPTIVE SCALES

Social Skills	47
Leadership	49
Study Skills	55
Adaptive Skills Composite	51

Behavior Assessment System for Children—Self-Report of Personality (BASC-SRP)

CLINICAL SCALES	T-SCORES
Attitude to School	39
Attitude to Teachers	41
Sensation Seeking	36
School Maladjustment Composite	36
Atypicality	39
Locus of Control	39
Somatization	37
Social Stress	39
Anxiety	38
Clinical Maladjustment Composite	37
Depression	44
Sense of Inadequacy	39
Emotional Symptoms Index	38

ADAPTIVE SCALES

Relations with Parents	49
Interpersonal Relations	56
Self-Esteem	57
Self-Reliance	59
Personal Adjustment Composite	59
F Index—acceptable	
V Index—acceptable	
L Index—caution to extreme caution	

CHAPTER SUMMARY

- Screeners of intelligence and academic achievement are useful for numerous purposes when the administration of comprehensive instruments is not feasible.

- The PPVT-III is considered to be a screening measure of verbal ability. This test is designed for use with individuals ages 2 years, 6 months to 90+ years of age.

- The SIT-R was designed to provide a quick estimate of crystallized intelligence for individuals between the ages of 4 and 18+ years.

- The K-BIT is a comparatively new instrument designed to provide a brief measure of both verbal and nonverbal intelligence for persons from 4 to 90 years of age.

- The WASI is a recent instrument intended to assess verbal and performance abilities for individuals 6 to 89 years of age.

- Academic achievement screeners survey a broad range of content areas such as reading, mathematics, and writing at a wide range of skill levels. Diagnostic achievement tests are given to probe an academic area in-depth.

- The WRAT-3 is a brief screener of achievement designed for use with individuals ages 5 to 74 years, 11 months.

- The MBA is a relatively new brief screener of achievement intended for use with children and adults ages 4 through 95 years.

- The DAS ACH consists of three school achievement tests as a part of the Differential Ability Scales. These tests are to be used with children ages 6 years to 17 years, 11 months.

- The PIAT-R is an individually administered achievement test designed to cover six content areas for children ages 5 years to 18 years, 11 months.

- The K-TEA is an achievement test that consists of a Brief and a Comprehensive form, and is intended for use with children ages 6 years to 18 years, 11 months.

- As a part of the WJ-R, the WJ-R ACH is an individually administered test of academic achievement designed for use with individuals ages 4 to 95. The third edition of the Woodcock-Johnson Psycho-Educational Battery is due to be published in the fall of 2000.

- The WIAT is a relatively new broadband measure of academic achievement. This test is intended for use with individuals ages 5 years to 19 years, 11 months. The second edition of the WIAT is expected to be on the test market in the spring of 2001.

CHAPTER 15

Infant and Preschool Methods

Normative scales like the [Bayley Scales of Infant Development] BSID-II may be useful for monitoring changes in the mental or motor status of children participating in early intervention programs, but they are not appropriate as instruments for identifying behavior goals for intervention. (Dunst, 1998, p. 92)

CHAPTER QUESTIONS

What are the special reliability and validity issues associated with the assessment of young children?

What are some strengths and weaknesses of the Bayley Scales?

Infant and preschool measures, which are usually associated with the age range of 1 year to 6 years, differ from other intelligence tests in scope. Infant measures in particular are usually multidimensional. Infant tests, for example, frequently assess cognitive and motor domains simultaneously. The McCarthy Scales of Children's Abilities (McCarthy, 1972), for example, is designed for ages 2½ through 8 and includes a motor domain. Motor domains are even more common for infant measures. Some measures also assess behavioral, temperamental, and emotional status. The Battelle Developmental Inventory (Newborg, Stock, Wnek, Guidubaldi, & Svinicki, 1984) is a broad-based diagnostic measure that assesses personal-social, adaptive, motor, communication, and cognitive skills.

Many tests for young children also focus on screening (see Chapter 14). Usually, cutoff scores for at-risk status are rather generous in order to err in the direction of more false positives (children identified by the screener as at-risk who are subsequently found to not be at-risk) than false negatives (children who were not identified as at-risk by the screener who may in fact have developmental problems). Screeners are brief by definition and more prone to measurement error. Screeners are designed for use by professionals or trained paraprofessionals and are multidimensional. These measures are designed for the screening of large numbers of young children in a variety of settings ranging from neonatal clinics to prekindergarten school screening. These devices have brief intellectual/cognitive tests, and in some cases the cognitive component is not emphasized any more than any other part of the battery. The Developmental Indicators for Assessment of Learning—Revised (DIAL-R) and the Denver Developmental Screening Tests are examples of multidimensional screening measures.

This chapter focuses on comprehensive measures. It discusses intelligence test batteries that emphasize the assessment of cognitive functions and that are typically used for making diagnostic, as opposed to screening, decisions.

ISSUES IN PRESCHOOL ASSESSMENT

United States Public Law 99-457

Just as IDEA provided impetus for increased assessment of children and adolescents by the public schools, PL 99-457 is a major extension of these services for preschool children and infants. The major provisions of the law are twofold. It mandates the extension of services under IDEA downward to the 3- to 5-year-old age group. Preschoolers with disabilities are entitled to a free and appropriate public education beginning in the 90–91 school year. The second component is the creation of a new federal Handicapped Infants and Toddlers Program for children from birth to 2 years of age. Children are eligible for the birth to 2 program if they are experiencing developmental delays, have a physical or mental condition that places them at risk for later delays (e.g., Down syndrome), or are at risk for physical or emotional delays. These provisions have renewed interest in the assessment and

diagnosis of very young children, and there has been an associated increase in the number of available instruments for the cognitive assessment of this age group.

Sources of Items

There is a notable lack of differentiation between the item pools of infant measures. Most of the widely used tests of infant intelligence can trace their roots to a single item pool, that of Arnold Gesell, the famous developmentalist.

This item similarity among preschool instruments was formally evaluated by Lewis and - Sullivan (1985), who compared the items of 11 different tests spanning 50 years of test development. The tests that they reviewed are listed below.

Gesell Developmental Schedules (1939)

Uzgiris-Hunt (1976)

Denver Developmental Screening Test (1976)

Iowa Tests for Young Children (1936)

Merrill-Palmer (1926)

Kuhlman-Binet (1922)

Minnesota Pre-School Scale (1932)

Kuhlman Tests of Mental Development (1939)

Cattell Infant Intelligence Scale (1940)

Bayley Scales of Infant Development (1969)

Griffiths Mental Development Scale (1945–70)

Lewis and Sullivan (1985) noted remarkable similarity among the items in these tests, and most of the items could be traced to the pioneering work of Gesell. This situation is reminiscent of the rush to copy Binet early in the last century. At that time there were numerous adaptations of the original Binet scales, all of them bearing striking similarities to the original. If, in fact, imitation is a sincere form of flattery, then Gesell's work on measuring mental development has had a substantial impact on the measurement of infant intelligence.

Intelligence versus Developmental Status

It is interesting that Arnold Gesell, while providing the basis for so many test development activities, *did not believe that intelligence could be assessed.* He was more interested in measuring the general maturation of the child (Goodman, 1990). Gesell conducted his important research as a contemporary of Terman, Goddard, Binet, and other early workers. These were the "heady" days when intelligence testing had become known as the major practical contribution of psychology. Many scientists of the day believed that Binet's test measured only or primarily biologically determined intelligence (see Chapter 1). Others, such as Gesell, believed that while intelligence was a construct worth studying, direct measures of this biological entity were not yet available and likely not to be discovered for some time. This idea is similar to the widely held view today that intelligence tests measure psychometric intelligence (Hebb's Intelligence B, 1949; Eysenck's Psychometric Intelligence, 1986), not biological intelligence.

This view, that infant tests measure a multidetermined general developmental status, has been carried forward by Nancy Bayley, the author of the respected Bayley Scales of Infant Development (1969). Bayley (1969) did not use the word *intelligence* in the title of her original test nor in her manual. She referred to her test as a measure of developmental status. She stated further that there are not "factors" of intelligence for preschoolers but rather clusters of abilities that differentiate at school age. As Bayley stated, ". . . any classification of abilities into parallel arrays purporting to designate different factors that develop concurrently is artificial and serves no useful purpose" (1969, p. 3). This point of

view appears to be supported by subsequent factor analyses of preschool measures such as the Binet-4 where numerous researchers identified only one factor for 2- and 3-year-olds. The Bayley was also not devised to make inferences about past history or etiology. It was intended only as a measure of the current status of a child's cognitive development. The Bayley and the Gesell, by the way, did not offer "IQ" scores.

Gesell, Bayley, and Binet were all cautious about the interpretation of their scales as measures of intelligence. Does this caution have anything to do with their experiences with young children? Perhaps, but these viewpoints are currently important as *they emphasize the fairly low level of inference that is appropriate for all intelligence measures.* According to these great researchers, modern-day psychologists should regard preschool intelligence assessment as the evaluation of developmental status in the cognitive domain.

Assessing "Developmental Status" at All Ages

Sandra Scarr (1981) provided a theoretical framework for the viewpoint of these early workers, and she advanced the idea that assessment of older children follow the lead of the early childhood tests by emphasizing the assessment of multiple domains. Analogous to the term *developmental status,* Scarr proposed that clinicians measure "intellectual competence" (as opposed to intelligence). Scarr concluded that school personnel in particular measure three domains: cognitive (similar to current intelligence tests), motivation, and adjustment. She summarized her argument for broadening intellectual assessment by offering that:

Whenever one measures a child's cognitive functioning, one is also measuring cooperation, attention, persistence, ability to sit still, and social responsiveness to an assessment situation. This is certainly not an original thought; David Wechsler, for one, said this for nearly 50 years. Binet, before him, was aware that testing sampled far more than cognitive development. (p. 1161)

In many ways Scarr described the history of the practice of early childhood assessment where there is a longer tradition of not placing one domain of development at a higher premium than others. Why did this orientation not take a foothold in the assessment of school-age children? The reasons are likely multitudinous and speculative. It is clear, however, that the intelligence test has historically been the loadstar of the school-age child's evaluation whereas many cautioned against the same for preschoolers.

Stability Revisited

One of the unusual aspects of preschool intellectual assessment is that psychologists cannot depend on these measures to show strong evidence of stability (of past and future intelligence test scores; see Chapter 3). Stability research with preschoolers also differs in that there are significant differences in stability for normal developing and developmentally delayed infants and preschoolers.

The typical stability coefficients for intelligence tests hover in the .70s range and higher when tests are first administered at ages 6–7 or above and a second test is given about a year later (see Chapter 3). For normal developing children evaluated between birth and 2½ years of age the correlation with scores obtained at ages 3 to 8 range from .01 to .59 (Goodman, 1990). These coefficients are particularly unimpressive given that the correlation between parental intelligence or SES and child's scores on the Bayley approximate these values with coefficients as high as .50 for normal developing children. The trend, however, does differ for children showing developmental delays.

Developmentally delayed young children's intelligence test scores are considerably more stable. Whereas stability coefficients between early (taken below 2 years of age) and later tests (taken at age 4–5 or above) for nonchallenged children reach .50 at their zenith, stability coefficients for handicapped children are in the .70s to .90s range for children tested at 1 year of age and older. There is

a substantial likelihood that a child diagnosed as developmentally delayed during the first 2 years of life will retain such a diagnosis (Goodman, 1990) (see Chapter 3). Although infant cognition is predictive of later cognitive development, the causes of continuity and change are unknown (Slater, 1995).

Inadequate Theory

Some of the same problems that have plagued all of intellectual assessment of course also apply to the assessment of infants and preschoolers. Since most of the items currently in use can be traced to the pioneering work of Arnold Gesell in the 1920s, the item content of many of these measures is not specified by a theory unique to each test author. Early developers of infant tests were driven by the same empiricism as Binet, who sought high correlations with school achievement. Infant and preschool test developers used the same approach but gave attention to a different type of validity. These test developers were seeking strong evidence of age differentiation validity. Goodman (1990) eloquently states the problem:

> From today's distance, one wonders why the one fundamental criterion for item selection was goodness of fit with evolving age. Apparently no effort was made to predefine the nature of intelligence and then to select items that most adequately fit the construct(s), regardless of how smoothly they paralleled age changes. Theories of mental growth were generated by, rather than generating, item development. (p. 187)

Some tests that are designed for wide age ranges may make some theoretical contributions to preschool assessment. The K-ABC, W-J Cog, and DAS have tried to develop theory-based items down to age 2 years.

Preschool and Infant Assessment as Specialty

In many instances infant and preschool intellectual assessment is full of pitfalls for the clinician. The test instruments offer choices ranging from

Box 15.1   Preschool Escapades

Preschoolers are so cute that they may seem to be an appealing audience to many people. Hence, I think that a few cautions are in order. When I worked as a school psychologist, I was charged with reevaluating high-risk kindergarteners annually as part of an experimental intervention program. I gave the McCarthy scales to about 40 children each winter, and I was always ill with an upper respiratory infection until spring break! I tried washing my hands psychopathologically, taking vitamins, sitting farther away from the kids, everything short of wearing a mask, but it was of no avail. I was miserably sick for 3 months every year.

In addition to the colds, I was orthopedically impaired for these same 3 months. This difficulty was due to my having to sit every day in a preschooler's chair, or on the floor, in order to conduct the evaluations. At 6 foot 3 inches tall and inflexible, I had great difficulty adjusting to talking through my knees.

There was no escaping the little cuties. At the time I had a preschooler at home, and a vengeful one at that. I'll never forget the day that she became angry at her older sister and used her sister's shoe for her bowel movement in lieu of the commode. I vividly remember her proudly walking out of the bathroom with her sister's shoe full of you know what.

Yes, young children can be delightful, in the hands of the right clinician, which apparently was not me!

---

the psychometrically inadequate to the antique. The usual thinking regarding predictive validity and stability does not apply to these measures, and the challenges presented by this age group, ranging from adorable manipulation to soiled pants, require a skilled clinician.

Given that intellectual assessment of preschoolers requires a different set of knowledge and skills than for older children, there seems to be a need for specialized training in this area. It is akin to the assessment of children with hearing impairments, children from cultures vastly different from that of the examiner, and other children which require new sets of knowledge and skills. While formal guidelines for the training of individuals to assess young children are lacking, it seems wise for clinicians to seek specialized coursework and supervised practica before conducting evaluations of young children (see Box 15.1).

ASSESSING INFANTS

The assessment of children under 24 months of age typically involves some modifications in the standard assessment procedure. While tests administered to older children are to be administered in prescribed order, this is not the case for younger children. Standardized procedures for infants are more of a "guide" than a rigid set of rules. Examiners should feel free to violate the prescribed test's sequence in order to maintain the infant's interest in the tasks. Scoring may be flexible as well. On the Bayley, for example, an item may be scored correct if the child demonstrates the criterion behavior outside the test session (e.g., in the waiting room).

It is also conventional wisdom that mothers or other caretakers are not to be present for intellectual evaluations. Not only are mothers "allowed" to be present for the testing of preschoolers, they may also administer some items if the infant is more likely to respond to the mother (Bayley, 1969). It is therefore important that the examiner develop a good rapport with the mother as well as with the baby. In fact, rapport with the mother is probably equally important. In this setting the word *doctor* may not be wise to use when introducing oneself to the child's mother since it may remind the child of some painful medical procedure. Rapport with the mother will be facilitated by making eye contact, smiling, and approaching her in a direct and friendly manner. The reason for the assessment and/or more neutral topics such as the weather and parking difficulties may provide good material for an opening conversation. It is also important to explain the testing procedures thoroughly to the mother (or father or other caregiver as the case may be) and to continue to explain procedures as the evaluation unfolds.

The child should not be approached abruptly (Bayley, 1969). The examiner may place a toy or other object near the child, then speak with the child's caregiver for a brief time or arrange the test setting. The examiner may then gradually approach the child while interacting with the parent. Approaching the child with the parent will help allay the baby's fears.

The examiner should be aware of the context surrounding the individual testing session. This awareness is particularly important when testing infants because the examiner has the opportunity to provide the parent with some information about his or her child. For example, the examiner may use the session to model appropriate interaction with an infant for a parent whose parenting skills need strengthening, or may highlight the child's capabilities in order to reassure an overly anxious parent.

Scheduling is a crucial consideration with infants. Young infants may have only an hour or two of alert time each day, and it is imperative that examiners attempt to schedule testing for this time (Bayley, 1969). Unfortunately, predicting these alert times is often difficult and thus makes the testing of infants very tricky indeed. A testing session should never be scheduled during a regular nap or feeding time. Breaks may also be taken for feeding, nursing, or changing diapers as needed.

Recommendations regarding the environment differ for infants and preschoolers compared to older children. The floor should be carpeted or otherwise be made comfortable, and there should be homelike places for the young infant—a blanket on the floor or an infant seat, for example. If infant seats are not available, a car seat or stroller seat can be used instead. Some preschoolers may respond better to an examiner sitting across the

table as opposed to beside the child (Bayley, 1969). This arrangement may work better for the reticent child who may feel uncomfortable if the examiner comes too close.

Because infants have such brief periods when they are happy and alert, the examiner must pace the session carefully and be extremely flexible. The pace of the session must be rapid in order to catch as much optimal behavior as possible *and* very calm and gentle in order not to overstimulate the baby. As Bayley (1969) aptly stated, "Hurry yourself but do not hurry the child" (p. 27). Too many repetitions of an item or too many items in too little time can cause the baby to be overwhelmed and fall apart. Flexibility is also necessary—the examiner may have to follow a toddler around the room administering whatever item seems most likely to attract the child's attention. Generally, young children respond better when the session begins with manipulatives such as blocks or other test toys (Bayley, 1969). Oral questions or items involving following instructions should be administered after working with a few manipulatives. Finally, as the child tires and needs a break from sitting, gross and fine motor activities may be optimal.

The key to flexible, swift, yet relaxed administration of a test is a thorough knowledge of the test and total familiarity with the materials. This knowledge enables the examiner to move rapidly from one item to another while focusing on the child and maximizing the likelihood that the child will perform up to the level of his or her true capability. Test familiarity will also allow the examiner to collect valuable nontest data for domains such as parent–child interaction, parenting skill, and child temperament.

Comprehension of Instructions

Some children may simply not be able to understand the instructions given them, which may preclude the psychologist from validly assessing a preschooler's cognitive development (Flanagan, Alfonso, Kaminer, & Rader, 1995). Flanagan et al. (1995) reviewed the incidence of basic concepts in test directions for the Wechsler Preschool and Primary Scale of Intelligence—Revised (WPPSI-R), Binet-4, DAS, W-JRCog, and Bayley Scales of Infant Development—Second Edition (BSID-II, Bayley, 1993) and found numerous incidents of the use of difficult-to-understand basic concepts in the test directions. Basic concepts such as "on, big, red, missing, all, without, together, over, same, alike, etc." all have known difficult indices for 3- and 4-year-old children, thanks to the availability of norming data from the Bracken Basic Concepts Scale and the Boehm. Thus, Flanagan et al. (1995) were able to estimate the comprehensibility of test instructions to the typical preschooler.

They concluded that the DAS and W-JR Cog were among the worst offenders, but even the BSID-II included 28 concepts such as "red, one, like, in, on, big, and with" (pp. 356–357). These results suggest that many children may simply misunderstand the directions given them, precluding the examiner from obtaining an estimate of the child's cognitive development. Moreover, the problem may be exacerbated during the evaluation of preschoolers with limited English proficiency.

One of the very reasonable suggestions offered by Flanagan et al. (1995) is that *knowledge of basic concepts should be assessed for all children prior to administration of one of the popular preschool intelligence tests.* This procedure will allow the clinician to more accurately gauge the veracity of the child's results.

INFANT TESTS

Bayley Scales

The most popular of infant cognitive developmental status measures is the Bayley Scales of Infant Development—Second Edition (BSID-II; Bayley, 1993). The latest version of this venerable scale extends from 1 to 42 months of age and includes a Mental Scale, Motor Scale, and Behavior Rating Scale. Nancy Bayley's original test was somewhat unique in that it was the result of a long career of research on the mental development of children, primarily with the Berkeley Growth Study. Based on this research, Bayley concluded that infant's mental development was highly unstable and that no general factor of intelligence existed (Goodman, 1990).

The original Bayley scales differed from other infant tests of its day because of its technical superiority. It, for example, broke with tradition by offering standard scores instead of the ratio IQ that was typical of its predecessors. This tradition of psychometric quality continues with the BSID-II, as will be noted later.

The two Bayley composite scores of interest are the Mental Development Index (MDI) and the Psychomotor Development Index (PDI). The Mental and Motor scales of the BSID-II have been enhanced considerably in this edition with new stimulus materials, new items, and more extensive content coverage (Fugate, 1998). The MDI and PDI are normalized standard scores using the familiar mean of 100 and standard deviation of 15. Their values only range as low as 50, making it difficult to make differential diagnostic decisions for children with severe disabilities (Dunst, 1998). These are not, however, IQs or meant to serve as meaures of intelligence per se, but rather as measures of developmental status. According to Bayley (1969), the three scales serve as "a tripartite basis for the evaluation of a child's developmental status in the first two and one half years of life" (p. 3).

Virtually all infant and preschool tests are difficult to administer in standardized fashion given the behavioral characteristics of this age group, especially the difficulties in gaining and sustaining their attention. Consequently, test developers make heavy use of manipulatives, resulting in test kits that resemble toy boxes and weigh nearly as much. All parents know how difficult it is to find the toy you want in a toy box! Finding and using the test materials of the Bayley and other scales is similarly difficult. The Bayley requires extraordinary familiarity with its materials in order to administer it properly.

The BSID capitalizes on new developments in measurement theory by utilizing latent trait theory in a manner similar to that employed by the DAS. Like the DAS, children of a specific age are administered uniform sets of items. One must administer every item in the first set appropriate for the child's age in order to obtain a basal of 5 items correct on the Mental Scale and 4 items correct on the Motor Scale. A ceiling is obtained when a child makes at least 3 errors in a set on the Mental Scale and 2 on the Motor Scale. Of course, flexibility is built into the BSID-II, which allows testing below the basal for children suspected of developmental delays and above the ceiling as needed to ensure full assessment of the child's abilities. The use of item sets is relatively new to the work of psychologists, some of whom may find it disquieting to give a youngster credit for a failed item that is within a set of items that was passed (Schock & Buck, 1995). Examiners may think that this procedure could serve to produce less accurate scores, as has been intimated by some (Mayes, 1994).

Schock and Buck (1995) conducted an informal survey of early BSID-II adopters and reported the following impressions regarding the practical aspects of the scale.

1. *Practitioners appreciate the flexibility of the order of item administration within an item set.*

2. *Considerable familiarity with the items, and their associated materials, is required prior to administration.*

3. *BSID-II record forms are well organized and instructions explicit.*

4. *The* Infant Behavior Record *was viewed as superior to its predecessor. Its parent report form and the availability of percentile ranks for specific domains were also perceived to be advantages.*

5. *The increased age range is a significant advantage.*

6. *Prepublication research with children with prenatal drug exposure, Down syndrome, and premature birth provides guidance to practitioners regarding the "potential needs and responses" of examinees beforehand.*

7. *The new stimulus materials are more appealing and realistic to children, durable, washable, and generally easier for the examiner to manage.*

8. *Improved scoring criteria and more succinct norming conversion tables compared to its predecessor. (p. 12)*

Standardization

The BSID-II was normed on a sample of 1,700 (100 per month) infants and preschoolers aged 1 to 42 months in 1991 and 1992. The sample was a good match to the 1988 U.S. Census data (Flanagan & Alfonso, 1995).

Reliability

Internal consistency coefficients for the MDI hover at about .90. This level of reliability is somewhat lower than that obtained for other measures cited in this chapter, however, one should keep in mind that the Bayley attempts to assess much younger children than the others. In fact, a test-retest coefficient of .91 for the MDI over an average 4-day interval is impressive for such young children.

Validity

There is clear evidence to support Bayley's (1969) point that the abilities assessed by the MDI change *qualitatively* over time. Fugate (1998) points out these developmental differences by noting:

> *The mental scale should not be considered an "IQ" measure as the items are not generally concerned with the functions generally measured by intelligences scales. Prior to 12 months of age, the Mental scale of the BSID-II essentially measures [the] sensory and perceptual development. Items are highly dependent upon auditory and visual skills, although early vocalization, memory, and social skill development are also assessed. Beyond 12 months, the mental scale becomes more oriented toward vocalization and language skill development, problem solving, generalization, classification, social skills, and the development of early number concepts. (p. 93)*

These was one study of the relationship between the Stanford-Binet L-M and the Bayley reported in the original Bayley (1969) manual. At age 24 months the correlation between the two measures was .53, at 27 months .64, and at 30 months it was .47. These relationships showed some independence of the two measures. The BSID-II manual shows stronger relationships for the MDI with other products developed by the same publisher (e.g., WPPSI-R = .73), but the relationship of the MDI to many infant and preschool tests is still unknown.

It is especially curious that factor analytic data are presented for the BRS and not for the Mental or Motor scales in the BSID-II manual. A rationale for this decision is not given but sorely needed since the publisher has access to a larger and more representative sample than anyone else. Overall, BSID-II validity evidence, however, is meager when one considers that this scale is so widely used (Fugate, 1998). Specifically, predictive and factor analytic validity evidence are generally lacking (Flanagan & Alfonso, 1995).

Summary

The original Bayley was generally considered an important psychometric achievement in the development of infant tests. The BSID-II extends this reputation by providing good evidence of norming and reliability (Dunst, 1998). The validity evidence available for the BSID-II is currently insufficient for some applications (Fugate, 1998). For example, no studies of the use of the Bayley with children from various cultural and linguisitc groups are currently available (Black & Matula, 2000).

Regardless of its psychometric properties, psychologists who use the Bayley have to continually remind themselves of the undifferentiated and less stable nature of the cognitive skills of young children and the limitations of formal psychometric assessment with this age range. To this end, Dunst (1998) lauded the psychometric properties of the BSID-II and yet concluded:

This reviewer has administered hundreds of Bayley Scales and has overseen the administration of the scales by psychologists with children participating in several early intervention programs, and the scales simply have limited value as a tool for informing practice. (p. 92).

Measures of Infant Information Processing

Tests of infant mental processing skills have received considerable attention as a potential breakthrough in the assessment of infant intelligence. These "tests," although many of these measures are experimental in nature, have received attention because of claims of stronger predictive validity coefficients, even for nondisabled children. They measure attention, retrieval, encoding, and other processing skills, using a variety of paradigms.

One of the well-known information processing characteristics of infants is habituation. Most of these paradigms present face-like stimuli to infants. As the child becomes familiar with the visual stimulus, his or her interest in it and attention to it begins to wain. This decrement in attention to a familiar stimulus signifies "habituation." In other words, more capable children direct less attention to the familiar stimulus.

Another habitation method is to measure recovery of attention when a novel stimulus (e.g., face-like pattern) is introduced. This paradigm, commonly referred to as novelty preference or dishabituation, measures the attention that a child gives to a newly introduced stimulus. Children with impaired intelligence do not recognize or respond to the novel stimulus as quickly in such procedures.

A novelty preference task was used by Fagan (1984b) who tested 36 suburban nondisabled children on a novelty preference task at age 7 months. Each infant was shown pairs of pictures (black and white) of women and babies until a child fixated on one of the faces for 20 seconds. The child was then shown this face again paired with a novel face for two 5-second test intervals to determine the child's preference for novelty. The children were then evaluated again at 3 years on a recognition memory task and the PPVT-R. The children were given these same tests again at 5 years of age.

The reliability of the novelty preference measures was quite low at .32. The predictive validity of the novelty preference task at 7 months for PPVT-R scores at age 5 was higher at .42. The recognition memory scores at age 3 were more highly correlated with PPVT-R scores at age 5 (r = .66) than novelty preference at age 7 months. These are all modest stability and validity coefficients that do not differ significantly from the data for more traditional measures.

The finding of significant predictive validity coefficients for the novelty preference task is robust (Fagan, 1984b). A novelty preference task has also been found effective for differentiating low birth weight and high-risk monkeys (Gunderson, Grant-Webster, & Fagan, 1987; Gunderson, Grant-Webster, & Sackett, 1989) from normal monkeys. This line of research has resulted in the Fagan Test of Infant Intelligence (Joseph F. Fagan, Department of Psychology, Case Western Reserve University, Cleveland, OH, 44106). Fagan (1984) also draws theoretical implications from his work suggesting that visual preference and visual recognition tasks measure developmentally continuous intellectual skills that may shed light on the nature of "g."

Goodman (1990) is critical of Fagan's work on a variety of levels. She notes that there are reliability problems with these types of tasks because of the difficulties involved in measuring infants' attention. Typical reliability coefficients are in the .40s. Predictive validity coefficients for normal children are higher than those of tests such as the Bayley, but coefficients for samples of children with disabilities are similar to those for traditional tests (Goodman, 1990). After a thorough review of the data on measures of infant information processing, including Fagan's work, Goodman (1990) concluded:

Until we have more predictors and criteria, it will remain unclear just what the visual recognition tasks are

measuring and how much reliance can be placed on them. (p. 199)

Ross (1989) assessed the practical utility of Fagan's and similar approaches and draws two conclusions: (1) information processing approaches are less satisfactory from a clinical standpoint, and (2) their predictive validity advantage is insignificant for clinical cases. The narrow set of skills assessed by information processing measures results in less of an information yield than that obtained from traditional measures that sample a larger variety of infant behavior.

The predictive superiority of information processing measures is insignificant for challenged infants when ranges of scores are utilized. Ranges may include broad categories such as >85 (normal), 70–85 (at risk), and < 70 (handicapped). These ranges correspond to typical diagnostic practice where children are classified or diagnosed based on the range in which their scores lie. Ross (1989) found a correct classification rate of 87% using the Bayley with a sample of 94 preterm infants. Siegel (1979) obtained an 84% correct classification rate when using the Bayley. Fagan, Singer, and Montie (1986) found a classification rate of 86% with preterm infants when a novelty preference task was used.

The novelty preference task, however, does show more consistent superiority when used to predict the performance of nondisabled children (Ross, 1989). The information processing approaches of Fagan and similar methodologies are promising (Colombo, 1993). More large-scale investigations and greater attention to issues of norming, reliability, and validity are necessary before clinical application is warranted.

Battelle Developmental Inventory

The Battelle Developmental Inventory (BDI) was developed as part of a large-scale federal research program concerned with planning and evaluating intervention programs for at-risk infants, toddlers, and preschoolers. The BDI was published in 1984 and manual and norms were updated in 1988. The BDI was designed for children from birth to 8 years of age, and it includes five major domains. These domains include Cognitive, Personal-Social, Adaptive, Motor, and Communication. Each domain is comprised of numerous sub-domains. Consequently, the BDI is extremely comprehensive, capable of producing a profile of 30 scores. These scores include:

1. Adult Interaction
2. Expression of Feeling-Affect
3. Self-concept
4. Peer Interactions
5. Coping
6. Social Role
7. Personal-Social Total
8. Attention
9. Eating
10. Dressing
11. Personal Responsibility
12. Toileting
13. Adaptive Total
14. Muscle Control
15. Body Coordination
16. Locomotion
17. Gross Motor
18. Fine Muscle
19. Perceptual Motor
20. Fine Motor
21. Motor Total
22. Receptive
23. Expressive
24. Communication Total
25. Perceptual Discrimination
26. Memory
27. Reasoning and Academic Skills
28. Conceptual Development
29. Cognitive Total
30. Total Battery

The BDI is in many ways similar to the Bayley Scales because of its multidimensional emphasis and because it does include a cognitive domain, which is the focus of this review.

Administration and Scoring

The BDI, because of its comprehensive nature, is somewhat more lengthy to administer than many preschool and infant test batteries. A study by Bailey, Vandiviere, Dellinger, and Munn (1987) evaluated several practical aspects of BDI administration and scoring. They included a study of 76 teachers who had administered the BDI to 247 handicapped preschoolers as part of a statewide study evaluating the use of the BDI. One of the findings of this implementation study was that the BDI required on the average 2½ sessions to administer. Average administration time was 93.4 minutes and the mean amount of scoring time was 34.4 minutes. Hence, the BDI, on average, will require 2 hours of examiner time.

The BDI offers a variety of scores, including percentile ranks, age equivalents, and developmental quotients (DQ) (standard scores with a mean of 100 and SD of 15). One of the problems identified with BDI scoring is the difficulty in obtaining extreme DQ values for domains. In the Cognitive domain, for example, the lowest value available for the DQ is 65. The manual, however, provides a procedure for calculating (extrapolating) DQs below this level. This procedure, however, is somewhat cumbersome and has resulted in what appear to be spurious values (Bailey et al., 1987). McClinden (1989) clarified the nature of the problem of calculating extreme BDI scores. Apparently, it is possible to obtain negative developmental quotients. In the implementation study by Bailey et al., 28% of the children obtained a negative developmental quotient. In addition, McClinden (1989) has criticized the wide age ranges used in developing the norms. It was noted, for example, that a toddler tested at 23 months of age with a total raw score of 243 would receive a DQ of 99. If this same child was tested *one month later* at 24 months of age, and again obtained a raw score of 243, the developmental quotient would be 65. Norms for lower functioning levels and ceiling effects are frequently cited problems with the BDI (Oehler-Stinnett, 1989).

The BDI also requires a considerable number of manipulatives in the administration process. Many of the manipulatives have to be produced by the examiner. The examiner, for example, must cut out puzzles and pictures for administration purposes—materials that may show considerable wear and tear (Paget, 1989).

Standardization

Standardization of the BDI was conducted from December 1982 to March 1983. A stratified national sample was collected consisting of 800 children, approximately 50 boys and 50 girls at each 1-year age level. The sample was constructed so as to reflect 1980 Census Bureau statistics. The sample, however, was not specifically stratified for socioeconomic status, leading to some question about the accuracy of the sampling program (McClinden, 1989).

Reliability

Reliability coefficients for the BDI are extremely high. A study of 183 children involved in a test-retest reliability study produced coefficients ranging from .71 to .99, with a .99 also being yielded for the BDI total score. Interrater reliability coefficients for the BDI are similarly high. Several authors have cited the small standard errors of measurement of the BDI as a potential strength of the instrument (Oehler-Stinnett, 1989; Paget, 1989). McClinden (1989), however, challenges the values for the standard errors of measurement included in the BDI manual. McClinden suggests that the test authors used the incorrect formula to calculate the SEMs. It appears that the authors of the BDI used the formula for the standard error of the mean as opposed to the formula for SEM. Correctly computed SEMs for the BDI are reported in an article by McClinden (1989), and they are considerably more realistic and larger than the "SEMs" reported in the manual.

Validity

An early concurrent validity study by Guidubaldi and Perry (1984) showed substantial correlations between BDI Cognitive DQ scores and other cognitive measures in a sample of first-grade children. In this investigation, the BDI Cognitive DQ correlated .38 with the PPVT-R and .31 with the Stanford-Binet Third Edition Vocabulary subtest. A similar investigation by Mott (1987) was conducted on 20 children diagnosed as having significant speech-language disorders. For this small sample, the BDI Cognitive DQ correlated .32 with the PPVT-R.

A classification study by McLean, McCormick, Baird, and Mayfield (1987) involved 30 handicapped and 35 nonhandicapped children between the ages of 7 months and 72 months. The handicapped sample included primarily children diagnosed as developmentally delayed or multihandicapped. A small number of children were diagnosed as hearing impaired or behaviorally disordered. This study compared the diagnostic agreement between the BDI screening test (a short form of the BDI) and the Denver Developmental Screening Test—Revised. These authors found that the Denver and the BDI disagreed substantially in identifying children for follow-up evaluation. Specifically, "Out of a group of 35 children with no prior indication of exceptionality, the BDI identified 22 as needing further testing while the Denver Developmental Screening Test—Revised identified all as normal" (McClean et al., 1987 p. 19). An interesting investigation by Sexton, McLean, Boyd, Thompson, and McCormick (1988) compared the BDI to the Bayley Scales for a sample of 70 handicapped children who were less than 30 months old. The correlation between the BDI Cognitive and Bayley Mental Score was quite high at .93. This high coefficient lead Sexton et al. to conclude that "The correlation coefficients . . . indicate that the scales within both measures tend to place the 70 children in roughly the same order. The results strongly support the concurrent validity of the newly developed BDI" (p. 22).

Oehler-Stinnett (1989) concluded that correlational studies of the BDI and other popular intelligence tests have produced modest evidence of criterion-related validity. She observed:

Lower than expected correlations betweeen the BDI Cognitive domain and the S-B [Stanford-Binet] and WISC-R would suggest this domain is not, for the most part, measuring the same cognitive skills assessed by these IQ tests. (p. 67)

One of the frequently cited strengths of the BDI is its content validity (Paget, 1989). The final BDI item pool was selected from an initial pool of 4,000 items that were derived from other tests and evaluated carefully in two preliminary studies.

The factor structure of the BDI in an early investigation suggests some correspondence between the five domains of this measure and its factor structure for children from birth to 5 years of age. At ages 6 through 8 more than five factors were yielded suggesting that factorial support is strongest for younger age groups (Newman & Guidubaldi, 1981).

Summary

Although a relatively new entrant into the field of preschool assessment, the BDI has been noted as having several strengths. Among these assets are its careful selection of item content, comprehensive sampling of preschool and infant behavior, extended age range, administration flexibility, and concurrent validity with the prior version of the Bayley Scales. Negative aspects of the BDI include questionable scaling, lack of SES stratification for the norming sample, mediocre concurrent validity with well-known cognitive measures such as the WISC-R and Stanford-Binet (Oehler-Stinnett, 1989), and lengthy administration time.

It is perhaps reasonable and predictable for the BDI to not show a close correspondence with multisubtest measures of intelligence at the preschool level. The domains assessed by the BDI are frequently not assessed by intelligence measures (e.g., adaptive behavior), which could adversely affect the correlation between BDI total score and traditional intelligence measures. In addition, the Cognitive domain of the BDI is somewhat brief in comparison to other preschool measures, which again could adversely affect its correlational relationship with well-known competitors. The BDI differs in concept to such a substantial extent from many multisubtest measures of intelligence that one has to evaluate the utility of the BDI in a much larger context. The decision regarding selection of the BDI has more to do with the nature of the assessment purpose that the clinician has in mind. Clinicians have to decide how the BDI or its competitors in a particular age range fit into the larger context of the assessment of an infant or preschooler. The bar, however, continues to be raised, and the revision of the Bayley (BSID-II) and other measures may make them better options.

PRESCHOOL TESTS

McCarthy Scales of Children's Abilities

The McCarthy Scales (McCarthy, 1972) have been the recipient of considerable research attention (Kaufman, 1982; Valencia, 1990). There is even a well-written textbook on the use of the McCarthy (Kaufman & Kaufman, 1977). The McCarthy warrants consideration by all clinicians who evaluate children because of its long research tradition and other strengths. These strengths include a design that considers the developmental needs and interests of preschoolers, use of cognitive developmental research and theory in test design, and utility for diagnostic decision making (Kaufman & Kaufman, 1977).

The McCarthy consists of 18 subtests designed for use with children between the ages of 2½ and 8½. This brief age range may be a hindrance to the popularity of the McCarthy since it does limit opportunities for continuity of follow-up assessment. The subtests of the McCarthy are then combined to produce six composite scores. The Verbal, Perceptual-Performance, and Quantitative scales assess important content or knowledge, whereas the Memory and Motor scales are designed to assess how well a child processes information (Valencia, 1990). The subtests of the McCarthy, and their scale membership, are shown in Table 15.1 in their order of administration. The sixth scale of the McCarthy is an overall composite score called a General Cognitive Index (GCI) (Mean = 100, SD = 16). The GCI is comprised of 15 subtests from all of the scales (three of the motor tests are omitted from the GCI and two are retained).

The McCarthy is designed so that all of the tests are to be administered to all children (with the exception of Right-Left Orientation, which is only administered at ages 5 and above). This may sound lengthy to a novice, but the McCarthy subtests are designed to be relatively short so as to hold the child's interest. The brevity of the subtests precludes subtest interpretation for the McCarthy. The subtests also vary in terms

TABLE 15.1   Subtests of the McCarthy scales of children's abilities

Subtest	Scale (s)
Block Building	Perc-Perf, GCI
Puzzle Solving	Perc-Perf, GCI
Pictorial Memory	Ver, Mem, GCI
Word Knowledge	Ver, GCI
Number Questions	Quant, GCI
Tapping Sequence	Perc-Perf, Mem, GCI
Verbal Memory	Ver, Mem, GCI
Right-Left Orientation*	Perc-Perf, GCI
Leg Coordination	Motor
Arm Coordination	Motor
Imitative Action	Motor
Draw-A-Design	Perc-Perf, Motor, GCI
Draw-A-Child	Perc-Perf, Motor, GCI
Numerical Memory	Quant, Mem, GCI
Verbal Fluency	Ver, GCI
Counting and Sorting	Quant, GCI
Opposite Analogies	Ver, GCI
Conceptual Grouping	Perc-Perf, GCI

*This test is only administered at age 5 and above.

of motor activity (i.e., gross motor tasks are included that allow the child to get out of his or her seat), which is clearly congruent with the activity level of young children. The McCarthy is one of the few tests that has these built-in "breathers" for young children. This design can be seen in Table 15.1, where the motor subtests are administered halfway through the evaluation; thus, the child is provided with a reprieve from sitting.

Standardization

The standardization sample consisted of 1,032 boys and girls divided equally among 10 age groups ranging from 2½ to 8½ years. The sample was selected based on 1970 U.S. Census statistics. Stratification variables included gender, age, father's occupation, ethnicity, geographic region, and urban/rural residence. The standardization sample used sophisticated procedures for its day (Nagle, 1979); however, it cannot be considered to be representative of the national population of young children today.

Reliability

The McCarthy scales show good evidence of reliability for the six composite scores (Kaufman, 1982). Valencia (1990) reviewed five studies of the internal consistency reliability of the McCarthy and eight studies of stability. Internal consistency estimates were generally high across investigations with most of them being in the .80s and .90s, which is commendable given the lower reliabilities that are associated with preschool assessment. The Motor scale was an exception to this trend in that coefficients for this scale were typically lower, in the .60s and .70s. Test-retest studies produced lower reliabilities overall. Of the eight studies reported by Valencia (1990) only one produced a GCI test-retest reliability of .90—the remainder were primarily in the .80s. The Motor scale again had lower reliabilities with coefficients ranging from .33 to .77. These results suggest that McCarthy scores, while highly stable for many children, will be unstable for a few children. This is likely to be a particular problem for some of the composites other than the GCI. It is also predictable from previous research on preschoolers that stability will be an even greater problem with children toward the bottom of the McCarthy age range.

Validity

Factor analytic studies of the McCarthy have produced inconsistent results (Valencia, 1990). Some studies have produced a large first or "g" factor (Kaufman & Hollenbeck, 1973; Keith & Bolen, 1980), whereas others have not (Kaufman & DiCuio, 1975; Teeter, 1984). There has been consistent evidence, however, of factors that correspond to the Verbal, Motor, and Perceptual-Performance scales (Kaufman, 1982; Valencia, 1990). The Quantitative and Memory scales, in contrast, do not show consistent factorial support (Kaufman, 1982; Valencia, 1990). This sounds vaguely familiar, does it not? These results are strikingly consistent with the Binet-4 findings, indicating a lack of factor analytic support for its Quantitative and Short-Term Memory scores, and the DAS data, which showed no indication of a separate memory scale. In the light of these findings for other tests, the McCarthy results seem predictable and reasonable.

Valencia (1990) concluded that there is strong evidence for the concurrent validity of the McCarthy. He reviewed the available correlational studies comparing the McCarthy with the Binet, WPPSI, and other scales and found a mean correlation of .74, a substantial correlation. The greater controversy regarding the McCarthy deals with the issue of mean differences between McCarthy GCI and overall composite scores of other measures, notably the WISC-R Full Scale score (see the discussion of the difference between correlation and agreement in Chapter 5). Many studies have addressed this issue, and the conclusion across investigations is that the GCI underestimates intelligence test scores from the Wechsler scales and the Binet LM (which is now superseded by the Binet-4) by about 4 standard score

points. This finding has led some clinicians to view the McCarthy skeptically. Unfortunately, this difference between the McCarthy and the WISC-R and the Binet LM cannot be explained by differences in dates of norming sample as one would predict since all were normed in the early 1970s. An interesting finding is that the McCarthy and K-ABC agree more closely (Valencia, 1990).

Evidence for the predictive validity of the McCarthy is strong, with coefficients from most studies being in the .60s and .70s. This type of validity evidence is of particular relevance for a preschool instrument designed to identify children at risk for educational problems. The McCarthy has also piqued interest in predictive validity issues because of its well-known screening short form, the McCarthy Screening Test (MST; The Psychological Corporation, 1978).

Lyon and Smith (1986) compared the McCarthy and the K-ABC performance of groups of repeating and nonrepeating preschoolers. One group had been recommended for kindergarten (N=27) and a second group of children had been recommended for retention in the preschool program (N=13). Both the McCarthy and K-ABC scores discriminated between the two groups. The mean GCI for the repeaters was 67.0, whereas for the nonrepeaters, the mean GCI was 86.5. In parallel fashion the MPC for the repeaters was 76.2 as opposed to 91.4 for the nonrepeaters. It is noteworthy in this study that the McCarthy scores are lower for both the repeater and nonrepeater groups. This finding is consistent with other research showing that the McCarthy tends to produce lower scores than other tests (Valencia, 1988).

McCarthy Screeners

The MST consists of six subtests, including Right-Left Orientation, Draw-A-Design, Numerical Memory (Parts 1 and 2), Verbal Memory (Part 1), Leg Coordination, and Conceptual Grouping. In lieu of a GCI or other total score, the MST offers two decision points: at risk at one of three cutoffs of the 10th, 20th, or 30th percentile rank, and "failure" of one, two, or three subtests.

There has been some controversy regarding the construction of the MST, which has resulted in the development of alternative screening forms of the MST (Taylor, Slocumb, & O'Neill, 1979). The most serious challenge to the MST is the Kaufman short form (Kaufman, 1977; hereafter referred to as the KSF). This short form for screening purposes also includes six McCarthy subtests: Puzzle Solving, Word Knowledge, Numerical Memory, Verbal Fluency, Counting and Sorting, and Conceptual Grouping. The KSF has impressive psychometric properties with correlations with complete GCI being in the low .90s in the majority of investigations (Valencia, 1990). Perhaps because of these impressive psychometric properties, the KSF has spawned a number of studies comparing the MST and the KSF (see Valencia, 1990, for an excellent review of the McCarthy research, including screener investigations). The available research has been somewhat more supportive of the KSF. Based on his extensive and insightful review Valencia (1990) concludes:

> Taken together, the available research on the three McCarthy short forms clearly points to the Kaufman SF as the instrument of choice, and thus I endorse it as a useful screening tool. Both psychometric and "hands-on" studies speak to its effectiveness as a screening tool. (p. 233)

Summary

The McCarthy is a unique instrument that is especially suited to assessing the emerging cognitive abilities of preschool and young school-age children. Research abounds on the use of the McCarthy and its various screeners as predictors of later academic problems. The McCarthy is well constructed and alluring to young children. It is gamelike, which can place some demands for motor skill on the part of the examiner.

The McCarthy could benefit from greater floor. While the materials are childlike, there are not enough easy items for 2½ year olds. Evidence of this problem is the fact that for 11 of the 17 subtests the raw score standard deviation at age 2½ is *larger* than the mean raw score.

Although the McCarthy norms may need updating, the extensive supportive research base of the McCarthy suggests that every clinician who assesses the intelligence of young children should become familiar with this scale. The well-known psychometrician Cronbach (1989) rates the McCarthy highly by saying: "The McCarthy scales, despite out-of-date norms, appear to be the instrument of choice at early ages" (p. 775).

Binet-4

The release of the Binet-4 was generally not greeted with enthusiasm by those who assess preschoolers. In comparison to previous editions, the Binet-4 lacked manipulatives (toys, dogs, cats, scissors, etc.), and clinicians thought that it would be less likely to hold preschooler's interest. Anastasi (1989) notes this poor early acceptance among clinicians by stating that "At this stage, its principal limitation centers on communication with test users, especially in clinical settings" (p. 772). Cronbach (1989) echoed some of the concerns of clinicians when he observed, "My impression is that the SB4 is less game-like than some other individual tests and will be less attractive to children" (p. 773).

I also question the arrangement of Binet-4 subtests for preschoolers. Pattern Analysis, for example, uses three different item types and the child shifts abruptly from one to the other as the test becomes more difficult (see Chapter 9). This procedure complicates the examiner's duty to administer a variety of item types correctly.

Practical problems and concerns aside, the Binet-4 is being used with preschoolers, and it has a number of positive attributes to recommend its use. The continuity of measurement with the Binet-4 is one admirable characteristic. Its wide age range and extended standard score scale (to a low of 35) make it a useful tool for assessing developmentally delayed young children and following them through their school years.

The psychometric properties of the Binet-4 are also excellent (see Chapter 9).

Reliability

Internal consistency coefficients for the Binet-4 for preschoolers are excellent (see Chapter 9). Furthermore, test-retest coefficients reported in the Binet-4 *Technical Manual* (Thorndike et al., 1986) are also impressive. The test-retest reliability of the composite scores ranges from a low of .71 for Quantitative Reasoning to a high of .91 for the Composite. These findings are sensible given the robust factor analytic support for the Composite score and validity problems of the Quantitative area score. Most of the Binet-4 subtests have test-retest coefficients in the .70s for preschoolers except for Bead Memory, which had a coefficient of .56 (Thorndike et al., 1986). One can imagine how preschoolers' eagerness to play with the beads may have adversely affected their performance on this test.

Validity

Given the availability of the Binet-4 since 1986, it is surprising to find so little research available on the use of the test with preschoolers. One concurrent validity study is available in the *Technical Manual* (Thorndike et al., 1986) that used the old WPPSI with 5-year-olds. The correlation between the two composite scores was high at .80.

Factor analytic data for preschoolers shows that the four area score model is a poor fit for this age group. Thorndike (1990), Kline (1989), and Sattler (1988) used a variety of methods but came to the same conclusions. The composite score is the most important to interpret for preschoolers because of a strong "g" factor. The Verbal and Abstract/Visual area scores are the only two with any substantial support. This leads one to consider altering the administration of the Binet-4 for this age group. Is it wise to merely administer the Verbal and Abstract/Visual domains and only administer the other domains for supplementary information? This is an important topic that I hope someone will address.

Summary

The advantages of the Binet-4 for preschool assessment include a large age range that supports continuity of measurement, an extended standard score scale, factor analytic validity evidence to support the composite score, relative brevity, and strong concurrent validity. Disadvantages include area scores that lack validity, less game-like materials, and a limited research base. More than anything else the Binet-4 is in need of more research with this population.

K-ABC

The K-ABC enjoys considerable popularity for use with preschoolers (Kamphaus, Kaufman & Harrison, 1990). The Kaufmans had young children clearly in mind when developing the K-ABC, and they included several characteristics that make the test useful for this age group.

The K-ABC differs greatly in its appearance from many widely used tests. The K-ABC was designed to attract the interest of preschoolers by using colorful and true-to-life materials, not unlike the McCarthy scales. Tests such as Magic Window, Face Recognition, Expressive Vocabulary, and Arithmetic use either full-color artwork or photographs. As Telzrow (1984) notes: "Unlike other measures of preschool intelligence . . . the K-ABC utilizes marvelous color photographs in place of static (and too often unfamiliar) line drawings" (p. 312). On the other hand, although the K-ABC is attractive to young children, it could benefit from more manipulatives, which tend to pique the interest of children at the youngest age levels. Some clinicians bemoan the fact, for example, that the Triangles subtest is not administered until age 4. Additionally, Telzrow (1984) remarks:

> *The easel format facilitates the direction of attention where it should be—on the child—instead of on myriad boxes, manuals, and test materials. And the child's attention is easy to maintain, given the attractiveness of the materials and their appeal to the children.* (pp. 311–312)

The K-ABC authors also took great care to ensure that young children are able to understand the test instructions. This feat was accomplished by removing potentially difficult verbal concepts from the examiner instructions. Such concepts as "middle" and "after," which Boehm (1967) had found to be difficult for young disadvantaged children, appear commonly in the directions spoken by the examiner when administering various standardized preschool instruments (Kaufman, 1978). Many examiners have asked why, for example, the Photo Series instructions do not use the words *sequence* or *order*. These words were not used because it was believed that they would be difficult for some 6-year-olds to understand. In the K-ABC, however, there is an additional fall-back position if a young child does not understand even these simplified directions: Sample and Teaching Items.

Telzrow (1984) described several potential uses of the K-ABC with preschoolers. She proposed that the Nonverbal scale is a needed addition for preschoolers. She noted the deficiencies in other nonverbal measures and suggested that the Nonverbal scale should be given a trial by those charged with the evaluation of hearing-impaired and severely speech-impaired preschoolers. Telzrow cautioned that some severely language-disordered children may be misidentified, possibly as mentally retarded, by many existing measures of intelligence that depend heavily on the assessment of verbal skills and knowledge.

Telzrow (1984) also argued that the K-ABC offers two advantages in the identification of preschool gifted children. One of these advantages is the availability of an achievement scale that is normed down to age 2½. She noted that academic achievement has been proposed as an important measure of early academic potential and that the K-ABC is unusual in that it possesses one of the few achievement scales that is appropriate for this age group.

Reliability

The test-retest coefficients for the K-ABC are generally in the middle .80s for the Mental Processing Composite scales for preschool children. The test-retest coefficients are generally higher (in the middle .90s) for the Achievement scale. This is an interesting finding in that the K-ABC Achievement scale is similar to traditional measures of verbal intelligence (Kamphaus & Reynolds, 1987). Furthermore, the K-ABC Achievement scale is the test's best predictor of future achievement. Since prediction of future achievement is one of the central purposes of preschool intelligence testing, it is fortuitous for practitioners that the best predictor on the K-ABC clearly possesses the best reliability.

Lyon and Smith (1986) assessed the long-term stability of the K-ABC with at-risk preschoolers. The K-ABC was administered at a 9-month interval to 53 children between the ages of 49 and 73 months who had been referred for early intervention. The stability coefficients ranged from .84 for the MPC to .73 for the Sequential scale. The coefficient was .76 for the Simultaneous scale and .82 for the Achievement scale. While these results support the overall accuracy of the K-ABC, an equally useful finding for practitioners was the level of gain over this time period. The Simultaneous scale was the big gainer (87.9 on test 1 to 97.2 on test 2) which is consistent with the test-retest data presented in the K-ABC *Interpretive Manual* (Kaufman & Kaufman, 1983b). The Sequential and Achievement scales each improved by about 3 points. The MPC improved by about 8 points over the 9-month time period.

In fact, the Achievement scale of the K-ABC yields comparable or higher stability coefficients at the preschool level than do the composite scores of tests such as the Stanford-Binet—Fourth Edition, WPPSI-R, and McCarthy scales (see Bracken, 1987, for a review of the stability of preschool tests).

Validity

The K-ABC Achievement scale, like the Verbal scale of the WISC-R, is the best predictor of subsequent school achievement (Kamphaus &

Reynolds, 1987). This finding is an important reminder to psychologists that measures of achievement, basic concepts, readiness skills, and related measures are likely to be better predictors of future school achievement than intelligence measures. I recommend that the Achievement scale be routinely administered when assessing preschoolers. This is consistent with the recommendations of Kaufman and Kaufman (1983b) that the Achievement scale always be administered in conjunction with the Mental Processing scales of the K-ABC.

Other research with at-risk preschoolers compares the K-ABC to other popular tests. Lyon and Smith (1986) compared the K-ABC, Stanford-Binet Form L-M, and McCarthy scales for a group of 72 children referred for early intervention. The children ranged in age from 49 to 73 months. The correlations between the K-ABC and the other tests were moderate; .59 with the GCI and .45 with the Binet IQ. The correlation between the K-ABC Achievement scale and the GCI was also .59. The correlation between the Achievement scale and the Binet IQ, however, was considerably higher (.71). In this study, the K-ABC MPC (M=85.9) and McCarthy GCI were highly consistent (M=86.3). The Binet mean IQ of 82.4 was somewhat lower.

Factor analytic studies of the K-ABC for preschoolers are consistent with the three-factor-structure identified for older ages (see Chapter 10) but less robust. The distinctiveness of the Achievement factor is particularly lacking with the Achievement subtests having numerous significant coloadings on Sequential and Simultaneous factors. These results suggest that the Achievement scale in particular may not be interpreted as a distinct entity with confidence (Kamphaus & Reynolds, 1987).

Summary

The K-ABC has some floor problems. As a result, K-ABC users have to be wary of obtaining too many zero raw scores when assessing handicapped children. The K-ABC has plenty of difficulty to challenge precocious preschoolers, especially beginning at age 4½ where tests such as Reading/Decoding can be administered via the out-of-level norms procedure.

The K-ABC has a number of characteristics to recommend its use with preschoolers. At present, the K-ABC is among the most frequently used tests in handicapped children's early education programs (HCEEP) (Thurlow, Ysseldyke, Lehr, & Nania, 1988), and in programs for preschool children with learning disabilities (Esterly & Griffin, 1987).

Wechsler Preschool and Primary Scale of Intelligence—Revised

The WPPSI-R (1989) is a revision of Wechsler's WPPSI (1967). There were several test development goals for this revision, including updating the norms, improving the appeal of the content to young children, and expanding the original age range of the WPPSI so that it now applies to children aged 3 years, 0 months through 7 years, 3 months (Gyurke, 1991). It should be noted, however, that highly intelligent kindergarten and first-grade children may find the test too easy (Kaplan, 1992).

The WPPSI-R follows loyally in the original Wechsler-Bellevue tradition by emphasizing intelligence as a global capacity, but having Verbal and Performance scales as two methods for assessing this global entity. The subtests of the WPPSI-R consist primarily of adaptations of Wechsler-Bellevue subtests. The subtests of the WPPSI-R are shown in Table 15.2

The content of the WPPSI-R subtests has changed substantially in an effort to be more attractive to children. This change reminds me of the controversy over the "colorization" of old movies that were filmed in half-tones. The WPPSI-R, in effect, is a "colorized" version of its predecessor that is more appropriate for young children.

A new feature of the WPPSI-R is in line with modern tests of intelligence such as the K-ABC

TABLE 15.2 WPPSI-R subtests

Verbal Tests

- *Information*: The information subtest of the WPPSI-R is a simplified version of the traditional Wechsler information test in that it requires the child to initially point to a picture to answer a question and later give oral responses to questions from the examiner.

- *Comprehension*: The child is required to give oral responses to questions about common place, actions, or consequences of events.

- *Arithmetic*: The child must demonstrate elementary counting, number concept, and computation skills on pictorial item types and word problems.

- *Vocabulary*: The child has to orally identify pictures of objects. On more difficult items the child has to provide verbal definitions of words.

- *Similarities*: There are three item types on this test. The first requires the child to choose a group of objects that is most similar to another group of objects that share a common feature. The second part requires the child to orally complete a sentence that reflects an analogy. The last portion of the test is similar to the traditional Wechsler item type which requires the child to orally identify commonality among verbal concepts.

- *Sentences*: The child has to repeat sentences from memory in the same manner as dictated by the examiner.

Performance Tests

- *Object Assembly*: The child has to assemble colorful puzzles.

- *Geometric Design*: The first part of the task requires the child to look at a design and find a similar one to match it. The second part of the task requires the child to draw a geometric figure based on a model.

- *Block Design*: The child uses flat two-colored chips to construct patterns based on a model. This is a timed task.

- *Mazes*: The child uses pencil and paper to trace mazes. This is a timed task.

- *Picture Completion*: The child has to identify a missing element of pictures of common events or objects.

- *Animal Pegs*: Much in the same manner as the coding test for other versions of the Wechsler scales, the child has to match particular color pegs to a series of pictured animals. This is also a speeded test.

---

and the DAS. Examiners are allowed to give extra help on early items of subtests in order to ensure that the young child understands what is expected of him or her. This practice is vitally important for testing preschoolers, especially the reticent ones. The only subtest that does not allow for this type of assistance is the Arithmetic test.

Computation of WPPSI-R scores is familiar to Wechsler users. Subtest scores are provided with a mean of 10 and standard deviation of 3. These in turn are converted to Verbal, Performance and Full Scale IQs with a mean of 100 and standard deviation of 15. In addition, the WPPSI manual is considerably more comprehensive than previous editions of the Wechsler scales. Interpretive tables are provided that allow the examiner to determine the statistical significance and clinical rarity of Verbal and Performance score differences, determining strengths and weaknesses on WPPSI-R subtests, and in making pairwise comparisons among WPPSI-R subtests. These interpretive data are likely to be extremely helpful to the new WPPSI-R user.

Norming

The WPPSI-R norming sample was obtained via a stratified sampling procedure based on 1986 U.S. Census Bureau estimates. The sample included 1,700 children. The stratification variables included gender, race (White, Black, Hispanic, other), geographic region, parental occupation, and parental education. The 1,700 cases were divided among nine age groups that included 200 children in each. The 7-year-old age group was the lone exception in that it included only 100 children. There is generally good correspondence between the sample statistics and the Census statistics.

Reliability

The WPPSI-R appears to be highly reliable. The average Verbal, Performance, and Full Scale internal consistency coefficients across age groups are .95, .92, and .96, respectively. The internal consistency estimates are slightly lower at age 7, where it is recommended that the WPPSI-R is most appropriate for below-average children and the WISC-III is generally recommended for use with other children.

The reliability coefficients for the individual subtests vary substantially from an average internal consistency coefficient of .86 for the Similarities subtest to an average of .63 for the Object Assembly subtest. As is typically the case, stability estimates are somewhat lower than internal consistency estimates. A test-retest investigation of 175 children from the standardization sample yielded coefficients in the high .80s and low .90s. The test-retest coefficient for the Full Scale was .91.

Validity

While the WPPSI-R manual goes much further than the older WPPSI or other Wechsler scale manuals in providing validity evidence, it still comes up short in relationship to newer measures such as the DAS, K-ABC, and Binet-4. For example, no predictive validity data are included in the WPPSI-R manual.

Exploratory factor analytic investigations reported in the manual show generally good congruence with the well-known verbal and nonverbal dimensions from the research literature. The data, however, may not be as clearcut as they first appear. The Arithmetic subtest, for example (see Table 64 in the WPPSI-R manual), has a substantial loading of .57 on the verbal factor and .44 on the performance factor. Similarly, Picture Completion loads .39 on the verbal factor and .53 on the performance factor. The Animal Peg subtest does not have a particularly strong loading on either factor with a .25 on the verbal factor and a .41 on the performance factor. The factor structure of the WPPSI-R will likely be better understood when additional analyses are conducted by independent researchers. For example, the notion of the WISC-R third factor was not explored thoroughly in the analysis conducted in the WPPSI-R manual. Similarly, confirmatory factor analyses would be helpful in clarifying the nature of the WPPSI-R structure.

There are a number of concurrent validity studies showing correlations between the WPPSI-R and other well-known measures of intelligence. The correlation between WPPSI and WPPSI-R Full Scale IQs was reported at .87, and the correlation between WPPSI-R and WISC-R IQs for a sample of 50 children was reported at .85. The correlations between the WPPSI-R and other preschool cognitive measures is somewhat lower than the .80s, which is to be expected. The correlation of the composites from the WPPSI-R with the Stanford-Binet is .74, with the McCarthy .81, and with the K-ABC .55. The low correlation of .49 with the K-ABC is curious and inconsistent with the study correlating the K-ABC and the old WPPSI (Kaufman & Kaufman, 1983b). Otherwise, these concurrent validity coefficients provide strong evidence for the construct validity of the WPPSI-R.

A predictive validity study with middle- and high-SES children (FSIQ = 114) produced considerable evidence for the predictive validity of the Verbal IQ with no additional contribution to the prediction of academic achievement for the PIQ (Kaplan, 1993). Children were assessed prior to kindergarten and their achievement in Listening, Reading, Math, and Word Analysis was assessed at the end of first grade.

Correlations between VIQ and these four areas ranged from .44 to .71, whereas the PIQ correlations were in the range of .38 to .65. When VIQ was entered into a multiple regression equation first as a predictor of achievement, the subsequent addition of the PIQ added nothing to the prediction. Kaplan (1993) advised that recommending children for an accelerated curriculum based on a strong WPPSI-R PIQ and weak VIQ is ill-advised.

Summary

The WPPSI-R is a major update and improvement of its predecessor, the 1967 WPPSI. Strengths of the WPPSI-R include more attractive materials than its predecessor. The use of materials that are more intrinsically interesting to young children should improve child interest and motivation. The flexible administration allowing examiners to teach the tasks should also improve the utility of the test with young children. Other practical features of the WPPSI-R include the extended age range and a more comprehensive and well-written manual.

The psychometric quality of the WPPSI-R is unimpeachable, including the updated standardization sample. The reliablity and validity evidence was carefully gathered, and it buttresses the quality of the instrument (Bracken & Delugach, 1990).

The WPPSI-R, however, is burdened by its heritage. Its primary weaknesses are due to the fact that it is inextricably linked to the work of Wechsler in adult intellectual assessment. Potential weaknesses include the fact that it clings to the individual subtest format that Wechsler popularized in the 1930s. The use of subtests that are

in and of themselves reliable and interpretable is most appropriate for the more patient and cooperative adult client. For extremely young children, however, the use of brief sets of items as was popularized by the original Binet and intelligence tests such as the Bayley and McCarthy scales is more suitable to the attention spans of young children. In addition, the WPPSI-R still suffers from a limited age range. A broader age range extending down to 2½ years of age is offered by numerous other tests including the Binet-4, K-ABC, McCarthy scales, and Differential Ability Scales. In addition, the WPPSI-R competitors also have upper age limits beyond that of the WPPSI-R.

Another holdover from the Wechsler tradition that makes the test more cumbersome for use with preschoolers is the use of 10 subtests as the standard battery. The WPPSI-R has always been known for its high reliability; however, this reliability has always come at a price, and the price is having to push a young child through a minimum of 10 subtests. Block Design itself could theoretically take 25 minutes to administer (Slate & Saddler, 1990). Other preschool measures such as the Binet-4 (abbreviated battery), Woodcock-Johnson Revised, McCarthy scales, K-ABC, and DAS are much more realistic in their demands on the attention of preschool children. With these caveats and strengths in mind, the WPPSI-R should be considered a contribution to preschool assessment that warrants consideration for use by clinicians who work with young children.

Differential Ability Scales

The DAS has a battery of tests designed specifically for preschoolers beginning at age 2½. The core and diagnostic (supplementary) subtests for the DAS are shown in Table 15.3. The Block Building, Verbal Comprehension, Picture Similarities, and Naming Vocabulary tests contribute to the GCA (General Conceptual Ability) score at ages 2½ through 3½. Block Building is not used in the GCA at the remaining preschool ages and Early Number Concepts, Copying, and Pattern

Box 15.2   Case Study

This is a case study for a young child who was evaluated with the WPPSI-R and the Binet-4. One interesting aspect of this case is that the examiner hypothesized that this highly active child enjoyed taking the Binet-4 more than the WPPSI-R.

Reason for Referral

Matt is a 4-year-old preschooler who was referred for evaluation at his parents' request due to attentional problems at preschool. He is considered hyperactive at home and demanding of adult attention.

Medical History

Information provided by the parents suggested that Matt's condition at birth was good. He was delivered by Caesarean section with a birth weight of 6 lbs., 5 oz. No difficulties were noted in Matt's early developmental history. His medical history is significant for asthma, which seems to be improving, and scarlet fever at age 3. Frequent rashes around Matt's mouth are treated with hydrocortisone cream. Parental report indicates that Matt passed vision and hearing screenings administered at school within the last year.

Background Information

Matt lives with both parents and one sister, age 11. Matt's sister has been previously diagnosed as having an attention deficit disorder, and Matt's father reported having experienced similar difficulty in school: "daydreaming" and an inability to complete tasks. A psychoeducational evaluation was desired as part of a comprehensive assessment.

Parents report that their most difficult problems with Matt involve discipline. Although very loving, Matt can be stubborn, and he "talks back." When he doesn't get his way, he becomes angry, whines, and cries. Matt reportedly loves preschool, but last year, he had difficulty listening, following directions, and making wise use of his time. He often screamed or made other loud noises, disrupted the activities of other children, and demanded attention.

Behavioral Observations

Matt was nicely dressed in casual clothes and appeared comfortable. He was brought to the testing session by his father and mother. Throughout the evaluation Matt was responsive and candid in his responses. He demonstrated fair to low task persistence yet seemed to try hard on some tasks presented. Rapport was established and maintained throughout the testing session. At times Matt cooperated fully with the examiner, but for the most part he was uncooperative, and he was very difficult to keep in his seat. Matt was able to be redirected.

Assessment Results

Matt was evaluated with the Stanford-Binet Intelligence Scale—Fourth Edition (SB—IV). Matt obtained a Test Composite Score of 90 ± 6. The chances are 95 out of 100 that Matt's scores meet or exceed 16% to 40% of the children his age. This estimate of his current cognitive functioning classifies him in the average to low-average range. On the Wechsler Preschool and Primary Scale of Intelligence—Revised (WPPSI-R) his Full Scale Score was slightly lower. He obtained a score of 80 ± 6, which means that the chances are 95 out of 100 that Matt's scores meet or exceed 4% to 18% of the children his age. This estimate classifies him in the low-average range. This lower score may be due in part to fatigue, inattention, and overactivity level, which were more evident during administration of the WPPSI-R than during the Stanford-Binet.

Matt demonstrated a weakness in his ability to mentally compute arithmetic problems and to complete visual-motor tasks. His weakness in perceptual-motor skills was mainly due to his lack of attention and concentration on tasks that demanded tedious and accurate work. Matt demonstrated strengths in his verbal ability to comprehend words and verbal concept formation.

The Developmental Test of Visual Motor Integration (VMI), a measure of the degree to which visual perception and motor behavior are integrated, yielded a Standard Scaled score of 80. This score is consistent with Matt's ability scores and his weakness in visual-motor coordination.

Box 15.2   Case Study (Continued)

The Bracken Basic Concepts Scale provides a measure of readiness skills in the areas of basic concept knowledge. The results indicate that his Total Test Standard Score of 97 classifies him as meeting or exceeding 42% of the children his age on basic readiness skills.

Matt's mother completed the Parenting Stress Index. The total stress score and the parent domain score were within normal limits. The overall child domain score was high. This suggests that this family would be viewed as experiencing a normal amount of stress and that characteristics of the child that may need to be the focus of intervention include demandingness (compliance), child mood (crying, fussing), and distractibility/hyperactivity. These results are consistent with referral concerns.

Both parents and Matt's preschool teacher completed the Achenbach CBCL. Parental ratings reflected social competence within normal limits, including Matt's participation and performance in activities, social relationships, and school performance. Teacher reports of adaptive functioning suggest that Matt is working much less than his classmates and he is behaving somewhat less appropriately. He was, however, considered to be happy and learning at an average rate. No difficulties were noted by the teacher in Matt's attainment of readiness skills.

The teacher and the mother's ratings on the behavior problem scales suggest that Matt's characteristics are more externalizing (undercontrolled) than internalizing. Both parents' responses reflect similar concerns with primary elevations on the Hyperactive scale and on the scale labeled Delinquent. Only Matt's mother's ratings exceeded the upper limit of the normal range in these two areas (T > 70). His mother indicated that she handles most of the child management in the home. Items endorsed on the Delinquent scale reflect Matt's disobedience at school and destructiveness of things.

On the Structured Interview for Diagnostic Assessment of Children (SIDAC) Matt's behavior was rated as being characteristic of attention deficit hyperactivity disorder.

On the Family Kinetic Drawing his visual-motor coordination was shown to be consistent with the other measures of perceptual-motor integration. Although he seems to have a weakness in this area, caution should be taken in interpreting these results because of his young age.

During the child interview the examiner noted many inconsistencies in Matt's description of his environment. Matt was constantly changing facts, especially when talking about his behavior at the preschool.

Diagnosis

Matt's behavior is characteristic of children diagnosed as having attention deficit hyperactivity disorder—combined type.

Summary

Matt is a 4-year-old boy who will soon be entering kindergarten. He is very active and inattentive at times. Current assessment data suggest that Matt's cognitive functioning is in the average to low-average range, but this should be considered merely an "estimate" because of his youth and inattentiveness. Matt's basic concept scores are commensurate with his cognitive ability.

Psychometric Summary

Binet-4

SUBTESTS	STANDARD AGE SCORE
Vocabulary	54
Comprehension	50
Absurdities	49
Verbal Reasoning	102
Pattern Analysis	41
Copying	49

(Continues)

Box 15.2   Case Study (Continued)

SUBTESTS	STANDARD AGE SCORE
Abstract/Visual Reasoning	87
Quantitative	39
Quantitative Reasoning	78
Bead Memory	54
Memory for Sentences	45
Short-Term Memory	99
Test Composite	90

WPPSI-R

SUBTESTS	SCALED SCORE	IQ
Object Assembly	6	
Geometric Design	5	
Block Design	6	
Mazes	7	
Picture Completion	7	
Animal Pegs	9	
Performance		76
Information	8	
Comprehension	7	
Arithmetic	7	
Vocabulary	7	
Similarities	11	
Sentences	11	
Verbal		87
Full Scale		80

Construction subtests are added to the aforementioned core subtests to create a battery of six subtests for 3½ through 6-year-olds. The four diagnostic subtests shown in Table 15.3 are also available for various young age groups. The preschool battery gets equal emphasis with the school-age battery of the DAS and it has its own record form.

The item types on the DAS are well known, most of them being variants of Binet-type tasks. Tests such as Block Building, Verbal Comprehension, Naming Vocabulary, and Copying are reminiscent of similar items on previous editions of the Binet. The use of toy-like objects for the Verbal Comprehension test is most similar to the earlier Binet editions. Given that these are tried-and-true item types for these age groups, one would predict that they should work well with young children. One unknown aspect of the DAS is its interest level to young children. New clinicians should make an effort to consult DAS users to assess this variable as it is crucial for the successful use of the DAS with this age group.

The DAS also offers some administration flexibility at this age range. Most of the subtests allow for out-of-level testing so that an examiner

TABLE 15.3   Differential ability scale preschool subtests

Ages	Core Subtests	Diagnostic Subtests
2–6 to 3–5	Block Building	Recall of Digits
	Picture Similarities	Recognition of Pictures
	Naming Vocabulary	
	Verbal Comprehension	
3–6 to 5–11	Copying (NV)	Block Building
	Pattern Construction (NV)	Matching Letter-like Forms
	Picture Similarities (NV)	
	Naming Vocabulary (V)	Recall of Digits
	Verbal Comprehension (V)	Recall of Objects (V)
	Early Number Concepts	Recognition of Pictures

could give a test that is ordinarily too difficult for an age group to a precocious child, and conversely, give a subtest that is normally too easy for an age group to a developmentally delayed child.

Norming and Reliability

The psychometric properties of the DAS are commendable, including its standardization program (see Chapter 13). Some of the subtests do not have an extraordinary amount of floor. If, for example, a child obtains a raw score of only 1 on Block Building, the corresponding T score is 37, which is slightly less than $1\frac{1}{2}$ standard deviations below the mean. The GCA, on the other hand, appears to have plenty of evidence of floor.

Both internal consistency and test-retest reliabilites for the GCA are strong, rarely dipping below .90. A rather unusual feature of the manual is to report reliability estimates separately for ability levels for the purposes of out-of-level testing. This practice shows clearly the amount of confidence an examiner may place in a test that is administered out of level. Pattern Construction, a test that is relatively difficult for young children, has a slightly positively skewed distribution for 3-year-olds. Because of this fact the test is less reliable for low-achieving 3-year-olds (T score < 40) because it does not have enough easy items to measure these children

well (.47). It is for this reason that Pattern Construction is not part of the regular battery for this age. For high-ability 3-year-olds (T score > 60), however, the reliability of the test is considerably better (.93). The opposite is true where there are ceiling effects (negatively skewed). These reliability data for out-of-level testing are reported on page 183 of the DAS *Introductory and Technical Handbook* (Elliott, 1990b).

The DAS manual (p. 191) also reports subtest specificity values for the preschool subtests. Some of the subtests with the most specificity and correspondingly low error variances include Pattern Construction, Copying, and Recall of Digits. The ratio of specificity to error variance is lowest for Naming Vocabulary, which has a mean specificity of .34 and error variance of .22.

Validity

Intercorrelations of the subtests and composites at the preschool-age level (p. 199 of the *Handbook*, Elliott, 1990b) suggest that the memory tests, particularly Recall of Objects Immediate and Delayed, are least likely to covary with the GCA. In addition, Matching Letter-Like Forms and Block Building have relatively low correlations with the GCA. Block Building does have a higher correlation with GCA at ages $2\frac{1}{2}$ to $3\frac{1}{2}$. The core subtests clearly have the higher correlations with the GCA, which is their reason for inclusion in the GCA (see Chapter 13).

The "g" factor at ages $2\frac{1}{2}$ through $3\frac{1}{2}$ is marked by Verbal Comprehension and Naming Vocabulary with loadings of .80 and .74, respectively. The remaining four subtests have loadings only in the .50s (Elliott, 1990b). Subtests with high first-factor loadings (using a one-factor confirmatory model) at ages 4 and 5 include Verbal Comprehension, Naming Vocabulary, and Early Number Concepts. Subtests with low loadings on this factor included Recall of Digits and Recall of Objects. These results, therefore, parallel the intercorrelation matrices cited earlier and show which subtests are not likely to align themselves with the GCA.

Based on factor analytic evidence Elliott (1990a) concluded that at ages $2\frac{1}{2}$ through $3\frac{1}{2}$ a single general factor was the most appropriate explanation for the intercorrelation matrix. At ages 4 through 5–11 a two-factor model was proposed as the best fit to the data. These two factors were labeled as verbal and nonverbal.

Concurrent validity studies reported in the *Handbook* (Elliott, 1990b) show strong and lawful correlations between the DAS and other popular preschool tests. In a variety of studies of preschoolers the GCA of the DAS correlated .89 and .81 in two studies with the WPPSI-R Full Scale, .77 with the Binet-4 Composite, .76 and .82 with the McCarthy GCI, and .68 with the K-ABC MPC. There was also a consistent trend for the GCA to be 1 to 4 standard score points lower than these other measures. It is a small difference, but it occured in every study. The GCA was considerably lower than the McCarthy GCI, being about 8 points lower in two separate studies. One plausible explanation for this substantial difference is the age of the McCarthy norms, although this is somewhat surprising given the concern about the McCarthy scoring lower than other tests (Valencia, 1990).

Summary

The DAS possesses a number of characteristics of good measures of preschool intelligence, including provisions for teaching, familiar and attractive item types, factor analytic support, good reliability and concurrent validity, good norming, out-of-level testing, and strong manuals. Some questions remain about the ability of the DAS to hold the interest of young children and ease of administration. The DAS now needs to be "road tested" with clinicians who assess preschoolers.

CONCLUSIONS

The state of the art in infant and preschool intelligence testing is changing rapidly. While there are few current competitors for the Bayley, there are likely some under development. Generally speaking there have been many practical improvements in preschool testing technology in particular. While lack of adequately easy items remains a problem for many scales, evidence of test-retest reliability (Flanagan & Alfonso, 1995) and better quality norming samples make the BSID-II, DAS, and other measures clearly superior to their predecessors.

In addition, new procedures based on cognitive science research may eventually change the face of infant testing. Until that time we are destined to utilize the existing technology that, improvements in psychometrics aside, still does not help significantly clarify our understanding of the nature of infant and preschool cognition and its developmental course.

A convening of a U.S. governmental committee in 1997–1998 produced a booklet with some practical advice for those who assess preschoolers (Shepard, Kagan, & Wurtz, 1998). Some of the general principles emanating from this panel represent sound practical advice for the psychologist who assesses infants and preschoolers. Much of this advice is consistent with points made in this chapter. In abbreviated form the panel recommends:

1. *Assessment should bring about benefits for children.*

2. *Assessments should be tailored to a specific purpose and should be reliable, valid, and fair for that purpose.*

3. *Assessment policies should be designed recognizing that reliability and validity of assessments increase with children's age.*

4. *Assessments should be age-appropriate in both content and the method of data collection.*

5. *Assessments should be linguistically appropriate, recognizing that to some extent all assessments are measures of language.*

6. *Parents should be a valued source of assessment information, as well as an audience for assessment results. (pp. 5–6)*

CHAPTER SUMMARY

- Infant measures of intelligence are usually multidimensional.

- PL 99-457 is a major extension of the provision of educational services for preschool children and infants.

- Lewis and Sulllivan (1985) noted remarkable similarity among the items in infant tests and most of the items could be traced to the pioneering work of Arnold Gesell.

- Arnold Gesell, while providing the basis for so many test development activities, *did not believe that intelligence could be assessed.*

- For normal children evaluated between birth and 2½ years of age the correlation with scores obtained at ages 3 to 8 range from .01 to .59 (Goodman, 1990).

- Stability coefficients between early and later tests for normal children reach .50 at their best, but stability coefficients for handicapped children are in the .70s to .90s range.

- Specialized training for child clinicians who assess infants and preschoolers might include strong coursework in normal and handicapped child development, preschool assessment coursework, and supervised experience in an early childhood setting.

- The assessment of children under 24 months of age typically involves some modifications in the standard assessment procedure.

- The most popular and respected of infant intelligence measures is the Bayley Scales of Infant Development—Second Edition (Bayley, 1993).

- Tests of infant information processing skills have received considerable attention lately as a potential breakthrough in the assessment of infant intelligence.

- The McCarthy scales (McCarthy, 1972) have been the recipient of considerable research attention (Kaufman, 1982; Valencia, 1990).

- There has been some controversy regarding the construction of the McCarthy Screening Test, which has resulted in the development of alternative screening forms of the MST (Taylor et. al., 1979).

- Although the McCarthy norms may need updating, the extensive supportive research base of the McCarthy suggests that every clinician who assesses the intelligence of young children should become familiar with this scale.

- Cronbach concluded that the Binet-4 was likely to be as interesting to preschoolers as its predecessor or as other measures.

- The K-ABC enjoys considerable popularity for use with preschoolers and it possesses a strong research base.

- The WPPSI-R (1989) is a revision of Wechsler's WPPSI (1967).

- The Differential Ability Scales (DAS) possesses a number of characteristics of good measures of preschool intelligence including provisions for teaching, familiar and attractive item types, factor analytic support, good reliability and concurrent validity, good norming, out-of-level testing, and strong manuals.

CHAPTER 16

Nonverbal Tests

". . . the Performance IQ corresponds most closely to G_v, broad visual perception." (Carroll, 1994, p. 139)

CHAPTER QUESTIONS

What are some common problems with "nonverbal measures"?

What cognitive abilities are typically assessed by nonverbal tests?

The variety of intelligence tests currently available is befuddling. Along with newer comprehensive, individually administered tests, there are brief measures, nonverbal tests, group tests, and adaptations for various linguistic groups. Since this book clearly emphasizes comprehensive, individually administered measures, this chapter will focus on broad-based rather than screening nonverbal measures.

There is a long history, especially in the United States, of the use of nonverbal intelligence tests.

The need for nonverbal measures of the intelligence construct has been present since the early days of World War I (see Chapter 1). In fact, Wechsler (1939) clearly recognized this need for a nonverbal measure by including the Performance scale as part of his original test battery. Over the past 70 years, the assessment of nonverbal intelligence has continued to evolve. Now, there are numerous measures that were designed specifically to serve as nonverbal measures of intelligence.

THE CONSTRUCT(S)

Prior to the discussion of individual tests, one conceptual issue regarding nonverbal intelligence testing requires consideration. An important first question is, what is nonverbal intelligence? Some suggest (Naglieri & Prewett, 1990) that "nonverbal intelligence tests are those that are designed to measure a theoretical construct called nonverbal intelligence" (p. 348). Others have argued that there is not such a construct as nonverbal intelligence (Glaub & Kamphaus, 1991). These individuals have proposed that the use of the word *nonverbal* simply describes a methodology for accessing the same general intelligence that has always been of interest to psychologists since the early part of the last century.

Traditionally, most nonverbal measures were considered to be primarily perceptual. Thus, many tests were not considered capable of assessing higher-order intellectual abilities that correlated more substantially with "g." In fact, Wechsler's assumption that the Performance scale provided a "language" through which "g" could be assessed is untrue. Decades of research has shown that the PIQ is simply a modest correlate of various measures of academic achievement and occupational success. On the contrary, the Verbal scale correlates significantly better with such criterion measures.

In effect, many traditional nonverbal measures were probably measuring abilities similar to the Performance scale or Carroll's Stratum II Visualization/Spatial ability factor which, predictably, is less related to general intelligence than reasoning, verbal, or memory abilities. Hence, newer nonverbal measures tout themselves as measuring these higher-order mental abilities that are both more correlated with general intelligence and more predictive of important life outcomes. We will see if this is the case.

U.S. Needs

The development of nonverbal scales of intelligence seems to have come full circle since the time of Wechsler. Wechsler included the more nonverbal Performance scale as an integral part of his intellectual assessment battery. Subsequent to this development, many authors prepared nonverbal intelligence tests that were designed exclusively as nonverbal measures. These include tests such as the Hiskey-Nebraska Tests of Learning Aptitude and the Leiter International Performance Scale. Now intelligence test developers

are reverting back to the practice of Wechsler. Many test batteries offer nonverbal intelligence tests or scales as supplemental scales or specialized short forms. Tests of this variety are multipurpose test batteries such as the K-ABC and the Differential Ability Scales. This chapter will also discuss these nonverbal measures that are part of other comprehensive measures.

More comprehensive measures such as the WISC were not deemed as ideal for use with a variety of populations in which language/hearing variables loom as confounds. The WISC-III oral instructions to examinees, for example, are exceedingly wordy for tests such as Coding. Popular nonverbal (or perhaps a better term is *less verbal*) tests such as the Hiskey-Nebraska and the Leiter include nonverbal instructions and use pantomime as part of the administration process. This method allows these measures to be used with children with hearing impairments with a greater degree of confidence.

Nonverbal intelligence measures later became popular for use with children who do not speak English (the most popular language used by test developers). While English is the dominant language in the United States, for example, the United States continues to be a multilingual society. Just as the Army Beta was used to assess the intelligence of waves of immigrants after World War I, so too modern nonverbal tests of intelligence are attractive to psychologists who work in areas of the United States with large non-English-speaking populations.

Nonverbal measures can also be helpful for assessing children with significant speech or language impairments. A child or adolescent who may have lost speech due to a head injury may be a good candidate for the use of nonverbal measures of intelligence. These three audiences—children who are non-English-speaking, hearing-impaired, and speech-impaired—provide a healthy demand for the use of nonverbal measures.

There is also a cadre of nonverbal intelligence assessment screeners. Some of the more well-known names here are the Raven Progressive

Matrices and Columbia Mental Maturity Scale. An overview of several multi-subtest measures follows.

UNIVERSAL NONVERBAL INTELLIGENCE TEST (UNIT)

The UNIT exemplifies the new genre of nonverbal tests that purports to assess higher-level cognitive abilities than the typical assessment of visualization/spatial/perceptual abilities (Bracken & McCallum, 1998). The theoretical model underlying the UNIT is hierarchical in nature with "g" at the apex. Their general intelligence is defined as "the ability to solve problems using memory and reasoning" (p. 12). The UNIT assess two abilities at the next level of the hierarchy (Stratum II, if you will); namely, memory and reasoning, two familiar factors on intelligence test batteries. Overall, Bracken and MacCallum are clearly trying to differentiate the UNIT from its predecessors by emphasizing the assessment of cognitive abilities that are closer to many theoretical traditions that posit a hierarchical arrangement of abilities with at least two strata.

Another clever attempt made by the UNIT is to differentiate abilities into "symbolic" and "nonsymbolic" domains. Symbolic subtests are simply those that use nonverbal stimuli and, yet, are amenable to or encourage verbal mediation (e.g., utilizing concrete stimuli in an analogical reasoning task). Nonsymbolic subtests then utilize abstract figural stimuli.

Standardization

The UNIT was standardized on a nationally representative sample of 2,100 children between the ages of 5 years, 0 months and 17 years, 11 months, 30 days. Stratification was accomplished using 1995 U.S. Census estimates. Stratification variables included child sex, race, Hispanic origin, geographic region, community size, classroom placement, special education services, and parental educational attainment as a measure of SES. Altogether 108 sites in 38 states were utilized (Bracken & McCallum, 1998). Overall match to stratification statistics was good, giving one confidence in the obtained scores.

Normalized standard scores are offered for subtests (mean = 10, SD = 3), and Memory, Reasoning, Symbolic, Nonsymbolic, and Full Scale composite scores (mean = 100, SD = 15).

Three administration options are offered; Abbreviated Battery (2 subtests), Standard Battery (4 subtests), or Extended Battery (6 subtests). The manual offers good detail regarding the oft-complex nonverbal administration procedures along with a thorough and clear treatise of scoring rules. A videotape gives thorough information regarding administration gestures and pantomime.

Reliability

Subtest internal consistency is good with coefficients typically in the .80s. Estimates for Mazes are the lowest (average = .64) with Object Memory second to lowest (.76). Cube Design has the highest average coefficient at .91, which is not surprising given the tried-and-true nature of the Block Design task. Separate internal consistency coefficients are provided for children with learning disabilities, mental retardation, intellectual giftedness, and speech and language impairments. Full Scale composite score internal consistency estimates are very good with a .96 for the Abbreviated Battery, .98 Standard Battery, and .98 Extended Battery.

Test-retest stability coefficients are lower, yielding a .79 Full Scale for the Abbreviated Battery, .84 Standard Battery, and .81 Extended Battery (coefficients corrected for restriction of range are higher). These coefficients likely more realistically reflect the stability that will be obtained in clinical practice. A finding of particular importance is that the stability of the Abbreviated Battery may be greater with increasing age. In fact, this battery was essentially unreliable between ages 8 and 10, where it yielded a Full Scale reliability coefficient of only .64. The Abbreviated Battery did yield a .81 at ages 5 to 7. For the most part other composite score stability coefficients are acceptable or quite good. Subtest stability coefficients can be quite variable for some age groups, occasionally yielding coefficients in the .60s. In fact, four of the subtest coefficients were in the .60s at ages 5 to 7 and one was .70. These results give one pause when making subtest interpretations, particularly for younger children.

Validity

Bracken and McCallum (1998) have written an easily readable and relatively thorough manual that provides at least the basic validity evidence. Several internal validity studies utilizing exploratory and confirmatory methods are included. Of greatest importance is that these studies subtantially inform interpretive practice. The most compelling finding from the confirmatory studies (which I think are the most relevant in this case since the authors clearly had an a prior structure in mind) is that a one-factor, general intelligence, model accounts well for the data. Therefore, in the interest of parsimony, the Full Scale composite should be valued more than others when interpreting the UNIT. It should be noted, however, that a Memory and Reasoning model also fit the data well, suggesting that this dichotomy may be relevant for some cases. These findings, however, do not reveal much about the nature of the Memory and Reasoning scales without comparisons to other measures of like constructs.

The theoretical model of the UNIT suggests several key criterion-related validity questions:

1. Does the Full Scale correlate at about .70 or greater with other composite scores from intelligence tests suggesting that it is a good measure of "g"?

2. Does the Memory scale correlate highly, at about .70 or greater with other memory composites?

3. Does the Reasoning scale correlate highly with other reasoning composites?

4. Does the Symbolic composite correlate significantly better with verbal composites than the nonsymbolic composite?

The answer to question 1 is a preliminary "yes." UNIT Full Scale correlates .71 (Extended Battery) with WISC-III Full Scale for a sample of children with LD, .72 for a sample with MR, .54 for a sample of Gifted (although this sample was severely restricted, so the corrected correlation of .88 is probably more accurate), and .53 for a Native American Sample. Moreover, UNIT scores correlated with W-J achievement scores at nearly the same level as WISC-III Full Scale for three samples. It should also be noted that UNIT Full Scale composite mean scores tend to be very similar to those of other intelligence tests used in these studies.

The answers to questions 2 and 3 are difficult to ascertain because correlational studies are offered for criterion tests that do not possess well-validated measures of memory (i.e., WISC-III, W-J Cog, K-BIT) or reasoning. One study stands as an exception in that the Raven's Progressive Matrices is considered to be the "gold standard" for cross-cultural studies of reasoning ability. The UNIT Extended Battery Full Scale correlated .71 with Raven's Total Test Score for a small sample of 27 children from Ecuador. Clearly, much more evidence needs to be gathered.

The WISC-III VCI serves as a good criterion measure for answering question 4. The obtained correlations for the four special samples identified earlier suggest that the symbolic/nonsymbolic distinction is questionable at the moment. The correlations between the Symbolic and VCI composites for the four samples were .45, .43, .00, and .40, whereas the correlations for the nonsymbolic and VCI were .37, .52, .28, and .32.

Summary

The UNIT is a promising addition to the armamentarium of psychologists who have to deal with an increasingly diverse audience of clients. While promising, the UNIT is in need of further validation in order to gain wide acceptance. The need for nonverbal instruments is, however, so substantial that the UNIT will likely find a number of uses even if all of its derived scores are not supported by future validation studies.

These future studies are more important for ensuring proper interpretation of the battery. At the moment the overall composite score appears to have enough evidence to be used routinely for interpretation. The other composite and subtest scores, while intuitively appealing, are not yet well enough understood to be routinely utilized in clinical practice.

Hiskey-Nebraska Tests of Learning Aptitude (HNTLA or Hiskey)

The Hiskey was designed specifically to assess the cognitive skills of deaf children and adolescents (Hiskey, 1966). The Hiskey-Nebraska age range extends from 2½ years through 17½ years. The Hiskey suggests the use of pantomined instructions for hearing-impaired individuals. There are five subtests that are administered to ages 3 to 10 and four subtests that are specific to ages 11 to 17. There are three subtests on the Hiskey that extend across all age ranges. Administration of the Hiskey takes approximately 45-50 minutes for an experienced examiner.

The procedures that were used for the selection of items were specified prior to test development and explicitly stated. Item selection criteria included:

1. Tasks should be similar to those that young children encounter in school.

2. The item had to be adaptable for use in a nonverbal test.

3. The item had to be able to be presented in such a way that directions could be given through simple pantomime.

4. The item had to be one that in previous research has been shown to yield high correlations with acceptable criteria of intelligence or learning ability.

5. The item had to be capable of being constructed and presented in such a way that the child could make a definite response, thus making the scoring objective and easily done.

6. The item had to be appealing and attactive to children.

7. The item should be capable of being scored without the score being based on time.

8. The difficulty of the item should appear to be within the age range of the standardization group.

9. The item had to be likely to show high discriminative capacity.

The seventh point about time is an interesting one. This criterion makes the Hiskey more of a power test than the WISC. It is in contrast to tests such as Object Assembly, where the only means of obtaining a high score is through quick performance. Hiskey clearly differentiated his test development philosophy from Wechsler on this point. The Hiskey does, however, use tried-and-true items. No attempts were made to develop novel item types. The use of novel items would not have been consistent with item specification 4. One weakness of the Hiskey may be a lack of creativity in item development.

The Hiskey is designed to be a broad-based measure of intellectual skills. For this reason, the test consists of a number of subtests as opposed to using only one- or two-item formats to assess a child's intelligence. In this way the Hiskey is analogous to the WISC in that numerous types of "languages" may be used by the child or adolescent to express his or her intelligence.

The subtests of the Hiskey include the following:

1. Bead Patterns—ages 3–10
2. Memory for Color—ages 3–10
3. Picture Identification—ages 3–10

4. Picture Association—ages 3–10

5. Paper Folding—ages 3–10

6. Visual Attention Span—all ages

7. Block Patterns—all ages

8. Completion of Drawings—all ages

9. Memory for Digits—ages 11 and above

10. Puzzle Blocks—ages 11 and above

11. Picture Analogy—ages 11 and above

12. Spatial Reasoning—ages 11 and above

Standardization

The Hiskey was standardized on 1,079 deaf children and 1,074 hearing children between the ages of 2½ years and 17½ years. Specific information on the standardization sample of the Hiskey is lacking. An attempt was made to stratify the hearing sample based on the 1960 U.S. Census data using parental occupation. Beyond that, there is little evidence that systematic efforts were made to match Census Bureau or other statistics for gender, type or severity of hearing impairment, geographic region, or ethnic group or race. The normative sample of the Hiskey is lacking by modern standards.

The scaling of the Hiskey is consistent with the early Binet tradition. Early versions of the Binet emphasized the interpretation of mental ages (or learning ages for hearing-impaired children) for interpretive purposes. Hiskey (1966) argued that mental ages were more readily understood and interpreted than standard scores or percentile ranks. This statement was perhaps true back in the 1960s as the Binet at that time also emphasized mental ages in computing scores. Mental ages are derived for each of the Hiskey subtests and a median mental age is computed as an overall rating of intelligence. This median age rating can then be converted to a deviation IQ (DIQ), which uses the traditional Binet metric of a mean of 100 and standard deviation of 16. The computation of scores is slightly different when the deaf norms are used. For the deaf norms, the median learning age in this case can be converted to a learning quotient (LQ) using the old ratio IQ approach, the forerunner of modern standard scores (see Chapter 5). The formula for computing a LQ is LQ = LA/CA × 100. As is apparent, the Hiskey scaling technology is also far behind current standards.

Reliability

Split-half reliability coefficients are reported in the Hiskey manual with the use of the Spearman-Brown correction formula (Hiskey, 1966). Split-half internal consistency coefficients are generally very high. The lowest one reported for the composite score is .90. Test-retest data for the Hiskey is not reported in the manual nor is information on standard errors of measurement or individual subtest reliability. One study that evaluated the use of the Hiskey for 41 hearing-impaired children and adolescents produced a test-retest coefficient for the composite score of .79 after a 1-year interval (Watson, 1983).

Validity

The manual produces strong evidence of concurrent validity for the Hiskey for hearing children. The 1966 manual reports a correlation of .82 with the 1949 WISC and .86 for younger children and .78 for older children with Form LM the 1960 edition of the Stanford-Binet. Further information on validity is not provided in the manual. A recent study by Phelps and Branyan (1988) with 31 hearing-impaired children ages 6 through 10 yielded LQ correlations of .66 with the WISC-R Performance score, .57 with the K-ABC Nonverbal scale, and .67 with the Leiter. An investigation by Watson and Goldgar (1985) with 71 hearing-impaired children ages 5 through 18 yielded a correlation of .85 between the LQ and the WISC-R Full Scale. The Hiskey yielded a greater number of extreme scores (scores < 70 and > 119), which caused the authors to advise cautious use of the Hiskey.

Kennedy and Hiltonsmith (1988) correlated the Hiskey with the K-ABC Nonverbal scale and the Pictorial Test of Intelligence (PTI). The Hiskey correlation with the K-ABC was .72 and with the PTI .80. The Hiskey yielded 10 scores above a standard score of 116. The K-ABC yielded the lowest scores, but the authors stated that this result is to be expected because of the out-of-date (and, therefore, softer) Hiskey and PTI norms. An independent factor analytic investigation by Bolton (1978) found that the factor structures of the Hiskey differed for hearing and deaf children for the 3- to 10-year-old age group. Specifically, the Memory for Colors and Block pattern subtest loaded on different factors for the hearing and deaf children. Unfortunately the Hiskey does not seem to be the recipient of a great deal of recent research interest.

Summary

The Hiskey-Nebraska Test of Learning Aptitude is a multisubtest comprehensive intellectual assessment battery designed specifically for hearing-impaired children and adolescents between the ages of 2½ and 17½ years. The Hiskey is primarily an adaptation of earlier editions of the Stanford-Binet. In fact, some of the items can be traced directly to the Binet scales. The Hiskey was the first of its genre in that it was specifically defined for the deaf population, making it particularly attractive for use with this group of children. In many ways, however, the Hiskey is also wedded to earlier intelligence tests and earlier Stanford-Binet assessment technology in particular. The standardization and scaling procedures used by the Hiskey would not be acceptable today. The manual may have been adequately prepared for the 1960s, but does not meet modern standards of assessment practices. For all practical purposes, in the light of current developments in noverbal intellectual assessment, the Hiskey is psychometrically inadequate and cannot be recommended for use. It is primarily of historical interest in that it was the most broad-based nonverbal assessment battery available. There are currently available other broad-based nonverbal measures that are

excellent alternatives to the Hiskey, such as the Leiter-R described next.

LEITER INTERNATIONAL PERFORMANCE SCALE— REVISED (LEITER-R)

The Leiter-R (Roid & Miller, 1997) is one of the most venerable of nonverbal intelligence tests. This measure was revised in 1948 and most recently in 1997 (Roid & Miller, 1997). The Leiter-R, like the UNIT and many other new tests, attempts to capitalize on the recent work of theoreticians who emphasize hierarchical approaches to intelligence. The new measure assesses "g" as well as visualization, reasoning, memory, and attention abilities via 20 subtests. Reasoning subtests include Classification, Sequential Order, Repeated Patterns, and Design Analogies. Visualization subtests include Matching, Figure-Ground, Form Completion, Picture Context, Paper Folding, and Figure Rotation. Memory subtests include Memory Span (forward), Memory Span (reverse), Spatial Memory, Visual Coding (symbol and digit), Associative Memory, Associative Delayed Memory, Immediate Recognition, and Delayed Recognition. The Attention subtests are twofold, including Attention-Sustained and Attention-Divided. This total battery clearly represents the most broad-based assessment of cognitive abilities via nonverbal means. The battery is made more manageable by separating the Visualization and Reasoning Battery (VR) from the Attention and Memory Battery (AM). Of course, a complete Leiter-R assessment requires more time. Completion of all four domains probably requires well over an hour, and perhaps an hour and a half or more of administration time.

Further testimony to the broad-based nature of the Leiter-R is its inclusion of four behavior rating scales for the examinee, parents, teachers, and a self-report for the examinee. Some of the subscales of these measures, which differ by informant, include Attention, Activity Level, Sociability, Energy and Feelings, Mood and Regulation, Anxiety, Adaptation, Organization/ Impulsivity, and Temperament.

The Leiter-R offers all of the traditional scores expected, including subtest (mean = 10, SD = 3), domain composite (mean = 100, SD = 15), and overall composite (mean = 100, SD = 15). This scale does, however, also offer latent trait derived scaled scores (called "growth" scores) for assessing change over the course of development. These scores are conceptually similar to age equivalents, or other developmental scores, with the noteworthy exception that they have interval as opposed to ordinal scale properties (see Chapter 5). The interval scale characteristics of this metric thus allow the clinician to gauge whether or not a child's *rate of cognitive development* is stable, accelerating, or decelerating. This metric may be particularly useful for children with disabilities who are closely monitored for progress in intensive intervention programs (e.g., residential care).

Of course, the stimulus content of the Leiter-R is far more modern than that of its predecessors. Moreover, the now prototypical easel administration format is utilized.

Standardization

The Leiter-R was standardized in the 1990s based on 1993 U.S. Census population estimates. The sample included 1,719 children ranging in age from 2 years, 0 months to 20 years, 11 months. The typical stratification variables were utilized including sex, race, age, and SES with a relatively close match to population estimates being obtained. In addition, data were collected on 692 children with special needs (e.g., children with speech impairment, hearing impairment, motor impairment, cognitive delay, ADHD, LD, and ESL students) in order to collect numerous validation studies, including those aimed at diagnostic differentation between these children and children without special needs.

Reliability

Psychometric properties for the Leiter-R are "competitive" in that internal consistency and stability estimates are similar to those for other tests such as the UNIT. Domain and overall composite IQ score internal consistency coefficients are generally in the high .80s to low .90s. Subtest internal consistency coefficients are typically in the .80s as well.

Test-retest coefficients for the domains and overall composite are generally high as well. These same coefficients for the Memory and Attention composites are somewhat lower, but generally sufficient for clinical purposes. The Memory Process value was .78 and the Attention composite was .85.

Validity

Correlations between the original Leiter and intelligence scales such as the Stanford-Binet Form LM have always been consistently high. In a review of literature, Ratcliffe and Ratcliffe (1979) found a median correlation of .77 for 13 concurrent validity investigations.

The Leiter-R manual provides a generous amount of validity evidence that is competitive with the UNIT and others. Several studies of classification accuracy including children with mental retardation, academic giftedness, learning disabilities, and ADHD are provided. These studies, however, only tried to determine the ability of the scale to accurately classify cases in comparison to the norm, not in comparison to one another. In other words, the more difficult classification task of differentiating clinical samples was not studied. Given this limited mission the Leiter-R did an excellent job of differentiating mental retardation from normality and was relatively poor at differentiating LD from typical development. This latter finding, however, is consistent with the well-known difficulty that all clinicians and instruments have in identifying this population. As expected, the cognitive scales did not do a good job of classifying cases of learning disability, but the addition of the Examiner Rating Scale Cognitive/Social Composite significantly improved the correct classification rate. Clearly, behavior rating scales are better than intelligence tests for making the ADHD diagnosis. Taken altogether, these classification studies suggest that the Leiter-R is similar to well-known and valued intelligence tests.

A very strong correlation of .86 between the Leiter-R and WISC-III Full Scale IQ is reported in the manual for a sample of 122 cases. In addition, the Leiter-R mean in this study only differed by 3 points (lower) from the WISC-III, which is within the realm of predictability given the Flynn effect (see Chapter 3). Unfortunately, the correlation between the other Leiter-R composites and the WISC-III Index scores is not reported. In similar fashion the correlations between the Leiter-R Full IQ and WIAT, WJ-R, and WRAT-3 achievement test results are also high, ranging from .62 to .82 for several small samples. Correlations with group-administered achievement tests are somewhat lower. Again, however, we are prevented from knowing the criterion-related validity of the various Leiter-R composites as they were also not reported for these samples.

Exploratory factor analytic results are reported but the value of this procedure seems questionable since the Leiter-R is clearly based on a priori theory. Fortunately, some confirmatory models were also tested. Generally speaking these results echo those of the UNIT in that the one-factor model consistently emerges across age groups as a relatively good fit to the data. These results, combined with those of the criterion-related validity studies, suggest that the Leiter-R is a good measure of psychometric "g" through nonverbal means.

In direct contrast, support for the other composites is less compelling. We have no evidence available from the criterion-related validity studies and a four-factor hierarchical CFA model (Fluid Reasoning, Broad Visualization, Attention, and Memory with "g") did not "fit" as well. Three five-factor models also did not fit significantly better than a one-factor model. I should

make it clear, however, that my interpretation of these results may differ from those of the authors, which is not unreasonable, given the lack of hard-and-fast rules for interpreting various CFA fit indices and residuals.

We are seeing a trend here. Both the UNIT and Leiter-R need additional criterion-related validity studies, utilizing the equivalent of "gold standard" measures of reasoning, visualization, memory, and so on, in order to help clarify the results of CFA studies. Still other validation approaches may be conducted to give clinicians greater confidence that the domain composite scores are measuring that which they purport to measure.

Exploratory factor analyses of the Examiner, Parent, Teacher, and Self-Rating scales suggest that two factors underly these instruments. The authors named the factors Cognitive/Social and Emotions/Regulation. It is difficult to imagine, however, that four rating scales utilizing different informants could produce the same two factors given the differences in factor structure commonly found between adult and child ratings and the known differences in contexts and accuracy of raters (Kamphaus & Frick, 1996). More validity evidence would be welcomed for the rating scales. For example, no criterion-related validity studies are reported.

The authors did make efforts to identify and eliminate problems with bias. A study by Flemmer and Roid (1997) studied 10 Leiter-R subtests and found significant differences on 3 between adolescents identified as either "Euro-American" or Hispanic.

Summary

This version of the Leiter is far superior to its predecessors. The Leiter-R is clearly based on a thorough and thoughtful test-development process that attempted to establish fairness and expand the range of abilities and behaviors assessed. It is a complex instrument; in fact, it may be more appropriately described as a system that possesses a large package of stimulus materials and easels and numerous record and rating forms.

Although daunting at first the examiner in need of such an assessment should try to master at least a portion of the Leiter-R.

On the other hand, this version is so different from its predecessor that much needs to be learned about its validity. While the overall composite produces a measure of general intelligence comparable to other multi-subtest intelligence batteries, the validity of its various domains, and subtests for that matter, requires much more study in order to guide appropriate interpretive practice.

COMPREHENSIVE TEST OF NONVERBAL INTELLIGENCE (CTONI)

The CTONI (Hammill, Pearson, & Wiederholt, 1996) seems streamlined in comparison to both the UNIT and Leiter-R. This impression is immediate upon lifting the test kit, which is efficiently packaged in a lightweight cardboard box. It seems efficient compared to the substantial canvas bags needed to hold all of the pieces of the aforementioned competitors. The CTONI is normed for ages 6 years, 0 months through 18 years, 11 months.

In this small package, however, is included six subtests designed to measure three abilities: analogical reasoning, categorical classification, and sequential reasoning. All of these constructs could be easily subsumed under fluid abilities. The six subtests of the CTONI—Pictorial Analogies, Geometric Analogies, Pictorial Categories, Geometric Categories, Pictorial Sequences, and Geometric Sequences—provide a balance between pictorial and abstract stimuli. The composites offered are the overall Nonverbal Intelligence, Pictorial Nonverbal Intelligence, and Geometric Nonverbal Intelligence. Both subtest and composite standard scores utilize the familiar means of 10 and 100 and standard deviations of 3 and 15, respectively.

Administration of the CTONI is efficient. There are no manipulatives to be concerned with, keeping administration time to far less than an hour.

Standardization

The test was normed on 2,129 children from 23 states. Sex, ethnicity, community size, family income, parental educational attainment, disability status, and geographic region were utilized as stratification variables in order to match U.S. Census estimates. The match to U.S. Census data was generally good (van Lingen, 1998).

Reliability

Internal consistency and test-retest reliability estimates tend to be in the .80s and .90s as is the case for similar measures. Internal consistency estimates also did not vary for several ethnic and disability status groups, nor did they differ by sex.

Validity

Criterion-related validity was studied for a sample of 43 children with LD who were administered the WISC-III and PPVT-R. The correlation between the Nonverbal Intelligence composite and WISC-III Full Scale was very high at .81; however, the mean scores for the sample are not reported so conclusions about *agreement* cannot be made. This lack of information is very problematic for the practitioner.

Generally speaking, I perceive the validity section of the CTONI manual as inadequate compared to those of the UNIT or Leiter-R. The sections on concurrent and factor analytic validity could not even be described as minimal. Alternatively, it should be noted that the CTONI is intuitively appealing causing external reviewers to suggest that the measure holds promise.

Summary

Aylward, for example, (1998) concluded:

The combination of pictorial and geometric content, absence of purely perceptual-performance matching or gestalt closure tasks, or better normative data are potential advantages over existing nonverbal tests such as

Raven's Progressive Matrices . . . or Martix Analogies Test—Extended Form. (p. 312)

Van Lingen (1998) also sees promise by concluding:

Both manual and record forms are well designed for ease of use. . . . Other issues, such as limited evidence on validity, will be amended as investigators conduct further research using the CTONI. (p. 314)

I only wish that other validity research had come to light prior to this writing. It has not, meaning that the clinician has to decide, based on local experience, whether or not the use of the CTONI can be supported by acumen in lieu of evidence.

WISC-III
Performance Scale

The WISC-R Performance Scale has traditionally been one of the most popular tests for use in the assessment of children with hearing impairments (Levine, 1974). This fact is congruent with the original design of the Wechsler series. Wechsler appears to be well aware of the fact that an intelligence test had to provide flexible administration options especially in assessing individuals in a multicultural society. According to Sullivan and Burley (1990), "the WISC-R performance scale is an excellent test for use with school-aged hearing impaired children" (p. 784).

It is typically recommended that six or seven subtests of the Performance scale be administered when assessing a hearing-impaired child. Hearing-impaired children seem to have particular difficulty with the Picture Arrangement and Coding subtests. This fact is not surprising given the lengthy oral instructions on these tests, particularly those on Coding, which require a good deal of verbal comprehension. The problem of verbal comprehension may also interfere with valid administration of the Symbol Search test.

It has been recommended that if these tests seem inappropriate that the Performance score may be prorated so that the Performance scale is effectively serving as a four-subtest nonverbal short form (Sullivan & Burley, 1990).

Standardization

Typically the regular WISC-III norms are used for computing the Performance IQ when the Performance scale is used as a nonverbal test of intelligence. Alternatively, a nonrepresentative but large sample of norms collected for hearing-impaired children is available for the WISC-R and has been used (Anderson & Sisco, 1977). The utility of these hearing-impaired norms, however, has been questioned and their practical utility not clarified (Sullivan & Burley, 1990).

Reliability and Validity

Separate validity evidence for the use of the WISC-R for hearing-impaired children has typically been supportive. The mean WISC-R Performance score for hearing-impaired children, however, is somewhat lower than for the standardization sample (standard score = 95). This mean is also slightly lower than, for example, the average K-ABC Nonverbal scale for hearing-impaired children (median = 98). The more substantial level of verbal comprehension that is required on the part of the child on tests such as Coding may account for this small difference (Sullivan & Burley, 1990).

The only study available for the WISC-III produced higher PIQ scores (Wechsler, 1991). This relatively small sample of 30 children with severe and profound hearing impairments achieved a Verbal score of 81.1, Performance score of 105.8, and Full Scale of 92.2. The Coding and Symbol Search subtests did yield lower scores than many of the Performance subtests, resulting in a Perceptual Organization Index of 106.0 and Processing Speed Index of 101.4. It remains to be seen whether or not these data will be replicated.

Summary

The WISC-III Performance Scale is likely to continue to be a popular nonverbal test of intelligence. One caution is that the WISC-III Performance subtests do seem to require substantially more verbalization on the part of the examiner and verbal comprehension on the part of the child than some nonverbal measures. More importantly, little validity evidence is available to support the use of the PIQ with children with hearing impairments.

K-ABC
Nonverbal Scale

Analogous to the inclusion of the Performance scale in the Wechsler series, the Kaufmans (Kaufman & Kaufman, 1983b) included a Nonverbal scale as part of the K-ABC development process. The K-ABC Nonverbal scale is a subset of K-ABC Mental Processing subtests that spans the ages of 4 to 12½ years. It is considered a "special short form of the mental processing composite, one that correlates quite well with this total score" (Kaufman & Kaufman, 1983c, p. 35). The test is designed for use with "deaf, hearing-impaired, speech or language-disordered, autistic, and non-English-speaking children" (Kaufman & Kaufman, 1983b, p. 35).

The subtests comprising the K-ABC Nonverbal scale include Face Recognition (age 4 only), Hand Movements, Triangles, Matrix Analogies, Spatial Memory, and Photo Series (ages 6 and up only).

Given that the instructions to the K-ABC require litle oral expression on the part of the examiner and verbal comprehension on the part of the child, this test can be administered readily using pantomime and gestures. Several studies (Porter & Kirby, 1986; Ulissi, Brice, & Gibbons, 1985) have shown no specific problems with the administration of the Nonverbal scale to hearing-impaired children.

Standardization

The K-ABC Nonverbal scale norms are derived from the same national standardization sample that was selected so as to meet 1980 U.S. Census data (see Chapter 10). The featured score for the K-ABC nonverbal scale is a composite with the mean of 100 and standard deviation of 15. Other derived scores for the Nonverbal scale such as percentile ranks are also included as part of the regular K-ABC manuals and software.

Reliability

Internal consistency coefficients for the K-ABC Nonverbal scale are strong, ranging from a .87 coefficient for 4-year-olds to a .94 for a number of the older age groups. The average coefficient for school-aged children is .93. One study of the test-retest reliability of the K-ABC Nonverbal scale reported a coefficient of .87 (Kaufman & Kaufman, 1983b).

Validity

There is substantial evidence from the K-ABC *Interpretive Manual* (Kaufman & Kaufman, 1983b) that the Nonverbal scale correlates highly with the Mental Processing composite of the K-ABC. This finding holds true even when the coefficients are corrected for spurious overlap. Correlations between the nonverbal short form and the Mental Processing composite range from .88 at age 4 to .94 at several of the older age groups. Studies by Ulyssi et al. (1985), Ham (1985), and Porter & Kirby (1986) all yielded significant correlations (typically in the .60s and above) between the K-ABC and other nonverbal intelligence measures. These three investigations also yielded mean K-ABC Nonverbal composites for hearing-impaired children ranging from 97 to 101, suggesting that the normal distribution of intelligence for hearing-impaired children is strikingly similar to that of the population at large when using the K-ABC Nonverbal scale.

Although the samples for these studies were relatively small, the trend is clear. Hearing-impaired children have relatively normal IQs as assessed by the K-ABC Nonverbal scale.

The Porter and Kirby study also tested the utility of pantomimed versus sign language administrations of the K-ABC Nonverbal scale. The means for the pantomimed and sign language administration groups were 98.8 and 96.8, respectively. For this relatively small sample, this difference was not statistically significant. These results argue for using the K-ABC Nonverbal scale as it was originally designed, in pantomime.

Summary

The K-ABC Nonverbal scale carries on the tradition of using portions of a larger intelligence test battery as nonverbal intelligence measures. The K-ABC Nonverbal scale holds promise as a nonverbal intelligence measure for a variety of populations (Kamphaus & Reynolds, 1987). The relevance of the nearly 20-year-old K-ABC norms, however, is questionable.

DIFFERENTIAL ABILITY SCALES

The DAS takes a similar route to the K-ABC by including a Nonverbal scale as part of a larger test battery. The rationale for use of the DAS Nonverbal scale is given in the following quote:

> *If the examiner judges that subtests involving verbal presentation or response may not be reliable and valid measures of a particular child's ability, a briefer battery may be administered in order to obtain a special nonverbal composite score in place of the GCA score. . . . shy preschoolers, those reluctant to talk to an unfamiliar adult, children with delayed language or speech problems, elective mutes, children from culturally different backgrounds, children whose primary language is not English, and children with middle ear infections or suspected hearing loss frequently are referred for assessment. Directions for the subtests of the special nonverbal scale may be conveyed through gestures, and the child's responses require only pointing, drawing, or manipulation of objects. (Elliott, Daniel, & Guiton, 1990, p. 17)*

The DAS subtests that may be used to compute a Nonverbal composite at each age include the following:

1. Ages 2.6 through 4.11—Block Building, Picture Similarities
2. Ages 3.6 through 7.11—Pattern Construction, Copying, Picture Similarities (i.e., the Nonverbal cluster)
3. Ages 5.0 through 17.11—Pattern Construction, Recall of Designs, Matrices, Sequential and Quantitative Reasoning

Standardization

The norms for the special nonverbal composite (SNV) are derived from the regular DAS norming program. The Nonverbal composite yields a standard score with a mean of 100 and standard deviation of 15. (See the earlier parts of Chapter 13 for a detailed description of the DAS normative sample and the various scores available for the DAS.)

Reliability and Validity

Special Nonverbal composite score reliabilities are generally high. The mean Nonverbal composite reliability coefficient for ages 3.6 through 5.11 is .89; for ages 6 through 17, the mean is .94. The reliability of the two-subtest composite for age 2.6 through 4.11 is somewhat lower, averaging .81. The SNV is a high correlate of the GCA. Correlations between the SNV and GCA scores at their lowest are .85 for ages 2.6 through 3.5 and .88 for ages 3.6 through 5.11 suggesting good concurrent validity for the SNV score (Elliott, 1990b). Separate validity evidence for the Special Nonverbal composite particularly for hearing-impaired or non-English-speaking children is currently lacking.

Summary

As a Nonverbal scale of intelligence, the Special Nonverbal scale of the DAS is relatively brief at some ages yet it remains as a multisubtest battery with a variety of item types that may be used for assessing intelligence and limiting the confounding effects of verbal and hearing issues. Early reliability studies of this specialized composite are favorable. Given the recency of the publication of the DAS, it is not suprising that validity evidence is lacking. Given the norming and reliability properties of the DAS Nonverbal scale, this scale requires further study and consideration for at least trial clinical use. At this point, the DAS nonverbal scale does show promise as another useful alternative in the area of Nonverbal intellectual assessment.

COLUMBIA MENTAL MATURITY SCALE

The Columbia Mental Maturity Scale (Burgemeister, Blumm, & Lorge, 1972) is designed to assess the "general reasoning ability" of children from 3½ to 9 years, 11 months of age. The test is designed for children who may have communication or motor problems, including those with problems, such as mental retardation, hearing loss, speech impairment, or cerebral palsy. The test does not require the child to read or speak English and so it is advised as a nonverbal measure for assessing intelligence. The test consists of 92 items each presented on cards with 3 to 5 drawings per card. These items are divided among eight levels where the child is administered a set of items at an appropriate level designed for his or her chronological age. However, additional levels of items may be administered depending upon the child's score earned on the first level administered. The stimulus cards used depict drawings where the child is asked which drawing does not belong in the set. The objects used on the cards are intended to be familiar to American children.

The feature score of the Columbia is an age deviation score (ADS). The ADS is a standard score with mean of 100 and standard deviation of 16. ADS scores may be converted to percentile ranks and stanines. The Columbia also offers a maturity index (MI). This is in effect an age equivalent developmental norm.

Standardization

The Columbia standardization sample is now somewhat dated, since it was collected in the late 1960s and early 1970s and based on 1960s U.S. Census data. At the time, the standardization sample of the Columbia was first rate, consisting of 2,600 children, which in turn included 200 children in each age group of the Columbia. The sample was stratified based on geographic region, race, sex, and parental occupation.

Reliability

Considering that this is a single subtest measure, reliability estimates for the Columbia are quite good. Split-half reliability coefficients are high for most age groups, ranging from .85 to .91. They are more consistently in the mid-80s range between the ages of 6 and 9 years. Test-retest reliability coefficients are slightly lower, ranging from .84 at ages 5 and 6 to .86 at age 4.

Validity

The Columbia depends primarily on correlations of other tests as evidence of its validity. An extensive study in the manual showing correlations between the Columbia and the 1964 edition of the Stanford Achievement Test showed moderate correlations between the two batteries. Most of these correlations were in the 40s, 50s, and 60s. Correlations between the Columbia and the Stanford-Binet Intelligence Scale Form LM for a sample of 52 preschool and first-grade pupils yielded a coefficient of .84.

Summary

The Columbia is a rather unique single subtest measure of "reasoning ability" for children of ages 3½ to 9 years of age. At the time of its publication in 1972, this test typically exceeded standards of psychometric quality for clinical instruments. At this point, however, the Columbia is thoroughly in need of revision. It would be especially desireable to have a revised standardization sample.

RAVEN'S PROGRESSIVE MATRICES

As the name implies, the Raven's is comprised of a set of figural matrices that may be used as a measure of general intelligence. In fact, the Raven's is the defacto standard for cross-cultural and cross-national studies of intelligence (see Chapter 3). Given the minimal language involvement and requirement of this item type, this test is particularly suited to assessing the intelligence of individuals with hearing impairment, language disabilities, and children whose native language is not English.

The two most popular matrices are the Standard and the Coloured. The Coloured Progressive Matrice includes 30 items and the Standard Progressive Matrices contain 60 items. Each item consists of 2×2 or 3×3 figural matrices presented in a multiple-choice format where the child has to identify the missing element.

The Standard and Coloured matrices raw scores can be converted to percentile ranks. These percentile conversions are available for ages $6\frac{1}{2}$ to $16\frac{1}{2}$. Percentile ranks can also be converted to other derived scores such as standard scores. This conversion, however, is not very effective at the tails of the distribution. This conversion of percentile ranks to standard scores will not yield a very wide range of standard scores below 70 and above 130.

Standardization

Both the Standard and Coloured Progressive Matrices were recently renormed in the United States (Raven, 1986). This renorming, however, was somewhat unusual in the sense that this 1986 publication does not describe a set of national norms for the Raven but rather a collection of norm tables from 10 local norming investigations conducted in various areas of the United States. There was an attempt to provide combined norms for the United States for the Standard and Coloured matrices. However, descriptions of how these norms were derived, including descriptions of socioeconomic status, geographic, racial, age, gender, and other representations of the samples, are not included in the manual. The description given by Raven (1986), with its lack of detail, leads one to believe that these were more or less "convenience" samples. Certainly, more detail is needed on the description of these samples to help clinicians understand the value of using these norm tables.

Reliability

Reliability data are now presented in the 1986 Raven manual showing adequate reliability for research purposes, which is the primary use of this measure.

Validity

Validity evidence for the Raven's extends primarily from correlational studies with other tests. A correlational study with the California Achievement Test yielded a coefficient of .76 with the Standard Progressive Matrices. A correlation of .69 was found with the Standard Matrices and WISC-R Full Scale score and .61 between the Coloured Matrices and WISC-R Full Scale score for a sample of Mexican American students.

Summary

Although the Raven Standard and Coloured Matrices have a long history, they have not been the beneficiary of continuing sophisticated psychometric development. The 1986 Compendium of local norms is an example of this problem. These norms may be perfectly adequate for users of the Raven. However, there is not enough information provided to determine whether or not this is the case. Given such a paucity of technical information, the Raven should likely be considered as a research instrument, an area in which it has enjoyed a great deal of historical popularity. This status should change, however, once the psychometric properties and/or information on the Raven's become more compelling.

MATRIX ANALOGIES TEST

Yet another variation on the Raven's theme is this modern version of a figural matrices test by Naglieri (1985d). There are two forms of the Matrix Analogies Test: a short form consisting of 34 multiple-choice items and an expanded form consisting of 64 multiple-choice items. The age range of the Matrix Analogies Test is from 5 through 16.

The uses for this measure are the same as those for tests of figural matrices mentioned earlier. Raw scores on the expanded form of the Matrix Analogies Test can be converted to standard scores with a mean of 100 and standard deviation of 15. These scores in turn can be converted to age equivalents and percentile ranks. Raw scores on the short form can be converted to percentiles, stanines, and age equivalents.

Standardization

The expanded form was administered to 5,718 children in the United States in the early 1980s. The sample was stratified according to U.S. Census statistics by race, sex, age, geographic region, community size, and socioeconomic status. The match between the sample and Census statistics is adequate.

Reliability

Internal consistency reliability of the expanded form is generally high, ranging from .88 to .95.

As is the case with several of the measures discussed previously, test-retest coefficients are considerably lower. Test-retest reliability of the total test score over a 1-month interval is only .77.

Validity

The validity of the expanded form has been assessed primarily via correlations of other tests such as the WISC-R. Correlations with the WISC-R for a sample of normal children were .41, for Native American children .43, and for hearing-impaired children, .68. Expanded form correlations with the Wide Range Achievement Test Reading test were .45. Several have found the expanded form to produce consistently lower scores than the WISC-R Performance Scale score. The trend across studies is for the expanded form to score about 10 points lower than the Performance score of the WISC-R (Naglieri & Prewett, 1990).

Summary

The Matrix Analogies Test, particularly the expanded form, follows in the tradition of the use of figural matrices as a means of assessing the intelligence of children with communication problems, motor problems, and children for whom English is not their first language. The Matrix Analogies Test, however, is considerably more modern than many of its predecessors. Its norming sample is more recent, larger, and more psychometrically sophisticated. If one is going to use single subtest screeners of intelligence for a particular purpose, or is interested in conducting research on the mental processing of figural matrices by children, the Matrix Analogies Test expanded form would be a viable candidate for such endeavors.

CONCLUSIONS

Much has changed in the nonverbal intelligence assessment field—for the good. Several new comprehensive measures are available, all with some preliminary validity evidence. Certainly, newer measures take a broader sampling of cognitive abilities, and norming evidence and reliability evidence is impressive. Clinicians can now have greater confidence in the use of such measures for limited English speakers in the United States and children with speech, hearing, and language impairments.

The major question remaining to be answered is whether or not the new measures adequately measure multiple intellectual abilities such as memory and reasoning. It is too early to know the answer to this question. In the interim, one can interpret the composite scores of many of these new tests as measures of general intelligence. This development alone is a substantial improvement over the technology available previously.

Some of the newer nonverbal tests such as the Leiter-R and UNIT and nonverbal short forms of tests such as the DAS and K-ABC are clearly better alternatives than utilizing the Performance scale of the WISC-III. The availability of high-quality nonverbal measures makes the tendency to use the Wechsler scales as the default measure with all referrals a practice to be abandoned.

CHAPTER SUMMARY

- Nonverbal intelligence tests are best considered as simply a clever and unusual means for assessing the same general intelligence, not a different "nonverbal intelligence" construct.

- The Hiskey was designed specifically to assess the cognitive skills of deaf children and adolescents.

- The UNIT purports to assess higher level cognitive abilities such as reasoning.

- The standardization and scaling procedures used by the Hiskey would not be acceptable today. The manual may have been adequately prepared for the 1960s, but it is in dire need of revision in order to meet modern standards of assessment practice.

- The psychometric properties of the Leiter International Performance Scale—Revised generally meet modern standards.

- The K-ABC Nonverbal Scale holds promise as a nonverbal intelligence measure for a variety of populations although its norms are dated.

- Given the strong norming and reliability properties of the DAS Nonverbal Scale, this scale warrants further study and consideration for at least trial clinical use.

- The WISC-III Performance scale is likely the most popular nonverbal test of intelligence in spite of its limitations. Now the sheer number of modern alternatives suggest that this practice should be abandoned.

CHAPTER 17

Modern Interpretation Methods

We observe that it is a warm day, and there is not much doubt about it until we read the thermometer. Then we find that our impression of warmth is modified by humidity, air currents, amount of clothing, time of day, degree of activity, season, and the like. A warm day in winter would be a cold one in summer. A warm day in between two cooler days is pyschologically warmer than one between two hotter days. Altitude makes a difference, as does one's mental or physical state at the time. A day too warm for office work may be cool enough for tennis; one cool enough for hiking may be too cool for sailing. We re-examine the (ordinary) thermometer. We thought it was reasonably accurate; but it is not so accurate as a clinical thermometer, nor so sensitive as the delicate thermopiles of the physics laboratory. We find it is difficult to estimate temperature without regard to altitude, barometric pressure, humidity and other related variables. Nevertheless, we return to the original conclusion, that it is a warm day, and this general observation is agreed to by those present with due regard for the degree of accuracy warranted by the circumstances, then, that governs the crudity of the refinement of the measurement for the purpose in hand. It becomes important to effect a compromise between that degree of crudity which allows too wide a margin of error of observation

and judgment on the one hand, and that degree of refinement which makes such observation and judgment impracticable on the other. (Doll, 1953, p. 60)

CHAPTER QUESTIONS

How important is background information for the useful interpretation of scores?

How can the validity of interpretations be maximized by using psychological science?

How valid are commonly made intelligence test interpretations?

The extent of "crudity" to employ in test interpretation remains the central conundrum for the psychologist. And was said well by Doll (1953), the special circumstances of each assessment, such as the differing needs for diagnosis, treatment planning, and establishing prognosis, all must be met. In addition, the context of the client's life, akin to the relationship of humidity to perceptions of temperature, affects interpretation. The fourth child in a family of academically gifted children may be perceived as cognitively delayed if his overall intelligence composite is a mere 100. On the contrary, a hard-working person of average general intellectual ability may seem precocious if she attends a college with an easy curriculum. In other words, we must carefully consider contextual variables such as career choice, educational aspirations, educational history, curriculum demands, peer competitors, sibling performance, cultural demands, linguistic competencies, medical history, and numerous other qualitative variables prior to judging the appropriate "crudity" of our conclusions. For this reason I use the term *integrative* or *integrate* with some frequency throughout this chapter in order to emphasize the necessity of making interpretations in the light of knowledge of environmental contexts.

Psychologists have often been criticized for failure to consider context and for reifying intelligence test results (Stanovich, 1999). This latter tendency causes us to be more likely to error in the direction of overinterpretation of results. We may be tempted, or in fact solicited, to infer causality (etiology), prognosis, genetic or environmental contributions to test scores, potential curriculum choices, job placement, life-long enduring profiles or abilities, and capacity for happiness among other issues. We must now be more humble about our intelligence test results in order to prevent a public backlash that has already occured in some fields, such as learning disabilities (Stanovich, 1999)—a field where intelligence tests are falling into disuse for diagnostic purposes. One way of remaining humble and making interpretations that are consistent with the current state of technology is to try to achieve parsimony in the interpretive process, where the law of parsimony as it is applied to test interpretation is defined as: *in explaining an assessment result, no more assumptions should be made than necessary*. One way of striving for parsimony is to reduce the number of statistical and logical gyrations involved in the interpretive process. Another way of avoiding the overinterpretation

tendency is to more closely join our clinical decision making with measurement, developmental, cognitive, and intelligence science.

Test score inferences can be based on a continuum where theory-based inferences (be they formal psychological or informal theories born of everyday experiences and biases) are made at one extreme and scientifically based interpretations are made at the other. This chapter encourages the reader to move toward the scientific end point of this continuum. In doing so, I hope to create greater respect for intelligence test interpretive work. Clinical acumen that is the product of years of careful observation and rigorous habits of thought remains important. Such acumen, however, can be strengthened substantially by giving the clinician access to the results of thousands of additional cases that cannot be seen in several lifetimes of work. Realistically speaking, it is difficult for us to maintain rigorous thought processes in our everyday work. Our perspectives, and norms perhaps, are shaped and skewed by our clientele, which usually represents a limited range of typical abilities, referral problems, SES, ethnicity, geographic region, and other characteristics. I will now try to convince the reader to adopt an interpretive system that is integrative, parsimonius, and science-based.

HISTORICAL PRECEDENTS

Substandard Practices

Matarazzo (1990) identified some disturbing problems in the interpretive aspect of the assessment process, including a lack of knowledge of the psychometric properties of the tests that psychologists use (a science-based practice problem) and a lack of congruence between test results and other information about the client (an integration problem). Matarazzo (1990) offered the example of neuropsychologists who would conclude that a cognitive deficit was due to some traumatic injury without carefully checking the individual's prior academic records. He noted that these records sometimes revealed that patient test scores subsequent to an injury were low, just as had been the case when they were in school, long before the occurrence of the supposed insult. Matarazzo (1990) explained why substandard interpretion of psychological assessment instruments cannot continue to be widespread.

> These congressional and judicial decisions had a clear message for psychology: Given the human costs involved, in the event a mistake was made, society now wanted firmer evidence of the validity of opinions offered by psychologists in job hiring and in the schools. Society had spoken out 25 years ago that turning down a job applicant or placing a minority child or a poor child in a special education class for slow learners entailed human costs that were too high to be based solely on the professional belief of the consulting psychologist (or technician surrogate) that the tests, which formed a core part of his or her assessment decision, had been adequately validated. (p. 1001)

Many concerns are leading to the need to change traditional test development, selection, and interpretation practices. Now, for example, psychologists have to also consider the *consequences* of their conclusions (Messick, 1989). In fact, even the most reliable and valid measure of intelligence may still be used in a manner that does harm (Anastasi, 1988; Jensen, 1980; Matarazzo, 1990; Thorndike, 1990). In addition, the science of psychology and the politics of health care delivery and reimbursement are creating a need for practitioners to have demonstrated validity evidence for their interpretations (see Chapter 7). Hence, the groundwork has been laid for a movement toward science-based interpretive practice.

Acting "in the Absence of Evidence"

Elsewhere, I have suggested that we pursue a greater reliance on a scientific approach to test interpretation (Kamphaus, 1998). This proposal was far from new—I was simply reinforcing the call of scientists (Dawes, 1995) and practice leaders (Bush, 1997) to return "back to the future" of test interpretation by reembracing the 1948 "Boulder scientist/practitioner model" of clinical psychology. One way of implementing a scientist/practitioner model is to develop practice guidelines for intellectual assessment just as has been attempted for psychotherapy practice (Clinton, McCormick, & Besteman, 1994). Practice guidelines for intelligence testing are probably not in our near future, but the revised *Standards for Educational and Psychological Testing* (AERA, APA, NCME, 1999) may be perceived as a significant step in that direction. In fact, the mere use of the term *standards* in the title of this respected document suggests that these are more than aspirational. We could conceivably be found in violation of these "standards" for assessment as case law accumulates. Consequently, this publication provides even more impetus for science-based practice.

There are additional reasons to argue for some variant of the scientist/practitioner model as the ideal for intelligence test interpretation. Quality of care, the need to practice "defensive medicine," accountability for outcomes, and the desire to preserve the guild are a few reasons to ensure that intelligence test interpretation is grounded in scientific rigor. These rationales are also interrelated. The logic is frequently offered, for example, that quality of care can only be provided by skilled providers, necessitating preservation and enhancement of the guild.

Current intellectual assessment practice relies primarily on the theories and experiences of the practicum and internship supervisors and professors who train each new generation of practitioners. Unfortunately, some of the rules handed down to the new generation of professionals are questionable if not invalid.

Russell (1994) noted that physicians also conduct numerous medical assessment practices (e.g., prostate screening) on the basis of common sense and good intentions rather than because of strong scientific evidence. She elucidates the problem by demonstrating the dubious value of widespread prostate screening in order to trigger the delivery of expensive therapeutic or preventive interventions (e.g., radical prostatectomy). One research study involved 58 men in the United States, where expensive medical and surgical procedures are often delivered once cancer is diagnosed, and 58 in Sweden, where the men were typically "followed" in the absence of intervention, whose screening test results identified cancer (Russell, 1994). She noted that at 10-year follow-up the morbidity rate of the two samples was virtually identical, in spite of dramatic differences in treatment approaches between the two countries. Consequently, the utility of prostate screening, which often triggers expensive and invasive surgery in the United States, is called into question by some (Russell, 1994). Psychologists probably acquire their assessment knowledge in the same manner as physcians and other professionals, which may, in turn, hinder the integration of science and practice. Professional psychologists likely depend heavily on the recommendations of "experts" such as their professors, valued colleagues, practicum, and internship supervisors. Physician assessment practices are then altered, "correctly or incorrectly" (Russell, 1994), by subsequent clinical experiences.

Given this scenario it is a difficult task indeed for the "typical" psychologist to systematically use scientific findings to interpret intelligence tests. Science-based practice is made more unlikely given the dearth of high-quality research. I propose that the scientific basis for many popular intellgence test interpretations is more perception than reality. I often hear the refrain that the use of the Wechsler scales is supported by hundreds of research studies. Well, as it turns out, many of the studies are of dubious quality (e.g., small samples with inadequate designs) while others suggest that popular interpretations have been proven wrong in numerous studies. This observation led me to more systematically tally the high-quality research studies that are available for popular intelligence tests. Some of the results of my WISC-III Picture

Arrangement review (reported in part in Kamphaus, 1998) follow.

Picture Arrangement as Exemplar

Psychologists continue to presume that Wechsler subtests assess "specific capacities" (Lipsitz, Dworkin, & Erlenmeyer-Kimling, 1993). Most Wechsler subtests, however, have little research to either support or refute popular subtest interpretations (Kamphaus, 1998). The Picture Arrangement (PA) subtest is unusual in that some research has been devoted to identifying the latent trait (or specific capacity) that is unique to PA. The preponderance of evidence suggests that performance on PA is determined by a single cognitive ability (see Appendix A). The difficult issue is reaching consensus regarding a label for this ability. Several researchers have suggested that the PA subtest measures a construct requiring some type of visual/spatial ability (Carroll, 1993; Cohen, 1959). The common labels for this ability include perceptual organization, visualization, spatial:mechanical, and simultaneous processing. Furthermore, Carroll's (1993) reanalysis of some WISC-R data sets suggests that this subtest measures the same ability as a broad visualization factor and that PA cannot be easily categorized as either fluid or crystallized ability.

There has also been some research that identifies the abilities that are not assessed by PA. In particular, the theory that PA measures social judgment has been tested in at least four studies (see Lipsitz et al., 1993, for a review). In a detailed study of the relationship of the PA subtest to criterion measures of social adjustment, Lipsitz et al. (1993) drew the following conclusion:

The absence of a positive association between performance on the Picture Arrangement subtest and either social adjustment measure is consistent with earlier negative findings in both clinical (Johnson, 1969) and normal (Krippner, 1964; Simon & Evans, 1980) samples.

Moreover, in this investigation, comparisons using Picture Arrangement scatter scores suggest that normal adolescents for whom the Picture subtest was a relative strength (positive Picture Arrangement scatter) in fact had greater deficits in social adjustment. Brannigan (1975) has observed that even if Picture Arrangement performance does reflect sensitivity in the social environment, this is not synonymous with positive social adjustment or competence. (p. 435)

There remain many untested hypotheses regarding the central ability assessed by PA (see Appendix A). Some of these hypotheses include integrated brain functioning, convergent production and evaluation of semantic stimuli, planning, common sense, distinguishing essential from nonessential details, and synthesis. Some of these hypotheses could be subsumed under the general PA ability of visualization (e.g., synthesis, distinguishing essential from nonessential details). Until proven otherwise, the semantic aspects of this task are secondary or of minimal importance in the determination of PA factor loadings. Moreover, tasks of the PA variety are not identified as markers of reasoning ability or speed of mental processing in the numerous factor studies conducted by Carroll (1993).

Untested Interpretations Abound

The current body of PA evidence suggests two implications for WISC-III scientist practitioners: (a) interpretation of a PA score as a measure of some variation of visualization/spatial ability constitutes a case of interpretation that is supported by some scientific evidence, whereas (b) making an inference regarding social adjustment/judgment based on PA scores is contraindicated by research.

A review of research provided in Appendix A leads inevitably to the conclusion that the Wechsler tests measure fewer constructs than are typically suggested in most textbooks that are used to train practitioners (including this one).

An essential conclusion to make, however, is that most of the presumed abilities that are offered for Wechsler interpretation are just that: presumptions that are not supported by a preponderance of scientific evidence. The number of untested hypothesized abilities is far larger than the list of tested ones.

Some Wechsler subtests, however, are more frequently studied. There are a few studies, for example, of the information processing components of the Block Design task (e.g., Royer, 1984; Schorr, Bower, & Kiernan, 1982). This series of studies, however, has not led to agreement regarding the central processes that are assessed by the Block Design task, but to the development of new stimuli that better isolate cognitive processes (Royer, 1984).

The Digit Span subtest has also generated much research. The results of this research, however, have not clarified the nature of the underlying ability being assessed. A central impediment to the understanding of Digit Span performance is the finding that the forward and backward spans measure different traits (Reynolds, in press). Yes, hundreds of studies have been conducted, but many aspects of even our most popular intelligence tests are unknown and some routine interpretations are refuted.

Interpretation History

There are identifiable trends in test interpretation practice (Kamphaus, Petoskey, & Morgan, 1997). During the early part of the 1900s psychologists emphasized quantification of a general intellectual level. After World War II and the publication of the first of the Wechsler scales, interpretive practice became dominated by profile analysis. In addition, specific profiles and subtest results were linked to diagnoses. A relative strength on the Object Assembly test, for example, was specifically linked to the diagnosis of "simple schizophrenia" (Kamphaus et. al., 1997). Profile analysis changed in the 1970s due to the ready availability of factor analysis. Many factor analyses yielded the familiar WISC-R three factors that served as alternatives to interpreting clinically derived subtest profiles or the overall IQs. This psychometric approach to intelligence test interpretation was accompanied by an emphasis on using numerous calculations to identify significant profiles and factors.

The current wave of intelligence test interpretation identifies theory as central to interpretation. The works of John Carroll (three-stratum theory) and John Horn ("g" fluid/"g" crystallized theory) are noteworthy examples of an emphasis on theoretical approaches to deriving score meaning (McGrew & Flanagan, 1998).

Moving Forward: Science-Based Practice

I aspire to build on the research compendium included in my 1998 book chapter by compiling the results of major intelligence test research findings in Appendix A. Such a compendium is a necessary precursor to science-based practice. You, the practitioner, may consult Appendix A as needed to determine if you are making your interpretation based on research findings, or your clinical experience, or that of mentors or colleagues. I am not suggesting that psychologists abandon making interpretations that are based primarily on their experience or other sources of information. Moreover, *I do not wish to incapacitate the practitioner by discouraging innovation or the application of skilled clinical acumen*. I think, however, that it is important for the practitioner to know the basis for his or her conclusions. In this way the clinician can continue to engage in a process of continuing professional development based on the dissemination of new research findings. It is also important for the consumer to know the basis of the clinician's reasoning in order to allow each client to make informed decisions about his or her treatment. With these premises in mind I constructed Appendix A. Furthermore, in an effort to ensure some semblance of quality for the research presented I adopted specific criteria for study inclusion, interpreta-

tion of the results, and application of the results to assessment practice (see Appendix A).

I seek to integrate background information, referral questions, theory, psychometric principles, and most importantly, scientific findings with an individual's test results. My advice for doing so is described next.

PREPARATION FOR INTERPRETATION

I choose the term *integrative* for my interpretive approach in order to ensure that I consider the patient's context. The term *integrate* has been defined as "to make into a whole by bringing all parts together; unify" (American Heritage Dictionary, New College Edition). Granted it is difficult for the new clinician to make all pieces of data (quantitative and qualitative) for a client fit together to make sensible and practical interpretations and recommendations. One byproduct of this difficulty is that it leads to the temptation to ignore one's own observations and intuitions, preferring instead to derive "the answer" to a child's profile from a textbook such as this one. Here is a concrete example. Given a Digit Span weakness, a clinician might conclude that the child has an auditory short-term memory deficit. This conclusion is what many textbooks would suggest as a plausible one. In fact, the clinician may make this conclusion based on the writings of others without considering the fact that the child was more inattentive during this test than during any others. New clinicians in particular will favor the textbook interpretation in this case and ignore, or fail to integrate, the relevant observations that provide a defensible interpretation of the subtest score. I have observed that my students are even more likely to fail to integrate findings with other data if the interpretive textbook they are using requires numerous calculations and manipulation of statistical and interpretive tables as part of the interpretive process. I keep calculations to a minimum in my interpretive work in order to avoid taking quantitative interpretation to its illogical extreme and to prevent new examiners from getting bogged down in calculations. I have seen many of my students focus so much on the calculations involved in test interpretation that they overlook their own experiences with the child and other important pieces of qualitative information. Besides, software programs make whatever calculations that may be needed easily accessible. In keeping with this philosophy of minimal calculation, only average values are used in the interpretive process. Hence, the integrative approach described herein attempts to unify all test- and non-test-based data for a child in order to draw conclusions and to deemphasize statistical calculations or other machinations that dissuade examiners from integrating assessment results and, hopefully, achieve parsimony.

An integrative approach to interpretation takes time. As a general rule, *I advise examiners to not draw premature conclusions because of time or other pressures in a nonemergency case.* An analogous situation would be for a pediatrician to examine a child with stomach problems, collect a history, and conclude that the child has an ulcer without seeing X rays or other test results. Similarly, the psychologist should feel equally free to "order" (to use medical parlance) additional diagnostic tests before a definitive diagnosis is offered.

Taking the time to engage in this "iterative" process is especially useful when surprising findings occur. A clear understanding that this type of detective work is often necessary has the additional advantage of precluding clinicians from making premature and potentially erroneous conclusions.

The interpretive approach described next is basically a codification of what has always been considered sound clinical assessment practice. There are several hallmarks of sophisticated assessment practice, including an emphasis on the collection of multiple data sources in order to consider context, searching for hypotheses that can be corroborated by more than one source of data, making the most parsimonius conclusions, and supporting conclusions with scientifically based theory and research.

Integrate Multiple Data Sources and Referral Questions

Intelligence test interpretation is fraught with problems when these tests are interpreted in isolation. The integrative approach emphasizes collecting data from a variety of sources so that intelligence test results can be checked against other sources of information. Consider the case of an adolescent who obtained a relative weakness (a lower subtest score than on any other subtest) on the Arithmetic subtest. The clinician may conclude, based solely on WISC-III performance, that the child shows arithmetic difficulties. A clinician could look foolish if he or she cited a mathematics problem in the report, which could easily happen, if the examiner lacked information from the child's teacher regarding school performance. It may be that the child excels in math in school. Matarazzo (1990) gives a similar example, from a neuropsychological evaluation, of the failure to integrate test results with background information.

> *There is little that is more humbling to a practitioner who uses the highest one or two Wechsler subtest scores as the only index of a patient's "premorbid" level of intellectual functioning and who therefore interprets concurrently obtained lower subtest scores as indexes of clear "impairment" and who is then shown by the opposing attorney elementary and high school transcripts that contain several global IQ scores, each of which were at the same low IQ levels as are suggested by the currently obtained lowest Wechsler subtest scaled scores. (p. 1003)*

All intelligence test results should be integrated with other information about the individual to portray a more valid picture of a person's intelligence. This "integration" can only be accomplished if multiple data sources are available.

Furthermore, failure to consider all data sources (qualitative as well as quantitative) leads to a most common interpretive and logical error—the failure to consider information that is contrary to the clinician's hypothesis. Harkness and Lilienfeld (1997) refer to the problem of ignoring relevant data as violation of Carnap's (1962) "requirement of total evidence" for hypothesis testing. In their words, "If relevant facts X, Y, and Z are available, induction will be flawed if one decides to ignore Z and only use one's favorite facts, X and Y" (p. 349). If we decide to adopt a single theory of intelligence, perhaps focusing exlusively on Stratum II of Carroll's three-stratum theory, we may systematically fail to recognize relevant Stratum I hypotheses. Let us propose that Price (a sample case) has problems with verbal skills that result in verbal ability scores being lower than other Stratum II scores. In order to incorporate the principle of total evidence and, to achieve integration, we review subtest scores only to find that subtests requiring keen auditory skills (e.g., phonological coding tasks administered by his teacher, tests of auditory discrimination administered by an audiologist), are his worst performances. Upon further qualitative data collection we discover that he has always suffered from ear infections, has had pus aspirated from his ear on numerous occasions, and still frequently displays symptoms of sinusitis. Our favorite facts (i.e., X) provide ample evidence of a verbal ability deficit, but other facts (i.e., Y and Z) yield evidence in support of an auditory discrimination deficit that adversely impacts cognitive performances, especially verbal ones. Consequently, the conceptualization and treatment of Price's problems in the workplace would differ substantially if the totality of evidence was not considered.

I am not advocating that each client should be administered multiple intelligence measures in order to obtain the corroborating evidence necessary for interpretive integration. On the contrary, I propose that psychologists make greater use of the numerous test and nontest data sources such as background information, observations during testing, and parent and teacher reports. The integration of these various quantitative and qualitative sources of evidence is demonstrated in case studies throughout this text. In order to implement the desire to integrate multiple data sources I propose the concrete rule of thumb that *each conclusion drawn in a psychological report should be supported by at least two data sources.*

A clinician, for example, may conclude that a child's composite score of 84 (below average) means that she possesses below average general intelligence. Even this seemingly obvious conclusion should be corroborated by two external sources of information. If the majority of the child's achievement scores are in this range, and her teacher says that she seems to be progressing more slowly than the majority of the children in her class, then the conclusion of below-average intelligence has been corroborated by two sources of information external to the intelligence test.

The criterion of two pieces of corroborating information sounds stringent although this is not the case in actual practice. Frequently, substantial evidence for corroborating hypotheses may be obtained from caretakers, other clinicians, and teachers, let alone prior test results.

Integrative interpretation also requires testing and matching intepretations to the referral questions of interest. Most referral questions are, frankly speaking, Stratum III questions, for example, "I want to know my IQ." Other Stratum III questions might include:

Does he possess mental retardation?

Should he be in the gifted class?

Can he avoid the death penalty because of the diagnosis of mental retardation?

Is her intelligence at least average?

He has bipolar disorder; can you rule out an intelligence problem?

These questions are best answered with overall composite scores. Furthermore, when these questions are the focus of assessment, Stratum I or II interpretations are of little importance unless there are compelling findings. Other strata may need to be interpreted only if there is such scatter in the profile that Stratum III interpretation is inappropriate. Specifically, a 40-point difference between Verbal Reasoning and Abstract/Visual Reasoning area scores on the Binet-4 would necessitate effectively changing the referral question to a Stratum II question that was unanticipated. In other words, the referral question would change from "Does she have mental retardation," to "What are the educational implications of her having average spatial skills with verbal skills in the mental retardation range?"

Stratum II referral questions many include:

My child wishes to attend medical school as I did but she also may have my same weakness in geometry and chemistry. I suffered from weak spatial skills in these courses and we want to see if she has the same weakness.

I want to better understand my child's abilities in order to help choose his high school coursework.

I've always struggled with my writing and I want to know why.

These referral questions are notably different from Stratum III questions in that they are more appropriate for the application of Stratum II tests to assess functioning in areas of concern. An estimate of general intelligence will likely be found wanting as a response to these questions. The same can be said, however, for the following Stratum I questions where Stratum II assessment may be found lacking. Some sample questions include:

I've had memory problems since my automobile accident. I took a leave from law school for a year, but I do not think that I am back to normal yet. Please tell me what sort of problem I have and what I can do about it.

I want to know if my child has a reading disability.

Does my child have a writing disability?

These referral questions cannot be answered by Stratum II or III assessment measures. An individual with memory problems is not likely to be satisfied with knowing that their general intelligence is average or that they possess a weakness in memory abilities. This individual will want to know the specific nature of his memory difficulties (short versus long term, visual or aural, concrete versus abstract stimuli, effects of distractors, etc.), which is not capable of being answered by popular intelligence tests that, at best, provide Stratum II assessment of memory with very limited assessment of Stratum I memory abilities. The necessary assessment of Stratum I abilities will have to be conducted with a dedicated memory assessment battery such as those discussed in detail in Chapter 19.

In like manner the emerging consensus in reading disability assessment is that the core deficit for the most prevalent reading disorder, phonetic coding, is a Stratum I ability rendering Stratum II or III assessment of limited, if any, value (Siegel, 1988, 1990, 1992; Stanovich, 1999). Most intelligence measures do not possess phonetic coding subtests or, if they do, they do not possess the content validity necessary to conduct the necessary error analyses (Siegel, 1999). Significantly more achievment measures assess this ability, as was revealed in Chapter 14. Stanovich (1999), Siegel (1999), and others in the learning disability field review considerable data showing that intelligence assessment is not necessary to diagnose learning disability. They find that, regardless of overall intelligence composite score, individuals with phonetic coding deficits all read words in the same flawed manner. This point of view is akin to saying that whether of tall or small stature, all individuals with breast cancer experience similar pathogenesis, or regardless of overall intelligence or Stratum II ability profile, all children with cleft palate have similar speech difficulties. The same thinking holds true with the phonetic coding deficits associated with reading disabilities. Children with above- or below-average general intelligence, intact or impaired verbal or auditory processing abilities, or other profiles all read similarly if they have phonetic coding (i.e., Stratum I) deficits. In effect then, for most individuals with reading disabilities, *impaired Stratum III or II abilities are a comorbidity not a cause of reading disabilities.* Kline, Snyder, and Castellanos (1996) provide a model for reading disability assessment where an ability/achievement distinction is not made. In their model, Stratum II verbal, visual-spatial, and memory cognitive abilities are merely contributors to early letter-word recognition skills along with phonological processing and listening comprehension skills. In this model intellectual abilities are not viewed as necessarily causal but as co-occuring. More information on this topic is provided in Chapter 20.

As can be seen from these examples, the focus of intellectual assessment is dictated by the referral questions offered. This fact necessitates that clinicians learn enough intelligence, achievement, and related tests to be able to answer questions at all three strata and integrate results with the referral question(s). An alternative approach is to work collaboratively with professionals who have complementary expertise.

Apply Psychological Science

Empirical Findings

The "clinical impressions" of examiners are no longer adequate for supporting interpretations of an individual's intelligence test scores (Matarazzo, 1990). Consider again the example above in which the child with persistent school problems obtained a composite score of 84. Given the data showing the positive relationship between intelligence and achievement scores, the results seem consistent with the research literature and lend support to the interpretation of below-average intelligence. If necessary, the clinician could give testimony citing studies supporting the correlational relationship between intelligence and achievement test scores to support the conclusion of below-average intelligence (see Appendix A). As is stated clearly in the *Test Standards*, all conclusions that are made based on intelligence tests should have empirical support.

This advice is not intended to communicate that clinicians have to routinely give formal written citations supporting their conclusions (e.g., Kamphaus, 1993). While this practice is desirable, it is too burdensome for most purposes. Clinicians should simply retrieve whatever theory or research knowledge they have regarding a conclusion that they draw about an individual's intelligence. Even without formal citations, this recommendation at least fosters the practice of clinicians checking their results with their knowledge base regarding intelligence research and theory.

Theory

Knowledge of theory is important above and beyond research findings because theory allows the clinician to do a better job of conceptualizing a child's scores. Having a clear conceptualization of the child's cognitive status then allows the clinician to better explain the child's results to parents, teachers, colleagues, and other consumers of the test findings. Parents will often want to know the etiology of the child's scores. They will question, "Is it my fault for not sending her to a more academically demanding preschool?" or "Did he inherit this problem? My brother had the same problems when he was in school." Clinicians will find themselves unprepared to give plausible answers to such questions without adequate theoretical knowledge.

Unfortunately, much of our research is not directly applicable to the individual. We do not, for example, have research-based plausible explanations for the child who changes composite intelligence test scores by 15 points or more upon retesting (see Chapter 3). The reason for change, on the other hand, is quite obvious in the case of the child who has lower scores subsequent to a traumatic head injury. Given the lack of applicability of much research to the individual the clinician has to become an "intelligent tester" (Kaufman, 1979b) who has the breadth and depth of knowledge to apply numerous theories and research findings to explain the child's scores. This individualized approach lies in contrast to making the child's scores fit the theory of the particular test or the clinician's most valued theory. Individualized interpretation requires considerable skill and flexibility on the part of the examiner.

I try to accomplish this goal of individualized interpretation by using the names of individuals who are associated with particular theories or research studies to help me conceptualize the child's performance. Even while testing a child, I will make remarks to myself such as, "Sternberg would love to see this child; she cannot allocate her time resources. This inability is dramatically lowering her Performance IQ." Clinicians can refer to Chapters 2, 3, and similar sources to acquire the knowledge requisite for individualized interpretation of a child's scores.

Psychometrics

Integration of test findings with psychometric theory may also increase the validity of obtained results. The hierarchical aspects of Kaufman's (1979b) approach to WISC-R interpretation has proven popular for two decades. This approach emphasizes drawing conclusions based on the most reliable and valid scores yielded by intelligence tests. At its essence, psychometric theory suggests that larger samples of behavior are more likely to have good evidence of reliability and, of course, reliability is a necessary but insufficient condition for the establishment of validity.

Conversely, poor reliability makes validity unobtainable.

From a psychometric standpoint Stratum III scores are likely to have better measurement properties than either Stratum II or Stratum I scores or shared abilities (see Chapter 8) due to their increased reliability, which gives them a better opportunity to demonstrate validity. A conceptualization of this psychometric hierarchy is shown in the table below.

Adherence to this hierarchy may also produce interpretation that achieves parsimony. An adult may, for example, have the following WAIS-III scores: Full Scale = 78, Verbal Conceptualization = 83, Perceptual Organization = 82, Working Memory = 84, and Processing Speed = 69. One could say that this woman has a weakness in Processing Speed that adversely affects her cognitive performances. If, on the other hand, one appealed to Kaufman's hierarchy the conclusion more likely to have evidence of validity would be subaverage general intelligence, a deficit that is more likely to adversely affect a variety of cognitive performances. Additionally, the conclusion of subaverage general intelligence is also parsimonius.

Although Stratum II has received considerable research attention since the publication of Carroll's landmark work, many of the Stratum II constructs lack validity evidence. McGrew and Flanagan (1998) provide a comprehensive view of the criterion-related validity of Horn's "g_f"–"g_c" factors (which are in many cases similar to Carroll's). I was struck, after reviewing their compilation of prior criterion-related studies, by the

Source of Conclusion	Definition	Reliability	Validity
Overall Composite Scores	Stratum III	Good	Good
Composite Scale Scores	Stratum II	Good	Fair to Good
Shared Subtest Scores	Two or more subtests	Fair to Good	Fair to Good
Single Subtest Scores	Stratum I	Fair to Good	Poor to Good

fact that several of the Stratum II-like abilities were virtually unvalidated. Specifically, in their Table 2.1, which provides a summary of numerous studies of the relationship between "g_f"–"g_c" intellectual abilities and reading skill, there were no studies that attempted to validate the visual processing factor. Even more remarkable was that only one study was devoted to the fluid, short-term memory, and long-term storage and retrieval abilities. They cite many related studies but few of these are direct tests of the "g_f"–"g_c" model, and most of these were conducted by McGrew and his colleagues. Similarly, mathematics achievement has not been studied in terms of its relationship to either visual processing or long-term storage and retrieval abilities, and other ability factors have only been studied in two investigations by McGrew, Flanagan, and colleagues (see their Table 2.2). Finally, McGrew and Flanagan were only able to identify nine studies that correlated "g_f"–"g_c" abilities with occupations. Most of these studies attempted to validate visual-processing-like abilities. Only two studies, by contrast, were devoted to studying the relationship of fluid abilities to occupations. I conclude that Carroll's Stratum II factors have impressive evidence of internal validity, especially when one takes into account the cumulative findings of the Vernon, Horn-Cattell, and related research traditions aimed at identifying ability factors beneath "g." On the other hand, external validity—specifically, criterion-related validity—has not been well established to date despite the substantial number of "related" research studies. This state of affairs is not surprising given that Carroll's relatively recent work served as the primary work to stimulate research of these abilities. My advice to clinicians is to review carefully the evidence provided by McGrew and Flanagan (1998) and prepare to integrate new evidence into one's practice as it becomes available. In the interim, the relationship between Stratum II abilities and many achievements is either unknown or preliminary in nature, requiring further validation. The criterion-related validity

problem is even more acute for shared subtest hypotheses, as is shown next.

Interpretation of shared subtest hypotheses or profiles has proved especially problematic. For the purposes of this discussion a subtest profile consists of a pattern of subtest strengths (high subtest scores) and weaknesses (low subtest scores) that are considered distinctive for a particular person or clinical sample thereby warranting interpretation. The centerpiece of profile analysis is ipsative interpretation—the process of discovering intra-individual strengths and weaknesses in cognitive areas. In ipsative interpretation the patient is used as his or her own standard or norm. In contrast, in normative-based interpretation a patient's score is compared to that of a reference group of his/her peers. An example of a hypothesis from a normative approach would be, "James has above-average intelligence as measured by the WISC-III." An ipsative interpretation would be something like, "James's mathematics skills are better than his reading skills."

One of the most popular methods of ipsative interpretation involves interpreting clusters of subtests that are relatively high or low in relation to the other subtests. A conclusion based on two or more subtests that are deviant from the remainder of the profile has been referred to as shared abilities or hypotheses (Kaufman, 1979b; Sattler, 1988). The crucial problem with interpreting shared hypotheses is their lack of validity evidence (Lyman, 1998). Unfortunately, the validity of many combinations of subtests as shared hypotheses is not known because it simply has not been studied. One of the few shared hypotheses that has been studied is the regrouping of WISC-R subtests proposed by Bannatyne (1974). His recategorizations are shown in the table on the next page.

Matheson, Mueller, and Short (1984) studied the validity of Bannatyne's recategorization of the WISC-R using a multiple group factor analysis procedure with three age ranges of the WISC-R and data from the WISC-R standard-

Spatial	Conceptualization	Sequencing	Acquired Knowledge
Block Design	Vocabulary	Digit Span	Information
Object Assembly	Similarities	Coding	Arithmetic
Picture Completion	Comprehension	Arithmetic	Vocabulary
		Picture Arrangement	

ization sample. They found that the acquired knowledge, conceptualization, sequencing, and spatial categories of the WISC-R had high reliabilities but problems with validity. Matheson et al. (1984) found, for example, that while the acquired knowledge category had sufficiently high reliabilities, it was not independent of the other three categories, particularly conceptualization. This finding is sensible given that the conceptualization and acquired knowledge categories have one subtest in common (Vocabulary) and that previous factor analytic studies of the WISC-R revealed three not four factors. The subtests from the conceptualization and acquired knowledge categories form the large first factor, labeled verbal comprehension. As a result, Matheson et al. (1984) advise that the acquired knowledge category not be interpreted as a unique entity. Said another way, these results suggest that the acquired knowledge and conceptualization categories are best interpreted as one measure of verbal intelligence, which is more consistent with the factor analytic research on the WISC-R.

In a similar investigation Naglieri, Kamphaus, and Kaufman (1983) tried to test the accuracy of Kaufman's (1979b) recategorizations of the WISC-R into successive and simultaneous tests based on Luria's theory (see Chapter 2). They met with mixed results. While there was some support for Kaufman's recategorization, it was not robust. Mazes, for example, was hypothesized to be a strong sequential test, yet it had its highest loadings on the simultaneous factor. Again, a recategorization of the WISC-R subtests failed to

gain validity support as strong as that which has been found for the three-factor structure of the WISC-R.

In one sense the Matheson et al. (1984) and Naglieri et al. (1983) investigations support the hierarchical aspects of the integrative method of interpretation proposed in this chapter, whereby interpretation of the composite scores, in this case the Verbal and Performance scales, receives primacy over interpretation of recategorizations such as Bannatyne's. Fortunately, the validity of Bannatyne's and Kaufman's recategorizations has at least been tested. The vast majority of other proposed recategorizations that will be discussed in upcoming sections have not been tested to determine the extent of their validity (see also McDermott, Fantuzzo, & Gluttings [1990], and Anastasi [1985], for a discussion of measurement issues in profile analysis). Most importantly, clinicians need to be aware of the fact that *shared subtest profile analysis depends exclusively on the clinical acumen of the examiner not on a sound research base.*

I concur with the views of Kline et al. (1996) with regard to shared subtest and individual subtest interpretations. They observed:

> Instead, we recommend that subtests be viewed as observed variables in the technique of confirmatory factor analysis: fallible (not perfectly reliable) means to measure underlying abilities that are not expressed in a single, direct way. Thus, the lowest level of profile analysis, if conducted at all, should concern scale or composite scores. (p. 14)

An individual's profile simply cannot be matched to some of the theoretical profiles mentioned in the literature. Nor can a valid conclusion be drawn without the integration of other pieces of evidence. Similarly, *a clinical diagnosis should never be made solely on the basis of a subtest profile.*

A related scientific and conceptual problem is the false distinction between ability (a capacity) and achievements (an accomplishment) (Kaufman, 1994; Wesman, 1968). The distinction between ability and achievement measures has never been empirically demonstrated. In fact, dissimilar interpretations can be made of the same measures. The same item, a mathematics addition item, when placed on the Wechsler scale Arithmetic subtest is deemed a measure of quantitative reasoning, but when the identical item is placed on a mathematics test, it is interpreted as a measure of knowledge acquired.

A similar problem is encountered in personality assessment when some of the same items are assigned, via empirical means, to more than one scale. It is not uncommon to find that "worry" items are found on both depression and anxiety scales (Kamphaus & Frick, 1996). This lack of differentiated item content, whether it be on intelligence or personality measures results in considerable interpretive confusion. Alas, however, the distinction between constructs is primarily theoretical, although empirical analyses are of some value. Recent analyses have been able to better differentiate the item content of depression and anxiety child behavior rating scales (Reynolds & Kamphaus, 1992). Similarly, Carroll's (1993) compendium has delimited reading skills to serve as but one indicator of crystallized abilities and not other Stratum II factors. In addition, he did not find adequeate support for a Stratum II quantitative factor that obviated the need to have mathematics measures serve as indicators of Stratum II abilities. Moreover, measures of reading are not required to assess crystallized abilities.

At least a theoretical distinction could be made between abilities and achievements where item content is kept distinct, as was the case for the K-ABC, and has been done in some cases in personality assessment. Conceptual confusion

reigns, however, if clinicians think that certain achievements are in large part determined by intellectual abilities. Psychologists are likely to consider this proposition true, especially if they have little experience with achievement tests. For this reason a chapter on achievement testing is included in this volume (see Chapter 14). In cases of referrals for academic problems I consider ability and achievement tests to be coequals. In other words, abilities may cause achievements and achievements may cause abilities, but we do not have adequate scientific evidence to date to always know the direction of the causal arrow. Kline et al. (1996), based on a review of relevant research, make a convincing case that the reading-related abilities often assessed on achievement measures are the causal variables for reading disabilities, and intellectual abilities are not core deficits, although they may be co-occurring problems.

A child may, for example, be a gifted reader and yet have general intelligence test scores in the average range. In direct contrast, a gifted child may possess basic reading skills in the average range. It follows that if a clinician is testing a child who is referred for academic problems, then the core deficits in achievement should be the primary focus of assessment and intellectual abilities the secondary aim. A framework for such reading disability assessments is provided by Kline et al. (1996).

Psychologists would also be hard pressed to defend conclusions about the relationship between intelligence and various achievements. It is as difficult to defend a conclusion that a person's reading problems were caused by her poor verbal skills as it is to propose the opposite—that her verbal intelligence has been adversely impacted by reading problems (Stanovich, 1999). Much more research is needed to establish the direction of causality between the intelligence and achievement constructs. At this point in time I prefer to emphasize the delineation of functional deficits and strengths (to be discussed in the next section) and engage in "therapeutic testing," which may eventually allow for making inferences about causality.

Until more research regarding causality or co-occurrence becomes available *I treat intelligence and achievement tests as measures of differing types of achievements that have reciprocal influences upon one another*. Intelligence and achievement measures are considered as coequals by doing so. This juxtaposition of intellgence and academic achievement essentially brings us back to Binet's original notion (see Chapter 1) that the only meaningful distinction between intelligence and achievement tests is the test content (i.e., psychological versus pedagogical, respectively). If, however, we do treat the two sets of constructs as equals, then we are less likely to be concerned about making causal inferences between the two. Kline et al. (1996) provide a similar conceptual model for the case of reading disability assessment. Their model, reproduced in Figure 17.1, treats both achievement and intelligence measures as precursors to the development of reading skills. A research study by Vellutino, Scanlon, Sipay, Small, Pratt, Chen, and Denckla (1996) further demonstrates the equality of intelligence and achievement testing in the reading disability diagnostic process.

Velluttino et al. (1996) conducted one of the few empirical tests of the stimulability of children

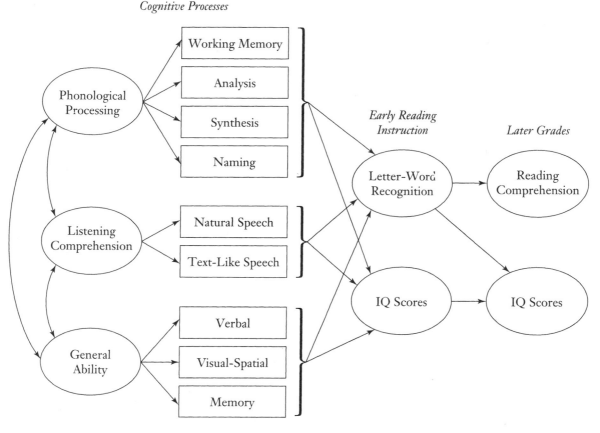

FIGURE 17.1

Conceptual model of assessment for poor readers

SOURCE: Adapted from Kline et al. (1996) with permission.

with poor basic reading skills where, coincidentally, they showed that children with a great variety of reading skills may have average intelligence test scores. They formed six groups of children for the purposes of their study, two groups of normal readers and four groups of children with reading problems who responded differently to a 15-week tutorial intervention. The six groups were formed according to scores on the Woodcock Reading Master Tests—Revised (Woodcock, 1987) Word Identification and Word Attack subtests. According to the authors, "The Word Identification subtest evaluates facility in naming printed words individually and the Word Attack subtest evaluates the child's knowledge of letter-sound correspondences by having him or her sound out pseudowords" (p. 605). All children were drawn from a large community sample and a minimum WISC-R Full Scale IQ of 90 was required for all. The groups were formed according to their Word Attack and Word Identification scores in the following manner:

Group 1. Normal readers had both Word Attack and Word Identification scores above the 15th percentile rank and they represented the lower half of the normal reader's intelligence test score distribution.

Group 2. Normal readers had both Word Attack and Word Identification scores above the 15th percentile rank and they represented the upper half of the normal reader's intelligence test score distribution.

Group 3. Very low group had either Word Attack and Word Identification scores at or below the 15th percentile rank, intelligence test composite scores of 90 or above, and

they had the poorest response of four poor reader groups to 15 weeks sessions (70 to 80) of tutoring.

Group 4. Low group had either Word Attack and Word Identification scores at or below the 15th percentile rank, intelligence test composite scores of 90 or above, and they had the second poorest response of four poor reader groups to 15 weeks sessions (70 to 80) of tutoring.

Group 5. Good group had either Word Attack or Word Identification scores at or below the 15th percentile rank, intelligence test composite scores of 90 or above, and they had the second best response of four poor reader groups to 15 weeks sessions (70 to 80) of tutoring.

Group 6. Very good group had either Word Attack or Word Identification scores at or below the 15th percentile rank, intelligence test composite scores of 90 or above, and they had the best response of four poor reader groups to 15 weeks (about 70 to 80 half hour sessions) of tutoring.

The mean overall intelligence test results and Word Attack and Word Identification raw scores for these groups at the beginning of the study show (below, adapted from Table 1 of Vellutino et al., 1996) that poor readers exist throughout the intelligence test score distribution, and response to reading intervention is better predicted by initial reading scores than by intelligence test sccores.

These results suggest that initial reading score is by far the best predictor of response to intervention. However, response to intervention is best predicted by the delivery of intervention not

Measure	Group 1	Group 2	Group 3	Group 4	Group 5	Group 6
WISC-R Full Scale IQ	107	123	101	102	106	106
Word Identification	37	39	4	7	12	12
Word Attack	13	14	.7	1.1	.8	1.3

by passive prediction with a test score. It is also noteworthy that none of these groups had significant verbal/performance discrepancies. Finally, and of utmost importance for interpretation, these results show that significant functional cognitive impairment can be present when average or better intelligence test results are obtained. The relationship of functional impairment to test interpretation is explicated next.

Identify Functional Impairments and Strengths

Our conclusions necessarily lack importance for understanding patient function if they are reflective of individual differences but they do not reflect functional impairment or strength. When referring to functional impairment, I am referring to the concept that an individual difference in cognitive abilities is causing a patient to exhibit habitual behavior that is impaired in comparison to his or her peers. In the case of the Americans with Disabilities Act it is referred to as the "average person" standard (Gordon, Lewandowski, & Keiser, 1999). This definition necessarily embraces a broad definition of behavior that may include academic or other "cognitive" performances. Consider the following example, which is a disguised actual case.

Ashonte' is a 17-year-old attending a private school. Her parents are seeking an updated psychological evaluation prior to making application to college. Ashonte' has a long history of academic problems dating back to the fourth grade when she was first cited by parents as having academic problems. Her pediatrician at the time suggested a diagnosis of attention deficit hyperactivity disorder. She was evaluated by a psychologist in the fifth grade who made the diagnoses of ADHD, Adjustment Disorder with Mixed Features, and Reading Disorder. Her teachers, however, did not report any concerns with inattention or learning problems until the sixth grade. She began taking Ritalin in the sixth grade and she remains on this medication to this day.

Ashonte' is considered to be performing adequately in high school by her teachers where she receives primarily grades of B with course averages in the 80s.

Ashonte' achieved cognitive ability test scores in the average range on the Stanford-Binet Fourth Edition. Her scores were Verbal Reasoning = 90, Abstract/Visual Reasoning = 114, Quantitative Reasoning = 92, Short-Term Memory = 89, and Test Composite = 96. Ashonte's achievement test scores ranged from a low of 94 on Applied Problems to a high of 117 on Passage Comprehension of the Woodcock-Johnson Tests of Achievement. Similarly, her Woodcock Reading Mastery Tests—Revised (WRMT) scores included a 93 on Word Attack and 109 on Passage Comprehension. Finally, she achieved a Listening Comprehension score on the OWLS of 93.

All of Ashonte's behavior rating scale results were unremarkable with the exception of significant ratings of hyperactivity and inattention by her parents. Teacher and self-ratings were within normal limits. A structured diagnostic interview revealed that she did not meet diagnostic criteria for a psychiatric disorder including ADHD or an Adjustment Disorder. Moreover, the clinician concluded that there was not adequate evidence of a learning disability.

Typical intelligence test interpretive practice in the case of Ashonte' may be to conclude that she has a relative strength in spatial/visualization abilities, and/or weaknesses in verbal, quantitative, or memory abilities. If, on the other hand, we were interpreting behavior ratings we may simply conclude, as was done in this case, that there is no evidence of behavioral problems that produce functional impairment—an interpretation based on a lack of rating scale results that are significantly deviant from the average. Interpretation of the rating scale results, then, emphasize interpretation of "level" over "type" whereas intelligence test results have often been interpreted in relation to one another—a "type" interpretation.

In Ashonte's case we could simply emphasize her level of performance by saying that her intelligence test results are within normal limits since no scores are significantly high enough to identify them as strengths in comparison to her peers and none are low enough to produce functional impairment. In sum, we would do well to ask ourselves if an interpretation of a score as a relative strength or weakness is warranted. *Such an interpretation is more likely warranted if it is deviant by level, which is an indicator of a functional impairment or strength.* If all of Ashonte's scores were in the 60s and 70s or the 120s and 130s her intelligence test results would be of greater importance and, correspondingly, an interpretation of "within normal limits" would be insufficient.

The next logical question is to inquire as to guidelines for identifying a deviant "level." It is rather easy to agree that scores at two or more standard deviations from the mean indicate a deviant level. Such a criterion seems too stringent, however, for clinical interpretation, particularly in the light of the research suggesting that reading scores that are about one standard deviation or more below the mean may indicate functional impairment (Siegel, 1999). In the light of these considerations, I suggest the following guide.

Scores that are in the *extreme 10% (approximately) of the population (standard score of 80 or less and 120 or more where mean = 100 and SD = 15) indicate a deviant level where functional impairment or strength is probably present,* thus warranting interpretation due to the likelihood that these results are producing functional impairment or reflect a strength.

Standard scores that are *between 80 and 89 and 111 and 119 are in the marginal range, which may indicate a deviant level if there is ample evidence of functional impairment or strength.* Normally, scores between 90 and 110 do not indicate functional impairment or strength.

As the case of Ashonte' exemplifies, level interpretation will normally take priority over type unless highly unusual circumstances are present. It is conceivable, for example, for an individual with a reading disability to possess phonological coding problems combined with a global verbal ability deficit. This individual may have intelligence test scores in the average range save verbal

intelligence and reading skill scores in the 80s. Even a 15-point discrepancy may be highly meaningful in this case, causing one to interpret both level and type although the level hypothesis is not particularly deviant from average. This interpretation is made due to the finding that reading and related scores at this level (i.e. <90) do result in functional impairment in reading (Stanovich, 1999). It is equally conceivable, however, for a type interpretation to be made when all scores are within the average range. *Type interpretation, however, is most meaningful when it is also associated with a deviant level.*

Kline, Snyder, and Castellanos (1996), in like manner, suggest that intelligence tests possess the greatest utility for individuals with scores that indicate functional impairment. They offer the following, highly similar point of view.

> *There can be little doubt that the general verbal, visual-spatial, and memory skills measured by tests such as the K-ABC, the Wechlser scales, or the Stanford-Binet are factors in school success. But the estimation of very general, broadband competencies may be the only real value of IQ tests. Certainly, very low IQ scores indicate high risk for poor scholastic performance and possible cognitive and developmental disorders, such as mental retardation. Likewise, very high IQ scores may evince the capability to benefit from an accelerated academic program. Between these two extremes, however, the potential value of the information provided by IQ tests is very limited for perhaps most children for reasons already reviewed. Kaufman (1994) reported that Wechsler once said: "My scales are meant for people with average or near-average intelligence, clinical patients who score between 70 and 130." Many of the research results cited earlier, however, suggest just the opposite: IQ test results may be least informative for children who score more or less in the normal range. (p. 12)*

I expand on the observations of Kline et al. (1996) by noting that it is, for example, only of interest to know the type of ADHD if a child possesses the level of disruptive behavior problems needed to warrant the diagnosis. Similarly, when we take our car to a mechanic for a routine checkup, we are not as interested in whether or not our engine is in better condition than our automobile body if the machanic tells us that there are "no problems." In like manner, we become much more interested in the types of investments we possess if we have considerable wealth to invest. And finally, the track and field team member differs from most of the population in level of athletic ability, making judgments regarding preferred competition specialty a decision of type. Thus, *in many spheres of endeavor level takes primacy over type.*

A CLASS EXERCISE

I use the a priori interpretive method espoused in the first edition of this text (Kamphaus, 1993) as a method for ensuring that trainees apply their theortical and scientific knowledge from the domains of psychometrics, cognition, development, and others to intelligence test interpretation. I have found that the process of offering a priori hypotheses prior to the calculation of a client's scores is a powerful method for encouraging the integration of test results with other information. The word *a priori* is defined as "proceeding from a known or assumed cause to a necessarily related effect; deductive . . . Based on a hypothesis or theory rather than on experiment or experience" (American Heritage Dictionary, 1981). This definition is in contrast to the term *a posteriori*, which is defined as "denoting reasoning from facts or particulars to general principles, or from effects to causes; inductive; empirical" (American Heritage Dictionary, 1981). In this case a posteriori is meant specifically to refer to the latter parts of the above definition, which emphasize inferring causes from effects.

A priori hypotheses are based on previous information about the client, including reports from teachers, clinicians, and parents; previous school grades; medical and developmental histories; and observations during the test session. The clinician, for example, may observe that a child entered the test session begrudgingly because she

had to leave her favorite playmate to attend the test session. She had a noticeable scowl on her face during administration of the Information subtest, and she offered minimal effort with no elaboration of her answers. After the Information subtest the examiner was able to more firmly establish rapport and the child's effort improved substantially thereafter. The examiner may then hypothesize based on these observations that the child will score lower on the Information subtest than on others because of her poor motivation. If, in fact, this finding obtains, then the examiner can feel confident that the a priori hypothesis is confirmed. This method virtually guarantees integration of intelligence test results with other findings since the hypotheses are already based on other findings.

The a priori approach also forces consideration of research and theory because the clinician is operating on the basis of research and theory when the hypothesis is drawn. Another example will clarify the element of previous research. A child is referred for psychological evaluation because of a failure to make academic gains in first grade. He does not yet know his letters and numbers and he is being retained in grade one while receiving remedial assistance. Based on the known correlation between intelligence and academic achievement (see Chapter 3) the examiner hypothesizes that below-average intelligence test scores will be the result. If the child obtains a WISC-III Full Scale of 89 or below, the hypothesis would be confirmed and, additionally, the examiner's conclusion would be based on research findings.

Yet another example demonstrates the link between a priori hypotheses and theory. A child is referred subsequent to a brain injury with complaints of short-term memory deficits and declining school performance. The child's grades have deteriorated from primarily As to mainly Cs. The psychologist conducting the evaluation may hypothesize that Digit Span would be a weakness on the WISC-III because of the reported short-term memory deficits. In addition, the psychologist may also hypothesize that the child will show a lower

WISC-III Full Scale than would be predicted (in the average as opposed to the above-average range) based on the child's previous academic record. Borkowski theorizes (see Chapter 2) that the architectural system must be intact for the executive system to work adequately. This theory may lead the psychologist to predict an overall deficit (in comparison to previous estimates) in intelligence test scores due to damage to the architectural system which in turn damages the executive system. If one of the child's lowest scores is on Digit Span and his Full Scale falls somewhere in the average range or below, then the clinician's hypotheses may again be confirmed.

This approach to interpretation is analogous to one of the differences between exploratory and confirmatory factor analysis, wherein the latter procedure theories about the factor structure are offered a priori (see Chapter 5). Traditional "exploratory" methods of interpretation give the clinician a data set (i.e., Wechsler scores) and ask the clinician to make sense of them, which is similar to what a researcher does by labeling exploratory factors post hoc. I have found this exploratory method of interpretation to be difficult for new students because it is bereft of theory, and it does not emphasize the integration of intelligence test results with other findings. New trainees, in particular, feel very insecure about "naming factors" or drawing conclusions post hoc, causing them to sometimes revert to cookbook methods of interpretation that are far from insightful or helpful. *A priori hypotheses should receive priority in the interpretive process because these hypotheses are already based on substantial information suggesting that they are likely to be highly meaningful in the context of the child's referring problem(s).*

Listed below are some examples of hypotheses that emanate from data acquired prior to the calculation of scores. The hypotheses are based on research and theory cited earlier.

Background Information

Elizabeth is starting school and has a prior diagnosis of a genetic abnormality that is frequently associated with mental retardation such as Down Syndrome or Fragile X syndrome.

Hypothesis

Significantly below-average measures of "g."

Background Information

Greg's mother reports that his language developmental milestones were delayed. He did not use single words until 2 years of age.

Hypothesis

Average to below-average verbal ability scores.

Background Information

Chloe's mother complains of a decline in school performance subsequent to a head injury that occurred when her daughter was struck by a car while riding a bicycle.

Hypothesis

Lower intelligence test scores than premorbid levels (i.e., her scores may be lower than estimates of her intelligence prior to the accident).

Background Information

Beda was referred for evaluation for a second opinion. Some of the previous evaluation data (i.e., achievement test scores at the 99th percentile) suggested that she would be a good candidate for the gifted program, other data were inconsistent.

Hypothesis

Significantly above-average measures of "g."

Background Information

Rowanda has a history of a mild hearing deficit and chronic otitis media (ear infections). She is also receiving speech therapy for articulation difficulties.

Hypothesis

Relative weakness on measures of verbal ability, auditory processing, and auditory short-term memory tasks.

Background Information

Caroline has made poor progress in school. She is currently in the third grade and was retained in both the first and second grades. She has lived in foster care since she was 3 years of age. She was taken from her parents because of evidence of paternal child sexual abuse and parental neglect.

Hypothesis

Average to below-average intelligence test scores.

Background Information

Charles is 2½ years old and virtually all of his developmental milestones are delayed. His mother was addicted to alcohol during pregnancy. He was born premature and he has a previous diagnosis of fetal alcohol syndrome.

Hypothesis

Below-average to significantly below-average intelligence test scores.

Background Information

A teacher notes that Ricky's retention of facts is poor. Information does not seem to "stick with him."

Hypothesis

Two hypotheses may be drawn here. One is that measures of "g" may be below average and the other is that scores on tests requiring long- or short-term memory may be poor.

Background Information

Pilar's academic performance is uneven in the first grade this year. One of her problems is very poor motor skills. She is clumsy, has an odd gait, and her written work is messy and disorganized. She

does express herself well in class and she conversed readily and competently with the examiner.

Hypothesis

Relative weakness on visualization, processing speed, or rate of test-taking tasks that have a motor component.

Background Information

Antonio was highly distractible when observed in the classroom. Similarly, he was highly distracted during the WISC-III Comprehension, Digit Span, Picture Arrangement, Block Design, Coding, and Symbol Search subtests.

Hypothesis

Relative weaknesses on the WISC-III Comprehension, Digit Span, Picture Arrangement, Block Design, Coding, and Symbol Search subtests.

Background Information

Ashley gave up easily on the Coding subtest. She did not seem willing to work quickly on this test.

Hypothesis

Relative weaknesses on processing speed and rate of test-taking subtests.

Background Information

Kristin is 16 years old. She has a history of poor school performance and truancy. She is on probation for automobile theft, and she has run away from home for weeks at a time.

Hypothesis

Below-average scores.

It is noteworthy that the vast majority of the hypotheses drawn above pertain to the Full Scale, Verbal, and Performance scores and few are ipsative (single subtests or profiles) in nature. This is the case because the composite scores have the most research associated with them. Of course, a priori hypotheses, on the other hand, should also be tested against alternative hypotheses in order to ensure that they fit well with other information about the client.

We have been accused of routinely failing to entertain alternative hypotheses for our findings. In the case of diagnostic practice, Dawes (1995) concluded that

> We often make diagnoses consistent only with the numerator in the likelihood ratio form of Bayes' theorem—thereby making what is technically termed a pseudo-diagnostic judgment as a result of evaluating only the degree to which evidence supports a particular hypothesis, rather than comparing that support to the degree to which the evidence supports alternative hypotheses as well. (p. 38)

An example may serve to elucidate Dawes's point. A psychologist may draw the conclusion that a child who is having academic problems may show an intelligence decline and be functioning "beneath his potential" due to the effects of protracted parental fighting over custody and poverty subsequent to parental divorce. The current composite score estimate may be a standard score of 90. Well, a careful review of this child's school records may reveal that his academic achievement scores and the results of a group-administered intelligence screener prior to the family strife and change in SES were virtually identical to current findings. In this case the alternative hypothesis of no significant change in intellectual functioning is supported. Personally, in this case, I would assess behavioral changes related to family functioning (e.g., failure to complete homework) as explanatory variables for this child's academic difficulties.

FIVE EASY STEPS APPLIED TO A SAMPLE CASE (BOX 17.1)

The following five steps will be discussed in turn for the Michael case. The results obtained are real but every other aspect of the case has been disguised far beyond recognition.

Step 1. Collect adequate qualitative and quantitative data from numerous sources.

There is probably an excess of data that has been collected for this case, far beyond that which is necessary for most clinical work. In this sense Michael's case is unrealistic. However, the thorough treatise of developmental history is crucial. Clearly, Michael's parents have already identified his learning disabilities in the language areas. In fact, they have already put educational remediation in place. This information leads us to begin by hypothesizing the existence of a learning disability, which influenced test selection. Specifically, more reading and other achievement tests were necessary for this evaluation. In addition, the application of several intelligence measures allows the clinician to determine the extent of cognitive deficits. It would be interesting to see if his learning disabilities also affected Stratum II and Stratum III abilities. In this case Stratum I abilities are primarily affected.

Step 2. List all scores that may indicate functional impairment or strength and draw hypotheses for each score.

Virtually all of Michael's intelligence scores reflect functional strengths. In fact, this result is so obvious that it is not necessary to list all of these. Some potential weaknesses that may be listed include the Freedom from Distractibility Index score (109) and Coding score (8). Upon reflection, however, the FDI score of 109 should not be listed because it does not indicate funcional impairment. This score is merely relatively lower that his other WISC-III index scores. In addition, his Coding score borders on the average range. There are not any indicators here of functional impairment; in contrast, there are numerous indicators of functional strength. We may have great news for Michael's parents.

Step 3. Integrate all information and draw conclusions that are contextually valid,

parsimonious, and consistent with the state of scientific knowledge.

Well, Michael's results are quite easy to support with background information. He has long been suspected of possessing strong intellectual abilities while simultaneously struggling with reading and writing. These impressions fit well within the context of his daily functioning. He is recognized by all as having good general intellectual abilities and, yet, inexplicably struggling in some academic areas.

His intellectual abilities are quite easily summed up with the composite scores of the DAS and WISC-III. This conclusion is parsimonious.

Lastly, his case fits well with the emerging scientific evidence that reading disabilities are modular and unrelated to estimates of general intelligence or intelligence test profiles (Siegel, 1999). In summary, my preferences for contextual validity, parsimony, and scientific evidence appears to have been achieved.

Step 4. Develop and test rival hypotheses.

One, however, should not be hasty; hence, some rival hypothesis could be offered. A rival hypothesis is that his general intellectual ability is not above average. It could be that he does not have a learning disability but rather just below-average intellectual abilities overall. We can test this hypothesis by searching for convincing evidence to support it. His reading and writing performance in school may support this rival alternative hypothesis. His record of average to above-average achievement in mathematics, the consistent results of two individually administered intelligence tests, and parental and teacher perceptions of above-average general intellectual ability based on long-term knowledge of him all argue against this rival hypothesis.

Step 5. Include remaining conclusions in all oral and written communcation regarding the case.

One singular conclusion remains regarding Michael's intellectual abilities. Michael's current estimates of general intellectual ability are clearly above average in comparison to his same-age peers.

Box 17.1   Sample Case

SCHOOL PSYCHOLOGY SERVICES
CONFIDENTIAL

Name: Michael
Gender: Male
Age: 8 years, 1 month
Grade: 2nd

Assessment Procedures

Differential Ability Scale (DAS)

Wechsler Intelligence Scale for Children—Third Edition (WISC-III)

Kaufman Test of Education Achievement (K-TEA)

Peabody Picture Vocabulary Test—Revised (PPVT-R)

Test of Written Language—Second Edition (TOWL-2)

Woodcock-Johnson Tests of Achievement—Revised (WJ-R)

Woodcock Reading Mastery Tests—Revised (WRMT-R)

Achenbach Child Behavior Checklist—Parent Form (CBCL-P)

(Continues)

Box 17.1   Sample Case (Continued)

Teacher Report Form (TRF)

Behavior Assessment System for Children (BASC)

Parent Rating Scale (PRS)

Structured Developmental History (SDH) (Interview)

Student Observation System (SOS)

Teacher Rating Scale (TRS)

Parenting Stress Index (PSI)

Reynold's Child Depression Scale (RCDS)

Sentence Completion

Teacher Interview

Test of Visual-Motor Integration (VMI)

Torrance Tests of Creative Thinking

Referral Question

This evaluation was requested by Mr. Perla for assessment of Michael's reading difficulties. Mr. Perla expressed concern that Michael is able to recognize words in isolation, but not within the context of a sentence. As a result, a psychoeducational evaluation was conducted in order to assess the need for appropriate school placement and supporting therapies.

Background Information

Michael is the third child born to Lee and Beverly Perla. Michael has two brothers, ages 13 and 6, and one sister, age 10. Michael's father works for a gas company. Michael's mother is currently a waitress. Mr. and Mrs. Perla both have a high school diploma. Mr. Perla did report, however, that he did not learn to read until he was 19 and his father exhibited similar difficulties. Currently, Mr. Perla notes that he does not read very often, although Mrs. Perla reads to the children 3 or 4 times a week. According to Mr. Perla, Mrs. Perla experienced severe swelling during her pregnancy with Michael. She often had to keep her legs elevated and wrapped with towels in order to minimize swelling. Michael was carried full-term but complications at birth included anoxic blue skin tone. Mr. Perla reported that this constriction seemed to last for approximately one minute. According to Michael's father, Michael was within normal limits in reaching his developmental milestones. Mr. Perla does report, however, that numerous respiratory problems have been experienced since he was 1 month old. He currently has asthma and is prescribed Ventolin and Prednisone. Mr. Perla also reported that Michael has been admitted to the hospital on numerous occasions for his asthma. In conjunction with his asthma and allergies, Mr. Perla reports that Michael has experienced frequent ear infections.

Michael's father reported that Michael had pneumonia when he was 4 or 5 and was in the hospital for approximately 9 days. Michael also has had pneumonia one or two times since. In addition, Mr. Perla reported that Michael has choked on food on numerous occasions. Michael's tonsils often swell up when he comes in contact with allergens (e.g., cats, dust, mold). Since Michael's tonsils are already somewhat enlarged because of numerous infections, this allergic swelling has caused some life-threatening incidents. For example, Michael's father reports that in July 1995, Michael choked on a hot dog and "went limp" before his father applied the Heimlich maneuver to dislodge the food. According to Mr. Perla, similar incidents have occurred on 11 occasions. He also reported that previous doctors were hesitant to remove Michael's tonsils. However, Michael's current physician has indicated he will have them removed if another choking incident occurs.

Michael attended kindergarten and is enrolled in the second grade. Mr. Perla reported that he is pleased with Michael's school and current teacher. When Mr. Perla originally referred Michael to the Clinic, he reported that Michael may be retained in the second grade. However, during the interview for this evaluation, Michael's father

Box 17.1 Sample Case (Continued)

noted that Michael would be promoted to the third grade according to his teacher. Mr. Perla further notes that Michael has had high grades in everything but reading. Michael currently attends a special reading class twice a week for 45 minutes. As a result of a teacher referral for these reading problems, a Kaufman Brief Intelligence Test (K-BIT) was administered by the school psychologist at Michael's school. The results revealed average intelligence, which is consistent with Michael's latest Iowa Tests of Basic Skills (ITBS) scores. In addition, Michael has been receiving private tutoring in reading. Both Mr. Perla and Ms. Doyle reported that Michael's confidence toward reading has improved dramatically since initiation of these services.

Teacher Interview

Michael's father indicated that his major concern about Michael was his reading skills. For example, Michael's third quarter report card indicates that he earned grades of Satisfactory (Ss) in every subject but reading, in which he earned Ns (i.e., Need Improvement). His teacher added that Michael often becomes frustrated when he is trying to read. She noted that he is usually able to recognize and say a word that is printed on a flashcard, but is unable to recognize and say the same word when it is within the context of a sentence. She also indicated that the speech and language pathologist recently assessed Michael's hearing, with findings within normal limits. Lastly, his teacher reported that Michael is "very intelligent," but that she often has to redirect him, especially in reading. Nevertheless, she does not consider his behavior within the classroom to be a problem.

Classroom Observation

Michael was observed at school in his classroom. His seat in the classroom is in the front and center of the room. Reading a story about Pecos Bill was the first activity observed. Throughout the activity Michael remained attentive and involved. He answered promptly and correctly when the teacher called on him. The next activity involved completion of basic addition problems, and then calling out the answer when called on. Again, Michael participated appropriately and responded correctly. The last activity observed was a calendar activity using questions about the days and months of the year in order to practice math. The children sat on the floor for this activity. Michael followed the teacher's directions, and sat quietly with the group. Overall, Michael's behavior and academic performance was not distinct from his peers. His teacher indicated that Michael's behavior during the observation was typical of his presentation on most days.

Behavioral Observations

Michael was friendly, talkative, and cooperative throughout the testing sessions. Rapport was easily established and maintained and Michael appeared eager to relate stories and interact with the examiners. Moreover, he seemed exceptionally friendly and asked one of the examiners if he wanted to go to one of his baseball games. In addition, Michael was very persistent on tasks as they became increasingly more difficult. When off-task, he often self-monitored himself and said to the examiner that "they better get back to work." Michael also commented numerous times that he was fidgety and restless because of the medicine, Prednisone, which he started taking a few days before the testing. He reported that he did not like the way it made him feel. Although he was somewhat "fidgety" during the testing sessions, neither examiner experienced significant problems with his behavior.

Test Results and Interpretation

Intelligence
According to Michael's performance on the Differential Ability Scales (DAS), his current level of intellectual functioning is in the above-average to well-above-average range. There is a 90% probability that Michael's General Cognitive Ability score, an overall estimate of intelligence, meets or exceeds that of 84% to 96% of his agemates. Michael's Verbal scores were in the well-above-average range, while his Spatial and Nonverbal scores were in the above-average range. Michael's performance on the Weschler Intelligence Scale for Children—Third Edition

(Continues)

Box 17.1   **Sample Case** (Continued)

(WISC-III) indicates that his overall estimate of intellectual functioning, the Full Scale score, falls in the above-average to well-above-average range. There is a 90% probability that his overall score meets or exceeds that of 81% to 93% of his agemates.

These results are consistent with test results from his school. For example, both the ITBS and K-BIT indicate that Michael has at least average intelligence.

Language

Michael's performance on the PPVT-R was in the above-average to well-above-average range. These results indicate that he has a well-developed ability to understand and comprehend words that are read to him. These results are consistent with above-average PPVT-R scores provided by his private tutor.

Achievement

Michael was administered the Kaufman Test of Educational Achievement (K-TEA). Michael's overall estimate of achievement, the Battery Composite score, indicates that his performance is in the below-average range. There is a significant difference, however, between his mathematics and reading scores. Michael's mathematics composite score was in the average range, while his reading composite score was well-below-average. These findings are consistent with information provided by Michael's teacher.

In addition, Michael was also administered the Woodcock-Johnson Tests of Achievement—Revised (WJ-R). On this instrument Michael was administered subtests that assessed his broad mathematics and reading skills. Similar to his performance on the K-TEA, Michael's math and reading scores were significantly different. His broad mathematics score was of average to above-average quality, while his broad reading score was in the well-below-average to below-average range.

To further assess Michael's reading ability, the Wookcock Reading Mastery Tests—Revised (WRMT-R) was administered. Michael's Total Reading Cluster score was in the well-below-average range. Similarly, his performance on the Word Identification, Passage Comprehension, Letter Identification, and Word Attack subtests was significantly deficient. Michael's performance on the Visual Auditory Learning subtest, however, was inconsistent with these findings and found to be in the upper extreme range. This subtest requires memorizing symbols that correspond to words. The examinee reads a sentence by using these memorized symbols. Findings from this subtest suggest that Michael's above-average intellectual ability and memory skills enabled him to score well on this subtest. Overall, the results on the WRMT-R are consistent with Michael's well-below-average to below-average reading performance on both the K-TEA and WJ-R.

The Test of Written Language—Third Edition (TOWL-3) was administered to Michael to assess his written language skills. Michael was administered the Spontaneous Writing Section of the TOWL-3, which yielded a score in the well-below-average range. These results are also consistent with Michael's reading difficulties.

Social/Emotional/Behavioral

Michael's mother and father completed the Behavior Assessment System for Children—Parent Rating Scale (BASC-PRS), and the Achenbach Child Behavior Checklist (CBCL). These instruments assess the parents' view of their child's behavior, emotional functioning, and social competence.

On the BASC-PRS, Mr. and Mrs. Perla both indicated significant problems on the Somatization scale. This scale assesses the child's tendency to have numerous medical (somatic) complaints. These results are consistent with Michael's history of chronic health problems. Michael's father and mother indicated no significant problems on the CBCL.

Michael's second grade teacher completed the Behavior Assessment System for Children—Teacher Rating Scale (BASC-TRS) and the Achenbach Teacher Report Form (TRF). On the BASC-TRS, his teacher also endorsed significant problems on the Somatization scale, which is consistent with ratings provided by Michael's parents. Michael's teacher indicated no significant problems on the TRF. Mr. and Mrs. Perla also completed the Parenting Stress Index (PSI). The PSI is designed to assess the overall stress in the parent's life. The only significant area indicated by

Box 17.1   Sample Case (Continued)

Michael's parents was on the Restriction of Role subscale. Parents in this category see themselves as being controlled and dominated by their children's demands and needs. These results are consistent with the stress of parenting a chronically ill child in a family of three other children.

Summary

Michael is an 8-year-old male who was referred by his father for an evaluation due to his reading difficulties. Mr. Perla reported that Michael was being considered for retention in second grade due to his reading problems. School officials have since indicated that he will be promoted to the third grade. Mr. Perla and Michael's teacher reported that Michael is performing in an acceptable manner in all of his subjects except reading. Administration of the intellectual test measures indicated that Michael's current level of intellectual functioning is in the above-average to well-above-average range. On tests of academic proficiency, Michael's achievement scores on both instruments were consistent with indications of his reading and mathematics abilities within the classroom. As such, a significant scholastic discrepancy is noted with reading scores in the well-below-average to below-average range, while math scores were average to above-average. Social/Emotional/Behavioral assessment indicated significant somatic complaints and parental restriction of role. Both of these results are consistent with Michael's chronic health problems and associated stress on Michael's parents and siblings. As a result of these findings, it is highly recommended that Michael be considered eligible for Specific Learning Disability (SLD) placement in the areas of reading comprehension, reading recognition, and written expression.

Diagnoses

Learning Disability
Reading Recognition
Reading Comprehension
Written Expression

Recommendations

1. It is strongly recommended that Michael not be retained in second grade. In the light of his Learning Disability, no benefit would be derived from a retention of this nature.

2. It is strongly recommended that Michael's school communicate with his private teacher in order to determine what has and has not been effective in promoting Michael's reading skills. His tutor has compiled a list of areas that Michael has not mastered: (a) consonant blends; (b) consonant digraphs; (c) long vowels; (d) R-controlled vowels; (e) double vowels; (f) variant/irregular vowels; (g) syllabication.

3. It is recommended that a number of reading approaches be explored with Michael, including whole-language, phonetics, and so on, in order to find the instructional methodology that is most effective in assisting Michael with his reading deficits.

4. Michael should utilize a computer and software designed to increase his reading, spelling, and overall language skills. Fun and interesting programs are available for teaching children decoding, phoneme awareness, and blending skills as well as others.

5. It is recommended that Michael's teachers evaluate the manner in which they assess what Michael has learned. Oral tests or tests on a computer are strongly encouraged given his significant deficit with written expression skills.

6. It is recommended that Michael's parents encourage reading at home. For example, playing games could make reading fun for Michael while increasing his vocabulary. The use of flashcards can be continued with multiple variations. Michael could have a Word Bank using flashcards. The words could be written on one side of the card, while Michael could draw a picture about the word on the other side. These cards could be kept in a box for Michael so that he could practice and drill with them in school and at home.

7. A study skills training program is recommended for Michael (e.g., how to outline, take tests, and complete homework).

(Continues)

Box 17.1   **Sample Case** (Continued)

Psychometric Summary

Differential Ability Scales (DAS)

The DAS is an individually administered intelligence test consisting of six "core subtest" and several diagnostic subtests. Only the core subtests are used in the calculation of the General Cognitive Ability (GCA) score, an estimate of overall intelligence. The DAS core subtests are also used to calculate composite scores for verbal abilities, nonverbal reasoning, and spatial abilities.

The following composite standard scores have a mean of 100 and a standard deviation of 15. Scores between 90 and 110 are considered average. Scores between 110 and 120 are considered above average, scores between 120 and 130 are considered well above average, and scores above 130 are considered extremely high.

	STANDARD SCORE	90% CONFIDENCE BAND
GCA	121	115–126
Verbal	123	113–130
Nonverbal	112	104–119
Spatial	117	109–123

The following *T* scores have a mean of 50 and a standard deviation of 10. Scores between 40 and 60 are in the average range. Scores between 60 and 70 are above average, and scores above 70 are very high.

VERBAL	*T* SCORES
Word definitions	63
Similarities	68

NONVERBAL	*T* SCORES
Matrices	55
Sequential & Quantitative Reasoning	59

SPATIAL	*T* SCORES
Recall of Designs	55
Pattern Construction	66

Wechsler Intelligence Scale for Children—Third Edition (WISC-III)

The WISC-III is an individually administered clinical instrument for assessing the intellectual ability of children aged 6 years through 16 years, 11 months. The child's performance on 12 subtests is summarized in an overall intelligence score called the Full Scale standard score. The WISC-III also yields scores for Verbal and Performance scores. Verbal activities included defining words, answering factual as well as commonsense questions, and doing arithmetic problems without pencil and paper. Performance activities include putting together puzzles and picture sequences, making designs with blocks, and pointing out missing parts of a picture.

The following subtest scores have a mean score = 10 with a standard deviation = 3. Scores between 7 and 13 are considered average.

Box 17.1   Sample Case (Continued)

Verbal	SS	Performance	SS
Information	11	Picture Completion	13
Similarities	13	Coding	8
Arithmetic	11	Picture Arrangement	14
Vocabulary	13	Block Design	14
Comprehension	13	Object Assembly	14
(Digit Span)	12	(Symbol Search)	12

The following composite scores have a mean score = 100 with a standard deviation = 15. Scores between 85 and 115 are considered average.

Composite score	SS	90% Confidence Bands
Verbal Score	113	107–118
Performance Score	120	111–125
Full Scale Score	118	113–122

Factor scores	SS	90% Confidence Bands
Verbal Comprehension	114	107–119
Perceptual Organization	126	116–130
FD (Third Factor)	109	100–116
Processing Speed	111	101–117

Peabody Picture Vocabulary Test—Revised (PPVT-R)

The PPVT-R is an individually administered, norm-referenced, wide-range, power test of hearing vocabulary. The following standard score has a mean of 100 and a standard deviation of 15.

Standard Score: 120   Percentile Rank: 91

Kaufman Test of Educational Achievement (K-TEA)

The K-TEA is an individually administered measure of the school achievement. It yields standard scores with a mean = 100 and a standard deviation = 15. Standard scores between 90 and 110 are considered average.

	Standard scores	90% Confidence bands	Description
Math Applications	108	100–116	Average
Math Computation	97	87–107	Average
Math Composite	103	96–110	Average
Reading Decoding	77	72–82	Well Below Average
Reading Comprehension	80	74–86	Well Below Average
Reading Composite	77	73–81	Well Below Average
Battery Composite	86	82–90	Below Average

(Continues)

Box 17.1   Sample Case (Continued)

Test of Written Language—3 (TOWL-3)

The TOWL-3 was designed as a comprehensive measure of writing ability that can be used to identify students achieving significantly below their peers and to determine strengths and weaknesses in writing. For the Spontaneous Writing Section of the TOWL-3, the child is asked to write a story that tells about the picture presented.

The following subtest scores have a mean = 10 with a standard deviation = 3. Scores between 7 and 13 are considered average.

	SUBTEST STANDARD SCORES
Thematic Maturity	6
Contextual Vocabulary	8
Syntactic Maturity	6
Contextual Spelling	3
Contextual Style	10

The following quotients have a mean = 100 with a standard deviation = 15. Quotients between 85 and 115 are considered average.

Spontaneous Writing Quotient	77

Woodcock-Johnson Tests of Achievement—Revised (WJ-R)

The Woodcock-Johnson is an individually administered achievement test. It is made up of a number of subtests the results of which are combined into composite scores: Broad Reading, Basic Reading Skills, Broad Mathematics, Broad Written Language, and Broad Knowledge.

The Woodcock-Johnson yields standard scores with a mean = 100 and a standard deviation = 15. Standard scores between 90 and 110 are considered average.

	STANDARD SCORES	CONFIDENCE BANDS
Visual-Auditory Learning	130	123–138
Letter Identification	82	77–87
Word Identification	71	69–73
Word Attack	84	81–87
Passage Comprehension	74	71–77
Basic Skills Cluster	73	71–75
Total Reading Cluster	72	70–74

Achenbach Child Behavior Checklist—Parent Form (CBCL-P)

The Achenbach CBCL is a questionnaire that is completed by parents in order to report behavior and emotional problems of their children. The Achenbach yields T scores with a mean of 50 and a standard deviation of 10. Scores between 67 and 70 are considered borderline significant. A score above 70 is indicative of significant problems.

Box 17.1 **Sample Case** (Continued)

	T scores	
	Mother	**Father**
Withdrawn	54	58
Somatic Complaints	50	64
Anxious/Depressed	50	50
Social Problems	50	50
Thought Problems	50	57
Attention Problems	50	50
Delinquent Behavior	50	50
Aggressive Behavior	50	50
Internalizing Composite	43	53
Externalizing Composite	43	49
Total Composite Score	40	47

Achenbach Teacher Report Form (TRF)

The TRF is a questionnaire to be completed by teachers in order to report behavior and emotional problems. The TRF yields T scores with a mean of 50 and standard deviation of 10. Scores between 64 and 70 are considered to be borderline significant. A score above 70 is clinically significant.

	T scores
Withdrawn	55
Somatic Complaints	50
Anxious/Depressed	51
Social Problems	55
Thought Problems	50
Attention Problems	56
Delinquent Behavior	57
Aggressive Behavior	50
Internalizing Composite	51
Externalizing Composite	48
Total Composite Score	53

Behavior Assessment System for Children—Parent Rating Scales (BASC-PRS)

The BASC-PRS is a questionnaire that is filled out by parents in order to assess the behavior problems, emotional problems, and social competence of their children. The BASC-PRS yields T scores with a mean = 50 and a standard deviation = 10. Scores between 65 and 70 are indicative of some difficulty, and scores above 70 are considered significant problems.

	T scores	
	Father	**Mother**
Hyperactivity	52	41
Aggression	55	46
Conduct Problems	49	52

(Continues)

Box 17.1   Sample Case (Continued)

	T scores	
	FATHER	MOTHER
Externalizing Problems Composite	52	46
Anxiety	59	38
Depression	51	43
Somatization	73	79
Internalizing Problems Composite	64	54
Attention Problems	50	45
Atypicality	46	38
Withdrawal	57	50
Behavioral Symptoms Index	53	38

Scores below 30 on the adaptive scales are considered significantly low.

Adaptability	41	47
Social Skills	50	48
Leadership	41	48
Adaptive Skills Composite	43	47

Behavior Assessment System for Children—Teacher Rating Scale (BASC-TRS)

The BASC-TRS is a questionnaire completed by teachers to obtain ratings of adaptive skills, and behavior and emotional problems of students. The BASC-TRS yields T-Scores with a mean = 50 and a standard deviation of 10. Scores between 60 and 70 indicate some difficulty. Scores above 70 are considered significantly high.

	T scores
Hyperactivity	44
Aggression	41
Conduct Problems	47
Externalizing Problems Composite	44
Anxiety	59
Depression	48
Somatization	72
Internalizing Problems Composite	62
Attention Problems	60
Learning Problems	59
School Problems Composite	60
Atypicality	47
Withdrawal	45
Behavioral Symptoms Index	

<u>**Box 17.1   Sample Case**</u> (Continued)

Scores below 30 on the adaptive scales are considered significantly low.

Adaptability	43
Social Skills	53
Leadership	55
Study Skills	41
Adaptive Skills Composite	48

Parenting Stress Index (PSI)

The PSI was designed as an overall measure of stress in the parent's life. Two domains are sampled: stress associated with parenting this particular child, and stress in other parts of the parent's life. The composite scores (Total Stress, Child Domain, and Parent Domain) are the most reliable scores for interpretation. Percentile scores above 90 are considered indicative of a problem.

	PERCENTILE	
	FATHER	MOTHER
Adaptability	65	65
Acceptability	70	70
Demandingness	45	25
Mood	60	75
Distractibility/Hyperactivity	10	10
Reinforces Parent	45	45
Child Domain Score	35	33
Depression	20	20
Attachment	1	1
Restriction of Role	92	92
Sense of Competence	7	7
Social Isolation	75	75
Relationship with Spouse	75	75
Parent Health	65	65
Parent Domain Score	42	42
Total Stress Score	36	35

SOME PRACTICAL INTERPRETIVE ISSUES

Failure to Draw Conclusions

Psychologists do not gain by pretending to know answers when they do not. Admitting to unclear findings is not symptomatic of incompetence, but rather, such acknowledgements typically signify that the examiner is thoughtful, careful, and concerned.

Clinicians can also make tentative conclusions in a report if further data are required to test a theory or hypothesis. If an uncorroborated Information subtest weakness is found, for example, an examiner should not feel compelled to overinterpret the finding or ignore it. The examiner, in this case, could write, a clear explanation for Al's lower score on the Information subtest is not yet apparent. A second Information-like measure should be obtained to see if this is a reliable finding. One source of additional information could be scores on file such as Al's scores on the science, history, and social science sections of the achievement test used by his school.

Inferring Cause-and-Effect Relationships

A particularly disconcerting problem of assessment reports is the tendency to offer cause-and-effect relationships between intelligence test profiles and a child's school or other problems. For example, concluding that a child cannot write because of poor visual-motor skills seems sensible but it is, nevertheless, a supposition of unknown validity.

The examiner who offers such conclusions is inferring etiology, a tricky proposition at best. A similar temptation occurs in medical diagnosis. When a pediatrician diagnoses a problem, parents often ask questions such as, "How did he get this?" If a child were diagnosed with leukemia, a physician would be unlikely to say that the child acquired the condition from the chemical waste dump down the street. While this may be true, it would be difficult to prove given the multiple etiologies of leukemia. Similarly, the argument that a child's visual-motor weakness, as identified on Block Design or similar tests, is the cause of a reading problem is a high-inference enterprise. It is entirely possible that these two problems exist but are not related.

Other examples of inferring cause-and-effect relationships include the following.

"Jason's mathematics problem is due to his problem with psychomotor speed."

"Michelle's inattentiveness is caused by her school failure, which is adversely affected by her poor verbal intelligence."

"Aaron's writing problem is the result of his spatial processing problem."

Of course, the psychologist's (and the physician's) job in many cases is to infer cause-and-effect relationships. The point that I wish to make is that psychologists should at least clearly recognize when they are making such a conclusion so that they think critically about these inferences before making them. Examiners should also *label an inference as such when offering it as a conclusion*.

Retesting

In some cases a psychologist may feel that the current intelligence test results are invalidated by other factors. In these instances there are basically two choices. The psychologist can make an estimate of the client's intelligence or retest the child. An example of using background information to help gauge if a client's scores were valid may help explicate the issue of retesting further.

A 15-year-old female was hospitalized in a psychiatric unit of a general hospital for severe depression with psychotic features. This young woman was suffering from visual hallucinations and an inability to "slow down" her thought processes. She had also slit her wrists in a suicide attempt just prior to admission. This young lady was the product of a very supportive family background. Her father was an engineer and her mother a school teacher. She had nearly a straight A average in her high school advanced placement program.

On the WISC-III this woman obtained a Full Scale of 115, which corresponds to the 84th percentile rank. While this score is above average there is considerable evidence that her score could have been adversely affected by her mental illness. In this case the client should be tested again once her depressive and psychotic symptoms were under better control. Unfortunately, inaccurate intelligence test scores can remain in an individual's records for some time and potentially result in misperceptions of that individual's skills.

Conclusions

The integrative method of interpretation offered in this chapter is empirically based and emphasizes interpretation of intelligence test scores in the larger context of the person's life. One of the hallmarks of this approach is an emphasis on the corroboration of intelligence test results with other data. The case studies in this chapter emphasized the use of intelligence tests as one component of the diagnostic decision-making process where sometimes the intelligence test results are primary and in other cases they are not as relevant. Clinicians must remember that *intelligence tests do not make decisions about an individual's life, professionals do* (Kaufman, 1990). In this more limited context intelligence tests are much less likely to be overused and more likely to be of value for helping to understand an individual's cognitive abilities.

McDermott et al. (1990) assail the age-old practice of investigating strengths and weaknesses in a child's subtest profile by revealing measurement flaws underlying the practice.

The outcome of these and other criticisms is that clinicians' interpretations of intelligence tests are now held to a higher standard. Put in psychometric terms, *we strive to ensure that our interpretations of intelligence test results routinely have demonstrated validity*. While this point now seems axiomatic, this has frequently not been the case.

Chapter Summary

- Matarazzo (1990) identified some disturbing problems in the interpretive aspect of the assessment process, including a lack of knowledge of the psychometric properties of the tests that psychologists use (a science-based practice problem) and a lack of congruence between test results and other information about the client (an integration problem).

- Russell (1994) noted that physicians also conduct numerous medical assessment practices on the basis of common sense and good intentions rather than because of strong scientific evidence.

- In the early days of psychological assessment, a premium was placed on interpretation of subtests and composite scores and subtest profiles (Rapport, Gill, & Schafer, 1945–46). The Wechsler scales were instrumental in fostering this emphasis because of the provision of subtest scores.

- The three core characteristics advised for intelligence test interpretation include striving for contextual relevance, parsimony, and consistency with psychological science.

- The five steps offered for intelligence test interpretation include:

Step 1. Collect adequate qualitative and quantitative data from numerous sources.

Step 2. List all scores that may indicate functional impairment or strength and draw hypotheses for each score.

Step 3. Integrate all information and draw conclusions that are contextually valid, parsimonious, and consistent with the state of scientific knowledge.

Step 4. Develop and test rival hypotheses.

Step 5. Include remaining conclusions in all oral and written communcation regarding the case.

- *Two pieces of evidence* are generally adequate to corroborate or reject a hypothesis.

- Psychometric science suggests that we always *try to subsume less reliable and valid hypotheses under more reliable and valid ones*. By doing so examiners are erroring in the direction of drawing hypotheses based on greater evidence of reliability and validity.

- Always attempt to offer research and theory to support conclusions.
- Clinicians should consider deferring offering conclusions prematurely.

- Examiners should "order a retest" if there is reason to believe that current intelligence test results were invalidated by other factors.

CHAPTER 18

Report Writing
and Oral Reporting

CHAPTER QUESTIONS

What is the best way to tell parents of their child's test results?

What are the common mistakes made in report writing?

Effective report writing is taking on increased importance for practicing psychologists. Psychological reports are routinely made available to parents, judges, lawyers, and other nonpsychologists, creating the opportunity for improper interpretation of the results by untrained individuals. Oftentimes, misconceptions, such as parents or others who cling to the notion that the IQ is an entirely genetically based and fixed entity, about intellectual assessment and the nature of intelligence tests make it imperative that psychologists communicate clearly, both orally and in writing.

In addition, psychological reports remain particularly useful to other clinicians who evaluate a patient who has previously been seen by a psychologist. A previous psychological report could be extremely valuable in a case of brain injury, for example, if a child was given an intelligence test prior to the injury. The previous psychological report could be crucial as a measure of premorbid status. Estimates of premorbid status are extremely valuable because they allow the psychologist to determine the extent of cognitive impairment that may be due to brain insult (see Chapter 19). As Glasser and Zimmerman (1967) correctly recognize, "The clarity of the original presentation will determine the use made of the examination at a later date." The written psychological report often becomes an extremely important piece of information for treatment planning and diagnosis because of its role in clarifying the nature of the obtained scores.

Despite its importance, the topic of report writing is a neglected one in the research literature (Ownby & Wallbrown, 1986). While a number of treatises are available on this topic (Tallent, 1988; Teglasi, 1983), little research has been done on the effects of report writing on important outcomes such as the likelihood that a recommendation will be followed (Ownby & Wallbrown, 1986).

The conclusions of Ownby and Wallbrown (1986) are still pertinent today. They observed that psychological reports

1. are considered useful to some extent by consumers such as psychiatrists and social workers,
2. are frequently criticized by these professional groups on both content and stylistic grounds, and
3. may (or may not) make substantial contributions to patient management.

In addition to psychiatrists and social workers, a number of studies have assessed teachers' satisfaction with psychological reports, and the news is not good (Ownby & Wallbrown, 1986). Researchers have found that teachers are frequently dissatisfied with psychological reports (Ownby & Wallbrown, 1986).

One can get a sense of why teachers and other professionals are dissatisfied with psychological reports by reading the following excerpt that was taken verbatim from a psychological report that was given to me several years ago by a colleague. Keep in mind that all of the conclusions drawn by the evaluator in this case *were based on one test requiring the child to simply reproduce 9 designs with pencil and paper*.

> *The Bender-Visual Motor Gestalt test suggests delinquency and an acting out potential. He is anxious, confused, insecure and has a low self-esteem. He may have difficulties in interpersonal relationships and tends to isolate himself when problems arise. . . . (He) also seems to have a lot of anxiety and tension over phallic sexuality and may be in somewhat of a homosexual panic.*

This examiner was probably using an antiquated cookbook approach to interpretation in order to prepare this report. Needless to say, a report that makes extraordinary inferences based on limited data is of no help to anyone, especially not the client being evaluated.

One of the difficulties with report writing is that different audiences require different reports. For example, a psychometric summary (a psychometric summary is a portion of the report that presents only test scores and is usually given as an appendix at the end of a report) given out of context is likely to be of little use to parents, but of great potential use to colleagues and perhaps teachers. An important decision that each psychologist must make prior to report writing is to determine the primary audience for the report. A psychometric summary is more appropriate in a clinic situation where it is imperative that a psychologist communicate effectively with knowledgeable colleagues.

PITFALLS OF REPORT WRITING

As Tallent (1988) observed, "That many psychological reports are written so as not to be very useful, so as not to contribute to decision making, is a complaint that just won't go away." Norman Tallent's (1988) textbook on report writing summarizes the literature on the strengths and weaknesses of reports as identified by psychologist's colleagues in mental health care, most notably social workers and psychiatrists. Some of the highlights of Tallent's (1988) review will be summarized next.

Vocabulary Problems

The problem of using vague or imprecise language in report writing persists. The colloquial term used to describe such language is *psychobabble*. Siskind (1967), for example, studied the level of agreement between psychologists and psychiatrists in defining words such as the following.

Abstract	Compulsive	Depressive
Affective	Constriction	Hostility
Aggression	Control	Immaturity
Anxiety	Defense	Impulsive
Bizarre	Dependent	Emotional
Bright Normal	Depressive	

The results of the study showed very little correspondence between the definitions proffered by the two groups of professionals.

Harvey (1989) explained how this problem of vague or imprecise language applies to school psychologists, who probably do the greatest amount of assessment work with children and adolescents. She also pointed out that because of the passing of the "Buckley Amendment" and the increasingly common practice of giving reports to parents, that the educational level of the typical consumer of psychological reports is lower than in the past. While many writers of psychological reports use language consistent with their graduate-level training, such language may be at a reading level far beyond the capability of the target audience, particularly if the audience is parents or even adolescents. Harvey (1989) noted that even respected magazines are written at a high school level. The *Atlantic Monthly* is written at a 12th-grade level, and *Time* and *Newsweek* at 11th-grade levels (Harvey, 1989).

Tallent (1988) referred to one aspect of this problem with language as "exhibitionism," which seems to be a frequent criticism of reports, particularly on the part of other psychologists. One commentator stated, "They are written in stilted psychological terms to boost the ego of the psychologist."

Other pertinent observations (Tallent, 1988) on the use of language by psychologists in reports include:

"Often padded with meaningless multisyllabic words to lengthen report."

"Gobbledygook."

"Semantics have a tendency to creep in, and the phenomenon of 'verbal diarrhea' occurs too often."

"They are too often written in a horrible psychologese—so that clients 'manifest overt aggressive hostility in an impulsive manner'—when, in fact—they punch you on the nose."

"They are not frequently enough written in lay language. I believe it requires clear thinking to write without use of technical terms."

And my personal favorite is:

"Scores have little meaning even to the psychologist who understands their rationale, unless he knows how they fit together in terms of cause and effect regarding behavior. To cover up his ignorance he resorts to the reporting of percentages, ratios, etc., and overwhelms his reader with such technical language that little information is conveyed."

Actually, I have one more favorite.

"They are not clear enough to be wrong."

Of course, psychologists cannot be singled out as the only profession with a preference for its own idiosyncratic terminology, as anyone who reads a physician's report or legal contract will admit.

Eisegesis

This is the problem of "faulty interpretation based on personal ideas, bias, and what not" (Tallent, 1988). It is most readily seen in reports where the psychologist is clearly using the same theories or drawing the same conclusions in every report. A psychologist may conclude that all children's problems are due to poor ego functioning, neuropsychological problems, or family system failure. Psychologists who aspire exclusively to behavioral principles, for example, will attribute all child problems to faulty reinforcement histories. The savvy consumer of this psychologist's reports will eventually become wary of the skill of the psychologist, as the relevance of this theory to some cases is questionable. One can imagine the skepticism that may be engendered by a psychologist who concludes that a child whose school performance has just deteriorated subsequent to a traumatic head injury merely needs more "positive reinforcement" to bring his grades up to pretrauma levels.

The problem of eisegesis may also occur if a psychologist draws conclusions that are clearly in conflict with the data collected. I have seen an extraordinarily large number of students who never seemed capable of assessing intelligence accurately, because they always found some mitigating circumstance. Either the child was not sitting still, the room was too hot, or the child just did not seem motivated to take the test. If a child obtained a low standard score (which is typical because children are usually referred because of problems), it was considered invalid and the conclusion drawn that the child's "true ability" was undoubtedly considerably higher. Teachers who receive this interpretation consistently from the same psychologist may eventually pay more attention to the data presented in the reports and ignore the psychologist's conclusions.

Report Length

Psychologists, more so than other groups, complain about the excessive length of reports (Tallent, 1988). However, length may not be the real issue. Perhaps long reports are used to disguise incompetence, fulfill needs for accountability, or impress others. The possibility that length is a cover for other ills is offered in the following quote (Tallent, 1988).

> *A certain business executive likes to relate the anecdote about the occasion when he assigned a new employee to prepare a report for him. In due time a voluminous piece of writing was returned. Dismayed, the executive pointed out that the required information could be presented on one, certainly not more than two, pages. "But sir," pleaded the young man, "I don't know that much about the matter you assigned me to." (p. 72)*

It may also be worth considering that the Ten Commandments are expressed in 297 words, the Declaration of Independence in 300 words, and the Gettysburg Address in 266 words (Tallent, 1988).

A Number Emphasis

Psychologists are also infamous for having sections of their report entitled something like "Test Results." In this part of the report, the reader usually gets the sense that the child is of secondary importance and the numbers are of greatest importance (Tallent, 1988). The psychologist needs to keep clearly in mind that the child is the loadstar of the evaluation, and the numbers obtained from intelligence tests and the like are only worthy of emphasis if they contribute to the understanding of the child being evaluated. All too frequently, the numbers take precedence in assessment results sections. One way to think of the scores is as a means to an end, the end being better understanding of the child. The same numbers for two children can mean two quite different things. Just as a high temperature reading can be symptomatic of a host of disorders from influenza to appendicitis, so, too a low intelligence test score can reveal a host of possible conditions.

One horrendous error made often in reporting test scores is when a psychologist reports a child's IQ and then says that it's invalid. Then why report it (Tallent, 1988)? If a test score is invalid, how does it serve the child to have this score as part of a permanent record? Is it to record for all time the lack of logic on the part of the psychologist? This purpose seems to be the only one served by reporting scores in which the clinician has little, if any, faith. Reporting invalid scores is akin to a physician making a diagnostic decision based on a fasting blood test where the patient violated the fasting requirements. In all likelihood the flawed results would not be reported, rather the patient would be required to retake the test. My rule of thumb is that *one does not have to report scores for a test just because it was administered.*

Failure to Address Referral Questions

Tallent (1988) points out that psychologists too often fail to demand clear referral questions and, as a result, their reports appear vague and unfocused. This very obvious point is all too frequently overlooked. Psychologists should insist that referral sources present their questions clearly and, if not, the psychologist should meet with the referring person to obtain further detail on the type of information that is expected from the evaluation (Tallent, 1988). Many agencies use referral forms to assist in this process of declaring assessment goals. A form similar to those used by hospitals is shown in Figure 18.1, and one suitable for use by school systems is given in Figure 18.2.

THE CONSUMER'S VIEW

A few studies have evaluated psychological reports from the viewpoint of the consumer (Brandt & Giebink, 1968; Mussman, 1964; Rucker, 1967). One rather clever recent study evaluated teacher preferences for and comprehension of varying report formats (Wiener, 1985). This study required a group of elementary school teachers to read and rate their comprehension of and preferences for three different reports for the same child.

The three reports used were a "short form," "the psychoeducational report," and "question and answer." The short form report was one page, single spaced. It used some jargon, such as acronyms, to shorten length, conclusions were drawn without reference to a data source, and recommendations were given without elaboration. The psychoeducational report format was $3\frac{1}{2}$ single-spaced pages. It used headings such as reason for referral, learning style, mathematics, conclusions, and recommendations. Observations were stated in behavioral terms with examples used freely. Recommendations were given and elaborated, and acronyms and other jargon were only used when they were defined in text. The question-and-answer report was similar to the psychoeducational report in many ways, but it did not use headings per se. This report listed referral questions and then answered each question in turn. This report was $4\frac{1}{2}$ pages long.

Now the time has come to crown the winner! Was it the short form, the psychoeducational, or the question-and-answer format? Amazingly enough, in this study *length* was preferred. First, teachers comprehended the two longer reports better. Secondly, of the two longer reports, the teachers preferred the question-and-answer report over the psychoeducational report. The short form was clearly preferred least.

Patient Name _____   Medical Record Number _____

Attending Physician _____

Type of Consultation _____

Signed _____   Title _____   Date _____

Results of Consultation:

Date of Consultation_____

Signature of Consultant _____ Title _____ Date _____

FIGURE 18.1

Referral for consultation

School District _____ Referring School _____

Student's Name _____ Date of Referral _____

Address _____ Phone _____ Birth date _____

Grade _____ Grade Repeated _____ Attendance (days absent) _____

Is the student now receiving speech therapy? ____ yes ____ no

	Never	Sometimes	Often
Communications Problems			
Expressive Language (Problems in grammar, limited vocabulary)	____	____	____
Receptive Language (Comprehension, not following directions)	____	____	____
Speech (Poor enunciation, lisps, stutters, omits sounds, infantile speech)	____	____	____
Physical Problems			
Gross Motor Coordination (Awkward, clumsy, poor balance)	____	____	____
Fine Motor Coordination (Eye-hand, manual dexterity)	____	____	____
Visual (Cannot see blackboard, squints, rubs eyes, holds book too close)	____	____	____
Hearing (Unable to discriminate sounds, asks to have instructions repeated, turns ear to speaker, often has earaches)	____	____	____
Health (Example: epilepsy, respiratory problems, etc.) _____	____	____	____
Medication: ____ yes ____ no Type: _____	____	____	____
Classroom Behavior			
Overly energetic, talks out, out of seat	____	____	____
Very quiet, uncommunicative	____	____	____
Acting out (Aggressive, hostile, rebellious, destructive, cries easily)	____	____	____
Inattentive (Short attention span, poor on-task behavior)	____	____	____
Doesn't appear to notice what is happening in the immediate environment	____	____	____
Poor Peer Relationships (Few friends, rejected, ignored, abused by peers)	____	____	____
Academic Problems			
Reading (Word attack, comprehension)	____	____	____
Writing (Illegible, reverses letters, doesn't write)	____	____	____
Spelling (Cannot spell phonetically, omits or adds letters)	____	____	____
Mathematics (computation, concepts, application)	____	____	____
Social Science, Sciences (Doesn't handle concepts, doesn't understand relationships, poor understanding of cause and effect)	____	____	____

Other Problems _____

What methods/materials have you tried to solve the problems? _____
_____

_____   _____
Signature and Position of referring person   Chairperson/School Position

FIGURE 18.2

Sample student referral

These are interesting results in that they hint that length may be overrated as a problem in report writing and that teachers may prefer a question-and-answer report format. This finding is interesting to me because I have never seen anyone use this format in my entire career as a psychologist!

Do parents have different preferences from teachers? In a follow-up study with parents, using the same methodology, Wiener and Kohler (1986) found that teachers and parents have similar preferences. In this second study, the same three report formats were used. As was the case with teachers, parents comprehended the two longer reports significantly better than the short form report. An interesting additional finding was that parents with a college education comprehended reports better than parents with a high school diploma. Parents also tended to prefer the question-and-answer format to the other two formats, although the difference in preference scores between the psychoeducational and question-and-answer reports failed to reach statistical significance.

Taken together, these two studies suggested that the two most frequent consumers of child and adolescent psychological reports, parents and teachers, consider the clarity of reports to be more important than their absolute length. They also show a preference for reports that have referral questions as their focus. The importance of referral questions has also been emphasized by Tallent (1988). These two findings should be kept clearly in mind by all psychologists who write reports for children and adolescents.

SUGGESTED PRACTICES

Report Only Pertinent Information

One of the most difficult decisions to make when writing a report involves gauging the relevance of information included (Teglasi, 1983). Examiners happen onto a great deal of information during the course of an evaluation, some of which is tangential. Say, for example, a child is referred for an evaluation of a suspected learning disability. During the course of an interview with the child's mother, she recounts at length her disappointment in her husband. She tells the examiner that he is dating other women, and she believes that he is not spending adequate time with their son.

In writing the report for this case, the clinician has to determine whether or not this information is pertinent to the learning-disability evaluation. This example is used because it is rather obvious that the husband's infidelity is not directly linked with learning disabilities, and the mother's report about her husband may or may not be able to be corroborated. In most cases, however, the decision is not so obvious. If, for example, the above case were a referral for behavioral problems at home, the parent's marital satisfaction might be of relevance to the referral problem. Clinicians must think critically about the information that they include in reports and consider its relevance to the case. If information is not relevant to the referral problem, and it is very personal information, the psychologist should consider carefully the decision to invade the families' privacy and include the information in the report.

Define Abbreviations and Acronyms

Acronyms are part of the idiosyncratic language of psychological assessment. They can greatly facilitate communication among psychologists but hinder communication with nonpsychologists. Psychologists, just as other professionals, need to use nontechnical language to communicate with parents, teachers, and other colleagues in the mental health field. A pediatrician would not ask a mother if her child had an emesis; rather, the physician would inquire whether or not the child vomited.

When writing a report, psychologists should try to *avoid using acronyms*, at least undefined ones. To simply use the acronym "WISC-III" is inappropriate. On the other hand, the use of the complete name, the "Wechsler Intelligence Scale for Children—Third Edition," repeatedly throughout a report seems clumsy and laborious. *Acronyms and short forms can be used effectively if they are defined.* However, short form names (abbreviations) of tests should be used for reports geared toward parents and teachers, and acronyms should be used in reports for mental health care colleagues who are used to receiving test scores. Examples of how one could define abbreviations or acronyms for later reference in a report are shown below.

- Wechsler Intelligence Scale for Children—Third Edition (Wechsler Scale)
- Wechsler Intelligence Scale for Children—Third Edition (WISC-III)

At later points in the report, the psychologist can then refer to the WISC-III or Wechsler Scale.

Emphasize Words Rather Than Numbers

Particularly in the test results section of a report, clinicians must resist the "wizardry of numbers" (Zimmerman & Woo Sam, 1967). Words communicate more effectively than numbers because they communicate more directly. The typical question is not what the child obtained on the WISC-III, but rather determining how the child's intelligence compares to others. As an example, instead of saying, "Demetrius obtained a Full Scale standard score of 106," say something like "Demetrius' intelligence is in the average range."

Reduce Difficult Words

This issue is by now an obvious one. The difficult part for report writers is following through on this advice. Consider the following two paragraphs that differ greatly. The first one uses a level of vocabulary that is too high for most consumers

of reports. The second example is a rewrite of the first paragraph that uses a lower vocabulary level:

> *There is also evidence from the cognitive test data to suggest that Pam is very obdurate in response to anxiety.*
>
> *She may also tend to be very concrete and not notice some of the subtleties of interpersonal discourse. Given these idiosyncrasies, she may find it difficult to generate effective social problem-solving strategies and strategies for coping with life's stressors.*

The next paragraph tries to communicate more clearly by using, among other things, simpler language.

> *Pam responds to stress by withdrawing from others (e.g., in her room, or leaving a group of friends on a social outing), which seems to be the only method she uses for dealing with stress. She also has trouble understanding and responding to messages given by others in social situations (e.g., body language or verbal hints). Because of these behavior patterns, Pam has trouble keeping friends.*

Related to the use of difficult words is the issue of using the correct person. I have occasionally seen reports where instead of using the child's name, he or she was referred to as "the child" or "the subject." This usage sounds too mechanistic and impersonal for a psychological report. In most cases the use of the child's name is better. In a sentence such as the following: "The child scowled at the examiner," I suggest this alternative: "Sandy scowled at the examiner."

Describe the Tests Used

In many cases, it is safe to assume that the reader of the report has little knowledge of the tests being used. For this reason I suggest that report writers describe the nature of the assessment devices. Prior to the ready availability of personal computers, this task would have been onerous. Now it is relatively easy to store, retrieve, and insert a description of a test in the body of a report or in the psychometric summary so as to avoid requiring the reader to encounter the description prior to seeing the results of interest. I occasionally use the following descriptive paragraph for the WISC-III in my psychometric summary.

> (Child's Name) *was evaluated with the Wechsler Intelligence Scale for Children—III (WISC-III). This test is a popular scale made up of 12 subtests that assess various aspects of intelligence. The tests are divided into two types: Verbal and Performance. Verbal tests have items such as defining vocabulary words, answering commonsense questions, and answering factual questions on topics such as science. The Performance tests have items such as constructing puzzles and abstract designs, and identifying missing parts of a picture. The WISC-III produces three scores: Verbal, Performance, and Full Scale, where the Full Scale is based on the sum of the scores on all of the tests.*

An introductory paragraph for a test such as the WISC-III is probably not as crucial because of the WISC's long-standing popularity. Even so, the WISC-III is not well known to most parents. An introductory paragraph describing the intelligence test being used is even more appropriate for newer tests such as the DAS and WJ-R, since these tests are not as widely used as the WISC-III.

The naive reader of a report will also be helped by descriptors of the nature of a subtest that is being discussed. This observation is particularly true for tests that are not adequately described by their names. Take, for example, the Coding subtest of the WISC-III. The name "Coding" could conjure up a variety of images in a report reader's mind. In this case the examiner should try to describe the nature of the task. Instead of concluding that a child had a weakness in coding, the report writer could state that the child had a weakness on a test that required using a pencil to copy as many geometric symbols (that are to follow a code given at the top of the page) as possible in a 2-minute period. On verbal tests examples of items may be given to communicate the nature of a task. One example may be to say that a child showed a wide range

of knowledge that was demonstrated on the Information subtest (sample item: Who was Pablo Picasso?) of the WISC-III. When sample items are used, however, they should be analogous items and not actual test items. This suggestion is in keeping with the ethical guidelines of the American Psychological Association that charge psychologists with maintaining the security of test items (see Chapter 7).

Edit the Report at Least Once

I have found that a number of my students do not take a critical eye toward editing their own work. Editing is necessary to ensure the most accurate communication in the least amount of space. Tallent (1988) provides the following excellent example of how an editor thinks:

> *There is the tale of the young man who went into the fish business. He rented a store, erected a sign, FRESH FISH SOLD HERE, and acquired merchandise. As he was standing back admiring his market and his sign, a friend happened along. Following congratulations, the friend gazed at the sign and read aloud, "FRESH FISH SOLD HERE. Of course it's here. You wouldn't sell it elsewhere, would you?" Impressed with such astuteness, the young man painted over the obviously superfluous word. The next helpful comment had to do with the word* sold. *"You aren't giving it away?" Again impressed, he eliminated the useless word. Seemingly that was it, but the critic then focused on the word* fresh. *"You wouldn't sell stale fish, would you?" Once more our hero bowed to the strength of logic. But finally he was relieved that he had a logic-tight sign for his business; FISH. His ever alert friend, however, audibly sniffing the air for effect, made a final observation: "You don't need a sign." (p. 88)*

Psychologists do not need to engage in such severe editing, but they should at least make an attempt to think critically about their word usage in order to reduce report, sentence, and paragraph length. The problem with editing is that for some people it can become a "neurosis" in itself, as was the case in the smelly fish story above. Despite this downside, judicious editing can go a long way toward clarifying meaning in a report.

An examiner could conclude, for example, that, "Roy performed in a manner on the WISC-III that is indicative of intelligence in the average range when compared to his peers." An editor might suggest the following alternative for this statement: "Roy's intelligence is average."

Sometimes new examiners are not accustomed to critiquing their own writing. One readily available option is to have a colleague read reports. Confidentiality, however, should be kept in mind if an editor is used.

Use Headings and Lists Freely

Headings and lists can serve to enhance the clarity of communication (Harvey, 1989). If, for example, an examiner draws a number of conclusions about a child, these can sometimes lose their impact if they are embedded in paragraphs. Here is an example.

> *Shirley has a specific learning disability in mathematics reasoning. In addition to this, she is having difficulty interacting with her peers. She appears to have a social skills deficit. Shirley exhibits strong reading skills and a great deal of interest in reading for pleasure.*

These conclusions could have an increased impact if headings and lists were used as shown below.

CONCLUSIONS

1. Shirley has a specific learning disability in mathematics reasoning.
2. Shirley has social skills problems that are adversely affecting relationships with her peers.
3. Shirley's strength is in reading, which she nourishes with a great deal of leisure reading.

As one would predict, the use of headings and lists to excess has a downside. A report that uses too many lists, for example, becomes stilted, and it may not communicate all of the texture and subtleties of the child's performance. Report writers should consider using additional headings

if a section of their report stretches for nearly a page (single spaced) without a heading. Examiners should consider lists if they want to add impact to statements that they want to ensure the reader remembers.

Use Examples of Behavior to Clarify Meaning

Since there is some disagreement as to the meanings of particular words, report writers should clarify meaning in order to ensure accuracy. Words that may conjure up a variety of interpretations include anxiety, cooperation, dependent, hyperactive, and low self-esteem. One way to foster clarity is to use examples of the child's behavior. Here, for example, are two ways to say that Emilio was anxious.

1. "Emilio exhibited considerable anxiety during the testing."
2. "Emilio appeared anxious during the testing. He frequently asked whether or not he had solved an item correctly, he would occasionally look at the ticking stopwatch during an item and then hurry, and his face became flushed when it was obvious to him that he did not know the answer to a question."

An additional benefit of using examples of behavior generously is that it forces the psychologist to consider the extent of supporting evidence for a conclusion about a child's behavior. If a psychologist writes that a child is anxious but cannot think of behaviors to help explain this, then the conclusion should not be drawn as it is unsupportable.

Direct quotes are also very helpful in clarifying meaning. If a clinician concludes that an adolescent is "suicidal," a quote from the child may help clarify this statement considerably. The child may have said, "I thought about taking some pills once" or "I feel like I want to run out in front of a car tonight and if that doesn't work, I will steal my father's gun and kill myself." These are obviously varying degrees of suicidal intent that are most clearly differentiated by knowing what the child or adolescent actually said.

Reduce Report Length

Tallent (1988) gives the following instances as indices of undue length. A report is too long when

1. the psychologist is concerned that it took too long to write it.

2. the psychologist has difficulty organizing all of the details for presentation.

3. some of the content is not clear or useful.

4. the detail is much greater than can be put to good use.

5. speculations are presented without a good rationale for them.

6. when the writing is unnecessarily repetitious.

7. when the organization does not represent "tightness."

8. when the reader is irritated by the length or reads only a few sections such as the summary or recommendations sections.

The issue of length is primarily a concern of other psychologists, and it is intertwined with other issues, such as clarity. Hence, the psychologist in training should not assume that shorter is better. Quality may be a more important issue than quantity. At this point the new report writer should keep the issue of length in mind while writing reports. Concerns about length, however, should never interfere with the need to portray a child's performance accurately.

Check Scoring Accuracy

An all too frequent and grievous error is to report scores that are incorrect. Psychological expertise and clerical skill may not be highly correlated variables. One major breakthrough that is helping with this problem is computerized scoring. In fact, if the facilities are available, *I suggest that each test protocol that is scored by hand be checked against computer scoring*. If this is not possible, the test scores should at least be double checked prior to finalizing a report. Having to recant scores because an error was caught by someone else is a very embarrassing experience.

One way of checking scores is to be alert to inconsistencies. If a child who was referred for possible mental retardation obtains a score in the average range, then the score should be double checked to see if a scoring error is the source of the incongruity. Other situations that may make an examiner suspicious would include a child suspected of a learning disability in math whose Arithmetic score is the child's highest score on the WISC-III, a child with a 50-point discrepancy between Verbal and Performance IQs, or the case where the examiner thought that the child was doing rather well on a test and yet it turned out to be the lowest score in the profile. The clinician, then, needs to be ever vigilant in order to avoid scoring errors. If a score doesn't seem sensible, then the examiner should always check for a scoring error in order to rule out this possibility.

Use Software Spelling and Grammar Checks

Another problem with reports that detracts from the credibility of the examiner is the presence of spelling errors. Spelling and grammatical errors in a written report reduce the likelihood of readers crediting an examiner with sage wisdom.

Avoid Stating Etiologies Routinely

An often-confused aspect of interpretation is the difference between inferring *etiologies versus consistencies*. It is clear from research findings, for example, that low SES is associated with lower intelligence test scores (as it is with health problems and other difficulties). It is quite a different matter to conclude that low SES *causes* low scores for a particular child. It is more sensible to conclude that if a child from a low-SES background obtains a high score that this finding is *inconsistent* with research on the relationship between SES and intelligence test scores. Similarly, if this same child obtains a slightly below-average Full Scale score, one may conclude that this score is *consistent* with research findings which suggests the Full Scale score is a predictable finding. In this case, however, the clinician should not conclude that the child's low SES circumstances *caused* the lower-than-average scores. It could be that a brain injury *caused* the lower scores independent of SES.

Often psychologists will be asked to infer etiologies in court testimony or other forums. These occasions require careful study, exhaustive data collection, and presentation of results with appropriate caveats. Often consumers of intelligence test data want simple answers regarding etiologies, but these are indeed rare in everyday practice. Often children experience multiple insults (as will be shown in many of the case studies herein), making the determination of a single insult as *the* etiological agent a veritable impossibility. These comments are not intended to convey the idea that the assessment of cognitive development or skills lacks utility; to the contrary, knowledge of cognitive status can be revealing. *These cautions are given to discourage the routine determination of intelligence etiology in oral or written psychological reports when substantial evidence is lacking.*

Adapting Reports to Audience and Setting

It is probably a truism that no report format is optimal. I find that I am always having to adapt my reports to meet the needs of an ever-changing audience. Different audiences have different characteristics, such as literacy levels, but more importantly, different audiences have different questions.

In a school setting, where most of the psychological assessment of children is conducted, the most frequent referral is for a learning problem.

As such, the intelligence test results are of great concern and are usually the featured aspect of the report. Teachers are also seeking information to assist them in curriculum decisions.

In a psychiatric hospital setting, the most frequent referrals are likely to be for problems such as depression, conduct disorder, and alcohol or drug abuse. In this setting, intelligence test results are frequently of little concern to the treatment team. Of greater concern are issues such as suicide potential, personality structure, and coping strategies. These questions are very different than those of the school setting, requiring a focus on topics other than intelligence.

Parents are yet another audience with different questions. When conducting an evaluation for parents in a private practice setting, the emphasis is on what the parents can do to effect a change in their child's behavior. The three reports given next reflect the variety of report writing styles that may be used in different settings.

Private Practice—Parents

This report was written for the adolescent being evaluated and for the parents (who paid for the evaluation). Both the parents and client were looking for explanations and assistance in dealing with the client's difficulties in high school.

School—Educators/Parents

This report is pitched to teachers who are making a special education classification decision and are interested in curricular planning. In this case, parents will likely review the report.

Other Report Writing Issues

Confidence Bands

It is customary practice to always report confidence bands to represent the amount of error associated with intelligence test scores (Kamphaus & Reynolds, 1987). These have been included

Psychological evaluation for Harry (confidential)

NAME: Harry
DATE OF BIRTH: 3/28/70
AGE: 16 years, 2 months
GRADE: 12
SCHOOL: Valley Preparatory School

Assessment Procedures

Wechsler Intelligence Scale for Children—Third Edition (Wechsler)

Diagnostic Interview

Mental Status Exam

Sentence Completion Test

Kaufman Test of Educational Achievement—Comprehensive Form (K-TEA)

Family History (By mail)

Minnesota Multiphasic Personality Inventory—Adolescent (MMPI-A)

Referral Information

Harry's father initiated the evaluation process. He was referred by a local tutoring service. Harry is having some difficulty with his coursework at the residential high school he attends. Harry also expressed an interest in determining whether or not he has a learning disability and in deciding whether or not to attend college.

Background Information

Harry grew up in a large eastern city with his parents and his older sister. His father and mother both have some college education. His father is a manager, and his mother is a nurse.

Harry's parents describe his developmental history as normal. He was also described as having school problems at an early age. During elementary school, he had difficulty with reading, writing, and arithmetic, and a generally slow rate of learning. His parents provided for tutoring beginning in the fourth grade. Harry also had ear surgery when he was 9 years old to correct a mild hearing loss. His parents were told by his teachers that he had a reading comprehension problem. His mother also reported being told that Harry had a below-average IQ and that he would probably never be able to succeed in college. He was never retained.

Harry had many friends in grammar school, but he has had some problems with social relationships in high school. Harry describes himself as being rebellious during his teenage years. He obtained primarily average grades. He stated that he did not like himself until his junior year when he read a self-help book. When he was 10, he was seriously injured in a train wreck. He has a large scar on his cheek that he said is the result of being thrown into a seat during the accident. Harry reported that he was unconscious for about a week. Harry was in a rehabilitation program at University Hospital for about a month, where he received speech and physical therapy. Harry said that he had to learn how to write and speak all over again. He said that his school grades were about the same before and after the accident. He did miss a great deal of school because of the accident.

At school Harry lives in a dormitory. He had particular problems this past year with a political science class, for which he received tutoring. He has also received poor grades in the sciences, mathematics, and history. He has received better grades in art, physical education, and music. His cumulative grade point average is now a 2.0 (where 2.0 = C). He has scored poorly on college entrance exams. He reports that "studying does not help."

Harry is involved in other student activities including a French club and band. He likes dancing, conversation, "hanging out with friends," and parties. Harry expressed some concern about not having a girlfriend.

(Continues)

Psychological evaluation for Harry (confidential) (Continued)

Behavioral Observations and Interview Data

Harry appeared very open and honest in the interview situation. He maintained excellent eye contact and did not hesitate before responding to questions. Harry said that he enjoyed being interviewed.

Harry's behavior during testing was similarly exemplary. He tried very hard on all of the tests. He was so reluctant to give up when faced with test items too difficult for him that the testing session lasted longer than one would anticipate for an individual his age. At one point during the testing he said, "I'm slow." His overall test behavior was cooperative and hard working.

Test Results and Conclusions

Harry was evaluated with the Wechsler Intelligence Scale for Children—Third Edition (WISC-III). This popular scale is made up of several subtests (usually 12 tests are used) that assess various aspects of intelligence. The tests are divided into two types: Verbal and Performance. Verbal tests have items such as defining vocabulary words, answering commonsense questions, and answering factual questions on topics such as science. The Performance tests have items such as constructing puzzles and abstract designs, and identifying missing parts of a picture. The WISC-III produces three scores: Verbal, Performance, and Full Scale, which is based on the sum of the scores on all of the tests.

Harry's performance on the WISC-III indicates that overall he is currently functioning in the well-below-average range of intelligence. There is a 90% probability that his performance meets or exceeds that of approximately 3 to 12% of his age mates. While this is a low estimate of intelligence in comparison to the general population, it is of particular concern when one considers the fact that his prep school competitors are typically more intelligent than the population at large.

This overall intelligence score is, however, something of a misrepresentation of his skills in that on some subtests he scored in the average range, while on others his performance was well below average. He performed in the average range on tests of vocabulary (knowledge of word meanings) and short-term memory for strings of numbers. By contrast, he performed very poorly on a test requiring him to construct puzzles and one requiring him to solve practical, everyday problems (e.g., what to do if someone steals your wallet). A complete summary of Harry's Wechsler performance is attached. Generally, he performed better on tests that were familiar to him or on tests requiring only rote learning. Harry had greater difficulty on more novel or unfamiliar tasks.

Harry was administered the K-TEA in order to obtain more diagnostic information regarding his school problems. His K-TEA profile is somewhat consistent with his measured intelligence in that his scores in mathematics applications, calculation, and reading comprehension are below what one would expect for his age. On the other hand, his performance in spelling and word decoding was considerably better. In these two areas he performed in the average range. Again, Harry is capable of performing in the average range for his age when the task is amenable to rote or overlearning. On cognitive tasks that require more conceptual skills or an ability to deal with novel problems, he has great difficulty.

A K-TEA error analysis was conducted for the three weak areas. The error analysis for the two mathematics tests shows that Harry makes similar errors whether the problem is applied or calculation. He had particular problems with fractions on both mathematics subtests. He also had problems with advanced number concepts and with algebraic equations. On the reading comprehension test, Harry showed problems with both literal and inferential comprehension. This difficulty is probably one of Harry's major stumbling blocks in college preparatory level work, since in many classes test performance is a direct reflection of the student's ability to read and comprehend textbooks.

Harry's personality functioning seems to be well within normal limits at the present time. His responses to interview questions, the MMPI-A, and the sentence completion blank showed stable personality functioning. Harry does seem to be sensitive to interpersonal feedback and desirous of close interpersonal relationships. His family is a very important source of support for him.

Psychological evaluation for Harry (confidential) (Continued)

Recommendations

1. Harry requires an approach to tutoring that minimizes his weaknesses and maximizes his strengths. He learns best in a situation where he can apply his language skills to familiar problems. He also seems to thrive on warm personal attention. These factors should be considered in designing any intervention program. For example, in preparing for college entrance examinations, he should work with a tutor that is not only competent but also personable in order to help maintain his motivation. He should also receive instruction on tasks very similar to those included on the examination. If the task on the examination is to read a paragraph about a topic and answer multiple-choice questions, then he should practice taking this type of test. This procedure will make the administration of the exam a more familiar problem-solving situation for him and will avoid problems with transfer of training. Language skills may also be used to help him understand areas such as mathematics. He could, for example, memorize verbal rules for solving mathematics problems involving fractions. Harry's interpersonal strengths also argue for the use of study groups. He may learn more by discussing a topic with his peers than by solitary study.

2. For certain areas where Harry may receive tutoring, some further diagnostic testing may be necessary. Writing is a curricular area in which further assessment may be required. His tutors in a particular content area should be able to conduct any further academic testing that is necessary.

3. Harry should take only the minimum number of classes required to stay enrolled. To date he has been able to overcome some significant cognitive weaknesses with relatively few signs of undue stress. However, Harry should not overly commit himself. Given his academic weaknesses, he is going to have to take extra time to complete his degree.

4. Harry should consult with the adult learning disabilities clinic at the university where he intends to enroll. He may be able to access appropriate services from the university to help him complete his degree.

5. If it appears that Harry is going to have difficulty completing his high school degree, he should seek counseling from the high school counseling service.

Summary

Harry is a 16-year-old male who has a history of academic problems. His language ability, ability to solve familiar problems, and rote learning ability are in the average to low average range. By contrast, his ability to solve unfamiliar problems and his higher cognitive skills are in the well-below-average range. Recommendations for Harry include that he take a reduced course load and receive tutoring that capitalizes on his rote learning, interpersonal, and language strengths and does not depend on transfer of training, and consult with the learning disabilities clinic at the university he attends.

Wechsler Intelligence Scale for Children—Third Edition

SCORE SUMMARY

Full Scale Score	76
Performance	74
Verbal	81

VERBAL TESTS

Information	5
Similarities	9
Arithmetic	6
Vocabulary	10

(Continues)

Psychological evaluation for Harry (confidential) (Continued)

VERBAL TESTS (CONT.)

Comprehension	5
Digit Span	8

PERFORMANCE TESTS

Picture Completion	6
Coding	10
Picture Arrangement	5
Block Design	5
Object Assembly	5
Symbol Search	9

Clinic/Hospital—Colleagues

This report attempts to follow the guidelines of Tallent (1988) for a "case-focused report." In this case the audience consists of the treatment team at the hospital, which includes the attending psychiatrist, nurses, aides, teachers, and social workers.

Psychological evaluation for Natalie (confidential)

Natalie is a 13-year-old female who was admitted to the hospital yesterday for treatment and evaluation of suicidal threats and oppositional behavior at home. This evaluation was designed to assess for suicidal risk and to pinpoint her coping strategies and personality structure in order to assist the treatment team in designing interventions for her.

Natalie was evaluated with the Wechsler Intelligence Scale for Children—III (WISC-III), the Comprehensive form of the Kaufman Test of Educational Achievement (K-TEA), Kinetic Family Drawing, Sentence Completion Test, Reynolds Adolescent Depression Scale (RADS), and Suicidal Ideation Questionnaire. Information was also gathered from Natalie's chart and from a diagnostic interview.

Natalie's assessment results portray her as a shy and anxious adolescent who is responding poorly to the stresses associated with early adolescence. Most problematic for her is her self-effacing nature. Because of this characteristic, she would rather meet the needs of others to the exclusion of her own. She is likely, for example, to be extremely compliant at home until she becomes so frustrated with not being able to spend as much time with friends as she would like that she eventually explodes with a verbal tirade and breaks rules such as curfews. Similarly, she has a very low tolerance for interpersonal conflict. She ruminates unduly about any conflict between herself and her parents or peers, all of which contributes to cognitions associated with depression such as thoughts of worthlessness and hopelessness.

Natalie's personality structure has proved inadequate for dealing with the emotionally charged early adolescent years, resulting in her experiencing significant depression. While formerly a good student, her academic achievement has declined dramatically over the last year to primarily failing grades. This decline cannot be explained by intellectual reasons, since the current estimate of her intellectual skills is in the average range (WISC-III Full Scale of 103, Performance scale of 101, and Verbal scale of 106). She has also reported having severe crying spells two to three times a week, irritability, mood swings, feelings of sadness, poor appetite, difficulty sleeping, and a tendency to withdraw by spending increasingly more time in her room. Recently, her depression has exacerbated to a point that she has thought of suicide. She was unable, however, to produce a "plan" for how she would attempt suicide, and she currently denies such ideation.

Psychological evaluation for Natalie (confidential) (Continued)

Natalie expresses an interest in receiving treatment. Her treatment should focus on helping her develop skills for dealing with others, especially in emotionally charged situations. Depending on what is discovered in the psychotherapeutic process, she may benefit from approaches such as cognitive behavior therapy aimed at controlling ruminations and other maladaptive cognitions (Aaron Beck's approach should be considered) that reinforce feelings of depression. She is also a good candidate for assertiveness training and social skills training aimed at developing interpersonal coping skills. In the latter area, strategies from the skillstreaming series used on the unit would likely be of benefit.

A diagnosis of major depression, single episode, moderate (296.22) seems most appropriate given all of the information collected to date.

Psychological evaluation for Shawn (confidential)

NAME:	Shawn
DATE OF BIRTH:	9/3/69
AGE:	15 yrs, 6 months
GRADE:	9th
SCHOOL:	Washington High School
CLASS:	Educable Mentally Retarded with one-third of his time in regular education classes

Assessment Procedures

Wechsler Intelligence Scale for Children—Third Edition (Wechsler)

Vineland Adaptive Behavior Scales—Survey Form (Vineland)

Basic Achievement Skills Individual Screener (BASIS)

Clinical Interview

Teacher Interview

Record Review

Classroom Observation

Referral Information

Shawn was referred by the Director of Psychological Services for a 3-year reevaluation to determine whether or not his educational placement was still appropriate.

Background Information

Shawn's mother describes his early development as uneventful. She did note, however, that many of his early milestones were delayed. He did not speak in sentences until about age 5. She describes him as a compliant child who has not presented any significant behavior problems.

Similarly, his special education teacher describes him as hard working and polite. She also reports that he is well liked by the other students and is a leader in the class. She does wonder if he sometimes does not work up to his ability.

(Continues)

Psychological evaluation for Shawn (confidential) (Continued)

According to Shawn's school, he seems to be the product of a normal developmental history. His last evaluation 3 years ago yielded a WISC-III Verbal of 82, a Performance of 91, and a Full Scale of 85. Six years ago, he obtained a Stanford-Binet IQ of 79, and 9 years ago he obtained a WISC-III IQ of 74. Shawn has recently had a vocational evaluation.

Behavioral Observations and Interview Data

Shawn was somewhat skeptical of the testing situation at the outset. His special education teacher indicated that he had a previous bad experience with a mental health professional. Hence, she told Shawn that the examiner was doing vocational testing as opposed to psychological testing. While somewhat reserved for the first 5 to 10 minutes of the testing situation, Shawn eventually warmed up. Once he was assured that this experience was not going to be negative, he cooperated fully in the evaluation process. In fact, Shawn was delightful to work with. He was cooperative and consistently gave his best efforts.

One did get the sense from working with Shawn that he was conscious of his history of poor academic achievement. When faced with an academic task that was difficult for him, he began to tremble slightly when responding.

Test Results and Conclusions

On the WISC-III Shawn obtained a Full Scale IQ in the below-average range, with a 90% probability that his IQ falls between the standard scores of 73 and 83. He obtained a Verbal IQ in the well-below-average range, and a Performance IQ in the low-average range. There is a 90% probability that Shawn's Verbal and Performance IQs fall within the standard score ranges of 66 to 78, and 80 to 96, respectively. The percentile rank confidence bands, indicating the percentage of age mates Shawn's performance met or exceeded, for the Full Scale, Verbal, and Performance IQs were 4 to 13, 1 to 7, and 9 to 39, respectively.

Shawn's performance on the WISC-III is indicative of an individual who suffers from a lack of acquired knowledge. His lowest scores on the WISC-III were on the Information, Arithmetic, and Vocabulary subtests. All three of these subtests are heavily dependent on both school learning and out-of-school intellectual stimulation. In addition to the subtests requiring a good deal of acquired information, he also performed very poorly on one subtest of high-level nonverbal reasoning skills. This result is consistent with his overall Full Scale standard score, which is in the below-average range. In direct contrast, Shawn's performance on many of the WISC-III tasks that require "practical reasoning skills" was in the average range. For example, on a puzzle-solving task his performance was even slightly above average for his age.

Hence, Shawn's performance on the WISC-III does indicate that he is currently functioning in the below-average range of intelligence. On the other hand, he shows good potential in practical problem-solving situations. This relative strength makes one optimistic about his vocational possibilities. His academic deficits in acquired information/academic achievement, however, also need to be addressed in order to enhance the probability of his eventual vocational success.

Shawn achieved the following age-based percentile ranks on the BASIS: mathematics 1, reading 1, and spelling 1. Shawn's performance in mathematics indicated that he had only successfully acquired basic addition and subtraction skills involving one- and two-digit numerals. On items requiring addition and subtraction of three- and four-digit numbers, multiplication or division, his performance waned. His mathematics performance indicates that he possesses only rudimentary skills, which are not adequate for functioning as an adult. Shawn's performance in reading, although only at the first percentile, was closer to a literate level. He showed adequate comprehension at about the third- or fourth-grade levels but considerable problems with decoding several words. He was unable to decode the following words: *creatures, suggested, dwarfed, despair, successful, gasped,* and *bugs.* His comprehension could seemingly improve even further if he were better able to decode words in context. Finally, Shawn's spelling performance was also at a rudimentary level. He was able to spell words such as *wall, left, child, apple, near,* and *butter.* In contrast, he was unable to spell the following words: *woke, rubber, corner,* and *month.*

Psychological evaluation for Shawn (confidential) (Continued)

In summary, his BASIS performance indicates that he possesses a very rudimentary level of academic skills. Most importantly, his academic skills are not up to par with his intelligence test scores on the Full Scale, Verbal, or Performance scales of the WISC-III. Based on these results, he may need more intensive intervention accompanied by higher academic standards for his performance.

On the Survey form of the Vineland, Shawn obtained standard scores of 95, 105, and 111 on the Socialization, Communication, and Daily Living Skills Domains, respectively. Shawn seems to possess many adaptive skills that are important for independent functioning as an adult. Generally, his adaptive behavior as measured by the Vineland indicates that his adaptive functioning is well within the average range. This finding precludes Shawn from obtaining a dual deficit in intelligence and adaptive behavior indicative of the mildly mentally retarded child. In other words, Shawn's level of adaptive functioning indicates that he clearly is not functioning in the mild level of mental retardation outside the school environment.

Summary

Shawn seems to be a congenial adolescent who is functioning in the well-below-average range intellectually and possesses an average level of adaptive behavior skills. He shows particular strengths in practical problem-solving and adaptive life skills. These skills are most critical for vocational success. However, his vocational success could be hindered drastically by his lack of academic achievement. Therefore, his vocational plans should be addressed as soon as possible by giving him appropriate training for a career. Also, his academic program should be intensified to bring his academic skills up to par with his intellectual skills. Once he has accomplished this goal, Shawn shows potential for responsible and independent functioning as an adult.

Recommendations

1. Shawn's vocational plans should be considered as an entry on his individual educational plan. He should begin working with vocational rehabilitation personnel in order to plan career training for him. His individual education plan should be adjusted so as to be congruent with his career objectives.

2. Shawn's academic expectations should be raised. He shows more intellectual and adaptive behavior potential than he is applying to the academic situation. He may respond, because of his very pleasant personality, to tutoring by peers. This practice would have the added benefit of allowing him to interact with positive peer models.

3. An attempt should be made to get Shawn involved in extracurricular school activities. Indications are from Shawn, and the peer group that he interacts with, that he may be tempted to drop out of school prior to high school graduation. Involvement in extracurricular activities would perhaps provide the immersion necessary to keep him in school through graduation.

4. Shawn should be referred to the dropout prevention program for evaluation.

---

when reporting intelligence test results in a variety of ways. Some examples of how report writers have included confidence bands are shown below.

"Janie obtained a WISC-III Full Scale standard score of 109 ± 3."

"Janie obtained a WISC-III Full Scale standard score of 109 ± 3.19."

"Janie obtained a WISC-III Full Scale standard score of 109 (106–112)."

"There is a 68% probability that Janie's three Full Scale standard scores lie within the range of scores of 106–112."

Report writers also use differing levels of confidence. While the above examples use 1 SEM (68%), many report writers adhere to Kaufman's

(1979b) advice and use a 90% confidence band. Of course, the decision is up to the examiner, who must consider factors such as the nature of his or her audience. In order to promote this flexibility, most test manuals offer 68%, 85%, 90%, 95%, and 99% confidence bands. One of the examples above uses decimals although most manuals use only whole numbers for simplicity of calculation.

This text will use 90% confidence bands because of Kaufman's (1979b) precedent, but also because this book emphasizes using percentile ranks in report writing. Higher levels of confidence (95% and 99%) produce such large percentile rank bands that the scores look grossly inexact. This is an artifact of the nature of the percentile rank scale and its unequal intervals (see Chapter 5).

Score Classification Schemes

Some of the systems used today are very old and in need of revision in the light of changes in terminology. The Wechsler-Binet classification systems can be traced to the early part of last century. They are very similar to descriptive schemes proposed by writers such as Pintner (1923) and Levine and Marks (1928). Pintner's (1923, p. 77) early classification scheme is shown below.

CLASSIFICATION	INTELLIGENCE QUOTIENTS
Feebleminded	0–69
Borderline	70–79
Backward	80–89
Normal	90–109
Bright	110–119
Very Bright	120–129
Very Superior	130 and above

The classification system of Levine and Marks (1928, p.131) is as follows:

LEVEL	RANGE IN IQ
Idiots	0–24
Imbeciles	25–49
Morons	50–74
Borderline	75–84
Dull	85–94
Average	95–104
Bright	105–114
Very Bright	115–124
Superior	125–149
Very Superior	150–174
Precocious	175 and over

The typical procedure used by modern psychologists is to place the Full Scale standard score into the Wechsler classification system given in the WISC-R manual (Wechsler, 1974). This classification system is given below. This system is very similar to that of Levine and Marks (1928).

CLASSIFICATION	FULL SCALE STANDARD SCORE
Very Superior	130 and above
Superior	120–129
Above Average (bright)	110–119
Average	90–109
Below Average (dull)	80–89
Borderline	70–79
Mentally Deficient	69 and below

Using the classification system of Wechsler, if a child obtains a score of 105, he or she is classified as average, 84 as below average, 126 as superior, etc. What is to be said, however, if a child obtains a score of 109? It does not seem fair, given what we know about the standard error of measurement, to assign this child to the "average" classification. In order to address this problem I have devised a rule for my own students. Given that the standard error of measurement for the Full Scale standard score of the WISC-III rounds to about 3 standard score points at most age ranges, I recommend that *if a child's composite score is within 3 standard score points of the next classification, both bordering classifications should be given*. For example, a Full Scale standard score of 93 would be classified as average, whereas a score of 92 would be given two classifications, below average to average.

Although the Wechsler classification system for intelligence test scores is by far the most popular, it may not be the most appropriate (Reynolds & Kaufman, 1990). The Wechsler classification system does use a great deal of antiquated terminology. This includes terminology such as "bright" and "dull" to describe the performance of children. By the way, these two classifications are not parallel. Should it not be "bright" and "dim"?

Besides its age, there are other problems with the use of the Wechsler classification system that may lead to inappropriate use. For example, scores of 69 or below are classified as "mentally deficient," an older term for mental retardation. The reader of a psychological report that describes the child's performance as in the mentally deficient range may interpret the report as indicating, in fact, that the child is mentally retarded. Intelligence tests were designed for use as the sole criterion for the diagnosis of mental retardation. This practice, however, is no longer appropriate since most modern diagnostic systems, such as DSM-IV and Public Law 94-142, require dual deficits in intelligence *and* adaptive behavior in order to make the diagnosis of mental retardation. Further, describing a child's score as being in the borderline range may be potentially confusing because of the existence of diagnoses such as Borderline Personality Disorder from DSM-IV. Examiners need to be careful when using Wechsler's classification system because it may lead to some confusion on the part of the reader of the psychological report, especially parents and teachers.

The WISC-III offers an update of the WISC-R classification system that addresses some of these criticisms. The new classification system is listed in the next column.

CLASSIFICATION	FULL SCALE STANDARD SCORE
Very Superior	130 and above
Superior	120–129
High Average	110–119
Average	90–109
Low Average	80–89
Borderline	70–79
Intellectually Deficient	69 and below

An alternative classification system proposed by Lyman (1998, p. 177) is shown below. This system may be adequate for some purposes, but it is still too evaluative as opposed to descriptive. The use of terms such as *weak* or *excellent* should be avoided.

PERCENTILE RANKS	DESCRIPTIVE TERMS
95 or above	Very high; Superior
85–95	High; Excellent
75–85	Above average; Good
25–75	About average; Satisfactory or fair
15–25	Below average; Fair or slightly weak
5–15	Low; Weak
5 or below	Very low; Very weak

Another alternative system of classification was proposed by Kaufman and Kaufman (1983b). This system is more in keeping with modern practice in that it uses parallel terminology above and below the mean, and it describes a level of performance without promoting diagnostic confusion. Their system is as follows:

Upper extreme	130 and above
Well above average	120–129
Above average	110–119
Average	90–109
Below average	80–89
Well below average	70–79
Lower extreme	69 and below

Yet another nonevaluative classification system is offered by the Differential Ability Scales (DAS; Elliott, 1990b).

Fish (1990) offered an intelligence classification scheme that is also descriptive and yet is not easily confused with diagnostic categories. Fish's scheme includes the following score ranges and classifications (where M=100 and SD=15).

Significantly below average	69 and below
Moderately below average	70–79
Below average	80–89
Average	90–109
Above average	110–119
Moderately above average	120–129
Significantly above average	130 and above

I have used the Kaufman and Kaufman (1983b) and Fish (1990) systems throughout most of this book because, in my opinion, these seem less evaluative.

Undoubtedly, psychologists will find that other systems are more appropriate for particular settings. The point being made by offering so many different classification schemes is that the decision to use a particular system should be made by the psychologist writing the report. The psychologist should choose a system based upon the setting in which the report is being written, the purpose(s) of the evaluation, the audience for the report, and other factors. Clinicians should not use a system just because it is written in a test manual, particularly if the system is likely to promote confusion or even inappropriate practice.

Reporting Scores

Another debate in report writing is the issue of whether or not, or how, to report scores. Some professors argue that IQs should never be given in a report because they are prone to misinterpretation, particularly overinterpretation, by parents and others. Yet other professors and supervisors do not see including scores in the report as an issue at all. I am sympathetic to the point of view that parents do tend to take scores too seriously. Much to my chagrin, I have even seen IQ scores used by parents to play "one upmanship" at cocktail parties. On the other hand, test scores can enhance the clarity of communication. If I were told that my child was below average, I would not be satisfied with that. I would want to know exactly how far below average.

One option is to effect a compromise by reporting scores, but also clearly stating the error associated with them. The score that many prefer is the percentile rank, as this score seems to be the most easily understood by parents (Lyman, 1998). In addition, Lyman (1998) suggested using percentile rank confidence bands. This practice is consistent with my bias of gearing reports to the least sophisticated audience. If a psychologist can communicate effectively with an unsophisticated audience, then he or she will have no difficulty with other audiences. In addition, percentile ranks are less apt to produce inaccurate reactions that are more typically associated with IQ scores (Kellerman & Burry, 1981). A sample sentence from a report using these guidelines may read something like this:

> "Laura's intelligence test scores fell in the average range.
>
> Her performance exceeded that of anywhere from 25 to 50 percent of the children her age."

This practice is in contrast to the more traditional practice of giving the obtained score with a confidence band. This approach would read something like:

> "Laura obtained a WISC-III Full Scale IQ of 95 ± 5."

An excellent example of using percentile rank confidence bands to communicate with parents is available for the Peabody Individual Achievement Test—Revised (PIAT-R; Markwardt, 1991) report to parents. The following quote is taken directly from the PIAT-R report to parents.

Results on each part of the test . . . are reported as percentile ranks. This type of score tells what percentage of other students at the same grade or age level scored below your child's score. In other words, a percentile rank of 50 indicates achievement above that of 50 percent of students at the same level. . . .

A common way to interpret percentile ranks is shown in the chart below. For example, a percentile rank of 50 could be interpreted as indicating average performance.

PERCENTILE RANKS OF	ARE CONSIDERED
1 to 5	low
6 to 24	below average
25 to 75	average
76 to 94	above average
95 to 99	high

Because no test score can be perfectly accurate and any student might score higher or lower if tested again on another day, it is said that the "true" score can only be estimated. To account for the possible variation in test results, a range of scores has been calculated for your child. (This range is written in parentheses following the test score obtained by your child.) In interpreting the test results, you should think of your child's score as falling somewhere in that range. (p. 2)

A Proposed Format for New Students

That which follows is intended as a rudimentary beginning at report writing. Consequently, there are several characteristics of the proposed report format that need to be made explicit. First, the report is intended for an unsophisticated audience. Secondly, the format is highly structured in order to satisfy the need of many new students for explicit guidance. Each section of the report will now be discussed in turn.

Identifying Information

Most report formats provide some identifying information on the top of the first page of the report. This section can include information such as name of the child, age, grade, birth date, and perhaps the name of the school or agency where the child is currently attending or being served. Also, most reports identify that the nature of the report content is confidential.

A sample of the identifying information section of a report for Connie (from Chapter 8) is shown in Figure 18.3.

Assessment Procedures

I prefer to use these terms to describe the tests administered because in everyday practice not all of the assessment devices used in an evaluation are tests per se. Evaluation procedures can and frequently do include interviews, reviews of records, and classroom or other observations. A sample of this type of section is also shown in Figure 18.3.

Referral Questions

This section is all too often overlooked (Tallent, 1988). It is crucial because the referral questions dictate the design of the evaluation. In addition, the lack of clear referral questions may lead to consumer or referral source dissatisfaction with the report. As Tallent (1988) suggests, psychologists may have to contact the referral source in order to clarify the nature of the question(s). Again, a sample is given for Connie in Figure 18.3.

Background Information

This section should include all of the pertinent information that may affect interpretation of a child's scores. The key word here is *pertinent*. The clinician should report only information that is relevant to the current evaluation, not information

Psychological Report
CONFIDENTIAL

Name: Connie P.
Birth date: 7/31/73
Age: 16 years, 2 months
Date of Report: 10/6/89
Gender: female
Grade: 11
Evaluated by: Ashley S. Kamphaus, B.A., psychology practicum student

Assessment Procedures

Wechsler Intelligence Scale for Children—Third Edition (WISC-III)

Referral Questions

This evaluation was requested by Connie's treatment team coordinator at the psychiatric hospital while she was being treated as an inpatient. Specifically, the treatment team wanted to rule out mental retardation as a possible contributory factor to her depression.

Background Information

Connie has had a tumultuous family background. She has never known her biological father. For the first 3 years of her life she was reared by foster parents. Since that time she has lived with her biological mother. Her mother has married and divorced three times. Consequently, Connie has moved and changed schools frequently, resulting in her missing a considerable amount of school. Her mother currently works as an administrative secretary.

Connie has always been cited by her teachers as being an underachiever. Although she has never failed a grade, she reportedly tends to do just the minimum to get by. Her grades have ranged from Bs to Ds.

According to her mother, Connie's current problems with alcohol abuse can be traced to the 8th grade. During this year, she moved to a less-than-desirable neighborhood. She began to associate with a group of older children who were heavy users of alcohol and drugs. For some reason, Connie has avoided significant drug use in spite of peer influence. She has been drinking beer and/or hard liquor at least 5 days a week since the 8th grade.

Observations and Interview Results

Connie seemed highly motivated to achieve a high score on the WISC-III. She frequently asked, "How'd I do?" Connie complained bitterly when she was unable to solve an item correctly. She also tried to hurry in order to obtain bonus points. No urging was required on the part of the examiner.

Connie seemed quite capable of expressing herself. She appeared to thrive on conversation and spoke freely and often throughout the assessment process.

Assessment Results and Interpretation

Connie was evaluated with the Wechsler Intelligence Scale for Children—Third Edition (WISC-III). This popular scale is made up of several subtests (usually 12 tests are used) that assess various aspects of intelligence. The tests are divided into two types: Verbal and Performance. Verbal tests have items such

FIGURE 18.3

Sample psychological report for Connie

Psychological Report (Continued)

as defining vocabulary words, answering common sense questions, and answering factual questions on topics such as science. The Performance tests have items such as constructing puzzles and abstract designs, and identifying missing parts of a picture. The WISC-III produces three scores, Verbal, Performance, and Full Scale, which is based on the sum of the scores on all of the tests.

Connie's overall estimate of intelligence, the Full Scale, places her in the average to above-average range. Taking measurement error into account, this score indicates that her performance meets or exceeds anywhere from 61% to 82% of the children her age. An estimate of her intelligence in the above-average range is consistent with a number of pieces of information about Connie. Her teachers have always argued that she does not use her ability in school, and she displayed an interest in getting items correct, suggesting that she has some confidence in her cognitive skills.

This description of her intelligence test performance, however, is not complete because she obtained a Verbal score in the above-average to well-above-average range, and a considerably lower Performance score—in the average range. Again, taking measurement error into account, Connie's Verbal score indicates that she exceeds anywhere from 81% to 95% of the adolescents her age, whereas on the Performance scale she exceeds 23% to 58% of her peers. Her relatively stronger verbal skills were even reflected on one of the Performance scale subtests. On the only Performance subtest requiring a verbal response, she obtained her highest subtest score on the scale. As mentioned earlier, her relative verbal strength was also evident during the evaluation, in which she showed excellent conversational skills and ability to express herself verbally.

These test results all rule out a problem with mental retardation. Even her relative weakness in Performance scale skills is still in the average range compared to other 16-year-olds.

Summary

Connie is a 16-year-old-female who was evaluated while receiving inpatient treatment for alcohol abuse. She has a history of alcohol abuse and academic underachievement dating back to the 8th grade. The purpose of this evaluation was to rule out mental retardation. Connie exhibited a high level of cooperation and motivation during the administration of the WISC-III. Her Full Scale and Verbal standard scores were in the above-average range and her Performance standard score was in the average range. Her relative strength on Verbal subtests was pervasive in that it appeared to even help her on one of the Performance tests. This strength is also consistent with her conversational skills. These findings effectively rule out a diagnosis of mental retardation.

Recommendations

1. Connie's verbal strength should be tapped to assist her with difficult school subjects. She could be advised by teachers to use verbal encoding and rehearsal strategies even for subjects that are more nonverbal, such as mathematics. She could, for example, be required to verbally rehearse the steps involved in solving algebraic equations.

2. Connie's enjoyment of conversation suggests that this high-frequency activity may serve as a good reinforcing stimulus for her. If she completes a satisfactory amount of schoolwork, for example, she might be allowed to converse with someone.

Ashley S. Kamphaus, B.A.
Psychology Practicum Student

FIGURE 18.3

(Continued)

Psychological Report (Continued)

Psychometric Summary for Connie

Wechsler Intelligence Scale for Children—Third Edition (WISC-III)

Composite scores

Full Scale Standard Score	108
Verbal Standard Score	117
Performance Standard Score	96

Subtest scores

Verbal scale

Information	13
Similarities	13
Arithmetic	13
Vocabulary	12
Comprehension	13
Digit Span	13

Performance scale

Picture Completion	14
Coding	4
Picture Arrangement	10
Block Design	10
Object Assembly	10
Symbol Search	9

FIGURE 18.3

(Continued)

that is superfluous or an undue invasion of privacy (Teglasi, 1983). Material should only be included if it has some potential impact on the interpretation of the child's scores in order to answer the referral question(s).

While parental occupation and marital status are generally private subjects, these may be important pieces of information, given what is currently known about the effects of SES and parental strife (divorce) on a child's cognitive functioning (see Chapter 3). A sample of how background information may be written in a report is provided in Figure 18.3.

The report writer should also be clear about the sources of information. If the father views his son as lazy, then this statement should be attributed to the father. Statements that could be used for making such attributions include the following:

"According to . . ."

"His father/mother said . . ."

"His mother's/father's opinion is . . ."

"His teacher's view of the situation is . . ."

"_____ reports that . . ."

"_____ acknowledges that . . ."

If care is not taken to make clear the sources of information, questions may arise at the time that feedback is given to involved parties.

Sensitive background information should also be corroborated, or excluded from the report if it is inflammatory and cannot be corroborated. For example, a 5-year-old may say something like "mother shoots people," and later the psychologist discovers that the child's mother is a police officer.

Previous assessment results should also be included in this section (Teglasi, 1983). Also, previous experiences with psychological or educational interventions should be noted here.

If several evaluations are already available, the report writer can simply refer the reader to another source (Zimmerman & Woo-Sam, 1967). This practice can substantially reduce bulk.

Observations and Interview Results

In this section the behaviors that the child exhibits during the assessment are recorded. The behaviors that may be significant were cited in Chapters 3 and 5. When writing this section, the number of observations made, the setting where the observations were made (e.g., school, clinic, etc.), and the person who made the observations should be included (Teglasi, 1983). Observations for Connie are shown in Figure 18.3.

This section is also the place to enter interview results that may assist in the process of corroborating or rejecting hypotheses.

Assessment Results and Interpretation

This section is where the intelligence test results for the child are reported. For the beginning report writer who is trying to communicate with parents, the following sequence for reporting intelligence test results is suggested.

First paragraph

1. Introduction to the WISC-III
2. Global composite score (e.g., Full Scale or overall composite from other tests) classification, conclusions, and supporting evidence

3. Global composite score percentile rank confidence bands

Second paragraph

4. Area score (e.g., Verbal, Performance, or other composite scores based on two or more subtests) classification, conclusions, and supporting evidence
5. Area score percentile rank confidence bands

Third paragraph

6. Shared subtest conclusions and supporting evidence

Fourth paragraph

7. Single subtest conclusions and supporting evidence

This outline, of necessity, may promote stilted writing at first. It is intended to ensure that students apply the same interpretive logic to their report writing that they applied to interpretation. At this point in the report the intelligence test results should also be integrated with other findings, as "the IQ score . . . does not exist in a vacuum" (Kellerman & Burry, 1981).

Less stilted usage of this and similar report formats is demonstrated in several of the chapters. A sample of this section of a report is given in Figure 18.3.

Summary

The final section of the report is intended to give an overview of the major findings (see Figure 18.3). This review helps ensure that the reader understands the major points made in the report. A rule of thumb for writing summaries is to use one sentence to summarize each section of the report. In addition, a sentence should be devoted to each major finding presented in the test results section and to each recommendation. In some cases, one sentence can be used to summarize multiple findings and recommendations, as was done for the sample report given in Figure 18.3.

One of the common pitfalls in preparing summaries is including new information in the summary section. If an examiner introduces a new finding in the summary, then the reader is lost. The reader has no idea as to the source or rationale behind the conclusion. I suggest that students read their draft summaries carefully and check every conclusion made in the summary against the body of the report.

Signatures

Reports typically require signatures in order to attest to their authenticity. It is important for clinicians to use titles that represent them accurately. Some states, for example, do not have specialty licensure, and as such the use of a title such as licensed pediatric psychologist is not appropriate. In this case, a more generic term such as licensed psychologist should be utilized.

Students should also be careful to represent themselves accurately. A title such as practicum student, intern, trainee, or something similar should be used. Psychological custom also determines the inclusion of the highest degree obtained by the clinician.

Writing Recommendations

This part of a report is often the most difficult for new clinicians to write. It is difficult primarily because it requires them to draw on information from a host of graduate training, practicum, and internship experiences. Fortunately, the age of the Internet has eased this process. Numerous Web sites offer suggested interventions and remediation strategies. Obviously, the quality of these suggestions is uneven and unregulated. The clinician can be selective about Web sites used or merely use experience to determine the quality of suggestions offered. A list of some potentially useful sources of recommendations is provided in Figure 18.4.

SPECIAL EDUCATION	
Special Education Resources on the Internet	http://www.hood.edu/seri/serihome.htm
User-Friendly Mental Health Information and Resource Directory service for consumers and professionals	http://www.mental-health-matters.com/
Addressing Student Problem Behavior	http://www.air-dc.org/cecp/resources/ problembehavior/main.htm
ANXIETY	
The Anxiety Panic Internet resource (tAPir)	http://www.algy.com/anxiety/index.html
ADHD	
Consensus Statement Overview: Diagnosis and Treatment of Attention Deficit Disorder	http://odp.od.nih.gov/consensus/cons/110/ 110_intro.htm
Children and Adults with Attention Deficit Disorder (CHADD)	http://www.chadd.org/

FIGURE 18.4

Internet resources for report writing

LEARNING DISABILITIES

Learning Disability Policy	http://www.ets.org/distest/ldpolicy.html
LD Online	http://www.ldonline.org/

MISC.

Empirically Supported Treatment Documents	http://www.apa.org/divisions/div12/est/est.htm
Healthy People 2000 home page	http://odphp.osophs.dhhs.gov/pubs/hp2000/default.htm
CEC ERIC Clearinghouse on Disabilities and Gifted Education	http://www.cec.sped.org/er-menu.htm
At Risk Institute, USF—Home Page	http://ari.coedu.usf.edu/kat/
Child Growth and Development	http://www.coe.ilstu.edu/mbgraham/c&i210/cogni.html
GROUP-PSYCHOTHERAPY HOMEPAGE	http://freud.tau.ac.il/~haimw/group2.html
Temperament.com and b-di.com	http://www.temperament.com/
Information on Specific Mental Disorders, Their Diagnosis and Treatment	http://www.nimh.nih.gov/publist/specific.htm
The Preschooler's Project	http://www.childmmc.edu/CMHWeb/CMH Depts/PsychWeb/PreschoolersHome.html
Intl. Soc. Infant Studies	http://isisweb.org/
Health-Psychology.base.org	http://health-psychology.base.org/
Clinical Psychology Resources: Psychotherapy	http://www.psychologie.unibonn.de/kap/links/li_pt.htm

PROFESSIONAL ASSOCIATIONS

Division 17 APA Division 17—Counseling Psychology	http://www.div17.org/
Phi Delta Kappa	http://www.pdkintl.org/
American School Counselor Association	http://www.schoolcounselor.org/
American Counseling Association	http://www.counseling.org/
National Association of Child Development	http://www.nacd.org/
American Medical Association	http://www.ama-assn.org/
American Psychological Association	http://www.apa.org/
National Association of School Psychologists	http://www.naspweb.org
American Psychiatric Association	http://www.psych.org/
APA—Division 16—School Psychology	http://www.gse.utah.edu/apa/d16.htm

FIGURE 18.4

(Continued)

PROFESSIONAL ASSOCIATIONS (Cont.)

American Academy of Pediatrics (AAP)	http://www.aap.org
Assoc. for Supervision & Curriculum Dev. (ASCD)	http://www.ascd.org
Association for Specialists in Group Work (ASGW)	http://www.uc.edu/~wilson/sgw/index.html
American Educational Research Association (AERA)	http://www.aera.net
American Academy of Child & Adolescent Psychiatry (AACAP)	http://www.aacap.org/web/aacap/
Council for Exceptional Children	http://www.cec.sped.org/
American Federation of Teachers	http://www.aft.org/
National Education Association	http://www.nea.org
Parent Teacher Association	http://www.pta.org
American Public Health Association	http://www.apha.org
Division 40 of APA—Clinical Neuropsychology	http://www.div40.org/

FEDERAL SITES

United States Department of Education	http://www.ed.gov/
National Institute of Health	http://www.nih.gov/
HOME PAGE: U.S. Dept. of Health & Human Services	http://www.hhs.gov/

PROFESSIONAL RESOURCES

Education Week	http://www.edweek.org
Making the Grade	http://www.gwu.edu/~mtg/
National Mental Health Association	http://www.nmha.org
Zero to Three	http://www.zerotothree.org
School Mental Health Project	http://www.smhp.psych.ucla.edu
CDC's Adolescent and School Health Information	http://www.cdc.gov/nccdphp/dash/
School Psychology Resources Online	http://www.bcpl.lib.md.us/~sandyste/school _psych.html
Adolescents Online	http://education.indiana.edu/cas/adol/adol.html
KidSource online	http://www.kidsource.com
The divorce page	http://hughson.com/
Gifted and Talented Page	http://www.eskimo.com/~user/kids.html
PsychWeb	http://www.gasou.edu/psychweb/psychweb.htm
Center for the study of Autism	http://www.autism.org
National Alliance for the Mentally Ill	http://www.nami.org

FIGURE 18.4

(Continued)

PROFESSIONAL RESOURCES (Cont.)

Obsessive-Compulsive Disorder	http://www.fairlite.com/ocd/
Adult Children Resources	http://www.intac.com/%7Ewoy/drwoititz/source.htm
Anorexia	http://www.neca.com/%7Ecwildes/
LD Online	http://www.ldonline.org/
Conflict Resolution/Peer Mediation Research Project	http://www.coe.ufl.edu/CRPM/CRPMhome.html
Teachers for Teachers	http://www.pacificnet/~mandel/
Pathways to School Improvement	http://www.ncrel.org/sdrs/pathwayg.htm
The Well-Connected Educator	http://www.gsh.org/wce
EDscape	http://www.edscape.com
Education World	http://www.education-world.com
Family Education Network	http://www.families.com
Center for Multilingual Multicultural Research	http://www-rcf.usc.edu/~cmmr/
Babies Can't Wait	http://www.doas.state.ga.us/Departments/DHR/facba.html
The National Center for Education in Maternal & Child Health	http://www.ncemch.org/
Clinical Child Psychology	http://freud.psy.fsu.edu/~clinical_child/
ERIC Clearinghouse on Assessment and Evaluation	http://ericae.net/
PSYCHOLOGICAL ASSESSMENT ONLINE	http://wso.net/assessment/
ERIC Clearinghouse on Disabilities and Gifted Ed	http://www.cec.sped.org/ericec.htm
Pharmaceutical Information Network Home Page	http://www.pharminfo.com/
Centers for Disease Control and Prevention Home Page	http://www.cdc.gov/

PEDIATRICS

Society of Pediatric Psychology	http://129.171.43.143/spp/
National Organization for Rare Disorders, Inc. (NORD)	http://www.pcnet.com/~orphan/
AAP—The Best of the Pediatric Internet	http://www.aap.org/bpi/default.htm
Virtual Children's Hospital Home Page	http://indy.radiology.uiowa.edu/VCH/
MedWeb: Robert W. Woodruff Health Science Center Library of Emory University	http://WWW.MedWeb.Emory.Edu/MedWeb/
Developmental and Behavioral Pediatrics Home Page	http://www.dbpeds.org/welcome.html

FIGURE 18.4

(Continued)

NEUROPSYCHOLOGY

Neuropsychology Central	http://www.premier.net/~cogito/neuropsy.html
National Academy of Neuropsychology	http://nan.drexel.edu/
The Neuropsychology Center/Neuropsychology Links	http://www.neuropsych.com/Links.htm
NIMH Human Genetics Initiative	http://www-srb.nimh.nih.gov/gi.html
Child Neurology Frames Page	http://www.waisman.wisc.edu/child-neuro/index.html
Folkstone Design Anatomy Resources	http://www.sunshine.net/folkstone/anatomist/anatomy/
Neurosciences on the Internet Table of Contents	http://www.neuroguide.com/toc.html
Neonatal Diseases and Abnormalities	http://www.mic.ki.se/Diseases/c16.html
Brain Injury Glossary	http://www.waiting.com/glossary.html
Genetic Conditions / Rare Conditions Information	http://www.kumc.edu/gec/support/groups.html
Office of Rare Diseases (ORD)	http://cancernet.nci.nih.gov/ord/
Epilepsy FAQ	http://debra.dgbt.doc.ca/~andrew/epilepsy/FAQ.html#basic
Society for Neuroscience	http://www.sfn.org/
Physiology and Endocrinology Neuroscience	http://www.mcg.edu/som/PhyEndo/NEUROLNK.htm
Strathearn Neurological Access Point	http://www.sol.co.uk/k/keir/snap1.htm
The Whole Brain Atlas	http://count51.med.harvard.edu/AANLIB/home.html
Mental Health Net—Neurosciences and Neuropsychology	http://cmhcsys.com/guide/pro10.htm

NATIONAL CENTERS

CDC Division of Adolescent & School Health	http://www.cdc.gov/nccdphp/dash
National Information Center for Children & Youth w/Disabilities (NICHCY)	http://www.nichcy.org
Center for Effective Collaboration & Practice	http://www.air-dc.org/cecp/
Autism Society of America	http://www.autism-society.org
Internet Mental Health	http://www.mentalhealth.com
American Academy of Pediatrics	http://www.aap.org
American School Counselor Association	http://www.schoolcounselor.org
National Alliance for the Mentally Ill	http://www.nami.org
National Mental Health Association	http://www.nmha.org

FIGURE 18.4

(Continued)

NATIONAL CENTERS (Cont.)	
Center for Mental Health Services (SAMHSA)	http://www.samhsa.gov/cmhs/cmhs.htm
National Clearinghouse on Child Abuse & Neglect Info	http://www.caleb.com/nccanch/
Attention Deficit Disorders	http://www.add.org/main/abc/basic.htm
LD Association of America	http://www.ldanatl.org
Pediatric Psychiatry Pamphlets	http://www.klis.com/chandler/
National Depressive & Manic-depressive Association	http://www.ndmda.org
National Clearinghouse for Alcohol & Drug Information	http://www.health.org
National Institute of Mental Health's Public Information	http://www.nimh.nih.gov/publicat/
Psych Central—Dr. Grohol's Mental Health Page	http://www.psychcentral.com
U.S. Dept. of Education	http://www.ed.gov
Publications for Parents	http://www.ed.gov/pubs/parents

NOTE: This information was compiled by A. Shayne Abelkop.

FIGURE 18.4

(Continued)

Regardless of the source of knowledge for writing recommendations, some principles may be followed. Recommendations should be specific and clear (Teglasi, 1983). Writing a recommendation for "extra drill and practice" may be difficult to carry out if the curriculum content area and other aspects of the recommendation are not made explicit. Some recommendations may also not be easy to communicate succinctly in writing. In almost all cases, the examiner should relay recommendations in person to teachers, parents, and colleagues (Teglasi, 1983) in order to ensure that they are followed.

Another way of offering suggestions in a way that they will be carried out is to offer a "sliding scale" (Zimmerman & Woo Sam, 1967). If, for example, special class placement is warranted but not practical, then perhaps tutoring should be recommended in lieu of school intervention services.

Psychometric Summary

Some clinicians include a listing of all of the child's obtained scores with the report. While this summary will be of limited value to the less knowledgeable reader, it may be of great value to another examiner who reviews the report. This summary is best placed on a separate sheet, typically sheets, of paper, which makes it convenient for the examiner to be selective about who receives it. A report writing self-test is provided in Figure 18.5.

COMMUNICATING RESULTS ORALLY

Parent Conferences

Imparting intelligence test results to parents requires considerable savvy, as the individual differences between families are multitudinous.

In order to help report writers think critically about their work, the following checklist is offered. This "test" can be completed periodically to help ensure that reports are carefully prepared.

Item	True	False
		(circle one)
1. Was the report edited?	T	F
2. Are there unnecessary invasions of privacy?	T	F
3. Is the referral question(s) explicitly stated?	T	F
4. Is the referral question answered?	T	F
5. Does the report emphasize numbers over words?	T	F
6. Can a person with a high school education understand the wording used?	T	F
7. Is the report so long that the major findings are lost?	T	F
8. Are the conclusions drawn without undue hedging?	T	F
9. Do the conclusions fit the data?	T	F
10. Are questionable results presented?	T	F
11. Are percentile ranks included for the benefit of parents and client?	T	F
12. Was spelling and grammar checked?	T	F
13. Are supporting data integrated with conclusions?	T	F
14. Are the recommendations clear and specific?	T	F
15. Are headings and lists used as needed to enhance impact?	T	F
16. Are acronyms defined?	T	F
17. Are acronyms overused?	T	F
18. Is new information included in the summary?	T	F
19. Were scores double-checked?	T	F
20. Are examples of behavior used to clarify meaning?	T	F
21. Are test instruments described adequately?	T	F
22. Is a conference scheduled to accompany the written report?	T	F
23. Was written parental consent obtained for minor children prior to releasing the report to interested agencies or parties?	T	F
24. Is a feedback session scheduled with the child or adolescent?	T	F

FIGURE 18.5

Report writing self-test

Ricks (1959) summarizes the heart of the dilemma.

The audience of parents to which our test-based information is to be transmitted includes an enormous range and variety of minds and emotions. Some are ready and able to absorb what we have to say. Reaching others may be as hopeless as reaching TV watchers with an AM radio broadcast. Still others may hear what we say, but clothe the message with their own special needs, ideas, and predilections. (p. 4)

Regardless of the potential pitfalls, parents must be informed of the results of a psychological evaluation of their child (the legal, ethical, and regulatory mandates for this practice are given in Chapter 7).

Hints for communicating intelligence test results to parents include (see also Research Report 18.1):

1. Avoid excessive hedging or deceit. I have seen many students get into trouble with parents by trying to dupe them. The problem with excessive hedging or failure to report the "bad" news is that many parents sense this deceit and respond to the psychologist with great mistrust. Honesty on the part of the clinician is also easily sensed by parents, which ultimately enhances the credibility of the clinician.

2. Use percentile ranks heavily when describing levels of performance.

3. Instead of lecturing, allow parents opportunities to participate by asking about things such as their opinion of the results and how they fit with their knowledge of their child.

4. Anticipate questions prior to the interview and prepare responses. How would a psychologist answer the question, "Will my son's intelligence get better?" One way of preparing would be to reread Chapter 3 of this book.

5. Schedule adequate time for the interview. Parent conferences often become more involved than one has planned. I once had a session turn into therapeutic counseling for the mother, who had just separated from the child's father. I suggest allowing 2 hours for such a session with parents. If it does not take this long, then the clinician can take a long lunch or, even less likely, see another child earlier than planned.

6. Practice communicating with parents from a variety of backgrounds. Some parents can be addressed as colleagues, while others may have only a limited education. Sometimes translators may be needed.

7. Never make an overly explicit prediction (Lyman, 1998). A phrase to be avoided would be something like, "She will never go to college," or "She will always have trouble with school." These types of statements can be very offensive to parents, not to mention very inaccurate.

8. Use good basic counseling skills. Every parent likes to talk about the trials, successes, and tribulations of raising a child. Give parents at least some opportunity to do this, as it allows you to show interest in the child by your listening to the parent's story.

9. Do not engage in counseling that is beyond your level of expertise (Lyman, 1998). Parents are often very eager to obtain advice from a professional. It is inappropriate (and unethical by most standards) for a psychologist to provide services for which he or she is not trained. If, for example, a parent requests marital counseling and you have no training in this area, you should inform the parent of this fact and offer a referral. In fact, the psychologist will be helped by having referral sources readily available for such eventualities.

10. Be aware that some parents are not "ready" to accept some test results. Some parents will impugn your skills because psychologically they cannot accept the fact that their child has a severe disability. They may leave the session angry, and you may feel inept. The hope that every parent conference will end on a happy note is unrealistic. Examine your skills critically in response to parent

RESEARCH REPORT 18.1

Interacting with Parents

Tuma and Elbert (1990) have offered some advice for understanding and dealing with parents in the assessment process. Children are often referred by their parents. If a parent defines a problem or set of problem behaviors, then the psychologist must deal directly with these problems in the assessment process. Parents are most concerned about child problems that increase the child's demands on them. However, parents may be less responsive to a child's problems at school and prefer to attribute these problems to the teacher or school situation. Parents of a delinquent child may have other issues requiring consideration in the assessment process. These parents may be unwilling or reluctant to obtain an evaluation and complain that they have been compelled by some authority to seek help with their child or adolescent.

Guilt is another issue that may arise with parents. Sometimes parents are racked with guilt about their child's behavior problems, assuming perhaps too much responsibility for the etiology of them. Another group of parents that may be difficult to deal with in the assessment situation is the parent who is reluctant to become involved for fear that his or her own problems, learning disabilities, or psychopathology may be discovered. These parents may delay seeking help for their child until late adolescence or early adulthood when they are seeking help primarily in order to get the child to leave the "nest."

Tuma and Elbert (1990) go on to identify four important phases of the parent feedback conference. The four components are:

1. the initial conference analysis, where parents are asked for their own observations, impressions, and/or concerns about the child's behavior during an evaluation or any other concerns about the assessment process,

2. the problem discussion, where the psychologist presents the various assessment findings and discusses the implications of the assessment results,

3. the consultation process, where recommendations and intervention planning are considered and recommendations may include those related to family, the child, the clinical facility, or the child's school, and

4. the summary, where the examiner reiterates the nature of the referral, significant assessment findings, and the recommendations and interventions to be carried out.

Tuma and Elbert (1990) further recommend that if a psychologist also has to present findings at the child's school where a large meeting will be called, it is incumbent upon the examiner to meet with the parents prior to the larger school conference. This allows parents and the psychologist to discuss aspects of the evaluation that would be inappropriate in a larger meeting because some topics may be invasions of the child's (or parents) privacy and confidentiality.

---

feedback, but realize that some parents simply will not accept the results because of their own personal issues. I have encountered this problem on numerous occasions, particularly if a parent had a subtle disability. If a parent was labeled "slow" and ridiculed by peers, then this parent may become defensive and angry at the suggestion that their child may have a disability. The session with such a parent will likely end on a tense note. In many of these cases, however, the parent will accept the bad news after a number of evaluations of the child reveal the same results. Thus, the parent may be able to interact more positively with the clinician on their next encounter.

Teacher Conferences

Many of the principles used in parent conferences will apply to teachers also. Two nuances, however, are outlined below.

1. Be aware that teachers get few breaks in a day. Most do get a brief lunch where they prefer to unwind with colleagues and prepare for the remainder of the day. A clinician is unlikely to command a teacher's undivided attention during this lunch break. If a teacher has an additional free (e.g., planning) period, it may be a good time for a conference. After school is frequently the best time to get a teacher's undivided attention for a meeting. Teachers are generally very busy people, so the pace of the meeting will be quicker than is the case for parents.

2. Teachers are interested in schooling issues. The diagnosis of conduct disorder is of less concern to teachers than getting specific recommendations for helping the child in the classroom (Teglasi, 1983). If an examiner is not trained and/or has little experience in teacher consultation, then the assistance of someone like a qualified school psychologist should be enlisted to assist with the teacher conference.

The most important thing to remember about teacher conferences is that they should take place (Zimmerman & Woo Sam, 1967; Teglasi, 1983). Such a conference is desirable because teachers are usually involved somehow in the treatment of children and adolescents. An accurate portrayal of the child's intelligence can assist teachers in designing interventions to assist a child in school.

Child Feedback

This session may be the most challenging for many clinicians, but it is a skill that must be acquired nonetheless. The practice of giving a child feedback about an evaluation has received more emphasis recently.

The major decision that a clinician need make before giving feedback to a child is to determine the type of information that is appropriate for a child's developmental level. Clearly, the kind of feedback given to parents is inappropriate for a 5- or 6-year-old who may have extraordinary difficulty understanding the concept of a percentile rank. A child this age, however, may be able to understand the consequences of the evaluation. In this situation the child may be able to understand something like, "Remember those tests I gave you? Well, your scores were low on a couple of them. Because of this I suggested to your parents that you be tutored after school. So now, you will be going to visit a teacher after school who will help you with schoolwork."

The older the child, the more similar the feedback session becomes to the one for parents. Another dramatic difference, however, is that negative feedback to a child or adolescent can have the opposite of the intended effect. That is, in most cases the goal is to improve variables such as academic achievement. A child who is told that he or she has low intelligence test scores may decide to stop trying in school. In some cases the examiner's honesty could harm the child. A few options are available in cases where an examiner is concerned about such negative consequences. One option is to have someone who knows the child well and has a positive relationship with him or her help the psychologist communicate the results in a nonthreatening manner to the child. A good person to fill this role is a teacher. A second possibility is to have the child's primary therapist or counselor eventually share the results with the child in a counseling session. The counselor or therapist would then be able to help the child cope with the results in a supportive setting.

In all cases involving feedback to children or adolescents, it is advisable to consult with a fellow professional who knows the child extremely well.

CONCLUSIONS

Report writing and oral reporting are central, not ancillary considerations in the assessment process. The most insightful and elegant of evaluations is lost if not translated to useable information in written reports and treatment team meetings. Unfortunately, these central assessment skills are easily overlooked in the training of clinicians who are left to acquire these skills through trial-and-error practice. Clinicians should seek out expert supervision in this area if it is not readily offered. In addition, most clinicians should enlist the aid of a competent and preferably brutal editor to review their written work. Writing is not easy. Writing skills, however, can be acquired with diligence and patience. George Orwell described the writing process well when stating why he writes. Orwell said that writing a book "is a horrible, exhausting struggle, like a long bout of some painful illness." Unfortunately, writing good assessment reports can be just as laborious.

CHAPTER SUMMARY

- Psychological reports are essentially public domain as they are frequently made available to parents, judges, lawyers, and other non-psychologists, creating the opportunity for improper interpretation of the results by untrained individuals.

- Psychological reports can be useful to other clinicians who evaluate a child who has previously been seen by a psychologist.

- Ownby and Wallbrown (1986) concluded that psychological reports
  1. are considered useful to some extent by consumers such as psychiatrists and social workers,
  2. are frequently criticized by these professional groups on both content and stylistic grounds, and

  3. may (or may not) make substantial contributions to patient management.

- Different audiences require different types of written reports.

- Some of the common problems with report writing include:

  Vocabulary problems

  Eisegesis

  Report length

  A number emphasis

  Failure to address referral questions

- Some research has shown that teachers prefer a question-and-answer report format.

- Parents also tend to prefer a question-and-answer format to other formats, although the difference in preference scores between the psychoeducational and question-and-answer reports in one study failed to reach statistical significance.

- Suggested report writing practices include:

  Report only pertinent information

  Define abbreviations and acronyms

  Emphasize words rather than numbers

  Reduce difficult words

  Describe the tests used

  Edit the report at least once

  Use headings and lists freely

  Use examples of behavior to clarify meaning

  Reduce report length

  Check scores

  Use software spelling and grammar checks

- Some of the score classification systems used today are old and in need of revision in the light of changes in terminology. The Wechsler-Binet classification systems can be traced to the early part of this century.

- If a child's composite score is within 3 standard score points of the next classification, both bordering classifications should be given.

- A continuing debate regarding report writing is the issue of whether or not, or how, to report scores.
- Percentile ranks are less apt to produce inaccurate reactions that are more typically associated with IQ scores.
- A proposed report format for new students includes the following headings.

  Identifying Information

  Assessment Procedures

  Referral Questions

  Background Information

  Observations and Interview Results

  Assessment Results and Interpretation

  Summary

  Signatures

  Recommendations

  Psychometric Summary

- Hints for communicating intelligence test results to parents include:

  Avoid excessive hedging or deceit.

  Use percentile ranks heavily when describing levels of performance.

  Allow parents opportunities to participate.

  Anticipate questions prior to the interview and prepare responses.

  Schedule adequate time for the interview.

  Practice communicating with parents from a variety of backgrounds.

  Never make an overly explicit prediction.

  Use good basic counseling skills.

  Do not engage in counseling that is beyond your level of expertise.

  Be aware that some parents are not ready to accept some test results.

- The most important thing to remember about teacher conferences is that they should take place.
- The major decision that a clinician needs to make before giving feedback to a child is to determine the type of information that is appropriate for a child's developmental level.

Neuropsychological Assessment and Intellectual Function in Children

Mary Kral

The University of Georgia

NEUROPSYCHOLOGICAL ASSESSMENT AND INTELLECTUAL FUNCTION IN CHILDREN

As a cognitive process, intelligence involves primarily the perception of relations, or to use Spearman's more precise phrase, the eduction of correlates, and this process is independent of the specific modality in which the terms are perceived. For effective functioning intelligence may depend more upon the intactness of some rather than other portions of the brain, but in no sense can it be said to be mediated by any single part of it. Intelligence has no locus. (Wechsler, 1958)

Recently, the American Psychological Association appointed a task force to define and describe the study of "intelligence" (Neisser et al., 1996). Any more, intelligence is no longer conceptualized singularly as performance on an intelligence test, but rather this construct is understood more broadly to include basic, underlying processes, such as attention, memory, learning, and processing speed (Beaumont, 1983; Lezak, 1995).

The field of neuropsychology, which has gained eminence within the last 30 years, seeks to address these underlying brain processes as expressed in observable behaviors, including, but not limited to, performance on intelligence tests. Aided by recent technological advances (e.g., positron emission tomography, computerized axial tomography, and magnetic resonance imaging), efforts in the field of neuropsychology are primarily aimed toward elucidation of the neuroanatomical substrates of brain–behavior relationships. Within a developmental context, child neuropsychology has emerged as a field distinct from adult neuropsychology and is characterized by inquiry into such areas as hemispheric specialization, development of frontal lobe function, and plasticity of function. To this end, child neuropsychology attempts to address not only the neurocognitive sequelae of brain injury, but also the neuroanatomical correlates of a broad spectrum of disorders, including psychopathology, developmental disabilities, and various pediatric syndromes. Neuropsychological findings in the areas of learning disabilities and disorders of attention, for example, offer much promise for both theory and remediation (Cohen, Branch, Willis, Weyandt, & Hynd,1992; Goldstein, 1992; Obrzut & Hynd, 1986).

Characterized by investigation of underlying brain processes, the field of neuropsychology holds the potential to contribute substantially to current theories of intelligence. The explanatory power of this field of inquiry may be particularly relevant to the developing organism. While a thorough treatise of the field is beyond the scope of this chapter, an attempt will be made to tie current trends in neuropsychological assessment to the development and assessment of intellectual function in children.

NEUROPSYCHOLOGICAL THEORIES OF INTELLECTUAL FUNCTION

Although the study of brain–behavior relationships dates back to Aristotle (Beaumont, 1983), several theoretical models have shaped the field, both in terms of empirical investigation and instrumentation. The contributions of Ward Halstead and Aleksandr Luria have been particularly formative. These and other theories are briefly described, with particular attention directed toward theoretical application to intellectual function.

Halstead's "Biological Intelligence"

Regarded as the first proponent of systematic neuropsychological evaluation, Ward Halstead is arguably the father of clinical neuropsychology (Reitan, 1994). Primarily an experimental, physiological psychologist, Halstead was critical of prefrontal lobotomies, a widely practiced intervention during his day. His objection was leveled primarily against the nonstandardized methodology of this procedure. On the other hand, Halstead looked with equal disfavor upon traditional psychometric tests of intelligence. While well standardized, he cogently argued that these measures essentially assessed verbal ability, and as such, served primarily as criterion measures of academic success. Halstead poignantly expressed this contention in the following statement: "It is my belief that psychometric intelligence, as reflected by the IQ, does not adequately indicate the 'wisdom' of the healthy nervous system or of its alteration in the pathological nervous system. We have repeatedly found normal or superior IQs in neurosurgical patients lacking up to one-fourth of the total cerebrum following frontal lobectomy" (cited in Reitan, 1994, p. 55).

Consequently, Halstead (1947) attempted to deliver a comprehensive theory of intelligence in which he made a distinction between "biological intelligence," or innate ability, and "psychological intelligence," that which is measured by more traditional tests of intellectual function. While both types of intelligence were regarded as distinct, they are, nonetheless, interdependent. Halstead devoted much of his research efforts toward uncovering the neuroanatomical correlates of biological intelligence. Based upon factor analytic techniques, Halstead identified four basic components of biological intelligence, which he labeled C, A, P and D. These factors are briefly described below:

- C, *the central integrative field factor*, comprises the ability to flexibly adapt to new circumstances and to integrate novel information and stimuli into new symbols and frames of reference. The C factor enables the individual to assimilate the constant and varied bombardment of external stimuli as an internalized sense of order.

- A, *the abstraction factor*, represents the ability to think abstractly or to synthesize a series of seemingly unrelated stimuli into a meaningful assemblage or idea. This factor affords the ability to find similarity among differences, and, conversely, uniqueness within homogenous elements.

- *P, the power factor*, is described as the "reserve" energy within the brain required for thinking. This mental energy correlates with the rate of neuronal firing and is coordinated by the frontal lobes.

- *D, the directional factor*, was the most difficult component of biological intelligence to substantiate with factor analysis. Halstead, nonetheless, maintained that *D* is the primary mode of expression for innate ability, including, for example, reading, writing, speaking, or artistic mediums. Also, *D* is characterized by attentional processes. That is, in order to express intellectual ability, focused attention or sustained mental effort is required.

Having established these components of biological intelligence, Halstead's work turned to the discovery of their neuroanatomical correlates. This seminal work served as the very foundation of contemporary neuropsychology (Reynolds, 1981b). To this end, he developed a battery of tests to assess the *C, A, P* and *D* factors. This battery lead to the development of the well-known Halstead Impairment Index, as performance on these measures reliably discriminated among individuals who had suffered brain insult from those who had not. Also premonitory, Halstead maintained that the components of biological intelligence were differentially represented throughout the cerebral cortex, although primacy was attributed to the frontal lobes, the seat of higher cognitive function:

> *Biological intelligence is a basic function of the brain and is essential for many forms of adaptive behavior of the human organism. While it is represented throughout the cerebral cortex, its representation is not equal throughout. It is distributed in a gradient with its maximal representation occurring in the cortex of the frontal lobes. The nuclear structure of biological intelligence comprises four basic factors which, in unified fashion, enter into all cognitive activities. While these factors make possible the highest reaches of human intellect, their dysfunction, as produced by brain damage, may yield progressively maladaptive forms of behavior, or "biological neurosis." The frontal lobes,*

> *long regarded as silent areas, are the portion of the brain most essential to biological intelligence. They are the organs of civilization—the basis of man's despair and of his hope for the future. (Halstead, 1947, pp. 148–149)*

While neither Halstead's factor structure nor the alleged coordinating function of the frontal lobes have been substantiated in subsequent research, his work provided a significant foundation for the clinical assessment of neurocognitive impairment because, it appeared, his tests provided the best means to differentiate "organic" from "nonorganic" explanations of behavior. In particular, his battery of tests have emerged as a standard core battery, as evidenced in the Halstead-Reitan Neuropsychological Batteries (Reitan, 1994; Reynolds, 1981b).

Luria's "Functional Systems Model"

Aleksandr Luria, a soviet neuropsychologist and prolific researcher, offered an alternative model of intellectual function from a neuropsychological perspective. In accord with Halstead, Luria ascribed a central role to the frontal lobes in mediating intellectual function. However, influenced by the work of Karl Lashley, Luria offered an integrationist model, or the functional systems model (Luria, 1966, 1973, 1980). As such, this model suggests that behavior is the result of coordinated efforts among three hierarchically organized functional units:

1. The first functional unit, *the subcortical unit*, is subserved by the brainstem, reticular formation and midbrain (including areas of the limbic system and hippocampus). This unit functions as the conscious base, organizing and regulating the functions of the other units. The subcortical unit, therefore, mediates arousal, regulates the energy level or "cortical tone" of the brain, and supports functions such as orientation, learning, and memory.

2. The second functional unit, *the posterior cortical unit*, is located in the parietal, occipital and temporal lobes, including projections radiating from the thalamus. Compared to the general arousal function of the first unit, the second unit subserves very specific functions (e.g., auditory processing in the temporal region, visual processing in the occipital region, and tactile processing in the parietal region). Frequently referred to as the association areas of the cortex, most cognitive information processing occurs in this unit, including reception, storage, and analysis of sensory input.

3. The third functional unit, *the anterior cortical unit*, is comprised of the remainder of the cortex anterior to the central sulcus (principally the frontal lobes and their projections). Involved in every complex, higher-order behavior, this unit activates the brain; regulates attention and concentration; and plans, initiates, and monitors behavior and mental activity. In short, this third unit serves an "executive function" for the entire system.

Figure 19.1 offers a pictorial view of Luria's functional systems model. Intelligent behavior, according to Luria, "is not a property of only one of these functional parts, but requires the coordination of all three functional units, each of them playing its own, highly specific role, in the organization of behavioral processes" (Luria, 1973, p. 5).

Luria (1966) also described two modes of information processing that are primarily accomplished by the second functional unit, in concert with the first and third units. *Successive processing* involves sequential, temporally based, linear processing. Serial tasks, such as learning to write, in which the elements are related to one another in a linear fashion, involve successive processing. Luria maintained that this type of information processing was subserved by the frontal and temporal lobes. Conversely, *simultaneous processing* is employed when all elements of a stimulus can be surveyed at the same time. For example, visual-spatial tasks involve this type of information processing,

such as block design and puzzles. Neuroanatomical correlates of this type of processing are located in the parietal and occipital lobes. Luria maintained that these two methods of information processing are not modality specific. That is, both verbal and nonverbal stimuli may be processed either successively or simultaneously. However, one or the other mode is more efficient for certain stimuli (e.g., language is most efficiently processed via successive means, where as figure drawing is most effectively processed simultaneously).

Neuropsychological evaluation, following from this integrationist view, was described as "synthesis analysis" (Luria, 1970). Following from this perspective, impairment in one unit will necessarily affect the integrity of the whole, interconnected system. However, failure in a particular unit may also produce specific disturbances in behavior. For example, a focal lesion may produce specific impairment, depending upon the systems involved (e.g., a focal lesion in the occipital region may produce visual disorientation). Luria was therefore critical of quantitative, norm-referenced assessment, which tends to erroneously categorize function and reduce disparate information into summary scores (Jorgensen & Christensen, 1995). Instead, Luria adopted a more qualitative approach, involving careful analysis of individual performance and observation of problem-solving behaviors on a variety of tests. Additionally, a pattern analysis was preferred to single test performance, as emphasized within the quantitative tradition. Luria was also critical of the emphasis placed on reliability of results in standardized testing, calling attention to the varied performance of patients who suffer brain injury. Reliability, according to Luria, occurs when a similar functional deficit associated with a particular syndrome is manifested consistently on several tests that purportedly assess the same function. The Luria Nebraska Neuropsychological Battery (LNNB) was developed from this qualitative approach (Golden, 1997). The psychometric properties of this instrument will be further detailed in subsequent sections.

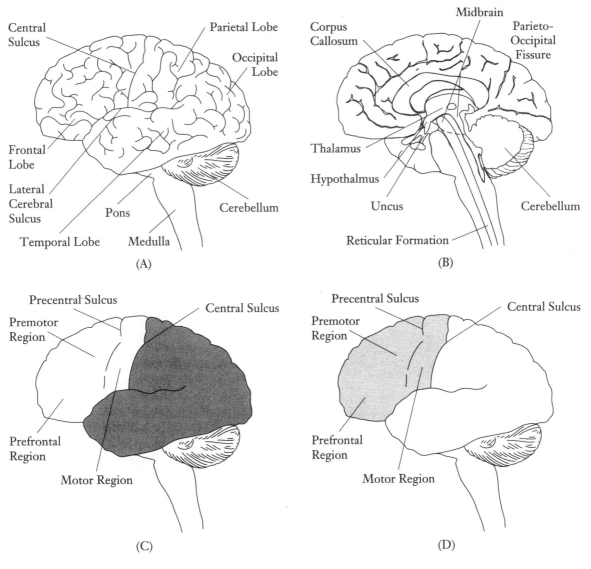

FIGURE 19.1

Depiction of Luria's "functional systems" of the brain. A. Gross anatomy of the human brain, left hemisphere view. The remaining depictions identify the three major units of the brain involved in the organization of behavior. B. The *subcortical unit* includes the brain stem and evolutionarily "old cortex." It serves a regulatory function in wakefulness and responsiveness to stimuli. C. The *posterior cortical unit* includes regions of the association cortex posterior to the central sulcus (parietal, occipital, and temporal lobes), as illustrated by the shaded areas. These cortical regions mediate the analysis, coding, and storage of information. D. The shaded area denotes the *anterior cortical unit*, comprised of the regions anterior to the central sulcus (i.e., the frontal lobes, including the motor strip). This region is involved in the formation of intentions and planning.

SOURCE: Adapted from Luria (1970).

According to Luria (1980), development follows an "ontogenetic course," suggesting that development is complete for the subcortical unit at birth, for the posterior cortical unit several months following birth, and for the anterior cortical unit during the first few years of life. This hypothesis may explain why brain injuries suffered early in development result in generalized deficits due to impairment of brain regions that form the critical foundation for other cortical areas. Conversely, brain damage suffered at a relatively later time in childhood may result in more focal impairment. Beyond this general description of neural maturation, particular behaviors subserved by Luria's functional units, particularly the third unit (i.e., the prefrontal cortex), are little understood in the context of development. "Executive function," which enables future-oriented planning and flexibility of thought, has been implicated in current theories of attention deficit hyperactivity disorder (ADHD, Barkley, 1997); however, the nature of impairment or developmental disturbance is not well understood. Luria's astute understanding of developmental processes has, however, been empirically substantiated. Research suggests that executive functions, which are subserved by the prefrontal cortical regions, are present at birth but continue to mature until around age 12 (Cohen et al., 1992).

According to some critics (e.g., Telzrow, 1990), Luria's theory has been characterized as too broad to encompass a model of intelligence. However, authors of the Kaufman Assessment Battery for Children (K-ABC) and the Das-Naglieri Cognitive Assessment System (CAS) developed these instruments based primarily upon Lurian theory. Specifically, both batteries emphasize a cognitive processing approach to the assessment of intellectual function in children, predicated upon a distinction between simultaneous and successive processing. The interested reader is directed to Chapter 10 for a more thorough description of the K-ABC. Further discussion of the CAS requires an exploration of the PASS model.

The PASS Model

Based on Luria's functional systems model, Das, Naglieri and colleagues (Naglieri & Das, 1988, 1990; Das, Naglieri, & Kirby, 1994) developed a neuropsychological theory of intellectual function. The planning-attention-simultaneous-successive (PASS) model is an attempt to empirically define the cognitive processes subserved by Luria's functional units. The *attention unit*, the first functional unit, maintains the cortical energy and tone necessary for higher levels of function. *Simultaneous* and *successive coding* correspond with Luria's second functional unit, which receives, processes, and stores information. Finally, the third functional unit, *planning*, programs, regulates, and verifies mental activity. Following from Luria's emphasis on frontal lobe mediation of higher-order behavior, planning within the PASS model is localized within this cortical region. Recall that the functional systems model was predicated upon distinct, yet highly interdependent and dynamic units, or regions, within the brain. Attentional systems, for example, subserved by such structures as the reticular formation located in the brain stem, maintain the "cortical tone" throughout the brain via ascending and descending projections. It follows, therefore, that planning is integrally tied to the arousal function; selective inhibition of attention to certain stimuli and focused attention on certain other stimuli influence the manner in which information is coded. The interrelationship among these components is depicted in Figure 19.2.

The authors also contend that the PASS model accounts for developmental changes: "There is a developmental consideration in discussing the relationship between coding and planning. Obviously if coding should be developed to an adequate level before planning can emerge clearly as a mental function, then before that level is reached, coding and planning will not be found to be independent. Luria has indicated that probably planning does not develop until ages 4 to 5" (Das, 1980, p. 149). That is, Luria's functional

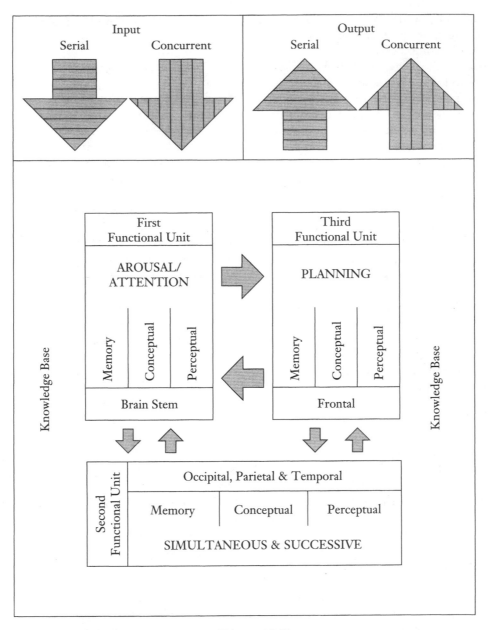

FIGURE 19.2

The PASS model of intellectual function. Based upon Luria's theory of "functional units," the PASS model purports that attention, simultaneous and successive processing, and planning, while subserved by distinct regions in the brain, are interrelated components of cognition. These units operate concertedly in the knowledge acquisition process. In addition, prior learning, or one's knowledge base, influences the learning process and moderates on-going processing of information.

SOURCE: Naglieri & Das, 1990, p. 316. Originally appeared in Das, Naglieri, & Kirby, 1994. Reprinted with permission.

units form a dynamic, interrelated system within the PASS model, where each unit responds to the developmental changes and experiences of an individual, and yet concurrently maintain distinct functions. In this sense, experience or a knowledge base is the product of the interrelated activity of these functional units.

The authors of the PASS model contend that constructs such as "intelligence" and "IQ" are obsolete and should be replaced by the assessment of "cognitive processes." That is, tested models of cognitive processing should be utilized when attempting to measure intellectual function: "The PASS view of cognitive processes opposes general ability as a real entity and questions its value as an average or composite measure of a set of processes. This concept is limited because it does not adequately recognize that human cognitive functioning is comprised of varied cognitive processes. The conception of general intelligence does not describe adequately the processes by which intelligent action is produced, nor does it suggest a means to enhance performance" (Naglieri & Das, 1990, p. 331). Moreover, Naglieri and Das (1988) maintain that two important aspects of intellectual function—namely, planning and attention—are missing from more traditional measures of intelligence, possibly accounting for the fact that IQ tests are not good discriminators of frontal lobe damage or sensitive to differences characterized by exceptional populations, particularly children with learning disabilities (Naglieri & Das, 1990; Lezak, 1995).

Based on the PASS model, the Das-Naglieri Cognitive Assessment System (CAS; Naglieri & Das, 1997) is offered as an alternative test of intelligence. Standardized with a nationally representative group of 2,200 children and adolescents, the CAS is normed for ages 5 years through 17 years, 11 months. Unlike the atheoretical nature of more traditional tests of intelligence, the CAS is comprised of four scales following from Luria's functional systems model. The tasks comprising the four scales were designed to assess basic cognitive processes, as opposed to cognitive abilities, which are sensitive to educational experience. The structure of the CAS offers a 12-subtest standard battery and an abbreviated 8-subtest basic battery. The subtests associated with each of the PASS scales are listed below.

The CAS yields standard scores for the subtests and composite scores for the PASS scales, which combine to yield a full scale score. The authors report reliability coefficients ranging from .95 to .97 for the Standard Battery Full Scale score, and the following coefficients for the PASS scale scores: .88 (Planning), .88 (Attention), .93 (Simultaneous), and .93 (Successive).

While the authors of the CAS have presented considerable research with various populations, particularly factor analytic support for the validity of a four-factor solution (e.g., Das, Mensink, & Mishra, 1990; Naglieri & Das, 1987; Naglieri, Das, Stevens, & Ledbetter, 1991), further empirical exploration concerning reliability and validity is needed by independent investigators. Preliminary review of the CAS highlighted the inconsistent use of different subtests that purportedly measure the PASS components across separate empirical investigations, resulting in compromised factor analytic results (Telzrow, 1990).

Planning	Attention	Simultaneous	Successive
Matching Numbers*	Expressive Attention*	Nonverbal Matrices*	Word Series*
Planned Codes*	Number Detection*	Verbal-Spatial Relations*	Sentence Repetition*
Planned Connections	Receptive Attention	Figure Memory	Speech Rate (ages 5–7)
			Sentence Questions (ages 8–17)

*denotes subtests that comprise the Basic Battery

Additionally, Lambert (1990) suggested that this factor analytic research was erroneously considered apart from the contribution of general intellectual ability, or "g." More recently, Carroll (1995) and Kranzler and Weng (1995a, 1995b) reanalyzed the data from many of these factor analytic studies. These investigators concluded that the PASS model does not provide an adequate "fit" for the obtained correlational structure. For example, the Planning and Attention scales proved to be highly correlated and, thus, indistinguishable. Instead, an underlying neurological process, such as speed of information processing, may be shared by the timed subtests of these scales. Moreover, subtests from each of the PASS scales loaded significantly on a general ability factor, "g," accounting for more variance on the CAS than on more traditional measures of intelligence. In sum, while commendation should be extended to the authors of the CAS for their attempt to develop a battery firmly grounded in neuropsychological theory, further empirical validation of the constructs purportedly assessed by this measure is necessary.

Cerebral Lateralization

Not unlike the theoretical basis for the PASS model, research in the area of cerebral lateralization draws heavily from information processing theory and cognitive psychology. As such, it may very well hold the potential to integrate all three previously outlined models (Reynolds, 1981b). The theory of cerebral lateralization finds its basis in Sperry's classic "split-brain" studies, which involved an operation that severed the commissural connections between the hemispheres. Independent functioning of the two cerebral hemispheres was the presumed result, affording the study of the relative specialization of each hemisphere for the processing of various tasks. Theories of cerebral lateralization, therefore, concern *functional asymmetries*, or the relative specialization of one hemisphere for a particular function (Hynd & Willis, 1988).

Far from the overpopularized and oversimplified notions of "right-brain" and "left-brain" function, this field of research is sizable and complex. No attempt will be made here to present a thorough overview of the literature; a description of the research will necessarily be concise. Contemporary research, which followed from examination of split-brain patients, has utilized a number of highly specialized tasks to examine perceptual asymmetries and to localize specialization of function (e.g., dichotic listening tasks, tachistoscopic visual-perceptual tasks, and haptic identification tasks). General agreement exists within the literature to suggest that the left hemisphere is specialized for linguistic, serial, and analytic tasks, as demonstrated in patients with aphasic disorders (i.e., disorders of speech), or patients with unilateral damage to the left hemisphere. Conversely, unilateral damage to the right hemisphere revealed the relative specialization of this cerebral region for visual-spatial processes, face recognition, music perception and perception of affective components of speech (Bryden & Saxby, 1986; Spreen, Rissell, & Edgell, 1995). Rather than viewing these relative specializations as strictly dichotomous, the widely held view contends that functional asymmetries exist along a continuum, the difference between hemispheric function being one of quantity rather than quality (Hahn, 1987).

Whether cerebral lateralization is present at birth or results from developmental changes has been the target of much empirical investigation and theorizing in neuropsychology. The work of Karl Lashley and others suggest that the immature brain possesses "equipotentiality," and specialization of hemispheric function is the result of a developmental process. For example, damage to the left hemisphere at an early age may result in compensatory specialization for language within the right hemisphere (Hahn, 1987). Conversely, Kinsbourne (1982) offered the selective activation hypothesis, maintaining that hemispheric asymmetries are "hard wired" both anatomically and functionally from birth and remain constant throughout development. Because there is contralateral representation of sensory information in the cerebral cortex, perhaps differential activation of these pathways accounts for hemispheric dominance for different perceptual abilities. In the statement to follow, Kinsbourne underscores the interconnection, via commissural pathways, between these specialized cerebral regions that operate concertedly to produce behavior:

> *Lateralization provides neural distance, not between alternative mutually exclusive acts, but between complementary component processes that combine to program a unitary pattern of behavior. (p. 413)*

As concerns cerebral lateralization and intellectual function, there is a sizable literature exploring the anatomical localization of specific higher-order cognitive processes; however, it is replete with inconsistencies. Considering Luria's theory of functional systems, suggesting the interdependence of cortical function, this makes sense. Much empirical investigation, however, has been devoted to how deficiencies in reading ability, language skills, or cognitive abilities can be attributed to abnormal lateralization. The prototypical paradigm involves studies of the interrelationships between cerebral dominance, cognitive function, and lateralized motor preference (e.g., handedness), as right-handed individuals typically express left cerebral dominance for language. Moreover, measures of lateral preference have been integrated into many neuropsychological batteries. There is, as yet, little evidence in support of significant changes in cerebral lateralization after the age of 2 or 3 years. Roughly 92% of the population demonstrates a right-hand preference and left-hemisphere dominance for language. With the exception of major injury, these patterns of cerebral lateralization will likely persist into adulthood. Additionally, the relationship between cerebral lateralization and cognitive ability remains speculative (Bryden & Saxby, 1986; Hahn, 1987; Spreen, Rissell & Edgell, 1995). In a longitudinal study of 93 children, Sulzbacher, Thomson, Farwell, Temkin, and Holubkov (1994) report negligible correlations between lateral preferences and measures of intelligence (.08) and achievement (ranging from –.04 to .02). The authors conclude, "children who demonstrated inconsistencies in hand, eye and foot lateral preference at an early age did not subsequently demonstrate intellectual or academic deficits. In fact no relationship was found between early lateral consistency and later intellectual performance or academic achievement" (p. 477).

NEURODEVELOPMENTAL CONSIDERATIONS

While the aforementioned neuropsychological theories afford an important theoretical framework, an accurate conceptualization of higher-order cognitive processes in children cannot simply be a generalization of adult-based models. Understanding the neurological substrates of intelligence in children must necessarily incorporate principles of cognitive development and the maturing nervous system. For example, children experience different sources of brain insult (e.g., epilepsy, anoxia, birth trauma, postnatal infections, closed head injuries) as compared to those of adults (e.g., cerebral vascular accidents, intracerebral tumors, and dementing conditions). Additionally, it has been fairly well-established that children suffer greater generalized rather than localized brain damage (Kinsbourne, 1974). The reverse is often true among adult populations, and, by comparison, the resultant neuropsychological profiles for these two age groups will likely appear quite different (Hynd & Obrzut, 1986). In this regard, Tramontana and Hooper (1988) proffer an important charge to child neuropsychologists:

Not only do children differ in the types of brain insult commonly experienced, they also differ with respect to the specificity of behavioral effects manifested, the pattern and course of (re)acquisition of function after injury, the modifying effects of ongoing developmental change, and the extent to which deficits sometimes can be delayed or "silent" until later developmental periods. Developmentalists argue that a child should never be viewed as simply a scaled-down version of an adult. Likewise, an appropriate assessment of brain-behavior relationships in children cannot be based simply on scaled-down versions of assessment methods used with adults. (p. 4)

The relationship of brain injury within the context of development is, therefore, multivariate and a complex interaction. Obrzut and Hynd (1986) highlight several developmental variables that must be considered in the context of neuropsychological assessment with children. Among these variables, *age of onset of injury* may likely constitute the developmental factor that elicits the greatest debate. In children, the age at which brain injury is acquired plays a critically important role when attempting to untangle the complex interactions of stage of brain development, environmental demands at the time of injury, and nature of the brain injury. "Plasticity" of brain function and critical periods for "transfer of function" are relevant issues in this regard (see Box 19.1 for more information). Also, Hynd and Willis (1988) reference the extant literature in cognitive psychology, which suggests that children may perform differently on similar tasks at different developmental stages, employing different cognitive strategies at each stage. Finally, children who experience brain insult at an early age may not demonstrate deficits until certain cognitive functions that rely upon the impaired cortical regions reach maturity at a later age (Williams & Boll, 1997). The issue of *organicity vs. ontogenetic development* poses an often nebulous distinction between neurodevelopmental anomalies and individual differences in the rate and pattern of development. That is, making a distinction between developmental lag versus abnormal cortical development is a mercurial undertaking.

Still, the contribution of a number of other variables highlights the complex nature of child neuropsychological assessment (Obrzut & Hynd, 1986). *Neurological variables*, such as the presence and length of unconsciousness, type of treatment following injury (e.g., surgery, irradiation, or chemotherapy), type and size of lesion, and the extent and location of brain damage, also must be considered. *Cognitive factors*, namely the specific mental activities implicated in brain insult and the cognitive complexity of such functions, are important considerations as well. As highlighted previously, the onset of symptoms associated with neurological impairment may be delayed due to development. *Environmental variables*, such as socioeconomic status and educational attainment have demonstrated sizable contributions to the outcome of neurological trauma. And, finally, *premorbid functioning* is a critically important part of neuropsychological assessment, especially when establishing a decrement in function subsequent to brain insult. Very often, however, a referential baseline, such as intelligence test scores, is not available, and in these cases premorbid functioning must be estimated (Crawford, 1992).

Assessing Premorbid Level of Functioning

Estimation of premorbid function, or establishing a referential baseline of preinjury ability, has historically been a difficult endeavor. In recent years, while investigation of the predictive accuracy of several methods has been on the rise, there remains no consensus regarding a superior method for estimating premorbid functioning (Johnstone, Slaughter, Schoop, McAllister, Schwake, & Luebbering, 1997). Moreover, there remains a paucity of empirical efforts aimed specifically toward the estimation of children's premorbid ability (Franzen, Burgess, & Smith-Seemiller, 1997). As previously stated, premorbid functioning is an integral component of neuropsychological assessment. In most cases, a defensible decrement

Box 19.1   Plasticity and Intellectual Function

The concept of *plasticity*, or the capacity of the immature brain to recover, and possibly compensate for, brain insult follows from research conducted by Kennard (1936, 1942) with primates. This researcher noted less detrimental effects for motor behavior following early brain insult as compared to damage suffered during adulthood. The resultant "Kennard principle" suggests that the central nervous system evidences greater "plasticity," or recovery of neural and/or behavioral function, early in development. Subsequent research has challenged this relatively simplistic notion of brain recovery, pointing to the dynamic and interrelated variables that contribute to recovery following brain injury. Several of these variables are discussed with regard to developmental considerations in the section entitled Neurodevelopmental Considerations. Additionally, evidence suggests that considerable cerebral specialization at the time of birth may also place limits on plasticity. It is fairly well established that injury, regardless of whether it occurs to the right or left hemisphere and whether it is relatively localized, tends to produce more generalized decrements in ability among children as compared with adults.

There is no question, however, that the central nervous system continues to develop and mature dramatically, especially during the first year of life. Beardsworth and Harding (1996) offer a brief description of these early neurodevelopmental changes:

> The period from six months from conception to several years after birth is called the period of organization. During this time several processes are being completed: the alignment, orientation and layering of cortical neurons; the elaboration of dendrites and axons; contacts between synapses; elective elimination of many cells; and glial proliferation and differentiation. Relatively little is known about the primary disorders at this time, with the exception of response to trauma (such as birth injury). The final stage is myelination. This is most rapid immediately after birth but continues to adulthood. Again, primary disturbances of this stage are little documented, but certainly some of the effects of malnutrition in early infancy can be attributed to interference with this process. (pp. 17–18)

While substantial empirical evidence would seem to challenge the concept of brain plasticity, the aforementioned neurodevelopmental scene sheds some light on the potential vulnerability and resilience of the developing brain.

Depending upon the nature of injury, the effect of early brain insult on intellectual function is variable. In a study of children with unilateral lesion sustained prior to 6 months of age, Aram, Ekelman, Rose, and Whitaker (1985) report little decrement in intellectual function when assessed between the ages of 18 months to 8 years postinjury. Conversely, Nass and Peterson (1989) report greater deficits in intellectual function among a group of children with right-hemisphere congenital injury. The authors suggest that early right-hemisphere damage results in more severe deficits in overall intellectual function, as compared with early left-hemisphere damage. Similarly, in a summarization of research findings concerning the effects of early damage to the frontal lobes, Kolb and Fantie (1997) conclude, "Although there are likely differences in etiology and extent of injuries in the children in different studies, the overriding conclusion that intelligence is severely compromised by early frontal injuries is inescapable" (p. 36). In general, nature seems to confer a preferential sparing of certain functions (especially language) subsequent to brain injury sustained very early in life. However, this sparing of function is often not without cost to other functional domains.

Banich, Levine, Kim, and Huttenlocher (1990) investigated the differential effects of congenital lesion on Vocabulary and Block Design subtest scores of the WISC-R over time. Congenital conditions are those conditions present at birth, the etiology of which is not attributable to genetic factors. The results of this study suggest that length of recovery period has a significant effect on intellectual functioning. At age 6, children with congenital lesion performed similarly to age-matched controls on measures of verbal (Vocabulary) and nonverbal (Block Design) abilities. However, with increasing age these children demonstrated progressive decrements in function (see figure on next page). The authors offer tentative hypotheses that relate directly to plasticity of function:

> The reorganizational capacity of the young lesioned brain is adequate to support early developing functions, but not more complex functions that typically develop later, as the normal brain matures. Early

(Continues)

Box 19.1   Plasticity and Intellectual Function (Continued)

damage may attenuate the ability of the brain to undergo normal developmental changes, thus limiting the computational and/or storage capacities necessary to master the skills normally acquired during development. Assuming that the cognitive skills acquired at one point during development are necessary to maintain a normal rate of subsequent intellectual growth (scaffolding model), the disparity in intellectual functioning between children with early brain damage and normal, age-matched controls would be expected to increase with age. (p. 44)

A graphic representation of differential performance on both WISC-R Vocabulary and Block Design subtests over time appears below.

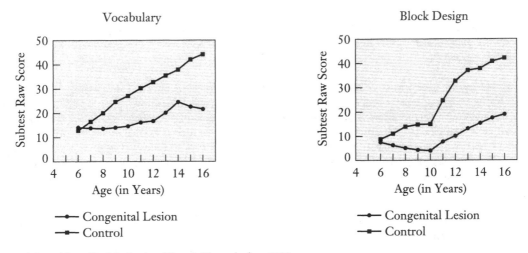

SOURCE: Adapted from Banich, Levine, Kim, & Huttenlocher, 1990.

in neuropsychological functioning as a result of brain insult or injury is tantamount, not only for diagnosis, but also for appropriate rehabilitative planning. More often than not, valid and reliable indicators of ability prior to the onset of neurological trauma are not available, and the neuropsychologist must rely on the available arsenal of estimation methodologies (Crawford, 1992). To this end, premorbid ability has primarily been estimated with measures of intellectual ability, generating a need for estimates of other abilities (e.g., memory) in neuropsychological assessment. This later point may be of particular relevance for children, as IQ in this population tends to covary with maturation, education, and development (Klesges, 1982). Currently, the

most widely utilized methods of estimation appear to be downward extensions of adult measures, including "hold–don't hold" methods, demographically based regression formulas, and clinical judgment.

"Hold–don't hold" methods are based on abilities that are presumed to be relatively resistant to impairment. Such abilities generally include performance on Wechsler Intelligence subtests and performance on word reading tests. Performance on the Wechsler scales is derived from the Wechsler Deterioration Index (WDI), which subtracts scaled scores on "hold" subtests (Vocabulary, Information, Object Assembly, and Picture Completion) from those achieved on "don't hold" subtests (Digit Span, Similarities,

Coding, and Block Design), to yield the following equation:

$$WDI = \frac{hold-don't\ hold}{hold}$$

Performance on the "hold" subtests was presumed to be free from impairment or deterioration following brain injury, as compared with performance on "don't hold" subtests, which was thought to reflect marked decrements in cognitive function (Crawford, 1992). Estimates of premorbid function based on "hold–don't hold" formulas have proven to be "notoriously unreliable" (Klesges, Fisher, Vasey, & Pheley, 1985). Neuropsychological theories of intellectual function may shed some light on this empirical finding. This method assumes equal functioning across all cognitive domains prior to injury, an erroneous assumption particularly for the developing brain. Also, empirical investigation suggests that some "hold" subtests (e.g., Vocabulary) are differentially affected by neurological trauma, depending upon the size and extent of injury, than previously presumed. Additional criticism of this estimation formula includes the failure to account for regression effects and measurement error, leading to overestimations of premorbid function in many cases (Franzen et al., 1997).

Demographically based regression formulas were offered as an alternative to the "hold–don't hold" formula (e.g., Reynolds & Gutkin, 1979). Variables such as age, sex, socioeconomic status, and education were utilized in multiple regression formulas with the original WISC-R standardization sample. Due to high correlations between education and intelligence, and the fact that demographic variables are impervious to neurologic trauma, these variables comprise potentially useful estimates of premorbid ability. Correlations between the demographic variables and performance on the WISC-R Verbal, Performance, and Full Scale IQ scores were reported as .44, .37, and .44, respectively. Unfortunately, subsequent cross-validation studies failed to replicate this significant level of correlation with samples of children

with and without brain impairment (Klesges, 1982; Klesges & Sanchez, 1981). Moreover, Franzen et al. (1997) suggest that the clinical utility of regression formulas is suspect, as the obtained correlation provides information about the linear relationship between demographic variables and IQ, as opposed to providing information about the accuracy of IQ estimates.

Clinical judgement is often utilized in the absence of a standard and reliable method for predicting premorbid intellectual function, relying upon clinical acumen and the synthesis of multiple sources of information (e.g., school records, standardized tests of achievement, parent interview, medical records and developmental history) to determine a decline in function. According to a recent survey of neuropsychologists, the most frequently used method was indeed clinical judgment (Smith-Seemiller, Franzen, Burgess, & Prieto, 1997). In an empirical investigation designed to compare the predictive validity of clinical judgment versus demographic regression formulas, clinician's IQ estimates approximated those obtained with multiple regression formulas, producing significantly narrower confidence intervals, in fact, than those derived from the regression formulas (Kareken & Williams, 1994). These authors recommend cautious application of this estimation methodology, favoring the use of actuarial methods that may minimize sources of bias, such as failure to consider such variables as regression to the mean when making an estimate. A child with a premorbid IQ of 130, who loses 20–25 IQ points subsequent to head trauma, may be missed because they appear "normal" (Reynolds, 1997). Cases such as this underscore the need for standardized procedures for estimating premorbid function.

NEUROPSYCHOLOGICAL ASSESSMENT WITH CHILDREN

Following from the previously detailed developmental concerns, child neuropsychological assessment must necessarily consist of more than

Box 19.2   Neuropsychological Screening and Neurological "Soft Signs"

For psychologists engaged in psychometric assessment, knowing when to refer for a complete neurological evaluation is important. This may become increasingly more relevant given the current definitions of behavioral and learning disorders that implicate a neurological basis, but no "hard" neurological signs, and the trend to elucidate the neuroanatomical correlates of psychopathology. Careful observation of possible minor neurological abnormalities is indicated, as these so-called *neurological soft signs* have been detected in the nonnormative performance of children on neurological exams in the absence of known brain insult. Additionally, early detection of soft signs have been variously associated with subsequent behavioral disturbances, such as hyperactivity and conduct disorders, and emotional and cognitive disorders (Tupper, 1986). As such, presence of these neurological soft signs may indicate the need for further neuropsychological evaluation.

While the detection of neurological soft signs seems a pertinent endeavor, these signs are difficult to evaluate and often produce poor interrater reliabilities. For example, a classification system has been offered, dividing soft signs into two different categories (Spreen, Risser, & Edgell, 1995). The *developmental soft signs* include behaviors that are considered abnormal beyond a certain developmental period. This category includes the delayed onset of certain age-appropriate behaviors (e.g., late onset of walking) or the persistence of behaviors beyond expected developmental periods (e.g., delayed suppression of the Babkin reflex). Comparatively, the *soft signs of abnormality* are those behaviors that are considered to be abnormal at any age, although they are not characteristic of neurological disease (e.g., significant incoordination; nystagmus or spasmodic, involuntary eye movements). These signs may reflect more subtle manifestations of underlying central nervous system dysfunction. Empirical investigation of soft signs often fail to uniformly apply such classification systems. Additionally, much research is needed to provide developmental norms for these signs. Taken together, the methodological problems in this area of research seriously compromise the validity of inference (Ardila & Rosselli, 1996).

Efforts to provide standardized measurement of neurological soft signs are evident, nonetheless, in the development of early childhood screening instruments. *Neuropsychological screening* is concerned with early detection of children at risk for subsequent neurological or behavioral disability. The goal, therefore, is to identify among large groups those with a predisposition for neuropsychological abnormality, and referral of these individuals for a more comprehensive diagnostic evaluation. Empirical investigation in this realm is fraught with methodological problems, including sampling inconsistencies, suspect psychometric properties of the screening instruments, and a lack of longitudinal data (Pine, Scott, Busner, Davies, Fried, Parides, & Shaffer, 1996).

While longitudinal data is limited in this area, one such study offered by Shaffer and colleagues (1985) reported that soft signs of motor incoordination present in childhood were predictive of subsequent psychopathology in adulthood, particularly anxiety disorders. Additionally, soft signs at age 7 were associated with lower IQ at age 17. Comparatively, Huttenlocher, Levine, Huttenlocher, and Gates (1990) studied the predictive validity of neurological soft signs and predisposition for subsequent learning disabilities. In this investigation, a standardized neuropsychological screening battery was administered to 200 at-risk children and age-matched controls, ages 3 through 5. A significant, negative correlation was found between children identified as at risk during early neuropsychological screening and subsequent performance on the WISC-R at age 7. The graph below depicts this linear relationship. In this graph, IQ scores at age 7 are plotted against neurological test scores at age 5 (test score represents number of items failed on a neuropsychological screener, ranging from 0 to 10).

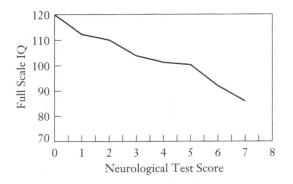

SOURCE: Adapted from Huttenlocher, Levine, Huttenlocher, & Gates, 1990.

Box 19.2   Neuropsychological Screening and Neurological "Soft Signs" (Continued)

The authors conclude that neurological screening reliably identified children who manifested a developmental lag involving cognitive ability, motor function, and sensory discrimination. Accordingly, this group of children required special education services at age 7. More recently, Hall and Kramer (1995) provide empirical data that question the predictive validity of neurological soft signs detected in childhood. In this study, the authors followed the developmental trajectory of 135 boys demonstrating a large number of neurological soft signs during childhood. The findings suggest that the performance of these children was indistinguishable from a comparison group demonstrating low incidence of soft signs on a broad range of cognitive and behavioral measures administered in adulthood.

In summary, neurological soft signs remain a controversial prognostic indicator of subsequent disability. Further empirical investigation is needed to refine the psychometric properties of neuropsychological screening instruments. Additionally, continued longitudinal study is required to substantiate the stable influence of neurological soft signs and subsequent deficits in function. These limitations notwithstanding, the potential importance of this area of neuropsychological assessment for early remediation and prevention is evident. In the absence of reliable, standardized measures, the examiner must rely upon clinical judgment. Such data as a positive medical history of neurological disorder (e.g., seizure disorder) and observation of soft signs during examination may warrant referral for a more comprehensive neuropsychological exam. The interested reader is referred to Tupper (1987) for a thorough description of neurological soft signs. Additionally, the Bender-Gestalt Test of Visual-Motor Integration is purportedly utilized as a neurological screener among school-aged children, as this instrument taps a broad range of neurologically relevant behaviors (Tupper, 1986). In general, the astute clinician will corroborate a conclusion to refer with multiple data sources.

"downward extensions" of adult measures. Unfortunately, many of the currently available batteries are just this—renormed adult tests for children that lack adequate national, cross-sectional norming and tasks that are age appropriate (Tramontana & Hooper, 1988). There is a need for neuropsychological measures capable of assessing normal cognitive development at different age-referenced points. For example, research suggests the presence of a "general memory factor," as children's performance on tests of memory stabilize with increasing age, implicating, perhaps, development of various memory strategies (Morra, 1994). Clearly, more research is needed to understand normal development in this area. Additionally, Hynd and Obrzut (1986) maintain that developmental considerations, such as short attention span and the tendency for an idiosyncratic presentation of deficits among children, may warrant a more flexible approach, as compared to neuropsychological assessment with adults. And finally, to date, there exists no formalized nosology or diagnostic classification system in child neuropsychological assessment. Again, this issue may reflect the unique profile produced by developing neurocognitive abilities, especially in concert with socioeducational factors.

The general purposes of child neuropsychological evaluation center around diagnosis and remediation. Lezak (1995) suggests that the diagnostic function of neuropsychological assessment may have been more important in the early history of this discipline, as neuroimaging technology has increasingly assumed this role. However, fine diagnostic discriminations remain the purview of neuropsychological assessment. Cases such as mild head trauma or toxic encephalopathy are exemplary of the discriminative accuracy of neuropsychological measures. Additionally, neuropsychological assessment aids in diagnostic screening (see Box 19.2 for more information). Finally, Hynd and Willis (1988) highlight the importance of neuropsychological assessment for the purpose of differential diagnosis in several important areas: (1) functional versus organic disorders; (2) areas of deficit versus areas of strength in children with "organic" disorders; and (3) subtypes of neurodevelopmental disorders. In this regard, neuropsychological assessment is becoming increasingly important in the realm of developmental disorders such as developmental learning disabilities and ADHD.

General Components of Neuropsychological Assessment

The goal of neuropsychological assessment is the evaluation of the behavioral expression of brain function. As such, no single psychometric test can adequately assess this brain–behavior relationship. Instead, neuropsychological assessment constitutes a wide range of standardized tests that assess several cognitive, perceptual, and behavioral domains. In general, neuropsychological assessment with children typically involves the following functional areas:

1. *General intelligence* is perhaps the area most impacted following the many sources of brain insult or injury. "Following brain damage, the patient is not as bright as he or she was before. Problems are solved less effectively, goal-directed behavior becomes less well organized, and there is impairment of a number of specific skills such as solving arithmetic problems or interpreting proverbs" (Goldstein, 1990, p. 198).

2. *Memory* constitutes the next most common manifestation of brain impairment. More often than not recent memory manifests greater decline than memory for remote events (Goldstein, 1990). Table 19.1 describes several currently available tests of memory designed for use with children.

3. *Perceptual ability (visual, auditory, and tactile)* may manifest as an inability to perceive embedded figures with accuracy or to recognize objects that are displayed in some unusual manner. Many brain-damaged patients also have deficits in the areas of auditory and tactile perception. Agnosia, for example, involves "perception without meaning," implying the intactness of the primary sense modality but loss of the ability to comprehend incoming information (Lezak, 1995).

4. *Visual-spatial/visual-motor functions* are often assessed as speed and accuracy of psychomotor activity. Neuropsychological impairment often results in decrements in psychomotor speed, either in motor speed or speed involved in the mental coordination of a skilled movement. For example, on block design tasks, the configuration of the internal pattern may be reproduced inaccurately (Goldstein, 1990). Fine and gross motor skills are also assessed during a comprehensive neuropsychological evaluation.

5. *Attention* is an essential function to assess as part of the neuropsychological examination, as this domain influences all other functional areas. Deficits in attention may manifest during tests of vigilance or subtly affect performance on tasks requiring sustained levels of mental effort (e.g., Picture Completion) (Goldstein, 1990).

6. *Communication and language skills* may be variously affected by brain insult. The aphasic disorders are a common example.

Measures of academic achievement and social-emotional and behavioral functioning are also commonly included in neuropsychological assessment with children. Various instruments that assess the general components of a neuropsychological evaluation appear in Table 19.2.

Assessment Approaches

There are currently available several approaches to neuropsychological assessment and interpretation with children. Selection of a particular approach is usually driven by the theoretical orientation of the neuropsychologist, the primary referral question, and constraints of the testing setting (Williams & Boll, 1997). Arguably, the most important consideration when selecting an approach to neuropsychological assessment is the rehabilitative demands (Batchelor & Dean, 1996). The following is a brief description of the fixed battery, flexible battery, and process approaches.

TABLE 19.1   Several currently available tests of memory designed for use with children

	Children's Memory Scale	Test of Memory and Learning	Wide Range Assessment of Memory and Learning
Authors	Morris J. Cohen, Ph.D.	Cecil R. Reynolds, Ph.D. Erin D. Bigler, Ph.D.	David Sheslow, Ph.D. Wayne Adams, Ph.D.
Copyright	1997	1994	1990
Publishers	The Psychological Corporation	PRO-ED	Jastar Associates
Standardization Sample	1,000 children stratified sampling	1,342 children stratified sampling	2,300 children nationally representative
Age Range	5–16	5.0–19.11	5–17

Domains Assessed Scales	*Auditory/Verbal Learning and Memory*
	  Stories
	  Word Pairs
	  Word Lists*
	Visual/Nonverbal Learning and Memory (Visual)
	  Dot Locations
	  Faces
	  Family Pictures*
	Attention/Concentration
	  Numbers
	  Sequences
	  Picture Locations*
		Verbal Memory
		  Memory for Stories
		  Word Selective Reminding
		  Object Recall
		  Digits Forward
		  Paired Recall
		  Letters Forward*
		  Digits Backward*
		  Letters Backward*
		Nonverbal Memory
		  Facial Memory
		  Visual Selective Reminding
		  Abstract Visual Memory
		  Visual Sequential Memory
		  Memory for Location
		  Manual Imitation*
			Verbal Memory
			  Number/Letter Memory
			  Sentence Memory
			  Story Memory
			Visual Memory
			  Finger Windows
			  Design Memory
			  Picture Memory
			Learning
			  Verbal Learning
			  Visual Learning
			  Sound Symbol
			*Delayed Recall**

Derived Scores	scaled scores (subtest scores) standard scores (index scores) percentile ranks	scaled scores (subtest scores) standard scores (index scores) percentile ranks	scaled scores (subtest) standard scores (General Memory Index)
Administration time	30–35 minutes (core battery)	45 minutes	45–60 minutes
Reliability	.70–.93 (index scores)	.80–.98 (index scores)	.84 (test-retest reliability)

Validity	content validity
	construct validity
	  3-factor solution
	criterion-related validity
	  WISC-III, WPPSI-R,
	  DAS, OLSAT, WIAT,
	  WCST, CELF-3
	concurrent validity
	  WMS-III; WRAML;
	  CVLT-C
		content validity
		construct validity
		  4-factor solution
		criterion-related validity
		  WISC-R, K-ABC,
		  WRAT-R, K-ABC Ach
			criterion-related validity
			  McCarthy Scales;
			  Stanford Binet

*Supplemental subtests

TABLE 19.2   Select instruments that assess the general components of a neuropsychological evaluation

Functional Domains	Assessment Instruments
Abstract Reasoning/ Executive Function	Children's Category Test (CCT) Raven's Progressive Matrices Wisconsin Card Sorting Test
Attention	Cancellation tasks Continuous Performance Tasks (CPTs) Matching Familiar Figures Task (MFFT) Test of Variables of Attention (TOVA)
Communication/ Language skills	Boston Naming Test (BNT) Comprehensive Test of Phonological Processing (CTOPP) Clinical Evaluation of Language Functions - Third Edition (CELF-3) Oral and Written Language Scales (OWLS) Peabody Picture Vocabulary Test—Third Edition (PPVT-III) Rapid Automatized Naming (RAN) Test of Language Competence (TLC)
Memory and Learning	Benton Memory for Faces California Verbal Learning Test—Children's Version (CVLT-C) Children's Memory Scale (CMS) Test of Memory and Learning (TOMAL) Wide Range Assessment of Memory and Learning (WRAML)
Perceptual ability (visual, auditory, and tactile)	Beery-Buktenica Developmental Test of Visual-Motor Integration (VMI) Bender Visual-Motor Gestalt Test Benton Judgment of Line Orientation (JLO) Rey-Osterrieth Complex Figure Test (ROCF) Tactual Performance Test of the HRNB-C
Sensory-Motor	Grip Strength Test, Finger Oscillation, and Finger Tapping speeded subtests of the HRNB-C Purdue Pegboard Reitan-Klove Sensory Perceptual Examination

The *fixed battery approach*, characterized also as the "quantitative" approach to neuropsychological assessment, is rooted in the American psychometric tradition. As such, it is "actuarial" (i.e., statistical) in emphasis. Advantages of this orientation include objective, standardized procedures and empirically defined, scaled products that can be compared across tests. The very strengths of this approach have also been the target of criticism, in that the statistically driven essence of this orientation may produce results in a "psychological vacuum" (Lezak, 1995). Two widely utilized batteries that are characterized by this assessment approach are the Halstead-Reitan Batteries for Children and the Luria-Nebraska Neuropsychological Battery—Children's Revision.

The Halstead-Reitan Neuropsychological Battery for Children (HRNB-C), developed for children ages 9 to 14, and the Reitan-Indiana Neuropsychological Test Battery for Children (RINTB), developed for children ages 5 to 8, are modified versions of the adult battery. Based upon Halstead's theory of biological intelligence, these batteries were designed to assess the biological basis of behavior and to infer brain function from performance on these measures. Both batteries are often administered in conjunction with a standardized test of intelligence and an achievement measure. Table 19.3 provides an overview of the subtests that comprise both batteries. Criticism of the Halstead-Reitan batteries includes the lack of specifically labeled tests of memory and language (Williams & Boll, 1997).

TABLE 19.3   Subtests of the Halstead-Reitan Neuropsychological Test Batteries for Children and Adolescents (HRNB-C) and the Reitan-Indiana Neuropsychological Test Battery (RINTB).

Subtest	Primary abilities assessed	HRNB-C Ages 9–14	RINTB-C Ages 5–8
Category Test	Complex concept formation, reasoning abilities	√	√
Tactual Performance Test	Right/left-sided sensory perception, sensory recognition, spatial memory, manual dexterity	√	√
Finger Tapping Test	Right/left-sided manual speed	√	√
Aphasia Screening Test	Letter identification, follow directions regarding right-left hands, copy abilities, basic arithmetic abilities	√	√
Grip Strength Test	Right/left-sided muscle strength	√	√
Lateral Dominance	Right/left-sided preference	√	√
Sensory-Perceptual Examination	Tactile, auditory, and visual sensory recognition, perception, and localization (minor differences in administration for two age groups)	√	√
Tactile Finger Localization Test	Perceive and localize sensory stimulation	√	√
Fingertip Number/Symbol Writing Test	Perceive written numbers (or symbols) on finger tips (graphesthesia) (Xs and Os are the symbols used for the 5–8 age group)	√	√
Tactile Form Recognition Test	Sensory recognition, tactile-visual integration (stereognosis)	√	√
Seashore Rhythm Test	Sustained auditory attention; perceive and match auditory rhythmic sequences	√	
Speech Sounds Perception Test	Sustained attention, auditory perception, auditory-visual integration	√	
Trail Making Test	Cognitive set shifting, sequencing, psychomotor speed, attention	√	
Color Form Test	Cognitive flexibility, sequential reasoning		√
Progressive Figures Test	Visual-spatial reasoning, cognitive flexibility, sequential reasoning		√
Matching Pictures Test	Perceptual generalization, ability to categorize		√
Target Test	Pattern perception, ability to attend to and copy visual-spatial configurations		√
Individual Performance Test	Visual perception, visual-motor integration		√
Marching Test	Visual-motor integration, coordination		√

SOURCE: Originally appeared in Hynd, 1988. Reprinted with permission.

Additionally, the batteries do not provide transformation of raw scores to scaled scores, making meaningful comparisons among scales difficult (Reynolds, 1997).

In addition to the diagnostic accuracy (validity) of the RINTB and the HRNB-C for the identification of children with brain damage, these measures are more commonly utilized to assess a child's behavioral strengths and weaknesses, such as sensory functioning, motor abilities, auditory processing, attention, visual-motor abilities, conceptual processing, sequential processing, and language function (Nussbaum & Bigler, 1997). For example, Batchelor, Sowles, Dean, and Fischer (1991) studied the effect of age on factor solutions for the HRNB-C, WISC-R, and WRAT among a sample of 1,236 students with learning disabilities. The results yielded a six-factor solution for the 9- to 10-year-old group and a seven-factor solution for the 11- to 12-year-old and 13- to 14-year-old groups. The authors suggest that the different factor solutions as a function of age group may reflect an increased complexity or sophistication of neuropsychological ability with development. As such, the authors concluded that the HRNB-C is an appropriate measure to utilize for psychoeducational purposes.

The Luria-Nebraska Neuropsychological Battery—Children's Revision (LNNB-CR) was designed for use with children ages 8 to 12. In accordance with Lurian theory of neuropsychological development, the adult version of the LNNB is administered to children ages 13 and older, as performance of this age group was found to be similar to that of adults. Also consistent with the Lurian theoretical foundation of this measure, pattern analysis is the primary interpretive method utilized. As highlighted previously, this method is characterized by careful, qualitative analysis of test performance, as opposed to the more traditional psychometric approach that emphasizes comparisons between products of performance (i.e., scaled scores). The LNNB-CR attempts, therefore, to provide a marriage between the qualitative, pattern analysis approach of Luria and the psychometric soundness afforded by the quantitative approach (Golden, 1997). Table 19.4 provides an overview of the subtests that comprise the LNNB-CR.

Although the LNNB-CR was designed to provide a measure sensitive to developmental changes, the battery has been criticized as a downsized version of the adult battery, including similar tests that are simply modified for use with children. Additionally, while the LNNB-CR includes a memory scale, its coverage of the memory construct is allegedly limited and inadequate. Moreover, performance variability may be accounted for by general intellectual ability, or "g," compromising its clinical utility with brain-injured populations (Williams & Boll, 1997). Finally, Reynolds (1997) suggests that the products of the LNNB-CR, T scores, are problematic psychometrically.

Beyond the psychometric issues that plague the HRNB-C and LNNB-CR, neither battery has been normed for use with preschool children. Hartlage and Telzrow (1981) suggest that "one factor which has delayed the development of neuropsychological assessment batteries for very young children is uncertainty over the extent to which stable neuropsychological patterns can be measured in young children" (p. 41). Additionally, assessment of higher-order cognitive function in children prior to complete language formation is also problematic. One recent attempt to include the assessment of very young children is the NEPSY (Korkman, Kirk, & Kemp, 1998). The name of this battery is derived from the NE in *neuro* and the PSY in *psychology*, in order to facilitate its utilization cross-culturally.

The NEPSY was standardized with a nationally representative group of 1,000 children and is normed for ages 3–12. This battery consists of 27 subtests designed to assess neuropsychological development across five functional domains: (1) attention and executive function; (2) language; (3) sensorimotor ability; (4) visuospatial processing; and (5) memory and learning. Table 19.5 provides a description of the subtests that comprise the NEPSY. The complete battery may be

TABLE 19.4   Subtests of the Luria-Nebraska Neuropsychological Battery—Children's Revision for use with children ages 8–12.

Scales	Primary abilities assessed
Motor Skills	Motor speed, coordination, ability to imitate motor movements
Rhythm	Perceive and repeat rhythmic patterns, sing a song from memory
Tactile	Finger localization, arm localization, 2-point discrimination, movement discrimination, shape discrimination, stereognosis
Visual	Visual recognition, visual discrimination
Receptive Speech	Follow simple commands, comprehend verbal directions, decode phonemes
Expressive Language	Ability to read and repeat words and simple sentences, name objects from description, use automated speech
Writing	Analyze letter sequences, spell, write from dictation
Reading	Letter and word recognition, sentence and paragraph reading, nonsense syllable reading
Arithmetic	Simple arithmetic abilities, number writing and number recognition
Memory	Verbal and nonverbal memory
Intelligence	Vocabulary development, verbal reasoning, picture comprehension, social reasoning, deductive reasoning

SOURCE: Originally appeared in Hynd, 1988. Reprinted with permission.

administered for a comprehensive neuropsychological evaluation, or the core battery may be administered for an abbreviated overview of a child's abilities. Both assessments yield a profile of results representative of a pattern of relative strengths and weaknesses across the five functional domains. The NEPSY yields scaled scores for each of the subtests and composite scores for each of the five functional domains. The authors report the following reliability coefficients for the 5–12 core domain scores: .82 (Attention/Executive), .87 (Language), .79 (Sensorimotor), .83 (Visuospatial), and .87 (Memory and Learning). This developmental neuropsychological battery is purportedly sensitive to abilities affected by learning disabilities, ADHD, traumatic brain injury, and various other developmental disorders. While a promising addition to child neuropsychological assessment, further empirical investigation is needed to substantiate the clinical utility and psychometric properties of the NEPSY.

The *flexible battery ("eclectic") approach*, in contrast to the fixed battery approach, has been characterized as the "qualitative" approach to neuropsychological assessment. Not unlike the fixed battery approach, the flexible battery approach also emphasizes standardized test procedures for the measurement of cognitive and behavioral functioning. However, this approach emphasizes the "flexible" selection of measures in an attempt to tailor the battery of tests to the specific purposes of the examination and suspected deficits. As such, this approach begins with a core battery of tests, assessing broad domains of cognitive function. Performance on this battery then informs selection of additional measures. The result is both a comprehensive and individualized assessment (Williams & Boll, 1997).

TABLE 19.5   Subtests of the NEPSY: A developmental neuropsychological assessment for use with children ages 3–12

Functional Domain/ Scales	Primary abilities assesses	3–4 Core	5–12 Core
Attention/Executive Functions			
Tower	Planning, monitoring, self-regulation, problem-solving		√
Auditory Attention and Response Set	Vigilance, selective auditory attention, cognitive flexibility, and set shifting		√
Visual Attention	Speed and accuracy of visual localization	√	√
Statue	Inhibition and motor persistence		√
Design Fluency	Ability to generate novel designs given an array of dots		
Knock and Tap	Self-regulation and ability to inhibit motoric responses to visual stimuli that conflict with verbal directions		
Language			
Body Part Naming	Naming, expressive vocabulary	√	
Phonological Processing	Phonological segmentation, identification of visual stimuli from word segments	√	√
Speeded Naming	Rapid naming by size, color, and shape		√
Comprehension of Instructions	Processing and responding to instructional sets of increasing syntactic complexity	√	√
Repetition of Nonsense Words	Phonological encoding and decoding, articulation of complex nonsense words		
Verbal Fluency	Ability to generate words in semantic or phonemic categories		
Oromotor Sequences	Rhythmic oromotor coordination, repetition of sound sequences		
Sensorimotor Functions			
Fingertip Tapping	Finger dexterity, lateralized manual speed		√
Imitating Hand Positions	Imitation of hand positions, motor coordination	√	√
Visuomotor Precision	Fine motor skills, visual-motor integration	√	√
Manual Motor Sequences	Perception and imitation of rhythmic motor sequences		
Finger Discrimination	Tactile perception unaided by visual cues		
Visuospatial Processing			
Design Copying	Visual-motor integration, ability to copy	√	√
Arrows	Visual-spatial ability, judgment of line orientation		√
Block Construction	Visual-spatial and motor integration		
Route Finding	Visual-spatial reasoning, directionality and orientation	√	
Memory and Learning			
Memory for Faces	Visual memory		√
Memory for Names	Auditory and visual memory		√
Narrative Memory	Ability to recall a story under free and cued recall conditions	√	√
Sentence Repetition	Auditory memory	√	
List Learning	Supraspan memory, resistance to interference		

SOURCE: Korkman, Kirk, & Kemp, 1988.

This approach to neuropsychological assessment evolved from the clinical–theoretical approach of Luria (1980), who emphasized careful, intensive observation within the context of single case studies. Accordingly, the flexible battery approach is "exploratory" and "hypothesis testing" in nature. Its advantages include the capability of capturing the uniqueness of the individual and the allowance for discriminating, flexible, and imaginative use of examination techniques. For example, the child's history, present circumstances, and attitudes toward the assessment are all considered when selecting pertinent instruments. The selection of instruments and the order in which each is administered may vary, therefore, from one evaluation to another (Jorgensen & Christensen, 1995). Additionally, as it allows for the revision of batteries as new and improved tests become available, this approach is commonly practiced (Williams & Boll, 1997).

One of the more recent orientations in neuropsychological assessment, the *process approach*, is an outgrowth of the flexible approach in its emphasis on both *nomothetic* (i.e., norm-referenced, standardized procedures) and *idiographic* (i.e., single case study) information. This approach begins with norm-referenced, standardized measures designed to assess broad domains of cognitive functioning. The resultant profile of strengths and weaknesses is utilized to formulate hypotheses about specific deficit processes that contribute to observed decrements in performance. The term *satellite tests* is often used to describe the instruments selected to further assess the hypothesized deficits, as these measures are generally characterized by greater specificity (Williams & Boll, 1997). The qualitative aspect of this assessment approach involves careful observation of an individual's approach to a task. In this regard, one hallmark of the process approach is the dissection of a task into its component cognitive processes. The Block Design subtest of the Wechsler scales is one such task that has been analyzed according to these processing steps. "Testing the limits" is an additional feature of the process approach that enables the detection of pathognomonic signs of neurological damage (e.g., perseverative errors, hemi-inattention, and particular errors on constructional tasks) (White & Rose, 1997). One purported advantage of the process approach is the reduction of type II error (i.e., no significant change identified, when in fact there has been significant change), as this approach allows for finer discriminant analyses via testing of clinical limits (Kaplan, 1988).

Perhaps the true difference between the above-mentioned assessment approaches is one of subtle distinction. Given that the neuropsychological batteries in current use (e.g., HRNB and LNNB) resemble the original versions only slightly, Goldstein (1997) maintains that, indeed, there is no true difference. More often than not, the "flexible" approach generally employs an initial standard battery, rather than a unique selection for each case. And application of a "fixed battery approach," by definition, generally only occurs in research settings, where protocol dictates a delimited procedure. Moreover, there are no data that favor the relative efficacy of one approach over another, based upon such criteria as accuracy of diagnosis, efficacy of rehabilitation outcomes, or predictive validity of prognosis. The superiority of any one approach has not been clearly demonstrated with children, either (Lezak, 1995). As a general rule, both qualitative and quantitative data are required for accurate diagnosis and remediation in neuropsychological assessment—quantitative data for reliable and valid measures, qualitative data for patient-specific information. To this end, practicing clinicians likely use a combination of both fixed and flexible battery approaches, depending upon the particular demands of an individual case. In a recent survey of 133 licensed practitioners, the most widely utilized instruments with children included the WISC-R as a single measure (100% of the respondents); the WRAT-R as a broadband achievement test (82%); and the Trail Making Test, a component of the HRNB (70%). The HRNB was reported as the most popular formal battery; 30% reportedly utilize this battery, as compared with 16% reported usage of the LNNB (Sellers & Nadler, 1992).

Reliability and Validity Issues in Neuropsychological Assessment

Neuropsychological assessment presents unique challenges to the development of reliable and valid measures. Brain damage and subsequent decrements in performance often do not present a one-to-one correspondence. Numerous studies underscore the varieties of "type-locus" interactions, or the dynamic interplay between the location and extent of lesion and the behaviors that these particular regions subserve. Neuropsychological theory, such as the functional systems model, would suggest that the pervasiveness and pattern of behavioral deficits will vary to a large extent based upon the nature of the brain injury. In spite of advances in medical technology, neuropsychological assessment measures have historically been more sensitive than their validating criteria (i.e., neurological indices) in terms of diagnostic accuracy. However, with increasing sophistication in brain imaging technology, these neurological indices are quickly overtaking the diagnostic role of neuropsychological assessment and are also providing increasingly sensitive validation criteria for both neuropsychological assessment and theory. While neuropsychological instruments have demonstrated remarkable ability to predict the degree of recovery or response to treatment, predictive validity remains problematic due to the paucity of longitudinal studies to date. Finally, construct validity remains the focus of the majority of research efforts in neuropsychology, as this field centers around such theoretical concepts as memory, attention, and executive function. Factor analytic studies are often employed when construct validity is in question. For example, factor analytic investigation may address the extent to which memory subtests load on a "memory" factor versus factors more accurately labeled "general intellectual ability" or "attention" (Goldstein, 1990; Lezak, 1995).

As with issues of validity, the reliability of instruments available for use in neuropsychological assessment is subject to some problems not shared by other psychometric measures. The unpredictable nature of brain impairment imposes serious limitations on determination of reliability coefficients through, for example, test-retest methods. Additionally, split-half reliability coefficients are often precluded by the frequently small item samples comprising many neuropsychological subtests (Goldstein, 1990). Batchelor and Dean (1996) suggest that pervasive individual differences in brain development during childhood may account for poor reliability coefficients for neuropsychological measures administered specifically at young ages. Finally, Reynolds (1997) reports that "even in the research literature, reliability data are seldom presented and the most frequently used of the various batteries, the HRNB, does not even have a discussion of reliability in the manual. Reliability of the LNNB is reported but is based on highly heterogeneous groups, across a too wide age span, and is likely spuriously inflated" (p. 187).

NEUROPSYCHOLOGICAL ASSESSMENT AND "G"

Traditionally, neuropsychological assessment instruments have been utilized to detect the presence or absence of brain damage. While the diagnostic accuracy of such test batteries as the LNNB and HRNB has been well established, there is increasing concern that standard neuropsychological batteries for children assess "g," general cognitive ability, as opposed to distinct neuropsychological processes (Obrzut & Hynd, 1986). Although Lurian theory would predict correlations between "g" and other neuropsychological functions, redundancy has been noted in comparative studies of the Wechsler scales with the HRNB and the LNNB (Kane, Parsons & Goldstein, 1985). The pertinent question then becomes one of validity: What distinguishes neuropsychological assessment from assessment of intellectual ability? Hynd and Willis (1988) suggest that this question is especially important to answer for children, whose short attention span may warrant an abbreviated assessment battery, such as that offered by tests of intelligence. Kelly, Arceneaux, Dean, and Anderson (1994) empirically addressed the issue of redundancy by comparing summary scores on the WISC-R (PIQ, VIQ, and FSIQ) and the HRNB-C for 423 children with learning disabilities. Results of multivariate analyses indicated that the WISC-R summary scores and HRNB-C subtest scores shared 29% of common variability. The authors conclude that while both measures share some commonality, accounted for by general intellectual ability, both instruments also provide unique information.

As early as 1949, Hebb described a case in which nearly one-third of the cerebral cortex had been surgically removed. The intellectual ability of this patient was surprisingly reported to be within the superior range (cited in Lezak, 1995)! This and subsequent empirical evidence seemed to suggest that while traditional tests of intellectual ability may produce reliable capability to detect generalized brain impairment, these measures possess far less sensitivity to detect focal lesions. In particular, the Wechsler scales have not demonstrated an ability to reliably localize or even lateralize the site of brain insult. Reitan (1994) maintains that traditional tests of intellectual ability are not good discriminators of neurologic impairment, as they are designed typically to predict academic achievement as opposed to the biological condition of the brain: "IQ measures, which relate more closely to academic success, also appear to be influenced heavily by environmental and cultural advantages. On the other hand, tests developed specifically to evaluate impairment of brain functions seem to be fairer (unbiased) in terms of cultural and environmental experiences and advantages" (p. 62). Comparatively, the sensitivity of some neuropsychological measures to detect focal deficits remains suspect. Perhaps the difference between these sets of measures depends upon the func-

tional domain targeted in the assessment (e.g., language function versus motor skills). In summary, reliable and comprehensive neuropsychological measures designed to assess distinct brain–behavior relationships are needed to inform both diagnosis and effective educational planning (Reynolds, 1981a; Tramontana & Hooper, 1988).

NEUROCOGNITIVE CORRELATES OF VARIOUS PEDIATRIC SYNDROMES

In addition to the diagnostic accuracy of various neuropsychological instruments in detecting brain impairment, there are other reasons for the increasing relevance and importance of developmental neuropsychology. First, legislation, such as the Individuals with Disabilities Education Act (the latest amendment of the Education for All Handicapped Children Act; PL 94–142) requires that all states provide adequate educational services for all handicapped children. Addressing the presumed neuropsychological origin of learning disabilities and other developmental disorders, this legislation implicates the necessary role of neuropsychological assessment in diagnosis, prognosis, and educational planning (e.g., IEP) for children with acquired brain injury or neurodevelopmental disorders (Riccio, Hynd, & Cohen, 1993). Sexson and Madan-Swain (1995) suggest that the increased survival rates of children with neurological trauma due to advances in medical technology, along with concomitantly increasing incidence rates, further substantiate the need for appropriate psychoeducational assessment. Moreover, there is mounting evidence suggestive of a neurological basis for various developmental learning and behavioral disorders (Denckla, 1996; Hynd & Semrud-Clikeman, 1989; Hynd, Semrud-Clikeman, Lorys, Novey, & Eliopulus, 1990). While the scope of this chapter precludes a thorough review of the spectrum of childhood disorders with consequent neurocognitive sequelae, several syndromes with relatively prevalent occurrence rates will be covered. Additionally, this review will focus primarily on intellectual sequelae.

Traumatic Brain Injury

The rough and tumble play associated with childhood often results in minor head injuries, such as bumps and bruises, that are usually inconsequential to normal brain function. However, when such events are of sufficient force to cause total or partial impairment of the brain's regulatory function, they are classified as *traumatic brain injury (TBI)*. An estimated one million pediatric TBIs occur annually, accounting for the leading cause of death and the single greatest source of neurological disability in children (Ryan, Lamarche, Barth, & Boll, 1996). Also, the epidemiology of TBI is different for children as compared with adults. Whereas adults are more likely to experience TBI as a result of motor vehicle accidents, TBI during childhood is commonly the result of the following sources, in decreasing order of occurrence: pedestrian car accidents, falls, and child abuse (Dalby & Obrzut, 1991). Additionally, males in all age groups suffer a higher incidence of TBI than their female cohort, with some estimates suggesting a more than two-to-one ratio (Boll & Stanford, 1997). Finally, this epidemiology of pediatric head injury does not seem to be characterized by random data. Rather, several risk factors, such as psychosocial adversity, poor parental supervision, and a variety of impulsive, risk-taking behaviors have been positively correlated with the occurrence of pediatric head injury (Rutter, Chadwick, & Shaffer, 1983). Recent empirical evidence confirms the role of preinjury psychiatric disorders and behavior problems in the increased risk for TBI among children (e.g., Max et al., 1997).

Head injury is a complex phenomenon and best viewed along a continuum of cerebral impairment and consequent deficit of neurocognitive function. Assessment of premorbid function is critically important for accurate diagnosis and prognosis. As noted in the earlier section addressing developmental considerations, prediction of outcome is predicated upon a number of highly interactive and complex factors: (1) age at onset and impact on neurological development; (2) preexisting conditions, such as premorbid intellectual function, psychiatric disorder, and/or learning disability; (3) type of injury, referring to focal, lateralized, or diffuse; (4) severity of injury, often measured by length of coma and posttraumatic amnesia; (5) age at the time of assessment, as deficits may not manifest until a later developmental period; and (6) sensitivity of the instruments utilized to detect brain impairment (Boll & Stanford, 1997; Ryan et al., 1996; Williams & Boll, 1997).

Interest in TBI grew out of the literature concerning *plasticity*, as pediatric head injury offers a window for observation of the interrelated effects of cerebral damage on the developing brain (Dalby & Obrzut, 1991; see also Box 19.1). In this regard, Jaffe and colleagues (1992) suggest that TBI may interrupt previously established abilities. However, depending upon the site of the injury, the effects of TBI may not manifest behaviorally until a later time, when more mature cognitive skills call upon the impaired region of the brain. This may be especially true in cases of early frontal lobe damage (Kolb & Fantie, 1997). Recall Luria's theory of cortical development, suggesting that the frontal lobes are not fully developed until around ages 12 to 14. Early damage to this cerebral region may not evidence impairment in function until a later age, when development of higher-order cognitive function is completed. In contrast, early and diffuse head injury may result in impressive compensatory mechanisms. Nonetheless, plasticity of function is not equally likely throughout brain. For example, early damage to the visual cortex may produce irreversible deficits, compared with compensatory responses to focal damage in other cortical areas, such as the language centers (Williams & Boll, 1997). As neuroimaging procedures may provide less-sensitive indices of impairment, Lord-Maes and Obrzut (1996) highlight the importance of neuropsychological assessment, especially with child populations. Children who suffer TBI often appear normal physically. However, underlying subtle deficits in cognitive function may interfere with academic and psychosocial function.

Depending on the extent and severity of damage and length of coma, neurocognitive sequelae following pediatric TBI may include impairment in the following functional domains: disturbances in memory and learning (particularly verbal memory); slowed rate of information processing; deficits in motor ability (e.g., fine motor speed, dexterity, and strength), visual-spatial skills, attention, speech and language; and impaired cognitive function (Ryan et al., 1996). In a seminal investigation conducted by Chadwick, Rutter, Brown, Shaffer, and Traub (1981, cited in Rutter, Chadwick, & Shaffer, 1983), performance on the WISC was compared between children ages 5 to 14 having suffered either mild or severe TBI (based upon length of posttraumatic amnesia) to that of matched controls, who had suffered orthopedic injury. Assessment was conducted immediately following injury, and at intervals of 4 months, 1 year, and 2½ years postinjury. By directly assessing recovery of function, the authors attempted to investigate the causal role of TBI in neurocognitive impairment. Results indicated greater impairment on timed measures of visual-motor and visual-spatial function (e.g., Performance scale subtests of the WISC), as compared with performance on measures of verbal ability. Additionally, this impairment was more pronounced immediately following injury for the severe group, as compared with the performance of subjects with mild head injury. Figure 19.3 offers a graphic depiction of the course of recovery for head injured and control subjects. The investigators concluded: "It is evident that there *was* a marked cognitive recovery phase in the severe-head-injury group but *none* in the mild-injury group. We conclude that *severe* head injuries did indeed *cause* intellectual impairment, but equally that mild injuries did not" (p. 88).

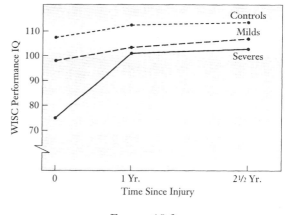

FIGURE 19.3

Cognitive recovery following mild versus severe traumatic brain injury

SOURCE: Rutter, Chadwick, & Shaffer, 1983. Reprinted with permission.

In a more recent study, Jaffe et al. (1992) attempted to control for several important premorbid differences that have been associated with outcome in pediatric TBI populations. In a prospective study, 98 children ages 6 to 15 with mild, moderate, and severe TBI were individually matched to control for premorbid characteristics, such as demographic background, perinatal risk factors, preinjury scholastic achievement, and psychosocial indicators. Results of this investigation yielded a *dose-response relationship* between magnitude of injury severity and associated degree of neurocognitive impairment, as measured by the WISC-R, the WRAT, and several neuropsychological measures selected from the HRNB. In particular, this study replicated previous findings suggestive of statistically significant decrements in PIQ, as a function of both injury severity and matched control cases. These decrements were attributed to the nature of the WISC-R nonverbal subtests—timed tasks involving tactual, cognitive, and motor problem-solving abilities. While the moderate and severe TBI cases manifested the greatest degree of impairment, results of this study also yielded small but significant decrements in performance on tasks of speeded motor ability and long-term verbal memory among children with mild TBI. The authors concluded: "Because of our close matching overall and within severity groups, the difference in outcome between cases and controls is most likely attributable to the brain injury" (p. 545).

In general, the finding that children who suffer moderate to severe traumatic brain injury evidence subsequent decline in intellectual function is well-supported in the literature. Degree of impairment (e.g., postinjury IQ) seems to be correlated with severity of injury, with the greatest impairment immediately following onset of injury and a period of recovery lasting anywhere from 1 to 2 years postinjury (Donders, 1997; Rutter et al., 1983). In fact, Beardsworth and Harding (1996) contend that the

> *WISC-III Full Scale IQ (FSIQ) before discharge has been found to be the best single predictor of outcome in a study including a wide variety of other investigations. Deficits in FSIQ are largely due to a lowering of Performance IQ (PIQ). This is rarely because of any real loss of spatial ability, but because the child is slowed down, and so is penalized for this on non-verbal tests which are timed. Recovery in IQ can continue for several years post-injury. Although many aspects of neuropsychological test scores after head injury can be accounted for by a general loss of ability and slower information processing, specific deficits in verbal memory and in other measures of verbal ability, such as verbal fluency and naming, have been reported. (p. 25)*

More severe and persistent deficits in Performance IQ scores, relative to Verbal IQ, may also result from the fact that Verbal subtests require past learning and Performance subtests are more reliant on new learning, speed of information processing, and problem-solving skills—functions most commonly affected by head injury (Williams & Boll, 1997). Returning to the issue of plasticity of function, the literature is also suggestive of critical periods of development for intellectual function. Unilateral brain damage seems to produce differential effects, depending

upon the age at which the injury occurred. For example, right-hemisphere damage, if suffered early in the child's development, results in greater risk of intellectual impairment (Aran & Eisele, 1994). Comparatively, left hemisphere damage suffered at a relatively later time in childhood interferes with the normal development of language, producing delays in expressive language, slower rates of speech, and deficits in phonological processing (Lord-Maes & Obrzut, 1996).

While formal tests of intellectual function often prove to be sensitive indicators of brain impairment, a note of caution is in order. These instruments do not assess the range of neurocognitive abilities implicated in TBI (e.g., attention, memory, motor). This is especially important to remember in cases when the child performs in the average range on intelligence tests, but evidences impairment in other areas critical to school performance (e.g., attention, memory, or executive function). An additional consideration, Farmer and Peterson (1995) suggest that the artificially structured nature of the assessment setting may in fact overestimate attentional function in this pediatric population. Finally, in consideration of the aforementioned assessment issues, Kinsella and colleagues (1995) echo the importance of neuropsychological assessment to guide individualized educational programming for children with TBI. Flexible allocation of special education services is also advised, in concert with varying rates of recovery.

Seizure Disorders

An estimated 8 out of every 1,000 children experience seizure activity, constituting the most common neurological disorder for this population. *Seizures*, or random electrical disturbance of the nervous system, are the observed phenomena of epilepsy. When seizure activity occurs with repeated frequency, the syndrome is either called a seizure disorder or epilepsy (Bennett & Ro, 1997). Dodrill and Warner (1996) summarize the three major classifications of seizures, as defined by the Commission on Classification and Terminology of the International League Against Epilepsy. *Parital seizures* are limited to seizure activity within an area, or "part," of one cerebral hemisphere. In contrast, *generalized seizures* are characterized by approximately equal seizure activity within both hemispheres and are further classified as convulsive or nonconvulsive. *Unclassified seizures* include seizure activity that cannot be clearly classified as either partial or general. Of interest, neonatal seizure activity is often categorized as unclassified. As this summarization does not include further subdivisions of these categories, or an account of unique seizure disorders of childhood, the interested reader is directed to Tharp (1987) for a more thorough discussion of pediatric epilepsy.

Not unlike TBI, seizure disorders and the associated neurocognitive features form a very complex interaction. Hartlage and Hartlage (1997) suggest that among children such factors as premorbid brain dysfunction, anticonvulsant medication, and psychosocial factors interact in a complex fashion to produce variable neuropsychological outcome. As such, the mercurial nature of pediatric seizure disorders poses a considerable methodological obstacle to research. Sampling bias, for example, often favors selection of more severely disordered children who participate in epilepsy programs and clinics. Perhaps the most prevalent confounding factor in pediatric seizure disorder research is the unique contribution of antiepileptic medication to outcome. Surprisingly, there is a paucity of research on *medication-performance interactions*, although the vast majority of children referred for neuropsychological assessment are managed with medication, and results of limited empirical investigation tend to yield equivocal findings. In an important prospective study, Bourgeois and colleagues (1983) compared the performance of children with epilepsy to that of their nonepileptic siblings on measures of intellectual ability, from the time of diagnosis through a period up to 6 years. The results did not yield significant

group differences for FSIQ at any time during the study; IQ scores did not decline appreciably with time for the epilepsy group. However, a subset of the epilepsy group, characterized by higher incidence of drug levels in the toxic range, greater difficulty with seizure management, and early onset of seizure activity, did yield a statistically significant decline in FSIQ of 10 points or more. Subsequent research seems to tentatively point to a similar relationship between some medications and certain neurocognitive abilities. Namely, barbiturates (e.g., phenobarbital and primidone) have been most frequently associated with negative effects, whereas carbamazepine (Tegretol) yielded the most favorable results (see Dodrill & Warner, 1996, for a review).

Following from the aforementioned interactive factors, formal studies of neurocognitive correlates of pediatric epilepsy have not yielded a specific profile or pattern of impairment (Hartlage & Hartlage, 1997). Deficits in attention, memory, perceptual-motor skills, and learning (due to auditory or visual processing deficits) are common correlates of pediatric seizure disorder. Language skills have also been variously affected, perhaps resulting in difficulties in learning to read. In their recent research, McCarthy, Richman, and Yarbrough (1995) suggest that

> problems with sustained attention may be partially related to medication, whereas problems with selective attention have been associated with generalized, early-onset seizures. . . . Short-term memory deficits are commonly reported in individuals with partial seizures of temporal lobe origin, especially left temporal lobe. Verbal memory deficits have tended to occur more often in individuals with left temporal lobe foci, whereas visual memory deficits have tended to occur more often in individuals with right temporal lobe foci. (pp. 72–73)

Williams, Sharp, Lange, Bates, Griebel, Spence, and Thomas (1996) provide further investigation of memory and attentional sequelae in children with epilepsy. No statistically significant deficits in memory or attentional skills were reported, based on seizure type, although mean scores on measures sensitive to attention and concentration (e.g., WISC-R Digit Span and Coding) were slightly lower than other subtest scores. The investigators note that scores on Digit Span Forward and Digit Span Backward were equally depressed in the epileptic group, pointing to an overall deficit in attention and encoding (versus working memory, a distinguishing skill required for Digit Span Backwards). Additionally, management of seizure activity with more than one medication was associated with significant deficits on verbal and visual memory skills and auditory inattention. While this difference may be confounded by underlying neurologic pathology and cannot, therefore, be attributed to a medication-performance interaction, the investigators contend that this study offers empirical support for subtle attentional difficulties among children with various levels of epilepsy severity.

There is some evidence to suggest that for some children with epilepsy, average IQ scores may range from one standard deviation below the mean. Age of onset, seizure type and frequency, and drug-related variables have all been negatively correlated with IQ. While age at onset may covary with duration and frequency of seizure activity, this variable is perhaps the most salient predictor of subsequent intellectual ability. Evidence suggests that onset of seizure activity prior to age 5 yields greater risk than onset at older ages (Beardsworth & Harding, 1996; Bennett & Ho, 1997; Hartlage & Hartlage, 1997). In a study of 118 children with epilepsy, Farwell, Dodrill, and Batzel (1985) reported a significant negative correlation between seizure type, years of seizure activity, and degree of medical management and FSIQ, as measured by the WISC-R. Additionally, regardless of seizure type, children with epilepsy differed from age-matched controls in distribution of FSIQ: 63% of children with epilepsy produced FSIQ scores less than or equal to 100, as compared with 50% of the controls. More recently, Forceville, Dekker, Aldenkamp, Alpherts, and Schelvis (1992) found a significant VIQ > PIQ split for children

with epilepsy. Decrements in scores on Information, Digit Span, and Coding versus relatively higher scores on Picture Completion and Picture Arrangement accounted for the verbal/performance discrepancy. The authors also note subsequent depression of the third factor, Freedom from Distractibility, which may be substantially affected by working memory.

In summary, a positive history of seizure-related activity may affect performance on various psychometric measures. In particular, Beardsworth and Harding (1996) suggest that measures of general intellectual ability are typically insensitive measures of medication-performance interactions, whereas motor and speeded tasks may be more useful. Similarly, Dodrill and Troupin (1975) caution that the Wechsler scales may be more affected by antiepileptic medications than many other neuropsychological measures, implicating the reliability of these instruments. These factors should be considered when interpreting test results for this population of children. Also, the skilled examiner will carefully observe the child during performance of assessment tasks for any overt signs of seizure activity and consider such observations during interpretation of test results.

Leukemia

Leukemia, the most prevalent form of malignancy diagnosed during childhood, is a disease in which there is an abnormal proliferation of lymphoblasts, a certain type of white blood cell, in bone marrow. This abnormal growth of white blood cells results in symptoms of anemia, bone pain, fatigue, and easy bruising. The incidence of leukemia is reportedly greater for boys than for girls and peaks around age 4. Sequelae of leukemia have received increasing empirical emphasis, as treatment has greatly enhanced the survival rate of children with this disease. Such treatment commonly includes cranial irradiation, intrathecal methotrexate (i.e., chemotherapy injected directly into the spinal fluid), or a combination of the two. Treatments are primarily administered prophylactically to prevent disease relapse and the spread of leukemic cells to the central nervous system (CNS). While the advantages of such treatment for survival are clear, they are not without cost. Research indicates that cranial irradiation and intrathecal methotrexate have possible neurotoxic effects, damaging glial cells, which are abundant in CNS white matter. This side effect may be particularly deleterious in younger children, as myelination is not completed until ages 8 to 9. Young children, therefore, who are treated with cranial irradiation and intrathecal methotrexate are at risk for CNS damage and consequent learning and behavioral problems (Berg & Linton, 1997; Brown et al., 1992a; Williams & Williams, 1996).

Results of research investigating the neurocognitive sequelae of various forms of treatment are equivocal, with some evidence for deficits following cranial irradiation therapy, but not following intrathecal chemotherapies (Dowell, Copeland, & Judd, 1989). Similar to the methodological problems characteristic of research in the areas of pediatric TBI and epilepsy, investigation of the neurocognitive sequelae of cranial irradiation and intrathecal methotrexate is subject to such limitations as small sample size, variability in treatment regime, lack of appropriate comparison groups, and differences in age at the time of diagnosis and assessment across studies (Butler & Copeland, 1993). In spite of these limitations, a review of 20 years of published investigations of children treated both with cranial irradiation and intrathecal methotrexate is suggestive of neurocognitive deficits in fine motor skills, visual-spatial abilities, somatosensory functioning, attention-concentration skills, and verbal and nonverbal memory (see Stehbens et al., 1991, for a review). Copeland and associates (1988) conducted a comparative study of treatment modality (cranial irradiation and/or intrathecal chemotherapy) and treatment status (newly diagnosed versus long-term survivors). Results of neuropsychological assessment in this investigation were indicative of significantly

lower scores on measures of intellectual function, visual-motor and fine motor skills, nonverbal memory, and arithmetic achievement for the long-term survivor group receiving cranial irradiation and intrathecal chemotherapy. This group was also distinguished by significantly lower scores on the Freedom from Distractibility factor of the WISC-R. The authors attribute this difference to increased distractibility. Comparatively, newly diagnosed groups, receiving either treatment modality, demonstrated decrements in fine motor and visual-motor skills only. Conversely, Stehbens and colleagues (1994) provide a comparative study of the effect of type of CNS prophylaxis on neurocognitive outcome at 9 months postdiagnosis. This study of 42 children diagnosed after age 6 did not yield significant group differences. The performance of children treated with cranial irradiation plus intrathecal methotrexate was similar to those receiving prophylaxis intrathecal methotrexate alone on measures of general intellectual ability, academic achievement, memory, language, motor function, and perceptual-motor abilities. More recently, MacLean and associates (1995) investigated the acute neuropsychological effects of leukemia and various forms of treatment at 9 months postdiagnosis for a cohort of children ages 3 through 6½ years. Results indicated greater risk for children treated with both cranial irradiation and intrathecal methotrexate before age 5. In sum, a general consensus in the literature is suggestive of more pronounced deficits in intellectual function, attention, and memory for children diagnosed before age 5 (Berg & Linton, 1997).

Findings specifically implicating general intellectual function among children diagnosed with leukemia covary with age at diagnosis and prophylactic CNS treatment. Williams and Williams (1996) contend that most findings report intellectual performance of children with leukemia in the average range. Where statistical differences are reported, the leukemic group often performed in the average range as compared to the above-average performance of the control group. The authors qualify this generalization by noting the deleterious effects of repeated high doses of CNS prophylaxis: "The best predictors of IQ following treatment were the number of radiation therapy courses, age, and the presence of cerebral pathology measured by computed tomography (CT)" (p. 256). Brown and colleagues (1992b) compared performance among three groups of children with leukemia on the K-ABC. Group 1 was comprised of children recently diagnosed. Group 2 consisted of children with leukemia 1 year postdiagnosis who were receiving CNS prophylactic chemotherapy. And group 3 included children with leukemia 3 years postdiagnosis who were also receiving CNS prophylactic chemotherapy. Children who had been receiving treatment for 3 years demonstrated significantly greater impairment on tasks of simultaneous processing than other treatment groups or healthy sibling controls. Recall from previous discussions of the K-ABC, the Simultaneous scale is a purported measure of right-hemisphere function.

In an investigation of the long-term effects of CNS prophylactic treatment (intrathecal methotrexate) on neuropsychological functioning, Brown, Sawyer, Antoniou, Toogood, Rice, Thompson, and Madan-Swain (1996) provide a prospective study of a cohort of 63 children with leukemia followed 3 years from time of diagnosis. Children diagnosed with other types of cancer comprised the control group. Surprisingly, no significant decline in intellectual ability was found over the 3-year interval, substantiating previous findings that the neurotoxic effects of chemotherapy are less severe for children receiving this type of prophylactic therapy than for children receiving CNS radiation. However, the CNS-treated group evidenced a significant discrepancy between achievement test scores and intellectual function, with lower scores in the areas of reading, spelling, and arithmetic as compared to FSIQ at the year 3 follow-up evaluation. While replication with larger samples of children is needed, the authors suggest that these findings indicate perhaps greater impair-

ments in learning than general intellectual function for children receiving CNS prophylactic treatment.

In summary, children treated for leukemia with CNS-prophylaxis may experience subtle deterioration of neuropsychological function that is delayed several years subsequent to diagnosis. These late effects underscore the need for periodic reevaluations of function. Additionally, traditional measures of general intellectual function may not provide sufficient sensitivity to detect subtle late effects of the illness and its treatment. Finally, empirical investigation to date highlights the predictive value of age at diagnosis, as well as the specific and enduring effects of prophylactic CNS treatment. Box 19.3 presents a case study illustrative of several neuropsychological sequelae associated with pediatric leukemia.

Sickle Cell Anemia

Sickle cell anemia is a hereditary disease that affects 1 out of every 400 African Americans (Brown et al., 1993). This lifelong, chronic illness ensues from a genetic defect in the gene that codes for hemoglobin. Red blood cells assume a sickle shape, which compromises the efficient delivery of oxygen throughout the system. The resultant ischemia, or decreased blood supply to vital organs and tissue, can produce a variety of deleterious effects, including recurrent painful crises, cardiomegaly, liver dysfunction, respiratory complications, and small physical stature due to delayed growth (Fowler et al., 1988). Additionally, central nervous system effects result, including cerebral vascular accidents (CVA), or stroke. An estimated 5% to 10% of individuals with sickle cell disease experience stroke, with the average age of onset around 6 years (Cohen, Branch, McKie, & Adams, 1994). Moreover, recent MRI investigations reveal that a significant proportion of children with sickle cell disease experience "silent cerebral infarcts" that are not associated with overt neurological symptoms (DeBaun et al., 1998).

Box 19.3   Case study

Background and Referral Information

Molly, an 8 year, 7-month-old girl, was referred for a psychoeducational evaluation due to concerns about the effects of her medical history on school performance. Molly was diagnosed with acute lymphocytic leukemia (ALL) one month after her fifth birthday and received intrathecal chemotherapy intermittently for a $2\frac{1}{2}$ year period. During this time, she reportedly suffered from complications related to this treatment, such as liver dysfunction and cerebral white matter degeneration. Subsequently, Molly has demonstrated difficulty in school, particularly related to academic skills and distractibility. She is currently repeating the second grade, in compliance with recommendations from school personnel. In spite of some initial embarrassment, Molly is reportedly adjusting well socially and performing on grade level in all academic areas. Her parents express concern, however, that the increasing complexity of curricular material in advanced grades will reveal, as yet, undetected learning difficulties.

Educational History

Molly was evaluated at age 6 for academic and attention-related difficulties. At that time, she had received chemotherapy for 21 months. She was reportedly functioning in the average range academically, although she worked slowly and evidenced difficulty following directions and sitting still. Assessment results indicated that Molly was functioning in the average range on measures of general intellectual ability (WISC-III FSIQ, 99; VIQ, 104; PIQ, 95) and academic achievement (Wechsler Individual Achievement Tests standard scores ranging from 89–116). While a diagnosis of specific learning disability was not given at that time, a recommendation was made to monitor visual-perceptual ability, memory for rote and abstract information, and abstract processing skills in future assessments of Molly's abilities. Molly did, however, receive a diagnosis of ADHD-NOS, as well as anxiety disorder. A trial of Ritalin was pursued, with no reported improvement in inattentive and hyperactive behaviors. Subsequently, this medication has been discontinued.

Test Behavior and Observations

Although initially shy, Molly quickly established rapport with the examiner and completed all tasks presented to her. While she moved about in her seat throughout the assessment period, Molly approached each task with focused attention. Lateral dominance was firmly established in the right hand, with no apparent graphomotor difficulties.

Test Results and Interpretation

On this administration, Molly achieved scores generally within the low average range on many measures of cognitive ability. (The results of several measures are detailed in the psychometric summary.) Relying on the *integrative interpretative approach*, the psychometric data reveals relative deficits in the areas of visual-spatial processing and visual immediate memory. The tasks of greatest difficulty for Molly required memory for visually presented information, such as geometric figures. The difficulty of these tasks was further compounded when a motor component was involved, such as arranging blocks to form a pattern or drawing geometric patterns from memory. Scores on the VMI, a test of visual-motor integration, and memory tasks on the CMS that required reproduction of visually presented patterns, corroborate those attained on the tests of intellectual ability (e.g., Coding). Comparatively, Molly demonstrated a relative strength on verbal tasks, such as word definitions or word comparisons.

In general, Molly's performance on tasks of academic achievement were commensurate with her general intellectual ability, placing her in the average range. On tests of written language, however, her performance falls in the below-average range. Persistent spelling errors and some apparent difficulty in understanding directions on writing tasks may account for depressed scores in this functional domain. On tests measuring mathematics ability, Molly indicated difficulty in understanding the concept of money, implicating a deficit in problem solving with abstract information. Additionally, she struggled with arithmetic problems involving two or more digits. Her noted visual perceptual deficits likely impact upon spelling and mathematics tasks, as well. As manipulation of

(Continues)

Box 19.3   Case study (Continued)

numbers becomes increasingly more complex in subsequent grades, these tasks may become more challenging for Molly.

In summary, Molly's overall intellectual functioning is in the low average range. Academically, Molly's performance is commensurate with her general cognitive ability, although this assessment indicates some weakness in spelling, as well as problem-solving ability with abstract information. While the results of this evaluation do not indicate a specific learning disability, there is evidence to suggest that Molly's reported learning difficulties may be attributed to deficits in visual-spatial processing and integration, and visual memory. Moreover, according to teacher and parent rating scales, Molly displays significantly high levels of inattention and hyperactivity. This data, along with the observed test behavior, confirm a previous diagnosis of Attention Deficit Hyperactivity Disorder, Combined Type. According to the research findings presented earlier in this chapter, the source of these difficulties may be tied to Molly's illness and treatment.

Psychometric Summary

Wechsler Intelligence Scale for Children—Third Edition (WISC-III)

Verbal	SS	Performance	SS
Information	7	Picture Completion	8
Similarities	12	Coding	5
Arithmetic	8	Picture Arrangement	10
Vocabulary	8	Block Design	9
Comprehension	11	Object Assembly	8
(Digit Span)	(12)	(Symbol Search)	(9)

Composite scores	SS	90% CI	Factor Scores	SS	90% CI
Verbal IQ	95	89–100	Verbal Comprehension	98	92–104
Performance IQ	87	81–95	Perceptual Organization	93	87–101
Full Scale IQ	91	87–96	Freedom from Distractibility	101	93–109
			Processing Speed	86	80–96

Differential Ability Scales (DAS)

Verbal	SS	Nonverbal	SS	Spatial	SS
Word Definitions	40	Matrices	47	Recall of Designs	28
Similarities	47	Sequential & Quantitative Reasoning	41	Pattern Construction	33

Composite scores	SS	90% CI
GCA	78	73-84
Verbal	89	81–98
Nonverbal	89	82–97
Spatial	67	61–76

Beery-Buktenica Developmental Test of Visual-Motor Integration (VMI)

Standard Score 82   Percentile 25

Peabody Picture Vocabulary Test—Third Edition (PPVT-III)

Standard Score 91   Percentile 27

Box 19.3   Case study (Continued)

Children's Memory Scale (CMS)

	INDEX SCORE	PERCENTILE RANK
Visual Immediate	76	5
Visual Delay	91	27
Verbal Immediate	109	73
Verbal Delay	109	73
General Memory	95	37
Attention/Concentration	106	66
Learning	103	58
Delayed Recall	115	84

Woodcock-Johnson Tests of Achievement—Revised (WJ-R)

	SS	PERCENTILE RANK
Letter Word Identification	101	52
Passage Comprehension	111	77
Broad Reading	*105*	*62*
Calculation	103	58
Applied Problems	92	30
Broad Mathematics	*96*	*39*
Dictation	89	23
Writing Samples	77	6
Broad Written Language	*85*	*16*
Word Attack	88	21
Reading Vocabulary	105	63
Reading Comprehension	107	69

Oral and Written Language Scales (OWLS)

SS	PERCENTILE RANK
Written Expression Scale 101	39

Key Math Diagnostic Arithmetic Test—Revised

	SCALED SCORE	STANDARD SCORE	PERCENTILE RANK
Numeration	5		
Geometry	14		
Basic Concepts Area		*92*	*30*
Addition	11		
Subtraction	6		
Multiplication	9		
Division	12		
Mental Computation	7		
Operations Area		*95*	*37*
Measurement	12		
Time and Money	9		
Estimation	11		
Interpreting Data	6		
Problem Solving	9		
Applications Area		*94*	*34*
Total Test		94	34

In a recent review of the literature, Goonan, Goonan, Brown, Buchanan, and Eckman (1994) highlight not only the paucity of research, but also the multitude of methodological problems in this line of research. The astute reader will recognize many of the same methodological limitations that plague the empirical investigation of other pediatric illnesses. The list includes the lack of a developmental focus; heterogeneous subjects across studies; suspect assessment instruments (i.e., questionable reliability and validity); poor control for demographic variables (e.g., SES); and, in general, a poor understanding of the contribution of various aspects of the disease to a decline in performance across functional domains. A logical outcome of these methodological issues would include inconsistent findings across studies. These limitations notwithstanding, preliminary evidence is suggestive of neurocognitive deficits in visual-motor tasks and attention/concentration among children with sickle cell disease. Additionally, given the "silent" neurological course of sickle cell disease, these deficits may very well prove to be cumulative over the course of development.

In an early investigation of the neuropsychological correlates of pediatric sickle cell disease, Fowler and colleagues (1988) compared 28 children with sickle cell anemia to age-, sex-, and SES-matched controls on measures of general intellectual ability, academic achievement, visual-motor integration, and attention. No significant differences were found between groups on the composite scores of the WISC-R, with the exception of scores on the Coding subtest. Deficits on this scale among the sickle cell group were attributed to a decline in visual-motor ability and psychomotor speed. This finding was corroborated by visual-motor deficits on the VMI, yielding, on average, scores $3\frac{1}{2}$ years below developmental expectations. Sickle cell children also performed significantly poorer on a measure of attention, demonstrating a tendency for impulsive and inaccurate responding, and on academic achievement measures, particularly in the areas of reading and spelling. As concerns the hypothesized cumulative effect of this illness, older children in the sickle cell group performed more poorly on the WISC-R Digit Span subtest and on visual-motor tasks. The investigators concluded that children with sickle cell disease constitute an at-risk group for learning difficulties, particularly in the areas of reading, visual-motor ability, and attentional skills. Following from this pioneering study, Swift, Cohen, Hynd, Wisenbaker, McKie, Makari, and McKie (1989) investigated the neuropsychological functioning of 21 children with sickle cell anemia, excluding cases with a known history of CVA, compared with the performance of healthy sibling controls. Results of this investigation were suggestive of subtle cognitive impairment, as the sickle cell group produced scores that were roughly one standard deviation below the sibling group on most cognitive measures. For example, performance of the sickle cell group on the WISC-R yielded a mean FSIQ of 77.7, compared to a mean score of 94.3 for the sibling group. Also, in agreement with the Fowler et al. study, the sickle cell group produced significantly lower scores on measures of verbal function, perceptual organization, attention/distractibility, memory, and academic learning, as compared to sibling controls.

More recently, Brown, Buchanan, Doepke, Eckman, Baldwin, Goonan, and Schoenherr (1993), in response to the potential SES effects of previous studies, implemented a study designed to control for the effects of age, illness severity, and socioeconomic factors. In this investigation, the performance of 70 children, ages $2\frac{1}{2}$ to 17, on measures of neurocognitive and academic abilities, was compared to their healthy siblings. While the findings suggest generally normal intelligence for both groups, the sickle cell group evidenced greater impairment on tasks measuring sustained attention and academic achievement, in agreement with the aforementioned studies. Specifically, deficits among the children with sickle cell disease seemed to be related to the areas of attention, concentration, and reading decoding. An age effect was also reported, as older children with sickle cell disease demonstrated greater declines in performance on measures of sustained attention and visual-motor function. The authors speculate that these findings may suggest early interference in frontal lobe neurodevelopment due to the course of the illness.

Evidence for decline in general intellectual function among children with sickle cell disease has been equivocal. Generally, overall lower intellectual performance has been reported for children with sickle cell disease, as compared to age- and sex-matched controls (Berg & Linton, 1997). These findings seem to be particularly relevant to children who have suffered CVAs. In a study of 10 sickle cell children receiving transfussion therapy following stroke, Cohen, Branch, McKie, and Adams (1994) subdivided this group based on lateralization of stroke. Findings indicated that left-hemisphere involvement resulted in general impairment on intelligence testing, including measures of verbal, nonverbal, and spatial ability. Comparatively, stroke lateralized within the right hemisphere resulted in impairment of nonverbal/spatial abilities only.

Based upon the results of this study, children with left hemisphere stroke demonstrated a global decline on intelligence testing with a very small VIQ-PIQ discrepancy in favor of PIQ (4 points). In contrast, the children with right hemisphere stroke demonstrated a marked decline in PIQ only, resulting in a large (13 point) VIQ-PIQ discrepancy in favor of VIQ. (p. 522)

Additional neurocognitive findings included impairment across measures of language, which was significantly lower in the area of expressive vocabulary only, visual-spatial construction, auditory/verbal memory, immediate visual/spatial memory, and all academic areas (consistent with IQ) among children sustaining left-hemisphere involvement. Visual-spatial construction, immediate visual/spatial memory, and arithmetic were compromised among children with a history of stroke localized within the right hemisphere. The authors conclude that these results are similar to findings with adult stroke patients, challenging studies that support plasticity of language function and "shifting" of dominance for language from the left hemisphere to the right.

HIV Infection

Pediatric acquired immunodeficiency syndrome (AIDS) is the direct result of a retrovirus, *human immunodeficiency virus (HIV)*, now the ninth leading cause of death in children (Wolters, Brouwers, & Moss, 1995). Improvements in medical technology and treatment, and higher incidence rates, reportedly contribute to the exponential growth in the number of children with HIV infection. The transmission of HIV infection may take several routes, most commonly including exposure to the virus *in utero* by infected mothers or through infected blood transfusions. Symptomatology of the illness is, in some ways, not unlike adults, characterized by opportunistic infections and/or Karposi's sarcoma. However, among infants the illness differs in its course due to the immature nature of the immune system and presence of maternal antibodies in the infant's circulatory system. As a result, the central nervous system may be the most vulnerable target of the infection, particularly the regions of the basal ganglia, pyramidal tracts, extrapyramidal tracts, and cerebellum. Neurological sequelae include microcephaly, brain atrophy, encephalopathy, and other abnormalities in neurological development (e.g., neoplasms such as lymphoma of the CNS). Children who are born infected are often small for their gestational age and demonstrate numerous developmental complications, including failure to thrive (Llorente, LoPresti, & Satz, 1997; Williams & Williams, 1996).

Although the neurologic complications of pediatric HIV infection have been well researched, the neuropsychological complications are less clear. Pediatric HIV infection constitutes a new area of investigation. As such, it is characterized by a paucity of research and many of the same methodological problems associated with the empirical investigation of other pediatric syndromes. These issues may be particularly troublesome for investigators of pediatric HIV, as the progression of this illness is complex and, in many cases, its onset is prenatal (Williams & Williams, 1996). These methodological obstacles notwithstanding, neurocognitive areas reportedly affected by CNS HIV infection include deficits in motor skills, perceptual motor ability, attention, and expressive language. However, as concerns problems of inattention, the etiology is not clearly the direct result of HIV (Berg & Linton, 1997; Moss, Wolters, Brouwers, Hendricks, & Pizzo, 1996).

Overall lowering of cognitive functioning among children with HIV infection is generally documented by empirical investigation. Given that the CNS is the primary target during the progression of the virus, cognitive decline is a likely result. In a study of 99 children with symptomatic HIV disease who had received no antiretroviral therapy, Brouwers, Tudor-Williams, DeCarli, Moss, Wolters, Civitello, and Pizzo (1995) report a mean FSIQ of 85.9 $\pm$2.5, with a range from 39 to 131. Additionally, children who acquired the virus prenatally demonstrated significantly lower levels of functioning than a transfusion-infected group. In conclusion, the authors state that "this study shows that advanced immune dysfunction and elevated viral burden as markers of disease progression place children at increased risk for the development of HIV-related CNS manifestations" (p. 719). In an attempt to study the effects of HIV infection acquired during childhood, Smith, Minden, Netley, Read, King, and Blanchette (1997) conducted a 3-year longitudinal investigation of the neurocognitive sequelae of transfusion-infected children. In contrast to the aforementioned study, these authors report no significant differences on measures of general intellectual function, memory, motor function, and language abilities among children infected with HIV and hemophilia, children with hemophilia who were

not infected with HIV, and healthy sibling controls over time. The performance of the HIV-infected group on measures of academic achievement was lower than would be predicted by their assessed cognitive ability. The authors conclude that these results are not suggestive of progressive cognitive decline in asymptomatic HIV-infected children, and that age at infection is a significant prognostic indicator.

CONCLUSIONS

This chapter has attempted to present the reader with an introductory review of neuropsychological assessment with children. In particular, a brief overview of theories of intellectual function from a neuropsychological framework, as well as several approaches to neuropsychological assessment, was presented. As such, recent advances not only in neurodiagnostic imaging of brain function, but also in psychometric instrumentation hold much promise for a broader understanding of intellectual function in children.

CHAPTER SUMMARY

1. Neuropsychology, which has gained eminence within the last thirty years, seeks to define and describe brain processes, which subserve such unitary constructs as intelligence.

2. Early pioneers in the field of neuropsychology, such as Ward Halstead and Aleksandr Luria, developed neuropsychological theories of intelligence. Such theories ascribed central importance to the role of the frontal lobes. Similarly, modern neuropsychological researchers advance a cognitive processing approach to intellectual function. Additionally, studies of cerebral lateralization suggest that the hemispheres operate concertedly to produce "intelligent" behavior.

3. The nature of the developing brain poses considerable challenge to child neuropsychologists, who must consider multiple and interactive variables when evaluating the impact of early brain insult.

4. Just as a child's brain should not be viewed as a down-sized version of the adult brain, assessment of brain-behavior relationships in children cannot be based simply on down-sized versions of adult measures. As such, the state of child neuropsychological assessment is in its infancy, with a need for the development of measures designed to assess normal cognitive development at different age-referenced stages.

5. Neuropsychological assessment with children typically involves the functional domains of general intelligence, memory, perceptual ability, visual-spatial function, attention, communication and language skills, academic achievement, and social-emotional function.

6. Several approaches to child neuropsychological assessment include the fixed battery approach, the flexible battery approach, and the process approach. Battery selection is driven by the purpose of the assessment or the referral question, and rehabilitative demands.

7. While neuropsychological measures share some common variance with measures of intelligence (i.e., psychometric g), neuropsychological measures do provide unique information about brain-behavior relationships.

8. The neuropsychological sequelae of various pediatric syndromes underscore the necessity for measures characterized by greater sensitivity and specificity, as compared to traditional tests of intelligence, for detection of subtle functional deficits.

CHAPTER 20

Mental Retardation and Learning Disabilities

CHAPTER QUESTIONS

How are intelligence tests used in the diagnosis of mental retardation?

How diagnostic are Wechsler subtest profiles?

How should intelligence tests be used when diagnosing important and prevalent childhood disorders? The range of presenting problems of children is enormous, requiring the intelligence test user to be aware of a variety of issues presented by exceptional children. Some children may be "untestable," and others may require specialized measures. Clinicians require specialized knowledge to use intelligence measures effectively with such groups.

MENTAL RETARDATION

Since intelligence tests were designed originally to diagnose mental retardation (see Chapter 1), it

is eminently appropriate that this group be discussed first. Mental retardation (MR) has been recognized by societies for some time—at least since the Roman Empire. It has been said that Roman parents often threw their children with mental retardation into the Tiber River in order to not have to care for them, and Spartans killed or abandoned mentally retarded individuals. It was not until the Middle Ages that some societies began to care for these individuals' needs (Weiss & Weisz, 1986). Given such potential dire consequences, one cannot help but wonder about the accuracy of the diagnoses that were made in those days!

Most modern diagnostic systems are based on the criteria set by the American Association on Mental Retardation (AAMR; 1992). The influential AAMR definition is:

Mental Retardation *refers to substantial limitations in present functioning. It is characterized by significantly subaverage intellectual functioning, existing concurrently with related limitations in two or more of the fol-*

lowing applicable adaptive skill areas: communication, self-care, home living, socials skills, community use, self-direction, health and safety, functional academics, leisure and work. Mental retardation manifests itself before age 18. (p. iii)

The AAMR has for some time considered mental retardation as a condition that can only be diagnosed if *dual deficits* in intelligence and adaptive behavior exist during the developmental period (usually considered to be 18 by most diagnostic systems). All of the major diagnostic systems have adopted the view that an intelligence deficit is at best only one of the core deficits of mental retardation. Most diagnostic systems also mimic the DSM-IV by defining significantly below-average intelligence as a standard score (M=100, SD=15 or 16) of about 70 or below. Often individual state departments of education also stipulate, in their IDEA implementation regulations, that the standard error of measurement may be taken into account. Specifically, scores of about 67 to 73 may be considered as either qualifying or disqualifying a child for the diagnosis of mental retardation when other variables, such as adaptive behavior and age of onset, are taken into account.

The core logic of the criteria for the diagnosis of mental retardation can be simplistically applied to the following examples.

Case	Intelligence Composite	Adaptive Behavior	Onset Age	Mental Retardation
1	55	62	27	No
2	60	81	2	No
3	84	63	7	No
4	58	59	2	Yes

The sample cases above, while oversimplifications of the diagnostic principles involved in mental retardation diagnosis, do give some indication of the general parameters that are considered in making the diagnosis. Case 1 is probably the trickiest because the sole reason that the di-

agnosis cannot be made is because the age of onset is outside that which is typically considered the developmental period.

With regard to intellectual assessment, the AAMR provides the following guidelines:

1. Determination of subaverage intellectual functioning requires the use of global measures that include different types of items and different factors of intelligence. The instruments more commonly used include The Stanford Binet Intelligence Scale, one of the Wechsler scales (WISC-III, WAIS-R [now III]), or the Kaufman Assessment Battery for Children.

2. If a valid IQ is not possible, significantly subaverage intellectual capabilities means a level of performance that is less than that observed in the vast majority (approximately 97 percent) of persons of comparable background.

3. In order to be valid, the assessment of cognitive performance must be free from errors caused by motor, sensory, emotional, or cultural factors. (p. 1)

These guidelines have several sensible implications for assessment practice. First, screening measures are discouraged. Second, it is recognized that a standardized assessment of IQ is not always possible. Later I will suggest that an adaptive measure be used for the intelligence measure in these extreme cases. Third, psychologists must use good common sense and rule out nonintellective causes for low intelligence test scores.

Adaptive Behavior Scales

Adaptive behavior scales assess the degree to which an individual meets the standards of personal independence and social responsibility expected for a child's age or cultural group (Grossman, 1983). This construct is more variable than intelligence since the standards of behavior and achievement are determined by an individual's society. For example, adult expectations to vote may be relevant to some societies and not others. Cooking skills may be deemed necessary for some cultural groups and not for others. As it turns out, however, there are some standards of adaptive behavior that are relatively universal, such as toilet training, control of aggression, and respect for authority figures. These skills are the ones typically assessed by adaptive behavior scales.

One of the oldest and premier measures of adaptive behavior is the *Vineland Adaptive Behavior Scale* (Sparrow, Balla, & Cicchetti, 1984). The latest *Vineland* is a revision of the *Vineland Social Maturity Scale* that was developed by Edgar Doll in the 1930s. Doll essentially founded the field of adaptive behavior assessment by noting that although all of his patients at the Vineland (NJ) State Training School suffered from intellectual problems, there were vast differences in their day-to-day life and coping skills. If, for example, two children have intelligence test composite scores of 60, and one is toilet trained and the other is frequently incontinent, these children would place considerably different demands on an adult's time. The toilet-trained child is more mobile and can be involved in many more activities than the incontinent child who requires considerably more attention and care (see Box 20.1).

Levels of Mental Retardation

A standard score of less than 70 has long been accepted as a criterion of mental retardation (Flynn, 1985). To date there are very few who have questioned the ability of the WISC-III or other intelligence tests to provide a meaningful criterion of mental retardation. This acceptance exists although the research of Flynn (1985), in an interesting investigation, showed how sampling problems and changes in norms over time have served to effectively change the numbers of individuals (the percentage of the population) that are identified by the standard score = 70 criterion. He found the criterion of mental retardation (Standard score=70) to vary as much as a full standard deviation on the particular Wechsler scale selected. Among other results, Flynn (1985) concluded that in order to have a coherent and consistent cut score for mental retardation, the Psychological Corporation would have to renorm the WISC-III every 7 years. Despite such contrary findings, a WISC-III standard score of less than 70 will likely be used as a cutoff for some time.

Different levels of mental retardation used to be recognized by most diagnostic systems. The newest version of the AAMR diagnostic manual

---

Box 20.1   The difference between intelligence and adaptive behavior

I learned to appreciate the difference between intelligence and adaptive behavior early in my career. My third job after completing college (yes, I had trouble finding a job I liked with a bachelor's degree in psychology) was a temporary position as Rehabilitation Workshop Supervisor in a modern version of a state mental hospital. I helped patients build birdhouses and stools, and I served as the favorite target for the adolescents who felt the need to throw paint at someone—but that is another story. I vividly recall an experience with a young man, about age 30, who was in the hospital for alcoholism treatment. I remember this man so well because he was well groomed, mannered, and pleasant. We had many enjoyable conversations about his family and his work, and I looked forward to his visits to the workshop. I also remember being stunned when one of the staff members from the alcoholism treatment unit told me that the young man was diagnosed with mild mental retardation. I remember feeling a sense of empathy and also wishing that all of the clients who did not have cognitive deficits would be as polite and enjoyable to work with as this man.

has eschewed this practice by emphasizing the assessment of patient needs in a variety of domains. Some descriptions of the various levels of mental retardation that have served as conventions in the past are given below. These criteria are adapted from Weiss and Weisz (1986).

- **Mild Mental Retardation** (standard score range 55 to 69)

  This group constitutes approximately 80% of the cases of mental retardation. In most cases, these individuals look relatively normal and often are not identified until they begin school and experience considerable difficulty. They can develop social and basic life skills and achieve up to about a sixth-grade level in some academic areas. Mildly retarded individuals usually become self-supporting, but the jobs that they do may be viewed by most as tiresome (see Box 20.1).

- **Moderate Mental Retardation** (standard score range 40 to 54)

  About 12% of the mental retardation cases fall into this range. These children often have obvious physical abnormalities and appear awkward or clumsy. They frequently show language delays in the preschool years and do not obey social conventions. These individuals may be able to work in a sheltered workshop setting but rarely live independently.

- **Severe Mental Retardation** (standard score range 25 to 39)

  This group constitutes approximately 7% of the mental retardation cases. During early childhood, they show significant speech and motor delays. Their schooling focuses on the development of personal hygiene and basic communication skills. As adults, these individuals can only perform simple occupational tasks under close supervision.

- **Profound Mental Retardation** (standard score less than 25)

  Individuals in this 1% of mentally retarded individuals suffer from physical abnormalities and neurological problems that often preclude them from walking and speaking. They require constant supervision and lifelong custodial care. (p. 349)

It is in the differentiation of levels of mental retardation that psychologists have come face to face with the limitations of intelligence tests. The scholastic nature of many of the items does not provide easy enough items for children with severe impairments. Infant and some preschool tests do have enough easy items because intelligence is defined differently, more globally, for these ages. Motor scales, for example, are common and contribute to developmental indices (see Chapter 15). Some individuals have advised using infant scales such as the Bayley with children who are beyond the test's age range and yet have mental ages that are within the age range (Sullivan & Burley, 1990). Differentiating between severe and profound levels of retardation remains a murky area where the intelligence testing technology usually fails. In fact, the AAMR approach, which places less emphasis on the differentiation of levels, may be of greater value for clinical assessment purposes with severely disabled populations.

Profile Research

Some research on the use of the intelligence tests with children has focused on identifying characteristic composite score or subtest profiles. Kaufman (1979b) identified a WISC-R profile in which mildly mentally retarded children obtained relative strengths on spatial tests such as Block Design, Picture Completion, and Object Assembly and relative weaknesses on school related tests such as Arithmetic, Vocabulary, and Information. While this profile suggests that there may be a characteristic P>V profile, this does not appear to be the case. As Kaufman (1979b) emphasized, the WISC-R profile is merely a *trend* in the data.

It is now clear that a mild P>V pattern and the aforementioned subtest profile are only trends that are potentially theoretically significant but *useless for making differential diagnoses*. In the majority of studies conducted with the WISC-R, the P>V profile was only in the 8- to 10-point range (Kaufman & Van Hagen, 1977; Gutkin, 1979; Naglieri, 1979; Thompson, 1980). *A V/P difference of this magnitude is not reliable enough for individual assessment purposes* and therefore, not a valuable group trend that may be used as a diagnostic sign.

Why did this mild subtest and P>V pattern occur in so many studies? It certainly makes sense that children with mental retardation would have a deficit in school-related skills such as those assessed by the Arithmetic and Vocabulary subtests, since the diagnosis of mental retardation is usually made by schools and children who are referred for suspected mental retardation are likely referred because of substantial school failure (Kaufman, 1979b). It is also conceivable that the cumulative deficit phenomenon (see Chapter 3) comes into play and adversely affects school achievement. This proposition may be particularly true for mathematics tests since later skill development is dependent on prerequisite skill acquisition. The relative strength on nonverbal tasks with a strong spatial component may be explained similarly. This profile could be affected by the nature of mild mental retardation. Most mild mental retardation (about 75% of cases) is described as familial (Weiss & Weisz, 1986), where problems such as poverty and illiteracy are associated with the syndrome. Perhaps Block Design, Object Assembly, and Picture Completion are less affected by adverse cultural conditions. Yet another possibility is that some mentally retarded children exhibit subtle neurological differences from the population at large that could be due to prenatal or postnatal factors.

Reynolds and Kaufman (1990) have also summarized the extent of WISC-R subtest scatter (intercomposite or intersubtest differences) that has been found for populations of children with mental retardation. They found that subtest scatter in the typical investigation was in the 6- to 7-

point range (when the lowest subtest score is subtracted from the highest subtest score). This finding is well within the range of 7 + or − 2 points, which was found to be within the average range for the WISC-R standardization sample (Kaufman, 1979b).

Overall, neither composite score or subtest profiles for children with mental retardation have been of significant theoretical or practical value. The overall composite score offered by intelligence tests has, however, been shown to be of some value for predicting important phenomena. For example, several studies have shown that psychostimulant therapy is ineffective for children with ADHD and mental retardation if their overall IQ score is very low (i.e., about 55 or less) (Brown, Dreelin, & Dingle, 1997).

Selecting a Score for Mental Retardation (MR) Diagnosis

An important issue regarding the use of intelligence tests for the purposes of mental retardation diagnosis is the decision about which composite score to use in making a diagnosis when there is a composite score (e.g., V/P) difference and one of these scores is outside that which is typically considered to be the mental retardation range. A child, for example, could obtain a WISC-III Verbal score of 78 and a Performance score of 65. In this scenario, the Full Scale score of 70 is not too problematic. If the child's adaptive behavior composite score is also about 70 or less, the diagnosis of mental retardation becomes more likely as dual deficits in intelligence and adaptive behavior are clearly documented.

What if, however, a more difficult case with a large V/P discrepancy is considered? A good example of this latter situation would be a child who obtains a Performance score of 88, Verbal score of 60, Full Scale score of 72, and adaptive behavior composite score of 71. This case is more difficult to decide based on scores alone, forcing logic and prior research to come into play. This case is also a good example of why *rigid cut scores should not be used when making diagnoses based on intelligence test results* (Kaufman, 1990). One may make quite different diagnostic decisions with this same set of scores, depending on other information about the child. This child may be diagnosed with mental retardation given information that he or she

1. is 9 years old and has failed most academic subjects every school year despite the fact that his or her parents have hired tutors and he or she seems to be putting forth great effort in school;

2. was born in the United States and speaks English as his or her native language; and

3. has a developmental history indicating that he or she achieved major language and motor milestones considerably later than normal.

A child with the scores cited above may just as well not be diagnosed with mental retardation if he or she

1. is 7 years old, has lived in the United States for only 1 year, and Spanish was his or her first language acquired;

2. has failed only language arts subjects; and

3. was reared in a high-SES family environment where his or her needs were met by others, and the acquisition of adaptive life skills was not emphasized or deemed necessary (e.g., the household employed both a maid and a cook). This privileged environment resulted in a very low score on the Daily Living Skills domain of the Vineland with other domain scores being considerably higher.

Since background information, other test scores, developmental history, and other factors are so important in making diagnostic decisions with intelligence tests, perhaps the most reasonable approach is to consider developmental history, other test scores, and related information as *central to the mental retardation diagnostic process*. In cases where there are composite score differences, with some scores within the mental retardation range and others outside this range, *the examiner should explain why the diagnostic decision was made*, whatever that decision may be. This practice at least allows for peer review and collaboration. If the reason is defensible to other professionals who know the child's circumstances, then the clinician can feel more comfortable with the decision made. Writing the rationale for the diagnosis has an additional benefit in that it may also help the clinician clarify his or her thought processes regarding the diagnostic decision.

Unfortunately, the use of intelligence tests in isolation has been reinforced by statutory guidelines such as those offered by some state departments of education and U.S. federal agencies such as the Social Security Administration. A cutoff score of 70 has been identified by various agencies to decide everything from special education class placement to eligibility for monetary benefits. One can imagine the ire of physicians if the use of medical diagnostic tests were similarly regulated. What if some governmental body decided that a person had to have a cholesterol level of 200 (LDL) to be eligible to receive medicine to reduce serum cholesterol (a practice that is now more likely due to the ubiquitous nature of managed care)? The patients with levels of 195 would likely be very angry at being denied treatment, and those patients with levels of 205 who wanted to treat themselves with diet modifications would be similarly angry. This situation is not far removed from current mental retardation diagnostic practice that occurs with school-aged children under the aegis of various governmental regulatory bodies. If intelligence tests are going to be used in a larger context for decision making, then clinicians have to use discretion as opposed to rigid cut scores or diagnostic formulas. To do otherwise is to promote the simplistic and inappropriate use of intelligence tests, which serves no one.

Intelligence and Adaptive Behavior Revisited

The relationship between adaptive behavior scales and intelligence scales should also be kept in mind for appropriate use of intelligence tests in diagnosing MR (Kamphaus, 1987). I found that the correlation between the WISC-R and the K-ABC and adaptive behavior scales such as the Vineland Adaptive Behavior Scales, where parents serve as the informant, is moderate to low in most studies (i.e., correlations in the .20 to .60 range). This finding has several practical implications for the use of an intelligence test along with an adaptive behavior scale in the diagnosis of mental retardation. These implications include:

1. Psychologists should not expect intelligence and parent-reported adaptive behavior scores to show a great deal of agreement, especially when the child is outside the mental retardation range.
2. The limited correlation of these measures with intelligence tests suggests that adaptive behavior scales are adding information to the diagnostic process that is different from that of intelligence tests (Kamphaus, 1987).
3. The correlation between intelligence tests and adaptive behavior scores as rated by teachers may be somewhat higher (Kamphaus, 1987). Teacher-rated adaptive behavior, therefore, may not be considered as a substitute for parent-reported adaptive behavior and vice versa.

All of these findings also support the notion that adaptive behavior is likely to become more central to the diagnosis of mental retardation and to treatment plan design (DeStefano & Thompson, 1990). In fact, the latest AAMR (1992) criteria emphasize the assessment of adaptive behavior in 10 domains in order to establish need for services.

These same AAMR criteria have expanded the advised diagnostic procedures to include two new assessment domains. First, clinicians are ad-

monished to systematically assess the "individual's health and physical well-being." Second, the "elements of an individiual's current environment" are to be assessed to determine any factors that restrict or assist an individual's current level of daily functioning. Consideration of these new domains should aid further in the habilitation process.

Regression Effects

Yet another issue to consider in the diagnosis of mental retardation is the likelihood of regression effects. Since intelligence tests are not perfectly reliable, one can expect the composite score means for samples of mentally retarded children to move toward the normative mean. A good example of this is a study by Spitz (1983) where the original mean for the MR group was 55 (54.96) at age 13 and 58 (58.33) at age 15. This fact can make diagnosis very difficult, especially if a child moves from a score of 68 to 74. Is this child still appropriately diagnosed as mentally retarded? At least a few of the possibilities to consider include:

1. The child's first evaluation was conducted under less than ideal circumstances, and the first test results were inordinately low.
2. The second score is higher primarily due to regression effects. This hypothesis is especially plausible when the difference between the first and second scores is rather small (e.g., less than 10 points or so).
3. Practice effects could play a role in the second score being higher. This result could also be obtained when the difference between tests is very small—about 6 points or less—and there is greater gain on nonverbal/spatial/simultaneous tests that are more prone to practice effects.
4. The second score could reflect gains in cognitive development. This explanation is more likely when the first evaluation was conducted

when the child was very young—in the preschool years. The child's intellectual skills could have simply unfolded during the early school years when cognitive development is fairly rapid. Another possibility is that the child has been the beneficiary of an effective intervention program. An effective intervention program may have succeeded in placing an impoverished child back onto a favorable "creode" (see Chapter 2).

These possibilities and others should be considered when evaluating a child's gain on retest. However, equally important are the child's scores on measures of other traits. If a child's overall composite is 74 on retest and his achievement and adaptive behavior test scores are both 69 and below, then it is more difficult to argue that there has been a substantial and important cognitive change for the better that is not due to regression and practice effects. On the other hand, if a child with this same composite on retest has achievement test and adaptive behavior scores that have also moved above 70, then retaining the diagnosis of mental retardation becomes questionable.

Another finding that could mitigate against regression effects is the cumulative deficit phenomenon (see Chapter 3). If a child scores lower on retesting and is the product of an impoverished environment, then the effects of the impoverishment may accumulate over ontongeny (Haywood, 1986, refers to this as the "MA deficit"), resulting in a child achieving increasingly lower *standard* scores with increasing age in comparison to chronological age peers. The child's raw scores may be increasing over the course of development but a relatively flat developmental trajectory makes the child look like he is loosing ground when standard scores are computed. It may be that children without early cognitive delay are developing at a faster rate, which serves to make the norm-referenced standard scores look like no growth or reversal of cognitive growth is occurring for the developmentally delayed child.

The Range of Scores Issue

A common complaint about intelligence tests is their inability to differentiate between the various levels of mental retardation. Few intelligence tests offer standard scores that go so low as to be able to differentiate between moderate, severe, and profound levels of retardation. Many popular scales only produce standard scores as low as 45 or 50 (the DAS is a notable exception in this regard).

It is first important to consider the psychometric limitations inherent in this situation. One limitation is the availability of data for calculating norms for these groups. If, for example, a test has collected only 200 cases at age 7 for norming purposes, then there are only going to be about 4 cases, or data points, below a standard score of 70 (the 2nd percentile). Consequently, the calculation of norms below the 2nd percentile may be based more on the computer algorithms used for calculating the norms than actual data for disabled children.

Even if this psychometric limitation is conquered with statistical or sampling procedures, the practice may still may be questionable. At the very low levels of functioning, the type of scholastic intelligence assessed by most intelligence tests is less relevant. Adaptive behavior issues such as ambulation, speech, toileting, and eating skills are more important at these low levels of functioning. Reschly (1980) recognized this difference between mild and other levels of mental retardation by pointing out that mild retardation is not characterized by physical abnormalities, it is usually only apparent in school settings, and it may not be permanent. It may well be that not only does the nature of mental retardation differ across levels, but also the relative importance of adaptive behavior and intelligence tests changes across the levels of mental retardation. Intelligence tests may be important for differentiating between mild and moderate levels of mental retardation. Adaptive behavior scales, however, such as the Vineland do produce standard scores as low as 20. Adaptive behavior scales are also more likely to produce much more important information for intervention design than intelligence scales. It is also theoretically defensible to *use adaptive behavior scales as measures of intelligence* with the severely disabled, because the content domain at low levels of adaptive behavior scales is strikingly similar to that of infant intelligence tests such as the Bayley. Motor skills are part of intelligence scales for preschoolers; why can't they be part of a developmental assessment for the older child or adolescent who has a significant cognitive impairment? My opinion is that *adaptive behavior scales are the tests of choice for differentiating among moderate, severe, and profound levels of mental retardation or developmental disability.*

Unfortunately, some regulatory agencies still insist that every child diagnosed with MR have a recent intelligence test score on record. This requirement results in psychologists engaging in questionable practices such as using preschool tests to obtain a mental age for mentally retarded adolescents, and using the old ratio IQ formula (MA/CA × 100 = IQ) to produce an IQ score. *An intelligence test should never be used outside its age range to produce a norm-referenced score to be used in making diagnostic decisions.* If an intelligence test is used in this manner, it is likely no better, and it may be worse, than an educated guess by a skilled professional. The sample case for Kent (in this chapter) shows how a credible evaluation of a severely disabled child may be completed without using an intelligence test.

Other Diagnostic Issues

With problems and limitations duly recognized (Spitz, 1988, 1983, 1986a), intelligence tests will likely continue to play an important role in the diagnosis of mental retardation. The potential for misuse of intelligence tests in making the mental retardation diagnosis, however, looms large, especially when intelligence test scores are interpreted in isolation without giving due consideration to adaptive behavior evaluations and background information. A good example is the case of Daniel Hoffman who was diagnosed by a school board psychologist as mentally retarded (Payne & Patton, 1981). He spent *12* years in a class for the mentally retarded before it was discovered that the initial diagnosis was incorrect. He, in fact, was above average intellectually, but he had a severe speech defect. Remarkably, he had even accepted the fact that he was mentally retarded.

The reasons for making the diagnosis of mental retardation, since it does depend so heavily on the use of intelligence test results, *should be explained in writing.* Simply reporting scores that are 70 or below and concluding that a child has MR is not adequate for modern assessment practice. Above all, intelligence test results should not be used rigidly in making mental retardation diagnoses. The use of strict cut scores serves to place too much emphasis on those very scores and cause evaluators to lose sight of the child's full spectrum of strengths and weaknesses. Gone are the days when the diagnosis of mental retardation is based solely on one measure—intelligence tests. The practice of using intelligence tests in isolation is analogous to using only the LDL serum cholesterol level to diagnose risk for heart disease. It is now clear that other factors (e.g., HDL) must be considered. The AAMR (1992) diagnostic manual has provided compelling empirical evidence and logical arguments to support the identification of adaptive behavior, emotional functioning, health, and intellectual abilities as part of MR diagnosis and treatment planning.

Case Study

This case study (see Box 20.2) is interesting in that it is clearly a difficult case. This child provided the ultimate challenge for the examiner in that he was young, medically involved, severely developmentally delayed, and could not communicate with anyone other than his mother. Kent lacked school experience, making it even

Box 20.2   Psychological report involving mental retardation

NAME: Kent
SEX: Male
GRADE: Preschool—not attending a formal program
CHRONOLOGICAL AGE: 4 years, 7 months
ORDINAL POSITION (birth order): 2nd
SIBLINGS: 1 older brother

Referral Question(s)

Kent was referred for assessment to determine an appropriate educational placement for the next school year. Questions to be addressed were:

At what developmental level is Kent currently functioning?

Will Kent require special class placement?

If so, what type of placement is appropriate for Kent's needs?

Background Information

Health and Physical Development

The pregnancy with Kent was complicated by hemorrhaging in the first 6 weeks, followed by a high fever that resolved without treatment. His mother reported experiencing mild PET (toxemia) near term. Kent was born at term via an elective caesarian section; birth weight 5 pounds, 12 ounces.

According to his mother, a milk allergy was diagnosed at 2 days of age. Kent continued to experience vomiting and diarrhea from 10 days to 6 weeks of age. In addition, a ventricular septal defect was diagnosed at 10 days of age, which later closed spontaneously. At 2 months of age, Kent's pediatrician queried deafness and blindness. In addition, Kent was again experiencing vomiting and diarrhea. Kent's mother reported that he exhibited "strange shaking of the feet, arms, and grimacing of the face" around $2\frac{1}{2}$ months,of age. An EEG was performed at 5 months of age and Kent was diagnosed as having hypsarrhythmia (infantile spasms). At the present time, additional diagnostic problems, as specified by the pediatric neurologist, include probable Cerebral Dysgenesis, Mental Retardation, Cerebral Palsy: Mild Spastic Diplegia, Microcephaly, Seizure Disorder, Congenital Renal Problems, and Recurrent Otitis Media.

According to his mother, Kent held up his head at 3–4 months, sat at 10 months, pulled to a stand and crawled at 12 months, and walked at 23 months of age. However, due to subsequent heel cord lengthening operations, Kent again walked independently at 3 years of age. His mother reports that Kent has an expressive language vocabulary of 15–20 words.

Kent wears corrective lenses for astigmatism. His hearing was assessed at Children's Hospital, and he was diagnosed as having "functional hearing for communication purposes." At the present time, Kent undergoes physical and occupational therapy and is on a waiting list for kindergarten.

Family Background

Kent is the youngest of two children, the first being a boy also. The family is intact, and relationships appear to be healthy. His mother was observed to verbally reprimand Kent when he played inappropriately. This discipline technique was appropriate for the situation. Both parents appeared to interact and cope with their handicapped child at a high degree of proficiency. The social worker at the Child Development Center expressed concern that his parents are overly involved with Kent's handicap such that their requests for services are, at times, unreasonable. Although his parents intensely inquired about school district services, their questions were appropriate and indicative of considerable thought and insight.

(Continues)

Box 20.2   **Psychological report involving mental retardation** (Continued)

Previous Test Results

Kent underwent psychological assessments at Children's Hospital at ages 2 and 2 1/2. Test results from the Bayley Scales of Infant Development were as follows:

Age	Mental Age	Motor Scale
2	13 months (below 50)	16 months (below 50)
$2^{1/2}$	15 months (below 50)	16 months (below 50)

Current Psychoeducational Assessment

Formal psychological assessment was attempted, but reliable and valid results were unobtainable due to the extensive nature of Kent's communication disorder. Kent appeared to be at the exploratory level of functioning and was unable to point to any object upon command or sit at an activity for a sustained period of time.

Observations

Due to Kent not being presently engaged in a preschool program, observations were made at the evaluation center and at Kent's home. Each observation was approximately 1 hour in duration.

Mobility

Kent walked independently, although he exhibited awkward gait and tended to lean forward with his arms stretched forward while walking. Kent walked independently up and down stairs. His mother reported that Kent is unable to run, jump, hop, or catch a ball.

Speech and Language

Kent did not attempt any vocalizations at home. However, he frequently gestured and whined for a coloring book at home. These behaviors appeared to be an attempt to communicate with others. Kent did not voice any discernable words during either observation.

Awareness of Environment and Exploratory Behavior

Kent demonstrated awareness (visual and auditory) of his environment. He was interested in watching and attempting to engage in activities being conducted within his immediate visual field. He responded to loud noises by visually orienting to the sound source. Kent wore glasses during both observations. Kent also actively explored his surrounding environment. When at the center, Kent took objects from their container and replaced them upon command from his mother. He actively sought new toys. When at home, Kent attempted to color in a coloring book. He held the crayon incorrectly within his fist. When reprimanded for not completing his task, Kent left the room and searched for a photograph album. His mother reported that Kent is unable to cut with scissors.

Interaction with Others

Kent attempted to solicit the examiner's attention on a variety of occasions. He readily approached the examiner upon initial meeting and appeared pleased (i.e., smiled) when placed on the examiner's lap.

Following Instructions and Attending to Tasks

When requested by his mother to color on the page instead of the table, Kent readily complied. Kent did not follow instructions provided by the examiner.

Peabody Picture Vocabulary Test—Revised

This receptive vocabulary test was administered, but Kent was unable to produce a satisfactory pointing response. He appeared to point at the pictures at random.

Brigance Inventory of Early Development

Self Help Skills: His mother answered these questions. The ratings assigned by his mother are as follows:

Box 20.2   Psychological report involving mental retardation (Continued)

Feeding and Eating—approximately a 2-year developmental level

Undressing and Dressing—approximately a 2-year developmental level

Fastening and Unfastening—approximately a 2-year developmental level

Toileting—approximately a 2-year developmental level (verbalizes toilet needs consistently)

Bathing—approximately a 2-year developmental level (washes face with assistance)

Grooming—approximately a 3-year developmental level (brushes teeth with assistance)

Household Chores—approximately a 2-year developmental level (imitates housework but does not avoid hazards)

General Knowledge and Comprehension

Kent did not perform these tasks due to his inability to provide a reliable pointing response and his inability to remain at this task.

Vineland Adaptive Behavior Scales (Expanded Form)

This instrument was administered to Kent's mother to obtain additional information for program development.

Domain	Standard Score	Adaptive Level	Age Equivalent
Communication	53 ± 4	Low	1-5
Daily Living Skills	58 ± 4	Low	1-6
Socialization	59 ± 4	Low	1-6
Motor Skills	46 ± 8	Low	1-7

Adaptive Behavior Composite 50 ± 3
(Mean=100, SD=15)

On the basis of these test results, when compared to his same-age peers, Kent is presently functioning 3–4 standard deviations below the mean, which is indicative of a Severe/Profound Mentally Handicapped child. (Please refer to the protocol for an analysis of Kent's behavioral strengths and weaknesses.)

Summary of Assessment Results

Due to the nature and severity of Kent's handicapping condition, a formal standardized assessment was not possible. However, based on interviews with his parents and observations at school and at home, it appears that Kent's overall developmental level is within the 1- to 2-year range. In most respects, Kent is presently at the exploratory stage of development.

Response to Referral Questions

At what developmental level is Kent currently functioning? On the basis of the present assessment, Kent appears to be functioning at the 1- to 2-year developmental level.

Will Kent require special class placement? If so, what type of placement is appropriate for his needs? Based on the current evaluation, Kent will require special class placement. Kent meets the entrance criteria for the Special Learning Resource classroom: performance of 4 or more standard deviations below the mean on a test of intelligence and an adaptive behavior profile that is below the moderately mentally handicapped range.

Recommendations

1. Kent should be referred for consideration for entrance into Special Education.

2. An individualized program should be developed by the appropriate teacher and school psychologist. Kent's parents should participate in program development.

less likely that he would respond to a stranger. Suggestions for evaluating challenging children like Kent are given in Box 20.3.

This case is also instructive in that it makes the diagnosis of mental retardation without appealing to questionable assessment practices. It would have been tempting to use an intelligence test outside its age range or simply make an educated guess as to the child's "IQ" (e.g., "some-where below 20"). Instead, *the examiner focused more on determining the child's needs*, making appropriate programming recommendations, and developing appropriate answers to the referral questions, rather than expending great effort to produce "the IQ." This report also follows the guideline that a good report presents and answers referral questions in a straightforward manner (see Chapter 18).

Box 20.3   Procedures for assessing individuals with severe and profound disabilities

Listed below are some unusual aspects that should be considered when assessing the intelligence of substantially disabled children and adolescents. Children such as Kent (see sample case) require special skills to evaluate with intelligence tests or other measures. Some ideas for assessing significantly impaired children are given below.

1. Sometimes severely disabled individuals are disrupted by new individuals in their environment. For this reason, examiners should always observe the child first before introducing themselves. Frequently, repetitive, stereotypic, or self-stimulatory behavior will increase in response to a new person or a new environment (e.g., a testing room). A child's home or classroom may be the best setting to use for the test session, as these children may be adversely affected by novel surroundings. In addition, the child's teacher, teacher assistant, or a parent may be used to administer some portions of the evaluation.

2. Many intelligence measures will not have a large enough number of low difficulty items to assess these significantly impaired children. Examiners should broaden their focus to assess language, gross motor, fine motor, adaptive behavior, and other skills that are at least somewhat related to cognitive development. Examiners may also need to make a dedicated attempt to describe what the child *can* do. Behavioral competencies should not be overlooked in the evaluation of the intelligence of these individuals.

3. Attentional problems are frequently present in these children. This difficulty may result in the need for more than one test session. Ideally, a second examiner or assistant should be present to record the child's responses and take notes while the examiner is testing and interacting with the child.

4. Observe the child's teacher or parents in order to determine a method for communicating with the child. Communication methods may include pantomime, gestures, sign language, eye blinking, or any other method the child may use to signify at least a yes or no response.

5. A physically disabled child may require the assistance of a physical therapist, occupational therapist, or aide to be placed in position for the testing to occur. Similarly, children should have their physical assistance devices and communication devices (e.g., a computer) at their disposal.

6. These children may require considerable rewards in order to perform up to their potential. Primary reinforcers such as food may be necessary. Similarly, it may be necessary to reinforce successive approximations to terminal behaviors in order to encourage the child to continue responding.

7. Be observant for physical limitations, illnesses, prosthetics, or medications that may be affecting intelligence test performance. An exhaustive developmental history including medical information is central for appropriate interpretation of these children's intelligence test scores.

8. Some of these children and adolescents will not possess even rudimentary skills such as imitation that are necessary to take tests. In this case, clinicians may work with the child's teacher in order to develop test-taking skills prior to an eventual evaluation.

LEARNING DISABILITIES

Definitions

The term *learning disability* (LD) is used to refer to a class of academic problems that interfere with a child's ability to acquire a particular academic skill such as reading or mathematics. Although the concept of learning disabilities has been part of the professional parlance for over a century now, this set of academic disorders still remains somewhat enigmatic, and there is considerable disagreement regarding definition of the population (Hammill, 1990; Smith, 1983). Moreover, the condition is very difficult to diagnosis because of its low base rate (see Box 20.4).

Samual Kirk (1962) offered one popular early definition of LD as follows:

> *A learning disability refers to a retardation, disorder, or delayed development in one or more of the processes of speech, language, reading, writing, arithmetic, or other school subject resulting from a psychological handicap caused by a possible cerebral dysfunction and/or emotional or behavioral disturbances. It is not the result of mental retardation, sensory deprivation, or cultural and instructional factors. (p. 263)*

Hammill (1990) reviewed the various definitions of learning disabilities and concluded that there is increasing agreement on a definition of this set of disorders. He reviewed 11 well-known definitions of learning disabilities and identified similarities. Some of the commonalities in these definitions included (Hammill, 1990):

1. *Academic underachievement.* Children with learning disabilities do not achieve up to their intellectual potential in at least one academic area.

2. *Central nervous system dysfunction.* Several of the definitions cited by Hammill (1990) presume that the etiology of the disorder is due to some neurological dysfunction.

3. *Existence of the disorder in children and adults.* Several definitions do not limit the presence of a learning disability to childhood.

Hammill concluded that the chances of agreeing on the definition of learning disabilities are now greatly improved. He predicted that the definition offered by the National Joint Committee on Learning Disabilities (NJCLD) was the one that is most likely to gain widespread acceptance:

> *Learning disabilities is a general term that refers to a heterogeneous group of disorders manifested by significant difficulties in the acquisition and use of listening, speaking, reading, writing, reasoning, or mathematical abilities. These disorders are intrinsic to the individual, presumed to be due to central nervous system dysfunc-*

Box 20.4   **The nature of the diagnosis of rare mild handicaps**

Shepard (1989) elucidates a number of difficulties in the diagnosis of mild handicapping conditions such as learning disabilities (LD). She concludes that misclassification in LD diagnosis will inevitably occur because we are attempting to detect a rare disorder with imperfect criteria. Using a validity coefficient of .75, a cross-tabulation table would reveal that 94% of the classification decisions made were accurate, but what about the 5% of the population that were classified as LD?

In this example, over half the children labeled LD were normal. Shepard (1989) amplifies this by saying that in a group of 1,000 children classified LD only 400 would actually have the disorder!

Adapted from Shepard (1989).

tion, and may occur across the life span. Problems in self-regulatory behaviors, social perception, and social interaction may exist with learning disabilities but do not by themselves constitute a learning disability. Although learning disabilities may occur concomitantly with other handicapping conditions (for example, sensory impairment, mental retardation, serious emotional disturbance) or with extrinsic influences (such as cultural differences, insufficient or inappropriate instruction), they are not the result of those conditions or influences. (NJCLD, 1988, p. 1)

This definition was the product of a committee comprised of members of several important organizations including the American Speech-Language-Hearing Association (ASHA), the Council for Learning Disabilities (CLD), the Division for Children with Communication Disorders (DCCD), the Division for Learning Disabilities (DLD), the International Reading Association (IRA), the Learning Disability Association of America (LDA), the National Association of School Psychologists (NASP), and the Orton Dyslexia Society (ODS).

The 1992 *Federal Register* contains the regulations for identifying and defining students with specific learning disabilities under the current Individuals with Disabilities Education Act legislation so that they may receive special education and related services. It is this definition that serves as the foundation for state department of education regulations regarding special education eligibility. The definition is:

"Specific learning disability" means a disorder in one or more of the basic psychological processes involved in understanding or in using language, spoken or written, that may manifest itself in an imperfect ability to listen, think, speak, read, write, spell or to do mathematical calculations. The term includes such conditions as perceptual disabilities, brain injury, minimal brain dysfunction, dyslexia and developmental aphasia. The term does not apply to students who have learning problems that are primarily the result of visual, hearing, or motor disabilities, intellectual disabilities, emotional or behavioral disorders, or environmental, cultural, or economic disadvantage. (U.S. Office of Education, 1992)

Reading Disability

Perhaps the most well-known learning disability is developmental dyslexia (now referred to as reading disability), which is characterized by extraordinary difficulty acquiring basic reading skills (see Box 20.5). This disorder was first isolated in the late 1800s (Hinshelwood, 1986; Shaywitz & Waxman, 1987). There is a long history of conceptualizing this disorder as neurologically based, although documentation of flawed neurological makeup on the part of these children has not been well documented (Stanovich, 1999).

Neuropsychological research has been fostered by the availability of more sophisticated brain-imaging technologies. Prior to the existence of sophisticated noninvasive diagnostic procedures the primary sources of evidence of neurological problems in children with learning disabilities came from more crude imaging procedures or the rare autopsy study. There is evidence emerging from recent studies that some of the neurological structures of reading-disabled children may be different from those of normal readers, and that dyslexia is by no means a visual-spatial but rather a language-based disability that adversely affects the phonological coding of information (Hynd & Semrud-Clikeman, 1989).

While the affected neurological structures remain open to debate, there is considerable consensus that the core psychological processing deficit is in phonological coding (Siegel, 1999; Stanovich, 1999).

Siegel (1999) offers the following definition of dyslexia:

Dyslexia involves difficulties with phonological processing, including knowing the relationship between letters and sounds. Over the years, a consensus has emerged that one core deficit in dyslexia is a severe difficulty with phonological processing. (p. 306)

She goes on to propose that reading disabilities are so intertwined with spelling and written language problems that a separate written expression disability cannot be demonstrated. The commingling of reading and other problems is

Box 20.5   Severe reading disability

This psychometric summary is for a child with a severe reading disability. He was evaluated in the first grade, having been retained because of failure to read. Note the vast difference between his WISC-R scores and WRMT-R scores. All of his Wechsler composite scores were average or above and yet his Woodcock Reading Mastery Tests scores were below average. His basic reading skill, or ability to identify words, reflects functional impairment with a standard score of 66. Also of interest is the fact that his mother did not learn to read until about the sixth grade.

Wechsler Intelligence Scale for Children— Revised (WISC-R)

Verbal	SS	Performance	SS
Information	9	Picture Completion	10
Similarities	12	Picture Arrangement	12
Arithmetic	9	Block Design	18
Vocabulary	9	Object Assembly	17
Comprehension	14	Coding	9
(Digit Span)	10		
Verbal Scale = 103			
Performance Scale = 123			
Full Scale = 113			

Woodcock Reading Mastery Tests— Revised (WRMT-R)

Subtest	Percentile	SS
Visual Auditory Learning	12	82
Letter Identification	0.1	34
Word Identification	1	66
Word Attack	11	82
Word Comprehension	15	84
Passage Comprehension	2	69
Readiness Cluster	0.1	54
Basic Skills Cluster	4	73
Reading Comprehension Cluster	3	72
Total Reading	3	72

represented in a definition of dyslexia offered by Padget, Knight, and Sawyer (1996, cited in Siegel, 1999, p. 306), who proposed the following definition.

> Dyslexia is a language-based learning disorder that is biological in origin and primarily interferes with the acquisition of print literacy (reading, writing, and spelling). Dyslexia is characterized by poor decoding and spelling abilities as well as deficit in phonological manipulation. These primary characteristics may co-occur with spoken language difficulties and deficits in short-term memory. Secondary characteristics may include poor reading comprehension (due to the decoding and memory difficulties) and poor written expression, as well as difficulty organizing information for study and retrieval. (p. 55)

Siegel proposes further that there is a second type of learning disability, which she refers to as "writing-arithmetic" or "output failure" disability and is defined as

> difficulty with computational arithmetic and written language, typically in the absence of reading difficulties, although, this disability can co-occur with dyslexia. They often have difficulties with spelling, fine-motor coordination, visual-spatial processing, and short-term and long-term memory (e.g., multiplication tables), but usually have good oral language skills. (p. 306)

Subtypes of either reading disability or writing-arithmetic disability have not been found consistently in the literature (Siegel, 1999). It is now clear, based on the emerging consensus referred to by Siegel, that current intelligence tests are not of value for the diagnosis of a learning disability. Just in case the reader doubts this proposition, a review of the history of failed attempts at using intelligence test results to identify LD is presented next.

Ability/Achievement Discrepancies

In opposition to the evidence currently available, intelligence tests still play a central role in the diagnosis of learning disabilities in that they are frequently used to determine whether or not there is an ability/achievement discrepancy where intelligence tests serve as the "ability" measure. The rationale for this practice goes something like this: If a child is inexplicably not achieving at a level that would be expected for his or her ability level, then a learning disability may be the culprit. An example of a significant discrepancy would be the case in which a child has an intelligence test composite score at the 98th percentile and a basic word reading test score at the 2nd percentile. The issue that is somewhat open to debate is the size of the difference required to denote a discrepancy as "significant" or "severe." Most state education agencies trying to implement the IDEA have selected a discrepancy in the range of about 1½ standard deviations (18 to 22 standard score points) as a cutoff (see Reynolds, 1984a, for an overview of the various methods used for determining severe discrepancies). In other words, if a child obtains an ability/achievement discrepancy of this magnitude or larger, then it can be considered severe. The rationale for using a discrepancy of about 1½ SD is that this would theoretically identify approximately five percent of the population as having a severe ability/achievement discrepancy.

Reynolds (1984a) has identified numerous problems with many of the methods of determining a severe discrepancy. One of the common methods is to use a single cut score regardless of intelligence level. This method is referred to as the simple standard score method by Reynolds (1984a). A criterion discrepancy of 20 points, for example, would be required if the child had an intelligence test score of 120 or 85. This method, while simple to apply, appears to by systematically biased against children with below-average intelligence test scores. In other words, it is much easier to receive the diagnosis of

LD if a child has an intelligence test score of 120 versus 85 (Shepard, 1989; Braden, 1987). One can easily imagine that it would be much more likely to obtain a reading score of less than 100 for a child with an intelligence test score of 120 than for a child with an intelligence test score of 85 to obtain a reading score of less than 65. This bias in the use of simple standard score discrepancy models is due to not taking into account the regression of achievement on intelligence (Reynolds, 1984a). If the relationship of these variables is considered, then a smaller discrepancy (<20) is required for children with low intelligence test scores and a larger discrepancy (>20) is required for children with high intelligence test scores. Use of such a "regression" model for identifying ability/achievement discrepancies for the purposes of learning disability diagnosis merely evens out the probabilities that a child of any intelligence level will be identified as having a severe discrepancy. The child with low intelligence test scores is equally likely to be diagnosed with a severe discrepancy as a child with high intelligence test scores.

Use of a statutorily defined cut score (ability/achievement discrepancy) is similar to mental retardation diagnosis in that qualifying sets of scores have been specified by many regulatory agencies. In addition to specifying the size of the ability/achievement discrepancy required to make the diagnosis of LD, many state education agencies have also specified a minimal level of intelligence (or at least one may not be mentally retarded) to be eligible for the learning disability diagnosis. Usually minimum intelligence test scores must be in the below-average range or higher (e.g., > 85). What if a severe (rare) discrepancy is found for a child? Reynolds (1984a) concluded that the presence of a severe discrepancy merely indicates that the child has an unusual difference that *may* be caused by a learning disability.

Deciding Which Composite to Use

Another interesting issue is the case in which there is a significant difference between the composite scales. What if a child obtained a Wechsler

Verbal score of 82 and Performance score of 102? Which score should be used as the criterion of intelligence for making the comparison between ability and achievement? In all likelihood the Full Scale is an average that may have little psychological meaning for the child. Some states have guidelines for deciding when the higher score can be used as the test of intelligence. Cutoff scores in many cases, however, are too rigid and do not encourage an in-depth understanding of the child being evaluated. A large V/P or other composite score discrepancy often suggests that the child's cognitive skills cannot be understood in simplistic terms. One procedure for investigating a composite score discrepancy further is to administer a second intelligence measure. While intelligence tests correlate rather highly, they do measure distinct content, which may cause them to disagree in individual cases. Administration of a second test would also help the clinician rule out situational and other confounding behavioral factors.

If a second test results in another large discrepancy in composite scores (e.g., K-ABC Seq = 84 and Sim = 108), then the examiner remains in a diagnostic quandary even though light has been shed on the child's profile of skills. One still must choose an "ability" measure—or must one? In this case the child's profile should be evaluated for consistency with other data and the diagnostic decision based on knowledge of the etiology, course, and prognosis for LD temporarily *disregarding any regulations that foster simplistic discrepancy methods.*

This heretical statement is not meant to encourage civil disobedience, but rather to emphasize that the child's needs should take precedence in making the diagnostic decision. Consider the following profile of scores.

WISC-III FS = 102, V = 82, P = 119

Binet-4 Composite = 100, V/R = 81, A/V = 117, Quant = 96, S-T   M = 98.

Word Reading standard score = 83

The profile above could be problematic for a clinician who is advised to comply with a rigid discrepancy formula of a 20-point difference between a composite intelligence test score and an academic area test score. In this case the composite scores are uninsightful, but the profile is clear. This child may suffer from *a pervasive language-based learning disability that affects intelligence and academic achievement test scores.* If background and other information supports such a diagnosis, then the intelligence composite scores are moot.

It has often been argued that the PIQ should be used as the measure of educational potential in such a case because the VIQ is tainted by the child's disability. This conclusion is, however, illogical if one is interested in predicting school achievement. I have already revealed mounds of evidence in previous chapters to show that the PIQ is a poor predictor of school achievement in comparison to the VIQ. Stanovich (1999) criticizes the entire "educational potential" concept and the over reliance on intelligence tests by saying:

> We seem to find it difficult to use this crude cognitive probe, an IQ Score, as a circumscribed behavioral index without loading social, and indeed metaphysical (Scheffler, 1985), baggage onto it. If these tests are mere predictors of school performance, let's treat them as such. If we do, performance IQ is manifestly not the predictor that we want to use, at least in the domain of literacy-based educational prediction. (p. 355)

Other Antiquated Diagnostic Practices

Early Profile Research

Profile analysis has encountered difficulty since the inception of the practice. Rapaport, Gill, and Schaffer (1945–46) began research on profile analysis in the 1940s shortly after the publication of the Wechsler-Bellevue Scales. These authors worked at the famed Meninger Clinic with adult psychiatric populations. Their text was the product of years of research aimed at using the Wechsler-Bellevue to make differential diagnoses of conditions such as schizophrenia and depression. In their classic text, *Manual of Diagnostic Psychological Testing* (Rapaport, Gill, & Schaffer, 1945–1946), which summarized their findings, the authors noted that the Wechsler scale would likely never yield characteristic profiles because of its psychometric properties. They observed:

> An ideal test for scatter analysis should contain perfectly reliable subtests completely homogeneous and factorially simple, each of which would be as independent as possible of the others. . . . Some of the publications that have appeared in the past 20 years concerning the (Wechsler-Bellevue) and the Wechsler Adult Intelligence Scale . . . has shown how far from this ideal either of the Wechsler tests is. The standardization of the W-B left a great deal to be desired so that the average scatter-grams of normal college students, Kansas highway patrolmen . . . and applicants to the Meninger School of Psychiatry . . . all deviated from a straight line in just about the same ways. (p. 161)

This early concern about the utility of profile analysis for diagnosing psychiatric populations is an important early failure that was predictive of later research seeking profiles for LD children. Some of the impetus to find characteristic profiles for LD children was provided by the implementation of PL 94-142 and the associated "child find" effort. This law created the need to search for accurate means of identifying children with learning disabilities so that all of these children could receive appropriate special education services. The WISC-R was caught up in this effort, and there was an almost feverish search to find a profile, or set of profiles, that could serve as a marker for this group of children. Many researchers focused not on ability/achievement discrepancies but on finding scatter *within the WISC-R* that could signify the presence of a learning disability. There is an enduring diagnostic controversy regarding the utility of using WISC-R profiles (V/P or shared subtest groupings) to diagnose the presence of a learning disability (Reynolds & Kaufman, 1990).

In the 1970s there was optimism that such a "marker" profile could be identified. Kaufman's (1979b) text noted some consistency in the literature regarding the ACID profile. This profile is made up of the Wechsler Arithmetic, Coding, Information, and Digit Span subtests. Kaufman (1979b) noted a tendency for samples of children with learning disabilities to score more poorly on these Wechsler subtests. Similarly, the Bannatyne categorization (see Chapter 8) seemed promising for diagnosing the presence of a learning disability. Kaufman's own enthusiasm for Wechsler profiles waned as he stated in his now-classic text.

> . . . the extreme similarity in the relative strengths and weaknesses of the typical profiles for mentally retarded, reading-disabled, and learning-disabled children renders differential diagnosis based primarily on WISC-R subtest patterns a veritable impossibility. (p. 206)

Kaufman (1979b) found Wechsler profiles more useful for theory building and testing than for clinical diagnosis of LD. A review of the problems associated with profile analysis, particularly regarding LD diagnosis, supports Kaufman's cautious stance regarding the distinctiveness of LD profiles.

WISC-R Profile Research for LD Samples

One of the more well known investigations of WISC-R profiles for LD children is the meta-analysis conducted by Kavale and Forness (1984). These researchers performed an exhaustive analysis of the ability of WISC-R profiles to differentiate samples of normal children and children with learning disabilities. They included an impressive number of studies, 94 to be exact, and they assessed the ability of a variety of profiles to differentiate learning disabled from normal children. One profile investigated by these researchers was the aforementioned ACID profile. Kavale and Forness (1984) compared the performance of normal and LD children on the ACID profile for the 94 samples included in the meta-analysis. Despite the fact that the ACID profile had been proposed as being diagnostic of learning disabilities, Kavale and Forness found the ACID profile to produce a very small effect size for differentiating normal children from those with learning disabilities. The authors found that the magnitude of the effect size of the 94 investigations produced an average scaled score equivalent for the four subtests in the ACID profile of 8.66. Given that many diagnosticians consider a significant deviation from the mean scale score of 10 to be 3 points, a deviation of 1.4 points from the average for the ACID profile hardly seems to be diagnostic of a pervasive weakness on the part of LD children.

Kavale and Forness (1984) also evaluated several possible recategorizations in addition to the ACID profile. In some cases there was a slight depression of scores for children with learning disabilities, but there was nothing that would usually be considered as approaching clinically significant.

Among other findings from the Kavale and Forness (1984) investigation was the finding of no significant differences between the normal and learning disability samples on WISC-R factor scores or on Bannatyne's recategorization of the WISC. Finally, this study debunked the myth of children with learning disabilities exhibiting more scatter than normal children (Reynolds & Kaufman, 1990), where scatter is defined as the difference between the child's highest and lowest WISC-R subtest score. The authors found *a trend for normal children to exhibit slightly more scatter than children with learning disabilities.*

Reynolds and Kaufman (1990) reiterated these findings in a review by concluding that samples of LD children exhibited about the same amount of subtest scatter as was found for the WISC-R standardization sample—about 7 to 8 scaled score points (Anderson, Kaufman, & Kaufman, 1976; Gutkin, 1979; Naglieri, 1979; Stevenson, 1979; Tabachnik, 1979; Thompson, 1980; Ryckman 1981).

Similarly, Verbal and Performance scale differences for samples of LD children have been in the 10- to 12-point range, oftentimes with a P>V profile (Anderson, Kaufman, & Kaufman, 1976; Gutkin, 1979; Naglieri, 1979; Stevenson, 1979; Thompson, 1980). While these V/P differences are potentially statistically reliable, they are by no means unusual in comparison to the V/P differences of the WISC-R nondisabled standardization sample. Differences of 10 to 12 standard score

points occurred for approximately 34% to 43% of the standardization sample (Kaufman, 1979b).

The Question of Heterogeneity

Critics of nonsupportive studies of WISC-R profile analysis of children with learning disabilities have argued, however, that many of the samples used in such investigations are too heterogeneous. They say that, for example, the learning-disability sample was made up of children with mathematics, reading, oral expression, and other types of disabilities or perhaps children who were misdiagnosed.

Unfortunately, the heterogeneity argument also does not seem valid. A well-controlled study by Semrud-Clikeman (1990) mitigates again this argument. In this study well-defined groups of normal readers, reading-disabled children, and children with attention deficit hyperactivity disorder were selected. The reading-disabled group was carefully selected from clinic cases. The reading-disabled sample was selected so as to have a history of reading failure, a difference of 20 standard score points between the WISC-R Full Scale standard score and a reading measure (with the WISC-R being the higher score), a Full Scale standard score > 85, and no history of seizure disorder, head injury, or other neurological history. It is noteworthy how even for this homogeneous sample of reading-disabled children a V/P pattern does not emerge (they were virtually identical).

There was, however, one glaringly apparent pattern that did result, and that was the difference between the WISC-R and the WRMT-R. In this study, relatively low reading achievement was a clear marker for the LD group.

Measurement Problems

McDermott, Fantuzzo, and Glutting (1990) provided a detailed review of measurement problems with profile analysis, some of which are a more sophisticated explication of the Rapaport et al. (1945–1946) concerns. Most importantly, McDermott et al. (1990) provided some insight into the reasons why so many of the LD profiling studies have produced equivocal results. McDermott et al. (1990) initially make the argument that ipsatized scores are inherently problematic. An ipsatized score is the difference score representing the difference between a child's score on a subtest and the child's mean subtest score. These are the same scores that were computed as part of the process of determining subtest strengths and weaknesses as described in Chapter 8. McDermott et al. (1990) cite numerous problems with these scores and conclude that "ipsative assessment has not been well researched, and there is ample evidence to militate against its current applications" (see Chapter 8). Composite scores such as the Verbal, Sequential, or Abstract/Visual have some evidence of factorial (construct) validity. Similarly, most of these composite scores have evidence of predictive validity, but ipsatized scores did not (McDermott et al., 1990). Finally, by virtue of their being difference scores, ipsatized scores also lack strong evidence of reliability (McDermott et al., 1990).

The Ubiquity of Scatter

Comparison to an adequate null hypothesis was another criticism of profile research (McDermott et al., 1990). One can crudely evaluate the utility of profiles for LD diagnosis by comparing the profiles of LD children to those of other groups, especially normal samples, to determine their distinctiveness from the null. There is a trend for LD children to score slightly below the normative mean, and for them to exhibit a P>V pattern. Performance-like subtests on the K-ABC are also slightly higher than other composites. Specifically, the Simultaneous scale of the K-ABC is somewhat higher than the Sequential scale (usually less than 6 points).

Implications of Profile Research

The results of LD profile analysis research suggest several implications for practice. First, the questionable and inconsistent results reiterate the necessity to deemphasize drawing shared-subtest and single-subtest conclusions. If such conclusions are offered, *it should be understood that they are likely offered based on the clinician's acumen and not on any sound research base.* Profile-based conclusions will be warranted in some cases and for such purposes the requirement of having two pieces of corroborating evidence to draw such conclusions seem minimal, especially in the context of the typical amount of data collected in an evaluation. Second, it must be concluded that intelligence test profiles remain virtually useless for diagnosing LD or its various theoretical subtypes. Third, although profiling provides no easy answers for diagnosis, it may still be beneficial for research purposes and theory building. Profiles may be statistically significant but not clinically meaningful. Such a profile could be helpful for testing a theory, even though it is too indistinctive to be clinically meaningful. Fourth, given the lack of validity and reliability evidence for profiles, one should be wary of interpreting them in causal fashion. Statements such as those below are at a high level of inference and therefore should be avoided.

"He has a cause-and-effect relationship problem that is the likely etiology of his mathematics disability."

"His spatial processing difficulty is at the root of his reading disorder."

"Her long-term memory weakness explains her mathematics problem."

Such cause-and-effect statements made on the basis of profiles are exceedingly risky and inappropriate without overwhelming corroborating evidence. Even with corroboration the clinician is making these statements without substantial, if any, research support.

LD Diagnosis Trends

Siegel (1990) concluded that intelligence tests are unnecessary for making an LD diagnosis and advises the use of reading-like processing tests in isolation. Siegel (1990) found little relationship between reading and intelligence test scores, which she maintains supports her conclusion that intelligence tests contribute little to the diagnostic process. A decade later the data to support Siegel's point of view were even more convincing.

Siegel (1992) later found that "both these groups [reading disabled (dyslexic) and poor readers] deserve the label of reading disabled and have similar problems in reading and spelling and significant problems in phonological processing, memory, and language" (p. 627). Similarly, Fletcher, Francis, Rourke, S. Shaywitz, and B. Shaywitz (1992) tested the validity of discrepancy-based definitions of reading disabilities by comparing the performances of four groups of children classified as reading disabled according to four different methods, with one group of nondisabled children on a battery of neuropsychological tests. They found no significant differences among the "disabled" children, thus calling into question the "validity of segregating children with reading deficiencies according to discrepancies with IQ scores" (p. 555). Stanovich and Siegel (1994) subsequently tested Stanovich's phonological-core variable-difference model of reading disability, again finding that "garden variety" poor readers did not differ from reading-disabled readers on measures of phonological, word recognition, and language skills. They concluded:

> If there is a special group of children with reading disabilities who are behaviorally, cognitively, genetically, or neurologically different, it is becoming increasingly unlikely that they can be easily identified by using IQ discrepancy as a proxy for the genetic and neurological differences themselves. Thus, the basic assumption that underlies decades of classification in research and educational practice regarding reading disabilities is becoming increasingly untenable. (p. 48)

In the light of this research the dominant emerging proposal is to use academic achievement tests, such as those discussed in Chapter 14, to make the diagnosis of a learning, especially reading, disability. Moreover, the consensus seems to be that the cut score for a reading disability should be set at about a standard score of 85 with some flexibility built in (Stanovich, 1999). This proposal is both revolutionary and parsimonious. First, it disavows the use of intelligence tests for making the diagnostic decision. Second, and of great political interest, this methodology requires that each individual considered as LD show functional impairment (see Gordon, Lewandowski, & Keiser, 1999). Specifically, by abandoning the notion of severe discrepancy, individuals with average or better reading scores can no longer be considered LD just because of having high intelligence test results. The effects of such a change would be enormous in that the "gifted LD" field would disappear and university students would find it more difficult to obtain the diagnosis of LD and receive accommodations in school (see Gordon et al., 1999, for a thorough discussion of these issues). Third, LD would be capable of being diagnosed with a simple word reading test (e.g., K-TEA Reading Decoding, WRAT-3 Reading, etc.). This prospect may cause concern about the qualifications of examiners.

Based on current evidence, I have concluded that intelligence tests are most appropriately used in a learning disability evaluation to *identify cognitive comorbidities that may affect educational achievement*. Some intelligence tests may be well suited to identifying the short- and long-term memory, spatial/visualization, or other cognitive problems that are not core deficits of LD but, rather, affect prognosis and response to remediation. In a similar fashion the sphygmomanometer, cardiac stress test, and other measures are not central to the diagnosis of diabetes in adulthood. These tests are crucial, however, for ruling out some of the common comorbidities such as high blood pressure and heart disease. Just as an individual with diabetes and heart disease has a poorer prognosis due to the comorbidity, it would seem reasonable that an individual with LD with long-term memory deficits would be at greater risk for poor educational outcomes.

CONCLUSIONS

This chapter reviewed research on the use of intelligence tests with individuals with mental retardation and learning disabilities with a focus on identifying distinct diagnostic profiles. This search was predictably futile. Modern diagnostic standards require a broader assessment in cases of MR, and the LD field is moving forward with proposals to disentangle intelligence testing altogether from the LD diagnostic process. Intelligence tests will continue to be useful adjuncts to the LD assessment process just as behavior rating scales are useful for ruling out comorbid psychopathology. Intelligence tests will still be needed, if for no other reason, to rule out comorbidities such as MR.

CHAPTER SUMMARY

- Most modern diagnostic systems for mental retardation are based on the criteria set by the American Association on Mental Retardation (1992).

- Mental retardation is a condition marked by *dual deficits* in intelligence and adaptive behavior.

- Most diagnostic systems mimic the DSM-IV by defining significantly below-average intelligence as a standard score (M=100, SD=15 or 16) of about 70 or below.

- Adaptive behavior scales assess the degree to which an individual meets the standards of personal independence and social responsibility expected for a child's age or cultural group (Grossman, 1983).

- One of the oldest and most widely used measures of adaptive behavior is the Vineland Adaptive Behavior Scale (Sparrow et al., 1984).

- Intelligence test composite score profiles are *useless for making differential diagnoses* of MR and reading disability.

- *Rigid cut scores should not be used when making diagnoses based on intelligence test results.*

- In cases in which there are composite score differences with some scores within the mental retardation range and others are outside this range, *the examiner should explain why the diagnostic decision was made*, whatever that decision may be.

- Psychologists should not expect intelligence and parent-reported adaptive behavior scores to show a great deal of agreement, especially when the child is outside the mental retardation range.

- *Adaptive behavior scales are the tests of choice for differentiating between levels of mental retardation.*

- *An intelligence test should never be used outside its age range to produce a norm-referenced score to be used in making diagnostic decisions.*

- The term *learning disability* is used to refer to a class of academic problems that interfere with a child's ability to acquire a particular academic skill.

- Developmental dyslexia, which is characterized by extraordinary difficulty acquiring basic reading skills, was first isolated in the late 1800s.

- Intelligence tests currently play a central role in the diagnosis of learning disabilities, where they are used to determine whether or not there is an ability/achievement discrepancy.

- Profile analysis has encountered difficulty since the inception of the practice.

- Kaufman (1979b) found Wechsler profiles more useful for theory building and testing than for clinical diagnosis of LD.

- Kavale and Forness found the ACID profile to produce a very small effect size for differentiating normal children from those with learning disabilities.

- Reynolds and Kaufman (1990) concluded that samples of children with learning disabilities exhibit about the same amount of subtest scatter as was found for the WISC-R standardization sample—about 7 to 8 scaled score points.

- McDermott, Fantuzzo, and Glutting (1990) provided a detailed review of measurement problems with profile analysis, some of which are a more sophisticated explication of the Rapaport et al. (1945–1946) concerns.

- New methods for diagnosing learning disabilities are evolving, and the role of intelligence tests in this diagnostic process may be changed dramatically as the discrepancy-based diagnostic model is called into question.

Intelligence Test Interpretation Research

SCIENTIFIC CONSIDERATIONS AND ASSUMPTIONS (SEE CHAPTER 17)

Study Selection

The majority of studies included in Appendix A were aimed at identifying the latent traits underlying test scores, and profiles are typically factor analytic. Therefore, criteria for identifying technically adequate factor analyses had to be addressed. The considerations that I used for including factor analytic studies were:

Sample Size

I chose primarily large, national standardization samples where N equaled approximately 200 or greater.

Sample Composition

I selected both exceptional and nationally representative samples for inclusion.

Differing Interpretations of the Same Results

I favored a "preponderance-of-evidence" criterion when alternative interpretations needed to be reconciled. In his landmark factor analytic study of nearly 500 data sets, Carroll (1993) found that several Stratum I reading, spelling, and writing abilities loaded with the "g_c" (crystallized ability) factor for several data sets. In one large-scale factor analytic investigation, McGrew (1997) found a reading/writing factor that differed from a "g_c" factor. I think that Carroll's findings represent a preponderance of evidence in comparison to the single study of McGrew

(1997). Consequently, I subsume reading and writing abilities under the Stratum II "g_c" ability.

Differing Results Given the Same Interpretations

An example of this scenario is as follows. On one hand, Cohen (1959) labels the third WISC factor as Freedom from Distractibility; he characterizes it so "primarily due to the loadings of subtests which clearly do not involve memory (Mazes, Picture Arrangement, Object Assembly), but which it seems reasonable to suppose are quite vulnerable to the effects of distractibility" (p. 288). On the other hand, Blaha and Wallbrown (1996) assign the same label as Cohen to the third factor with significant loadings only for the Arithmetic and Digit Span subtests. Again, I invoke the preponderance-of-evidence rule to make a decision regarding the conclusion to be drawn. Most studies have found the Arithmetic and Digit Spans subtests to load on this factor. They have also, however, found little evidence that inattention/distractibility is likely to be the central latent trait assessed by this factor (Kamphaus, 1998).

Types of Evidence

There is not a clear consensus on the issue of weighting evidence differentially. Although it may seem that factor analytic studies have been reified to a special status in the evaluation of intelligence test validity, other forms of validity may be equally if not more important depending on the issue under study. If, for example, the research question deals with the issue of using an intelligence test for differential diagnosis, then I would weigh research on various diagnostic groups more heavily than factor analytic findings.

The Preponderance of Evidence

This premise means that Carroll's multisample factor analytic work will be proportionally more influential than single factor analytic investiga-

tions when disagreements arise between studies. When referring to identification of the latent trait assessed by the WISC-III third factor again, for example, Carroll (1994) asserts that "the WISC-III was not designed for factor analysis because the various factors that it may measure—at least beyond the Verbal and Performance factors—are not represented adequately by the multiple measures of those factors" (p. 138). I agree that the measure of inattention/distractibility via the third factor is unsupportable. Drawing conclusions, however, is clouded by scenarios where both positive and negative findings exist. In this case I make an arbitrary decision.

Exploratory versus Confirmatory Methods

Generally speaking, confirmatory factor analytic methods have gained considerable popularity over exploratory methods in modern factor analysis. I think that confirmatory methods may also result in more scientifically useful tests of factor structure (see Kamphaus, Benson, Hutchinson, & Platt, 1994, for an example). Therefore, I prefer such methods over traditional factor analysis.

Myopic Research Evidence

Carroll (1993) makes a compelling argument that factor analyses of tests such as the WISC-III are likely to produce noncontributory results because of the nature of the scale. I try, whenever possible, to draw conclusions regarding research that is consistent with findings of other disciplines (e.g., cognitive psychology).

Lack of Evidence

I appreciate that some intelligence test interpretations are not necessarily invalid in the absence of research. They could be found valid if they are studied. Clearly, psychology is no different from medicine and other professions where professionals have to take action or make nonscientifically based interpretations in unusual cases and circumstances. A lack of evidence should not be allowed to limit experimentation. I have and will draw interpretations that are case specific and untested.

Theoretical Evidence

Some test interpretations may be untested, and yet they may be based on a theory that has some empirical support. McGrew and Flanagan (1998), for example, provide a comprehensive test interpretation manual that, of necessity, often theorizes about the fit of intelligence test subtests and scales with Horn's version of "g_f-g_c" theory. They posit, for example, about the Stratum II and Stratum III abilities measured by numerous tests, including the WAIS-III and WPPSI-R. Their speculation about the abilities measured by the WAIS-III, for example, is essentially theoretical since the WAIS-III has not been factor analyzed jointly with well-validated measures of Horn's theory. Such theoretical propositions are of primary assistance to researchers and of potential assistance to practitioners. In fact, speculation based on considerable prior research and explicit theory is likely better than speculation based on idiosyncratic theories or from a poorly articulated theory that is untestable. Nevertheless, I give theoretical evidence less weight than the results of research evidence.

Incorporating New Evidence

My summary of extant interpretive research is outdated on its date of publication. We have the good fortune now to be part of the Internet, which provides for quicker dissemination and updates of findings. Readers of this text should assume incompleteness and build on the research summarized here with continuing education activities. Having presented this caveat, it is also clear that some research findings have stood the test of time. One would be hard-pressed, for example, to find new evidence that vocabulary measures are, in fact, measures of spatial abilities.

Applicability of Research from Previous Editions

Fortunately, even the venerable Wechsler scales are evolving in a manner that precludes automatic generalization of previous findings to current editions. I think that some findings, such as the futility of using the PA subtest to measure social judgment, are applicable to the WISC-III and WAIS-III. The addition of the Symbol Search subtest, however, may make factor analytic evidence for the WISC-R less relevant for understanding the WISC-III third and fourth factors.

Definition of Terms

Intelligence testing research is characterized by similar sounding terms that are offered without operational definitions. For instance, I do not know the extent to which terms such as *Spatial:Mechanical*, *Visualization*, *Perceptual Organization*, and *Spatial Organization without Essential Motor Activity* are interchangeable. Moreover, I admit to not having a sound working definition of terms such as *integrated brain functioning*, which precludes me from using such a term for interpretation. *Do not make interpretations for which you do not have a working definition.*

Summary Table of Intelligence Test Research Findings

Test	Solutions	Summary	Conclusion
WISC-III	Two factor	The consistency of the WISC-III and the WPPSI-R Verbal Comprehension and Perceptual Organization factors was investigated using cross-validation of covariance structure models applied to the data from the respective normative samples of the tests (Allen & Thorndike, 1995b).	This study extended the examination of factor invariance to a larger number of age groups within the WISC-III and the WPPSI-R, as well as utilized contemporary, advanced methodology to this end. In summary, the two-factor structure consisting of Verbal Comprehension and Perceptual Organization was confirmed (Allen & Thorndike, 1995).
	Three factor	The WISC-III was factor analyzed for the national standardization sample without including the Symbol Search subtest (Reynolds & Ford, 1994).	With the Symbol Search subtest deleted from the analyses, the third factor, Freedom from Distractibility, appeared to be as stable on the WISC-III as on the WISC-R. A three-factor solution is therefore supported, with the third factor being comprised of Arithmetic, Digit Span, and Coding (Reynolds & Ford, 1994).
	Four factor	The WISC-III was factor analyzed for the national standardization sample (Wechsler, 1991).	The four-factor (corresponding to the index scores) solution was deemed most appropriate based on a variety of criteria, including confirmatory factor analytic fit statistics (Wechsler, 1991).
	WISC-III vs. WISC-R	The WISC-III was administered to 257 children who were administered the WISC-R earlier. The sample was comprised of 118 children with specific learning disabilities, 79 with mental retardation, and 60 who were not classified (Slate & Saarnio, 1995).	The data showed that the WISC-III Full Scale, Verbal, and Performance IQs were 7.2, 5.8, and 7.5 points lower than the corresponding WISC-R scores (Slate & Saarnio, 1995).
	WISC-III Cluster subtypes	Representative cluster subtypes based on factor Index scores were examined in the standardization sample of the WISC-III (Donders, 1996).	In this study, five primary cluster subtypes were found. Further, the results indicated support for the presence of the fourth factor, Processing Speed (Donders, 1996).
	WISC-III Index vs. IQ scores	This study tabulated the frequency distributions of standard score discrepancies between the WISC-III IQ and Index scores for 202, 115, and 159 children who were identified as having	In this study, it was found that IQ and Index score discrepancies were present, but not significant enough to be practical indicators of abnormalities. Further, as with prior research

Summary Table of Intelligence Test Research Findings (continued)

Test	Solutions	Summary	Conclusion
	WISC-III Index vs. IQ scores (cont.)	a specific learning disability, mental retardation, or no specific classification (Slate, 1995).	related to the WISC-R, it was found that Performance IQ scores were higher than Verbal IQ scores for each of the three groups (Slate, 1995).
	WISC-III vs. WISC-R	A sample of 61 children with learning impairments were administered the WISC-III 2.5 to 3 years subsequent to administration of the WISC-R (Bolen, Aichinger, Hall, & Webster, 1995).	As a result, all WISC-III IQs were significantly lower than their WISC-R counterparts. The mean differences were 5.20 for VIQ, 9.21 for PIQ, and 7.95 for FSIQ (Bolen, Aichinger, Hall, & Webster, 1995).
	Short-form WISC-III	The effectiveness of the Vocabulary/Block Design subtest short form as an estimate of the WISC-III Full Scale IQ was examined for 197 special education students in public school settings (Herrera-Graf, Dipert, & Hinton, 1996).	The findings indicated that the Vocabulary/Block Design short form correlated highly with FSIQs, but that they had little value for special education classification purposes or for prediction (Herrera-Graf, Dipert, & Hinton, 1996).
WISC-R	One factor	The factor structure of the WISC-R was studied in a sample of 829 children having Full Scale IQs equal to or above 120. The described factorial solutions were determined by parallel and minimum average partial analyses (Macmann, Placket, Barnett, & Siler, 1991).	Although the data yielded some support for a two-factor solution for the WISC-R, analyses indicated stronger support for a one-factor solution representing verbal, as opposed to general, ability (Macmann, Placket, Barnett, & Siler, 1991).
	One factor	Confirmatory factor analysis was used to assess the validity of the WISC-R for the normative sample and for 11 additional samples (O'Grady, 1989).	The data indicated that the practice of interpreting a third factor, Freedom from Distractibility, is not supported. Further, although no single factor solution was clearly favored, it was found that a sizable proportion of performance on the WISC-R can be attributed to a general intellectual factor (O'Grady, 1989).
	Two factor	The WISC-R was factor analyzed using subjects from the standardization sample for both upper and lower SES groups (Carlson, Reynolds, & Gutkin, 1983).	The data demonstrated a strong degree of similarity between the upper and lower SES groups as well as support for the existence of a Verbal Comprehension and Perceptual Organization factor (Carlson, Reynolds, & Gutkin, 1983).

(Continues)

Summary Table of Intelligence Test Research Findings (continued)

Test	Solutions	Summary	Conclusion
	Two factor (Language Comprehension and Visual-Spatial Organization)	The WISC-R was factor analyzed for a sample of 368 deaf and hard-of-hearing children ranging in age from 6 to 16 years (Sullivan & Schulte, 1992).	The results of this study yielded a two-factor solution for hearing-impaired children on the WISC-R. The factors were named Language Comprehension (l) and Visual-Spatial Organization (v-s). Also, among this sample, the Arithmetic and Digit Span subtests loaded on the l factor, and Coding loaded on the v-s factor (Sullivan & Schulte, 1992).
	Three factor	Confirmatory factor analysis was used to test one-, two-, three-, and four-factor models of the WISC-R for psychiatric and standardization samples (Anderson & Dixon, 1995).	The results of this study provided confirmatory factor analytic support of Kaufman's three-factor model of the WISC-R (Verbal Comprehension, Perceptual Organization, and Freedom from Distractibility) which has had previous support from exploratory factor analyses (Anderson & Dixon, 1995).
	Three factor	This study conducted confirmatory factor analyses of the WISC-R and the Hong Kong-Wechsler Intelligence Scale for Children (HK-WISC) using the normative samples of the respective tests (Lee & Lam, 1988).	The results of this study suggested that the three-factor model is applicable to American and Hong Kong Chinese children, as well as the across-the-age cohorts of 7, 10, and 13 for the HK-WISC. The invariance of the factor structure across cultures and age groups lent support to the use of the Wechsler scales for differing cultures and age groups as long as the test is normed and adapted for use with a particular group (Lee & Lam, 1988)
	Five factor (Language, Academic Achievement, Visual Spatial, Attention & Memory, Motor Speed)	Psychoeducational test scores from the records of 360 children were factor analyzed. The results were compared to factors cited as characterizing neuropsychological test batteries such as the Luria–Nebraska and the Halstead-Reitan. The psychoeducational battery yielded five factors: Language, Academic Achievement, Visual Spatial, Attention and Memory, and Motor Speed (Sutter, Bishop, & Battin, 1986).	In this study, the Language factor was comprised mostly of the WISC-R Verbal scale. Academic Achievement, the second factor, had highest loadings on language arts subtests such as reading, grammar, and spelling. Each test that loaded on the Visual Spatial factor involved positioning objects or shapes in space, similar to such factors on neuropsychological tests. Attention and Memory, the fourth factor, consisted of tests used to measure short-term

Summary Table of Intelligence Test Research Findings (continued)

Test	Solutions	Summary	Conclusion
	Five factor (cont.)		attention and retention. The Freedom from Distractibility factor subtests on the WISC-R did not appear in this factor for this analysis, as Arithmetic and Coding probably loaded more closely on other factors. The fifth factor, Motor Speed, only had two tests load on it, but it was clear that a fine motor speed skill using paper and pencil (e.g., Coding) was being tapped (Sutter, Bishop, & Battin, 1986).
	Third factor (Freedom from Distractibility)	This study investigated the characteristics of the third factor, Freedom from Distractibility, of the WISC-R by comparing it to constructs believed to underlie certain neuropsychological instruments using combined factor analysis (Ownby & Matthews, 1985).	The results of this study suggested that a number of various cognitive abilities may be related to Freedom from Distractibility. Thus, this finding indicates that the term *Freedom from Distractibility* is inappropriate in that it oversimplifies the ability measured by this third factor (Ownby & Matthews, 1985).
	Third factor criterion related validity	The relationship among the Conners Teacher Rating Scale, the Revised Conners Parent Rating Scale, the Revised Problem Behavior Checklist, and the Freedom from Distractibility factor of the WISC-R was investigated for a sample of 135 children newly referred to a pediatric neurology learning disabilities clinic (Cohen, Becker, & Campbell, 1990).	The results indicated only one significant, expected correlation for the ADHD-related subscales used in the study. There was a moderate, negative correlation between the Freedom from Distractibility factor on the WISC-R and the ADD/H subscale on the Conners Teacher Rating Scale when the Verbal Comprehension and Perceptual Organization factors were controlled. Thus, as this was the only relationship found, it appears that Freedom from Distractibility is not a solid measure of attention deficit (Cohen, Becker, & Campbell, 1990).
	Third factor & ACID Pattern	The ACID profile (deficits jointly on Arithmetic, Coding, Information, and Digit Span subtests) and the factor structure of the WISC-R was studied for a sample of 526 children who were treated at a psychiatric hospital: 151 inpatients, 307 outpatients, and 68	Results indicated that even though the ACID pattern was present for the total psychiatric population and was more significant in the day-hospital patients, only three children showed this pattern. Further, the data suggested that a deficit in the Freedom from Distractibility

(Continues)

Summary Table of Intelligence Test Research Findings (continued)

Test	Solutions	Summary	Conclusion
	Third factor & ACID Patterns (cont.)	day-hospital patients (Greenblatt, Mattis, & Trad, 1991).	factor can be found across different psychiatric disorders. The number was lowest for the ADD and ADD/H group, and also seemed to occur with about equal frequency for the remainder of the psychiatric groups. Thus, the findings suggest that attention as tapped by the WISC-R is not specific to diagnoses of ADD or ADD/H as it is found across different psychiatric groups. Further, the authors found Block Design to have a significant loading on the Freedom from Distractibility factor (Greenblatt, Mattis, & Trad, 1991).
	Block Design	The Dutch adaptation of the WISC-R was administered to 770 children in the Netherlands. Stimulus characteristics of the Block Design tasks were varied to determine if analytic versus synthetic problem-solving strategies were used (Spelberg, 1987).	Results indicated that in all subgroups at each age level, the subjects mostly used an analytic problem-solving strategy on this subtest, although it is not impossible that a synthetic strategy could be used. This was determined from the presence of a strong relationship between the number of interior edges and item performance (Spelberg, 1987).
	WISC-R Subtest Reliability	This study assessed the test-retest reliability of the WISC-R over a 3-year period for a sample of children classified as learning disabled (Truscott, Narrett, & Smith, 1994).	The reliabilities for the first to third testing for the Verbal IQ, Performance IQ, and Full Scale IQ were .72, .72, and .81. Further, the subtest reliabilities over 6 years range from .21 to .81 with a median of .54. Picture Arrangement (.21) was found to be the most unreliable subtest across that total sample as well as the subsample, with a range from .21 to .40. Block Design only had consistently high reliabilities across all analyses, ranging from .78 to .81 (Truscott, Narrett, & Smith, 1994).
	WISC-R & Adaptive Behavior	The WISC-R factor deviation quotients (DQ) were calculated for Verbal Comprehension (VCDQ), Perceptual Organization (PODQ), and Freedom from Distractibility (FDDQ)	The VCDQ and Verbal IQ scores were fundamentally equal predictors of adaptive behavior, but the PODQ and Performance IQ scores were not. Thus, the findings suggest that

Summary Table of Intelligence Test Research Findings (continued)

Test	Solutions	Summary	Conclusion
	WISC–R & Adaptive Behavior (cont.)	factors for 83 referred children. These scores were then compared to scores on the Adaptive Behavior Scale—School Edition (ABS-SE) (Huberty, 1986).	verbal comprehension is a common construct that underlies the WISC-R and the ABS-SE (Huberty, 1986).
	WISC–R Correlation with PIC	The WISC-R was correlated with the Personality Inventory for Children (PIC) for a sample of 129 children, some of whom were receiving special education (Wielkiewicz & Daood, 1993).	Modest, negative correlations were obtained between the WISC-R IQS and the Achievement, Intellectual Screening, and Development scores of the PIC (range = .27 to .49). The PIC Anxiety scale correlated .22 with the Full Scale IQs (Wielkiewicz & Daood, 1993).
	WISC–R Stability	The WISC-R was administered to 130 children who had received the WISC-R from 1 to 5 years earlier. All children were referred for continuing academic difficulties (Bauman, 1991).	Results showed that the mean IQ scores for the first administration of the WISC-R were 86.50, 90.14, and 87.39 respectively, for the VIQ, PIQ, and FSIQ. Retest scores were 82.41, 91.79, and 85.71. Thus, there were significant losses for VIQ and FSIQ, indicating that IQs of children with learning difficulties are not as stable as once believed (Bauman, 1991).
WISC	Bannatyne's (1974) Pattern	This study evaluated the predictive validity of Bannatyne's (1974) Spatial, Conceptual, and Sequential categorization of the WISC subtests for a sample of 179 children (McKay, Neale, & Thompson, 1985).	The findings of this study lent some support to the belief that low-ability readers typically demonstrate poor performance on the Sequential category of the WISC. However, results also indicated that Bannatyne's scheme was of little use in differentiating students with and without learning disabilities (McKay, Neale, & Thompson, 1985).
WAIS–R	One factor	In this study, a simultaneous maximum likelihood confirmatory factor analysis of the intercorrelations among the 11 subsets of the WAIS-R was conducted for the nine age groups in the standardization sample (O'Grady, 1983).	The results suggest that a single-factor structure best fits the WAIS-R across age groups. None of the multifactor models fit the data any better, leading to the conclusion that the WAIS-R consists of a single general intellectual factor (O'Grady, 1983).
	Cluster analysis	This study analyzed the intercorrelations among the subtests of the WAIS-R for the nine	Results of the cluster analysis showed that a single-factor solution was as adequate as two-

(Continues)

Summary Table of Intelligence Test Research Findings (continued)

Test	Solutions	Summary	Conclusion
	Cluster analysis (cont.)	age groups in the standardization sample (Silverstein, 1985).	and three-factor solutions. Hence, it was recommended that for practical reasons, the WAIS-R be regarded as measuring a single, general intellectual factor (Silverstein, 1985).
	Two factor	In this study, WAIS-R scores for 234 incarcerated persons were factor analyzed (Faulstich, Mcanulty, Gresham, Veitia, Moore, Bernard, Waggoner, & Howell, 1986).	The results of this investigation identified two factors, Perceptual Organization and Verbal Comprehension. These findings support the interpretation of Performance and Verbal IQs on the WAIS-R for incarcerated populations (Faulstich et al., 1986).
	Two factor	The standardization samples for the WAIS and the WAIS-R were factor analyzed (Silverstein, 1982c).	Results of the analyses supported the presence of two factors, Verbal Comprehension and Perceptual Organization (Silverstein, 1982c).
	Two factor	In this study, the factor structure of the WAIS and the WAIS-R was investigated using two samples of 198 and 276 neuropsychiatric patients (Warner, Ernst, & Townes, 1986).	The results of this study supported similar two-factor solutions for both the WAIS and the WAIS-R. Freedom from Distractibility, the third factor, accounted for only a small portion of the total variances. Further, the composition of the third factor was inconsistent between samples, thus showing weak, if any support for the third factor (Warner, Ernst, & Townes, 1986).
	Two factor	In this study, an exploratory principal axis factor analysis was conducted on the WAIS-R performance of 345 persons receiving vocational guidance services (Athanasou, 1993).	Results of this investigation yielded a two-factor solution, one consisting of Verbal subtests, and the other of Performance subtests (Athanasou, 1993).
	Two factor	This study used data reported in three previous factor analytic studies of the WAIS-R for the purpose of further studying its factor structure. The researchers used an alternative factor analytic technique, FACTOREP, which reduces the influences of the general factor and error variance (Siegert, Patten, Taylor, & McCormick, 1988).	The results of this study indicated strong support for two factors on the WAIS-R and little evidence to support the presence of a third factor (Siegert, Patten, Taylor, & McCormick, 1988).

Summary Table of Intelligence Test Research Findings (continued)

Test	Solutions	Summary	Conclusion
	Two factor	Factor analyses of the WAIS-R standardization sample were conducted for samples grouped by sex and race (Kaufman, McLean, & Reynolds, 1991).	The analyses supported the division of the WAIS-R into Verbal and Performance factors. Further, differences pertaining to sex-related findings in patients with unilateral brain damage were found in the factor structures for males and females across ages. Results also indicated that Black females and males may use differing strategies to solve verbal and nonverbal tasks on the WAIS-R (Kaufman, McLean, & Reynolds, 1991).
	Two factor (Verbal Comprehension Deviation Quotient and Perceptual Organization Deviation Quotient)	The WAIS-R was investigated using orthogonal and oblique factor analyses on the standardization sample (Gutkin, Reynolds, & Galvin, 1984).	As a result, the researchers found a two-factor solution for the WAIS-R. However, the first factor (typically termed as Verbal Comprehension) was redefined as the Verbal Comprehension Deviation Quotient, which contains the Information, Vocabulary, Comprehension, and Similarities subtests. The second factor (typically termed as Perceptual Organization) was redefined as the Perceptual Organization Deviation Quotient, which consists of the Block Design and Object Assembly subtests (Gutkin, Reynolds, & Galvin, 1984).
	Two factor (Verbal Comprehension Deviation Quotient and Perceptual Organization Deviation Quotient)	In this study, a modified confirmatory factor analysis was conducted to refine factor analytic solutions found by Plake, Gutkin, and Kroeten (1984) to provide a more complete comparison of the factor solutions offered by Wechsler (1981) and Gutkin, Reynolds, & Galvin (1984) (Plake, Gutkin, Wise, & Kroeten, 1987).	The results of the study support Gutkin, Reynolds, and Galvin's (1984) proposed model for the factor structure of the WAIS-R. In this model, the verbal factor is represented by the scores on the Information, Vocabulary, Comprehension, and Similarities subtests. The performance factor is represented by scores on the Block Design and Object Assembly subtests (Plake, Gutkin, Wise, & Kroeten, 1987).
	Three factor	In this study, WAIS-R scores for 204 persons with low intelligence were factor analyzed (Atkinson & Cyr, 1988).	As a result, the researchers found that the three-factor structure is stable with regards to those in the lower end of intellectual ability (Atkinson & Cyr, 1988).

(Continues)

Summary Table of Intelligence Test Research Findings (continued)

Test	Solutions	Summary	Conclusion
	Three factor	The dimensional structure of the WAIS-R was examined using multisample confirmatory factor analytic procedures for samples of 200 Anglo and 200 Mexican American adults (Geary & Whitworth, 1988).	This study supported the presence of a three-factor solution for the WAIS-R (Verbal Comprehension, Perceptual Organization, and Freedom from Distractibility). Further, it was found that performance on the Freedom from Distractibility and Perceptual Organization factors was not affected by cultural differences between the Anglo and Mexican American samples. However, performance on the Verbal Comprehension tasks may have been affected by the bilingualism of the Mexican American sample (Geary & Whitworth, 1988).
	Three factor	In this article, ten factor analytic studies done on the WAIS-R standardization sample and various patient samples were reviewed for the purpose of drawing conclusions pertaining to the WAIS-R factor structure based on these findings (Leckliter, Matarazzo, & Silverstein, 1986).	The reviewers concluded that although the results of each study varied depending on the author's theoretical orientation and methodology, a three-factor solution (Verbal Comprehension, Perceptual Organization, and Memory/Freedom from Distractibility) appears to offer the best source of hypotheses for cognitive ability (Leckliter, Matarazzo, & Silverstein, 1986).
	Three factor	In this study, the factor structure of the WAIS-R was examined using a series of restricted factor analyses on the nine cohorts of the WAIS-R standardization sample (Waller & Waldman, 1990).	As a result, it was found that a three-factor model (Verbal Comprehension, Perceptual Organization, and Memory/Freedom from Distractibility) best fits the WAIS-R for eight out of the nine standardization cohorts (Waller & Waldman, 1990).
	Three factor	In this study, the factor structure of the WAIS-R was examined in a sample of 200 general medical patients and a sample of 271 psychiatric patients and then compared to that of the WAIS-R normative sample and a sample of 84 vocational counseling patients as well as an additional sample of 114 psychiatric patients (Beck, Horwitz, Seidenberg, Parker, & Frank, 1985).	A three-factor solution (Verbal Comprehension, Perceptual Organization, and Freedom from Distractibility) was supported across all of the studied samples, suggesting that the WAIS-R has a robust factor structure and that a three-factor solution is applicable to psychiatric and medical populations (Beck, Horwitz, Seidenberg, Parker, & Frank, 1985).

Summary Table of Intelligence Test Research Findings (continued)

Test	Solutions	Summary	Conclusion
	Three factor	In this study, the WAIS-R was factor analyzed across the nine age cohorts in the standardization sample (Parker, 1983).	As a result, it was found that a three-factor structure (Verbal Comprehension, Perceptual Organization, and Freedom from Distractibility) was supported (Parker, 1983).
	Three factor	Cross-validation of covariance structure models were used to test the stability of the Verbal Comprehension, Perceptual Organization, and Freedom from Distractibility factors of the WAIS-R and the WISC-III (Allen & Thorndike, 1995a).	As a result, it was concluded that the original three-factor structure of the WAIS-R and WISC-III is robust and stable across age groups (Allen & Thorndike, 1995a).
	Three factor	The three-factor solution for the WAIS-R in a sample of 260 adults with suspected head injury was compared with neuropsychological tests measuring similar abilities (Sherman, Strauss, Spellacy, & Hunter, 1995).	Results indicated that the three-factor solution of the WAIS-R presented relatively good construct validity based on correlations with neuropsychological tests (Sherman, Strauss, Spellacy, & Hunter, 1995).
	Two factor and Three factor	In this study, six objective methods for determining the number of factors in the structure of the WAIS-R were utilized and examined (Naglieri & Kaufman, 1983).	As a result, it was determined that two- and three-factor solutions were most appropriate for the WAIS-R (Naglieri & Kaufman, 1983).
	One factor, Two & Three factor	This study utilized six hierarchical clustering methods for each of the nine age cohorts in the WAIS-R standardization sample (Fraboni & Saltstone, 1992).	As a result, varying degrees of support were found for one- ("g"), two- (Verbal Comprehension, Perceptual Organization), and three- (Verbal Comprehension, Perceptual Organization, Freedom from Distractibility) factor solutions for the WAIS-R, suggesting that there might be three reasonable solutions (Fraboni & Saltstone, 1992).
	Vernon's model ("g," v:ed, k)	A hierarchical factor analysis was conducted on the nine age groups of the WAIS-R standardization sample (Blaha & Wallbrown, 1982).	The researchers found a structural arrangement based on Vernon's model at all age levels of the WAIS-R standardization sample. The hierarchical model consisted of a strong general ("g") factor, a major group factor akin to the verbal-educational (v:ed) dimension, and a minor group factor analogous to the spatial-perceptual (k) dimensions from Vernon's

(Continues)

Summary Table of Intelligence Test Research Findings (continued)

Test	Solutions	Summary	Conclusion
	Vernon's model ("g," v:ed, k) (cont.)		paradigm. These findings support the validity of the WAIS-R as a measure of "g," and support the division of Verbal and Performance IQs (Blaha & Wallbrown, 1982).
	Vernon's model ("g," k:m, VC, FD)	A hierarchical factor analysis was conducted on a sample of 232 learning-disabled adults' scores on the WAIS-R (Blaha, Mandes, & Swisher, 1987).	The researchers found a structural arrangement based on Vernon's paradigm for this sample. The hierarchical model consisted of a somewhat weak general ("g") factor, and a primary level including spatial-perceptual-mechanical (k:m), verbal comprehension (VC), and Freedom from Distractibility (FD) factors (Blaha, Mandes, & Swisher, 1987).
Digit Span		This article describes major research findings pertaining to the Wechsler Digit Span subtests in relation to psychoeducational assessment (Mishra, Ferguson, & King, 1985).	Conclusions state that forward and backward components can be looked at separately. Further, it was found that Digit Span is not only a measure of memory, but also attention, sequencing, numerical skills, mnemonic strategy use, and speed of item identification (Mishra, Ferguson, & King, 1985).
Demographic variables		In this study, the WAIS-R standardization sample was analyzed to determine relationships between intellectual abilities and demographic variables (Chastain & Joe, 1987).	The analyses yielded a general factor representing crystallized ability (Cattell, 1943) with high loadings on all 11 subtests of the WAIS-R, race, occupation, and education. A performance factor representing fluid ability was found with loadings on the Performance subtests of the WAIS-R, age, and single marital status. A third factor indicated a manual dexterity factor for males on the Block Design subtests (Chastain & Joe, 1987).
Speed of Performance		The effect of response time on WAIS-R subtest scores of 213 normal individuals age 75 years or older was investigated using principal components analysis on the 11 subtest scores, response time scores (obtained from the Picture	Results yielded three factors: Verbal Comprehension, Perceptual Organization, and Response Time (consisting of Block Design, Picture Arrangement, and Object Assembly). A second principal components analysis was

Summary Table of Intelligence Test Research Findings (continued)

Test	Solutions	Summary	Conclusion
	Speed of Performance (cont.)	Arrangement, Block Design, and Object Assembly subtests), and age (Ryan, Bohac, & Trent, 1994).	conducted controlling for time, but these results were ambiguous, indicating that the first analysis was more sound (Ryan, Bohac, & Trent, 1994).
WAIS	Two factor	A principal-components factor analysis was conducted on the standardization sample of the original WAIS and the Spanish version, the Escala de Inteligencia Wechsler para Adultos (EIWA) (Gomez, Piedmont, & Fleming, 1992).	The results of this study supported a two-factor solution representing the Verbal and Performance scales on the EIWA and the WAIS (Gomez, Piedmont, & Fleming, 1992).
	Two factor and Three factor	A factor analysis was conducted on the urban standardization sample (n=2,029) and the rural standardization sample (n=992) of the mainland Chinese version of the WAIS, the Wechsler Adult Intelligence Scale—Revised for China (WAIS-RC) (Dai, Gong, & Zhong, 1990).	As a result, a two-factor solution was supported for the urban sample (Verbal Comprehension and Perceptual Organization) and a three-factor solution was supported for the rural sample (Verbal Comprehension, Perceptual Organization, and Freedom from Distractibility) (Dai, Gong, & Zhong, 1990).
	Gender differences	Men and women from the standardization sample (n=1,406) of the Wechsler Adult Intelligence Scale—Revised for China (WAIS-RC) were matched on variables of education, age, and vocation to investigate gender differences on performance on the WAIS-RC (Dai, Ryan, Paolo, & Harrington, 1991).	Results of the study showed that men scored higher than women on Verbal, Performance, and Full Scale IQs and presented a different pattern of subtest scores. Although the differences were statistically significant, the score distributions for males and females were similar, calling into question clinical significance. Further, both genders produced a two-factor solution (Verbal Comprehension and Perceptual Organization) per factor analysis (Dai, Ryan, Paolo, & Harrington, 1991).
	Third factor (Freedom from Distractibility)	WAIS scores of 111 mentally retarded individuals were factor analyzed. The results of this factor analysis were correlated with the individuals' scores on the Adaptive Behavior Scale (ABS) to assess the validity of the term *Freedom from Distractibility* for the third factor	The results failed to support any of the author's hypotheses. Instead of assessing attention, it appeared that the third factor was more cognitive in nature, perhaps measuring memory or numerical ability. Thus, it was concluded that Freedom from Distractibility may not be an

(Continues)

Summary Table of Intelligence Test Research Findings (continued)

Test	Solutions	Summary	Conclusion
	Third factor (Freedom from Distractibility) (cont.)	of the WAIS. The author hypothesized that if this third factor was a measure of attention, it would have a strong relationship with the Hyperactive Tendencies domain of the ABS, have lower correlations with the cognitive domains of the ABS, and have a lower correlation with the general factor of the WAIS (Roszkowski, 1983).	appropriate term for the third factor of the WAIS (Roszkowski, 1983).
	Subtests	This study utilized the Parker, Hanson, and Hunsley (1988) meta-analytic procedures to estimate the validities for the WAIS subtests across a variety of measures related to intelligence (Hanson, Hunsley, & Parker, 1988).	The most reliable WAIS composite, the Full Scale IQ can be expected to predict approximately 42% of the variance in relevant criterion measures, and the WAIS subtests can be expected to predict about 20% of the variance (Hanson, Hunsley, & Parker, 1988).
KAIT	Two factor	In this study, results on the Kaufman Adolescent and Adult Intelligence Test (KAIT) for samples of Whites (n=1,535), African Americans (n=226), and Hispanics (n=140) were factor analyzed (Kaufman, A, Kaufman, J., & McLean, 1995).	Results yielded "g," fluid, and crystallized factors across race/ethnic groups (Kaufman, A., Kaufman, J., & McLean, 1995).
K-ABC	One factor	In this study, confirmatory factor analysis was used on the standardization sample to investigate the factor structure of the K-ABC, specifically to test the hypothesis that the factors that make up the test are only moderately correlated (Strommen, 1988).	The results showed that the factors (Simultaneous Processing, Sequential Processing, and Achievement) comprising the K-ABC are substantially intercorrelated. Thus, this indicated that the K-ABC cannot distinguish these constructs in a distinct manner, making interpretation of the K-ABC factors questionable (Strommen, 1988).
	Two factor	Results of K-ABC administrations for 61 individuals age 50 and above with severe intellectual impairment were factor analyzed (Hogg & Moss, 1995).	The factor analysis yielded two factors: Simultaneous Processing and Sequential Processing, similar to the factor structure that has been demonstrated for younger children. The Achievement subtests loaded on these two

Summary Table of Intelligence Test Research Findings (continued)

Test	Solutions	Summary	Conclusion
	Two factor (cont.)		factors instead of creating a separate factor (Hogg & Moss, 1995).
	Three factor	This study investigated the factor structure of the K-ABC as used with 172 Egyptian children. Confirmatory and exploratory factor analyses were conducted with this sample and results were compared to that of the standardization sample (Elwan, 1996).	Results indicated that the factor structure of the K-ABC for the Egyptian children was similar to the specified structure of the K-ABC (Simultaneous Processing, Sequential Processing, and Achievement) (Elwan, 1996).
	Three factor	The K-ABC standardization sample in addition to samples of White (n=887) and African American (n=345) children were analyzed using four statistical methods for the purpose of assessing the congruence of the factor structure of the K-ABC for these two groups (Fan, Willson, & Reynolds, 1995).	Results indicated that the factor structure of the K-ABC is similar for groups of White and African American children, thus supporting the validity of interpreting K-ABC scores for children of different ethnicities. These results also provide support for the construct validity of the K-ABC for these two groups of children (Fan, Willson, & Reynolds, 1995).
	Construct bias	In this study, multisample confirmatory factor analysis was used to test for construct bias across groups of Black (n=486) and White (n=813) children (Keith, Fugate, DeGraff, Diamond, Shadrach, & Stevens, 1995).	Results suggested that the K-ABC measures indistinguishable abilities in Black and White children at ages 7 through 8, but that some differences existed between Black and White children at ages 9 through 12. Upon reexamination of the second group, it was found that the differences were due to measurement issues, as opposed to true construct differences (Keith, Fugate, DeGraff, Diamond, Shadrach, & Stevens, 1995).
	Low vs. High functioning	In this study, the K-ABC and the Stanford-Binet, Form L-M were administered to 93 preschool children at risk for learning problems. These children were divided into lower and higher ability groups per median split on the Stanford-Binet (Bloom, Allard, Zelko, Brill, Topinka, & Pfohl, 1988).	Results showed that the Stanford-Binet and K-ABC yielded close to identical results for the higher ability group, but that scores on the K-ABC for the lower ability group were significantly higher than those on the Stanford-Binet. Thus, the ability of the K-ABC to discriminate among preschoolers at risk for learning problems is called into question (Bloom, Allard, Zelko, Brill, Topinka, & Pfohl, 1988).

(Continues)

Summary Table of Intelligence Test Research Findings (continued)

Test	Solutions	Summary	Conclusion
	Cognitive Complexity	This study evaluated the complexity of abilities measured by the K-ABC and the WISC-R for a sample of 146 children referred for special services (Kline, Guilmette, Snyder, & Castellanos, 1992).	Findings indicated that the abilities tapped by the Mental Processing scale of the K-ABC are not as complex as those measured by the WISC-R. However, the K-ABC Achievement scales appear to assess skills as complex as those on the WISC-R. Thus, the relative cognitive complexity of the K-ABC and WISC-R seems to be similar as long as all subtests of the K-ABC are given (Kline, Guilmette, Snyder, & Castellanos, 1992).
	Hemispheric functioning	The relationship between the K-ABC and neuropsychological ability in 79 neurologically impaired children was studied in an attempt to interpret K-ABC results in the light of a hemispheric specialization model. Hemispheric functioning was assessed by finding the mean performance level on several neuropsychological measures of lateralized function. The relationship between the WISC-R and neuropsychological performance was also examined for comparison (Morris & Bigler, 1987).	The results of this study provided some support for a hemispheric model of interpreting K-ABC Simultaneous and Sequential Processing scores. The correlation between Simultaneous Processing (K-ABC) and right-hemisphere functioning was stronger than the correlation between Performance IQ (WISC-R) and right-hemisphere functioning, but the correlation between Sequential Processing (K-ABC) and left-hemisphere functioning was not as strong as the correlation between Verbal IQ (WISC-R) and left-hemisphere functioning (Morris & Bigler, 1987).
	Profile variability index	The profile variability index (PVI), a measure of IQ subtest variability, was evaluated for external validity. A sample of 146 referred children were each given the K-ABC, SB-IV, and the WISC-R, and PVIs were calculated for each child for each instrument (Kline, Snyder, Guilmette, & Castellanos, 1993).	As a result, the profile variability as measured by the PVI on the K-ABC and the WISC-R had essentially no external validity. That is, the relationship between the PVIs on the K-ABC and WISC-R and the children's achievement, as well as discrepancies between their actual and predicted achievement levels were all nonsignificant. Further, on the SB-IV, variability had a positive relationship with higher academic achievement rather than indicating poor achievement (Kline, Snyder, Guilmette, & Castellanos, 1993).

Summary Table of Intelligence Test Research Findings (continued)

Test	Solutions	Summary	Conclusion
	K-ABC and Attention	Results of the scores of 52 referred children on the K-ABC and the Continuous Performance Test (CPT) were analyzed to determine the relationship between attention and performance on the K-ABC (Gordon, Thomason, & Cooper, 1990).	As a result, significant interrelationships were found among the K-ABC and the CPT. This study suggests that since about 25% of the variance in this sample was accounted for by the CPT, the function of attention in intellectual ability needs to be further investigated (Gordon, Thomason, & Cooper, 1990).
DAS	DAS & LD	In this study, the DAS was administered to 53 children with learning disabilities approximately 3 years after each child had been given the WISC-III. The relationship between the results of these two tests was analyzed (Dumont, Cruse, Price, & Whelley, 1996).	As a result, it was found that the General Conceptual Ability (GCA), Verbal Cluster, and Spatial Cluster scores of the DAS were not significantly different from the Full Scale, Verbal, and Performance scores of the WISC-III. The Nonverbal Reasoning Cluster scores of the DAS were significantly different from the Verbal and Performance scores of the WISC-III. In addition, it was found that congruent constructs on the two tests were highly correlated. Further, 96% of the children classified as learning disabled from the WISC-III received an analogous classification on the DAS (Dumont, Cruse, Price, & Whelley, 1996).
	DAS & LD	In this study, the performance characteristics of 83 children classified as learning disabled on the DAS were investigated (Shapiro, Buckhalt, & Herod, 1995).	Results showed that this group of children scores low on many subtests of the DAS in comparison to the normative sample. The validity of the DAS scores was also demonstrated by significant correlations with children's past scores on the WISC-R and achievement tests (Shapiro, Buckhalt, & Herod, 1995).
	DAS and core profile types	In this study, cluster analytic procedures were used to determine the core ability profiles that are most representative of the school-age norm group from the standardization sample on the DAS (Holland & McDermott, 1996).	As a result, seven core profile types described in terms of ability level, achievement, subtest configuration, and demographic trends were discovered: high, above average, slightly above average, slightly below average with higher verbal, slightly below average with higher spatial, below average, and low (Holland & McDermott, 1996).

(Continues)

Summary Table of Intelligence Test Research Findings (continued)

Test	Solutions	Summary	Conclusion
WJ-R	Uniqueness and General Factor Characteristics of the WJTCA-R	This study examined the uniqueness and general factor characteristics of the Woodcock-Johnson Tests of Cognitive Ability—Revised (WJTCA-R) using selected subjects from the standardization sample (McGrew & Murphy, 1995).	As a result, it was found that only 2 of the 19 subtests of the WJTCA-R had low general factor loadings (Visual Closure and Incomplete Words). Further, only 2 of the 19 subtests had low uniqueness (Listening Comprehension and Cross Out). The remaining subtests had medium to high uniqueness and general factor loadings (McGrew & Murphy, 1995).
	Intracognitive scatter on the WJ-R	This study examined the relationship between school achievement and the number of significant intracognitive strengths and/or weaknesses (scatter) on the Woodcock-Johnson Psycho-Educational Battery—Revised (WJ-R) using 2,974 school-age subjects from the standardization sample (McGrew & Knopik, 1996).	Results of this study suggest that an individual's total number of significant intracognitive strengths and/or weaknesses on the WJ-R has little diagnostic importance with regards to low or underachievement in mathematics, reading, and/or written language (McGrew & Knopik, 1996).
	"g_f-g_c" clusters & writing achievement	This study investigated the relationship between the seven "g_f-g_c" cognitive clusters of the WJTCA-R (Long-Term Retrieval, Short-Term Memory, Visual Processing, Auditory Processing, Processing Speed, Comprehension-Knowledge, Fluid Reasoning) and written language achievement as measured by the Basic Writing Skills and Written Expression clusters of the WJ-R using the standardization sample (McGrew & Knopik, 1993).	Results indicated that performance on the Processing Speed, Auditory Processing, Comprehension-Knowledge, and Fluid Reasoning WJTCA-R cognitive clusters was significantly related to performance on measures of writing mechanics and fluency of written expression as measured by the Basic Writing Skills and Written Expression clusters of the WJ-R. Thus, it appears that measures of vocabulary knowledge and speed of mental processing are most related to writing achievement across the life span (McGrew & Knopik, 1993).
	"g_f-g_c" clusters & math achievement	This study investigated the relationship between the seven "g_f-g_c" cognitive clusters of the WJTCA-R (Long-Term Retrieval, Short-Term Memory, Visual Processing, Auditory Processing, Processing Speed, Comprehension-Knowledge, Fluid Reasoning) and mathematics achievement as measured by the Basic Mathematics Skills and Mathematics Reasoning	Results indicated that performance on the Processing Speed, Comprehension-Knowledge, and Fluid Reasoning WJTCA-R cognitive clusters was significantly related to performance on measures of mathematics calculation and basic knowledge and mathematics problem solving and applications as measured by the Basic Mathematics Skills and Mathematics

Summary Table of Intelligence Test Research Findings (continued)

Test	Solutions	Summary	Conclusion
	"g_f–g_c" clusters & math achievement (cont.)	clusters of the WJ-R using the standardization sample (McGrew & Hessler, 1995).	Reasoning clusters of the WJ-R. Thus, it appears that measures of fluid reasoning, verbal knowledge, and speed of mental processing are most related to mathematics achievement across the life span (McGrew & Hessler, 1995).
	Three-stratum theory of cognitive abilities	This study used hierarchical confirmatory factor analysis to test the three-stratum theory of intelligence as measured by the WJ-R. Developmental changes across the life span in the structure of cognitive abilities were also examined (Bickley, Keith, & Wolfle, 1995).	Results of the study indicated that no significant changes in the structure of intelligence develop with age. Further, the findings support the three-stratum theory as being an adequate model for conceptualizing intelligence (Bickley, Keith, & Wolfle, 1995).
	WJTCA factor solutions	Exploratory factor analyses were conducted using the school-age standardization samples of the Woodcock-Johnson Tests of Cognitive Ability (WJTCA). In addition, parallel analyses using two samples of referred public school children (n=251, n=210) were conducted (McGrew, 1987).	As a result of this study, it was found that there are a number of alternative factor solutions for the WJTCA. Overall, a two-factor structure is supported as the simplest solution. Three- and four-factor analyses suggest the existence of three factors: reasoning, verbal, and speeded visual perceptual. This solution may provide for more meaningful interpretation of the WJTCA although it changes by school grade level. The four-factor standardization solution also produced an auditory and/or sequential factor. However, interpretation of this fourth factor is questionable, as it was found to be weak (McGrew, 1987).
	W-J/COG factor structure	In this study, the Woodcock-Johnson Cognitive Battery (W-J/COG) was factor analyzed using data from the standardization sample for ages preschool through adulthood (Kaufman & O'Neal, 1988).	Results suggested that there is only one meaningful factor present for the preschool group, but that there are three factors present for grades 1 through 12 and ages 20–65+, named Verbal Ability, Perceptual Speed, and Reasoning. Also, loadings on the general ("g") factor were found to increase through adulthood (Kaufman & O'Neal, 1988).

(Continues)

Summary Table of Intelligence Test Research Findings (continued)

Test	Solutions	Summary	Conclusion
	WJ-R Tests of Achievement factor structure	Exploratory factor analysis was conducted to examine the factor structure of the Woodcock-Johnson—Revised Tests of Achievement using the standardization data (Sinnett, Rogg, Benton, Downey, & Whitfill, 1993).	As a result, two factors, as opposed to the several factors posited by the authors of the WJ-R, were found. The major factor, use and comprehension of language, is thought to represent general intellectual ability. Number skill, the second factor, was somewhat small in comparison. Thus, it was concluded that the use of discrepancies amongst the WJ-R scores and discrepancies between the WJ-R and intelligence scores is not warranted for evaluating individuals for learning disabilities (Sinnett, Rogg, Benton, Downey, & Whitfill, 1993).
SB-IV	Factor structure	The factor structure of the SB-IV was studied using confirmatory factor analytic procedures on a sample of 50 children aged 2–6 years and 137 children aged 7–11 years who were not a part of the standardization sample. The factor models proposed by the test authors and by Sattler (1988) were tested (Gridley & McIntosh, 1991).	As a result of this investigation, it was found that the four-factor model as proposed by the authors of the SB-IV was not supported for either age group. This finding is similar to that found in earlier factor analyses (e.g., Keith et al., 1988; Kline, 1989; Ownby & Carmen, 1988; Reynolds et al., 1987). The Verbal, Quantitative, Abstract/Visual, and Memory area scores were not supported for the children aged 2–6 years. The authors propose that either a two- or three-factor model may better fit the structure of the SB-IV for this group. For the children aged 7–11 years, neither the four-factor model proposed by the test authors or Sattler's three-factor model fit the structure for this group. However, the authors proposed that a modified four-factor model may better fit this age group, allowing some subtests of the SB-IV to load on more than one factor (Gridley & McIntosh, 1991).
	SB-IV factor structure for 3-year-olds	In this study, the factor structure of the SB-IV was examined for a sample of 50 three-year-old children. Further, the relationship between the verbal scores on the SB-IV and the verbal scores	The results of this study indicate that the four-factor model described by the test authors of the SB-IV is not accurate for 3-year-old children. In this study, factor analyses identified only verbal

Summary Table of Intelligence Test Research Findings (continued)

Test	Solutions	Summary	Conclusion
	SB-IV factor structure for 3-year-olds (cont.)	from the McCarthy Scales of Children's Abilities was studied (Molfese, Yaple, Helwig, Harris, & Connell, 1992).	and nonverbal factors, but the subtest construction of these two factors is as of yet uncertain. However, it was found that the verbal scores of the SB-IV do correlate strongly with the McCarthy verbal scores (Molfese, Yaple, Helwig, Harris, & Connell, 1992).
	Elevation, Shape, & Variability of SB-IV & WISC-R and K-ABC	In this study, numerical indices of profile elevation, shape, and variability were calculated on a sample of 146 referred children's scores on the SB-IV, K-ABC, and WISC-R. This was done to assess whether the validity of scatter information for predicting achievement is any greater for the SB-IV and the K-ABC than the WISC-R (Kline, Snyder, Guilmette, & Castellanos, 1992).	Results of this study indicated that elevation was the most important predictor of achievement in the SB-IV, K-ABC, and WISC-R. Profile variability had no validity for this purpose for any of the intelligence measures. Further, profile shape had only moderate predictive properties for the WISC-R. Thus, it appears that profile shape and variability have little or no predictive value for achievement in any of the intelligence measures examined (Kline, Snyder, Guilmette, & Castellanos, 1992).
	Concurrent validity of SB-IV with the MAT-SF & KTEA	In this study, the relationship between the Matrix Analogies Test—Short Form (MAT-SF), the SB-IV, and academic achievement as assessed by the Kaufman Test of Educational Achievement—Brief Form (KTEA-BF) was investigated in 71 referred children (Prewett & Farhney, 1994).	Results of this study supported the concurrent and criterion-related validity of the MAT-SF. More specifically, the MAT-SF correlated significantly with the SB-IV Area and Test Composite scores, and with the Mathematics, Reading, and Spelling scores of the KTEA-BF (Prewett & Farhney, 1994).
	Comparison of WISC-III and SB-IV scores	In this study, the WISC-III and SB-IV were administered to 73 referred inner-city students having low socioeconomic status for the purpose of comparing their performance on each of these measures (Prewett & Matavich, 1994).	Results of this study indicated that although the WISC-III and SB-IV were highly correlated, they did not give the same diagnostic impressions with this sample of children. On average, the scores on the WISC-III Full Scale IQ were 9.4 points lower than on the SB-IV Test Composite. Thus, there could be differences in diagnosis with this population. Specifically, only 7 of 34 children diagnosed with mental retardation (IQ below 70) on the WISC-III obtained scores in this range on the

(Continues)

Summary Table of Intelligence Test Research Findings (continued)

Test	Solutions	Summary	Conclusion
	Comparison of WISC-III and SB-IV scores (cont.)		SB-IV. However, caution should be taken in interpreting these results, as they may not necessarily generalize to other populations (Prewett & Matavich, 1994).
	Validity of the Composite SAS	In this study, the validity of the Composite Standard Age Score (SAS) of the SB-IV was investigated in a sample of 119 persons as an adequate measure of intellectual ability in persons with mental retardation (Spruill, 1996).	As a result of this investigation, it appears that the Composite SAS of the SB-IV is not an accurate reflection of the overall intellectual abilities of many persons with mental retardation. More specifically, in cases where there is a discrepancy among the four Area SASs (Verbal Reasoning, Abstract/Visual Reasoning, Quantitative Reasoning, and Short-Term Memory), the Composite SAS is closest to the lowest Area SAS score as opposed to representing an aggregate of all four Area SASs (Spruill, 1996).
	Comparison of SB-IV and Form L-M	This study examined the floors of the SB-IV and the Stanford-Binet Form L-M for persons with mental retardation (Wilson, 1992).	As a result of this study, the author concluded that the high floor of the SB-IV makes it inadequate for the assessment of children under age 5 who are believed to have mild mental retardation, or for any person thought to have severe or profound mental retardation. As the Stanford-Binet Form L-M has had a history of successful use with such populations, it is recommended that this form be used until a more adequate test is created (Wilson, 1992).

REFERENCES

Ackerman, P. T., Dykman, R. A., & Oglesby, D. M. (1983). Sex and group differences in reading and attention disordered children with and without hyperkinesis. *Journal of Learning Disabilities, 16*(7), 407–415.

Ackerman, P. T., Dykman, R. A., & Peters, J. E. (1976). Hierarchal factor patterns on the WISC as related to areas of processing deficit. *Perceptual and Motor Skills, 42*, 381–386.

Alexander, H. B. (1922). A comparison of ranks of American states in Army Alpha and in social-economic status. *School and Society, 16*, 388–392.

Algozzine, B., Ysseldyke, J., & Shinn, M. (1982). Identifying children with learning disabilities: When is a discrepancy severe? *Journal of School Psychology, 20*, 299–305.

Allen, S. R., & Thorndike, R. M. (1995a). Stability of the WAIS-R and WISC-III factor structure using cross-validation of covariance structures. *Journal of Clinical Psychology, 51*(5), 648–657.

Allen, S. R., & Thorndike, R. M. (1995b). Stability of the WPPSI-R and WISC-III factor structure using cross-validation of covariance structure models. *Journal of Psychoeducational Assessment, 13*, 3–20.

American Educational Research Association, American Psychological Association, and National Council on Measurement in Education. (1999). *Standards for educational and psychological testing*. Washington, DC: Author.

American Psychiatric Association. (1994). *Diagnostic and statistical manual of mental disorders* (4th ed.). Washington, DC: Author.

American Psychological Association. (1965). Pickets at APA headquarters protest psychological tests. *American Psychologist, 20*, 871–872.

American Psychological Association. (1985). *Standards for educational and psychological testing*. Washington, DC: Author.

American Psychological Association (APA) Committee on Professional Standards and Committee on Psychological Tests and Assessment. (1986). *Guidelines for computer-based tests and interpretations*. Washington, DC: Author.

American Psychological Association. (1992). *Ethical principles of psychologists*. Washington, DC: Author.

Amrine, M. (1965). The 1965 congressional inquiry into testing. *American Psychologist, 20*, 859–861.

Anastasi, A. (1983). *Review of the Kaufman Assessment Battery for Children*. [Machine-readable data file]. Latham, NY: Buros Review Service.

Anastasi, A. (1984). The K-ABC in historical and contemporary perspective. *Journal of Special Education, 18*, 357–366.

Anastasi, A. (1985). Testing the test: Interpreting the scores from multiscore batteries. *Journal of Counseling and Development, 64*, 84–86.

Anastasi, A. (1986). Intelligence as a quality of behavior. In R. J. Sternberg & D. K. Detterman (Eds.), *What is intelligence: Contemporary viewpoints on its nature and definition*. Norwood, NJ: Ablex. pp. 19–21.

Anastasi, A. (1988). *Psychological testing* (6th ed.). New York: Macmillan.

Anastasi, A. (1989). Review of the Stanford-Binet Intelligence Scales: Fourth Edition. *Tenth mental measurements yearbook*. Lincoln, NE: Buros Institute.

Anastasi, A., & Urbina, S. (1998). *Psychological testing* (7th ed). New York: Prentice-Hall.

Anderson, R. J., & Sisco, F. H. (1977). *Standardization of the WISC-R Performance scale for deaf children*. Washington, DC: Gallaudet University, Office of Demographic Studies.

Anderson, T., & Dixon, W. E., Jr. (1995). Confirmatory factor analysis of the Wechsler Intelligence Scale for Children—

Revised with normal and psychiatric adolescents. *Journal of Research on Adolescence, 5*(3), 319–332.

Angoff, W. H. (1988). The nature-nurture debate, aptitudes, and group differences. *American Psychologist, 43,* 713–720.

Applegate, B., & Kaufman, A. S. (1989). Short form of K-ABC sequential and simultaneous processing for research and screening. *Journal of Clinical Child Psychology, 18*(4), 305–313.

Aram, D. M., & Eisele, J. A. (1994). Intellectual stability in children with unilateral brain lesions. *Neuropsychologia, 32,* 85–95.

Aram, D. M., Ekelman, B. L., Rose, D. F., & Whitaker, H. A. (1985). Verbal and cognitive sequelae following unilateral lesions acquired in early childhood. *Journal of Clinical and Experimental Neuropsychology, 7,* 55–78.

Archer, R. P., Maruish, M., Imhof, E. A., & Piotrowski, C. (1991). Psychological test usage with adolescent clients: 1990 survey findings. *Professional Psychology: Research and Practice, 22,* 247–252.

Ardila, A., & Rosselli, M. (1996). Soft neurological signs in children: A normative study. *Developmental Neuropsychology, 12,* 181–200.

Arthur, G. A. (1947). *Point Scale of Performance Tests: Form II*(rev.). New York: The Psychological Corporation.

Arthur, G. (1950). *The Arthur Adaptation of the Leiter International Performance Scale.* Chicago: Stoelting.

Athanasou, J. A. (1993). Patterns of performance on the Verbal and Performance subtests of the Wechsler Adult Intelligence Scale—Revised; Some Australian data. *Journal of Clinical Psychology, 49*(1), 102–108.

Atkinson, L., & Cyr, J. J. (1988). Low IQ samples and WAIS-R factor structure. *American Journal on Mental Retardation, 93*(3), 278–282.

Atkinson, R. C., & Shiffrin, R. M. (1971). The control of short-term memory. *Scientific American, 225,* 82–90.

Avery, R. O., Slate, J. R., & Chovan, W. (1989). A longitudinal study of WISC-R and WAIS-R scores with students who are Educable Mentally Handicapped. *Education of Training of the Mentally Retarded, 24*(1), 28–31.

Aylward, G. P. (1992). Review of the Differential Ability Scales. In J. J. Kramer & J. C. Impara (Eds.), *The eleventh mental measurements yearbook* (pp. 281–282). Lincoln: University of Nebraska Press.

Aylward, G. P., & MacGruder, R. W. (1986). *Test Behavior Checklist (TBC).* Brandon, VT: Clinical Psychology Publishing.

Ayres, R. R., Cooley, E. J., & Severson, H. H. (1988). Educational translation of the Kaufman Assessment Battery for Children: A construct validity study. *School Psychology Review, 17*(1), 113–124.

Baddeley, A., & Gathercole, S. (1999). Individual differences in learning and memory: Psychometrics and the single case.

In P. L. Ackerman, P. C. Kyllonen, & R. D. Roberts (Eds.), *Learning and individual differences: Process, trait, and content determinants* (pp. 31–54). Washington, DC: Author.

Bagnato, S. J., & Neisworth, J. T. (1989). *System to plan early childhood services.* Circle Pines, MN: American Guidance Service.

Bailey, D. B., Jr., Vandiviere, P., Dellinger, J., & Munn, D. (1987). The Battelle Developmental Inventory: Teacher perceptions and implementation data. *Journal of Psychoeducational Assessment, 3,* 217–226.

Baltes, P. B. (1986). Notes on the concept of intelligence. In R. J. Sternberg & D. K. Detterman (Eds.), *What is intelligence? Contemporary viewpoints on its nature and definition* (pp. 23–27). Norwood, NJ: Ablex.

Banich, M. T., Levine, S. C., Kim, H., & Huttenlocher, P. (1990). The effects of developmental factors on IQ in hemiplegic children. *Neuropsychologia, 28,* 35–47.

Bannatyne, A. (1974). Diagnosis: A note on recategorization of the WISC scale scores. *Journal of Learning Disabilities, 7,* 272–274.

Barber, T. X. (1973). Pitfalls in research: Vine investigator and experimenter effects. In R. M. W. Travers (Ed.), *Second handbook of research on teaching* (pp. 382–404). Chicago: Rand McNally.

Bardos, A. N., Naglieri, J. A., & Prewett, P. N. (1992). Gender differences on planning, attention, simultaneous, and successive cognitive processing tasks. *Journal of School Psychology, 30,* 293–305.

Bardos, A. N., Softas, B. C., & Petrogiannis, R. K. (1989). Comparison of the Goodenough-Harris and Naglieri's Draw-a-Person scoring systems for Greek children. *School Psychology International, 10,* 205–209.

Barkley, R. A. (1988). Attention. In M. Tramontana & S. Hooper (Eds.), *Issues in child clinical neuropsychology* (pp. 145–176). New York: Plenum Press.

Barkley, R. A. (1989). Attention deficit-hyperactivity disorder. In E. J. Mash & R. A. Barkley (Eds.), *Treatment of childhood disorders* (pp. 39–72). New York: Guilford.

Barkley, R. A. (1997). Attention-deficit/hyperactivity disorder, self-regulation, and time: Toward a more comprehensive theory. *Journal of Developmental and Behavioral Pediatrics, 18,* 271–279.

Barnes, T., & Forness, S. (1982). Learning characteristics of children and adolescents with various psychiatric diagnoses. In R. Rutherford (Ed.), *Severe behavior disorders of children and youth* (pp. 32–41). Austin, TX: Pro-Ed.

Barry, B. J. (1983). *Validity study of the Kaufman Assessment Battery for Children compared to the Stanford-Binet, Form L-M, in the identification of gifted nine- and ten-year-olds.* Unpublished master's thesis, National College of Education, Chicago, IL.

Barry, B., Klanderman, J., & Stripe, D. (1983). Study number one. In A. S. Kaufman & N. L. Kaufman (Eds.), *Kaufman Assessment Battery for Children: Interpretive manual* (p. 94). Circle Pines, MN: American Guidance Service.

Batchelor, E. S., & Dean, R. S. (Eds.). (1996). *Pediatric neuropsychology: Interfacing assessment and treatment for rehabilitation.* Needham Heights, MA: Simon & Schuster.

Batchelor, E., Sowles, G., Dean, R. S., & Fischer, W. (1991). Construct validity of the Halstead-Reitan Neuropsychological Battery for Children with learning disorders. *Journal of Psychoeducational Assessment, 9,* 16–31.

Bauer, J. J., & Smith, D. K. (1988, April). *Stability of the K-ABC and the S-B:4 with preschool children.* Paper presented at the meeting of the National Association of School Psychologists, Chicago.

Bauman, E. (1991). Stability of WISC-R scores in children with learning difficulties. *Psychology in the Schools, 28*(2), 95–100.

Bayley, N. (1969). *Bayley scales of infant development.* New York: Psychological Corporation.

Beardsworth, E., & Harding, L. (1996). Developmental neuropsychology and the assessment of children. In L. Harding & J. R. Beech (Eds.), *Assessment in neuropsychology* (pp. 16–46). New York: Routledge.

Beaumont, J. G. (1983). *Introduction to neuropsychology.* New York: Guilford Press.

Beck. F. W., & Lindsey, J. D. (1986). Visually impaired students' degree of visual acuity and their verbal intelligence quotients. *Educational and Psychological Research, 6*(1), 49–53.

Beck, N. C., Horwitz, E., Seidenberg, M., Parker, J., & Frank, R. (1985). WAIS-R factor structure in psychiatric and general medical patients. *Journal of Consulting and Clinical Psychology, 53*(3), 402–405.

Beitchman, J. H., Patterson, P., Gelfand, B., & Minty, G. (1982). IQ and child psychiatric disorder. *Canadian Journal of Psychiatry, 27,* 23–28.

Belmont, J. M. (1989). Cognitive strategies and strategic learning: The socio-instructional approach. *American Psychologist, 44,* 142–148.

Bender, W. N. (1995). *Learning disabilities: Characteristics, identification, and teaching strategies* (2nd ed.). Boston: Allyn & Bacon.

Bennett, T. L., & Ho, M. R. (1997). The neuropsychology of pediatric epilepsy and antiepileptic drugs. In C. R. Reynolds & E. Fletcher-Janzen (Eds.), *Handbook of clinical child neuropsychology* (2nd ed., pp. 517–538). New York: Plenum Press.

Bennett, T. L., & Krein, L. K. (1989). The neuropsychology of epilepsy: Psychological and social impact. In C. R. Reynolds and E. Fletcher-Janzen (Eds.), *Handbook of clinical child neuropsychology* (pp. 419–441). New York: Plenum Press.

Benson, J. (1998). Developing a strong program of construct validation: A test anxiety example. *Educational Measurement: Issues and Practice, 17,* 10–22.

Benton, A. L. (1980). The neuropsychology of facial recognition. *American Psychologist, 35,* 176–186.

Benton, A. L., Hamsher, K., Varney, N. R., & Spreen, O. (1983). *Contributions to neuropsychological assessment: A clinical manual.* New York: Oxford University Press.

Berg, R. A., & Linton, J. C. (1997). Neuropsychological sequelae of chronic medical disorders in children and youth. In C. R. Reynolds & E. Fletcher-Janzen (Eds.), *Handbook of clinical child neuropsychology* (2nd ed., pp. 663–687). New York: Plenum Press.

Berk, R. A. (1982). *Handbook of methods for detecting test bias.* Baltimore: Johns Hopkins University Press.

Berninger, V. W., & Abbott, R. D. (1994). Redefining learning disabilities: Moving beyond aptitude-achievement discrepancies to failure to respond to validated treatment protocols. In G. Reid Lyon (Ed.), *Frames of reference for the assessment of learning disabilities: New views on measurement issues.* Baltimore: Paul H. Brookes Publishing.

Beutler, L. E., & Davison, E. H. (1995). What standards should we use? In S. C. Hayes, V. M. Follette, R. M. Dawes, & K. E. Grady (Eds.), *Scientific standards of psychological practice: Issues and recommendations* (pp. 11–24). Reno, NV: Context Press.

Beutler, L. E., Williams, R. E., Wakefield, P. J., & Entwistle, S. R. (1995). Bridging scientist and practitioner perspectives in clinical psychology. *American Psychologist, 50,* 984–994.

Bever, T. G. (1975). Cerebral asymmetries in humans are due to the differentiation of two incompatible processes: Holistic and analytic. In D. Aaronson & R. Rieber (Eds.), *Developmental psycholinguistics and communication disorders.* New York: New York Academy of Sciences.

Bickley, P. G., Keith, T. Z., & Wolfle, L. M. (1995). The three-stratum theory of cognitive abilities: Test of the structure of intelligence across the life-span. *Intelligence, 20*(3), 309–328.

Bigler, E. D. (1988). The role of neuropsychological assessment in relation to other types of assessment with children. In M. G. Tramontana & S. R. Hooper (Eds.), *Assessment issues in child neuropsychology* (pp. 67–91). New York: Plenum Press.

Binet, A., & Simon, T. (1905). New methods for the diagnosis of the intellectual level of subnormals. *L'Anne'e Psychologique, 11,* 191–244.

Binet, A., & Simon, T. (1908). The development of intelligence in the child. *L'Anee'e Psychologique, 14,* 1–90.

Bing, S., & Bing, J. (1984, April). *Relationship between the K-ABC and PPVT-R for preschoolers.* Paper presented at the meeting of the National Association of School Psychologists, Philadelphia, PA.

Bing, S. B., & Bing, J. R. (1985, February). *Comparison of the Kaufman Assessment Battery for Children and the Stanford Early School Achievement Test for non-referred kindergarten children*. Paper presented at the meeting of the Eastern Educational Research Association, Virginia Beach, VA.

Bjorklund, D. F. (1989). *Children's thinking: Developmental function and individual differences*. Pacific Grove, CA: Brooks/Cole.

Blaha, J., Mandes, E., & Swisher, C. W. (1987). The hierarchical factor structure of the WAIS-R for learning-disabled adults. *Journal of Clinical Psychology, 43*(2), 280–286.

Blaha, J., & Wallbrown, F. H. (1982). Hierarchical factor structure of the Wechsler Adult Intelligence Scale—Revised. *Journal of Consulting and Clinical Psychology, 50*(5), 652–660.

Blaha, J., & Wallbrown, F. H. (1996). Hierarchical factor structure of the Wechsler Intelligence Scale for Children—III. *Psychological Assessment, 8*, 214–218.

Bloom, A. S., Allard, A. M., Zelko, F. A. J., Brill, W. J., Topinka, C. W., & Pfohl, W. (1988). Differential validity of the K-ABC for lower functioning preschool children versus those of higher ability. *American Journal on Mental Retardation, 93*(3), 273–277.

Bloom, B. S. (1964). *Stability and change in human characteristics*. New York: Wiley.

Bogen, J. E. (1969). The other side of the brain: Parts I, II, and I. *Bulletin of the Los Angeles Neurological Society, 34*, 73–105, 135–162, 191–203.

Bogen, J. E., Dezure, R., Tenouten, W., & Marsh, J. (1972). The other side of the brain: IV. *Bulletin of the Los Angeles Neurological Society, 37*, 49–61.

Bolen, L. M., Aichinger, K. S., Hall, C. W., & Webster, R. W. (1995). A comparison of the performance of cognitively disabled children on the WISC-R and WISC-III. *Journal of Clinical Psychology, 51*(1), 89–94.

Boll, T. J. (1974). Behavioral correlates of cerebral damage in children aged 9 through 14. In R. M. Reitan & L. A. Davison (Eds.), *Clinical neuropsychology: Current status and applications* (pp. 91–120). Washington, DC: V. H. Winston & Sons.

Boll, T. J., & Stanford, L. D. (1997). Pediatric brain injury. In C. R. Reynolds & E. Fletcher-Janzen (Eds.), *Handbook of clinical child neuropsychology* (2nd ed., pp. 140–156). New York: Plenum Press.

Bolton, B. (1978). Differential ability structure in deaf and hearing children. *Applied Psychological Measurement, 2*, 147–149.

Boring, E. G. (1929). *A history of experimental psychology*. New York: The Century Company.

Borkowski, J. G. (1985). Signs of intelligence: Strategy generalization and metacognition. In S. R. Yussen (Ed.), *The growth of reflection in children* (pp. 105–144). New York: Academic Press.

Bouchard, T. J., & McGue, M. (1981). Familial studies of intelligence: A review. *Science, 212*, 1055–1059.

Bouchard, T. J., Jr., & Segal, N. L. (1985). Environment and IQ. In B. B. Wolman (Ed.), *Handbook of intelligence: Theories, measurements, and applications* (pp. 391–464). New York: Wiley.

Bourgeois, B. F. D., Prensky, A. L., Palkes, H. S., Talent, B. K., & Busch, S. G. (1983). Intelligence in epilepsy: A prospective study in children. *Annals of Neurology, 14*, 438–444.

Boyle, G. J. (1989). Confirmation of the structural dimensionality of the Stanford-Binet Intelligence Scale (4th ed.). *Personality and Individual Differences, 10*, 709–715.

Bracken, B. A. (1985). A critical review of the Kaufman Assessment Battery for Children (K-ABC). *School Psychology Review, 14*, 21–36.

Bracken, B. A. (1987). Limitations of preschool instruments and standards for minimal levels of technical adequacy. *Journal of Psychoeducational Assessment, 5*, 313–326.

Bracken, B. A., & Delugach, R. R. (1990, October). Changes improve test. *Communique, 21*.

Bracken, B. A., & Fagan, T. K. (1988). Abilities assessed by the K-ABC Mental Processing subtests: The perceptions of practitioners with varying degrees of experience. *Psychology in the Schools, 25*(1), 22–34.

Bracken, B. A., & McCalllum, R. S. (1998). Universal nonverbal intelligence test—Examiner's manual. Itasca, IL: Riverside Publishing.

Bracken, B. A., Prasse, D. P., & McCallum, R. S. (1984). Peabody Picture Vocabulary Test—Revised: An appraisal and review. *School Psychology Review, 13*, 49–60.

Braden, J. P. (1984a). LPAD applications to deaf populations. In D. S. Martin (Ed.), *International symposium on cognition, education, and deafness: Working papers*. Washington, DC: Gallaudet College Press.

Braden, J. P. (1984b). The factorial similarity of the WISC-R Performance scale in deaf and hearing samples. *Personal Individual Differences, 5*(4), 403–410.

Braden, J. P. (1985a). The structure of nonverbal intelligence in deaf and hearing subjects. *American Annals of the Deaf, 130*, 496–501.

Braden, J. P. (1985b). WISC-R deaf norms reconsidered. *Journal of School Psychology, 23*, 375–382.

Braden, J. P. (1987). A comparison of regression and standard score discrepancy methods for learning disabilities identification: On racial representation. *Journal of School Psychology, 25*, 23–29.

Brandt, H. M., & Giebink, J. W. (1968). Concreteness and congruence in psychologists' reports to teachers. *Psychology in the Schools, 5,* 87–89.

Brody, N. (1985). The validity of tests of intelligence. In B. B. Wolman (Ed.), *Handbook of intelligence* (pp. 353–389). New York: Wiley.

Brouwers, P., Tudor-Williams, G., DeCarli, C., Moss, H. A., Wolters, P. L., Civitello, L. A., & Pizzo, P. A. (1995). Relation between stage of disease and neurobehavioral measures in children with symptomatic HIV disease. *AIDS, 9,* 713–720.

Brown, D. T. (1994). Review of the Kaufman Adolescent and Adult Intelligence Test (KAIT). *Journal of School Psychology, 32,* 85–99.

Brown, G., Chadwich, O., Shaffer, D., Rutter, M., & Traub, M. (1981). A prospective study of children with head injuries: III. Psychiatric sequelae. *Psychological Medicine, 11,* 63–78.

Brown, R. T., Buchanan, I., Doepke, K., Eckman, J. R., Baldwin, K., Goonan, B., & Schoenherr, S. (1993). Cognitive and academic functioning in children with sickle-cell disease. *Journal of Clinical Child Psychology, 22,* 207–218.

Brown, R. T., Madan-Swain, A., Pais, R., Lambert, R. G., Baldwin, K., Casey, R., Frank, N., Sexson, S. B., Ragab, A., & Kamphaus, R. (1992). Cognitive status of children treated with central nervous system prophylactic chemotherapy for acute lymphocytic leukemia. *Archives of Clinical Neuropsychology, 7,* 481–497.

Brown, R. T., Madan-Swain, A., Pais, R., Lambert, R. G., Sexson, S. B., & Ragab, A. (1992). Chemotherapy for acute lymphocytic leukemia: Cognitive and academic sequelae. *Journal of Pediatrics, 121,* 885–889.

Brown, R. T., Sawyer, M. B., Antoniou, G., Toogood, I., Rice, M., Thompson, N., & Madan-Swain, A. (1996). A 3-year follow-up of the intellectual and academic functioning of children receiving central nervous system prophylactic chemotherapy for leukemia. *Journal of Developmental and Behavioral Pediatrics, 17,* 392–398.

Bryden, M., & Saxby, L. (1986). Developmental aspects of cerebral lateralization. In J. E. Obrzut & G. W. Hynd (Eds.), *Child neuropsychology: Vol. 1. Theory and research* (pp. 73–94). Orlando, FL: Academic Press.

Burchinal, M. R., Campbell, F. A., Bryant, D. M., Wasik, B. H., & Ramey, C. T. (1997). Early intervention and mediating processes in cognitive performance of children of low-income African American families. *Child Development, 68(5),* 935–954.

Buros, O. K. (1961). *Tests in print: A comprehensive bibliography of tests for use in education, psychology, and industry.* Highland Park, NJ: Gryphon Press.

Bush, J. W. (1997). It's time we stuck up for the Boulder model. *American Psychologist, 52,* 181.

Butler, R. W., & Copeland, D. R. (1993). Neuropsychological effects of central nervous system prophylactic treatment in childhood leukemia: Methodological considerations. *Journal of Pediatric Psychology, 18,* 319–338.

Campbell, D. T. (1996). Unresolved issues in measurement validity: An autobiographical overview. *Psychological Assessment, 8(4),* 363–368.

Canivez, G. L. (1995). Validity of the Kaufman Brief Intelligence Test: Comparisons with the Wechsler Intelligence Scale for Children—Third Edition. *Assessment, 2(2),* 101–111.

Canivez, G. L. (1996). Validity and diagnostic efficiency of the Kaufman Brief Intelligence Test in reevaluating students with learning disability. *Journal of Psychoeducational Assessment, 14,* 4–19.

Carlson, L., Reynolds, C. R., & Gutkin, T. B. (1983). Consistency of the factorial validity of the WISC-R for upper and lower SES groups. *Journal of School Psychology, 21(4),* 319–326.

Carroll, J. B. (1993). *Human cognitive abilities: A survey of factor analytic studies.* New York: Cambridge University Press.

Carroll, J. B. (1994). What abilities are measured by the WISC-III? *Journal of Psychoeducational Assessment-Monograph,* 134–143.

Carroll, J. B. (1995). Review of J. P. Das, J. A. Naglieri & J. R. Kirby, Assessment of cognitive processes: The PASS theory of intelligence. *Journal of Psychoeducational Assessment, 13,* 397–409.

Caruso, J. C., & Cliff, N. (1999). The properties of equally and differentially weighted WAIS-III factor scores. *Psychological Assessment, 11(2),* 198–206.

Carvajal, H., & Pauls, K. K. (1995). Relationships among graduate record examination scores, Wechsler Adult Intelligence Scale—Revised IQs and undergraduate grade point average. *College Student Journal, 29,* 414–416.

Cassidy, L. C. (1997). The stability of WISC-III scores: For whom are triennial reevaluations necessary? *Dissertation Abstracts, International Section B: The Sciences & Engineering Vol. 58(8–B),* p. 4514.

Chastain, R. L., & Joe, G. W. (1987). Multidimensional relations between intellectual abilities and demographic variables. *Journal of Educational Psychology, 79(3),* 323–325.

Chen, J-Q, & Gardner, H. (1997). Alternative assessment from a multiple intelligences theoretical perspective. In D. Flanagan, J. L. Genshaft, & P. L. Harrison (Eds.), *Contemporary intellectual assessment: Theories, tests, and issues* (pp. 105–121). New York: Guilford.

Cicchetti, D. V. (1994). Guidelines, criteria, and rules of thumb for evaluating normed and standardized assessment instruments in psychology. *Psychological Assessment, 6(4),* 284–290.

Cleary, T. A., Humphreys, L. G., Kendrick, S. A., & Wesman, A. (1975). Educational uses of tests with disadvantaged students. *American Psychologist, 30,* 15–41.

Clinton, J. J., McCormick, K., & Besteman, J. (1994). Enhancing clinical practice: The role of practice guidelines. *American Psychologist, 49,* 30–33.

Cohen, J. (1952). A factor-analytically based rationale for the Wechsler-Bellevue. *Journal of Consulting Psychology, 16,* 272–277.

Cohen, J. (1957). A factor-analytically based rationale for the Wechsler Adult Intelligence Scale. *Journal of Consulting Psychology, 21,* 451–457.

Cohen, J. (1959). The factorial structure of the WISC at ages 7–6, 10–6, and 13–6. *Journal of Consulting Psychology, 23,* 285–299.

Cohen, L. G., & Spenciner, L. J. (1998). *Assessment of children and youth.* New York: Addison Wesley Longman.

Cohen, M., Becker, M. G., & Campbell, R. (1990). Relationships among four methods of assessment of children with attention deficit-hyperactivity disorder. *Journal of School Psychology, 28*(3), 189–202.

Cohen, M. J., Branch, W. B., McKie, V. C., & Adams, R. J. (1994). Neuropsychological impairment in children with sickle cell anemia and cerebrovascular accidents. *Clinical Pediatrics, 33,* 517–524.

Cohen, M. J., Branch, W. B., Willis, W. G., Weyandt, L. L., & Hynd, G. W. (1992). Childhood. In A. E. Puente & R. J. McCaffrey (Eds.), *Handbook of neuropsychological assessment: A biopsychosocial perspective* (pp. 49–80). New York: Plenum Press.

Colombo, J. (1993). *Infant cognition: Predicting later intellectual functioning.* Newbury Park, CA: Sage.

Copeland, D. R., Dowell, R. E., Fletcher, J. M., Bordeaux, J. D., Sullivan, M. P., Jaffe, N., Frankel, L. S., Ried, H. L., & Cangir A. (1988). Neuropsychological effects of childhood cancer treatment. *Journal of Child Neurology, 3,* 53–62.

Costenbader, V. K., & Adams, J. W. (1991). A review of the psychometric and administrative features of the PIAT-R: Implications for the practitioner. *Journal of School Psychology, 29,* 219–228.

Crawford, J. R. (1992). Current and premorbid intelligence measures in neuropsychological assessment. In J. R. Crawford, D. M. Parker, & W. W. McKinlay (Eds.), *A handbook of neuropsychological assessment* (pp. 21–49). Hillsdale, NJ: Lawrence Erlbaum Associates.

Dai, X., Gong, Y., & Zhong, L. (1990). Factor analysis of the Mainland Chinese version of the Wechsler Adult Intelligence Scale. *Psychological Assessment, 2*(1), 31–34.

Dai, X., Ryan, J. J., Paolo, A. M., & Harrington, R. G. (1991). Sex differences on the Wechsler Adult Intelligence Scale—Revised for China. *Psychological Assessment, 3*(2), 282–284.

Dalby, P. R., & Obrzut, J. E. (1991). Epidemiologic characteristics and sequelae of closed head-injured children and adolescents: A review. *Developmental Neuropsychology, 7,* 35–68.

Daniel, M. H. (1997). Intelligence testing: Status and trends. *American Psychologist, 52,* 1038–1045.

Das, J. P. (1973). Structure of cognitive abilities: Evidence for simultaneous and successive processing. *Journal of Educational Psychology, 65,* 103–108.

Das, J. P. (1980). Planning: Theoretical considerations and empirical evidence. *Psychological Research, 41,* 141–151.

Das, J. P. (1988). Intelligence: A view from neuropsychology. *The Alberta Journal of Educational Research, 34,* 76–82.

Das, J. P., Kirby, J. R., & Jarman, R. F. (1975). Simultaneous and successive synthesis: An alternative model for cognitive abilities. *Psychological Bulletin, 82,* 87–103.

Das, J. P., Kirby, J. R., & Jarman, R. F. (1979). *Simultaneous and successive cognitive processes.* New York: Academic Press.

Das, J. P., Mensink, D., & Mishra, R. K. (1990). Cognitive processes separating good and poor readers when IQ is covaried. *Learning and Individual Differences, 2,* 423–436.

Das, J. P., & Naglieri, J. A. (1997). *Cognitive Assessment System.* Chicago: Riverside.

Das, J. P., Naglieri, J. A., & Kirby, J. R. (1994). *Assessment of cognitive processes: The PASS theory of intelligence.* Needham Heights, MA: Allyn & Bacon.

Das, J. P., Naglieri, J. A., & Kirby, J. R. (1994). *Assessment of cognitive processes: The PASS theory of intelligence.* Needham Heights, MA: Allyn & Bacon.

Das, J. P., & Varnhagen, C. K. (1986). Neuropsychological functioning and cognitive processing. In J. E. Obrzut & G. W. Hynd (Eds.), *Child neuropsychology: Vol. 1. Theory and research* (pp. 117–140). Orlando, FL: Academic Press.

Daub, D., & Colarusso, R. P. (1996). The validity of the WJ-R, PIAT-R, and DAB-2 reading subtests with students with learning disabilities. *Learning Disabilities Research and Practice, 11*(2), 90–95.

Dawes, R. M. (1995). Standards of practice. In S. C. Hayes, V. M. Follette, R. M. Dawes, & K. E. Grady (Eds.), *Scientific standards of psychological practice: Issues and recommendations* (pp. 31–43). Reno, NV: Context Press.

Deary, I. J., & Stough, C. (1996). Intelligence and inspection time: Achievements, prospects, and problems. *American Psychologist, 51,* 599–608.

DeBaun, M. R., Schatz, J., Siegel, M. J., Koby, M., Craft, S., Resar, L., Chu, J. Y., Launius, G., Dadash-Zadey, M., Lee, R. B., & Noetzel, M. (1998). Cognitive screening examinations for silent cerebral infarcts in sickle cell disease. *Neurology, 50,* 1678–1682.

Denckla, M. B. (1996). Biological correlates of learning and attention: What is relevant to learning disability and attention-deficit hyperactivity disorder? *Developmental and Behavioral Pediatrics, 17,* 114–119.

Dodrill, C. B., & Troupin, A. S. (1975). Effects of repeated administrations of a comprehensive neuropsychological battery among chronic epileptics. *Journal of Nervous and Mental Disease, 161,* 185–190.

Dodrill, C. B., & Troupin, A. S. (1977). Psychotropic effects of carbamazepine in epilepsy: A double-blind comparison with phenytoin. *Neurology, 27,* 1023–1028.

Dodrill, C. B., & Warner, M. H. (1996). Seizure disorders. In L. S. Batchelor & R. S. Dean (Eds.), *Pediatric neuropsychology* (pp. 303–324). Needham Heights, MA: Allyn & Bacon.

Donders, J. (1992). Validity of the Kaufman Assessment Battery for Children when employed with children with traumatic brain injury. *Journal of Clinical Psychology, 48,* 225–230.

Donders, J. (1996). Cluster subtypes in the WISC-III standardization sample: Analysis of factor index scores. *Psychological Assessment, 8*(3), 312–318.

Donders, J. (1997). Sensitivity of the WISC-III to injury severity in children with traumatic head injury. *Assessment, 4,* 107–109.

Dowell, R. E., Copeland, D. R., & Judd, B. W. (1989). Neuropsychological effects of chemotherapeutic agents. *Developmental Neuropsychology, 5,* 17–24.

Dumont, R., Cruse, C. L., Price, L., & Whelley, P. (1996). The relationship between the Differential Ability Scales (DAS) and the Wechsler Intelligence Scale for Children—Third Edition (WISC-III) for students with learning disabilities. *Psychology in the Schools, 33*(3), 203–209.

Dunn, L. M. (1959). *Peabody Picture Vocabulary Test.* Circle Pines, MN: American Guidance Service.

Dunn, L. M., & Dunn, L. M. (1981). *Peabody Picture Vocabulary Test—Revised.* Circle Pines, MN: American Guidance Service.

Dunn, L. M., & Dunn, L. M. (1997a). *Examiner's manual for the Peabody Picture Vocabulary Test—Third Edition.* Circle Pines, MN: American Guidance Service.

Dunn, L. M., & Dunn, L. M. (1997b). *Norms booklet for the Peabody Picture Vocabulary Test—Third Edition.* Circle Pines, MN: American Guidance Service.

Dunn, L. M., Lugo, D. E., Padilla, E. R., & Dunn, L. M. (1986). *Test de Vocabulario en Imágenes Peabody.* Circle Pines, MN: American Guidance Service.

Dunn, L. M., & Markwardt, F. C. (1970). *Peabody Individual Achievement Test.* Circle Pines, MN: American Guidance Service.

Edelman, S. (1996). A review of the Wechsler Intelligence Scale for Children—Third Edition (WISC-III). *Measurement and Evaluation in Counseling and Development, 28*(4), 219–224.

Edwards, B. T., & Klein, M. (1984). Comparison of the WAIS and the WAIS-R with Ss of high intelligence. *Journal of Clinical Psychology, 40,* 300–302.

Elliott, C. D. (1990a). *Administration and scoring manual for the Differential Ability Scales.* New York: Psychological Corporation.

Elliott, C. D. (1990b). *Introductory and technical handbook for the Differential Ability Scales.* New York: Psychological Corporation.

Elliott, C. D. (1990c). *Differential Ability Scales.* San Antonio, TX: Psychological Corporation.

Elliott, C. D. (1990d). The nature and structure of children's abilities: Evidence from the Differential Ability Scales. *Journal of Psychoeducational Assessment, 8,* 376–390.

Elliott, C. D., Daniel, M. H., & Guiton, G. W. (1990). Preschool cognitive assessment with the Differential Ability Scales. In B. A. Bracken (Ed.), *The psychoeducational assessment of preschool children* (pp. 133–153). Needham Heights, MA: Allyn & Bacon.

Elliott, C. D., Murray, D. J., & Pearson, L. S. (1979). *British Ability Scales.* Windsor, England: National Foundation for Educational Research.

Elliott, R. (1987). *Litigating intelligence: IQ tests, special education, and social science in the courtroom.* Dover, MA: Auburn House.

Elwan, F. Z. (1996). Factor structure of the Kaufman Assessment Battery for Children with Egyptian schoolchildren. *Psychological Reports, 78*(1), 99–110.

Epps, E. G. (1974). Situational effects in testing. In L. P. Miller (Ed.), *The testing of black students* (pp. 41–51). Englewood Cliffs, NJ: Prentice Hall.

Esters, I. G., Ittenbach, R. F., & Han, K. (1997). Today's IQ tests: Are they really better than their historical predecessors? *School Psychology Review, 26,* 211–223.

Eysenck, H. J. (1988). The concept of 'intelligence': Useful or useless? *Intelligence, 12,* 1–16.

Eysenck, H. J., & Kamin, L. (1981). *The intelligence controversy.* New York: John Wiley.

Fagan, J. F. (1984). The intelligent infant: Theoretical implications. *Intelligence, 8,* 1–9.

Fagan, J. F., III. (1984). The relationship of novelty preferences during infancy to later intelligence and later recognition memory. *Intelligence, 8,* 339–346.

Fagan, J. F., Singer, L. T., Montie, J. E., & Shepherd, P. A. (1986). Selective screening device for the early detection of normal or delayed cognitive development in infants at risk for later mental retardation. *Pediatrics, 78,* 1021–1026.

Fan, X., Willson, V. L., & Reynolds, C. R. (1995). Assessing the similarity of the factor structure of the K-ABC for

African-American and white children. *Journal of Psychoeducational Assessment, 13*(2), 120–131.

Farmer, J. E., & Peterson, L. (1995). Pediatric traumatic brain injury: Promoting successful school reentry. *School Psychology Review, 24,* 230–243.

Farwell, J. R., Dodrill, C. B., & Batzel, L. W. (1985). Neuropsychological abilities of children with epilepsy. *Epilepsia, 26,* 395–400.

Faulstich, M., Mcanulty, D., Gresham, F., Veitia, M., Moore, J., Bernard, B., Waggoner, C., & Howell, R. (1986). Factor structure of the WAIS-R for an incarcerated population. *Journal of Clinical Psychology, 42*(2), 369–371.

Felton, R. H., Wood, F. B., Brown, I. S., Campbell, S. K., & Harter, R. (1987). Separate verbal memory and naming deficits in attention deficit disorder and reading disability. *Brain and Language, 31,* 171–184.

Feuerstein, R. (1979). *The dynamic assessment of retarded persons.* Baltimore, MD: University Park Press.

Feuerstein, R., Rand, Y., & Hoffman, M. B. (1979). *The dynamic assessment of retarded performers: The learning potential -assessment device, theory, instruments, and techniques.* Baltimore, MD: University Park Press.

Field, D., Schaie, K. W., & Leino, E. Z. (1988). Continuity in intellectual functioning: The role of self-reported health. *Psychology and Aging, 3,* 385–392.

Figueroa, R. A. (1989, May). Using interpreters in assessments. *National Association of School Psychologists Communique, 19.*

Figueroa, R. A. (1990). Assessment of linguistic minority group children. In C. R. Reynolds & R. W. Kamphaus (Eds.), *Handbook of psychological and educational assessment of children: Vol. 1. Intelligence and achievement* (pp. 671–696). New York: Guilford.

Figueroa, R. A., & Sassenrath, J. M. (1989). A longitudinal study of the predictive validity of the System of Multicultural Pluralistic Assessment (SOMPA). *Psychology in the Schools, 26,* 1–19.

Filipek, P. A., Kennedy, D. N., Caviness, V. S., Rossnick, S. L., Spraggins, T. A., & Starewicz, P. M. (1989). Magnetic resonance imaging-based brain morphometry: Development and application to normal subjects. *Annals of Neurology, 25,* 61–67.

Finch, A. J., Jr., Blount, R. L., Saylor, C. F., Wolfe, V. V., Pallmeyer, T. P., McIntosh, J. A., Griffin, J. M., & Careh, D. J. (1988). Intelligence and emotional/behavioral factors as correlates of achievement in child psychiatric inpatients. *Psychological Reports, 63,* 163–170.

Finegan, J. K., Zucher, K. J., Bradley, S. J., & Doering, R.W. (1982). Pattern of intellectual functioning and spatial ability in boys with gender identity disorder. *Canadian Journal of Psychiatry, 27,* 135–139.

Fish, J. M. (1988). Reinforcement in testing: Research with children and adolescents. *Professional School Psychology, 3,* 203–218.

Fish, J. M. (1990). IQ terminology: Modification of current schemes. *Journal of Psychoeducational Assessment, 8,* 527–530.

Flanagan, D. P., & Alfonso, V. C. (1995). A critical review of the technical characteristics of new and recently revised American intelligence tests for preschool children. *Journal of Psychoeducational Assessment, 13,* 66–90.

Flanagan, D. P., Alfonso, V. C., & Flanagan, R. (1994). A review of the Kaufman Adolescent and Adult Intelligence Test: An advancement in cognitive assessment? *School Psychology Review, 23,* 512–525.

Flanagan, D. P., Alfonso, V. C., Kaminer, T., & Rader, D. E. (1995). Incidence of basic concepts in the directions of new and recently revised American intelligence tests for preschool children. *School Psychology International, 16,* 345–364.

Flaugher, R. L. (1974). Some points of confusion in discussing the testing of black students. In L. P. Miller (Ed.), *The testing of black students: A symposium* (p. 74). New York: Prentice Hall.

Flavell, J. H., & Wellman, H. M. (1977). Metamemory. In R. V. Kail, Jr. & J. W. Hagen (Eds.), *Perspectives on the development of memory and cognition* (pp. 3–33). Hillsdale, NJ: Erlbaum.

Fletcher, J. M., Francis, D. J., Rourke, B. P., Shaywitz, S. E., & Shaywitz, B. A. (1992). The validity of discrepancy-based definitions of reading disabilities. *Journal of Learning Disabilities, 25*(9), 555–561.

Flynn, J. R. (1984). The mean IQ of Americans: Massive gains 1932 to 1978. *Psychological Bulletin, 95,* 29–51.

Flynn, J. R. (1985). Wechsler Intelligence Tests: Do we really have a criterion of mental retardation? *American Journal of Mental Deficiency, 90,* 236–244.

Flynn, J. R. (1987). Massive IQ gains in 14 nations: What IQ tests really measure. *Psychological Bulletin, 101,* 171–191.

Flynn, J. R. (1998). IQ gains over time: Toward finding the causes. In U. Neisser (Ed.), *The rising curve: Long-term gains in IQ and related measures* (pp. 25–66). Washington, DC: American Psychological Association.

Follette, V. M., & Naugle, A. E. (1995). Discussion of Beutler and Davidson: Psychology's failure to educate. In S. C. Hayes, V. M. Follette, R. M. Dawes, & K. E. Grady (Eds.), *Scientific standards of psychological practice: Issues and recommendations* (pp. 25–30). Reno, NV: Context Press.

Foorman, B. R., Sadowski, B. R., & Basen, J. A. (1985). Children's solutions for figural matrices: Developmental differences in strategies and effects of matrix characteristics. *Journal of Experimental Child Psychology, 39,* 107–130.

Forceville, E. J. M., Dekker, M. J. A., Aldenkampt, A. P., Alpherts, W. C. J., & Schelvis, A. J. (1992). Subtest profiles of the WISC-R and WAIS in mentally retarded patients with epilepsy. *Journal of Intellectual Disability Research, 36,* 45–59.

Fourqurean, J. M. (1987). A K-ABC and WISC-R comparison for Latino learning-disabled children of limited English proficiency. *Journal of School Psychology, 25,* 15–21.

Fowler, M. G., Whitt, J. K., Lallinger, R. R., Nash, K. B., Atkinson, S. S., Wells, R. J., & McMillan, C. (1988). Neuropsychological and academic functioning of children with sickle cell anemia. *Developmental and Behavioral Pediatrics, 9,* 213–220.

Fraboni, M., & Saltstone, R. (1992). The WAIS-R number of factors quandary: A cluster analytic approach to construct validation. *Educational and Psychological Measurement, 52(3),* 603–613.

Franzen, M. D., Burgess, E. J., & Smith-Seemiller, L. (1997). Methods of estimating premorbid functioning. *Archives of Clinical Neuropsychology, 12,* 711–738.

Frederiksen, N. (1986). Toward a broader conception of human intelligence. *American Psychologist, 41,* 445–452.

Freeman, B. J., Lucas, J. C., Forness, S. R., & Ritvo, E. R. (1985). Cognition processing of high-functioning autistic children: Comparing the K-ABC and the WISC-R. *Journal of Psychoeducational Assessment, 3,* 357–362.

French, J. L. (1964). *Pictorial test of intelligence.* Boston: Houghton-Mifflin.

French, J. L., & Hale, R. L. (1990). A history of the development of psychological and educational testing. In C. R. Reynolds & R. W. Kamphaus (Eds.), *Handbook of psychological and educational assessment of children* (pp. 3–28). New York: Guilford.

Frick, P. J., Kamphaus, R. W., Lahey, B. B., Loeber, R., Christ, M. G., Hart, E. L., & Tannenbaum, L. E. (1991). Academic underachievement and the disruptive behavior disorders. *Journal of Consulting and Clinical Psychology, 59,* 289–294.

Fuller, G. B., Goh, D. S., (1981). Intelligence, achievement, and visual-motor performance among learning disabled and emotionally impaired children. *Psychology in the Schools, 18,* 261–268.

Gaddes, W. H. (1981). An examination of the validity of neuropsychological knowledge in educational diagnosis and remediation. In G. W. Hynd & J. E. Obrzut (Eds.), *Neuropsychological assessment of the school-aged child: Issues and procedures.* New York: Grune & Stratton.

Galton, F. (1883). *Inquiries into human faculty and its development.* London: Macmillan.

Galton, F. (1952). *Hereditary genius: An inquiry into its laws and consequences.* New York: Horizon Press.

Galton, F. H. (1978). *Hereditary genius.* New York: St. Martin's. (Original work published 1869)

Gardner, H. (1993). *Multiple intelligences: The theory in practice.* New York: Basic Books.

Gardner, J. F. (1993). The era of optimism, 1850–1870: A preliminary reappraisal. *Mental Retardation, 31,* 89–95.

Garrett, H. E. (1961). A developmental theory of intelligence. In J. J. Jenkins & D. G. Paterson (Eds.), *Studies in individual differences: The search for intelligence* (pp. 572–581). New York: Appleton-Century-Crofts. (Reprinted from *The American Psychologist,* 1946, *1,* 372–378).

Gazzaniga, M. S. (1970). *The bisected brain.* New York: Appleton-Century-Crofts.

Gazzaniga, M. S. (1974). Cerebral dominance viewed as a decision system. In S. Dimond & J. Beaumont (Eds.), *Hemispheric functions in the human brain.* London: Halstead Press.

Gazzaniga, M. S. (1975). Recent research on hemispheric lateralization of the human brain: Review of the split brain. *UCLA Educator, 17,* 9–12.

Geary, D. C., & Whitworth, R. H. (1988). Dimensional structure of the WAIS-R: A simultaneous multi-sample analysis. *Educational and Psychological Measurement, 48(4),* 945–956.

Gellis, S., & Kagan, B. (1976). *Current pediatric therapy.* Philadelphia: W. B. Saunders.

Gentry, N., Sapp, G. L., & Daw, J. L. (1995). Scores on the Wechsler Individual Achievement Test and the Kaufman Test of Educational Achievement—Comprehensive Form for emotionally conflicted adolescents. *Psychological Reports, 76,* 607–610.

Gerken, K. C. (1978). Performance of Mexican American children on intelligence tests. *Exceptional Children, 44,* 438–443.

Gibbins, S., Ulissi, S. M., & Brice, P. (in press). The use of the Kaufman Assessment Battery for Children with the hearing impaired. *American Annals of the Deaf.*

Gibbs, J. T., & Huang, L. N. (1989). *Children of Color.* San Francisco, CA: Jossey Bass Publishers.

Glasser, A. J., & Zimmerman, I. L. (1967). *Clinical interpretation of the Wechsler Intelligence Scale for Children.* New York: Grune & Stratton.

Glaub, V. E., & Kamphaus, R. W. (1991). Construction of a nonverbal adaptation of the Stanford-Binet: Fourth Edition. *Educational and Psychological Measurement, 51,* 231–241.

Glaxer, R. (1984). Education and thinking: The role of knowledge. *American Psychologist, 39(2),* 93–104.

Glutting, J. J. (1986). Potthoff bias analysis of K-ABC MPC and non-verbal scale IQs among Anglo, Black, and Puerto

Rican kindergarten children. *Professional School Psychology, 4,* 225–234.

Glutting, J. J., & Kaplan, D. (1990). Stanford-Binet Intelligence Scale: Fourth Edition: Making the case for reasonable interpretations. In C. R. Reynolds & R. W. Kamphaus (Eds.), *Handbook of psychological and educational assessment of children* (pp. 277–295). New York: Guilford.

Glutting, J. J., & McDermott, P. A. (1990). Principles and problems in learning potential. In C. R. Reynolds & R. W. Kamphaus (Eds.), *Handbook of psychological and educational assessment of children* (pp. 277–295). New York: Guilford.

Glutting, J. J., Oakland, T., & McDermott, P. A. (1989). Observing child behavior during testing: Constructs, validity, and situational generality. *Journal of School Psychology, 27,* 155–164.

Glutting, J. J., Youngstrom, E. A., Ward, T., Ward, S., & Hale, R. L. (1997). Incremental efficacy of WISC-III factor scores in predicting achievement: What do they tell us? *Psychological Assessment, 9*(3), 295–301.

Goddard, H. H. (1912). Echelle metrique de l'intelligence de Binet-Simon. *Annee psychol., 18,* 288–326.

Golden, C. J. (1981). The Luria-Nebraska Children's Battery: Theory and initial formulation. In G. Hynd & S. Obrzut (Eds.), *Neuropsychological assessment and the school age child: Issues and procedures* (pp. 277–302). New York: Grune & Stratton.

Golden, C. J. (1997). The Nebraska Neuropsychological Children's Battery. In C. R. Reynolds & E. Fletcher-Janzen (Eds.), *Handbook of clinical child neuropsychology* (2nd ed., pp. 237–251). New York: Plenum Press.

Goldman, J., Stein, C. L., & Querry, S. (1983). *Psychological methods of child assessment.* New York: Brunner/Mazel.

Goldstein, D., Parell, G. G., & Sanfilippo-Cohn, S. (1985). Depression and achievement in subgroups of children with learning disabilities. *Journal of Allied Development Psychology, 6,* 263–275.

Goldstein, G. (1990). Comprehensive neuropsychological assessment batteries. In G. Goldstein & M. Hersen (Eds.), *Handbook of psychological assessment* (2nd ed., pp. 197–227). New York: Pergamon Press.

Goldstein, G. (1992). Historical perspectives. In A. E. Puente & R. J. McCaffrey (Eds.), *Handbook of neuropsychological assessment: A biopsychosocial perspective* (pp. 1–12). New York: Plenum Press.

Goldstein, G. (1997). The clinical utility of standardized or flexible battery approaches to neuropsychological assessment. In G. Goldstein & T. Incagnoli (Eds.), *Contemporary approaches to neuropsychological assessment* (pp. 67–91). New York: Plenum Press.

Goldstein, S., & Goldstein, M. (1990). *Managing attention disorders in children: A guide for practitioners.* New York: John Wiley.

Gomez, F. C., Jr., Piedmont, R. L., & Fleming, M. Z. (1992). Factor analysis of the Spanish version of the WAIS: The Escala de Inteligencia Wechsler para Adultos (EIWA). *Psychological Assessment, 4*(3), 317–321.

Goodenough, F. L. (1926). *Measurement of intelligence by drawings.* New York: Harcourt Brace & World.

Goodman, J. F. (1990). Infant intelligence: Do we, can we, should we assess it? In C. R. Reynolds & R. W. Kamphaus (Eds.), *Handbook of psychological and educational assessment of children* (pp. 183–208). New York: Guilford.

Goonan, B. T., Goonan, L. J., Brown, R. T., Buchanan, I., & Eckman, J. R. (1994). Sustained attention and inhibitory control in children with sickle cell syndrome. *Archives of Clinical Neuropsychology, 9,* 89–104.

Gordon, M., Thomason, D., & Cooper, S. (1990). To what extent does attention affect K-ABC scores? *Psychology in the Schools, 27*(2), 144–147.

Gorsuch, R. L. (1988). *Factor analysis* (3rd ed.). Hillsdale, NJ: Erlbaum Associates.

Gottfried, A. W. (1973). Intellectual consequences of perinatal anoxia. *Psychological Bulletin, 80,* 231–242.

Gottling, S. (1985). *Comparison of the reliability of the Goodenough-Harris Draw-a-Man Test with the Naglieri Draw-a-Person: A Quantitative System.* Unpublished master's thesis, Ohio State University.

Grace, W. C. (1986). Equivalence of the WISC-R and WAIS-R in delinquent males. *Journal of Psychoeducational Assessment, 4,* 155–162.

Grady, J. (1980). Opinion. *PASE v. Hannon. Federal Supplement 506,* 831–883.

Greenblatt, E., Mattis, S., & Trad, P. V. (1991). The ACID pattern and the freedom from distractibility factor in a child psychiatric population. *Developmental Neuropsychology, 7*(2), 121–130.

Greene, A. C., Sapp. G. L., & Chisson, B. (1990). Validation of the Stanford-Binet Intelligence Scale Fourth Edition with exceptional black male students. *Psychology in the Schools, 27*(1), 35–41.

Greenfield, P. M. (1998). The cultural evolution of IQ. In U. Neiser (Ed.), *The rising curve: Long-term gains in IQ and related measures* (pp. 81–123). Washington, DC: American Psychological Association.

Gresham, F. M., & Reschly, D. J. (1986). Social skills deficits and low peer acceptance of mainstreamed learning disabled children. *Learning Disability Quarterly, 9,* 23–31.

Gribbin, K., Schaie, K. W., & Parham, I. A. (1975). *Cognitive complexity and maintenance of intellectual abilities.* Paper presented at the 10th International Congress of Gerontology, Jerusalem, Israel.

Gridley, B. E., & McIntosh, D. E. (1991). Confirmatory factor analysis of the Stanford-Binet: Fourth Edition for a normal sample. *Journal of School Psychology, 29*(3), 237–248.

Griggs v. Duke Power Co., 401 U. S. 424 (1971).

Grossman, H. J. (1983). *Classification in mental retardation.* Washington, DC: American Association of Mental Deficiency.

Grottfried, A. W. (1973). Intellectual consequences of perinatal anoxia. *Psychological Bulletin, 80,* 213–242.

Guidubaldi, J., & Perry, J. D. (1984). Concurrent and predictive validity of the Battelle Development Inventory at the first grade level. *Educational and Psychological Measurement, 44,* 977–985.

Guilford, J. P. (1967). *The nature of human intelligence.* New York: McGraw-Hill.

Guilford, J. P. (1979). Intelligence isn't what it used to be: What to do about it. *Journal of Research and Development in Education, 12*(2), 33–46.

Guilford, J. P. (1985). The structure-of-intellect model. In B. B. Wolman (Ed.), *Handbook of intelligence* (pp. 225–266). New York: John Wiley.

Gunderson, V. M., Grant-Webster, K. S., & Fagan, J. F., III. (1987). Visual recognition memory in high- and low-risk infant pigtailed macaques (Macaca Nemestrina). *Developmental Psychology, 23,* 671–675.

Gunderson, V. M., Grant-Webster, K. S., & Sackett, G. P. (1989). Deficits in visual recognition in low birth weight infant pigtailed monkeys (Macaca Nemestrina). *Child Development, 60,* 119–127.

Gutkin, T. B. (1978). Some useful statistics for the interpretation of the WISC-R. *Journal of Consulting and Clinical Psychology, 46,* 1561–1563.

Gutkin, T. B. (1979). The WISC-R verbal comprehension, perceptual organization, and freedom from distractibility deviation quotients: Data for practitioners. *Psychology in the Schools, 16,* 359–360.

Gutkin, T. B. (1982). WISC-R deviation quotients vs. traditional IQs: An examination of the standardization sample and some implications for scores interpretation. *Journal of Clinical Psychology, 38,* 179–182.

Gutkin, T. B., & Reynolds, C. R. (1980). Factorial similarity of the WISC-R for Anglos and Chicanos referred for psychological services. *Journal of School Psychology, 18,* 34–39.

Gutkin, T. B., & Reynolds, C. R. (1981). Factorial similarity of the WISC-R for white and black children from the standardization sample. *Journal of Educational Psychology, 73,* 227–231.

Gutkin, T. B., Reynolds, C. R., Galvin, G. A. (1984). Factor analysis of the Wechsler Adult Intelligence Scale—Revised (WAIS-R): An examination of the standardization sample. *Journal of School Psychology, 22*(1), 83–93.

Gutterman, J. E., Ward, M., & Genshaft, J. (1985). Correlations of scores of low vision children on the Perkins-Binet Tests of Intelligence for the Blind, the WISC-R and the WRAT. *Journal of Visual Impairment & Blindness, 79,* 55–58.

Gyurke, J. S. (1991). The assessment of preschool children with the Wechsler Preschool Primary Scale of Intelligence—Revised. In B. A. Bracken (Ed.), *The psychoeducational assessment of preschool children* (2nd ed., pp. 86–106). Needham Heights, MA: Allyn & Bacon.

Haddad, F. A. (1986). Concurrent validity of the test of nonverbal intelligence with learning disabled children. *Psychology in the Schools, 23,* 361–364.

Haensly, P. A., & Torrance, E. P. (1990). Assessment of creativity in children and adolescents. In C. R. Reynolds & R. W. Kamphaus (Eds.), *Handbook of psychological and educational assessment: Children intelligence & achievement* (pp. 697–722). New York: Guilford Press.

Hahn, W. K. (1987). Cerebral lateralization of function: From infancy through childhood. *Psychological Bulletin, 101,* 376–392.

Hales, R. L. (1983). Intellectual assessment. In M. Hersen, A. Kazdin, & A. Bellack (Eds.), *The clinical psychology handbook* (pp. 345–376). New York: Pergamon.

Hales, R. L., Landino, S. A. (1981). Utility of WISC-R subtest analysis in discriminating among groups of conduct-problem, withdrawn, mixed and nonproblem boys. *Journal of Consulting and Clinical Psychology, 49,* 91–95.

Hall, G. C. N., Bansal, A., & Lopez, I. R. (1999). Ethnicity and psychopathology: A meta-analytic review of 31 years of comparative MMPI/MMPI-2 research. *Psychological Assessment, 11*(2), 186–197.

Hall, L. E., & Kramer, J. R. (1995). Neurological soft signs in childhood do not predict neuropsychological dysfunction in adulthood. *Developmental Neuropsychology, 11,* 223–235.

Hall, L. P., & LaDriere, L. (1969). Patterns of performance on WISC Similarities in emotionally disturbed and brain-damaged children. *Journal of Consulting and Clinical Psychology, 33,* 357–364.

Hallahan, D. P., Kauffman, J. M., & Lloyd, J. W. (1996). *Introduction to learning disabilities.* Boston: Allyn & Bacon.

Halstead, W. C. (1947). *Brain and intelligence: A quantitative study of the frontal lobes.* Chicago: University of Chicago Press.

Ham, S. J. (1985). *A validity study of recent intelligence tests on a deaf population.* (Available from Sandra J. Ham, School Psychologist, North Dakota School for the Deaf, Devils Lake, ND 58301.)

Hammill, D. D. (1990). On defining learning disabilities: An emerging consensus. *Journal of Learning Disabilities, 23,* 74–84.

Hammill, D. D., Pearson, N. A., & Wiederholt, J. L. (1997). *Examiner's manual: Comprehensive test of nonverbal intelligence.* Austin, TX: Pro-Ed.

Hanson, R. A. (1975). Consistency and stability of home environmental measures related to IQ. *Child Development, 46,* 470–480.

Hanson, R. K., Hunsley, J., Parker, K. C. H. (1988). The relationship between WAIS subtest reliability, "g" loadings, and meta-analytically derived validity estimates. *Journal of Clinical Psychology, 44*(4), 557–563.

Harnad, S., Doty, R. W., Goldstein, L., Jaynes, J., & Krauthamer, G. (Eds.). (1977). *Lateralization in the nervous system.* New York: Academic Press.

Harnqvist, K. (1968). Relative changes in intelligence from 13 to 18. *Scandinavian Journal of Psychology, 9,* 50–64.

Harrison, P. L., Flanagan, D. P., & Genshaft, J. L. (1997). An integration and synthesis of contemporary theories, tests, and issues in the field of intellectual assessment. In D. P. Flanagan, J. L. Genshaft, & P. L. Harrison (Eds.), *Contemporary intellectual assessment* (pp. 533–561). New York: Guilford Press.

Harrison, P. L., & Kamphaus, R. W. (1984, April). *Comparison between the K-ABC and Vineland Adaptive Behavior Scales.* Paper presented at the meeting of the National Association of School Psychologists, Philadelphia, PA.

Harrison, P. L., Kaufman, A. S., Hickman, J. A., & Kaufman, N. L. (1988). A survey of tests used for adult assessment. *Journal of Psychoeducational Assessment, 6,* 188–198.

Hartlage, L. C., & Hartlage, P. L. (1989). Neuropsychological aspects of epilepsy: Introduction and overview. In C. R. Reynolds & E. Fletcher-Janzen (Eds.), *Handbook of clinical child neuropsychology* (pp. 409–417). New York: Plenum.

Hartlage, L. C., & Telzrow, C. F. (1981). Neuropsychological assessment of young children. *Clinical Neuropsychology, 3,* 41–43.

Hartlage, L. C., & Telzrow, C. F. (1983). The neuropsychological basis of educational intervention. *Journal of Learning Disabilities, 16,* 521–528.

Hartlage, P. L., & Hartlage, L. C. (1997). The neuropsychology of epilepsy: Overview and psychosocial aspects. In C. R. Reynolds & E. Fletcher-Janzen (Eds.), *Handbook of clinical child neuropsychology* (2nd ed., pp. 506–516). New York: Plenum Press.

Hartwig, S. S., Sapp, G. L., & Clayton, G. A. (1987). Comparison of the Stanford-Binet Intelligence Scale: Form L-M and the Stanford-Binet Intelligence Scale Fourth Edition. *Psychological Reports, 60,* 1215–1218.

Harvey, V. S. (1989, March). Eschew obfuscation: Support of clear writing. *Communique, 12.*

Hasegawa, C. (1989). The unmentioned minority. In C. J. Maker & S. W. Schiever (Eds.), *Defensive programs for cultural and ethnic minorities (Vol. 2).* Austin, TX: Pro-Ed.

Haskins, R. (1989). Beyond metaphor: The efficacy of early childhood education. *American Psychologist, 44,* 274–282.

Hauser, W. A. (1994). The prevalence and incidence of convulsive disorders in children. *Epilepsia, 35* (Suppl. 2), S1–S6.

Hayden, D. C., Furlong, M. J., & Linnemeyer, S. (1988). A comparison of the Kaufman Assessment Battery for Children and the Stanford-Binet IV for the assessment of gifted children. *Psychology in the Schools, 22,* 133–141.

Hayes, S. C. (1999). Comparison of the Kaufman Brief Intelligence Test and the Matrix Analogies Test—Short Form in an adolescent forensic population. *Psychological Assessment, 11*(1), 108–110.

Hayes, S. P. (1941). *Contributions to a psychology of blindness.* New York: American Foundation for the Blind.

Haynes, J. P., & Bensch, M. (1981). The P>V sign on the WISC-R and recidivism in delinquents. *Journal of Consulting and Clinical Psychology, 49,* 480–481.

Hays, J. R., & Smith, A. L. (1980). Comparison of the WISC-R and culture-fair intelligence tests for three ethnic groups of juvenile delinquents. *Psychological Reports, 46,* 931–934.

Haywood, H. C. (1986). *A transactional approach to intellectual and cognitive development.* Prepared for presentation at university de Provence, Aix-en-Provence, France, Conference on Cognitive Development.

Haywood, H. C., & Switzky, H. N. (1986). The malleability of intelligence: Cognitive processes as a function of polygenic-experiential interaction. *School Psychology Review, 15,* 245–255.

Haywood, H. C., Tzuriel, D., & Vaught, S. (1992). Psychoeducational assessment from a transactional perspective. In H. C. Haywood & D. Tzuriel (Eds.), *Interactive assessment* (pp. 38–63). New York: Springer-Verlag.

Hebb, D. O. (1949). *The organization of behavior.* New York: Wiley.

Heber, R. (1961). A manual on terminology and classification in mental retardation (rev. ed.). *American Journal of Mental Deficiency,* Monograph (Suppl. 64).

Herrera-Graf, M., Dipert, Z. J., & Hinton, R. N. (1996). Exploring the effective use of the vocabulary/block design short form with a special school population. *Educational and Psychological Measurement, 56*(3), 522–528.

Herskowitz, J., & Rosman, N. P. (1982). *Pediatrics, neurology, and psychiatry—common ground.* New York: Macmillan.

Hertzog, C., Schaie, K. W., & Gribbin, K. (1978). Cardiovascular disease and changes in intellectual functioning from middle to old age. *Journal of Gerontology, 33,* 872–883.

Hickman, J. A., & Stark, K. D. (1987, April). *Relationship between cognitive impulsivity and information processing abilities in children: Implications for training programs.* Paper presented at the meeting of the National Association of School Psychologists, New Orleans, LA.

Hilliard, A. G. (1989). Back to Binet: The case against the use of IQ tests in the schools. *Diagnostique, 2,* 125–135.

Hinshelwood, J. (1986). A case of dyslexia: A peculiar form of word blindness. *Lancet, 2,* 1451.

Hiskey, M. S. (1966). *Hiskey-Nebraska Test of Learning Aptitude.* Lincoln, NE: Union College Press.

Hobson v. Hansen, 269 F. Supp. 401 (D. C. 1967).

Hofmann, R. (1988, May). Comparability of Binet (4th) Full Scale and abbreviated IQs. *National Association of School Psychologists: Communique, 27.*

Hoge, R. D. (1988, October). Issues in the definition and measurement of the giftedness construct. *Educational Researcher,* 12–16.

Hogg, J., & Moss, S. (1995). The applicability of the Kaufman Assessment Battery for Children (K-ABC) with older adults (50+ years) with moderate, severe, and profound intellectual impairment. *Journal of Intellectual Disability Research, 39*(3), 167–176.

Holland, A. M., & McDermott, P. A. (1996). Discovering core profile types in the school-age standardization sample of the Differential Ability Scales. *Journal of Psychoeducational Assessment, 14*(2), 131–146.

Hollenbeck, G. P., & Kaufman, A. S. (1973). Factor analysis of the Wechsler Preschool and Primary Scale of Intelligence (WPPSI). *Journal of Clinical Psychology, 29,* 41–45.

Honzik, M. P., Macfarlane, J. W., & Allen, L. (1948). The stability of mental test performance between two and eighteen years. *Journal of Experimental Psychology, 17,* 309–324.

Hopkins, K. D., & Glass, G. V. (1978). *Basic statistics for the behavioral sciences.* Englewood Cliffs, NJ: Prentice-Hall.

Hooper, S. R., & Hynd, G. W. (1985). Differential diagnosis of subtypes of developmental dyslexia with the Kaufman Assessment Battery for Children (K-ABC). *Journal of Clinical Child Psychology, 14,* 145–152.

Horn, J. L. (1979). The rise and fall of human abilities. *Journal of Research and Development in Education, 12*(2), 59–78.

Horn, J. L. (1994). Theory of fluid and crystallized intelligence. In R. J. Sternberg (Ed.), *Encyclopedia of human intelligence* (pp. 443–451). New York: Macmillan.

Horn, J. L., & Cattell, R. B. (1966). Refinement and test of the theory of fluid and crystallized general intelligences. *Journal of Educational Psychology, 57,* 253–270.

Horn, J. L., & Noll, J. (1997). Human cognitive capabilities: Gf-Gc theory. In D. P. Flanagan, J. L. Genshaft, & P. L. Harrison (Eds.), *Contemporary intellectual assessment* (pp. 53–91). New York: Guilford Press.

Horney, K. (1939). *New ways in psychoanalysis.* New York: Norton.

Horowitz, F. D., & O'Brien, M. (1989). A reflective essay on the state of our knowledge and the challenges before us. *American Psychologist, 44,* 441–445.

Hubble, L. M., & Groff, M. (1981). Magnitude and direction of WISC-R Verbal-Performance IQ discrepancies among adjudicated male delinquents. *Journal of Youth and Adolescence, 10,* 179–184.

Huberty, T. J. (1986). Relationship of the WISC-R factors to the Adaptive Behavior Scale—School Edition in a referral sample. *Journal of School Psychology, 24*(2), 155–162.

Humphreys, L. G., & Parsons, C. K. (1979). Piagetian tasks measure intelligence and intelligence tests assess cognitive development: A reanalysis. *Intelligence, 3,* 369–382.

Hunt, E. (1999a). Intelligence and human resources: Past, present, and future. In P. L. Ackerman, P. C. Kyllonen, & R. D. Roberts (Eds.), *Learning and individual differences: Process, trait, and content determinants* (pp. 3–30). Washington, DC: Author.

Hunt, J. M. (1961). *Intelligence and experience.* New York: Ronald Press.

Hunter, J. E., & Schmidt, F. L. (1976). Critical analysis of the statistical and ethical implications of various definitions of test bias. *Psychological Bulletin, 83,* 1053–1071.

Hunter, J. E., Schmidt, F. L., & Rauschenberger, J. (1984). Methodological, statistical, and ethical issues in the study of bias in psychological tests. In C. R. Reynolds & R. T. Brown (Eds.), *Perspectives on bias in mental testing* (pp. 41–99). New York: Plenum.

Hutchens, T., & Thomas, M. G. (1990). The effects of vocal intonation in digit span testing. *Journal of Psychoeducational Assessment, 8,* 150–154.

Huttenlocher, P. R., Levine, S. C., Huttenlocher, J., & Gates, J. (1990). Discrimination of normal and at-risk preschool children on the basis of neurological tests. *Developmental Medicine and Child Neurology, 32,* 394–402.

Hynd, G. W. (1988). *Neuropsychological assessment in clinical child psychology.* Newbury Park, CA: Sage.

Hynd, G. W., & Obrzut, J. E. (1986). Clinical child neuropsychology: Issues and perspectives. In J. E. Obrzut & G. W. Hynd (Eds.), *Child neuropsychology: Vol. 2. Clinical practice* (pp. 3–14). Orlando, FL: Academic Press.

Hynd, G. W., & Semrud-Clikeman, M. (1989). Dyslexia and brain morphology. *Psychological Bulletin, 106,* 447–482.

Hynd, G. W., & Semrud-Clikeman, M. (1990). Neuropsychological assessment. In A. S. Kaufman (Ed.), *Assessing adolescent and adult intelligence* (pp. 638–695). Boston, MA: Allyn & Bacon.

Hynd, G. W., Semrud-Clikeman, M., Lorys, A. R., Novey, E. S., & Eliopulus, D. (1990). Brain morphology in developmental dyslexia and attention deficit disorder/hyperactivity. *Archives of Neurology, 47*, 919–926.

Hynd, G. W., & Willis, W. G. (1985). Neurological foundations of intelligence. In B. B. Wolman (Ed.), *Handbook of intelligence* (pp. 119–158). New York: Wiley.

Hynd, G. W., & Willis, W. G. (1988). *Pediatric neuropsychology*. Orlando, FL: Grune & Stratton.

Inclan, J. E., & Herron, D. G. (1989). Puerto Rican adolescents. In G. T. Gibbs & L. N. Huang (Eds.), *Children of color* (pp. 251–277). San Francisco: Jossey-Bass Publications.

Ingram, G., & Hakari, L. (1985). Validity of the Woodcock-Johnson Test of Cognitive Ability for Gifted Children: A comparison with the WISC-R. *Journal for the Education of the Gifted, 9*, 11–23.

Ipsen, S. M., McMillan, J. H., & Fallen, N. H. (1983). An investigation of the reported discrepancy between the Woodcock-Johnson Tests of Cognitive Ability and the Wechsler Intelligence Scale for Children-Revised. *Diagnostique, 9*, 32–44.

Jacklin, C. N. (1989). Female and male: Issues of gender. *American Psychologist, 44*, 127–133.

Jacob, S., & Brantley, J. C. (1987). Ethical-legal problems with computer use and suggestions for best practices: A national survey. *School Psychology Review, 16*, 69–77.

Jaffe, K. M., Fay, G. C., Polissar, N. L., Martin, K. M., Shurtleff, H., Rivara, J. B., & Winn, H. R. (1992). Severity of pediatric traumatic brain injury and early neurobehavioral outcome: A cohort study. *Archives of Physical Medicine and Rehabilitation, 73*, 540–547.

Jastrow, J. (1901). Some currents and undercurrents in psychology. *The Psychological Review, 8*, 1–26.

Jenkins, J. J., & Paterson, D. G. (Eds.). (1961). *Studies in individual differences*. New York: Appleton-Century-Crofts.

Jensen, A. R. (1969). How much can we boost IQ and scholastic achievement? *Harvard Educational Review, 39*, 1–123.

Jensen, A. R. (1974). Cumulative deficit: A testable hypothesis. *Developmental Psychology, 10*, 996–1019.

Jensen, A. R. (1976). Test bias and construct validity. *Phi Delta Kappan, 58*, 340–346.

Jensen, A. R. (1977). Cumulative deficit in IQ of blacks in the rural south. *Developmental Psychology, 13*, 184–191.

Jensen, A. R. (1980). *Bias in mental testing*. New York: Free Press.

Jensen, A. R. (1982). Reaction time and psychometric *g*. In R. J. Sternberg (Ed.), *A model for intelligence* (pp. 93–132). Heidelberg: Springer-Verlag.

Jensen, A. R. (1984). The black-white difference on the K-ABC: Implications for future tests. *The Journal of Special Education, 18*, 377–408.

Jensen, A. R. (1986). g: Artifact or reality. *Journal of Vocational Behavior, 29*, 301–331.

Jensen, A. R. (1987). Intelligence as a fact of nature. *Zeitschrift fur Padagogische Psychologie, 3*, 157–169.

Johnstone, B., Slaughter, J., Schoop, L., McAllister, J., Schwake, C., & Luebbering, A. (1997). Determining neuropsychological impairment using estimates of premorbid intelligence: Comparing methods based on level of education versus reading scores. *Archives of Clinical Neuropsychology, 12*, 591–601.

Joreskog, K. G., & Sorbom, D. (1984). *LISREL VI: Analysis of linear structural relationships by the method of maximum likelihood: User's guide*. Mooresville, IN: Scientific Software.

Joreskog, K. G., & Sorbom, D. (1987). *Lisrel 6.13: User's reference guide*. Chicago, IL: Scientific Software.

Jorgensen, K., & Christensen, A. (1995). The approach of A. R. Luria to neuropsychological assessment. In R. L. Mapou & J. Spector (Eds.), *Clinical neuropsychological assessment: A cognitive approach* (pp. 217–236). New York: Plenum Press.

Juliano, J. M., Haddad, F. A., & Carroll, J. L. (1988). Three year stability of the WISC-R factor scores for black and white, female and male children classified as learning disabled. *Journal of School Psychology, 26*, 317–325.

Kagan, J., & Klein, R. E. (1973). Cross-cultural perspectives on early development. *American Psychologist, 28*, 947–961.

Kagan, J., & Salkind, N. J. (1965). *Matching familiar figures test*. (Available from Jerome Kagan, Harvard University, 33 Kirkland Street, 1510 William James Hall, Cambridge, MA 02138).

Kagan, V. E. (1981). Nonprocess autism in children: A comparative etiopathogenic study. *Soviet Neurology and Psychiatry, 14*, 25–30.

Kamin, L. J. (1974). *The science and politics of IQ*. Potomac, MD: Lawrence Erlbaum.

Kamphaus, R. W. (1983, August). *The relationship of the Kaufman Assessment Battery for Children (K-ABC) to diagnostic measures of academic achievement*. Paper presented at the meeting of the American Psychological Association, Anaheim, CA.

Kamphaus, R. W. (1987). Conceptual and psychometric issues in the assessment of adaptive behavior. *Journal of Special Education, 21*, 27–36.

Kamphaus, R. W. (1990). K-ABC theory in historical and current contexts. *Journal of Psychoeducational Assessment, 8*, 356–368.

Kamphaus, R. W. (1991, October). Multicultural expertise. *Child Assessment News*, pp. 1, 8–10.

Kamphaus, R. W. (1993). *Clinical assessment of children's intelligence*. Boston: Allyn & Bacon.

Kamphaus, R. W. (1995). Review of the Slosson Intelligence Test [1991 Edition]. In J. C. Conoley & J. C. Impara (Eds.), *The twelfth mental measurements yearbook* (pp. 954–956). Lincoln: University of Nebraska Press.

Kamphaus, R. W., Benson, J., Hutchinson, S., & Platt, L. O. (1994). Identification of factor models for the WISC-III. *Educational and Psychological Measurement, 54,* 174–186.

Kamphaus, R. W., Dresden, J., & Kaufman, A. S. (1993). Clinical and psychometric considerations in the assessment of preschool children. In D. J. Willis & J. L. Culbertson (Eds.), *Testing young children*. Austin, TX: Pro Ed. Allyn & Bacon.

Kamphaus, R. W., & Kaufman, A. S. (1986). Factor analysis of the Kaufman Assessment Battery for Children (K-ABC) for separate groups of boys and girls. *Journal of Clinical Child Psychology, 3,* 210–213.

Kamphaus, R. W., Kaufman, A. S. & Kaufman, N. L. (1982, August). *A cross-validation study of sequential-simultaneous processing at 2 ½ to 12 ½ using the Kaufman Assessment Battery for Children*. Paper presented at the meeting of the American Psychological Association, Washington, DC.

Kamphaus, R. W., & Lozano, R. (1981). Developing local norms for individually administered tests. *School Psychology Review, 13,* 491–498.

Kamphaus, R. W., Morgan, A. W., Cox, M. R., & Powell, R. M. (1995). Personality and intelligence in the psychodiagnostic process: The emergence of diagnostic schedules. In D. H. Saklofske & M. Zeidner (Eds.), *International handbook of personality and intelligence* (pp. 525–544). New York: Plenum Press.

Kamphaus, R. W., & Pleiss, K. (1991). Draw-a-person techniques: Tests in search of a construct. *Journal of School Psychology, 29,* 395–401.

Kamphaus, R. W., & Reynolds, C. R. (1984). Development and structure of the Kaufman Assessment Battery for Children. *The Journal of Learning Education, 18* (3), 213–228.

Kamphaus, R. W., & Reynolds, C. R. (1987). *Clinical and research applications of the K-ABC*. Circle Pines, MN: American Guidance Service.

Kamphaus, R. W., Reynolds, C. R., & Imperato-McCammon, C. (1999). Diagnosis and classification in school psychology. In C. R. Reynolds & T. B. Gutkin (Eds.), *Handbook of school psychology* (3rd ed.). New York: Wiley.

Kamphaus, R. W., & Stanton, H. (1988, August). *Reliability of the parent rating scale of the Behavior Assessment System for Children (BASC)*. Paper presented at the meeting of the American Psychological Association, Atlanta, GA.

Kane, R. L., Parsons, O. A., & Goldstein, G. (1985). Statistical relationships and discriminative accuracy of the Halstead-Reitan, Luria-Nebraska, and Wechsler IQ scores in the identification of brain damage. *Journal of Clinical and Experimental Neuropsychology, 7,* 211–223.

Kaplan, C. (1992). Ceiling effects in assessing high-IQ children with the WPPSI-R. *Journal of Clinical Child Psychology, 21*(4), 403–406.

Kaplan, C. (1993). Predicting first-grade achievement from pre-kindergarten WPPSI-R scores. *Journal of Psychoeducational Assessment, 11,* 133–138.

Kaplan, E. (1988). A process approach to neuropsychological assessment. In T. Boll & B. K. Bryant (Eds.), *Clinical neuropsychology and brain function: Research, measurement and practice* (pp. 125–167). Washington, DC: American Psychological Association.

Kaplan, R. J., & Klanderman, J. W. (1984, April). *Neuropsychological profile of T.M.H. youngsters assessed with the K-ABC*. Paper presented at the meeting of the National Association of School Psychologists, Philadelphia, PA.

Kareken, D. A. (1997). Judgment pitfalls in estimating premorbid intellectual function. *Archives of Clinical Neuropsychology, 12,* 701–709.

Kareken, D. A., & Williams, J. M. (1994). Human judgment and estimation of premorbid intellectual function. *Psychological Assessment, 6,* 83–91.

Karnes, F. A., Edwards, R. P., & McCallum, R. S. (1986). Normative achievement assessment of gifted children: Comparing the K-ABC, WRAT, and CAT. *Psychology in the Schools, 23,* 361–364.

Kaufman, A. S. (1972, May). *Restriction of range: Questions and answers* (Test Service Bulletin No. 59). San Antonio, TX: The Psychological Corporation.

Kaufman, A. S. (1975a). Factor analysis of the WISC-R at 11 age levels between 6-1/2 and 16-1/2 years. *Journal of Consulting and Clinical Psychology, 43,* 135–147.

Kaufman, A. S. (1975b). Factor structure of the McCarthy Scales at five age levels between 2-1/2 and 8-1/2. *Educational and Psychological Measurement, 35,* 641–656.

Kaufman, A. S. (1976a). Verbal-Performance IQ discrepancies on the WISC-R. *Journal of Consulting and Clinical Psychology, 44,* 739–744.

Kaufman, A. S. (1976b). A four-test short form of the WISC-R. *Contemporary Educational Psychology, 1,* 180–196.

Kaufman, A. S. (1977). A McCarthy short form for rapid screening of preschool, kindergarten, and first-grade children. *Contemporary Educational Psychology, 2,* 149–157.

Kaufman, A. S. (1978). The importance of basic concepts in the individual assessment of preschool children. *Journal of School Psychology, 16,* 207–211.

Kaufman, A. S. (1979a). Cerebral specialization and intelligence testing. *Journal of Research and Development in Education, 12,* 96–107.

Kaufman, A. S. (1979b). *Intelligent testing with the WISC-R.* New York: Wiley-Interscience.

Kaufman, A. S. (1979c). Role of speed on WISC-R Performance across the age range. *Journal of Consulting and Clinical Psychology, 47,* 595–597.

Kaufman, A. S. (1982). An integrated review of almost a decade of research of the McCarthy Scales. In T. R. Kratochwill (Ed.), *Advances in school psychology* (Vol. 2, pp. 119–169). Hillsdale, NJ: Erlbaum.

Kaufman, A. S. (1983). Some questions and answers about the Kaufman Assessment Battery for Children (K-ABC). *Journal of Psychoeducational Assessment, 1,* 205–218.

Kaufman, A. S. (1984). K-ABC and controversy. *The Journal of Special Education, 18,* 409–444.

Kaufman, A. S. (1990). *Assessing adolescent and adult intelligence.* Needham, MA: Allyn & Bacon.

Kaufman, A. S. (1992). Dr. Wechsler remembered. *The School Psychologist, 46(2),* 4–5, 17.

Kaufman, A. S. (1994). *Intelligent testing with the WISC-III.* New York: Wiley.

Kaufman, A. S., & Applegate, B. (1988). Short forms of the K-ABC Mental Processing and Achievement scales at ages 4 to 12-1/2 years for clinical and screening purposes. *Journal of Clinical Child Psychology, 17,* 359–369.

Kaufman, A. S., & DiCuio, R. F. (1975). Separate factor analysis of the McCarthy Scales for groups of black and white children. *Journal of School Psychology, 13,* 10–17.

Kaufman, A. S., & Doppelt, J. E. (1976). Analysis of WISC-R standardization data in terms of the stratification variables. *Child Development, 47,* 165–171.

Kaufman, A. S., & Hollenbeck, G. P. (1973). Factor analysis of the standardization edition of the McCarthy Scales. *Journal of Clinical Psychology, 29,* 358–362.

Kaufman, A. S., & Hollenbeck, G. P. (1974). Comparative structure of the WPPSI for blacks and whites. *Journal of Clinical Psychology, 13,* 10–18.

Kaufman, A. S., & Kamphaus, R. W. (1984). Factor analysis of the Kaufman Assessment Battery for Children (K-ABC) for ages 2-1/2 through 12-1/2 years. *Journal of Educational Psychology, 76(4),* 623–637.

Kaufman, A. S., Kamphaus, R. W., & Kaufman, N. L. (1985). The Kaufman Assessment Battery for Children (K-ABC). In C. S. Newmark (Ed.), *Major psychological assessment instruments* (pp. 249–275). Newton, MA: Allyn & Bacon.

Kaufman, A. S., & Kaufman, N. L. (1977). *Clinical evaluation of young children with the McCarthy Scales.* New York: Grune & Stratton.

Kaufman, A. S., & Kaufman, N. L. (1983a). *Administration and scoring manual for the Kaufman Assessment Battery for Children.* Circle Pines, MN: American Guidance Service.

Kaufman, A. S., & Kaufman, N. L. (1983b). *Interpretive manual for the Kaufman Assessment Battery for Children.* Circle Pines, MN: American Guidance Service.

Kaufman, A. S., & Kaufman, N. L. (1985a). *Brief Form manual for the Kaufman Test of Educational Achievement.* Circle Pines, MN: American Guidance Service.

Kaufman, A. S., & Kaufman, N. L. (1985b). *Comprehensive Form manual for the Kaufman Test of Educational Achievement.* Circle Pines, MN: American Guidance Service.

Kaufman, A. S., & Kaufman, N. L. (1990). *Manual for the Kaufman Brief Intelligence Test.* Circle Pines, MN: American Guidance Service.

Kaufman, A. S., & Kaufman, N. L. (1993). *Kaufman Adolescent and Adult Intelligence Test.* Circle Pines, MN: American Guidance Service.

Kaufman, A. S., & Kaufman, N. L. (1997a). *Brief Form manual for the Kaufman Test of Educational Achievement: Normative update.* Circle Pines, MN: American Guidance Service.

Kaufman, A. S., & Kaufman, N. L. (1997b). *Comprehensive Form manual for the Kaufman Test of Educational Achievement: Normative update.* Circle Pines, MN: American Guidance Service.

Kaufman, A. S., Kaufman, J. C., Chen, T.-H., Kaufman, N. L. (1996). Differences on six horn abilities for 14 age groups between 15–16 and 75–94 years. *Psychological Assessment, 8(2),* 161–171.

Kaufman, A. S., Kaufman, J. C., & McLean, J. E. (1995). Factor structure of the Kaufman Adolescent and Adult Intelligence Test (KAIT) for whites, African Americans, and Hispanics. *Educational and Psychological Measurement, 55(3),* 365–376.

Kaufman, A. S., Kaufman, N. L., Kamphaus, R. W., Naglieri, J. A. (1982). Sequential and simultaneous factors at ages 3–12-1/2: Developmental changes in neuropsychological dimensions. *Clinical Neuropsychology, 4,* 74–81.

Kaufman, A. S., & Lichtenberger, E. O. (1999). *Essentials of WAIS-III assessment,* New York: John Wiley & Sons.

Kaufman, A. S., Long, S. W., & O'Neal, M. R. (1986). Topical review of the WISC-R for pediatric neuroclinicians. *Journal of Child Neurology, 1,* 89–98.

Kaufman, A. S., & McLean, J. E. (1986). K-ABC/WISC-R factor analysis for a learning disabled population. *Journal of Learning Disabilities, 19,* 145–153.

Kaufman, A. S., & McLean, J. E. (1987). Joint factor analysis of the K-ABC and WISC-R with normal children. *Journal of School Psychology, 25 (2),* 105–118.

Kaufman, A. S., McLean, J. E., & Reynolds, C. R. (1991). Analysis of WAIS-R factor patterns by sex and race. *Journal of Clinical Psychology, 47*(4), 548–557.

Kaufman, A. S., & O'Neal, M. R. (1988). Factor structure of the Woodcock-Johnson cognitive subtests from preschool to adulthood. *Journal of Psychoeducational Assessment, 6*(1), 35–48.

Kaufman, A. S., O'Neal, M. R., Avant, A. H., & Long, S. W. (1987). Introduction to the Kaufman Assessment Battery for Children (K-ABC) for pediatric neuroclinicians. *Journal of Child Neurology, 2*, 3–16.

Kaufman, A. S., Reynolds, C. R., & McLean, J. E. (1989). Age and WAIS-R intelligence in a national sample of adults in the 20- to 74-year range: A cross-sectional analysis with education level controlled. *Intelligence, 13*, 235–253.

Kavale, K. A., & Forness, S. R. (1984). A meta-analysis of the validity of Wechsler Scale profiles and recategorizations: Patterns or parities. *Learning Disabilities Quarterly, 7*, 136–156.

Keith, T. Z. (1985). Questioning the K-ABC: What does it measure? *School Psychology Review, 14*, 9–20.

Keith, T. Z. (1990). Confirmatory and hierarchical confirmatory analysis of the Differential Ability Scales. *Journal of Psychoeducational Assessment, 8*, 391–405.

Keith, T. Z. (1994). Intelligence is important, intelligence is complex. *School Psychology Quarterly, 9*, 209–221.

Keith, T. Z., & Bolen, L. M. (1980). Factor structure of the McCarthy Scales for children experiencing problems in school. *Psychology in the Schools, 17*, 320–326.

Keith, T. Z., Cool, V. A., Novak, C. G., White, L. J., & Pottebaum, S. M. (1988). Confirmatory factor analysis of the Stanford-Binet Fourth Edition: Testing the theory-test match. *Journal of School Psychology, 26*, 253–274.

Keith, T. Z., & Dunbar, S. B. (1984). Hierarchical factor analysis of the K-ABC: Testing alternate models. *Journal of Special Education, 18* (3), 367–375.

Keith, T. Z., Fehrmann, P. G., Harrison, P. L., & Pottebaum, S. M. (1986). The relation between adaptive behavior and intelligence: Testing alternative explanations. *Journal of School Psychologists, 25*, 31–43.

Keith, T. Z., Fugate, M. H., DeGraff, M., Diamond, C. M., Shadrach, E. A., & Stevens, M. L. (1995). Using multi-sample confirmatory factor analysis to test for construct bias: An example using the K-ABC. *Journal of Psychoeducational Assessment, 13*(4), 347–364.

Keith, T. Z., Hood, C., Eberhart, S., & Pottebaum, S. M. (1985, April). *Factor structure of the K-ABC for referred school children.* Paper presented at the meeting of the National Association of School Psychologists, Las Vegas, NV.

Keith, T. Z., & Witta, E. L. (1997). Hierarchical and cross-age confirmatory factor analysis of the WISC-III: What does it measure? *School Psychology Quarterly, 12*(2), 89–107.

Kellerman, H., & Burry, A. (1981). *Handbook of psychodiagnostic testing.* New York: Grune & Stratton.

Kelly, M. D., Arceneaux, J. M., Dean, R. S., & Anderson, J. L. (1994). Neuropsychological significance of IQ summary scores. *International Journal of Neuroscience, 75*, 175–179.

Kelly, R. R., & Tomlinson-Keasey C. (1976). Information processing of visually presented picture and word simulation by young hearing-impaired children. *Journal of Speech Hearing Resource, 19*, 628–638.

Kennard, M. (1936). Age and other factors in motor recovery from precentral lesions in monkeys. *Journal of Neurophysiology, 1*, 447–496.

Kennard, M. (1942). Cortical reorganization of motor function: Studies on series of monkeys of various ages from infancy to maturity. *Archives of Neurology and Psychiatry, 47*, 227–240.

Kennedy, M. H., & Hiltonsmith, R. W. (1988). Relationship among the K-ABC Nonverbal Scale, the Pictorial Test of Intelligence, and the Hiskey-Nebraska Test of Learning Aptitude for speech- and language-disabled preschool children. *Journal of Psychoeducational Assessment, 6*, 49–54.

Kinsbourne, M. (1974). Mechanisms of hemispheric interaction in man. In M. Kinsbourne & W. L. Smith (Eds.), Hemispheric disconnection and cerebral function (pp. 260–285). Springfield, IL: Charles C. Thomas.

Kinsbourne, M. (1975). Cerebral dominance, learning, and cognition. In H. R. Myklebust (Ed.), *Progress in learning disabilities* v.3 (pp. 201–218). New York: Grune & Stratton.

Kinsbourne, M. (1978). Biological determinants of functional bisymmetry and asymmetry. In M. Kinsbourne (Ed.), *Asymmetrical function of the brain* (pp. 3–13). London: Cambridge University Press.

Kinsbourne, M. (1982). Hemispheric specialization and the growth of human understanding. *American Psychologist, 37*, 411–420.

Kinsella, G., Prior, M., Sawyer, M., Murtagh, D., Eisenmajer, R., Anderson, V., Bryan, D., & Klug, G. (1995). Neuropsychological deficit and academic performance in children and adolescents following traumatic brain injury. *Journal of Pediatric Psychology, 20*, 753–767.

Kirk, S. A. (1962). *Educating exceptional children.* New York: Houghton Mifflin.

Kirk, S. A., Gallagher, J. J., & Anastasiow, N. J. (1997). *Educating exceptional children* (8th ed.). New York: Houghton Mifflin.

Klanderman, J. W., Perney, J., & Kroeschell, Z. B. (1984, April). *Comparisons of the K-ABC and WISC-R for LD Children.* Paper presented at the meeting of the National Association of School Psychologists, Philadelphia, PA.

Klanderman, J. W., Perney, J., & Kroeschell, Z. B. (1985a, April). *Comparisons of the K-ABC and WISC-R for LD children.* Paper presented at the meeting of the National Association of School Psychologists, Las Vegas, NV.

Klanderman, J. W., Perney, J., & Kroeschell, Z. B. (1985b). Comparisons of the K-ABC and WISC-R for LD children. *Journal of Learning Disabilities, 18*(9), 524–527.

Klesges, R. C. (1982). Establishing premorbid levels of intellectual functioning in children: An empirical investigation. *Clinical Neuropsychology, 4,* 15–17.

Klesges, R. C., Fisher, L., Vasey, M., & Pheley, A. (1985). Predicting adult premorbid functioning levels: Another look. *Clinical Neuropsychology, 7,* 1–3.

Klesges, R. C., & Sanchez, V. C. (1981). Cross-validation of an index of premorbid functioning in children. *Journal of Clinical and Consulting Psychology, 49,* 141.

Kline, R. B. (1991). Latent variable path analysis in clinical research: A beginner's tour guide. *Journal of Clinical Psychology, 47,* 471–484.

Kline, R. B. (1989). Is the Fourth Edition Stanford-Binet a four-factor test? Confirmatory analysis of alternative models for ages 2 through 23. *Journal of Psychoeducational Assessment,* pp. 7, 4–13.

Kline, R. B., Guilmette, S., Snyder, J., & Castellanos, M. (1992). Relative cognitive complexity of the Kaufman Assessment Battery for Children (K-ABC) and the WISC-R. *Journal of Psychoeducational Assessment, 10*(2), 141–152.

Kline, R. B., Snyder, J., Guilmette, S., & Castellanos, M. (1992). Relative usefulness of elevation, variability, and shape information from WISC-R, K-ABC, and Fourth Edition Stanford-Binet profiles in predicting achievement. *Psychological Assessment, 4*(4), 426–432.

Kline, R. B., Snyder, J., Guilmette, S., & Castellanos, M. (1993). External validity of the profile variability index for the K-ABC, Stanford-Binet, and WISC-R: Another cul-de-sac. *Journal of Learning Disabilities, 26*(8), 557–567.

Knight, R. M., & Bakker, D. J. (1980). *Treatment of hyperactive and learning disordered children: Current research.* Baltimore: University Park Press.

Kohs, S. C. (1923). *Intelligence measurement: A psychological and statistical study based upon the Block-Design Test.* New York: Macmillan.

Kohs, S. C. (1927). *Intelligence measurement.* New York: Macmillan.

Kolb, B., & Fantie, B. (1997). Development of the child's brain and behavior. In C. R. Reynolds & E. Fletcher-Janzen (Eds.), *Handbook of clinical child neuropsychology* (2nd ed., pp. 17–41). New York: Plenum Press.

Kolb, B., & Whishaw, I. Q. (1985). *Fundamentals of human neuropsychology* (2nd ed.). San Francisco: Freeman.

Koppitz, E. M. (1963). *Psychological evaluation of children's human figure drawings.* New York: Grune & Stratton.

Korkman, M., Kirk, U., & Kemp, S. (1998). *NEPSY: A developmental neuropsychological assessment.* San Antonio, TX: Psychological Corporation.

Kranzler, J. H. (1997). What does the WISC-III measure? Comments on the relationship between intelligence, working memory capacity, and information processing speed and efficiency. *School Psychology Quarterly, 12*(2), 110–116.

Kranzler, J. H., & Weng, L. (1995a). Factor structure of the PASS cognitive tasks: A reexamination of Naglieri et al. (1991). *Journal of School Psychology, 33,* 143–157.

Kranzler, J. H., & Weng, L. (1995b). Reply to the commentary by Naglieri and Das on the factor structure of a battery of PASS cognitive tasks. *Journal of School Psychology, 33,* 169–176.

Krug, D., Dean, R. S., & Anderson, J. L. (1995). Factor analysis of the Halstead-Reitan neuropsychological Test Battery for Older Children. *International Journal of Neuroscience, 83,* 131–134.

Kunen, S., Overstreet, S., & Salles, C. (1996). Concurrent validity study of the Slosson Intelligence Test—Revised in mental retardation testing. *Mental Retardation, 34*(6), 380–386.

Kyllonen, P., & Alluisi, E. (1987). Learning and forgetting facts and skills. In G. Salvendy (Ed.), *Handbook of human factors* (pp. 124–153). New York: John Wiley & Sons.

Kyllonen, P. C. (1996). Is working memory capacity Spearman's g? In Dennis & P. Tapsfield (Eds.) *Human abilities: Their nature and measurement* (pp. 49–75). Mahwah, NJ: Erlbaum.

LaBuda, M. C., DeFries, J. C., Plomin, R., & Fulker, D. W. (1986). Longitudinal stability of cognitive ability from infancy to early childhood: Genetic and environmental etiologies. *Child Development, 57,* 1142–1150.

Lambert, N. M. (1981). Psychological evidence in Larry P. v. Wilson Riles: An evaluation by a witness for the defense. *American Psychologist, 36,* 937–952.

Lambert, N. M. (1990). Consideration of the Das-Naglieri Cognitive Assessment System. *Journal of Psychoeducational Assessment, 8,* 338–343.

Lampley, D. A., & Rust, J. O. (1986). Validation of the Kaufman Assessment Battery for Children with a sample of preschool children. *Psychology in the Schools, 23,* 131–137.

Landers, S. (1986, December). Judge reiterates I.Q. test ban. *Monitor.* Washington, DC: American Psychological Association.

Larry P. v. Riles, 495 F. Supp. 926 (N. D. Cal. 1979).

Larry P. et al v. Riles. (1979, October). United States District Court for the Northern District of California, C-71–227O RFP.

Larry P. v. Riles. (1986). United States District Count for the Northern District of California, C-71–2270 RFP. Order Modifying Judgment.

Lavin, C. (1996a). Scores on the Wechsler Intelligence Scale for Children—Third Edition and Woodcock-Johnson Test of Achievement—Revised for a sample of children with emotional handicaps. *Psychological Reports, 79*, 1291–1295.

Lavin, C. (1996b). The relationship between the Wechsler Intelligence Scales for Children—Third Edition and the Kaufman Test of Educational Achievement. *Psychology in the Schools, 33*, 119–123.

Leark, R. A., Snyder, T., Grove, T., & Golden, C. J. (1983, August). *Comparison of the K-ABC to standardized neuropsychological batteries: Preliminary results.* Paper presented at the meeting of the American Psychological Association, Anaheim, CA.

Leckliter, I. N., Matarazzo, J. D., & Silverstein, A. B. (1986). A literature review of factor analytic studies of the WAIS-R. *Journal of Clinical Psychology, 42*(2), 332–342.

Lee, L. P., & Lam, Y. R. (1988). Confirmatory factor analyses of the Wechsler Intelligence Scale for Children—Revised and the Hong Kong—Wechsler Intelligence Scale for Children. *Educational and Psychological Measurement, 48*(4), 895–903.

Lee, S. W. (1995). Review of the Woodcock-Johnson Psycho-Educational Battery—Revised. In J. C. Conoley & J. C. Impara (Eds.), *The twelfth mental measurements yearbook* (pp. 1116–1117). Lincoln: University of Nebraska Press.

Leiter, R. G. (1979). *Leiter International Performance Scale: Instruction manual.* Chicago: Stoelting.

Leiter, R. G., & Arthur, G. (1948). *Leiter International Performance Scale.* Chicago: Stoelting.

Lennon, R. T. (1985). Group tests of intelligence. In B. B. Wolman (Ed.), *Handbook of intelligence: Theories, measurements, and applications* (pp. 825–845). New York: Wiley.

Levine, A. J., & Marks, L. (1928). *Testing intelligence and achievement.* New York: MacMillan.

Levine, E. S. (1974). Psychological tests and practices with the deaf: A survey of the state of the art. *The Volta Review, 76*, 298–319.

Levine, M. D., Busch, B., & Aufsuser, C. (1982). The dimension of inattention among children with school problems. *Pediatrics, 70*, 387–395.

Levine, S. C., Huttenlock, P., Banich, M. T., & Duda, C. (1987). Factors affecting cognitive functioning in hemiplegic children. *Developmental Medicine and Child Neurology, 29*, 27–35.

Levy, J. (1974). Psychobiological implications of bilateral asymmetry. In S. Dimond & G. Beaumont (Eds.), *Hemispheric functioning in the human brain.* New York: Halsted Press.

Lewandowski, L. J., & de Rienzo, P. J. (1985). WISC-R and K-ABC performances of hemiplegic children. *Journal of Psychoeducational Assessment, 3*(3), 215–221.

Lewis, M. L., & Johnson, J. J. (1985). Comparison of the WAIS and WAIS-R IQs from two equivalent college populations. *Journal of Psychoeducational Assessment, 3*, 55–60.

Lezak, M. (1995). *Neuropsychological assessment* (3rd ed.). New York: Oxford University Press.

Liaw, F., & Brooks-Gunn, J. (1994). Cumulative familial risks and low-birthweight children's cognitive and behavioral development. *Journal of Clinical Child Psychology, 23*, 360–372.

Lidz, C. S. (1983). Issues in assessing preschool children. In K. D. Paget & B. A. Bracken (Eds.), *The psychoeducational assessment of preschool children* (pp. 17–27). New York: Grune & Stratton.

Lidz, C. S., & Mearig, J. S. (1989). A response to Reynolds. *Journal of School Psychology, 27*, 81–86.

Lindley, R. H., & Smith, W. R. (1992). Coding tests as measures of IQ: Cognition or motivation? *Personality and Individual Differences, 13*(1), 25–29.

Linn, R. L. (1983). Pearson selection formulas: Implications for studies of predictive bias and estimates of educational effects in selected samples. *Journal of Educational Measurement, 20*, 1–15.

Lipsitz, J. D., Dworkin, R. H., & Erlenmeyer-Kimling, L. (1993). Wechsler Comprehension and Picture Arrangement subtests and social adjustment. *Psychological Assessment, 5*, 430–437.

Little, A. J., Templer, D. I., Persel, C. S., & Ashley, M. J. (1996). Feasibility of the neuropsychological spectrum in prediction of outcome following head injury. *Journal of Clinical Psychology, 52*, 455–460.

Little, S. G. (1991, October). Is the WISC-III factor structure valid? (Letter to the editor). *Communique, 24.*

Llorente, A. M., LoPresti, C. M., & Satz, P. (1997). Neuropsychological and neurobehavioral sequelae associated with pediatric HIV infection. In C. R. Reynolds & E. Fletcher-Janzen (Eds.), *Handbook of clinical child neuropsychology* (2nd ed., pp. 634–650). New York: Plenum Press.

Locurto, C. (1990). The malleability of IQ as judged from adoption studies. *Intelligence, 14*, 275–292.

Lohman, D. F. (1999). Minding our p's and q's: On finding relationships between learning and intelligence. In P. L. Ackerman, P. C. Kyllonen, & R. D. Roberts (Eds.), *Learning and individual differences: Process, trait, and content determinants* (pp. 55–76). Washington, DC: Author.

López, S. R. (1999). Teaching culturally informed psychological assessment. In R. H. Dana (Ed.), *Handbook of cross-cultural/multicultural personality assessment* (pp. 669–687). Hillsdale, NJ: Erlbaum.

Lord-Maes, J., & Obrzut, J. E. (1996). Neuropsychological consequences of traumatic brain injury in children and adolescents. *Journal of Learning Disabilities, 29,* 609–617.

Lowman, M. G., Schwanz, K. A., & Kamphaus, R. W. (1997). WISC-III third factor: Critical measurement issues. *Canadian Journal of School Psychology 12*(1), 15–22.

Lufi, D., Cohen, A., & Parish-Plass, J. (1990). Identifying attention deficit hyperactivity disorder with the WISC-R and the Stroop Color and Word Test. *Psychology in the Schools, 27*(1), 28–34.

Lukens, J. (1988). Comparison of the Fourth Edition and the L-M Edition of the Stanford-Binet used with mentally retarded persons. *Journal of School Psychology, 26,* 87–89.

Luria, A. R. (1966a). *Higher cortical functions in man.* New York: Basic Books.

Luria, A. R. (1966b). *Human brain and psychological processes.* New York: Harper & Row.

Luria, A. R. (1970). The functional organization of the brain. *Scientific American, 222,* 66–78.

Luria, A. R. (1973). *The working brain.* London: Penguin.

Luria, A. R. (1980). *Higher cortical functions in man* (2nd ed.). New York: Basic Books.

Luria, A. R., & Majovski, L. V. (1977). Basic approaches used in American and Soviet clinical neuropsychology. *American Psychologist, 32,* 959–968.

Lyman, H. (1963). *Test scores and what they mean.* Englewood Cliffs, NJ: Prentice-Hall.

Lynn, R. (1977). The intelligence of the Japanese. *Bulletin of the British Psychological Society, 30,* 69–72.

Lyon, G. Reid (Ed.). (1994). *Frames of references for the assessment of learning disabilities: New views on measurement issues.* Baltimore: Paul H. Brookes Publishing.

Lyon, G. Reid (1996). Learning disabilities. In E. J. Mash & R. A. Barkley (Eds.), *Child psychopathology* (pp. 390–435). New York: Guilford Press.

Lyon, M. A., & Smith, D. K. (1986). A comparison of at-risk preschool children's performance on the K-ABC, McCarthy Scales, and Stanford-Binet. *Journal of Psychoeducational Assessment, 4,* 35–43.

Mabry, L. (1995). Review of the Wide Range Achievement Test-3. In J. C. Conoley & J. C. Impara (Eds.), *The twelfth mental measurements yearbook* (pp. 1108–1110). Lincoln: University of Nebraska Press.

MacLean, W. E., Noll, R. B., Stehbens, J. A., Kaleita, T. A., Schwartz, E., Whitt, K., Cantor, N. J., Waskerwitz, M., Ruymann, R., Novak, L. J., Woodard, A., & Hammond, D. (1995). Neuropsychological effects of cranial irradiation in young children with acute lymphoblastic leukemia 9 months after diagnosis. *Archives of Neurology, 52,* 156–160.

Macmann, G. M., Plasket, C. M., Barnett, D. W., & Siler, R. F. (1991). Factor structure of the WISC-R for children of superior intelligence. *Journal of School Psychology, 29*(1), 19–36.

Madan-Swain, A., & Brown, R. T. (in press). Cognitive and psychosocial sequelae for children with acute lymphocytic leukemia and their families. *Clinical Psychology Review, 11,* 267–294.

Majovski, L. (1984). The K-ABC: Theory and applications for child neuropsychological assessment and research. *Journal of Special Education, 18,* 257–268.

Maker, C. J., & Schiever, S. W. (1989). *Volume II: Defensible programs for cultural and ethnic minorities.* Austin, TX: Pro-Ed.

Malgady, R. G., & Costantino, G. (1998). Symptom severity in bilingual Hispanics as a function of clinician ethnicity and language of interview. *Psychological Assessment, 10*(2), 120–127.

Markwardt, F. C., Jr. (1989). *Manual for the Peabody Individual Achievement Test—Revised.* Circle Pines, MN: American Guidance Service.

Markwardt, F. C., Jr. (1997). *Manual for the Peabody Individual Achievement Test—Revised: Normative update.* Circle Pines, MN: American Guidance Service.

Martin, R. P. (1988). *The temperament assessment battery for children.* Brandon, VT: Clinical Psychology Publishing.

Maruish, M. E. (1994). Introduction. In M. E. Maruish (Ed.), *The use of psychological testing for treatment planning and outcome assessment* (pp. 3–21). Hillsdale, NJ: Lawrence Erlbaum Associates.

Mash, E. J., & Barkley, R. A. (Eds.). (1996). *Child psychopathology.* New York: Guilford Press.

Matarazzo, J. D. (1972). *Wechsler's measurement and appraisal of adult intelligence.* Baltimore: Williams & Wilkins.

Matarazzo, J. D. (1990). Psychological assessment versus psychological testing: Validation from Binet to the school, clinic, and courtroom. *American Psychologist, 45*(9), 999–1017.

Matarazzo, J. D., & Herman, D. O. (1984). Relationship of education and IQ in the WAIS-R standardization sample. *Journal of Consulting and Clinical Psychology, 52,* 631–634.

Mather, N. (1984). *Performance of learning disability subjects and gifted subjects on the Woodcock-Johnson Psycho-Educational Battery and the Wechsler Intelligence Scale for Children—Revised.* Unpublished doctoral dissertation, University of Arizona, Tucson.

Matheson, D. W., Mueller, H. H., & Short, R. H. (1984). The validity of Bannatyne's acquired knowledge category as a separate construct. *Journal of Psychoeducational Assessment, 2,* 279–291.

Max, J. E., Lindgren, S. D., Robin, D. A., Smith, W. L., Sato, Y., Mattheis, P. J., Castillo, C. S., & Stierwalt, J. A. (1997). Traumatic brain injury in children and adolescents:

Psychiatric disorders in the second three months. *Journal of Nervous and Mental Disease, 185,* 394–401.

Mayer, J. D., & Salovey, P. (1993). The intelligence of emotional intelligence. *Intelligence, 17,* 433–442.

Mayer, J. D., & Salovey, P. (1995). Emotional intelligence and the construction and regulation of feelings. *Applied and Preventive Psychology, 4,* 197–208.

Mayes, S. D. (1994). Questions about the Bayley Scales. *Communiqué, 22*(7).

McCall, R. B. (1983). A conceptual approach to early mental development. In M. Lewis (Ed.), *Origins of intelligence* (2nd ed. pp. 107–133). New York: Plenum.

McCallum, R. S., Karnes, F. A., & Edwards, R. P. (1984). The test of choice for assessment of gifted children: A comparison of the K-ABC, WISC-R, and Stanford-Binet. *Journal of Psychoeducational Assessment, 2,* 57–63.

McCarthy, A. M., Richman, L. C., & Yarbrough, D. (1995). Memory, attention, and school problems in children with seizure disorders. *Developmental Neuropsychology, 11,* 71–86.

McCarthy, D. (1972). *McCarthy Scales of Children's Abilities.* New York: Psychological Corporation.

McDermott, P. A., Fantuzzo, J. W., & Glutting, J. J. (1990). Just say no to subtest analysis: A critique on Wechsler theory and practice. *Journal of Psychoeducational Assessment, 8,* 290–302.

McDermott, P. A., Fantuzzo, J. W., Glutting, J. J., Watkins, M. W., & Baggaley, A. R. (1992). Illusions of meaning in the ipsative assessment of children's ability. *Journal of Special Education, 25,* 504–526.

McDermott, P. A., Glutting, J. J., Jones, J. N., Watkins, M. W., & Kush, J. (1989). Core profile types in the WISC-R national sample: Structure, membership, and applications. *Psychological Assessment, 1,* 292–299.

McFali, R. M. (1995). Models of training and standards of care. In S. C. Hayes, V. M. Follette, R. M. Dawes, & K. E. Grady (Eds.), *Scientific standards of psychological practice: Issues and recommendations* (pp. 125–137). Reno, NV: Context Press.

McGrew, K. S. (1987). Exploratory factor analysis of the Woodcock-Johnson Tests of Cognitive Ability. *Journal of Psychoeducational Assessment, 5*(3), 200–216.

McGrew, K. S. (1994). *Clinical interpretation of the Woodcock-Johnson Tests of Cognitive Ability* (rev. ed.). Needham Heights, MA: Allyn & Bacon.

McGrew, K. S. (1997). Analysis of the major intelligence batteries according to a proposed comprehensive Gf-Gc framework. In D. P. Flanagan, J. L. Genshaft, & P. L. Harrison (Eds.), *Contemporary intellectual assessment* (pp. 151–179). New York: Guilford Press.

McGrew, K. S., & Flanagan, D. F. (1996). General factor and uniqueness characteristics of the Kaufman Adolescent and Adult Intelligence Test (KAIT). *Journal of Educational Assessment, 14,* 208–219.

McGrew, K. S., Flanagan, D. F., Keith, T. Z., Vanderwood, M. (1997). Beyond g: The impact of Gf-Gc specific cognitive abilities research on the future use and interpretation of intelligence tests in the schools. *School Psychology Review, 26,* 189–210.

McGrew, K. S., & Hessler, G. L. (1995). The relationship between the WJ-R Gf-Gc cognitive clusters and mathematics achievement across the life-span. *Journal of Psychoeducational Assessment, 13*(1), 21–38.

McGrew, K. S., & Knopik, S. N. (1993). The relationship between the WJ-R Gf-Gc cognitive clusters and writing achievement across the life-span. *School Psychology Review, 22*(4), 687–695.

McGrew, K. S., & Knopik, S. N. (1996). The relationship between intra-cognitive scatter on the Woodcock-Johnson Psycho-Educational Battery—Revised and school achievement. *Journal of School Psychology, 34*(4), 351–364.

McGrew, K. S., & Murphy, S. (1995). Uniqueness and general factor characteristics of the Woodcock-Johnson Tests of Cognitive Ability—Revised. *Journal of School Psychology, 33*(3), 235–245.

McGrew, K. S., & Pehl, J. (1988). Prediction of future achievement by the Woodcock-Johnson Psycho-Educational Battery and the WISC-R. *Journal of School Psychology, 26,* 275–281.

McGrew, · K. S., Werder, J. K., & Woodcock, R. W. (1991). *WJ-R technical manual.* Allen, TX: DLM Teaching Resources.

McKay, H., Sinisterra, L., McKay, A., Gomez, H., & Lloreda, P. (1978). Improving cognitive ability in chronically deprived children. *Science, 200,* 270–278.

McKay, M. F., Neale, M. D., & Thompson, G. B. (1985). The predictive validity of Bannatyne's WISC categories for later reading achievement. *British Journal of Educational Psychology, 55*(3), 280–287.

McLean, M., McCormick, K., Baird, S., & Mayfield, P. (1987). Concurrent validity of the Battelle Developmental Inventory Screening Test. *Diagnostique, 13,* 10–20.

McLinden, S. E. (1989). An evaluation of the Battelle Developmental Inventory for determining special education eligibility. *Journal of Psychoeducational Assessment, 7,* 66–73.

McLoughlin, C. S., & Ellison, C. L. (1984, April). *Comparison of scores for normal preschool children on the Peabody Picture Vocabulary Test—Revised and the Achievement Scale of the Kaufman Assessment Battery for Children.* Paper presented at the meeting of the National Association of School Psychologists, Philadelphia, PA.

McManis, D. L., Figley, C., Richert, M., & Fabre, T. (1978). Memory for Designs, Bender Gestalt, Trailmaking Test, and

WISC-R performance of retarded inadequate readers. *Perceptual and Motor Skills, 46,* 443–450.

Mealor, D., Livesay, K. K., & Finn, M. H. (1983). Study Number 27. In A. S. Kaufman & N. L. Kaufman (Eds.), *Kaufman Assessment Battery for Children: Interpretive Manual* (p. 97). Circle Pines, MN: American Guidance Service.

Mercer, J. R. (1979). *The System of Multicultural Pluralistic Assessment: Conceptual and technical manual.* New York: Psychological Corporation.

Mercer, J. R., & Lewis, J. E. (1978). *Adaptive Behavior Inventory for Children.* New York: Psychological Corporation.

Merrill, K. W., & Shinn, M. R. (1990). Critical variables in the learning disabilities identification process. *School Psychology Review, 19*(1), 74–82.

Messick, S. (1992). Multiple intelligences or multilevel intelligence? Selective emphasis on distinctive parts of hierarchy: On Gardner's *Frames of Mind* and Sternberg's *Beyond IQ* in the context of theory and research on the structure of human abilities. *Psychological Inquiry, 3,* 365–384.

Michael, W. B. (1998). Review of the Woodcock-McGrew-Werder Mini-Battery of Achievement. In J. C. Impara & B. S. Plake (Eds.), *The thirteenth mental measurements yearbook* (pp. 1140–1142). Lincoln: University of Nebraska Press.

Mille, F. (1979). Cultural bias in the WISC. *Intelligence, 3,* 149–164.

Miller, L. J. (1982). *Miller Assessment for Preschoolers.* Littleton, CO: Foundation for Knowledge and Development.

Miller, M. D. (1995). Review of the Kaufman Brief Intelligence Test. In J. C. Conoley & J. C. Impara (Eds.), *The twelfth mental measurements yearbook* (pp. 533–534). Lincoln: University of Nebraska Press.

Miller, T. L., & Reynolds, C. R. (1984). Special issue . . . The K-ABC. *The Journal of Special Education, 18*(3), 207–448.

Minton, H. L., & Schneider, F. W. (1980). *Differential psychology.* Monterey, CA: Brooks/Cole.

Mishra, S. P., Ferguson, B. A., & King, P. V. (1985). Research with the Wechsler Digit Span subtest: Implications for assessment. *School Psychology Review, 14*(1), 37–47.

Misra, G. (1983). Deprivation and development: A review of Indian studies. *Indian Educational Review,* 12–32.

Molfese, V., Yaple, K., Helwig, S., Harris, L., & Connell, S. (1992). Stanford-Binet Intelligence Scale (Fourth Edition): Factor structure and verbal subscale scores for three-year-olds. *Journal of Psychoeducational Assessment, 10*(1), 47–58.

Moores, D. F. (1987). *Educating the deaf: Psychology, principles, and practices* (3rd ed.). Boston: Houghton Mifflin.

Moreland, K. L., Fowler, R. D., & Honaker, L. M. (1994). Future directions in the use of psychological assessment for treatment planning and outcome assessment: Predictions and recommendations. In M. E. Maruish (Ed.), *The use of psychological testing for treatment planning and outcome assessment* (pp. 581–602). Hillsdale, NJ: Lawrence Erlbaum Associates.

Morgan, A. W., Sullivan, S. A., Darden, C., & Gregg, N. (1997). Measuring the intelligence of college students with learning disabilities: A comparison of results obtained on the WAIS-R and the KAIT. *Journal of Learning Disabilities, 30,* 560–565.

Morra, S. (1994). Issues in working memory measurement: Testing for M capacity. *International Journal of Behavioral Development, 17,* 143–159.

Morris, J. D., Evans, J. G., & Pearson, D. D. (1978). The WISC-R subtest profile of a sample of severely emotionally disturbed children. *Psychological Reports, 42,* 319–325.

Morris, J. M., & Bigler, E. D. (1985, January). *An investigation of the Kaufman Assessment Battery for Children (K-ABC) with neurologically impaired children.* Paper presented at the meeting of the International Neuropsychological Society, San Diego, CA.

Morris, J. M., & Bigler, E. D. (1987). Hemispheric functioning and the Kaufman Assessment Battery for Children: Results in the neurologically impaired. *Developmental Neuropsychology, 3*(1), 67–79.

Morris, R., Blashfield, R., & Satz, P. (1986). Developmental classification of reading-disabled children. *Journal of Clinical and Experimental Neuropsychology, 8,* 371–392.

Moss, H. A., Wolters, P. L., Brouwers, P., Hendricks, M. L., & Pizzo, P. A. (1996). Impairment of expressive behavior in pediatric HIV-infected patients with evidence of CNS disease. *Journal of Pediatric Psychology, 21,* 379–400.

Mott, S. E. (1987). Concurrent validity of the Battelle Developmental Inventory for speech and language disordered children. *Psychology in the Schools, 24,* 215–220.

Murray, A., & Bracken, B. A. (1984). Eleven-month predictive validity of the Kaufman Assessment Battery for Children. *Journal of Psychoeducational Assessment, 2,* 225–232.

Mussman, M. C. (1964). Teacher's evaluations of psychological reports. *Journal of School Psychology, 3,* 35–37.

Myklebust, H. R. (1960). *The psychology of deafness: Sensory deprivation, learning, and adjustment.* New York: Grune & Stratton.

Naeye, R. L., Diener, M. M., Dellinger, W. S., & Blanc, W. A. (1969). Urban poverty: Effect on prenatal nutrition. *Science, 166,* 1026.

Nagle, R. J. (1979). The McCarthy Scale of Children's Abilities: Research implications for the assessment of young children. *School Psychology Review, 8,* 319–326.

Naglieri, J. A. (1981a). Extrapolated developmental indices for the Bayley Scales of Infant Development. *American Journal of Mental Deficiencies, 85,* 548–550.

Naglieri, J. A. (1981b). Factor structure of the WISC-R for children identified as learning disabled. *Psychological Reports, 49,* 891–895.

Naglieri, J. A. (1984). Concurrent and predictive validity of the Kaufman Assessment Battery for Children with a Navajo sample. *Journal of School Psychology, 22,* 373–380.

Naglieri, J. A. (1985a). Use of the WISC-R and K-ABC with learning disabled, borderline mentally retarded, and normal children. *Psychology in the Schools, 22,* 133–141.

Naglieri, J. A. (1985b). Assessment of mentally retarded children with the Kaufman Assessment Battery for Children. *American Journal of Mental Deficiency, 89,* 367–371.

Naglieri, J. A. (1985c). Normal children's performance on the McCarthy Scales, Kaufman Assessment Battery, and Peabody Individual Achievement Test. *Journal of Psychoeducational Assessment, 3,* 123–129.

Naglieri, J. A. (1986). WISC-R and K-ABC comparison for matched samples of black and white children. *Journal of School Psychology, 24,* 81–88.

Naglieri, J. A. (1988a). Interpreting area score variation on the Fourth Edition of the Stanford-Binet Scale of Intelligence. *Journal of Clinical Child Psychology, 17,* 224–228.

Naglieri, J. A. (1988b). Interpreting the subtest profile on the Fourth Edition of the Stanford-Binet Scale of Intelligence. *Journal of Clinical Child Psychology, 17,* 62–65.

Naglieri, J. A. (1988c). *Draw-a-Person: A quantitative system.* New York: Psychological Corporation.

Naglieri, J. A., & Anderson, D. F. (1985). Comparison of the WISC-R and K-ABC with gifted students. *Journal of Psychoeducational Assessment, 3,* 175–179.

Naglieri, J. A., & Bardos, A. N. (1987, March). *Draw-a-Person and Matrix Analogies Test cross-culture validity.* Paper presented at the annual meeting of the National Association of School Psychologists, New Orleans.

Naglieri, J. A., & Bardos, A. N. (1988). Canadian children's performance on the Matrix Analogies Test. *School Psychology International, 9,* 309–313.

Naglieri, J. A., & Das, J. P. (1987). Construct and criterion-related validity of planning, simultaneous and successive cognitive processing tasks. *Journal of Psychoeducational Assessment, 4,* 353–363.

Naglieri, J. A., & Das, J. P. (1988). Planning-arousal-simultaneous-successive (PASS): A model for assessment. *Journal of School Psychology, 26,* 35–48.

Naglieri, J. A., & Das, J. P. (1990). Planning, attention, simultaneous, and successive (PASS) cognitive processes as a model for intelligence. *Journal of Psychoeducational Assessment, 8,* 303–337.

Naglieri, J. A., & Das, J. P. (1997). *Das-Naglieri Cognitive Assessment System.* Itasca, IL: Riverside Publishing.

Naglieri, J. A., Das, J. P., Stevens, J. J., & Ledbetter, M. F. (1991). Confirmatory factor analysis of planning, attention, simultaneous, and successive cognitive processing tasks. *Journal of School Psychology, 29,* 1–17.

Naglieri, J. A., & Haddad, F. (1984). Learning disabled children's performance on the Kaufman Assessment Battery for Children: A concurrent validity study. *Journal of Psychoeducational Assessment, 2,* 49–56.

Naglieri, J. A., & Jensen, A. R. (1987). Comparison of black-white differences on the WISC-R and the K-ABC: Spearman's hypothesis. *Intelligence, 11,* 21–43.

Naglieri, J. A., & Kamphaus, R. W. (in press). Interpreting the subtest profile on the Kaufman Assessment Battery for Children. *Clinical Neuropsychology.*

Naglieri, J. A., Kamphaus, R. W., & Kaufman, A. S. (1983). The Luria-Das simultaneous-successive model applied to the WISC-R. *Journal of Psychoeducational Assessment, 1,* 25–34.

Naglieri, J. A., Kaufman, A. S., Kaufman, N. L., & Kamphaus, R. W. (1981). Cross-validation of Das' simultaneous and successive processes with novel tasks. *Alberta Journal of Educational Research, 27,* 264–271.

Naglieri, J. A., & Prewett, P. N. (1990). Nonverbal intelligence measures: A selected review of instruments and their use. In C. R. Reynolds & R. W. Kamphaus (Eds.), *Handbook of psychological and educational assessment of children: Intelligence and achievement* (pp. 348–370). New York: Guilford.

Naglieri, J. A., & Wisniewski, J. J. (1988). Clinical use of the WISC-R, MAT-EF, and PPVT-R. *Journal of Psychoeducational Assessment, 6,* 390–395.

Narrett, C. M. (in press). Review of the Kaufman Assessment Battery for Children (K-ABC). *The Reading Teacher.*

Nass, R., & Peterson, H. D. (1989). Differential effects of congenital left and right brain injury on intelligence. *Brain and Cognition, 9,* 258–266.

Nass, R., Peterson, H. D., & Koch, D. (1989). Differential effects of congenital left and right brain injury on intelligence. *Brain and Cognition, 9,* 258–266.

National Association of School Psychologists. (1985). *Principles for professional ethics.* Silver Springs, MD: Author.

Naugle, R. I., Chelune, G. J., & Tucker, G. D. (1993). Validity of the Kaufman Brief Intelligence Test. *Psychological Assessment, 3*(2), 182–186.

Nebes, R. D. (1974). Hemispheric specialization in commisurotomized man. *Psychological Bulletin, 81,* 1–14.

Neisser, U. (1967). *Cognitive psychology.* New York: Appleton-Century-Crofts.

Neisser, U. (1979). The concept of intelligence. *Intelligence, 3,* 217–227.

Neisser, U., Boodoo, G., Bouchard, J. T., Jr., Boykin, A. W., Brody, N., Ceci, S. J., Halpern, D. F., Loehlin, J. C., Perloff, R., Sternberg, R. J., & Urbina, S. (1996). Intelligence: Knowns and unknowns. *American Psychologist, 51,* 77–101.

Neisworth, J. T., & Butler, R. J. (1990). Review of the Draw-a-Person: A quantitative scoring system. *Journal of Psychoeducational Assessment, 8,* 190–194.

Nelson, R. B., Obrzut, A., & Cummings, J. (1984). *Construct and predictive validity of the K-ABC with EMR children*. (Available from R. Brett Nelson, Weld County School District #6, Greeley, CO 80631.)

Newborg, J., Stock, J. R., Wnek, L., Guidubaldi, J., & Svinicki, J. (1984). *Battelle Developmental Inventory*. Allen, TX: DLM/Teaching Resources.

Newman, I., & Guidubaldi, J. (1981, April). *Factor validity estimate of the Battelle Developmental Inventory for three age groupings*. Paper presented at the meeting of the National Association of School Psychologists, Houston.

Nihira, K., Foster, R., Shellhaas, M., Leland, H., Lambert, N., & Windmiller, M. (1981). *AAMD Adaptive Behavior Scale, School Edition*. Monterey, CA: Publisher's Test Service.

Nitko, A. (1983). *Educational tests and measurement: An introduction*. New York: Harcourt, Brace, Jovanovich.

Nussbaum, N. L., & Bigler, E. D. (1989). Halstead-Reitan Neuropsychological Test Batteries for Children. In C. R. Reynolds & E. Fletcher-Janzen (Eds.), *Handbook of clinical child neuropsychology* (pp. 181–191). New York, NY: Plenum.

Nussbaum, N. L., & Bigler, E. D. (1997). Halstead-Reitan Neuropsychological Test Batteries for Children. In C. R. Reynolds & E. Fletcher-Janzen (Eds.), *Handbook of clinical child neuropsychology* (2nd ed., pp. 219–236). New York: Plenum Press.

Oakland, T. (1979). Research on the Adaptive Behavior Inventory for Children and the Estimated Learning Potential. *School Psychology Digest, 8*, 63–70.

Oakland, T. (1983). Joint use of adaptive behavior and IQ to predict achievement. *Journal of Consulting and Clinical Psychology, 51*, 298–301.

Oakland, T., & Dowling, L. (1983). The Draw-a-Person test: Validity properties for nonbiased assessment. *Learning Disability Quarterly, 6*, 526–534.

Oakland, T., & Feigenbaum, D. (1979). Multiple sources of test bias on the WISC-R and the Bender-Gestalt Test. *Journal of Consulting and Clinical Psychology, 47*, 968–974.

Oakman, S., & Wilson, B. (1988). Stability of WISC-R intelligence scores: Implication for 3-year reevaluations of learning disabled students. *Psychology in the Schools, 25*(2), 118–120.

Obringer, S. J. (1988, November). *A survey of perceptions by school psychologists of the Stanford-Binet IV*. Paper presented at the meeting of the Mid-South Educational Research Association, Louisville, KY.

Obrzut, A., Nelson, R. B., & Obrzut, J. E. (in press). Construct validity of the K-ABC with mildly mentally retarded students. *American Journal of Mental Deficiency*.

Obrzut, A., Obrzut, J., & Shaw, D. (1984). Construct validity of the Kaufman Assessment Battery for Children with learning disabled and mentally retarded. *Psychology in the Schools, 4*, 417–424.

Obrzut, J. E., & Hynd, G. W. (1986). Child neuropsychology: An introduction to theory and research. In J. E. Obrzut & G. W. Hynd (Eds.), *Child neuropsychology: Vol. 1. Theory and research* (pp. 1–12). Orlando, FL: Academic Press.

Oehler-Stinnett, J. (1989). Review of the Battelle Developmental Inventory. In J. C. Conoley & J. J. Kramer (Eds.). *The tenth mental measurements yearbook* (pp. 66–70). Lincoln: University of Nebraska Press.

O'Grady, K. (1983). A confirmatory maximum likelihood factor analysis of the WAIS-R. *Journal of Consulting and Clinical Psychology, 51*(6), 826–831.

O'Grady, K. (1989). Factor structure of the WISC-R. *Multivariate Behavioral Research, 24*(2), 177–193.

Ornstein, R., Johnstone, J., Herron, J., & Swencionis, C. (1980). Differential right hemisphere engagement in visuospatial tasks. *Neuropsychologia, 18*, 49–64.

Osborne, A. F. (1963). *Applied imagination* (3rd ed.). New York: Scribner.

Osborne, R. T. (1980). *Twins, black and white*. Athens, GA: Foundation for Human Understanding.

Ownby, R. L., & Carmin, C. N. (1988). Confirmatory factor analysis of the Stanford-Binet Intelligence Scale, Fourth Edition. *Journal of Psychoeducational Assessment, 6*, 331–340.

Ownby, R. L., & Matthews, C. G. (1985). On the meaning of the WISC-R third factor: Relations to selected neuropsychological measures. *Journal of Consulting and Clinical Psychology, 53*(4), 531–534.

Ownby, R. L., & Wallbrown, F. (1986). Improving report writing in school psychology. In T. R. Kratochwill (Ed.), *Advances in school psychology*, Vol. V (pp. 7–49). Hillsdale, NJ: Lawrence Erlbaum Associates.

Paget, K. D. (1983). The individual examining situation: Basic considerations for preschool children. In K. D. Paget & B. A. Bracken (Eds.), *The psychoeducational assessment of preschool children* (pp. 51–61). New York: Grune & Stratton.

Paget, K. D. (1989). Review of the Battelle Developmental Inventory. In J. C. Conoley & J. J. Kramer (Eds.). *The tenth mental measurements yearbook* (pp. 70–72). Lincoln: University of Nebraska Press.

Paramesh, C. R. (1982). Relationship between Quick Test and WISC-R and reading ability as used in a juvenile setting. *Perceptual and Motor Skills, 55*, 881–882.

Parker, K. (1983). Factor analysis of the WAIS-R at nine age levels between 16 and 74 years. *Journal of Consulting and Clinical Psychology, 51*(2), 302–308.

PASE: Parents in Action on Special Education et al, v. Hannon et al. (1980, July). United States District Court for the Northern District of Illinois, Eastern Division, C-74–3586RFP, slip opinion.

Payne, J. S., & Patton, J. R. (1981). *Mental retardation.* Columbus, OH: Charles E. Merrill.

Pearson, K. (1901). On lines and planes of closest fit to systems of points in space. *Philosophical Magazine (Series 6), 2,* 559–572.

Peckham, R. F. (1972). Opinion, *Larry P. v. Riles. Federal Supplement 343,* 1306–1315.

Peckham, R. F. (1979). Opinion, *Larry P. v. Riles. Federal Supplement 495,* 926–992.

Pellegrino, J. W. (1986). Intelligence: The interaction of culture and cognitive processes. In R. J. Sternberg & D. K. Detterman (Eds.), *What is intelligence? Contemporary viewpoints on its nature and definition* (pp. 113–116). Norwood, NJ: Ablex Publishing.

Perrine, J. (1989). Situational identification of gifted Hispanic students. In C. J. Maker & S. W. Schiever (Eds.), *Critical issues in gifted education (Vol. 2), Defensible programs of cultural and ethnic minorities.* Austin, TX: Pro-Ed.

Petersen, N. S., Kolen, M. J., & Hoover, H. D. (1989). Scaling, norming, and equating. In R. L. Linn (Ed.), *Educational measurement* (3rd ed., pp. 221–262). New York: Macmillan.

Phelps, L., Bell, M. C., & Scott, M. J. (1988). Correlations between the Stanford-Binet: Fourth Edition and the WISC-R with a learning disabled population. *Psychology in the Schools, 25,* 380–382.

Phelps, L., & Branyan, L. T. (1988). Correlations among the Hiskey, K-ABC Nonverbal Scale, Leiter, and WISC-R Performance scale with public school deaf children. *Journal of Psychoeducational Assessment, 6,* 354–358.

Phelps, L., & Rosso, M. (1985). Validity assessment of the Woodcock-Johnson Broad Cognitive Ability and scholastic ability cluster scores for behavior-disordered adolescents. *Psychology in the Schools, 22,* 398–403.

Phelps, L., Rosso, M., & Falasco, S. L. (1985). Multiple regression data using the WISC-R and the Woodcock-Johnson Tests of Cognitive Ability. *Psychology in the Schools, 22,* 46–49.

Pine, D. S., Scott, M. R., Busner, C., Davies, M., Fried, J. A., Parides, M., & Shaffer, D. (1996). Psychometrics of neurological soft signs. *Journal of the American Academy of Child and Adolescent Psychiatry, 35,* 509–515.

Pintner, R. (1923). *Intelligence testing.* New York: Henry Holt and Company.

Plake, B. S., Gutkin, T. B., Wise, S. L., & Kroeten, T. (1987). Confirmatory factor analysis of the WAIS-R: Competition of models. *Journal of Psychoeducational Assessment, 5*(3), 267–272.

Plomin, R. (1988). The nature and nurture of cognitive abilities. In R. J. Sternberg (Ed.), *Advances in the psychology of human intelligence* (Vol. 4, pp. 1–33). Hillsdale, NJ: Lawrence Erlbaum.

Plomin, R. (1989). Environment and genes: Determinants of behavior. *American Psychologist, 44,* 105–111.

Plotkin, L. (1974). Research, education, and public policy: Heredity v. environment in Negro intelligence. In L. P. Miller (Ed.), *The testing of Black students: A symposium.* New York: Prentice Hall.

Pommer, L. T. (1986). Seriously emotionally disturbed children's performance on the Kaufman Assessment Battery for Children: A concurrent validity study. *Journal of Psychoeducational Assessment, 4,* 155–162.

Porter, L. J., & Kirby, E. A. (1986). Effects of two instructional sets on the validity of the Kaufman Assessment Battery for Children—Nonverbal Scale with a group of severely hearing impaired children. *Psychology in the Schools, 23,* 1–6.

Posner, M. I., Petersen, S. E., Fox, P. T., & Raichle, M. E. (1988). Localization of cognitive operations in the human brain. *Science, 240,* 1627–1631.

Potthoff, R. F. (1966). *Statistical aspects of the problem of biases in psychological tests.* (Institute of Statistics Mimeo Series No. 479). Chapel Hill: University of North Carolina, Department of Statistics.

Prewett, P. N. (1992a). The relationship between the Kaufman Brief Intelligence Test (K-BIT) and the WISC-R with incarcerated juvenile delinquents. *Educational and Psychological Measurement, 52,* 977–982.

Prewett, P. N. (1992b). The relationship between the Kaufman Brief Intelligence Test (K-BIT) and the WISC-R with referred students. *Psychology in the Schools, 29,* 25–27.

Prewett, P. N. (1995). A comparison of two screening tests (the Matrix Analogies Test—Short Form and the Kaufman Brief Intelligence Test) with the WISC-III. *Psychological Assessment, 7*(1), 69–72.

Prewett, P. N., Bardos, A. N., & Naglieri, J. A. (1989). Assessment of mentally retarded children with the Matrix Analogies Test—Short Form, Draw-a-Person: A Quantitative Scoring System, and the Kaufman Test of Educational Achievement. *Psychology in the Schools, 26,* 254–260.

Prewett, P. N., & Farhney, M. R. (1994). The concurrent validity of the Matrix Analogies Test—Short Form with the Stanford-Binet: Fourth Edition and KTEA-BF (Academic Achievement). *Psychology in the Schools, 31*(1), 20–25.

Prewett, P. N., & Giannuli, M. M. (1991). The relationship among the reading subtests of the WJ-R, PIAT-R, K-TEA, and WRAT-R. *Journal of Psychoeducational Assessment, 9,* 166–174.

Prewett, P. N., & Matavich, M. A. (1994). A comparison of referred students' performance on the WISC-III and the Stanford-Binet Intelligence Scale: Fourth Edition. *Journal of Psychoeducational Assessment, 12*(1), 42–48.

Pribram, K. (1971). *Language of the brain.* Englewood Cliffs, NJ: Prentice-Hall.

Price, J. R., Mount, G. R., & Coles, E. A. (1987, January). Evaluating the visually impaired: Neuropsychological techniques. *Journal of Visual Impairment & Blindness*, 28–30.

Psychological Corporation. (1978). *The McCarthy Screening Test*. San Antonio, TX: Author.

Puente, A. E. (1989). Historical perspectives in the development of neuropsychology as a professional psychological specialty. In C. R. Reynolds & E. Fletcher-Janzen (Eds.), *Handbook of clinical child neuropsychology* (pp. 3–16). New York: Plenum.

Quereshi, M. Y., & McIntire, D. H. (1984). The comparability of the WISC, WISC-R, and WPPSI. *Journal of Clinical Psychology, 40*(4), 1036–1043.

Rafferty, Y., & Shinn, M. (1991). The impact of homelessness on children. *American Psychologist, 46*, 1170–1179.

Raguet, M. L., Campbell, D. A., Berry, D. T. R., Schmitt, F. A., & Smith, T.S. (1996). Stability of intelligence and intellectual predictors in older persons. *Psychological Assessment, 8*(2), 154–160.

Ranganath, V. M., & Ranganath, V. K. (1997). Asian Indian children. In G. Johnson-Powell & J. Yamamoto (Eds.), *Transcultural child development: Psychological assessment and treatment* (pp. 103–123). New York: Wiley.

Rapaport, D., Gill, M., & Schafer, R. (1945–1946). *Diagnostic psychological testing* (2 vols.). Chicago: Year Book Publishers.

Ratcliffe, K. J., & Ratcliffe, M. W. (1979). The Leiter Scales: A review of validity findings. *American Annals of the Deaf, 124*, 38–45.

Rattan, A. I., Rattan, G., Dean, R. S., & Gray, J. W. (1989). Assessing the commonality of the WISC-R and the Halstead-Reitan Neuropsychological Test Battery with learning-disordered children. *Journal of Psychoeducational Assessment, 7*, 296–303.

Raven, J. (1948). *Progressive matrices*. New York: Psychological Corporation.

Raven, J. C. (1947a). *Standard progressive matrices*. London: H. K. Lewis.

Raven, J. C. (1947b). *Coloured progressive matrices*. London: H. K. Lewis.

Raven, J. C. (1965). *Raven's progressive matrices*. New York: The Psychological Corporation.

Raven, J. C. (1986). A compendium of North American normative and validity studies. New York: Psychological Corporation.

Ray, S. (1979). *Wechsler's Intelligence Scales for Children—Revised: For the Deaf*. Baton Rouge, LA: Author.

Reilly, T. P., Drudge, O. W., Rosen, J. C., Loew, D. E., & Fischer, M. (1985). Concurrent and predictive validity of the WISC-R, McCarthy Scales, Woodcock-Johnson, and academic achievement. *Psychology in the Schools, 22*, 380–382.

Reitan, R. M. (1955). Certain differential effects of left and right cerebral lesions in human adults. *Journal of Comparative and Physiological Psychology, 48*, 474–477.

Reitan, R. M. (1981). *Halstead-Reitan Neuropsychological Test Battery*. Tucson, AZ: Reitan Neuropsychological Laboratories.

Reitan, R. M. (1994). Ward Halstead's contributions to neuropsychology and the Halstead-Reitan Neuropsychological Test Battery. *Journal of Clinical Psychology, 50*, 47–70.

Reitan, R. M., & Davison, L. A. (1974). *Clinical neuropsychology: Current status and applications*. Washington, DC: Winston.

Reschly, D. J. (1978). WISC-R factor structures among Anglos, Blacks, Chicanos, and Native-American Papagos. *Journal of Consulting and Clinical Psychology, 46*, 417–422.

Reschly, D. J. (1980). Psychological evidence in the Larry P. opinion: A case of right problem—wrong solution? *School Psychology Review, 9*, 123–135.

Reschly, D. J. (1987). Marshall v. Georgia. In C. R. Reynolds & L. Mann (Eds.), *Encyclopedia of special education* (Vol. 2. pp. 989–992). New York: Wiley-Interscience.

Reschly, D. J. (1990). Found: Our intelligences: What do they mean? *Journal of Psychoeducational Assessment, 8*, 259–267.

Reschly, D. J., & Saber, D. L. (1979). Analysis of test bias in four groups with the regression definition. *Journal of Educational Measurement, 16*, 1–9.

Rethazi, M., & Wilson, A. K. (1988). The Kaufman Assessment Battery for Children (K-ABC) in the assessment of learning disabled children. *Psychology in the Schools, 25*(4), 131–137.

Reynolds, C. R. (1997). Forward and backward memory span should not be combined for clinical analysis. *Archives of Clinical Neuropsychology, 12*, 29–40.

Reynolds, C. R. (1981a). Neuropsychological assessment and the habilitation of learning: Considerations in the search for the aptitude x treatment interaction. *School Psychology Review, 10*, 343–349.

Reynolds, C. R. (1981b). The neuropsychological basis of intelligence. In G. W. Hynd & J. E. Obrzut (Eds.), *Neuropsychological assessment and the school-age child* (pp. 87–124). New York: Grune & Stratton.

Reynolds, C. R. (1982a). The importance of norms and other psychometric concepts to assessment in clinical neuropsychological. In R. N. Malatesha & L. C. Hartlage (Eds.), *Neuropsychology and cognition* (Vol. 2, pp. 55–76). The Hague, Netherlands: Martinus Nijhoff.

Reynolds, C. R. (1982b). The problem of bias in psychological assessment. In C. R. Reynolds & T. B. Gutkin (Eds.), *The handbook of school psychology* (pp. 178–208). New York: Wiley.

Reynolds, C. R. (1984a). Critical measurement issues in learning disabilities. *Journal of Special Education, 18*, 451–476.

Reynolds, C. R. (1984b). K-ABC. Special issue of *Journal of Special Education*, *18*, (3).

Reynolds, C. R. (1986). Transactional models of intellectual development, yes. Deficit models of process remediation, no. *School Psychology Review*, *15*, 256–260.

Reynolds, C. R. (1987). Playing IQ roulette with the Stanford-Binet, 4th edition. *Measurement and Evaluation in Counseling and Development*, *20*, 139–141.

Reynolds, C. R. (1990). Conceptual and technical problems in learning disability diagnosis. In C. R. Reynolds & R. W. Kamphaus (Eds.), *Handbook of psychological and educational assessment of children* (pp. 571–592). New York: Guilford.

Reynolds, C. R. (1997). Measurement and statistical problems in neuropsychological assessment of children. In C. R. Reynolds & E. Fletcher-Janzen (Eds.), *Handbook of clinical child neuropsychology* (2nd ed., pp. 180–203). New York: Plenum Press.

Reynolds, C. R., Chastain, R. L., Kaufman, A. S., & McLean, J. E. (1987). Demographic characteristics and IQ among adults: Analysis of the WAIS-R standardization sample as a function of the stratification variables. *Journal of School Psychology*, *25*, 323–342.

Reynolds, C. R., & Clark, J. H. (Eds.). (1983). *Assessment and programming for children with low incidence handicaps*. New York: Plenum.

Reynolds, C. R., & Clark, J. H. (1984, November). *Profile analysis of standardized intelligence test performance of high IQ children*. Paper presented to the annual meeting of the National Association for Gifted Children, St. Louis.

Reynolds, C. R., & Clark, J. H. (1985). Profile analysis of standardized intelligence test performance of very low functioning individuals. *Journal of School Psychology*, *23*, 277–283.

Reynolds, C. R., & Clark, J. H. (1986). Profile analysis of standardized intelligence test performance of very high IQ children. *Psychology in the Schools*, *23*, 5–12.

Reynolds, C. R., & Ford, L. (1994). Comparative three-factor solutions of the WISC-III and WISC-R at 11 age levels between 6-1/2 and 16-1/2 years. *Archives of Clinical Neuropsychology*, *9*(6), 553–570.

Reynolds, C. R., & Gutkin, T. B. (1979). Predicting the premorbid intellectual status of children using demographic data. *Clinical Neuropsychology*, *1*, 36–38.

Reynolds, C. R., & Gutkin, T. B. (1980a). Stability of the WISC-R factor structure across sex at two age levels. *Journal of Clinical Psychology*, *36*(3), 775–777.

Reynolds, C. R., & Gutkin, T. B. (1980b, September). *WISC-R performance of blacks and whites matched on four demographic variables*. Paper presented at the annual meeting of the American Psychological Association, Montreal.

Reynolds, C. R., & Gutkin, T. B. (1980c). A regression analysis of test bias on the WISC-R for Anglos and Chicanos referred to psychological services. *Journal of Abnormal Child Psychology*, *8*, 237–243.

Reynolds, C. R., & Gutkin, T. B. (1980d). Stability of the WISC-R factor structure across sex at two age levels. *Journal of Clinical Psychology*, *36*, 775–777.

Reynolds, C. R., Gutkin, T. B., Dappen, L., & Wright, D. (1979). Differential validity of the WISC-R for boys and girls referred for psychological services. *Perceptual and Motor Skills*, *48*, 868–879.

Reynolds, C. R., & Kaiser, S. (1990). Test bias in psychological assessment. In C. R. Reynolds & Kamphaus, R. W. (Eds.), *Handbook of psychological and educational assessment of children* (2nd ed., pp. 487–525). New York: Guilford.

Reynolds, C. R., Kamphaus, R. W., & Rosenthal, B. (1988). Factor analysis of the Stanford-Binet Fourth Edition for ages 2 through 23. *Measurement and Evaluation in Counseling and Development*, *21*, 52–63.

Reynolds, C. R., Kamphaus, R. W., Rosenthal, B. L., & Hiemenz, J. R. (1997). Applications of the Kaufman Assessment Battery for Children (K-ABC) in neuropsychological assessment. In C. R. Reynolds & E. Fletcher-Janzen (Eds.), *Handbook of clinical child neuropsychology* (2nd ed., pp. 252–269). New York: Plenum Press.

Reynolds, C. R., & Kaufman, A. S. (1990). Assessment of children's intelligence with the Wechsler Intelligence Scale for Children—Revised (WISC-R). In C. R. Reynolds & R. W. Kamphaus (Eds.), *Handbook of psychological and educational assessment of children: Intelligence and achievement* (pp. 127–165). New York: Guilford.

Reynolds, C. R., & Willson, V. L. (1984, April). *Factorial consistency of simultaneous and sequential cognitive processing for whites and blacks ages 3 to 12 1/2*. Paper presented at the meeting of the National Council on Measurement in Education, New Orleans, LA.

Reynolds, C. R., Willson, V. L., & Chatman, S. P. (1983, March). *Relationships between age and raw score increases on the Kaufman Assessment Battery for Children*. Paper presented at the meeting of the National Association of School Psychologists, Detroit, MI.

Reynolds, C. R., Willson, V. L., & Chatman, S. P. (1984). Relationships between age and raw score increases on the Kaufman Assessment Battery for Children. *Psychology in the Schools*, *21*, 19–24.

Reynolds, C. R., Willson, V. L., & Chatman, S. P. (1985). Regression analyses of bias on the Kaufman Assessment Battery for Children. *Journal of School Psychology*, *23*, 195–204.

Reynolds, C. R., & Wright, D. (1981). A comparison of the criterion-related validity (academic achievement of the WPPSI and the WISC-R). *Psychology in the Schools*, *18*, 20–23.

Riccio, C. A., Cohen, M. J., Hall, J., & Ross, C. M. (1997). The third and fourth factors of the WISC-III: What they don't measure. *Journal of Psychoeducational Assessment, 15*, 27–39.

Riccio, C. A., Hynd, G. W., & Cohen, M. J. (1993). Neuropsychology in the schools: Does it belong? *School Psychology International, 14*, 291–315.

Richardson, K., & Bynner, J. M. (1984). Intelligence: Past and future. *International Journal of Psychology, 19*, 499–526.

Richters, J. E. (1997). The hubble hypothesis and the developmentalist's dilemma. *Development and Psychopathology, 9*, 193–229.

Ricks, J. H. (1959). On telling parents about test results. *Test Service Bulletin, 54*, 1–4.

Rie, E. D., & Yeh, J. W. (1982). Block Design and neurocognitive impairment in children. *Journal of Learning Disabilities, 15*, 28–32.

Ripple, C. H., Gilliam, W. S., Chanana, N., & Zigler, E. (1999). Will fifty cooks spoil the broth? The debate over entrusting Head Start to the states. *American Psychologist, 54*(5), 327–343.

Rogers, B. G. (1992). Review of the Peabody Individual Achievement Test—Revised. In J. J. Kramer & J. C. Impara (Eds.), *The eleventh mental measurements yearbook* (pp. 652–654). Lincoln: University of Nebraska Press.

Roid, G. H. (1986). Computer technology in testing. In B. S. Plake, J. C. Witt, & J. V. Mitchell, Jr. (Eds.), *The future of testing: Buros-Nebraska Symposium on Measurement and Testing* (pp. 29–69). Hillsdale, NJ: Erlbaum.

Roid, G. H. (1990, August). Historical continuity in intelligence assessment: Goals of the WISC-III standardization. In *Development of the Wechsler Intelligence Scale for Children—3rd ed.* Symposium conducted at the meeting of the American Psychological Association, Boston.

Roid, G. H., & Gorsuch, R. L. (1984). Development and clinical use of test interpretive programs on microcomputers. In M. D. Schwartz (Ed.), *Using computers in clinical practice: Psychotherapy and mental health applications* (pp. 141–149). New York: Haworth Press.

Roid, G. H., & Miller, L. J. (1997). Leiter International Performance Scale—Revised: Examiner's Manual. Wood Dale, IL: Stoelting Co.

Rosenthal, B. L., & Kamphaus, R. W. (1988). Interpretive tables for test scatter on the Stanford-Binet Intelligence Scale: Fourth Edition. *Journal of Psychoeducational Assessment, 6*, 359–370.

Ross, G. R. (1989). Some thoughts on the value of infant tests for assessing and predicting mental ability. *Journal of Developmental and Behavioral Pediatrics, 10*, 44–47.

Roszkowski, M. J. (1983). The freedom-from-distractibility factor: An examination of its adaptive behavior correlates. *Journal of Psychoeducational Assessment, 1*(3), 285–297.

Rothlisberg, B. A. (1987). Comparing the Stanford-Binet, Fourth Edition to the WISC-R: A concurrent validity study. *Journal of School Psychology, 25*, 193–196.

Rothlisberg, B. A., & McIntosh, D. E. (1991). Performance of a referred sample on the Stanford-Binet IV and the K-ABC. *Journal of School Psychology, 29*, 367–370.

Rousey, A. (1990). Factor structure of the WISC-R Mexicano. *Educational and Psychological Measurement, 50*(2), 351–357.

Royer, F. L. (1984). Stimulus variables in the Block Design task: A commentary on Schorr, Bower, and Kiernan. *Journal of Consulting and Clinical Psychology, 52*, 700–704.

Ruchala, E., Schalt, E., & Bogel, F. (1985). Relations between mental performance and reaction time: New aspects of an old problem. *Intelligence, 9*, 189–205.

Rucker, C. N. (1967). Technical language in the school psychologists' report. *Psychology in the Schools, 4*, 146–150.

Rules and Regulations for Implementing Education for All Handicapped Children Act of 1975, P.L. 94–142, 42 Fed. Reg. 42474 (1977).

Rudner, L. M. (1983). Individual assessment accuracy. *Journal of Educational Measurement, 20*(3), 207–219.

Russell, L. B. (1994). *Educated guesses: Making policy about medical screening tests.* Berkeley: University of California Press.

Rutter, M. (1978). Diagnosis and definition of childhood autism. *Journal of Autism and Childhood Schizophrenia, 8*, 139–161.

Rutter, M., Chadwick, O., & Shaffer, D. (1983). Head injury. In M. Rutter (Ed.), *Developmental neuropsychiatry* (pp. 83–111). New York: Guilford Press.

Ryan, J. J., Bohac, D. L., & Trent, D. (1994). Speed of performance on the WAIS-R among persons 75 years of age and older. *Journal of Psychoeducational Assessment, 12*(4), 351–356.

Ryan, J. J., Dai, X., & Zheng, L. (1994). Psychological test usage in the People's Republic of China. *Journal of Psychoeducational Assessment, 12*, 324–330.

Ryan, J. J., Nowak, T. J., & Geisser, M. E. (1987). On the comparability of the WAIS and WAIS-R: Review of the research and implications for clinical practice. *Journal of Psychoeducational Assessment, 5*, 15–30.

Ryan, T. V., Lamarche, J. A., Barth, J. T., & Boll, T. J. (1996). Neuropsychological consequences and treatment of pediatric head trauma. In L. S. Batchelor & R. S. Dean (Eds.), *Pediatric neuropsychology* (pp. 117–137). Needham Heights, MA: Allyn & Bacon.

Saco-Pollitt, C., Pollitt, E., & Greenfield, D. (1985). The cumulative deficit hypothesis in the light of cross-cultural evidence. *International Journal of Behavioral Development, 8,* 75–97.

Salovey, P., & Mayer, J. D. (1989–90). Emotional intelligence. *Imagination, Cognition, and Personality, 9,* 185–211.

Salvia, J., & Hritcko, T. (1984). The K-ABC and ability training. *Journal of Special Education, 18*(3), 345–356.

Sandoval, J. (1979). The WISC-R and internal evidence of test bias with minority groups. *Journal of Consulting and Clinical Psychology, 47*(5), 919–927.

Sandoval, J., & Irvin, M. G. (1990). Legal and ethical issues in the assessment of children. In C. R. Reynolds & R. W. Kamphaus (Eds.), *Handbook of psychological and educational assessment: Children's intelligence and achievement* (pp. 86–104). New York: Guilford Press.

Sandoval, J., & Mille, M. (1979, September). *Accuracy judgements of WISC-R item difficulty for minority groups.* Paper presented at the annual meeting of the American Psychological Association, New York.

Sarasan, S. B. (1954). *The clinical interaction.* New York: Harper & Brothers.

Sattler, J. M. (1988). *Assessment of children* (3rd ed.). San Diego, CA: J. M. Sattler.

Sattler, J. M., & Covin, T. M. (1986). Comparison of the Slosson Intelligence Test, Revised Norms and WISC-R for children with learning problems and for gifted children. *Psychology in the Schools, 23,* 259–264.

Sattler, J. M., & Ryan, J. J. (1998). *Assessment of children: Revised and updated third edition WAIS-III supplement.* San Diego, CA: Author.

Satz, P., Strauss, E., & Whitaker, H. (1990). The ontogeny of hemispheric specialization: Some old hypotheses revisited. *Brain and Language, 38.*

Scarr, S. (1981). *Social class, race and individual differences in intelligence.* New York: Plenum.

Scarr, S., & Weinberg, R. A. (1976). IQ test performance of black children adopted by white families. *American Psychologist, 31,* 726–739.

Scarr, S., & Weinberg, R. A. (1978). The influence of "family background" on intellectual attainment. *American Sociological Review, 43,* 674–692.

Schaie, K. W., & Hertzog, C. (1983). Fourteen-year cohort-sequential analyses of adult intellectual development. *Developmental Psychology, 32,* 1118–1120.

Schaie, K. W., & Parham, I. A. (1977). Cohort-sequential analyses of adult intellectual development. *Developmental Psychology, 13,* 649–653.

Schaughency, E. A., Lahey, B. B., Hynd, G. W., Stone, P. A., Piacentini, J. C., & Frick, P. J. (1989). Neuropsychological test performance and the attention deficit disorders: Clinical utility of the Luria-Nebraska Neuropsychological Battery—Children's Revision. *Journal of Consulting and Clinical Psychology, 57*(1), 112–116.

Schinka, J. A., Haley, J. A., Vanderploeg, R. D., & Greblo, P. (1998). Frequency of WISC-III and WAIS-R pairwise subtest differences. *Psychological Assessment, 10*(2), 171–175.

Schinka, J. A., Vanerploeg, R. D., & Curtiss, G. (1997). WISC-III subtest scatter as a function of highest subtest scaled score. *Psychological Assessment, 9*(2), 83–88.

Schock, H. H., & Buck, K. (1995, November). The Bayley Scales of Infant Development. *Child Assessment News, 5*(2).

Schooler, C. (1998). Environmental complexity and the Flynn effect. In U. Neisser (Ed.), *The rising curve: Long-term gains in IQ and related measures* (pp. 67–79). Washington, DC: American Psychological Association.

Schorr, D., Bower, G. H., & Kiernan, R. (1982). Stimulus variables in the block design task. *Journal of Consulting and Clinical Psychology, 50,* 479–487.

Schuerger, J. M., & Witt, A. C. (1989). The temporal stability of individually tested intelligence. *Journal of Clinical Psychology, 45,* 294–302.

Schwartz, G. E., Davidson, R. J., & Mear, F. (1975). Right hemisphere lateralization for emotion in the human brain: Interactions with cognition. *Science, 190,* 286–288.

Seashore, H. G. (1951). Differences between verbal and performance IQ's on the WISC. *Journal of Consulting Psychology, 15,* 62–67.

Sechenov, I. (1965). *Reflexes of the brain.* Cambridge, MA: MIT Press. (Original work published in 1863.)

Segalowitz, S. J., & Gruber, F. A. (Eds.). (1977). *Language development and neurological theory.* New York: Academic Press.

Seidenberg, M., Giordani, B., Berent, S., & Boll, T. J. (1983). IQ level and performance on the Halstead-Reitan Neuropsychological Test Battery for older children. *Journal of Consulting and Clinical Psychology, 51,* 406–413.

Sellers, A. H., & Nadler, J. D. (1992). A survey of current neuropsychological assessment procedures used for different age groups. *Psychotherapy in Private Practice, 11,* 47–57.

Semrud-Clikeman, M. (1990). *Dyslexia and brain morphology: Contributions to disturbances in phonological coding, naming, and reading.* Unpublished doctoral dissertation, University of Georgia, Athens, Georgia.

Sexson, S., & Madan-Swain, A. (1995). The chronically ill child in the school. *School Psychology Quarterly, 10,* 359–368.

Sexton, D., McLean, M., Boyd, R. D., Thompson, B., & McCormick, K. (1988). Criterion-related validity of a new standardized developmental measure for use with infants who are handicapped. *Measurement and Evaluation in Counseling and Development, 21,* 16–24.

Shaffer, D., Schonfeld, R., O'Connor, P. A., Stokman, C., Trautman, P., Shafer, S., & Ng, S. (1985). Neurological soft signs. *Archives of General Psychiatry, 42*, 342–351.

Shah, A., & Holmes, N. (1985). Brief report: The use of the Leiter International Performance Scale with autistic children. *Journal of Autism and Developmental Disorders, 15*(2), 195–203.

Shapiro, E. G., & Dotan, N. (1985, October). *Neurological findings and the Kaufman Assessment Battery for Children*. Paper presented at the National Association of Neuropsychologists, Philadelphia, PA.

Shapiro, E. G., & Dotan, N. (1986). Neurological findings and the Kaufman Assessment Battery for Children. *Developmental Neuropsychology, 2*(1), 51–64.

Shapiro, S. K., Buckhalt, J. A., & Herod, L. A. (1995). Evaluation of learning-disabled students with the Differential Ability Scales (DAS). *Journal of School Psychology, 33*(3), 247–263.

Shaywitz, B. A., & Waxman, S. G. (1987). Dyslexia. *New England Journal of Medicine, 316*, 1268–1270.

Shaywitz, S. E., Shaywitz, B. A., Fletcher, J., & Shupack, H. (1986). Evaluation of school performance: Dyslexia and attention deficit disorder. *Pediatrician, 13*, 96–107.

Shellenberger, S., & Lachterman, T. (1976, March). *Usability of the McCarthy Scales of Children's Abilities in the intellectual assessment of the Puerto Rican child*. Paper presented at the meeting of the National Association of School Psychologists, Kansas City, Mo.

Shephard, L. A. (1989). Identification of mild handicaps. In R. L. Linn (Ed.), *Educational measurement* (3rd ed. pp. 545–572). New York: Macmillan.

Shephard, L. A., Smith, M. L., & Vojir, C. P. (1983). Characteristics of pupils identified as learning disabled. *American Educational Research Journal, 20*, 309–331.

Sherman, E. M. S., Strauss, E., Spellacy, F., & Hunter, M. (1995). Construct validity of WAIS-R factors: Neuropsychological test correlates in adults referred for evaluation of possible head injury. *Psychological Assessment, 7*(4), 440–444.

Sherman, M., & Key, C. V. (1932). The intelligence scores of isolated mountain children. *Child Development, 3*, 279–290.

Shure, G. H., & Halstead, W. C. (1959). Cerebral lateralization of individual processes. *Psychological Monographs: General and Applied, 72* (12).

Siegel, L. (1992). An evaluation of the discrepancy definition of dyslexia. *Journal of Learning Disabilities, 25*(10), 618–629.

Siegel, L. S. (1979). Infant perceptual, cognitive, and motor behaviors as predictors of subsequent cognitive and language development. *Canadian Journal of Psychology, 33*, 382–395.

Siegel, L. S. (1988). Evidence that IQ scores are irrelevant to the definition and analysis of reading disability. *Canadian Journal of Psychology, 42*, 201–215.

Siegel, L. S. (1990). IQ and learning disabilities: R.I.P. In H. L. Swanson & B. Keogh (Eds.), *Learning disabilities: Theoretical and research issues* (pp. 111–128). Hillsdale, NJ: Lawrence Erlbaum Associates

Siegel, L. S. (1999). Issues in the definition and diagnosis of learning disabilities: A perspective on Guckenberger V. Boston University, *Journal of Learning Disabilities, 32*, 304–319.

Siegert, R. J., Patten, M. D., Taylor, A. J. W., & McCormick, I. A. (1988). Factor analysis of the WAIS-R using the factor replication procedure, FACTOREP. *Multivariate Behavioral Research, 23*(4), 481–489.

Silverstein, A. B. (1974). A short-short form of the WISC-R for screening purposes. *Psychological Reports, 35*, 817–818.

Silverstein, A. B. (1976). Comparison of two criteria for determining the number of factors. *Psychological Reports, 41*, 387–390.

Silverstein, A. B. (1980). Cluster analysis of the Wechsler Intelligence Scale for Children—Revised. *Educational and Psychological Measurement, 40*, 51–54.

Silverstein, A. B. (1981). Reliability and abnormality of test score differences. *Journal of Clinical Psychology, 37*(2), 392–394.

Silverstein, A. B. (1982a). Alternative multiple-group solutions for the WISC and the WISC-R. *Journal of Clinical Psychology, 38*, 166–168.

Silverstein, A. B. (1982b). Pattern analysis as simultaneous statistical inference. *Journal of Consulting and Clinical Psychology, 50*, 234–240.

Silverstein, A. B. (1982c). Factor structure of the Wechsler Adult Intelligence Scale—Revised. *Journal of Consulting and Clinical Psychology, 50*(5), 661–664.

Silverstein, A. B. (1983a). Full scale IQ equivalents for a two-subtest short form of the Wechsler Preschool and Primary Scale of Intelligence and the Wechsler Intelligence Scale for Children—Revised. *Psychological Reports, 53*, 16–18.

Silverstein, A. B. (1983b). Validity of random short forms: III. Wechsler's intelligence scales. *Perceptual and Motor Skills, 56*, 572–574.

Silverstein, A. B. (1985). Cluster analysis of the Wechsler Adult Intelligence Scale—Revised. *Journal of Clinical Psychology, 41*(1), 98–100.

Silverstein, A. B., & Legutki, G. (1982). Direct comparisons of the factor structures of the WISC and the WISC-R. *Psychology in the Schools, 19*, 5–7.

Simon, C. L., & Clopton, J. R. (1984). Comparison of WAIS and WAIS-R scores of mildly and moderately mentally retarded adults. *American Journal of Mental Deficiency, 89*, 301–303.

Sinclair, E., Forness, S. R., & Alexson, J. (1985). Psychiatric diagnosis: A study of its relationship to school needs. *Journal of Special Education, 19*(3), 333–344.

Sinnett, E. R., Rogg, K. L., Benton, S. L., Downey, R. G., & Whitfill, J. M. (1993). The Woodcock-Johnson Revised—Its factor structure. *Educational and Psychological Measurement, 53*(3), 763–769.

Siskind, G. (1967). Fifteen years later: A replication of "a semantic study of concepts of clinical psychologists and psychiatrists." *Journal of Psychology, 65*, 3–7.

Slate, J. R. (1994). WISC-III correlations with the WIAT. *Psychology in the Schools, 31*, 278–285.

Slate, J. R. (1995). Discrepancies between IQ and index scores for a clinical sample of students: Useful diagnostic indicators? *Psychology in the Schools, 32*(2), 103–108.

Slate, J. R., & Chick, D. (1989). WISC-R examiner errors: Cause for concern. *Psychology in the Schools, 26*, 78–83.

Slate, J. R., & Saarnio, D. A. (1995). Differences between WISC-III and WISC-R IQS: A preliminary investigation. *Journal of Psychoeducational Assessment, 13*(4) 340–346.

Slate, J. R., & Saddler, C. D. (1990, October). Improved but not perfect. *NASP Communique*, p. 20.

Slosson, R. L. (1963). *Slosson Intelligence Test.* East Aurora, NY: Slosson Educational Publications.

Slosson, R. L. (1981). *Slosson Intelligence Test.* East Aurora, NY: Slosson Educational Publications.

Slosson, R. L. (1991a). *Manual for the Slosson Intelligence Test—Revised.* East Aurora, NY: Slosson Educational Publications.

Slosson, R. L. (1991b). *Norms tables and technical manual for the Slosson Intelligence Test—Revised.* East Aurora, NY: Slosson Educational Publications.

Smith, C. R. (1983). *Learning disabilities: The interaction of learner, task, and setting.* Boston: Little, Brown.

Smith, D. K., Klass, P. D., & Stovall, D. L. (1992, August). *Relationship of the K-BIT and SIT-R in a gifted sample.* Paper presented at the annual meeting of the American Psychological Association, Washington, DC.

Smith, D. K., Lyon, M. A., Hunter, E., & Boyd, R. (1986, April). Relationship between the K-ABC and WISC-R for students referred for severe learning disabilities. *Journal of Learning Disabilities, 21*(8), 509–513.

Smith, M. L., Minden, D., Netley, C., Read, S. E., King, S. M., & Blanchette, V. (1997). Longitudinal investigation of neuropsychological functioning in children and adolescents with hemophilia and HIV infection. *Developmental Neuropsychology, 13*, 69–85.

Smith, T. D., Smith, B. L., & Smithson, M. M. (1995). The relationship between the WISC-III and the WRAT-3 in a sample of rural referred children. *Psychology in the Schools, 32*, 291–295.

Smith-Seemiller, L., Franzen, M. D., Burgess, E. J., & Prieto, L. R. (1997). Neuropsychologists' practice patterns in assessing premorbid intelligence. *Archives of Clinical Neuropsychology, 12*, 739–744.

Snyder, T. J., Leark, R. A., Golden, C. J., Grove, T., & Allison, R. (1983, March). *Correlations of the K-ABC, WISC-R, and Luria-Nebraska Children's Battery for Exceptional children.* Paper presented at the meeting of the National Association of School Psychologists, Detroit, MI.

Snyderman, M., & Rothman, S. (1986). Science, politics and the IQ controversy. *The Public Interest, 83*, 79–97.

Snyderman, M., & Rothman, S. (1987). Survey of expert opinion on intelligence and aptitude testing. *American Psychologist, 42*, 137–144.

Sparrow, S. S., Balla, D. A., & Cicchetti, D. V. (1984). *Vineland Adaptive Behavior Scales.* Circle Pines, MN: American Guidance Service.

Spearman, C. (1927). *The abilities of man.* New York: Macmillan.

Spearman, C., & Jones, L. (1950). *Human abilities.* London: Macmillan.

Spelberg, H. C. L. (1987). Problem-solving strategies on the block-design task. *Perceptual and Motor Skills, 65*(1), 99–104.

Sperry, R. W. (1968). Hemispheric deconnection and unity in conscious awareness. *American Psychologist, 23*, 723–733.

Sperry, R. W. (1970a). Cerebral dominance in perception. In F. A. Young & D. B. Lindsley (Eds.), *Early experience and visual information processing in perceptual and reading disorders* (pp. 167–178). Washington, DC: National Academy of Sciences.

Sperry, R. W. (1970b). Perception in the absence of the neocortical commissures. *Research Publication, Association for Research in Nervous and Mental Diseases (Perception and Its Disorders), 68*, 123.

Sperry, R. W. (1974). Lateral specialization in the surgically separated hemispheres. In F. O. Schmitt & F. G. Worden (Eds.), *The neurosciences: Third study program* (pp. 5–9). Cambridge, MA: MIT Press.

Sperry, R. W., Gazzaniga, M. S., & Bogan, J. E. (1969). Interhemispheric relationships: The neocortical commissures: Syndromes of hemispheric disconnection. In P. Vinken & G. W. Bruyn (Eds.), *Handbook of clinical neurology* (Vol. 4., pp. 273–290). New York: Wiley-Interscience.

Spitz, H. H. (1983). Intratest and intertest reliability and stability of the WISC, WISC-R, and WAIS full scale IQS in a mentally retarded population. *Journal of Special Education, 17*, 69–80.

Spitz, H. H. (1986a). *The raising of intelligence.* Hillsdale, NJ: Lawrence Erlbaum Associates.

Spitz, H. H. (1986b). Disparities in mentally retarded persons' IQs derived from different intelligence tests. *American Journal of Mental Deficiency, 90*, 588–591.

Spitz, H. H. (1988). Inverse relationship between the WISC-R/WAIS-R score disparity and IQ level in the lower range of intelligence. *American Journal of Mental Deficiency, 92*, 376–378.

Spreen, O., Rissell, A. H., & Edgell, D. (1995). *Developmental neuropsychology.* New York: Oxford University Press.

Springer, S. P., & Deutsch, G. (1981). *Left brain, right brain.* San Francisco: W. H. Freeman.

Spruill, J. (1988). Two types of tables for use with the Stanford-Binet Intelligence Scale: Fourth Edition. *Journal of Psychoeducational Assessment, 6*, 78–86.

Spruill, J. (1996). Composite SAS of the Stanford-Binet Intelligence Scale, Fourth Edition: Is it determined by only one area SAS? *Psychological Assessment, 8*(3), 328–330.

Stanovich, K. E. (1986). Cognitive processes and the reading problems of learning disabled children: Evaluating the assumption of specificity. In J. Torgesen & B. Wong (Eds.), *Psychological and educational perspectives on learning disabilities* (pp. 87–131). New York: Academic Press.

Stanovich, K. E. (1988). Explaining the differences between the dyslexic and the garden-variety poor reader: The phonological-core variable-difference model. *Journal of Learning Disabilities, 21*(10), 590–604.

Stanovich, K. E. (1991). Discrepancy definitions of reading disability: Has intelligence led us astray? *Reading Research Quarterly, 26*(1), 7–29.

Stanovich, K. E. (1993). A model for studies of reading disability. *Developmental Review, 13*(3), 225–245.

Stanovich, K. E., & Siegel, L. S. (1994). Phenotypic performance profile of children with reading disabilities: A regression-based test of the phonological-core variable-difference model. *Journal of Educational Psychology, 86*(1), 24–53.

Starr, R. W. (1983). Split-brain IQ test. *Omni, 5*(10), 35.

Staton, R. D., Wilson, H., & Brumbach, R. A. (1981). Cognitive improvement associated with tricyclic antidepressant treatment of childhood major depressive illness. *Perceptual and Motor Skills, 53*, 219–234.

Stehbens, J. A., Kaleita, T. A., Noll, R. B., MacLean, W. E. & O'Brien, R. T. (1991). CNS prophylaxis of childhood leukemia: What are the long-term, neurological, neuropsychological, and behavioral effects? *Neuropsychology Review, 2*, 147–177.

Stehbens, J. A., MacLean, W. E., Kaleita, T. A., Noll, R. B., Schwartz, W., Cantor, N. L., Woodard, A., Whitt, J. K., Waskerwitz, M. J., Ruymann, F. B., & Hammond, G. D. (1994). Effects of CNS prophylaxis on the neuropsychological performance of children with acute lymphblastic leukemia: Nine months postdiagnosis. *Children's Health Care, 23*, 231–250.

Steinberg, L., Dornbusch, S. M., & Brown, B. B. (1992). Ethnic differences in adolescent achievement: An ecological perspective. *American Psychologist, 47*(6), 725–729.

Stern, W. (1914). *The psychological methods for testing intelligence.* Baltimore, MD: Warwick & York.

Sternberg, R., Conway, G., Ketron, J., & Bernsetin, M. (1981). People's conceptions of intelligence. *Journal of Personality and Social Psychology, 4*, 37–55.

Sternberg, R. J. (1984). The Kaufman Assessment Battery for Children: An information-processing analysis and critique. *Journal of Special Education, 18*, 269–279.

Sternberg, R. J. (1985a). Cognitive approaches to intelligence. In B. B. Wolman (Ed.), *Handbook of intelligence* (pp. 59–117). New York: Wiley.

Sternberg, R. J. (1985b). *Beyond IQ: A triarchic theory of intelligence.* New York: Cambridge University Press.

Sternberg, R. J. (1987). Synopsis of a triarchic theory of human intelligence. In S. H. Irvine & S. E. Newstead (Eds.), *Intelligence and cognition: Contemporary frames of reference* (pp. 141–175). Boston: Martinus Nijhoff.

Sternberg, R. J. (1997). The triarchic theory of intelligence. In Flanagan, D.P. et al (Eds.). *Contemporary intellectual assessment: Theories, tests, and issues* (pp. 92–104). New York: Guilford Press 1997.

Sternberg, R. J., & Detterman, D. K. (1986). *What is intelligence? Contemporary viewpoints on its nature and definition.* Norwood, NJ: Ablex.

Sternberg, R. J., & Kaufman, J. C. (1996). Innovation and intelligence testing: The curious case of the dog that didn't bark. *European Journal of Psychological Assessment, 12*(3), 175–182.

Stevenson, H. W., Stigler, J. W., Lee, S., Lucker, G. W., Kitamura, S., & Hsu, C. (1985). Cognitive performance and academic achievement of Japanese, Chinese, and American children. *Child Development, 56*, 718–734.

Strauss, E., Loring, D., Chelune, G., Hunter, M., Hermann, B., Perrine, K., Westerveld, M., Trenerry, M., & Barr, W. (1995). Predicting cognitive impairment in epilepsy: Findings from the Bozeman Epilepsy Consortium. *Journal of Clinical and Experimental Neuropsychology, 17*, 909–917.

Street, R. F. (1931). A gestalt completion test. *Contributions to Education, 481*, vii–65. New York: Bureau of Publications, Teachers College, Columbia University.

Stricker, G. (1997). Are science and practice commensurable? *American Psychologist, 52*, 442–448.

Strommen, E. (1988). Confirmatory factor analysis of the Kaufman Assessment Battery for Children: A reevaluation. *Journal of School Psychology, 26*(1), 13–23.

Stutsman, R. (1931). *Merrill-Palmer Scale of Mental Tests*. Chicago: Stoelting.

Sue, S., & Abe, J. (1988). *Predictors of academic achievement among Asian American and White students* (Report No. 88–11). New York: College Entrance Examination Board.

Sue, S., & Okazaki, S. (1990). Asian-American educational achievements: A phenomena in search of an explanation. *American Psychologist, 45*, 913–920.

Sullivan, G. S., Mastropieri, M. A., & Scruggs, T. E. (1995). Reasoning and remembering: Coaching students with learning disabilities to think. *Journal of Special Education, 29*(3), 310–322.

Sullivan, P. M., & Burley, S. K. (1990). Mental testing of the hearing-impaired child. In C. R. Reynolds & R. W. Kamphaus (Eds.), *Handbook of psychological and educational assessment of children* (pp. 761–788). New York: Guilford.

Sullivan, P. M., & Schulte, L. E. (1992). Factor analysis of WISC-R with deaf and hard-of-hearing children. *Psychological Assessment, 4*(4), 537–540.

Sulzbacher, S., Thomson, J., Farwell, J., Temkin, N., & Holubkov, A. (1994). Crossed dominance and its relationship to intelligence and academic achievement. *Developmental Neuropsychology, 10*, 473–479.

Sutter, E. G., Bishop, P. C., & Battin, R. R. (1986). Factor similarities between traditional psychoeducational and neuropsychological test batteries. *Journal of Psychoeducational Assessment, 4*(1), 73–82.

Swanson, H. L., Brandenburg-Ayers, S., & Wallace, S. (1989). Construct validity of the K-ABC with gifted children. *Journal of Special Education, 23*(10), 342–352.

Swift, A. V., Cohen, M. J., Hynd, G. W., Wisenbaker, J. M., McKie, K. M., Makari, G., & McKie, V. C. (1989). Neuropsychological impairment in children with sickle cell anemia. *Pediatrics, 84*, 1077–1085.

Szatmari, P., Offord, D. R., & Boyle, M. H. (1989). Ontario child health study: Prevalence of attention deficit disorder with hyperactivity. *Journal of Child Psychology and Psychiatry, 2*, 219–230.

Tabachnick, B. G. (1979). Test scatter on the WISC-R. *Journal of Learning Disabilities, 12*, 626–628.

Tallent, N. (1988). *Psychological report writing* (3rd ed.). Englewood Cliffs, NJ: Prentice-Hall.

Tarnopol, L., & Tarnopol, M. (1977). Introduction to neuropsychology. In L. Tarnopol & M. Tarnopol (Eds.), *Brain function and reading disabilities* (pp. 1–47). Baltimore: University Park Press.

Taylor, R. L., Slocumb, P. R., & O'Neill, J. (1979). A short form of the McCarthy Scales of Children's Abilities: Methodological and clinical applications. *Psychology in the Schools, 16*, 347–350.

Teare, J. F., & Thompson, R. W. (1982). Concurrent validity of the Perkins-Binet Tests of Intelligence for the Blind. *Journal of Visual Impairment and Blindness, 76*, 279–280.

Teeter, P. A. (1984). Cross validation of the factor structure of the McCarthy Scales for kindergarten children. *Psychology in the Schools, 21*, 158–164.

Teglasi, H. (1983). Report of a psychological assessment in a school setting. *Psychology in the Schools, 20*, 466–479.

Telzrow, C. F. (1990). Does PASS pass the test? A critique of the Das-Naglieri Cognitive Assessment System. *Journal of Psychoeducational Assessment, 8*, 344–355.

Telzrow, C. F., Century, E., Harris, B., & Redmond, C. (1985, April). *Relationship between neuropsychological processing models and dyslexia subtypes*. Paper presented at the National Association of School Psychologists, Las Vegas, NV.

Telzrow, C. F., Redmond, C., & Zimmerman, B. (1984, October). *Dyslexic subtypes: A comparison of the Bannatyne, Boder, and Kaufman models*. Paper presented at the meeting of the National Academy of Neuropsychologists, San Diego, CA.

Terman, L. M. (1916). *The measurement of intelligence*. Cambridge, MA: Riverside Press.

Terman, L. M., & Merrill, M. A. (1960). *Stanford-Binet Intelligence Scale*. Boston: Houghton Mifflin.

Terman, L., & Merrill, M. (1973). *Technical manual for the Stanford-Binet Intelligence Scale: 1972 norms edition*. Boston: Houghton Mifflin.

Tharp, B. R. (1987). An overview of pediatric seizure disorders and epileptic syndromes. *Epilepsia, 28* (Suppl. 1), S36–S45.

The National Education Goals Panel. (1998). *Principles and recommendations for early childhood assessments*. Washington, DC: Author.

The Psychological Corporation. (1992). *Manual for the Wechsler Individual Achievement Test*. San Antonia, TX: Psychological Corporation.

The Psychological Corporation. (1997). *WAIS-III–WMS-III technical manual*. San Antonio, TX: Psychological Corporation.

The Psychological Corporation (1999). *Wechsler Abbreviated Scale of Intelligence*. San Antonio, TX: Psychological Corporation.

Thorndike, E. L., Bregman, E. O., Cobb, M. V., & Woodyard, E. (1927). *The measurement of intelligence*. New York: Columbia University, Teachers College.

Thorndike, R. L. (1971). Concepts of culture-fairness. *Journal of Educational Measurement, 8*, 63–70.

Thorndike, R. L., & Hagen, E. P. (1977). *Measurement and evaluation in psychology and education* (4th ed.). New York: Wiley.

Thorndike, R. L., Hagen, E. P., & Sattler, J. M. (1986). *Technical manual for the Stanford-Binet Intelligence Scale: Fourth Edition.* Chicago: Riverside Publishing.

Thorndike, R. M. (1990). Would the real factors of the Stanford-Binet Fourth Edition please come forward? *Journal of Psychoeducational Assessment, 8,* 412–435.

Thorndike, R. M. (1997). The early history of intelligence testing. In D. P. Flanagan, J. L. Genshaft, & P. L. Harrison (Eds.), *Contemporary intellectual assessment* (pp. 53–91). New York: Guilford Press.

Thorndike, R. M., & Lohman, D. F. (1990). *A century of ability testing.* Chicago: Riverside.

Thurstone, L. L. (1938). *Primary mental abilities.* Chicago: Chicago University Press.

Thurstone, L. L., & Thurstone, T. (1941). *The Chicago Tests of Primary Mental Abilities.* Chicago: Science Research Associates.

Thurstone, T. W. (1951). Primary mental abilities of children. In J. J. Jenkins & D. G. Paterson (Eds.), *Studies in individual differences: The search for intelligence* (pp. 527–533). New York: Appleton-Century-Crofts. (Reprinted from *Educational and Psychological Measurement,* 1941, *1,* 105–116).

Tomlinson-Keasey, C., & Clarkson-Smith, L. (1980, February). *What develops in hemispheric specialization?* Paper presented at the meeting of the International Neuropsychological Society, San Francisco.

Torrance, E. P. (1965). *Rewarding creative behavior.* Englewood Cliffs, NJ: Prentice-Hall.

Tramontana, M. G., & Hooper, S. R. (1988). *Assessment issues in child neuropsychology.* New York: Plenum Press.

Tramontana, M. G., & Hooper, S. R. (1989). Neuropsychology of child psychopathology. In C. R. Reynolds & E. Fletcher-Janzen (Eds.), *Handbook of clinical child neuropsychology* (pp. 87–106). New York: Plenum.

Truscott, S. D., Narrett, C. M., & Smith, S. E. (1994). WISC-R subtest reliability over time: Implications for practice and research. *Psychological Reports, 74*(1), 147–156.

Tulsky, D. S., Zhu, J., & Prifitera, A. (1996, August). *An introduction to the Wechsler Adult Intelligence Scale, Third Edition (WAIS-III).* Paper presented at the annual convention of the American Psychological Association, Toronto.

Tuma, J. M., & Elbert, J. C. (1990). Critical issues and current practice in personality assessment of children. In C. R. Reynolds & R. W. Kamphaus (Eds.), *Handbook of psychological and educational assessment of children: Personality, behavior, and context* (pp. 3–26). New York: Guilford.

Tupper, D. E. (1986). Neuropsychological screening and soft signs. In J. E. Obrzut & G. W. Hynd (Eds.), *Child neuropsychology: Vol. 2. Clinical practice* (pp. 139–186). Orlando, FL: Academic Press.

Tupper, D. E. (Ed.). (1987). *Soft neurological signs.* Orlando, FL: Grune & Stratton.

Ulissi, S. M., Brice, P. J., & Gibbons, S. (1985, April). *The use of the Kaufman Assessment Battery for Children with the hearing impaired.* Paper presented at the meeting of the National Association of School Psychologists, Las Vegas, NV.

U.S. Department of Education. (1992). *Fourteenth annual report to Congress on the implementation of the Individuals with Disabilities Education Act.* Washington, DC: Author.

U.S. Department of Education. (1994). *Sixteenth annual report to Congress on the implementation of the Individuals with Disabilities Education Act.* Washington, DC: Author.

U.S. Office of Education. (1992). Definition and criteria for defining students as learning disabled. *Federal Register, 57*(189). Washington DC: Author.

Uzgiris, I. C., & Hunt, J. McV. (1989). *Assessment in infancy: Ordinal scales of psychological development.* Urbana: University of Illinois.

Valencia, R. R. (1985). Concurrent validity of the Kaufman Assessment Battery for Children in a sample of Mexican-American children. *Educational and Psychological Measurement, 44,* 365–372.

Valencia, R. R. (1990). Clinical assessment of young children with the McCarthy Scales of Children's Abilities. In C. R. Reynolds & R. W. Kamphaus (Eds.), *Handbook of psychological and educational assessment of children: Intelligence and achievement* (pp. 209–258). New York: Guilford.

Valencia, R. R., & Rankin, R. J. (1985). Evidence of content bias on the McCarthy Scales with Mexican American children: Implications for test translation and nonbiased assessment. *Journal of Educational Psychology, 77,* 197–207.

Valencia, R. R., & Rankin, R. (1986). Factor analysis of the K-ABC for groups of Anglo and Mexican-American children. *Journal of Educational Measurement, 23,* 209–219.

Valsiner, J. (1984). Conceptualizing intelligence: From an internal static attribution to the study of the process structure of organism-environment relationships. *International Journal of Psychology, 19,* 363–389.

Vance, B., & Fuller, G. B. (1995). Relation of scores on the WISC-III and the WRAT-3 for a sample of referred children and youth. *Psychological Reports, 76,* 371–374.

Vance, B., Hankins, N., & Brown, N. (1986). The relationship among the test of Nonverbal Intelligence, Ammons' Quick Test, and Wechsler Intelligence Scale for Children—Revised. *Diagnostique, 12*(1), 47–52.

Vance, B., Kitson, D., & Singer, M. (1983). Further investigation of comparability of the WISC-R and PPVT-R for children and youth referred for psychological services. *Psychology in the Schools, 20,* 307–310.

Vance, H. B., Fuller, G. B., & Ellis, R. (1983). Discriminant function analysis of LD/BD children scores on the WISC-R. *Journal of Clinical Psychology, 39*(5), 749–753.

Vance, H. B., & Wallbrown, F. H. (1978). The structure of intelligence for black children: A hierarchical approach. *Psychological Record, 28,* 31–39.

Van den Berg, A. R. (1986). *The problems of measuring intelligence in a heterogeneous society and possible solutions to some of these problems.* Pretoria: Institute for Psychological and Edumetric Research, Human Sciences Research Council.

Vandenberg, S. G., & Vogler, G. P. (1985). Genetic determinants of intelligence. In B. B. Wolman, (Ed.), *Handbook of intelligence: Theories, research and applications* (pp. 3–57). New York: Wiley.

Vanderploeg, R. D., Schinka, J. A., Baum, K. M., Tremont, G., & Mittenberg, W. (1998). WISC-III premorbid prediction strategies: Demographic and best performance approaches. *Psychological Assessment, 10(3),* 277–284.

Vellutino, F. R., Scanlon, D. M., Sipay, E. R., Small, S. G., Pratt, A., Chen, R., & Denckla, M. B. (1996). Cognitive profiles of difficult to remediate and readily remediated poor readers: Toward distinguishing between constitutionally and experientially based causes of reading disability. *Journal of Educational Psychology, 88*(4), 601–638.

Vernon, P. A. (1985). Individual differences in general cognitive ability. In L. C. Hartlage & C. F. Telzrow (Eds.), *The neuropsychology of individual differences.* New York: Plenum

Vernon, P. E. (1950). *The structure of human abilities.* New York: Wiley.

Vernon, P. E. (1979). *Intelligence: Heredity and environment.* San Francisco: W. H. Freeman.

Vernon, P. E. (1984). Intelligence, cognitive styles, and brain lateralization. *International Journal of Psychology, 19,* 435–455.

von Mayrhauser, R. T. (1992). The mental testing community and validity. *American Psychologist, 47,* 244–253.

Vygotsky, L. S. (1978). *Mind in society.* (M. Cole, V. John-Steiner, S. Scribner, & E. Souberman, Eds.). Cambridge, MA: Harvard University Press.

Wada, J., Clarke, R., & Hamm, A. (1975). Cerebral hemisphere asymmetry in humans. *Archives of Neurology, 37,* 234–246.

Wallbrown, F., Blaha, J., Wallbrown, J., & Engin, A. (1975). The hierarchical factor structure of the Wechsler Intelligence Scale for Children—Revised. *Journal of Psychology, 89,* 223–235.

Wallbrown, F. H., Blaha, J., & Wherry, R. J. (1973). The hierarchical factor structure of the Wechsler Preschool and Primary Scale of Intelligence. *Journal of Consulting and Clinical Psychology, 41,* 356–362.

Waller, N. G., & Waldman, I. D. (1990). A reexamination of the WAIS-R factor structure. *Psychological Assessment, 2*(2), 139–144.

Ward, M. E., & Genshaft, J. (1983, February). The Perkins-Binet Tests: A critique and recommendations for administration. *Exceptional Children,* 450–452.

Warner, M. H., Ernst, J., & Townes, B. D. (1986). Comparison of WAIS and WAIS-R factor structure for neuropsychiatric patients. *Psychological Reports, 59*(2), 715–720.

Watson, B. U. (1983). Test-retest stability of the Hiskey-Nebraska Test of Learning Aptitude in a sample of hearing-impaired children and adolescents. *Journal of Speech and Hearing Disorders, 48,* 145–149.

Watson, B. U., & Goldgar, D. E. (1985). A note on the use of the Hiskey-Nebraska Test of Learning Aptitude with deaf children. *Language, Speech, and Hearing Services in Schools, 16,* 53–57.

Watson, T. S. (1995). Review of the Slosson Intelligence Test [1991 Edition]. In J. C. Conoley & J. C. Impara (Eds.), *The twelfth mental measurements yearbook* (pp. 956–958). Lincoln: University of Nebraska Press.

Weschler, D. (1939). *The measurement of adult intelligence.* Baltimore: Williams & Wilkins.

Wechsler, D. (1952). *The range of human capacities.* Baltimore: Williams & Wilkins.

Wechsler, D. (1955). *Wechsler Adult Intelligence Scale.* New York: Psychological Corporation.

Wechsler, D. (1958). *The measurement and appraisal of adult intelligence* (4th ed.). Baltimore: Williams & Wilkins.

Wechsler, D. (1974). *Manual for the Wechsler Intelligence Scale for Children—Revised (WISC-R).* New York: Psychological Corporation.

Wechsler, D. (1981). *Manual for the Wechsler Adult Intelligence Scale—Revised (WAIS-R).* San Antonio, TX: Psychological Corporation.

Wechsler, D. (1991). *Wechsler Intelligence Scale for Children—Third Edition: Manual.* New York: Psychological Corporation.

Wechsler, D. (1997a). *Wechsler Adult Intelligence Scale—Third Edition.* San Antonio, TX: Psychological Corporation.

Wechsler, D. (1997b). *Wechsler Memory Scale—Third Edition.* San Antonio, TX: Psychological Corporation.

Weiner, P. S. (1971). Stability and validity of two measures of intelligence used with children whose language development is delayed. *Journal of Speech and Hearing Research, 14,* 254–261.

Weiss, B., & Weisz, J. R. (1986). General cognitive deficits: Mental retardation. In R. T. Brown & C. R. Reynolds (Eds.), *Psychological perspectives on childhood exceptionality* (pp. 344–390). New York: Wiley.

Weiss, L. G. (1991, December). WISC-III: The revision of the WISC-R. *Child Assessment News*, pp. 1, 9.

Weiss, L. G., Prifitera, A., & Roid, G. (1993). The WISC-III and the fairness of predicting achievement across ethnic and gender groups [Monograph]. *Journal of Psychoeducational Assessment, Advances in psychoeducational assessment.* Bracken, B. A., McCallum, R. S. (Ed.), *Wechsler Intelligence Scale for Children: Third Edition*, pp. 35–42.

Wesman, A. G. (1968). Intelligent testing. *American Psychologist, 23*, 267–274.

West, S. (1982). A smarter test for intelligence? *Science, 823*(9), 14.

Wherry, R. J., & Wherry, R. J., Jr. (1969). WHEWH program. In R. J. Wherry (Ed.), *Psychology department computer programs.* Columbus: Ohio State University, Department of Psychology.

White, R. F., & Rose, F. E. (1997). The Boston process approach: A brief history and current practice. In G. Goldstein & T. Incagnoli (Eds.), *Contemporary approaches to neuropsychological assessment* (pp. 171–211). New York: Plenum Press.

Whitehouse, C. C. (1983). Analysis of WISC-R Coding performance of normal and dyslexic readers. *Perceptual and Motor Skills, 57*, 951–960.

Whitworth, R. H., & Chrisman, S. B. (1987). Validation of the Kaufman Assessment Battery for Children comparing Anglo and Mexican-American preschoolers. *Educational and Psychological Measurement, 47*, 695–702.

Wielkiewicz, R. M., & Daood, C. J. (1993). Correlations between WISC-R subtests and scales of the Personality Inventory for Children. *Psychological Reports, 73*(3, Pt 2), 1343–1346.

Wiener, J. (1985). Teachers' comprehension of psychological reports. *Psychology in the Schools, 22*, 60–64.

Wiener, J., & Kohler, S. (1986). Parents' comprehension of psychological reports. *Psychology in the Schools, 23*, 265–270.

Wilkinson, G. S. (1993). *Administration and scoring manual for the Wide Range Achievement Test–3.* Wilmington, DE: Jastak Associates.

Williams, J., & Dykman, R. A. (1994). Nonverbal factors derived from children's performance on neuropsychological tests instruments. *Developmental Neuropsychology, 10*, 19–26.

Williams, J., Sharp, G., Lange, B., Bates, S., Griebel, M., Spence, G. T., & Thomas, P. (1996). The effects of seizure type, level of seizure control and antiepileptic drugs on memory and attention skills in children with epilepsy. *Developmental Neuropsychology, 12*, 241–253.

Williams, K. S., & Williams, J. M. (1996). Childhood medical conditions impacting on central nervous system function. In L. S. Batchelor & R. S. Dean (Eds.), *Pediatric neuropsychology* (pp. 249–268). Needham Heights, MA: Allyn & Bacon.

Williams, M. A., & Boll, T. J. (1997). Recent advances in neuropsychological assessment of children. In G. Goldstein & T. Incagnoli (Eds.), *Contemporary approaches to neuropsychological assessment* (pp. 231–276). New York: Plenum Press.

Willson, V. L., & Reynolds, C. R. (1984). Regression effects on part scores based on whole-score selected samples. *Educational and Psychological Measurement, 44*, 95–99.

Willson, V. L., Reynolds, C. R., Chatman, S. P., & Kaufman, A. S. (1985). Confirmatory analysis of simultaneous, sequential, and achievement factors on the K-ABC at 11 age levels ranging from 2-1/2 to 12-1/2 years. *Journal of School Psychology, 23*, 261–269.

Wilson, W. M. (1992). The Stanford-Binet: Fourth Edition and Form L-M in assessment of young children with mental retardation. *Mental Retardation, 30*(2), 81–84.

Winick, M., Meyer, K., & Harris, R. C. (1975). Malnutrition and environmental enrichment by early adoption. *Science, 190*, 1173–1175.

Wisniewski, J. J., & Naglieri, J. A. (1989). Validity of the Draw-a-Person: A quantitative scoring system with the WISC-R. *Journal of Psychoeducational Assessment, 7*, 346–351.

Wissler, C. (1901). The correlation of mental and physical tests. *Psychological Review Monograph Supplement, 3*(6), pp. 1–62.

Witelson, S. F. (1985). On hemisphere specialization and cerebral plasticity from birth: Mark II. In C. T. Best (Ed.), *Hemispheric function and collaboration in the child* (pp. 33–85). New York: Academic Press, Inc.

Witelson, S. F. (1987). Neurobiological aspects of language in children. *Child Development, 58*, 653–688.

Witmer, L. (1911). *The special class for backward children.* Philadelphia: Psychological Clinic Press.

Witt, J. C., & Gresham, F. M. (1985). Review of Wechsler Intelligence Scale for Children—Revised. In J. V. Mitchell (Ed.), *The ninth mental measurement yearbook: Vol. II* (pp. 1715–1716). Lincoln, NE: Buros Institute of Mental Measurements.

Wittrock, M. C. (1980). *The brain and psychology.* New York: Academic Press.

Wolf, T. H. (1961). An individual who made a difference. *American Psychologist, 16*, 245–248.

Wolf, T. H. (1964). Alfred Binet: A time of crisis. *American Psychologist, 19*, 762–771.

Wolf, T. H. (1966). Intuition and experiment: Alfred Binet's first efforts in child psychology. *Journal of History of Behavioral Sciences, 2*, 233–239.

Wolman, B. (1985). *Handbook of intelligence.* New York: Wiley-Interscience.

Wolters, P. L., Brouwers, P., & Moss, H. A. (1995). Pediatric HIV disease: Effect on cognition, learning, and behavior. *School Psychology Quarterly, 10*, 305–328.

Woodcock, R. W. (1984). A response to some questions raised about the WOODCOCK-JOHNSON 1. The mean score discrepancy issue. *School Psychology Review, 13*(3), 342–354.

Woodcock, R. W. (1990). Theoretical foundations of the WJ-R Measures of Cognitive Ability. *Journal of Psychoeducational Assessment, 8*, 231–258.

Woodcock, R. W., & Johnson, M. B. (1977). *Woodcock-Johnson Psycho-Educational Battery*. Allen, TX: DLM Teaching Resources.

Woodcock, R. W., & Johnson, M. B. (1989a). *Woodcock-Johnson Psycho-Educational Battery—Revised*. Allen, TX: DLM Teaching Resources.

Woodcock, R. W., & Johnson, M. B. (1989b). *Woodcock-Johnson Tests of Cognitive Ability—Revised*. Chicago: Riverside.

Woodcock, R. W., & Mather, N. (1989a). WJ-R Tests of Achievement: Examiner's Manual. In R. W. Woodcock & M. B. Johnson, *Woodcock-Johnson Psycho-Educational Battery—Revised*. Allen, TX: DLM Teaching Resources.

Woodcock, R. W., & Mather, N. (1989b). WJ-R Tests of Cognitive Ability—Standard and Supplemental Batteries: Examiner's manual. In R. W. Woodcock & M. B. Johnson, *Woodcock-Johnson Psycho-Educational Battery—Revised*. Allen, TX: DLM Teaching Resources.

Woodcock, R. W., McGrew, K. S., & Werder, J. K. (1994). *Woodcock-McGrew-Werder Mini-Battery of Achievement*. Chicago: Riverside Publishing.

Woodcock, R. W., & Munoz-Sandoval, A. F. (1996). *Bateria Woodcock-Munoz-Revisada*. Chicago: Riverside Publishing.

Worthington, C. F. (1987). Testing the test: Kaufman Test of Educational Achievement, Comprehensive Form and Brief Form. *Journal of Counseling and Development, 65*, 325–327.

WPPSI-R poll results. (1991, October). *Child Assessment News*, p. 11.

Wright, J. S. (1967). Opinion, *Hobson v. Hansen. Federal Supplement 269*, 401–510.

Ysseldyke, J. E. (1990). Goodness of fit of the Woodcock-Johnson Psycho-Educational Battery—Revised to the Horn-Cattell Gf-Gc theory. *Journal of Psychoeducational Assessment, 8*, 268–275.

Zachary, R. A. (1990). Weschler's intelligence scales: Theoretical and practical considerations. *Journal of Psychoeducational Assessment, 8*, 276–289.

Zajonc, R. B., & Marcus, G. B. (1975). Birth order and intellectual development. *Psychological Review, 82*, 74–88.

Zarantonello, M. M. (1988). Comparability of the WAIS and WAIS-R: A consideration of level of neuropsychological impairment. *Journal of Consulting & Clinical Psychology, 56*, 295–297.

Zimmerman, I. L., & Woo-Sam, J. M. (1967). Reporting results. In A. J. Glasser & I. L. Zimmerman (Ed.), *Clinical interpretation of the Wechsler Intelligence Scale for Children (WISC)* (pp. 20–35). New York: Grune & Stratton.

Zimmerman, I. L., & Woo-Sam, J. M. (1985). Clinical applications. In B. B. Wolman (Ed.), *Handbook of intelligence: Theories, measurements, and applications* (pp. 873–898). New York: Wiley.

Zins, J. E., & Barnett, D. W. (1983). The Kaufman Assessment Battery for Children and school achievement: A validity study. *Journal of Psychoeducational Assessment, 1*, 235–241.

Zins, J. E., & Barnett, D. W. (1984). A validity study of the K-ABC, the WISC-R, and the Stanford-Binet with nonreferred children. *Journal of School Psychology, 22*, 369–371.

Zuckerman, M. (1990). Some dubious premises in research and theory on racial differences: Scientific, social, and ethical issues. *American Psychologist, 45*, 1297–1303.